COLLINS

COMPACT ENGLISH THESAURUS IN A-Z FORM

HarperCollins*Publishers*

First Published 1993
© HarperCollins Publishers 1993

ISBN 0 00 470288 - 3

A catalogue record for this book is
available from the British Library.

NOTE

Entered words that we have reason to
believe constitute trademarks have
been designated as such. However,
neither the presence nor absence of
such designation should be regarded as
affecting the legal status of any trademark.

Computer typeset by Barbers Ltd
Wrotham, England

Printed in Great Britain by
HarperCollins *Manufacturing*
PO Box, Glasgow G4 0NB

EDITORIAL STAFF

Managing Editor
Marian Makins

Chief Lexicographer
Diana Adams

Senior Editor
Lorna Knight

Editors
John Widdowson
Alice Grandison, Danielle McGinley,
Thomas Shearer

Editorial Assistance
Anne Young

Foreword

The name 'thesaurus' comes from a Greek word meaning treasure, treasury, or storehouse, and the Thesaurus is so named because it is a treasury or storehouse of words. Its purpose is to provide lists of words which mean the same, or almost the same, as the word which the user of the book has in mind, so that an alternative can be chosen.

There are many reasons why an alternative word might be sought. It may be that the original word is felt to be inappropriate in some way – perhaps it is too formal or too colloquial, perhaps it is not quite precise in conveying the intended meaning, or somehow does not suit the tone of the piece of writing. Perhaps it is a perfectly suitable word in its context, but one that has already been used – the desire to avoid repetition is a frequent reason for consulting a thesaurus. Sometimes a word that is known to exist just will not come to mind; on such occasions the elusive word can be discovered by looking up an equivalent term in the Thesaurus. For these, and many other purposes which the user will soon discover, the Thesaurus is an invaluable help to anyone interested in improving their command of the English language.

The Collins Compact Thesaurus is arranged, like a dictionary, in a single alphabetical listing of main-entry words. If the main-entry word has more than one meaning, synonyms for the different meanings are found at the one entry. The full range of alternatives is thus available at a glance, and the user of the book can choose the appropriate word from the entry without the need to refer to an index.

The main-entry words have been selected with the needs of today's user in mind. They represent the core of modern English – those that are most likely to be looked up. The lists of synonyms provided, however, cover the whole range of usage and style, from slang and informal to literary and archaic, and the choice is generous, with an average of seventeen alternatives for every main-entry word. Labels identify synonyms that have a specialist or restricted sense in the context of the main-entry word.

English, being derived from so many sources, is particularly rich in terms that are synonymous or nearly so; however, true synonyms, those that are substitutable in all contexts, are rare – a fact that gives the language interest and dimension. In preparing this book, therefore, care was taken to ensure that all the synonyms given were genuinely interchangeable with the main-entry word in some context. The precise usage or shade of meaning of any synonym unfamiliar to the user of the book may be checked by using a good dictionary as a companion to the Thesaurus.

Finally, it should not be forgotten that the *Collins Compact Thesaurus*, as well as providing practical help, can be used purely for fun. It is invaluable in preparing or solving word games, and a marvellous aid for crossword addicts. Or it can, quite simply, be used to browse through, leading the reader on a fascinating journey through the highways and byways of the English language.

Explanatory Notes

1. Under each main-entry word, the synonyms are arranged alphabetically. When a word has distinctly separate meanings, separate numbered lists are given for the different senses, eg

> **distinct 1.** apparent, clear, clear-cut...
> **2.** detached, different, discrete...

2. Where it is helpful to distinguish between different parts of speech, labels have been added as follows: *n.* (noun), *v.* (verb), *adj.* (adjective), *adv.* (adverb), *pron.* (pronoun), *conj.* (conjunction), *prep.* (preposition), *interj.* (interjection). When a headword has more than one meaning and can function as more than one part of speech, a new part-of-speech function is shown by a large swung dash (~), eg

> **local** *adj.* **1.** community, district...
> **2.** confined, limited...~ *n.*
> **3.** character (*Inf.*), inhabitant...

3. Usually the synonyms for a particular part of speech are grouped together. For instance, in the entry *catch* synonyms for all the verb senses are given first, followed by synonyms for all the noun senses. Sometimes, however, noun and verb functions are very closely associated in specific meanings, and where this is the case the synonyms are grouped by meanings, as in the entry for *cover*.

4. Much-used phrases appear as main entries; for instance, *act for* comes after *act*. Expressions such as *en route*, and compounds such as *highly-strung* or *high-spirited*, are also given as main entries within the alphabetical listing. Short idiomatic phrases are entered under their key word and are to be found either at the end of the entry or immediately following the sense with which they are associated. Thus, the phrase *take a dim view* appears as sense 7 of the entry *dim*, since the synonyms in sense 6 most closely approximate to the meaning of the phrase.

5. Plural forms that have a distinctly separate meaning, such as *provisions*, are entered at their own alphabetical position, while those with a less distinct difference, such as *extremities*, are given as a separate sense under the singular form, eg

> **extremity** ...**4.** *Plural* ...

6. A label in brackets applies only to the synonym preceding it, while one which is not bracketed relates to the whole of that particular sense. Labels have been abbreviated when a readily understandable shortened form exists, such as *Sl.* (Slang), *Inf.* (Informal), and *Fig.* (Figurative).

7. The small swung dash symbol (~) is used to show that a word has been broken merely because it happens to fall at the end of a line, while the conventional sign (-) is used to distinguish a word which is always written with a hyphen, as in the entry for *adversity*:

> **adversity** affliction, bad luck, ca~
> lamity, catastrophe, disaster, dis~
> tress, hardship, hard times, ill-
> fortune, ill-luck, misery, misfor~
> tune, mishap, reverse, sorrow, suf~
> fering, trial, trouble, woe, wretch~
> edness

A

abandon *v.* 1. desert, forsake, jilt, leave, leave behind 2. evacuate, quit, vacate, withdraw from 3. abdicate, cede, give up, relinquish, renounce, resign, surrender, waive, yield 4. desist, discontinue, drop, forgo ~*n.* 5. careless freedom, dash, recklessness, unrestraint, wantonness, wild impulse, wildness

abandoned 1. cast aside, cast away, cast out, derelict, deserted, discarded, dropped, forlorn, forsaken, jilted, left, neglected, outcast, rejected, relinquished, unoccupied, vacant 2. corrupt, debauched, depraved, dissipated, dissolute, profligate, reprobate, sinful, wanton, wicked 3. uncontrolled, uninhibited, unrestrained, wild

abandonment 1. dereliction, desertion, forsaking, jilting, leaving 2. evacuation, quitting, withdrawal from 3. abdication, cession, giving up, relinquishment, renunciation, resignation, surrender, waiver 4. desistance, discontinuation, dropping

abbey cloister, convent, friary, monastery, nunnery, priory

abbreviate abridge, abstract, clip, compress, condense, contract, curtail, cut, digest, epitomize, précis, reduce, shorten, summarize, trim, truncate

abbreviation abridgment, abstract, clipping, compendium, compression, condensation, conspectus, contraction, curtailment, digest, epitome, précis, reduction, résumé, shortening, summary, synopsis, trimming, truncation

abdicate abandon, abjure, abnegate, cede, forgo, give up, quit, relinquish, renounce, resign, retire, surrender, vacate, waive, yield

abdication abandonment, abjuration, abnegation, cession, giving up, quitting, relinquishment, renunciation, resignation, retiral

(*esp. Scot.*), retirement, surrender, waiver, yielding

abdominal gastric, intestinal, stomachic, stomachical, visceral

abduct carry off, kidnap, make off with, run away with, run off with, seize, snatch (*Sl.*)

abet 1. aid, assist, back, condone, connive at, help, promote, sanction, second, succour, support, sustain, uphold 2. egg on, encourage, incite, prompt, spur, urge

abeyance 1. adjournment, deferral, discontinuation, inactivity, intermission, postponement, recess, reservation, suspense, suspension, waiting 2. **in abeyance** hanging fire, on ice (*Inf.*), pending, shelved, suspended

abhor abominate, detest, execrate, hate, loathe, recoil from, regard with repugnance *or* horror, shrink from, shudder at

abhorrent abominable, detestable, disgusting, distasteful, execrable, hated, hateful, heinous, horrible, horrid, loathsome, obnoxious, odious, offensive, repellent, repugnant, repulsive, revolting

abide 1. accept, bear, brook, endure, put up with, stand, stomach, submit to, suffer, tolerate 2. dwell, linger, live, lodge, reside, rest, sojourn, stay, stop, tarry, wait 3. continue, endure, last, persist, remain, survive

abide by 1. acknowledge, agree to, comply with, conform to, follow, obey, observe, submit to 2. adhere to, carry out, discharge, fulfil, hold to, keep to, persist in, stand by

abiding constant, continuing, durable, enduring, eternal, everlasting, fast, firm, immortal, immutable, indissoluble, lasting, permanent, persistent, persisting, steadfast, surviving, tenacious, unchanging, unending

ability adeptness, aptitude, capability, capacity, competence, competency, dexterity, endowment, energy, expertise, expertness, facility, faculty, flair, force, gift, knack, know-how (*Inf.*), potentiality, power, proficiency, qualification, skill, talent

abject 1. base, contemptible, cringing, debased, degraded, despicable, dishonourable, fawning, grovelling, humiliating, ignoble, ignominious, low, mean, servile, slavish, sordid, submissive, vile, worthless 2. deplorable, forlorn, hopeless, miserable, outcast, pitiable, wretched

abjectness 1. abjection, baseness, contemptibleness, debasement, degradation, dishonour, humbleness, humiliation, ignominy, lowness, meanness, servility, slavishness, sordidness, submissiveness, vileness, worthlessness 2. destitution, forlornness, hopelessness, misery, pitiableness, pitifulness, squalor, wretchedness

ablaze 1. afire, aflame, alight, blazing, burning, fiery, flaming, ignited, lighted, on fire 2. aglow, brilliant, flashing, gleaming, glowing, illuminated, incandescent, luminous, radiant, sparkling 3. angry, aroused, enthusiastic, excited, fervent, frenzied, fuming, furious, impassioned, incensed, passionate, raging, stimulated

able accomplished, adept, adequate, adroit, capable, clever, competent, effective, efficient, experienced, expert, fit, fitted, gifted, highly endowed, masterful, masterly, powerful, practised, proficient, qualified, skilful, skilled, strong, talented

able-bodied firm, fit, hale, hardy, healthy, hearty, lusty, powerful, robust, sound, staunch, stout, strapping, strong, sturdy, vigorous

abnormal aberrant, anomalous, atypical, curious, deviant, eccentric, erratic, exceptional, extraordinary, irregular, monstrous, odd, peculiar, queer, singular, strange, uncommon, unexpected, unnatural, untypical, unusual, weird

abnormality aberration, anomaly, atypicalness, bizarreness, deformity, deviation, eccentricity, exception, extraordinariness, flaw, irregularity, monstrosity, oddity, peculiarity, queerness, singularity, strangeness, uncommonness, unexpectedness, unnaturalness, untypicalness, unusualness, weirdness

abolish abrogate, annihilate, annul, blot out, cancel, destroy, do away with, eliminate, end, eradicate, expunge, exterminate, extinguish, extirpate, invalidate, nullify, obliterate, overthrow, overturn, put an end to, quash, repeal, repudiate, rescind, revoke, stamp out, subvert, suppress, terminate, vitiate, void, wipe out

abolition abrogation, annihilation, annulment, blotting out, cancellation, destruction, elimination, end, ending, eradication, expunction, extermination, extinction, extirpation, invalidation, nullification, obliteration, overthrow, overturning, quashing, repeal, repudiation, rescission, revocation, stamping out, subversion, suppression, termination, vitiation, voiding, wiping out, withdrawal

abominable abhorrent, accursed, atrocious, base, contemptible, despicable, detestable, disgusting, execrable, foul, hateful, heinous, hellish, horrible, horrid, loathsome, nauseous, obnoxious, odious, repellent, reprehensible, repugnant, repulsive, revolting, terrible, vile, villainous, wretched

abominate abhor, detest, execrate, hate, loathe, recoil from, regard with repugnance, shudder at

abomination 1. abhorrence, antipathy, aversion, detestation, disgust, distaste, execration, hate, hatred, horror, loathing, odium, repugnance, revulsion 2. anathema, *bête noire*, bugbear, curse, disgrace, evil, horror, plague, shame, torment

aboriginal ancient, autochthonous, earliest, first, indigenous, native, original, primary, primeval, primitive, primordial, pristine

abound be jammed with, be packed with, be plentiful, crowd, flourish, increase, infest, luxuriate, overflow, proliferate, superabound, swarm, swell, teem, thrive

abounding abundant, bountiful, copious, filled, flourishing, flowing, flush, full, lavish, luxuriant, over~ flowing, plenteous, plentiful, pro~ fuse, prolific, rank, replete, rich, superabundant, teeming

about *prep.* 1. anent (*Scot.*), as re~ gards, concerned with, concerning, connected with, dealing with, on, re, referring to, regarding, relating to, relative to, respecting, touch~ ing, with respect to 2. adjacent, beside, circa (*used with dates*), close to, near, nearby 3. around, encircling, on all sides, round, sur~ rounding 4. all over, over, through, throughout ~*adv.* 5. almost, ap~ proaching, approximately, around, close to, more or less, nearing, nearly, roughly 6. from place to place, here and there, hither and thither, to and fro ~*adj.* 7. active, around, astir, in motion, present, stirring

about to intending to, on the point of, on the verge *or* brink of, ready to

above *prep.* 1. atop, beyond, ex~ ceeding, higher than, on top of, over, upon ~*adv.* 2. atop, in heav~ en, on high, overhead ~*adj.* 3. aforementioned, aforesaid, earlier, foregoing, preceding, previous, prior 4. before, beyond, exceeding, prior to, superior to, surpassing

aboveboard 1. *adv.* candidly, forthrightly, frankly, honestly, honourably, openly, overtly, straightforwardly, truly, truthfully, uprightly, veraciously, without guile 2. *adj.* candid, fair and square, forthright, frank, guileless, honest, honourable, legitimate, open, overt, square, straight, straightforward, true, trustworthy, truthful, upright, veracious

abrasion 1. *Medical* chafe, graze, scrape, scratch, scuff, surface in~ jury 2. abrading, chafing, erosion, friction, grating, rubbing, scouring, scraping, scratching, scuffing, wearing away, wearing down

abrasive *adj.* 1. chafing, erosive, frictional, grating, rough, scraping, scratching, scratchy, scuffing 2. annoying, biting, caustic, cutting, galling, grating, hurtful, irritating, nasty, rough, sharp, unpleasant ~*n.* 3. abradant, burnisher, grinder, scarifier, scourer

abreast 1. alongside, beside, level, shoulder to shoulder, side by side 2. acquainted, *au courant, au fait,* conversant, familiar, informed, in touch, knowledgeable, up to date

abridge abbreviate, abstract, clip, compress, concentrate, condense, contract, curtail, cut, cut down, decrease, digest, diminish, epito~ mize, lessen, précis, reduce, short~ en, summarize, synopsize (*U.S.*), trim

abridgment abbreviation, ab~ stract, compendium, condensation, conspectus, contraction, curtail~ ment, cutting, decrease, digest, di~ minishing, diminution, epitome, lessening, limitation, outline, pré~ cis, reduction, restraint, restric~ tion, résumé, shortening, sum~ mary, synopsis

abroad 1. beyond the sea, in for~ eign lands, out of the country, overseas 2. about, at large, away, circulating, current, elsewhere, extensively, far, far and wide, forth, in circulation, out, out-of-doors, outside, publicly, widely, without

abrupt 1. blunt, brisk, brusque, curt, direct, discourteous, gruff, impolite, rough, rude, short, snap~ pish, snappy, terse, unceremoni~ ous, uncivil, ungracious 2. precipi~ tous, sharp, sheer, steep, sudden 3. hasty, headlong, hurried, precipi~ tate, quick, sudden, surprising, swift, unanticipated, unexpected, unforeseen 4. broken, disconnect~ ed, discontinuous, irregular, jerky, uneven

abscond bolt, clear out, decamp, disappear, do a bunk (*Sl.*), escape, flee, flit (*Inf.*), fly, make off, run off, slip away, sneak away, steal away

absence 1. absenteeism, non~appearance, nonattendance, truancy 2. default, defect, deficiency, lack, need, nonexistence, omission, privation, unavailability, want 3. absent-mindedness, abstraction, distraction, inattention, preoccupation, reverie

absent *adj.* 1. away, elsewhere, gone, lacking, missing, nonattendant, nonexistent, not present, out, truant, unavailable, wanting 2. absent-minded, absorbed, abstracted, bemused, blank, daydreaming, distracted, dreamy, empty, faraway, heedless, inattentive, musing, oblivious, preoccupied, unaware, unconscious, unheeding, unthinking, vacant, vague ~*v.* 3. **absent oneself** abscond, depart, keep away, play truant, remove, stay away, truant, withdraw

absently absent-mindedly, abstractedly, bemusedly, blankly, distractedly, dreamily, emptily, heedlessly, inattentively, obliviously, unconsciously, unheedingly, vacantly, vaguely

absent-minded absent, absorbed, abstracted, bemused, distracted, dreaming, dreamy, engrossed, faraway, forgetful, heedless, in a brown study, inattentive, musing, oblivious, preoccupied, unaware, unconscious, unheeding, unthinking

absolute 1. complete, consummate, downright, entire, out-and-out, outright, perfect, pure, sheer, thorough, total, unadulterated, unalloyed, unmitigated, unmixed, unqualified, utter 2. actual, categorical, certain, conclusive, decided, decisive, definite, exact, genuine, infallible, positive, precise, sure, unambiguous, unequivocal, unquestionable 3. absolutist, arbitrary, autarchical, autocratic, autonomous, despotic, dictatorial, full, peremptory, sovereign, supreme, tyrannical, unbounded, unconditional, unlimited, unqualified, unquestionable, unrestrained, unrestricted

absolutely 1. completely, consum~mately, entirely, fully, perfectly, purely, thoroughly, totally, unmitigatedly, utterly, wholly 2. actually, categorically, certainly, conclusively, decidedly, decisively, definitely, exactly, genuinely, infallibly, positively, precisely, surely, truly, unambiguously, unequivocally, unquestionably 3. arbitrarily, autocratically, autonomously, despotically, dictatorially, fully, peremptorily, sovereignly, supremely, tyrannically, unconditionally, unquestionably, unrestrainedly

absoluteness 1. consummateness, entirety, perfection, purity, thoroughness, totality, unmitigatedness, wholeness 2. assuredness, certainty, certitude, conclusiveness, correctness, decidedness, decisiveness, definiteness, exactitude, genuineness, infallibility, positiveness, precision, sureness, surety, truth, unambiguousness, unequivocalness 3. arbitrariness, autonomy, despotism, dictatorialness, fullness, peremptoriness, supremacy, tyranny, unboundedness, unquestionability, unrestrainedness, unrestrictedness

absolution acquittal, amnesty, deliverance, discharge, dispensation, exculpation, exemption, exoneration, forgiveness, freeing, indulgence, liberation, mercy, pardon, release, remission, setting free, shriving, vindication

absolutism absoluteness, arbitrariness, autarchy, authoritarianism, autocracy, despotism, dictatorship, totalitarianism, tyranny

absolutist arbiter, authoritarian, autocrat, despot, dictator, totalitarian, tyrant

absolve acquit, clear, deliver, discharge, exculpate, excuse, exempt, exonerate, forgive, free, let off, liberate, loose, pardon, release, remit, set free, shrive, vindicate

absorb 1. assimilate, consume, devour, digest, drink in, exhaust, imbibe, incorporate, ingest, osmose, receive, soak up, suck up, take in 2. captivate, engage, engross, enwrap, fascinate, fill, fill up, fix, hold, immerse, monopolize, occupy, preoccupy, rivet

absorbed 1. captivated, concentrating, engaged, engrossed, fascinated, fixed, held, immersed, involved, lost, occupied, preoccupied, rapt, riveted, wrapped up 2. assimilated, consumed, devoured, digested, exhausted, imbibed, incorporated, received

absorbing arresting, captivating, engrossing, fascinating, gripping, interesting, intriguing, preoccupying, riveting, spellbinding

abstain avoid, cease, decline, deny (oneself), desist, forbear, forgo, give up, keep from, refrain, refuse, renounce, shun, stop, withhold

abstemious abstinent, ascetic, austere, continent, frugal, moderate, self-denying, sober, sparing, temperate

abstention abstaining, abstinence, avoidance, desistance, eschewal, forbearance, nonindulgence, refraining, refusal, self-control, self-denial, self-restraint

abstinence abstemiousness, asceticism, avoidance, continence, forbearance, moderation, refraining, self-denial, self-restraint, soberness, sobriety, teetotalism, temperance

abstinent abstaining, abstemious, continent, forbearing, moderate, self-controlled, self-denying, self-restraining, sober, temperate

abstract *adj.* 1. abstruse, arcane, complex, conceptual, deep, general, generalized, hypothetical, indefinite, intellectual, nonconcrete, occult, philosophical, profound, recondite, separate, subtle, theoretic, theoretical, unpractical, unrealistic ~*n.* 2. abridgment, compendium, condensation, digest, epitome, essence, outline, précis, recapitulation, résumé, summary, synopsis ~*v.* 3. abbreviate, abridge, condense, digest, epitomize, outline, précis, shorten, summarize, synopsize (*U.S.*) 4. detach, dissociate, extract, isolate, remove, separate, steal, take away, take out, withdraw

abstracted 1. absent, absent-minded, bemused, daydreaming, dreamy, faraway, inattentive, preoccupied, remote, withdrawn, woolgathering 2. abbreviated, abridged, condensed, digested, epitomized, shortened, summarized, synopsized (*U.S.*)

abstraction 1. absence, absent-mindedness, bemusedness, dreaminess, inattention, pensiveness, preoccupation, remoteness, woolgathering 2. concept, formula, generality, generalization, hypothesis, idea, notion, theorem, theory, thought

abstruse abstract, arcane, complex, dark, deep, enigmatic, esoteric, hidden, incomprehensible, mysterious, mystical, obscure, occult, perplexing, profound, puzzling, recondite, subtle, unfathomable, vague

absurd crazy (*Inf.*), daft (*Inf.*), farcical, foolish, idiotic, illogical, incongruous, irrational, laughable, ludicrous, meaningless, nonsensical, preposterous, ridiculous, senseless, silly, stupid, unreasonable

absurdity craziness (*Inf.*), daftness (*Inf.*), farce, farcicality, farcicalness, folly, foolishness, idiocy, illogicality, illogicalness, incongruity, irrationality, joke, ludicrousness, meaninglessness, nonsense, preposterousness, ridiculousness, senselessness, silliness, stupidity, unreasonableness

abundance 1. affluence, ampleness, bounty, copiousness, exuberance, fullness, heap (*Inf.*), plenitude, plenteousness, plenty, profusion 2. affluence, fortune, opulence, riches, wealth

abundant ample, bounteous, bountiful, copious, exuberant, filled, full, lavish, luxuriant, overflowing, plenteous, plentiful, profuse, rank, rich, teeming, well-provided, well-supplied

abuse *v.* 1. damage, exploit, harm, hurt, ill-treat, impose upon, injure, maltreat, manhandle, mar, misapply, misuse, oppress, spoil, take advantage of, wrong 2. calumniate, castigate, curse, defame, disparage, insult, inveigh against, libel, malign, revile, scold, slander, smear, swear at, traduce, upbraid, vilify, vituperate ~n. 3. damage, exploitation, harm, hurt, ill-treatment, imposition, injury, maltreatment, manhandling, misapplication, misuse, oppression, spoiling, wrong 4. blame, calumniation, castigation, censure, contumely, curses, cursing, defamation, derision, disparagement, insults, invective, libel, opprobrium, reproach, revilement, scolding, slander, swearing, tirade, traducement, upbraiding, vilification, vituperation 5. corruption, crime, delinquency, fault, injustice, misconduct, misdeed, offence, sin, wrong, wrongdoing

abusive 1. calumniating, castigating, censorious, contumelious, defamatory, derisive, disparaging, insulting, invective, libellous, maligning, offensive, opprobrious, reproachful, reviling, rude, scathing, scolding, slanderous, traducing, upbraiding, vilifying, vituperative 2. brutal, cruel, destructive, harmful, hurtful, injurious, rough

abysmal bottomless, boundless, complete, deep, endless, extreme, immeasurable, incalculable, infinite, profound, thorough, unending, unfathomable, vast

abyss abysm, bottomless depth, chasm, crevasse, fissure, gorge, gulf, pit, void

academic adj. 1. bookish, campus, college, collegiate, erudite, highbrow, learned, lettered, literary, scholarly, scholastic, school, studious, university 2. abstract, conjectural, hypothetical, impractical, notional, speculative, theoretical ~n. 3. academician, don, fellow, lecturer, master, professor, pupil, scholar, scholastic, schoolman, student, tutor

accede 1. accept, acquiesce, admit, agree, assent, comply, concede, concur, consent, endorse, grant, yield 2. assume, attain, come to,

enter upon, inherit, succeed, succeed to (as heir)

accelerate advance, expedite, forward, further, hasten, hurry, pick up speed, precipitate, quicken, speed, speed up, spur, step up (Inf.), stimulate

acceleration expedition, hastening, hurrying, quickening, speeding up, spurring, stepping up (Inf.), stimulation

accent n. 1. beat, cadence, emphasis, force, pitch, rhythm, stress, timbre, tonality 2. articulation, enunciation, inflection, intonation, modulation, pronunciation, tone ~v. 3. accentuate, emphasize, stress, underline, underscore

accentuate accent, draw attention to, emphasize, highlight, stress, underline, underscore

accept 1. acquire, gain, get, have, obtain, receive, secure, take 2. accede, acknowledge, acquiesce, admit, adopt, affirm, agree to, approve, believe, concur with, consent to, cooperate with, recognize, swallow (Inf.) 3. bear, bow to, brook, defer to, put up with, stand, submit to, suffer, take, yield to 4. acknowledge, admit, assume, avow, bear, take on, undertake

acceptable 1. agreeable, delightful, grateful, gratifying, pleasant, pleasing, welcome 2. adequate, admissible, all right, fair, moderate, passable, satisfactory, so-so (Inf.), standard, tolerable

acceptance 1. accepting, acquiring, gaining, getting, having, obtaining, receipt, securing, taking 2. accedence, accession, acknowledgment, acquiescence, admission, adoption, affirmation, agreement, approbation, approval, assent, belief, compliance, concession, concurrence, consent, cooperation, credence, O.K. (Inf.), permission, recognition, stamp or seal of approval 3. deference, standing, submission, taking, yielding 4. acknowledgment, admission, assumption, avowal, taking on, undertaking

accepted acceptable, acknowledged, admitted, agreed, agreed upon, approved, authorized, common, confirmed, conventional, customary, established, normal, received, recognized, regular, sanctioned, standard, time-honoured, traditional, universal, usual

access 1. admission, admittance, approach, avenue, course, door, entering, entrance, entrée, entry, gateway, key, passage, passageway, path, road 2. *Medical* attack, fit, onset, outburst, paroxysm

accessibility 1. approachability, attainability, availability, handiness, nearness, obtainability, possibility, readiness 2. affability, approachability, conversableness, cordiality, friendliness, informality 3. exposedness, openness, susceptibility

accessible 1. achievable, at hand, attainable, available, get-at-able (*Inf.*), handy, near, nearby, obtainable, on hand, possible, reachable, ready 2. affable, approachable, available, conversable, cordial, friendly, informal 3. exposed, liable, open, subject, susceptible, vulnerable, wide-open

accessory *n.* 1. abettor, accomplice, assistant, associate (*in crime*), colleague, confederate, helper, partner 2. accent, accompaniment, addition, adjunct, adornment, aid, appendage, attachment, component, convenience, decoration, extension, extra, frill, help, supplement, trim, trimming ~*adj.* 3. abetting, additional, aiding, ancillary, assisting in, auxiliary, contributory, extra, secondary, subordinate, supplemental, supplementary

accident 1. blow, calamity, casualty, chance, collision, crash, disaster, misadventure, mischance, misfortune, mishap, pile-up 2. chance, fate, fluke, fortuity, fortune, hazard, luck

accidental adventitious, casual, chance, contingent, fortuitous, haphazard, inadvertent, incidental, inessential, nonessential, random,

uncalculated, uncertain, unessential, unexpected, unforeseen, unintended, unintentional, unlooked-for, unplanned, unpremeditated, unwitting

accidentally adventitiously, by accident, by chance, by mistake, casually, fortuitously, haphazardly, inadvertently, incidentally, randomly, unconsciously, undesignedly, unexpectedly, unintentionally, unwittingly

acclaim 1. *v.* applaud, approve, celebrate, cheer, clap, commend, eulogize, exalt, extol, hail, honour, laud, praise, salute, welcome 2. *n.* acclamation, applause, approbation, approval, celebration, cheering, clapping, commendation, eulogizing, exaltation, honour, laudation, plaudits, praise, welcome

acclamation acclaim, adulation, approbation, cheer, cheering, cheers, enthusiasm, laudation, loud homage, ovation, plaudit, praise, salutation, shouting, tribute

acclimatization acclimation, accommodation, acculturation, adaptation, adjustment, habituation, inurement, naturalization

acclimatize accommodate, acculture, accustom, adapt, adjust, become seasoned to, get used to, habituate, inure, naturalize

accommodate 1. billet, board, cater for, entertain, harbour, house, lodge, put up, quarter, shelter 2. afford, aid, assist, furnish, help, oblige, provide, serve, supply 3. accustom, adapt, adjust, comply, compose, conform, fit, harmonize, modify, reconcile, settle

accommodating complaisant, considerate, cooperative, friendly, helpful, hospitable, kind, obliging, polite, unselfish, willing

accommodation 1. adaptation, adjustment, compliance, composition, compromise, conformity, fitting, harmony, modification, reconciliation, settlement 2. board, digs (*Inf.*), harbouring, house, housing, lodging(s), quartering, quarters, shelter, sheltering 3. aid, assistance, help, provision, service, supply

accompany 1. attend, chaperon, conduct, convoy, escort, go with, squire, usher 2. belong to, coexist with, coincide with, come with, follow, go together with, join with, occur with, supplement

accompanying accessory, added, additional, appended, associate, associated, attached, attendant, complementary, concomitant, concurrent, connected, fellow, joint, related, supplemental, supplementary

accomplice abettor, accessory, ally, assistant, associate, coadjutor, collaborator, colleague, confederate, helper, henchman, partner

accomplish achieve, attain, bring about, bring off (*Inf.*), carry out, complete, conclude, consummate, do, effect, effectuate, execute, finish, fulfil, manage, perform, produce, realize

accomplished 1. achieved, attained, brought about, carried out, completed, concluded, consummated, done, effected, executed, finished, fulfilled, managed, performed, produced, realized 2. adept, consummate, cultivated, expert, gifted, masterly, polished, practised, proficient, skilful, skilled, talented

accomplishment 1. achievement, attainment, bringing about, carrying out, completion, conclusion, consummation, doing, effecting, execution, finishing, fulfilment, management, performance, production, realization 2. achievement, act, attainment, coup, deed, exploit, feat, stroke, triumph 3. ability, achievement, art, attainment, capability, gift, proficiency, skill, talent

accord v. 1. agree, assent, be in tune (*Inf.*), concur, conform, correspond, fit, harmonize, match, suit, tally 2. allow, bestow, concede, confer, endow, give, grant, present, render, tender, vouchsafe ~n. 3. accordance, agreement, concert, concurrence, conformity,

congruence, correspondence, harmony, rapport, sympathy, unanimity

accordance 1. accord, agreement, assent, concert, concurrence, conformity, congruence, correspondence, harmony, rapport, sympathy, unanimity 2. according, allowance, bestowal, concession, conferment, conferral, endowment, gift, giving, granting, presentation, rendering, tendering

accordingly 1. appropriately, correspondingly, fitly, properly, suitably 2. as a result, consequently, ergo, hence, in consequence, so, therefore, thus

according to 1. commensurate with, in proportion, in relation 2. as believed by, as maintained by, as stated by, in the light of, on the authority of, on the report of 3. after, after the manner of, consistent with, in accordance with, in compliance with, in conformity with, in harmony with, in keeping with, in line with, in obedience to, in step with, in the manner of, obedient to

account n. 1. chronicle, description, detail, explanation, history, narration, narrative, recital, record, relation, report, statement, story, tale, version 2. *Commerce* balance, bill, book, books, charge, computation, inventory, invoice, ledger, reckoning, register, score, statement, tally 3. advantage, benefit, consequence, distinction, esteem, honour, import, importance, merit, note, profit, rank, repute, significance, standing, use, value, worth 4. basis, cause, consideration, ground, grounds, interest, motive, reason, regard, sake, score (*Inf.*) ~v. 5. appraise, assess, believe, calculate, compute, consider, count, deem, esteem, estimate, explain, gauge, hold, judge, rate, reckon, regard, think, value, weigh

accountability 1. answerability, chargeability, culpability, liability, responsibility 2. comprehensibility, explainability, explicability, intelligibility, understandability

accountable 1. amenable, answerable, charged with, liable, obligated, obliged, responsible 2. comprehensible, explainable, explicable, intelligible, understandable

account for 1. answer for, clarify, clear up, elucidate, explain, illuminate, justify, rationalize 2. destroy, incapacitate, kill, put out of action

accredit 1. appoint, authorize, certify, commission, depute, empower, endorse, entrust, guarantee, license, recognize, sanction, vouch for 2. ascribe, assign, attribute, credit

accredited appointed, authorized, certified, commissioned, deputed, deputized, empowered, endorsed, guaranteed, licensed, official, recognized, sanctioned, vouched for

accrue accumulate, amass, arise, be added, build up, collect, enlarge, ensue, flow, follow, grow, increase, issue, spring up

accumulate accrue, amass, build up, collect, cumulate, gather, grow, hoard, increase, pile up, stockpile, store

accumulation aggregation, augmentation, build-up, collection, conglomeration, gathering, growth, heap, hoard, increase, mass, pile, stack, stock, stockpile, store

accuracy accurateness, authenticity, carefulness, closeness, correctness, exactitude, exactness, faithfulness, faultlessness, fidelity, meticulousness, niceness, nicety, precision, strictness, truth, truthfulness, veracity, verity

accurate authentic, careful, close, correct, exact, faithful, faultless, just, meticulous, nice, precise, proper, regular, right, scrupulous, spot-on (*Inf.*), strict, true, truthful, unerring, veracious

accurately authentically, carefully, closely, correctly, exactly, faithfully, faultlessly, justly, meticulously, nicely, precisely, properly, regularly, rightly, scrupulously, strictly, truly, truthfully, unerringly, veraciously

accursed 1. bedevilled, bewitched, condemned, cursed, damned, doomed, hopeless, ill-fated, ill-omened, jinxed, luckless, ruined, undone, unfortunate, unlucky, wretched 2. abominable, despicable, detestable, execrable, hateful, hellish, horrible

accusation allegation, arraignment, attribution, charge, citation, complaint, denunciation, impeachment, imputation, incrimination, indictment, recrimination

accuse allege, arraign, attribute, blame, censure, charge, cite, denounce, impeach, impute, incriminate, indict, recriminate, tax

accustom acclimatize, acquaint, adapt, discipline, exercise, familiarize, habituate, inure, season, train

accustomed 1. acclimatized, acquainted, adapted, disciplined, exercised, familiar, familiarized, given to, habituated, in the habit of, inured, seasoned, trained, used 2. common, conventional, customary, established, everyday, expected, fixed, general, habitual, normal, ordinary, regular, routine, set, traditional, usual, wonted

ace *n.* 1. *Cards, dice, etc.* one, single point 2. *Inf.* adept, champion, dab hand (*Inf.*), expert, genius, master, star, virtuoso, winner, wizard (*Inf.*) ~*adj.* 3. *Inf.* brilliant, champion, excellent, expert, fine, great, masterly, outstanding, superb, virtuoso

ache *v.* 1. hurt, pain, pound, smart, suffer, throb, twinge 2. agonize, grieve, mourn, sorrow, suffer 3. covet, crave, desire, hanker, hunger, long, need, pine, yearn ~*n.* 4. hurt, pain, pang, pounding, smart, smarting, soreness, suffering, throb, throbbing 5. anguish, grief, mourning, sorrow, suffering 6. craving, desire, hankering, hunger, longing, need, pining, yearning

achieve accomplish, acquire, attain, bring about, carry out, complete, consummate, do, earn, effect, execute, finish, fulfil, gain, get, obtain, perform, procure, reach, realize, win

achievement 1. accomplishment, acquirement, attainment, completion, execution, fulfilment, performance, production, realization 2. accomplishment, act, deed, effort, exploit, feat, stroke

acid 1. acerbic, acidulous, acrid, biting, pungent, sharp, sour, tart, vinegarish, vinegary 2. acerbic, acid, biting, bitter, caustic, cutting, harsh, hurtful, mordant, pungent, sharp, stinging, trenchant, vitriolic

acidity 1. acerbity, acidulousness, acridity, acridness, bitterness, pungency, sharpness, sourness, tartness, vinegariness, vinegarishness 2. acerbity, acridity, acridness, bitterness, causticity, causticness, harshness, hurtfulness, mordancy, pungency, sharpness, trenchancy

acknowledge 1. accede, accept, acquiesce, admit, allow, concede, confess, declare, grant, own, profess, recognize, yield 2. address, greet, hail, notice, recognize, salute 3. answer, notice, react to, recognize, reply to, respond to, return

acknowledged accepted, accredited, admitted, answered, approved, conceded, confessed, declared, professed, recognized, returned

acknowledgment 1. acceptance, accession, acquiescence, admission, allowing, confession, declaration, profession, realization, yielding 2. addressing, greeting, hail, hailing, notice, recognition, salutation, salute 3. answer, appreciation, credit, gratitude, reaction, recognition, reply, response, return, thanks

acme apex, climax, crown, culmination, height, high point, optimum, peak, pinnacle, summit, top, vertex, zenith

acquaint advise, announce, apprise, disclose, divulge, enlighten, familiarize, inform, let (someone) know, notify, reveal, tell

acquaintance 1. associate, colleague, contact 2. association, awareness, cognizance, companionship, conversance, conversancy, experience, familiarity, fellowship, intimacy, knowledge, relationship, social contact, understanding

acquainted alive to, apprised of, *au fait,* aware of, cognizant of, conscious of, conversant with, experienced in, familiar with, informed of, in on, knowledgeable about, privy to, versed in

acquiesce accede, accept, agree, allow, approve, assent, bow to, comply, concur, conform, consent, give in, go along with, submit, yield

acquiescence acceptance, accession, agreement, approval, assent, compliance, concurrence, conformity, consent, giving in, obedience, submission, yielding

acquire achieve, amass, attain, buy, collect, earn, gain, gather, get, obtain, pick up, procure, realize, receive, secure, win

acquisition 1. buy, gain, possession, prize, property, purchase 2. achievement, acquirement, attainment, gaining, learning, obtainment, procurement, pursuit

acquisitive avaricious, avid, covetous, grabbing, grasping, greedy, predatory, rapacious

acquisitiveness avarice, avidity, avidness, covetousness, graspingness, greed, predatoriness, rapaciousness, rapacity

acquit 1. absolve, clear, deliver, discharge, exculpate, exonerate, free, fulfil, liberate, release, relieve, vindicate 2. discharge, pay, pay off, repay, satisfy, settle 3. bear, behave, comport, conduct, perform

acquittal absolution, clearance, deliverance, discharge, exculpation, exoneration, freeing, liberation, release, relief, vindication

acquittance acknowledgment, discharge, payment, receipt, release, settlement, settling

acrid 1. acid, astringent, biting, bitter, burning, caustic, harsh, irritating, pungent, sharp, stinging 2. acrimonious, biting, bitter, caustic, cutting, harsh, mordant, nasty,

sarcastic, sharp, trenchant, vitriol~
ic

acrimonious acerbic, astringent,
biting, bitter, caustic, censorious,
churlish, crabbed, cutting, iras~
cible, mordant, peevish, petulant,
pungent, rancorous, sarcastic, se~
vere, sharp, spiteful, splenetic, tart,
testy, trenchant

acrimony acerbity, asperity, as~
tringency, bitterness, churlishness,
harshness, ill will, irascibility,
mordancy, peevishness, rancour,
sarcasm, spleen, tartness, trench~
ancy, virulence

act n. 1. accomplishment, achieve~
ment, action, blow, deed, doing,
execution, exertion, exploit, feat,
move, operation, performance,
step, stroke, undertaking 2. bill,
decree, edict, enactment, law,
measure, ordinance, resolution,
statute 3. affectation, attitude,
counterfeit, dissimulation, fake,
feigning, front, performance, pose,
posture, pretence, sham, show,
stance 4. performance, routine,
show, sketch, turn ~v. 5. acquit,
bear, behave, carry, carry out,
comport, conduct, do, enact, ex~
ecute, exert, function, go about,
make, move, operate, perform, re~
act, serve, strike, take effect,
undertake, work 6. affect, assume,
counterfeit, dissimulate, feign,
imitate, perform, pose, posture,
pretend, put on, seem, sham 7. act
out, characterize, enact, imper~
sonate, mime, mimic, perform,
personate, personify, play, play or
take the part of, portray, represent

act for cover for, deputize for, fill in
for, function in place of, replace,
represent, serve, stand in for, sub~
stitute for, take the place of

acting adj. 1. interim, pro tem,
provisional, substitute, surrogate,
temporary ~n. 2. characterization,
dramatics, enacting, impersona~
tion, performance, performing,
playing, portrayal, portraying,
stagecraft, theatre 3. assuming,
counterfeiting, dissimulation,
feigning, imitating, imitation, im~
posture, play-acting, posing, pos~

turing, pretence, pretending, put~
ting on, seeming, shamming

action 1. accomplishment,
achievement, act, blow, deed, ex~
ercise, exertion, exploit, feat,
move, operation, performance,
step, stroke, undertaking 2. activ~
ity, energy, force, liveliness, spirit,
vigour, vim, vitality 3. activity, ef~
fect, effort, exertion, force, func~
tioning, influence, motion, move~
ment, operation, power, process,
work, working 4. battle, combat,
conflict, fighting, warfare 5. affray,
battle, clash, combat, contest, en~
counter, engagement, fight, fray,
skirmish, sortie 6. case, cause,
lawsuit, litigation, proceeding,
prosecution, suit

actions bearing, behaviour, com~
portment, conduct, demeanour,
deportment, manners, ways

activate actuate, animate, arouse,
energize, galvanize, impel, initiate,
mobilize, motivate, move, prompt,
propel, rouse, set going, set in mo~
tion, set off, start, stimulate, stir,
switch on, trigger (off), turn on

active 1. acting, astir, at work, do~
ing, effectual, functioning, in ac~
tion, in force, in operation, live,
moving, operative, running, stir~
ring, working 2. bustling, busy, en~
gaged, full, hard-working, involved,
occupied, on the go (Inf.), on the
move, strenuous 3. alert, animated,
diligent, energetic, industrious,
lively, nimble, on the go (Inf.),
quick, spirited, sprightly, spry, vi~
brant, vigorous, vital, vivacious 4.
activist, aggressive, ambitious, as~
sertive, committed, devoted, ener~
getic, engaged, enterprising, en~
thusiastic, forceful, forward, hard-
working, industrious, militant,
zealous

activity 1. action, activeness, ani~
mation, bustle, enterprise, exer~
cise, exertion, hurly-burly, hustle,
labour, life, liveliness, motion,
movement, stir, work 2. act, avo~
cation, deed, endeavour, enter~
prise, hobby, interest, job, labour,
occupation, pastime, project, pur~

suit, scheme, task, undertaking, venture, work

act on, act upon 1. act in accordance with, carry out, comply with, conform to, follow, heed, obey, yield to 2. affect, alter, change, influence, modify, sway, transform

actor 1. actress, dramatic artist, leading man, performer, playactor, player, Thespian, tragedian, trouper 2. agent, doer, executor, factor, functionary, operative, operator, participant, participator, performer, perpetrator, practitioner, worker

actress actor, dramatic artist, leading lady, performer, playactor, player, starlet, Thespian, tragedienne, trouper

actual 1. absolute, categorical, certain, concrete, corporeal, definite, factual, indisputable, indubitable, physical, positive, real, substantial, tangible, undeniable, unquestionable 2. authentic, confirmed, genuine, real, realistic, true, truthful, verified 3. current, existent, extant, live, living, present, present-day, prevailing

actually absolutely, as a matter of fact, de facto, essentially, indeed, in fact, in point of fact, in reality, in truth, literally, really, truly, veritably

actuate animate, arouse, cause, dispose, drive, excite, impel, incite, induce, influence, inspire, instigate, motivate, move, prompt, quicken, rouse, spur, stimulate, stir, urge

act up be naughty, carry on, cause trouble, give bother, give trouble, horse around (*Inf.*), malfunction, mess about, misbehave, play up (*Brit. inf.*)

act upon *see* ACT ON

acumen acuteness, astuteness, cleverness, discernment, ingenuity, insight, intelligence, judgment, keenness, penetration, perception, perspicacity, perspicuity, sagacity, sharpness, shrewdness, smartness, wisdom, wit

acute 1. astute, canny, clever, discerning, discriminating, incisive, ingenious, insightful, intuitive, keen, observant, penetrating, perceptive, perspicacious, piercing, sensitive, sharp, smart, subtle 2. critical, crucial, dangerous, decisive, essential, grave, important, serious, severe, sudden, urgent, vital 3. cutting, distressing, excruciating, exquisite, fierce, intense, overpowering, overwhelming, piercing, poignant, powerful, racking, severe, sharp, shooting, shrill, stabbing, sudden, violent 4. cuspate, needle-shaped, peaked, pointed, sharp, sharpened

acuteness 1. acuity, astuteness, canniness, cleverness, discernment, discrimination, ingenuity, insight, intuition, intuitiveness, keenness, perception, perceptiveness, perspicacity, sensitivity, sharpness, smartness, subtleness, subtlety, wit 2. criticality, criticalness, cruciality, danger, dangerousness, decisiveness, essentiality, gravity, importance, seriousness, severity, suddenness, urgency, vitalness 3. distressingness, exquisiteness, fierceness, intenseness, intensity, poignancy, powerfulness, severity, sharpness, shrillness, suddenness, violence 4. pointedness, sharpness

adamant 1. determined, firm, fixed, immovable, inexorable, inflexible, insistent, intransigent, obdurate, resolute, rigid, set, stiff, stubborn, unbending, uncompromising, unrelenting, unshakable, unyielding 2. adamantine, flinty, hard, impenetrable, indestructible, rock-hard, rocky, steely, stony, tough, unbreakable

adapt acclimatize, accommodate, adjust, alter, apply, change, comply, conform, familiarize, fashion, fit, habituate, harmonize, make, match, modify, prepare, qualify, remodel, shape, suit, tailor

adaptability adaptableness, adjustability, alterability, changeability, compliancy, convertibility, flexibility, malleability, modifiability, plasticity, pliability, pliancy, resilience, variability, versatility

adaptable adjustable, alterable, changeable, compliant, conformable, convertible, easy-going, flexible, malleable, modifiable, plastic, pliant, resilient, variable, versatile

adaptation 1. adjustment, alteration, change, conversion, modification, refitting, remodelling, reworking, shift, transformation, variation, version 2. acclimatization, accustomedness, familiarization, habituation, naturalization

add 1. adjoin, affix, amplify, annex, append, attach, augment, enlarge by, include, increase by, supplement 2. add up, compute, count up, reckon, sum up, total, tot up

addendum addition, adjunct, affix, appendage, appendix, attachment, augmentation, codicil, extension, extra, postscript, supplement

addict 1. dope-fiend (*Sl.*), fiend (*Inf.*), freak (*Sl.*), head (*Sl.*), junkie (*Sl.*), user (*Inf.*) 2. adherent, buff (*Sl.*), devotee, enthusiast, fan, follower, freak (*Sl.*), nut (*Sl.*)

addicted absorbed, accustomed, dedicated, dependent, devoted, disposed, fond, habituated, hooked (*Sl.*), inclined, obsessed, prone

addiction craving, dependence, enslavement, habit, obsession

addition 1. accession, adding, adjoining, affixing, amplification, annexation, attachment, augmentation, enlargement, extension, inclusion, increasing 2. addendum, additive, adjunct, affix, appendage, appendix, extension, extra, gain, increase, increment, supplement 3. adding up, computation, counting up, reckoning, summation, summing up, totalling, totting up 4. **in addition (to)** additionally, also, as well (as), besides, into the bargain, moreover, over and above, to boot, too, withal

additional added, affixed, appended, extra, fresh, further, increased, more, new, other, over-and-above, spare, supplementary

address *n.* 1. abode, domicile, dwelling, home, house, location, lodging, place, residence, situation, whereabouts 2. direction, inscription, superscription 3. discourse, disquisition, dissertation, harangue, lecture, oration, sermon, speech, talk 4. adroitness, art, dexterity, discretion, expertness, ingenuity, skilfulness, skill, tact ~*v.* 5. accost, apostrophize, approach, greet, hail, invoke, salute, speak to, talk to 6. discourse, give a speech, give a talk, harangue, lecture, orate, sermonize, speak, talk 7. **address (oneself) to** apply (oneself) to, attend to, concentrate on, devote (oneself) to, engage in, focus on, knuckle down to, look to, take care of, take up, turn to, undertake

adduce advance, allege, cite, designate, mention, name, offer, present, quote

add up 1. add, compute, count, count up, reckon, sum up, total, tot up 2. amount, come to, imply, indicate, mean, reveal, signify 3. be plausible, be reasonable, hold water, make sense, ring true, stand to reason

adept 1. *adj.* able, accomplished, adroit, dexterous, expert, masterful, masterly, practised, proficient, skilful, skilled, versed 2. *n.* dab hand (*Inf.*), expert, genius, master

adequacy capability, commensurateness, competence, fairness, requisiteness, satisfactoriness, sufficiency, suitability, tolerability

adequate capable, commensurate, competent, enough, fair, passable, requisite, satisfactory, sufficient, suitable, tolerable

adhere 1. attach, cement, cleave, cling, cohere, fasten, fix, glue, glue on, hold fast, paste, stick, stick fast, unite 2. abide by, be attached, be constant, be devoted, be faithful, be loyal, be true, cleave to, cling, follow, fulfil, heed, keep, keep to, maintain, mind, obey, observe, respect, stand by, support

adherent 1. *n.* admirer, advocate, devotee, disciple, fan, follower, hanger-on, partisan, sectary, supporter, upholder, votary 2. *adj.* adhering, adhesive, clinging, gluey, glutinous, gummy, holding, muci~

laginous, sticking, sticky, tacky, tenacious

adhesive 1. *adj.* adhering, attaching, clinging, cohesive, gluey, glutinous, gummy, holding, mucilaginous, sticking, sticky, tacky, tenacious 2. *n.* cement, glue, gum, mucilage, paste

adieu congé, farewell, goodbye, leave-taking, parting, valediction

adjacent abutting, adjoining, alongside, beside, bordering, close, contiguous, near, neighbouring, next door, touching

adjoin abut, add, affix, annex, append, approximate, attach, border, combine, communicate with, connect, couple, impinge, interconnect, join, link, neighbour, touch, unite, verge

adjoining abutting, adjacent, bordering, connecting, contiguous, impinging, interconnecting, joined, joining, near, neighbouring, next door, touching, verging

adjourn defer, delay, discontinue, interrupt, postpone, prorogue, put off, recess, stay, suspend

adjournment deferment, deferral, delay, discontinuation, interruption, postponement, prorogation, putting off, recess, stay, suspension

adjudge adjudicate, allot, apportion, assign, award, decide, declare, decree, determine, distribute, judge, order, pronounce

adjudicate adjudge, arbitrate, decide, determine, judge, referee, settle, umpire

adjudication adjudgment, arbitration, conclusion, decision, determination, finding, judgment, pronouncement, ruling, settlement, verdict

adjust acclimatize, accommodate, accustom, adapt, alter, arrange, compose, dispose, fit, fix, harmonize, make conform, measure, modify, order, reconcile, rectify, redress, regulate, remodel, set, settle, suit, tune (up)

adjustable adaptable, alterable, flexible, malleable, modifiable, mouldable, movable, tractable

adjustment 1. adaptation, alteration, arrangement, arranging, fitting, fixing, modification, ordering, rectification, redress, regulation, remodelling, setting, tuning 2. acclimatization, harmonization, orientation, reconciliation, settlement, settling in

ad-lib 1. *v.* extemporize, improvise, make up, speak extemporaneously, speak impromptu, speak off the cuff 2. *adj.* extemporaneous, extempore, extemporized, impromptu, improvised, made up, off-the-cuff (*Inf.*), unprepared, unrehearsed 3. *adv.* extemporaneously, extempore, impromptu, off the cuff, off the top of one's head (*Inf.*), without preparation, without rehearsal

administer 1. conduct, control, direct, govern, manage, oversee, run, superintend, supervise 2. apply, contribute, dispense, distribute, execute, give, impose, mete out, perform, provide

administration 1. administering, application, conduct, control, direction, dispensation, distribution, execution, governing, government, management, overseeing, performance, provision, running, superintendence, supervision 2. executive, governing body, government, management, ministry, term of office

administrative directorial, executive, governmental, gubernatorial, (*Chiefly U.S.*), management, managerial, organizational, regulatory, supervisory

admirable choice, commendable, estimable, excellent, exquisite, fine, laudable, meritorious, praiseworthy, rare, superior, valuable, wonderful, worthy

admiration adoration, affection, amazement, appreciation, approbation, approval, astonishment, delight, esteem, pleasure, praise, regard, respect, surprise, veneration, wonder, wonderment

admire 1. adore, appreciate, approve, esteem, idolize, look up to, praise, prize, respect, think highly of, value, venerate, worship 2. appreciate, delight in, marvel at, take pleasure in, wonder at

admirer 1. beau, boyfriend, lover, suitor, sweetheart, wooer 2. adherent, devotee, disciple, enthusiast, fan, follower, partisan, supporter, votary, worshipper

admissible acceptable, allowable, allowed, passable, permissible, permitted, tolerable, tolerated

admission 1. acceptance, access, admittance, entrance, entrée, entry, ingress, initiation, introduction 2. acknowledgment, admitting, affirmation, allowance, avowal, concession, confession, declaration, disclosure, divulgence, profession, revelation

admit 1. accept, allow, allow to enter, give access, initiate, introduce, let in, receive, take in 2. acknowledge, affirm, avow, concede, confess, declare, disclose, divulge, profess, reveal 3. agree, allow, grant, let, permit, recognize

admittance acceptance, access, admitting, allowing, entrance, entry, letting in, passage, reception

admonish advise, berate, caution, censure, check, chide, counsel, enjoin, exhort, forewarn, rebuke, reprimand, reprove, scold, tell off (*Inf.*), upbraid, warn

admonition advice, berating, caution, chiding, counsel, rebuke, remonstrance, reprimand, reproach, reproof, scolding, telling off (*Inf.*), upbraiding, warning

admonitory admonishing, advisory, cautionary, rebuking, reprimanding, reproachful, reproving, scolding, warning

adolescence 1. boyhood, girlhood, juvenescence, minority, teens, youth 2. boyishness, childishness, girlishness, immaturity, juvenility, puerility, youthfulness

adolescent 1. *adj.* boyish, girlish, growing, immature, juvenile, puerile, teenage, young, youthful 2. *n.* juvenile, minor, teenager, youngster, youth

adopt 1. accept, appropriate, approve, assume, choose, embrace, endorse, espouse, follow, maintain,

ratify, select, support, take on, take over, take up 2. foster, take in

adoption 1. acceptance, approbation, appropriation, approval, assumption, choice, embracing, endorsement, espousal, following, maintenance, ratification, selection, support, taking on, taking over, taking up 2. adopting, fosterage, fostering, taking in

adorable appealing, attractive, captivating, charming, darling, dear, delightful, fetching, lovable, pleasing, precious

adoration admiration, esteem, estimation, exaltation, glorification, honour, idolatry, idolization, love, reverence, veneration, worship, worshipping

adore admire, bow to, cherish, dote on, esteem, exalt, glorify, honour, idolize, love, revere, reverence, venerate, worship

adorn array, beautify, bedeck, deck, decorate, embellish, emblazon, enhance, enrich, garnish, grace, ornament, trim

adornment 1. accessory, decoration, embellishment, frill, frippery, ornament, trimming 2. beautification, decorating, decoration, embellishment, ornamentation, trimming

adrift 1. afloat, drifting, unanchored, unmoored 2. aimless, directionless, goalless, purposeless 3. amiss, astray, off course, wrong

adroit able, adept, apt, artful, clever, cunning, deft, dexterous, expert, ingenious, masterful, neat, nimble, proficient, quick-witted, skilful, skilled

adroitness ability, ableness, address, adeptness, aptness, artfulness, cleverness, cunning, deftness, dexterity, expertise, ingeniousness, ingenuity, masterfulness, mastery, nimbleness, proficiency, quick-wittedness, skilfulness, skill

adulation blandishment, bootlicking (*Inf.*), extravagant flattery, fawning, fulsome praise, servile flattery, sycophancy, worship

adulatory blandishing, bootlicking (*Inf.*), fawning, flattering, obsequious, praising, servile, slavish, sycophantic, worshipping

adult 1. *adj.* full grown, fully developed, fully grown, grown-up, mature, of age, ripe 2. *n.* grown *or* grown-up person (man *or* woman), grown-up, person of mature age

adulterate 1. *v.* attenuate, bastardize, contaminate, corrupt, debase, depreciate, deteriorate, devalue, make impure, mix with, thin, vitiate, water down, weaken 2. *adj.* adulterated, attenuated, bastardized, contaminated, corrupt, debased, depreciated, deteriorated, devalued, mixed, thinned, vitiated, watered down, weakened

adumbrate 1. delineate, indicate, outline, silhouette, sketch, suggest 2. augur, forecast, foreshadow, foretell, portend, predict, prefigure, presage, prognosticate, prophesy 3. bedim, darken, eclipse, obfuscate, obscure, overshadow

adumbration 1. delineation, draft, indication, outline, rough, silhouette, sketch, suggestion 2. augury, forecast, foreshadowing, foretelling, omen, portent, prediction, prefiguration, prefigurement, presage, prognostication, prophecy, sign 3. bedimming, cloud, darkening, darkness, eclipse, eclipsing, obfuscation, obscuring, overshadowing, shadow

advance *v.* 1. accelerate, bring forward, bring up, come forward, elevate, go ahead, go forward, go on, hasten, move onward, move up, press on, proceed, progress, promote, send forward, send up, speed, upgrade 2. benefit, further, grow, improve, multiply, prosper, thrive 3. adduce, allege, cite, offer, present, proffer, put forward, submit, suggest 4. increase (*price*), lend, pay beforehand, raise (*price*), supply on credit ~*n.* 5. advancement, development, forward movement, headway, onward movement, progress 6. advancement, amelioration, betterment, breakthrough, furtherance, gain, growth, improvement, progress,

promotion, step 7. appreciation, credit, deposit, down payment, increase (*in price*), loan, prepayment, retainer, rise (*in price*) 8. **advances** approach, approaches, moves, overtures, proposals, proposition ~*adj.* 9. beforehand, early, foremost, forward, in front, leading, prior 10. **in advance** ahead, beforehand, earlier, in the forefront, in the lead, in the van, previously

advanced ahead, avant-garde, extreme, foremost, forward, higher, late, leading, precocious, progressive

advancement 1. advance, forward movement, headway, onward movement, progress 2. advance, amelioration, betterment, gain, growth, improvement, preferment, progress, promotion, rise

advantage aid, ascendancy, asset, assistance, avail, benefit, blessing, boon, convenience, dominance, edge, gain, good, help, interest, lead, precedence, pre-eminence, profit, service, start, superiority, sway, upper hand, use, utility, welfare

advantageous 1. dominant, dominating, favourable, superior 2. beneficial, convenient, helpful, of service, profitable, useful, valuable, worthwhile

advent appearance, approach, arrival, coming, entrance, occurrence, onset, visitation

adventitious accidental, casual, chance, extraneous, foreign, fortuitous, incidental, nonessential, unexpected

adventure 1. *n.* chance, contingency, enterprise, experience, exploit, hazard, incident, occurrence, risk, speculation, undertaking, venture 2. *v.* dare, endanger, hazard, imperil, jeopardize, risk, venture

adventurer 1. daredevil, hero, heroine, knight-errant, soldier of fortune, swashbuckler, traveller, venturer, voyager, wanderer 2. charlatan, fortune-hunter, gambler, mercenary, opportunist, rogue, speculator

adventurous adventuresome, audacious, bold, dangerous, dare~ devil, daring, enterprising, fool~ hardy, hazardous, headstrong, in~ trepid, rash, reckless, risky, tem~ erarious (*Rare*), venturesome

adversary antagonist, competitor, contestant, enemy, foe, opponent, opposer, rival

adverse antagonistic, conflicting, contrary, detrimental, disadvanta~ geous, hostile, inexpedient, inimi~ cal, injurious, inopportune, nega~ tive, opposing, opposite, reluctant, repugnant, unfavourable, unfortu~ nate, unfriendly, unlucky, unpropi~ tious, unwilling

adversity affliction, bad luck, ca~ lamity, catastrophe, disaster, dis~ tress, hardship, hard times, ill~ fortune, ill-luck, misery, misfor~ tune, mishap, reverse, sorrow, suf~ fering, trial, trouble, woe, wretch~ edness

advertise advise, announce, ap~ prise, blazon, declare, display, flaunt, inform, make known, notify, plug (*Inf.*), praise, proclaim, pro~ mote, promulgate, publicize, pub~ lish, puff, push (*Inf.*), tout

advertisement ad (*Inf.*), advert (*Inf.*), announcement, bill, blurb, circular, commercial, display, no~ tice, placard, plug (*Inf.*), poster, promotion, publicity, puff

advice 1. admonition, caution, counsel, guidance, help, injunction, opinion, recommendation, sugges~ tion, view 2. information, instruc~ tion, intelligence, notice, notifica~ tion, warning, word

advisability appropriateness, apt~ ness, desirability, expediency, fit~ ness, judiciousness, profitability, propriety, prudence, seemliness, soundness, suitability, wisdom

advisable appropriate, apt, desir~ able, expedient, fit, fitting, judi~ cious, politic, profitable, proper, prudent, recommended, seemly, sensible, sound, suggested, suitable, wise

advise 1. admonish, caution, com~ mend, counsel, enjoin, recom~ mend, suggest, urge 2. acquaint, apprise, inform, make known, no~ tify, report, tell, warn

adviser aide, authority, coach, confidant, consultant, counsel, counsellor, guide, helper, lawyer, mentor, right-hand man, solicitor, teacher, tutor

advisory advising, consultative, counselling, helping, recommend~ ing

advocate v. 1. advise, argue for, campaign for, champion, counte~ nance, defend, encourage, favour, hold a brief for (*Inf.*), justify, plead for, press for, promote, propose, recommend, speak for, support, uphold, urge ~n. 2. apologist, apostle, backer, campaigner, champion, counsellor, defender, pleader, promoter, proponent, proposer, speaker, spokesman, supporter, upholder 3. *Law.* attor~ ney, barrister, counsel, lawyer, so~ licitor

aegis advocacy, auspices, backing, favour, guardianship, patronage, protection, shelter, sponsorship, support, wing

affability amiability, amicability, approachability, benevolence, be~ nignity, civility, congeniality, cor~ diality, courtesy, friendliness, ge~ niality, good humour, good nature, graciousness, kindliness, mildness, obligingness, pleasantness, socia~ bility, urbanity, warmth

affable amiable, amicable, ap~ proachable, benevolent, benign, civil, congenial, cordial, courteous, friendly, genial, good-humoured, good-natured, gracious, kindly, mild, obliging, pleasant, sociable, urbane, warm

affair 1. activity, business, circum~ stance, concern, episode, event, happening, incident, interest, mat~ ter, occurrence, proceeding, proj~ ect, question, subject, transaction, undertaking 2. amour, intrigue, liaison, relationship, romance

affect 1. act on, alter, bear upon, change, concern, impinge upon, influence, interest, involve, modify, prevail over, regard, relate to, sway, transform **2.** disturb, impress, move, overcome, perturb, stir, touch, upset **3.** adopt, aspire to, assume, contrive, counterfeit, feign, imitate, pretend, put on, sham, simulate

affectation act, affectedness, appearance, artificiality, assumed manners, façade, fakery, false display, insincerity, mannerism, pose, pretence, pretension, pretentiousness, sham, show, simulation, unnatural imitation

affected 1. afflicted, altered, changed, concerned, damaged, deeply moved, distressed, hurt, impaired, impressed, influenced, injured, melted, stimulated, stirred, touched, troubled, upset **2.** artificial, assumed, conceited, contrived, counterfeit, feigned, insincere, la-di-da (*Inf.*), mannered, mincing, phoney (*Inf.*), pompous, precious, pretended, pretentious, put-on, sham, simulated, spurious, stiff, studied, unnatural

affecting moving, pathetic, piteous, pitiable, pitiful, poignant, sad, saddening, touching

affection amity, attachment, care, desire, feeling, fondness, friendliness, good will, inclination, kindness, liking, love, passion, propensity, tenderness, warmth

affectionate attached, caring, devoted, doting, fond, friendly, kind, loving, tender, warm, warmhearted

affiliate ally, amalgamate, annex, associate, band together, combine, confederate, connect, incorporate, join, unite

affiliation alliance, amalgamation, association, banding together, coalition, combination, confederation, connection, incorporation, joining, league, merging, relationship, union

affinity 1. alliance, analogy, closeness, compatibility, connection, correspondence, kinship, likeness, relation, relationship, resemblance, similarity **2.** attraction, fondness, inclination, leaning, liking, partiality, rapport, sympathy

affirm assert, asseverate, attest, aver, avouch, avow, certify, confirm, declare, maintain, pronounce, ratify, state, swear, testify

affirmation assertion, asseveration, attestation, averment, avouchment, avowal, certification, confirmation, declaration, oath, pronouncement, ratification, statement, testimony

affirmative agreeing, approving, assenting, concurring, confirming, consenting, corroborative, favourable, positive

afflict beset, burden, distress, grieve, harass, hurt, oppress, pain, plague, rack, smite, torment, trouble, try, wound

affliction adversity, calamity, cross, curse, depression, disease, distress, grief, hardship, misery, misfortune, ordeal, pain, plague, scourge, sickness, sorrow, suffering, torment, trial, tribulation, trouble, woe, wretchedness

affluence abundance, exuberance, fortune, opulence, plenty, profusion, prosperity, riches, wealth

affluent 1. loaded (*Sl.*), moneyed, opulent, prosperous, rich, wealthy, well-heeled (*Inf.*), well-off, well-to-do **2.** abundant, copious, exuberant, plenteous, plentiful

afford 1. bear, spare, stand, sustain **2.** bestow, furnish, give, grant, impart, offer, produce, provide, render, supply, yield

affront 1. *v.* abuse, anger, annoy, displease, insult, offend, outrage, pique, provoke, slight, vex **2.** *n.* abuse, indignity, injury, insult, offence, outrage, provocation, slap in the face (*Inf.*), slight, slur, vexation, wrong

aflame 1. ablaze, afire, alight, blazing, burning, fiery, flaming, ignited, lighted, lit, on fire **2.** afire, aroused, excited, fervent, impassioned, passionate, stimulated **3.** aglow, flushed, inflamed, red, ruddy

afoot about, abroad, afloat, astir, brewing, circulating, current, going on, hatching, in preparation, in progress, in the wind, on the go (*Inf.*), operating, up (*Inf.*)

afraid 1. alarmed, anxious, apprehensive, cowardly, faint-hearted, fearful, frightened, intimidated, nervous, reluctant, scared, suspicious, timid, timorous 2. regretful, sorry, unhappy

afresh again, anew, newly, once again, once more, over again

after afterwards, behind, below, following, later, subsequently, succeeding, thereafter

aftermath after-effects, consequences, effects, end, outcome, results, upshot

again 1. afresh, anew, another time, once more 2. also, besides, furthermore, in addition, moreover, on the contrary, on the other hand

against 1. counter, hostile to, in contrast to, in defiance of, in opposition to, in the face of, opposed to, opposing, resisting, versus 2. abutting, close up to, facing, fronting, in contact with, on, opposite to, touching, upon 3. in anticipation of, in expectation of, in preparation for, in provision for

age *n.* 1. date, day(s), duration, epoch, era, generation, lifetime, period, span, time 2. advancing years, decline (*of life*), majority, maturity, old age, senescence, senility, seniority ~*v.* 3. decline, deteriorate, grow old, mature, mellow, ripen

aged age-old, ancient, antiquated, antique, elderly, getting on, grey, hoary, old, senescent, superannuated

agency 1. action, activity, auspices, efficiency, force, influence, instrumentality, intercession, intervention, means, mechanism, mediation, medium, operation, power, work 2. bureau, business, department, office, organization

agenda calendar, diary, list, plan, programme, schedule, timetable

agent 1. advocate, deputy, emissary, envoy, factor, go-between, negotiator, rep (*Inf.*), representative, substitute, surrogate 2. actor,

author, doer, executor, mover, officer, operative, operator, performer, worker 3. agency, cause, force, instrument, means, power, vehicle

aggravate 1. exacerbate, exaggerate, heighten, increase, inflame, intensify, magnify, make worse, worsen 2. *Inf.* annoy, exasperate, get on one's nerves (*Inf.*), irk, irritate, needle (*Inf.*), nettle, pester, provoke, tease, vex

aggravation 1. exacerbation, exaggeration, heightening, increase, inflaming, intensification, magnification, worsening 2. *Inf.* annoyance, exasperation, irksomeness, irritation, provocation, teasing, vexation

aggregate 1. *v.* accumulate, amass, assemble, collect, combine, heap, mix, pile 2. *n.* accumulation, agglomeration, amount, assemblage, body, bulk, collection, combination, heap, lump, mass, mixture, pile, sum, total, whole 3. *adj.* accumulated, added, assembled, collected, collective, combined, composite, corporate, cumulative, mixed, total

aggression 1. assault, attack, encroachment, injury, invasion, offence, offensive, onslaught, raid 2. aggressiveness, antagonism, belligerence, destructiveness, hostility, pugnacity

aggressive 1. belligerent, destructive, hostile, offensive, pugnacious, quarrelsome 2. assertive, bold, dynamic, energetic, enterprising, forceful, militant, pushing, pushy (*Inf.*), vigorous, zealous

aggressor assailant, assaulter, attacker, invader

aggrieved afflicted, distressed, disturbed, harmed, hurt, ill-used, injured, peeved (*Inf.*), saddened, unhappy, woeful, wronged

aghast afraid, amazed, appalled, astonished, astounded, awestruck, confounded, frightened, horrified, horror-struck, shocked, startled, stunned, thunder-struck

agile active, acute, alert, brisk, clever, limber, lithe, lively, nimble, prompt, quick, quick-witted, sharp, sprightly, spry, supple, swift

agility activity, acuteness, alertness, briskness, cleverness, litheness, liveliness, nimbleness, promptitude, promptness, quickness, quick-wittedness, sharpness, sprightliness, spryness, suppleness, swiftness

agitate 1. beat, churn, convulse, disturb, rock, rouse, shake, stir, toss 2. alarm, arouse, confuse, disconcert, disquiet, distract, disturb, excite, ferment, fluster, incite, inflame, perturb, rouse, ruffle, stimulate, trouble, upset, work up, worry 3. argue, debate, discuss, dispute, examine, ventilate

agitation 1. churning, convulsion, disturbance, rocking, shake, shaking, stir, stirring, tossing, turbulence 2. alarm, arousal, clamour, commotion, confusion, discomposure, disquiet, distraction, disturbance, excitement, ferment, flurry, fluster, incitement, lather (*Inf.*), outcry, stimulation, trouble, tumult, turmoil, upset, worry 3. argument, controversy, debate, discussion, disputation, dispute, ventilation

agitator agent provocateur, demagogue, firebrand, inciter, instigator, rabble-rouser, revolutionary, troublemaker

agog avid, curious, eager, enthralled, enthusiastic, excited, expectant, impatient, in suspense, keen

agony affliction, anguish, distress, misery, pain, pangs, suffering, throes, torment, torture, woe

agree 1. accede, acquiesce, admit, allow, assent, be of the same mind, comply, concede, concur, consent, engage, grant, permit, see eye to eye, settle 2. accord, answer, chime, coincide, conform, correspond, fit, get on (together), harmonize, match, square, suit, tally

agreeable 1. acceptable, delightful, enjoyable, gratifying, pleasant, pleasing, pleasurable, satisfying, to one's liking, to one's taste 2. appropriate, befitting, compatible, consistent, fitting, in keeping, proper, suitable 3. acquiescent, amenable, approving, complying, concurring, consenting, in accord, responsive, sympathetic, well-disposed, willing

agreement 1. accord, accordance, affinity, analogy, compatibility, compliance, concert, concord, concurrence, conformity, congruity, consistency, correspondence, harmony, similarity, suitableness, union 2. arrangement, bargain, compact, contract, covenant, deal (*Inf.*), pact, settlement, treaty, understanding

agriculture agronomics, agronomy, cultivation, culture, farming, husbandry, tillage

aground ashore, beached, foundered, grounded, high and dry, on the rocks, stranded, stuck

ahead along, at an advantage, at the head, before, forwards, in advance, in front, in the foreground, in the lead, in the vanguard, leading, on, onwards, to the fore, winning

aid v. 1. abet, assist, befriend, encourage, favour, help, promote, relieve, second, serve, subsidize, succour, support, sustain ~n. 2. assistance, benefit, encouragement, favour, help, relief, service, succour, support 3. abettor, adjutant, aide, aide-de-camp, assistant, helper, second, supporter

aim 1. *v.* aspire, attempt, design, direct, draw a bead (on), endeavour, intend, level, mean, plan, point, propose, purpose, resolve, seek, set one's sights on, sight, strive, take aim (at), train, try, want, wish 2. *n.* ambition, aspiration, course, design, desire, direction, end, goal, intent, intention, mark, object, objective, plan, purpose, scheme, target, wish

aimless chance, directionless, erratic, frivolous, goalless, haphazard, pointless, purposeless, random, stray, undirected, unguided, unpredictable, vagrant, wayward

air n. 1. atmosphere, heavens, sky 2. blast, breath, breeze, draught, puff,

waft, whiff, wind, zephyr 3. ambi~
ence, appearance, atmosphere,
aura, bearing, character, demean~
our, effect, feeling, flavour, im~
pression, look, manner, mood,
quality, style, tone 4. circulation,
display, dissemination, exposure,
expression, publicity, utterance,
vent, ventilation 5. aria, lay, melo~
dy, song, tune ~v. 6. aerate, ex~
pose, freshen, ventilate 7. circu~
late, communicate, declare, dis~
close, display, disseminate, divulge,
exhibit, expose, express, give vent
to, make known, make public, pro~
claim, publicize, reveal, tell, utter,
ventilate, voice

airily 1. animatedly, blithely,
breezily, buoyantly, gaily, happily,
high-spiritedly, jauntily, light-
heartedly 2. daintily, delicately,
ethereally, gracefully, lightly

airiness 1. breeziness, draughti~
ness, freshness, gustiness, light~
ness, openness, windiness 2. ethe~
reality, immateriality, incorpo~
reality, insubstantiality, lightness,
weightlessness 3. animation,
blitheness, breeziness, buoyancy,
gaiety, happiness, high spirits,
jauntiness, light-heartedness,
lightness of heart

airing 1. aeration, drying, freshen~
ing, ventilation 2. excursion, jaunt,
outing, promenade, stroll, walk 3.
circulation, display, dissemination,
exposure, expression, publicity,
utterance, vent, ventilation

airless breathless, close, heavy,
muggy, oppressive, stale, stifling,
stuffy, suffocating, sultry, unventi~
lated

airs affectation, affectedness, arro~
gance, haughtiness, hauteur, pom~
posity, pretensions, supercilious~
ness, swank (Inf.)

airy 1. blowy, breezy, draughty,
fresh, gusty, light, lofty, open, spa~
cious, uncluttered, well-ventilated,
windy 2. aerial, delicate, ethereal,
fanciful, flimsy, illusory, imagi~
nary, immaterial, incorporeal, in~
substantial, light, vaporous, vision~
ary, weightless, wispy 3. animated,
blithe, buoyant, cheerful, cheery,

debonair, frolicsome, gay, grace~
ful, happy, high-spirited, jaunty,
light, light-hearted, lively, merry,
nonchalant, sprightly

aisle corridor, gangway, lane, pas~
sage, passageway, path

alarm v. 1. daunt, dismay, distress,
frighten, give (someone) a turn
(Inf.), panic, put the wind up
(someone) (Inf.), scare, startle,
terrify, unnerve 2. alert, arouse,
signal, warn ~n. 3. anxiety, appre~
hension, consternation, dismay,
distress, fear, fright, nervousness,
panic, scare, terror, trepidation,
unease, uneasiness 4. alarm-bell,
alert, bell, danger signal, distress
signal, siren, tocsin, warning 5. Ar~
chaic call to arms

alarming daunting, dismaying, dis~
tressing, disturbing, dreadful,
frightening, scaring, shocking,
startling, terrifying, unnerving

alcoholic 1. adj. brewed, distilled,
fermented, hard, inebriant, inebri~
ating, intoxicating, spirituous,
strong, vinous 2. n. bibber, boozer
(Inf.), dipsomaniac, drunk, drunk~
ard, hard drinker, inebriate, soak
(Inf.), sot, sponge (Inf.), tippler,
toper, tosspot (Inf.), wino (Inf.)

alcove bay, bower, compartment,
corner, cubbyhole, cubicle, niche,
nook, recess

alert 1. adj. active, agile, attentive,
brisk, careful, circumspect, heed~
ful, lively, nimble, observant, on
guard, on one's toes, on the ball
(Inf.), on the lookout, on the watch,
perceptive, quick, ready, spirited,
sprightly, vigilant, wary, watchful,
wide-awake 2. n. alarm, signal, si~
ren, warning 3. v. alarm, forewarn,
inform, notify, signal, warn

alertness activeness, agility, at~
tentiveness, briskness, carefulness,
circumspection, heedfulness, live~
liness, nimbleness, perceptiveness,
promptitude, quickness, readiness,
spiritedness, sprightliness, vigi~
lance, wariness, watchfulness

alias 1. adv. also called, also known
as, otherwise, otherwise known as
2. n. assumed name, *nom de*

guerre, nom de plume, pen name, pseudonym, stage name

alibi defence, excuse, explanation, justification, plea, pretext, reason

alien 1. *adj.* adverse, conflicting, contrary, estranged, exotic, foreign, inappropriate, incompatible, incongruous, not native, not naturalized, opposed, outlandish, remote, repugnant, separated, strange, unfamiliar 2. *n.* foreigner, newcomer, outsider, stranger

alienate 1. break off, disaffect, divert, divorce, estrange, make unfriendly, separate, set against, turn away, withdraw 2. *Law* abalienate, convey, transfer

alienation 1. breaking off, disaffection, diversion, divorce, estrangement, indifference, remoteness, rupture, separation, setting against, turning away, withdrawal 2. *Law* abalienation, conveyance, transfer

alight¹ *v.* come down, come to rest, descend, disembark, dismount, get down, get off, land, light, perch, settle, touch down

alight² *adj.* 1. ablaze, aflame, blazing, burning, fiery, flaming, flaring, ignited, lighted, lit, on fire 2. bright, brilliant, illuminated, lit up, shining

align 1. arrange in line, coordinate, even, even up, line up, make parallel, order, range, regulate, straighten 2. affiliate, agree, ally, associate, cooperate, join, side, sympathize

alignment 1. adjustment, arrangement, coordination, evening, evening up, line, lining up, order, ranging, regulating, sequence, straightening up 2. affiliation, agreement, alliance, association, cooperation, sympathy, union

alike 1. *adj.* akin, analogous, corresponding, duplicate, equal, equivalent, even, identical, parallel, resembling, similar, the same, uniform 2. *adv.* analogously, correspondingly, equally, evenly, identically, similarly, uniformly

alive 1. animate, breathing, having life, in the land of the living (*Inf.*), living, subsisting 2. active, existent,

existing, extant, functioning, in existence, in force, operative, unquenched 3. active, alert, animated, awake, brisk, cheerful, eager, energetic, full of life, lively, quick, spirited, sprightly, spry, vigorous, vital, vivacious, zestful

alive to alert to, awake to, aware of, cognizant of, eager for, sensible of, sensitive to, susceptible to

all 1. *adj.* every bit of, the complete, the entire, the sum of, the totality of, the total of, the whole of 2. each, each and every, every, every one of, every single 3. complete, entire, full, greatest, perfect, total, utter ~*n.* 4. aggregate, entirety, everything, sum, sum total, total, total amount, totality, utmost, whole, whole amount ~*adv.* 5. altogether, completely, entirely, fully, totally, utterly, wholly

allegation accusation, affirmation, assertion, asseveration, averment, avowal, charge, claim, declaration, deposition, plea, profession, statement

allege advance, affirm, assert, asseverate, aver, avow, charge, claim, declare, depose, maintain, plead, profess, put forward, state

alleged 1. affirmed, asserted, averred, declared, described, designated, stated 2. doubtful, dubious, ostensible, professed, purported, so-called, supposed, suspect, suspicious

allegorical emblematic, figurative, parabolic, symbolic, symbolizing

allegory apologue, emblem, fable, myth, parable, story, symbol, symbolism, tale

allergic 1. affected by, hypersensitive, sensitive, sensitized, susceptible 2. *Inf.* antipathetic, averse, disinclined, hostile, loath, opposed

allergy 1. antipathy, hypersensitivity, sensitivity, susceptibility 2. *Inf.* antipathy, aversion, disinclination, dislike, hostility, loathing, opposition

alley alleyway, backstreet, lane, passage, passageway, pathway, walk

alliance affiliation, affinity, agreement, association, coalition, combination, compact, concordat, confederacy, confederation, connection, federation, league, marriage, pact, partnership, treaty, union

allied affiliated, amalgamated, associated, bound, combined, confederate, connected, hand in glove (*Inf.*), in cahoots (*U.S. inf.*), in league, joined, joint, kindred, leagued, linked, married, related, unified, united, wed

allocate allot, apportion, appropriate, assign, budget, designate, earmark, mete, set aside, share out

allocation allotment, allowance, apportionment, appropriation, grant, lot, measure, portion, quota, ration, share, stint

allot allocate, apportion, appropriate, assign, budget, designate, earmark, mete, set aside, share out

allotment 1. allocation, allowance, apportionment, appropriation, grant, lot, measure, portion, quota, ration, share, stint 2. kitchen garden, patch, plot, tract

all-out complete, determined, exhaustive, full, full-scale, maximum, optimum, resolute, supreme, thorough, thoroughgoing, total, undivided, unlimited, unremitting, unrestrained, unstinted, utmost

allow 1. acknowledge, acquiesce, admit, concede, confess, grant, own 2. approve, authorize, bear, brook, endure, give leave, let, permit, put up with (*Inf.*), sanction, stand, suffer, tolerate 3. allocate, allot, assign, deduct, give, grant, provide, remit, spare

allowable acceptable, admissible, all right, appropriate, approved, permissible, sanctionable, sufferable, suitable, tolerable

allowance 1. allocation, allotment, amount, annuity, apportionment, grant, lot, measure, pension, portion, quota, ration, remittance, share, stint, stipend, subsidy 2. admission, concession, sanction, sufferance, toleration 3. concession, deduction, discount, rebate, reduction

allow for arrange for, consider,

foresee, keep in mind, make allowances for, make concessions for, make provision for, plan for, provide for, set (something) aside for, take into account, take into consideration

alloy *n.* 1. admixture, amalgam, blend, combination, composite, compound, hybrid, mixture ~*v.* 2. admix, amalgamate, blend, combine, compound, fuse, mix 3. adulterate, debase, devalue, diminish, impair

all right *adj.* 1. acceptable, adequate, average, fair, O.K. (*Inf.*), passable, satisfactory, standard, unobjectionable 2. hale, healthy, safe, sound, unharmed, unimpaired, uninjured, well, whole ~*adv.* 3. acceptably, adequately, O.K. (*Inf.*), passably, satisfactorily, unobjectionably, well enough

allure 1. *v.* attract, beguile, cajole, captivate, charm, coax, decoy, enchant, entice, inveigle, lead on, lure, persuade, seduce, tempt, win over 2. *n.* appeal, attraction, charm, enchantment, enticement, glamour, lure, persuasion, seductiveness, temptation

allusion casual remark, glance, hint, implication, indirect reference, innuendo, insinuation, intimation, mention, suggestion

ally 1. *n.* abettor, accessory, accomplice, associate, coadjutor, collaborator, colleague, confederate, co-worker, friend, helper, partner 2. *v.* affiliate, associate, band together, collaborate, combine, confederate, connect, join, join forces, league, marry, unify, unite

almighty 1. absolute, all-powerful, invincible, omnipotent, supreme, unlimited 2. *Inf.* awful, desperate, enormous, excessive, great, intense, loud, severe, terrible

almost about, all but, approximately, as good as, close to, just about, nearly, not far from, not quite, on the brink of, practically, virtually, well-nigh

alone 1. abandoned, apart, by itself, by oneself, deserted, desolate, de~

tached, forlorn, forsaken, isolated, lonely, lonesome, only, separate, single, single-handed, sole, solitary, unaccompanied, unaided, unassisted, unattended, uncombined, unconnected, unescorted 2. incomparable, matchless, peerless, singular, unequalled, unique, unparalleled, unsurpassed

aloof 1. chilly, cold, cool, detached, distant, forbidding, formal, haughty, indifferent, remote, reserved, standoffish, supercilious, unapproachable, unfriendly, uninterested, unresponsive, unsociable, unsympathetic 2. above, apart, at a distance, away, distanced, distant

aloud 1. audibly, clearly, distinctly, intelligibly, out loud, plainly 2. clamorously, loudly, noisily, vociferously

already as of now, at present, before now, by now, by that time, by then, by this time, even now, heretofore, just now, previously

also additionally, along with, and, as well, as well as, besides, further, furthermore, in addition, including, into the bargain, moreover, on top of that, plus, to boot, too

alter adapt, adjust, amend, change, convert, diversify, metamorphose, modify, recast, reform, remodel, reshape, revise, shift, transform, transmute, turn, vary

alteration adaptation, adjustment, amendment, change, conversion, difference, diversification, metamorphosis, modification, reformation, remodelling, reshaping, revision, shift, transformation, transmutation, variance, variation

alternate v. 1. act reciprocally, alter, change, follow in turn, follow one another, interchange, intersperse, oscillate, rotate, substitute, take turns, vary ~adj. 2. alternating, every other, every second, interchanging, rotating 3. alternative, another, different, second, substitute

alternative 1. n. choice, option, other (of two), preference, recourse, selection, substitute 2. adj. alternate, another, different, other, second, substitute

alternatively as an alternative, by way of alternative, if not, instead, on the other hand, or, otherwise

although albeit, despite the fact that, even if, even supposing, even though, notwithstanding, though, while

altitude elevation, height, loftiness, peak, summit

altogether 1. absolutely, completely, fully, perfectly, quite, thoroughly, totally, utterly, wholly 2. all in all, all things considered, as a whole, collectively, generally, in general, in toto, on the whole 3. all told, everything included, in all, in sum, in toto, taken together

always consistently, constantly, continually, eternally, ever, everlastingly, evermore, every time, forever, in perpetuum, invariably, perpetually, repeatedly, unceasingly, without exception

amalgamate alloy, ally, blend, coalesce, combine, commingle, compound, fuse, incorporate, integrate, intermix, merge, mingle, unite

amalgamation admixture, alliance, alloy, amalgam, amalgamating, blend, coalition, combination, commingling, composite, compound, fusion, incorporation, integration, joining, merger, mingling, mixing, mixture, union

amass accumulate, aggregate, assemble, collect, compile, garner, gather, heap up, hoard, pile up, rake up, scrape together

amateur dabbler, dilettante, layman, nonprofessional

amateurish amateur, bungling, clumsy, crude, inexpert, unaccomplished, unprofessional, unskilful

amaze alarm, astonish, astound, bewilder, bowl over (Inf.), confound, daze, dumbfound, electrify, flabbergast, shock, stagger, startle, stun, stupefy, surprise

amazement admiration, astonishment, bewilderment, confusion, marvel, perplexity, shock, stupefaction, surprise, wonder

ambassador agent, consul, deputy, diplomat, emissary, envoy, legate, minister, plenipotentiary, representative

ambiguity doubt, doubtfulness, dubiety, dubiousness, enigma, equivocacy, equivocality, equivocation, inconclusiveness, indefiniteness, indeterminateness, obscurity, puzzle, tergiversation, uncertainty, unclearness, vagueness

ambiguous cryptic, doubtful, dubious, enigmatic, enigmatical, equivocal, inconclusive, indefinite, indeterminate, obscure, puzzling, uncertain, unclear, vague

ambition 1. aspiration, avidity, desire, drive, eagerness, enterprise, get-up-and-go (*Inf.*), hankering, longing, striving, yearning, zeal 2. aim, aspiration, desire, dream, end, goal, hope, intent, objective, purpose, wish

ambitious 1. aspiring, avid, desirous, driving, eager, enterprising, hopeful, intent, purposeful, striving, zealous 2. arduous, bold, challenging, demanding, difficult, elaborate, energetic, exacting, formidable, grandiose, hard, impressive, industrious, pretentious, severe, strenuous

amble dawdle, meander, mosey (*Inf.*), ramble, saunter, stroll, walk, wander

ambush 1. *n.* ambuscade, concealment, cover, hiding, hiding place, lying in wait, retreat, shelter, trap, waylaying 2. *v.* ambuscade, bushwhack (*U.S.*), ensnare, surprise, trap, waylay

amenable 1. able to be influenced, acquiescent, agreeable, open, persuadable, responsive, susceptible, tractable 2. accountable, answerable, chargeable, liable, responsible

amend alter, ameliorate, better, change, correct, enhance, fix, improve, mend, modify, rectify, reform, remedy, repair, revise

amendment 1. alteration, amelioration, betterment, change, correction, enhancement, improvement, mending, modification, rec-

tification, reform, remedy, repair, revision 2. addendum, addition, adjunct, alteration, attachment, clarification

amends apology, atonement, compensation, expiation, indemnity, recompense, redress, reparation, requital, restitution, restoration, satisfaction

amenity 1. advantage, comfort, convenience, facility, service 2. affability, agreeableness, amiability, complaisance, courtesy, mildness, pleasantness (*of situation*), politeness, refinement, suavity

amiable affable, agreeable, attractive, benign, charming, cheerful, delightful, engaging, friendly, genial, good-humoured, good-natured, kind, kindly, lovable, obliging, pleasant, pleasing, sociable, sweet-tempered, winning, winsome

amicable amiable, brotherly, civil, cordial, courteous, fraternal, friendly, good-humoured, harmonious, kind, kindly, neighbourly, peaceable, peaceful, polite, sociable

amid amidst, among, amongst, in the middle of, in the midst of, in the thick of, surrounded by

amiss 1. *adj.* awry, confused, defective, erroneous, fallacious, false, faulty, improper, inaccurate, inappropriate, incorrect, mistaken, out of order, unsuitable, untoward, wrong 2. *adv.* as an insult, as offensive, erroneously, faultily, improperly, inappropriately, incorrectly, mistakenly, out of turn, unsuitably, wrongly

ammunition armaments, cartridges, explosives, materiel, munitions, powder, rounds, shells, shot, shot and shell

amnesty absolution, condonation, dispensation, forgiveness, general pardon, immunity, oblivion, remission (*of penalty*), reprieve

amok *see* AMUCK

among, amongst 1. amid, in association with, in the middle of, in the midst of, in the thick of, midst, surrounded by, together with, with 2. between, to each of 3. in the class of, in the company of, in the group of, in the number of, out of **4.** by all of, by the joint action of, by the whole of, mutually, with one another

amorous affectionate, amatory, ardent, attached, doting, enamoured, erotic, fond, impassioned, in love, lovesick, loving, lustful, passionate, tender

amount 1. bulk, expanse, extent, lot, magnitude, mass, measure, number, quantity, supply, volume **2.** addition, aggregate, entirety, extent, lot, sum, sum total, total, whole **3.** full effect, full value, import, result, significance

amount to add up to, aggregate, become, come to, develop into, equal, grow, mean, purport, total

ample abounding, abundant, big, bountiful, broad, capacious, commodious, copious, enough and to spare, expansive, extensive, full, generous, great, large, lavish, liberal, plenteous, plentiful, plenty, profuse, rich, roomy, spacious, substantial, unrestricted, voluminous, wide

amplify augment, boost, deepen, develop, dilate, elaborate, enlarge, expand, expatiate, extend, flesh out, go into detail, heighten, increase, intensify, lengthen, magnify, raise, round out, strengthen, stretch, supplement, widen

amply abundantly, bountifully, capaciously, completely, copiously, extensively, fully, generously, greatly, lavishly, liberally, plenteously, plentifully, profusely, richly, substantially, thoroughly, unstintingly, well

amputate curtail, cut off, lop, remove, separate, sever, truncate

amuck, amok berserk, destructively, ferociously, frenziedly, in a frenzy, insanely, madly, maniacally, murderously, savagely, uncontrollably, violently, wildly

amuse beguile, charm, cheer, delight, divert, enliven, entertain, gladden, gratify, interest, occupy, please, recreate, regale, tickle (*Inf.*)

amusement 1. beguilement, cheer, delight, diversion, enjoyment, entertainment, fun, gladdening, gratification, hilarity, interest, laughter, merriment, mirth, pleasing, pleasure, recreation, regalement, sport **2.** distraction, diversion, entertainment, game, hobby, joke, lark, pastime, prank, recreation, sport

amusing charming, cheerful, cheering, comical, delightful, diverting, droll, enjoyable, entertaining, facetious, funny, gladdening, gratifying, humorous, interesting, jocular, laughable, lively, merry, pleasant, pleasing, witty

anaemic ashen, bloodless, characterless, colourless, dull, enervated, feeble, frail, infirm, pale, pallid, sickly, wan, weak

anaesthetic 1. *n.* analgesic, anodyne, narcotic, opiate, painkiller, sedative, soporific, stupefacient, stupefactive **2.** *adj.* analgesic, anodyne, deadening, dulling, narcotic, numbing, opiate, pain-killing, sedative, sleep-inducing, soporific, stupefacient, stupefactive

analogy agreement, comparison, correlation, correspondence, equivalence, homology, likeness, parallel, relation, resemblance, similarity, similitude

analyse 1. assay, estimate, evaluate, examine, interpret, investigate, judge, test **2.** anatomize, break down, consider, dissect, dissolve, divide, resolve, separate, study, think through

analysis 1. anatomization, anatomy, assay, breakdown, dissection, dissolution, division, enquiry, examination, investigation, resolution, scrutiny, separation, sifting, test **2.** estimation, evaluation, finding, interpretation, judgment, opinion, reasoning, study

analytic, analytical detailed, diagnostic, discrete, dissecting, explanatory, expository, inquiring, inquisitive, interpretative, interpretive, investigative, logical, organized, problem-solving, ques-

tioning, rational, searching, studi~
ous, systematic, testing

anarchist insurgent, nihilist, rebel,
revolutionary, terrorist

anarchy chaos, confusion, disorder,
disorganization, lawlessness, mis~
government, misrule, rebellion,
revolution, riot

anathema 1. ban, condemnation,
curse, damnation, denunciation,
excommunication, execration, im~
precation, malediction, proscrip~
tion, taboo 2. abomination, bane,
bête noire, bugbear, enemy, pariah

anathematize abominate, ban,
condemn, curse, damn, denounce,
excommunicate, execrate, impre~
cate, proscribe

anatomize analyse, break down,
dissect, dissolve, divide, examine,
resolve, scrutinize, separate, study

anatomy 1. analysis, dismember~
ment, dissection, division, enquiry,
examination, investigation, study
2. build, composition, frame,
framework, make-up, structure

ancestor forebear, forefather,
forerunner, precursor, predeces~
sor, progenitor

ancestry ancestors, antecedents,
blood, derivation, descent, extrac~
tion, family, forebears, forefathers,
genealogy, house, line, lineage,
origin, parentage, pedigree, pro~
genitors, race, stock

ancient aged, age-old, antediluvian,
antiquated, antique, archaic, by~
gone, early, hoary, obsolete, old,
olden, old-fashioned, outmoded,
out-of-date, primeval, primordial,
superannuated, timeworn

ancillary accessory, additional,
auxiliary, contributory, extra, sec~
ondary, subordinate, subsidiary,
supplementary

and along with, also, as well as,
furthermore, in addition to, in~
cluding, moreover, plus, together
with

anecdote reminiscence, short sto~
ry, sketch, story, tale, yarn

anew afresh, again, another time,
from scratch, from the beginning,
once again, once more, over again

angel 1. archangel, cherub, divine

messenger, guardian spirit, seraph,
spiritual being 2. *Inf.* beauty, dar~
ling, dear, dream, gem, ideal, jew~
el, paragon, saint, treasure

angelic 1. celestial, cherubic, ethe~
real, heavenly, seraphic 2. ador~
able, beatific, beautiful, entranc~
ing, innocent, lovely, pure, saintly,
virtuous

anger 1. *n.* annoyance, antagonism,
choler, displeasure, exasperation,
fury, ill humour, ill temper, indig~
nation, ire, irritability, irritation,
outrage, passion, pique, rage, re~
sentment, spleen, temper, vexa~
tion, wrath 2. *v.* affront, annoy, an~
tagonize, displease, enrage, exas~
perate, excite, fret, gall, incense,
infuriate, irritate, madden, nettle,
offend, outrage, pique, provoke,
rile, vex

angle *n.* 1. bend, corner, crook,
crotch, cusp, edge, elbow, inter~
section, knee, nook, point 2. ap~
proach, aspect, outlook, perspec~
tive, point of view, position, side,
slant, standpoint, viewpoint ~*v.* 3.
cast, fish

angry annoyed, antagonized, chol~
eric, displeased, enraged, exasper~
ated, furious, heated, hot, hot under
the collar (*Inf.*), ill-tempered, in~
censed, indignant, infuriated, iras~
cible, irate, ireful, irritable, irritat~
ed, mad (*Inf.*), nettled, outraged,
passionate, piqued, provoked, rag~
ing, resentful, riled, splenetic, tu~
multuous, uptight (*Sl.*), wrathful

anguish agony, distress, grief,
heartache, heartbreak, misery,
pain, pang, sorrow, suffering,
throe, torment, torture, woe

angular bony, gaunt, lank, lanky,
lean, rangy, rawboned, scrawny,
skinny, spare

animal *n.* 1. beast, brute, creature
2. *Applied to a person* barbarian,
beast, brute, monster, savage, wild
man ~*adj.* 3. bestial, bodily, brut~
ish, carnal, fleshly, gross, physical,
sensual

animate *v.* 1. activate, embolden,
encourage, energize, enliven, ex~
cite, fire, gladden, impel, incite,
inspire, inspirit, instigate, invigor~

ate, kindle, move, quicken, revive, rouse, spark, spur, stimulate, stir, urge, vitalize, vivify ~*adj.* 2. alive, breathing, live, living, moving 3. gay, lively, spirited, vivacious

animated active, airy, ardent, brisk, buoyant, dynamic, ebullient, elated, energetic, enthusiastic, ex~ cited, fervent, gay, lively, passion~ ate, quick, spirited, sprightly, vi~ brant, vigorous, vital, vivacious, vivid, zealous, zestful

animation action, activity, airiness, ardour, briskness, buoyancy, dy~ namism, ebullience, elation, ener~ gy, enthusiasm, excitement, ex~ hilaration, fervour, gaiety, high spirits, life, liveliness, passion, pep, sparkle, spirit, sprightliness, verve, vibrancy, vigour, vitality, vivacity, zeal, zest, zing (*Inf.*)

animosity acrimony, animus, an~ tagonism, antipathy, bad blood, bitterness, enmity, hate, hatred, hostility, ill will, malevolence, malice, malignity, rancour, re~ sentment, virulence

annals accounts, archives, chroni~ cles, history, journals, memorials, records, registers

annex 1. add, adjoin, affix, append, attach, connect, fasten, join, sub~ join, tack, unite 2. acquire, appro~ priate, arrogate, conquer, expro~ priate, occupy, seize, take over

annexe 1. ell, extension, sup~ plementary building, wing 2. ad~ dendum, addition, adjunct, affix, appendix, attachment, supplement

annihilate abolish, destroy, eradi~ cate, erase, exterminate, extin~ guish, extirpate, liquidate, nullify, obliterate, root out, wipe out

annihilation abolition, destruction, eradication, erasure, extermina~ tion, extinction, extinguishing, ex~ tirpation, liquidation, nullification, obliteration, rooting out, wiping out

annotate commentate, comment on, elucidate, explain, footnote, gloss, illustrate, interpret, make observations, note

annotation comment, commen~ tary, elucidation, exegesis, expla~ nation, explication, footnote, gloss, illustration, interpretation, note, observation

announce 1. advertise, broadcast, declare, disclose, divulge, give out, intimate, make known, proclaim, promulgate, propound, publish, re~ port, reveal, tell 2. augur, betoken, foretell, harbinger, herald, por~ tend, presage, signal, signify

announcement advertisement, broadcast, bulletin, communiqué, declaration, disclosure, divulgence, intimation, proclamation, promul~ gation, publication, report, revela~ tion, statement

announcer anchor man, broad~ caster, commentator, master of ceremonies, newscaster, news reader, reporter

annoy anger, badger, bedevil, bore, bother, bug (*Inf.*), displease, dis~ turb, exasperate, gall, get (*Inf.*), harass, harry, incommode, irk, ir~ ritate, madden, molest, needle (*Inf.*), nettle, peeve, pester, plague, provoke, rile, ruffle, tease, trouble, vex

annoyance 1. aggravation, anger, bedevilment, bother, displeasure, disturbance, exasperation, harass~ ment, irritation, nuisance, provo~ cation, trouble, vexation 2. bind (*Inf.*), bore, bother, nuisance, pain (*Inf.*), pain in the neck (*Inf.*), pest, plague, tease

annoying aggravating, bedevilling, boring, bothersome, displeasing, disturbing, exasperating, galling, harassing, irksome, irritating, maddening, peeving (*Inf.*), pro~ voking, teasing, troublesome, vexatious

annual once a year, yearlong, yearly

annually by the year, each year, every year, once a year, per an~ num, per year, year after year, yearly

annul abolish, abrogate, cancel, countermand, declare *or* render null and void, invalidate, negate, nullify, recall, repeal, rescind, re~ tract, reverse, revoke, void

annulment abolition, abrogation,

cancellation, countermanding, in~
validation, negation, nullification,
recall, repeal, rescindment, re~
scission, retraction, reversal,
revocation, voiding

anodyne 1. *n*. analgesic, narcotic,
painkiller, painreliever, palliative
2. *adj*. analgesic, deadening, dull~
ing, narcotic, numbing, pain~
killing, pain-relieving, palliative

anoint 1. daub, embrocate, grease,
oil, rub, smear, spread over 2.
anele (*Archaic*), bless, consecrate,
hallow, sanctify

anomalous aberrant, abnormal,
atypical, bizarre, deviating, eccen~
tric, exceptional, incongruous, in~
consistent, irregular, odd, peculiar,
rare, unusual

anomaly aberration, abnormality,
departure, deviation, eccentricity,
exception, incongruity, inconsist~
ency, irregularity, oddity, peculi~
arity, rarity

anonymous 1. incognito, innomi~
nate, nameless, unacknowledged,
unattested, unauthenticated, un~
credited, unidentified, unknown,
unnamed, unsigned 2. character~
less, nondescript, unexceptional

answer *n.* 1. acknowledgment,
comeback, defence, explanation,
plea, reaction, refutation, rejoin~
der, reply, report, resolution, re~
sponse, retort, return, riposte, so~
lution, vindication ~*v.* 2. acknowl~
edge, explain, react, refute, rejoin,
reply, resolve, respond, retort, re~
turn, solve 3. conform, correlate,
correspond, do, fill, fit, fulfil,
measure up, meet, pass, qualify,
satisfy, serve, suffice, suit, work

answerable 1. accountable, ame~
nable, chargeable, liable, respon~
sible, subject, to blame 2. explain~
able, refutable, resolvable, solv~
able

answer back argue, be cheeky, be
impertinent, cheek (*Inf.*), contra~
dict, disagree, dispute, rebut, re~
tort, talk back

answer for 1. be accountable for,
be answerable for, be chargeable
for, be liable for, be responsible
for, be to blame for, take the rap

for (*Sl.*) 2. atone for, make amends
for, pay for, suffer for

answer to 1. be accountable to, be
answerable to, be responsible to,
be ruled by, obey 2. agree, con~
firm, correspond, fit, match, meet

antagonism antipathy, competi~
tion, conflict, contention, discord,
dissension, friction, hostility, oppo~
sition, rivalry

antagonist adversary, competitor,
contender, enemy, foe, opponent,
opposer, rival

antagonistic adverse, antipathet~
ic, at odds, at variance, averse,
conflicting, contentious, hostile, ill-
disposed, incompatible, in dispute,
inimical, opposed, unfriendly

antagonize 1. alienate, anger, an~
noy, disaffect, estrange, insult, ir~
ritate, offend, repel, rub (someone)
up the wrong way (*Inf.*) 2. contend
with, counteract, neutralize, op~
pose, struggle with, work against

antecedent anterior, earlier, fore~
going, former, preceding, precur~
sory, preliminary, previous, prior

antecedents 1. ancestors, ances~
try, blood, descent, extraction,
family, forebears, forefathers, ge~
nealogy, line, progenitors, stock 2.
background, history, past

antediluvian 1. prehistoric, pri~
meval, primitive, primordial 2. an~
cient, antiquated, antique, archaic,
obsolete, old-fashioned, out-of-date,
out of the ark (*Inf.*), passé

anteroom antechamber, foyer,
lobby, outer room, reception room,
vestibule, waiting room

anthem 1. canticle, chant, chorale,
hymn, psalm 2. paean, song of
praise

anthology analects, choice, collec~
tion, compendium, compilation,
digest, garland, miscellany, selec~
tion, treasury

anticipate 1. apprehend, await,
count upon, expect, forecast, fore~
see, foretell, hope for, look for,
look forward to, predict, prepare
for 2. antedate, beat (someone) to
it (*Inf.*), forestall, intercept, pre~
vent

anticipation apprehension, await~

ing, expectancy, expectation, fore~ sight, foretaste, forethought, hope, preconception, premonition, pres~ cience, presentiment

anticlimax bathos, comedown (*Inf.*), disappointment, letdown

antics buffoonery, capers, clown~ ing, escapades, foolishness, frolics, larks, mischief, monkey tricks, playfulness, pranks, silliness, sky~ larking, stunts, tomfoolery, tricks

antidote antitoxin, antivenin, cor~ rective, counteragent, counter~ measure, cure, neutralizer, pre~ ventive, remedy, specific

antipathy abhorrence, animosity, animus, antagonism, aversion, bad blood, contrariety, disgust, dislike, distaste, enmity, hatred, hostility, ill will, incompatibility, loathing, opposition, rancour, repugnance, repulsion

antiquated 1. antediluvian, an~ tique, archaic, dated, obsolete, old-fashioned, old hat, outmoded, out-of-date, outworn, passé 2. aged, ancient, elderly, hoary, old, super~ annuated

antique *adj.* 1. aged, ancient, el~ derly, old, superannuated 2. ar~ chaic, obsolete, old-fashioned, out~ dated 3. antiquarian, classic, olden, vintage ~*n.* 4. bygone, heirloom, object of virtu, relic

antiquity 1. age, ancientness, el~ derliness, old age, oldness 2. an~ cient times, distant past, olden days, time immemorial 3. antique, relic, ruin

antiseptic 1. *adj.* aseptic, clean, germ-free, hygienic, pure, sanitary, sterile, uncontaminated, unpollut~ ed 2. *n.* bactericide, disinfectant, germicide, purifier

antisocial 1. alienated, asocial, misanthropic, reserved, retiring, uncommunicative, unfriendly, un~ sociable, withdrawn 2. antagonis~ tic, belligerent, disorderly, dis~ ruptive, hostile, menacing, rebel~ lious

anxiety angst, apprehension, care, concern, disquiet, disquietude, dis~ tress, foreboding, fretfulness, mis~ giving, nervousness, restlessness, solicitude, suspense, tension, un~ ease, uneasiness, watchfulness, worry

anxious 1. apprehensive, careful, concerned, disquieted, distressed, disturbed, fearful, fretful, in sus~ pense, nervous, overwrought, rest~ less, solicitous, taut, tense, trou~ bled, uneasy, unquiet (*Chiefly lit~ erary*), watchful, worried 2. ardent, avid, desirous, eager, expectant, impatient, intent, itching, keen, yearning

apart 1. afar, alone, aloof, aside, away, by itself, by oneself, cut off, distant, distinct, divorced, exclud~ ed, independent, independently, isolated, piecemeal, separate, separated, separately, singly, to it~ self, to oneself, to one side 2. asun~ der, in bits, in pieces, into parts, to bits, to pieces 3. **apart from** aside from, besides, but, except for, ex~ cluding, not counting, other than, save

apartment accommodation, chambers, compartment, flat (*U.S.*), living quarters, penthouse, quarters, room, rooms, suite

apathetic cold, cool, emotionless, impassive, indifferent, insensible, listless, passive, phlegmatic, slug~ gish, stoic, stoical, torpid, uncon~ cerned, unemotional, unfeeling, uninterested, unmoved, unrespon~ sive

apathy coldness, coolness, emo~ tionlessness, impassibility, impas~ sivity, indifference, insensibility, listlessness, passiveness, passivity, phlegm, sluggishness, stoicism, torpor, unconcern, unfeelingness, uninterestedness, unresponsive~ ness

ape affect, caricature, copy, counterfeit, echo, imitate, mimic, mirror, mock, parody, parrot

aperture breach, chink, cleft, crack, eye, eyelet, fissure, gap, hole, interstice, opening, orifice, passage, perforation, rent, rift, slit, slot, space

aphorism adage, apothegm, axiom, dictum, gnome, maxim, precept, proverb, saw, saying

apiece each, for each, from each, individually, respectively, separately, severally, to each

aplomb balance, calmness, composure, confidence, coolness, equanimity, level-headedness, poise, sang-froid, self-assurance, self-confidence, self-possession, stability

apocryphal doubtful, dubious, equivocal, fictitious, legendary, mythical, questionable, spurious, unauthenticated, uncanonical, unsubstantiated, unverified

apologetic contrite, penitent, regretful, remorseful, rueful, sorry

apologize ask forgiveness, beg pardon, express regret, say one is sorry, say sorry

apology 1. acknowledgment, confession, defence, excuse, explanation, extenuation, justification, plea, vindication 2. caricature, excuse, imitation, makeshift, mockery, stopgap, substitute, travesty

apostle 1. evangelist, herald, messenger, missionary, preacher, proselytizer 2. advocate, champion, pioneer, propagandist, propagator, proponent

apotheosis deification, elevation, exaltation, glorification, idealization, idolization

appal alarm, astound, daunt, dishearten, dismay, frighten, harrow, horrify, intimidate, outrage, petrify, scare, shock, terrify, unnerve

appalling alarming, astounding, awful, daunting, dire, disheartening, dismaying, dreadful, fearful, frightening, frightful, ghastly, grim, harrowing, hideous, horrible, horrid, horrific, horrifying, intimidating, petrifying, scaring, shocking, terrible, terrifying, unnerving

apparatus 1. appliance, contraption (*Inf.*), device, equipment, gear, implements, machine, machinery, materials, means, mechanism, outfit, tackle, tools, utensils 2. bureaucracy, chain of command, hierarchy, network, organization, setup, structure, system

apparent 1. clear, conspicuous, discernible, distinct, evident, indubitable, manifest, marked, obvious, open, overt, patent, plain, understandable, unmistakable, visible 2. ostensible, outward, seeming, specious, superficial

apparently it appears that, it seems that, on the face of it, ostensibly, outwardly, seemingly, speciously, superficially

apparition 1. appearance, manifestation, materialization, presence, vision, visitation 2. chimera, ghost, phantom, revenant, shade (*Literary*), spectre, spirit, spook (*Inf.*), visitant, wraith

appeal *n.* 1. adjuration, application, entreaty, invocation, petition, plea, prayer, request, solicitation, suit, supplication 2. allure, attraction, attractiveness, beauty, charm, engagingness, fascination, interestingness, pleasingness ~*v.* 3. adjure, apply, ask, beg, beseech, call, call upon, entreat, implore, petition, plead, pray, refer, request, resort to, solicit, sue, supplicate 4. allure, attract, charm, engage, entice, fascinate, interest, invite, please, tempt

appear 1. arise, arrive, attend, be present, come forth, come into sight, come into view, come out, come to light, crop up (*Inf.*), develop, emerge, issue, loom, materialize, occur, show (*Sl.*), show up (*Inf.*), surface, turn out, turn up 2. look (like *or* as if), occur, seem, strike one as 3. be apparent, be clear, be evident, be manifest, be obvious, be patent, be plain 4. become available, be created, be developed, be invented, be published, come into being, come into existence, come out 5. act, be exhibited, come on, come onstage, enter, perform, play, play a part, take part

appearance 1. advent, appearing, arrival, coming, debut, emergence, introduction, presence, showing up (*Inf.*), turning up 2. air, aspect, bearing, demeanour, expression, face, figure, form, image, look, looks, manner, mien (*Literary*) 3.

front, guise, illusion, image, impression, outward show, pretence, semblance

appease allay, alleviate, assuage, blunt, calm, compose, conciliate, diminish, ease, lessen, lull, mitigate, mollify, pacify, placate, quell, quench, quiet, satisfy, soften, soothe, subdue, tranquillize

appeasement 1. acceding, accommodation, compromise, concession, conciliation, placation, propitiation 2. abatement, alleviation, assuagement, blunting, easing, lessening, lulling, mitigation, mollification, pacification, quelling, quenching, quieting, satisfaction, softening, solace, soothing, tranquillization

append add, adjoin, affix, annex, attach, fasten, hang, join, subjoin, tack on, tag on

appendage 1. accessory, addendum, addition, adjunct, affix, ancillary, annexe, appendix, appurtenance, attachment, auxiliary, supplement 2. *Zool.* extremity, limb, member, projection, protuberance

appendix addendum, addition, adjunct, appendage, codicil, postscript, supplement

appertain *Usually with* to apply, bear upon, be characteristic of, be connected, belong, be part of, be pertinent, be proper, be relevant, have to do with, inhere in, pertain, refer, relate, touch upon

appetite appetence, appetency, craving, demand, desire, hankering, hunger, inclination, liking, longing, passion, proclivity, propensity, relish, stomach, taste, willingness, yearning, zeal, zest

appetizer 1. antipasto, canapé, cocktail, hors d'oeuvre, titbit 2. apéritif, cocktail 3. foretaste, sample, taste

appetizing appealing, delicious, inviting, mouthwatering, palatable, savoury, scrumptious (*Inf.*), succulent, tasty, tempting

applaud acclaim, approve, cheer, clap, commend, compliment, encourage, eulogize, extol, laud, magnify (*Archaic*), praise

applause acclaim, acclamation, accolade, approbation, approval, cheering, cheers, commendation, eulogizing, hand, hand-clapping, laudation, ovation, plaudit, praise

appliance apparatus, device, gadget, implement, instrument, machine, mechanism, tool

applicable apposite, appropriate, apropos, apt, befitting, fit, fitting, germane, pertinent, relevant, suitable, suited, to the point, to the purpose, useful

applicant aspirant, candidate, claimant, inquirer, petitioner, postulant, suitor, suppliant

application 1. appositeness, exercise, function, germaneness, pertinence, practice, purpose, relevance, use, value 2. appeal, claim, inquiry, petition, request, requisition, solicitation, suit 3. assiduity, attention, attentiveness, commitment, dedication, diligence, effort, hard work, industry, perseverance, study 4. balm, cream, dressing, emollient, lotion, ointment, poultice, salve, unguent

apply 1. administer, assign, bring into play, bring to bear, carry out, employ, engage, execute, exercise, implement, practise, put to use, use, utilize 2. appertain, be applicable, be appropriate, bear upon, be fitting, be relevant, fit, pertain, refer, relate, suit 3. anoint, bring into contact with, cover with, lay on, paint, place, put on, smear, spread on, touch to 4. appeal, claim, inquire, make application, petition, put in, request, requisition, solicit, sue 5. address, be assiduous, be diligent, be industrious, buckle down (*Inf.*), commit, concentrate, dedicate, devote, direct, give, make an effort, pay attention, persevere, study, try, work hard

appoint 1. allot, arrange, assign, choose, decide, designate, determine, establish, fix, set, settle 2. assign, choose, commission, delegate, elect, install, name, nominate, select 3. command, decree, direct, enjoin, ordain 4. equip, fit out, furnish, provide, supply

appointed 1. allotted, arranged, assigned, chosen, decided, designated, determined, established, fixed, set, settled **2.** assigned, chosen, commissioned, delegated, elected, installed, named, nominated, selected **3.** commanded, decreed, directed, enjoined, ordained **4.** equipped, fitted out, furnished, provided, supplied

appointment 1. arrangement, assignation, consultation, date, engagement, interview, meeting, rendezvous, session, tryst (*Archaic*) **2.** allotment, assignment, choice, choosing, commissioning, delegation, designation, election, installation, naming, nomination, selection **3.** assignment, berth (*Inf.*), job, office, place, position, post, situation, station **4.** appointee, candidate, delegate, nominee, office-holder, representative **5.** *Usually plural* accoutrements, appurtenances, equipage, fittings, fixtures, furnishings, gear, outfit, paraphernalia, trappings

apportion allocate, allot, assign, deal, dispense, distribute, divide, dole out, measure out, mete out, parcel out, ration out, share

apportionment allocation, allotment, assignment, dealing out, dispensing, distribution, division, doling out, measuring out, meting out, parcelling out, rationing out, sharing

apposite appertaining, applicable, appropriate, apropos, apt, befitting, germane, pertinent, proper, relevant, suitable, suited, to the point, to the purpose

appraisal 1. assessment, estimate, estimation, evaluation, judgment, opinion, sizing up (*Inf.*) **2.** assay, pricing, rating, reckoning, survey, valuation

appreciable ascertainable, clear-cut, considerable, definite, detectable, discernible, distinguishable, evident, marked, material, measurable, noticeable, obvious, perceivable, perceptible, pronounced, recognizable, significant, substantial, visible

appreciate 1. be appreciative, be grateful for, be indebted, be obliged, be thankful for, give thanks for **2.** acknowledge, be alive to, be aware (cognizant, conscious) of, comprehend, estimate, know, perceive, realize, recognize, sympathize with, take account of, understand **3.** admire, cherish, enjoy, esteem, like, prize, rate highly, regard, relish, respect, savour, treasure, value **4.** enhance, gain, grow, improve, increase, inflate, raise the value of, rise

appreciation 1. acknowledgment, gratefulness, gratitude, indebtedness, obligation, thankfulness, thanks **2.** admiration, appraisal, assessment, awareness, cognizance, comprehension, enjoyment, esteem, estimation, knowledge, liking, perception, realization, recognition, regard, relish, respect, responsiveness, sensitivity, sympathy, understanding, valuation **3.** enhancement, gain, growth, improvement, increase, inflation, rise **4.** acclamation, criticism, critique, notice, praise, review, tribute

appreciative 1. beholden, grateful, indebted, obliged, thankful **2.** admiring, aware, cognizant, conscious, enthusiastic, in the know (*Inf.*), knowledgeable, mindful, perceptive, pleased, regardful, respectful, responsive, sensitive, supportive, sympathetic, understanding

apprehend 1. arrest, bust (*Inf.*), capture, catch, collar (*Inf.*), nab (*Inf.*), nick (*Sl.*), pinch (*Inf.*), run in (*Sl.*), seize, take, take prisoner **2.** appreciate, believe, comprehend, conceive, grasp, imagine, know, perceive, realize, recognize, think, understand **3.** be afraid of, dread, fear

apprehension 1. alarm, anxiety, apprehensiveness, concern, disquiet, doubt, dread, fear, foreboding, misgiving, mistrust, premonition, suspicion, unease, uneasiness, worry **2.** arrest, capture, catching, seizure, taking **3.** awareness, comprehension, grasp, intellect, intelligence, ken, knowledge, perception, understanding 4. belief, concept, conception, conjecture, idea, impression, notion, opinion, sentiment, thought, view

apprehensive afraid, alarmed, anxious, concerned, disquieted, doubtful, fearful, foreboding, mistrustful, suspicious, uneasy, worried

apprentice beginner, learner, neophyte, novice, probationer, pupil, student, tyro

approach v. 1. advance, catch up, come close, come near, come to, draw near, gain on, meet, move towards, near, push forward, reach 2. appeal to, apply to, broach the matter with, make advances to, make a proposal to, make overtures to, sound out 3. begin, begin work on, commence, embark on, enter upon, make a start, set about, undertake 4. approximate, be comparable to, be like, come close to, come near to, compare with, resemble ~n. 5. access, advance, advent, arrival, avenue, coming, drawing near, entrance, nearing, passage, road, way 6. approximation, likeness, semblance 7. *Often plural* advance, appeal, application, invitation, offer, overture, proposal, proposition 8. attitude, course, manner, means, method, mode, modus operandi, procedure, style, technique, way

approachable 1. accessible, attainable, come-at-able (*Inf.*), get-at-able (*Inf.*), reachable 2. affable, congenial, cordial, friendly, open, sociable

appropriate adj. 1. adapted, applicable, apposite, appurtenant, apropos, apt, becoming, befitting, belonging, congruous, correct, felicitous, fit, fitting, germane, meet (*Archaic*), opportune, pertinent, proper, relevant, right, seemly, suitable, to the point, to the purpose, well-suited, well-timed ~v. 2. allocate, allot, apportion, assign, devote, earmark, set apart 3. annex, arrogate, assume, commandeer, confiscate, expropriate, im-

pound, pre-empt, seize, take, take over, take possession of, usurp 4. embezzle, filch, misappropriate, pilfer, pocket, steal

appropriateness applicability, appositeness, aptness, becomingness, congruousness, correctness, felicitousness, felicity, fitness, fittingness, germaneness, opportuneness, pertinence, properness, relevance, rightness, seemliness, suitability, timeliness, well-suitedness

appropriation 1. allocation, allotment, apportionment, assignment, earmarking, setting apart 2. annexation, arrogation, assumption, commandeering, confiscation, expropriation, impoundment, preemption, seizure, takeover, taking, usurpation

approval 1. acquiescence, agreement, assent, authorization, blessing, compliance, concurrence, confirmation, consent, countenance, endorsement, imprimatur, leave, licence, mandate, O.K. (*Inf.*), permission, ratification, recommendation, sanction, the go-ahead (*Inf.*), the green light (*Inf.*), validation 2. acclaim, admiration, applause, appreciation, approbation, commendation, esteem, favour, good opinion, liking, praise, regard, respect

approve 1. acclaim, admire, applaud, appreciate, be pleased with, commend, esteem, favour, have a good opinion of, like, praise, regard highly, respect, think highly of 2. accede to, accept, advocate, agree to, allow, assent to, authorize, bless, concur in, confirm, consent to, countenance, endorse, give the go-ahead (*Inf.*), give the green light (*Inf.*), go along with, mandate, O.K. (*Inf.*), pass, permit, ratify, recommend, sanction, second, subscribe to, uphold, validate

approximate adj. 1. almost accurate, almost exact, close, near 2. estimated, inexact, loose, rough 3. analogous, close, comparable, like, near, relative, similar, verging on 4. adjacent, bordering, close together, contiguous, near, nearby, neighbouring ~*v.* 5. approach, border on, come close, come near, reach, resemble, touch, verge on

approximately about, almost, around, circa (*used with dates*), close to, generally, in the neigh~ bourhood of, in the region of, in the vicinity of, just about, loosely, more or less, nearly, not far off, relatively, roughly

approximation 1. conjecture, esti~ mate, estimation, guess, guess~ work, rough calculation, rough idea 2. approach, correspondence, likeness, resemblance, semblance

apron pinafore, pinny (*Inf.*)

apropos *adj.* 1. applicable, appo~ site, appropriate, apt, befitting, be~ longing, correct, fit, fitting, ger~ mane, meet (*Archaic*), opportune, pertinent, proper, related, rel~ evant, right, seemly, suitable, to the point, to the purpose ~*adv.* 2. appropriately, aptly, opportunely, pertinently, relevantly, suitably, timely, to the point, to the purpose 3. by the bye, by the way, inciden~ tally, in passing, parenthetically, while on the subject

apropos of *prep.* in respect of, on the subject of, re, regarding, re~ specting, with reference to, with regard to, with respect to

apt 1. applicable, apposite, appro~ priate, apropos, befitting, correct, fit, fitting, germane, meet (*Archa~ ic*), pertinent, proper, relevant, seemly, suitable, timely, to the point, to the purpose 2. disposed, given, inclined, liable, likely, of a mind, prone, ready 3. astute, bright, clever, expert, gifted, in~ genious, intelligent, prompt, quick, sharp, skilful, smart, talented, teachable

aptitude 1. bent, disposition, incli~ nation, leaning, predilection, pro~ clivity, proneness, propensity, ten~ dency 2. ability, aptness, capabil~ ity, capacity, cleverness, faculty, flair, gift, giftedness, intelligence, knack, proficiency, quickness, tal~ ent 3. applicability, appositeness,

appropriateness, fitness, rel~ evance, suitability, suitableness

aptness 1. applicability, apposite~ ness, appropriateness, becoming~ ness, congruousness, correctness, felicitousness, felicity, fitness, fit~ tingness, germaneness, oppor~ tuneness, pertinence, properness, relevance, rightness, seemliness, suitability, timeliness, well~ suitedness 2. aptitude, bent, dispo~ sition, inclination, leaning, liability, likelihood, likeliness, predilection, proclivity, proneness, propensity, readiness, tendency 3. ability, ca~ pability, capacity, cleverness, fac~ ulty, fitness, flair, gift, giftedness, intelligence, knack, proficiency, quickness, suitability, talent

arable cultivable, farmable, fecund, fertile, fruitful, ploughable, pro~ ductive, tillable

arbiter 1. adjudicator, arbitrator, judge, referee, umpire 2. authority, controller, dictator, expert, gover~ nor, lord, master, pundit, ruler

arbitrariness 1. capriciousness, fancifulness, inconsistency, ran~ domness, subjectivity, unreason~ ableness, whimsicality, wilfulness 2. absoluteness, despotism, dicta~ torialness, dogmatism, domineer~ ingness, high-handedness, imperi~ ousness, magisterialness, over~ bearingness, peremptoriness, summariness, tyrannicalness, tyr~ annousness, tyranny, uncon~ trolledness, unlimitedness, unre~ strainedness

arbitrary 1. capricious, chance, discretionary, erratic, fanciful, in~ consistent, optional, personal, ran~ dom, subjective, unreasonable, whimsical, wilful 2. absolute, auto~ cratic, despotic, dictatorial, dog~ matic, domineering, high-handed, imperious, magisterial, overbear~ ing, peremptory, summary, tyran~ nical, tyrannous, uncontrolled, un~ limited, unrestrained

arbitrate adjudge, adjudicate, de~ cide, determine, judge, pass judg~ ment, referee, settle, sit in judg~ ment, umpire

arbitration adjudication, arbitra~

ment, decision, determination, judgment, settlement

arbitrator adjudicator, arbiter, judge, referee, umpire

arc arch, bend, bow, crescent, curve, half-moon

arch[1] *n.* 1. archway, curve, dome, span, vault 2. arc, bend, bow, curvature, curve, semicircle ~*v.* 3. arc, bend, bow, bridge, curve, embow, span

arch[2] 1. accomplished, chief, consummate, expert, finished, first, foremost, greatest, highest, leading, main, major, master, preeminent, primary, principal, top 2. artful, frolicsome, knowing, mischievous, pert, playful, roguish, saucy, sly, waggish, wily

archaic ancient, antiquated, antique, behind the times, bygone, obsolete, old, olden (*Archaic*), old-fashioned, old hat, outmoded, out of date, passé, primitive, superannuated

arched curved, domed, embowed, vaulted

archer bowman (*Archaic*), toxophilite (*Formal*)

archetype classic, exemplar, form, ideal, model, original, paradigm, pattern, prime example, prototype, standard

architect 1. designer, master builder, planner 2. author, contriver, creator, deviser, engineer, founder, instigator, inventor, maker, originator, planner, prime mover, shaper

architecture 1. architectonics, building, construction, design, planning 2. construction, design, framework, make-up, structure, style

archives 1. annals, chronicles, documents, papers, records, registers, rolls 2. museum, record office, registry, repository

arctic 1. far-northern, hyperborean, polar 2. *Inf.* chilly, cold, freezing, frigid, frost-bound, frosty, frozen, gelid, glacial, icy

ardent avid, eager, enthusiastic, fervent, fervid, fierce, fiery, hot, hot-blooded, impassioned, intense,

keen, lusty, passionate, spirited, vehement, warm, warm-blooded, zealous

ardour avidity, devotion, eagerness, earnestness, enthusiasm, feeling, fervour, fierceness, fire, heat, intensity, keenness, passion, spirit, vehemence, warmth, zeal

arduous backbreaking, burdensome, difficult, exhausting, fatiguing, formidable, gruelling, hard, harsh, heavy, laborious, onerous, painful, punishing, rigorous, severe, steep, strenuous, taxing, tiring, toilsome, tough, troublesome, trying

area 1. district, domain, locality, neighbourhood, patch, plot, realm, region, sector, sphere, stretch, territory, tract, zone 2. breadth, compass, expanse, extent, range, scope, size, width 3. arena, department, domain, field, province, realm, sphere, territory 4. part, portion, section, sector 5. sunken space, yard

arena 1. amphitheatre, bowl, coliseum, field, ground, park (*Inf.*), ring, stadium, stage 2. area, battlefield, battleground, domain, field, field of conflict, lists, province, realm, scene, scope, sector, sphere, territory, theatre

argot cant, dialect, idiom, jargon, lingo (*Inf.*), parlance, patois, slang, vernacular

argue 1. altercate, bandy words, bicker, disagree, dispute, fall out (*Inf.*), feud, fight, have an argument, quarrel, squabble, wrangle 2. assert, claim, contend, controvert, debate, discuss, dispute, expostulate, hold, maintain, plead, question, reason, remonstrate 3. convince, persuade, prevail upon, talk into, talk round 4. demonstrate, denote, display, evince, exhibit, imply, indicate, manifest, point to, show, suggest

argument 1. altercation, barney (*Inf.*), bickering, clash, controversy, difference of opinion, disagreement, dispute, falling out (*Inf.*), feud, fight, quarrel, row, squabble, wrangle 2. assertion, claim, contention, debate, discussion, dispute, expostulation, plea, pleading, questioning, remonstrance, re~monstration 3. argumentation, case, defence, dialectic, ground(s), line of reasoning, logic, polemic, reason, reasoning 4. abstract, gist, outline, plot, story, story line, sub~ject, summary, synopsis, theme

argumentative 1. belligerent, combative, contentious, contrary, disputatious, litigious, opinionated, quarrelsome 2. contentious, controversial, disputed

arid 1. barren, desert, dried up, dry, moistureless, parched, sterile, wa~terless 2. boring, colourless, dreary, dry, dull, flat, jejune, life~less, spiritless, tedious, uninteresting, vapid

aright accurately, appropriately, aptly, correctly, duly, exactly, fitly, in due order, justly, properly, rightly, suitably, truly, without er~ror

arise 1. appear, begin, come into being, come to light, commence, crop up (*Inf.*), emanate, emerge, ensue, follow, happen, issue, occur, originate, proceed, result, set in, spring, start, stem 2. get to one's feet, get up, go up, rise, stand up, wake up 3. ascend, climb, lift, mount, move upward, rise, soar, tower

aristocracy body of nobles, elite, gentry, *haut monde,* nobility, no~blesse (*Literary*), patricians, pa~triciate, peerage, ruling class, up~per class, upper crust (*Inf.*)

aristocrat grandee, lady, lord, no~ble, nobleman, noblewoman, pa~trician, peer, peeress

aristocratic 1. blue-blooded, elite, gentle (*Archaic*), gentlemanly, highborn, lordly, noble, patrician, titled, upper-class, well-born 2. courtly, dignified, elegant, fine, haughty, polished, refined, snob~bish, stylish, well-bred

arm[1] *n.* 1. appendage, limb, upper limb 2. bough, branch, department, detachment, division, extension, offshoot, projection, section, sector 3. branch, channel, estuary, firth,

inlet, sound, strait, tributary 4. authority, command, force, might, potency, power, strength, sway

arm[2] *v.* 1. *Esp. with weapons* ac~coutre, array, deck out, equip, fur~nish, issue with, outfit, provide, rig, supply 2. mobilize, muster forces, prepare for war, take up arms 3. brace, equip, forearm, fortify, gird one's loins, guard, make ready, outfit, prepare, prime, protect, strengthen

armada fleet, flotilla, navy, squad~ron

armaments ammunition, arms, guns, materiel, munitions, ord~nance, weaponry, weapons

armed accoutred, arrayed, carry~ing weapons, equipped, fitted out, forearmed, fortified, furnished, girded, guarded, in arms, pre~pared, primed, protected, provid~ed, ready, rigged out, strength~ened, supplied, under arms

armistice ceasefire, peace, sus~pension of hostilities, truce

armour armour plate, covering, protection, sheathing, shield

armoured armour-plated, bomb~proof, bulletproof, ironclad, mailed, protected, steel-plated

armoury ammunition dump, arms depot, arsenal, magazine, ord~nance depot

arms 1. armaments, firearms, guns, instruments of war, ordnance, weaponry, weapons 2. blazonry, crest, escutcheon, heraldry, insig~nia

army 1. armed force, host (*Archa~ic*), land forces, legions, military, military force, soldiers, soldiery, troops 2. *Fig.* array, horde, host, multitude, pack, swarm, throng, vast number

aroma bouquet, fragrance, odour, perfume, redolence, savour, scent, smell

aromatic balmy, fragrant, odorif~erous, perfumed, pungent, redo~lent, savoury, spicy, sweet-scented, sweet-smelling

around *prep.* 1. about, encircling, enclosing, encompassing, environ~ing, on all sides of, on every side of,

surrounding 2. about, approxi~
mately, circa (*used with dates*),
roughly ~*adv.* 3. about, all over,
everywhere, here and there, in all
directions, on all sides, throughout,
to and fro 4. at hand, close, close at
hand, close by, near, nearby, nigh
(*Archaic or dialect*)

arouse agitate, animate, awaken,
call forth, enliven, excite, foment,
foster, goad, incite, inflame, insti~
gate, kindle, move, provoke,
quicken, rouse, sharpen, spark,
spur, stimulate, stir up, summon
up, waken, wake up, warm, whet,
whip up

arrange 1. align, array, class, clas~
sify, dispose, file, form, group, line
up, marshal, order, organize, posi~
tion, put in order, range, rank, set
out, sort, sort out (*Inf.*), systema~
tize, tidy 2. adjust, agree to, come
to terms, compromise, construct,
contrive, determine, devise, fix up
(*Inf.*), organize, plan, prepare,
project, schedule, settle 3. adapt,
instrument, orchestrate, score

arrangement 1. alignment, array,
classification, design, display, dis~
position, form, grouping, line-up,
marshalling, order, ordering, or~
ganization, ranging, rank, setup
(*Inf.*), structure, system 2. *Often
plural* adjustment, agreement,
compact, compromise, construc~
tion, deal, devising, organization,
plan, planning, preparation, provi~
sion, schedule, settlement, terms 3.
adaptation, instrumentation, inter~
pretation, orchestration, score,
version

array *n.* 1. arrangement, collection,
display, disposition, exhibition,
formation, line-up, marshalling,
muster, order, parade, show, sup~
ply 2. *Poetic* apparel, attire,
clothes, dress, finery, garb, gar~
ments, raiment (*Archaic*), regalia
~*v.* 3. align, arrange, display, dis~
pose, draw up, exhibit, form up,
group, line up, marshal, muster,
order, parade, place in order,
range, set in line (*Military*), show
4. accoutre, adorn, apparel (*Ar~
chaic*), attire, bedeck, caparison,
clothe, deck, decorate, dress,

equip, fit out, garb, outfit, robe,
supply, wrap

arrest *v.* 1. apprehend, bust (*Inf.*),
capture, catch, collar (*Inf.*), detain,
lay hold of, nab (*Inf.*), nick (*Sl.*),
pinch (*Inf.*), run in (*Sl.*), seize, take,
take into custody, take prisoner 2.
block, check, delay, end, halt, hin~
der, hold, inhibit, interrupt, ob~
struct, restrain, retard, slow, stall,
stay, stop, suppress 3. absorb,
catch, engage, engross, fascinate,
grip, hold, intrigue, occupy ~*n.* 4.
apprehension, bust (*Inf.*), capture,
cop (*Sl.*), detention, seizure 5.
blockage, check, delay, end, halt,
hindrance, inhibition, interruption,
obstruction, restraint, stalling,
stay, stoppage, suppression

arresting conspicuous, engaging,
extraordinary, impressive, notice~
able, outstanding, remarkable,
striking, stunning, surprising

arrival 1. advent, appearance, ar~
riving, coming, entrance, happen~
ing, occurrence, taking place 2.
arriver, caller, comer, entrant, in~
comer, newcomer, visitant, visitor

arrive 1. appear, attain, befall,
come, enter, get to, happen, occur,
reach, show up (*Inf.*), take place,
turn up 2. *Inf.* achieve recognition,
become famous, make good, make
it (*Inf.*), make the grade (*Inf.*),
reach the top, succeed

arrogance bluster, conceit, con~
ceitedness, contemptuousness, dis~
dainfulness, haughtiness, hauteur,
high-handedness, imperiousness,
insolence, loftiness, lordliness,
overweeningness, pomposity,
pompousness, presumption, pre~
tension, pretentiousness, pride,
scornfulness, superciliousness,
swagger, uppishness (*Brit. inf.*)

arrogant assuming, blustering,
conceited, contemptuous, disdain~
ful, haughty, high and mighty
(*Inf.*), high-handed, imperious, in~
solent, lordly, overbearing, over~
weening, pompous, presumptuous,
pretentious, proud, scornful,
supercilious, swaggering, uppish
(*Brit. inf.*)

arrogation appropriation, assump~

tion, commandeering, demand, expropriation, presumption, seizure, usurpation

arrow 1. bolt, dart, flight, quarrel, reed (*Archaic*), shaft (*Archaic*) 2. indicator, pointer

arsenal ammunition dump, armoury, arms depot, magazine, ordnance depot, stock, stockpile, store, storehouse, supply

art 1. adroitness, aptitude, artifice (*Archaic*), artistry, craft, craftsmanship, dexterity, expertise, facility, ingenuity, knack, knowledge, mastery, method, profession, skill, trade, virtuosity 2. artfulness, artifice, astuteness, craftiness, cunning, deceit, duplicity, guile, trickery, wiliness

artful adept, adroit, clever, crafty, cunning, deceitful, designing, dexterous, foxy, ingenious, intriguing, masterly, politic, proficient, resourceful, scheming, sharp, shrewd, skilful, sly, smart, subtle, tricky, wily

article 1. commodity, item, object, piece, substance, thing, unit 2. composition, discourse, essay, feature, item, paper, piece, story, treatise 3. branch, clause, count, detail, division, head, heading, item, matter, paragraph, part, particular, passage, piece, point, portion, section

articulate *adj.* 1. clear, coherent, comprehensible, eloquent, expressive, fluent, intelligible, lucid, meaningful, understandable, vocal, well-spoken ~*v.* 2. enounce, enunciate, express, pronounce, say, speak, state, talk, utter, verbalize, vocalize, voice 3. connect, couple, fit together, hinge, join, joint

artifice 1. contrivance, device, dodge, expedient, hoax, machination, manoeuvre, ruse, stratagem, subterfuge, tactic, trick, wile 2. artfulness, chicanery, craft, craftiness, cunning, deception, duplicity, guile, scheming, slyness, trickery 3. adroitness, cleverness, deftness, facility, finesse, ingenuity, invention, inventiveness, skill

artificer 1. artisan, craftsman, mechanic 2. architect, builder, contriver, creator, designer, deviser, inventor, maker, originator

artificial 1. man-made, manufactured, non-natural, plastic, synthetic 2. bogus, counterfeit, ersatz, fake, imitation, mock, phoney (*Inf.*), sham, simulated, specious, spurious 3. affected, assumed, contrived, false, feigned, forced, hollow, insincere, meretricious, phoney (*Inf.*), pretended, spurious, unnatural

artillery battery, big guns, cannon, cannonry, gunnery, ordnance

artisan artificer, craftsman, handicraftsman, journeyman, mechanic, skilled workman, technician

artistic aesthetic, beautiful, creative, cultivated, cultured, decorative, elegant, exquisite, graceful, imaginative, ornamental, refined, sensitive, stylish, tasteful

artistry accomplishment, art, artistic ability, brilliance, craftsmanship, creativity, finesse, flair, genius, mastery, proficiency, sensibility, skill, style, talent, taste, touch, virtuosity, workmanship

artless 1. candid, direct, fair, frank, genuine, guileless, honest, open, plain, sincere, straightforward, true, undesigning 2. humble, natural, plain, pure, simple, unadorned, unaffected, uncontrived, unpretentious 3. awkward, bungling, clumsy, crude, incompetent, inept, maladroit, primitive, rude, unskilled, untalented 4. childlike, ingenuous, innocent, jejune, naive, trustful, trusting, unsophisticated

as *conj.* 1. at the time that, during the time that, just as, when, while 2. in the manner that, in the way that, like 3. that which, what 4. because, considering that, seeing that, since 5. in the same manner with, in the same way that, like 6. for instance, like, such as ~*prep.* 7. being, in the character of, in the role of, under the name of 8. **as for** as regards, in reference to, on the subject of, with reference to, with regard to, with respect to 9. **as it**

were in a manner of speaking, in a way, so to say, so to speak

ascend climb, float up, fly up, go up, lift off, mount, move up, rise, scale, slope upwards, soar, take off, tower

ascendancy, ascendency authority, command, control, dominance, domination, dominion, hegemony, influence, mastery, power, predominance, pre-eminence, prevalence, reign, rule, sovereignty, superiority, supremacy, sway, upper hand

ascendant, ascendent *adj.* 1. ascending, climbing, going upwards, mounting, rising 2. authoritative, commanding, controlling, dominant, influential, powerful, predominant, pre-eminent, prevailing, ruling, superior, supreme, uppermost ~*n.* 3. **in the ascendant** ascending, climbing, commanding, dominant, dominating, flourishing, growing, increasing, mounting, on the rise, on the way up, prevailing, rising, supreme, up-and-coming, uppermost, winning

ascent 1. ascending, ascension, clambering, climb, climbing, mounting, rise, rising, scaling, upward movement 2. acclivity, gradient, incline, ramp, rise, rising ground, upward slope

ascertain confirm, determine, discover, establish, ferret out, find out, fix, identify, learn, make certain, settle, verify

ascetic 1. *n.* abstainer, anchorite, hermit, monk, nun, recluse, self-denier 2. *adj.* abstemious, abstinent, austere, celibate, frugal, harsh, plain, puritanical, rigorous, self-denying, self-disciplined, severe, Spartan, stern

asceticism abstemiousness, abstinence, austerity, celibacy, frugality, harshness, mortification of the flesh, plainness, puritanism, rigorousness, rigour, self-abnegation, self-denial, self-discipline, self-mortification

ascribe assign, attribute, charge, credit, impute, put down, refer, set down

ashamed abashed, bashful, blushing, chagrined, conscience-stricken, crestfallen, discomfited, distressed, embarrassed, guilty, humbled, humiliated, mortified, prudish, reluctant, remorseful, shamefaced, sheepish, shy, sorry

ashore aground, landwards, on dry land, on land, on the beach, on the shore, shorewards, to the shore

aside 1. *adv.* alone, alongside, apart, away, beside, in isolation, in reserve, on one side, out of mind, out of the way, privately, separately, to one side, to the side 2. *n.* departure, digression, excursion, excursus, interpolation, interposition, parenthesis, tangent

asinine brainless, daft (*Inf.*), dunderheaded, fatuous, foolish, gormless (*Inf.*), halfwitted, idiotic, imbecile, imbecilic, inane, moronic, obstinate, senseless, silly, stupid, thickheaded, thick-witted

ask 1. inquire, interrogate, query, question, quiz 2. appeal, apply, beg, beseech, claim, crave, demand, entreat, implore, petition, plead, pray, request, seek, solicit, sue, supplicate 3. bid, invite, summon

askance 1. awry, indirectly, obliquely, out of the corner of one's eye, sideways, with a side glance 2. disapprovingly, distrustfully, doubtfully, dubiously, mistrustfully, sceptically, suspiciously

askew *adv./ adj.* aslant, awry, cockeyed (*Inf.*), crooked, crookedly, lopsided, oblique, obliquely, off-centre, to one side

asleep crashed out (*Sl.*), dead to the world (*Inf.*), dormant, dozing, fast asleep, napping, sleeping, slumbering, snoozing (*Inf.*), sound asleep

aspect 1. air, appearance, attitude, bearing, condition, countenance, demeanour, expression, look, manner, mien (*Literary*) 2. bearing, direction, exposure, outlook, point of view, position, prospect, scene, situation, view 3. angle, facet, feature, side

asperity acerbity, acrimony, bitterness, churlishness, crabbedness, crossness, harshness, irascibility, irritability, moroseness, peevishness, roughness, ruggedness, severity, sharpness, sourness, sullenness

asphyxiate choke, smother, stifle, strangle, strangulate, suffocate, throttle

aspirant 1. *n.* applicant, aspirer, candidate, hopeful, postulant, seeker, suitor 2. *adj.* ambitious, aspiring, eager, endeavouring, hopeful, longing, striving, wishful

aspiration aim, ambition, craving, desire, dream, eagerness, endeavour, goal, hankering, hope, longing, object, objective, wish, yearning

aspire aim, be ambitious, be eager, crave, desire, dream, hanker, hope, long, pursue, seek, wish, yearn

aspiring *adj.* ambitious, aspirant, eager, endeavouring, hopeful, longing, striving, wishful, would-be

ass 1. donkey, jennet, moke (*Sl.*) 2. blockhead, bonehead (*Sl.*), dolt, dope (*Sl.*), dunce, fool, halfwit, idiot, jackass, nincompoop, ninny, nitwit, numskull, simpleton, twerp (*Inf.*), twit (*Inf.*)

assail 1. assault, attack, beset, charge, encounter, fall upon, invade, lay into, maltreat, set about, set upon 2. abuse, berate, criticize, impugn, malign, revile, vilify

assassin eliminator (*Sl.*), executioner, hatchet man (*Sl.*), hit man (*Sl.*), killer, liquidator, murderer, slayer

assassinate eliminate (*Sl.*), hit (*U.S. sl.*), kill, liquidate, murder, slay

assault 1. *n.* aggression, attack, charge, incursion, invasion, offensive, onset, onslaught, storm, storming, strike 2. *v.* assail, attack, beset, charge, fall upon, invade, lay into, set about, set upon, storm, strike at

assay *v.* 1. analyse, appraise, assess, evaluate, examine, inspect, investigate, prove, test, try, weigh ~*n.* 2. *Archaic* attempt, endeavour, essay, try, venture 3. analysis, examination, inspection, investigation, test, trial

assemble 1. accumulate, amass, bring together, call together, collect, come together, congregate, convene, convoke, flock, forgather, gather, marshal, meet, muster, rally, round up, summon 2. build up, connect, construct, erect, fabricate, fit together, join, make, manufacture, piece together, put together, set up

assembly 1. accumulation, aggregation, assemblage, body, collection, company, conclave, conference, congregation, convocation, council, crowd, diet, flock, gathering, group, mass, meeting, multitude, rally, synod, throng 2. building up, connecting, construction, erection, fabrication, fitting together, joining, manufacture, piecing together, putting together, setting up

assent 1. *v.* accede, accept, acquiesce, agree, allow, approve, comply, concur, consent, fall in with, go along with, grant, permit, sanction, subscribe 2. *n.* acceptance, accession, accord, acquiescence, agreement, approval, compliance, concurrence, consent, permission, sanction

assert 1. affirm, allege, asseverate, attest, aver, avouch (*Archaic*), avow, contend, declare, maintain, predicate, profess, pronounce, state, swear 2. claim, defend, insist upon, press, put forward, stand up for, stress, uphold, vindicate 3. **assert oneself** exert one's influence, make one's presence felt, put oneself forward

assertion 1. affirmation, allegation, asseveration, attestation, avowal, contention, declaration, predication, profession, pronouncement, statement 2. defence, insistence, maintenance, stressing, vindication

assertive aggressive, confident, decided, decisive, demanding, dogmatic, domineering, emphatic, firm, forceful, forward, insistent, overbearing, positive, pushy (*Inf.*), self-assured, strong-willed

assess 1. appraise, compute, determine, estimate, evaluate, fix, gauge, judge, rate, size up (*Inf.*), value, weigh **2.** demand, evaluate, fix, impose, levy, rate, tax, value

assessment 1. appraisal, computation, determination, estimate, estimation, evaluation, judgment, rating, valuation **2.** charge, demand, duty, evaluation, fee, impost, levy, rate, rating, tariff, tax, taxation, toll, valuation

asset 1. advantage, aid, benefit, blessing, boon, help, resource, service **2.** *Plural* capital, estate, funds, goods, holdings, means, money, possessions, property, reserves, resources, valuables, wealth

assiduous attentive, constant, diligent, hard-working, indefatigable, industrious, laborious, persevering, persistent, sedulous, steady, studious, unflagging, untiring, unwearied

assign 1. appoint, choose, delegate, designate, name, nominate, select **2.** allocate, allot, apportion, consign, distribute, give, give out, grant, make over **3.** appoint, appropriate, determine, fix, set apart, stipulate **4.** accredit, ascribe, attribute, put down

assignment 1. appointment, charge, commission, duty, job, mission, position, post, responsibility, task **2.** allocation, allotment, appointment, apportionment, appropriation, ascription, assignation (*Law, chiefly Scot.*), attribution, choice, consignment, delegation, designation, determination, distribution, giving, grant, nomination, selection, specification, stipulation

assist abet, aid, back, benefit, boost, collaborate, cooperate, expedite, facilitate, further, help, reinforce, relieve, second, serve, succour, support, sustain, work for, work with

assistance abetment, aid, backing, benefit, boost, collaboration, cooperation, furtherance, help, helping hand, reinforcement, relief,

service, succour, support, sustenance

assistant abettor, accessory, accomplice, aide, aider, ally, associate, auxiliary, backer, coadjutor (*Rare*), collaborator, colleague, confederate, cooperator, helper, helpmate, henchman, partner, right-hand man, second, supporter

associate *v.* **1.** affiliate, ally, combine, confederate, conjoin, connect, correlate, couple, identify, join, league, link, lump together, mix, pair, relate, think of together, unite, yoke **2.** accompany, befriend, be friends, consort, fraternize, hang about, hang out (*Inf.*), hobnob, mingle, mix, run around (*Inf.*) ~*n.* **3.** ally, collaborator, colleague, companion, compeer, comrade, confederate, confrère, co-worker, follower, friend, mate, partner

association 1. affiliation, alliance, band, clique, club, coalition, combine, company, confederacy, confederation, cooperative, corporation, federation, fraternity, group, league, organization, partnership, society, syndicate, union **2.** companionship, comradeship, familiarity, fellowship, fraternization, friendship, intimacy, partnership, relations, relationship **3.** blend, bond, combination, concomitance, connection, correlation, identification, joining, juxtaposition, linkage, linking, lumping together, mixing, mixture, pairing, relation, tie, union, yoking

assort arrange, array, categorize, classify, dispose, distribute, file, grade, group, range, rank, sort, type

assorted 1. different, diverse, diversified, heterogeneous, miscellaneous, mixed, motley, sundry, varied, variegated, various **2.** arranged, arrayed, categorized, classified, disposed, filed, graded, grouped, ranged, ranked, sorted, typed

assortment 1. array, choice, collection, diversity, farrago, hotchpotch, jumble, medley, *mélange*, miscellany, mishmash, mixed bag (*Inf.*), mixture, potpourri, salmagundi, selection, variety 2. arrangement, categorizing, classification, disposition, distribution, filing, grading, grouping, ranging, ranking, sorting, typing

assume 1. accept, believe, expect, fancy, guess (*Inf., chiefly U.S.*), imagine, infer, presume, presuppose, suppose, surmise, suspect, take for granted, think 2. adopt, affect, counterfeit, feign, imitate, impersonate, mimic, pretend to, put on, sham, simulate 3. accept, acquire, attend to, begin, don, embark upon, embrace, enter upon, put on, set about, shoulder, take on, take over, take responsibility for, take up, undertake 4. acquire, appropriate, arrogate, commandeer, expropriate, pre-empt, seize, take, take over, usurp

assumed 1. affected, bogus, counterfeit, fake, false, feigned, fictitious, imitation, made-up, make-believe, phoney (*Inf.*), pretended, pseudonymous, sham, simulated, spurious 2. accepted, expected, hypothetical, presumed, presupposed, supposed, surmised, taken for granted 3. appropriated, arrogated, pre-empted, seized, usurped

assuming *adj.* arrogant, bold, conceited, disdainful, domineering, egotistic, forward, haughty, imperious, overbearing, presumptuous, pushy (*Inf.*), rude

assumption 1. acceptance, belief, conjecture, expectation, fancy, guess, hypothesis, inference, postulate, postulation, premise, premiss, presumption, presupposition, supposition, surmise, suspicion, theory 2. acceptance, acquisition, adoption, embracing, entering upon, putting on, shouldering, takeover, taking on, taking up, undertaking 3. acquisition, appropriation, arrogation, expropriation, pre-empting, seizure, takeover, taking, usurpation 4. arrogance, conceit, imperiousness, presumption, pride, self-importance

assurance 1. affirmation, assertion, declaration, guarantee, oath, pledge, profession, promise, protestation, vow, word, word of honour 2. aggressiveness, assuredness, boldness, certainty, certitude, confidence, conviction, coolness, courage, faith, firmness, nerve, poise, positiveness, security, self-confidence, self-reliance, sureness 3. arrogance, effrontery, gall (*Inf.*), impudence, nerve (*Inf.*), presumption

assure 1. comfort, convince, embolden, encourage, hearten, persuade, reassure, soothe 2. affirm, attest, certify, confirm, declare confidently, give one's word to, guarantee, pledge, promise, swear, vow 3. clinch, complete, confirm, ensure, guarantee, make certain, make sure, seal, secure

assured 1. beyond doubt, clinched, confirmed, dependable, ensured, fixed, guaranteed, indubitable, irrefutable, made certain, sealed, secure, settled, sure, unquestionable 2. assertive, audacious, bold, brazen, certain, complacent, confident, overconfident, poised, positive, pushy (*Inf.*), self-assured, self-confident, self-possessed, sure of oneself

astonish amaze, astound, bewilder, confound, daze, dumbfound, flabbergast (*Inf.*), stagger, stun, stupefy, surprise

astonishing amazing, astounding, bewildering, breathtaking, impressive, staggering, striking, stunning, stupefying, surprising

astonishment amazement, awe, bewilderment, confusion, consternation, stupefaction, surprise, wonder, wonderment

astounding amazing, astonishing, bewildering, breathtaking, impressive, staggering, striking, stunning, stupefying, surprising

astray *adj./adv.* 1. adrift, afield, amiss, lost, off, off course, off the mark, off the right track, off the subject 2. into error, into sin, to the bad, wrong

astronaut cosmonaut, spaceman,

space pilot, space traveller, space~
woman

astute adroit, artful, bright, calcu~
lating, canny, clever, crafty, cun~
ning, discerning, foxy, insightful,
intelligent, keen, knowing, pen~
etrating, perceptive, politic, saga~
cious, sharp, shrewd, sly, subtle,
wily

astuteness acumen, adroitness,
artfulness, brightness, canniness,
cleverness, craftiness, cunning,
discernment, foxiness, insight, in~
telligence, keenness, knowledge,
penetration, perceptiveness, sa~
gacity, sharpness, shrewdness, sly~
ness, subtlety, wiliness

asylum 1. harbour, haven, pre~
serve, refuge, retreat, safety,
sanctuary, shelter 2. *Old-fashioned*
funny farm (*Sl.*), hospital, institu~
tion, loony bin (*Sl.*), madhouse
(*Inf.*), mental hospital, nuthouse
(*Sl.*), psychiatric hospital

atheism disbelief, freethinking,
godlessness, heathenism, infidelity,
irreligion, nonbelief, paganism,
scepticism, unbelief

atheist disbeliever, freethinker,
heathen, infidel, irreligionist, non~
believer, pagan, sceptic, unbeliev~
er

athlete competitor, contender,
contestant, games player, gym~
nast, player, runner, sportsman,
sportswoman

athletic 1. *adj.* able-bodied, active,
brawny, energetic, fit, herculean,
husky (*Inf.*), lusty, muscular, pow~
erful, robust, sinewy, strapping,
strong, sturdy, vigorous, well-
proportioned 2. *pl. n.* contests, ex~
ercises, games of strength, gym~
nastics, races, sports, track and
field events

atmosphere 1. aerosphere, air,
heavens, sky 2. air, ambience,
aura, character, climate, environ~
ment, feel, feeling, flavour, mood,
quality, spirit, surroundings, tone

atom bit, crumb, dot, fragment,
grain, iota, jot, mite, molecule,
morsel, mote, particle, scintilla
(*Rare*), scrap, shred, speck, spot,
tittle, trace, whit

atone 1. *With* **for** answer for, com~
pensate, do penance for, make
amends for, make redress, make
reparation for, make up for, pay
for, recompense, redress 2. ap~
pease, expiate, make expiation for,
propitiate, reconcile, redeem

atrocious 1. barbaric, brutal, cruel,
diabolical, fiendish, flagrant, hei~
nous, infamous, infernal, inhuman,
monstrous, nefarious, ruthless,
savage, vicious, villainous, wicked
2. appalling, detestable, execrable,
grievous, horrible, horrifying,
shocking, terrible

atrocity 1. abomination, act of sav~
agery, barbarity, brutality, crime,
cruelty, enormity, evil, horror,
monstrosity, outrage, villainy 2.
atrociousness, barbarity, barba~
rousness, brutality, cruelty, enor~
mity, fiendishness, grievousness,
heinousness, horror, infamy, inhu~
manity, monstrousness, nefarious~
ness, ruthlessness, savagery,
shockingness, viciousness, villain~
ousness, wickedness

attach 1. add, adhere, affix, annex,
append, bind, connect, couple, fas~
ten, fix, join, link, make fast, se~
cure, stick, subjoin, tie, unite 2. ac~
company, affiliate, associate, be~
come associated with, combine,
enlist, join, join forces with, latch
on to, sign on with, sign up with,
unite with 3. ascribe, assign, asso~
ciate, attribute, connect, impute,
invest with, lay, place, put 4. allo~
cate, allot, appoint, assign, consign,
designate, detail, earmark, second,
send

attached 1. affectionate towards,
devoted, fond of, full of regard for,
possessive 2. accompanied, en~
gaged, married, partnered, spoken
for

attachment 1. adapter, bond,
clamp, connection, connector,
coupling, fastener, fastening, joint,
junction, link, tie 2. affection, af~
finity, attraction, bond, devotion,
fidelity, fondness, friendship, lik~
ing, love, loyalty, partiality, pos~
sessiveness, predilection, regard,
tenderness 3. accessory, accou~

trement, adapter, addition, ad~ junct, appendage, appurtenance, auxiliary, extension, extra, fitting, fixture, supplement, supplementa~ ry part

attack n. 1. aggression, assault, charge, foray, incursion, inroad, invasion, offensive, onset, on~ slaught, raid, rush, strike 2. abuse, blame, calumny, censure, criti~ cism, denigration, impugnment, vilification 3. access, bout, convul~ sion, fit, paroxysm, seizure, spasm, spell, stroke ~v. 4. assail, assault, charge, fall upon, invade, lay into, raid, rush, set about, set upon, storm, strike (at) 5. abuse, berate, blame, censure, criticize, impugn, malign, revile, vilify

attacker aggressor, assailant, as~ saulter, intruder, invader, raider

attain accomplish, achieve, ac~ quire, arrive at, bring off, com~ plete, earn, effect, fulfil, gain, get, grasp, obtain, procure, reach, re~ alize, reap, secure, win

attainment 1. accomplishment, achievement, acquirement, acqui~ sition, arrival at, completion, feat, fulfilment, gaining, getting, obtain~ ing, procurement, reaching, reali~ zation, reaping, winning 2. ability, accomplishment, achievement, art, capability, competence, gift, mastery, proficiency, skill, talent

attempt 1. n. assault, attack, bid, crack (Inf.), effort, endeavour, es~ say, experiment, go, shot (Inf.), trial, try, undertaking, venture 2. v. endeavour, essay, experiment, have a crack (go, shot) (Inf.), seek, strive, tackle, take on, try, try one's hand at, undertake, venture

attend 1. appear, be at, be here, be present, be there, frequent, go to, haunt, make one (Archaic), put in an appearance, show oneself, show up (Inf.), turn up, visit 2. care for, look after, mind, minister to, nurse, take care of, tend 3. follow, hear, hearken (Archaic), heed, listen, look on, mark, mind, note, notice, observe, pay attention, pay heed, regard, take to heart, watch 4. ac~ company, arise from, be associat~

ed with, be connected with, be consequent on, follow, go hand in hand with, issue from, occur with, result from 5. With to apply one~ self to, concentrate on, devote oneself to, get to work on, look after, occupy oneself with, see to, take care of 6. accompany, chap~ eron, companion, convoy, escort, guard, squire, usher 7. be in the service of, serve, wait upon, work for

attendance 1. appearance, at~ tending, being there, presence 2. audience, crowd, gate, house, number present, turnout

attendant 1. n. aide, assistant, auxiliary, chaperon, companion, custodian, escort, flunky, follower, guard, guide, helper, lackey, me~ nial, servant, steward, underling, usher, waiter 2. adj. accessory, ac~ companying, associated, concomi~ tant, consequent, related

attention 1. concentration, consid~ eration, contemplation, delibera~ tion, heed, heedfulness, intentness, mind, scrutiny, thinking, thought, thoughtfulness 2. awareness, con~ sciousness, consideration, notice, observation, recognition, regard 3. care, concern, looking after, mini~ stration, treatment 4. Often plural assiduities, care, civility, compli~ ment, consideration, courtesy, def~ erence, gallantry, mindfulness, po~ liteness, regard, respect, service

attentive 1. alert, awake, careful, concentrating, heedful, intent, lis~ tening, mindful, observant, re~ gardful, studious, watchful 2. ac~ commodating, civil, conscientious, considerate, courteous, devoted, gallant, gracious, kind, obliging, polite, respectful, thoughtful

attic garret, loft

attitude 1. approach, disposition, frame of mind, mood, opinion, out~ look, perspective, point of view, position, posture, stance, standing, view 2. air, aspect, bearing, car~ riage, condition, demeanour, man~ ner, mien (Literary), pose, posi~ tion, posture, stance

attract allure, appeal to, bewitch,

captivate, charm, decoy, draw, en~
chant, endear, engage, entice, fas~
cinate, incline, induce, interest, in~
vite, lure, pull (*Inf.*), tempt

attraction allure, appeal, attrac~
tiveness, bait, captivation, charm,
come-on (*Inf.*), draw, enchant~
ment, endearment, enticement,
fascination, inducement, interest,
invitation, lure, magnetism, pull
(*Inf.*), temptation, temptingness

attractive agreeable, alluring, ap~
pealing, beautiful, captivating,
charming, comely, engaging, en~
ticing, fair, fascinating, fetching,
good-looking, gorgeous, handsome,
interesting, inviting, lovely, mag~
netic, pleasant, pleasing, prepos~
sessing, pretty, seductive, tempt~
ing, winning, winsome

attribute 1. *v.* apply, ascribe, as~
sign, blame, charge, credit, impute,
lay at the door of, put down to,
refer, set down to, trace to 2. *n.*
aspect, character, characteristic,
facet, feature, idiosyncrasy, indi~
cation, mark, note, peculiarity,
point, property, quality, quirk, sign,
symbol, trait, virtue

auburn chestnut-coloured, copper-
coloured, henna, nutbrown,
reddish-brown, russet, rust-
coloured, tawny, Titian red

audacious 1. adventurous, bold,
brave, courageous, daredevil, dar~
ing, dauntless, death-defying, en~
terprising, fearless, intrepid, rash,
reckless, risky, valiant, venture~
some 2. assuming, brazen, cheeky,
defiant, disrespectful, forward, im~
pertinent, impudent, insolent, pert,
presumptuous, rude, shameless

audacity 1. adventurousness,
audaciousness, boldness, bravery,
courage, daring, dauntlessness,
enterprise, fearlessness, guts (*Sl.*),
intrepidity, nerve, rashness, reck~
lessness, valour, venturesomeness
2. audaciousness, brass neck (*Inf.*),
cheek, defiance, disrespectfulness,
effrontery, forwardness, gall (*Inf.*),
impertinence, impudence, inso~
lence, nerve, pertness, presump~
tion, rudeness, shamelessness

audible clear, detectable, discern~
ible, distinct, hearable, perceptible

audience 1. assemblage, assembly,
congregation, crowd, gallery,
gathering, house, listeners, on~
lookers, spectators, turnout, view~
ers 2. devotees, fans, following,
market, public 3. consultation,
hearing, interview, meeting, re~
ception

au fait abreast of, *au courant,* clued
up (*Sl.*), conversant, expert, fa~
miliar, fully informed, in the know,
in touch, knowledgeable, on the
ball (*Inf.*), well-acquainted, well up

augment add to, amplify, boost,
build up, dilate, enhance, enlarge,
expand, extend, grow, heighten,
increase, inflate, intensify, magni~
fy, multiply, raise, reinforce,
strengthen, swell

augmentation accession, addition,
amplification, boost, build-up, dila~
tion, enhancement, enlargement,
expansion, extension, growth,
heightening, increase, inflation,
intensification, magnification,
multiplication, reinforcement, rise,
strengthening, swelling

augur 1. *n.* auspex, diviner, harus~
pex, oracle, prophet, seer, sooth~
sayer 2. *v.* be an omen of, bespeak
(*Archaic*), betoken, bode, fore~
shadow, harbinger, herald, por~
tend, predict, prefigure, presage,
promise, prophesy, signify

augury 1. divination, prediction,
prophecy, soothsaying 2. auspice,
forerunner, forewarning, harbin~
ger, herald, omen, portent, pre~
cursor, presage, prognostication,
promise, prophecy, sign, token,
warning

august dignified, exalted, glorious,
grand, high-ranking, imposing, im~
pressive, kingly, lofty, magnificent,
majestic, monumental, noble, re~
gal, solemn, stately, superb

auspice *n.* 1. *Usually plural* advo~
cacy, aegis, authority, backing,
care, championship, charge, con~
trol, countenance, guidance, influ~
ence, patronage, protection, spon~
sorship, supervision, support 2.
augury, indication, omen, portent,

prognostication, prophecy, sign, token, warning

auspicious bright, encouraging, favourable, felicitous, fortunate, happy, hopeful, lucky, opportune, promising, propitious, prosperous, rosy, timely

austere 1. cold, exacting, forbidding, formal, grave, grim, hard, harsh, inflexible, rigorous, serious, severe, solemn, stern, stiff, strict, stringent, unfeeling, unrelenting 2. abstemious, abstinent, ascetic, chaste, continent, economical, exacting, puritanical, rigid, self-denying, self-disciplined, sober, solemn, Spartan, strait-laced, strict, unrelenting 3. bleak, economical, plain, severe, simple, spare, Spartan, stark, subdued, unadorned, unornamented

austerity 1. coldness, exactingness, forbiddingness, formality, gravity, grimness, hardness, harshness, inflexibility, rigour, seriousness, severity, solemnity, sternness, stiffness, strictness 2. abstemiousness, abstinence, asceticism, chasteness, chastity, continence, economy, exactingness, puritanism, rigidity, self-denial, self-discipline, sobriety, solemnity, Spartanism, strictness 3. economy, plainness, severity, simplicity, spareness, Spartanism, starkness

authentic accurate, actual, authoritative, bona fide, certain, dependable, factual, faithful, genuine, legitimate, original, pure, real, reliable, simon-pure (*Rare*), true, true-to-life, trustworthy, valid, veritable

authenticity accuracy, actuality, authoritativeness, certainty, dependability, factualness, faithfulness, genuineness, legitimacy, purity, realness, reliability, trustworthiness, truth, truthfulness, validity, veritableness, verity

author architect, composer, creator, designer, doer, fabricator, father, founder, framer, initiator, inventor, maker, mover, originator, parent, planner, prime mover, producer, writer

authoritarian 1. *adj.* absolute, autocratic, despotic, dictatorial, disciplinarian, doctrinaire, dogmatic, domineering, harsh, imperious, rigid, severe, strict, tyrannical, unyielding 2. *n.* absolutist, autocrat, despot, dictator, disciplinarian, tyrant

authority 1. ascendancy, charge, command, control, domination, dominion, force, government, influence, jurisdiction, might, power, prerogative, right, rule, say-so, strength, supremacy, sway, weight 2. the authorities administration, government, management, officialdom, police, powers that be, the establishment 3. authorization, justification, licence, permission, permit, sanction, say-so, warrant 4. arbiter, bible, connoisseur, expert, judge, master, professional, scholar, specialist, textbook 5. attestation, avowal, declaration, evidence, profession, say-so, statement, testimony, word

authorization 1. ability, authority, power, right, say-so, strength 2. approval, credentials, leave, licence, permission, permit, sanction, say-so, warrant

authorize 1. accredit, commission, empower, enable, entitle, give authority 2. accredit, allow, approve, confirm, countenance, give authority for, give leave, license, permit, ratify, sanction, vouch for, warrant

autocrat absolutist, despot, dictator, tyrant

autocratic absolute, all-powerful, despotic, dictatorial, domineering, imperious, tyrannical, tyrannous, unlimited

automatic 1. automated, mechanical, mechanized, push-button, robot, self-acting, self-activating, self-moving, self-propelling, self-regulating 2. habitual, mechanical, perfunctory, routine, unconscious 3. instinctive, instinctual, involuntary, mechanical, natural, reflex, spontaneous, unconscious, unwilled 4. assured, certain, inescapable, inevitable, necessary, routine, un~avoidable

autonomous free, independent, self-determining, self-governing, self-ruling, sovereign

autonomy freedom, home rule, in~dependence, self-determination, self-government, self-rule, sover~eignty

autopsy dissection, necropsy, postmortem, postmortem exami~nation

auxiliary 1. *adj.* accessory, aiding, ancillary, assisting, back-up, emergency, helping, reserve, sec~ondary, subsidiary, substitute, sup~plementary, supporting 2. *n.* ac~cessory, accomplice, ally, assis~tant, associate, companion, con~federate, helper, partner, reserve, subordinate, supporter

available accessible, applicable, at hand, at one's disposal, attainable, convenient, free, handy, obtain~able, on hand, on tap, ready, ready for use, to hand, vacant

avalanche 1. landslide, landslip, snow-slide, snow-slip 2. barrage, deluge, flood, inundation, torrent

avant-garde *adj.* experimental, far-out (*Sl.*), innovative, innova~tory, pioneering, progressive, un~conventional, way-out (*Inf.*)

avaricious acquisitive, close-fisted, covetous, grasping, greedy, mean, miserable, miserly, niggardly, parsimonious, penny-pinching, pe~nurious, rapacious, stingy

avenge even the score for, get even for, punish, repay, requite, retaliate, revenge, take satisfac~tion for, take vengeance

avenue access, alley, approach, boulevard, channel, course, drive, driveway, entrance, entry, pass, passage, path, pathway, road, route, street, thoroughfare, way

average *n.* 1. common run, mean, medium, midpoint, norm, normal, par, rule, run, run of the mill, standard 2. **on average** as a rule, for the most part, generally, nor~mally, typically, usually ~*adj.* 3. common, commonplace, fair, gen~eral, indifferent, mediocre, mid~

dling, moderate, normal, not bad, ordinary, passable, regular, run-of-the-mill, so-so (*Inf.*), standard, tol~erable, typical, undistinguished, unexceptional, usual 4. intermedi~ate, mean, median, medium, mid~dle ~*v.* 5. balance out to, be on average, do on average, even out to, make on average

averse antipathetic, backward, disinclined, hostile, ill-disposed, in~disposed, inimical, loath, opposed, reluctant, unfavourable, unwilling

aversion abhorrence, animosity, antipathy, detestation, disgust, dis~inclination, dislike, distaste, hate, hatred, horror, hostility, indisposi~tion, loathing, odium, opposition, reluctance, repugnance, repulsion, revulsion, unwillingness

aviation aeronautics, flight, flying, powered flight

aviator aeronaut, airman, flier, pi~lot

avid 1. ardent, devoted, eager, en~thusiastic, fanatical, fervent, in~tense, keen, passionate, zealous 2. acquisitive, athirst, avaricious, covetous, grasping, greedy, hun~gry, insatiable, rapacious, raven~ous, thirsty, voracious

avoid avert, bypass, circumvent, dodge, duck (out of) (*Inf.*), elude, escape, eschew, evade, fight shy of, keep aloof from, keep away from, prevent, refrain from, shirk, shun, sidestep, steer clear of

avoidance circumvention, dodging, eluding, escape, eschewal, evasion, keeping away from, prevention, refraining, shirking, shunning, steering clear of

avowed acknowledged, admitted, confessed, declared, open, pro~fessed, self-proclaimed, sworn

await 1. abide, anticipate, expect, look for, look forward to, stay for, wait for 2. attend, be in readiness for, be in store for, be prepared for, be ready for, wait for

awake *v.* 1. awaken, rouse, wake, wake up 2. activate, alert, animate, arouse, awaken, call forth, enliven, excite, fan, incite, kindle, provoke, revive, stimulate, stir up, vivify

~*adj.* 3. alert, alive, aroused, at~ tentive, awakened, aware, con~ scious, heedful, not sleeping, ob~ servant, on guard, on the alert, on the lookout, vigilant, wakeful, waking, watchful, wide-awake

awaken activate, alert, animate, arouse, awake, call forth, enliven, excite, fan, incite, kindle, provoke, revive, rouse, stimulate, stir up, vivify, wake

awakening *n.* activation, animat~ ing, arousal, awaking, birth, enliv~ ening, incitement, kindling, provo~ cation, revival, rousing, stimula~ tion, stirring up, vivification, wak~ ing, waking up

award *v.* 1. accord, adjudge, allot, apportion, assign, bestow, confer, decree, distribute, endow, gift, give, grant, present, render ~*n.* 2. adjudication, allotment, bestowal, conferment, conferral, decision, decree, endowment, gift, order, presentation 3. decoration, gift, grant, prize, trophy, verdict

aware acquainted, alive to, appre~ ciative, apprised, attentive, *au courant,* cognizant, conscious, conversant, enlightened, familiar, hip (*Sl.*), informed, knowing, knowledgeable, mindful, sensible, sentient, wise (*Inf.*)

awareness acquaintance, appre~ ciation, attention, cognizance, consciousness, enlightenment, fa~ miliarity, knowledge, mindfulness, perception, realization, recogni~ tion, sensibility, sentience, under~ standing

away *adv.* 1. abroad, elsewhere, from here, from home, hence, off 2. apart, at a distance, far, remote 3. aside, out of the way, to one side 4. continuously, incessantly, inter~ minably, relentlessly, repeatedly, uninterruptedly, unremittingly ~*adj.* 5. abroad, absent, elsewhere, gone, not at home, not here, not present, not there, out ~*interj.* 6. beat it (*Inf.*), begone, be off, get lost (*Inf.*), get out, go, go away, on your way

awe 1. *n.* admiration, amazement, astonishment, dread, fear, horror,

respect, reverence, terror, ven~ eration, wonder 2. *v.* amaze, astonish, cow, daunt, frighten, hor~ rify, impress, intimidate, stun, ter~ rify

awe-inspiring amazing, astonish~ ing, awesome, breathtaking, daunting, fearsome, impressive, intimidating, magnificent, stunning (*Inf.*), wonderful, wondrous

awe-stricken, awe-struck afraid, amazed, astonished, awed, awe-inspired, cowed, daunted, dumbfounded, fearful, frightened, horrified, impressed, intimidated, shocked, struck dumb, stunned, terrified, wonder-stricken, wonder- struck

awful 1. alarming, appalling, de~ plorable, dire, distressing, dreadful, fearful, frightful, ghastly, grue~ some, harrowing, hideous, horren~ dous, horrible, horrific, horrifying, nasty, shocking, terrible, tremen~ dous, ugly, unpleasant, unsightly 2. *Archaic* amazing, awe-inspiring, awesome, dread, fearsome, majes~ tic, portentous, solemn

awfully 1. badly, disgracefully, dis~ reputably, dreadfully, inadequate~ ly, reprehensibly, shoddily, unfor~ givably, unpleasantly, wickedly, woefully, wretchedly 2. *Inf.* badly, dreadfully, exceedingly, excep~ tionally, excessively, extremely, greatly, immensely, quite, terribly, very, very much

awhile briefly, for a little while, for a moment, for a short time, for a while

awkward 1. all thumbs, artless, blundering, bungling, clownish, clumsy, coarse, gauche, gawky, graceless, ham-fisted, ham-handed, ill-bred, inelegant, inept, inexpert, lumbering, maladroit, oafish, rude, skill-less, stiff, uncoordinated, un~ couth, ungainly, ungraceful, unpol~ ished, unrefined, unskilful, un~ skilled 2. cumbersome, difficult, inconvenient, troublesome, un~ handy, unmanageable, unwieldy 3. compromising, delicate, difficult, embarrassed, embarrassing, ill at ease, inconvenient, inopportune, painful, perplexing, sticky (*Inf.*), thorny, ticklish, troublesome, try~ing, uncomfortable, unpleasant, untimely 4. annoying, bloody-minded (*Inf.*), difficult, disobliging, exasperating, hard to handle, in~tractable, irritable, perverse, prickly, stubborn, touchy, trouble~some, trying, uncooperative, un~helpful, unpredictable, vexatious, vexing 5. chancy (*Inf.*), dangerous, difficult, hazardous, perilous, risky

awkwardness 1. artlessness, clownishness, clumsiness, coarse~ness, gaucheness, gaucherie, gawkiness, gracelessness, ill-breeding, inelegance, ineptness, inexpertness, maladroitness, oaf~ishness, rudeness, skill-lessness, stiffness, uncoordination, uncouth~ness, ungainliness, unskilfulness, unskilledness 2. cumbersomeness, difficulty, inconvenience, trouble~someness, unhandiness, unman~ageability, unwieldiness 3. delica~cy, difficulty, discomfort, embar~rassment, inconvenience, inoppor~tuneness, painfulness, perplexing~ness, stickiness (*Inf.*), thorniness, ticklishness, unpleasantness, un~timeliness 4. bloody-mindedness (*Inf.*), difficulty, disobligingness, intractability, irritability, perver~sity, prickliness, stubbornness, touchiness, uncooperativeness, unhelpfulness, unpredictability 5. chanciness (*Inf.*), danger, difficul~ty, hazardousness, peril, perilous~ness, risk, riskiness

axe *n.* 1. chopper, hatchet 2. **an axe to grind** grievance, personal con~sideration, pet subject, private ends, private purpose, ulterior motive 3. **the axe** *Inf.* cancellation, cutback, discharge, dismissal, ter~mination, the boot (*Sl.*), the chop (*Sl.*), the sack (*Inf.*), wind-up ~*v.* 4. chop, cut down, fell, hew 5. *Inf.* cancel, cut back, discharge, dis~miss, dispense with, eliminate, fire (*Inf.*), get rid of, remove, sack (*Inf.*), terminate, throw out, turn off (*Inf.*), wind up

axiom adage, aphorism, apo~phthegm, dictum, fundamental, gnome, maxim, postulate, precept, principle, truism

axiomatic 1. absolute, accepted, apodictic, assumed, certain, fun~damental, given, granted, indubi~table, manifest, presupposed, self-evident, understood, unquestioned 2. aphoristic, apophthegmatic, epi~grammatic, gnomic, pithy, terse

axis 1. axle, centre line, pivot, shaft, spindle 2. alliance, bloc, coalition, compact, entente, league, pact

axle arbor, axis, mandrel, pin, piv~ot, rod, shaft, spindle

B

babble 1. *v.* blab, burble, cackle, chatter, gabble, gibber, gurgle, jabber, mumble, murmur, mutter, prate, prattle 2. *n.* burble, clamour, drivel, gabble, gibberish, murmur

babe 1. baby, bairn (*Scot.*), child, infant, nursling, suckling 2. babe in arms, ingénue, innocent

baby 1. *n.* babe, bairn (*Scot.*), child, infant, newborn child 2. *adj.* diminutive, dwarf, little, midget, mini, miniature, minute, pygmy, small, tiny, wee 3. *v.* coddle, cosset, humour, indulge, mollycoddle, overindulge, pamper, pet, spoil, spoon-feed

babyish baby, childish, foolish, immature, infantile, juvenile, namby-pamby, puerile, silly, sissy, soft (*Inf.*), spoiled

back *v.* 1. abet, advocate, assist, champion, countenance, encourage, endorse, favour, finance, sanction, second, side with, sponsor, subsidize, support, sustain, underwrite 2. backtrack, go back, move back, regress, retire, retreat, reverse, turn tail, withdraw ~*n.* 3. backside, end, far end, hind part, hindquarters, posterior, rear, reverse, stern, tail end ~*adj.* 4. end, hind, hindmost, posterior, rear, tail 5. *From an earlier time* delayed, earlier, elapsed, former, overdue, past, previous 6. **behind one's back** covertly, deceitfully, secretly, sneakily, surreptitiously

backbone 1. *Medical* spinal column, spine, vertebrae, vertebral column 2. bottle (*Sl.*), character, courage, determination, firmness, fortitude, grit, hardihood, mettle, moral fibre, nerve, pluck, resolution, resolve, stamina, steadfastness, strength of character, tenacity, toughness, will, willpower 3. basis, foundation, mainstay, support

backbreaking arduous, crushing, exhausting, gruelling, hard, killing, laborious, punishing, strenuous, toilsome, wearing, wearying

back down accede, admit defeat, back-pedal, concede, give in, surrender, withdraw, yield

backer advocate, angel (*Inf.*), benefactor, patron, promoter, second, sponsor, subscriber, supporter, underwriter, well-wisher

backfire boomerang, disappoint, fail, flop, miscarry, rebound, recoil

background breeding, circumstances, credentials, culture, education, environment, experience, grounding, history, milieu, preparation, qualifications, tradition, upbringing

backhanded ambiguous, double-edged, equivocal, indirect, ironic, oblique, sarcastic, sardonic, two-edged

backing abetment, accompaniment, advocacy, aid, assistance, championing, encouragement, endorsement, funds, grant, moral support, patronage, sanction, seconding, sponsorship, subsidy, support

backlash backfire, boomerang, counteraction, counterblast, kickback, reaction, recoil, repercussion, resentment, resistance, response, retaliation, retroaction

backlog accumulation, excess, hoard, reserve, reserves, resources, stock, supply

back out abandon, cancel, chicken out (*Inf.*), give up, go back on, recant, renege, resign, retreat, withdraw

backslide fall from grace, go astray, go wrong, lapse, regress, relapse, renege, retrogress, revert, sin, slip, stray, weaken

backslider apostate, deserter, recidivist, recreant, renegade, reneger, turncoat

back up aid, assist, bolster, confirm, corroborate, reinforce, second, stand by, substantiate, support

backward *adj.* 1. bashful, diffident, hesitating, late, reluctant, shy, sluggish, tardy, unwilling, wavering 2. behind, behindhand, dense, dull, retarded, slow, stupid, subnormal, underdeveloped, undeveloped ~*adv.* 3. aback, behind, in reverse, rearward

backwoods 1. *adj.* hick (*Inf., chiefly U.S.*), isolated, remote, rustic, uncouth 2. *n.* back of beyond, outback, sticks (*Inf.*)

bacteria bacilli, bugs (*Sl.*), germs, microbes, microorganisms, pathogens, viruses

bad 1. defective, deficient, erroneous, fallacious, faulty, imperfect, inadequate, incorrect, inferior, poor, substandard, unsatisfactory 2. damaging, dangerous, deleterious, detrimental, harmful, hurtful, injurious, ruinous, unhealthy 3. base, corrupt, criminal, delinquent, evil, immoral, mean, sinful, vile, villainous, wicked, wrong 4. disobedient, mischievous, naughty, unruly 5. decayed, mouldy, off, putrid, rancid, rotten, sour, spoiled 6. disastrous, distressing, grave, harsh, painful, serious, severe, terrible 7. ailing, diseased, ill, sick, unwell 8. apologetic, conscience-stricken, contrite, guilty, regretful, remorseful, sad, sorry, upset 9. adverse, discouraged, discouraging, distressed, distressing, gloomy, grim, melancholy, troubled, troubling, unfortunate, unpleasant 10. **not bad** all right, average, fair, fair to middling (*Inf.*), moderate, O.K. (*Inf.*), passable, respectable, so-so (*Inf.*), tolerable

badge brand, device, emblem, identification, insignia, mark, sign, stamp, token

badger bully, chivvy, goad, harass, harry, hound, importune, nag, pester, plague, torment

badly 1. carelessly, defectively, erroneously, faultily, imperfectly, inadequately, incorrectly, ineptly, poorly, shoddily, wrong, wrongly 2. unfavourably, unfortunately, unsuccessfully 3. criminally, evilly, immorally, improperly, naughtily, shamefully, unethically, wickedly 4. acutely, deeply, desperately, exceedingly, extremely, gravely, greatly, intensely, painfully, seriously, severely

baffle 1. amaze, astound, bewilder, confound, confuse, daze, disconcert, dumbfound, elude, flummox, mystify, nonplus, perplex, puzzle, stump, stun 2. balk, check, defeat, foil, frustrate, hinder, thwart, upset

bag *v.* 1. balloon, bulge, droop, sag, swell 2. acquire, capture, catch, gain, get, kill, land, shoot, take, trap

baggage accoutrements, bags, belongings, equipment, gear, impedimenta, luggage, paraphernalia, suitcases, things

baggy billowing, bulging, droopy, floppy, ill-fitting, loose, oversize, roomy, sagging, seated, slack

bail[1] *n.* bond, guarantee, guaranty, pledge, security, surety, warranty

bail[2], **bale** *v.* dip, drain off, ladle, scoop

bail out, bale out 1. aid, help, relieve, rescue 2. escape, quit, retreat, withdraw

bait *n.* 1. allurement, attraction, bribe, decoy, enticement, inducement, lure, snare, temptation ~*v.* 2. annoy, gall, harass, hound, irk, irritate, needle (*Inf.*), persecute, provoke, tease, torment 3. allure, beguile, entice, lure, seduce, tempt

baked arid, desiccated, dry, parched, scorched, seared, sun-baked

balance *v.* 1. level, match, parallel, poise, stabilize, steady 2. adjust, compensate for, counteract, counterbalance, counterpoise, equalize, equate, make up for, neutralize, offset 3. assess, compare, consider, deliberate, estimate, evaluate, weigh 4. calculate, compute, settle, square, tally, total ~*n.* 5. correspondence, equilibrium, equipoise, equity, equivalence, evenness, parity, symmetry 6. composure, equanimity, poise, self-control, self-possession, stability, steadiness 7. difference, remainder, residue, rest, surplus

balanced disinterested, equitable, even-handed, fair, impartial, just, unbiased, unprejudiced

balance sheet account, budget, credits and debits, ledger, report, statement

balcony 1. terrace, veranda 2. gallery, gods, upper circle

bald 1. baldheaded, baldpated, depilated, glabrous (*Biol.*), hairless 2. barren, bleak, exposed, naked, stark, treeless, uncovered 3. bare, blunt, direct, downright, forthright, outright, plain, severe, simple, straight, straightforward, unadorned, unvarnished

balderdash bunk (*Inf.*), bunkum, claptrap (*Inf.*), drivel, gibberish, nonsense, poppycock (*Inf.*), rot, rubbish, tommyrot, trash, twaddle

baldness 1. alopecia (*Pathology*), baldheadedness, baldpatedness, glabrousness (*Biol.*), hairlessness 2. barrenness, bleakness, nakedness, sparseness, starkness, treelessness 3. austerity, bluntness, plainness, severity, simplicity, spareness

balk 1. demur, dodge, evade, flinch, hesitate, jib, recoil, refuse, resist, shirk, shrink from 2. baffle, bar, check, counteract, defeat, disconcert, foil, forestall, frustrate, hinder, obstruct, prevent, thwart

ball 1. drop, globe, globule, orb, pellet, sphere, spheroid 2. ammunition, bullet, grapeshot, pellet, shot, slug

ballast balance, counterbalance, counterweight, equilibrium, sandbag, stability, stabilizer, weight

balloon *v.* belly, billow, bloat, blow up, dilate, distend, enlarge, expand, inflate, puff out, swell

ballot election, poll, polling, vote, voting

ballyhoo 1. babble, commotion, fuss, hubbub, hue and cry, hullabaloo, noise, racket, to-do 2. advertising, build-up, hype (*Sl.*), promotion, propaganda, publicity

balm 1. balsam, cream, embrocation, emollient, lotion, ointment, salve, unguent 2. anodyne, comfort, consolation, curative, palliative, restorative, solace

balmy 1. clement, mild, pleasant, summery, temperate 2. *Also* barmy crazy, daft, foolish, idiotic, insane, loony (*Sl.*), nuts (*Sl.*), nutty (*Sl.*), odd, silly, stupid

bamboozle 1. cheat, con (*Sl.*), deceive, defraud, delude, dupe, fool, hoax, hoodwink, swindle, trick 2. baffle, befuddle, confound, confuse, mystify, perplex, puzzle, stump

ban 1. *v.* banish, bar, debar, disallow, exclude, forbid, interdict, outlaw, prohibit, proscribe, restrict, suppress 2. *n.* boycott, censorship, embargo, interdiction, prohibition, proscription, restriction, stoppage, suppression, taboo

banal clichéd, cliché-ridden, commonplace, everyday, hackneyed, humdrum, old hat, ordinary, pedestrian, platitudinous, stale, stereotyped, stock, threadbare, tired, trite, unimaginative, unoriginal, vapid

banality bromide (*Inf.*), cliché, commonplace, platitude, triteness, trite phrase, triviality, truism, vapidity

band¹ *n.* bandage, belt, binding, bond, chain, cord, fetter, fillet, ligature, manacle, ribbon, shackle, strap, strip, tie

band² *n.* 1. assembly, association, body, clique, club, company, coterie, crew (*Inf.*), gang, horde, party, society, troop 2. combo, ensemble, group, orchestra ~*v.* 3. affiliate, ally, consolidate, federate, gather, group, join, merge, unite

bandage 1. *n.* compress, dressing, gauze, plaster 2. *v.* bind, cover, dress, swathe

bandit brigand, crook, desperado, footpad, freebooter, gangster, gunman, highwayman, hijacker, marauder, outlaw, pirate, racketeer, robber, thief

bandy 1. *v.* barter, exchange, interchange, pass, shuffle, swap, throw, toss, trade 2. *adj.* bandy-legged, bent, bowed, bow-legged, crooked, curved

bane affliction, *bête noir*, blight,

baneful baleful, calamitous, deadly, deleterious, destructive, disastrous, fatal, harmful, hurtful, injurious, noxious, pernicious, pestilential, ruinous, venomous

bang n. 1. boom, burst, clang, clap, clash, detonation, explosion, peal, pop, report, shot, slam, thud, thump 2. blow, box, bump, cuff, hit, knock, punch, smack, stroke, wallop (*Inf.*), whack ~v. 3. bash (*Inf.*), beat, bump, clatter, crash, hammer, knock, pound, pummel, rap, slam, strike, thump 4. boom, burst, clang, detonate, drum, echo, explode, peal, resound, thump, thunder ~adv. 5. abruptly, hard, headlong, noisily, precisely, slap, smack, straight, suddenly

banish 1. deport, drive away, eject, evict, exclude, excommunicate, exile, expatriate, expel, ostracize, outlaw, shut out, transport 2. ban, cast out, discard, dislodge, dismiss, dispel, eliminate, eradicate, get rid of, oust, remove, shake off

banishment deportation, exile, expatriation, expulsion, proscription, transportation

banisters balusters, balustrade, handrail, rail, railing

bank[1] 1. n. accumulation, depository, fund, hoard, repository, reserve, reservoir, savings, stock, stockpile, store, storehouse 2. v. deal with, deposit, keep, save, transact business with

bank[2] n. 1. banking, embankment, heap, mass, mound, pile, ridge 2. brink, edge, margin, shore, side ~v. 3. amass, heap, mass, mound, pile, stack 4. camber, cant, incline, pitch, slant, slope, tilt, tip

bank on assume, believe in, count on, depend on, lean on, look to, rely on, trust

bankrupt broke (*Inf.*), depleted, destitute, exhausted, failed, impoverished, insolvent, lacking, ruined, spent

bankruptcy disaster, exhaustion, failure, indebtedness, insolvency, lack, liquidation, ruin

banner banderole, burgee, colours, ensign, fanion, flag, gonfalon, pennant, pennon, standard, streamer

banquet dinner, feast, meal, repast, revel, treat

banter 1. v. chaff, deride, jeer, jest, joke, kid (*Inf.*), make fun of, rib (*Inf.*), ridicule, taunt, twit 2. n. badinage, chaff, chaffing, derision, jeering, jesting, joking, kidding (*Inf.*), mockery, persiflage, pleasantry, raillery, repartee, ribbing (*Inf.*), ridicule, wordplay

baptism 1. christening, immersion, purification, sprinkling 2. beginning, debut, dedication, initiation, introduction, launching, rite of passage

baptize 1. besprinkle, cleanse, immerse, purify 2. admit, enrol, initiate, recruit 3. call, christen, dub, name, title

bar n. 1. batten, crosspiece, paling, pole, rail, rod, shaft, stake, stick 2. barricade, barrier, deterrent, hindrance, impediment, obstacle, obstruction, rail, railing, stop 3. boozer (*Inf.*), canteen, counter, inn, lounge, pub (*Inf.*), public house, saloon, tavern 4. bench, court, courtroom, dock, law court 5. *Law* barristers, body of lawyers, counsel, court, judgment, tribunal ~v. 6. barricade, bolt, fasten, latch, lock, secure 7. ban, exclude, forbid, hinder, keep out, obstruct, prevent, prohibit, restrain

barb 1. bristle, point, prickle, prong, quill, spike, spur, thorn 2. affront, cut, dig, gibe, insult, rebuff, sarcasm, scoff, sneer

barbarian n. 1. brute, hooligan, lout, ruffian, savage, vandal, yahoo 2. bigot, boor, ignoramus, illiterate, lowbrow, philistine ~adj. 3. boorish, crude, lowbrow, philistine, primitive, uncouth, uncultivated, uncultured, unsophisticated, vulgar

barbaric 1. primitive, rude, uncivilized, wild 2. barbarous, boorish, brutal, coarse, crude, cruel, fierce, inhuman, savage, uncouth, vulgar

barbarism 1. coarseness, crudity, savagery, uncivilizedness 2. atrocity, barbarity, enormity, outrage 3. corruption, misusage, misuse, solecism, vulgarism

barbarity brutality, cruelty, inhumanity, ruthlessness, savagery, viciousness

barbarous 1. barbarian, brutish, primitive, rough, rude, savage, uncivilized, uncouth, wild 2. barbaric, brutal, cruel, ferocious, heartless, inhuman, monstrous, ruthless, vicious 3. coarse, crude, ignorant, uncultured, unlettered, unrefined, vulgar

bare 1. denuded, exposed, naked, nude, peeled, shorn, stripped, unclad, unclothed, uncovered, undressed 2. barren, blank, empty, lacking, mean, open, poor, scanty, scarce, unfurnished, vacant, void, wanting 3. austere, basic, basic, cold, essential, hard, literal, plain, severe, sheer, simple, spare, stark, unadorned, unembellished, unvarnished

barefaced 1. audacious, bold, brash, brazen, impudent, insolent, shameless 2. bald, blatant, flagrant, glaring, manifest, naked, obvious, open, palpable, patent, transparent, unconcealed

barely almost, hardly, just, only just, scarcely

bargain n. 1. agreement, arrangement, business, compact, contract, convention, engagement, negotiation, pact, pledge, promise, stipulation, transaction, treaty, understanding 2. (cheap) purchase, discount, giveaway, good buy, good deal, good value, reduction, snip (Inf.) ~v. 3. agree, contract, covenant, negotiate, promise, stipulate, transact 4. barter, buy, deal, haggle, sell, trade, traffic

bargain for anticipate, contemplate, expect, foresee, imagine, look for, plan for

bargain on assume, bank on, count on, depend on, plan on, rely on

barge canal boat, flatboat, lighter, narrow boat, scow

barge in break in, burst in, butt in, infringe, interrupt, intrude, muscle in (Inf.)

barge into bump into, cannon into, collide with, hit, push, shove

bark¹ 1. n. casing, cortex (Anat., bot.), covering, crust, husk, rind, skin 2. v. abrade, flay, rub, scrape, shave, skin, strip

bark² 1. n./v. bay, growl, howl, snarl, woof, yap, yelp 2. v. Fig. bawl, bawl at, berate, bluster, growl, shout, snap, snarl, yell

barmy 1. Also **balmy** crazy, daft, foolish, idiotic, insane, loony (Sl.), nuts (Sl.), nutty (Sl.), odd, silly, stupid 2. fermenting, foamy, frothy, spumy, yeasty

baroque bizarre, convoluted, elaborate, extravagant, flamboyant, florid, grotesque, ornate, overdecorated

barracks billet, camp, cantonment, casern, encampment, garrison, quarters

barrage 1. battery, bombardment, cannonade, curtain of fire, fusillade, gunfire, salvo, shelling, volley 2. assault, attack, burst, deluge, hail, mass, onslaught, plethora, profusion, rain, storm, stream, torrent

barren 1. childless, infecund, infertile, sterile, unprolific 2. arid, desert, desolate, dry, empty, unfruitful, unproductive, waste 3. boring, dull, flat, fruitless, lacklustre, stale, uninformative, uninspiring, uninstructive, uninteresting, unrewarding, useless, vapid

barricade 1. n. barrier, blockade, bulwark, fence, obstruction, palisade, rampart, stockade 2. v. bar, block, blockade, defend, fortify, obstruct, protect, shut in

barrier 1. bar, barricade, blockade, boundary, ditch, fence, fortification, obstacle, obstruction, railing, rampart, stop, wall 2. Fig. check, difficulty, drawback, handicap, hindrance, hurdle, impediment, limitation, obstacle, restriction, stumbling block

barter bargain, exchange, haggle, sell, swap, trade, traffic

base¹ n. 1. bed, bottom, foot, foundation, groundwork, pedestal, rest, stand, support 2. basis, core, essence, essential, fundamental, heart, key, origin, principal, root, source 3. camp, centre, headquarters, home, post, settlement, starting point, station ~*v.* 4. build, construct, depend, derive, establish, found, ground, hinge, locate, station

base² 1. abject, contemptible, corrupt, depraved, despicable, dishonourable, disreputable, evil, ignoble, immoral, infamous, scandalous, shameful, sordid, vile, villainous, vulgar, wicked 2. downtrodden, grovelling, low, lowly, mean, menial, miserable, paltry, pitiful, poor, servile, slavish, sorry, subservient, worthless, wretched 3. adulterated, alloyed, counterfeit, debased, fake, forged, fraudulent, impure, inferior, pinchbeck, spurious

baseless groundless, unconfirmed, uncorroborated, unfounded, ungrounded, unjustifiable, unjustified, unsubstantiated, unsupported

baseness 1. contemptibility, degradation, depravation, depravity, despicability, disgrace, ignominy, infamy, notoriety, obloquy, turpitude 2. lowliness, meanness, misery, poverty, servility, slavishness, subservience, vileness, worthlessness, wretchedness 3. adulteration, debasement, fraudulence, phoneyness (*Sl.*), pretence, speciousness, spuriousness

bash 1. *v.* biff (*Sl.*), break, crash, crush, hit, punch, slosh (*Sl.*), smash, sock (*Sl.*), strike, wallop (*Inf.*) 2. *n.* attempt, crack, go, shot, stab, try

bashful abashed, blushing, confused, constrained, coy, diffident, easily embarrassed, nervous, overmodest, reserved, reticent, retiring, self-conscious, self-effacing, shamefaced, sheepish, shrinking, shy, timid, timorous

basic central, elementary, essential, fundamental, indispensable, inherent, intrinsic, key, necessary, primary, underlying, vital

basically at bottom, at heart, *au*

fond, essentially, firstly, fundamentally, inherently, in substance, intrinsically, mostly, primarily, radically

basics brass tacks (*Inf.*), core, essentials, facts, fundamentals, hard facts, necessaries, nitty-gritty (*Sl.*), nuts and bolts (*Inf.*), practicalities, principles, rudiments

basis 1. base, bottom, footing, foundation, ground, groundwork, support 2. chief ingredient, core, essential, fundamental, heart, premise, principal element, principle, theory

bask 1. laze, lie in, loll, lounge, relax, sunbathe, swim in, toast oneself, warm oneself 2. delight in, enjoy, indulge oneself, luxuriate, relish, revel, savour, take pleasure, wallow

bass deep, deep-toned, grave, low, low-pitched, resonant, sonorous

bastard 1. *n.* illegitimate (child), love child, natural child 2. *adj.* adulterated, baseborn, counterfeit, false, illegitimate, imperfect, impure, inferior, irregular, misbegotten, sham, spurious

bastion bulwark, citadel, defence, fastness, fortress, mainstay, prop, rock, stronghold, support, tower of strength

bat bang, hit, rap, smack, strike, swat, thump, wallop (*Inf.*), whack

batch accumulation, aggregation, amount, assemblage, bunch, collection, crowd, group, lot, pack, quantity, set

bath 1. *n.* ablution, cleansing, douche, douse, scrubbing, shower, soak, soaping, sponging, tub, wash, washing 2. *v.* bathe, clean, douse, lave (*Archaic*), scrub down, shower, soak, soap, sponge, tub, wash

bathe 1. *v.* cleanse, cover, dunk, flood, immerse, moisten, rinse, soak, steep, suffuse, wash, wet 2. *n.* dip, swim

bathing costume bathing suit, bikini, swimming costume, swimsuit, trunks

bathos anticlimax, false pathos, mawkishness, sentimentality

baton club, mace, rod, staff, stick, truncheon, wand

battalion army, brigade, company, contingent, division, force, horde, host, legion, multitude, regiment, squadron, throng

batten[1] board up, clamp down, cover up, fasten, fasten down, fix, nail down, secure, tighten

batten[2] fatten, flourish, gain, grow, increase, prosper, thrive, wax

batter 1. assault, bash, beat, belabour, break, buffet, dash against, lash, pelt, pound, pummel, smash, smite, thrash, wallop (*Inf.*) 2. bruise, crush, deface, demolish, destroy, disfigure, hurt, injure, mangle, mar, maul, ruin, shatter, shiver

battered beaten, broken-down, bruised, crushed, damaged, dilapidated, injured, ramshackle, squashed, weather-beaten

battery 1. chain, ring, sequence, series, set, suite 2. assault, attack, beating, mayhem, onslaught, physical violence, thumping 3. artillery, cannon, cannonry, gun emplacements, guns

battle *n.* 1. action, attack, combat, encounter, engagement, fight, fray, hostilities, skirmish, war, warfare 2. agitation, campaign, clash, conflict, contest, controversy, crusade, debate, disagreement, dispute, strife, struggle ~*v.* 3. agitate, argue, clamour, combat, contend, contest, dispute, feud, fight, strive, struggle, war

battle cry catchword, motto, slogan, war cry, war whoop, watchword

battlefield battleground, combat zone, field, field of battle, front

battleship capital ship, gunboat, man-of-war, ship of the line, warship

batty barmy (*Sl.*), bats (*Sl.*), bonkers (*Sl.*), cracked (*Sl.*), crackers (*Sl.*), cranky (*Inf.*), crazy, daft, dotty (*Sl.*), eccentric, insane, loony (*Sl.*), lunatic, mad, nuts (*Sl.*), nutty (*Sl.*), odd, peculiar, potty (*Inf.*), queer, screwy (*Inf.*), touched

bauble bagatelle, gewgaw, gimcrack, kickshaw, knick-knack, plaything, toy, trifle, trinket

bawd brothel-keeper, madam, pimp, procuress, prostitute, whore

bawdy blue, coarse, dirty, erotic, gross, indecent, indecorous, indelicate, lascivious, lecherous, lewd, libidinous, licentious, lustful, obscene, prurient, ribald, risqué, rude, salacious, suggestive, vulgar

bawl 1. bellow, call, clamour, halloo, howl, roar, shout, vociferate, yell 2. blubber, cry, sob, squall, wail, weep

bay[1] bight, cove, gulf, inlet, natural harbour, sound

bay[2] alcove, compartment, embrasure, niche, nook, opening, recess

bay[3] 1. bark, bell, clamour, cry, growl, howl, yelp 2. at bay caught, cornered, trapped

bayonet *v.* impale, knife, run through, spear, stab, stick, transfix

bazaar 1. exchange, market, marketplace, mart 2. bring-and-buy, fair, fête

be 1. be alive, breathe, exist, inhabit, live 2. befall, come about, come to pass, happen, occur, take place, transpire (*Inf.*) 3. abide, continue, endure, last, obtain, persist, prevail, remain, stand, stay, survive

beach coast, littoral, margin, sands, seaboard (*Chiefly U.S.*), seashore, seaside, shingle, shore, strand, water's edge

beachcomber forager, loafer, scavenger, scrounger, tramp, vagabond, vagrant, wanderer

beached abandoned, aground, ashore, deserted, grounded, high and dry, marooned, stranded, wrecked

beacon beam, bonfire, flare, lighthouse, pharos, rocket, sign, signal, signal fire, smoke signal, watchtower

bead blob, bubble, dot, drop, droplet, globule, pellet, pill, spherule

beads chaplet, choker, necklace, necklet, pearls, pendant, rosary

beak 1. bill, mandible, neb (*Archaic or dialect*), nib 2. nose, proboscis, snout 3. *Naut.* bow, prow, ram, rostrum, stem

beam *n.* 1. girder, joist, plank, raft~ er, spar, support, timber 2. bar, emission, gleam, glimmer, glint, glow, radiation, ray, shaft, streak, stream ~*v.* 3. broadcast, emit, glare, gleam, glitter, glow, radiate, shine, transmit 4. grin, laugh, smile

beaming 1. beautiful, bright, bril~ liant, flashing, gleaming, glisten~ ing, glittering, radiant, scintillat~ ing, shining, sparkling 2. cheerful, grinning, happy, joyful, smiling, sunny

bear 1. bring, carry, convey, move, take, tote, transport 2. cherish, en~ tertain, exhibit, harbour, have, hold, maintain, possess, shoulder, support, sustain, uphold, weigh upon 3. abide, admit, allow, brook, endure, permit, put up with (*Inf.*), stomach, suffer, tolerate, undergo 4. beget, breed, bring forth, devel~ op, engender, generate, give birth to, produce, yield

bearable admissible, endurable, manageable, passable, sufferable, supportable, sustainable, tolerable

beard 1. *n.* bristles, five-o'clock shadow, stubble, whiskers 2. *v.* brave, confront, dare, defy, face, oppose

bearded bewhiskered, bristly, bushy, hairy, hirsute, shaggy, stub~ bly, unshaven, whiskered

beardless 1. barefaced, clean-shaven, hairless, smooth, smooth-faced 2. callow, fresh, green, im~ mature, inexperienced

bear down 1. burden, compress, encumber, press down, push, strain, weigh down 2. advance on, approach, attack, close in, con~ verge on, move in

bearer 1. agent, carrier, conveyor, messenger, porter, runner, servant 2. beneficiary, consignee, payee

bearing 1. air, aspect, attitude, be~ haviour, carriage, demeanour, de~ portment, manner, mien, posture 2. *Naut.* course, direction, point of compass 3. application, connec~ tion, import, pertinence, reference, relation, relevance, significance

bearings aim, course, direction, location, orientation, position, situation, track, way, whereabouts

bear on affect, appertain to, belong to, concern, involve, pertain to, re~ fer to, relate to, touch upon

bear out confirm, corroborate, en~ dorse, justify, prove, substantiate, support, uphold, vindicate

bear up bear the brunt, carry on, endure, grin and bear it (*Inf.*), per~ severe, suffer, withstand

bear with be patient, forbear, make allowances, put up with (*Inf.*), suffer, tolerate, wait

beast 1. animal, brute, creature 2. barbarian, brute, fiend, monster, ogre, sadist, savage, swine

beastly 1. barbarous, bestial, bru~ tal, brutish, coarse, cruel, de~ praved, inhuman, monstrous, re~ pulsive, sadistic, savage 2. awful, disagreeable, foul, mean, nasty, rotten, terrible, unpleasant

beat *v.* 1. bang, batter, break, bruise, buffet, cane, cudgel, drub, flog, hit, knock, lash, maul, pelt, pound, punch, strike, thrash, thwack, whip 2. best, conquer, de~ feat, excel, outdo, outrun, outstrip, overcome, overwhelm, subdue, surpass, vanquish 3. fashion, forge, form, hammer, model, shape, work 4. flap, flutter, palpitate, pound, pulsate, pulse, quake, quiver, shake, throb, thump, tremble, vi~ brate ~*n.* 5. blow, hit, lash, punch, shake, slap, strike, swing, thump 6. flutter, palpitation, pulsation, pulse, throb 7. accent, cadence, measure, metre, rhythm, stress, time 8. cir~ cuit, course, path, rounds, route, way ~*adj.* 9. *Sl.* exhausted, fa~ tigued, tired, wearied, worn out

beaten 1. baffled, cowed, defeated, disappointed, disheartened, frus~ trated, overcome, overwhelmed, thwarted, vanquished 2. forged, formed, hammered, shaped, stamped, worked 3. much trav~ elled, trampled, trodden, well-trodden, well-used, worn 4. blend~ ed, foamy, frothy, mixed, stirred, whipped, whisked

beating 1. belting (*Inf.*), caning, chastisement, corporal punish~

ment, flogging, slapping, smacking, thrashing, whipping 2. conquest, defeat, downfall, overthrow, rout, ruin

beat up assault, attack, batter, do over (*Sl.*), duff up (*Sl.*), fill in (*Sl.*), knock about or around, thrash

beau 1. admirer, boyfriend, escort, fiancé, lover, suitor, swain, sweet~ heart 2. cavalier, coxcomb, dandy, fop, gallant, ladies' man, popinjay, swell (*Inf.*)

beautiful alluring, appealing, at~ tractive, charming, comely, de~ lightful, exquisite, fair, fine, good-looking, gorgeous, graceful, hand~ some, lovely, pleasing, radiant, ravishing, stunning (*Inf.*)

beautify adorn, array, bedeck, deck, decorate, embellish, en~ hance, garnish, gild, glamorize, grace, ornament

beauty 1. allure, attractiveness, bloom, charm, comeliness, el~ egance, exquisiteness, fairness, glamour, grace, handsomeness, loveliness, pulchritude, seemliness, symmetry 2. belle, charmer, cracker (*Sl.*), goddess, good-looker, lovely (*Sl.*), stunner (*Inf.*), Venus 3. advantage, asset, attraction, ben~ efit, blessing, boon, excellence, feature, good thing

becalmed motionless, settled, still, stranded, stuck

because as, by reason of, in that, on account of, owing to, since, thanks to

beckon 1. bid, gesticulate, gesture, motion, nod, signal, summon, wave at 2. allure, attract, call, coax, draw, entice, invite, lure, pull, tempt

becloud bedim, befog, complicate, confuse, darken, muddle, obfus~ cate, obscure, overcast, screen, veil

become 1. alter to, be transformed into, change into, develop into, evolve into, grow into, mature into, metamorphose into, ripen into 2. embellish, enhance, fit, flatter, grace, harmonize, ornament, set off, suit

becoming 1. attractive, comely,

enhancing, flattering, graceful, neat, pretty, tasteful 2. appropri~ ate, befitting, *comme il faut*, com~ patible, congruous, decent, deco~ rous, fit, fitting, in keeping, meet (*Archaic*), proper, seemly, suit~ able, worthy

bed *n.* 1. bedstead, berth, bunk, cot, couch, divan, pallet 2. area, border, garden, patch, plot, row, strip 3. base, bottom, foundation, ground~ work, substratum ~*v.* 4. base, em~ bed, establish, fix, found, implant, insert, plant, settle, set up

bedazzle amaze, astound, bewilder, blind, captivate, confuse, daze, dazzle, dumbfound, enchant, over~ whelm, stagger, stun

bedclothes bedding, bed linen, blankets, coverlets, covers, eider~ downs, pillowcases, pillows, quilts, sheets

bed down lie, retire, settle down, sleep, turn in (*Inf.*)

bedeck adorn, array, bedight (*Ar~ chaic*), bedizen (*Archaic*), deco~ rate, embellish, festoon, garnish, ornament, trim

bedevil afflict, annoy, confound, distress, fret, frustrate, harass, irk, irritate, pester, plague, torment, torture, trouble, vex, worry

bedlam chaos, clamour, commo~ tion, confusion, furore, hubbub, madhouse (*Inf.*), noise, pandemo~ nium, tumult, turmoil, uproar

bedraggled dirty, dishevelled, dis~ ordered, drenched, dripping, messy, muddied, muddy, sodden, soiled, stained, sullied, unkempt, untidy

bedridden confined, confined to bed, flat on one's back, incapaci~ tated, laid up (*Inf.*)

bedrock 1. bed, bottom, foundation, nadir, rock bottom, substratum, substructure 2. basics, basis, core, essentials, fundamentals, roots

beef 1. *Inf.* brawn, flesh, heftiness, muscle, physique, robustness, sin~ ew, strength 2. *Sl.* complaint, criti~ cism, dispute, grievance, gripe (*Inf.*), grouse, grumble, objection, protestation

beefy *Inf.* 1. brawny, bulky, burly,

hulking, muscular, stalwart, stocky, strapping, sturdy 2. chubby, corpulent, fat, fleshy, heavy, obese, overweight, paunchy, plump, podgy, portly, pudgy, rotund

beetle, beetling *adj.* jutting, leaning over, overhanging, pendent, projecting, protruding, sticking out, swelling over

befall bechance, betide, chance, come to pass, ensue, fall, follow, happen, materialize, occur, supervene, take place, transpire (*Inf.*)

befitting appropriate, becoming, fit, fitting, meet (*Archaic*), proper, right, seemly, suitable

before 1. *adv.* ahead, earlier, formerly, in advance, in front, previously, sooner 2. *prep.* earlier than, in advance of, in front of, in the presence of, prior to

beforehand ahead of time, already, before, before now, earlier, in advance, in anticipation, previously, sooner

befriend advise, aid, assist, back, benefit, encourage, favour, help, patronize, side with, stand by, succour, support, sustain, uphold, welcome

befuddled confused, dazed, fuddled, groggy (*Inf.*), inebriated, intoxicated, muddled, woozy (*Inf.*)

beg 1. beseech, crave, desire, entreat, implore, importune, petition, plead, pray, request, solicit, supplicate 2. cadge, call for alms, scrounge, seek charity, solicit charity, sponge on 3. *As in* beg the question avoid, dodge, duck (*Inf.*), equivocate, eschew, evade, fend off, hedge, parry, shirk, shun, sidestep

beggar *n.* 1. cadger, mendicant, scrounger (*Inf.*), sponger (*Inf.*), supplicant, tramp, vagrant 2. bankrupt, down-and-out, pauper, starveling ~*v.* 3. *As in* beggar description baffle, challenge, defy, surpass

beggarly abject, base, contemptible, despicable, destitute, impoverished, inadequate, indigent, low, meagre, mean, miserly, needy, niggardly, pitiful, poor, poverty-stricken, stingy, vile, wretched

begin 1. commence, embark on, inaugurate, initiate, instigate, institute, prepare, set about, set on foot, start 2. appear, arise, be born, come into being, come into existence, commence, crop up (*Inf.*), dawn, emerge, happen, originate, spring, start

beginner amateur, apprentice, fledgling, freshman, greenhorn (*Inf.*), initiate, learner, neophyte, novice, recruit, starter, student, tenderfoot, trainee, tyro

beginning 1. birth, commencement, inauguration, inception, initiation, onset, opening, origin, outset, preface, prelude, rise, rudiments, source, start, starting point 2. embryo, fountainhead, germ, root, seed

begrime besmirch, blacken, dirty, muddy, smear, smirch, soil, spatter, stain, sully, tarnish

begrudge be jealous, be reluctant, be stingy, envy, grudge, resent

beguile 1. befool, cheat, deceive, delude, dupe, fool, hoodwink, impose on, mislead, trick 2. amuse, charm, cheer, delight, distract, divert, engross, entertain, occupy, solace

beguiling alluring, attractive, bewitching, captivating, charming, diverting, enchanting, entertaining, enthralling, interesting, intriguing

behalf account, advantage, benefit, defence, good, interest, part, profit, sake, side, support

behave 1. act, function, operate, perform, run, work 2. act correctly, conduct oneself properly, mind one's manners

behaviour 1. actions, bearing, carriage, comportment, conduct, demeanour, deportment, manner, manners, ways 2. action, functioning, operation, performance

behest bidding, charge, command, commandment, decree, dictate, direction, expressed desire, injunction, instruction, mandate, order, precept, wish

behind *prep.* 1. after, at the back of, at the rear of, following, later than 2. at the bottom of, causing, initiating, instigating, responsible for 3. backing, for, in agreement, on the side of, supporting ~*adv.* 4. after, afterwards, following, in the wake (of), next, subsequently 5. behindhand, in arrears, in debt, overdue ~*n.* 6. bottom, buttocks, posterior, rump, seat

behindhand backward, behind time, dilatory, late, remiss, slow, tardy

behold 1. *v.* consider, contemplate, discern, eye, look at, observe, perceive, regard, scan, survey, view, watch, witness 2. *interj.* lo, look, mark, observe, see, watch

beholden bound, grateful, indebted, obligated, obliged, owing, under obligation

beige biscuit, buff, *café au lait*, camel, cinnamon, coffee, cream, ecru, fawn, khaki, mushroom, neutral, oatmeal, sand, tan

being 1. actuality, animation, existence, life, living, reality 2. entity, essence, nature, soul, spirit, substance 3. animal, beast, body, creature, human being, individual, living thing, mortal, thing

belabour 1. batter, beat, flog, lambaste, thrash, whip 2. attack, berate, castigate, censure, criticize, flay, lay into

belated behindhand, behind time, delayed, late, overdue, tardy

belch 1. burp (*Inf.*), eruct, eructate, hiccup 2. discharge, disgorge, emit, erupt, give off, gush, spew forth, vent, vomit

beleaguered badgered, beset, besieged, bothered, harassed, nagged, persecuted, plagued, put upon, set upon, vexed

belief 1. admission, assent, assurance, confidence, conviction, credit, feeling, impression, judgment, notion, opinion, persuasion, presumption, reliance, theory, trust, view 2. credence, credo, creed, doctrine, dogma, faith, ideology, principles, tenet

believable acceptable, authentic, credible, creditable, imaginable, likely, plausible, possible, probable, reliable, trustworthy

believe 1. accept, be certain of, be convinced of, count on, credit, depend on, have faith in, hold, place confidence in, presume true, rely on, swear by, trust 2. assume, conjecture, consider, gather, guess, imagine, judge, maintain, postulate, presume, reckon, speculate, suppose, think

believer adherent, convert, devotee, disciple, follower, proselyte, supporter, upholder, zealot

bellow bawl, call, clamour, cry, howl, roar, scream, shout, shriek, yell

belly 1. *n.* abdomen, breadbasket (*Sl.*), corporation (*Inf.*), gut, insides (*Inf.*), paunch, potbelly, stomach, tummy, vitals 2. *v.* billow, bulge, fill, spread, swell, swell out

belong 1. *With* to be at the disposal of, be held by, be owned by, be the property of 2. *With* to be affiliated to, be allied to, be a member of, be associated with, be included in 3. attach to, be connected with, be fitting, be part of, fit, go with, have as a proper place, pertain to, relate to

belonging acceptance, affinity, association, attachment, fellowship, inclusion, kinship, loyalty, rapport, relationship

belongings accoutrements, chattels, effects, gear, goods, paraphernalia, personal property, possessions, stuff, things

beloved admired, adored, cherished, darling, dear, dearest, loved, pet, precious, prized, revered, sweet, treasured, worshipped

below *adv.* 1. beneath, down, lower, under, underneath ~*prep.* 2. inferior, lesser, less than, subject, subordinate, unworthy of 3. **below par** below average, imperfect, inferior, off colour, off form, poor, second-rate, unfit

belt 1. band, cincture, cummerbund, girdle, girth, sash, waistband 2. *Geog.* area, district, layer, region, stretch, strip, tract, zone 3.

below the belt cowardly, foul, not playing the game (*Inf.*), unfair, unjust, unscrupulous, unsporting, unsportsmanlike

bemused absent-minded, bewildered, confused, dazed, engrossed, fuddled, half-drunk, muddled, perplexed, preoccupied, stunned, stupefied, tipsy

bench 1. form, pew, seat, settle, stall 2. board, counter, table, trestle table, workbench, worktable 3. court, courtroom, judge, judges, judiciary, magistrate, magistrates, tribunal

bend *v.* 1. bow, buckle, contort, crouch, curve, deflect, diverge, flex, incline, incurvate, lean, stoop, swerve, turn, twist, veer, warp 2. compel, direct, influence, mould, persuade, shape, subdue, submit, sway, yield ~*n.* 3. angle, arc, bow, corner, crook, curve, hook, loop, turn, twist, zigzag

beneath 1. *adv.* below, in a lower place, underneath 2. *prep.* below, inferior to, less than, lower than, unbefitting, underneath, unworthy of

beneficial advantageous, benign, favourable, gainful, healthful, helpful, profitable, salubrious, salutary, serviceable, useful, valuable, wholesome

benefit 1. *n.* advantage, aid, asset, assistance, avail, betterment, blessing, boon, favour, gain, good, help, interest, profit, use 2. *v.* advance, advantage, aid, ameliorate, assist, avail, better, enhance, further, improve, profit, promote, serve

bent *adj.* 1. angled, arched, bowed, crooked, curved, hunched, stooped, twisted 2. *With* on determined, disposed, fixed, inclined, insistent, predisposed, resolved, set ~*n.* 3. ability, aptitude, facility, faculty, flair, forte, inclination, knack, leaning, penchant, preference, proclivity, propensity, talent, tendency

bequeath bestow, commit, endow, entrust, give, grant, hand down, impart, leave to by will, pass on, transmit, will

bequest bequeathal, bestowal, dower, endowment, estate, gift, heritage, inheritance, legacy, settlement, trust

bereave afflict, deprive of kindred, dispossess, divest, make destitute, strip, take away from, widow

bereavement affliction, death, deprivation, loss, misfortune, tribulation

berserk crazy, enraged, frantic, frenzied, insane, mad, maniacal, manic, rabid, raging, uncontrollable, violent, wild

berth *n.* 1. bed, billet, bunk, cot (*Naut.*), hammock 2. anchorage, dock, harbour, haven, pier, port, quay, slip, wharf 3. appointment, employment, job, living, position, post, situation ~*v.* 4. *Naut.* anchor, dock, drop anchor, land, moor, tie up

beseech adjure, ask, beg, call upon, crave, entreat, implore, importune, petition, plead, pray, solicit, sue, supplicate

beside 1. abreast of, adjacent to, alongside, at the side of, close to, near, nearby, neighbouring, next door to, next to, overlooking 2. **beside oneself** apoplectic, berserk, crazed, delirious, demented, deranged, distraught, frantic, frenzied, insane, mad, out of one's mind, unbalanced, uncontrolled, unhinged

besides 1. *adv.* also, as well, further, furthermore, in addition, moreover, otherwise, too, what's more 2. *prep.* apart from, barring, excepting, excluding, in addition to, other than, over and above, without

besiege 1. beleaguer, beset, blockade, confine, encircle, encompass, environ, hedge in, hem in, invest (*Rare*), lay siege to, shut in, surround 2. badger, bother, harass, harry, hound, importune, nag, pester, plague, trouble

besotted 1. befuddled, drunk, intoxicated, stupefied 2. doting, hypnotized, infatuated, smitten, spell-

bound 3. confused, foolish, mud~
dled, witless

best *adj.* 1. chief, finest, first, first-
class, first-rate, foremost, highest,
leading, most excellent, outstand~
ing, perfect, pre-eminent, princi~
pal, superlative, supreme, unsur~
passed 2. advantageous, apt, cor~
rect, golden, most desirable, most
fitting, right 3. greatest, largest,
most ~*adv.* 4. advantageously, at~
tractively, excellently, most fortu~
nately 5. extremely, greatly, most
deeply, most fully, most highly ~*n.*
6. choice, cream, elite, favourite,
finest, first, flower, pick, prime, top
7. hardest, highest endeavour, ut~
most ~*v.* 8. beat, conquer, defeat,
get the better of, lick (*Inf.*), out~
class, outdo, surpass, thrash, tri~
umph over, trounce

bestial animal, barbaric, barba~
rous, beastlike, beastly, brutal,
brutish, carnal, degraded, de~
praved, gross, inhuman, low, sav~
age, sensual, sordid, vile

bestow accord, allot, apportion,
award, commit, confer, donate,
entrust, give, grant, honour with,
impart, lavish, present, render to

bestride bestraddle, bridge, domi~
nate, extend, mount, span, step
over, straddle, tower over

bet 1. *n.* ante, gamble, hazard, long
shot, pledge, risk, speculation,
stake, venture, wager 2. *v.* chance,
gamble, hazard, pledge, punt
(*Brit.*), put money on, risk, specu~
late, stake, venture, wager

bête noir abomination, anathema,
aversion, bugbear, pet hate

betide bechance, befall, chance,
come to pass, crop up (*Inf.*), ensue,
happen, occur, overtake, super~
vene, take place, transpire (*Inf.*)

betimes anon, beforehand, before
long, early, first thing, in good
time, punctually, seasonably, soon

betoken augur, bespeak, bode, de~
clare, denote, evidence, indicate,
manifest, mark, portend, presage,
prognosticate, promise, represent,
signify, suggest, typify

betray 1. be disloyal (treacherous,
unfaithful), break one's promise,

break with, double-cross (*Inf.*), in~
form on *or* against, sell down the
river (*Inf.*), sell out (*Inf.*) 2. blurt
out, disclose, divulge, evince, ex~
pose, give away, lay bare, let slip,
manifest, reveal, show, tell, tell on,
uncover, unmask 3. beguile, cor~
rupt, deceive, delude, dupe, en~
snare, entrap, lead astray, mislead,
undo 4. abandon, desert, forsake,
jilt, walk out on

betrayal 1. deception, disloyalty,
double-cross (*Inf.*), double-dealing,
duplicity, falseness, perfidy, sell~
out (*Inf.*), treachery, treason,
trickery, unfaithfulness 2. blurting
out, disclosure, divulgence, giving
away, revelation, telling

better *adj.* 1. bigger, excelling, fin~
er, fitter, greater, higher quality,
larger, more appropriate (desir~
able, expert, fitting, suitable, use~
ful, valuable), preferable, superior,
surpassing, worthier 2. cured, fit~
ter, fully recovered, healthier, im~
proving, less ill, mending, more
healthy, on the mend (*Inf.*), pro~
gressing, recovering, stronger,
well 3. bigger, greater, larger,
longer ~*adv.* 4. in a more excellent
manner, in a superior way, more
advantageously (attractively,
competently, completely, effec~
tively, thoroughly), to a greater
degree ~*v.* 5. advance, ameliorate,
amend, correct, enhance, forward,
further, improve, meliorate, mend,
promote, raise, rectify, reform 6.
beat, cap (*Inf.*), exceed, excel, im~
prove on *or* upon, outdo, outstrip,
surpass, top 7. get the better of
beat, best, defeat, get the upper
hand, outdo, outsmart (*Inf.*), outwit,
prevail over, score off, surpass,
triumph over, worst

between amidst, among, betwixt,
halfway, in the middle of, mid

beverage draught, drink, libation
(*Facetious*), liquid, liquor, potable,
potation, refreshment

bevy 1. band, bunch (*Inf.*), collec~
tion, company, crowd, gathering,
group, pack, troupe 2. covey, flight,
flock

bewail bemoan, cry over, deplore,

express sorrow, grieve for, keen, lament, moan, mourn, regret, repent, rue, wail, weep over

beware avoid, be careful (cautious, wary), guard against, heed, look out, mind, refrain from, shun, steer clear of, take heed, watch out

bewilder baffle, befuddle, bemuse, confound, confuse, daze, mix up, mystify, perplex, puzzle, stupefy

bewildered awed, baffled, confused, disconcerted, dizzy, giddy, mystified, perplexed, puzzled, speechless, startled, stunned, surprised, taken aback, uncertain

bewitch allure, attract, beguile, captivate, charm, enchant, enrapture, entrance, fascinate, hypnotize, spellbind

bewitched charmed, enchanted, entranced, mesmerized, possessed, spellbound, transformed, under a spell, unrecognizable

beyond above, apart from, at a distance, away from, before, farther, out of range, out of reach, over, past, remote, superior to, yonder

bias *n.* 1. bent, bigotry, favouritism, inclination, intolerance, leaning, narrow-mindedness, one-sidedness, partiality, penchant, predilection, predisposition, prejudice, proclivity, proneness, propensity, tendency, turn, unfairness 2. angle, cross, diagonal line, slant ~*v.* 3. distort, influence, predispose, prejudice, slant, sway, twist, warp, weight

biased distorted, embittered, jaundiced, one-sided, partial, predisposed, prejudiced, slanted, swayed, twisted, warped, weighted

bicker argue, disagree, dispute, fight, quarrel, row (*Inf.*), scrap (*Inf.*), spar, squabble, wrangle

bid *v.* 1. offer, proffer, propose, submit, tender 2. call, greet, say, tell, wish 3. ask, call, charge, command, desire, direct, enjoin, instruct, invite, require, solicit, summon, tell ~*n.* 4. advance, amount, offer, price, proposal, proposition, submission, sum, tender 5. attempt, crack (*Inf.*), effort, endeavour, try, venture

bidding 1. behest, call, charge, command, demand, direction, injunction, instruction, invitation, order, request, summons 2. auction, offer, offers, proposal, tender

big 1. bulky, burly, colossal, considerable, enormous, extensive, gigantic, great, huge, hulking, immense, large, mammoth, massive, ponderous, prodigious, sizable, spacious, substantial, vast, voluminous 2. eminent, important, influential, leading, main, momentous, paramount, powerful, prime, principal, prominent, serious, significant, valuable, weighty 3. adult, elder, grown, grown-up, mature 4. altruistic, benevolent, generous, gracious, heroic, magnanimous, noble, princely, unselfish 5. arrogant, boastful, bragging, conceited, haughty, inflated, pompous, pretentious, proud

bigot dogmatist, fanatic, persecutor, sectarian, zealot

bigoted biased, dogmatic, illiberal, intolerant, narrow-minded, obstinate, opinionated, prejudiced, sectarian, twisted, warped

bigotry bias, discrimination, dogmatism, fanaticism, ignorance, injustice, intolerance, mindlessness, narrow-mindedness, prejudice, provincialism, racialism, racism, sectarianism, sexism, unfairness

bigwig big cheese (*Sl.*), big gun (*Sl.*), big noise (*Sl.*), big shot (*Sl.*, *chiefly U.S.*), celebrity, dignitary, heavyweight (*Inf.*), nob (*Sl.*), notability, notable, panjandrum, personage, somebody, V.I.P.

bile anger, bitterness, churlishness, ill humour, irascibility, irritability, nastiness, peevishness, rancour, spleen

bilious 1. liverish, nauseated, out of sorts, queasy, sick 2. bad-tempered, crabby, cross, crotchety, grouchy, grumpy, irritable, nasty, peevish, short-tempered, testy, touchy

bilk bamboozle, cheat, con (*Sl.*), deceive, defraud, do (*Sl.*), fleece, rook (*Sl.*), swindle, trick

bill[1] *n.* 1. account, charges, invoice,

note of charge, reckoning, score, statement, tally 2. advertisement, broadsheet, bulletin, circular, handbill, handout, leaflet, notice, placard, playbill, poster 3. agenda, card, catalogue, inventory, list, listing, programme, roster, schedule, syllabus 4. measure, piece of legislation, projected law, proposal ~v. 5. charge, debit, figure, invoice, reckon, record 6. advertise, announce, give advance notice of, post

bill² beak, mandible, neb (*Archaic or dialect*), nib

billet 1. *n.* accommodation, barracks, lodging, quarters 2. *v.* accommodate, berth, quarter, station

billow *n.* 1. breaker, crest, roller, surge, swell, tide, wave 2. cloud, deluge, flood, outpouring, rush, surge, wave ~v. 3. balloon, belly, puff up, rise up, roll, surge, swell

billowy heaving, rippling, rolling, surging, swelling, swirling, undulating, waving, wavy

bind *v.* 1. attach, fasten, glue, hitch, lash, paste, rope, secure, stick, strap, tie, tie up, truss, wrap 2. compel, constrain, engage, force, necessitate, obligate, oblige, prescribe, require 3. confine, detain, hamper, hinder, restrain, restrict 4. bandage, cover, dress, encase, swathe, wrap 5. border, edge, finish, hem, trim ~n. 6. *Inf.* bore, difficulty, dilemma, nuisance, predicament, quandary

binding *adj.* compulsory, conclusive, imperative, indissoluble, irrevocable, mandatory, necessary, obligatory, unalterable

binge bender (*Sl.*), blind (*Sl.*), bout, fling, jag (*Sl.*), orgy, spree

biography account, life, life history, life story, memoir, profile

birth 1. childbirth, delivery, nativity, parturition, 2. beginning, emergence, fountainhead, genesis, origin, rise, source 3. ancestry, background, blood, breeding, derivation, descent, extraction, forebears, genealogy, line, lineage, nobility, noble extraction, parentage, pedigree, race, stock, strain

bisect bifurcate, cross, cut across, cut in half, cut in two, divide in two, halve, intersect, separate, split, split down the middle

bishopric diocese, episcopacy, episcopate, primacy, see

bit¹ 1. atom, chip, crumb, fragment, grain, iota, jot, mite, morsel, mouthful, part, piece, scrap, segment, slice, small piece, speck, tittle, whit 2. instant, jiffy (*Inf.*), little while, minute, moment, period, second, spell, tick (*Inf.*), time

bit² 1. brake, check, curb, restraint, snaffle 2. **take the bit in** *or* **between one's teeth** defy, disobey, get stuck into (*Sl.*), get to grips with, rebel, resist, revolt, run amok, rush into, set about

bitchy catty (*Inf.*), cruel, malicious, mean, nasty, rancorous, snide, spiteful, venomous, vindictive, vixenish

bite *v.* 1. champ, chew, clamp, crunch, crush, cut, gnaw, grip, hold, masticate, nibble, nip, pierce, pinch, rend, seize, snap, tear, wound 2. burn, corrode, eat away, eat into, erode, smart, sting, tingle, wear away ~n. 3. itch, nip, pinch, prick, smarting, sting, tooth marks, wound 4. food, light meal, morsel, mouthful, piece, refreshment, snack, taste 5. edge, kick (*Inf.*), piquancy, punch (*Inf.*), pungency, spice

biting 1. bitter, blighting, cold, cutting, freezing, harsh, nipping, penetrating, piercing, sharp 2. caustic, cutting, incisive, mordant, sarcastic, scathing, severe, stinging, trenchant, withering

bitter 1. acid, acrid, astringent, sharp, sour, tart, unsweetened, vinegary 2. acrimonious, begrudging, crabbed, embittered, hostile, morose, rancorous, resentful, sore, sour, sullen, with a chip on one's shoulder 3. calamitous, cruel, dire, distressing, galling, grievous, harsh, heartbreaking, merciless, painful, poignant, ruthless, savage, vexatious 4. biting, fierce, freezing, intense, severe, stinging

bitterness 1. acerbity, acidity,

sharpness, sourness, tartness, vin~
egariness 2. animosity, grudge,
hostility, pique, rancour, resent~
ment 3. acrimoniousness, asperity,
sarcasm, venom, virulence

bizarre comical, curious, eccentric,
extraordinary, fantastic, freakish,
grotesque, ludicrous, odd, off-beat,
outlandish, outré, peculiar, queer,
ridiculous, strange, unusual, weird

blab blurt out, disclose, divulge,
gossip, let slip, reveal, tattle, tell,
tell on

blabber 1. *n.* busybody, gossip, in~
former, rumour-monger, scandal~
monger, talebearer, tattler, telltale
2. *v.* blather, blether (*Scot.*), chat~
ter, gab (*Inf.*), jabber, prattle

black *adj.* 1. coal-black, dark,
dusky, ebony, inky, jet, murky,
pitchy, raven, sable, starless, styg~
ian, swarthy 2. *Fig.* atrocious, de~
pressing, dismal, distressing, dole~
ful, foreboding, funereal, gloomy,
hopeless, horrible, lugubrious,
mournful, ominous, sad, sombre 3.
dingy, dirty, filthy, grimy, grubby,
soiled, sooty, stained 4. angry, furi~
ous, hostile, menacing, resentful,
sullen, threatening 5. bad, evil, in~
iquitous, nefarious, villainous,
wicked ~*v.* 6. ban, bar, blacklist,
boycott 7. **in the black** in credit, in
funds, solvent, without debt

blackball *v.* ban, bar, blacklist, de~
bar, drum out, exclude, expel, os~
tracize, oust, repudiate, snub, vote
against

blacken 1. befoul, begrime, cloud,
darken, grow black, make black,
smudge, soil 2. calumniate, decry,
defame, defile, denigrate, dishon~
our, malign, slander, smear,
smirch, stain, sully, taint, tarnish,
traduce, vilify

blackguard bastard (*Offensive*),
blighter (*Inf.*), bounder (*Brit. inf.*),
miscreant, rascal, rogue, scoun~
drel, swine, villain, wretch

blacklist *v.* ban, bar, blackball,
boycott, debar, exclude, expel, os~
tracize, preclude, proscribe, reject,
repudiate, snub, vote against

black magic black art, diabolism,

necromancy, sorcery, voodoo,
witchcraft, wizardry

blackmail 1. *n.* bribe, exaction, ex~
tortion, hush money (*Sl.*), intimi~
dation, milking, pay-off (*Inf.*), pro~
tection (*Inf.*), ransom, slush fund 2.
v. bleed (*Inf.*), bribe, coerce, com~
pel, demand, exact, extort, force,
hold to ransom, milk, squeeze,
threaten

blackness darkness, duskiness,
gloom, inkiness, melanism, murki~
ness, nigrescence, nigritude,
swarthiness

blackout *n.* 1. coma, faint, loss of
consciousness, oblivion, swoon,
syncope (*Pathology*), unconscious~
ness 2. power cut, power failure 3.
censorship, noncommunication,
radio silence, secrecy, suppression,
withholding news

black out *v.* 1. conceal, cover,
darken, eclipse, obfuscate, shade 2.
collapse, faint, flake out (*Inf.*), lose
consciousness, pass out, swoon

black sheep disgrace, ne'er-do-
well, outcast, prodigal, renegade,
reprobate, wastrel

blame *n.* 1. accountability, cul~
pability, fault, guilt, incrimination,
liability, onus, rap (*Inf.*), respon~
sibility 2. accusation, castigation,
censure, charge, complaint, con~
demnation, criticism, recrimina~
tion, reproach, reproof ~*v.* 3. ac~
cuse, admonish, censure, charge,
chide, condemn, criticize, disap~
prove, express disapprobation, find
fault with, hold responsible, repre~
hend, reproach, reprove, tax, up~
braid

blameless above suspicion, clean,
faultless, guiltless, immaculate,
impeccable, innocent, in the clear,
irreproachable, perfect, stainless,
unblemished, unimpeachable, un~
offending, unspotted, unsullied, un~
tarnished, upright, virtuous

blameworthy discreditable, dis~
reputable, indefensible, inexcus~
able, iniquitous, reprehensible, re~
proachable, shameful

bland 1. boring, dull, flat, humdrum,
insipid, monotonous, tasteless, te~
dious, undistinctive, unexciting,

uninspiring, uninteresting, un~ stimulating, vapid, weak 2. affable, amiable, congenial, courteous, friendly, gentle, gracious, smooth, suave, unemotional, urbane 3. balmy, calm, mild, mollifying, nonirritant *or* non-irritating (*Medical*), soft, soothing, temper~ ate

blandishments blarney, cajolery, coaxing, compliments, fawning, flattery, ingratiation, inveiglement, soft soap (*Inf.*), soft words, sweet talk (*Inf., chiefly U.S.*), wheedling, winning caresses

blank *adj.* 1. bare, clean, clear, empty, plain, spotless, uncomplet~ ed, unfilled, unmarked, void, white 2. deadpan, dull, empty, expres~ sionless, hollow, impassive, inane, lifeless, poker-faced (*Inf.*), vacant, vacuous, vague 3. at a loss, bewil~ dered, confounded, confused, dis~ concerted, dumbfounded, muddled, nonplussed, uncomprehending 4. absolute, complete, outright, thor~ ough, unqualified, utter ~*n.* 5. emptiness, empty space, gap, nothingness, space, tabula rasa, vacancy, vacuity, vacuum, void

blanket *n.* 1. afghan, cover, cover~ let, rug 2. carpet, cloak, coat, coat~ ing, covering, envelope, film, layer, mantle, sheet, wrapper, wrapping ~*adj.* 3. across-the-board, all-inclusive, comprehensive, overall, sweeping, wide-ranging ~*v.* 4. cloak, cloud, coat, conceal, cover, eclipse, hide, mask, obscure, sup~ press, surround

blare blast, boom, clamour, clang, honk, hoot, peal, resound, roar, scream, sound out, toot, trumpet

blarney blandishment, cajolery, coaxing, exaggeration, flattery, honeyed words, overpraise, soft soap (*Inf.*), sweet talk (*Inf., chiefly U.S.*), wheedling

blasé apathetic, bored, cloyed, glutted, indifferent, jaded, luke~ warm, nonchalant, offhand, satiat~ ed, surfeited, unconcerned, unex~ cited, uninterested, unmoved, weary, world-weary

blaspheme abuse, anathematize,

curse, damn, desecrate, execrate, profane, revile, swear

blasphemous godless, impious, ir~ religious, irreverent, profane, sac~ rilegious, ungodly

blasphemy cursing, desecration, execration, impiety, impiousness, indignity (*to God*), irreverence, profanation, profaneness, profan~ ity, sacrilege, swearing

blast *n./v.* 1. blare, blow, clang, honk, peal, scream, toot, wail ~*n.* 2. bang, blow-up, burst, crash, detonation, discharge, eruption, explosion, outburst, salvo, volley 3. gale, gust, squall, storm, strong breeze, tempest. ~*v.* 4. blow up, break up, burst, demolish, destroy, explode, ruin, shatter 5. blight, kill, shrivel, wither 6. attack, castigate, criticize, flay, rail at

blasted blighted, desolated, de~ stroyed, devastated, ravaged, ruined, shattered, spoiled, wasted, withered

blastoff *n.* discharge, expulsion, firing, launch, launching, lift-off, projection, shot

blatant 1. bald, brazen, conspicu~ ous, flagrant, flaunting, glaring, naked, obtrusive, obvious, ostenta~ tious, outright, overt, prominent, pronounced, sheer, unmitigated 2. clamorous, deafening, ear-splitting, harsh, loud, noisy, piercing

blaze *n.* 1. bonfire, conflagration, fire, flame, flames 2. beam, bril~ liance, flare, flash, glare, gleam, glitter, glow, light, radiance 3. blast, burst, eruption, flare-up, fury, outbreak, outburst, rush, storm, torrent ~*v.* 4. beam, burn, fire, flame, flare, flash, glare, gleam, glow, shine 5. boil, explode, flare up, fume, seethe

bleach blanch, etiolate, fade, grow pale, lighten, peroxide, wash out, whiten

bleached achromatic, etiolated, faded, lightened, peroxided, stone-washed, washed-out

bleak 1. bare, barren, chilly, cold, desolate, exposed, gaunt, open, raw, unsheltered, weather-beaten, windswept, windy 2. cheerless, comfortless, depressing, discour~ aging, disheartening, dismal, dreary, gloomy, grim, hopeless, joyless, sombre, unpromising

bleary blurred, blurry, dim, fogged, foggy, fuzzy, hazy, indistinct, misty, murky, rheumy, watery

bleed 1. exude, flow, gush, lose blood, ooze, run, seep, shed blood, spurt, trickle, weep 2. deplete, drain, draw *or* take blood, exhaust, extort, extract, fleece, leech, milk, phlebotomize (*Medical*), reduce, sap, squeeze 3. ache, agonize, feel for, grieve, pity, suffer, sympathize

blemish 1. *n*. blot, blotch, blur, de~ fect, disfigurement, disgrace, dis~ honour, fault, flaw, imperfection, mark, smudge, speck, spot, stain, taint 2. *v*. blot, blotch, blur, dam~ age, deface, disfigure, flaw, impair, injure, mar, mark, smirch, smudge, spoil, spot, stain, sully, taint, tar~ nish

blend *v*. 1. amalgamate, coalesce, combine, compound, fuse, inter~ mix, merge, mingle, mix, synthe~ size, unite 2. complement, fit, go well, go with, harmonize, suit ~*n*. 3. alloy, amalgam, amalgamation, combination, composite, com~ pound, concoction, fusion, mix, mixture, synthesis, union

bless 1. anoint, consecrate, dedi~ cate, exalt, extol, give thanks to, glorify, hallow, invoke happiness on, magnify, ordain, praise, sancti~ fy, thank 2. bestow, endow, favour, give, grace, grant, provide

blessed 1. adored, beatified, divine, hallowed, holy, revered, sacred, sanctified 2. endowed, favoured, fortunate, granted, lucky 3. blissful, contented, glad, happy, joyful, joy~ ous

blessedness beatitude, bliss, blissfulness, content, felicity, hap~ piness, heavenly joy, pleasure, sanctity, state of grace, *summum bonum*

blessing 1. benediction, benison, commendation, consecration, dedication, grace, invocation, thanksgiving 2. approbation, ap~ proval, backing, concurrence,

consent, favour, good wishes, leave, permission, regard, sanc~ tion, support 3. advantage, benefit, boon, bounty, favour, gain, gift, godsend, good fortune, help, kind~ ness, profit, service, windfall

blight *n*. 1. canker, decay, disease, fungus, infestation, mildew, pest, pestilence, rot 2. affliction, bane, contamination, corruption, curse, evil, plague, pollution, scourge, woe ~*v*. 3. blast, destroy, injure, nip in the bud, ruin, shrivel, taint with mildew, wither 4. *Fig*. annihi~ late, crush, dash, disappoint, frus~ trate, mar, nullify, ruin, spoil, wreck

blind *adj*. 1. destitute of vision, eye~ less, sightless, stone-blind, unsee~ ing, unsighted, visionless 2. *Fig*. careless, heedless, ignorant, inat~ tentive, inconsiderate, indifferent, indiscriminate, injudicious, insen~ sitive, morally darkened, neglect~ ful, oblivious, prejudiced, thought~ less, unaware of, unconscious of, uncritical, undiscerning, unmindful of, unobservant, unreasoning 3. hasty, impetuous, irrational, mind~ less, rash, reckless, senseless, un~ controllable, uncontrolled, un~ thinking, violent, wild 4. closed, concealed, dark, dead-end, dim, hidden, leading nowhere, obscured, obstructed, without exit ~*n*. 5. camouflage, cloak, cover, façade, feint, front, mask, masquerade, screen, smoke screen

blindly 1. aimlessly, at random, confusedly, frantically, indiscrimi~ nately, instinctively, madly, pur~ poselessly, wildly 2. carelessly, heedlessly, impulsively, inconsid~ erately, passionately, recklessly, regardlessly, senselessly, thought~ lessly, unreasonably, wilfully

blink 1. bat, flutter, glimpse, nic~ tate, nictitate, peer, squint, wink 2. flash, flicker, gleam, glimmer, scintillate, shine, sparkle, twinkle, wink 3. *Fig*. condone, connive at, disregard, ignore, overlook, pass by, turn a blind eye to 4. **on the blink** *Inf*. faulty, malfunctioning, not working (properly), out of ac~ tion, out of order, playing up

bliss beatitude, blessedness, bliss~ fulness, ecstasy, euphoria, felicity, gladness, happiness, heaven, joy, paradise, rapture

blissful delighted, ecstatic, elated, enchanted, enraptured, euphoric, happy, heavenly (*Inf.*), in ecstasies, joyful, joyous, rapturous

blister abscess, blain, bleb, boil, bubble, canker, carbuncle, cyst, furuncle (*Pathology*), pimple, pus~ tule, sore, swelling, ulcer, welt, wen

blithe 1. animated, buoyant, care~ free, cheerful, cheery, debonair, gay, gladsome, happy, jaunty, light- hearted, merry, mirthful, sprightly, sunny, vivacious 2. careless, cas~ ual, heedless, indifferent, noncha~ lant, thoughtless, unconcerned, untroubled

blitz assault, attack, blitzkrieg, bombardment, offensive, on~ slaught, raid, strike

blizzard blast, gale, snowstorm, squall, storm, tempest

bloat balloon, blow up, dilate, dis~ tend, enlarge, expand, inflate, puff up, swell

blob ball, bead, bubble, dab, dew~ drop, drop, droplet, glob, globule, lump, mass, pearl, pellet, pill

bloc alliance, axis, cabal, clique, coalition, combine, entente, fac~ tion, group, league, ring, union, wing

block *n.* 1. bar, brick, cake, chunk, cube, hunk, ingot, lump, mass, piece, square 2. bar, barrier, blockage, hindrance, impediment, jam, obstacle, obstruction, stop~ page ~*v.* 3. bung up (*Inf.*), choke, clog, close, obstruct, plug, stop up 4. arrest, bar, check, deter, halt, hinder, impede, obstruct, stop, thwart

blockade barricade, barrier, clo~ sure, encirclement, hindrance, im~ pediment, obstacle, obstruction, restriction, siege, stoppage

blockage block, blocking, impedi~ ment, obstruction, occlusion, stop~ page, stopping up

blockhead bonehead (*Sl.*), dolt, dullard, dunce, fool, idiot, ignora~ mus, numskull

blond, blonde fair, fair-haired, fair-skinned, flaxen, golden-haired, light, light-coloured, light- complexioned, tow-headed

blood 1. gore, lifeblood, vital fluid 2. ancestry, birth, consanguinity, de~ scendants, descent, extraction, family, kindred, kinship, lineage, noble extraction, relations 3. *Fig.* anger, disposition, feeling, passion, spirit, temper

bloodcurdling appalling, chilling, dreadful, fearful, frightening, hair- raising, horrendous, horrifying, scaring, spine-chilling, terrifying

bloodless 1. cold, languid, lifeless, listless, passionless, spiritless, tor~ pid, unemotional, unfeeling 2. anaemic, ashen, chalky, colourless, pale, pallid, pasty, sallow, sickly, wan

bloodshed blood bath, bloodletting, butchery, carnage, gore, killing, massacre, murder, slaughter, slay~ ing

bloodthirsty barbarous, brutal, cruel, ferocious, inhuman, mur~ derous, ruthless, savage, vicious, warlike

bloody 1. bleeding, blood-soaked, blood-spattered, bloodstained, gaping, raw, unstaunched 2. cruel, ferocious, fierce, sanguinary, sav~ age

bloom *n.* 1. blossom, blossoming, bud, efflorescence, flower, opening (*of flowers*) 2. *Fig.* beauty, blush, flourishing, flush, freshness, glow, health, heyday, lustre, perfection, prime, radiance, rosiness, vigour ~*v.* 3. blossom, blow, bud, burgeon, open, sprout 4. develop, fare well, flourish, grow, prosper, succeed, thrive, wax

blossom *n.* 1. bloom, bud, floret, flower, flowers ~*v.* 2. bloom, bur~ geon, flower 3. *Fig.* bloom, devel~ op, flourish, grow, mature, pro~ gress, prosper, thrive

blot *n.* 1. blotch, mark, patch, smear, smudge, speck, splodge, spot 2. blemish, blur, defect, dis~ grace, fault, flaw, spot, stain, taint

~*v.* 3. bespatter, disfigure, dis~
grace, mark, smudge, spoil, spot,
stain, sully, tarnish 4. absorb, dry,
soak up, take up 5. **blot out** cancel,
darken, destroy, efface, erase, ex~
punge, obliterate, obscure, shadow

blow[1] *v.* 1. blast, breathe, exhale,
fan, pant, puff, waft 2. flow, rush,
stream, whirl 3. bear, buffet, drive,
fling, flutter, sweep, waft, whirl,
whisk 4. blare, mouth, pipe, play,
sound, toot, trumpet, vibrate ~*n.* 5.
blast, draught, flurry, gale, gust,
puff, strong breeze, tempest, wind

blow[2] *n.* 1. bang, bash (*Inf.*), belt
(*Inf.*), buffet, clomp (*Sl.*), clout
(*Inf.*), clump (*Sl.*), knock, punch,
rap, slosh (*Sl.*), smack, sock (*Sl.*),
stroke, thump, wallop (*Inf.*), whack
2. *Fig.* affliction, bolt from the blue,
bombshell, calamity, catastrophe,
comedown (*Inf.*), disappointment,
disaster, jolt, misfortune, reverse,
setback, shock, upset

blow out 1. extinguish, put out,
snuff 2. burst, erupt, explode, rup~
ture, shatter

blow over be forgotten, cease, die
down, disappear, end, finish, pass,
pass away, subside, vanish

blow up 1. bloat, distend, enlarge,
expand, fill, inflate, puff up, pump
up, swell 2. blast, bomb, burst,
detonate, dynamite, explode, go
off, rupture, shatter 3. enlarge, en~
large on, exaggerate, heighten,
magnify, overstate 4. *Inf.* become
angry, become enraged, erupt, go
off the deep end (*Inf.*), hit the roof
(*Inf.*), lose one's temper, rage

bludgeon *n.* 1. club, cudgel, shil~
lelagh, truncheon ~*v.* 2. beat, beat
up, club, cudgel, knock down,
strike 3. browbeat, bulldoze (*Inf.*),
bully, coerce, force, hector,
steamroller

blue 1. azure, cerulean, cobalt,
cyan, navy, sapphire, sky-coloured,
ultramarine 2. *Fig.* dejected, de~
pressed, despondent, dismal,
downcast, down-hearted, down in
the dumps (*Inf.*), fed up, gloomy,
glum, low, melancholy, sad, un~
happy 3. *Inf.* bawdy, dirty, inde~
cent, lewd, naughty, near the

knuckle (*Inf.*), obscene, risqué,
smutty, vulgar

blueprint design, draft, layout, out~
line, pattern, pilot scheme, plan,
project, prototype, scheme, sketch

blues dejection, depression, de~
spondency, doldrums, dumps (*Inf.*),
gloom, gloominess, glumness, low
spirits, melancholy, moodiness

bluff 1. *v.* deceive, defraud, delude,
fake, feign, humbug, lie, mislead,
pretend, sham 2. *n.* bluster, boast,
braggadocio, bragging, bravado,
deceit, deception, fake, feint, fraud,
humbug, idle boast, lie, mere show,
pretence, sham, show, subterfuge

blunder *n.* 1. error, fault, inaccura~
cy, mistake, oversight, slip, slip-up
(*Inf.*) 2. boob (*Sl.*), clanger (*Inf.*),
faux pas, gaffe, gaucherie, howler
(*Inf.*), impropriety, indiscretion,
mistake ~*v.* 3. botch, bungle, err,
slip up (*Inf.*) 4. bumble, confuse,
flounder, misjudge, stumble

blunt *adj.* 1. dull, dulled, edgeless,
pointless, rounded, unsharpened 2.
Fig. bluff, brusque, discourteous,
explicit, forthright, frank, impolite,
outspoken, plain-spoken, rude,
straightforward, tactless, trench~
ant, uncivil, unpolished ~*v.* 3.
dampen, deaden, dull, numb, sof~
ten, take the edge off, water down,
weaken

blur *v.* 1. becloud, bedim, befog,
cloud, darken, dim, fog, make hazy,
make indistinct, make vague,
mask, obscure, soften 2. blot,
smear, smudge, spot, stain ~*n.* 3.
blear, blurredness, cloudiness,
confusion, dimness, fog, haze, in~
distinctness, obscurity 4. blot,
smear, smudge, spot, stain

blurred bleary, blurry, faint, foggy,
fuzzy, hazy, ill-defined, indistinct,
lacking definition, misty, nebulous,
out of focus, unclear, vague

blurt out babble, blab, cry, disclose,
exclaim, gush, reveal, spill, spout
(*Inf.*), sputter, tattle, utter suddenly

blush 1. *v.* colour, crimson, flush,
redden, turn red, turn scarlet 2. *n.*
colour, flush, glow, pink tinge, red~
dening, rosiness, rosy tint, ruddi~
ness

bluster 1. *v.* boast, brag, bulldoze, bully, domineer, hector, rant, roar, roister, storm, swagger, swell, vaunt 2. *n.* bluff, boasting, boisterousness, bombast, bragging, bravado, crowing, swagger, swaggering

blustery blusterous, boisterous, gusty, squally, stormy, tempestuous, violent, wild

board *n.* 1. panel, piece of timber, plank, slat, timber 2. daily meals, food, meals, provisions, victuals 3. advisers, advisory group, committee, conclave, council, directorate, directors, panel, trustees ~*v.* 4. embark, embus, enplane, enter, entrain, mount 5. accommodate, feed, house, lodge, put up, quarter, room

boast *v.* 1. blow one's own trumpet, bluster, brag, crow, exaggerate, puff, strut, swagger, talk big (*Sl.*), vaunt 2. be proud of, congratulate oneself on, exhibit, flatter oneself, possess, pride oneself on, show off ~*n.* 3. avowal, brag, gasconade (*Rare*), rodomontade (*Literary*), swank (*Inf.*), vaunt 4. gem, joy, pride, pride and joy, source of pride, treasure

boastful bragging, cocky, conceited, crowing, egotistical, puffed-up, swaggering, swanky (*Inf.*), swollen-headed, vainglorious, vaunting

bob bounce, duck, hop, jerk, leap, nod, oscillate, quiver, skip, waggle, weave, wobble

bode augur, betoken, forebode, foreshadow, foretell, forewarn, impart, omen, portend, predict, presage, prophesy, signify, threaten

bodiless disembodied, ghostly, immaterial, incorporeal, insubstantial, spectral, spiritual, supernatural

bodily 1. *adj.* actual, carnal, corporal, corporeal, fleshly, material, physical, substantial, tangible 2. *adv.* altogether, as a body, as a group, collectively, completely, en masse, entirely, fully, totally, wholly

body 1. build, figure, form, frame, physique, shape, torso, trunk 2. cadaver, carcass, corpse, dead body, relics, remains, stiff (*Sl.*) 3. being, creature, human, human being, individual, mortal, person 4. bulk, essence, main part, mass, material, matter, substance 5. association, band, bloc, collection, company, confederation, congress, corporation, society 6. crowd, horde, majority, mass, mob, multitude, throng 7. consistency, density, firmness, richness, solidity, substance

bog fen, marsh, marshland, mire, morass, moss (*Northern Eng. & Scot.*), peat bog, quagmire, slough, swamp, wetlands

bog down delay, halt, impede, sink, slow down, slow up, stall, stick

bogey 1. apparition, bogeyman, goblin, hobgoblin, imp, spectre, spirit, spook (*Inf.*), sprite 2. *bête noire*, bugaboo, bugbear, nightmare

boggle 1. be alarmed (confused, surprised, taken aback), shy, stagger, startle, take fright 2. demur, dither, doubt, equivocate, falter, hang back, hesitate, hover, jib, shillyshally (*Inf.*), shrink from, vacillate, waver

boggy fenny, marshy, miry, muddy, oozy, quaggy, soft, spongy, swampy, waterlogged, yielding

bogus artificial, counterfeit, dummy, fake, false, forged, fraudulent, imitation, phoney (*Sl.*), pseudo (*Inf.*), sham, spurious

bohemian 1. *adj.* alternative, artistic, arty (*Inf.*), avant-garde, eccentric, exotic, left bank, nonconformist, offbeat, unconventional, unorthodox, way-out (*Inf.*) 2. *n.* beatnik, dropout, hippie, iconoclast, nonconformist

boil[1] *v.* 1. agitate, bubble, churn, effervesce, fizz, foam, froth, seethe 2. be angry, be indignant, foam at the mouth (*Inf.*), fulminate, fume, rage, rave, storm

boil[2] *n.* blain, blister, carbuncle, furuncle (*Pathology*), gathering, pustule, tumour, ulcer

boisterous 1. bouncy, clamorous, disorderly, impetuous, loud, noisy, obstreperous, riotous, rollicking, rowdy, rumbustious, unrestrained, unruly, uproarious, vociferous, wild 2. blustery, gusty, raging, rough, squally, stormy, tempestuous, tumultuous, turbulent

bold 1. adventurous, audacious, brave, courageous, daring, dauntless, enterprising, fearless, gallant, heroic, intrepid, lion-hearted, valiant, valorous 2. barefaced, brash, brazen, cheeky, confident, forward, fresh (*Inf.*), impudent, insolent, pert, rude, saucy, shameless 3. bright, colourful, conspicuous, eye-catching, flashy, forceful, lively, loud, prominent, pronounced, showy, spirited, striking, strong, vivid

bolster aid, assist, boost, brace, buoy up, buttress, cushion, help, hold up, maintain, pillow, prop, reinforce, shore up, stay, strengthen, support

bolt *n.* 1. bar, catch, fastener, latch, lock, sliding bar 2. peg, pin, rivet, rod 3. bound, dart, dash, escape, flight, rush, spring, sprint 4. arrow, dart, missile, projectile, shaft, thunderbolt ~*v.* 5. bar, fasten, latch, lock, secure 6. cram, devour, gobble, gorge, gulp, guzzle, stuff, swallow whole, wolf 7. abscond, bound, dash, escape, flee, fly, hurtle, jump, leap, make a break (for it), run, run for it, rush, spring, sprint

bomb 1. *n.* bombshell, charge, device, explosive, grenade, mine, missile, projectile, rocket, shell, torpedo 2. *v.* attack, blow up, bombard, destroy, shell, strafe, torpedo

bombard 1. assault, blast, blitz, bomb, cannonade, fire upon, open fire, pound, shell, strafe 2. assail, attack, barrage, batter, beset, besiege, harass, hound, pester

bombardment assault, attack, barrage, blitz, bombing, cannonade, fire, flak, fusillade, shelling, strafe

bona fide actual, authentic, genu-ine, honest, lawful, legal, legitimate, real, true

bond *n.* 1. band, binding, chain, cord, fastening, fetter, ligature, link, manacle, shackle, tie 2. affiliation, affinity, attachment, connection, link, relation, tie, union 3. agreement, compact, contract, covenant, guarantee, obligation, pledge, promise, word ~*v.* 4. bind, connect, fasten, fix together, fuse, glue, gum, paste

bonny 1. beautiful, comely, fair, handsome, lovely, pretty, sweet 2. bouncing, buxom, chubby, fine, plump, rounded, shapely 3. blithe, cheerful, cheery, gay, joyful, merry, sunny, winsome

bonus benefit, bounty, commission, dividend, extra, gift, gratuity, handout, honorarium, plus, premium, prize, reward

bony angular, emaciated, gangling, gaunt, lanky, lean, rawboned, scrawny, skinny, thin

book *n.* 1. manual, publication, roll, scroll, textbook, tome, tract, volume, work 2. album, diary, exercise book, jotter, notebook, pad ~*v.* 3. arrange for, bill, charter, engage, line up, make reservations, organize, procure, programme, reserve, schedule 4. enrol, enter, insert, list, log, mark down, note, post, put down, record, register, write down

bookish academic, donnish, erudite, intellectual, learned, literary, pedantic, scholarly, studious

boom *v.* 1. bang, blast, crash, explode, resound, reverberate, roar, roll, rumble, thunder 2. develop, expand, flourish, gain, grow, increase, intensify, prosper, spurt, strengthen, succeed, swell, thrive ~*n.* 3. bang, blast, burst, clap, crash, explosion, roar, rumble, thunder 4. advance, boost, development, expansion, gain, growth, improvement, increase, jump, push, spurt, upsurge, upswing, upturn

boomerang backfire, come back, come home to roost, rebound, recoil, return, reverse, ricochet

boon 1. *n.* advantage, benefaction, benefit, blessing, donation, favour, gift, godsend, grant, gratuity, present, windfall 2. *adj.* close, intimate, special

boorish awkward, barbaric, bearish, churlish, clownish, coarse, crude, gross, gruff, ill-bred, loutish, lubberly, oafish, rude, rustic, uncivilized, uncouth, uneducated, unrefined, vulgar

boost *n.* 1. encouragement, help, improvement, praise, promotion 2. heave, hoist, lift, push, raise, shove, thrust 3. addition, expansion, improvement, increase, increment, jump, rise ~*v.* 4. advance, advertise, assist, encourage, foster, further, improve, inspire, plug (*Inf.*), praise, promote, support, sustain 5. elevate, heave, hoist, lift, push, raise, shove, thrust 6. add to, amplify, develop, enlarge, expand, heighten, hoick, increase, jack up, magnify, raise

boot *v.* 1. drive, drop-kick, kick, knock, punt, shove 2. *Inf.* dismiss, eject, expel, kick out, oust, sack (*Inf.*), throw out

border *n.* 1. bound, boundary, bounds, brim, brink, confine, confines, edge, hem, limit, limits, lip, margin, rim, skirt, verge 2. borderline, boundary, frontier, line, march ~*v.* 3. bind, decorate, edge, fringe, hem, rim, trim

borderline *adj.* ambivalent, doubtful, equivocal, indecisive, indefinite, indeterminate, inexact, marginal, unclassifiable

bore[1] 1. *v.* burrow, drill, gouge out, mine, penetrate, perforate, pierce, sink, tunnel 2. *n.* borehole, calibre, drill hole, hole, shaft, tunnel

bore[2] 1. *v.* annoy, be tedious, bother, exhaust, fatigue, jade, pall on, pester, send to sleep, tire, trouble, vex, wear out, weary, worry 2. *n.* bother, drag (*Sl.*), dull person, headache (*Inf.*), nuisance, pain (*Inf.*), pain in the neck (*Inf.*), pest, tiresome person, wearisome talker

boredom apathy, doldrums, dullness, ennui, flatness, irksomeness, monotony, sameness, tedium, tediousness, weariness, world-weariness

boring dead, dull, flat, humdrum, insipid, monotonous, repetitious, routine, stale, tedious, tiresome, tiring, unexciting, uninteresting, unvaried, wearisome

borrow 1. cadge, scrounge (*Inf.*), take and return, take on loan, use temporarily 2. acquire, adopt, appropriate, copy, filch, imitate, obtain, pilfer, pirate, plagiarize, simulate, steal, take, use, usurp

bosom *n.* 1. breast, bust, chest 2. affections, emotions, feelings, heart, sentiments, soul, spirit, sympathies 3. centre, circle, core, midst, protection, shelter ~*adj.* 4. boon, cherished, close, confidential, intimate, very dear

boss[1] 1. *n.* administrator, chief, director, employer, executive, foreman, gaffer (*Inf.*), governor (*Inf.*), head, leader, manager, master, overseer, owner, superintendent, supervisor 2. *v.* administrate, command, control, direct, employ, manage, oversee, run, superintend, supervise, take charge

boss[2] knob, nub, nubble, point, protuberance, stud, tip

bossy arrogant, authoritarian, despotic, dictatorial, domineering, high-handed, imperious, lordly, overbearing, tyrannical

botch 1. *v.* blunder, bungle, butcher, cobble, fumble, mar, mend, mess, mismanage, muff, patch, spoil 2. *n.* blunder, bungle, bungling, failure, fumble, hash, mess, miscarriage

bother 1. *v.* alarm, annoy, concern, dismay, distress, disturb, harass, inconvenience, irritate, molest, nag, pester, plague, put out, trouble, upset, vex, worry 2. *n.* aggravation, annoyance, bustle, difficulty, flurry, fuss, inconvenience, irritation, molestation, nuisance, perplexity, pest, problem, strain, trouble, vexation, worry

bothersome aggravating, annoying, distressing, exasperating, inconvenient, irritating, tiresome, troublesome, vexatious, vexing

bottleneck block, blockage, congestion, hold-up, impediment, jam, obstacle, obstruction

bottle up check, contain, curb, keep back, restrict, shut in, suppress, trap

bottom n. 1. base, basis, bed, deepest part, depths, floor, foot, foundation, groundwork, lowest part, pedestal, support 2. lower side, sole, underneath, underside 3. backside, behind (*Inf.*), bum (*Sl.*), buttocks, fundament, posterior, rear, rear end, rump, seat, tail (*Inf.*) 4. base, basis, cause, core, essence, ground, heart, mainspring, origin, principle, root, source, substance ~adj. 5. base, basement, basic, fundamental, ground, last, lowest, undermost

bottomless boundless, deep, fathomless, immeasurable, inexhaustible, infinite, unfathomable, unlimited

bounce v. 1. bob, bound, bump, jounce, jump, leap, rebound, recoil, resile, ricochet, spring, thump 2. *Sl.* boot out (*Inf.*), eject, fire (*Inf.*), kick out (*Inf.*), oust, throw out ~n. 3. bound, elasticity, give, rebound, recoil, resilience, spring, springiness 4. animation, dynamism, energy, go (*Inf.*), life, liveliness, pep, vigour, vitality, vivacity, zip (*Inf.*)

bouncing blooming, bonny, healthy, robust, thriving, vigorous

bound[1] adj. 1. cased, fastened, fixed, pinioned, secured, tied, tied up 2. certain, destined, doomed, fated, sure 3. beholden, committed, compelled, constrained, duty-bound, forced, obligated, obliged, pledged, required

bound[2] v./n. bob, bounce, caper, frisk, gambol, hurdle, jump, leap, pounce, prance, skip, spring, vault

bound[3] n. 1. *Usually plural* border, boundary, confine, edge, extremity, fringe, limit, line, march, margin, pale, periphery, rim, termination, verge 2. **out of bounds** banned, barred, forbidden, off-limits (*Chiefly U.S. military*), prohibited, taboo ~v. 3. circumscribe, confine, define, delimit, demar-

cate, encircle, enclose, hem in, limit, restrain, restrict, surround, terminate

boundary barrier, border, borderline, bounds, brink, confines, edge, extremity, fringe, frontier, limits, march, margin, precinct, termination, verge

boundless endless, illimitable, immeasurable, immense, incalculable, inexhaustible, infinite, limitless, measureless, unbounded, unconfined, unending, unlimited, untold, vast

bountiful 1. abundant, ample, bounteous, copious, exuberant, lavish, luxuriant, plenteous, plentiful, prolific 2. beneficent, bounteous, generous, liberal, magnanimous, munificent, open-handed, princely, unstinting

bouquet 1. boutonniere, bunch of flowers, buttonhole, corsage, garland, nosegay, posy, spray, wreath 2. aroma, fragrance, perfume, redolence, savour, scent

bourgeois conventional, hidebound, materialistic, middle-class, traditional

bout 1. course, fit, period, round, run, session, spell, spree, stint, stretch, term, time, turn 2. battle, boxing match, competition, contest, encounter, engagement, fight, match, set-to, struggle

bovine dense, dull, slow, sluggish, stolid, stupid, thick

bow[1] v. 1. bend, bob, droop, genuflect, incline, make obeisance, nod, stoop 2. accept, acquiesce, comply, concede, defer, give in, kowtow, relent, submit, surrender, yield 3. cast down, conquer, crush, depress, overpower, subdue, subjugate, vanquish, weigh down ~n. 4. bending, bob, genuflexion, inclination, kowtow, nod, obeisance, salaam

bow[2] *Naut.* beak, fore, head, prow, stem

bowdlerize blue-pencil, censor, clean up, expurgate, mutilate

bowels 1. entrails, guts, innards (*Inf.*), insides (*Inf.*), intestines, viscera, vitals 2. belly, core, deep, depths, hold, inside, interior 3. *Archaic* compassion, mercifulness, mercy, pity, sympathy, tenderness

bowl 1. *n.* basin, deep dish, vessel 2. *v.* fling, hurl, pitch, revolve, roll, rotate, spin, throw, trundle, whirl

bowl over 1. amaze, astonish, astound, dumbfound, stagger, startle, stun, surprise 2. bring down, fell, floor, knock down, overthrow, overturn

box¹ 1. *n.* carton, case, chest, container, pack, package, portmanteau, receptacle, trunk 2. *v.* pack, package, wrap

box² *v.* 1. exchange blows, fight, spar 2. buffet, butt, clout (*Inf.*), cuff, hit, punch, slap, sock (*Sl.*), strike, thwack, wallop (*Inf.*), whack ~*n.* 3. blow, buffet, clout (*Inf.*), cuff, punch, slap, stroke, thumping, wallop (*Inf.*)

boxer fighter, prizefighter, pugilist, sparrer, sparring partner

box in cage, confine, contain, coop up, enclose, hem in, isolate, shut in, surround, trap

boxing fisticuffs, prizefighting, pugilism, sparring, the fight game (*Inf.*), the ring

boy fellow, junior, lad, schoolboy, stripling, youngster, youth

boycott ban, bar, black, blackball, blacklist, embargo, exclude, ostracize, outlaw, prohibit, proscribe, refrain from, refuse, reject, spurn

boyfriend admirer, beau, date, follower, lover, man, steady, suitor, swain, sweetheart, young man

brace 1. *n.* bracer, bracket, buttress, prop, reinforcement, stanchion, stay, strut, support, truss 2. *v.* bandage, bind, bolster, buttress, fasten, fortify, hold up, prop, reinforce, shove, shove up, steady, strap, strengthen, support, tie, tighten

bracing brisk, chilly, cool, crisp, energizing, exhilarating, fortifying, fresh, invigorating, lively, refreshing, restorative, reviving, rousing, stimulating, tonic, vigorous

brag blow one's own trumpet, bluster, boast, crow, swagger, talk big (*Sl.*), vaunt

braggart bigmouth (*Sl.*), bluffer, blusterer, boaster, brag, braggadocio, bragger, show-off, swaggerer, swashbuckler

braid entwine, interlace, intertwine, interweave, lace, plait, ravel, twine, weave

brain egghead (*Inf.*), genius, highbrow, intellect, intellectual, mastermind, prodigy, pundit, sage, scholar

brainless foolish, idiotic, inept, mindless, senseless, stupid, thoughtless, unintelligent, witless

brainy bright, brilliant, clever, intelligent, smart

brake 1. *n.* check, constraint, control, curb, rein, restraint 2. *v.* check, decelerate, halt, moderate, reduce speed, slacken, slow, stop

branch 1. arm, bough, limb, offshoot, prong, ramification, shoot, spray, sprig 2. chapter, department, division, local office, office, part, section, subdivision, subsection, wing

branch out add to, develop, diversify, enlarge, expand, extend, increase, multiply, proliferate, ramify, spread out

brand *n.* 1. cast, class, grade, kind, make, quality, sort, species, type, variety 2. emblem, hallmark, label, mark, marker, sign, stamp, symbol, trademark 3. blot, disgrace, infamy, mark, reproach, slur, smirch, stain, stigma, taint ~*v.* 4. burn, burn in, label, mark, scar, stamp 5. censure, denounce, discredit, disgrace, expose, mark, stigmatize

brandish display, exhibit, flaunt, flourish, parade, raise, shake, swing, wield

brash 1. audacious, foolhardy, hasty, impetuous, impulsive, indiscreet, precipitate, rash, reckless 2. bold, brazen, cocky, forward, heedless, impertinent, impudent, insolent, rude

brass audacity, cheek, effrontery, gall, impertinence, impudence, insolence, nerve (*Inf.*), presumption, rudeness

bravado bluster, boast, boastfulness, boasting, bombast, brag, braggadocio, fanfaronade (*Rare*), swagger, swaggering, swashbuckling, vaunting

brave 1. *adj.* bold, courageous, daring, dauntless, fearless, gallant, heroic, intrepid, plucky, resolute, undaunted, valiant, valorous 2. *v.* bear, beard, challenge, confront, dare, defy, endure, face, stand up to, suffer, withstand

bravery boldness, courage, daring, dauntlessness, doughtiness, fearlessness, fortitude, gallantry, grit, guts (*Inf.*), hardihood, hardiness, heroism, indomitability, intrepidity, mettle, pluck, pluckiness, spirit, spunk (*Inf.*), valour

bravura animation, audacity, boldness, brilliance, brio, daring, dash, display, élan, energy, exhibitionism, ostentation, panache, punch (*Inf.*), spirit, verve, vigour, virtuosity

brawl 1. *n.* affray (*Law*), altercation, argument, battle, broil, clash, disorder, dispute, donnybrook, fight, fracas, fray, free-for-all (*Inf.*), melee, punch-up (*Sl.*), quarrel, row (*Inf.*), ruckus (*Inf.*), rumpus, scrap (*Inf.*), scuffle, squabble, tumult, uproar, wrangle 2. *v.* altercate, argue, battle, dispute, fight, quarrel, row (*Inf.*), scrap (*Inf.*), scuffle, tussle, wrangle, wrestle

brawn beef (*Inf.*), beefiness, brawniness, flesh, might, muscle, muscles, muscularity, power, robustness, strength, vigour

brawny athletic, beefy (*Inf.*), bulky, burly, fleshy, hardy, hefty (*Inf.*), herculean, husky (*Inf.*), muscular, powerful, robust, sinewy, stalwart, strapping, strong, sturdy, thewy, vigorous, well-knit

breach 1. aperture, break, chasm, cleft, crack, fissure, gap, hole, opening, rent, rift, rupture, split 2. contravention, disobedience, infraction, infringement, noncompliance, nonobservance, offence, transgression, trespass, violation 3. alienation, difference, disaffection, disagreement, dissension, division, estrangement, falling-out (*Inf.*),

parting of the ways, quarrel, schism, separation, severance, variance

bread 1. aliment, diet, fare, food, necessities, nourishment, nutriment, provisions, subsistence, sustenance, viands, victuals 2. *Sl.* cash, dough (*Sl.*), finance, funds, money

breadth 1. beam (*of a ship*), broadness, latitude, span, spread, wideness, width 2. amplitude, area, compass, comprehensiveness, dimension, expanse, extensiveness, extent, magnitude, measure, range, reach, scale, scope, size, space, spread, sweep, vastness 3. broad-mindedness, freedom, latitude, liberality, open-mindedness, openness, permissiveness

break *v.* 1. batter, burst, crack, crash, demolish, destroy, disintegrate, divide, fracture, fragment, part, rend, separate, sever, shatter, shiver, smash, snap, splinter, split, tear 2. breach, contravene, disobey, disregard, infract (*Law*), infringe, renege on, transgress, violate 3. cow, cripple, demoralize, dispirit, enervate, enfeeble, impair, incapacitate, subdue, tame, undermine, weaken 4. abandon, cut, discontinue, give up, interrupt, pause, rest, stop, suspend 5. bust (*Inf.*), degrade, demote, discharge, dismiss, humiliate, impoverish, make bankrupt, reduce, ruin 6. announce, come out, disclose, divulge, impart, inform, let out, make public, proclaim, reveal, tell 7. *Of a record, etc.* beat, better, cap (*Inf.*), exceed, excel, go beyond, outdo, outstrip, surpass, top 8. appear, burst out, come forth suddenly, emerge, erupt, happen, occur 9. cut and run (*Inf.*), dash, escape, flee, fly, get away, run away 10. cushion, diminish, lessen, lighten, moderate, reduce, soften, weaken ~*n.* 11. breach, cleft, crack, division, fissure, fracture, gap, gash, hole, opening, rent, rift, rupture, split, tear 12. breather (*Inf.*), halt, hiatus, interlude, intermission, interruption, interval, letup (*Inf.*), lull, pause, recess, respite, rest, suspension 13. alienation, breach, disaffection, dispute, divergence, estrangement, rift, rupture, schism, separation, split 14. *Inf.* advantage, chance, fortune, opening, opportunity, stroke of luck

breakable brittle, crumbly, delicate, flimsy, fragile, frail, frangible, friable

break away 1. decamp, escape, flee, fly, make a break for it, make a run for it (*Inf.*), make off, run away 2. break with, detach, part company, secede, separate

breakdown 1. collapse, crackup (*Inf.*), disintegration, disruption, failure, mishap, stoppage 2. analysis, categorization, classification, detailed list, diagnosis, dissection, itemization

break down be overcome, collapse, conk out (*Sl.*), crack up (*Inf.*), fail, give way, go kaput (*Sl.*), go to pieces, seize up, stop, stop working

break-in breaking and entering, burglary, invasion, robbery

break in 1. barge in, burst in, butt in, interfere, interject, interpose, interrupt, intervene, intrude 2. break and enter, burgle, invade, rob 3. accustom, condition, get used to, habituate, initiate, prepare, tame, train

break into begin, burst into, burst out, commence, dissolve into, give way to, launch into

break off 1. detach, divide, part, pull off, separate, sever, snap off, splinter 2. cease, desist, discontinue, end, finish, halt, pause, stop, suspend, terminate

break out 1. appear, arise, begin, commence, emerge, happen, occur, set in, spring up, start 2. abscond, bolt, break loose, burst out, escape, flee, get free 3. burst out, erupt

breakthrough advance, development, discovery, find, gain, improvement, invention, leap, progress, quantum leap, step forward

break-up breakdown, breaking, crackup (*Inf.*), disintegration, dispersal, dissolution, divorce, ending, parting, rift, separation, split, splitting, termination, wind-up (*Inf., chiefly U.S.*)

break up adjourn, disband, dismantle, disperse, disrupt, dissolve, divide, divorce, end, part, scatter, separate, sever, split, stop, suspend, terminate

breakwater groyne, jetty, mole, sea wall, spur

breast 1. boob (*Sl.*), bosom, bust, chest, front, teat, thorax, udder 2. being, conscience, core, emotions, feelings, heart, seat of the affections, sentiments, soul, thoughts

breath 1. air, animation, breathing, exhalation, gasp, gulp, inhalation, pant, respiration, wheeze 2. aroma, odour, smell, vapour, whiff 3. break, breather, breathing-space, instant, moment, pause, respite, rest, second 4. faint breeze, flutter, gust, puff, sigh, slight movement, waft, zephyr 5. hint, murmur, suggestion, suspicion, undertone, whisper 6. animation, energy, existence, life, lifeblood, life force, vitality

breathe 1. draw in, gasp, gulp, inhale and exhale, pant, puff, respire, wheeze 2. imbue, impart, infuse, inject, inspire, instil, transfuse 3. articulate, express, murmur, say, sigh, utter, voice, whisper

breathless 1. choking, exhausted, gasping, gulping, out of breath, panting, short-winded, spent, wheezing, winded 2. agog, anxious, astounded, avid, eager, excited, flabbergasted (*Inf.*), on tenterhooks, open-mouthed, thunderstruck, with bated breath

breathtaking amazing, astonishing, awe-inspiring, awesome, exciting, heart-stirring, impressive, magnificent, moving, overwhelming, stunning (*Inf.*), thrilling

breed *v.* 1. bear, beget, bring forth, engender, generate, hatch, multiply, originate, procreate, produce, propagate, reproduce 2. bring up, cultivate, develop, discipline, educate, foster, instruct, nourish, nurture, raise, rear 3. arouse, bring about, cause, create, generate, give rise to, induce, make, occa~ sion, originate, produce, stir up ~*n.* 4. brand, class, extraction, family, ilk, kind, line, lineage, pedigree, progeny, race, sort, species, stamp, stock, strain, type, variety

breeding 1. ancestry, cultivation, development, lineage, nurture, raising, rearing, reproduction, training, upbringing 2. civility, conduct, courtesy, cultivation, cul~ ture, gentility, manners, polish, re~ finement, urbanity

breeze 1. *n.* air, breath of wind, capful of wind, current of air, draught, flurry, gust, light wind, puff of air, waft, whiff, zephyr 2. *v.* flit, glide, hurry, move briskly, pass, sail, sally, sweep, trip

breezy 1. airy, blowing, blowy, blusterous, blustery, fresh, gusty, squally, windy 2. airy, animated, blithe, buoyant, carefree, casual, cheerful, debonair, easy-going, free and easy, informal, jaunty, light, light-hearted, lively, sparkling, spirited, sprightly, sunny, vivacious

brevity 1. conciseness, concision, condensation, crispness, curtness, economy, pithiness, succinctness, terseness 2. briefness, ephemeral~ ity, impermanence, shortness, transience, transitoriness

brew *v.* 1. boil, ferment, infuse (*tea*), make (*beer*), prepare by fermentation, seethe, soak, steep, stew 2. breed, concoct, contrive, develop, devise, excite, foment, form, gather, hatch, plan, plot, project, scheme, start, stir up ~*n.* 3. beverage, blend, concoction, distillation, drink, fermentation, infusion, liquor, mixture, prepara~ tion

bribe 1. *n.* allurement, backhander (*Sl.*), boodle (*Sl., chiefly U.S.*), cor~ rupting gift, enticement, graft, hush money (*Sl.*), incentive, in~ ducement, kickback (*U.S.*), pay-off (*Inf.*), payola (*Inf.*), reward for treachery 2. *v.* buy off, corrupt, get at, grease the palm *or* hand of (*Sl.*), influence by gifts, lure, oil the palm of (*Inf.*), pay off (*Inf.*), re~ ward, square, suborn

bribery buying off, corruption, graft, inducement, palm-greasing (*Sl.*), payola (*Inf.*), protection, sub~ ornation

bridge *n.* 1. arch, flyover, overpass, span, viaduct 2. band, bond, con~ nection, link, tie ~*v.* 3. arch over, attach, bind, connect, couple, cross, cross over, extend across, go over, join, link, reach across, span, traverse, unite

bridle *v.* 1. check, constrain, con~ trol, curb, govern, keep in check, master, moderate, repress, re~ strain, subdue 2. be indignant, bristle, draw (oneself) up, get an~ gry, get one's back up, raise one's hackles, rear up ~*n.* 3. check, con~ trol, curb, restraint, trammels

brief *adj.* 1. compendious, com~ pressed, concise, crisp, curt, la~ conic, limited, pithy, short, succint, terse, thumbnail, to the point 2. ephemeral, fast, fleeting, hasty, little, momentary, quick, short, short-lived, swift, temporary, tran~ sitory 3. abrupt, blunt, brusque, curt, sharp, short, surly ~*n.* 4. abridgment, abstract, digest, epitome, outline, précis, sketch, summary, synopsis 5. argument, case, contention, data, defence, demonstration ~*v.* 6. advise, ex~ plain, fill in (*Inf.*), gen up (*Brit. inf.*), give (someone) a rundown, give (someone) the gen (*Brit. inf.*), inform, instruct, prepare, prime, put (someone) in the picture (*Inf.*)

briefing conference, directions, guidance, information, instruction, instructions, meeting, preamble, preparation, priming, rundown

briefly abruptly, briskly, casually, concisely, cursorily, curtly, fleet~ ingly, hastily, hurriedly, in a few words, in a nutshell, in brief, in outline, in passing, momentarily, precisely, quickly, shortly, tempo~ rarily

brigade band, body, company, con~ tingent, corps, crew, force, group, organization, outfit, party, squad, team, troop, unit

bright 1. beaming, blazing, brilliant, dazzling, effulgent, flashing, gleaming, glistening, glittering, glowing, illuminated, intense, lambent, luminous, lustrous, radiant, resplendent, scintillating, shimmering, shining, sparkling, twinkling, vivid 2. clear, clement, cloudless, fair, limpid, lucid, pellucid, pleasant, sunny, translucent, transparent, unclouded 3. acute, astute, aware, brainy, brilliant, clear-headed, clever, ingenious, intelligent, inventive, keen, quick, quick-witted, sharp, smart, wide-awake 4. auspicious, encouraging, excellent, favourable, golden, good, hopeful, optimistic, palmy, promising, propitious, prosperous, rosy 5. cheerful, gay, genial, glad, happy, jolly, joyful, joyous, light-hearted, lively, merry, vivacious 6. distinguished, famous, glorious, illustrious, magnificent, outstanding, remarkable, splendid

brighten 1. clear up, enliven, gleam, glow, illuminate, lighten, light up, make brighter, shine 2. become cheerful, buck up (*Inf.*), buoy up, cheer, encourage, enliven, gladden, hearten, make happy, perk up

brilliance, brilliancy 1. blaze, brightness, dazzle, effulgence, gleam, glitter, intensity, luminosity, lustre, radiance, refulgence, resplendence, sheen, sparkle, vividness 2. acuity, aptitude, braininess, cleverness, distinction, excellence, genius, giftedness, greatness, inventiveness, talent, wisdom 3. éclat, glamour, gorgeousness, grandeur, illustriousness, magnificence, splendour

brilliant 1. ablaze, bright, coruscating, dazzling, glittering, glossy, intense, luminous, lustrous, radiant, refulgent, resplendent, scintillating, shining, sparkling, vivid 2. celebrated, eminent, exceptional, famous, glorious, illustrious, magnificent, outstanding, splendid, superb 3. accomplished, acute, astute, brainy, clever, discerning, expert, gifted, intellectual, intelligent, inventive, masterly, penetrating, profound, quick, talented

brim 1. *n.* border, brink, circumfer-

ence, edge, lip, margin, rim, skirt, verge 2. *v.* fill, fill up, hold no more, overflow, run over, spill, well over

brimful brimming, filled, flush, full, level with, overflowing, overfull, packed, running over

bring 1. accompany, bear, carry, conduct, convey, deliver, escort, fetch, gather, guide, import, lead, take, transfer, transport, usher 2. cause, contribute to, create, effect, engender, inflict, occasion, produce, result in, wreak 3. compel, convince, dispose, force, induce, influence, make, move, persuade, prevail on *or* upon, prompt, sway 4. command, earn, fetch, gross, net, produce, return, sell for, yield

bring about accomplish, achieve, bring to pass, cause, compass, create, effect, effectuate, generate, give rise to, make happen, manage, occasion, produce, realize

bring down abase, cut down, drop, fell, floor, lay low, level, lower, overthrow, overturn, pull down, reduce, shoot down, undermine, upset

bring in accrue, bear, be worth, fetch, gross, produce, profit, realize, return, yield

bring off accomplish, achieve, bring home the bacon (*Inf.*), bring to pass, carry off, carry out, discharge, execute, perform, pull off, succeed

bring up 1. breed, develop, educate, form, nurture, raise, rear, support, teach, train 2. advance, allude to, broach, introduce, mention, move, propose, put forward, submit

brink border, boundary, brim, edge, fringe, frontier, limit, lip, margin, point, rim, skirt, threshold, verge

brisk 1. active, agile, alert, animated, bustling, busy, energetic, lively, nimble, no-nonsense, quick, speedy, sprightly, spry, vigorous, vivacious 2. biting, bracing, crisp, exhilarating, fresh, invigorating, keen, nippy, refreshing, sharp, snappy, stimulating

briskly actively, brusquely, coolly, decisively, efficiently, energetically, firmly, incisively, nimbly, promptly, quickly, rapidly, readily, smartly, vigorously

bristle *n.* 1. barb, hair, prickle, spine, stubble, thorn, whisker ~*v.* 2. horripilate, prickle, rise, stand on end, stand up 3. be angry, be infuriated, be maddened, bridle, flare up, get one's dander up (*Sl.*), rage, see red, seethe, spit (*Inf.*) 4. *With* with abound, be alive, be thick, crawl, hum, swarm, teem

brittle 1. breakable, crisp, crumbling, crumbly, delicate, fragile, frail, frangible, friable, shatterable, shivery 2. curt, edgy, irritable, nervous, prim, stiff, stilted, tense

broach 1. approach, bring up, hint at, introduce, mention, open up, propose, raise the subject, speak of, suggest, talk of, touch on 2. crack, draw off, open, pierce, puncture, start, tap, uncork

broad 1. ample, beamy (*of a ship*), capacious, expansive, extensive, generous, large, roomy, spacious, vast, voluminous, wide, widespread 2. all-embracing, comprehensive, encyclopedic, far-reaching, general, inclusive, nonspecific, sweeping, undetailed, universal, unlimited, wide, wide-ranging 3. *As in* broad daylight clear, full, obvious, open, plain, straightforward, undisguised 4. broad-minded, liberal, open, permissive, progressive, tolerant, unbiased 5. blue, coarse, gross, improper, indecent, indelicate, near the knuckle (*Inf.*), unrefined, vulgar

broadcast *v.* 1. air, beam, cable, put on the air, radio, relay, show, televise, transmit 2. advertise, announce, circulate, disseminate, make public, proclaim, promulgate, publish, report, spread ~*n.* 3. programme, show, telecast, transmission

broaden augment, develop, enlarge, expand, extend, fatten, increase, open up, spread, stretch, supplement, swell, widen

broad-minded catholic, cosmopolitan, dispassionate, flexible, free-thinking, indulgent, liberal, open-minded, permissive, responsive, tolerant, unbiased, unbigoted, undogmatic, unprejudiced

broadside abuse, assault, attack, battering, bombardment, censure, criticism, denunciation, diatribe, philippic

brochure advertisement, booklet, circular, folder, handbill, hand-out, leaflet, pamphlet

broke bankrupt, bust (*Inf.*), cleaned out (*Sl.*), flat broke (*Sl.*), impoverished, insolvent, on one's uppers, penniless, penurious, ruined, skint (*Brit. inf.*), stony-broke (*Sl.*)

broken 1. burst, demolished, destroyed, fractured, fragmented, rent, ruptured, separated, severed, shattered, shivered 2. defective, exhausted, feeble, imperfect, kaput (*Inf.*), not functioning, out of order, ruined, run-down, spent, weak 3. disconnected, discontinuous, disturbed, erratic, fragmentary, incomplete, intermittent, interrupted, spasmodic 4. beaten, browbeaten, crippled, crushed, defeated, demoralized, humbled, oppressed, overpowered, subdued, tamed, vanquished 5. dishonoured, disobeyed, disregarded, forgotten, ignored, infringed, isolated, retracted, traduced, transgressed 6. disjointed, halting, hesitating, imperfect, stammering

broken-down collapsed, dilapidated, in disrepair, inoperative, kaput (*Sl.*), not functioning, not in working order, old, on the blink (*Inf.*), out of commission, out of order, worn out

brokenhearted crestfallen, desolate, despairing, devastated, disappointed, disconsolate, grief-stricken, heartbroken, heart-sick, inconsolable, miserable, mournful, prostrated, sorrowful, wretched

broker agent, dealer, factor, go-between, intermediary, middleman, negotiator

bronze brownish, chestnut, copper, copper-coloured, metallic brown, reddish-brown, reddish-tan, rust, tan

brood *v.* 1. agonize, dwell upon, fret, meditate, mope, mull over, muse, ponder, repine, ruminate, think upon 2. cover, hatch, incu~ bate, set, sit upon ~*n*. 3. breed, chicks, children, clutch, family, hatch, infants, issue, litter, off~ spring, progeny, young

brook beck, burn, gill (*Dialect*), rill, rivulet, runnel (*Literary*), stream, streamlet, watercourse

brother 1. blood brother, kin, kins~ man, relation, relative, sibling 2. associate, chum (*Inf.*), colleague, companion, compeer, comrade, confrère, fellow member, mate, pal (*Inf.*), partner 3. cleric, friar, monk, regular, religious

brotherhood 1. brotherliness, ca~ maraderie, companionship, com~ radeship, fellowship, friendliness, kinship 2. alliance, association, clan, clique, community, coterie, fraternity, guild, league, society, union

brotherly affectionate, altruistic, amicable, benevolent, cordial, fra~ ternal, friendly, kind, neighbourly, philanthropic, sympathetic

brow 1. air, appearance, aspect, bearing, countenance, eyebrow, face, forehead, front, mien, temple 2. brim, brink, crown, edge, peak, rim, summit, tip, top, verge

browbeat badger, bulldoze (*Inf.*), bully, coerce, cow, domineer, dra~ goon, hector, intimidate, lord it over, oppress, overawe, overbear, threaten, tyrannize

brown 1. *adj.* auburn, bay, brick, bronze, bronzed, browned, bru~ nette, chestnut, chocolate, coffee, dark, donkey brown, dun, dusky, fuscous, ginger, hazel, nigger brown, rust, sunburnt, tan, tanned, tawny, toasted, umber 2. *v.* cook, fry, grill, sauté, seal, sear

browse 1. dip into, examine curso~ rily, flip through, glance at, leaf through, look round, look through, peruse, scan, skim, survey 2. crop, eat, feed, graze, nibble, pasture

bruise *v.* 1. blacken, blemish, con~ tuse, crush, damage, deface, dis~ colour, injure, mar, mark, pound, pulverize 2. displease, grieve, hurt, injure, insult, offend, pain, sting,

wound ~*n*. 3. black-and-blue mark, black mark, blemish, contusion, discoloration, injury, mark, swell~ ing

brunt burden, force, full force, im~ pact, pressure, shock, strain, stress, thrust, violence

brush[1] *n.* 1. besom, broom, sweeper 2. clash, conflict, confrontation, encounter, fight, fracas, scrap (*Inf.*), set-to (*Inf.*), skirmish, slight engagement, spot of bother (*Inf.*), tussle ~*v.* 3. buff, clean, paint, pol~ ish, sweep, wash 4. caress, contact, flick, glance, graze, kiss, scrape, stroke, sweep, touch

brush[2] *n.* brushwood, bushes, copse, scrub, shrubs, thicket, undergrowth, underwood

brush-off *n.* cold shoulder, cut, dis~ missal, go-by (*Sl.*), rebuff, refusal, rejection, repudiation, repulse, slight, snub

brush off *v.* cold-shoulder, cut, deny, disdain, dismiss, disown, dis~ regard, ignore, rebuff, refuse, re~ ject, repudiate, scorn, slight, snub, spurn

brush up cram, go over, polish up, read up, refresh one's memory, relearn, revise, study

brutal 1. barbarous, bloodthirsty, cruel, ferocious, heartless, inhu~ man, merciless, pitiless, remorse~ less, ruthless, savage, uncivilized, vicious 2. beastly, bestial, brute, brutish, carnal, coarse, crude, sen~ sual 3. bearish, callous, gruff, harsh, impolite, insensitive, rough, rude, severe, uncivil, unfeeling, unmannerly

brute *n.* 1. animal, beast, creature, wild animal 2. barbarian, beast, devil, fiend, monster, ogre, sadist, savage, swine ~*adj.* 3. bodily, car~ nal, fleshly, instinctive, mindless, physical, senseless, unthinking 4. bestial, coarse, depraved, gross, sensual

bubble *n.* 1. air ball, bead, blister, blob, drop, droplet, globule, vesicle 2. bagatelle, delusion, fantasy, illu~ sion, toy, trifle, vanity ~*v.* 3. boil, effervesce, fizz, foam, froth, per~ colate, seethe, sparkle 4. babble, burble, gurgle, murmur, purl, rip~ple, trickle, trill

bubbly 1. carbonated, curly, effer~vescent, fizzy, foamy, frothy, lath~ery, sparkling, sudsy 2. animated, bouncy, elated, excited, happy, lively, merry

buccaneer corsair, freebooter, pi~rate, privateer, sea-rover

buckle n. 1. catch, clasp, clip, fas~tener, hasp 2. bulge, contortion, distortion, kink, warp ~v. 3. catch, clasp, close, fasten, hook, secure 4. bend, bulge, cave in, collapse, con~tort, crumple, distort, fold, twist, warp

buckle down apply oneself, exert oneself, launch into, pitch in, put one's shoulder to the wheel, set to

buck up 1. get a move on, hasten, hurry up, shake a leg, speed up 2. brighten, cheer up, encourage, hearten, inspirit, perk up, rally, take heart

bud 1. n. embryo, germ, shoot, sprout 2. v. burgeon, burst forth, develop, grow, pullulate, shoot, sprout

budding beginning, burgeoning, developing, embryonic, fledgling, flowering, germinal, growing, in~cipient, nascent, potential, promis~ing

budge 1. dislodge, give way, inch, move, propel, push, remove, roll, shift, slide, stir 2. bend, change, convince, give way, influence, persuade, sway, yield

budget 1. n. allocation, allowance, cost, finances, financial statement, fiscal estimate, funds, means, re~sources 2. v. allocate, apportion, cost, cost out, estimate, plan, ra~tion

buff¹ 1. adj. sandy, straw, tan, yel~lowish, yellowish-brown 2. n. **in the buff** bare, in one's birthday suit (Inf.), in the altogether (Inf.), in the raw (Inf.), naked, nude, unclad, unclothed, with bare skin 3. v. brush, burnish, polish, rub, shine, smooth

buff² addict, admirer, aficionado, connoisseur, devotee, enthusiast, expert, fan, fiend (Inf.), freak (Sl.)

buffer bulwark, bumper, cushion, fender, intermediary, safeguard, screen, shield, shock absorber

buffet¹ n. café, cafeteria, cold table, counter, cupboard, refreshment-counter, salad bar, sideboard, snack bar

buffet² 1. v. bang, batter, beat, box, bump, clobber (Sl.), cuff, flail, knock, pound, pummel, push, rap, shove, slap, strike, thump, wallop (Inf.) 2. n. bang, blow, box, bump, cuff, jolt, knock, push, rap, shove, slap, smack, thump, wallop (Inf.)

buffoon clown, comedian, comic, droll, fool, harlequin, jester, joker, merry-andrew, silly billy (Inf.), wag

bug n. 1. Inf. bacterium, disease, germ, infection, microorganism, virus 2. craze, fad, mania, obses~sion, rage 3. blemish, catch, defect, error, failing, fault, flaw, gremlin, imperfection, snarl-up (Inf.) ~v. 4. Inf. annoy, badger, bother, disturb, get on (someone's) wick (Sl.), har~ass, irk, irritate, needle (Inf.), net~tle, pester, plague, vex 5. eaves~drop, listen in, spy, tap, wiretap

bugbear anathema, bane, bête noire, bogey, bugaboo, devil, dread, fiend, horror, nightmare, pet hate

build v. 1. assemble, construct, erect, fabricate, form, make, put up, raise 2. base, begin, constitute, establish, formulate, found, in~augurate, initiate, institute, origi~nate, set up, start 3. accelerate, amplify, augment, develop, en~large, escalate, extend, improve, increase, intensify, strengthen ~n. 4. body, figure, form, frame, phy~sique, shape, structure

building 1. domicile, dwelling, edi~fice, fabric, house, pile, structure 2. architecture, construction, erec~tion, fabricating, raising

build-up 1. accumulation, develop~ment, enlargement, escalation, expansion, gain, growth, increase 2. ballyhoo (Inf.), hype (Sl.), plug (Inf.), promotion, publicity, puff 3. accretion, accumulation, heap, load, mass, stack, stockpile, store

built-in essential, implicit, in-built,

included, incorporated, inherent, inseparable, integral, part and parcel of

bulge n. 1. bump, lump, projection, protrusion, protuberance, swelling 2. boost, increase, intensification, rise, surge ~v. 3. bag, dilate, distend, enlarge, expand, project, protrude, puff out, sag, stand out, stick out, swell, swell out

bulk 1. amplitude, bigness, dimensions, immensity, largeness, magnitude, massiveness, size, substance, volume, weight 2. better part, body, generality, lion's share, main part, majority, major part, mass, most, nearly all, plurality, preponderance 3. **bulk large** be important, carry weight, dominate, loom, loom large, preponderate, stand out, threaten

bulldoze 1. demolish, flatten, level, raze 2. drive, force, propel, push, shove, thrust 3. browbeat, bully, coerce, cow, hector, intimidate

bullet ball, missile, pellet, projectile, shot, slug

bulletin account, announcement, communication, communiqué, dispatch, message, news flash, notification, report, statement

bull-headed headstrong, inflexible, mulish, obstinate, pig-headed, stiffnecked, stubborn, stupid, tenacious, uncompromising, unyielding, wilful

bullish assured, bold, confident, expectant, improving, positive, rising

bully 1. n. big bully, browbeater, bully boy, coercer, intimidator, oppressor, persecutor, ruffian, tormentor, tough 2. v. bluster, browbeat, bulldoze (Inf.), bullyrag, coerce, cow, domineer, hector, intimidate, oppress, overbear, persecute, push around (Sl.), ride roughshod over, swagger, terrorize, tyrannize 3. adj. admirable, excellent, fine, nifty (Inf.), very good 4. interj. bravo, capital, good, grand, great, well done

bulwark 1. bastion, buttress, defence, embankment, fortification, outwork, partition, rampart, re-

doubt 2. buffer, guard, mainstay, safeguard, security, support

bump v. 1. bang, collide (with), crash, hit, knock, slam, smash into, strike 2. bounce, jar, jerk, jolt, jostle, jounce, rattle, shake 3. budge, dislodge, displace, move, remove, shift ~n. 4. bang, blow, collision, crash, hit, impact, jar, jolt, knock, rap, shock, smash, thud, thump 5. bulge, contusion, hump, knob, knot, lump, node, nodule, protuberance, swelling

bumper adj. abundant, bountiful, excellent, exceptional, jumbo (Inf.), massive, prodigal, spanking (Inf.), teeming, unusual, whacking (Inf.), whopping (Inf.)

bump into chance upon, come across, encounter, happen upon, light upon, meet, meet up with, run across, run into

bump off assassinate, dispatch, do away with, do in (Sl.), eliminate, finish off, kill, knock off (Sl.), liquidate, murder, remove, wipe out (Inf.)

bumptious arrogant, boastful, brash, cocky, conceited, egotistic, forward, full of oneself, impudent, overbearing, overconfident, presumptuous, pushy (Inf.), self-assertive, showy, swaggering, vainglorious, vaunting

bunch n. 1. assortment, batch, bouquet, bundle, clump, cluster, collection, heap, lot, mass, number, parcel, pile, quantity, sheaf, spray, stack, tuft 2. band, crew (Inf.), crowd, flock, gang, gathering, group, knot, mob, multitude, party, swarm, team, troop ~v. 3. assemble, bundle, cluster, collect, congregate, cram together, crowd, flock, group, herd, huddle, mass, pack

bundle n. 1. accumulation, assortment, batch, bunch, collection, group, heap, mass, pile, quantity, stack 2. bag, bale, box, carton, crate, pack, package, packet, pallet, parcel, roll ~v. 3. bale, bind, fasten, pack, package, palletize, tie, tie together, tie up, truss, wrap 4. With out, off, into, etc. hurry, hustle, push, rush, shove, throw, thrust 5. *With up* clothe warmly, muffle up, swathe, wrap up

bungle blunder, bodge (*Inf.*), botch, butcher, cock up (*Sl.*), foul up, fudge, louse up (*Sl.*), make a mess of, mar, mess up, miscalculate, mismanage, muff, ruin, screw up (*Inf.*), spoil

bungling awkward, blundering, botching, cack-handed (*Inf.*), clumsy, ham-fisted (*Inf.*), ham-handed (*Inf.*), incompetent, inept, maladroit, unskilful

bunk, bunkum balderdash, baloney (*Inf.*), bilge (*Inf.*), bosh (*Inf.*), garbage, havers (*Scot.*), hooey (*Sl.*), horsefeathers (*U.S. inf.*), nonsense, piffle (*Inf.*), poppycock (*Inf.*), rot, rubbish, stuff and nonsense, tarradiddle, tomfoolery, tommyrot, tosh (*Inf.*), trash, truck (*Inf.*), twaddle

buoy 1. *n.* beacon, float, guide, marker, signal 2. *v. With up* boost, cheer, cheer up, encourage, hearten, keep afloat, lift, raise, support, sustain

buoyant 1. afloat, floatable, floating, light, weightless 2. animated, blithe, bouncy, breezy, bright, carefree, cheerful, debonair, happy, jaunty, joyful, light-hearted, lively, peppy (*Inf.*), sunny, vivacious

burden *n.* 1. affliction, anxiety, care, clog, encumbrance, grievance, load, millstone, obstruction, onus, responsibility, sorrow, strain, stress, trial, trouble, weight, worry 2. *Naut.* cargo, freight, lading, tonnage ~*v.* 3. bother, encumber, handicap, load, oppress, overload, overwhelm, saddle with, strain, tax, weigh down, worry

bureau 1. desk, writing desk 2. agency, branch, department, division, office, service

bureaucracy 1. administration, authorities, civil service, corridors of power, directorate, government, ministry, officials, officialdom, the system 2. bumbledom, officialdom, officialese, red tape, regulations

bureaucrat administrator, appa-

ratchik, civil servant, functionary, mandarin, minister, office-holder, officer, official, public servant

burglar cat burglar, filcher, house~breaker, picklock, pilferer, robber, sneak thief, thief

burglary break-in, breaking and entering, filching, housebreaking, larceny, pilferage, robbery, stealing, theft, thieving

burial burying, entombment, ex~equies, funeral, inhumation, interment, obsequies, sepulture

buried 1. coffined, consigned to the grave, entombed, interred, laid to rest 2. dead and buried, dead and gone, in the grave, long gone, pushing up the daisies, six feet under 3. covered, forgotten, hidden, repressed, sunk in oblivion, suppressed 4. cloistered, concealed, hidden, private, sequestered, tucked away 5. caught up, committed, concentrating, devoted, engrossed, immersed, intent, lost, occupied, preoccupied, rapt

burlesque 1. *n.* caricature, mock, mockery, parody, satire, send-up (*Brit. inf.*), spoof (*Inf.*), takeoff (*Inf.*), travesty 2. *adj.* caricatural, comic, farcical, hudibrastic, ironical, ludicrous, mock, mock-heroic, mocking, parodic, satirical, travestying 3. *v.* ape, caricature, exaggerate, imitate, lampoon, make fun of, mock, parody, ridicule, satirize, send up (*Brit. inf.*), spoof, (*Inf.*), take off (*Inf.*), travesty

burly beefy, big, brawny, bulky, hefty, hulking, muscular, powerful, stocky, stout, strapping, strong, sturdy, thickset, well-built

burn 1. be ablaze, be on fire, blaze, flame, flare, flash, flicker, glow, smoke 2. brand, calcine, char, ignite, incinerate, kindle, light, parch, reduce to ashes, scorch, set on fire, shrivel, singe, toast, wither 3. bite, hurt, pain, smart, sting, tingle 4. be excited (angry, aroused, inflamed, passionate), blaze, desire, fume, seethe, simmer, smoulder, yearn 5. consume, eat up, expend, use

burning 1. blazing, fiery, flaming,

flashing, gleaming, glowing, hot, illuminated, scorching, smoulder~ ing 2. all-consuming, ardent, eager, earnest, fervent, fervid, frantic, frenzied, impassioned, intense, passionate, vehement, zealous 3. acrid, biting, caustic, irritating, painful, piercing, prickling, pun~ gent, reeking, smarting, stinging, tingling 4. acute, compelling, criti~ cal, crucial, essential, important, pressing, significant, urgent, vital

burrow 1. *n.* den, hole, lair, retreat, shelter, tunnel 2. *v.* delve, dig, ex~ cavate, hollow out, scoop out, tun~ nel

burst *v.* 1. blow up, break, crack, disintegrate, explode, fly open, fragment, puncture, rend asunder, rupture, shatter, shiver, split, tear apart 2. barge, break, break out, erupt, gush forth, run, rush, spout ~*n.* 3. bang, blast, blasting, blow~ out, blow-up, breach, break, crack, discharge, explosion, rupture, split 4. eruption, fit, gush, gust, out~ break, outburst, outpouring, rush, spate, spurt, surge, torrent ~*adj.* 5. flat, punctured, rent, ruptured, split

bury 1. consign to the grave, en~ tomb, inearth, inhume, inter, lay to rest, sepulchre 2. conceal, cover, cover up, enshroud, hide, secrete, shroud, stow away 3. drive in, em~ bed, engulf, implant, sink, sub~ merge 4. absorb, engage, engross, immerse, interest, occupy

bush 1. hedge, plant, shrub, shrub~ bery, thicket 2. backwoods, brush, scrub, scrubland, the wild, wood~ land

busily actively, assiduously, briskly, carefully, diligently, earnestly, en~ ergetically, industriously, intently, purposefully, speedily, strenuously

business 1. calling, career, craft, employment, function, job, line, métier, occupation, profession, pursuit, trade, vocation, work 2. company, concern, corporation, enterprise, establishment, firm, organization, venture 3. bargain~ ing, commerce, dealings, industry, manufacturing, merchandising, selling, trade, trading, transaction

4. affair, assignment, concern, duty, function, issue, matter, point, problem, question, responsibility, subject, task, topic

businesslike correct, efficient, matter-of-fact, methodical, orderly, organized, practical, professional, regular, routine, systematic, thor~ ough, well-ordered, workaday

businessman, businesswoman capitalist, employer, entrepreneur, executive, financier, industrialist, merchant, tradesman, tycoon

bust[1] bosom, breast, chest, torso

bust[2] *v.* 1. break, burst, fracture, rupture 2. bankrupt, break, crash, fail, impoverish, ruin 3. arrest, catch, collar (*Inf.*), cop (*Sl.*), nab (*Inf.*), raid, search 4. **go bust** be~ come insolvent, be ruined, break, fail, go bankrupt ~*n.* 5. arrest, capture, cop (*Sl.*), raid, search, sei~ zure

bustle 1. *v.* bestir, dash, flutter, fuss, hasten, hurry, rush, scamper, scramble, scurry, scuttle, stir, tear 2. *n.* activity, ado, agitation, com~ motion, excitement, flurry, fuss, haste, hurly-burly, hurry, pother, stir, to-do, tumult

busy *adj.* 1. active, assiduous, brisk, diligent, employed, engaged, en~ grossed, hard at work, industrious, in harness, occupied, on duty, per~ severing, slaving, working 2. ac~ tive, energetic, exacting, full, hec~ tic, hustling, lively, on the go (*Inf.*), restless, strenuous, tireless, tiring 3. fussy, inquisitive, interfering, meddlesome, meddling, nosy, offi~ cious, prying, snoopy, stirring, troublesome ~*v.* 4. absorb, employ, engage, engross, immerse, inter~ est, occupy

busybody eavesdropper, gossip, intriguer, intruder, meddler, nosy parker (*Inf.*), pry, scandalmonger, snoop, snooper, troublemaker

but 1. *sentence connector* further, however, moreover, nevertheless, on the contrary, on the other hand, still, yet 2. *conj.* bar, barring, ex~ cept, excepting, excluding, not~ withstanding, save, with the ex~

ception of 3. *adv.* just, merely, only, simply, singly, solely

butcher *n.* 1. destroyer, killer, murderer, slaughterer, slayer ~*v.* 2. carve, clean, cut, cut up, dress, joint, prepare, slaughter 3. assassinate, cut down, destroy, exterminate, kill, liquidate, massacre, put to the sword, slaughter, slay 4. bodge (*Inf.*), botch, destroy, mess up, mutilate, ruin, spoil, wreck

butchery blood bath, blood-letting, bloodshed, carnage, killing, massacre, mass murder, murder, slaughter

butt[1] 1. haft, handle, hilt, shaft, shank, stock 2. base, end, fag end (*Inf.*), foot, leftover, stub, tail, tip

butt[2] Aunt Sally, dupe, laughing stock, mark, object, point, subject, target, victim

butt[3] *v./n.* 1. *With or of the head or horns* ram, buck, buffet, bump, bunt, jab, knock, poke, prod, punch, push, ram, shove, thrust ~*v.* 2. abut, join, jut, meet, project, protrude 3. *With in or into* chip in (*Inf.*), cut in, interfere, interrupt, intrude, meddle, put one's oar in, stick one's nose in

butt[4] barrel, cask, pipe

buttonhole *v. Fig.* accost, bore, catch, detain in talk, grab, impor~

tune, persuade importunately, take aside, waylay

buttress 1. *n.* abutment, brace, mainstay, pier, prop, reinforce~ment, shore, stanchion, stay, strut, support 2. *v.* back up, bolster, brace, prop, prop up, reinforce, shore, shore up, strengthen, sup~port, sustain, uphold

buy *v.* 1. acquire, get, invest in, obtain, pay for, procure, purchase, shop for 2. *Often with off* bribe, corrupt, fix (*Inf.*), grease some~one's palm (*Inf.*), square, suborn ~*n.* 3. acquisition, bargain, deal, purchase

by *prep.* 1. along, beside, by way of, close to, near, next to, over, past, via 2. through, through the agency of, under the aegis of ~*adv.* 3. aside, at hand, away, beyond, close, handy, in reach, near, past, to one side

by and by before long, eventually, in a while, in the course of time, one day, presently, soon

bypass avoid, circumvent, depart from, detour round, deviate from, get round, go round, ignore, ne~glect, outflank, pass round

bystander eyewitness, looker-on, observer, onlooker, passer-by, spectator, viewer, watcher, wit~ness

C

cab hackney, hackney carriage, minicab, taxi, taxicab

cabin 1. berth, bothy, chalet, cot, cottage, crib, hovel, hut, lodge, shack, shanty, shed 2. berth, compartment, deckhouse, quarters, room

cabinet 1. case, chiffonier, closet, commode, cupboard, dresser, escritoire, locker 2. administration, assembly, council, counsellors, ministry 3. apartment, boudoir, chamber (*Archaic*)

cackle babble, blather, chatter, chuckle, cluck, crow, gabble, gibber, giggle, jabber, prattle, snicker, snigger, titter

cad bounder (*Brit. inf.*), churl, cur, dastard (*Archaic*), heel (*Sl.*), knave, rat (*Sl.*), rotter (*Sl.*)

caddish despicable, ill-bred, low, ungentlemanly, unmannerly

café cafeteria, coffee bar, coffee shop, lunchroom, restaurant, snack bar, tearoom

cage 1. *v.* confine, coop up, fence in, immure, impound, imprison, incarcerate, lock up, mew, restrain, shut up 2. *n.* corral (*U.S.*), enclosure, pen, pound

cajole beguile, coax, decoy, dupe, entice, entrap, flatter, inveigle, lure, manoeuvre, mislead, seduce, sweet-talk (*U.S. inf.*), tempt, wheedle

cake 1. *v.* bake, cement, coagulate, congeal, consolidate, dry, encrust, harden, inspissate (*Archaic*), ossify, solidify, thicken 2. *n.* bar, block, cube, loaf, lump, mass, slab

calamitous blighting, cataclysmic, catastrophic, deadly, devastating, dire, disastrous, fatal, pernicious, ruinous, tragic, woeful

calamity adversity, affliction, cataclysm, catastrophe, disaster, distress, downfall, hardship, misadventure, mischance, misfortune, mishap, reverse, ruin, scourge, tragedy, trial, tribulation, woe, wretchedness

calculate 1. adjust, compute, consider, count, determine, enumerate, estimate, figure, gauge, judge, rate, reckon, value, weigh, work out 2. aim, design, intend, plan

calculated considered, deliberate, intended, intentional, planned, premeditated, purposeful

calculating canny, cautious, contriving, crafty, cunning, designing, devious, Machiavellian, manipulative, politic, scheming, sharp, shrewd, sly

calculation 1. answer, computation, estimate, estimation, figuring, forecast, judgment, reckoning, result 2. caution, circumspection, contrivance, deliberation, discretion, foresight, forethought, planning, precaution

calibre 1. bore, diameter, gauge, measure 2. *Fig.* ability, capacity, distinction, endowment, faculty, force, gifts, merit, parts, quality, scope, stature, strength, talent, worth

call *v.* 1. announce, arouse, awaken, cry, cry out, hail, halloo, proclaim, rouse, shout, waken, yell 2. assemble, bid, collect, contact, convene, convoke, gather, invite, muster, phone, rally, ring up, summon, telephone 3. christen, denominate, describe as, designate, dub, entitle, label, name, style, term 4. announce, appoint, declare, decree, elect, ordain, order, proclaim, set apart 5. consider, estimate, judge, regard, think ~*n.* 6. cry, hail, scream, shout, signal, whoop, yell 7. announcement, appeal, command, demand, invitation, notice, order, plea, request, ring (*Brit. inf.*), summons, supplication, visit 8. cause, claim, excuse, grounds, justification, need, occasion, reason, right, urge

call for 1. demand, entail, involve,

necessitate, need, occasion, re~
quire, suggest 2. collect, fetch, pick
up, uplift (*Scot.*)

calling business, career, employ~
ment, life's work, line, métier,
mission, occupation, profession,
province, pursuit, trade, vocation,
walk of life, work

call on 1. drop in on, look in on,
look up, see, visit 2. appeal to, ask,
bid, call upon, entreat, invite, in~
voke, request, summon, supplicate

callous apathetic, case-hardened,
cold, hard-bitten, hard-boiled (*Inf.*),
hardened, hardhearted, heartless,
indifferent, indurated (*Rare*), in~
sensate, insensible, insensitive, in~
ured, obdurate, soulless, thick-
skinned, torpid, uncaring, unfeel~
ing, unresponsive, unsusceptible,
unsympathetic

calm *adj.* 1. balmy, halcyon, mild,
pacific, peaceful, placid, quiet,
restful, serene, smooth, still, tran~
quil, windless 2. collected, com~
posed, cool, dispassionate, equable,
impassive, imperturbable, relaxed,
sedate, self-possessed, undisturbed,
unemotional, unexcitable, unexcit~
ed, unflappable (*Inf.*), unmoved,
unruffled ~*v.* 3. hush, mollify, pla~
cate, quieten, relax, soothe ~*n.* 4.
calmness, hush, peace, peaceful~
ness, quiet, repose, serenity, still~
ness

calmness 1. calm, composure, eq~
uability, hush, motionlessness,
peace, peacefulness, placidity,
quiet, repose, restfulness, serenity,
smoothness, stillness, tranquillity
2. composure, cool (*Sl.*), coolness,
dispassion, equanimity, impassiv~
ity, imperturbability, poise, sang-
froid, self-possession

camouflage 1. *n.* blind, cloak, con~
cealment, cover, deceptive mark~
ings, disguise, false appearance,
front, guise, mask, masquerade,
mimicry, protective colouring,
screen, subterfuge 2. *v.* cloak, con~
ceal, cover, disguise, hide, mask,
obfuscate, obscure, screen, veil

camp[1] bivouac, camping ground,
camp site, cantonment (*Mil.*), en~
campment, tents

camp[2] affected, artificial, camped
up, campy (*Inf.*), effeminate, man~
nered, ostentatious, poncy (*Sl.*),
posturing

campaign attack, crusade, drive,
expedition, jihad (*Rare*), move~
ment, offensive, operation, push

cancel 1. abolish, abort, abrogate,
annul, blot out, call off, counter~
mand, cross out, delete, do away
with, efface, eliminate, erase, ex~
punge, obliterate, quash, repeal,
repudiate, rescind, revoke 2. bal~
ance out, compensate for,
counterbalance, make up for, neu~
tralize, nullify, offset, redeem

cancellation abandoning, aban~
donment, abolition, annulment,
deletion, elimination, quashing,
repeal, revocation

cancer blight, canker, carcinoma
(*Pathol.*), corruption, evil, growth,
malignancy, pestilence, rot, sick~
ness, tumour

candid 1. blunt, fair, forthright,
frank, free, guileless, impartial, in~
genuous, just, open, outspoken,
plain, sincere, straightforward,
truthful, unbiased, unequivocal,
unprejudiced 2. impromptu, infor~
mal, uncontrived, unposed

candidate applicant, aspirant,
claimant, competitor, contender,
contestant, entrant, nominee, pos~
sibility, runner, solicitant, suitor

candour artlessness, directness,
fairness, forthrightness, frankness,
guilelessness, honesty, impartial~
ity, ingenuousness, naïveté, open~
ness, outspokenness, simplicity,
sincerity, straightforwardness,
truthfulness, unequivocalness

canker 1. *v.* blight, consume, cor~
rode, corrupt, embitter, envenom,
inflict, poison, pollute, rot, rust,
waste away 2. *n.* bane, blight, blis~
ter, cancer, corrosion, corruption,
infection, lesion, rot, scourge, sore,
ulcer

cannon 1. artillery piece, big gun
(*Inf.*), field gun, gun, mortar 2. *Plu~
ral* artillery, battery, big guns,
cannonry, field guns, guns, ord~
nance

canny acute, artful, astute, careful,

cautious, circumspect, clever, judicious, knowing, perspicacious, prudent, sagacious, sharp, shrewd, subtle, wise, worldly-wise

canon catalogue, criterion, dictate, formula, list, precept, principle, regulation, roll, rule, standard, statute, yardstick

canopy awning, baldachin, covering, shade, sunshade, tester

cant *n.* 1. affected piety, humbug, hypocrisy, insincerity, lip service, pious platitudes, pretence, pretentiousness, sanctimoniousness, sham holiness 2. argot, jargon, lingo, slang, vernacular ~*v.* 3. angle, bevel, incline, rise, slant, slope, tilt

cantankerous bad-tempered, captious, choleric, contrary, crabby, cranky (*U.S. inf.*), crotchety (*Inf.*), crusty, difficult, disagreeable, grouchy (*Inf.*), grumpy, ill-humoured, irascible, irritable, peevish, perverse, quarrelsome, testy

canter *n.* amble, dogtrot, easy gait, jog, lope

canting hypocritical, insincere, Janus-faced, sanctimonious, two-faced

canvass *v.* 1. analyse, campaign, electioneer, examine, inspect, investigate, poll, scan, scrutinize, sift, solicit, solicit votes, study, ventilate 2. agitate, debate, discuss, dispute ~*n.* 3. examination, investigation, poll, scrutiny, survey, tally

canyon coulee (*U.S.*), gorge, gulch (*U.S.*), gulf, gully, ravine

cap *v.* beat, better, complete, cover, crown, eclipse, exceed, excel, finish, outdo, outstrip, overtop, surpass, top, transcend

capability ability, capacity, competence, facility, faculty, means, potential, potentiality, power, proficiency, qualification(s), wherewithal

capable able, accomplished, adapted, adept, adequate, apt, clever, competent, efficient, experienced, fitted, gifted, intelligent, masterly, proficient, qualified, skilful, suited, susceptible, talented

capacious ample, broad, comfortable, commodious, comprehensive, expansive, extended, extensive, generous, liberal, roomy, sizable, spacious, substantial, vast, voluminous, wide

capacity 1. amplitude, compass, dimensions, extent, magnitude, range, room, scope, size, space, volume 2. ability, aptitude, aptness, brains, capability, cleverness, competence, competency, efficiency, facility, faculty, forte, genius, gift, intelligence, power, readiness, strength 3. appointment, function, office, position, post, province, role, service, sphere

cape chersonese (*Poetic*), head, headland, ness (*Archaic*), peninsula, point, promontory

caper 1. *v.* bounce, bound, cavort, dance, frisk, frolic, gambol, hop, jump, leap, romp, skip, spring 2. *n.* antic, dido (*Inf.*), escapade, gambol, high jinks, hop, jape, jest, jump, lark (*Inf.*), leap, mischief, practical joke, prank, revel, shenanigan (*Inf.*), sport, stunt

capital *adj.* 1. cardinal, central, chief, controlling, essential, foremost, important, leading, main, major, overruling, paramount, pre-eminent, primary, prime, principal, prominent, vital 2. excellent, fine, first, first-rate, prime, splendid, superb ~*n.* 3. assets, cash, finance, finances, financing, funds, investment(s), means, money, principal, property, resources, stock, wealth, wherewithal

capitalism free enterprise, *laissez faire*, private enterprise, private ownership

capitulate come to terms, give in, give up, relent, submit, succumb, surrender, yield

capitulation accedence, submission, surrender, yielding

caprice changeableness, fad, fancy, fickleness, fitfulness, freak, humour, impulse, inconstancy, notion, quirk, vagary, whim, whimsy

capricious changeful, crotchety (*Inf.*), erratic, fanciful, fickle, fitful, freakish, impulsive, inconstant, mercurial, odd, queer, quirky, unpredictable, variable, wayward, whimsical

capsize invert, keel over, overturn, tip over, turn over, turn turtle, up~set

capsule 1. bolus, lozenge, pill, tab~let, troche (*Medical*) 2. case, peri~carp (*Bot.*), pod, receptacle, seed vessel, sheath, shell, vessel

captain boss, chief, chieftain, com~mander, head, leader, master, number one (*Inf.*), officer, (senior) pilot, skipper

captivate allure, attract, beguile, bewitch, charm, dazzle, enamour, enchant, enrapture, enslave, en~snare, enthral, entrance, fascinate, hypnotize, infatuate, lure, mes~merize, seduce, win

captive 1. *n.* bondservant, convict, detainee, hostage, internee, pris~oner, prisoner of war, slave 2. *adj.* caged, confined, enslaved, en~snared, imprisoned, incarcerated, locked up, penned, restricted, sub~jugated

captivity bondage, confinement, custody, detention, durance (*Ar~chaic*), duress, enthralment, im~prisonment, incarceration, intern~ment, restraint, servitude, slavery, thraldom, vassalage

capture 1. *v.* apprehend, arrest, bag, catch, collar (*Inf.*), lift (*Sl.*), nab (*Inf.*), secure, seize, take, take into custody, take prisoner 2. *n.* apprehension, arrest, catch, im~prisonment, seizure, taking, taking captive, trapping

car 1. auto (*U.S.*), automobile, ja~lopy (*Inf.*), machine, motor, motorcar, vehicle 2. buffet car, ca~ble car, coach, dining car, (rail~way) carriage, sleeping car, van

carcass body, cadaver (*Medical*), corpse, corse (*Archaic*), dead body, framework, hulk, remains, shell, skeleton

cardinal capital, central, chief, es~sential, first, foremost, fundamen~tal, greatest, highest, important, key, leading, main, paramount, pre-eminent, primary, prime, principal

care 1. affliction, anxiety, burden, concern, disquiet, hardship, inter~est, perplexity, pressure, respon~sibility, solicitude, stress, tribula~tion, trouble, vexation, woe, worry 2. attention, carefulness, caution, circumspection, consideration, di~rection, forethought, heed, man~agement, meticulousness, pains, prudence, regard, vigilance, watchfulness 3. charge, control, custody, guardianship, keeping, management, ministration, pro~tection, supervision, ward

career *n.* 1. calling, employment, life work, livelihood, occupation, pursuit, vocation 2. course, pas~sage, path, procedure, progress, race, walk ~*v.* 3. bolt, dash, hurtle, race, rush, speed, tear

care for 1. attend, foster, look after, mind, minister to, nurse, protect, provide for, tend, watch over 2. be fond of, desire, enjoy, find congen~ial, like, love, prize, take to, want

carefree airy, blithe, breezy, buoy~ant, careless, cheerful, cheery, easy-going, happy, happy-go-lucky, insouciant, jaunty, light-hearted, lightsome (*Archaic*), radiant, sun~ny, untroubled

careful 1. accurate, attentive, cau~tious, chary, circumspect, consci~entious, discreet, fastidious, heed~ful, painstaking, precise, prudent, punctilious, scrupulous, thoughtful, thrifty 2. alert, concerned, judi~cious, mindful, particular, protec~tive, solicitous, vigilant, wary, watchful

careless 1. absent-minded, cursory, forgetful, hasty, heedless, incau~tious, inconsiderate, indiscreet, negligent, perfunctory, regardless, remiss, thoughtless, unconcerned, unguarded, unmindful, unthinking 2. inaccurate, irresponsible, lacka~daisical, neglectful, offhand, slap~dash, slipshod, sloppy (*Inf.*) 3. art~less, casual, nonchalant, unstudied

carelessness inaccuracy, inatten~tion, inconsiderateness, indiscre~tion, irresponsibility, neglect, neg~ligence, omission, remissness, slackness, sloppiness (*Inf.*), thoughtlessness

caress 1. *v.* cuddle, embrace, fon~ dle, hug, kiss, nuzzle, pet, stroke 2. *n.* cuddle, embrace, fondling, hug, kiss, pat, stroke

caretaker 1. *n.* concierge, curator, custodian, janitor, keeper, porter, superintendent, warden, watch~ man 2. *adj.* holding, interim, short-term, temporary

cargo baggage, consignment, con~ tents, freight, goods, lading, load, merchandise, shipment, tonnage, ware

caricature 1. *n.* burlesque, cartoon, distortion, farce, lampoon, mimic~ ry, parody, pasquinade, satire, send-up (*Brit. inf.*), takeoff (*Inf.*), travesty 2. *v.* burlesque, distort, lampoon, mimic, mock, parody, ridicule, satirize, send up (*Brit. inf.*), take off (*Inf.*)

carnage blood bath, bloodshed, butchery, havoc, holocaust, mas~ sacre, mass murder, murder, shambles, slaughter

carnival celebration, fair, festival, fête, fiesta, gala, holiday, jambo~ ree, jubilee, Mardi Gras, merry~ making, revelry

carol canticle, canzonet, chorus, ditty, hymn, lay, noel, song, strain

carp cavil, censure, complain, criticize, find fault, hypercriticize, knock (*Inf.*), nag, pick holes (*Inf.*), quibble, reproach

carpenter cabinet-maker, joiner, woodworker

carriage 1. carrying, conveyance, conveying, delivery, freight, trans~ port, transportation 2. cab, coach, conveyance, vehicle 3. *Fig.* air, bearing, behaviour, comportment, conduct, demeanour, deportment, gait, manner, mien, posture, pres~ ence

carry 1. bear, bring, conduct, con~ vey, fetch, haul, lift, lug, move, re~ lay, take, transfer, transmit, trans~ port 2. accomplish, capture, effect, gain, secure, win 3. drive, impel, influence, motivate, spur, urge 4. bear, hold up, maintain, shoulder, stand, suffer, support, sustain, underpin, uphold 5. broadcast, communicate, display, dissemi~ nate, give, offer, publish, release, stock

carry on 1. continue, endure, keep going, last, maintain, perpetuate, persevere, persist 2. administer, manage, operate, run 3. *Inf.* create (*Sl.*), make a fuss, misbehave

carry out accomplish, achieve, carry through, consummate, dis~ charge, effect, execute, fulfil, im~ plement, perform, realize

carton box, case, container, pack, package, packet

cartoon animated cartoon, ani~ mated film, animation, caricature, comic strip, lampoon, parody, sat~ ire, sketch, takeoff

cartridge 1. capsule, case, cassette, container, cylinder, magazine 2. charge, round, shell

carve chip, chisel, cut, divide, en~ grave, etch, fashion, form, grave, hack, hew, incise, indent, mould, sculpt, sculpture, slash, slice, whit~ tle

cascade 1. *n.* avalanche, cataract, deluge, falls, flood, fountain, out~ pouring, shower, torrent, waterfall 2. *v.* descend, flood, gush, overflow, pitch, plunge, pour, spill, surge, tumble

case 1. box, cabinet, canister, cap~ sule, carton, cartridge, casket, chest, compact, container, crate, holder, receptacle, shell, suitcase, tray, trunk 2. capsule, casing, cov~ er, covering, envelope, folder, in~ tegument, jacket, sheath, wrapper, wrapping 3. circumstance(s), con~ dition, context, contingency, di~ lemma, event, plight, position, predicament, situation, state 4. ex~ ample, illustration, instance, occa~ sion, occurrence, specimen 5. *Law* action, cause, dispute, lawsuit, proceedings, process, suit, trial

cash banknotes, bread (*Sl.*), bullion, charge, coin, coinage, currency, dough (*Sl.*), funds, money, notes, payment, ready (*Inf.*), ready mon~ ey, resources, specie, wherewithal

cashier 1. *n.* accountant, bank clerk, banker, bursar, clerk, purs~ er, teller, treasurer 2. *v.* break,

cast off, discard, discharge, dismiss, drum out, expel

casket box, case, chest, coffer, jewel box, kist (*Scot.*)

cast *v.* 1. chuck, drive, drop, fling, hurl, impel, launch, lob, pitch, project, shed, shy, sling, throw, thrust, toss 2. bestow, deposit, diffuse, distribute, emit, give, radiate, scatter, shed, spread 3. allot, appoint, assign, choose, name, pick, select 4. add, calculate, compute, figure, forecast, reckon, total 5. form, found, model, mould, set, shape ~*n.* 6. fling, lob, throw, thrust, toss 7. air, appearance, complexion, demeanour, look, manner, mien, semblance, shade, stamp, style, tinge, tone, turn 8. actors, characters, company, dramatis personae, players, troupe

cast down deject, depress, desolate, discourage, dishearten, dispirit

caste class, estate, grade, lineage, order, race, rank, social order, species, station, status, stratum

castigate beat, berate, cane, censure, chasten, chastise, correct, criticize, discipline, dress down (*Inf.*), flail, flay, flog, haul over the coals (*Inf.*), lash, rebuke, reprimand, scold, scourge, whip

castle chateau, citadel, donjon, fastness, fortress, keep, mansion, palace, peel, stronghold, tower

casual 1. accidental, chance, contingent, fortuitous, incidental, irregular, occasional, random, serendipitous, uncertain, unexpected, unforeseen, unintentional, unpremeditated 2. apathetic, blasé, cursory, indifferent, informal, insouciant, lackadaisical, nonchalant, offhand, perfunctory, relaxed, unconcerned

casualty 1. loss, sufferer, victim 2. accident, calamity, catastrophe, chance, contingency, disaster, misadventure, misfortune, mishap

cat feline, grimalkin, malkin (*Archaic*), moggy (*Sl.*), mouser, puss (*Inf.*), pussy (*Inf.*), tabby

catalogue 1. *n.* directory, gazetteer, index, inventory, list, record, register, roll, roster, schedule 2. *v.* accession, alphabetize, classify, file, index, inventory, list, register

catapult 1. *n.* ballista, sling, slingshot (*U.S.*), trebuchet 2. *v.* heave, hurl, hurtle, pitch, plunge, propel, shoot, toss

cataract 1. cascade, deluge, downpour, falls, Niagara, rapids, torrent, waterfall 2. *Medical* opacity (*of the eye*)

catastrophe 1. adversity, affliction, blow, calamity, cataclysm, devastation, disaster, failure, fiasco, ill, mischance, misfortune, mishap, reverse, tragedy, trial, trouble 2. conclusion, culmination, curtain, debacle, dénouement, end, finale, termination, upshot, winding-up

catcall 1. *v.* boo, deride, gibe, give the bird to (*Inf.*), hiss, jeer, whistle 2. *n.* boo, gibe, hiss, jeer, raspberry, whistle

catch *v.* 1. apprehend, arrest, capture, clutch, ensnare, entangle, entrap, grab, grasp, grip, lay hold of, nab (*Inf.*), seize, snare, snatch, take 2. detect, discover, expose, find out, surprise, take unawares, unmask 3. bewitch, captivate, charm, delight, enchant, enrapture, fascinate 4. contract, develop, go down with, incur, succumb to, suffer from 5. apprehend, discern, feel, follow, grasp, hear, perceive, recognize, sense, take in, twig (*Inf.*) ~*n.* 6. bolt, clasp, clip, fastener, hasp, hook, hook and eye, latch, sneck, snib (*Scot.*) 7. disadvantage, drawback, fly in the ointment, hitch, snag, stumbling block, trap, trick

catching 1. communicable, contagious, infectious, infective, transferable, transmittable 2. attractive, captivating, charming, enchanting, fascinating, fetching, taking, winning

catch on comprehend, find out, grasp, see, see through, twig (*Inf.*), understand

catchword byword, motto, password, refrain, slogan, watchword

catchy captivating, haunting, memorable, popular

catechize cross-examine, drill, examine, grill (*Inf.*), interrogate, question

categorical absolute, direct, downright, emphatic, explicit, express, positive, unambiguous, unconditional, unequivocal, unqualified, unreserved

category class, classification, department, division, grade, grouping, head, heading, list, order, rank, section, sort, type

cater furnish, outfit, provide, provision, purvey, supply, victual

catholic all-embracing, all-inclusive, broad-minded, charitable, comprehensive, eclectic, ecumenical, general, global, liberal, tolerant, unbigoted, universal, unsectarian, whole, wide, world-wide

cattle beasts, bovines, cows, kine (*Archaic*), livestock, neat (*Archaic*), stock

catty backbiting, bitchy (*Sl.*), ill-natured, malevolent, malicious, mean, rancorous, spiteful, venomous

caucus assembly, conclave, convention, get-together (*Inf.*), meeting, parley, session

cause *n.* 1. agent, beginning, creator, genesis, mainspring, maker, origin, originator, prime mover, producer, root, source, spring 2. account, agency, aim, basis, consideration, end, grounds, incentive, inducement, motivation, motive, object, purpose, reason 3. attempt, belief, conviction, enterprise, ideal, movement, purpose, undertaking ~*v.* 4. begin, bring about, compel, create, effect, engender, generate, give rise to, incite, induce, lead to, motivate, occasion, precipitate, produce, provoke, result in

caustic 1. acrid, astringent, biting, burning, corroding, corrosive, keen, mordant 2. acrimonious, cutting, pungent, sarcastic, scathing, severe, stinging, trenchant, virulent

caution *n.* 1. alertness, care, carefulness, circumspection, deliberation, discretion, forethought, heed, heedfulness, prudence, vigilance, watchfulness 2. admonition, advice, counsel, injunction, warning ~*v.* 3. admonish, advise, tip off, urge, warn

cautious alert, cagey (*Inf.*), careful, chary, circumspect, discreet, guarded, heedful, judicious, prudent, tentative, vigilant, wary, watchful

cavalcade array, march-past, parade, procession, spectacle, train

cavalier *n.* 1. chevalier, equestrian, horseman, knight, royalist 2. beau, blade (*Archaic*), escort, gallant, gentleman ~*adj.* 3. arrogant, condescending, curt, disdainful, haughty, insolent, lofty, lordly, offhand, scornful, supercilious

cavalry horse, horsemen, mounted troops

cave cavern, cavity, den, grotto, hollow

caveat admonition, caution, warning

cavern cave, hollow, pothole

cavernous 1. concave, deep-set, hollow, sunken, yawning 2. echoing, resonant, reverberant, sepulchral

cavil carp, censure, complain, find fault, hypercriticize, object, quibble

cavity crater, dent, gap, hole, hollow, pit

cease break off, bring or come to an end, conclude, culminate, desist, die away, discontinue, end, fail, finish, halt, leave off, refrain, stay, stop, terminate

ceaseless constant, continual, continuous, endless, eternal, everlasting, incessant, indefatigable, interminable, never-ending, nonstop, perennial, perpetual, unending, unremitting, untiring

cede abandon, abdicate, allow, concede, convey, grant, hand over, make over, relinquish, renounce, resign, surrender, transfer, yield

celebrate bless, commemorate, commend, drink to, eulogize, exalt, extol, glorify, honour, keep, laud, observe, perform, praise, proclaim, publicize, rejoice, reverence, solemnize, toast

celebrated acclaimed, distinguished, eminent, famed, famous, glorious, illustrious, lionized, notable, outstanding, popular, preeminent, prominent, renowned, revered, well-known

celebration 1. carousal, festival, festivity, gala, jollification, jubilee, junketing, merrymaking, party, revelry 2. anniversary, commemoration, honouring, observance, performance, remembrance, solemnization

celebrity 1. big name, big shot (*Sl.*), bigwig (*Sl.*), dignitary, lion (*Inf.*), luminary, name, personage, personality, star, superstar, V.I.P. 2. distinction, éclat, eminence, fame, glory, honour, notability, popularity, pre-eminence, prestige, prominence, renown, reputation, repute, stardom

celestial angelic, astral, divine, elysian, empyrean, eternal, ethereal, godlike, heavenly, immortal, seraphic, spiritual, sublime, supernatural

cell 1. cavity, chamber, compartment, cubicle, dungeon, stall 2. caucus, coterie, group, nucleus, unit

cement 1. *v.* attach, bind, bond, cohere, combine, glue, gum, join, plaster, seal, solder, stick together, unite, weld 2. *n.* adhesive, binder, glue, gum, paste, plaster, sealant

cemetery burial ground, churchyard, God's acre, graveyard, necropolis

censor blue-pencil, bowdlerize, cut, expurgate

censorious captious, carping, cavilling, condemnatory, disapproving, disparaging, fault-finding, hypercritical, severe

censure 1. *v.* abuse, berate, blame, castigate, chide, condemn, criticize, denounce, rebuke, reprehend, reprimand, reproach, reprove, scold, upbraid 2. *n.* blame, castigation, condemnation, criticism, disapproval, dressing down (*Inf.*), obloquy, rebuke, remonstrance, reprehension, reprimand, reproach, reproof, stricture

central chief, essential, focal, fundamental, inner, interior, key, main, mean, median, mid, middle, primary, principal

centralize amalgamate, compact, concentrate, concentre, condense, converge, incorporate, rationalize, streamline, unify

centre 1. *n.* bull's-eye, core, crux, focus, heart, hub, mid, middle, midpoint, nucleus, pivot 2. *v.* cluster, concentrate, converge, focus, revolve

centrepiece cynosure, epergne, focus, highlight, hub, star

ceremonial 1. *adj.* formal, liturgical, ritual, ritualistic, solemn, stately 2. *n.* ceremony, formality, rite, ritual, solemnity

ceremonious civil, courteous, courtly, deferential, dignified, exact, formal, precise, punctilious, ritual, solemn, starchy (*Inf.*), stately, stiff

ceremony 1. commemoration, function, observance, parade, rite, ritual, service, show, solemnities 2. ceremonial, decorum, etiquette, form, formal courtesy, formality, niceties, pomp, propriety, protocol

certain 1. assured, confident, convinced, positive, satisfied, sure 2. ascertained, conclusive, incontrovertible, indubitable, irrefutable, known, plain, true, undeniable, undoubted, unequivocal, unmistakable, valid 3. bound, definite, destined, fated, ineluctable, inescapable, inevitable, inexorable, sure 4. decided, definite, established, fixed, settled 5. assured, constant, dependable, reliable, stable, steady, trustworthy, unfailing, unquestionable 6. express, individual, particular, precise, special, specific

certainty 1. assurance, authoritativeness, certitude, confidence, conviction, faith, indubitableness, inevitability, positiveness, sureness, trust, validity 2. fact, reality, sure thing (*Inf.*), surety, truth

certificate authorization, creden~
tial(s), diploma, document, licence,
testimonial, voucher, warrant

certify ascertain, assure, attest,
authenticate, aver, avow, confirm,
corroborate, declare, endorse,
guarantee, notify, show, testify,
validate, verify, vouch, witness

chafe abrade, anger, annoy, exas~
perate, fret, fume, gall, grate, in~
cense, inflame, irritate, offend,
provoke, rage, rasp, rub, ruffle,
scrape, scratch, vex, worry

chaff n. 1. dregs, glumes, hulls,
husks, refuse, remains, rubbish,
trash, waste 2. badinage, banter,
joking, persiflage, raillery, teasing
~v. 3. banter, deride, jeer, mock,
rib (Inf.), ridicule, scoff, taunt,
tease

chain v. 1. bind, confine, enslave,
fetter, gyve (Archaic), handcuff,
manacle, restrain, shackle, tether,
trammel, unite ~n. 2. bond, cou~
pling, fetter, link, manacle, shack~
le, union 3. concatenation, pro~
gression, sequence, series, set,
string, succession, train

chairman chairperson, chair~
woman, director, master of cer~
emonies, president, presider,
speaker, spokesman, toastmaster

challenge 1. v. accost, arouse,
beard, brave, call out, claim, con~
front, dare, defy, demand, dispute,
impugn, investigate, object to,
provoke, question, require, stimu~
late, summon, tax, test, throw
down the gauntlet, try 2. n. con~
frontation, dare, defiance, interro~
gation, provocation, question,
summons to contest, test, trial, ul~
timatum

chamber 1. apartment, bedroom,
cavity, compartment, cubicle, en~
closure, hall, hollow, room 2. as~
sembly, council, legislative body,
legislature

champion 1. n. backer, challenger,
conqueror, defender, guardian,
hero, nonpareil, patron, protector,
title holder, upholder, victor, vin~
dicator, warrior, winner 2. v. ad~
vocate, back, defend, espouse, fight
for, promote, support, uphold

chance n. 1. liability, likelihood,
occasion, odds, opening, opportu~
nity, possibility, probability, pros~
pect, scope, time 2. accident, casu~
alty, coincidence, contingency,
destiny, fate, fortuity, fortune, luck,
misfortune, peril, providence 3.
gamble, hazard, jeopardy, risk,
speculation, uncertainty ~v. 4. be~
fall, betide, come about, come to
pass, fall out, happen, occur 5. en~
danger, gamble, go out on a limb
(Inf.), hazard, jeopardize, risk,
stake, try, venture, wager ~adj. 6.
accidental, casual, contingent, for~
tuitous, inadvertent, incidental,
random, serendipitous, unforesee~
able, unforeseen, unintentional,
unlooked-for

chancy dangerous, dicey (Sl.),
dodgy (Inf.), hazardous, problem~
atical, risky, speculative, uncertain

change v. 1. alter, convert, diversi~
fy, fluctuate, metamorphose, mod~
erate, modify, mutate, reform, re~
model, reorganize, restyle, shift,
transform, transmute, vacillate,
vary, veer 2. alternate, barter,
convert, displace, exchange, inter~
change, remove, replace, substi~
tute, swap (Inf.), trade, transmit
~n. 3. alteration, difference, inno~
vation, metamorphosis, modifica~
tion, mutation, permutation, revo~
lution, transformation, transition,
transmutation, vicissitude 4. con~
version, exchange, interchange,
substitution, trade 5. break (Inf.),
diversion, novelty, variation, vari~
ety

changeable capricious, changeful,
chequered, erratic, fickle, fitful,
fluid, inconstant, irregular, kalei~
doscopic, labile (Chem.), mercu~
rial, mobile, mutable, protean,
shifting, uncertain, unpredictable,
unreliable, unsettled, unstable, un~
steady, vacillating, variable, ver~
satile, volatile, wavering

changeless abiding, consistent,
constant, everlasting, fixed, immu~
table, permanent, perpetual, regu~
lar, reliable, resolute, settled, sta~
tionary, steadfast, steady, unalter~

able, unchanging, uniform, un~
varying

channel *n.* 1. canal, chamber, con~
duit, duct, fluting, furrow, groove,
gutter, main, passage, route, strait
2. *Fig.* approach, artery, avenue,
course, means, medium, path,
route, way ~*v.* 3. conduct, convey,
direct, guide, transmit

chant 1. *n.* carol, chorus, melody,
psalm, song 2. *v.* carol, chorus,
croon, descant, intone, recite, sing,
warble

chaos anarchy, bedlam, confusion,
disorder, disorganization, entropy,
lawlessness, pandemonium, tumult

chaotic anarchic, confused, de~
ranged, disordered, disorganized,
lawless, purposeless, rampageous,
riotous, topsy-turvy, tumultuous,
uncontrolled

chap bloke (*Inf.*), character, cove
(*Sl.*), customer, fellow, guy (*Inf.*),
individual, person, sort, type

chaperon 1. *n.* companion, duenna,
escort, governess 2. *v.* accompany,
attend, escort, protect, safeguard,
shepherd, watch over

chapter clause, division, episode,
part, period, phase, section, stage,
topic

char carbonize, cauterize, scorch,
sear, singe

character 1. attributes, bent, cali~
bre, cast, complexion, constitution,
disposition, individuality, kidney,
make-up, marked traits, nature,
personality, quality, reputation,
temper, temperament, type 2.
honour, integrity, rectitude,
strength, uprightness 3. card (*Inf.*),
eccentric, oddball (*Inf.*), oddity,
original, queer fish (*Inf.*) 4. cipher,
device, emblem, figure, hiero~
glyph, letter, logo, mark, rune,
sign, symbol, type 5. part, persona,
portrayal, role 6. fellow, guy (*Inf.*),
individual, person, sort, type

characteristic 1. *adj.* distinctive,
distinguishing, idiosyncratic, indi~
vidual, peculiar, representative,
singular, special, specific, symbol~
ic, symptomatic, typical 2. *n.* at~
tribute, faculty, feature, idiosyn~

crasy, mark, peculiarity, property,
quality, trait

characterize brand, distinguish,
identify, indicate, inform, mark,
represent, stamp, typify

charade fake, farce, pantomime,
parody, pretence, travesty

charge *v.* 1. accuse, arraign, blame,
impeach, incriminate, indict, in~
volve ~*n.* 2. accusation, allegation,
imputation, indictment ~*v.* 3. as~
sail, assault, attack, rush, storm
~*n.* 4. assault, attack, onset, on~
slaught, rush, sortie ~*v.* 5. afflict,
burden, commit, entrust, tax ~*n.* 6.
burden, care, concern, custody,
duty, office, responsibility, safe~
keeping, trust, ward 7. amount,
cost, damage (*Inf.*), expenditure,
expense, outlay, payment, price,
rate ~*v.* 8. fill, instil, lade, load,
suffuse 9. bid, command, enjoin,
exhort, instruct, order, require ~*n.*
10. command, dictate, direction,
exhortation, injunction, instruction,
mandate, order, precept

charitable 1. beneficent, benevo~
lent, bountiful, eleemosynary, gen~
erous, kind, lavish, liberal, philan~
thropic 2. broad-minded, consider~
ate, favourable, forgiving, gra~
cious, humane, indulgent, kindly,
lenient, magnanimous, sympathet~
ic, tolerant, understanding

charity 1. alms-giving, assistance,
benefaction, contributions, dona~
tions, endowment, fund, gift, hand-
out, philanthropy, relief 2. affec~
tion, agape, altruism, benevolence,
benignity, bountifulness, bounty,
compassion, fellow feeling, gener~
osity, goodness, good will, human~
ity, indulgence, love, tender~
heartedness

charlatan cheat, con man (*Inf.*),
fake, fraud, impostor, mountebank,
phoney (*Sl.*), pretender, quack,
sham, swindler

charm *v.* 1. allure, attract, beguile,
bewitch, cajole, captivate, delight,
enamour, enchant, enrapture, en~
trance, fascinate, mesmerize,
please, win, win over ~*n.* 2. allure,
allurement, appeal, attraction, de~
sirability, enchantment, fascina~

tion, magic, magnetism, sorcery, spell 3. amulet, fetish, good-luck piece, lucky piece, periapt (*Rare*), talisman, trinket

charming appealing, attractive, bewitching, captivating, delec~ table, delightful, engaging, eye~ catching, fetching, irresistible, lovely, pleasant, pleasing, seduc~ tive, winning, winsome

chart 1. *n.* blueprint, diagram, graph, map, plan, table, tabulation 2. *v.* delineate, draft, graph, map out, outline, plot, shape, sketch

charter 1. *n.* bond, concession, con~ tract, deed, document, franchise, indenture, licence, permit, pre~ rogative, privilege, right 2. *v.* authorize, commission, employ, hire, lease, rent, sanction

chase 1. *v.* course, drive, drive away, expel, follow, hound, hunt, pursue, put to flight, run after, track 2. *n.* hunt, hunting, pursuit, race, venery (*Archaic*)

chassis anatomy, bodywork, frame, framework, fuselage, skel~ eton, substructure

chaste austere, decent, decorous, elegant, immaculate, incorrupt, innocent, modest, moral, neat, pure, quiet, refined, restrained, simple, unaffected, uncontaminat~ ed, undefiled, unsullied, vestal, vir~ ginal, virtuous, wholesome

chasten afflict, castigate, chastise, correct, cow, curb, discipline, humble, humiliate, repress, soften, subdue, tame

chastise beat, berate, castigate, censure, correct, discipline, flog, lash, punish, scold, scourge, up~ braid, whip

chastity celibacy, continence, in~ nocence, maidenhood, modesty, purity, virginity, virtue

chat 1. *n.* chatter, chinwag (*Brit. inf.*), confab (*Inf.*), gossip, heart-to-heart, natter, talk, tête-à-tête 2. *v.* chatter, chew the rag *or* fat (*Sl.*), gossip, jaw (*Sl.*), natter, rabbit (on) (*Brit. sl.*), talk

chatter *n./v.* babble, blather, chat, gab (*Inf.*), gossip, jabber, natter, prate, prattle, tattle, twaddle

chatty colloquial, familiar, friendly, gossipy, informal, newsy (*Inf.*), talkative

cheap 1. bargain, cut-price, eco~ nomical, economy, inexpensive, keen, low-cost, low-priced, reason~ able, reduced, sale 2. common, in~ ferior, paltry, poor, second-rate, shoddy, tatty, tawdry, worthless 3. base, contemptible, despicable, low, mean, scurvy, sordid, vulgar

cheapen belittle, debase, degrade, demean, denigrate, depreciate, derogate, devalue, discredit, dis~ parage, lower

cheat *v.* 1. bamboozle (*Inf.*), be~ guile, bilk, con (*Sl.*), deceive, de~ fraud, diddle (*Inf.*), do (*Sl.*), double-cross (*Inf.*), dupe, finagle (*Inf.*), fleece, fool, gull (*Archaic*), hoax, hoodwink, mislead, rip off (*Sl.*), swindle, take for a ride (*Inf.*), take in (*Inf.*), thwart, trick, victimize 2. baffle, check, defeat, deprive, foil, frustrate, prevent, thwart ~*n.* 3. artifice, deceit, deception, fraud, imposture, rip-off (*Sl.*), swindle, trickery 4. charlatan, cheater, con man (*Inf.*), deceiver, dodger, double-crosser (*Inf.*), impostor, knave (*Archaic*), rogue, shark, sharper, swindler, trickster

check *v.* 1. compare, confirm, en~ quire into, examine, inspect, in~ vestigate, look at, look over, make sure, monitor, note, probe, scruti~ nize, study, test, tick, verify 2. ar~ rest, bar, bridle, control, curb, de~ lay, halt, hinder, impede, inhibit, limit, nip in the bud, obstruct, pause, repress, restrain, retard, stop, thwart 3. blame, chide, give (someone) a row (*Inf.*), rate, re~ buff, rebuke, reprimand, reprove, scold, tell off (*Inf.*) ~*n.* 4. exami~ nation, inspection, investigation, research, scrutiny, test 5. con~ straint, control, curb, damper, hin~ drance, impediment, inhibition, limitation, obstruction, restraint, stoppage 6. blow, disappointment, frustration, rejection, reverse, set~ back

cheek audacity, brass neck (*Inf.*), brazenness, disrespect, effrontery, gall (*Inf.*), impertinence, impu~ dence, insolence, lip (*Sl.*), nerve, sauce (*Inf.*), temerity

cheeky audacious, disrespectful, forward, impertinent, impudent, insolent, insulting, pert, saucy

cheer v. 1. animate, brighten, buoy up, cheer up, comfort, console, elate, elevate, encourage, enliven, exhilarate, gladden, hearten, in~ cite, inspirit, solace, uplift, warm 2. acclaim, applaud, clap, hail, hur~ rah ~n. 3. animation, buoyancy, cheerfulness, comfort, gaiety, gladness, glee, hopefulness, joy, liveliness, merriment, merry~ making, mirth, optimism, solace 4. acclamation, applause, ovation, plaudits

cheerful animated, blithe, bright, bucked (*Inf.*), buoyant, cheery, contented, enlivening, enthusiastic, gay, glad, gladsome, happy, hearty, jaunty, jolly, joyful, light-hearted, lightsome (*Archaic*), merry, opti~ mistic, pleasant, sparkling, sprightly, sunny

cheerfulness buoyancy, exuber~ ance, gaiety, geniality, gladness, good cheer, good humour, high spirits, jauntiness, joyousness, light-heartedness

cheering auspicious, bright, com~ forting, encouraging, heartening, promising, propitious

cheerless austere, bleak, comfort~ less, dark, dejected, depressed, desolate, despondent, disconsolate, dismal, dolorous, drab, dreary, dull, forlorn, gloomy, grim, joyless, melancholy, miserable, mournful, sad, sombre, sorrowful, sullen, un~ happy, woebegone, woeful

cheer up brighten, buck up (*Inf.*), comfort, encourage, enliven, glad~ den, hearten, jolly along, perk up, rally, take heart

cheery breezy, carefree, cheerful, good-humoured, happy, jovial, lively, pleasant, sunny

chemical compound, drug, potion, synthetic

cherish care for, cleave to, cling to, comfort, cosset, encourage, enter~ tain, foster, harbour, hold dear, nourish, nurse, nurture, prize, shelter, support, sustain, treasure

cherubic adorable, angelic, heav~ enly, innocent, lovable, seraphic, sweet

chest box, case, casket, coffer, crate, strongbox, trunk

chew 1. bite, champ, crunch, gnaw, grind, masticate, munch 2. *Fig. Usually with over* consider, delib~ erate upon, meditate, mull (over), muse on, ponder, reflect upon, ru~ minate, weigh

chic elegant, fashionable, modish, smart, stylish, trendy (*Brit. inf.*)

chide admonish, berate, blame, censure, check, criticize, find fault, give (someone) a row (*Inf.*), lec~ ture, rebuke, reprehend, repri~ mand, reproach, reprove, scold, tell off (*Inf.*), upbraid

chief 1. *adj.* capital, cardinal, cen~ tral, especial, essential, foremost, grand, highest, key, leading, main, most important, outstanding, paramount, predominant, pre~ eminent, premier, prevailing, pri~ mary, prime, principal, superior, supreme, uppermost, vital 2. *n.* boss (*Inf.*), captain, chieftain, commander, director, governor, head, leader, lord, manager, mas~ ter, principal, ringleader, ruler, superintendent, suzerain

chiefly above all, especially, essen~ tially, in general, in the main, mainly, mostly, on the whole, pre~ dominantly, primarily, principally, usually

child babe, baby, bairn (*Scot.*), brat, chit, descendant, infant, issue, ju~ venile, kid (*Inf.*), little one, minor, nipper (*Inf.*), nursling, offspring, progeny, suckling, toddler, tot, wean (*Scot.*), youngster (*Inf.*)

childbirth accouchement, child- bearing, confinement, delivery, la~ bour, lying-in, parturition, travail

childhood boyhood, girlhood, im~ maturity, infancy, minority, schooldays, youth

childish boyish, foolish, frivolous, girlish, immature, infantile, ju~ venile, puerile, silly, simple, tri~ fling, weak, young

childlike artless, credulous, guile~
less, ingenuous, innocent, naive,
simple, trustful, trusting, unfeigned

chill *adj.* 1. biting, bleak, chilly,
cold, freezing, frigid, raw, sharp,
wintry 2. *Fig.* aloof, cool, depress~
ing, distant, frigid, hostile, stony,
unfriendly, ungenial, unresponsive,
unwelcoming ~*v.* 3. congeal, cool,
freeze, refrigerate 4. *Fig.* dampen,
deject, depress, discourage, dis~
hearten, dismay ~*n.* 5. bite, cold,
coldness, coolness, crispness, fri~
gidity, nip, rawness, sharpness

chilly 1. blowy, breezy, brisk, cool,
crisp, draughty, fresh, nippy, pen~
etrating, sharp 2. frigid, hostile,
unfriendly, unresponsive, unsym~
pathetic, unwelcoming

chime boom, clang, dong, jingle,
peal, ring, sound, strike, tinkle, tin~
tinnabulate, toll

china ceramics, crockery, porce~
lain, pottery, service, tableware,
ware

chink aperture, cleft, crack, cran~
ny, crevice, cut, fissure, flaw, gap,
opening, rift

chip 1. *n.* dent, flake, flaw, frag~
ment, nick, notch, paring, scrap,
scratch, shard, shaving, sliver, wa~
fer 2. *v.* chisel, damage, gash, nick,
whittle

chip in contribute, donate, go
Dutch (*Inf.*), interpose, interrupt,
pay, subscribe

chivalrous bold, brave, coura~
geous, courteous, courtly, gallant,
gentlemanly, heroic, high-minded,
honourable, intrepid, knightly,
magnanimous, true, valiant

chivalry courage, courtesy, courtli~
ness, gallantry, gentlemanliness,
knight-errantry, knighthood, po~
liteness

chivvy annoy, badger, harass, has~
sle (*Inf.*), hound, nag, pester,
plague, pressure (*Inf.*), prod, tor~
ment

choice 1. *n.* alternative, discrimi~
nation, election, option, pick, pref~
erence, say, selection, variety 2.
adj. best, dainty, elect, elite, excel~
lent, exclusive, exquisite, hand~
picked, nice, precious, prime,

prize, rare, select, special, superi~
or, uncommon, unusual, valuable

choke asphyxiate, bar, block, clog,
close, congest, constrict, dam, ob~
struct, occlude, overpower, smoth~
er, stifle, stop, strangle, suffocate,
suppress, throttle

choleric angry, bad-tempered,
fiery, hasty, hot, hot-tempered, ill-
tempered, irascible, irritable, pas~
sionate, petulant, quick-tempered,
testy, touchy

choose adopt, cull, designate, de~
sire, elect, espouse, fix on, opt for,
pick, predestine, prefer, see fit, se~
lect, settle upon, single out, take,
wish

choosy discriminating, exacting,
faddy, fastidious, finicky, fussy,
particular, selective

chop 1. *v.* axe, cleave, cut, fell,
hack, hew, lop, sever, shear, slash,
truncate 2. *n.* for the chop *Sl.* dismis~
sal, one's cards, sacking (*Inf.*), ter~
mination, the axe (*Inf.*), the boot
(*Sl.*), the sack (*Inf.*)

choppy blustery, broken, rough,
ruffled, squally, tempestuous

chop up cube, dice, divide, frag~
ment, mince

chore burden, duty, errand, fag
(*Inf.*), job, task

chortle cackle, chuckle, crow, guf~
faw

chorus 1. choir, choristers, ensem~
ble, singers, vocalists 2. burden,
refrain, response, strain 3. accord,
concert, harmony, unison

christen baptize, call, designate,
dub, name, style, term, title

chronic 1. confirmed, deep-rooted,
deep-seated, habitual, incessant,
incurable, ineradicable, ingrained,
inveterate, persistent 2. *Inf.* appal~
ling, atrocious, awful, dreadful

chronicle 1. *n.* account, annals,
diary, history, journal, narrative,
record, register, story 2. *v.* enter,
narrate, put on record, record, re~
count, register, relate, report, set
down, tell

chronicler annalist, diarist, histo~
rian, historiographer, narrator, re~
corder, reporter, scribe

chronological consecutive, his~

torical, in sequence, ordered, pro~
gressive, sequential

chubby buxom, flabby, fleshy,
plump, podgy, portly, rotund,
round, stout, tubby

chuck cast, discard, fling, heave,
hurl, pitch, shy, sling, throw, toss

chuckle chortle, crow, exult, gig~
gle, laugh, snigger, titter

chum companion, comrade, crony,
friend, mate (*Inf.*), pal (*Inf.*)

chunk block, dollop (*Inf.*), hunk,
lump, mass, piece, portion, slab,
wad, wodge (*Inf.*)

chunky beefy (*Inf.*), dumpy, stocky,
stubby, thickset

churlish 1. boorish, brusque, crab~
bed, harsh, ill-tempered, impolite,
loutish, morose, oafish, rude, sul~
len, surly, uncivil, unmannerly,
vulgar 2. close-fisted, illiberal, in~
hospitable, mean, miserly, nig~
gardly, unneighbourly, unsociable

churlishness boorishness, crass~
ness, crudeness, loutishness, oaf~
ishness, rudeness, surliness, un~
couthness

churn agitate, beat, boil, convulse,
foam, froth, seethe, stir up, swirl,
toss

cigarette cancer stick (*Sl.*), ciggy
(*Inf.*), coffin nail (*Sl.*), fag (*Sl.*),
gasper (*Sl.*), smoke

cinema big screen (*Inf.*), films,
flicks (*Sl.*), motion pictures,
movies, pictures

cipher 1. nil, nothing, nought, zero
2. nobody, nonentity 3. character,
digit, figure, number, numeral,
symbol 4. code, cryptograph 5. de~
vice, logo, mark, monogram

circle n. 1. band, circumference,
coil, cordon, cycle, disc, globe, lap,
loop, orb, perimeter, periphery,
revolution, ring, round, sphere,
turn 2. area, bounds, circuit, com~
pass, domain, enclosure, field, or~
bit, province, range, realm, region,
scene, sphere 3. assembly, class,
clique, club, company, coterie,
crowd, fellowship, fraternity,
group, school, set, society ~v. 4.
belt, circumnavigate, circum~
scribe, coil, compass, curve, encir~
cle, enclose, encompass, envelop,

gird, hem in, pivot, revolve, ring,
rotate, surround, tour, whirl

circuit 1. area, compass, course,
journey, orbit, perambulation,
revolution, round, route, tour,
track 2. boundary, bounding line,
bounds, circumference, compass,
district, limit, range, region, tract

circuitous ambagious (*Archaic*),
devious, indirect, labyrinthine,
meandering, oblique, rambling,
roundabout, tortuous, winding

circulate 1. broadcast, diffuse, dis~
seminate, distribute, issue, make
known, promulgate, propagate,
publicize, publish, spread 2. flow,
gyrate, radiate, revolve, rotate

circulation 1. currency, dissemi~
nation, distribution, spread, trans~
mission, vogue 2. circling, flow,
motion, rotation

circumference border, boundary,
bounds, circuit, edge, extremity,
fringe, limits, outline, perimeter,
periphery, rim, verge

circumscribe bound, confine, de~
fine, delimit, delineate, demarcate,
encircle, enclose, encompass, en~
viron, hem in, limit, mark off, re~
strain, restrict, surround

circumspect attentive, canny,
careful, cautious, deliberate, dis~
creet, discriminating, guarded,
heedful, judicious, observant, poli~
tic, prudent, sagacious, sage, vigi~
lant, wary, watchful

circumstance accident, condition,
contingency, detail, element,
event, fact, factor, happening, in~
cident, item, occurrence, particu~
lar, position, respect, situation

circumstances life style, means,
position, resources, situation, state,
state of affairs, station, status,
times

circumstantial conjectural, con~
tingent, detailed, founded on cir~
cumstances, hearsay, incidental,
indirect, inferential, particular,
presumptive, provisional, specific

cistern basin, reservoir, sink, tank,
vat

citadel bastion, fastness, fortifica~
tion, fortress, keep, stronghold,
tower

citation 1. commendation, excerpt, illustration, passage, quotation, quote, reference, source 2. award, commendation, mention

cite 1. adduce, advance, allude to, enumerate, evidence, extract, mention, name, quote, specify 2. *Law* call, subpoena, summon

citizen burgess, burgher, denizen, dweller, freeman, inhabitant, ratepayer, resident, subject, townsman

city 1. *n.* conurbation, megalopolis, metropolis, municipality 2. *adj.* civic, metropolitan, municipal, urban

civic borough, communal, community, local, municipal, public

civil 1. civic, domestic, home, interior, municipal, political 2. accommodating, affable, civilized, complaisant, courteous, courtly, obliging, polished, polite, refined, urbane, well-bred, well-mannered

civilization 1. advancement, cultivation, culture, development, education, enlightenment, progress, refinement, sophistication 2. community, nation, people, polity, society 3. customs, mores, way of life

civilize cultivate, educate, enlighten, humanize, improve, polish, refine, sophisticate, tame

civilized cultured, educated, enlightened, humane, polite, sophisticated, tolerant, urbane

claim 1. *v.* allege, ask, assert, call for, challenge, collect, demand, exact, hold, insist, maintain, need, pick up, profess, require, take, uphold 2. *n.* affirmation, allegation, application, assertion, call, demand, petition, pretension, privilege, protestation, request, requirement, right, title

clamber claw, climb, scale, scrabble, scramble, shin

clamour agitation, babel, blare, brouhaha, commotion, din, exclamation, hubbub, hullabaloo, noise, outcry, racket, shout, shouting, uproar, vociferation

clamp 1. *n.* bracket, fastener, grip, press, vice 2. *v.* brace, clinch, fasten, fix, impose, make fast, secure

clan band, brotherhood, clique, coterie, faction, family, fraternity, gens, group, house, race, sect, sept, set, society, sodality, tribe

clang 1. *v.* bong, chime, clank, clash, jangle, resound, reverberate, ring, toll 2. *n.* clangour, ding-dong, knell, reverberation

clap 1. acclaim, applaud, cheer 2. bang, pat, slap, strike gently, thrust, thwack, wallop (*Inf.*), whack

claptrap affectation, blarney, bombast, bunk (*Inf.*), drivel, flannel (*Inf.*), guff (*Sl.*), hot air (*Inf.*), humbug, insincerity, nonsense, rodomontade, rubbish

clarification elucidation, explanation, exposition, illumination, interpretation, simplification

clarify 1. clear up, elucidate, explain, illuminate, make plain, resolve, simplify, throw *or* shed light on 2. cleanse, purify, refine

clarity clearness, comprehensibility, definition, explicitness, intelligibility, limpidity, lucidity, obviousness, precision, simplicity, transparency

clash *v.* 1. bang, clang, clank, clatter, crash, jangle, jar, rattle 2. conflict, cross swords, feud, grapple, quarrel, war, wrangle ~*n.* 3. brush, collision, conflict, confrontation, difference of opinion, disagreement, fight, showdown (*Inf.*)

clasp *v.* 1. attack, clutch, concatenate, connect, embrace, enfold, fasten, grapple, grasp, grip, hold, hug, press, seize, squeeze ~*n.* 2. brooch, buckle, catch, clip, fastener, fastening, grip, hasp, hook, pin, snap 3. embrace, grasp, grip, hold, hug

class 1. *n.* caste, category, classification, collection, denomination, department, division, genre, genus, grade, group, grouping, kind, league, order, rank, set, sort, species, sphere, status, type, value 2. *v.* brand, categorize, classify, codify, designate, grade, group, rank, rate

classic *adj.* 1. best, consummate, finest, first-rate, masterly 2. archetypal, definitive, exemplary, ideal, master, model, paradigmatic, quintessential, standard 3. characteristic, regular, standard, time-honoured, typical, usual 4. abiding, ageless, deathless, enduring, immortal, lasting, undying ~n. 5. exemplar, masterpiece, masterwork, model, paradigm, prototype, standard

classical 1. chaste, elegant, harmonious, pure, refined, restrained, symmetrical, understated, well-proportioned 2. Attic, Augustan, Grecian, Greek, Hellenic, Latin, Roman

classification analysis, arrangement, cataloguing, categorization, codification, grading, sorting, taxonomy

classify arrange, catalogue, categorize, codify, dispose, distribute, file, grade, pigeonhole, rank, sort, systematize, tabulate

clause 1. article, chapter, condition, paragraph, part, passage, section 2. heading, item, point, provision, proviso, specification, stipulation

claw 1. n. nail, nipper, pincer, talon, tentacle, unguis 2. v. dig, graze, lacerate, mangle, maul, rip, scrabble, scrape, scratch, tear

clean adj. 1. faultless, flawless, fresh, hygienic, immaculate, laundered, pure, sanitary, spotless, unblemished, unsoiled, unspotted, unstained, unsullied, washed 2. antiseptic, clarified, decontaminated, natural, purified, sterile, sterilized, unadulterated, uncontaminated, unpolluted 3. chaste, decent, exemplary, good, honourable, innocent, moral, pure, respectable, undefiled, upright, virtuous 4. delicate, elegant, graceful, neat, simple, tidy, trim, uncluttered 5. complete, conclusive, decisive, entire, final, perfect, thorough, total, unimpaired, whole ~v. 6. bath, cleanse, deodorize, disinfect, do up, dust, launder, lave, mop, purge, purify, rinse, sanitize, scour, scrub, sponge, swab, sweep, vacuum, wash, wipe

clean-cut chiselled, clear, definite,

etched, neat, outlined, sharp, trim, well-defined

cleanse absolve, clean, clear, lustrate, purge, purify, rinse, scour, scrub, wash

cleanser detergent, disinfectant, purifier, scourer, soap, soap powder, solvent

clear¹ adj. 1. bright, cloudless, fair, fine, halcyon, light, luminous, shining, sunny, unclouded, undimmed 2. apparent, audible, coherent, comprehensible, conspicuous, definite, distinct, evident, explicit, express, incontrovertible, intelligible, lucid, manifest, obvious, palpable, patent, perceptible, plain, pronounced, recognizable, unambiguous, unequivocal, unmistakable, unquestionable 3. empty, free, open, smooth, unhampered, unhindered, unimpeded, unlimited, unobstructed 4. crystalline, glassy, limpid, pellucid, see-through, transparent 5. certain, convinced, decided, definite, positive, resolved, satisfied, sure 6. clean, guiltless, immaculate, innocent, pure, sinless, stainless, unblemished, undefiled, untarnished, untroubled

clear² v. 1. clean, cleanse, erase, purify, refine, sweep away, tidy (up), wipe 2. break up, brighten, clarify, lighten 3. absolve, acquit, excuse, exonerate, justify, vindicate 4. emancipate, free, liberate, set free 5. disengage, disentangle, extricate, free, loosen, open, rid, unblock, unclog, unload, unpack 6. jump, leap, miss, pass over, vault 7. acquire, earn, gain, make, reap, secure

clearance 1. authorization, consent, endorsement, go-ahead, green light, leave, O.K. (Inf.), permission, sanction 2. allowance, gap, headroom, margin 3. depopulation, emptying, evacuation, eviction, removal, unpeopling, withdrawal

clear-cut definite, explicit, plain, precise, specific, straightforward, unambiguous, unequivocal

clearly beyond doubt, distinctly,

evidently, incontestably, incontro~
vertibly, markedly, obviously,
openly, seemingly, undeniably, un~
doubtedly

clear out 1. empty, exhaust, get rid
of, sort, tidy up 2. beat it (*Sl.*),
decamp, depart, leave, make one~
self scarce, retire, take oneself off,
withdraw

clear up 1. answer, clarify, eluci~
date, explain, resolve, solve,
straighten out, unravel 2. order,
rearrange, tidy (up)

cleave crack, dissever, disunite, di~
vide, hew, open, part, rend, rive,
sever, slice, split, sunder, tear
asunder

clergy churchmen, clergymen,
clerics, ecclesiastics, first estate,
holy orders, ministry, priesthood,
the cloth

clergyman chaplain, cleric, curate,
divine, father, man of God, man of
the cloth, minister, padre, parson,
pastor, priest, rabbi, rector, rever~
end (*Inf.*), vicar

clerical 1. ecclesiastical, pastoral,
priestly, sacerdotal 2. book~
keeping, clerkish, clerkly, office,
secretarial, stenographic

clever able, adroit, apt, astute,
brainy (*Inf.*), bright, canny, ca~
pable, cunning, deep, dexterous,
discerning, expert, gifted, ingen~
ious, intelligent, inventive, keen,
knowing, knowledgeable, quick,
quick-witted, rational, resourceful,
sagacious, sensible, shrewd, skilful,
smart, talented, witty

cleverness ability, adroitness, as~
tuteness, brains, brightness, canni~
ness, dexterity, flair, gift, gumption
(*Inf.*), ingenuity, intelligence, nous
(*Sl.*), quickness, quick wits, re~
sourcefulness, sagacity, sense,
sharpness, shrewdness, smartness,
talent, wit

cliché banality, bromide, chestnut
(*Inf.*), commonplace, hackneyed
phrase, old saw, platitude, stereo~
type, truism

click *n./v.* 1. beat, clack, snap, tick
~*v.* 2. *Inf.* become clear, come
home (to), fall into place, make
sense 3. *Sl.* be compatible, be on

the same wavelength, feel a rap~
port, get on, go over (*Inf.*), hit it off
(*Inf.*), make a hit, succeed, take to
each other

client applicant, buyer, consumer,
customer, dependant, habitué, pa~
tient, protégé, shopper

clientele business, clients, custom~
ers, following, market, patronage,
regulars, trade

cliff bluff, crag, escarpment, face,
overhang, precipice, rock face,
scar, scarp

climactic climactical, critical, cru~
cial, decisive, paramount, peak

climate 1. clime, country, region,
temperature, weather 2. ambi~
ence, disposition, feeling, mood,
temper, tendency, trend

climax 1. *n.* acme, apogee, culmi~
nation, head, height, highlight, high
spot (*Inf.*), ne plus ultra, pay-off
(*Inf.*), peak, summit, top, zenith 2.
v. come to a head, culminate, top

climb ascend, clamber, mount, rise,
scale, shin up, soar, top

climb down 1. descend, dismount
2. back down, eat crow (*U.S. inf.*),
eat one's words, retract, retreat

clinch 1. assure, cap, conclude,
confirm, decide, determine, seal,
secure, set the seal on, settle, sew
up (*Inf.*), verify 2. bolt, clamp, fas~
ten, fix, make fast, nail, rivet, se~
cure 3. clutch, cuddle, embrace,
grasp, hug, squeeze

cling adhere, attach to, be true to,
clasp, cleave to, clutch, embrace,
fasten, grasp, grip, hug, stick, twine
round

clip[1] 1. *v.* crop, curtail, cut, cut
short, pare, prune, shear, shorten,
snip, trim 2. *n./v. Inf.* blow, box,
clout (*Inf.*), cuff, knock, punch,
skelp (*Dialect*), smack, thump,
wallop (*Inf.*), whack 3. *n. Inf.* gal~
lop, lick (*Inf.*), rate, speed, velocity

clip[2] *v.* attach, fasten, fix, hold, pin,
staple

clique circle, clan, coterie, crew
(*Inf.*), crowd, faction, gang, group,
mob, pack, set

cloak 1. *v.* camouflage, conceal,
cover, disguise, hide, mask, ob~
scure, screen, veil 2. *n.* blind, cape,

coat, cover, front, mantle, mask, pretext, shield, wrap

clog 1. *v.* block, burden, congest, dam up, hamper, hinder, impede, jam, obstruct, occlude, shackle, stop up 2. *n.* burden, dead weight, drag, encumbrance, hindrance, impediment, obstruction

cloistered cloistral, confined, hermitic, insulated, reclusive, restricted, secluded, sequestered, sheltered, shielded, shut off, withdrawn

close[1] *v.* 1. bar, block, choke, clog, confine, cork, fill, lock, obstruct, plug, seal, secure, shut, shut up, stop up 2. cease, complete, conclude, culminate, discontinue, end, finish, mothball, shut down, terminate, wind up (*Inf.*) 3. come together, connect, couple, fuse, grapple, join, unite

close[2] 1. adjacent, adjoining, approaching, at hand, handy, hard by, imminent, impending, near, nearby, neighbouring, nigh 2. compact, congested, cramped, cropped, crowded, dense, impenetrable, jam-packed, packed, short, solid, thick, tight 3. accurate, conscientious, exact, faithful, literal, precise, strict 4. alert, assiduous, attentive, careful, concentrated, detailed, dogged, earnest, fixed, intense, intent, keen, minute, painstaking, rigorous, searching, thorough 5. attached, confidential, dear, devoted, familiar, inseparable, intimate, loving 6. airless, confined, frowsty, fuggy, heavy, humid, muggy, oppressive, stale, stifling, stuffy, suffocating, sweltering, thick, unventilated 7. hidden, private, reticent, retired, secluded, secret, secretive, taciturn, uncommunicative, unforthcoming 8. illiberal, mean, mingy (*Inf.*), miserly, near, niggardly, parsimonious, penurious, stingy, tight-fisted, ungenerous

close[3] cessation, completion, conclusion, culmination, denouement, end, ending, finale, finish, termination

closed 1. fastened, locked, out of business, out of service, sealed, shut 2. concluded, decided, ended, finished, over, resolved, settled, terminated 3. exclusive, restricted

cloth dry goods, fabric, material, stuff, textiles

clothe accoutre, apparel, array, attire, bedizen (*Archaic*), caparison, cover, deck, doll up (*Sl.*), drape, dress, endow, enwrap, equip, fit out, garb, habit, invest, outfit, rig, robe, swathe

clothes, clothing apparel, attire, clobber (*Brit. sl.*), costume, dress, duds (*Inf.*), ensemble, garb, garments, gear (*Inf.*), get-up (*Inf.*), habits, outfit, raiment, rigout (*Inf.*), togs (*Inf.*), vestments, vesture, wardrobe, wear

cloud *n.* 1. billow, darkness, fog, gloom, haze, mist, murk, nebula, nebulosity, obscurity, vapour 2. crowd, dense mass, flock, horde, host, multitude, shower, swarm, throng ~*v.* 3. becloud, darken, dim, eclipse, obfuscate, obscure, overcast, overshadow, shade, shadow, veil 4. confuse, disorient, distort, impair, muddle

cloudy blurred, confused, dark, dim, dismal, dull, dusky, emulsified, gloomy, hazy, indistinct, leaden, lowering, muddy, murky, nebulous, obscure, opaque, overcast, sombre, sullen, sunless

clown *n.* 1. buffoon, comedian, dolt, fool, harlequin, jester, joker, merry-andrew, mountebank, pierrot, prankster, punchinello 2. boor, clodhopper (*Inf.*), hind, peasant, swain (*Archaic*), yahoo, yokel ~*v.* 3. act the fool, act the goat, jest, mess about

club 1. *n.* bat, bludgeon, cosh, cudgel, stick, truncheon 2. *v.* bash, baste, batter, beat, bludgeon, clobber (*Sl.*), clout (*Inf.*), cosh, hammer, pommel (*Rare*), pummel, strike 3. *n.* association, circle, clique, company, fraternity, group, guild, lodge, order, set, society, sodality, union

clue evidence, hint, indication, inkling, intimation, lead, pointer, sign, suggestion, suspicion, tip, tip-off, trace

clump 1. *n.* bunch, bundle, cluster, mass, shock 2. *v.* bumble, clomp, lumber, plod, stamp, stomp, stump, thud, thump, tramp

clumsy awkward, blundering, bumbling, bungling, cack-handed (*Inf.*), gauche, gawky, ham-fisted (*Inf.*), ham-handed (*Inf.*), heavy, ill-shaped, inept, inexpert, lumbering, maladroit, ponderous, uncoordi~ nated, uncouth, ungainly, unhandy, unskilful, unwieldy

cluster 1. *n.* assemblage, batch, bunch, clump, collection, gather~ ing, group, knot 2. *v.* assemble, bunch, collect, flock, gather, group

clutch catch, clasp, cling to, em~ brace, fasten, grab, grapple, grasp, grip, seize, snatch

clutches claws, control, custody, grasp, grip, hands, keeping, pos~ session, power, sway

clutter 1. *n.* confusion, disarray, disorder, hotchpotch, jumble, lit~ ter, mess, muddle, untidiness 2. *v.* litter, scatter, strew

coach *n.* 1. bus, car, carriage, charabanc, vehicle 2. instructor, teacher, trainer, tutor ~*v.* 3. cram, drill, instruct, prepare, train, tutor

coalesce amalgamate, blend, co~ here, combine, come together, commingle, commix, consolidate, fraternize, fuse, incorporate, inte~ grate, merge, mix, unite

coalition affiliation, alliance, amalgam, amalgamation, associa~ tion, bloc, combination, compact, confederacy, confederation, con~ junction, fusion, integration, league, merger, union

coarse 1. boorish, brutish, coarse-grained, foul-mouthed, gruff, lout~ ish, rough, rude, uncivil 2. bawdy, earthy, immodest, impolite, im~ proper, impure, indelicate, inel~ egant, mean, offensive, ribald, rude, smutty, vulgar 3. coarse-grained, crude, homespun, impure, rough-hewn, unfinished, unpol~ ished, unprocessed, unpurified, un~ refined

coarsen anaesthetize, blunt, cal~ lous, deaden, desensitize, dull, harden, indurate, roughen

coarseness bawdiness, boorish~ ness, crudity, earthiness, indelica~ cy, offensiveness, poor taste, rib~ aldry, roughness, smut, smuttiness, uncouthness, unevenness

coast 1. *n.* beach, border, coastline, littoral, seaboard, seaside, shore, strand 2. *v.* cruise, drift, freewheel, get by, glide, sail, taxi

coat *n.* 1. fleece, fur, hair, hide, pelt, skin, wool 2. coating, covering, layer, overlay ~*v.* 3. apply, cover, plaster, smear, spread

coating blanket, coat, covering, dusting, film, finish, glaze, lamina~ tion, layer, membrane, patina, sheet, skin, varnish, veneer

coax allure, beguile, cajole, decoy, entice, flatter, inveigle, persuade, prevail upon, soft-soap (*Inf.*), soothe, talk into, wheedle

cock 1. *n.* chanticleer, cockerel, rooster 2. *v.* perk up, prick, raise, stand up

cockeyed absurd, askew, asym~ metrical, awry, crazy, crooked, lopsided, ludicrous, nonsensical, preposterous, skewwhiff (*Brit. inf.*), squint (*Inf.*)

cocky arrogant, brash, cocksure, conceited, egotistical, lordly, swaggering, swollen-headed, vain

code 1. cipher, cryptograph 2. can~ on, convention, custom, ethics, eti~ quette, manners, maxim, regula~ tions, rules, system

cogent compelling, conclusive, convincing, effective, forceful, for~ cible, influential, irresistible, po~ tent, powerful, strong, urgent, weighty

cogitate consider, contemplate, deliberate, meditate, mull over, muse, ponder, reflect, ruminate, think

cogitation consideration, contem~ plation, deliberation, meditation, reflection, rumination, thought

cognate affiliated, akin, alike, al~ lied, analogous, associated, con~ nected, kindred, related, similar

cognition apprehension, aware~ ness, comprehension, discernment, insight, intelligence, perception, reasoning, understanding

coherent articulate, comprehensible, consistent, intelligible, logical, lucid, meaningful, orderly, organized, rational, reasoned, systematic

coil convolute, curl, entwine, loop, snake, spiral, twine, twist, wind, wreathe, writhe

coin 1. *v.* conceive, create, fabricate, forge, formulate, frame, invent, make up, mint, mould, originate, think up 2. *n.* cash, change, copper, money, silver, specie

coincide 1. be concurrent, coexist, occur simultaneously, synchronize 2. accord, harmonize, match, quadrate, square, tally 3. acquiesce, agree, concur, correspond

coincidence 1. accident, chance, eventuality, fluke, fortuity, happy accident, luck, stroke of luck 2. concomitance, concurrence, conjunction, correlation, correspondence, synchronism

coincidental 1. accidental, casual, chance, fluky (*Inf.*), fortuitous, unintentional, unplanned 2. coincident, concomitant, concurrent, simultaneous, synchronous

cold *adj.* 1. arctic, biting, bitter, bleak, brumal, chill, chilly, cool, freezing, frigid, frosty, frozen, gelid, icy, inclement, raw, wintry 2. benumbed, chilled, chilly, freezing, frozen to the marrow, numbed, shivery 3. aloof, apathetic, cold-blooded, dead, distant, frigid, glacial, indifferent, inhospitable, lukewarm, passionless, phlegmatic, reserved, spiritless, standoffish, stony, undemonstrative, unfeeling, unmoved, unresponsive, unsympathetic ~*n.* 4. chill, chilliness, coldness, frigidity, frostiness, iciness, inclemency

cold-blooded barbarous, brutal, callous, cruel, dispassionate, heartless, inhuman, merciless, pitiless, ruthless, savage, steely, stony-hearted, unemotional, unfeeling, unmoved

cold-hearted callous, detached, frigid, heartless, indifferent, inhuman, insensitive, stony-hearted, uncaring, unfeeling, unkind, unsympathetic

collaborate 1. cooperate, coproduce, join forces, participate, team up, work together 2. collude, conspire, cooperate, fraternize

collaboration alliance, association, concert, cooperation, partnership, teamwork

collaborator 1. associate, colleague, confederate, co-worker, partner, team-mate 2. collaborationist, fraternizer, quisling, traitor, turncoat

collapse 1. *v.* break down, cave in, come to nothing, crack up (*Inf.*), crumple, fail, faint, fall, fold, founder, give way, subside 2. *n.* breakdown, cave-in, disintegration, downfall, exhaustion, failure, faint, flop (*Sl.*), prostration, subsidence

collar *v.* apprehend, appropriate, capture, catch, grab, lay hands on, seize

colleague aider, ally, assistant, associate, auxiliary, coadjutor (*Rare*), collaborator, companion, comrade, confederate, confrère, fellow worker, helper, partner, team-mate, workmate

collect 1. accumulate, aggregate, amass, assemble, gather, heap, hoard, save, stockpile 2. assemble, cluster, congregate, convene, converge, flock together, rally 3. acquire, muster, obtain, raise, secure, solicit

collected calm, composed, confident, cool, placid, poised, self-possessed, serene, together (*Sl.*), unperturbable, unperturbed, unruffled

collection 1. accumulation, anthology, compilation, congeries, heap, hoard, mass, pile, set, stockpile, store 2. assemblage, assembly, assortment, cluster, company, congregation, convocation, crowd, gathering, group 3. alms, contribution, offering, offertory

collide clash, come into collision, conflict, crash, meet head-on

collision 1. accident, bump, crash, impact, pile-up, prang (*Inf.*), smash

2. clash, clashing, conflict, confrontation, encounter, opposition, skirmish

colloquial conversational, demotic, everyday, familiar, idiomatic, informal, vernacular

collusion cahoots (*Inf.*), complicity, connivance, conspiracy, craft, deceit, fraudulent artifice, intrigue, secret understanding

colonist colonial, colonizer, frontiersman, homesteader (*U.S.*), immigrant, pioneer, planter, settler

colonize open up, people, pioneer, populate, settle

colony community, dependency, dominion, outpost, possession, province, satellite state, settlement, territory

colossal Brobdingnagian, elephantine, enormous, gargantuan, gigantic, herculean, huge, immense, mammoth, massive, monstrous, monumental, mountainous, prodigious, titanic, vast

colour *n.* 1. colorant, coloration, complexion, dye, hue, paint, pigment, pigmentation, shade, tincture, tinge, tint 2. animation, bloom, blush, brilliance, flush, glow, liveliness, rosiness, ruddiness, vividness 3. *Fig.* appearance, disguise, excuse, façade, false show, guise, plea, pretence, pretext, semblance ~*v.* 4. colourwash, dye, paint, stain, tinge, tint 5. *Fig.* disguise, distort, embroider, exaggerate, falsify, garble, gloss over, misrepresent, pervert, prejudice, slant, taint 6. blush, burn, crimson, flush, go crimson, redden

colourful 1. bright, brilliant, intense, jazzy (*Sl.*), kaleidoscopic, motley, multicoloured, psychedelic, rich, variegated, vibrant, vivid 2. characterful, distinctive, graphic, interesting, lively, picturesque, rich, stimulating, unusual, vivid

colourless 1. achromatic, achromic, anaemic, ashen, bleached, drab, faded, neutral, sickly, wan, washed out 2. characterless, dreary, insipid, lacklustre, tame, uninteresting, unmemorable, vacuous, vapid

colours 1. banner, emblem, ensign, flag, standard 2. *Fig.* aspect, breed, character, identity, nature, stamp, strain

column 1. cavalcade, file, line, list, procession, queue, rank, row, string, train 2. caryatid, obelisk, pilaster, pillar, post, shaft, support, upright

columnist correspondent, critic, editor, gossip columnist, reporter, reviewer

coma drowsiness, insensibility, lethargy, oblivion, somnolence, stupor, torpor, trance, unconsciousness

comatose drowsy, drugged, insensible, lethargic, sleepy, sluggish, somnolent, soporose (*Medical*), stupefied, torpid, unconscious

comb *v.* 1. arrange, curry, dress, groom, untangle 2. *Of flax, wool, etc.* card, hackle, hatchel, heckle, tease, teasel, teazle 3. *Fig.* go through with a fine-tooth comb, hunt, rake, ransack, rummage, scour, screen, search, sift, sweep

combat 1. *n.* action, battle, conflict, contest, encounter, engagement, fight, skirmish, struggle, war, warfare 2. *v.* battle, contend, contest, cope, defy, do battle with, engage, fight, oppose, resist, strive, struggle, withstand

combatant 1. *n.* adversary, antagonist, belligerent, contender, enemy, fighter, fighting man, opponent, serviceman, soldier, warrior 2. *adj.* battling, belligerent, combating, conflicting, contending, fighting, opposing, warring

combination 1. amalgam, amalgamation, blend, coalescence, composite, connection, mix, mixture 2. alliance, association, cabal, cartel, coalition, combine, compound, confederacy, confederation, consortium, conspiracy, federation, merger, syndicate, unification, union

combine amalgamate, associate, bind, blend, bond, compound, connect, cooperate, fuse, incorporate, integrate, join (together), link, marry, merge, mix, pool, put together, synthesize, unify, unite

come 1. advance, appear, approach, arrive, become, draw near, enter, happen, materialize, move, move towards, near, occur, originate, show up (*Inf.*), turn out, turn up (*Inf.*) 2. appear, arrive, attain, enter, materialize, reach, show up (*Inf.*), turn up (*Inf.*) 3. fall, happen, occur, take place 4. arise, emanate, emerge, end up, flow, issue, originate, result, turn out 5. extend, reach 6. be available (made, offered, on offer, produced)

come about arise, befall, come to pass, happen, occur, result, take place, transpire (*Inf.*)

come across bump into (*Inf.*), chance upon, discover, encounter, find, happen upon, hit upon, light upon, meet, notice, stumble upon, unearth

come along develop, improve, mend, perk up, pick up, progress, rally, recover, recuperate

come apart break, come unstuck, crumble, disintegrate, fall to pieces, give way, separate, split, tear

come at 1. attain, discover, find, grasp, reach 2. assail, assault, attack, charge, fall upon, fly at, go for (*Inf.*), light into, rush, rush at

comeback 1. rally, rebound, recovery, resurgence, return, revival, triumph 2. rejoinder, reply, response, retaliation, retort, riposte

come back reappear, recur, re-enter, return

come between alienate, divide, estrange, interfere, meddle, part, separate, set at odds

come by acquire, get, lay hold of, obtain, procure, secure, take possession of, win

come clean acknowledge, admit, confess, make a clean breast, own up, reveal

comedian card (*Inf.*), clown, comic, funny man, humorist, jester, joker, laugh (*Inf.*), wag, wit

comedown anticlimax, blow, decline, deflation, demotion, disappointment, humiliation, letdown, reverse

come down 1. decline, degenerate, descend, deteriorate, fall, go downhill, reduce, worsen 2. choose, decide, favour, recommend

come down on criticize, dress down (*Inf.*), jump on (*Inf.*), rebuke, reprimand

come down to amount to, boil down to, end up as, result in

come down with be stricken with, catch, contract, fall ill, fall victim to, sicken, take, take sick

comedy chaffing, drollery, facetiousness, farce, fun, hilarity, humour, jesting, joking, light entertainment, sitcom (*Inf.*), slapstick, wisecracking, witticisms

come forward offer one's services, present *or* proffer oneself, volunteer

come in appear, arrive, cross the threshold, enter, finish, reach, show up (*Inf.*)

come in for acquire, bear the brunt of, endure, get, receive, suffer

come off go off, happen, occur, succeed, take place, transpire

come out 1. appear, be published (announced, divulged, issued, released, reported, revealed) 2. conclude, end, result, terminate

come out with acknowledge, come clean, declare, disclose, divulge, lay open, own, own up, say

come round 1. accede, acquiesce, allow, concede, grant, mellow, relent, yield 2. come to, recover, regain consciousness, revive 3. call, drop in, pop in, stop by, visit

come through 1. accomplish, achieve, prevail, succeed, triumph 2. endure, survive, weather the storm, withstand

come up arise, crop up, happen, occur, rise, spring up, turn up

comeuppance chastening, deserts, due reward, dues, merit, punishment, recompense, requital, retribution

come up to admit of comparison with, approach, compare with, equal, match, measure up to, meet, resemble, rival, stand *or* bear comparison with

come up with advance, create, discover, furnish, offer, present, produce, propose, provide, submit, suggest

comfort v. 1. alleviate, assuage, cheer, commiserate with, compassionate (*Archaic*), console, ease, encourage, enliven, gladden, hearten, inspirit, invigorate, reassure, refresh, relieve, solace, soothe, strengthen ~n. 2. aid, alleviation, cheer, compensation, consolation, ease, encouragement, enjoyment, help, relief, satisfaction, succour, support 3. cosiness, creature comforts, ease, luxury, opulence, snugness, wellbeing

comfortable 1. adequate, agreeable, ample, commodious, convenient, cosy, delightful, easy, enjoyable, homely, loose, loose-fitting, pleasant, relaxing, restful, roomy, snug 2. at ease, contented, gratified, happy, relaxed, serene 3. affluent, prosperous, well-off, well-to-do

comforting cheering, consolatory, consoling, encouraging, heart-warming, inspiriting, reassuring, soothing

comfortless 1. bleak, cheerless, cold, desolate, dismal, dreary 2. disconsolate, forlorn, inconsolable, miserable, sick at heart, woebegone, wretched

comic 1. *adj.* amusing, comical, droll, facetious, farcical, funny, humorous, jocular, joking, light, rich, waggish, witty 2. *n.* buffoon, clown, comedian, funny man, humorist, jester, wag, wit

comical absurd, amusing, comic, diverting, droll, entertaining, farcical, funny, hilarious, humorous, laughable, ludicrous, priceless, ridiculous, risible, side-splitting, silly, whimsical

coming adj. 1. approaching, at hand, due, en route, forthcoming, future, imminent, impending, in store, in the wind, near, next, nigh 2. aspiring, future, promising, up-and-coming ~n. 3. accession, advent, approach, arrival

command v. 1. bid, charge, compel, demand, direct, enjoin, order, require 2. control, dominate, govern, head, lead, manage, reign over, rule, supervise, sway ~n. 3. behest, bidding, commandment, decree, direction, directive, edict, fiat, injunction, instruction, mandate, order, precept, requirement, ultimatum 4. authority, charge, control, domination, dominion, government, grasp, management, mastery, power, rule, supervision, sway, upper hand

commandeer appropriate, confiscate, expropriate, hijack, requisition, seize, sequester, sequestrate, usurp

commander boss, captain, chief, C in C, C.O., commander-in-chief, commanding officer, director, head, leader, officer, ruler

commanding 1. advantageous, controlling, decisive, dominant, dominating, superior 2. assertive, authoritative, autocratic, compelling, forceful, imposing, impressive, peremptory

commemorate celebrate, honour, immortalize, keep, memorialize, observe, pay tribute to, remember, salute, solemnize

commemoration ceremony, honouring, memorial service, observance, remembrance, tribute

commemorative celebratory, dedicatory, in honour, in memory, in remembrance, memorial

commence begin, embark on, enter upon, inaugurate, initiate, open, originate, start

commend 1. acclaim, applaud, approve, compliment, eulogize, extol, praise, recommend, speak highly of 2. commit, confide, consign, deliver, entrust, hand over, yield

commendable admirable, creditable, deserving, estimable, exemplary, laudable, meritorious, praiseworthy, worthy

commendation acclaim, acclamation, approbation, approval, credit, encomium, encouragement, good opinion, panegyric, praise, recommendation

commensurate adequate, appropriate, coextensive, comparable, compatible, consistent, corresponding, due, equivalent, fit, fitting, in accord, proportionate, sufficient

comment *v.* 1. animadvert, interpose, mention, note, observe, opine, point out, remark, say 2. annotate, criticize, elucidate, explain, interpret ~*n.* 3. animadversion, observation, remark, statement 4. annotation, commentary, criticism, elucidation, explanation, exposition, illustration, note

commentary analysis, critique, description, exegesis, explanation, narration, notes, review, treatise, voice-over

commentator 1. commenter, reporter, special correspondent, sportscaster 2. annotator, critic, expositor, interpreter, scholiast

commerce 1. business, dealing, exchange, merchandising, trade, traffic 2. communication, dealings, intercourse, relations, socializing

commercial 1. business, mercantile, profit-making, sales, trade, trading 2. in demand, marketable, popular, profitable, saleable 3. exploited, materialistic, mercenary, monetary, pecuniary, profit-making, venal

commission *n.* 1. appointment, authority, charge, duty, employment, errand, function, mandate, mission, task, trust, warrant 2. allowance, brokerage, compensation, cut, fee, percentage, rake-off (*Sl.*) 3. board, body of commissioners, commissioners, committee, delegation, deputation, representative ~*v.* 4. appoint, authorize, contract, delegate, depute, empower, engage, nominate, order, select, send

commit 1. carry out, do, enact, execute, perform, perpetrate 2. commend, confide, consign, deliver, deposit, engage, entrust, give, hand over 3. align, bind, compromise, endanger, make liable, obligate, pledge, rank 4. confine, imprison, put in custody

commitment 1. duty, engagement, liability, obligation, responsibility, tie 2. adherence, dedication, devotion, involvement, loyalty 3. assurance, guarantee, pledge, promise, undertaking, vow, word

common 1. average, commonplace, conventional, customary, daily, everyday, familiar, frequent, general, habitual, humdrum, obscure, ordinary, plain, regular, routine, run-of-the-mill, simple, standard, stock, usual, workaday 2. accepted, general, popular, prevailing, prevalent, universal, widespread 3. collective, communal, community, popular, public, social 4. coarse, hackneyed, inferior, low, pedestrian, plebeian, stale, trite, undistinguished, vulgar

commonplace 1. *adj.* common, customary, everyday, humdrum, obvious, ordinary, pedestrian, stale, threadbare, trite, uninteresting, widespread, worn out 2. *n.* banality, cliché, platitude, truism

common-sense, **commonsensical** *adj.* astute, down-to-earth, hard-headed, judicious, level-headed, matter-of-fact, practical, realistic, reasonable, sane, sensible, shrewd, sound

common sense good sense, gumption (*Inf.*), horse sense, level-headedness, mother wit, native intelligence, nous (*Sl.*), practicality, prudence, reasonableness, sound judgment, soundness, wit

commotion ado, agitation, brouhaha, bustle, disorder, disturbance, excitement, ferment, furore, fuss, hubbub, hullabaloo, hurly-burly, perturbation, racket, riot, rumpus, to-do, tumult, turmoil, uproar

communal collective, communistic, community, general, joint, neighbourhood, public, shared

commune[1] *v.* 1. communicate, confer, confide in, converse, discourse, discuss, parley 2. contemplate, meditate, muse, ponder, reflect

commune² *n.* collective, community, cooperative, kibbutz

communicate acquaint, announce, be in contact, be in touch, connect, convey, correspond, declare, disclose, disseminate, divulge, impart, inform, make known, pass on, phone, proclaim, publish, report, reveal, ring up, signify, spread, transmit, unfold

communication 1. connection, contact, conversation, correspondence, dissemination, intercourse, link, transmission 2. announcement, disclosure, dispatch, information, intelligence, message, news, report, statement, word

communications 1. routes, transport, travel 2. information technology, media, publicity, public relations, telecommunications

communicative candid, chatty, conversable, expansive, forthcoming, frank, informative, loquacious, open, outgoing, talkative, unreserved, voluble

communion 1. accord, affinity, agreement, closeness, communing, concord, converse, fellowship, harmony, intercourse, participation, rapport, sympathy, togetherness, unity 2. *Church* Eucharist, Lord's Supper, Mass, Sacrament

communiqué announcement, bulletin, dispatch, news flash, official communication, report

communism Bolshevism, collectivism, Marxism, socialism, state socialism

communist Bolshevik, collectivist, Marxist, Red (*Inf.*), socialist

community 1. association, body politic, brotherhood, commonwealth, company, district, general public, locality, people, populace, population, public, residents, society, state 2. affinity, agreement, identity, likeness, sameness, similarity

commute 1. barter, exchange, interchange, substitute, switch, trade 2. *Law: of penalties, etc.* alleviate, curtail, mitigate, modify, reduce, remit, shorten, soften

commuter 1. *n.* daily traveller, straphanger, suburbanite 2. *adj.* suburban

compact¹ *adj.* 1. close, compressed, condensed, dense, firm, impenetrable, impermeable, pressed together, solid, thick 2. brief, compendious, concise, epigrammatic, laconic, pithy, pointed, succinct, terse, to the point ~*v.* 3. compress, condense, cram, pack down, stuff, tamp

compact² *n.* agreement, alliance, arrangement, bargain, bond, concordat, contract, covenant, deal, entente, pact, stipulation, treaty, understanding

companion 1. accomplice, ally, associate, buddy (*Inf.*), colleague, comrade, confederate, consort, crony, friend, mate (*Inf.*), partner 2. aide, assistant, attendant, chaperon, duenna, escort, squire 3. complement, counterpart, fellow, match, mate, twin

companionable affable, congenial, conversable, convivial, cordial, familiar, friendly, genial, gregarious, neighbourly, outgoing, sociable

companionship amity, camaraderie, company, comradeship, conviviality, esprit de corps, fellowship, fraternity, friendship, rapport, togetherness

company 1. assemblage, assembly, band, body, circle, collection, community, concourse, convention, coterie, crew, crowd, ensemble, gathering, group, league, party, set, throng, troop, troupe, turnout 2. association, business, concern, corporation, establishment, firm, house, partnership, syndicate 3. callers, companionship, fellowship, guests, party, presence, society, visitors

comparable 1. a match for, as good as, commensurate, equal, equivalent, in a class with, on a par, proportionate, tantamount 2. akin, alike, analogous, cognate, corresponding, related, similar

comparative approximate, by comparison, qualified, relative

compare 1. *With* with balance, collate, contrast, juxtapose, set against, weigh 2. *With* **to** correlate, equate, identify with, liken, parallel, resemble 3. *Be the equal of* approach, approximate to, bear comparison, be in the same class as, be on a par with, come up to, compete with, equal, hold a candle to, match, vie

comparison 1. collation, contrast, distinction, juxtaposition 2. analogy, comparability, correlation, likeness, resemblance, similarity

compartment 1. alcove, bay, berth, booth, carrel, carriage, cell, chamber, cubbyhole, cubicle, locker, niche, pigeonhole, section 2. area, category, department, division, section, subdivision

compass *n.* 1. area, bound, boundary, circle, circuit, circumference, enclosure, extent, field, limit, range, reach, realm, round, scope, sphere, stretch, zone ~*v.* 2. beset, besiege, blockade, circumscribe, encircle, enclose, encompass, environ, hem in, invest (*Rare*), surround 3. accomplish, achieve, attain, bring about, effect, execute, fulfil, perform, procure, realize

compassion charity, clemency, commiseration, compunction, condolence, fellow feeling, heart, humanity, kindness, mercy, ruth (*Archaic*), soft-heartedness, sorrow, sympathy, tenderheartedness, tenderness

compassionate benevolent, charitable, humane, humanitarian, indulgent, kind-hearted, kindly, lenient, merciful, pitying, sympathetic, tender, tender-hearted, understanding

compatibility affinity, agreement, amity, congeniality, empathy, harmony, like-mindedness, rapport, single-mindedness, sympathy

compatible accordant, adaptable, agreeable, congenial, congruent, congruous, consistent, consonant, harmonious, in harmony, in keeping, like-minded, reconcilable, suitable

compel bulldoze (*Inf.*), coerce, constrain, dragoon, drive, enforce, exact, force, hustle (*Sl.*), impel, make, necessitate, oblige, restrain, squeeze, urge

compelling 1. cogent, conclusive, convincing, forceful, irrefutable, powerful, telling, weighty 2. enchanting, enthralling, gripping, hypnotic, irresistible, mesmeric, spellbinding 3. binding, coercive, imperative, overriding, peremptory, pressing, unavoidable, urgent

compensate 1. atone, indemnify, make good, make restitution, recompense, refund, reimburse, remunerate, repay, requite, reward, satisfy 2. balance, cancel (out), counteract, counterbalance, countervail, make amends, make up for, offset, redress

compensation amends, atonement, damages, indemnification, indemnity, payment, recompense, reimbursement, remuneration, reparation, requital, restitution, reward, satisfaction

compete be in the running, challenge, contend, contest, emulate, fight, pit oneself against, rival, strive, struggle, vie

competence ability, adequacy, appropriateness, capability, capacity, competency, expertise, fitness, proficiency, skill, suitability

competent able, adapted, adequate, appropriate, capable, clever, endowed, equal, fit, pertinent, proficient, qualified, sufficient, suitable

competition 1. contention, contest, emulation, one-upmanship (*Inf.*), opposition, rivalry, strife, struggle 2. championship, contest, event, puzzle, quiz, tournament 3. challengers, field, opposition, rivals

competitive aggressive, ambitious, antagonistic, at odds, combative, cutthroat, dog-eat-dog, emulous, opposing, rival, vying

competitor adversary, antagonist, challenger, competition, contestant, emulator, opponent, opposition, rival

compile accumulate, amass, anthologize, collect, cull, garner,

gather, marshal, organize, put to~
gether

complacency contentment, grati~
fication, pleasure, satisfaction, self-
satisfaction, smugness

complacent contented, gratified,
pleased, pleased with oneself, sat~
isfied, self-assured, self-contented,
self-righteous, self-satisfied, serene,
smug, unconcerned

complain beef (*Sl.*), bellyache (*Sl.*),
bemoan, bewail, bitch (*Sl.*), carp,
deplore, find fault, fuss, grieve,
gripe (*Inf.*), groan, grouse, growl,
grumble, kick up a fuss (*Inf.*), la~
ment, moan, whine

complaint 1. accusation, annoy~
ance, beef (*Sl.*), bitch (*Sl.*), charge,
criticism, dissatisfaction, fault-
finding, grievance, gripe (*Inf.*),
grouse, grumble, lament, moan,
plaint, remonstrance, trouble, wail
2. affliction, ailment, disease, dis~
order, illness, indisposition, mala~
dy, sickness, upset

complement *n.* 1. companion,
completion, consummation, cor~
relative, counterpart, finishing
touch, rounding-off, supplement 2.
aggregate, capacity, entirety, quo~
ta, total, totality, wholeness ~*v.* 3.
cap (*Inf.*), complete, crown, round
off, set off

complementary companion,
completing, correlative, corre~
sponding, fellow, interdependent,
interrelating, matched, reciprocal

complete *adj.* 1. all, entire, faultless, full, intact, integral, plenary,
unabridged, unbroken, undivided,
unimpaired, whole 2. accom~
plished, achieved, concluded, end~
ed, finished 3. absolute, consum~
mate, dyed-in-the-wool, perfect,
thorough, thoroughgoing, total, ut~
ter ~*v.* 4. accomplish, achieve,
cap, close, conclude, crown, dis~
charge, do, end, execute, fill in,
finalize, finish, fulfil, perfect, per~
form, realize, round off, settle, ter~
minate, wrap up (*Inf.*)

completely absolutely, altogether,
down to the ground, en masse, en~
tirely, from A to Z, from beginning
to end, fully, heart and soul, hook,
line and sinker, in full, *in toto*, per~
fectly, quite, root and branch, sol~
idly, thoroughly, totally, utterly,
wholly

completion accomplishment, at~
tainment, close, conclusion, con~
summation, culmination, end, ex~
piration, finalization, fruition, ful~
filment, realization

complex *adj.* 1. circuitous, compli~
cated, convoluted, Daedalian (*Lit~
erary*), intricate, involved, knotty,
labyrinthine, mingled, mixed, tan~
gled, tortuous 2. composite, com~
pound, compounded, hetero~
geneous, manifold, multifarious,
multiple ~*n.* 3. aggregate, compo~
site, network, organization,
scheme, structure, synthesis, sys~
tem 4. fixation, fixed idea, *idée
fixe*, obsession, phobia, preoccupa~
tion

complexion 1. colour, colouring,
hue, pigmentation, skin, skin tone
2. appearance, aspect, cast, char~
acter, countenance, disposition,
guise, light, look, make-up, nature,
stamp

complexity complication, convo~
lution, elaboration, entanglement,
intricacy, involvement, multiplic~
ity, ramification

compliance acquiescence, agree~
ment, assent, complaisance, con~
cession, concurrence, conformity,
consent, deference, obedience, ob~
servance, passivity, submission,
submissiveness, yielding

complicate confuse, entangle,
interweave, involve, make intri~
cate, muddle, snarl up

complicated 1. Byzantine (*of atti~
tudes, etc.*), complex, convoluted,
elaborate, interlaced, intricate, in~
volved, labyrinthine 2. difficult, in~
volved, perplexing, problematic,
puzzling, troublesome

complication 1. combination,
complexity, confusion, entangle~
ment, intricacy, mixture, web 2.
aggravation, difficulty, drawback,
embarrassment, factor, obstacle,
problem, snag

complicity abetment, collabora~

tion, collusion, concurrence, con~
nivance

compliment 1. *n.* admiration, bou~
quet, commendation, congratula~
tions, courtesy, eulogy, favour,
flattery, honour, praise, tribute 2.
v. commend, congratulate, extol,
felicitate, flatter, laud, pay tribute
to, praise, salute, sing the praises
of, speak highly of, wish joy to

complimentary 1. appreciative,
approving, commendatory, con~
gratulatory, eulogistic, flattering,
laudatory, panegyrical 2. courtesy,
donated, free, free of charge, gra~
tis, gratuitous, honorary, on the
house

compliments good wishes, greet~
ings, regards, remembrances, re~
spects, salutation

comply abide by, accede, accord,
acquiesce, adhere to, agree to,
conform to, consent to, defer, dis~
charge, follow, fulfil, obey, ob~
serve, perform, respect, satisfy,
submit, yield

component 1. *n.* constituent, el~
ement, ingredient, item, part,
piece, unit 2. *adj.* composing, con~
stituent, inherent, intrinsic

compose 1. build, compound,
comprise, constitute, construct,
fashion, form, make, make up, put
together 2. contrive, create, de~
vise, frame, imagine, indite, invent,
produce, write 3. adjust, arrange,
reconcile, regulate, resolve, settle
4. appease, assuage, calm, collect,
control, pacify, placate, quell, qui~
et, soothe, still, tranquillize

composed at ease, calm, collected,
confident, cool, imperturbable,
level-headed, poised, relaxed, self-
possessed, serene, together (*Sl.*),
tranquil, unflappable, unruffled,
unworried

composite 1. *adj.* blended, com~
bined, complex, compound, con~
glomerate, mixed, synthesized 2. *n.*
amalgam, blend, compound, con~
glomerate, fusion, synthesis

composition 1. arrangement, con~
figuration, constitution, design,
form, formation, layout, make-up,
organization, structure 2. compila~

tion, creation, fashioning, forma~
tion, formulation, invention, mak~
ing, mixture, production 3. crea~
tion, essay, exercise, literary work,
opus, piece, study, work, writing 4.
arrangement, balance, concord,
consonance, harmony, placing,
proportion, symmetry

compost humus, mulch, organic
fertilizer

composure aplomb, calm, calm~
ness, collectedness, cool (*Sl.*),
coolness, dignity, ease, equanimity,
imperturbability, placidity, poise,
sang-froid, sedateness, self-
assurance, self-possession, seren~
ity, tranquillity

compound *v.* 1. amalgamate,
blend, coalesce, combine, concoct,
fuse, intermingle, mingle, mix,
synthesize, unite 2. add to, aggra~
vate, augment, complicate, exac~
erbate, heighten, intensify, magni~
fy, worsen 3. *Used of a dispute,
difference, etc.* adjust, arrange,
compose, settle ~*n.* 4. alloy, amal~
gam, blend, combination, compo~
site, composition, conglomerate,
fusion, medley, mixture, synthesis
~*adj.* 5. complex, composite, con~
glomerate, intricate, multiple, not
simple

comprehend 1. apprehend, as~
similate, conceive, discern, fath~
om, grasp, know, make out, per~
ceive, see, take in, understand 2.
comprise, contain, embody, em~
brace, enclose, encompass, in~
clude, involve, take in

comprehensible clear, coherent,
conceivable, explicit, graspable,
intelligible, plain, understandable

comprehension 1. conception,
discernment, grasp, intelligence,
judgment, knowledge, perception,
realization, sense, understanding 2.
compass, domain, field, limits,
province, range, reach, scope

comprehensive all-embracing, all-
inclusive, blanket, broad, catholic,
complete, encyclopedic, exhaus~
tive, extensive, full, inclusive,
sweeping, thorough, umbrella,
wide

compress abbreviate, compact,

concentrate, condense, constrict, contract, cram, crowd, crush, press, shorten, squash, squeeze, summarize, wedge

compressed abridged, compact, compacted, concentrated, concise, consolidated, constricted, flat~ tened, reduced, shortened, squashed, squeezed

compression condensation, con~ solidation, constriction, crushing, pressure, squeezing, wedging

comprise 1. be composed of, com~ prehend, consist of, contain, em~ brace, encompass, include, take in 2. compose, constitute, form, make up

compromise v. 1. adjust, agree, arbitrate, compose, compound, concede, give and take, go fifty-fifty (*Inf.*), meet halfway, settle, strike a balance ~n. 2. accommo~ dation, accord, adjustment, agree~ ment, concession, give-and-take, half measures, middle ground, set~ tlement, trade-off ~v. 3. discredit, dishonour, embarrass, expose, hazard, imperil, implicate, jeop~ ardize, prejudice, weaken

compulsion 1. coercion, con~ straint, demand, duress, force, ob~ ligation, pressure, urgency 2. drive, necessity, need, obsession, preoc~ cupation, urge

compulsive besetting, compelling, driving, irresistible, obsessive, overwhelming, uncontrollable, ur~ gent

compulsory binding, *de rigueur*, forced, imperative, mandatory, obligatory, required, requisite

compute add up, calculate, cast up, cipher, count, enumerate, esti~ mate, figure, figure out, measure, rate, reckon, sum, tally, total

comrade ally, associate, buddy (*Inf.*), colleague, companion, com~ patriot, compeer, confederate, co~ worker, crony, fellow, friend, mate (*Inf.*), pal (*Inf.*), partner

concave cupped, depressed, exca~ vated, hollow, hollowed, incurved, indented, scooped, sunken

conceal bury, camouflage, cover, disguise, dissemble, hide, keep dark, keep secret, mask, obscure, screen, secrete, shelter

concealed covered, hidden, incon~ spicuous, masked, obscured, screened, secret, secreted, tucked away, unseen

concealment camouflage, cover, disguise, hideaway, hide-out, hid~ ing, secrecy

concede 1. accept, acknowledge, admit, allow, confess, grant, own 2. cede, give up, hand over, relin~ quish, surrender, yield

conceit 1. amour-propre, arro~ gance, complacency, egotism, narcissism, pride, self-importance, self-love, swagger, vainglory, van~ ity 2. *Archaic* belief, fancy, fantasy, idea, image, imagination, judg~ ment, notion, opinion, quip, thought, vagary, whim, whimsy

conceited arrogant, bigheaded (*Inf.*), cocky, egotistical, immodest, narcissistic, overweening, puffed up, self-important, stuck up (*Inf.*), swollen-headed, vain, vainglorious

conceivable believable, credible, imaginable, possible, thinkable

conceive 1. appreciate, apprehend, believe, comprehend, envisage, fancy, grasp, imagine, realize, sup~ pose, understand 2. contrive, cre~ ate, design, develop, devise, form, formulate, produce, project, pur~ pose, think up 3. become impreg~ nated, become pregnant

concentrate 1. be engrossed in, consider closely, focus attention on, give all one's attention to, put one's mind to, rack one's brains 2. bring to bear, centre, cluster, con~ verge, focus 3. accumulate, cluster, collect, congregate, gather, huddle

concentrated 1. all-out (*Inf.*), deep, hard, intense, intensive 2. boiled down, condensed, evaporated, re~ duced, rich, thickened, undiluted

concentration 1. absorption, ap~ plication, heed, single-mindedness 2. bringing to bear, centralization, centring, combination, compres~ sion, consolidation, convergence, focusing, intensification 3. accu~ mulation, aggregation, cluster, collection, convergence, horde, mass

concept abstraction, conception, conceptualization, hypothesis, idea, image, impression, notion, theory, view

conception 1. concept, design, idea, image, notion, plan 2. beginning, birth, formation, inception, initiation, invention, launching, origin, outset 3. appreciation, clue, comprehension, impression, inkling, perception, picture, understanding 4. fertilization, germination, impregnation, insemination

concern v. 1. affect, apply to, bear on, be relevant to, interest, involve, pertain to, regard, touch ~n. 2. affair, business, charge, deportment, field, interest, involvement, job, matter, mission, occupation, responsibility, task, transaction 3. bearing, importance, interest, reference, relation, relevance ~v. 4. bother, disquiet, distress, disturb, make anxious, make uneasy, perturb, trouble, worry ~n. 5. anxiety, apprehension, attention, burden, care, consideration, disquiet, disquietude, distress, heed, responsibility, solicitude, worry 6. business, company, corporation, enterprise, establishment, firm, house, organization

concerned 1. active, implicated, interested, involved, mixed up, privy to 2. anxious, bothered, distressed, disturbed, exercised, troubled, uneasy, upset, worried 3. attentive, caring, interested, solicitous

concerning about, anent (*Scot.*), apropos of, as regards, as to, in the matter of, on the subject of, re, regarding, relating to, respecting, touching, with reference to

concert n. 1. accord, agreement, concord, concordance, harmony, unanimity, union, unison 2. in concert concertedly, in collaboration, in league, in unison, jointly, shoulder to shoulder, together, unanimously

concerted agreed upon, collaborative, combined, coordinated, joint, planned, prearranged, united

concession 1. acknowledgment, admission, assent, confession, surrender, yielding 2. adjustment, allowance, boon, compromise, grant, indulgence, permit, privilege

conciliate appease, disarm, mediate, mollify, pacify, placate, propitiate, reconcile, restore harmony, soothe, win over

conciliation appeasement, disarming, mollification, pacification, placation, propitiation, reconciliation, soothing

conciliatory appeasing, disarming, irenic, mollifying, pacific, peaceable, placatory, propitiative

concise brief, compact, compendious, compressed, condensed, epigrammatic, laconic, pithy, short, succinct, summary, synoptic, terse, to the point

conclude 1. bring down the curtain, cease, close, come to an end, complete, draw to a close, end, finish, round off, terminate, wind up (*Inf.*) 2. assume, decide, deduce, gather, infer, judge, reckon (*Inf.*), sum up, suppose, surmise 3. accomplish, bring about, carry out, clinch (*Inf.*), decide, determine, effect, establish, fix, pull off, resolve, settle, work out

conclusion 1. close, completion, end, finale, finish, result, termination 2. consequence, culmination, issue, outcome, result, upshot 3. agreement, conviction, decision, deduction, inference, judgment, opinion, resolution, settlement, verdict 4. in conclusion finally, in closing, lastly, to sum up

conclusive clinching, convincing, decisive, definite, definitive, final, irrefutable, ultimate, unanswerable, unarguable

concoct brew, contrive, cook up (*Inf.*), design, devise, fabricate, formulate, hatch, invent, make up, mature, plot, prepare, project, think up

concoction blend, brew, combination, compound, contrivance, creation, mixture, preparation concrete *adj.* 1. actual, definite, explicit, factual, material, real, sensible, specific, substantial, tangible 2. calcified, compact, compressed, conglomerated, consolidated, firm, petrified, solid, solidified ~*n.* 3. cement (*Not in technical usage*), concretion

concubine courtesan, kept woman, leman (*Archaic*), mistress, odalisque, paramour

concur accede, accord, acquiesce, agree, approve, assent, coincide, combine, consent, cooperate, harmonize, join

concurrent 1. coexisting, coincident, concerted, concomitant, contemporaneous, simultaneous, synchronous 2. confluent, convergent, converging, uniting 3. agreeing, at one, compatible, consentient, consistent, cooperating, harmonious, in agreement, in rapport, like-minded, of the same mind

concussion clash, collision, crash, impact, jarring, jolt, jolting, shaking, shock

condemn 1. blame, censure, damn, denounce, disapprove, reprehend, reproach, reprobate, reprove, upbraid 2. convict, damn, doom, pass sentence on, proscribe, sentence

condemnation 1. blame, censure, denouncement, denunciation, disapproval, reproach, reprobation, reproof, stricture 2. conviction, damnation, doom, judgment, proscription, sentence

condensation 1. abridgment, contraction, digest, précis, synopsis 2. condensate, deliquescence, distillation, liquefaction, precipitate, precipitation 3. compression, concentration, consolidation, crystallization, curtailment, reduction

condense 1. abbreviate, abridge, compact, compress, concentrate, contract, curtail, encapsulate, epitomize, précis, shorten, summarize 2. boil down, coagulate, concentrate, decoct, precipitate (*Chem.*), reduce, solidify, thicken

condensed 1. abridged, compressed, concentrated, curtailed, shortened, shrunken, slimmed down, summarized 2. boiled down, clotted, coagulated, concentrated, precipitated (*Chem.*), reduced, thickened

condescend 1. be courteous, bend, come down off one's high horse (*Inf.*), deign, humble *or* demean oneself, lower oneself, see fit, stoop, submit, unbend (*Inf.*), vouchsafe 2. patronize, talk down to

condescending disdainful, lofty, lordly, patronizing, snobbish, snooty (*Inf.*), supercilious, superior, toffee-nosed (*Sl.*)

condition *n.* 1. case, circumstances, plight, position, predicament, shape, situation, state, state of affairs, *status quo* 2. arrangement, article, demand, limitation, modification, prerequisite, provision, proviso, qualification, requirement, requisite, restriction, rule, stipulation, terms 3. fettle, fitness, health, kilter, order, shape, state of health, trim 4. ailment, complaint, infirmity, malady, problem, weakness 5. caste, class, estate, grade, order, position, rank, status, stratum ~*v.* 6. accustom, adapt, educate, equip, habituate, inure, make ready, prepare, ready, tone up, train, work out

conditional contingent, dependent, limited, provisional, qualified, subject to, with reservations

conditioned acclimatized, accustomed, adapted, adjusted, familiarized, habituated, inured, made ready, prepared, seasoned, trained, used

conditioning *n.* 1. grooming, preparation, readying, training 2. accustoming, familiarization, hardening, inurement, reorientation, seasoning ~*adj.* 3. astringent, toning

conditions circumstances, environment, milieu, situation, surroundings, way of life

condone disregard, excuse, forgive, let pass, look the other way, make allowance for, overlook, pardon, turn a blind eye to, wink at

conduct *n.* 1. administration, con~

trol, direction, guidance, leader~ ship, management, organization, running, supervision ~v. 2. admin~ ister, carry on, control, direct, govern, handle, lead, manage, or~ ganize, preside over, regulate, run, supervise 3. accompany, attend, chair, convey, escort, guide, pilot, preside over, steer, usher ~n. 4. attitude, bearing, behaviour, car~ riage, comportment, demeanour, deportment, manners, mien (*Lit~ erary*), ways ~v. 5. acquit, act, be~ have, carry, comport, deport

confederacy alliance, bund, coali~ tion, compact, confederation, con~ spiracy, covenant, federation, league, union

confederate 1. *adj.* allied, associ~ ated, combined, federal, federated, in alliance 2. *n.* abettor, accessory, accomplice, ally, associate, col~ league, partner 3. *v.* ally, amal~ gamate, associate, band together, combine, federate, merge, unite

confer 1. accord, award, bestow, give, grant, present, vouchsafe 2. consult, converse, deliberate, dis~ course, parley, talk

conference colloquium, congress, consultation, convention, convoca~ tion, discussion, forum, meeting, seminar, symposium, teach-in

confess 1. acknowledge, admit, al~ low, blurt out, come clean (*Inf.*), concede, confide, disclose, divulge, grant, make a clean breast of, own, own up, recognize 2. affirm, assert, attest, aver, confirm, declare, evince, manifest, profess, prove, reveal

confession acknowledgment, ad~ mission, avowal, disclosure, divul~ gence, exposure, revelation, un~ bosoming

confidant, confidante alter ego, bosom friend, close friend, crony, familiar, intimate

confide 1. admit, breathe, confess, disclose, divulge, impart, reveal, whisper 2. commend, commit, consign, entrust

confidence 1. belief, credence, de~ pendence, faith, reliance, trust 2. aplomb, assurance, boldness, courage, firmness, nerve, self~ possession, self-reliance 3. **in con~ fidence** between you and me (and the gatepost), confidentially, in se~ crecy, privately

confident 1. certain, convinced, counting on, positive, satisfied, se~ cure, sure 2. assured, bold, daunt~ less, fearless, self-assured, self~ reliant

confidential 1. classified, hush~ hush (*Inf.*), intimate, off the record, private, privy, secret 2. faithful, familiar, trusted, trustworthy, trusty

confidentially behind closed doors, between ourselves, in camera, in confidence, in secret, personally, privately, sub rosa

confine 1. *v.* bind, bound, cage, cir~ cumscribe, enclose, hem in, hold back, immure, imprison, incarcer~ ate, intern, keep, limit, repress, restrain, restrict, shut up 2. *n.* bor~ der, boundary, frontier, limit, pre~ cinct

confined 1. enclosed, limited, re~ stricted 2. in childbed, in child~ birth, lying-in

confinement 1. custody, detention, imprisonment, incarceration, in~ ternment 2. *accouchement*, child~ bed, childbirth, labour, lying-in, parturition, time, travail

confines boundaries, bounds, cir~ cumference, edge, limits, precincts

confirm 1. assure, buttress, clinch, establish, fix, fortify, reinforce, settle, strengthen 2. approve, authenticate, bear out, corrobo~ rate, endorse, ratify, sanction, sub~ stantiate, validate, verify

confirmation 1. authentication, corroboration, evidence, proof, substantiation, testimony, valida~ tion, verification 2. acceptance, agreement, approval, assent, en~ dorsement, ratification, sanction

confirmed chronic, dyed-in-the~ wool, habitual, hardened, in~ grained, inured, inveterate, long~ established, rooted, seasoned

confiscate appropriate, comman~ deer, expropriate, impound, seize, sequester, sequestrate

confiscation appropriation, expropriation, forfeiture, impounding, seizure, sequestration, takeover

conflict n. 1. battle, clash, collision, combat, contention, contest, encounter, engagement, fight, fracas, set-to (*Inf.*), strife, war, warfare 2. antagonism, bad blood, difference, disagreement, discord, dissension, divided loyalties, friction, hostility, interference, opposition, strife, variance ~v. 3. be at variance, clash, collide, combat, contend, contest, differ, disagree, fight, interfere, strive, struggle

conflicting antagonistic, clashing, contradictory, contrary, discordant, inconsistent, opposed, opposing, paradoxical

conform 1. adapt, adjust, comply, fall in with, follow, follow the crowd, obey, run with the pack, yield 2. accord, agree, assimilate, correspond, harmonize, match, square, suit, tally

conformation anatomy, arrangement, build, configuration, form, framework, outline, shape, structure

conformist n. Babbitt (*U.S.*), conventionalist, stick-in-the-mud (*Inf.*), traditionalist, yes man

conformity 1. allegiance, Babbittry (*U.S.*), compliance, conventionality, observance, orthodoxy 2. affinity, agreement, conformance, congruity, consonance, correspondence, harmony, likeness, resemblance, similarity

confound 1. amaze, astonish, astound, baffle, bewilder, confuse, dumbfound, flabbergast (*Inf.*), mix up, mystify, nonplus, perplex, startle, surprise 2. annihilate, contradict, demolish, destroy, explode, overthrow, overwhelm, refute, ruin

confront accost, beard, brave, bring face to face with, challenge, defy, encounter, face, face up to, oppose, stand up to

confrontation conflict, contest, crisis, encounter, set-to (*Inf.*), showdown (*Inf.*)

confuse 1. baffle, bemuse, bewilder, darken, mystify, obscure, perplex, puzzle 2. blend, confound, disarrange, disorder, intermingle, involve, jumble, mingle, mistake, mix up, muddle, snarl up (*Inf.*), tangle 3. abash, addle, demoralize, discomfit, discompose, disconcert, discountenance, disorient, embarrass, fluster, mortify, nonplus, rattle (*Inf.*), shame, throw off balance, upset

confused 1. at a loss, at sea, at sixes and sevens, baffled, bewildered, dazed, discombobulated (*Inf., chiefly U.S.*), disorganized, disorientated, flummoxed, muddled, muzzy (*U.S. inf.*), nonplussed, not with it (*Inf.*), perplexed, puzzled, taken aback, thrown off balance, upset 2. at sixes and sevens, chaotic, disarranged, disordered, disorderly, disorganized, higgledy-piggledy (*Inf.*), hugger-mugger (*Archaic*), in disarray, jumbled, mistaken, misunderstood, mixed up, out of order, topsy-turvy, untidy

confusing ambiguous, baffling, complicated, contradictory, disconcerting, inconsistent, misleading, muddling, perplexing, puzzling, unclear

confusion 1. befuddlement, bemusement, bewilderment, disorientation, mystification, perplexity, puzzlement 2. bustle, chaos, clutter, commotion, disarrangement, disorder, disorganization, hotchpotch, jumble, mess, muddle, shambles, tangle, turmoil, untidiness, upheaval 3. abashment, chagrin, demoralization, discomfiture, distraction, embarrassment, fluster, perturbation

congenial adapted, agreeable, companionable, compatible, complaisant, favourable, fit, friendly, genial, kindly, kindred, like-minded, pleasant, pleasing, suitable, sympathetic, well-suited

congenital 1. constitutional, inborn, inbred, inherent, innate, natural 2. *Inf.* complete, inveterate, thorough, utter

congested blocked-up, clogged,

crammed, crowded, jammed, overcrowded, overfilled, overflow~ ing, packed, stuffed, stuffed-up, teeming

congestion bottleneck, clogging, crowding, jam, mass, overcrowd~ ing, snarl-up (Inf.), surfeit

conglomerate 1. adj. amassed, clustered, composite, hetero~ geneous, massed 2. v. accumulate, agglomerate, aggregate, cluster, coalesce, snowball 3. n. agglomer~ ate, aggregate, multinational

conglomeration accumulation, aggregation, assortment, combi~ nation, composite, hotchpotch, mass, medley, miscellany, mish~ mash, potpourri

congratulate compliment, felici~ tate, wish joy to

congratulations best wishes, compliments, felicitations, good wishes, greetings

congregate assemble, collect, come together, concentrate, con~ vene, converge, convoke, flock, forgather, gather, mass, meet, muster, rally, rendezvous, throng

congregation assembly, brethren, crowd, fellowship, flock, host, laity, multitude, parish, parishioners, throng

congress assembly, chamber of deputies, conclave, conference, convention, convocation, council, delegates, diet, legislative assem~ bly, legislature, meeting, parlia~ ment, representatives

conic, conical cone-shaped, co~ noid, funnel-shaped, pointed, py~ ramidal, tapered, tapering

conjecture 1. v. assume, fancy, guess, hypothesize, imagine, infer, suppose, surmise, suspect, theorize 2. n. assumption, conclusion, fancy, guess, guesstimate (Inf.), guess~ work, hypothesis, inference, no~ tion, presumption, shot in the dark, speculation, supposition, surmise, theorizing, theory

conjugal bridal, connubial, hy~ meneal, marital, married, matri~ monial, nuptial, spousal, wedded

conjunction association, coinci~

dence, combination, concurrence, juxtaposition, union

conjure 1. juggle, play tricks 2. be~ witch, call upon, cast a spell, charm, enchant, fascinate, invoke, raise, rouse, summon up 3. adjure, appeal to, beg, beseech, crave, en~ treat, implore, importune, pray, supplicate

conjurer, conjuror magician, miracle-worker, sorcerer, thau~ maturge (Rare), wizard

conjure up bring to mind, contrive, create, evoke, produce as by mag~ ic, recall, recollect

connect affix, ally, associate, co~ here, combine, couple, fasten, join, link, relate, unite

connected 1. affiliated, akin, allied, associated, banded together, bracketed, combined, coupled, joined, linked, related, united 2. Of speech coherent, comprehensible, consecutive, intelligible

connection 1. alliance, association, attachment, coupling, fastening, junction, link, tie, union 2. affinity, association, bond, commerce, communication, correlation, cor~ respondence, intercourse, interre~ lation, link, marriage, relation, re~ lationship, relevance, tie-in 3. con~ text, frame of reference, reference 4. acquaintance, ally, associate, contact, friend, sponsor 5. kin, kin~ dred, kinsman, kith, relation, rela~ tive

connivance abetment, abetting, collusion, complicity, conspiring, tacit consent

connive 1. cabal, collude, conspire, cook up (Inf.), intrigue, plot, scheme 2. With at abet, aid, be an accessory to, be a party to, be in collusion with, blink at, disregard, lend oneself to, let pass, look the other way, overlook, pass by, shut one's eyes to, turn a blind eye to, wink at

connoisseur aficionado, apprecia~ tor, arbiter, authority, buff (Inf.), cognoscente, devotee, expert, judge, savant, specialist

conquer 1. beat, checkmate, crush, defeat, discomfit, get the better of, humble, master, overcome, overpower, overthrow, prevail, quell, rout, subdue, subjugate, succeed, surmount, triumph, vanquish 2. acquire, annex, obtain, occupy, overrun, seize, win

conqueror champion, conquistador, defeater, hero, lord, master, subjugator, vanquisher, victor, winner

conquest 1. defeat, discomfiture, mastery, overthrow, rout, triumph, vanquishment, victory 2. acquisition, annexation, appropriation, coup, invasion, occupation, subjection, subjugation, takeover 3. captivation, enchantment, enthralment, enticement, seduction 4. acquisition, adherent, admirer, catch, fan, feather in one's cap, follower, prize, supporter, worshipper

conscience 1. moral sense, principles, scruples, sense of right and wrong, still small voice 2. in all conscience assuredly, certainly, fairly, honestly, in truth, rightly, truly

conscience-stricken ashamed, compunctious, contrite, disturbed, guilty, penitent, remorseful, repentant, sorry, troubled

conscientious 1. careful, diligent, exact, faithful, meticulous, painstaking, particular, punctilious, thorough 2. high-minded, high-principled, honest, honourable, incorruptible, just, moral, responsible, scrupulous, straightforward, strict, upright

conscious 1. alert, alive to, awake, aware, cognizant, percipient, responsive, sensible, sentient, wise to (*Sl.*) 2. calculated, deliberate, intentional, knowing, premeditated, rational, reasoning, responsible, self-conscious, studied, wilful

consciousness apprehension, awareness, knowledge, realization, recognition, sensibility

consecrate dedicate, devote, exalt, hallow, ordain, sanctify, set apart, venerate

consecutive chronological, following, in sequence, in turn, running, sequential, seriatim, succeeding, successive, uninterrupted

consensus agreement, common consent, concord, concurrence, general agreement, harmony, unanimity, unity

consent 1. *v.* accede, acquiesce, agree, allow, approve, assent, comply, concede, concur, permit, yield 2. *n.* acquiescence, agreement, approval, assent, compliance, concession, concurrence, go-ahead (*Inf.*), O.K. (*Inf.*), permission, sanction

consequence 1. effect, end, event, issue, outcome, repercussion, result, upshot 2. account, concern, import, importance, interest, moment, note, portent, significance, value, weight 3. distinction, eminence, notability, rank, repute, standing, status 4. in consequence as a result, because, following

consequent ensuing, following, resultant, resulting, sequential, subsequent, successive

consequently accordingly, ergo, hence, necessarily, subsequently, therefore, thus

conservation custody, economy, guardianship, husbandry, maintenance, preservation, protection, safeguarding, safekeeping, saving, upkeep

conservative 1. *adj.* cautious, conventional, die-hard, guarded, hidebound, middle-of-the-road, moderate, quiet, reactionary, right-wing, sober, tory, traditional 2. *n.* middle-of-the-roader, moderate, reactionary, right-winger, stick-in-the-mud (*Inf.*), tory, traditionalist

conservatory glasshouse, greenhouse, hothouse

conserve go easy on (*Inf.*), hoard, husband, keep, nurse, preserve, protect, save, store up, take care of, use sparingly

consider 1. chew over, cogitate, consult, contemplate, deliberate, discuss, examine, meditate, mull over, muse, ponder, reflect, revolve, ruminate, study, turn over in one's mind, weigh 2. believe, deem, hold to be, judge, rate, regard as, think **3**. bear in mind, care for, keep in view, make allowance for, reckon with, regard, remember, respect, take into account

considerable 1. abundant, ample, appreciable, comfortable, goodly, great, large, lavish, marked, much, noticeable, plentiful, reasonable, sizable, substantial, tidy, tolerable **2**. distinguished, important, influential, noteworthy, renowned, significant, venerable

considerably appreciably, greatly, markedly, noticeably, remarkably, significantly, substantially, very much

considerate attentive, charitable, circumspect, concerned, discreet, forbearing, kind, kindly, mindful, obliging, patient, tactful, thoughtful, unselfish

consideration 1. analysis, attention, cogitation, contemplation, deliberation, discussion, examination, reflection, regard, review, scrutiny, study, thought **2**. concern, factor, issue, point **3**. concern, considerateness, friendliness, kindliness, kindness, respect, solicitude, tact, thoughtfulness **4**. fee, payment, perquisite, recompense, remuneration, reward, tip **5**. **take into consideration** bear in mind, make allowance for, take into account, weigh

considering all in all, all things considered, insomuch as, in the light of, in view of

consignment 1. *Act of consigning* assignment, committal, dispatch, distribution, entrusting, handing over, relegation, sending, shipment, transmittal **2**. *Something consigned* batch, delivery, goods, shipment

consist 1. *With* of be composed of, be made up of, amount to, comprise, contain, embody, include, incorporate, involve **2**. *With* in be expressed by, be found *or* contained in, inhere, lie, reside

consistent 1. constant, dependable, persistent, regular, steady, true to type, unchanging, undeviating **2**. accordant, agreeing, all of a piece, coherent, compatible, congruous, consonant, harmonious, logical

consolation alleviation, assuagement, cheer, comfort, ease, easement, encouragement, help, relief, solace, succour, support

console assuage, calm, cheer, comfort, encourage, express sympathy for, relieve, solace, soothe

consolidate 1. amalgamate, cement, combine, compact, condense, conjoin, federate, fuse, harden, join, solidify, thicken, unite **2**. fortify, reinforce, secure, stabilize, strengthen

consolidation alliance, amalgamation, association, compression, condensation, federation, fortification, fusion, reinforcement, strengthening

consort *n*. **1**. associate, companion, fellow, husband, partner, spouse (*of a reigning monarch*), wife ~*v*. **2**. associate, fraternize, go around with, hang about *or* around with, keep company, mingle, mix **3**. accord, agree, correspond, harmonize, square, tally

conspicuous 1. apparent, clear, discernible, easily seen, evident, manifest, noticeable, obvious, patent, perceptible, visible **2**. celebrated, distinguished, eminent, famous, illustrious, notable, outstanding, prominent, remarkable, signal, striking **3**. blatant, flagrant, flashy, garish, glaring, showy

conspiracy cabal, collusion, confederacy, frame-up (*Sl.*), intrigue, league, machination, plot, scheme, treason

conspirator cabalist, conspirer, intriguer, plotter, schemer, traitor

conspire 1. cabal, confederate, contrive, devise, hatch treason, intrigue, machinate, manoeuvre, plot, scheme **2**. combine, concur, conduce, contribute, cooperate, tend, work together

constancy decision, determination, devotion, fidelity, firmness, fixedness, permanence, perseverance, regularity, resolution, stability, steadfastness, steadiness, tenacity, uniformity

constant 1. continual, even, firm, fixed, habitual, immutable, invariable, permanent, perpetual, regular, stable, steadfast, steady, unalterable, unbroken, uniform, unvarying 2. ceaseless, continual, continuous, endless, eternal, everlasting, incessant, interminable, never-ending, nonstop, perpetual, persistent, relentless, sustained, uninterrupted, unrelenting, unremitting 3. determined, dogged, persevering, resolute, unflagging, unshaken, unwavering 4. attached, dependable, devoted, faithful, loyal, staunch, tried-and-true, true, trustworthy, trusty, unfailing

constantly all the time, always, continually, continuously, endlessly, everlastingly, incessantly, interminably, invariably, morning, noon and night, night and day, nonstop, perpetually, relentlessly

consternation alarm, amazement, anxiety, awe, bewilderment, confusion, dismay, distress, dread, fear, fright, horror, panic, shock, terror, trepidation

constituent adj. 1. basic, component, elemental, essential, integral ~n. 2. component, element, essential, factor, ingredient, part, principle, unit 3. elector, voter

constitute 1. compose, comprise, create, enact, establish, fix, form, found, make, make up, set up 2. appoint, authorize, commission, delegate, depute, empower, name, nominate, ordain

constitution 1. composition, establishment, formation, organization 2. build, character, composition, disposition, form, habit, health, make-up, nature, physique, structure, temper, temperament

constitutional adj. 1. congenital, inborn, inherent, intrinsic, organic 2. chartered, statutory, vested ~n. 3. airing, stroll, turn, walk

constrain 1. bind, coerce, compel, drive, force, impel, necessitate, oblige, pressure, pressurize, urge 2.

chain, check, confine, constrict, curb, hem in, restrain

constrained embarrassed, forced, guarded, inhibited, reserved, reticent, subdued, unnatural

constraint 1. coercion, compulsion, force, necessity, pressure, restraint 2. bashfulness, diffidence, embarrassment, inhibition, repression, reservation, restraint, timidity 3. check, curb, damper, deterrent, hindrance, limitation, restriction

construct assemble, build, compose, create, design, elevate, engineer, erect, establish, fabricate, fashion, form, formulate, found, frame, make, manufacture, organize, put up, raise, set up, shape

construction 1. assembly, building, composition, creation, edifice, erection, fabric, fabrication, figure, form, formation, shape, structure 2. explanation, inference, interpretation, reading, rendering

constructive helpful, positive, practical, productive, useful, valuable

consult 1. ask, ask advice of, commune, compare notes, confer, consider, debate, deliberate, interrogate, question, refer to, take counsel, turn to 2. consider, have regard for, regard, respect, take account of, take into consideration

consultant adviser, authority, specialist

consultation appointment, conference, council, deliberation, dialogue, discussion, examination, hearing, interview, meeting, session

consume 1. absorb, deplete, dissipate, drain, eat up, employ, exhaust, expend, finish up, fritter away, lavish, lessen, spend, squander, use, use up, utilize, vanish, waste, wear out 2. devour, eat, eat up, gobble (up), guzzle, polish off (Inf.), put away, swallow 3. annihilate, decay, demolish, destroy, devastate, lay waste, ravage 4. Often passive absorb, devour, dominate, eat up, engross, monopolize, obsess, preoccupy

consumer buyer, customer, pur~
chaser, shopper, user

consuming absorbing, compelling,
devouring, engrossing, excruciat~
ing, gripping, immoderate, over~
whelming, tormenting

consummate 1. *v.* accomplish,
achieve, carry out, compass, com~
plete, conclude, crown, effectuate,
end, finish, perfect, perform 2. *adj.*
absolute, accomplished, complete,
conspicuous, finished, matchless,
perfect, polished, practised, skilled,
superb, supreme, total, transcend~
ent, ultimate, unqualified, utter

consumption 1. consuming, decay,
decrease, depletion, destruction,
diminution, dissipation, exhaustion,
expenditure, loss, use, using up,
utilization, waste 2. *Medical* atro~
phy, emaciation, phthisis, T.B., tu~
berculosis

contact *n.* 1. association, commu~
nication, connection 2. approxi~
mation, contiguity, junction, juxta~
position, touch, union 3. acquaint~
ance, connection ~*v.* 4. approach,
call, communicate with, get *or* be
in touch with, get hold of, phone,
reach, ring (up), speak to, write to

contagious catching, communi~
cable, epidemic, epizootic (*Veteri~
nary medicine*), infectious, pestif~
erous, pestilential, spreading, tak~
ing (*Inf.*), transmissible

contain 1. accommodate, enclose,
have capacity for, hold, incorpo~
rate, seat 2. comprehend, com~
prise, embody, embrace, include,
involve 3. control, curb, hold back,
hold in, repress, restrain, stifle

container holder, receptacle, re~
pository, vessel

contaminate adulterate, befoul,
corrupt, defile, deprave, infect,
pollute, radioactivate, soil, stain,
sully, taint, tarnish, vitiate

contamination adulteration, con~
tagion, corruption, decay, defile~
ment, dirtying, filth, foulness, im~
purity, infection, poisoning, pollu~
tion, radioactivation, rottenness,
taint

contemplate 1. brood over, con~
sider, deliberate, meditate, medi~

tate on, mull over, muse over, ob~
serve, ponder, reflect upon, re~
volve *or* turn over in one's mind,
ruminate (upon), study 2. behold,
examine, eye, gaze at, inspect, re~
gard, scrutinize, stare at, survey,
view 3. aspire to, consider, design,
envisage, expect, foresee, have in
view *or* in mind, intend, mean,
plan, propose, think of

contemplation 1. cogitation, con~
sideration, deliberation, medita~
tion, musing, pondering, reflection,
reverie, rumination, thought 2. ex~
amination, gazing at, inspection,
looking at, observation, scrutiny,
survey, viewing

contemplative deep *or* lost in
thought, in a brown study, intent,
introspective, meditative, musing,
pensive, rapt, reflective, rumina~
tive, thoughtful

contemporary *adj.* 1. coetaneous
(*Rare*), coeval, coexistent, coex~
isting, concurrent, contempora~
neous, synchronous 2. à la mode,
current, in fashion, latest, modern,
newfangled, present, present-day,
recent, ultramodern, up-to-date,
up-to-the-minute, with it (*Inf.*) ~*n.*
3. compeer, fellow, peer

contempt 1. condescension, con~
tumely, derision, despite (*Archaic*),
disdain, disregard, disrespect,
mockery, neglect, scorn, slight 2. *A
state of contempt* disgrace, dis~
honour, humiliation, shame

contemptible abject, base, cheap,
degenerate, despicable, detestable,
ignominious, low, low-down (*Inf.*),
mean, paltry, pitiful, scurvy, shab~
by, shameful, vile, worthless

contemptuous arrogant, cavalier,
condescending, contumelious, de~
risive, disdainful, haughty, high
and mighty, insolent, insulting,
scornful, sneering, supercilious

contend 1. clash, compete, contest,
cope, emulate, grapple, jostle, liti~
gate, skirmish, strive, struggle, vie
2. affirm, allege, argue, assert,
aver, avow, debate, dispute, hold,
maintain

content[1] 1. *v.* appease, delight,
gladden, gratify, humour, indulge,

mollify, placate, please, reconcile, satisfy, suffice 2. *n.* comfort, contentment, ease, gratification, peace, peace of mind, pleasure, satisfaction 3. *adj.* agreeable, at ease, comfortable, contented, fulfilled, satisfied, willing to accept

content[2] 1. burden, essence, gist, ideas, matter, meaning, significance, substance, text, thoughts 2. capacity, load, measure, size, volume

contented at ease, at peace, cheerful, comfortable, complacent, content, glad, gratified, happy, pleased, satisfied, serene, thankful

contention 1. competition, contest, discord, dispute, dissension, enmity, feuding, hostility, rivalry, strife, struggle, wrangling 2. affirmation, allegation, argument, assertion, asseveration, belief, claim, declaration, ground, idea, maintaining, opinion, position, profession, stand, thesis, view

contentious argumentative, bickering, captious, cavilling, combative, controversial, cross, disputatious, factious, litigious, peevish, perverse, pugnacious, quarrelsome, querulous, wrangling

contentment comfort, complacency, content, contentedness, ease, equanimity, fulfilment, gladness, gratification, happiness, peace, pleasure, repletion, satisfaction, serenity

contents 1. constituents, elements, ingredients, load 2. chapters, divisions, subject matter, subjects, themes, topics

contest *n.* 1. competition, game, match, tournament, trial 2. affray, altercation, battle, combat, conflict, controversy, debate, discord, dispute, encounter, fight, shock, struggle ~*v.* 3. compete, contend, fight, fight over, strive, vie 4. argue, call in *or* into question, challenge, debate, dispute, doubt, litigate, object to, oppose, question

contestant aspirant, candidate, competitor, contender, entrant, participant, player

context 1. background, connection, frame of reference, framework, relation 2. ambience, circumstances, conditions, situation

continent abstemious, abstinent, ascetic, austere, celibate, chaste, self-restrained, sober

contingency accident, chance, emergency, event, eventuality, fortuity, happening, incident, juncture, possibility, uncertainty

contingent *adj.* 1. *With* on *or* upon conditional, controlled by, dependent, subject to 2. accidental, casual, fortuitous, haphazard, random, uncertain ~*n.* 3. batch, body, bunch (*Inf.*), deputation, detachment, group, mission, quota, section, set

continual constant, continuous, endless, eternal, everlasting, frequent, incessant, interminable, oft-repeated, perpetual, recurrent, regular, repeated, repetitive, unceasing, uninterrupted, unremitting

continually all the time, always, constantly, endlessly, eternally, everlastingly, forever, incessantly, interminably, nonstop, persistently, repeatedly

continuation 1. addition, extension, furtherance, postscript, sequel, supplement 2. maintenance, perpetuation, prolongation, resumption

continue 1. abide, carry on, endure, last, live on, persist, remain, rest, stay, stay on, survive 2. go on, keep at, keep on, keep the ball rolling, keep up, maintain, persevere, persist in, prolong, pursue, stick at, stick to, sustain 3. draw out, extend, lengthen, project, prolong, reach 4. carry on, pick up where one left off, proceed, recommence, resume, return to, take up

continuing enduring, in progress, lasting, ongoing, sustained

continuity cohesion, connection, flow, interrelationship, progression, sequence, succession, whole

continuous connected, constant, continued, extended, prolonged, unbroken, unceasing, undivided, uninterrupted

contour curve, figure, form, lines, outline, profile, relief, shape, silhouette

contraband 1. *n.* black-marketing, bootlegging, moonshine (*U.S.*), rum-running, smuggling, trafficking 2. *adj.* banned, black-market, bootleg, bootlegged, forbidden, hot (*Inf.*), illegal, illicit, interdicted, prohibited, smuggled, unlawful

contract *v.* 1. abbreviate, abridge, compress, condense, confine, constrict, curtail, dwindle, epitomize, lessen, narrow, purse, reduce, shrink, shrivel, tighten, wither, wrinkle 2. agree, arrange, bargain, clinch, close, come to terms, commit oneself, covenant, engage, enter into, negotiate, pledge, stipulate 3. acquire, be afflicted with, catch, develop, go down with (*Inf.*), incur ~*n.* 4. agreement, arrangement, bargain, bond, commission, commitment, compact, concordat, convention, covenant, deal (*Inf.*), engagement, pact, settlement, stipulation, treaty, understanding

contraction abbreviation, compression, constriction, diminution, drawing in, elision, narrowing, reduction, shortening, shrinkage, shrivelling, tensing, tightening

contradict be at variance with, belie, challenge, contravene, controvert, counter, counteract, deny, dispute, gainsay (*Archaic*), impugn, negate, oppose

contradiction conflict, confutation, contravention, denial, incongruity, inconsistency, negation, opposite

contradictory antagonistic, antithetical, conflicting, contrary, discrepant, incompatible, inconsistent, irreconcilable, opposed, opposite, paradoxical, repugnant

contraption apparatus, contrivance, device, gadget, mechanism, rig

contrary *adj.* 1. adverse, antagonistic, clashing, contradictory, counter, discordant, hostile, inconsistent, inimical, opposed, opposite, paradoxical 2. awkward, balky, cantankerous, cussed (*Inf.*), difficult, disobliging, froward, intractable, obstinate, perverse, stroppy (*Brit. sl.*), thrawn (*Northern dialect*), unaccommodating, wayward, wilful ~*v.* 3. antithesis, converse, opposite, reverse 4. **on the contrary** conversely, in contrast, not at all, on the other hand, quite the opposite *or* reverse

contrast 1. *n.* comparison, contrariety, difference, differentiation, disparity, dissimilarity, distinction, divergence, foil, opposition 2. *v.* compare, differ, differentiate, distinguish, oppose, set in opposition, set off

contribute 1. add, afford, bestow, chip in, donate, furnish, give, provide, subscribe, supply 2. be conducive, be instrumental, be partly responsible for, conduce, help, lead, tend

contribution addition, bestowal, donation, gift, grant, input, offering, subscription

contributor 1. backer, bestower, conferrer, donor, giver, patron, subscriber, supporter 2. correspondent, freelance, freelancer, journalist, reporter

contrite chastened, conscience-stricken, humble, in sackcloth and ashes, penitent, regretful, remorseful, repentant, sorrowful, sorry

contrivance 1. artifice, design, dodge, expedient, fabrication, formation, intrigue, inventiveness, machination, measure, plan, plot, project, ruse, scheme, stratagem, trick 2. apparatus, appliance, contraption, device, equipment, gadget, gear, implement, invention, machine, mechanism

contrive 1. concoct, construct, create, design, devise, engineer, fabricate, frame, improvise, invent, wangle (*Inf.*) 2. arrange, bring about, effect, hit upon, manage, manoeuvre, plan, plot, scheme, succeed

contrived artificial, elaborate, forced, laboured, overdone, planned, freelance, recherché, strained, unnatural

control *v.* 1. boss (*Inf.*), call the

tune, command, conduct, direct, dominate, govern, have charge of, hold the purse strings, lead, manage, manipulate, oversee, pilot, reign over, rule, steer, superintend, supervise 2. bridle, check, constrain, contain, curb, hold back, limit, master, rein in, repress, restrain, subdue 3. *Used of a machine, an experiment, etc.* counteract, determine, monitor, regulate, verify ~*n.* 4. authority, charge, command, direction, discipline, government, guidance, jurisdiction, management, mastery, oversight, rule, superintendence, supervision, supremacy 5. brake, check, curb, limitation, regulation, restraint

controls console, control panel, dashboard, dials, instruments

controversial at issue, contended, contentious, controvertible, debatable, disputable, disputed, open to question, under discussion

controversy altercation, argument, contention, debate, discussion, dispute, dissension, polemic, quarrel, squabble, strife, wrangle, wrangling

convalescence improvement, recovery, recuperation, rehabilitation, return to health

convalescent *adj.* getting better, improving, mending, on the mend, recovering, recuperating

convene assemble, bring together, call, come together, congregate, convoke, gather, meet, muster, rally, summon

convenience 1. accessibility, appropriateness, availability, fitness, handiness, opportuneness, serviceability, suitability, usefulness, utility 2. *A convenient time or situation* chance, leisure, opportunity, spare moment, spare time 3. accommodation, advantage, benefit, comfort, ease, enjoyment, satisfaction, service, use 4. *A useful device* amenity, appliance, comfort, facility, help, labour-saving device

convenient 1. adapted, appropriate, beneficial, commodious, fit, fitted, handy, helpful, laboursaving, opportune, seasonable, serviceable, suitable, suited, timely, useful, well-timed 2. accessible, at hand, available, close at hand, handy, just round the corner, nearby, within reach

convent convent school, nunnery, religious community

convention 1. assembly, conference, congress, convocation, council, delegates, meeting, representatives 2. code, custom, etiquette, formality, practice, propriety, protocol, tradition, usage 3. agreement, bargain, compact, concordat, contract, pact, protocol, stipulation, treaty

conventional 1. accepted, common, correct, customary, decorous, expected, formal, habitual, normal, ordinary, orthodox, prevailing, prevalent, proper, regular, ritual, standard, traditional, usual, wonted 2. bourgeois, commonplace, hackneyed, hidebound, pedestrian, prosaic, routine, run-of-the-mill, stereotyped, unoriginal

converge coincide, combine, come together, concentrate, focus, gather, join, meet, merge, mingle

conversant *Usually with with* acquainted, *au fait*, experienced, familiar, knowledgeable, practised, proficient, skilled, versed, well-informed, well up in (*Inf.*)

conversation chat, chinwag (*Brit. inf.*), colloquy, communication, communion, confab (*Inf.*), confabulation, conference, converse, dialogue, discourse, discussion, exchange, gossip, intercourse, powwow, talk, tête-à-tête

converse 1. *n.* antithesis, contrary, obverse, opposite, other side of the coin, reverse 2. *adj.* contrary, counter, opposite, reverse, reversed, transposed

conversion 1. change, metamorphosis, transfiguration, transformation, transmogrification (*Jocular*), transmutation 2. adaptation, alteration, modification, reconstruction, remodelling, reorganization 3. change of heart, proselytization, rebirth, reformation, regeneration

convert[1] v. 1. alter, change, interchange, metamorphose, transform, transmogrify (*Jocular*), transmute, transpose, turn 2. adapt, apply, appropriate, modify, remodel, reorganize, restyle, revise 3. baptize, bring to God, convince, proselytize, reform, regenerate, save

convert[2] n. catechumen, disciple, neophyte, proselyte

convex bulging, gibbous, out~ curved, protuberant, rounded

convey 1. bear, bring, carry, conduct, fetch, forward, grant, guide, move, send, support, transmit, transport 2. communicate, disclose, impart, make known, relate, reveal, tell 3. *Law* bequeath, cede, deliver, demise, devolve, grant, lease, transfer, will

conveyance 1. carriage, movement, transfer, transference, transmission, transport, transportation 2. transport, vehicle

convict 1. v. condemn, find guilty, imprison, pronounce guilty, sentence 2. n. con (*Sl.*), criminal, culprit, felon, jailbird, malefactor, old lag (*Sl.*), prisoner

conviction 1. assurance, certainty, certitude, confidence, earnestness, fervour, firmness, reliance 2. belief, creed, faith, opinion, persuasion, principle, tenet, view

convince assure, bring round, gain the confidence of, persuade, prevail upon, prove to, satisfy, sway, win over

convincing cogent, conclusive, credible, impressive, incontrovertible, likely, persuasive, plausible, powerful, probable, telling

convoy 1. n. armed guard, attendance, attendant, escort, guard, protection 2. v. accompany, attend, escort, guard, pilot, protect, shepherd, usher

convulse agitate, churn up, derange, disorder, disturb, shake, shatter, twist, work

convulsion 1. agitation, commotion, disturbance, furore, shaking, tumult, turbulence, upheaval 2. contortion, contraction, cramp, fit, paroxysm, seizure, spasm, throe (*Rare*), tremor

cool adj. 1. chilled, chilling, chilly, coldish, nippy, refreshing 2. calm, collected, composed, deliberate, dispassionate, imperturbable, level-headed, placid, quiet, relaxed, self-controlled, self-possessed, serene, together (*Sl.*), unemotional, unexcited, unruffled 3. aloof, apathetic, distant, frigid, incurious, indifferent, lukewarm, offhand, reserved, standoffish, uncommunicative, unconcerned, unenthusiastic, unfriendly, uninterested, unresponsive, unwelcoming 4. audacious, bold, brazen, cheeky, impertinent, impudent, presumptuous, shameless 5. *Inf.* cosmopolitan, elegant, sophisticated, urbane ~v. 6. chill, cool off, freeze, lose heat, refrigerate 7. abate, allay, assuage, calm (down), dampen, lessen, moderate, quiet, temper ~n. 8. *Sl.* calmness, composure, control, poise, self-control, self-discipline, self-possession, temper

coop 1. n. box, cage, enclosure, hutch, pen 2. v. cage, confine, immure, imprison, pen, shut up

cooperate abet, aid, assist, collaborate, combine, concur, conduce, conspire, contribute, coordinate, go along with, help, join forces, pitch in, play ball (*Inf.*), pool resources, pull together, work together

cooperation assistance, collaboration, combined effort, concert, concurrence, esprit de corps, give-and-take, helpfulness, participation, responsiveness, teamwork, unity

cooperative 1. accommodating, helpful, obliging, responsive, supportive 2. coactive, collective, combined, concerted, coordinated, joint, shared, unified, united

coordinate 1. v. correlate, harmonize, integrate, match, mesh, organize, relate, synchronize, systematize 2. adj. coequal, correlative, correspondent, equal, equivalent, parallel, tantamount cope 1. carry on, get by (*Inf.*), hold one's own, make out (*Inf.*), make the grade, manage, rise to the occasion, struggle through, survive 2. cope with contend, deal, dispatch, encounter, grapple, handle, struggle, tangle, tussle, weather, wrestle

copious abundant, ample, bounteous, bountiful, extensive, exuberant, full, generous, lavish, liberal, luxuriant, overflowing, plenteous, plentiful, profuse, rich, superabundant

copy n. 1. archetype, carbon copy, counterfeit, duplicate, facsimile, forgery, image, imitation, likeness, model, pattern, photocopy, Photostat (*Trademark*), print, replica, replication, representation, reproduction, transcription, Xerox (*Trademark*) ~v. 2. counterfeit, duplicate, photocopy, Photostat (*Trademark*), replicate, reproduce, transcribe, Xerox (*Trademark*) 3. ape, echo, emulate, follow, follow suit, follow the example of, imitate, mimic, mirror, parrot, repeat, simulate

cordial affable, affectionate, agreeable, cheerful, earnest, friendly, genial, heartfelt, hearty, invigorating, sociable, warm, warm-hearted, welcoming, wholehearted

cordiality affability, amiability, friendliness, geniality, heartiness, sincerity, warmth, wholeheartedness

cordon 1. n. barrier, chain, line, ring 2. v. cordon off close off, encircle, enclose, fence off, isolate, picket, separate, surround

core centre, crux, essence, gist, heart, kernel, nub, nucleus, pith

corner n. 1. angle, bend, crook, joint 2. cavity, cranny, hideaway, hide-out, hidey-hole (*Inf.*), hole, niche, nook, recess, retreat 3. hole (*Inf.*), pickle (*Inf.*), predicament, tight spot (*Inf.*) ~v. 4. bring to bay, run to earth, trap 5. As in corner the market engross, hog (*Sl.*), monopolize

cornerstone 1. quoin 2. basis, bedrock, key, premise, starting point

corny banal, commonplace, dull, feeble, hackneyed, maudlin, mawkish, old-fashioned, old hat, sentimental, stale, stereotyped, trite

corporal anatomical, bodily, carnal, corporeal (*Archaic*), fleshly, material, physical, somatic

corporate allied, collaborative, collective, combined, communal, joint, merged, pooled, shared, united

corporation 1. association, corporate body, society 2. civic authorities, council, municipal authorities, town council 3. *Inf.* beer belly, paunch, pod, pot, potbelly, spare tyre

corps band, body, company, contingent, crew, detachment, division, regiment, squad, squadron, team, troop, unit

corpse body, cadaver, carcass, remains, stiff (*Sl.*)

corpulent beefy (*Inf.*), bulky, burly, fat, fattish, fleshy, large, lusty, obese, overweight, plump, portly, roly-poly, rotund, stout, tubby, well-padded

correct v. 1. adjust, amend, cure, emend, improve, rectify, redress, reform, regulate, remedy, right 2. admonish, chasten, chastise, chide, discipline, punish, reprimand, reprove ~adj. 3. accurate, equitable, exact, faultless, flawless, just, O.K. (*Inf.*), precise, regular, right, strict, true 4. acceptable, appropriate, diplomatic, fitting, O.K. (*Inf.*), proper, seemly, standard

correction 1. adjustment, alteration, amendment, improvement, modification, rectification, righting 2. admonition, castigation, chastisement, discipline, punishment, reformation, reproof

corrective adj. 1. palliative, rehabilitative, remedial, restorative, therapeutic 2. disciplinary, penal, punitive, reformatory

correctly accurately, aright, perfectly, precisely, properly, right, rightly

correctness 1. accuracy, exactitude, exactness, faultlessness, fidelity, preciseness, precision, regularity, truth 2. *bon ton*, civility, decorum, good breeding, propriety, seemliness

correlate associate, compare, connect, coordinate, correspond, equate, interact, parallel, tie in

correlation alternation, correspondence, equivalence, interaction, interchange, interdependence, interrelationship, reciprocity

correspond 1. accord, agree, be consistent, coincide, complement, conform, correlate, dovetail, fit, harmonize, match, square, tally 2. communicate, exchange letters, keep in touch, write

correspondence 1. agreement, analogy, coincidence, comparability, comparison, concurrence, conformity, congruity, correlation, fitness, harmony, match, relation, similarity 2. communication, letters, mail, post, writing

correspondent *n.* 1. letter writer, pen friend *or* pal 2. contributor, gazetteer (*Archaic*), journalist, reporter, special correspondent ~*adj.* 3. analogous, comparable, like, parallel, reciprocal, similar

corresponding analogous, answering, complementary, correlative, correspondent, equivalent, identical, interrelated, matching, reciprocal, similar, synonymous

corridor aisle, hallway, passage, passageway

corroborate authenticate, back up, bear out, confirm, document, endorse, establish, ratify, substantiate, support, sustain, validate

corrode canker, consume, corrupt, deteriorate, eat away, erode, gnaw, impair, oxidize, rust, waste, wear away

corrosive 1. acrid, biting, caustic, consuming, corroding, erosive, virulent, wasting, wearing 2. caustic, cutting, incisive, mordant, sarcastic, trenchant, venomous

corrugated channelled, creased, crinkled, fluted, furrowed, grooved, puckered, ridged, rumpled, wrinkled

corrupt *adj.* 1. bent (*Sl.*), bribable, crooked (*Inf.*), dishonest, fraudulent, rotten, shady (*Inf.*), unethical, unprincipled, unscrupulous, venal 2. abandoned, debased, defiled, degenerate, demoralized, depraved, dishonoured, dissolute, profligate, vicious ~*v.* 3. bribe, debauch, demoralize, deprave, entice, fix (*Inf.*), grease (someone's) palm (*Sl.*), lure, pervert, square (*Inf.*), suborn, subvert ~*adj.* 4. adulterated, altered, contaminated, decayed, defiled, distorted, doctored, falsified, infected, polluted, putrescent, putrid, rotten, tainted ~*v.* 5. adulterate, contaminate, debase, defile, doctor, infect, putrefy, spoil, taint, tamper with, vitiate

corruption 1. breach of trust, bribery, bribing, crookedness (*Inf.*), demoralization, dishonesty, extortion, fiddling (*Inf.*), fraud, fraudulency, graft, jobbery, profiteering, shadiness, shady dealings (*Inf.*), unscrupulousness, venality 2. baseness, decadence, degeneration, degradation, depravity, evil, immorality, impurity, iniquity, perversion, profligacy, sinfulness, turpitude, vice, viciousness, wickedness 3. adulteration, debasement, decay, defilement, distortion, doctoring, falsification, foulness, infection, pollution, putrefaction, putrescence, rot, rottenness

corset 1. belt, bodice, corselet, foundation garment, girdle, panty girdle, stays (*Rare*) 2. *Fig.* check, curb, limitation, restriction

cosmetic *adj.* beautifying, nonessential, superficial, surface, touching-up

cosmic grandiose, huge, immense, infinite, limitless, measureless, universal, vast

cosmonaut astronaut, spaceman, space pilot

cosmopolitan 1. *adj.* catholic, sophisticated, universal, urbane, well-travelled, worldly, worldly-wise 2. *n.* cosmopolite, jetsetter, man *or* woman of the world, sophisticate

cost *n.* 1. amount, charge, damage (*Inf.*), expenditure, expense, figure, outlay, payment, price, rate, worth 2. damage, deprivation, detriment, expense, harm, hurt, injury, loss, penalty, sacrifice, suffering ~v. 3. come to, command a price of, sell at, set (someone) back (*Inf.*) 4. *Fig.* do disservice to, harm, hurt, injure, lose, necessitate

costly 1. dear, excessive, exorbitant, expensive, extortionate, highly-priced, steep (*Inf.*), valuable 2. gorgeous, lavish, luxurious, opulent, precious, priceless, rich, splendid, sumptuous 3. *Entailing loss or sacrifice* catastrophic, damaging, deleterious, disastrous, harmful, loss-making, ruinous, sacrificial

costs 1. budget, expenses, outgoings 2. **at all costs** at any price, no matter what, regardless, without fail

costume apparel, attire, clothing, dress, ensemble, garb, get-up (*Inf.*), livery, national dress, outfit, robes, uniform

cosy comfortable, comfy (*Inf.*), cuddled up, homely, intimate, secure, sheltered, snug, snuggled down, tucked up, warm

cottage but-and-ben (*Scot.*), cabin, chalet, cot, hut, lodge, shack

cough 1. *n.* bark, frog *or* tickle in one's throat, hack 2. *v.* bark, clear one's throat, hack, hawk, hem

cough up ante up (*Inf.*), come across, deliver, fork out (*Sl.*), give up, hand over, shell out (*Inf.*), surrender

council assembly, board, cabinet, chamber, committee, conclave, conference, congress, convention, convocation, diet, governing body, ministry, panel, parliament, synod

counsel *n.* 1. admonition, advice, caution, consideration, consultation, deliberation, direction, forethought, guidance, information, recommendation, suggestion, warning 2. advocate, attorney, barrister, lawyer, legal adviser, solicitor ~v. 3. admonish, advise, advocate, caution, exhort, instruct, recommend, urge, warn

count *v.* 1. add (up), calculate, cast up, check, compute, enumerate, estimate, number, reckon, score, tally, tot up 2. consider, deem, esteem, impute, judge, look upon, rate, regard, think 3. carry weight, cut any ice (*Inf.*), enter into consideration, matter, rate, signify, tell, weigh 4. include, number among, take into account *or* consideration ~n. 5. calculation, computation, enumeration, numbering, poll, reckoning, sum, tally

countenance *n.* 1. appearance, aspect, expression, face, features, look, mien, physiognomy, visage 2. aid, approval, assistance, backing, endorsement, favour, sanction, support ~v. 3. abet, aid, approve, back, champion, condone, encourage, endorse, help, sanction, support 4. brook, endure, put up with (*Inf.*), stand for (*Inf.*), tolerate

counter 1. *adv.* against, at variance with, contrarily, contrariwise, conversely, in defiance of, versus 2. *adj.* adverse, against, conflicting, contradictory, contrary, contrasting, obverse, opposed, opposing, opposite 3. *v.* answer, hit back, meet, offset, parry, resist, respond, retaliate, return, ward off

counteract annul, check, contravene, counterbalance, countervail, cross, defeat, foil, frustrate, hinder, invalidate, negate, neutralize, offset, oppose, resist, thwart

counterbalance balance, compensate, counterpoise, countervail, make up for, offset, set off

counterfeit 1. *v.* copy, fabricate, fake, feign, forge, imitate, impersonate, pretend, sham, simulate 2. *adj.* bogus, copied, ersatz, faked, false, feigned, forged, fraudulent, imitation, phoney (*Sl.*), pseud (*Inf.*), pseudo (*Inf.*), sham, simulated, spurious, supposititious 3. *n.* copy, fake, forgery, fraud, imitation, phoney (*Sl.*), reproduction, sham

countermand annul, cancel, override, repeal, rescind, retract, reverse, revoke

counterpart complement, copy, correlative, duplicate, equal, fel-

low, match, mate, opposite num~
ber, supplement, tally, twin

countless endless, immeasurable,
incalculable, infinite, innumerable,
legion, limitless, measureless,
multitudinous, myriad, numberless,
uncounted, untold

count on *or* **upon** bank on, believe
(in), depend on, lean on, pin one's
faith on, reckon on, rely on, take
for granted, take on trust, trust

count out disregard, except, ex~
clude, leave out, leave out of ac~
count, pass over

country *n.* 1. commonwealth, king~
dom, nation, people, realm, sover~
eign state, state 2. fatherland,
homeland, motherland, nationality,
native land, *patria* 3. land, part,
region, terrain, territory 4. citizen~
ry, citizens, community, electors,
grass roots, inhabitants, nation,
people, populace, public, society,
voters 5. backwoods, boondocks
(*U.S. sl.*), countryside, farmland,
green belt, outback (*Australian &
New Zealand*), outdoors, provinces,
rural areas, sticks (*Inf.*), the back
of beyond, the middle of nowhere,
wide open spaces (*Inf.*) ~*adj.* 6.
agrarian, Arcadian, bucolic, geor~
gic (*Literary*), landed, pastoral,
provincial, rural, rustic

countryman 1. bumpkin, country
dweller, farmer, hayseed (*U.S.
inf.*), hind, husbandman, peasant,
provincial, rustic, swain, yokel 2.
compatriot, fellow citizen

countryside country, farmland,
green belt, outback (*Australian &
New Zealand*), outdoors, panora~
ma, sticks (*Inf.*), view, wide open
spaces (*Inf.*)

count up add, reckon up, sum, tal~
ly, total

county 1. *n.* province, shire 2. *adj.*
huntin', shootin', and fishin' (*Inf.*),
plummy (*Inf.*), tweedy, upper-class,
upper-crust (*Inf.*)

coup accomplishment, action,
deed, exploit, feat, manoeuvre,
masterstroke, stratagem, stroke,
stroke of genius, stunt, *tour de
force*

couple 1. *n.* brace, duo, pair, span
(*of horses or oxen*), twain (*Archa~
ic*), twosome 2. *v.* buckle, clasp,
conjoin, connect, hitch, join, link,
marry, pair, unite, wed, yoke

coupon card, certificate, detach~
able portion, slip, ticket, token,
voucher

courage boldness, bottle (*Sl.*),
bravery, daring, dauntlessness,
fearlessness, firmness, fortitude,
gallantry, grit, guts (*Inf.*), hardi~
hood, heroism, intrepidity, lion~
heartedness, mettle, nerve, pluck,
resolution, spunk (*Inf.*), valour

courageous audacious, bold,
brave, daring, dauntless, fearless,
gallant, hardy, heroic, indomitable,
intrepid, lion-hearted, plucky,
resolute, stouthearted, valiant,
valorous

course *n.* 1. advance, advance~
ment, continuity, development,
flow, furtherance, march, move~
ment, order, progress, progression,
sequence, succession, unfolding 2.
channel, direction, line, orbit, pas~
sage, path, road, route, tack, track,
trail, trajectory, way 3. duration,
lapse, passage, passing, sweep,
term, time 4. behaviour, conduct,
manner, method, mode, plan, poli~
cy, procedure, programme, regi~
men 5. cinder track, circuit, lap,
race, racecourse, round 6. classes,
course of study, curriculum, lec~
tures, programme, schedule, stu~
dies ~*v.* 7. dash, flow, gush, move
apace, race, run, scud, scurry,
speed, stream, surge, tumble 8.
chase, follow, hunt, pursue 9. **in
due course** eventually, finally, in
the course of time, in the end, in
time, sooner or later 10. **of course**
certainly, definitely, indubitably,
naturally, obviously, undoubtedly,
without a doubt

court *n.* 1. cloister, courtyard, piaz~
za, plaza, quad (*Inf.*), quadrangle,
square, yard 2. hall, manor, palace
3. attendants, cortege, entourage,
retinue, royal household, suite,
train 4. bar, bench, court of justice,
lawcourt, seat of judgment, tribu~
nal 5. addresses, attention, hom~
age, respects, suit ~*v.* 6. chase,

date, go (out) with, go steady with (*Inf.*), keep company with, make love to, pay court to, pay one's addresses to, pursue, run after, serenade, set one's cap at, sue (*Archaic*), take out, walk out with, woo **7.** cultivate, curry favour with, fawn upon, flatter, pander to, seek, solicit **8.** attract, bring about, incite, invite, prompt, provoke, seek

courteous affable, attentive, ceremonious, civil, courtly, elegant, gallant, gracious, mannerly, polished, polite, refined, respectful, urbane, well-bred, well-mannered

courtesy **1.** affability, civility, courteousness, courtliness, elegance, gallantness, gallantry, good breeding, good manners, graciousness, polish, politeness, urbanity **2.** benevolence, consent, consideration, favour, generosity, indulgence, kindness

courtier attendant, follower, henchman, liegeman, pursuivant (*Historical*), squire, train-bearer

courtly affable, aristocratic, ceremonious, chivalrous, civil, decorous, dignified, elegant, flattering, formal, gallant, highbred, lordly, obliging, polished, refined, stately, urbane

courtship courting, engagement, keeping company, pursuit, romance, suit, wooing

courtyard area, enclosure, peristyle, playground, quad, quadrangle, yard

cove anchorage, bay, creek, firth *or* frith (*Scot.*), inlet, sound

covenant *n.* **1.** arrangement, bargain, commitment, compact, concordat, contract, convention, pact, promise, stipulation, treaty, trust **2.** bond, deed ~*v.* **3.** agree, bargain, contract, engage, pledge, stipulate, undertake

cover *v.* **1.** camouflage, cloak, conceal, cover up, curtain, disguise, eclipse, enshroud, hide, hood, house, mask, obscure, screen, secrete, shade, shroud, veil ~*n.* **2.** cloak, cover-up, disguise, façade, front, mask, pretence, screen, smoke screen, veil, window-dressing ~*v.* **3.** defend, guard, protect, reinforce, shelter, shield, watch over ~*n.* **4.** camouflage, concealment, defence, guard, hiding place, protection, refuge, sanctuary, shelter, shield, undergrowth, woods ~*v.* **5.** canopy, clothe, coat, daub, dress, encase, envelop, invest, layer, mantle, overlay, overspread, put on, wrap ~*n.* **6.** binding, canopy, cap, case, clothing, coating, covering, dress, envelope, jacket, lid, sheath, top, wrapper ~*v.* **7.** comprehend, comprise, consider, contain, deal with, embody, embrace, encompass, examine, include, incorporate, involve, provide for, refer to, survey, take account of **8.** double for, fill in for, relieve, stand in for, substitute, take over, take the rap for (*Sl.*) **9.** describe, detail, investigate, narrate, recount, relate, report, tell of, write up **10.** balance, compensate, counterbalance, insure, make good, make up for, offset ~*n.* **11.** compensation, indemnity, insurance, payment, protection, reimbursement ~*v.* **12.** cross, pass through *or* over, range, travel over, traverse **13.** engulf, flood, overrun, submerge, wash over

covering **1.** *n.* blanket, casing, clothing, coating, cover, housing, layer, overlay, protection, shelter, top, wrap, wrapper, wrapping **2.** *adj.* accompanying, descriptive, explanatory, introductory

cover-up complicity, concealment, conspiracy, front, smoke screen, whitewash (*Inf.*)

cover up **1.** conceal, cover one's tracks, feign ignorance, hide, hush up, keep dark, keep secret, keep silent about, keep under one's hat (*Inf.*), repress, stonewall, suppress, whitewash (*Inf.*) **2.** coat, cover, encrust, envelop, hide, plaster, slather (*U.S. sl.*), swathe

covet aspire to, begrudge, crave, desire, envy, fancy (*Inf.*), hanker after, have one's eye on, long for, lust after, thirst for, yearn for

covetous acquisitive, avaricious, close-fisted, envious, grasping, greedy, jealous, mercenary, rapacious, yearning

coward caitiff (*Archaic*), craven, dastard (*Archaic*), faint-heart, funk (*Inf.*), poltroon, recreant (*Archaic*), renegade, scaredy-cat (*Inf.*), skulker, sneak, yellow-belly (*Sl.*)

cowardly base, caitiff (*Archaic*), chicken (*Sl.*), chicken-hearted, craven, dastardly, faint-hearted, fearful, gutless (*Inf.*), lily-livered, pusillanimous, recreant (*Archaic*), scared, shrinking, soft, spineless, timorous, weak, weak-kneed (*Inf.*), white-livered, yellow (*Inf.*)

cowboy broncobuster (*U.S.*), cattleman, cowhand, cowpuncher (*U.S. inf.*), drover, gaucho (*S American*), herder, herdsman, rancher, ranchero (*U.S.*), stockman, wrangler (*U.S.*)

cower cringe, crouch, draw back, fawn, flinch, grovel, quail, shrink, skulk, sneak, tremble, truckle

coy arch, backward, bashful, coquettish, demure, evasive, flirtatious, kittenish, modest, overmodest, prudish, reserved, retiring, self-effacing, shrinking, shy, skittish, timid

crack *v.* 1. break, burst, chip, chop, cleave, crackle, craze, fracture, rive, snap, splinter, split ~*n.* 2. breach, break, chink, chip, cleft, cranny, crevice, fissure, fracture, gap, interstice, rift ~*v.* 3. burst, crash, detonate, explode, pop, ring, snap ~*n.* 4. burst, clap, crash, explosion, pop, report, snap ~*v.* 5. break down, collapse, give way, go to pieces, lose control, succumb, yield ~*v./n.* 6. *Inf.* buffet, clip (*Inf.*), clout (*Inf.*), cuff, slap, thump, wallop (*Inf.*), whack ~*v.* 7. decipher, fathom, get the answer to, solve, work out ~*n.* 8. *Inf.* attempt, go, opportunity, stab, try 9. *Sl.* dig, funny remark, gag, insult, jibe, joke, quip, smart-alecky remark, wisecrack, witticism ~*adj.* 10. *Sl.* ace, choice, elite, excellent, first-class, first-rate, hand-picked, superior

cracked 1. broken, chipped, crazed, damaged, defective, faulty, fissured, flawed, imperfect, split 2. *Sl.* bats (*Sl.*), batty (*Sl.*), crackbrained, crackpot (*Inf.*), crazy (*Inf.*), daft (*Sl.*), eccentric, insane, loony (*Sl.*), nuts (*Sl.*), nutty (*Sl.*), off one's head *or* nut (*Sl.*), out of one's mind, round the bend (*Sl.*), touched

cracked up blown up, exaggerated, hyped up (*Sl.*), overpraised, overrated, puffed up

crack up break down, collapse, come apart at the seams (*Inf.*), freak out (*Inf.*), go crazy (*Inf.*), go off one's rocker (*Sl.*), go out of one's mind, go to pieces, have a breakdown

cradle *n.* 1. bassinet, cot, crib, Moses basket 2. *Fig.* beginning, birthplace, fount, fountainhead, origin, source, spring, wellspring ~*v.* 3. hold, lull, nestle, nurse, rock, support 4. nourish, nurture, tend, watch over

craft 1. ability, aptitude, art, artistry, cleverness, dexterity, expertise, expertness, ingenuity, knack, know-how (*Inf.*), skill, technique, workmanship 2. artfulness, artifice, contrivance, craftiness, cunning, deceit, duplicity, guile, ruse, scheme, shrewdness, stratagem, subterfuge, subtlety, trickery, wiles 3. business, calling, employment, handicraft, handiwork, line, occupation, pursuit, trade, vocation, work 4. aircraft, barque, boat, plane, ship, spacecraft, vessel

craftiness artfulness, astuteness, canniness, cunning, deviousness, duplicity, foxiness, guile, shrewdness, slyness, subtlety, trickiness, wiliness

craftsman artificer, artisan, maker, master, skilled worker, smith, technician, wright

craftsmanship artistry, expertise, mastery, technique, workmanship

crafty artful, astute, calculating, canny, cunning, deceitful, designing, devious, duplicitous, foxy, fraudulent, guileful, insidious, knowing, scheming, sharp, shrewd, sly, subtle, tricksy, tricky, wily

crag aiguille, bluff, peak, pinnacle, rock, tor

cram 1. compact, compress, crowd, crush, fill to overflowing, force, jam, overcrowd, overfill, pack, pack in, press, ram, shove, squeeze, stuff 2. glut, gorge, gormandize, guzzle, overeat, overfeed, put or pack away, satiate, stuff 3. *Inf.* con, grind, mug up (*Sl.*), revise, study, swot, swot up

cramp[1] *v.* check, circumscribe, clog, confine, constrain, encumber, hamper, hamstring, handicap, hinder, impede, inhibit, obstruct, restrict, shackle, stymie, thwart

cramp[2] *n.* ache, contraction, convulsion, crick, pain, pang, shooting pain, spasm, stiffness, stitch, twinge

cramped 1. awkward, circumscribed, closed in, confined, congested, crowded, hemmed in, jammed in, narrow, overcrowded, packed, restricted, squeezed, uncomfortable 2. *Esp. of handwriting* crabbed, indecipherable, irregular, small

cranky bizarre, capricious, eccentric, erratic, freakish, freaky (*Sl.*), funny (*Inf.*), idiosyncratic, odd, peculiar, queer, quirky, strange, wacky (*Sl.*)

cranny breach, chink, cleft, crack, crevice, fissure, gap, hole, interstice, nook, opening

crash *n.* 1. bang, boom, clang, clash, clatter, clattering, din, racket, smash, smashing, thunder ~*v.* 2. break, break up, dash to pieces, disintegrate, fracture, fragment, shatter, shiver, smash, splinter 3. come a cropper (*Inf.*), dash, fall, fall headlong, give way, hurtle, lurch, overbalance, pitch, plunge, precipitate oneself, sprawl, topple 4. bang, bump (into), collide, crash-land (*an aircraft*), drive into, have an accident, hit, hurtle into, plough into, run together, wreck ~*n.* 5. accident, bump, collision, jar, jolt, pile-up (*Inf.*), prang (*Inf.*), smash, smash-up, thud, thump, wreck 6. bankruptcy, collapse, debacle, depression, downfall, failure, ruin, smash ~*v.* 7. be ruined, collapse, fail, fold, fold up, go broke (*Inf.*), go

bust (*Inf.*), go under, smash ~*adj.* 8. *Of a course of studies, etc.* emergency, intensive, immediate, round-the-clock, speeded-up, telescoped, urgent

crass asinine, blundering, boorish, bovine, coarse, dense, doltish, gross, indelicate, insensitive, lumpish, oafish, obtuse, stupid, unrefined, witless

crate 1. *n.* box, case, container, packing case, tea chest 2. *v.* box, case, encase, enclose, pack, pack up

crater depression, dip, hollow, shell hole

crave 1. be dying for, cry out for (*Inf.*), desire, fancy (*Inf.*), hanker after, hunger after, long for, lust after, need, pant for, pine for, require, sigh for, thirst for, want, yearn for 2. ask, beg, beseech, entreat, implore, petition, plead for, pray for, seek, solicit, supplicate

craving appetite, cacoethes, desire, hankering, hunger, longing, lust, thirst, urge, yearning, yen (*Inf.*)

crawl 1. advance slowly, creep, drag, go on all fours, inch, move at a snail's pace, move on hands and knees, pull or drag oneself along, slither, worm one's way, wriggle, writhe 2. be overrun (alive, full of, lousy), swarm, teem 3. abase oneself, cringe, fawn, grovel, humble oneself, toady, truckle

craze 1. *n.* enthusiasm, fad, fashion, infatuation, mania, mode, novelty, passion, preoccupation, rage, the latest (*Inf.*), thing, trend, vogue 2. *v.* bewilder, confuse, dement, derange, distemper, drive mad, enrage, infatuate, inflame, madden, make insane, send crazy or berserk, unbalance, unhinge

crazy 1. *Inf.* a bit lacking upstairs (*Inf.*), barmy (*Sl.*), batty (*Sl.*), berserk, bonkers (*Sl.*), cracked (*Sl.*), crazed, cuckoo (*Inf.*), daft (*Sl.*), delirious, demented, deranged, idiotic, insane, lunatic (*Inf. or archaic*), mad, mad as a hatter, mad as a March hare, maniacal, mental (*Sl.*), not all there (*Inf.*), nuts (*Sl.*), nutty (*Sl.*), nutty as a fruitcake

(*Inf.*), off one's head (*Sl.*), of un~
sound mind, potty (*Inf.*), round the
bend (*Sl.*), touched, unbalanced,
unhinged 2. bizarre, eccentric,
fantastic, odd, outrageous, pecu~
liar, ridiculous, silly, strange, weird
3. absurd, bird-brained (*Inf.*),
cockeyed (*Inf.*), derisory, fatuous,
foolhardy, foolish, half-baked (*Inf.*),
idiotic, ill-conceived, impracti~
cable, imprudent, inane, inappro~
priate, irresponsible, ludicrous,
nonsensical, potty (*Inf.*), prepos~
terous, puerile, quixotic, senseless,
short-sighted, unrealistic, unwise,
unworkable, wild 4. *Inf.* ardent,
beside oneself, devoted, eager, en~
amoured, enthusiastic, fanatical,
hysterical, infatuated, mad, pas~
sionate, smitten, very keen, wild
(*Inf.*), zealous

creak *v.* grate, grind, groan, rasp,
scrape, scratch, screech, squeak,
squeal

cream *n.* 1. cosmetic, emulsion, es~
sence, liniment, lotion, oil, oint~
ment, paste, salve, unguent 2. best,
crème de la crème, elite, flower,
pick, prime ~*adj.* 3. off-white,
yellowish-white

creamy buttery, creamed, lush,
milky, oily, rich, smooth, soft, vel~
vety

crease 1. *v.* corrugate, crimp, crin~
kle, crumple, double up, fold,
pucker, ridge, ruck up, rumple,
screw up, wrinkle 2. *n.* bulge, cor~
rugation, fold, groove, line, over~
lap, pucker, ridge, ruck, tuck,
wrinkle

create 1. beget, bring into being *or*
existence, coin, compose, concoct,
design, develop, devise, dream up
(*Inf.*), form, formulate, generate,
give birth to, give life to, hatch,
initiate, invent, make, originate,
produce, spawn 2. appoint, consti~
tute, establish, found, install, in~
vest, make, set up 3. bring about,
cause, lead to, occasion

creation 1. conception, formation,
generation, genesis, making, pro~
creation, siring 2. constitution,
development, establishment, for~
mation, foundation, inception, in~

stitution, laying down, origination,
production, setting up 3. achieve~
ment, brainchild (*Inf.*), *chef-
d'oeuvre*, concept, concoction,
handiwork, invention, *magnum
opus, pièce de résistance*, produc~
tion 4. all living things, cosmos,
life, living world, natural world,
nature, universe, world

creative artistic, clever, fertile,
gifted, imaginative, ingenious, in~
spired, inventive, original, produc~
tive, stimulating, visionary

creativity cleverness, fecundity,
fertility, imagination, imaginative~
ness, ingenuity, inspiration, inven~
tiveness, originality, productivity,
talent

creator architect, author, begetter,
designer, father, framer, God, ini~
tiator, inventor, maker, originator,
prime mover

creature 1. animal, beast, being,
brute, critter (*U.S. dialect*), dumb
animal, living thing, lower animal,
quadruped 2. body, character, fel~
low, human being, individual, man,
mortal, person, soul, wight (*Archa~
ic*), woman 3. dependant, hanger-
on, hireling, instrument (*Inf.*),
lackey, minion, puppet, retainer,
tool, wretch

credentials attestation, authoriza~
tion, card, certificate, deed, diplo~
ma, docket, letter of recommen~
dation *or* introduction, letters of
credence, licence, missive, pass~
port, recommendation, refer~
ence(s), testament, testimonial, ti~
tle, voucher, warrant

credibility believability, believ~
ableness, integrity, plausibility, re~
liability, tenability, trustworthiness

credible 1. believable, conceivable,
imaginable, likely, plausible, pos~
sible, probable, reasonable, sup~
posable, tenable, thinkable 2. de~
pendable, honest, reliable, sincere,
trustworthy, trusty

credit *n.* 1. acclaim, acknowledg~
ment, approval, commendation,
fame, glory, honour, kudos, merit,
praise, recognition, thanks, tribute
2. character, clout (*Inf.*), esteem,
estimation, good name, influence,

position, prestige, regard, reputa~ tion, repute, standing, status 3. be~ lief, confidence, credence, faith, reliance, trust 4. *As in* **be a credit to** feather in one's cap, honour, source of satisfaction *or* pride 5. **on credit** by deferred payment, by instalments, on account, on hire- purchase, on (the) H.P., on the slate (*Inf.*), on tick (*Inf.*) ~v. 6. *With* **with** accredit, ascribe to, as~ sign to, attribute to, chalk up to (*Inf.*), impute to, refer to 7. accept, bank on, believe, buy (*Inf.*), depend on, fall for, have faith in, rely on, swallow (*Inf.*), trust

creditable admirable, commend~ able, deserving, estimable, exem~ plary, honourable, laudable, meri~ torious, praiseworthy, reputable, respectable, worthy

credulity blind faith, credulous~ ness, gullibility, naiveté, silliness, simplicity, stupidity

credulous born yesterday (*Inf.*), dupable, green, gullible, naive, overtrusting, trustful, uncritical, unsuspecting, unsuspicious

creed articles of faith, belief, can~ on, catechism, confession, credo, doctrine, dogma, persuasion, prin~ ciples, profession (*of faith*), tenet

creek 1. bay, bight, cove, firth *or* frith (*Scot.*), inlet 2. *U.S., Canadian, & Australian* brook, rivulet, runnel, stream, streamlet, tributary, watercourse

creep v. 1. crawl, crawl on all fours, glide, insinuate, slither, squirm, worm, wriggle, writhe 2. approach unnoticed, skulk, slink, sneak, steal, tiptoe 3. crawl, dawdle, drag, edge, inch, proceed at a snail's pace 4. bootlick (*Inf.*), cower, cringe, fawn, grovel, kowtow, scrape, suck up to (*Inf.*), toady, truckle ~n. 5. *Sl.* bootlicker (*Inf.*), sneak, sycophant, toady 6. **give one the creeps** *or* **make one's flesh creep** disgust, frighten, horrify, make one flinch (quail, shrink, squirm, wince), make one's hair stand on end (*Inf.*), repel, repulse, scare, terrify, terrorize

creeper climber, climbing plant,

rambler, runner, trailing plant, vine (*Chiefly U.S.*)

creepy awful, direful, disgusting, disturbing, eerie, frightening, ghoulish, goose-pimply (*Inf.*), gruesome, hair-raising, horrible, macabre, menacing, nightmarish, ominous, scary (*Inf.*), sinister, ter~ rifying, threatening, unpleasant, weird

crescent n. 1. half-moon, meniscus, new moon, old moon, sickle, sickle- shape ~adj. 2. bow-shaped, curved, falcate, semicircular, sickle- shaped 3. *Archaic* growing, in~ creasing, waxing

crest 1. apex, crown, head, height, highest point, peak, pinnacle, ridge, summit, top 2. aigrette, car~ uncle (*Zoology*), cockscomb, comb, crown, mane, panache, plume, tassel, topknot, tuft 3. *Heraldry* badge, bearings, charge, device, emblem, insignia, symbol

crestfallen chapfallen, dejected, depressed, despondent, disap~ pointed, disconsolate, discouraged, disheartened, downcast, down~ hearted

crevice chink, cleft, crack, cranny, fissure, fracture, gap, hole, inter~ stice, opening, rent, rift, slit, split

crew 1. hands, (ship's) company, (ship's) complement 2. company, corps, gang, party, posse, squad, team, working party 3. *Inf.* assem~ blage, band, bunch (*Inf.*), company, crowd, gang, herd, horde, lot, mob, pack, set, swarm, troop

crib n. 1. bassinet, bed, cot 2. bin, box, bunker, manger, rack, stall 3. *Inf.* key, translation, trot (*U.S. sl.*) ~v. 4. *Inf.* cheat, pass off as one's own work, pilfer, pirate, plagiarize, purloin, steal 5. box up, cage, con~ fine, coop, coop up, enclose, fence, imprison, limit, pen, rail, restrict, shut in

crime 1. atrocity, fault, felony, malfeasance, misdeed, misde~ meanour, offence, outrage, trans~ gression, trespass, unlawful act, violation, wrong 2. corruption, de~ linquency, guilt, illegality, iniquity, lawbreaking, malefaction, miscon~

duct, sin, unrighteousness, vice, villainy, wickedness, wrong, wrongdoing

criminal *n.* **1.** con (*Sl.*), convict, crook (*Inf.*), culprit, delinquent, evildoer, felon, jailbird, lawbreaker, malefactor, offender, sinner, transgressor ~*adj.* **2.** bent (*Sl.*), corrupt, crooked (*Inf.*), culpable, felonious, illegal, illicit, immoral, indictable, iniquitous, lawless, nefarious, peccant (*Rare*), unlawful, unrighteous, vicious, villainous, wicked, wrong **3.** *Inf.* deplorable, foolish, preposterous, ridiculous, scandalous, senseless

cringe **1.** blench, cower, dodge, draw back, duck, flinch, quail, quiver, recoil, shrink, shy, start, tremble, wince **2.** bend, bootlick (*Inf.*), bow, crawl, creep, crouch, fawn, grovel, kneel, kowtow, sneak, stoop, toady, truckle

cripple *v.* **1.** debilitate, disable, enfeeble, hamstring, incapacitate, lame, maim, mutilate, paralyse, weaken **2.** bring to a standstill, cramp, damage, destroy, halt, impair, put out of action, ruin, spoil, vitiate

crippled bedridden, deformed, disabled, enfeebled, handicapped, housebound, incapacitated, laid up (*Inf.*), lame, paralysed

crisis **1.** climacteric, climax, confrontation, critical point, crunch (*Inf.*), crux, culmination, height, moment of truth, point of no return, turning point **2.** catastrophe, critical situation, dilemma, dire straits, disaster, emergency, exigency, extremity, mess, plight, predicament, quandary, strait, trouble

crisp **1.** brittle, crispy, crumbly, crunchy, firm, fresh, unwilted **2.** bracing, brisk, fresh, invigorating, refreshing **3.** brief, brusque, clear, incisive, pithy, short, succinct, tart, terse **4.** clean-cut, neat, orderly, smart, snappy, spruce, tidy, trig (*Dialect*), well-groomed, well-pressed

criterion bench mark, canon, gauge, measure, norm, principle, proof, rule, standard, test, touchstone, yardstick

critic **1.** analyst, arbiter, authority, commentator, connoisseur, expert, expositor, judge, pundit, reviewer **2.** attacker, carper, caviller, censor, censurer, detractor, faultfinder, knocker (*Inf.*), Momus, reviler, vilifier

critical **1.** captious, carping, cavilling, censorious, derogatory, disapproving, disparaging, faultfinding, nagging, niggling, nitpicking (*Inf.*) **2.** accurate, analytical, diagnostic, discerning, discriminating, fastidious, judicious, penetrating, perceptive, precise **3.** all-important, crucial, dangerous, deciding, decisive, grave, hairy (*Sl.*), high-priority, momentous, perilous, pivotal, precarious, pressing, psychological, risky, serious, urgent, vital

criticism **1.** animadversion, bad press, brickbats (*Inf.*), censure, critical remarks, disapproval, disparagement, fault-finding, flak (*Inf.*), knocking (*Inf.*), panning (*Inf.*), slam (*Sl.*), slating (*Inf.*), stricture **2.** analysis, appraisal, appreciation, assessment, comment, commentary, critique, elucidation, evaluation, judgment, notice, review

criticize **1.** animadvert on *or* upon, carp, censure, condemn, disapprove of, disparage, excoriate, find fault with, give (someone *or* something) a bad press, knock (*Inf.*), nag at, pan (*Inf.*), pass strictures upon, pick to pieces, slam (*Sl.*), slate (*Inf.*) **2.** analyse, appraise, assess, comment upon, evaluate, give an opinion, judge, pass judgment on, review

critique analysis, appraisal, assessment, commentary, essay, examination, review

croak *v.* **1.** caw, gasp, grunt, squawk, utter *or* speak harshly (huskily, throatily), wheeze **2.** *Inf.* complain, groan, grouse, grumble, moan, murmur, mutter, repine **3.** *Sl.* die, expire, hop the twig (*Inf.*), kick the bucket (*Inf.*), pass away, perish

crook 1. *n. Inf.* cheat, criminal, knave (*Archaic*), racketeer, robber, rogue, shark, swindler, thief, villain 2. *v.* angle, bend, bow, curve, flex, hook

crooked 1. anfractuous, bent, bowed, crippled, curved, deformed, deviating, disfigured, distorted, hooked, irregular, meandering, misshapen, out of shape, tortuous, twisted, twisting, warped, winding, zigzag 2. angled, askew, asymmetric, at an angle, awry, lopsided, off-centre, slanted, slanting, squint, tilted, to one side, uneven, unsymmetrical 3. *Inf.* bent (*Sl.*), corrupt, crafty, criminal, deceitful, dishonest, dishonourable, dubious, fraudulent, illegal, knavish, nefarious, questionable, shady (*Inf.*), shifty, treacherous, underhand, unlawful, unprincipled, unscrupulous

croon breathe, hum, purr, sing, warble

crop *n.* 1. fruits, gathering, harvest, produce, reaping, season's growth, vintage, yield ~*v.* 2. clip, curtail, cut, lop, mow, pare, prune, reduce, shear, shorten, snip, top, trim 3. bring home, bring in, collect, garner, gather, harvest, mow, pick, reap 4. browse, graze, nibble

crop up appear, arise, emerge, happen, occur, spring up, turn up

cross *adj.* 1. angry, annoyed, cantankerous, captious, churlish, crotchety (*Inf.*), crusty, disagreeable, fractious, fretful, grouchy (*Inf.*), grumpy, ill-humoured, ill-tempered, impatient, in a bad mood, irascible, irritable, out of humour, peeved (*Inf.*), peevish, pettish, petulant, put out, querulous, shirty (*Sl.*), short, snappish, snappy, splenetic, sullen, surly, testy, vexed, waspish ~*v.* 2. bridge, cut across, extend over, ford, meet, pass over, ply, span, traverse, zigzag 3. crisscross, intersect, intertwine, lace, lie athwart of 4. blend, crossbreed, cross-fertilize, cross-pollinate, hybridize, interbreed,

intercross, mix, mongrelize 5. block, deny, foil, frustrate, hinder, impede, interfere, obstruct, oppose, resist, thwart ~*n.* 6. affliction, burden, grief, load, misery, misfortune, trial, tribulation, trouble, woe, worry 7. crucifix, rood 8. crossing, crossroads, intersection, junction 9. amalgam, blend, combination, crossbreed, cur, hybrid, hybridization, mixture, mongrel, mutt (*Sl.*) ~*adj.* 10. crosswise, intersecting, oblique, transverse 11. adverse, contrary, opposed, opposing, unfavourable 12. *Involving an interchange* opposite, reciprocal

cross-examine catechize, grill (*Inf.*), interrogate, pump, question, quiz

cross out *or* **off** blue-pencil, cancel, delete, eliminate, strike off *or* out

crotch crutch, groin

crotchety awkward, bad-tempered, cantankerous, contrary, crabby, cross, crusty, curmudgeonly, difficult, disagreeable, fractious, grumpy, irritable, obstreperous, peevish, surly, testy

crouch 1. bend down, bow, duck, hunch, kneel, squat, stoop 2. abase oneself, cower, cringe, fawn, grovel, truckle

crow bluster, boast, brag, exult, flourish, gloat, glory in, strut, swagger, triumph, vaunt

crowd *n.* 1. army, assembly, company, concourse, flock, herd, horde, host, mass, mob, multitude, pack, press, rabble, swarm, throng, troupe 2. bunch (*Inf.*), circle, clique, group, lot, set 3. attendance, audience, gate, house, spectators ~*v.* 4. cluster, congregate, cram, flock, forgather, gather, huddle, mass, muster, press, push, stream, surge, swarm, throng 5. bundle, congest, cram, pack, pile, squeeze 6. batter, butt, elbow, jostle, shove 7. **the crowd** hoi polloi, masses, mob, people, populace, proletariat, public, rabble, rank and file, riffraff, vulgar herd

crowded busy, congested,

cramped, crushed, full, huddled, jam-packed, mobbed, overflowing, packed, populous, swarming, teeming, thronged

crown n. 1. chaplet, circlet, coronal (*Poetic*), coronet, diadem, tiara 2. bays, distinction, garland, honour, kudos, laurels, laurel wreath, prize, trophy 3. emperor, empress, king, monarch, monarchy, queen, *rex*, royalty, ruler, sovereign, sovereignty 4. acme, apex, crest, head, perfection, pinnacle, summit, tip, top, ultimate, zenith ~v. 5. adorn, dignify, festoon, honour, invest, reward 6. be the climax *or* culmination of, cap, complete, consummate, finish, fulfil, perfect, put the finishing touch to, round off, surmount, terminate, top 7. *Sl.* biff (*Sl.*), box, cuff, hit over the head, punch

crucial 1. central, critical, decisive, pivotal, psychological, searching, testing, trying 2. *Inf.* essential, high-priority, important, momentous, pressing, urgent, vital

crucify 1. execute, harrow, persecute, rack, torment, torture 2. *Sl.* lampoon, pan (*Inf.*), ridicule, tear to pieces, wipe the floor with (*Inf.*)

crude 1. boorish, coarse, crass, dirty, gross, indecent, lewd, obscene, smutty, tactless, tasteless, uncouth, vulgar 2. natural, raw, unmilled, unpolished, unprepared, unprocessed, unrefined 3. clumsy, makeshift, outline, primitive, rough, rough-hewn, rude, rudimentary, sketchy, undeveloped, unfinished, unformed, unpolished

crudely bluntly, clumsily, coarsely, impolitely, indecently, pulling no punches (*Inf.*), roughly, rudely, sketchily, tastelessly, vulgarly

crudity 1. coarseness, crudeness, impropriety, indecency, indelicacy, lewdness, loudness, lowness, obscenity, obtrusiveness, smuttiness, vulgarity 2. clumsiness, crudeness, primitiveness, roughness, rudeness

cruel 1. atrocious, barbarous, bitter, bloodthirsty, brutal, brutish, callous, cold-blooded, depraved, excruciating, fell (*Archaic*), ferocious, fierce, flinty, grim, hard, hard-hearted, harsh, heartless, hellish, implacable, inclement, inexorable, inhuman, inhumane, malevolent, painful, poignant, ravening, raw, relentless, remorseless, sadistic, sanguinary, savage, severe, spiteful, stony-hearted, unfeeling, unkind, unnatural, vengeful, vicious 2. merciless, pitiless, ruthless, unrelenting

cruelly 1. barbarously, brutally, brutishly, callously, ferociously, fiercely, heartlessly, in cold blood, mercilessly, pitilessly, sadistically, savagely, spitefully, unmercifully, viciously 2. bitterly, deeply, fearfully, grievously, monstrously, mortally, severely

cruelty barbarity, bestiality, bloodthirstiness, brutality, brutishness, callousness, depravity, ferocity, fiendishness, hardheartedness, harshness, heartlessness, inhumanity, mercilessness, murderousness, ruthlessness, sadism, savagery, severity, spite, spitefulness, venom, viciousness

cruise v. 1. coast, sail, voyage 2. coast, drift, keep a steady pace, travel along ~n. 3. boat trip, sail, sea trip, voyage

crumb atom, bit, grain, mite, morsel, particle, scrap, shred, sliver, snippet, *soupçon*, speck

crumble 1. bruise, crumb, crush, fragment, granulate, grind, pound, powder, pulverize, triturate 2. break up, collapse, come to dust, decay, decompose, degenerate, deteriorate, disintegrate, fall apart, go to pieces (*Inf.*), go to wrack and ruin, moulder, perish, tumble down

crumple 1. crease, crush, pucker, rumple, screw up, wrinkle 2. break down, cave in, collapse, fall, give way, go to pieces

crunch 1. *v.* champ, chew noisily, chomp, grind, masticate, munch 2. *n. Inf.* crisis, critical point, crux, emergency, hour of decision, moment of truth, test

crusade campaign, cause, drive, holy war, jihad, movement, push

crusader advocate, campaigner, champion, reformer

crush v. 1. bray, break, bruise, comminute, compress, contuse, crease, crumble, crumple, crunch, mash, pound, pulverize, rumple, smash, squeeze, wrinkle 2. conquer, extinguish, overcome, overpower, overwhelm, put down, quell, stamp out, subdue, vanquish 3. abash, browbeat, chagrin, dispose of, humiliate, mortify, put down (Sl.), quash, shame 4. embrace, enfold, hug, press, squeeze ~n. 5. crowd, huddle, jam, party

crust caking, coat, coating, concretion, covering, film, incrustation, layer, outside, scab, shell, skin, surface

crusty 1. brittle, crisp, crispy, friable, hard, short, well-baked, welldone 2. brusque, cantankerous, captious, choleric, crabby, cross, curt, gruff, ill-humoured, irritable, peevish, prickly, short, shorttempered, snappish, snarling, splenetic, surly, testy, touchy

cry v. 1. bawl, bewail, blubber, boohoo, greet (Scot.), howl one's eyes out, keen, lament, mewl, pule, shed tears, snivel, sob, wail, weep, whimper, whine, whinge (Inf.), yowl ~n. 2. bawling, blubbering, crying, greet (Scot.), howl, keening, lament, lamentation, plaint (Archaic), snivel, snivelling, sob, sobbing, sorrowing, wailing, weep, weeping ~v. 3. bawl, bellow, call, call out, ejaculate, exclaim, hail, halloo, holler (Inf.), howl, roar, scream, screech, shout, shriek, sing out, vociferate, whoop, yell ~n. 4. bawl, bellow, call, ejaculation, exclamation, holler (Inf.), hoot, howl, outcry, roar, scream, screech, shriek, squawk, whoop, yell, yelp, yoo-hoo ~v. 5. advertise, announce, bark (Inf.), broadcast, bruit, hawk, noise, proclaim, promulgate, publish, trumpet ~n. 6. announcement, barking (Inf.), noising, proclamation, publication ~v. 7. beg, beseech, clamour, entreat, implore, plead, pray ~n. 8. appeal, entreaty, petition, plea, prayer, supplication

cry down belittle, decry, denigrate, disparage, run down

cry off back out, beg off, excuse oneself, quit, withdraw, withdraw from

crypt catacomb, tomb, undercroft, vault

cub 1. offspring, whelp, young 2. babe (Inf.), beginner, fledgling, greenhorn (Inf.), lad, learner, puppy, recruit, tenderfoot, trainee, whippersnapper, youngster

cuddle canoodle (Sl.), clasp, cosset, embrace, fondle, hug, nestle, pet, snuggle

cuddly buxom, cuddlesome, curvaceous, huggable, lovable, plump, soft, warm

cudgel 1. n. bastinado, baton, bludgeon, club, cosh, shillelagh, stick, truncheon 2. v. bang, baste, batter, beat, bludgeon, cane, cosh, drub, maul, pound, pummel, thrash, thump, thwack

cue catchword, hint, key, nod, prompting, reminder, sign, signal, suggestion

cuff off the cuff ad lib, extempore, impromptu, improvised, offhand, off the top of one's head, on the spur of the moment, spontaneous, spontaneously, unrehearsed

cul-de-sac blind alley, dead end

culminate climax, close, come to a climax, come to a head, conclude, end, end up, finish, rise to a crescendo, terminate, wind up (Inf.)

culmination acme, apex, apogee, climax, completion, conclusion, consummation, crown, crowning touch, finale, height, ne plus ultra, peak, perfection, pinnacle, punch line, summit, top, zenith

culpable answerable, at fault, blamable, blameworthy, censurable, found wanting, guilty, in the wrong, liable, reprehensible, sinful, to blame, wrong

culprit criminal, delinquent, evildoer, felon, guilty party, malefactor, miscreant, offender, person responsible, rascal, sinner, transgressor, wrongdoer

cult 1. body, church faction, clique, denomination, faith, following, party, religion, school, sect 2. admiration, craze, devotion, idolization, reverence, veneration, worship

cultivate 1. bring under cultivation, farm, fertilize, harvest, plant, plough, prepare, tend, till, work 2. ameliorate, better, bring on, cherish, civilize, develop, discipline, elevate, enrich, foster, improve, polish, promote, refine, train 3. aid, devote oneself to, encourage, forward, foster, further, help, patronize, promote, pursue, support 4. associate with, butter up, consort with, court, dance attendance upon, run after, seek out, seek someone's company *or* friendship, take trouble *or* pains with

cultivation 1. agronomy, farming, gardening, husbandry, planting, ploughing, tillage, tilling, working 2. breeding, civility, civilization, culture, discernment, discrimination, education, enlightenment, gentility, good taste, learning, letters, manners, polish, refinement, taste 3. advancement, advocacy, development, encouragement, enhancement, fostering, furtherance, help, nurture, patronage, promotion, support 4. devotion to, pursuit, study

cultural artistic, broadening, civilizing, developmental, edifying, educational, educative, elevating, enlightening, enriching, humane, humanizing, liberal, liberalizing

culture 1. civilization, customs, life style, mores, society, stage of development, the arts, way of life 2. accomplishment, breeding, education, elevation, enlightenment, erudition, gentility, good taste, improvement, polish, politeness, refinement, urbanity 3. agriculture, agronomy, cultivation, farming, husbandry

cultured accomplished, advanced, educated, enlightened, erudite, genteel, highbrow, knowledgeable, polished, refined, scholarly, urbane, versed, well-bred, well-informed, well-read

culvert channel, conduit, drain, gutter, watercourse

cumbersome awkward, bulky, burdensome, clumsy, cumbrous, embarrassing, heavy, hefty (*Inf.*), incommodious, inconvenient, oppressive, unmanageable, unwieldy, weighty

cumulative accruing, accumulative, aggregate, amassed, collective, heaped, increasing, snowballing

cunning *adj.* 1. artful, astute, canny, crafty, devious, foxy, guileful, knowing, Machiavellian, sharp, shifty, shrewd, subtle, tricky, wily ~*n.* 2. artfulness, astuteness, craftiness, deceitfulness, deviousness, foxiness, guile, shrewdness, slyness, trickery, wiliness ~*adj.* 3. adroit, deft, dexterous, imaginative, ingenious, skilful ~*n.* 4. ability, adroitness, art, artifice, cleverness, deftness, dexterity, finesse, ingenuity, skill, subtlety

cup beaker, cannikin, chalice, cupful, demitasse, draught, drink, goblet, potion, teacup, trophy

cupboard ambry (*Obsolete*), cabinet, closet, locker, press

curb 1. *v.* bite back, bridle, check, constrain, contain, control, hinder, impede, inhibit, moderate, muzzle, repress, restrain, restrict, retard, subdue, suppress 2. *n.* brake, bridle, check, control, deterrent, limitation, rein, restraint

curdle clot, coagulate, condense, congeal, curd, thicken, turn sour

cure *v.* 1. alleviate, correct, ease, heal, help, make better, mend, rehabilitate, relieve, remedy, restore, restore to health ~*n.* 2. alleviation, antidote, corrective, healing, medicine, panacea, recovery, remedy, restorative, specific, treatment ~*v.* 3. dry, kipper, pickle, preserve, salt, smoke

curiosity 1. inquisitiveness, interest, nosiness (*Inf.*), prying, snooping (*Inf.*) 2. celebrity, freak, marvel, novelty, oddity, phenomenon, rarity, sight, spectacle, wonder 3.

bibelot, bygone, curio, knickknack, *objet d'art,* trinket

curious 1. inquiring, inquisitive, interested, puzzled, questioning, searching 2. inquisitive, meddling, nosy (*Inf.*), peeping, peering, prying, snoopy (*Inf.*) 3. bizarre, exotic, extraordinary, marvellous, mysterious, novel, odd, peculiar, puzzling, quaint, queer, rare, singular, strange, unconventional, unexpected, unique, unorthodox, unusual, wonderful

curl 1. *v.* bend, coil, convolute, corkscrew, crimp, crinkle, crisp, curve, entwine, frizz, loop, meander, ripple, spiral, turn, twine, twirl, twist, wind, wreathe, writhe 2. *n.* coil, curlicue, kink, ringlet, spiral, twist, whorl

curly corkscrew, crimped, crimpy, crinkly, crisp, curled, curling, frizzy, fuzzy, kinky, permed, spiralled, waved, wavy, winding

currency 1. bills, coinage, coins, medium of exchange, money, notes 2. acceptance, circulation, exposure, popularity, prevalence, publicity, transmission, vogue

current *adj.* 1. accepted, circulating, common, common knowledge, customary, general, going around, in circulation, in progress, in the air, in the news, ongoing, popular, present, prevailing, prevalent, rife, widespread 2. contemporary, fashionable, in, in fashion, in vogue, now (*Inf.*), present-day, trendy (*Inf.*), up-to-date, up-to-the-minute ~*n.* 3. course, draught, flow, jet, progression, river, stream, tide 4. atmosphere, drift, feeling, inclination, mood, tendency, trend, undercurrent

curse *n.* 1. blasphemy, expletive, oath, obscenity, swearing, swearword 2. anathema, ban, denunciation, evil eye, excommunication, execration, imprecation, jinx, malediction, malison (*Archaic*) 3. affliction, bane, burden, calamity, cross, disaster, evil, misfortune, ordeal, plague, scourge, torment, tribulation, trouble, vexation ~*v.* 4. be foul-mouthed, blaspheme, cuss

(*Inf.*), swear, take the Lord's name in vain, turn the air blue (*Inf.*), use bad language 5. accurse, anathematize, damn, excommunicate, execrate, fulminate, imprecate 6. afflict, blight, burden, destroy, doom, plague, scourge, torment, trouble, vex

cursed 1. accursed, bedevilled, blighted, cast out, confounded, damned, doomed, excommunicate, execrable, fey (*Scot.*), foredoomed, ill-fated, star-crossed, unholy, unsanctified, villainous 2. abominable, damnable, detestable, devilish, fell (*Archaic*), fiendish, hateful, infamous, infernal, loathsome, odious, pernicious, pestilential, vile

curt abrupt, blunt, brief, brusque, concise, gruff, offhand, pithy, rude, sharp, short, snappish, succinct, summary, tart, terse, unceremonious, uncivil, ungracious

curtail abbreviate, abridge, contract, cut, cut back, cut short, decrease, dock, lessen, lop, pare down, reduce, retrench, shorten, trim, truncate

curtailment abbreviation, abridgment, contraction, cutback, cutting, cutting short, docking, retrenchment, truncation

curtain 1. *n.* drape (*Chiefly U.S.*), hanging 2. *v.* conceal, drape, hide, screen, shroud, shut off, shutter, veil

curve 1. *v.* arc, arch, bend, bow, coil, hook, inflect, spiral, swerve, turn, twist, wind 2. *n.* arc, bend, camber, curvature, half-moon, loop, trajectory, turn

curved arced, arched, bent, bowed, crooked, humped, rounded, serpentine, sinuous, sweeping, turned, twisted

cushion 1. *n.* beanbag, bolster, hassock, headrest, pad, pillow, scatter cushion, squab 2. *v.* bolster, buttress, cradle, dampen, deaden, muffle, pillow, protect, soften, stifle, support, suppress

custody 1. aegis, auspices, care, charge, custodianship, guardianship, keeping, observation, preservation, protection, safekeeping, supervision, trusteeship, tutelage, ward, watch 2. arrest, confine~ment, detention, durance (*Archa~ic*), duress, imprisonment, incar~ceration

custom 1. habit, habitude (*Rare*), manner, mode, procedure, routine, way, wont 2. convention, etiquette, fashion, form, formality, matter of course, observance, observation, policy, practice, praxis, ritual, rule, style, unwritten law, usage, use 3. customers, patronage, trade

customarily as a rule, commonly, generally, habitually, in the ordi~nary way, normally, ordinarily, regularly, traditionally, usually

customary accepted, accustomed, acknowledged, common, con~firmed, conventional, established, everyday, familiar, fashionable, general, habitual, normal, ordi~nary, popular, regular, routine, traditional, usual, wonted

customer buyer, client, consumer, habitué, patron, prospect, pur~chaser, regular (*Inf.*), shopper

customs duty, import charges, tariff, taxes, toll

cut *v.* 1. chop, cleave, divide, gash, incise, lacerate, nick, notch, pen~etrate, pierce, score, sever, slash, slice, slit, wound 2. carve, chip, chisel, chop, engrave, fashion, form, saw, sculpt, sculpture, shape, whittle 3. clip, dock, fell, gather, hack, harvest, hew, lop, mow, pare, prune, reap, saw down, shave, trim 4. contract, cut back, decrease, ease up on, lower, rationalize, re~duce, slash, slim (down) 5. abbre~viate, abridge, condense, curtail, delete, edit out, excise, precis, shorten 6. *Often with* **through, off,** *or* **across** bisect, carve, cleave, cross, dissect, divide, interrupt, intersect, part, segment, sever, slice, split, sunder 7. avoid, cold-shoulder, freeze (someone) out (*Inf.*, *chiefly U.S.*), grieve, hurt, ig~nore, insult, look straight through (someone), pain, send to Coventry, slight, snub, spurn, sting, turn one's back on, wound ~*n.* 8. gash, graze,

groove, incision, laceration, nick, rent, rip, slash, slit, stroke, wound 9. cutback, decrease, decrement, diminution, economy, fall, lower~ing, reduction, saving 10. *Inf.* chop (*Sl.*), division, kickback (*Chiefly U.S.*), percentage, piece, portion, rake-off (*Sl.*), section, share, slice 11. configuration, fashion, form, look, mode, shape, style

cutback cut, decrease, economy, lessening, reduction, retrenchment

cut down 1. fell, hew, level, lop, raze 2. *Sometimes with* **on** de~crease, lessen, lower, reduce

cut in break in, butt in, interpose, interrupt, intervene, intrude, move in

cut off 1. disconnect, intercept, in~terrupt, intersect 2. bring to an end, discontinue, halt, obstruct, suspend 3. isolate, separate, sever 4. disinherit, disown, renounce

cut out cease, delete, extract, give up, refrain from, remove, sever, stop

cut-price bargain, cheap, cut-rate (*Chiefly U.S.*), reduced, sale

cut short abort, break off, bring to an end, check, halt, interrupt, leave unfinished, postpone, stop, terminate

cutting *adj.* 1. biting, bitter, chill, keen, numbing, penetrating, pierc~ing, raw, sharp, stinging 2. acid, acrimonious, barbed, bitter, caus~tic, hurtful, malicious, pointed, sarcastic, sardonic, scathing, se~vere, trenchant, wounding

cut up 1. carve, chop, dice, divide, mince, slice 2. injure, knife, lacer~ate, slash, wound

cycle aeon, age, circle, era, period, phase, revolution, rotation, round (*of years*)

cynic doubter, misanthrope, mis~anthropist, pessimist, sceptic, scoffer

cynical contemptuous, derisive, distrustful, ironic, misanthropic, misanthropical, mocking, pessi~mistic, sarcastic, sardonic, scepti~cal, scoffing, scornful, sneering, unbelieving

D

dabble 1. dip, guddle (*Scot.*), moisten, paddle, spatter, splash, sprinkle, wet 2. dally, dip into, play at, potter, tinker, trifle (with)

dabbler amateur, dilettante, potterer, tinkerer, trifler

dab hand ace (*Inf.*), adept, dabster (*Dialect*), expert, past master, wizard

dagger 1. bayonet, dirk, poniard, skean, stiletto 2. **at daggers drawn** at enmity, at loggerheads, at odds, at war, on bad terms, up in arms 3. **look daggers** frown, glare, glower, look black, scowl

daily *adj.* 1. circadian, diurnal, everyday, quotidian 2. common, commonplace, day-to-day, everyday, ordinary, quotidian, regular, routine ~*adv.* 3. constantly, day after day, day by day, every day, often, once a day, per diem, regularly

dainty *adj.* 1. charming, delicate, elegant, exquisite, fine, graceful, neat, petite, pretty 2. choice, delectable, delicious, palatable, savoury, tasty, tender, toothsome 3. choosy, fastidious, finical, finicky, fussy, mincing, nice, particular, refined, scrupulous ~*n.* 4. *bonne bouche*, delicacy, fancy, sweetmeat, titbit

dale bottom, coomb, dell, dingle, glen, strath (*Scot.*), vale, valley

dam 1. *n.* barrage, barrier, embankment, hindrance, obstruction, wall 2. *v.* barricade, block, block up, check, choke, confine, hold back, hold in, obstruct, restrict

damage *n.* 1. destruction, detriment, devastation, harm, hurt, impairment, injury, loss, mischief, mutilation, suffering 2. *Inf.* bill, charge, cost, expense, total 3. *Plural* compensation, fine, indemnity, reimbursement, reparation, satisfaction ~*v.* 4. deface, harm, hurt, impair, incapacitate, injure, mar,

mutilate, ruin, spoil, tamper with, weaken, wreck

damaging deleterious, detrimental, disadvantageous, harmful, hurtful, injurious, prejudicial, ruinous

dame baroness, dowager, *grande dame*, lady, matron (*Archaic*), noblewoman, peeress

damn *v.* 1. blast, castigate, censure, condemn, criticize, denounce, denunciate, excoriate, inveigle against, pan (*Inf.*), slam (*Sl.*), slate (*Inf.*) 2. abuse, anathematize, blaspheme, curse, execrate, imprecate, revile, swear 3. condemn, doom, sentence ~*n.* 4. brass farthing, hoot, iota, jot, tinker's damn (*Sl.*), two hoots, whit 5. **not give a damn** be indifferent, not care, not mind

damnable abominable, accursed, atrocious, culpable, cursed, despicable, detestable, execrable, hateful, horrible, offensive, wicked

damnation anathema, ban, condemnation, consigning to perdition, damning, denunciation, doom, excommunication, objurgation, proscription, sending to hell

damned 1. accursed, anathematized, condemned, doomed, infernal, lost, reprobate, unhappy 2. *Sl.* confounded, despicable, detestable, hateful, infamous, infernal, loathsome, revolting

damning accusatorial, condemnatory, damnatory, dooming, implicating, implicative, incriminating

damp *n.* 1. clamminess, dampness, darkness, dew, drizzle, fog, humidity, mist, moisture, muzziness, vapour ~*adj.* 2. clammy, dank, dewy, dripping, drizzly, humid, misty, moist, muggy, sodden, soggy, sopping, vaporous, wet ~*v.* 3. dampen, moisten, wet 4. *Fig.* allay, check, chill, cool, curb, dash, deaden, deject, depress, diminish, discourage, dispirit, dull, inhibit, moderate, restrain, stifle ~*n.* 5. *Fig.* check, chill, cold water, curb, damper, discour~ agement, gloom, restraint, wet blanket

damper chill, cloud, cold water, curb, discouragement, gloom, hin~ drance, kill-joy, pall, restraint, wet blanket

dance 1. *v.* bob up and down, caper, frolic, gambol, hop, jig, prance, rock, skip, spin, sway, swing, whirl 2. *n.* ball, dancing party, hop (*Inf.*), social

danger endangerment, hazard, in~ security, jeopardy, menace, peril, precariousness, risk, threat, ven~ ture, vulnerability

dangerous alarming, breakneck, chancy (*Inf.*), exposed, hairy (*Sl.*), hazardous, insecure, menacing, nasty, parlous (*Archaic*), perilous, precarious, risky, threatening, treacherous, ugly, unchancy (*Scot.*), unsafe, vulnerable

dangerously 1. alarmingly, care~ lessly, daringly, desperately, harmfully, hazardously, perilously, precariously, recklessly, riskily, unsafely, unsecurely 2. critically, gravely, seriously, severely

dangle *v.* 1. depend, flap, hang, hang down, sway, swing, trail 2. brandish, entice, flaunt, flourish, lure, tantalize, tempt, wave

dapper active, brisk, chic, dainty, natty (*Inf.*), neat, nice, nimble, smart, spruce, spry, stylish, trig (*Archaic*), trim, well-groomed, well turned out

dappled brindled, checkered, flecked, freckled, mottled, piebald, pied, speckled, spotted, stippled, variegated

dare *v.* 1. challenge, defy, goad, provoke, taunt, throw down the gauntlet 2. adventure, brave, en~ danger, gamble, hazard, make bold, presume, risk, stake, venture ~*n.* 3. challenge, defiance, provo~ cation, taunt

daredevil 1. *n.* adventurer, despe~ rado, exhibitionist, madcap, show~ off (*Inf.*), stunt man 2. *adj.* adven~ turous, audacious, bold, daring, death-defying, madcap, reckless

daring 1. *adj.* adventurous, auda~ cious, bold, brave, fearless, game (*Inf.*), impulsive, intrepid, plucky, rash, reckless, valiant, venture~ some 2. *n.* audacity, boldness, bot~ tle (*Sl.*), bravery, courage, derring~ do (*Archaic*), fearlessness, grit, guts (*Inf.*), intrepidity, nerve (*Inf.*), pluck, rashness, spirit, spunk (*Inf.*), temerity

dark *adj.* 1. black, brunette, dark~ skinned, dusky, ebony, sable, swarthy 2. cloudy, darksome (*Lit~ erary*), dim, dingy, indistinct, murky, overcast, pitch-black, pitchy, shadowy, shady, sunless, unlit 3. abstruse, arcane, con~ cealed, cryptic, deep, enigmatic, hidden, mysterious, mystic, ob~ scure, occult, puzzling, recondite, secret 4. bleak, cheerless, dismal, doleful, drab, gloomy, grim, joy~ less, morbid, morose, mournful, sombre 5. benighted, ignorant, un~ cultivated, unenlightened, unlet~ tered 6. atrocious, damnable, evil, foul, hellish, horrible, infamous, infernal, nefarious, satanic, sinful, sinister, vile, wicked 7. angry, dour, forbidding, frowning, glow~ ering, glum, ominous, scowling, sulky, sullen, threatening ~*n.* 8. darkness, dimness, dusk, gloom, murk, murkiness, obscurity, semi~ darkness 9. evening, night, night~ fall, night-time, twilight 10. *Fig.* concealment, ignorance, secrecy

darken 1. becloud, blacken, cloud up *or* over, deepen, dim, eclipse, make dark, make darker, make dim, obscure, overshadow, shade, shadow 2. become angry, become gloomy, blacken, cast a pall over, cloud, deject, depress, dispirit, grow troubled, look black, sadden

darkness 1. blackness, dark, dim~ ness, dusk, duskiness, gloom, murk, murkiness, nightfall, obscurity, shade, shadiness, shadows 2. *Fig.* blindness, concealment, ignorance, mystery, privacy, secrecy, un~ awareness

darling *n.* 1. beloved, dear, dearest, love, sweetheart, truelove 2. apple of one's eye, blue-eyed boy, fair~

haired boy (*U.S.*), favourite, pet, spoiled child ~*adj.* 3. adored, beloved, cherished, dear, precious, treasured 4. adorable, attractive, captivating, charming, enchanting, lovely, sweet

darn 1. *v.* cobble up, mend, patch, repair, sew up, stitch 2. *n.* invisible repair, mend, patch, reinforcement

dart 1. bound, dash, flash, flit, fly, race, run, rush, scoot, shoot, spring, sprint, start, tear, whistle (*Inf.*), whiz 2. cast, fling, hurl, launch, propel, send, shoot, sling, throw

dash *v.* 1. break, crash, destroy, shatter, shiver, smash, splinter 2. cast, fling, hurl, slam, sling, throw 3. bolt, bound, dart, fly, haste, hasten, hurry, race, run, rush, speed, spring, sprint, tear 4. abash, chagrin, confound, dampen, disappoint, discomfort, discourage 5. blight, foil, frustrate, ruin, spoil, thwart ~*n.* 6. bolt, dart, haste, onset, race, run, rush, sortie, sprint, spurt 7. brio, élan, flair, flourish, panache, spirit, style, verve, vigour, vivacity 8. bit, drop, flavour, hint, little, pinch, smack, *soupçon*, sprinkling, suggestion, tinge, touch

dashing 1. bold, daring, debonair, exuberant, gallant, lively, plucky, spirited, swashbuckling 2. dapper, dazzling, elegant, flamboyant, jaunty, showy, smart, sporty, stylish, swish (*Inf.*)

data details, documents, facts, figures, information, input, materials, statistics

date *n.* 1. age, epoch, era, period, stage, time 2. appointment, assignation, engagement, meeting, rendezvous, tryst 3. escort, friend, partner, steady (*Inf.*) 4. **out of date** antiquated, archaic, dated, obsolete, old, old-fashioned, passé 5. **to date** now, so far, up to now, up to the present, up to this point, yet 6. **up-to-date** à la mode, contemporary, current, fashionable, modern, trendy (*Inf.*), up-to-the-minute ~*v.* 7. assign a date to, determine the date of, fix the period of, put a date on 8. bear a date, belong to, come

from, exist from, originate in 9. become obsolete, be dated, obsolesce, show one's age

dated antiquated, archaic, *démodé*, obsolete, old-fashioned, old hat, out, outdated, outmoded, out of date, passé, unfashionable

daub *v.* 1. coat, cover, paint, plaster, slap on (*Inf.*), smear 2. bedaub, begrime, besmear, blur, deface, dirty, grime, smirch, smudge, spatter, splatter, stain, sully ~*n.* 3. blot, blotch, smear, splodge, splotch, spot, stain

daunt 1. alarm, appal, cow, dismay, frighten, frighten off, intimidate, overawe, scare, subdue, terrify 2. deter, discourage, dishearten, dispirit, put off, shake

daunted *adj.* alarmed, cowed, demoralized, deterred, discouraged, disillusioned, dismayed, dispirited, downcast, frightened, hesitant, intimidated, overcome, put off, unnerved

dauntless bold, brave, courageous, daring, doughty, fearless, gallant, heroic, indomitable, intrepid, lionhearted, resolute, stouthearted, undaunted, unflinching, valiant, valorous

dawdle dally, delay, dilly-dally (*Inf.*), fritter away, hang about, idle, lag, loaf, loiter, potter, trail, waste time

dawn *n.* 1. aurora (*Literary*), cockcrow, crack of dawn, dawning, daybreak, daylight, dayspring (*Poetic*), morning, sunrise, sunup ~*v.* 2. break, brighten, gleam, glimmer, grow light, lighten ~*n.* 3. advent, beginning, birth, dawning, emergence, genesis, inception, onset, origin, outset, rise, start, unfolding ~*v.* 4. appear, begin, develop, emerge, initiate, open, originate, rise, unfold 5. come into one's head, come to mind, cross one's mind, flash across one's mind, hit, occur, register (*Inf.*), strike

day 1. daylight, daylight hours, daytime, twenty-four hours, working day 2. age, ascendancy, cycle, epoch, era, generation, height,

heyday, period, prime, time, zenith
3. date, particular day, point in
time, set time, time 4. **call it a day**
Inf. end, finish, knock off (*Inf.*),
leave off, pack it in (*Sl.*), pack up
(*Inf.*), shut up shop, stop 5. **day
after day** continually, monoto~
nously, persistently, regularly, re~
lentlessly 6. **day by day** daily,
gradually, progressively, steadily

daybreak break of day, cockcrow,
crack of dawn, dawn, dayspring
(*Poetic*), first light, morning, sun~
rise, sunup

daydream n. 1. dream, imagining,
musing, reverie, stargazing, vision,
woolgathering 2. castle in the air
or in Spain, dream, fancy, fantasy,
figment of the imagination, fond
hope, pipe dream, wish ~v. 3.
dream, envision, fancy, fantasize,
hallucinate, imagine, muse, star~
gaze

daydreamer castle-builder,
dreamer, fantast, pipe dreamer,
visionary, Walter Mitty, wishful
thinker, woolgatherer

daylight 1. light of day, sunlight,
sunshine 2. broad day, daylight
hours, daytime 3. full view, light of
day, openness, public attention

daze v. 1. benumb, numb, paralyse,
shock, stun, stupefy 2. amaze,
astonish, astound, befog, bewilder,
blind, confuse, dazzle, dumbfound,
flabbergast (*Inf.*), perplex, stagger,
startle, surprise ~n. 3. bewilder~
ment, confusion, distraction, shock,
stupor, trance, trancelike state

dazed baffled, bemused, bewil~
dered, confused, disorientated, diz~
zy, dopey (*Sl.*), flabbergasted (*Inf.*),
fuddled, groggy (*Inf.*), light-headed,
muddled, nonplussed, numbed,
perplexed, punch-drunk, shocked,
staggered, stunned, stupefied,
woozy (*Inf.*)

dazzle v. 1. bedazzle, blind, blur,
confuse, daze 2. amaze, astonish,
awe, bowl over (*Inf.*), fascinate,
hypnotize, impress, overawe,
overpower, overwhelm, strike
dumb, stupefy ~n. 3. brilliance,
flash, glitter, magnificence, razzle-

dazzle (*Sl.*), razzmatazz (*Sl.*), spar~
kle, splendour

dazzling brilliant, glittering, glori~
ous, radiant, ravishing, scintillat~
ing, sensational, shining, sparkling,
splendid, stunning, sublime, su~
perb, virtuoso

dead adj. 1. deceased, defunct, de~
parted, extinct, gone, inanimate,
late, lifeless, passed away, per~
ished 2. apathetic, callous, cold,
dull, frigid, glassy, glazed, indiffer~
ent, inert, lukewarm, numb, para~
lysed, spiritless, torpid, unrespon~
sive, wooden 3. barren, inactive,
inoperative, not working, obsolete,
stagnant, sterile, still, unemployed,
unprofitable, useless 4. boring,
dead-and-alive, dull, flat, insipid,
stale, tasteless, uninteresting, vap~
id 5. *Fig.* absolute, complete,
downright, entire, outright, thor~
ough, total, unqualified, utter 6. *Inf.*
dead beat (*Inf.*), exhausted, spent,
tired, worn out ~n. 7. depth, mid~
dle, midst ~adv. 8. absolutely,
completely, directly, entirely, ex~
actly, totally

deaden abate, alleviate, anaesthe~
tize, benumb, blunt, check, cush~
ion, damp, dampen, diminish, dull,
hush, impair, lessen, muffle, mute,
numb, paralyse, quieten, reduce,
smother, stifle, suppress, weaken

deadlock cessation, dead heat,
draw, full stop, halt, impasse,
stalemate, standoff, standstill, tie

deadly 1. baleful, baneful, danger~
ous, death-dealing, deathly, de~
structive, fatal, lethal, malignant,
mortal, noxious, pernicious, poi~
sonous, venomous 2. cruel, grim,
implacable, mortal, ruthless, sav~
age, unrelenting 3. ashen, death~
like, deathly, ghastly, ghostly, pal~
lid, wan, white 4. accurate, effec~
tive, exact, on target, precise, sure,
true, unerring, unfailing 5. *Inf.*
boring, dull, monotonous, tedious,
uninteresting, wearisome

deaf adj. 1. hard of hearing, stone
deaf, without hearing 2. indiffer~
ent, oblivious, unconcerned, un~
hearing, unmoved

deafen din, drown out, make deaf, split *or* burst the eardrums

deafening booming, dinning, ear-piercing, ear-splitting, intense, overpowering, piercing, resounding, ringing, thunderous

deal v. 1. *With with* attend to, cope with, handle, manage, oversee, see to, take care of, treat 2. *With with* concern, consider, treat (of) 3. *With with* act, behave, conduct oneself 4. bargain, buy and sell, do business, negotiate, sell, stock, trade, traffic, treat (with) ~n. 5. *Inf.* agreement, arrangement, bargain, buy (*Inf.*), contract, pact, transaction, understanding ~v. 6. allot, apportion, assign, bestow, dispense, distribute, divide, dole out, give, mete out, reward, share ~n. 7. amount, degree, distribution, extent, portion, quantity, share, transaction 8. cut and shuffle, distribution, hand, round, single game

dealer chandler, marketer, merchandiser, merchant, trader, tradesman, wholesaler

dealings business, business relations, commerce, trade, traffic, transactions, truck

dear adj. 1. beloved, cherished, close, darling, esteemed, familiar, favourite, intimate, precious, prized, respected, treasured 2. at a premium, costly, expensive, high-priced, overpriced, pricey (*Inf.*) ~n. 3. angel, beloved, darling, loved one, precious, treasure ~adv. 4. at a heavy cost, at a high price, at great cost, dearly

dearly 1. extremely, greatly, profoundly, very much 2. affectionately, devotedly, fondly, lovingly, tenderly 3. at a heavy price, at a high price, at great cost, dear

death 1. bereavement, cessation, curtains (*Inf.*), decease, demise, departure, dissolution, dying, end, exit, expiration, loss, passing, quietus, release 2. annihilation, destruction, downfall, eradication, extermination, extinction, finish, grave, obliteration, ruin, ruination, undoing

deathless eternal, everlasting, immortal, imperishable, incorruptible, timeless, undying

deathly 1. cadaverous, deathlike, gaunt, ghastly, grim, haggard, pale, pallid, wan 2. deadly, extreme, fatal, intense, mortal, terrible

debacle catastrophe, collapse, defeat, devastation, disaster, downfall, fiasco, havoc, overthrow, reversal, rout, ruin, ruination

debase 1. abase, cheapen, degrade, demean, devalue, disgrace, dishonour, drag down, humble, humiliate, lower, reduce, shame 2. adulterate, bastardize, contaminate, corrupt, defile, depreciate, impair, pollute, taint, vitiate

debased 1. adulterated, depreciated, devalued, impure, lowered, mixed, polluted, reduced 2. abandoned, base, corrupt, debauched, degraded, depraved, fallen, low, perverted, sordid, vile

debasement 1. adulteration, contamination, depreciation, devaluation, pollution, reduction 2. abasement, baseness, corruption, degradation, depravation, perversion

debatable arguable, borderline, controversial, disputable, doubtful, dubious, in dispute, moot, open to question, problematical, questionable, uncertain, undecided, unsettled

debate v. 1. argue, contend, contest, controvert, discuss, dispute, question, wrangle ~n. 2. altercation, argument, contention, controversy, discussion, disputation, dispute, polemic ~v. 3. cogitate, consider, deliberate, meditate upon, mull over, ponder, reflect, revolve, ruminate, weigh ~n. 4. cogitation, consideration, deliberation, meditation, reflection

debilitate devitalize, enervate, enfeeble, exhaust, incapacitate, prostrate, relax, sap, undermine, weaken, wear out

debility decrepitude, enervation, enfeeblement, exhaustion, faintness, feebleness, frailty, incapacity, infirmity, languor, malaise, sickliness, weakness

debonair affable, buoyant, charming, cheerful, courteous, dashing, elegant, jaunty, light-hearted, re~ fined, smooth (*Inf.*), sprightly, suave, urbane, well-bred

debris bits, brash, detritus, dross, fragments, litter, pieces, remains, rubbish, rubble, ruins, waste, wreck, wreckage

debt 1. arrears, bill, claim, com~ mitment, debit, due, duty, liability, obligation, score 2. **in debt** ac~ countable, beholden, in arrears, in hock (*Inf., chiefly U.S.*), in the red (*Inf.*), liable, owing, responsible

debtor borrower, defaulter, insol~ vent, mortgagor

debunk cut down to size, deflate, disparage, expose, lampoon, mock, puncture, ridicule, show up

debut beginning, bow, coming out, entrance, first appearance, in~ auguration, initiation, introduction, launching, presentation

decadence corruption, debase~ ment, decay, decline, degenera~ tion, deterioration, dissipation, dis~ solution, fall, perversion, retro~ gression

decadent corrupt, debased, de~ bauched, decaying, declining, de~ generate, degraded, depraved, dis~ solute, immoral, self-indulgent

decapitate behead, execute, guil~ lotine

decay *v.* 1. atrophy, crumble, de~ cline, degenerate, deteriorate, dis~ integrate, dissolve, dwindle, moulder, shrivel, sink, spoil, wane, waste away, wear away, wither 2. corrode, decompose, mortify, per~ ish, putrefy, rot ~*n.* 3. atrophy, collapse, decadence, decline, de~ generacy, degeneration, deterio~ ration, dying, fading, failing, wast~ ing, withering 4. caries, cariosity, decomposition, gangrene, mortifi~ cation, perishing, putrefaction, pu~ trescence, putridity, rot, rotting

decayed bad, carious, carrion, corroded, decomposed, perished, putrefied, putrid, rank, rotten, spoiled, wasted, withered

decaying crumbling, deteriorating, disintegrating, gangrenous, per~

ishing, putrefacient, rotting, wast~ ing away, wearing away

decease 1. *n.* death, demise, de~ parture, dissolution, dying, release 2. *v.* cease, die, expire, pass away *or* on *or* over, perish

deceased *adj.* dead, defunct, de~ parted, expired, finished, former, gone, late, lifeless, lost

deceit 1. artifice, cheating, chican~ ery, craftiness, cunning, deceitful~ ness, deception, dissimulation, double-dealing, duplicity, fraud, fraudulence, guile, hypocrisy, im~ position, pretence, slyness, treach~ ery, trickery, underhandedness 2. artifice, blind, cheat, chicanery, deception, duplicity, fake, feint, fraud, imposture, misrepresenta~ tion, pretence, ruse, sham, shift, stratagem, subterfuge, swindle, trick, wile

deceitful counterfeit, crafty, de~ ceiving, deceptive, designing, dis~ honest, disingenuous, double-dealing, duplicitous, fallacious, false, fraudulent, guileful, hypo~ critical, illusory, insincere, knavish (*Archaic*), sneaky, treacherous, tricky, two-faced, underhand, un~ trustworthy

deceive 1. bamboozle (*Inf.*), be~ guile, betray, cheat, con (*Sl.*), co~ zen, delude, disappoint, double-cross (*Inf.*), dupe, ensnare, entrap, fool, hoax, hoodwink, impose upon, lead (someone) on (*Inf.*), mislead, outwit, pull a fast one (*Sl.*), pull the wool over (someone's) eyes, swin~ dle, take for a ride (*Inf.*), take in (*Inf.*), trick 2. **be deceived by** be made a fool of, be taken in (by), be the dupe of, bite, fall for, fall into a trap, swallow, swallow hook, line, and sinker (*Inf.*), take the bait

decency appropriateness, civility, correctness, courtesy, decorum, etiquette, fitness, good form, good manners, modesty, propriety, re~ spectability, seemliness

decent 1. appropriate, becoming, befitting, chaste, comely, *comme il faut*, decorous, delicate, fit, fitting, modest, nice, polite, presentable, proper, pure, respectable, seemly, suitable 2. acceptable, adequate, ample, average, competent, fair, passable, reasonable, satisfactory, sufficient, tolerable 3. accommo~ dating, courteous, friendly, gener~ ous, gracious, helpful, kind, oblig~ ing, thoughtful

deception 1. craftiness, cunning, deceit, deceitfulness, deceptive~ ness, dissimulation, duplicity, fraud, fraudulence, guile, hypocri~ sy, imposition, insincerity, leger~ demain, treachery, trickery 2. ar~ tifice, bluff, cheat, decoy, feint, fraud, hoax, illusion, imposture, leg-pull (*Brit. inf.*), lie, ruse, sham, snare, stratagem, subterfuge, trick, wile

deceptive ambiguous, deceitful, delusive, dishonest, fake, falla~ cious, false, fraudulent, illusory, misleading, mock, specious, spuri~ ous, unreliable

decide adjudge, adjudicate, choose, come to a conclusion, commit oneself, conclude, decree, deter~ mine, elect, end, make a decision, make up one's mind, purpose, reach *or* come to a decision, re~ solve, settle

decided 1. absolute, categorical, certain, clear-cut, definite, distinct, express, indisputable, positive, pronounced, unambiguous, unde~ niable, undisputed, unequivocal, unquestionable 2. assertive, deci~ sive, deliberate, determined, em~ phatic, firm, resolute, strong-willed, unfaltering, unhesitating

decidedly absolutely, certainly, clearly, decisively, distinctly, downright, positively, unequivo~ cally, unmistakably

deciding chief, conclusive, critical, crucial, decisive, determining, in~ fluential, prime, principal, signifi~ cant

decipher construe, crack, decode, deduce, explain, figure out (*Inf.*), interpret, make out, read, reveal, solve, understand, unfold, unravel

decision 1. arbitration, conclusion, finding, judgment, outcome, reso~ lution, result, ruling, sentence, set~ tlement, verdict 2. decisiveness,

determination, firmness, purpose, purposefulness, resoluteness, reso~ lution, resolve, strength of mind *or* will

decisive 1. absolute, conclusive, critical, crucial, definite, definitive, fateful, final, influential, momen~ tous, positive, significant 2. decid~ ed, determined, firm, forceful, in~ cisive, resolute, strong-minded, trenchant

deck *v.* 1. adorn, apparel (*Archaic*), array, attire, beautify, bedeck, be~ dight (*Archaic*), bedizen (*Archaic*), clothe, decorate, dress, embellish, festoon, garland, grace, ornament, trim 2. **deck up** *or* **out** doll up (*Sl.*), prettify, pretty up, prink, rig out, tog up *or* out, trick out

declaim 1. harangue, hold forth, lecture, orate, perorate, proclaim, rant, recite, speak, spiel (*Inf.*) 2. **declaim against** attack, decry, de~ nounce, inveigh, rail

declamation address, harangue, lecture, oration, rant, recitation, speech, tirade

declaration 1. acknowledgment, affirmation, assertion, attestation, averment, avowal, deposition, dis~ closure, protestation, revelation, statement, testimony 2. announce~ ment, edict, manifesto, notifica~ tion, proclamation, profession, promulgation, pronouncement, pronunciamento

declarative, declaratory af~ firmative, definite, demonstrative, enunciatory, explanatory, exposi~ tory, expressive, positive

declare 1. affirm, announce, assert, attest, aver, avow, certify, claim, confirm, maintain, proclaim, pro~ fess, pronounce, state, swear, tes~ tify, validate 2. confess, convey, disclose, make known, manifest, reveal, show

decline *v.* 1. avoid, deny, forgo, refuse, reject, say 'no', send one's regrets, turn down 2. decrease, di~ minish, dwindle, ebb, fade, fail, fall, fall off, flag, lessen, shrink, sink, wane ~*n.* 3. abatement, diminu~ tion, downturn, dwindling, falling off, lessening, recession, slump ~*v.*

4. decay, degenerate, deteriorate, droop, languish, pine, weaken, worsen ~*n.* 5. decay, decrepitude, degeneration, deterioration, enfeeblement, failing, senility, weakening, worsening 6. *Archaic* consumption, phthisis, tuberculosis ~*v.* 7. descend, dip, sink, slant, slope ~*n.* 8. declivity, hill, incline, slope

decompose 1. break up, crumble, decay, fall apart, fester, putrefy, rot, spoil 2. analyse, atomize, break down, break up, decompound, disintegrate, dissect, dissolve, distil, separate

decomposition atomization, breakdown, corruption, decay, disintegration, dissolution, division, putrefaction, putrescence, putridity, rot

décor colour scheme, decoration, furnishing style, ornamentation

decorate 1. adorn, beautify, bedeck, deck, embellish, enrich, grace, ornament, trim 2. colour, do up (*Inf.*), furbish, paint, paper, renovate, wallpaper 3. cite, honour, pin a medal on

decoration 1. adornment, beautification, elaboration, embellishment, enrichment, garnishing, ornamentation, trimming 2. arabesque, bauble, curlicue, falderal, flounce, flourish, frill, furbelow, garnish, ornament, scroll, spangle, trimmings, trinket 3. award, badge, colours, emblem, garter, medal, order, ribbon, star

decorative adorning, arty-crafty, beautifying, enhancing, fancy, nonfunctional, ornamental, pretty

decorous appropriate, becoming, befitting, comely, *comme il faut*, correct, decent, dignified, fit, mannerly, polite, proper, refined, sedate, seemly, staid, suitable, wellbehaved

decorum behaviour, breeding, courtliness, decency, deportment, dignity, etiquette, gentility, good grace, good manners, gravity, politeness, politesse, propriety, protocol, punctilio, respectability, seemliness

decoy 1. *n.* attraction, bait, ensnarement, enticement, inducement, lure, pretence, trap 2. *v.* allure, bait, deceive, ensnare, entice, entrap, inveigle, lure, seduce, tempt

decrease 1. *v.* abate, contract, curtail, cut down, decline, diminish, drop, dwindle, ease, fall off, lessen, lower, peter out, reduce, shrink, slacken, subside, wane 2. *n.* abatement, contraction, cutback, decline, diminution, downturn, dwindling, ebb, falling off, lessening, loss, reduction, shrinkage, subsidence

decree 1. *n.* act, command, dictum, edict, enactment, law, mandate, order, ordinance, precept, proclamation, regulation, ruling, statute 2. *v.* command, decide, determine, dictate, enact, lay down, ordain, order, prescribe, proclaim, pronounce, rule

decrepit 1. aged, crippled, debilitated, doddering, effete, feeble, frail, incapacitated, infirm, superannuated, wasted, weak 2. antiquated, battered, broken-down, deteriorated, dilapidated, ramshackle, rickety, run-down, tumbledown, weather-beaten, worn-out

decry abuse, belittle, blame, censure, condemn, criticize, cry down, denounce, depreciate, derogate, detract, devalue, discredit, disparage, rail against, run down, traduce, underestimate, underrate, undervalue

dedicate 1. commit, devote, give over to, pledge, surrender 2. address, assign, inscribe, offer 3. bless, consecrate, hallow, sanctify, set apart

dedicated committed, devoted, enthusiastic, given over to, purposeful, single-minded, sworn, wholehearted, zealous

dedication 1. adherence, allegiance, commitment, devotedness, devotion, faithfulness, loyalty, single-mindedness, wholeheartedness 2. address, inscription, message 3. consecration, hallowing, sanctification

deduce conclude, derive, draw, gather, glean, infer, reason, take to mean, understand

deduct decrease by, knock off (*Inf.*), reduce by, remove, subtract, take away, take from, take off, take out, withdraw

deduction 1. assumption, conclusion, consequence, corollary, finding, inference, reasoning, result 2. abatement, allowance, decrease, diminution, discount, reduction, subtraction, withdrawal

deed 1. achievement, act, action, exploit, fact, feat, performance, reality, truth 2. *Law* contract, document, indenture, instrument, title, title deed, transaction

deem account, believe, conceive, consider, esteem, estimate, hold, imagine, judge, reckon, regard, suppose, think

deep *adj.* 1. abyssal, bottomless, broad, far, profound, unfathomable, wide, yawning 2. abstract, abstruse, arcane, esoteric, hidden, mysterious, obscure, recondite, secret 3. acute, discerning, learned, penetrating, sagacious, wise 4. artful, astute, canny, cunning, designing, devious, insidious, knowing, scheming, shrewd 5. extreme, grave, great, intense, profound 6. absorbed, engrossed, immersed, lost, preoccupied, rapt 7. *Of a colour* dark, intense, rich, strong, vivid 8. *Of a sound* bass, booming, full-toned, low, low-pitched, resonant, sonorous ~*n.* 9. *Usually preceded by the* briny (*Inf.*), high seas, main, ocean, sea 10. culmination, dead, middle, mid point ~*adv.* 11. deeply, far down, far into, late

deepen 1. dig out, dredge, excavate, hollow, scoop out, scrape out 2. grow, increase, intensify, magnify, reinforce, strengthen

deeply 1. completely, gravely, profoundly, seriously, severely, thoroughly, to the heart, to the quick 2. acutely, affectingly, distressingly, feelingly, intensely, mournfully, movingly, passionately, sadly

deep-rooted *or* **deep-seated** confirmed, entrenched, fixed, in-

eradicable, ingrained, inveterate, rooted, settled, subconscious, unconscious

deface blemish, deform, destroy, disfigure, impair, injure, mar, mutilate, obliterate, spoil, sully, tarnish, vandalize

defacement blemish, damage, destruction, disfigurement, distortion, impairment, injury, mutilation, vandalism

de facto 1. *adv.* actually, in effect, in fact, in reality, really 2. *adj.* actual, existing, real

defamation aspersion, calumny, character assassination, denigration, disparagement, libel, obloquy, opprobrium, scandal, slander, slur, smear, traducement, vilification

defamatory abusive, calumnious, contumelious, denigrating, derogatory, disparaging, injurious, insulting, libellous, slanderous, vilifying, vituperative

defame asperse, belie, besmirch, blacken, calumniate, cast a slur on, cast aspersions on, denigrate, detract, discredit, disgrace, dishonour, disparage, libel, malign, slander, smear, speak evil of, stigmatize, traduce, vilify, vituperate

default 1. *n.* absence, defect, deficiency, dereliction, failure, fault, lack, lapse, neglect, nonpayment, omission, want 2. *v.* bilk, defraud, dodge, evade, fail, levant (*Brit.*), neglect, rat, swindle, welsh (*Sl.*)

defaulter delinquent, embezzler, levanter (*Brit.*), nonpayer, offender, peculator, welsher (*Sl.*)

defeat *v.* 1. beat, conquer, crush, overpower, overthrow, overwhelm, quell, repulse, rout, subdue, subjugate, vanquish 2. baffle, balk, confound, disappoint, discomfit, foil, frustrate, get the better of, ruin, thwart ~*n.* 3. beating, conquest, debacle, overthrow, repulse, rout, trouncing, vanquishment 4. disappointment, discomfiture, failure, frustration, rebuff, repulse, reverse, setback, thwarting

defeated balked, beaten, bested, checkmated, conquered, crushed, licked (*Inf.*), overcome, overpowered, overwhelmed, routed, thrashed, thwarted, trounced, vanquished, worsted

defeatist 1. *n.* pessimist, prophet of doom, quitter, submitter, yielder 2. *adj.* pessimistic

defect *n.* 1. blemish, blotch, error, failing, fault, flaw, foible, imperfection, mistake, spot, taint, want 2. absence, default, deficiency, frailty, inadequacy, lack, shortcoming, weakness ~*v.* 3. abandon, apostatize, break faith, change sides, desert, go over, rebel, revolt, tergiversate, walk out on (*Inf.*)

defection abandonment, apostasy, backsliding, dereliction, desertion, rebellion, revolt

defective 1. broken, deficient, faulty, flawed, imperfect, inadequate, incomplete, insufficient, not working, out of order, scant, short 2. abnormal, mentally deficient, retarded, subnormal

defector apostate, deserter, rat (*Inf.*), recreant (*Archaic*), renegade, runagate (*Archaic*), tergiversator, turncoat

defence 1. armament, cover, deterrence, guard, immunity, protection, resistance, safeguard, security, shelter 2. barricade, bastion, buckler, bulwark, buttress, fastness, fortification, rampart, shield 3. apologia, apology, argument, excuse, exoneration, explanation, extenuation, justification, plea, vindication 4. *Law* alibi, case, declaration, denial, plea, pleading, rebuttal, testimony

defenceless endangered, exposed, helpless, naked, powerless, unarmed, unguarded, unprotected, vulnerable, wide open

defend 1. cover, fortify, guard, keep safe, preserve, protect, safeguard, screen, secure, shelter, shield, ward off, watch over 2. assert, champion, endorse, espouse, justify, maintain, plead, speak up for, stand by, stand up for, support, sustain, uphold, vindicate

defendant appellant, defence, litigant, offender, prisoner at the bar, respondent, the accused

defender 1. bodyguard, escort, guard, protector 2. advocate, champion, patron, sponsor, supporter, vindicator

defensible 1. holdable, impregnable, safe, secure, unassailable 2. justifiable, pardonable, permissible, plausible, tenable, valid, vindicable

defensive averting, defending, on the defensive, opposing, protective, safeguarding, uptight (*Sl.*), watchful, withstanding

defensively at bay, in defence, in self-defence, on guard, on the defensive, suspiciously

defer[1] adjourn, delay, hold over, postpone, procrastinate, prorogue, protract, put off, put on ice, set aside, shelve, suspend, table

defer[2] accede, bow, capitulate, comply, give in, give way to, respect, submit, yield

deference 1. acquiescence, capitulation, complaisance, compliance, obedience, obeisance, submission, yielding 2. attention, civility, consideration, courtesy, esteem, homage, honour, obeisance, politeness, regard, respect, reverence, thoughtfulness, veneration

deferential civil, complaisant, considerate, courteous, dutiful, ingratiating, obedient, obeisant, obsequious, polite, regardful, respectful, reverential, submissive

deferment, deferral adjournment, delay, moratorium, postponement, putting off, stay, suspension

defiance challenge, confrontation, contempt, contumacy, disobedience, disregard, insolence, insubordination, opposition, provocation, rebelliousness, recalcitrance, spite

defiant aggressive, audacious, bold, challenging, contumacious, daring, disobedient, insolent, insubordinate, mutinous, provocative, rebellious, recalcitrant, refractory, truculent

deficiency 1. defect, demerit, failing, fault, flaw, frailty, imperfection, shortcoming, weakness 2. absence, dearth, deficit, inadequacy, insufficiency, lack, scantiness, scarcity, shortage

deficient 1. defective, faulty, flawed, impaired, imperfect, incomplete, inferior, unsatisfactory, weak 2. exiguous, inadequate, insufficient, lacking, meagre, scanty, scarce, short, skimpy, wanting

deficit arrears, default, deficiency, loss, shortage, shortfall

defiled besmirched, desecrated, dishonoured, impure, polluted, profaned, ravished, spoilt, tainted, unclean

define 1. characterize, describe, designate, detail, determine, explain, expound, interpret, specify, spell out 2. bound, circumscribe, delimit, delineate, demarcate, limit, mark out, outline

definite 1. clear, clear-cut, clearly defined, determined, exact, explicit, express, fixed, marked, obvious, particular, precise, specific 2. assured, certain, decided, guaranteed, positive, settled, sure

definitely absolutely, beyond any doubt, categorically, certainly, clearly, decidedly, easily, far and away, finally, indubitably, obviously, plainly, positively, surely, undeniably, unequivocally, unmistakably, unquestionably, without doubt, without fail, without question

definition 1. clarification, description, elucidation, explanation, exposition, statement of meaning 2. delimitation, delineation, demarcation, determination, fixing, outlining, settling 3. clarity, contrast, distinctness, focus, precision, sharpness

definitive absolute, authoritative, complete, conclusive, decisive, exhaustive, final, perfect, reliable, ultimate

deflate 1. collapse, contract, empty, exhaust, flatten, puncture, shrink, void 2. chasten, dash, debunk (*Inf.*), disconcert, dispirit, humble, humiliate, mortify, put down (*Sl.*), squash, take the wind out of (someone's) sails 3. *Economics* decrease, depreciate, depress, devalue, diminish, reduce

deflect bend, deviate, diverge, glance off, ricochet, shy, sidetrack, slew, swerve, turn, turn aside, twist, veer, wind

deflection aberration, bend, declination, deviation, divergence, drift, refraction, swerve, veer

deform 1. buckle, contort, distort, gnarl, malform, mangle, misshape, twist, warp 2. cripple, deface, disfigure, injure, maim, mar, mutilate, ruin, spoil

deformed 1. bent, blemished, crippled, crooked, disfigured, distorted, maimed, malformed, mangled, marred, misbegotten, misshapen 2. depraved, gross, offensive, perverted, twisted, warped

deformity 1. abnormality, defect, disfigurement, distortion, irregularity, malformation, misproportion, misshapenness, ugliness 2. corruption, depravity, grossness, hatefulness, vileness

defraud beguile, bilk, cheat, con (*Sl.*), cozen, delude, diddle (*Inf.*), do (*Sl.*), dupe, embezzle, fleece, gull (*Archaic*), gyp (*Sl.*), outwit, pilfer, pull a fast one on (*Inf.*), rip off (*Sl.*), rob, swindle, trick

deft able, adept, adroit, agile, clever, dexterous, expert, handy, neat, nimble, proficient, skilful

defunct 1. dead, deceased, departed, extinct, gone 2. a dead letter, bygone, expired, inoperative, invalid, nonexistent, not functioning, obsolete, out of commission

defy 1. beard, brave, challenge, confront, contemn, dare, despise, disregard, face, flout, hurl defiance at, provoke, scorn, slight, spurn 2. baffle, defeat, elude, foil, frustrate, repel, repulse, resist, thwart, withstand

degenerate 1. *adj.* base, corrupt, debased, debauched, decadent, degenerated, degraded, depraved, deteriorated, dissolute, fallen, immoral, low, mean, perverted 2. *v.* decay, decline, decrease, deteriorate, fall off, lapse, regress, retrogress, rot, sink, slip, worsen

degeneration debasement, de~
cline, degeneracy, descent, de~
terioration, dissipation, dissolution,
regression

degradation 1. abasement, de~
basement, decadence, decline, de~
generacy, degeneration, demotion,
derogation, deterioration, down~
grading, perversion 2. discredit,
disgrace, dishonour, humiliation,
ignominy, mortification, shame

degrade 1. cheapen, corrupt, de~
base, demean, deteriorate, dis~
credit, disgrace, dishonour, hum~
ble, humiliate, impair, injure, per~
vert, shame, vitiate 2. break, cash~
ier, demote, depose, downgrade,
lower, reduce to inferior rank 3.
adulterate, dilute, doctor, mix, thin,
water, water down, weaken

degraded abandoned, base, cor~
rupt, debased, debauched, deca~
dent, depraved, despicable, dis~
graced, disreputable, dissolute,
low, mean, profligate, sordid, vi~
cious, vile

degrading cheapening, contempt~
ible, debasing, demeaning, dis~
graceful, dishonourable, humiliat~
ing, infra dig (*Inf.*), lowering,
shameful, undignified, unworthy

degree 1. class, grade, level, order,
position, rank, standing, station,
status 2. division, extent, gradation,
grade, interval, limit, mark, meas~
ure, notch, point, rung, scale, stage,
step, unit 3. calibre, extent, inten~
sity, level, measure, proportion,
quality, quantity, range, rate, ratio,
scale, scope, severity, standard 4.
by degrees bit by bit, gently,
gradually, imperceptibly, inch by
inch, little by little, slowly, step by
step

deign condescend, consent, deem
worthy, lower oneself, see fit,
stoop, think fit

deity celestial being, divine being,
divinity, god, goddess, godhead,
idol, immortal, supreme being

dejected blue, cast down, crest~
fallen, depressed, despondent, dis~
consolate, disheartened, dismal,
doleful, down, downcast, down~
hearted, gloomy, glum, low, low-
spirited, melancholy, miserable,
morose, sad, woebegone, wretched

dejection blues, depression, des~
pair, despondency, doldrums,
downheartedness, dumps (*Inf.*),
gloom, gloominess, heavy~
heartedness, low spirits, melan~
choly, sadness, sorrow, unhappi~
ness

de jure according to the law, by
right, legally, rightfully

delay v. 1. defer, hold over, post~
pone, procrastinate, prolong, pro~
tract, put off, shelve, stall, suspend,
table, temporize ~n. 2. deferment,
postponement, procrastination,
stay, suspension ~v. 3. arrest, bog
down, check, detain, halt, hinder,
hold back, hold up, impede, ob~
struct, retard, set back, slow up,
stop ~n. 4. check, detention, hin~
drance, hold-up, impediment, in~
terruption, interval, obstruction,
setback, stoppage, wait ~v. 5.
dawdle, dilly-dally (*Inf.*), drag, lag,
linger, loiter, tarry ~n. 6. dawdling,
dilly-dallying (*Inf.*), lingering, loi~
tering, tarrying

delectable adorable, agreeable,
appetizing, charming, dainty, deli~
cious, delightful, enjoyable, entic~
ing, gratifying, inviting, luscious,
lush, pleasant, pleasurable, satisfy~
ing, scrumptious (*Inf.*), tasty,
toothsome, yummy (*Sl.*)

delegate n. 1. agent, ambassador,
commissioner, deputy, envoy, leg~
ate, representative, vicar ~v. 2.
accredit, appoint, authorize, com~
mission, depute, designate, em~
power, mandate 3. assign, consign,
devolve, entrust, give, hand over,
pass on, relegate, transfer

delegation 1. commission, contin~
gent, deputation, embassy, envoys,
legation, mission 2. assignment,
commissioning, committal, depu~
tizing, devolution, entrustment,
relegation

delete blot out, blue-pencil, cancel,
cross out, cut out, dele, edit, edit
out, efface, erase, expunge, oblit~
erate, remove, rub out, strike out

deliberate v. 1. cogitate, consider,
consult, debate, discuss, meditate,

mull over, ponder, reflect, think, weigh ~*adj.* 2. calculated, conscious, considered, designed, intentional, planned, prearranged, premeditated, purposeful, studied, thoughtful, wilful 3. careful, cautious, circumspect, heedful, measured, methodical, ponderous, prudent, slow, thoughtful, unhurried, wary

deliberately by design, calculatingly, consciously, determinedly, emphatically, in cold blood, intentionally, knowingly, on purpose, pointedly, resolutely, studiously, wilfully, wittingly

deliberation 1. calculation, care, carefulness, caution, circumspection, cogitation, consideration, coolness, forethought, meditation, prudence, purpose, reflection, speculation, study, thought, wariness 2. conference, consultation, debate, discussion

delicacy 1. accuracy, daintiness, elegance, exquisiteness, fineness, lightness, nicety, precision, subtlety 2. debility, flimsiness, fragility, frailness, frailty, infirmity, slenderness, tenderness, weakness 3. discrimination, fastidiousness, finesse, purity, refinement, sensibility, sensitiveness, sensitivity, tact, taste 4. *bonne bouche*, dainty, luxury, relish, savoury, titbit, treat

delicate 1. ailing, debilitated, flimsy, fragile, frail, sickly, slender, slight, tender, weak 2. choice, dainty, delicious, elegant, exquisite, fine, graceful, savoury, tender 3. faint, muted, pastel, soft, subdued, subtle 4. accurate, deft, detailed, minute, precise, skilled 5. considerate, diplomatic, discreet, sensitive, tactful 6. critical, difficult, precarious, sensitive, sticky (*Inf.*), ticklish, touchy 7. careful, critical, discriminating, fastidious, prudish, pure, refined, scrupulous, squeamish

delicately carefully, daintily, deftly, elegantly, exquisitely, fastidiously, finely, gracefully, lightly, precisely, sensitively, skilfully, softly, subtly, tactfully

delicious 1. ambrosial, appetizing, choice, dainty, delectable, luscious, mouthwatering, nectareous, palatable, savoury, scrumptious (*Inf.*), tasty, toothsome, yummy (*Sl.*) 2. agreeable, charming, delightful, enjoyable, entertaining, exquisite, pleasant, pleasing

delight *n.* 1. ecstasy, enjoyment, felicity, gladness, gratification, happiness, joy, pleasure, rapture, transport ~*v.* 2. amuse, charm, cheer, divert, enchant, gratify, please, ravish, rejoice, satisfy, thrill 3. *With* in appreciate, enjoy, feast on, glory in, indulge in, like, love, luxuriate in, relish, revel in, savour

delighted captivated, charmed, ecstatic, elated, enchanted, gladdened, happy, joyous, jubilant, overjoyed, pleased, thrilled

delightful agreeable, amusing, captivating, charming, congenial, delectable, enchanting, engaging, enjoyable, entertaining, fascinating, gratifying, heavenly, pleasant, pleasing, pleasurable, rapturous, ravishing, thrilling

delinquency crime, fault, misbehaviour, misconduct, misdeed, misdemeanour, offence, wrongdoing

delinquent criminal, culprit, defaulter, juvenile delinquent, lawbreaker, malefactor, miscreant, offender, wrongdoer, young offender

delirious 1. crazy, demented, deranged, incoherent, insane, lightheaded, mad, raving, unhinged 2. beside oneself, carried away, corybantic, ecstatic, excited, frantic, frenzied, hysterical, wild

delirium 1. aberration, derangement, hallucination, insanity, lunacy, madness, raving 2. ecstasy, fever, frenzy, fury, hysteria, passion, rage

deliver 1. bear, bring, carry, cart, convey, distribute, transport 2. cede, commit, give up, grant, hand over, make over, relinquish, resign, surrender, transfer, turn over, yield 3. acquit, discharge, emancipate, free, liberate, loose, ransom, redeem, release, rescue, save 4. announce, declare, give, give forth, present, proclaim, pronounce, publish, read, utter 5. administer, aim, deal, direct, give, inflict, launch, strike, throw 6. discharge, dispense, feed, give forth, provide, release, supply

deliverance emancipation, escape, liberation, ransom, redemption, release, rescue, salvation

delivery 1. consignment, convey~ ance, dispatch, distribution, hand~ ing over, surrender, transfer, transmission, transmittal 2. ar~ ticulation, elocution, enunciation, intonation, speech, utterance 3. *Medical* childbirth, confinement, labour, parturition 4. deliverance, escape, liberation, release, rescue

delude bamboozle (*Inf.*), beguile, cheat, con (*Sl.*), cozen, deceive, dupe, fool, gull (*Archaic*), hoax, hoodwink, impose on, lead up the garden path (*Inf.*), misguide, mis~ lead, take in (*Inf.*), trick

deluge *n.* 1. cataclysm, downpour, flood, inundation, overflowing, spate, torrent 2. *Fig.* avalanche, barrage, flood, rush, spate, torrent ~*v.* 3. douse, drench, drown, flood, inundate, soak, submerge, swamp 4. *Fig.* engulf, inundate, overload, overrun, overwhelm, swamp

delusion deception, error, fallacy, false impression, fancy, hallucina~ tion, illusion, misapprehension, misbelief, misconception, mistake, phantasm, self-deception

de luxe choice, costly, elegant, ex~ clusive, expensive, grand, luxuri~ ous, opulent, palatial, plush (*Inf.*), rich, select, special, splendid, sumptuous, superior

delve burrow, dig into, examine, explore, ferret out, investigate, look into, probe, ransack, research, rummage, search, unearth

demagogue agitator, firebrand, haranguer, rabble-rouser, soapbox orator

demand *v.* 1. ask, challenge, in~ quire, interrogate, question, re~ quest 2. call for, cry out for, in~ volve, necessitate, need, require, take, want 3. claim, exact, expect, insist on, order ~*n.* 4. bidding, charge, inquiry, interrogation, or~ der, question, request, requisition 5. call, claim, necessity, need, re~ quirement, want 6. **in demand** fashionable, in vogue, needed, popular, requested, sought after

demanding 1. challenging, diffi~ cult, exacting, exhausting, exigent, hard, taxing, tough, trying, wearing 2. clamorous, imperious, importu~ nate, insistent, nagging, pressing, urgent

demarcate define, delimit, deter~ mine, differentiate, distinguish be~ tween, fix, mark, separate

demarcation 1. bound, boundary, confine, enclosure, limit, margin 2. delimitation, differentiation, dis~ tinction, division, separation

demean abase, debase, degrade, descend, humble, lower, stoop

demeanour air, bearing, behav~ iour, carriage, comportment, con~ duct, deportment, manner, mien

demented crackbrained, crazed, crazy, daft (*Sl.*), deranged, dis~ traught, dotty (*Sl.*), foolish, fren~ zied, idiotic, insane, lunatic, mad, maniacal, manic, *non compos mentis*, unbalanced, unhinged

democracy commonwealth, gov~ ernment by the people, repre~ sentative government, republic

democratic autonomous, egalitar~ ian, popular, populist, representa~ tive, republican, self-governing

demolish 1. bulldoze, destroy, dis~ mantle, flatten, knock down, level, overthrow, pulverize, raze, ruin, tear down 2. *Fig.* annihilate, de~ feat, destroy, overthrow, overturn, undo, wreck 3. consume, devour, eat, gobble up, put away

demolition bulldozing, destruction, explosion, knocking down, level~ ling, razing, wrecking

demon 1. devil, evil spirit, fiend, goblin, malignant spirit 2. *Fig.* devil, fiend, monster, rogue, villain 3. ace (*Inf.*), addict, fanatic, fiend, go-getter (*Inf.*), master, wizard 4.

daemon, daimon, genius, guardian spirit, ministering angel, numen

demonic, demoniac, demoniacal 1. devilish, diabolic, diabolical, fiendish, hellish, infernal, satanic **2.** crazed, frantic, frenetic, frenzied, furious, hectic, like one possessed, mad, maniacal, manic

demonstrable attestable, axiomatic, certain, evident, evincible, incontrovertible, indubitable, irrefutable, obvious, palpable, positive, provable, self-evident, undeniable, unmistakable, verifiable

demonstrate 1. display, establish, evidence, evince, exhibit, indicate, manifest, prove, show, testify to **2.** describe, explain, illustrate, make clear, show how, teach **3.** march, parade, picket, protest, rally

demonstration 1. affirmation, confirmation, display, evidence, exhibition, expression, illustration, manifestation, proof, substantiation, testimony, validation **2.** description, explanation, exposition, presentation, test, trial **3.** march, mass lobby, parade, picket, protest, rally, sit-in

demonstrative 1. affectionate, effusive, emotional, expansive, expressive, gushing, loving, open, unreserved, unrestrained **2.** evincive, explanatory, expository, illustrative, indicative, symptomatic

demoralize 1. cripple, daunt, deject, depress, disconcert, discourage, dishearten, dispirit, enfeeble, rattle (*Inf.*), sap, shake, undermine, unnerve, weaken **2.** corrupt, debase, debauch, deprave, lower, pervert, vitiate

demoralized 1. broken, crushed, depressed, discouraged, disheartened, dispirited, downcast, subdued, unmanned, unnerved, weakened **2.** bad, base, corrupt, degenerate, depraved, dissolute, immoral, low, reprobate, sinful, wicked

demur 1. *v.* balk, cavil, disagree, dispute, doubt, hesitate, object, pause, protest, refuse, take exception, waver **2.** *n.* compunction, demurral, demurrer, dissent, hesita-

tion, misgiving, objection, protest, qualm, scruple

demure 1. decorous, diffident, grave, modest, reserved, reticent, retiring, sedate, shy, sober, staid, unassuming **2.** affected, bashful, coy, priggish, prim, prissy (*Inf.*), prudish, strait-laced

den 1. cave, cavern, haunt, hide-out, hole, lair, shelter **2.** cloister, cubbyhole, hideaway, retreat, sanctuary, sanctum, snuggery, study

denial adjuration, contradiction, disavowal, disclaimer, dismissal, dissent, negation, prohibition, rebuff, refusal, rejection, renunciation, repudiation, repulse, retraction, veto

denigrate belittle, besmirch, blacken, calumniate, decry, defame, disparage, impugn, malign, revile, run down, slander, vilify

denigration aspersion, backbiting, defamation, detraction, disparagement, obloquy, scandal, scurrility, slander, vilification

denomination 1. belief, communion, creed, persuasion, religious group, school, sect **2.** grade, size, unit, value **3.** body, category, class, classification, group **4.** appellation, designation, label, name, style, term, title

denote betoken, designate, express, imply, import, indicate, mark, mean, show, signify, typify

denounce accuse, arraign, attack, brand, castigate, censure, condemn, declaim against, decry, denunciate, impugn, proscribe, revile, stigmatize, vilify

dense 1. close, close-knit, compact, compressed, condensed, heavy, impenetrable, opaque, solid, substantial, thick, thickset **2.** blockish, crass, dull, obtuse, slow, slow-witted, stolid, stupid, thick, thick-witted

density 1. body, bulk, closeness, compactness, consistency, crowdedness, denseness, impenetrability, mass, solidity, thickness, tightness **2.** crassness, dullness, obtuseness,

slowness, stolidity, stupidity, thick~
ness

dent 1. *n.* chip, concavity, crater,
depression, dimple, dip, hollow,
impression, indentation, pit 2. *v.*
depress, dint, gouge, hollow, im~
print, make a dent in, make con~
cave, press in, push in

denude bare, divest, expose, lay
bare, strip, uncover

deny 1. contradict, disagree with,
disprove, gainsay, oppose, rebuff,
refute 2. abjure, disavow, discard,
disclaim, disown, recant, renounce,
repudiate, revoke 3. begrudge, de~
cline, disallow, forbid, negative,
refuse, reject, turn down, veto,
withhold

deodorant air freshener, antiper~
spirant, deodorizer, disinfectant,
fumigant

depart 1. absent (oneself), decamp,
disappear, escape, exit, go, go
away, leave, migrate, quit, remove,
retire, retreat, set forth, start out,
take (one's) leave, vanish, with~
draw 2. deviate, differ, digress, di~
verge, stray, swerve, turn aside,
vary, veer

departed dead, deceased, expired,
late

department 1. district, division,
province, region, sector 2. branch,
bureau, division, office, section,
station, subdivision, unit 3. area,
domain, function, line, province,
realm, responsibility, speciality,
sphere

departure 1. exit, exodus, going,
going away, leave-taking, leaving,
removal, retirement, withdrawal 2.
abandonment, branching off, de~
viation, digression, divergence,
variation, veering 3. branching out,
change, difference, innovation,
novelty, shift

depend 1. bank on, build upon, cal~
culate on, confide in, count on, lean
on, reckon on, rely upon, trust in,
turn to 2. be based on, be contin~
gent on, be determined by, be sub~
ject to, be subordinate to, hang on,
hinge on, rest on, revolve around

dependable faithful, reliable, re~

sponsible, steady, sure, trust~
worthy, trusty, unfailing

dependant *n.* child, client, hanger-
on, henchman, minion, minor,
protégé, relative, retainer, subor~
dinate, vassal

dependent *adj.* 1. counting on, de~
fenceless, helpless, immature, re~
liant, relying on, vulnerable, weak
2. conditional, contingent, depend~
ing, determined by, liable to, rela~
tive, subject to 3. feudal, subject,
subordinate, tributary

depict 1. delineate, draw, illustrate,
limn, outline, paint, picture, por~
tray, render, reproduce, sculpt,
sketch 2. characterize, describe,
detail, narrate, outline, sketch

deplete bankrupt, consume, de~
crease, drain, empty, evacuate,
exhaust, expend, impoverish, less~
en, milk, reduce, use up

depleted consumed, decreased,
depreciated, devoid of, drained,
emptied, exhausted, lessened, out
of, reduced, short of, spent, used
(up), wasted, weakened, worn out

depletion attenuation, consump~
tion, decrease, deficiency, diminu~
tion, dwindling, exhaustion, ex~
penditure, lessening, lowering, re~
duction, using up

deplorable 1. calamitous, dire, dis~
astrous, distressing, grievous,
heartbreaking, lamentable, mel~
ancholy, miserable, pitiable, re~
grettable, sad, unfortunate,
wretched 2. blameworthy, dis~
graceful, dishonourable, disrepu~
table, execrable, opprobrious, rep~
rehensible, scandalous, shameful

deplore 1. bemoan, bewail, grieve
for, lament, mourn, regret, rue,
sorrow over 2. abhor, censure,
condemn, denounce, deprecate,
disapprove of, object to

deploy arrange, dispose, extend,
position, redistribute, set out, set
up, spread out, station, use, utilize

deport 1. banish, exile, expatriate,
expel, extradite, oust 2. *Used re~
flexively* acquit, act, bear, behave,
carry, comport, conduct, hold

deportation banishment, eviction,

exile, expatriation, expulsion, extradition, transportation

deportment air, appearance, aspect, bearing, behaviour, carriage, cast, comportment, conduct, demeanour, manner, mien, posture, stance

depose 1. break, cashier, degrade, demote, dethrone, dismiss, displace, downgrade, oust, remove from office 2.*Law* avouch, declare, make a deposition, testify

deposit *v.* 1. drop, lay, locate, place, precipitate, put, settle, sit down 2. amass, bank, consign, entrust, hoard, lodge, save, store ~*n.* 3. down payment, instalment, money (*in bank*), part payment, pledge, retainer, security, stake, warranty 4. accumulation, alluvium, deposition, dregs, lees, precipitate, sediment, silt

deposition 1. dethronement, dismissal, displacement, ousting, removal 2. *Law* affidavit, declaration, evidence, sworn statement, testimony

depository depot, repository, safe-deposit box, store, storehouse, warehouse

depot 1. depository, repository, storehouse, warehouse 2. *Military* arsenal, dump 3. bus station, garage, terminus

deprave brutalize, corrupt, debase, debauch, degrade, demoralize, lead astray, pervert, seduce, subvert, vitiate

depraved abandoned, corrupt, debased, debauched, degenerate, degraded, dissolute, evil, immoral, lascivious, lewd, licentious, perverted, profligate, shameless, sinful, vicious, vile, wicked

depravity baseness, contamination, corruption, criminality, debasement, debauchery, degeneracy, depravation, evil, immorality, iniquity, profligacy, sinfulness, vice, viciousness, vitiation, wickedness

depreciate 1. decrease, deflate, devaluate, devalue, lessen, lose value, lower, reduce 2. belittle, decry, denigrate, deride, detract, disparage, look down on, ridicule, run down, scorn, sneer at, traduce, underestimate, underrate, undervalue

depreciation 1. deflation, depression, devaluation, drop, fall, slump 2. belittlement, deprecation, derogation, detraction, disparagement, pejoration

depress 1. cast down, chill, damp, daunt, deject, desolate, discourage, dishearten, dispirit, make despondent, oppress, sadden, weigh down 2. debilitate, devitalize, drain, enervate, exhaust, lower, sap, slow up, weaken 3. cheapen, depreciate, devaluate, devalue, diminish, downgrade, impair, lessen, lower, reduce 4. flatten, level, lower, press down, push down

depressed 1. blue, crestfallen, dejected, despondent, discouraged, dispirited, down, downcast, downhearted, fed up, glum, low, low-spirited, melancholy, moody, morose, pessimistic, sad, unhappy 2. concave, hollow, indented, recessed, set back, sunken 3. *Of an area, circumstances* deprived, destitute, disadvantaged, distressed, grey, needy, poor, poverty-stricken, run-down 4. cheapened, depreciated, devalued, impaired, weakened

depressing black, bleak, daunting, dejecting, depressive, discouraging, disheartening, dismal, dispiriting, distressing, dreary, gloomy, heartbreaking, hopeless, melancholy, sad, saddening, sombre

depression 1. dejection, despair, despondency, dolefulness, downheartedness, dumps (*Inf.*), gloominess, hopelessness, low spirits, melancholia, melancholy, sadness, the blues 2. *Commerce* dullness, economic decline, hard *or* bad times, inactivity, lowness, recession, slump, stagnation 3. bowl, cavity, concavity, dent, dimple, dip, excavation, hollow, impression, indentation, pit, sag, sink, valley

deprivation 1. denial, deprival, dispossession, divestment, expropriation, removal, withdrawal, withholding 2. destitution, detriment, disadvantage, distress, hardship, need, privation, want

deprive bereave, despoil, dispossess, divest, expropriate, rob, strip, wrest

deprived bereft, denuded, destitute, disadvantaged, forlorn, in need, in want, lacking, necessitous, needy, poor

depth 1. abyss, deepness, drop, extent, measure, profoundness, profundity 2. *Fig.* astuteness, discernment, insight, penetration, profoundness, profundity, sagacity, wisdom 3. abstruseness, complexity, obscurity, reconditeness 4. intensity, richness, strength 5. *Often plural* abyss, bowels of the earth, deepest (furthest, innermost, most intense, remotest) part, middle, midst, slough of despond 6. **in depth** comprehensively, extensively, intensively, thoroughly

deputation 1. commission, delegates, delegation, deputies, embassy, envoys, legation 2. appointment, assignment, commission, designation, nomination

deputize 1. commission, delegate, depute 2. act for, stand in for, take the place of, understudy

deputy 1. *n.* agent, ambassador, commissioner, delegate, legate, lieutenant, nuncio, proxy, representative, second-in-command, substitute, surrogate, vicegerent 2. *adj.* assistant, depute (*Scot.*), subordinate

derange 1. confound, confuse, disarrange, disarray, discompose, disconcert, disorder, displace, disturb, ruffle, unsettle, upset 2. craze, dement (*Rare*), drive mad, madden, make insane, unbalance, unhinge

deranged berserk, crazed, crazy, delirious, demented, distracted, frantic, frenzied, insane, irrational, lunatic, mad, maddened, unbalanced, unhinged

derelict *adj.* 1. abandoned, deserted, dilapidated, discarded, forsaken, neglected, ruined 2. careless, irresponsible, lax, negligent, remiss, slack ~*n.* 3. down-and-out,

good-for-nothing, ne'er-do-well, outcast, tramp, vagrant, wastrel

dereliction 1. delinquency, evasion, failure, faithlessness, fault, neglect, negligence, nonperformance, remissness 2. abandonment, abdication, desertion, forsaking, relinquishment, renunciation

deride chaff, contemn, detract, disdain, disparage, flout, gibe, insult, jeer, knock (*Inf.*), mock, poohpooh, ridicule, scoff, scorn, sneer, taunt

derisory contemptible, insulting, laughable, ludicrous, outrageous, preposterous, ridiculous

derivation 1. acquiring, deriving, extraction, getting, obtaining 2. ancestry, basis, beginning, descent, etymology, foundation, genealogy, origin, root, source

derivative *adj.* 1. acquired, borrowed, derived, inferred, obtained, procured, transmitted 2. copied, imitative, plagiaristic, plagiarized, rehashed, secondary, second-hand, uninventive, unoriginal ~*n.* 3. byproduct, derivation, descendant, off-shoot, outgrowth, spin-off

derive 1. collect, deduce, draw, elicit, extract, follow, gain, gather, get, glean, infer, obtain, procure, receive, trace 2. *With* **from** arise, descend, emanate, flow, issue, originate, proceed, spring from, stem from

derogatory belittling, damaging, defamatory, depreciative, detracting, discreditable, dishonouring, disparaging, injurious, offensive, slighting, uncomplimentary, unfavourable, unflattering

descend 1. alight, dismount, drop, fall, go down, move down, plummet, plunge, sink, subside, tumble 2. dip, gravitate, incline, slant, slope 3. be handed down, be passed down, derive, issue, originate, proceed, spring 4. abase oneself, condescend, degenerate, deteriorate, lower oneself, stoop 5. *Often with* **on** arrive, assail, assault, attack, come in force, invade, pounce, raid, swoop

descent 1. coming down, drop, fall, plunge, swoop 2. declination, declivity, dip, drop, incline, slant, slope 3. ancestry, extraction, family tree, genealogy, heredity, lineage, origin, parentage 4. debasement, decadence, decline, degradation, deterioration 5. assault, attack, foray, incursion, invasion, pounce, raid, swoop

describe 1. characterize, define, depict, detail, explain, express, illustrate, narrate, portray, recount, relate, report, specify, tell 2. delineate, draw, mark out, outline, trace

description 1. account, characterization, delineation, depiction, detail, explanation, narration, narrative, portrayal, report, representation, sketch 2. brand, breed, category, class, genre, genus, ilk, kidney, kind, order, sort, species, type, variety

descriptive circumstantial, depictive, detailed, explanatory, expressive, graphic, illustrative, pictorial, picturesque, vivid

desert[1] 1. *n.* solitude, waste, wasteland, wilderness, wilds 2. *adj.* arid, bare, barren, desolate, infertile, lonely, solitary, uncultivated, uninhabited, unproductive, untilled, waste, wild

desert[2] *v.* abandon, abscond, betray, decamp, defect, forsake, give up, go over the hill (*Military sl.*), jilt, leave, leave high and dry, leave (someone) in the lurch, leave stranded, maroon, quit, rat (on), relinquish, renounce, resign, run out on (*Inf.*), strand, throw over, vacate, walk out on (*Inf.*)

deserted abandoned, bereft, cast off, derelict, desolate, empty, forlorn, forsaken, godforsaken, isolated, left in the lurch, left stranded, lonely, neglected, solitary, unfriended, unoccupied, vacant

deserter absconder, apostate, defector, escapee, fugitive, rat (*Inf.*), renegade, runaway, traitor, truant

desertion abandonment, absconding, apostasy, betrayal, defection, departure, dereliction, escape, evasion, flight, forsaking, relinquishment, truancy

deserve be entitled to, be worthy of, earn, gain, justify, merit, procure, rate, warrant, win

deserved appropriate, condign, due, earned, fair, fitting, just, justifiable, justified, meet (*Archaic*), merited, proper, right, rightful, suitable, warranted, well-earned

deserving commendable, estimable, laudable, meritorious, praiseworthy, righteous, worthy

design *v.* 1. delineate, describe, draft, draw, outline, plan, sketch, trace ~*n.* 2. blueprint, delineation, draft, drawing, model, outline, plan, scheme, sketch ~*v.* 3. conceive, create, fabricate, fashion, invent, originate, think up ~*n.* 4. arrangement, configuration, construction, figure, form, motif, organization, pattern, shape, style ~*v.* 5. aim, contrive, destine, devise, intend, make, mean, plan, project, propose, purpose, scheme, tailor ~*n.* 6. enterprise, plan, project, schema, scheme, undertaking 7. aim, end, goal, intent, intention, meaning, object, objective, point, purport, purpose, target, view 8. *Often plural* conspiracy, evil intentions, intrigue, machination, plot, scheme

designate 1. call, christen, dub, entitle, label, name, nominate, style, term 2. allot, appoint, assign, choose, delegate, depute, nominate, select 3. characterize, define, denote, describe, earmark, indicate, pinpoint, show, specify, stipulate

designation 1. denomination, description, epithet, label, mark, name, title 2. appointment, classification, delegation, indication, selection, specification

designer 1. architect, artificer, couturier, creator, deviser, inventor, originator, stylist 2. conniver, conspirator, intriguer, plotter, schemer

designing artful, astute, conniving, conspiring, crafty, crooked (*Inf.*), cunning, deceitful, devious, in~

triguing, Machiavellian, plotting, scheming, sharp, shrewd, sly, treacherous, tricky, unscrupulous, wily

desirability advantage, benefit, merit, profit, usefulness, value, worth

desirable 1. advantageous, advisable, agreeable, beneficial, covetable, eligible, enviable, good, pleasing, preferable, profitable, worthwhile 2. adorable, alluring, attractive, fascinating, fetching, seductive, sexy (*Inf.*)

desire *v.* 1. aspire to, covet, crave, desiderate, fancy, hanker after, long for, set one's heart on, want, wish for, yearn for ~*n.* 2. appetite, aspiration, craving, hankering, longing, need, want, wish, yearning, yen (*Inf.*) ~*v.* 3. ask, entreat, importune, petition, request, solicit ~*n.* 4. appeal, entreaty, importunity, petition, request, solicitation, supplication 5. appetite, concupiscence, lasciviousness, lechery, libido, lust, lustfulness, passion

desired accurate, appropriate, correct, exact, expected, express, fitting, necessary, particular, proper, required, right

desirous ambitious, anxious, aspiring, avid, craving, desiring, eager, hopeful, hoping, keen, longing, ready, willing, wishing, yearning

desist abstain, break off, cease, discontinue, end, forbear, give over (*Inf.*), give up, have done with, leave off, pause, refrain from, stop, suspend

desolate *adj.* 1. bare, barren, bleak, desert, dreary, ruined, solitary, unfrequented, uninhabited, waste, wild ~*v.* 2. depopulate, despoil, destroy, devastate, lay low, lay waste, pillage, plunder, ravage, ruin ~*adj.* 3. abandoned, bereft, cheerless, comfortless, companionless, dejected, depressing, despondent, disconsolate, dismal, downcast, forlorn, forsaken, gloomy, lonely, melancholy, miserable, wretched ~*v.* 4. daunt, deject, depress, discourage, dishearten, dismay, distress, grieve

desolation 1. destruction, devastation, havoc, ravages, ruin, ruination 2. barrenness, bleakness, desolateness, forlornness, isolation, loneliness, solitariness, solitude, wildness 3. anguish, dejection, despair, distress, gloom, gloominess, melancholy, misery, sadness, unhappiness, woe, wretchedness

despair *v.* 1. despond, give up, lose heart, lose hope ~*n.* 2. anguish, dejection, depression, desperation, despondency, disheartenment, gloom, hopelessness, melancholy, misery, wretchedness 3. burden, cross, ordeal, pain, trial, tribulation

despairing anxious, brokenhearted, dejected, depressed, desperate, despondent, disconsolate, downcast, frantic, grief-stricken, hopeless, inconsolable, melancholy, miserable, suicidal, wretched

desperado bandit, criminal, cutthroat, gangster, gunman, hoodlum (*Chiefly U.S.*), lawbreaker, mugger, outlaw, ruffian, thug

desperate 1. audacious, dangerous, daring, death-defying, determined, foolhardy, frantic, furious, hasty, hazardous, headstrong, impetuous, madcap, precipitate, rash, reckless, risky, violent, wild 2. acute, critical, dire, drastic, extreme, great, urgent, very grave 3. despairing, despondent, forlorn, hopeless, inconsolable, irrecoverable, irremediable, irretrievable, wretched

desperately 1. badly, dangerously, gravely, perilously, seriously, severely 2. appallingly, fearfully, frightfully, hopelessly, shockingly

desperation 1. defiance, foolhardiness, frenzy, heedlessness, impetuosity, madness, rashness, recklessness 2. agony, anguish, anxiety, despair, despondency, distraction, heartache, hopelessness, misery, pain, sorrow, torture, trouble, unhappiness, worry

despicable abject, base, beyond contempt, cheap, contemptible, degrading, detestable, disgraceful, disreputable, hateful, ignominious, infamous, low, mean, pitiful, rep~ rehensible, scurvy, shameful, sor~ did, vile, worthless, wretched

despise abhor, contemn, deride, detest, disdain, disregard, flout, loathe, look down on, neglect, re~ vile, scorn, slight, spurn, under~ value

despite *prep.* against, even with, in contempt of, in defiance of, in spite of, in the face of, in the teeth of, notwithstanding, regardless of, un~ deterred by

despoil denude, deprive, destroy, devastate, dispossess, divest, loot, pillage, plunder, ravage, rifle, rob, strip, vandalize, wreak havoc upon, wreck

despondency dejection, depres~ sion, despair, desperation, discon~ solateness, discouragement, dis~ piritedness, downheartedness, gloom, hopelessness, low spirits, melancholy, misery, sadness, wretchedness

despondent blue, dejected, de~ pressed, despairing, disconsolate, discouraged, disheartened, dispir~ ited, doleful, down, downcast, downhearted, gloomy, glum, hope~ less, in despair, low, low-spirited, melancholy, miserable, morose, sad, sorrowful, woebegone, wretched

despot autocrat, dictator, mono~ crat, oppressor, tyrant

despotic absolute, arbitrary, arro~ gant, authoritarian, autocratic, dictatorial, domineering, imperi~ ous, monocratic, oppressive, ty~ rannical, unconstitutional

despotism absolutism, autarchy, autocracy, dictatorship, monocra~ cy, oppression, totalitarianism, tyranny

destination 1. harbour, haven, journey's end, landing-place, resting-place, station, stop, termi~ nus 2. aim, ambition, design, end, goal, intention, object, objective, purpose, target

destine allot, appoint, assign, con~ secrate, decree, design, devote, doom, earmark, fate, intend, mark out, ordain, predetermine, purpose, reserve

destined 1. bound, certain, de~ signed, doomed, fated, foreor~ dained, ineluctable, inescapable, inevitable, intended, meant, or~ dained, predestined, unavoidable 2. assigned, booked, bound for, di~ rected, en route, heading, on the road to, routed, scheduled

destiny cup, divine decree, doom, fate, fortune, karma, kismet, lot, portion

destitute 1. distressed, down and out, impecunious, impoverished, indigent, insolvent, moneyless, ne~ cessitous, needy, on one's uppers, on the breadline (*Inf.*), penniless, penurious, poor, poverty-stricken 2. bereft of, deficient in, depleted, deprived of, devoid of, drained, empty of, in need of, lacking, wanting, without

destitution beggary, dire straits, distress, impecuniousness, indi~ gence, neediness, pauperism, pen~ nilessness, penury, privation, utter poverty, want

destroy annihilate, blow to bits, break down, crush, demolish, desolate, devastate, dismantle, dis~ patch, eradicate, extinguish, extir~ pate, gut, kill, ravage, raze, ruin, shatter, slay, smash, torpedo, waste, wipe out, wreck

destruction annihilation, crushing, demolition, devastation, downfall, end, eradication, extermination, extinction, havoc, liquidation, massacre, overthrow, overwhelm~ ing, ruin, ruination, shattering, slaughter, undoing, wreckage, wrecking

destructive 1. baleful, baneful, ca~ lamitous, cataclysmic, catastroph~ ic, damaging, deadly, deleterious, detrimental, devastating, fatal, harmful, hurtful, injurious, lethal, noxious, pernicious, ruinous 2. ad~ verse, antagonistic, contrary, de~ rogatory, discouraging, discredit~ ing, disparaging, hostile, invalidat~ ing, negative, opposed, undermin~ ing, vicious

detach cut off, disconnect, disen~

gage, disentangle, disjoin, disunite, divide, free, isolate, loosen, re~move, segregate, separate, sever, tear off, uncouple, unfasten, un~hitch

detached 1. disconnected, discrete, disjoined, divided, free, loosened, separate, severed, unconnected 2. aloof, disinterested, dispassionate, impartial, impersonal, neutral, objective, reserved, unbiased, uncommitted, uninvolved, unprejudiced

detachment 1. aloofness, coolness, indifference, remoteness, uncon~cern 2. disinterestedness, fairness, impartiality, neutrality, nonparti~sanship, objectivity 3. disconnec~tion, disengagement, disjoining, separation, severing 4. *Military* body, detail, force, party, patrol, squad, task force, unit

detail *n.* 1. aspect, component, count, element, fact, factor, fea~ture, item, particular, point, re~spect, specific, technicality 2. *Plu~ral* fine points, minutiae, niceties, particulars, parts, trivia, trivialities 3. **in detail** comprehensively, ex~haustively, inside out, item by item, point by point, thoroughly 4. *Military* assignment, body, detach~ment, duty, fatigue, force, party, squad ~*v.* 5. catalogue, delineate, depict, describe, enumerate, indi~vidualize, itemize, narrate, par~ticularize, portray, recite, recount, rehearse, relate, specify 6. allo~cate, appoint, assign, charge, com~mission, delegate, detach, send

detailed blow-by-blow, circum~stantial, comprehensive, elaborate, exact, exhaustive, full, intricate, itemized, meticulous, minute, par~ticular, particularized, specific, thorough

detain 1. check, delay, hinder, hold up, impede, keep, keep back, re~tard, slow up (*or* down), stay, stop 2. arrest, confine, hold, intern, re~strain

detect 1. ascertain, catch, descry, distinguish, identify, note, notice, observe, recognize, scent, spot 2. catch, disclose, discover, expose, find, reveal, track down, uncover, unmask

detection discovery, exposé, ex~posure, ferreting out, revelation, tracking down, uncovering, un~earthing, unmasking

detective C.I.D. man, constable, cop (*Sl.*), copper (*Sl.*), dick (*Sl., chiefly U.S.*), gumshoe (*U.S. sl.*), investigator, private eye, private investigator, sleuth (*Inf.*)

detention confinement, custody, delay, hindrance, holding back, imprisonment, incarceration, keeping in, quarantine, restraint, withholding

deter caution, check, damp, daunt, debar, discourage, dissuade, frighten, hinder, inhibit from, in~timidate, prevent, prohibit, put off, restrain, stop, talk out of

detergent 1. *n.* cleaner, cleanser 2. *adj.* abstergent, cleaning, cleans~ing, detersive, purifying

deteriorate 1. corrupt, debase, de~cline, degenerate, degrade, de~prave, depreciate, go downhill (*Inf.*), go to pot, go to the dogs (*Inf.*), impair, injure, lower, spoil, worsen 2. be the worse for wear (*Inf.*), crumble, decay, decline, de~compose, disintegrate, ebb, fade, fall apart, lapse, weaken, wear away

deterioration atrophy, corrosion, debasement, decline, degenera~tion, degradation, dégringolade, depreciation, descent, dilapidation, disintegration, downturn, drop, fall, lapse, retrogression, slump, vitia~tion, worsening

determination 1. backbone, con~stancy, conviction, dedication, doggedness, drive, firmness, forti~tude, indomitability, perseverance, persistence, resoluteness, resolu~tion, resolve, single-mindedness, steadfastness, tenacity, willpower 2. conclusion, decision, judgment, purpose, resolve, result, settle~ment, solution, verdict

determine 1. arbitrate, conclude, decide, end, finish, fix upon, ordain, regulate, settle, terminate 2. as~certain, certify, check, detect, dis~

cover, find out, learn, verify, work out 3. choose, decide, elect, establish, fix, make up one's mind, purpose, resolve 4. affect, condition, control, decide, dictate, direct, govern, impel, impose, incline, induce, influence, lead, modify, regulate, rule, shape

determined bent on, constant, dogged, firm, fixed, intent, persevering, persistent, purposeful, resolute, set on, single-minded, steadfast, strong-minded, strong-willed, tenacious, unflinching, unwavering

determining conclusive, critical, crucial, deciding, decisive, definitive, essential, final, important, settling

deterrent n. check, curb, defensive measures, determent, discouragement, disincentive, hindrance, impediment, obstacle, restraint

detest abhor, abominate, despise, dislike intensely, execrate, feel aversion (disgust, hostility, repugnance) towards, hate, loathe, recoil from

detonate blast, blow up, discharge, explode, fulminate, set off, touch off

detonation bang, blast, blow-up, boom, discharge, explosion, fulmination, report

detour bypass, byway, circuitous route, deviation, diversion, indirect course, roundabout way

detract 1. devaluate, diminish, lessen, lower, reduce, take away from 2. deflect, distract, divert, shift

detraction abuse, aspersion, belittlement, calumny, defamation, denigration, deprecation, disparagement, innuendo, insinuation, misrepresentation, muckraking, running down, scandalmongering, scurrility, slander, traducement, vituperation

detractor backbiter, belittler, defamer, denigrator, derogator (*Rare*), disparager, muckraker, scandalmonger, slanderer, traducer

detriment damage, disadvantage,

disservice, harm, hurt, impairment, injury, loss, mischief, prejudice

detrimental adverse, baleful, damaging, deleterious, destructive, disadvantageous, harmful, inimical, injurious, mischievous, pernicious, prejudicial, unfavourable

devastate 1. demolish, desolate, despoil, destroy, lay waste, level, pillage, plunder, ravage, raze, ruin, sack, spoil, waste, wreck 2. *Inf.* chagrin, confound, discomfit, discompose, disconcert, floor (*Inf.*), nonplus, overpower, overwhelm, take aback

devastating caustic, cutting, deadly, destructive, effective, incisive, keen, mordant, overpowering, overwhelming, ravishing, sardonic, satirical, savage, stunning, trenchant, withering

devastation demolition, depredation, desolation, destruction, havoc, pillage, plunder, ravages, ruin, ruination, spoliation

develop 1. advance, cultivate, evolve, flourish, foster, grow, mature, progress, promote, prosper, ripen 2. amplify, augment, broaden, dilate upon, elaborate, enlarge, expand, unfold, work out 3. acquire, begin, breed, commence, contract, establish, form, generate, invent, originate, pick up, start 4. be a direct result of, break out, come about, ensue, follow, happen, result

development 1. advance, advancement, evolution, expansion, growth, improvement, increase, maturity, progress, progression, spread, unfolding, unravelling 2. change, circumstance, event, happening, incident, issue, occurrence, outcome, phenomenon, result, situation, turn of events, upshot

deviant 1. adj. aberrant, abnormal, bent (*Sl.*), deviate, devious, freaky (*Sl.*), heretical, kinky (*Sl.*), perverse, perverted, queer (*Inf.*), twisted, wayward 2. n. deviate, freak, misfit, odd type, pervert, queer (*Inf.*)

deviate avert, bend, deflect, de

part, differ, digress, diverge, drift, err, part, stray, swerve, turn, turn aside, vary, veer, wander

deviation aberration, alteration, change, deflection, departure, digression, discrepancy, disparity, divergence, fluctuation, inconsistency, irregularity, shift, variance, variation

device 1. apparatus, appliance, contraption, contrivance, gadget, gimmick, implement, instrument, invention, tool, utensil 2. artifice, design, dodge, expedient, gambit, improvisation, manoeuvre, plan, ploy, project, purpose, ruse, scheme, shift, stratagem, strategy, stunt, trick, wile 3. badge, colophon, crest, design, emblem, figure, insignia, logo, motif, motto, symbol, token

devil 1. *Sometimes cap.* Apollyon, archfiend, Beelzebub, Belial, Clootie (*Scot.*), demon, fiend, Lucifer, Old Harry (*Inf.*), Old Nick (*Inf.*), Prince of Darkness, Satan 2. beast, brute, demon, monster, ogre, rogue, savage, terror, villain 3. imp, monkey (*Inf.*), rascal, rogue, scamp, scoundrel 4. beggar, creature, thing, unfortunate, wretch 5. demon, enthusiast, fiend, go-getter (*Inf.*)

devilish accursed, atrocious, damnable, detestable, diabolic, diabolical, execrable, fiendish, hellish, infernal, satanic, wicked

devilry, deviltry 1. devilment, knavery, mischief, mischievousness, rascality, roguery 2. cruelty, evil, malevolence, malice, vice, viciousness, villainy, wickedness 3. black magic, diablerie, diabolism, sorcery

devious 1. calculating, crooked (*Inf.*), deceitful, dishonest, double-dealing, evasive, indirect, insidious, insincere, not straightforward, scheming, sly, surreptitious, treacherous, tricky, underhand, wily 2. circuitous, confusing, crooked, deviating, erratic, excursive, indirect, misleading, rambling, roundabout, tortuous, wandering

devise arrange, conceive, concoct, construct, contrive, design, dream up, form, formulate, frame, imagine, invent, plan, plot, prepare, project, scheme, think up, work out

devoid barren, bereft, deficient, denuded, destitute, empty, free from, lacking, sans (*Archaic*), unprovided with, vacant, void, wanting, without

devolution decentralization, delegation

devolve 1. be transferred, commission, consign, delegate, depute, entrust, fall upon *or* to, rest with, transfer 2. *Law* alienate, be handed down, convey

devote allot, apply, appropriate, assign, commit, concern oneself, consecrate, dedicate, enshrine, give, occupy oneself, pledge, reserve, set apart

devoted ardent, caring, committed, concerned, constant, dedicated, devout, faithful, fond, loving, loyal, staunch, steadfast, true

devotee addict, adherent, admirer, aficionado, disciple, enthusiast, fan, fanatic, follower, supporter, votary

devotion 1. adherence, allegiance, commitment, consecration, constancy, dedication, faithfulness, fidelity, loyalty 2. adoration, devoutness, godliness, holiness, piety, prayer, religiousness, reverence, sanctity, spirituality, worship 3. affection, ardour, attachment, earnestness, fervour, fondness, intensity, love, passion, zeal 4. *Plural* church service, divine office, prayers, religious observance

devour 1. bolt, consume, cram, dispatch, eat, gobble, gorge, gulp, guzzle, polish off (*Inf.*), stuff, swallow, wolf 2. annihilate, consume, destroy, ravage, spend, waste, wipe out 3. absorb, appreciate, be engrossed by, be preoccupied, delight in, drink in, enjoy, feast on, go through, read compulsively *or* voraciously, relish, revel in, take in

devouring consuming, excessive, insatiable, intense, overwhelming, passionate, powerful

devout 1. godly, holy, orthodox, pious, prayerful, pure, religious, reverent, saintly 2. ardent, deep, devoted, earnest, fervent, genuine, heartfelt, intense, passionate, profound, serious, sincere, zealous

devoutly fervently, heart and soul, profoundly, sincerely, with all one's heart

dexterity 1. adroitness, artistry, deftness, effortlessness, expertise, facility, finesse, handiness, knack, mastery, neatness, nimbleness, proficiency, skill, smoothness, touch 2. ability, address, adroitness, aptitude, aptness, art, cleverness, expertness, ingenuity, readiness, skilfulness, tact

diabolical appalling, atrocious, damnable, difficult, disastrous, dreadful, excruciating, fiendish, hellish, nasty, outrageous, shocking, tricky, unpleasant, vile

diagnose analyse, determine, distinguish, identify, interpret, investigate, pinpoint, pronounce, recognize

diagnosis 1. analysis, examination, investigation, scrutiny 2. conclusion, interpretation, opinion, pronouncement

diagonal *adj.* angled, catercornered (*U.S. inf.*), cornerways, cross, crossways, crosswise, oblique, slanting

diagonally aslant, at an angle, cornerwise, crosswise, obliquely, on the bias, on the cross

diagram chart, drawing, figure, layout, outline, plan, representation, sketch

dialect accent, idiom, jargon, language, lingo (*Inf.*), localism, patois, pronunciation, provincialism, speech, tongue, vernacular

dialectic 1. *adj.* analytic, argumentative, dialectical, logical, polemical, rational, rationalistic 2. *n. Often plural* argumentation, contention, discussion, disputation, logic, polemics, ratiocination, reasoning

dialogue 1. colloquy, communication, confabulation, conference, conversation, converse, discourse, discussion, duologue, interlocution 2. conversation, lines, script, spoken part

diametric, diametrical antipodal, antithetical, conflicting, contrary, contrasting, counter, opposed, opposite

diametrically absolutely, completely, entirely, utterly

diary appointment book, chronicle, daily record, day-to-day account, engagement book, journal

diatribe abuse, castigation, criticism, denunciation, disputation, harangue, invective, philippic, reviling, stream of abuse, stricture, tirade, verbal onslaught, vituperation

dicey chancy (*Inf.*), dangerous, difficult, risky, ticklish, tricky

dicky *adj.* fluttery, queer, shaky, unreliable, unsound, unsteady, weak

dictate *v.* 1. read out, say, speak, transmit, utter 2. command, decree, direct, enjoin, impose, lay down, ordain, order, prescribe, pronounce ~*n.* 3. behest, bidding, command, decree, direction, edict, fiat, injunction, mandate, order, ordinance, requirement, statute, ultimatum, word 4. code, dictum, law, precept, principle, rule

dictator absolute ruler, autocrat, despot, oppressor, tyrant

dictatorial 1. absolute, arbitrary, autocratic, despotic, totalitarian, tyrannical, unlimited, unrestricted 2. authoritarian, bossy (*Inf.*), dogmatical, domineering, imperious, iron-handed, magisterial, oppressive, overbearing

dictatorship absolute rule, absolutism, authoritarianism, autocracy, despotism, reign of terror, totalitarianism, tyranny

diction 1. expression, language, phraseology, phrasing, style, usage, vocabulary, wording 2. articulation, delivery, elocution, enunciation, fluency, inflection, intonation, pronunciation, speech

dictionary concordance, encyclopedia, glossary, lexicon, vocabulary, wordbook

die 1. breathe one's last, decease,

depart, expire, finish, give up the ghost, hop the twig (*Sl.*), kick the bucket (*Sl.*), pass away, perish, snuff it (*Sl.*) 2. decay, decline, disappear, dwindle, ebb, end, fade, lapse, pass, sink, subside, vanish, wane, wilt, wither 3. break down, fade out *or* away, fail, fizzle out, halt, lose power, peter out, run down, stop 4. ache, be eager, desire, hunger, languish, long, pine for, swoon, yearn 5. *Usually with* of be overcome, collapse, succumb to

die-hard 1. *n.* fanatic, intransigent, old fogy, reactionary, stick-in-the-mud (*Inf.*), ultraconservative, zealot 2. *adj.* dyed-in-the-wool, immovable, inflexible, intransigent, reactionary, ultraconservative, uncompromising, unreconstructed (*Chiefly U.S.*)

diet[1] *n.* 1. abstinence, dietary, fast, regime, regimen 2. aliment, comestibles, commons, edibles, fare, food, nourishment, nutriment, provisions, rations, subsistence, sustenance, viands, victuals ~*v.* 3. abstain, eat sparingly, fast, lose weight, reduce, slim

diet[2] chamber, congress, convention, council, legislative assembly, legislature, meeting, parliament, sitting

differ 1. be dissimilar, be distinct, contradict, contrast, depart from, diverge, run counter to, stand apart, vary 2. clash, contend, debate, demur, disagree, dispute, dissent, oppose, take issue

difference 1. alteration, change, contrast, deviation, differentiation, discrepancy, disparity, dissimilarity, distinction, distinctness, divergence, diversity, unlikeness, variation, variety 2. distinction, exception, idiosyncrasy, particularity, peculiarity, singularity 3. argument, clash, conflict, contention, contrariety, contretemps, controversy, debate, disagreement, discordance, dispute, quarrel, set-to (*Inf.*), strife, tiff, wrangle 4. balance, remainder, rest, result

different 1. altered, at odds, at variance, changed, clashing, con-

trasting, deviating, discrepant, disparate, dissimilar, divergent, diverse, inconsistent, opposed, unlike 2. another, discrete, distinct, individual, other, separate 3. assorted, divers (*Archaic*), diverse, manifold, many, miscellaneous, multifarious, numerous, several, some, sundry, varied, various 4. another story, atypical, bizarre, distinctive, extraordinary, out of the ordinary, peculiar, rare, singular, something else, special, strange, uncommon, unconventional, unique, unusual

differential 1. *adj.* diacritical, discriminative, distinctive, distinguishing 2. *n.* amount of difference, difference, discrepancy, disparity

differentiate 1. contrast, discern, discriminate, distinguish, make a distinction, mark off, separate, set off *or* apart, tell apart 2. adapt, alter, change, convert, make different, modify, transform

difficult 1. arduous, burdensome, demanding, formidable, hard, laborious, no picnic (*Inf.*), onerous, painful, strenuous, toilsome, uphill, wearisome 2. abstract, abstruse, baffling, complex, complicated, delicate, enigmatical, intricate, involved, knotty, obscure, perplexing, problematical, thorny, ticklish 3. demanding, fastidious, fractious, fussy, hard to please, intractable, obstreperous, perverse, refractory, rigid, tiresome, troublesome, trying, unaccommodating, unamenable, unmanageable 4. dark, full of hardship, grim, hard, straitened, tough, trying

difficulty 1. arduousness, awkwardness, hardship, laboriousness, labour, pain, painfulness, strain, strenuousness, tribulation 2. deep water, dilemma, distress, embarrassment, fix (*Inf.*), hot water, jam (*Inf.*), mess, perplexity, pickle (*Inf.*), plight, predicament, quandary, spot (*Inf.*), straits, trial, trouble 3. *Often plural* complication, hindrance, hurdle, impediment, objection, obstacle, opposition, pitfall, problem, protest

diffidence backwardness, bashfulness, constraint, doubt, fear, hesi~tancy, hesitation, humility, insecu~rity, lack of self-confidence, meek~ness, modesty, reluctance, reserve, self-consciousness, sheepishness, shyness, timidity, timidness, tim~orousness, unassertiveness

diffident backward, bashful, con~strained, distrustful, doubtful, hesi~tant, insecure, meek, modest, re~luctant, reserved, self-conscious, self-effacing, sheepish, shrinking, shy, suspicious, timid, timorous, unassertive, unassuming, unobtru~sive, unsure, withdrawn

diffuse *adj.* 1. circumlocutory, co~pious, diffusive, digressive, discur~sive, long-winded, loose, maunder~ing, meandering, prolix, rambling, vague, verbose, waffling (*Inf.*), wordy 2. dispersed, scattered, spread out, unconcentrated ~*v.* 3. circulate, dispel, dispense, dis~perse, disseminate, dissipate, dis~tribute, propagate, scatter, spread

diffusion 1. circulation, dispersal, dispersion, dissemination, dissipa~tion, distribution, expansion, propaganda, propagation, scatter~ing, spread 2. circuitousness, dif~fuseness, digressiveness, discur~siveness, long-windedness, prolix~ity, rambling, verbiage, verbosity, wandering, wordiness

dig *v.* 1. break up, burrow, delve, excavate, gouge, grub, hoe, hollow out, mine, penetrate, pierce, quar~ry, scoop, till, tunnel, turn over 2. drive, jab, poke, prod, punch, thrust 3. delve, dig down, go into, investigate, probe, research, search 4. *With* **out** *or* **up** bring to light, come across, come up with, discover, expose, extricate, find, retrieve, root (*Inf.*), rootle, uncov~er, unearth 5. *Inf.* appreciate, en~joy, follow, groove (*Sl.*), like, understand ~*n.* 6. jab, poke, prod, punch, thrust (*Sl.*), crack (*Sl.*), cutting remark, gibe, insult, jeer, quip, sneer, taunt, wisecrack (*Inf.*)

digest *v.* 1. absorb, assimilate, con~coct, dissolve, incorporate, macer~ate 2. absorb, assimilate, con, con~sider, contemplate, grasp, master,

meditate, ponder, study, take in, understand 3. arrange, classify, codify, dispose, methodize, sys~tematize, tabulate 4. abridge, com~press, condense, reduce, shorten, summarize ~*n.* 5. abridgment, ab~stract, compendium, condensation, epitome, précis, résumé, summary, synopsis

digestion absorption, assimilation, conversion, incorporation, inges~tion, transformation

dig in 1. defend, entrench, estab~lish, fortify, maintain 2. *Inf.* begin, set about, start eating, tuck in (*Inf.*)

dignified august, decorous, distin~guished, exalted, formal, grave, honourable, imposing, lofty, lordly, noble, reserved, solemn, stately, upright

dignify adorn, advance, aggrandize, distinguish, elevate, ennoble, exalt, glorify, grace, honour, promote, raise

dignitary *n.* high-up (*Inf.*), notabil~ity, notable, personage, pillar of society (the church, the state), public figure, V.I.P., worthy

dignity 1. courtliness, decorum, grandeur, gravity, hauteur, lofti~ness, majesty, nobility, propriety, solemnity, stateliness 2. elevation, eminence, excellence, glory, greatness, honour, importance, nobleness, rank, respectability, standing, station, status 3. *amour-propre*, pride, self-esteem, self-importance, self-possession, self-regard, self-respect

digress be diffuse, depart, deviate, diverge, drift, expatiate, get off the point *or* subject, go off at a tan~gent, ramble, stray, turn aside, wander

digression apostrophe, aside, de~parture, detour, deviation, diver~gence, diversion, footnote, obiter dictum, parenthesis, straying, wandering

dilapidated battered, broken-down, crumbling, decayed, decay~ing, decrepit, fallen in, falling apart, gone to wrack and ruin, in ruins, neglected, ramshackle, rickety, ruined, ruinous, run-down,

shabby, shaky, tumble-down, un~
cared for, worn-out

dilate 1. broaden, distend, enlarge,
expand, extend, puff out, stretch,
swell, widen 2. amplify, be profuse,
be prolix, descant, detail, develop,
dwell on, enlarge, expand, expati~
ate, expound, spin out

dilatory backward, behindhand,
dallying, delaying, laggard, linger~
ing, loitering, procrastinating, put~
ting off, slack, slow, sluggish, snail-
like, tardy, tarrying, time-wasting

dilemma 1. difficulty, embarrass~
ment, fix (*Inf.*), jam (*Inf.*), mess,
perplexity, pickle (*Inf.*), plight,
predicament, problem, puzzle,
quandary, spot (*Inf.*), strait, tight
corner 2. **on the horns of a dilemma** between Scylla and Charybdis,
between the devil and the deep
blue sea

dilettante aesthete, amateur, dab~
bler, nonprofessional, trifler

diligence activity, application, as~
siduity, assiduousness, attention,
attentiveness, care, constancy,
earnestness, heedfulness, industry,
intentness, laboriousness, per~
severance, sedulousness

diligent active, assiduous, atten~
tive, busy, careful, conscientious,
constant, earnest, hard-working,
indefatigable, industrious, labo~
rious, painstaking, persevering,
persistent, sedulous, studious, tire~
less

dilly-dally dally, dawdle, delay,
dither, falter, fluctuate, hesitate,
hover, linger, loiter, potter, pro~
crastinate, shillyshally (*Inf.*), trifle,
vacillate, waver

dilute v. 1. adulterate, cut, make
thinner, thin (out), water down,
weaken 2. *Fig.* attenuate, decrease,
diffuse, diminish, lessen, mitigate,
reduce, temper, weaken

dim *adj.* 1. caliginous (*Archaic*),
cloudy, dark, darkish, dusky, grey,
overcast, poorly lit, shadowy, ten~
ebrous, unilluminated 2. bleary,
blurred, faint, fuzzy, ill-defined, in~
distinct, obscured, shadowy, un~
clear 3. dense, doltish, dull, dumb
(*Inf.*), obtuse, slow, slow on the up~

take (*Inf.*), stupid, thick 4. con~
fused, hazy, imperfect, indistinct,
intangible, obscure, remote, shad~
owy, vague 5. dingy, dull, feeble,
lacklustre, muted, opaque, pale,
sullied, tarnished, weak 6. dashing,
depressing, discouraging, gloomy,
sombre, unfavourable, unpromis~
ing 7. **take a dim view** be dis~
pleased, be sceptical, disapprove,
look askance, reject, suspect, take
exception, view with disfavour ~v.
8. bedim, blur, cloud, darken, dull,
fade, lower, obscure, tarnish, turn
down

dimension *Often plural* 1. ampli~
tude, bulk, capacity, extent, meas~
urement, proportions, size, volume
2. bigness, extent, greatness, im~
portance, largeness, magnitude,
measure, range, scale, scope

diminish 1. abate, contract, curtail,
cut, decrease, lessen, lower, re~
duce, retrench, shrink, weaken 2.
decline, die out, dwindle, ebb, fade
away, peter out, recede, shrivel,
slacken, subside, wane 3. belittle,
cheapen, demean, depreciate, de~
value

diminution abatement, contrac~
tion, curtailment, cut, cutback, de~
cay, decline, decrease, deduction,
lessening, reduction, retrench~
ment, weakening

diminutive *adj.* bantam, Lilliputi~
an, little, midget, mini, miniature,
minute, petite, pocket(-sized), pyg~
my, small, tiny, undersized, wee

din 1. *n.* babel, clamour, clangour,
clash, clatter, commotion, crash,
hubbub, hullabaloo, noise, outcry,
pandemonium, racket, row, shout,
uproar 2. *v. Usually with* **into** drum
into, go on at, hammer into, incul~
cate, instil, instruct, teach

dine 1. banquet, eat, feast, lunch,
sup 2. *Often with* **on, off** *or* **upon**
consume, eat, feed on

dingy bedimmed, colourless, dark,
dim, dirty, discoloured, drab,
dreary, dull, dusky, faded, gloomy,
grimy, murky, obscure, seedy,
shabby, soiled, sombre, tacky

dinner banquet, beanfeast (*Inf.*),
blowout (*Sl.*), collation, feast, main

meal, meal, refection, repast, spread

dip *v.* 1. bathe, douse, duck, dunk, immerse, plunge, rinse, souse 2. decline, descend, disappear, droop, drop (down), fade, fall, lower, sag, set, sink, slope, slump, subside, tilt 3. ladle, scoop, spoon 4. *With* in *or* into browse, dabble, glance at, peruse, play at, run over, sample, skim, try 5. *With* in *or* into draw upon, reach into ~*n.* 6. douche, drenching, ducking, immersion, plunge, soaking 7. bathe, dive, plunge, swim 8. concoction, dilution, infusion, mixture, preparation, solution, suspension 9. basin, concavity, depression, hole, hollow, incline, slope 10. decline, fall, lowering, sag, slip, slump

diplomacy 1. international negotiation, statecraft, statesmanship 2. artfulness, craft, delicacy, discretion, finesse, savoir faire, skill, subtlety, tact

diplomat conciliator, go-between, mediator, moderator, negotiator, politician, public relations expert, tactician

diplomatic adept, discreet, polite, politic, prudent, sensitive, subtle, tactful

dire 1. alarming, appalling, awful, calamitous, cataclysmic, catastrophic, cruel, disastrous, horrible, horrid, ruinous, terrible, woeful 2. dismal, dreadful, fearful, gloomy, grim, ominous, portentous 3. critical, crucial, crying, desperate, drastic, exigent, extreme, pressing, urgent

direct[1] *v.* 1. administer, advise, conduct, control, dispose, govern, guide, handle, lead, manage, mastermind, oversee, preside over, regulate, rule, run, superintend, supervise 2. bid, charge, command, dictate, enjoin, instruct, order 3. guide, indicate, lead, point in the direction of, point the way, show 4. address, aim, cast, fix, focus, intend, level, mean, point, train, turn 5. address, label, mail, route, send, superscribe

direct[2] *adj.* 1. candid, frank, honest, man-to-man, matter-of-fact, open, outspoken, plain-spoken, sincere, straight, straightforward 2. absolute, blunt, categorical, downright, explicit, express, plain, pointblank, unambiguous, unequivocal 3. nonstop, not crooked, shortest, straight, through, unbroken, undeviating, uninterrupted 4. face-to-face, first-hand, head-on, immediate, personal

direction 1. administration, charge, command, control, government, guidance, leadership, management, order, oversight, superintendence, supervision 2. aim, bearing, course, line, path, road, route, track, way 3. bent, bias, current, drift, end, orientation, proclivity, tack, tendency, tenor, trend 4. address, label, mark, superscription

directions briefing, guidance, guidelines, indication, instructions, plan, recommendation, regulations

directive *n.* charge, command, decree, dictate, edict, injunction, instruction, mandate, notice, order, ordinance, regulation, ruling

directly 1. by the shortest route, exactly, in a beeline, precisely, straight, unswervingly, without deviation 2. as soon as possible, at once, dead, due, forthwith, immediately, in a second, instantaneously, instantly, presently, promptly, pronto (*Inf.*), quickly, right away, soon, speedily, straightaway 3. candidly, face-to-face, honestly, in person, openly, personally, plainly, point-blank, straightforwardly, truthfully, unequivocally, without prevarication

director administrator, boss (*Inf.*), chairman, chief, controller, executive, governor, head, leader, manager, organizer, principal, producer, supervisor

dirge coronach (*Scot. & Irish*), dead march, elegy, funeral song, lament, requiem, threnody

dirt 1. dust, excrement, filth, grime, impurity, mire, muck, mud, slime, smudge, stain, tarnish 2. clay,

earth, loam, soil 3. indecency, ob~
scenity, pornography, smut

dirty *adj.* 1. begrimed, filthy, foul,
grimy, grubby, messy, mucky,
muddy, nasty, polluted, soiled, sul~
lied, unclean 2. blue, indecent, ob~
scene, off-colour, pornographic,
risqué, salacious, smutty, vulgar 3.
clouded, dark, dull, miry, muddy,
not clear 4. corrupt, crooked, dis~
honest, fraudulent, illegal, treach~
erous, unfair, unscrupulous, un~
sporting 5. base, beggarly, con~
temptible, cowardly, despicable,
ignominious, low, low-down (*Inf.*),
mean, nasty, scurvy, shabby, sor~
did, squalid, vile 6. angry, annoyed,
bitter, indignant, offended, resent~
ful, scorching 7. *Of weather* gusty,
lowering, rainy, squally, stormy
~*v.* 8. begrime, blacken, defile,
foul, mess up, muddy, pollute,
smear, smudge, soil, spoil, stain,
sully

disability 1. affliction, ailment,
complaint, defect, disablement,
disorder, handicap, impairment,
infirmity, malady 2. disqualifica~
tion, impotency, inability, incapac~
ity, incompetency, unfitness,
weakness

disable 1. cripple, damage, debili~
tate, enfeeble, hamstring, handi~
cap, immobilize, impair, incapaci~
tate, paralyse, prostrate, put out of
action, render *hors de combat*,
render inoperative, unfit, unman,
weaken 2. disenable, disqualify, in~
validate, render *or* declare inca~
pable

disabled bedridden, crippled,
handicapped, incapacitated, in~
firm, lame, maimed, mangled,
mutilated, paralysed, weak, weak~
ened, wrecked

disadvantage 1. damage, detri~
ment, disservice, harm, hurt, inju~
ry, loss, prejudice 2. *Often plural*
burden, drawback, flaw, fly in the
ointment (*Inf.*), handicap, hard~
ship, hindrance, impediment, in~
convenience, liability, minus (*Inf.*),
nuisance, privation, snag, trouble,
weakness, weak point 3. at a dis~
advantage boxed in, cornered,
handicapped, in a corner, vulner~
able

disadvantageous adverse, dam~
aging, deleterious, detrimental,
harmful, hurtful, ill-timed, incon~
venient, inexpedient, injurious, in~
opportune, prejudicial, unfavour~
able

disaffected alienated, antagonis~
tic, discontented, disloyal, dissatis~
fied, estranged, hostile, mutinous,
rebellious, seditious, uncompliant,
unsubmissive

disaffection alienation, animosity,
antagonism, antipathy, aversion,
breach, disagreement, discontent,
dislike, disloyalty, dissatisfaction,
estrangement, hostility, ill will, re~
pugnance, resentment, unfriendli~
ness

disagree 1. be discordant, be dis~
similar, conflict, contradict, coun~
ter, depart, deviate, differ, diverge,
run counter to, vary 2. argue,
bicker, clash, contend, contest, de~
bate, differ (in opinion), dispute,
dissent, fall out (*Inf.*), have words
(*Inf.*), object, oppose, quarrel, take
issue with, wrangle 3. be injurious,
bother, discomfort, distress, hurt,
make ill, nauseate, sicken, trouble,
upset

disagreeable 1. bad-tempered,
brusque, churlish, contrary, cross,
difficult, disobliging, ill-natured, ir~
ritable, nasty, peevish, rude, surly,
unfriendly, ungracious, unlikable,
unpleasant 2. disgusting, displeas~
ing, distasteful, nasty, objection~
able, obnoxious, offensive, repel~
lent, repugnant, repulsive, uninvit~
ing, unpalatable, unpleasant, unsa~
voury

disagreement 1. difference, dis~
crepancy, disparity, dissimilarity,
dissimilitude, divergence, diver~
sity, incompatibility, incongruity,
unlikeness, variance 2. altercation,
argument, clash, conflict, debate,
difference, discord, dispute, dis~
sent, division, falling out, mis~
understanding, quarrel, squabble,
strife, wrangle 3. in disagreement
at daggers drawn, at loggerheads,

at odds, at variance, disunited, in conflict

disallow 1. abjure, disavow, disclaim, dismiss, disown, rebuff, refuse, reject, repudiate 2. ban, cancel, embargo, forbid, prohibit, proscribe, veto

disappear 1. be lost to view, depart, drop out of sight, ebb, escape, evanesce, fade away, flee, fly, go, pass, recede, retire, vanish from sight, wane, withdraw 2. cease, cease to be known, die out, dissolve, end, evaporate, expire, fade, leave no trace, melt away, pass away, perish, vanish

disappearance departure, desertion, disappearing, disappearing trick, eclipse, evanescence, evaporation, fading, flight, going, loss, melting, passing, vanishing, vanishing point

disappoint 1. chagrin, dash, deceive, delude, disenchant, disgruntle, dishearten, disillusion, dismay, dissatisfy, fail, let down, sadden, vex 2. baffle, balk, defeat, disconcert, foil, frustrate, hamper, hinder, thwart

disappointed balked, cast down, depressed, despondent, discontented, discouraged, disenchanted, disgruntled, disillusioned, dissatisfied, distressed, downhearted, foiled, frustrated, let down, saddened, thwarted, upset

disappointing depressing, disagreeable, disconcerting, discouraging, failing, inadequate, inferior, insufficient, lame, pathetic, sad, second-rate, sorry, unexpected, unhappy, unsatisfactory, unworthy, upsetting

disappointment 1. chagrin, discontent, discouragement, disenchantment, disillusionment, displeasure, dissatisfaction, distress, failure, frustration, ill-success, mortification, regret, unfulfilment 2. blow, calamity, disaster, failure, fiasco, letdown, miscarriage, misfortune, setback, washout (*Inf.*)

disapproval censure, condemnation, criticism, denunciation, deprecation, disapprobation, displeasure, dissatisfaction, objection, reproach

disapprove 1. *Often with* of blame, censure, condemn, deplore, deprecate, discountenance, dislike, find unacceptable, frown on, look down one's nose at (*Inf.*), object to, reject, take exception to 2. disallow, set aside, spurn, turn down, veto

disarmament arms limitation, arms reduction, de-escalation, demilitarization, demobilization

disarming charming, irresistible, likable, persuasive, winning

disarrange confuse, derange, discompose, disorder, disorganize, disturb, jumble (up), mess (up), scatter, shake (up), shuffle, unsettle, untidy

disarray 1. confusion, discomposure, disharmony, dismay, disorder, disorderliness, disorganization, disunity, indiscipline, unruliness, upset 2. chaos, clutter, dishevelment, jumble, mess, mix-up, muddle, shambles, tangle, untidiness

disaster accident, act of God, adversity, blow, calamity, cataclysm, catastrophe, misadventure, mischance, misfortune, mishap, reverse, ruin, ruination, stroke, tragedy, trouble

disastrous adverse, calamitous, cataclysmal, cataclysmic, catastrophic, destructive, detrimental, devastating, dire, dreadful, fatal, hapless, harmful, ill-fated, ill-starred, ruinous, terrible, tragic, unfortunate, unlucky, unpropitious, untoward

disbelief distrust, doubt, dubiety, incredulity, mistrust, scepticism, unbelief

disbeliever agnostic, atheist, doubter, doubting Thomas, questioner, sceptic, scoffer

disbelievingly askance, cynically, doubtingly, incredulously, mistrustfully, quizzically, sceptically, suspiciously, with a pinch of salt

discard abandon, cast aside, dispense with, dispose of, ditch (*Sl.*), drop, dump (*Inf.*), get rid of, jettison, reject, relinquish, remove, repudiate, scrap, shed, throw away *or* out

discerning acute, astute, clear-sighted, critical, discriminating, ingenious, intelligent, judicious, knowing, penetrating, perceptive, percipient, perspicacious, piercing, sagacious, sensitive, sharp, shrewd, subtle, wise

discharge *v.* 1. absolve, acquit, allow to go, clear, exonerate, free, liberate, pardon, release, set free ~*n.* 2. acquittal, clearance, exoneration, liberation, pardon, release, remittance ~*v.* 3. cashier, discard, dismiss, eject, expel, fire (*Inf.*), give (someone) the sack (*Inf.*), oust, remove, sack (*Inf.*) ~*n.* 4. congé, demobilization, dismissal, ejection, the boot (*Sl.*), the sack (*Inf.*) ~*v.* 5. detonate, explode, fire, let off, set off, shoot ~*n.* 6. blast, burst, detonation, discharging, explosion, firing, fusillade, report, salvo, shot, volley ~*v.* 7. disembogue, dispense, emit, empty, excrete, exude, give off, gush, leak, ooze, pour forth, release, void ~*n.* 8. emission, emptying, excretion, flow, ooze, pus, secretion, seepage, suppuration, vent, voiding ~*v.* 9. disburden, off-load, remove, unburden, unload ~*n.* 10. disburdening, emptying, unburdening, unloading ~*v.* 11. accomplish, carry out, do, execute, fulfil, observe, perform ~*n.* 12. accomplishment, achievement, execution, fulfilment, observance, performance ~*v.* 13. clear, honour, meet, pay, relieve, satisfy, settle, square up ~*n.* 14. payment, satisfaction, settlement

disciple adherent, apostle, believer, catechumen, convert, devotee, follower, learner, partisan, proselyte, pupil, student, supporter, votary

disciplinarian authoritarian, despot, drill sergeant, hard master, martinet, stickler, strict teacher, taskmaster, tyrant

discipline *n.* 1. drill, exercise, method, practice, regimen, regulation, training 2. conduct, control, orderliness, regulation, restraint, self-control, strictness 3. castigation, chastisement, correction, punishment 4. area, branch of knowledge, course, curriculum, field of study, specialty, subject ~*v.* 5. break in, bring up, check, control, drill, educate, exercise, form, govern, instruct, inure, train 6. castigate, chasten, chastise, correct, penalize, punish, reprimand, reprove

disclaim abandon, abjure, abnegate, decline, deny, disaffirm, disallow, disavow, disown, forswear, reject, renounce, repudiate

disclose 1. broadcast, communicate, confess, divulge, impart, leak, let slip, make known, make public, publish, relate, reveal, spill the beans about (*Inf.*), tell, unveil, utter 2. bring to light, discover, exhibit, expose, lay bare, reveal, show, uncover, unveil

disclosure acknowledgment, admission, announcement, broadcast, confession, declaration, discovery, divulgence, exposé, exposure, leak, publication, revelation, uncovering

discolour fade, mar, mark, rust, soil, stain, streak, tarnish, tinge

discomfort 1. *n.* ache, annoyance, disquiet, distress, hardship, hurt, inquietude, irritation, malaise, nuisance, pain, soreness, trouble, uneasiness, unpleasantness, vexation 2. *v.* discomfit, discompose, disquiet, distress, disturb, embarrass, make uncomfortable

discomposure agitation, anxiety, confusion, discomfiture, disquiet, disquietude, distraction, disturbance, embarrassment, fluster, inquietude, malaise, nervousness, perturbation, uneasiness

disconcert 1. abash, agitate, bewilder, discompose, disturb, flurry, fluster, nonplus, perplex, perturb, put out of countenance, rattle (*Inf.*), ruffle, shake up (*Inf.*), take aback, throw off balance, trouble, unbalance, unsettle, upset, worry 2. baffle, balk, confuse, defeat, disarrange, frustrate, hinder, put off, thwart, undo

disconcerted annoyed, bewil~ dered, caught off balance, con~ fused, distracted, disturbed, em~ barrassed, fazed (*U.S. inf.*), flur~ ried, flustered, mixed-up, non~ plussed, out of countenance, per~ turbed, rattled (*Inf.*), ruffled, shook up (*Inf.*), taken aback, thrown (*Inf.*), troubled, unsettled, upset

disconcerting alarming, awkward, baffling, bewildering, bothersome, confusing, dismaying, distracting, disturbing, embarrassing, off-putting (*Brit. inf.*), perplexing, up~ setting

disconnect cut off, detach, disen~ gage, divide, part, separate, sever, take apart, uncouple

disconnected confused, disjointed, garbled, illogical, incoherent, irra~ tional, jumbled, mixed-up, ram~ bling, uncoordinated, unintelli~ gible, wandering

disconnection cessation, cut-off, cutting off, discontinuation, dis~ continuity, interruption, separa~ tion, severance, stoppage, suspen~ sion

disconsolate crushed, dejected, desolate, despairing, forlorn, gloomy, grief-stricken, heart~ broken, hopeless, inconsolable, melancholy, miserable, sad, un~ happy, woeful, wretched

discontent *n.* discontentment, dis~ pleasure, dissatisfaction, envy, fretfulness, regret, restlessness, uneasiness, unhappiness, vexation

discontented brassed off (*Sl.*), cheesed off (*Brit. sl.*), complaining, disaffected, disgruntled, dis~ pleased, dissatisfied, exasperated, fed up, fretful, miserable, unhappy, vexed, with a chip on one's shoul~ der (*Inf.*)

discontinue abandon, break off, cease, drop, end, finish, give up, halt, interrupt, leave off, pause, put an end to, quit, refrain from, stop, suspend, terminate

discontinued abandoned, ended, finished, given up *or* over, halted, no longer made, terminated

discord 1. clashing, conflict, con~ tention, difference, disagreement, discordance, dispute, dissension, disunity, division, friction, incom~ patibility, lack of concord, opposi~ tion, rupture, strife, variance, wrangling 2. cacophony, din, dis~ harmony, dissonance, harshness, jangle, jarring, racket, tumult

discordant 1. at odds, clashing, conflicting, contradictory, contra~ ry, different, disagreeing, diver~ gent, incompatible, incongruous, inconsistent, opposite 2. cacopho~ nous, dissonant, grating, harsh, in~ harmonious, jangling, jarring, shrill, strident, unmelodious

discount *v.* 1. brush off, disbelieve, disregard, ignore, leave out of ac~ count, overlook, pass over 2. de~ duct, lower, mark down, rebate, reduce, take off ~*n.* 3. abatement, allowance, concession, cut, cut price, deduction, drawback, per~ centage (*Inf.*), rebate, reduction

discourage 1. abash, awe, cast down, cow, damp, dampen, dash, daunt, deject, demoralize, depress, dishearten, dismay, dispirit, fright~ en, intimidate, overawe, put a damper on, scare, unman, unnerve 2. check, curb, deprecate, deter, discountenance, disfavour, dis~ suade, divert from, hinder, inhibit, prevent, put off, restrain, talk out of, throw cold water on (*Inf.*)

discouraged crestfallen, dashed, daunted, deterred, disheartened, dismayed, dispirited, downcast, down in the mouth, glum, pessi~ mistic, put off

discouragement 1. cold feet (*Inf.*), dejection, depression, despair, de~ spondency, disappointment, dis~ comfiture, dismay, downhearted~ ness, hopelessness, loss of confi~ dence, low spirits, pessimism 2. constraint, curb, damper, deter~ rent, disincentive, hindrance, im~ pediment, obstacle, opposition, re~ buff, restraint, setback

discouraging dampening, daunt~ ing, depressing, disappointing, dis~ heartening, dispiriting, off-putting

(*Brit. inf.*), unfavourable, unpropitious

discourse *n.* **1.** chat, communication, conversation, converse, dialogue, discussion, speech, talk **2.** address, disquisition, dissertation, essay, homily, lecture, oration, sermon, speech, talk, treatise ~*v.* **3.** confer, converse, debate, declaim, discuss, expatiate, hold forth, speak, talk

discourteous abrupt, bad-mannered, boorish, brusque, curt, disrespectful, ill-bred, ill-mannered, impolite, insolent, offhand, rude, uncivil, uncourteous, ungentlemanly, ungracious, unmannerly

discourtesy 1. bad manners, disrespectfulness, ill-breeding, impertinence, impoliteness, incivility, insolence, rudeness, ungraciousness, unmannerliness **2.** affront, cold shoulder, insult, rebuff, slight, snub

discover 1. bring to light, come across, come upon, dig up, find, light upon, locate, turn up, uncover, unearth **2.** ascertain, descry, detect, determine, discern, disclose, espy, find out, get wise to (*Inf.*), learn, notice, perceive, realize, recognize, reveal, see, spot, uncover **3.** conceive, contrive, design, devise, invent, originate, pioneer

discoverer author, explorer, founder, initiator, inventor, originator, pioneer

discovery 1. ascertainment, detection, disclosure, espial, exploration, finding, introduction, locating, location, origination, revelation, uncovering **2.** bonanza, breakthrough, coup, find, findings, godsend, innovation, invention, secret

discredit *v.* **1.** blame, bring into disrepute, censure, defame, degrade, detract from, disgrace, dishonour, disparage, reproach, slander, slur, smear, vilify ~*n.* **2.** aspersion, censure, disgrace, dishonour, disrepute, ignominy, ill-repute, imputation, odium, reproach, scandal, shame, slur, smear, stigma ~*v.* **3.** challenge, deny, disbelieve, discount, dispute, distrust, doubt, mistrust, question ~*n.* **4.** distrust, doubt, mistrust, question, scepticism, suspicion

discreditable blameworthy, degrading, disgraceful, dishonourable, humiliating, ignominious, improper, infamous, reprehensible, scandalous, shameful, unprincipled, unworthy

discredited brought into disrepute, debunked, discarded, exploded, exposed, obsolete, outworn, refuted, rejected

discreet careful, cautious, circumspect, considerate, diplomatic, discerning, guarded, judicious, politic, prudent, reserved, sagacious, sensible, tactful, wary

discrepancy conflict, contrariety, difference, disagreement, discordance, disparity, dissimilarity, dissonance, divergence, incongruity, inconsistency, variance, variation

discretion 1. acumen, care, carefulness, caution, circumspection, consideration, diplomacy, discernment, good sense, heedfulness, judgment, judiciousness, maturity, prudence, sagacity, tact, wariness **2.** choice, disposition, inclination, liking, mind, option, pleasure, predilection, preference, responsibility, volition, will, wish

discretionary arbitrary (*Law*), elective, nonmandatory, open, open to choice, optional, unrestricted

discriminate 1. disfavour, favour, show bias, show prejudice, single out, treat as inferior, treat differently, victimize **2.** assess, differentiate, discern, distinguish, draw a distinction, evaluate, segregate, separate, sift, tell the difference

discriminating acute, astute, critical, cultivated, discerning, fastidious, keen, particular, refined, selective, sensitive, tasteful

discrimination 1. bias, bigotry, favouritism, inequity, intolerance, prejudice, unfairness **2.** acumen, acuteness, clearness, discernment, insight, judgment, keenness, penetration, perception, refinement, sagacity, subtlety, taste

discriminatory, discriminative 1. biased, favouring, inequitable, one-sided, partial, partisan, preferential, prejudiced, prejudicial, unjust, weighted 2. analytical, astute, differentiating, discerning, discriminating, perceptive, perspicacious

discuss argue, confer, consider, consult with, converse, debate, deliberate, examine, exchange views on, get together (*Inf.*), go into, reason about, review, sift, talk about, thrash out, ventilate, weigh up the pros and cons

discussion analysis, argument, colloquy, confabulation, conference, consideration, consultation, conversation, debate, deliberation, dialogue, discourse, examination, exchange, review, scrutiny, symposium

disdain 1. *v.* belittle, contemn, deride, despise, disregard, look down on, look down one's nose at (*Inf.*), misprize, pooh-pooh, reject, scorn, slight, sneer at, spurn, undervalue 2. *n.* arrogance, contempt, contumely, derision, dislike, haughtiness, hauteur, indifference, scorn, sneering, snobbishness, superciliousness

disdainful aloof, arrogant, contemptuous, derisive, haughty, high and mighty (*Inf.*), hoity-toity (*Inf.*), insolent, proud, scornful, sneering, supercilious, superior

disease 1. affliction, ailment, complaint, condition, disorder, ill health, illness, indisposition, infection, infirmity, malady, sickness, upset 2. *Fig.* blight, cancer, canker, contagion, contamination, disorder, malady, plague

diseased ailing, infected, rotten, sick, sickly, tainted, unhealthy, unsound, unwell, unwholesome

disembark alight, arrive, get off, go ashore, land, step out of

disembodied bodiless, ghostly, immaterial, incorporeal, intangible, phantom, spectral, spiritual, unbodied

disenchanted blasé, cynical, disappointed, disillusioned, indifferent, jaundiced, let down, out of love, sick of, soured, undeceived

disenchantment disappointment, disillusion, disillusionment, revulsion, rude awakening

disengage 1. disentangle, ease, extricate, free, liberate, loosen, release, set free, unloose, untie 2. detach, disconnect, disjoin, disunite, divide, separate, undo, withdraw

disengaged 1. apart, detached, free, loose, out of gear, released, separate, unattached, unconnected, uncoupled 2. at ease, at leisure, free, not busy, uncommitted, unoccupied, vacant

disengagement detachment, disconnection, disentanglement, division, separation, withdrawal

disentangle 1. detach, disconnect, disengage, extricate, free, loose, separate, sever, unfold, unravel, unsnarl, untangle, untwist 2. clarify, clear (up), resolve, simplify, sort out, work out

disfavour 1. disapprobation, disapproval, dislike, displeasure 2. *As in* fall into disfavour bad books (*Inf.*), discredit, disesteem, disgrace, doghouse (*Inf.*), shame, unpopularity 3. bad turn, discourtesy, disservice

disfigure blemish, damage, deface, deform, disfeature, distort, injure, maim, make ugly, mar, mutilate, scar

disfigurement blemish, defacement, defect, deformity, distortion, impairment, injury, mutilation, scar, spot, stain

disgrace *n.* 1. baseness, degradation, dishonour, disrepute, ignominy, infamy, odium, opprobrium, shame 2. aspersion, blemish, blot, defamation, reproach, scandal, slur, stain, stigma 3. contempt, discredit, disesteem, disfavour, obloquy ~*v.* 4. abase, bring shame upon, defame, degrade, discredit, disfavour, dishonour, disparage, humiliate, reproach, shame, slur, stain, stigmatize, sully, taint

disgraced branded, degraded, discredited, dishonoured, humiliated, in disgrace, in the doghouse (*Inf.*), mortified, shamed, stigmatized

disgraceful blameworthy, contemptible, degrading, detestable, discreditable, dishonourable, disreputable, ignominious, infamous, low, mean, opprobrious, scandalous, shameful, shocking, unworthy

disgruntled annoyed, cheesed off (*Brit. sl.*), discontented, displeased, dissatisfied, grumpy, irritated, malcontent, peeved, peevish, petulant, put out, sulky, sullen, testy, vexed

disguise v. 1. camouflage, cloak, conceal, cover, hide, mask, screen, secrete, shroud, veil 2. deceive, dissemble, dissimulate, fake, falsify, fudge, gloss over, misrepresent ~n. 3. camouflage, cloak, costume, cover, get-up (*Inf.*), mask, screen, veil 4. deception, dissimulation, façade, front, pretence, semblance, trickery, veneer

disguised camouflaged, cloaked, covert, fake, false, feigned, incognito, in disguise, masked, pretend, undercover, unrecognizable

disgust 1. v. cause aversion, displease, fill with loathing, nauseate, offend, outrage, put off, repel, revolt, sicken, turn one's stomach 2. n. abhorrence, abomination, antipathy, aversion, detestation, dislike, distaste, hatefulness, hatred, loathing, nausea, repugnance, repulsion, revulsion

disgusted appalled, nauseated, offended, outraged, repelled, repulsed, scandalized, sick and tired of (*Inf.*), sickened, sick of (*Inf.*)

disgusting abominable, detestable, distasteful, foul, gross, hateful, loathsome, nasty, nauseating, nauseous, objectionable, obnoxious, odious, offensive, repellent, repugnant, revolting, shameless, sickening, stinking, vile, vulgar

dish n. 1. bowl, plate, platter, salver 2. fare, food, recipe ~v. 3. *Sl.* finish, muck up (*Sl.*), ruin, spoil, torpedo, wreck

dishearten cast down, crush, damp, dampen, dash, daunt, deject, depress, deter, discourage, dismay, dispirit, put a damper on

disheartened crestfallen, crushed, daunted, dejected, depressed, disappointed, discouraged, dismayed, dispirited, downcast, downhearted

dishevelled bedraggled, blowzy, disarranged, disordered, frowzy, hanging loose, messy, ruffled, rumpled, tousled, uncombed, unkempt, untidy

dishonest bent (*Sl.*), cheating, corrupt, crafty, crooked (*Inf.*), deceitful, deceiving, deceptive, designing, disreputable, double-dealing, false, fraudulent, guileful, knavish (*Archaic*), lying, mendacious, perfidious, shady (*Inf.*), swindling, treacherous, unfair, unprincipled, unscrupulous, untrustworthy, untruthful

dishonesty cheating, chicanery, corruption, craft, criminality, crookedness, deceit, duplicity, falsehood, falsity, fraud, fraudulence, graft, improbity, mendacity, perfidy, sharp practice, stealing, treachery, trickery, unscrupulousness, wiliness

dishonour v. 1. abase, blacken, corrupt, debase, debauch, defame, degrade, discredit, disgrace, shame, sully 2. defile, deflower, pollute, rape, ravish, seduce ~n. 3. abasement, degradation, discredit, disfavour, disgrace, disrepute, ignominy, infamy, obloquy, odium, opprobrium, reproach, scandal, shame 4. abuse, affront, discourtesy, indignity, insult, offence, outrage, slight

dishonourable 1. base, contemptible, despicable, discreditable, disgraceful, ignoble, ignominious, infamous, scandalous, shameful 2. blackguardly, corrupt, disreputable, shameless, treacherous, unprincipled, unscrupulous, untrustworthy

dish out allocate, distribute, dole out, hand out, inflict, mete out

dish up ladle, prepare, present, produce, scoop, serve, spoon

disillusion v. break the spell, bring

down to earth, disabuse, disen~
chant, open the eyes of, shatter
one's illusions, undeceive

disillusioned disabused, disap~
pointed, disenchanted, enlight~
ened, indifferent, out of love, sad~
der and wiser, undeceived

disincentive damper, determent,
deterrent, discouragement, dis~
suasion, impediment

disinclination alienation, antipa~
thy, aversion, demur, dislike, hesi~
tance, lack of desire, lack of en~
thusiasm, loathness, objection, op~
position, reluctance, repugnance,
resistance, unwillingness

disinclined antipathetic, averse,
balking, hesitating, indisposed,
loath, not in the mood, opposed,
reluctant, resistant, unwilling

disinfect clean, cleanse, decon~
taminate, deodorize, fumigate, pu~
rify, sanitize, sterilize

disinfectant antiseptic, germicide,
sanitizer, sterilizer

disinherit cut off, cut off without a
penny, disown, dispossess, oust,
repudiate

disintegrate break apart, break
up, crumble, disunite, fall apart,
fall to pieces, reduce to fragments,
separate, shatter, splinter

disinterest candidness, detach~
ment, disinterestedness, dispas~
sionateness, equity, fairness, im~
partiality, justice, neutrality, unbi~
asedness

disinterested candid, detached,
dispassionate, equitable, even-
handed, free from self-interest,
impartial, impersonal, neutral,
outside, unbiased, uninvolved, un~
prejudiced, unselfish

disjointed 1. aimless, confused,
disconnected, disordered, fitful, in~
coherent, loose, rambling, spas~
modic, unconnected 2. disconnect~
ed, dislocated, displaced, disunited,
divided, separated, split

dislike 1. *n.* animosity, animus, an~
tagonism, antipathy, aversion, de~
testation, disapprobation, disap~
proval, disgust, disinclination, dis~
pleasure, distaste, enmity, hatred,
hostility, loathing, repugnance 2. *v.*

abhor, abominate, be averse to,
despise, detest, disapprove, disfa~
vour, disrelish, hate, have no taste
or stomach for, loathe, not be able
to bear *or* abide, object to, scorn,
shun

dislocate 1. disorder, displace, dis~
rupt, disturb, misplace, shift 2. dis~
articulate, disconnect, disengage,
disjoint, disunite, luxate (*Medical*),
put out of joint, unhinge

dislocation 1. disarray, disorder,
disorganization, disruption, dis~
turbance, misplacement 2. disar~
ticulation, disconnection, disen~
gagement, luxation (*Medical*), un~
hinging

disloyal apostate, disaffected,
faithless, false, perfidious, sedi~
tious, subversive, traitorous,
treacherous, treasonable, two-
faced, unfaithful, unpatriotic, un~
trustworthy

disloyalty betrayal of trust, breach
of trust, breaking of faith, deceit~
fulness, double-dealing, falseness,
falsity, inconstancy, infidelity, per~
fidy, Punic faith, treachery, trea~
son, unfaithfulness

dismal black, bleak, cheerless,
dark, depressing, despondent, dis~
couraging, dolorous, dreary, for~
lorn, funereal, gloomy, gruesome,
lonesome, lowering, lugubrious,
melancholy, sad, sombre, sorrow~
ful

dismay *v.* 1. affright, alarm, appal,
distress, fill with consternation,
frighten, horrify, paralyse, scare,
terrify, unnerve 2. daunt, disap~
point, discourage, dishearten, dis~
illusion, dispirit, put off ~*n.* 3. agi~
tation, alarm, anxiety, apprehen~
sion, consternation, distress, dread,
fear, fright, horror, panic, terror,
trepidation 4. chagrin, disappoint~
ment, discouragement, disillusion~
ment, upset

dismember amputate, anatomize,
cut into pieces, disjoint, dislimb,
dislocate, dissect, divide, mutilate,
rend, sever

dismiss 1. axe (*Inf.*), cashier, dis~
charge, fire (*Inf.*), give notice to,
lay off, oust, remove, sack (*Inf.*),

send packing (*Inf.*) 2. disband, dis~
perse, dissolve, free, let go, re~
lease, send away 3. banish, discard,
dispel, disregard, drop, lay aside,
pooh-pooh, put out of one's mind,
reject, relegate, ˙repudiate, set
aside, shelve, spurn

dismissal 1. adjournment, congé,
end, freedom to depart, permission
to go, release 2. discharge, expul~
sion, marching orders (*Inf.*), no~
tice, one's cards, removal, the boot
(*Sl.*), the push (*Sl.*), the sack (*Inf.*)

disobedience indiscipline, infrac~
tion, insubordination, mutiny, non~
compliance, nonobservance, re~
calcitrance, revolt, unruliness,
waywardness

disobedient contrary, contuma~
cious, defiant, disorderly, froward,
insubordinate, intractable, mis~
chievous, naughty, noncompliant,
nonobservant, obstreperous, re~
fractory, undisciplined, unruly,
wayward, wilful

disobey contravene, defy, disre~
gard, flout, go counter to, ignore,
infringe, overstep, rebel, refuse to
obey, resist, transgress, violate

disorderly 1. chaotic, confused,
disorganized, higgledy-piggledy
(*Inf.*), indiscriminate, irregular,
jumbled, messy, shambolic (*Inf.*),
unsystematic, untidy 2. boisterous,
disruptive, indisciplined, lawless,
obstreperous, rebellious, refrac~
tory, riotous, rowdy, stormy, tu~
multuous, turbulent, ungovernable,
unlawful, unmanageable, unruly

disorganize break up, confuse, de~
range, destroy, disarrange, dis~
compose, disorder, disrupt, disturb,
jumble, make a shambles of, mud~
dle, turn topsy-turvy, unsettle, up~
set

disorganized chaotic, confused,
disordered, haphazard, jumbled,
muddled, shuffled, unmethodical,
unorganized, unsystematic

disown abandon, abnegate, cast
off, deny, disallow, disavow, dis~
claim, refuse to acknowledge *or*
recognize, reject, renounce, repu~
diate

disparage belittle, criticize, decry,

defame, degrade, denigrate, dep~
recate, depreciate, deride, dero~
gate, detract from, discredit, dis~
dain, dismiss, malign, minimize,
ridicule, run down, scorn, slander,
traduce, underestimate, underrate,
undervalue, vilify

disparagement aspersion, belit~
tlement, condemnation, contempt,
contumely, criticism, debasement,
degradation, denunciation, depre~
ciation, derision, derogation, de~
traction, discredit, disdain, impair~
ment, lessening, prejudice, re~
proach, ridicule, scorn, slander,
underestimation

dispassionate 1. calm, collected,
composed, cool, imperturbable,
moderate, quiet, serene, sober,
temperate, unemotional, unexcit~
able, unexcited, unmoved, unruf~
fled 2. candid, detached, disinter~
ested, fair, impartial, impersonal,
indifferent, neutral, objective, un~
biased, uninvolved, unprejudiced

dispatch, despatch *v.* 1. acceler~
ate, consign, dismiss, express, for~
ward, hasten, hurry, quicken, re~
mit, send, transmit 2. conclude,
discharge, dispose of, expedite,
finish, make short work of (*Inf.*),
perform, settle 3. assassinate,
bump off (*Sl.*), butcher, eliminate
(*Sl.*), execute, finish off, kill, mur~
der, put an end to, slaughter, slay
~*n.* 4. alacrity, celerity, expedition,
haste, precipitateness, prompti~
tude, promptness, quickness, ra~
pidity, speed, swiftness 5. account,
bulletin, communication, commu~
niqué, document, instruction, item,
letter, message, missive, news,
piece, report, story

dispel allay, banish, chase away,
dismiss, disperse, dissipate, drive
away, eliminate, expel, resolve,
rout, scatter

dispensable disposable, expend~
able, inessential, needless, nones~
sential, superfluous, unnecessary,
unrequired, useless

dispensation 1. allotment, ap~
pointment, apportionment, be~
stowal, conferment, consignment,
dealing out, disbursement, distri~

bution, endowment, supplying 2. award, dole, part, portion, quota, share 3. administration, direction, economy, management, plan, regulation, scheme, stewardship, system 4. exception, exemption, immunity, indulgence, licence, permission, privilege, relaxation, relief, remission, reprieve

dispense 1. allocate, allot, apportion, assign, deal out, disburse, distribute, dole out, mete out, share 2. measure, mix, prepare, supply 3. administer, apply, carry out, direct, discharge, enforce, execute, implement, operate, undertake 4. except, excuse, exempt, exonerate, let off (*Inf.*), release, relieve, reprieve 5. *With* with abstain from, do without, forgo, give up, omit, relinquish, waive 6. *With* with abolish, brush aside, cancel, dispose of, disregard, do away with, get rid of, ignore, pass over, render needless, shake off

disperse 1. broadcast, circulate, diffuse, disseminate, dissipate, distribute, scatter, spread, strew 2. break up, disappear, disband, dismiss, dispel, dissolve, rout, scatter, send off, separate, vanish

dispirited crestfallen, dejected, depressed, despondent, discouraged, disheartened, down, downcast, gloomy, glum, in the doldrums, low, morose, sad

displace 1. derange, disarrange, disturb, misplace, move, shift, transpose 2. cashier, depose, discard, discharge, dismiss, fire (*Inf.*), remove, sack (*Inf.*) 3. crowd out, oust, replace, succeed, supersede, supplant, take the place of 4. dislocate, dislodge, dispossess, eject, evict, force out, unsettle

display *v.* 1. betray, demonstrate, disclose, evidence, evince, exhibit, expose, manifest, open, open to view, present, reveal, show, unveil 2. expand, extend, model, open out, spread out, stretch out, unfold, unfurl 3. boast, flash (*Inf.*), flaunt, flourish, parade, show off, vaunt ~*n.* 4. array, demonstration, exhibition, exposition, exposure, mani-

festation, presentation, revelation, show 5. flourish, ostentation, pageant, parade, pomp, show, spectacle

displease aggravate (*Inf.*), anger, annoy, disgust, dissatisfy, exasperate, gall, incense, irk, irritate, nettle, offend, pique, provoke, put out, rile, upset, vex

displeasure anger, annoyance, disapprobation, disapproval, disfavour, disgruntlement, dislike, dissatisfaction, distaste, indignation, irritation, offence, pique, resentment, vexation, wrath

disposable 1. biodegradable, compostable, decomposable, nonreturnable, paper, throwaway 2. at one's service, available, consumable, expendable, free for use, spendable

disposal 1. clearance, discarding, dumping (*Inf.*), ejection, jettisoning, parting with, relinquishment, removal, riddance, scrapping, throwing away 2. arrangement, array, dispensation, disposition, distribution, grouping, placing, position 3. assignment, bequest, bestowal, consignment, conveyance, dispensation, gift, settlement, transfer 4. *As in* at one's disposal authority, conduct, control, determination, direction, discretion, government, management, ordering, regulation, responsibility

dispose 1. adjust, arrange, array, determine, distribute, fix, group, marshal, order, place, put, range, rank, regulate, set, settle, stand 2. actuate, adapt, bias, condition, incline, induce, influence, lead, motivate, move, predispose, prompt, tempt

disposed apt, given, inclined, liable, likely, minded, of a mind to, predisposed, prone, ready, subject, tending towards

dispose of 1. deal with, decide, determine, end, finish with, settle 2. bestow, give, make over, part with, sell, transfer 3. destroy, discard, dump (*Inf.*), get rid of, jettison, scrap, throw out *or* away, unload

disposition 1. character, constitution, make-up, nature, spirit, tem~ per, temperament 2. bent, bias, habit, inclination, leaning, predis~ position, proclivity, proneness, propensity, readiness, tendency 3. adjustment, arrangement, classifi~ cation, disposal, distribution, grouping, ordering, organization, placement 4. control, direction, disposal, management, regulation

disproportion asymmetry, dis~ crepancy, disparity, imbalance, inadequacy, inequality, insuffi~ ciency, lopsidedness, unevenness, unsuitableness

disproportionate excessive, in~ commensurate, inordinate, out of proportion, too much, unbalanced, unequal, uneven, unreasonable

disprove confute, contradict, controvert, discredit, expose, give the lie to, invalidate, negate, prove false, rebut, refute

disputation argumentation, controversy, debate, dispute, dis~ sension, polemics

dispute v. 1. altercate, argue, brawl, clash, contend, debate, dis~ cuss, quarrel, squabble, wrangle 2. challenge, contest, contradict, controvert, deny, doubt, impugn, question ~n. 3. altercation, argu~ ment, brawl, conflict, disagree~ ment, discord, disturbance, feud, friction, quarrel, strife, wrangle 4. argument, contention, controversy, debate, discussion, dissension

disqualification 1. disability, dis~ ablement, incapacitation, incapac~ ity, unfitness 2. debarment, disen~ ablement, disentitlement, elimina~ tion, exclusion, incompetence, in~ eligibility, rejection

disqualified debarred, eliminated, ineligible, knocked out, out of the running

disqualify 1. disable, incapacitate, invalidate, unfit (Rare) 2. debar, declare ineligible, disentitle, pre~ clude, prohibit, rule out

disquiet 1. n. alarm, angst, anxiety, concern, disquietude, distress, dis~ turbance, fear, foreboding, fretful~ ness, nervousness, restlessness, trouble, uneasiness, unrest, worry 2. v. agitate, annoy, bother, con~ cern, discompose, distress, disturb, fret, harass, incommode, make uneasy, perturb, pester, plague, trouble, unsettle, upset, vex, worry

disquieting annoying, bothersome, disconcerting, distressing, disturb~ ing, irritating, perturbing, trou~ bling, unnerving, unsettling, upset~ ting, vexing, worrying

disregard v. 1. brush aside or away, discount, disobey, ignore, laugh off, leave out of account, make light of, neglect, overlook, pass over, pay no attention to, pay no heed to, take no notice of, turn a blind eye to 2. brush off (Sl.), cold-shoulder, contemn, despise, dis~ dain, disparage, slight, snub ~n. 3. brushoff (Sl.), contempt, disdain, disrespect, heedlessness, ignoring, inattention, indifference, neglect, negligence, oversight, slight, the cold shoulder

disrepair 1. collapse, decay, de~ terioration, dilapidation, ruination 2. in disrepair broken, bust (Inf.), decayed, decrepit, kaput (Inf.), not functioning, on the blink (Sl.), out of commission, out of order, worn out

disreputable 1. base, contempt~ ible, derogatory, discreditable, dis~ graceful, dishonourable, disorder~ ly, ignominious, infamous, louche, low, mean, notorious, opprobrious, scandalous, shady (Inf.), shameful, shocking, unprincipled, vicious, vile 2. bedraggled, dilapidated, dingy, dishevelled, down at heel, scruffy, seedy, shabby, threadbare, worn

disrepute discredit, disesteem, disfavour, disgrace, dishonour, ig~ nominy, ill favour, ill repute, infa~ my, obloquy, shame, unpopularity

disrespect contempt, discourtesy, dishonour, disregard, imperti~ nence, impoliteness, impudence, incivility, insolence, irreverence, lack of respect, lese-majesty, rudeness, unmannerliness

disrespectful bad-mannered, cheeky, contemptuous, discour~ teous, ill-bred, impertinent, impo~

lite, impudent, insolent, insulting, irreverent, misbehaved, rude, uncivil

disrupt 1. agitate, confuse, disorder, disorganize, disturb, spoil, throw into disorder, upset 2. break up *or* into, interfere with, interrupt, intrude, obstruct, unsettle, upset

disruption confusion, disarray, disorder, disorderliness, disturbance, interference, interruption, stoppage

disruptive confusing, disorderly, distracting, disturbing, obstreperous, troublemaking, troublesome, unruly, unsettling, upsetting

dissatisfaction annoyance, chagrin, disappointment, discomfort, discontent, dislike, dismay, displeasure, distress, exasperation, frustration, irritation, regret, resentment, unhappiness

dissatisfied disappointed, discontented, disgruntled, displeased, fed up, frustrated, not satisfied, unfulfilled, ungratified, unhappy, unsatisfied

dissect 1. anatomize, cut up *or* apart, dismember, lay open 2. analyse, break down, explore, inspect, investigate, scrutinize, study

dissection 1. anatomization, anatomy, autopsy, dismemberment, necropsy, postmortem (examination) 2. analysis, breakdown, examination, inspection, investigation, scrutiny

disseminate broadcast, circulate, diffuse, disperse, dissipate, distribute, proclaim, promulgate, propagate, publicize, publish, scatter, sow, spread

dissemination broadcasting, circulation, diffusion, distribution, promulgation, propagation, publication, publishing, spread

dissension conflict, conflict of opinion, contention, difference, disagreement, discord, discordance, dispute, dissent, friction, quarrel, strife, variance

dissent 1. *v.* decline, differ, disagree, object, protest, refuse, withhold assent *or* approval 2. *n.*

difference, disagreement, discord, dissension, dissidence, nonconformity, objection, opposition, refusal, resistance

dissenter disputant, dissident, nonconformist, objector, protestant

dissentient *adj.* conflicting, differing, disagreeing, dissenting, dissident, opposing, protesting

dissertation critique, discourse, disquisition, essay, exposition, thesis, treatise

disservice bad turn, disfavour, harm, ill turn, injury, injustice, unkindness, wrong

dissident 1. *adj.* differing, disagreeing, discordant, dissentient, dissenting, heterodox, nonconformist, schismatic 2. *n.* agitator, dissenter, protestor, rebel, recusant

dissimilar different, disparate, divergent, diverse, heterogeneous, mismatched, not alike, not capable of comparison, not similar, unlike, unrelated, various

dissimilarity difference, discrepancy, disparity, dissimilitude, distinction, divergence, heterogeneity, incomparability, nonuniformity, unlikeness, unrelatedness

dissipate 1. burn up, consume, deplete, expend, fritter away, indulge oneself, lavish, misspend, run through, spend, squander, waste 2. disappear, dispel, disperse, dissolve, drive away, evaporate, scatter, vanish

dissipated 1. abandoned, debauched, dissolute, intemperate, profligate, rakish, self-indulgent 2. consumed, destroyed, exhausted, scattered, squandered, wasted

dissipation 1. abandonment, debauchery, dissoluteness, drunkenness, excess, extravagance, indulgence, intemperance, lavishness, prodigality, profligacy, squandering, wantonness, waste 2. amusement, distraction, diversion, entertainment, gratification 3. disappearance, disintegration, dispersion, dissemination, dissolution, scattering, vanishing

dissociate 1. break off, disband, disrupt, part company, quit 2. detach, disconnect, distance, divorce, isolate, segregate, separate, set apart

dissolute abandoned, corrupt, debauched, degenerate, depraved, dissipated, immoral, lax, lewd, libertine, licentious, loose, profligate, rakish, unrestrained, vicious, wanton, wild

dissolution 1. breaking up, disintegration, division, divorce, parting, resolution, separation 2. death, decay, decomposition, demise, destruction, dispersal, extinction, overthrow, ruin 3. adjournment, conclusion, disbandment, discontinuation, dismissal, end, ending, finish, suspension, termination 4. corruption, debauchery, dissipation, intemperance, wantonness 5. disappearance, evaporation, liquefaction, melting, solution

dissolve 1. deliquesce, flux, fuse, liquefy, melt, soften, thaw 2. crumble, decompose, diffuse, disappear, disintegrate, disperse, dissipate, dwindle, evanesce, evaporate, fade, melt away, perish, vanish, waste away 3. break up, destroy, discontinue, dismiss, end, overthrow, ruin, suspend, terminate, wind up 4. break into or up, collapse, disorganize, disunite, divorce, loose, resolve into, separate, sever

dissuade advise against, deter, discourage, disincline, divert, expostulate, persuade not to, put off, remonstrate, talk out of, urge not to, warn

distance n. 1. absence, extent, gap, interval, lapse, length, range, reach, remoteness, remove, separation, space, span, stretch, width 2. aloofness, coldness, coolness, frigidity, reserve, restraint, stiffness 3. go the distance bring to an end, complete, finish, see through, stay the course 4. keep one's distance avoid, be aloof (indifferent, reserved), keep (someone) at arm's length, shun 5. in the distance afar, far away, far off, on the

horizon, yonder ~v. 6. dissociate oneself, put in proportion, separate oneself 7. leave behind, outdistance, outdo, outrun, outstrip, pass

distant 1. abroad, afar, far, faraway, far-flung, far-off, outlying, out-of-the-way, remote, removed 2. apart, disparate, dispersed, distinct, scattered, separate 3. aloof, ceremonious, cold, cool, formal, haughty, reserved, restrained, reticent, standoffish, stiff, unapproachable, unfriendly, withdrawn 4. faint, indirect, indistinct, obscure, slight, uncertain

distaste abhorrence, antipathy, aversion, detestation, disfavour, disgust, disinclination, dislike, displeasure, disrelish, dissatisfaction, horror, loathing, repugnance, revulsion

distasteful abhorrent, disagreeable, displeasing, loathsome, nauseous, objectionable, obnoxious, offensive, repugnant, repulsive, undesirable, uninviting, unpalatable, unpleasant, unsavoury

distend balloon, bloat, bulge, dilate, enlarge, expand, increase, inflate, puff, stretch, swell, widen

distended bloated, dilated, enlarged, expanded, inflated, puffy, stretched, swollen, tumescent

distil condense, draw out, evaporate, express, extract, press out, purify, rectify, refine, sublimate, vaporize

distillation elixir, essence, extract, quintessence, spirit

distinct 1. apparent, clear, clearcut, decided, definite, evident, lucid, manifest, marked, noticeable, obvious, palpable, patent, plain, recognizable, sharp, unambiguous, unmistakable, well-defined 2. detached, different, discrete, dissimilar, individual, separate, unconnected

distinction 1. differentiation, discernment, discrimination, penetration, perception, separation 2. contrast, difference, differential, division, separation 3. characteristic, distinctiveness, feature, individuality, mark, particularity, peculiarity, quality 4. account, celebrity, consequence, credit, eminence, excellence, fame, greatness, honour, importance, merit, name, note, prominence, quality, rank, renown, reputation, repute, superiority, worth

distinctive characteristic, different, distinguishing, extraordinary, idiosyncratic, individual, original, peculiar, singular, special, typical, uncommon, unique

distinctly clearly, decidedly, definitely, evidently, manifestly, markedly, noticeably, obviously, palpably, patently, plainly, precisely, sharply

distinctness 1. clarity, lucidity, obviousness, plainness, sharpness, vividness 2. detachment, difference, discreteness, disparateness, dissimilarity, dissociation, distinctiveness, individuality, separation

distinguish 1. ascertain, decide, determine, differentiate, discriminate, judge, tell apart, tell between, tell the difference 2. categorize, characterize, classify, individualize, make distinctive, mark, separate, set apart, single out 3. discern, know, make out, perceive, pick out, recognize, see, tell 4. celebrate, dignify, honour, immortalize, make famous, signalize

distinguishable clear, conspicuous, discernible, evident, manifest, noticeable, obvious, perceptible, plain, recognizable, well-marked

distinguished 1. acclaimed, celebrated, conspicuous, eminent, famed, famous, illustrious, notable, noted, renowned, well-known 2. conspicuous, extraordinary, marked, outstanding, signal, striking

distinguishing characteristic, different, differentiating, distinctive, individualistic, marked, peculiar, typical

distort 1. bend, buckle, contort, deform, disfigure, misshape, twist, warp, wrench, wrest 2. bias, colour, falsify, garble, misrepresent, pervert, slant, twist

distortion 1. bend, buckle, contor-

tion, crookedness, deformity, malformation, twist, twistedness, warp 2. bias, colouring, falsification, misrepresentation, perversion, slant

distract 1. divert, draw away, sidetrack, turn aside 2. amuse, beguile, engross, entertain, occupy 3. agitate, bewilder, confound, confuse, derange, discompose, disconcert, disturb, harass, madden, perplex, puzzle, torment, trouble

distracted 1. agitated, bemused, bewildered, confounded, confused, flustered, harassed, in a flap (*Inf.*), perplexed, puzzled, troubled 2. crazy, deranged, distraught, frantic, frenzied, grief-stricken, insane, mad, overwrought, raving, wild

distracting bewildering, bothering, confusing, disconcerting, dismaying, disturbing, off-putting (*Brit. inf.*), perturbing

distraction 1. abstraction, agitation, bewilderment, commotion, confusion, discord, disorder, disturbance 2. amusement, beguilement, diversion, divertissement, entertainment, pastime, recreation 3. disturbance, diversion, interference, interruption 4. aberration, alienation, delirium, derangement, desperation, frenzy, hallucination, incoherence, insanity, mania

distress *n.* 1. affliction, agony, anguish, anxiety, desolation, discomfort, grief, heartache, misery, pain, sadness, sorrow, suffering, torment, torture, woe, worry, wretchedness 2. adversity, calamity, destitution, difficulties, hardship, indigence, misfortune, need, poverty, privation, straits, trial, trouble ~*v.* 3. afflict, agonize, bother, disturb, grieve, harass, harrow, pain, perplex, sadden, torment, trouble, upset, worry, wound

distressed 1. afflicted, agitated, anxious, distracted, distraught, saddened, tormented, troubled, upset, worried, wretched 2. destitute, indigent, needy, poor, poverty-stricken, straitened

distressing affecting, afflicting, distressful, disturbing, grievous,

heart-breaking, hurtful, lamen~
table, nerve-racking, painful, sad,
upsetting, worrying

distribute 1. administer, allocate,
allot, apportion, assign, deal, dis~
pense, dispose, divide, dole out,
give, measure out, mete, share 2.
circulate, convey, deliver, hand
out, pass round 3. diffuse, disperse,
disseminate, scatter, spread, strew
4. arrange, assort, categorize,
class, classify, file, group

distribution 1. allocation, allot~
ment, apportionment, dispensa~
tion, division, dole, partition, shar~
ing 2. circulation, diffusion, disper~
sal, dispersion, dissemination,
propagation, scattering, spreading
3. arrangement, assortment, clas~
sification, disposition, grouping, lo~
cation, organization, placement 4.
Commerce dealing, delivery, han~
dling, mailing, marketing, trading,
transport, transportation

district area, community, locale,
locality, neighbourhood, parish,
quarter, region, sector, vicinity,
ward

distrust 1. *v.* be sceptical of, be
suspicious of, be wary of, disbe~
lieve, discredit, doubt, misbelieve,
mistrust, question, smell a rat
(*Inf.*), suspect, wonder about 2. *n.*
disbelief, doubt, lack of faith, mis~
giving, mistrust, qualm, question,
scepticism, suspicion, wariness

disturb 1. bother, butt in on, dis~
rupt, interfere with, interrupt, in~
trude on, pester, rouse, startle 2.
confuse, derange, disarrange, dis~
order, disorganize, muddle, unset~
tle 3. agitate, alarm, annoy, con~
found, discompose, distract, dis~
tress, excite, fluster, harass, per~
turb, ruffle, shake, trouble, unset~
tle, upset, worry

disturbance 1. agitation, annoy~
ance, bother, confusion, derange~
ment, disorder, distraction, hin~
drance, interruption, intrusion,
molestation, perturbation, upset 2.
bother (*Inf.*), brawl, commotion,
disorder, fracas, fray, hubbub, riot,
ruckus (*Inf.*), ruction (*Inf.*), tumult,
turmoil, uproar

disturbed 1. *Psychiatry* disor~
dered, maladjusted, neurotic, trou~
bled, unbalanced, upset 2. agitated,
anxious, apprehensive, bothered,
concerned, disquieted, troubled,
uneasy, upset, worried

disturbing agitating, alarming,
disconcerting, discouraging, dis~
maying, disquieting, distressing,
frightening, perturbing, startling,
threatening, troubling, unsettling,
upsetting, worrying

disuse abandonment, decay,
desuetude, discontinuance, idle~
ness, neglect, non-employment,
nonuse

ditch *n.* 1. channel, drain, dyke,
furrow, gully, moat, trench, water~
course ~*v.* 2. dig, drain, excavate,
gouge, trench 3. *Sl.* abandon, dis~
card, dispose of, drop, dump (*Inf.*),
get rid of, jettison, scrap, throw out
or overboard

dither 1. *v.* faff about (*Brit. inf.*),
falter, haver, hesitate, oscillate,
shillyshally (*Inf.*), swither (*Scot.*),
teeter, vacillate, waver 2. *n.* both~
er, flap (*Inf.*), fluster, flutter, poth~
er, stew (*Inf.*), tiz-woz (*Inf.*), tizzy
(*Inf.*), twitter

dive *v.* 1. descend, dip, disappear,
drop, duck, fall, go underwater,
jump, leap, nose-dive, pitch, plum~
met, plunge, submerge, swoop ~*n.*
2. dash, header (*Inf.*), jump, leap,
lunge, nose dive, plunge, spring 3.
Sl. honky-tonk (*U.S. sl.*), joint (*Sl.*),
sleazy bar

diverge 1. bifurcate, branch, di~
varicate, divide, fork, part, radiate,
separate, split, spread 2. be at
odds, be at variance, conflict, dif~
fer, disagree, dissent 3. depart, de~
viate, digress, stray, turn aside,
wander

divergence branching out, depar~
ture, deviation, difference, digres~
sion, disparity, divagation, ramifi~
cation, separation deflection,
varying

divergent conflicting, deviating,
different, differing, disagreeing,
dissimilar, diverging, diverse,
separate, variant

divers different, manifold, many,

multifarious, numerous, several, some, sundry, varied, various

diverse 1. assorted, diversified, miscellaneous, of every description, several, sundry, varied, various 2. different, differing, discrete, disparate, dissimilar, distinct, divergent, separate, unlike, varying

diversify alter, assort, branch out, change, expand, mix, modify, spread out, transform, variegate, vary

diversion 1. alteration, change, deflection, departure, detour, deviation, digression, variation 2. amusement, beguilement, delight, distraction, divertissement, enjoyment, entertainment, game, gratification, pastime, play, pleasure, recreation, relaxation, sport

diversity assortment, difference, dissimilarity, distinctiveness, divergence, diverseness, diversification, heterogeneity, medley, multiplicity, range, unlikeness, variance, variegation, variety

divert 1. avert, deflect, redirect, switch, turn aside 2. amuse, beguile, delight, entertain, gratify, recreate, regale 3. detract, distract, draw or lead away from, lead astray, sidetrack

diverting amusing, beguiling, enjoyable, entertaining, fun, humorous, pleasant

divest 1. denude, disrobe, doff, remove, strip, take off, unclothe, undress 2. deprive, despoil, dispossess, strip

divide 1. bisect, cleave, cut (up), detach, disconnect, part, partition, segregate, separate, sever, shear, split, subdivide, sunder 2. allocate, allot, apportion, deal out, dispense, distribute, divvy (up) (*Inf.*), dole out, measure out, portion, share 3. alienate, break up, cause to disagree, come between, disunite, estrange, set or pit against one another, set at variance or odds, sow dissension, split 4. arrange, categorize, classify, grade, group, put in order, separate, sort

dividend bonus, cut (*Inf.*), divvy (*Inf.*), extra, gain, plus, portion, share, surplus

divine *adj.* 1. angelic, celestial, godlike, heavenly, holy, spiritual, superhuman, supernatural 2. consecrated, holy, religious, sacred, sanctified, spiritual 3. beatific, blissful, exalted, mystical, rapturous, supreme, transcendent, transcendental, transmundane 4. *Inf.* beautiful, excellent, glorious, marvellous, perfect, splendid, superlative, wonderful ~*n.* 5. churchman, clergyman, cleric, ecclesiastic, minister, pastor, priest, reverend ~*v.* 6. apprehend, conjecture, deduce, discern, foretell, guess, infer, intuit, perceive, prognosticate, suppose, surmise, suspect, understand 7. *Of water or minerals* dowse

diviner 1. astrologer, augur, oracle, prophet, seer, sibyl, soothsayer 2. *Of water or minerals* dowser

divinity 1. deity, divine nature, godhead, godhood, godliness, holiness, sanctity 2. daemon, deity, genius, god, goddess, guardian spirit, spirit 3. religion, religious studies, theology

divisible dividable, fractional, separable, splittable

division 1. bisection, cutting up, detaching, dividing, partition, separation, splitting up 2. allotment, apportionment, distribution, sharing 3. border, boundary, demarcation, divide, divider, dividing line, partition 4. branch, category, class, compartment, department, group, head, part, portion, section, sector, segment 5. breach, difference of opinion, disagreement, discord, disunion, estrangement, feud, rupture, split, variance

divisive alienating, damaging, detrimental, discordant, disruptive, estranging, inharmonious, pernicious, troublesome, unsettling

divorce 1. *n.* annulment, breach, break, decree nisi, dissolution, disunion, rupture, separation, severance, split-up 2. *v.* annul, disconnect, dissociate, dissolve (*mar-*

riage), disunite, divide, part, separate, sever, split up, sunder

divulge betray, communicate, confess, declare, disclose, exhibit, expose, impart, leak, let slip, make known, proclaim, promulgate, publish, reveal, spill (*Inf.*), tell, uncover

dizzy 1. faint, giddy, light-headed, off balance, reeling, shaky, staggering, swimming, vertiginous, weak at the knees, wobbly, woozy (*Inf.*) 2. befuddled, bemused, bewildered, confused, dazed, dazzled, muddled 3. lofty, steep, vertiginous 4. *Inf.* capricious, fickle, flighty, foolish, frivolous, giddy, lightheaded, scatterbrained, silly

do *v.* 1. accomplish, achieve, act, carry out, complete, conclude, discharge, end, execute, perform, produce, transact, undertake, work 2. answer, be adequate, be enough, be of use, be sufficient, pass muster, satisfy, serve, suffice, suit 3. arrange, be responsible for, fix, get ready, look after, make, make ready, organize, prepare, see to, take on 4. decipher, decode, figure out, puzzle out, resolve, solve, work out 5. adapt, render, translate, transpose 6. bear oneself, behave, carry oneself, comport oneself, conduct oneself 7. fare, get along, get on, make out, manage, proceed 8. bring about, cause, create, effect, produce 9. *Of a play, etc.* act, give, perform, present, produce, put on 10. *Inf.* cover, explore, journey through *or* around, look at, stop in, tour, travel, visit 11. *Sl.* cheat, con (*Sl.*), cozen, deceive, defraud, dupe, fleece, hoax, swindle, take (someone) for a ride (*Inf.*), trick ~*n.* 12. *Inf.* affair, event, function, gathering, occasion, party 13. **do's and don'ts** *Inf.* code, customs, etiquette, instructions, regulations, rules, standards

do away with 1. bump off (*Sl.*), destroy, do in (*Sl.*), exterminate, kill, liquidate, murder, slay 2. abolish, discard, discontinue, eliminate, get rid of, put an end to, remove

docile amenable, biddable, compli-

ant, ductile, manageable, obedient, pliant, submissive, teachable (*Rare*), tractable

docility amenability, biddableness, compliance, ductility, manageability, meekness, obedience, pliancy, submissiveness, tractability

dock *n.* 1. harbour, pier, quay, waterfront, wharf ~*v.* 2. anchor, berth, drop anchor, land, moor, put in, tie up 3. *Of spacecraft* couple, hook up, join, link up, rendezvous, unite

docket 1. *n.* bill, certificate, chit, chitty, counterfoil, label, receipt, tab, tag, tally, ticket 2. *v.* catalogue, file, index, label, mark, register, tab, tag, ticket

doctor *n.* 1. general practitioner, G.P., medic (*Inf.*), medical practitioner, physician ~*v.* 2. apply medication to, give medical treatment to, treat 3. botch, cobble, do up (*Inf.*), fix, mend, patch up, repair 4. alter, change, disguise, falsify, fudge, misrepresent, pervert, tamper with 5. add to, adulterate, cut, dilute, mix with, spike, water down

doctrinaire *adj.* 1. biased, dogmatic, fanatical, inflexible, insistent, opinionated, rigid 2. hypothetical, ideological, impractical, speculative, theoretical, unpragmatic, unrealistic

doctrine article, article of faith, belief, canon, concept, conviction, creed, dogma, opinion, precept, principle, teaching, tenet

document 1. *n.* certificate, instrument, legal form, paper, record, report 2. *v.* authenticate, back up, certify, cite, corroborate, detail, give weight to, instance, particularize, substantiate, support, validate, verify

doddering aged, decrepit, doddery, faltering, feeble, floundering, infirm, senile, shaky, shambling, tottery, trembly, unsteady, weak

dodge *v.* 1. dart, duck, shift, sidestep, swerve, turn aside 2. avoid, deceive, elude, equivocate, evade, fend off, fudge, get out of, hedge, parry, shirk, shuffle, trick ~*n.* 3.

contrivance, device, feint, machi~
nation, ploy, ruse, scheme, strata~
gem, subterfuge, trick, wheeze
(*Sl.*), wile

dodger evader, shifty so-and-so,
shirker, slacker, slippery one, sly~
boots, trickster

doer achiever, active person, ac~
tivist, bustler, dynamo, go-getter
(*Inf.*), live wire (*Sl.*), organizer,
powerhouse (*Sl.*), wheeler-dealer
(*Inf.*)

doff 1. *Of a hat* lift, raise, remove,
take off, tip, touch 2. *Of clothing*
cast off, discard, remove, shed, slip
off, slip out of, take off, throw off,
undress

dog *n.* 1. bitch, canine, cur, hound,
man's best friend, mongrel, mutt
(*Sl.*), pooch (*Sl.*), pup, puppy, tyke
2. *Inf.* beast, blackguard, cur, heel
(*Sl.*), knave (*Archaic*), scoundrel,
villain 3. **dog-eat-dog** cutthroat,
ferocious, fierce, ruthless, vicious,
with no holds barred 4. **go to the
dogs** *Inf.* degenerate, deteriorate,
go down the drain, go to pot, go to
ruin ~*v.* 5. haunt, hound, plague,
pursue, shadow, tail (*Inf.*), track,
trail, trouble

dogged determined, firm, indefati~
gable, obstinate, persevering, per~
sistent, pertinacious, resolute,
single-minded, staunch, steadfast,
steady, stubborn, tenacious, un~
flagging, unshakable, unyielding

doggedness bulldog tenacity, de~
termination, endurance, obstinacy,
perseverance, persistence, perti~
nacity, relentlessness, resolution,
single-mindedness, steadfastness,
steadiness, stubbornness, tena~
ciousness, tenacity

dogma article, article of faith, be~
lief, credo, creed, doctrine, opin~
ion, precept, principle, teachings,
tenet

dogmatic 1. arbitrary, arrogant,
assertive, categorical, dictatorial,
doctrinaire, downright, emphatic,
imperious, magisterial, obdurate,
opinionated, overbearing, per~
emptory 2. authoritative, canoni~
cal, categorical, doctrinal, ex ca~
thedra, oracular, positive

dogmatism arbitrariness, arro~
gance, dictatorialness, imperious~
ness, opinionatedness, perempto~
riness, positiveness, presumption

dogsbody drudge, general facto~
tum, man *or* maid of all work, me~
nial, skivvy, slave

do in 1. butcher, dispatch, eliminate
(*Sl.*), execute, kill, liquidate, mur~
der, slaughter, slay 2. exhaust, fag
(*Inf.*), fatigue, shatter (*Inf.*), tire,
wear out, weary

doing achievement, act, action,
carrying out *or* through, deed, ex~
ecution, exploit, handiwork, im~
plementation, performance

doings actions, affairs, concerns,
dealings, deeds, events, exploits,
goings-on (*Inf.*), handiwork, hap~
penings, proceedings, transactions

doldrums apathy, blues, boredom,
depression, dullness, dumps (*Inf.*),
ennui, gloom, inertia, lassitude,
listlessness, malaise, stagnation,
tedium, torpor

dole *n.* 1. allowance, alms, benefit,
donation, gift, grant, gratuity,
modicum, parcel, pittance, portion,
quota, share 2. allocation, allot~
ment, apportionment, dispensa~
tion, distribution, division ~*v.* 3.
Usually with **out** administer, allo~
cate, allot, apportion, assign, deal,
dispense, distribute, divide, give,
hand out, mete, share

dolt ass, blockhead, booby, chump
(*Inf.*), clot (*Sl.*), dimwit (*Inf.*), dope
(*Sl.*), dullard, dunce, fool, idiot, ig~
noramus, nitwit, simpleton, thick~
head

domestic *adj.* 1. domiciliary, fami~
ly, home, household, private 2. do~
mesticated, home-loving, homely,
housewifely, stay-at-home 3. do~
mesticated, house, house-trained,
pet, tame, trained 4. indigenous,
internal, native, not foreign ~*n.* 5.
char (*Inf.*), charwoman, daily, dai~
ly help, help, maid, servant, wom~
an (*Inf.*)

domesticate 1. break, gentle,
house-train, tame, train 2. accli~
matize, accustom, familiarize, ha~
bituate, naturalize

domesticated 1. *Of plants or ani~*

mals broken (in), naturalized, tame, tamed 2. *Of people* domestic, home-loving, homely, house-trained (*Jocular*), housewifely

dominant 1. ascendant, assertive, authoritative, commanding, controlling, governing, leading, presiding, ruling, superior, supreme 2. chief, influential, main, outstanding, paramount, predominant, preeminent, prevailing, prevalent, primary, principal, prominent

dominate 1. control, direct, domineer, govern, have the upper hand over, have the whip hand over, keep under one's thumb, lead, lead by the nose (*Inf.*), master, monopolize, overbear, rule, tyrannize 2. bestride, loom over, overlook, stand head and shoulders above, stand over, survey, tower above 3. detract from, eclipse, outshine, overrule, overshadow, predominate, prevail over

domination 1. ascendancy, authority, command, control, influence, mastery, power, rule, superiority, supremacy, sway 2. despotism, dictatorship, oppression, repression, subjection, subordination, suppression, tyranny

domineer bluster, boss around *or* about (*Inf.*), browbeat, bully, hector, intimidate, lord (it) over, menace, overbear, ride roughshod over, swagger, threaten, tyrannize

domineering arrogant, authoritarian, autocratic, bossy (*Inf.*), coercive, despotic, dictatorial, high-handed, imperious, iron-handed, magisterial, masterful, oppressive, overbearing, tyrannical

dominion 1. ascendancy, authority, command, control, domination, government, jurisdiction, mastery, power, rule, sovereignty, supremacy, sway 2. country, domain, empire, kingdom, province, realm, region, territory

don clothe oneself in, dress in, get into, pull on, put on, slip on *or* into

donate bequeath, bestow, chip in (*Inf.*), contribute, gift, give, make a gift of, present, subscribe

donation alms, benefaction, boon, contribution, gift, grant, gratuity, largess, offering, present, subscription

done *adj.* 1. accomplished, completed, concluded, consummated, ended, executed, finished, over, perfected, realized, terminated, through 2. cooked, cooked enough, cooked sufficiently, cooked to a turn, ready 3. depleted, exhausted, finished, spent, used up 4. acceptable, conventional, *de rigueur,* proper 5. *Inf.* cheated, conned (*Sl.*), duped, taken for a ride (*Inf.*), tricked ~*interj.* 6. agreed, it's a bargain, O.K. (*Inf.*), settled, you're on (*Inf.*) 7. **done for** *Inf.* beaten, broken, dashed, defeated, destroyed, doomed, finished, foiled, lost, ruined, undone, wrecked 8. **done in** *or* **up** *Inf.* all in (*Sl.*), bushed (*Inf.*), dead (*Inf.*), dead beat (*Inf.*), dog-tired (*Inf.*), exhausted, fagged out (*Inf.*), knackered (*Sl.*), on one's last legs, ready to drop, tired out, worn out, worn to a frazzle (*Inf.*) 9. **have done with** be through with, desist, end relations with, finish with, give up, throw over, wash one's hands of

donnish bookish, erudite, formalistic, pedagogic, pedantic, precise, scholarly, scholastic

donor almsgiver, benefactor, contributor, donator, giver, grantor (*Law*), philanthropist

doom *n.* 1. catastrophe, death, destiny, destruction, downfall, fate, fortune, lot, portion, ruin 2. condemnation, decision, decree, judgment, sentence, verdict 3. Armageddon, Doomsday, end of the world, Judgment Day, the Last Day, the Last Judgment, the last trump ~*v.* 4. condemn, consign, damn, decree, destine, foreordain, judge, predestine, sentence, threaten

doomed bedevilled, bewitched, condemned, cursed, fated, hopeless, ill-fated, ill-omened, luckless, star-crossed

door 1. doorway, egress, entrance, entry, exit, ingress, opening 2. **lay at the door of** blame, censure, charge, hold responsible, impute to 3. **out of doors** alfresco, in the air, out, outdoors, outside 4. **show someone the door** ask to leave, boot out (*Inf.*), bounce (*Sl.*), eject, oust, show out

do out of balk, bilk, cheat, con (*Sl.*), deprive, diddle (*Inf.*), swindle, trick

dope n. 1. drugs, narcotic, opiate 2. blockhead, dimwit (*Inf.*), dolt, dunce, fool, idiot, simpleton 3. details, facts, gen (*Inf.*), info (*Inf.*), information, inside information, lowdown (*Inf.*), news, tip ~v. 4. anaesthetize, doctor, drug, inject, knock out, narcotize, sedate, stupefy

dormant asleep, comatose, fallow, hibernating, inactive, inert, inoperative, latent, quiescent, sleeping, sluggish, slumbering, suspended, torpid

dose dosage, draught, drench, measure, portion, potion, prescription, quantity

dot n. 1. atom, circle, dab, fleck, full stop, iota, jot, mark, mite, mote, point, speck, spot 2. **on the dot** exactly, on time, precisely, promptly, punctually, to the minute ~v. 3. dab, dabble, fleck, spot, sprinkle, stipple, stud

dotage 1. decrepitude, feebleness, imbecility, old age, second childhood, senility, weakness 2. doting, foolish fondness, infatuation

dote on or **upon** admire, adore, hold dear, idolize, lavish affection on, prize, treasure

doting adoring, devoted, fond, foolish, indulgent, lovesick

double adj. 1. binate (*Botany*), coupled, doubled, dual, duplicate, in pairs, paired, twice, twin, twofold 2. deceitful, dishonest, false, hypocritical, insincere, Janus-faced, knavish (*Archaic*), perfidious, treacherous, two-faced, vacillating ~v. 3. duplicate, enlarge, fold, grow, increase, magnify, multiply, plait, repeat ~n. 4. clone, copy, counterpart, dead ringer (*Sl.*), Doppelgänger, duplicate, fellow, impersonator, lookalike, mate, replica, ringer (*Sl.*), spitting image

(*Inf.*), twin 5. **at** or **on the double** at full speed, briskly, immediately, in double-quick time, p.d.q. (*Sl.*), posthaste, quickly, without delay

double-cross betray, cheat, defraud, hoodwink, mislead, swindle, trick, two-time (*Inf.*)

double-dealer betrayer, cheat, con man (*Inf.*), deceiver, dissembler, double-crosser (*Inf.*), fraud, hypocrite, rogue, swindler, traitor, two-timer (*Inf.*)

double-dealing 1. n. bad faith, betrayal, cheating, deceit, deception, dishonesty, duplicity, foul play, hypocrisy, mendacity, perfidy, treachery, trickery, two-timing (*Inf.*) 2. adj. cheating, crooked (*Inf.*), deceitful, dishonest, duplicitous, fraudulent, hypocritical, lying, perfidious, sneaky, swindling, treacherous, tricky, two-faced, two-timing (*Inf.*), underhanded, untrustworthy, wily

double entendre ambiguity, double meaning, innuendo, play on words, pun

doubt v. 1. discredit, distrust, fear, lack confidence in, misgive, mistrust, query, question, suspect ~n. 2. apprehension, disquiet, distrust, fear, incredulity, lack of faith, misgiving, mistrust, qualm, scepticism, suspicion ~v. 3. be dubious, be uncertain, demur, fluctuate, hesitate, scruple, vacillate, waver ~n. 4. dubiety, hesitancy, hesitation, indecision, irresolution, lack of conviction, suspense, uncertainty, vacillation 5. ambiguity, confusion, difficulty, dilemma, perplexity, problem, quandary 6. **no doubt** admittedly, assuredly, certainly, doubtless, doubtlessly, probably, surely

doubter agnostic, disbeliever, doubting Thomas, questioner, sceptic, unbeliever

doubtful 1. ambiguous, debatable, dubious, equivocal, hazardous, inconclusive, indefinite, indeterminate, obscure, precarious, problematic, questionable, unclear, unconfirmed, unsettled, vague 2. distrustful, hesitating, in two minds (*Inf.*), irresolute, perplexed, scep-

tical, suspicious, tentative, uncer~
tain, unconvinced, undecided, un~
resolved, unsettled, unsure, vacil~
lating, wavering 3. disreputable,
dubious, questionable, shady (*Inf.*),
suspect, suspicious

doubtless 1. assuredly, certainly,
clearly, indisputably, of course,
precisely, surely, truly, undoubted~
ly, unquestionably, without doubt 2.
apparently, most likely, ostensibly,
presumably, probably, seemingly,
supposedly

dour 1. dismal, dreary, forbidding,
gloomy, grim, morose, sour, sullen,
unfriendly 2. austere, hard, inflex~
ible, obstinate, rigid, rigorous, se~
vere, strict, uncompromising, un~
yielding

dovetail v. 1. fit, fit together, inter~
lock, join, link, mortise, tenon,
unite 2. accord, agree, coincide,
conform, correspond, harmonize,
match, tally

dowdy dingy, drab, frowzy, frump~
ish, frumpy, ill-dressed, old-
fashioned, scrubby (*Inf.*), shabby,
slovenly, tacky (*U.S. inf.*), unfash~
ionable

dower 1. dowry, inheritance, lega~
cy, portion, provision, share 2. en~
dowment, faculty, gift, talent

do without abstain from, dispense
with, forgo, get along without, give
up, manage without

down adj. 1. blue, dejected, de~
pressed, disheartened, downcast,
low, miserable, sad, unhappy ~v. 2.
bring down, fell, floor, knock down,
overthrow, prostrate, subdue,
tackle, throw, trip 3. *Inf.* drain,
drink (down), gulp, put away,
swallow, toss off ~n. 4. decline,
descent, drop, dropping, fall, fall~
ing, reverse 5. **have a down on** *Inf.*
be antagonistic or hostile to, bear a
grudge towards, be prejudiced
against, be set against, feel ill will
towards, have it in for (*Sl.*) 6. **down
with** away with, get rid of, kick out
(*Inf.*), oust, push out

down and out 1. adj. derelict, des~
titute, impoverished, penniless,
ruined 2. **down-and-out** n. beggar,
derelict, dosser (*Sl.*), loser, outcast,
pauper, tramp, vagabond, vagrant

downcast cheerless, crestfallen,
daunted, dejected, depressed, de~
spondent, disappointed, disconso~
late, discouraged, disheartened,
dismayed, dispirited, miserable,
sad, unhappy

downfall 1. breakdown, collapse,
comedown, comeuppance (*Sl.*),
debacle, descent, destruction, dis~
grace, fall, overthrow, ruin, un~
doing 2. cloudburst, deluge, down~
pour, rainstorm

downgrade 1. degrade, demote,
humble, lower or reduce in rank,
take down a peg (*Inf.*) 2. decry,
denigrate, detract from, disparage,
run down

downhearted blue, chapfallen,
crestfallen, dejected, depressed,
despondent, discouraged, dis~
heartened, dismayed, dispirited,
downcast, low-spirited, sad, sor~
rowful, unhappy

downpour cloudburst, deluge,
flood, inundation, rainstorm, tor~
rential rain

downright 1. absolute, blatant,
categorical, clear, complete, ex~
plicit, out-and-out, outright, plain,
positive, simple, thoroughgoing,
total, undisguised, unequivocal,
unqualified, utter 2. blunt, candid,
forthright, frank, honest, open,
outspoken, plain, sincere, straight~
forward, straight-from-the-
shoulder

down-to-earth common-sense,
hard-headed, matter-of-fact, mun~
dane, no-nonsense, plain-spoken,
practical, realistic, sane, sensible,
unsentimental

downward adj. declining, de~
scending, earthward, heading
down, sliding, slipping

doze 1. v. catnap, drop off (*Inf.*),
drowse, kip (*Sl.*), nap, nod, nod off
(*Inf.*), sleep, sleep lightly, slumber,
snooze (*Inf.*), zizz (*Inf.*) 2. n. cat~
nap, forty winks (*Inf.*), kip (*Sl.*),
little sleep, nap, shuteye (*Sl.*), sies~
ta, snooze (*Inf.*)

drab cheerless, colourless, dingy,
dismal, dreary, dull, flat, gloomy,

grey, lacklustre, shabby, sombre, uninspired, vapid

draft v. 1. compose, delineate, design, draw, draw up, formulate, outline, plan, sketch ~n. 2. abstract, delineation, outline, plan, preliminary form, rough, sketch, version 3. bill (of exchange), cheque, order, postal order

drag v. 1. draw, hale, haul, lug, pull, tow, trail, tug, yank 2. crawl, creep, go slowly, inch, limp along, shamble, shuffle 3. dawdle, draggle, lag behind, linger, loiter, straggle, trail behind 4. With on or out draw out, extend, keep going, lengthen, persist, prolong, protract, spin out, stretch out 5. **drag one's feet** Inf. block, hold back, obstruct, procrastinate, stall ~n. 6. Sl. annoyance, bore, bother, nuisance, pain (Inf.), pest

dragging boring, dull, going slowly, humdrum, monotonous, tedious, tiresome, wearisome

dragoon v. browbeat, bully, coerce, compel, constrain, drive, force, impel, intimidate, strong-arm (Inf.)

drain v. 1. bleed, draw off, dry, empty, evacuate, milk, pump off or out, remove, tap, withdraw 2. consume, deplete, dissipate, empty, exhaust, sap, strain, tax, use up, weary 3. discharge, effuse, exude, flow out, leak, ooze, seep, trickle, well out 4. drink up, finish, gulp down, quaff, swallow ~n. 5. channel, conduit, culvert, ditch, duct, outlet, pipe, sewer, sink, trench, watercourse 6. depletion, drag, exhaustion, expenditure, reduction, sap, strain, withdrawal 7. **down the drain** gone, gone for good, lost, ruined, wasted

drainage bilge (water), seepage, sewage, sewerage, waste

dram drop, glass, measure, shot (Inf.), slug, snort (Sl.), tot

drama 1. dramatization, play, show, stage play, stage show, theatrical piece 2. acting, dramatic art, dramaturgy, stagecraft, theatre, Thespian art 3. crisis, dramatics, excitement, histrionics, scene, spectacle, theatrics, turmoil

dramatic 1. dramaturgic, dramaturgical, theatrical, Thespian 2. breathtaking, climactic, electrifying, emotional, exciting, melodramatic, sensational, startling, sudden, suspenseful, tense, thrilling 3. affecting, effective, expressive, impressive, moving, powerful, striking, vivid

dramatist dramaturge, playwright, scriptwriter

dramatize act, exaggerate, lay it on (thick) (Sl.), make a performance of, overdo, overstate, playact, play to the gallery

drastic desperate, dire, extreme, forceful, harsh, radical, severe, strong

draught 1. Of air current, flow, influx, movement, puff 2. dragging, drawing, haulage, pulling, traction 3. cup, dose, drench, drink, potion, quantity

draw v. 1. drag, haul, pull, tow, tug 2. delineate, depict, design, map out, mark out, outline, paint, portray, sketch, trace 3. deduce, derive, get, infer, make, take 4. allure, attract, bring forth, call forth, elicit, engage, entice, evoke, induce, influence, invite, persuade 5. extort, extract, pull out, take out 6. attenuate, elongate, extend, lengthen, stretch 7. breathe in, drain, inhale, inspire, puff, pull, respire, suck 8. compose, draft, formulate, frame, prepare, write 9. choose, pick, select, single out, take ~n. 10. Inf. attraction, enticement, lure, pull (Inf.) 11. dead heat, deadlock, stalemate, tie

drawback defect, deficiency, detriment, difficulty, disadvantage, fault, flaw, fly in the ointment (Inf.), handicap, hindrance, hitch, impediment, imperfection, nuisance, obstacle, snag, stumbling block, trouble

draw back recoil, retract, retreat, shrink, start back, withdraw

drawing cartoon, delineation, depiction, illustration, outline, picture, portrayal, representation, sketch, study

drawl v. Of speech sounds drag out,

draw out, extend, lengthen, pro~ long, protract

drawling dragging, drawly, dron~ ing, dull, twanging, twangy

drawn fatigued, fraught, haggard, harassed, harrowed, pinched, sapped, strained, stressed, taut, tense, tired, worn

draw on employ, exploit, extract, fall back on, have recourse to, make use of, rely on, take from, use

draw out drag out, extend, length~ en, make longer, prolong, prolon~ gate, protract, spin out, stretch, string out

draw up 1. bring to a stop, halt, pull up, run in, stop, stop short 2. com~ pose, draft, formulate, frame, pre~ pare, write out

dread 1. *v.* anticipate with horror, cringe at, fear, have cold feet (*Inf.*), quail, shrink from, shudder, tremble 2. *n.* affright, alarm, ap~ prehension, aversion, awe, dismay, fear, fright, funk (*Inf.*), heebie~ jeebies (*Sl.*), horror, terror, trepi~ dation 3. *adj.* alarming, awe~ inspiring, awful, dire, dreaded, dreadful, frightening, frightful, horrible, terrible, terrifying

dreadful alarming, appalling, aw~ ful, dire, distressing, fearful, for~ midable, frightful, ghastly, griev~ ous, hideous, horrendous, horrible, monstrous, shocking, terrible, tragic, tremendous

dream *n.* 1. daydream, delusion, fantasy, hallucination, illusion, im~ agination, pipe dream, reverie, speculation, trance, vagary, vision 2. ambition, aspiration, design, de~ sire, goal, hope, notion, wish 3. beauty, delight, gem, joy, marvel, pleasure, treasure ~*v.* 4. build cas~ tles in the air *or* in Spain, conjure up, daydream, envisage, fancy, fantasize, hallucinate, have dreams, imagine, stargaze, think, visualize

dreamer daydreamer, Don Quix~ ote, fantasist, fantasizer, fantast, idealist, romancer, theorizer, uto~ pian, visionary

dreamland cloud-cuckoo-land, cloudland, dream world, fairyland, fantasy, illusion, land of dreams, land of make-believe, land of Nod, never-never land (*Inf.*), sleep

dream up concoct, contrive, cook up (*Inf.*), create, devise, hatch, im~ agine, invent, spin, think up

dreamy 1. fanciful, imaginary, im~ practical, quixotic, speculative, vague, visionary 2. chimerical, dreamlike, fantastic, intangible, misty, phantasmagoric, phantas~ magorical, shadowy, unreal 3. ab~ sent, abstracted, daydreaming, faraway, in a reverie, musing, pensive, preoccupied, with one's head in the clouds 4. calming, gen~ tle, lulling, relaxing, romantic, soothing

dreary 1. bleak, cheerless, com~ fortless, depressing, dismal, dole~ ful, downcast, drear, forlorn, gloomy, glum, joyless, lonely, lonesome, melancholy, mournful, sad, solitary, sombre, sorrowful, wretched 2. boring, colourless, drab, dull, humdrum, lifeless, mo~ notonous, routine, tedious, un~ eventful, uninteresting, wearisome

dregs 1. deposit, draff, dross, grounds, lees, residue, residuum, scourings, scum, sediment, trash, waste 2. *Sl. canaille,* down-and-outs, good-for-nothings, outcasts, rabble, ragtag and bobtail, riffraff, scum

drench 1. drown, duck, flood, im~ brue, inundate, saturate, soak, souse, steep, wet 2. *Veterinary* dose, physic, purge

dress *n.* 1. costume, ensemble, frock, garment, get-up (*Inf.*), gown, outfit, rigout (*Inf.*), robe, suit 2. ap~ parel, attire, clothes, clothing, cos~ tume, garb, garments, gear (*Sl.*), guise, habiliment, raiment (*Archa~ ic*), togs, vestment ~*v.* 3. attire, change, clothe, don, garb, put on, robe, slip on *or* into 4. adorn, ap~ parel (*Archaic*), array, bedeck, deck, decorate, drape, embellish, furbish, ornament, rig, trim 5. ad~ just, align, arrange, comb (out), dispose, do (up), fit, groom, pre~

pare, set, straighten 6. bandage, bind up, plaster, treat

dress down berate, carpet (*Inf.*), castigate, haul over the coals, rebuke, reprimand, reprove, scold, tear (someone) off a strip, tell off (*Inf.*), upbraid

dressmaker couturier, modiste, seamstress, sewing woman, tailor

dress up 1. doll up (*Sl.*), dress for dinner, dress formally, put on one's best bib and tucker (*Inf.*), put on one's glad rags (*Sl.*) 2. disguise, play-act, put on fancy dress, wear a costume 3. beautify, embellish, gild, improve, titivate, trick out *or* up

dribble 1. drip, drop, fall in drops, leak, ooze, run, seep, trickle 2. drip saliva, drivel, drool, slaver, slobber

drift *v.* 1. be carried along, coast, float, go (aimlessly), meander, stray, waft, wander 2. accumulate, amass, bank up, drive, gather, pile up ~*n.* 3. accumulation, bank, heap, mass, mound, pile 4. course, current, direction, flow, impulse, movement, rush, sweep, trend 5. *Fig.* aim, design, direction, gist, implication, import, intention, meaning, object, purport, scope, significance, tendency, tenor

drill *v.* 1. discipline, exercise, instruct, practise, rehearse, teach, train ~*n.* 2. discipline, exercise, instruction, practice, preparation, repetition, training ~*v.* 3. bore, penetrate, perforate, pierce, puncture, sink in ~*n.* 4. bit, borer, boring-tool, gimlet, rotary tool

drink *v.* 1. absorb, drain, gulp, guzzle, imbibe, partake of, quaff, sip, suck, sup, swallow, swig, swill, toss off, wash down, wet one's whistle (*Inf.*) 2. booze (*Inf.*), carouse, go on a binge *or* bender (*Inf.*), hit the bottle (*Inf.*), indulge, pub-crawl (*Chiefly Brit. sl.*), revel, tipple, tope, wassail ~*n.* 3. beverage, liquid, potion, refreshment, thirst quencher 4. alcohol, booze (*Inf.*), hooch (*Sl.*), liquor, spirits, the bottle (*Inf.*) 5. cup, draught, glass, gulp, sip, swallow, swig (*Inf.*), taste 6. **the drink** *Inf.* the briny (*Inf.*),

the deep, the main, the ocean, the sea

drinker alcoholic, bibber, boozer (*Inf.*), dipsomaniac, drunk, drunkard, guzzler, inebriate, lush (*Sl.*), soak (*Sl.*), sot, sponge (*Inf.*), tippler, toper, wino (*Sl.*)

drink in absorb, assimilate, be all ears (*Inf.*), be fascinated by, be rapt, hang on (someone's) words, hang on the lips of, pay attention

drink to pledge, pledge the health of, salute, toast

drip *v.* 1. dribble, drizzle, drop, exude, filter, plop, splash, sprinkle, trickle ~*n.* 2. dribble, dripping, drop, leak, trickle 3. *Inf.* milksop, ninny, softy (*Inf.*), weakling, weed (*Inf.*), wet (*Inf.*)

drive *v.* 1. herd, hurl, impel, propel, push, send, urge 2. direct, go, guide, handle, manage, motor, operate, ride, steer, travel 3. actuate, coerce, compel, constrain, force, goad, harass, impel, motivate, oblige, overburden, overwork, press, prick, prod, rush, spur 4. dash, dig, plunge, hammer, ram, sink, stab, thrust ~*n.* 5. excursion, hurl (*Scot.*), jaunt, journey, outing, ride, run, spin (*Inf.*), trip, turn 6. action, advance, appeal, campaign, crusade, effort, push (*Inf.*), surge 7. ambition, effort, energy, enterprise, get-up-and-go (*Inf.*), initiative, motivation, pressure, push (*Inf.*), vigour, zip (*Inf.*)

drive at aim, allude to, get at (*Inf.*), have in mind, hint at, imply, indicate, intend, intimate, mean, refer to, signify, suggest

drivel *v.* 1. dribble, drool, slaver, slobber 2. babble, blether, gab (*Inf.*), gas (*Inf.*), maunder, prate, ramble, waffle (*Inf.*) ~*n.* 3. balderdash, blah (*Sl.*), bosh (*Inf.*), bunk (*Inf.*), bunkum, fatuity, gibberish, nonsense, poppycock (*Inf.*), prating, rot, rubbish, stuff, twaddle, waffle (*Inf.*) 4. saliva, slaver, slobber

driving compelling, dynamic, energetic, forceful, galvanic, sweeping, vigorous, violent

drizzle 1. *n.* fine rain, Scotch mist 2.

v. mizzle (*Dialect*), rain, shower, spot *or* spit with rain, spray, sprinkle

droll amusing, clownish, comic, comical, diverting, eccentric, entertaining, farcical, funny, humorous, jocular, laughable, ludicrous, odd, quaint, ridiculous, risible, waggish, whimsical

drone[1] *n.* idler, leech, loafer, lounger, parasite, scrounger (*Inf.*), sluggard, sponger (*Inf.*)

drone[2] *v.* 1. buzz, hum, purr, thrum, vibrate, whirr 2. *Often with* on be boring, chant, drawl, intone, prose about, speak monotonously, talk interminably ~*n.* 3. buzz, hum, murmuring, purr, thrum, vibration, whirr, whirring

droop 1. bend, dangle, drop, fall down, hang (down), sag, sink 2. decline, diminish, fade, faint, flag, languish, slump, wilt, wither 3. despond, falter, give in, give up, give way, lose heart *or* hope

drop *n.* 1. bead, bubble, driblet, drip, droplet, globule, pearl, tear 2. dab, dash, mouthful, nip, pinch, shot (*Inf.*), sip, spot, taste, tot, trace, trickle 3. abyss, chasm, declivity, descent, fall, plunge, precipice, slope 4. cut, decline, decrease, deterioration, downturn, fall-off, lowering, reduction, slump ~*v.* 5. dribble, drip, fall in drops, trickle 6. decline, depress, descend, diminish, dive, droop, fall, lower, plummet, plunge, sink, tumble 7. abandon, cease, desert, discontinue, forsake, give up, kick (*Inf.*), leave, quit, relinquish, remit, terminate 8. *Inf.* disown, ignore, jilt, reject, renounce, repudiate, throw over 9. *Inf. Sometimes with* off deposit, leave, let off, set down, unload

drop in (on) blow in (*Inf.*), call, call in, go and see, look in (on), look up, pop in (*Inf.*), roll up (*Inf.*), stop, turn up, visit

drop off 1. decline, decrease, diminish, dwindle, fall off, lessen, slacken 2. allow to alight, deliver, leave, let off, set down 3. *Inf.* catnap, doze (off), drowse, fall asleep,

have forty winks (*Inf.*), nod (off), snooze (*Inf.*)

drop out abandon, back out, forsake, give up, leave, quit, renege, stop, withdraw

drought 1. aridity, dehydration, drouth (*Archaic or Scot.*), dryness, dry spell, dry weather, parchedness 2. dearth, deficiency, insufficiency, lack, need, scarcity, shortage, want

drove collection, company, crowd, flock, gathering, herd, horde, mob, multitude, press, swarm, throng

drown 1. deluge, drench, engulf, flood, go down, go under, immerse, inundate, sink, submerge, swamp 2. *Fig.* deaden, engulf, muffle, obliterate, overcome, overpower, overwhelm, stifle, swallow up, wipe out

drowse 1. *v.* be drowsy, be lethargic, be sleepy, doze, drop off (*Inf.*), nap, nod, sleep, slumber, snooze (*Inf.*) 2. *n.* doze, forty winks (*Inf.*), nap, sleep, slumber

drowsy 1. comatose, dazed, dopey (*Sl.*), dozy, drugged, half asleep, heavy, lethargic, nodding, sleepy, somnolent, tired, torpid 2. dreamy, lulling, restful, sleepy, soothing, soporific

drubbing beating, clobbering (*Sl.*), defeat, flogging, hammering (*Inf.*), licking (*Inf.*), pounding, pummelling, thrashing, trouncing, walloping (*Inf.*), whipping

drudge 1. *n.* dogsbody (*Inf.*), factotum, hack, maid *or* man of all work, menial, plodder, scullion (*Archaic*), servant, skivvy, slave, toiler, worker 2. *v.* grind (*Inf.*), keep one's nose to the grindstone, labour, moil (*Archaic or dialect*), plod, plug away (*Inf.*), slave, toil, work

drudgery chore, donkey-work, fag (*Inf.*), grind (*Inf.*), hack work, hard work, labour, menial labour, skivvying, slavery, slog, sweat (*Inf.*), sweated labour, toil

drug *n.* 1. medicament, medication, medicine, physic, poison, remedy 2. dope (*Sl.*), narcotic, opiate ~*v.* 3. administer a drug, dope (*Sl.*), dose, medicate, treat **4.** anaesthetize, deaden, knock out, numb, poison, stupefy

drugged comatose, doped (*Sl.*), dopey (*Sl.*), high (*Inf.*), on a trip (*Inf.*), spaced out (*Sl.*), stoned (*Sl.*), stupefied, turned on (*Sl.*), under the influence (*Inf.*), zonked (*Sl.*)

drum *v.* **1.** beat, pulsate, rap, reverberate, tap, tattoo, throb **2.** *With* **into** din into, drive home, hammer away, harp on, instil, reiterate

drum up attract, bid for, canvass, obtain, petition, round up, solicit

drunk 1. *adj.* bacchic, canned (*Sl.*), drunken, fu' (*Scot.*), fuddled, half seas over (*Inf.*), inebriated, intoxicated, maudlin, merry (*Inf.*), muddled, pie-eyed (*Sl.*), plastered (*Sl.*), sloshed (*Inf.*), soaked (*Inf.*), stewed (*Sl.*), stoned (*Sl.*), tiddly (*Sl.*), tight (*Inf.*), tipsy, tired and emotional (*Euphemistic*), under the influence (*Inf.*), well-oiled (*Sl.*) **2.** *n.* boozer (*Inf.*), drunkard, inebriate, lush (*Sl.*), soak (*Sl.*), sot, toper, wino (*Sl.*)

drunkard alcoholic, carouser, dipsomaniac, drinker, drunk, lush (*Sl.*), soak (*Sl.*), sot, tippler, toper, wino (*Sl.*)

drunken 1. bibulous, boozing (*Sl.*), drunk, (gin-)sodden, inebriate, intoxicated, red-nosed, sottish, tippling, toping, under the influence (*Inf.*) **2.** bacchanalian, bacchic, boozy (*Sl.*), debauched, dionysian, dissipated, orgiastic, riotous, saturnalian

drunkenness alcoholism, bibulousness, dipsomania, inebriety, insobriety, intemperance, intoxication, sottishness, tipsiness

dry *adj.* **1.** arid, barren, dehydrated, desiccated, dried up, juiceless, moistureless, parched, sapless, thirsty, torrid, waterless **2.** *Fig.* boring, dreary, dull, monotonous, plain, tedious, tiresome, uninteresting **3.** *Fig.* cutting, deadpan, droll, keen, low-key, quietly humorous, sarcastic, sharp, sly ~*v.* **4.** dehumidify, dehydrate, desiccate, drain, make dry, parch, sear **5.** *With* **out** *or* **up** become dry, become unproductive, harden, mummify, shrivel up, wilt, wither, wizen

dryness aridity, aridness, dehumidification, dehydration, drought, thirst, thirstiness

dual binary, coupled, double, duplex, duplicate, matched, paired, twin, twofold

dub 1. bestow, confer, confer knighthood upon, entitle, knight **2.** call, christen, denominate, designate, label, name, nickname, style, term

dubious 1. doubtful, hesitant, iffy (*Inf.*), sceptical, uncertain, unconvinced, undecided, unsure, wavering **2.** ambiguous, debatable, doubtful, equivocal, indefinite, indeterminate, obscure, problematical, unclear, unsettled **3.** fishy (*Inf.*), questionable, shady (*Inf.*), suspect, suspicious, undependable, unreliable, untrustworthy

duck 1. bend, bob, bow, crouch, dodge, drop, lower, stoop **2.** dip, dive, douse, dunk, immerse, plunge, souse, submerge, wet **3.** *Inf.* avoid, dodge, escape, evade, shirk, shun, sidestep

duct blood vessel, canal, channel, conduit, funnel, passage, pipe, tube

dud 1. *n.* failure, flop (*Inf.*), washout (*Inf.*) **2.** *adj.* broken, bust (*Inf.*), duff (*Sl.*), failed, inoperative, kaput (*Inf.*), not functioning, valueless, worthless

dudgeon 1. *Archaic* indignation, ire, resentment, umbrage, wrath **2.** **in high dudgeon** angry, fuming, indignant, offended, resentful, vexed

due *adj.* **1.** in arrears, outstanding, owed, owing, payable, unpaid **2.** appropriate, becoming, bounden, deserved, fit, fitting, just, justified, merited, obligatory, proper, requisite, right, rightful, suitable, well-earned **3.** adequate, ample, enough, plenty of, sufficient **4.** expected, expected to arrive, scheduled ~*n.* **5.** comeuppance (*Sl.*), deserts, merits, prerogative, privilege, right(s) ~*adv.* **6.** dead, direct, directly, exactly, straight, undeviatingly

duel *n.* 1. affair of honour, single combat 2. clash, competition, contest, encounter, engagement, fight, rivalry ~*v.* 3. clash, compete, contend, contest, fight, rival, struggle, vie with

dues charge, charges, contribution, fee, levy, membership fee

duffer blunderer, booby, bungler, clod, clot (*Sl.*), galoot (*Sl., chiefly U.S.*), lubber, lummox (*Inf.*), oaf

dull *adj.* 1. dense, dim, dim-witted (*Inf.*), doltish, slow, stolid, stupid, thick, unintelligent 2. apathetic, blank, callous, dead, empty, heavy, indifferent, insensible, insensitive, lifeless, listless, passionless, slow, sluggish, unresponsive, unsympathetic, vacuous 3. boring, commonplace, dreary, dry, flat, humdrum, monotonous, plain, prosaic, run-of-the-mill, tedious, tiresome, unimaginative, uninteresting, vapid 4. blunt, blunted, dulled, edgeless, not keen, not sharp, unsharpened 5. cloudy, dim, dismal, gloomy, leaden, opaque, overcast, turbid 6. depressed, inactive, slack, slow, sluggish, torpid, uneventful 7. drab, faded, feeble, indistinct, lacklustre, muffled, murky, muted, sombre, subdued, subfusc, toned-down ~*v.* 8. dampen, deject, depress, discourage, dishearten, dispirit, sadden 9. allay, alleviate, assuage, blunt, lessen, mitigate, moderate, palliate, paralyse, relieve, soften, stupefy, take the edge off 10. cloud, darken, dim, fade, obscure, stain, sully, tarnish

dullard blockhead, clod, dimwit (*Inf.*), dolt, dope (*Sl.*), dunce, nitwit, numskull, oaf

duly 1. accordingly, appropriately, befittingly, correctly, decorously, deservedly, fittingly, properly, rightfully, suitably 2. at the proper time, on time, punctually

dumb 1. at a loss for words, inarticulate, mum, mute, silent, soundless, speechless, tongue-tied, voiceless, wordless 2. *Inf.* dense, dim-witted (*Inf.*), dull, foolish, stupid, thick, unintelligent

dumbfound, dumfound amaze, astonish, astound, bewilder, bowl over (*Inf.*), confound, confuse, flabbergast (*Inf.*), nonplus, overwhelm, stagger, startle, stun, take aback

dumbfounded, dumfounded amazed, astonished, astounded, bewildered, bowled over (*Inf.*), breathless, confounded, confused, dumb, flabbergasted (*Inf.*), knocked for six (*Inf.*), knocked sideways (*Inf.*), nonplussed, overcome, overwhelmed, speechless, staggered, startled, stunned, taken aback, thrown, thunderstruck

dummy *n.* 1. figure, form, lay figure, manikin, mannequin, model 2. copy, counterfeit, duplicate, imitation, sham, substitute 3. *Sl.* blockhead, dimwit (*Inf.*), dolt, dullard, dunce, fool, numskull, simpleton ~*adj.* 4. artificial, bogus, fake, false, imitation, mock, phoney (*Sl.*), sham, simulated 5. mock, practice, simulated, trial

dump *v.* 1. deposit, drop, fling down, let fall, throw down 2. discharge, dispose of, ditch (*Sl.*), empty out, get rid of, jettison, scrap, throw away *or* out, tip, unload ~*n.* 3. junkyard, refuse heap, rubbish heap, rubbish tip, tip 4. *Inf.* hole (*Inf.*), hovel, joint (*Sl.*), mess, pigsty, shack, shanty, slum

dumps blues, dejection, depression, despondency, dolour, gloom, gloominess, low spirits, melancholy, mopes, sadness, unhappiness, woe

dun *v.* beset, importune, pester, plague, press, urge

dunce ass, blockhead, bonehead (*Sl.*), dimwit (*Inf.*), dolt, donkey, duffer (*Inf.*), dullard, dunderhead, goose (*Inf.*), halfwit, ignoramus, loon (*Inf.*), moron, nincompoop, numskull, simpleton, thickhead

dungeon cage, cell, donjon, lockup, oubliette, prison, vault

duplicate 1. *adj.* corresponding, identical, matched, matching, twin, twofold 2. *n.* carbon copy, clone, copy, double, facsimile, likeness, lookalike, match, mate, photocopy, Photostat (*Trademark*), replica, reproduction, ringer (*Sl.*), twin, Xerox (*Trademark*) 3. *v.* clone, copy, double, echo, photocopy, Photostat (*Trademark*), repeat, replicate, reproduce, Xerox (*Trademark*)

durability constancy, durableness, endurance, imperishability, last~ingness, permanence, persistence

durable abiding, constant, depend~able, enduring, fast, firm, fixed, hard-wearing, lasting, long-lasting, permanent, persistent, reliable, resistant, sound, stable, strong, sturdy, substantial, tough

dusk 1. dark, evening, eventide, gloaming, nightfall, sundown, sun~set, twilight 2. *Poetic* darkness, gloom, murk, obscurity, shade, shadowiness

dusky 1. dark, dark-complexioned, dark-hued, sable, swarthy 2. calig~inous (*Archaic*), cloudy, crepuscu~lar, darkish, dim, gloomy, murky, obscure, overcast, shadowy, shady, tenebrous, twilight, twilit, veiled

dust *n.* 1. fine fragments, grime, grit, particles, powder, powdery dirt 2. dirt, earth, ground, soil 3. *Inf.* commotion, disturbance, fuss, racket, row 4. **bite the dust** *Inf.* die, drop dead, expire, fall in bat~tle, pass away, perish 5. **lick the dust** *Inf.* be servile, bootlick (*Inf.*), demean oneself, grovel, kowtow, toady 6. **throw dust in the eyes of** con (*Sl.*), confuse, deceive, fool, have (someone) on, hoodwink, mislead, take in (*Inf.*) ~*v.* 7. cover, dredge, powder, scatter, sift, spray, spread, sprinkle

dusty 1. dirty, grubby, sooty, un~clean, undusted, unswept 2. chalky, crumbly, friable, granular, pow~dery, sandy

dutiful compliant, conscientious, deferential, devoted, docile, du~teous (*Archaic*), filial, obedient, punctilious, respectful, reverential, submissive

duty 1. assignment, business, call~ing, charge, engagement, function, mission, obligation, office, onus, province, responsibility, role, ser~vice, task, work 2. allegiance, def~erence, loyalty, obedience, respect, reverence 3. customs, due, excise, impost, levy, tariff, tax, toll 4. **do duty for** stand in, substitute, take the place of 5. **be the duty of** be~hove (*Archaic*), be incumbent upon, belong to, be (someone's) pi~geon (*Inf.*), be up to (*Inf.*), devolve upon, pertain to, rest with 6. **off duty** at leisure, free, off, off work, on holiday 7. **on duty** at work, busy, engaged

dwarf *n.* 1. bantam, homunculus, hop-o'-my-thumb, Lilliputian, manikin, midget, pygmy, Tom Thumb 2. gnome, goblin ~*adj.* 3. baby, diminutive, dwarfed, Lillipu~tian, miniature, petite, pocket, small, tiny, undersized ~*v.* 4. dim, diminish, dominate, minimize, overshadow, tower above *or* over 5. check, cultivate by bonsai, low~er, retard, stunt

dwell abide, establish oneself, hang out (*Inf.*), inhabit, live, lodge, quar~ter, remain, reside, rest, settle, so~journ, stay, stop

dwelling abode, domicile, dwelling house, establishment, habitation, home, house, lodging, quarters, residence

dwell on *or* **upon** be engrossed in, continue, elaborate, emphasize, expatiate, harp on, linger over

dye 1. *n.* colorant, colour, colouring, pigment, stain, tinge, tint 2. *v.* col~our, pigment, stain, tincture, tinge, tint

dyed-in-the-wool complete, con~firmed, deep-rooted, entrenched, established, inveterate, through-and-through

dying at death's door, ebbing, ex~piring, fading, failing, final, going, *in extremis,* moribund, mortal, passing, perishing, sinking

dynamic active, driving, electric, energetic, forceful, go-ahead, go-getting (*Inf.*), high-powered, lively, magnetic, powerful, vigorous, vital, zippy (*Inf.*)

dynasty ascendancy, dominion, empire, government, house, re~gime, rule, sovereignty, sway

E

each 1. *adj.* every **2.** *pron.* each and every one, each one, every one, one and all **3.** *adv.* apiece, for each, from each, individually, per capita, per head, per person, respectively, singly, to each

eager agog, anxious, ardent, athirst, avid, earnest, enthusiastic, fervent, fervid, greedy, hot, hungry, impatient, intent, keen, longing, raring, vehement, yearning, zealous

eagerness ardour, avidity, earnestness, enthusiasm, fervour, greediness, heartiness, hunger, impatience, impetuosity, intentness, keenness, longing, thirst, vehemence, yearning, zeal

ear *Fig.* **1.** attention, consideration, hearing, heed, notice, regard **2.** appreciation, discrimination, musical perception, sensitivity, taste

early *adj.* **1.** advanced, forward, premature, untimely **2.** primeval, primitive, primordial, undeveloped, young ~*adv.* **3.** ahead of time, beforehand, betimes (*Archaic*), in advance, in good time, prematurely, too soon

earn 1. bring in, collect, draw, gain, get, gross, make, net, obtain, procure, realize, reap, receive **2.** acquire, attain, be entitled to, be worthy of, deserve, merit, rate, warrant, win

earnest *adj.* **1.** close, constant, determined, firm, fixed, grave, intent, resolute, resolved, serious, sincere, solemn, stable, staid, steady, thoughtful **2.** ardent, devoted, eager, enthusiastic, fervent, fervid, heartfelt, impassioned, keen, passionate, purposeful, urgent, vehement, warm, zealous ~*n.* **3.** determination, reality, resolution, seriousness, sincerity, truth **4.** assurance, deposit, down payment, earnest money (*Law*), foretaste, guarantee, pledge, promise, security, token

earnings emolument, gain, income, pay, proceeds, profits, receipts, remuneration, return, reward, salary, stipend, takings, wages

earth 1. globe, orb, planet, sphere, terrestrial sphere, world **2.** clay, clod, dirt, ground, land, loam, mould, sod, soil, topsoil, turf

earthenware ceramics, crockery, crocks, pots, pottery, terra cotta

earthly 1. mundane, sublunary, tellurian, telluric, terrene, terrestrial, worldly **2.** human, material, mortal, non-spiritual, profane, secular, temporal, worldly **3.** base, carnal, fleshly, gross, low, materialistic, physical, sensual, sordid, vile **4.** *Inf.* conceivable, feasible, imaginable, likely, possible, practical

ease *n.* **1.** affluence, calmness, comfort, content, contentment, enjoyment, happiness, leisure, peace, peace of mind, quiet, quietude, relaxation, repose, rest, restfulness, serenity, tranquillity **2.** easiness, effortlessness, facility, readiness, simplicity **3.** flexibility, freedom, informality, liberty, naturalness, unaffectedness, unconstraint, unreservedness **4.** aplomb, composure, insouciance, nonchalance, poise, relaxedness ~*v.* **5.** abate, allay, alleviate, appease, assuage, calm, comfort, disburden, lessen, lighten, mitigate, moderate, mollify, pacify, palliate, quiet, relax, relent, relieve, slacken, soothe, still, tranquillize **6.** aid, assist, expedite, facilitate, forward, further, lessen the labour of, make easier, simplify, smooth, speed up **7.** edge, guide, inch, manoeuvre, move carefully, slide, slip, squeeze, steer

easily 1. comfortably, effortlessly, facilely, readily, simply, smoothly, with ease, without difficulty, without trouble **2.** absolutely, beyond question, by far, certainly, clearly, definitely, doubtlessly, far and away, indisputably, indubitably, plainly, surely, undeniably, undoubtedly, unequivocally, unquestionably, without a doubt 3. almost certainly, probably, well

easy 1. a piece of cake (*Inf.*), a pushover (*Sl.*), child's play (*Inf.*), clear, effortless, facile, light, no bother, not difficult, no trouble, painless, simple, smooth, straightforward, uncomplicated, undemanding 2. calm, carefree, comfortable, contented, cushy (*Sl.*), easeful, leisurely, peaceful, pleasant, quiet, relaxed, satisfied, serene, tranquil, undisturbed, untroubled, unworried, well-to-do 3. flexible, indulgent, lenient, liberal, light, mild, permissive, tolerant, unburdensome, unoppressive 4. affable, casual, easy-going, friendly, gentle, graceful, gracious, informal, mild, natural, open, pleasant, relaxed, smooth, tolerant, unaffected, unceremonious, unconstrained, undemanding, unforced, unpretentious 5. accommodating, amenable, biddable, compliant, docile, gullible, manageable, pliant, soft, submissive, suggestible, susceptible, tractable, trusting, yielding 6. comfortable, gentle, leisurely, light, mild, moderate, temperate, undemanding, unexacting, unhurried

easy-going amenable, calm, carefree, casual, complacent, easy, even-tempered, flexible, happy-go-lucky, indulgent, insouciant, laidback (*Inf.*), lenient, liberal, mild, moderate, nonchalant, permissive, placid, relaxed, serene, tolerant, unconcerned, uncritical, undemanding, unhurried

eat 1. chew, consume, devour, ingest, munch, scoff (*Sl.*), swallow 2. break bread, dine, feed, have a meal, take food, take nourishment 3. corrode, crumble, decay, dissolve, erode, rot, waste away, wear away 4. **eat one's words** abjure, recant, rescind, retract, take (statement) back

eavesdrop bug (*Inf.*), listen in, monitor, overhear, snoop (*Inf.*), spy, tap (*Inf.*)

ebb v. 1. abate, fall away, fall back, flow back, go out, recede, retire, retreat, retrocede, sink, subside, wane, withdraw ~n. 2. ebb tide, going out, low tide, low water, reflux, regression, retreat, retrocession, subsidence, wane, waning, withdrawal ~v. 3. decay, decline, decrease, degenerate, deteriorate, diminish, drop, dwindle, fade away, fall away, flag, lessen, peter out, shrink, sink, slacken, weaken ~n. 4. decay, decline, decrease, degeneration, deterioration, diminution, drop, dwindling, fading away, flagging, lessening, petering out, shrinkage, sinking, slackening, weakening

eccentric 1. *adj.* aberrant, abnormal, anomalous, bizarre, capricious, erratic, freakish, idiosyncratic, irregular, odd, outlandish, peculiar, queer (*Inf.*), quirky, singular, strange, uncommon, unconventional, weird, whimsical 2. *n.* case (*Inf.*), character (*Inf.*), crank (*Inf.*), freak (*Sl.*), nonconformist, odd fish (*Inf.*), oddity, weirdie *or* weirdo (*Inf.*)

eccentricity aberration, abnormality, anomaly, bizarreness, caprice, capriciousness, foible, freakishness, idiosyncrasy, irregularity, nonconformity, oddity, oddness, outlandishness, peculiarity, queerness (*Inf.*), quirk, singularity, strangeness, unconventionality, waywardness, weirdness, whimsicality, whimsicalness

ecclesiastic 1. *n.* churchman, clergyman, cleric, divine, holy man, man of the cloth, minister, parson, priest 2. *adj. Also* **ecclesiastical** church, churchly, clerical, divine, holy, pastoral, priestly, religious, spiritual

echo v. 1. repeat, resound, reverberate 2. ape, copy, imitate, mirror, parallel, parrot, recall, reflect, reiterate, reproduce, resemble, ring, second ~n. 3. answer, repetition, reverberation 4. copy, imitation, mirror image, parallel, reflection, reiteration, reproduction, ringing 5. allusion, evocation, hint, intimation, memory, reminder, suggestion, trace 6. *Often plural* aftereffect, aftermath, consequence, repercussion

eclipse *v.* 1. blot out, cloud, darken, dim, extinguish, obscure, overshadow, shroud, veil 2. exceed, excel, outdo, outshine, surpass, transcend ~*n.* 3. darkening, dimming, extinction, obscuration, occultation, shading 4. decline, diminution, failure, fall, loss

economic 1. business, commercial, financial, industrial, mercantile, trade 2. money-making, productive, profitable, profit-making, remunerative, solvent, viable 3. bread-and-butter (*Inf.*), budgetary, financial, fiscal, material, monetary, pecuniary 4. *Inf. Also* economical cheap, fair, inexpensive, low, low-priced, modest, reasonable

economical 1. cost-effective, efficient, money-saving, sparing, time-saving, unwasteful, work-saving 2. careful, economizing, frugal, prudent, saving, scrimping, sparing, thrifty 3. *Also* economic cheap, fair, inexpensive, low, low-priced, modest, reasonable

economize be economical, be frugal, be sparing, cut back, husband, retrench, save, scrimp, tighten one's belt

economy frugality, husbandry, parsimony, providence, prudence, restraint, retrenchment, saving, sparingness, thrift, thriftiness

ecstasy bliss, delight, elation, enthusiasm, euphoria, exaltation, fervour, frenzy, joy, rapture, ravishment, rhapsody, seventh heaven, trance, transport

ecstatic blissful, delirious, elated, enraptured, enthusiastic, entranced, euphoric, fervent, frenzied, in exaltation, in transports of delight, joyful, joyous, on cloud nine (*Inf.*), overjoyed, rapturous, rhapsodic, transported

eddy 1. *n.* counter-current, counterflow, swirl, vortex, whirlpool 2. *v.* swirl, whirl

edge *n.* 1. border, bound, boundary, brim, brink, contour, fringe, limit, line, lip, margin, outline, perimeter, periphery, rim, side, threshold, verge 2. acuteness, animation, bite, effectiveness, force, incisiveness, interest, keenness, point, pungency, sharpness, sting, urgency, zest 3. advantage, ascendancy, dominance, lead, superiority, upper hand 4. **on edge** apprehensive, eager, edgy, excited, ill at ease, impatient, irritable, keyed up, nervous, on tenterhooks, tense, uptight (*Inf.*) ~*v.* 5. bind, border, fringe, hem, rim, shape, trim 6. creep, ease, inch, sidle, steal, work, worm 7. hone, sharpen, strop, whet

edgy anxious, ill at ease, irascible, irritable, keyed up, nervous, on edge, restive, tense, touchy

edible comestible (*Rare*), digestible, eatable, esculent, fit to eat, good, harmless, palatable, wholesome

edict act, command, decree, dictate, dictum, enactment, fiat, injunction, law, mandate, manifesto, order, ordinance, proclamation, pronouncement, pronunciamento, regulation, ruling, statute, ukase (*Rare*)

edifice building, construction, erection, fabric (*Rare*), habitation, house, pile, structure

edify educate, elevate, enlighten, guide, improve, inform, instruct, nurture, school, teach, uplift

edit 1. adapt, annotate, censor, check, condense, correct, emend, polish, redact, rephrase, revise, rewrite 2. assemble, compose, put together, rearrange, reorder, select

edition copy, impression, issue, number, printing, programme (*TV, Radio*), version, volume

educate civilize, coach, cultivate, develop, discipline, drill, edify, enlighten, exercise, foster, improve, indoctrinate, inform, instruct, mature, rear, school, teach, train, tutor

educated 1. coached, informed, instructed, nurtured, schooled, taught, tutored 2. civilized, cultivated, cultured, enlightened, experienced, informed, knowledgeable, learned, lettered, literary, polished, refined, tasteful

education breeding, civilization, coaching, cultivation, culture, development, discipline, drilling, edification, enlightenment, erudition, improvement, indoctrination, instruction, knowledge, nurture, scholarship, schooling, teaching, training, tuition, tutoring

educational cultural, didactic, edifying, educative, enlightening, heuristic, improving, informative, instructive

educative didactic, edifying, educational, enlightening, heuristic, improving, informative, instructive

eerie awesome, creepy (*Inf.*), eldritch (*Poetic*), fearful, frightening, ghostly, mysterious, scary (*Inf.*), spectral, spooky (*Inf.*), strange, uncanny, unearthly, weird

efface 1. annihilate, blot out, cancel, cross out, delete, destroy, dim, eradicate, erase, excise, expunge, extirpate, obliterate, raze, rub out, wipe out 2. *Of oneself* be modest (bashful, diffident, retiring, timid, unassertive), humble, lower, make inconspicuous, withdraw

effect *n.* 1. aftermath, conclusion, consequence, event, fruit, issue, outcome, result, upshot 2. clout (*Inf.*), effectiveness, efficacy, efficiency, fact, force, influence, power, reality, strength, use, validity, vigour, weight 3. drift, essence, impact, import, impression, meaning, purport, purpose, sense, significance, tenor 4. action, enforcement, execution, force, implementation, operation 5. **in effect** actually, effectively, essentially, for practical purposes, in actuality, in fact, in reality, in truth, really, to all intents and purposes, virtually 6. **take effect** become operative, begin, come into force, produce results, work ~*v.* 7. accomplish, achieve, actuate, bring about, carry out, cause, complete, consummate, create, effectuate, execute,

fulfil, give rise to, initiate, make, perform, produce

effective 1. able, active, adequate, capable, competent, effectual, efficacious, efficient, energetic, operative, productive, serviceable, useful 2. cogent, compelling, convincing, emphatic, forceful, forcible, impressive, moving, persuasive, potent, powerful, striking, telling 3. active, actual, current, in effect, in execution, in force, in operation, operative, real

effectiveness capability, clout (*Inf.*), cogency, effect, efficacy, efficiency, force, influence, potency, power, strength, success, use, validity, vigour, weight

effects belongings, chattels, furniture, gear, goods, movables, paraphernalia, possessions, property, things, trappings

effeminacy delicacy, femininity, softness, tenderness, unmanliness, weakness, womanishness, womanliness

effeminate delicate, feminine, sissy, soft, tender, unmanly, weak, womanish, womanlike, womanly

effervesce bubble, ferment, fizz, foam, froth, sparkle

effervescence 1. bubbling, ferment, fermentation, fizz, foam, foaming, froth, frothing, sparkle 2. animation, buoyancy, ebullience, enthusiasm, excitedness, excitement, exhilaration, exuberance, gaiety, high spirits, liveliness, vim (*Sl.*), vitality, vivacity, zing (*Inf.*)

effervescent 1. bubbling, bubbly, carbonated, fermenting, fizzing, fizzy, foaming, foamy, frothing, frothy, sparkling 2. animated, bubbly, buoyant, ebullient, enthusiastic, excited, exhilarated, exuberant, gay, in high spirits, irrepressible, lively, merry, vital, vivacious, zingy (*Inf.*)

effete 1. corrupt, debased, decadent, decayed, decrepit, degenerate, dissipated, enervated, enfeebled, feeble, ineffectual, overrefined, spoiled, weak 2. burnt out, drained, enervated, exhausted, played out, spent, used up, wasted, worn out 3. barren, fruitless, infecund, infertile, sterile, unfruitful, unproductive, unprolific

efficacious active, adequate, capable, competent, effective, effectual, efficient, energetic, operative, potent, powerful, productive, serviceable, successful, useful

efficacy ability, capability, competence, effect, effectiveness, efficaciousness, efficiency, energy, force, influence, potency, power, strength, success, use, vigour, virtue, weight

efficiency ability, adeptness, capability, competence, economy, effectiveness, efficacy, power, productivity, proficiency, readiness, skilfulness, skill

efficient able, adept, businesslike, capable, competent, economic, effective, effectual, powerful, productive, proficient, ready, skilful, well-organized, workmanlike

effigy dummy, figure, guy, icon, idol, image, likeness, picture, portrait, representation, statue

effluent n. 1. effluvium, pollutant, sewage, waste 2. discharge, effluence, efflux, emanation, emission, exhalation, flow, outflow, outpouring ~adj. 3. discharged, emanating, emitted, outflowing

effort 1. application, endeavour, energy, exertion, force, labour, pains, power, strain, stress, stretch, striving, struggle, toil, travail (Literary), trouble, work 2. attempt, endeavour, essay, go, shot (Inf.), stab (Inf.), try 3. accomplishment, achievement, act, creation, deed, feat, job, product, production

effortless easy, facile, painless, simple, smooth, uncomplicated, undemanding, untroublesome

effulgent beaming, blazing, bright, brilliant, dazzling, flaming, fluorescent, fulgent (Poetic), glowing, incandescent, lucent, luminous, lustrous, radiant, refulgent (Literary), resplendent, shining, splendid, vivid

effusion 1. discharge, effluence, efflux, emission, gush, outflow, outpouring, shedding, stream 2. address, outpouring, speech, talk, utterance, writing

effusive demonstrative, ebullient, enthusiastic, expansive, extravagant, exuberant, free-flowing, fulsome, gushing, lavish, overflowing, profuse, talkative, unreserved, unrestrained, wordy

egg on encourage, exhort, goad, incite, prod, prompt, push, spur, urge

egocentric egoistic, egoistical, egotistic, egotistical, self-centred, selfish

egoism egocentricity, egomania, egotism, narcissism, self-absorption, self-centredness, self-importance, self-interest, selfishness, self-love, self-regard, self-seeking

egoist egomaniac, egotist, narcissist, self-seeker

egoistic, egoistical egocentric, egomaniacal, egotistic, egotistical, narcissistic, self-absorbed, self-centred, self-important, self-seeking

egotism conceitedness, egocentricity, egoism, egomania, narcissism, self-admiration, self-centredness, self-conceit, self-esteem, self-importance, self-love, self-praise, superiority, vainglory, vanity

egotist bighead (Inf.), blowhard (Inf.), boaster, braggadocio, braggart, egoist, egomaniac, self-admirer, swaggerer

egotistic, egotistical boasting, bragging, conceited, egocentric, egoistic, egoistical, egomaniacal, narcissistic, opinionated, self-admiring, self-centred, self-important, superior, vain, vainglorious

egress departure, emergence, escape, exit, exodus, issue, outlet, passage out, vent, way out, withdrawal

eject 1. cast out, discharge, disgorge, emit, expel, spew, spout, throw out, vomit 2. banish, boot out (Inf.), bounce (Sl.), deport, dispossess, drive out, evacuate, evict, exile, expel, oust, remove, throw out, turn out 3. discharge, dislodge, dis~ miss, fire (*Inf.*), get rid of, kick out (*Inf.*), oust, sack (*Inf.*), throw out

ejection 1. casting out, disgorge~ ment, expulsion, spouting, throw~ ing out 2. banishment, deportation, dispossession, evacuation, eviction, exile, expulsion, ouster (*Law*), re~ moval 3. discharge, dislodgement, dismissal, firing (*Inf.*), sacking (*Inf.*), the boot (*Sl.*), the sack (*Inf.*)

eke out 1. be economical with, be frugal with, be sparing with, economize on, husband, stretch out 2. add to, enlarge, increase, make up (with), supplement

elaborate *adj.* 1. careful, detailed, exact, intricate, laboured, minute, painstaking, perfected, precise, skilful, studied, thorough 2. com~ plex, complicated, decorated, de~ tailed, extravagant, fancy, fussy, involved, ornamented, ornate, os~ tentatious, showy ~*v.* 3. add detail, amplify, complicate, decorate, de~ velop, devise, embellish, enhance, enlarge, expand (upon), flesh out, garnish, improve, ornament, pol~ ish, produce, refine, work out

elapse glide by, go, go by, lapse, pass, pass by, roll by, roll on, slip away, slip by

elastic 1. ductile, flexible, plastic, pliable, pliant, resilient, rubbery, springy, stretchable, stretchy, sup~ ple, yielding 2. accommodating, adaptable, adjustable, complaisant, compliant, flexible, supple, toler~ ant, variable, yielding 3. bouncy, buoyant, irrepressible, resilient

elated animated, blissful, cheered, delighted, ecstatic, elevated, euphoric, excited, exhilarated, ex~ ultant, gleeful, in high spirits, joy~ ful, joyous, jubilant, overjoyed, proud, puffed up, roused

elation bliss, delight, ecstasy, euphoria, exaltation, exhilaration, exultation, glee, high spirits, joy, joyfulness, joyousness, jubilation, rapture

elbow *n.* 1. angle, bend, corner, joint, turn 2. **at one's elbow** at hand, close by, handy, near, to hand, within reach 3. **out at el~**

bow(s) beggarly, down at heel, impoverished, in rags, ragged, seedy, shabby, tattered 4. **rub el~ bows with** associate, fraternize, hang out (*Inf.*), hobnob, mingle, mix, socialize 5. **up to the elbows** absorbed, busy, engaged, en~ grossed, immersed, occupied, tied up, up to the ears, wrapped up ~*v.* 6. bump, crowd, hustle, jostle, knock, nudge, push, shoulder, shove

elbowroom freedom, latitude, lee~ way, play, room, scope, space

elder *adj.* 1. ancient, earlier born, first-born, older, senior ~*n.* 2. older person, senior 3. *Presbyterianism* church official, office bearer, presbyter

elect 1. *v.* appoint, choose, decide upon, designate, determine, opt for, pick, pick out, prefer, select, settle on, vote 2. *adj.* choice, cho~ sen, elite, hand-picked, picked, preferred, select, selected

election appointment, choice, choosing, decision, determination, judgment, preference, selection, vote, voting

elector chooser, constituent, selec~ tor, voter

electric *Fig.* charged, dynamic, exciting, rousing, stimulating, stir~ ring, tense, thrilling

electrify *Fig.* amaze, animate, astonish, astound, excite, fire, gal~ vanize, invigorate, jolt, rouse, shock, startle, stimulate, stir, take one's breath away, thrill

elegance, elegancy 1. beauty, courtliness, dignity, exquisiteness, gentility, grace, gracefulness, grandeur, luxury, polish, polite~ ness, refinement, sumptuousness 2. discernment, distinction, propriety, style, taste

elegant 1. à la mode, artistic, beautiful, chic, choice, comely, courtly, cultivated, delicate, ex~ quisite, fashionable, fine, genteel, graceful, handsome, luxurious, modish, nice, polished, refined, stylish, sumptuous, tasteful 2. ap~ propriate, apt, clever, effective, ingenious, neat, simple

elegy coronach (*Scot., Irish*), dirge, keen, lament, plaint (*Archaic*), requiem, threnody

element 1. basis, component, constituent, essential factor, factor, feature, hint, ingredient, member, part, section, subdivision, trace, unit 2. domain, environment, field, habitat, medium, milieu, sphere

elementary 1. clear, easy, facile, plain, rudimentary, simple, straightforward, uncomplicated 2. basic, elemental, fundamental, initial, introductory, original, primary, rudimentary

elements 1. basics, essentials, foundations, fundamentals, principles, rudiments 2. atmospheric conditions, atmospheric forces, powers of nature, weather

elevate 1. heighten, hoist, lift, lift up, raise, uplift, upraise 2. advance, aggrandize, exalt, prefer, promote, upgrade 3. animate, boost, brighten, buoy up, cheer, elate, excite, exhilarate, hearten, lift up, perk up, raise, rouse, uplift 4. augment, boost, heighten, increase, intensify, magnify, swell

elevated 1. dignified, exalted, grand, high, high-flown, high-minded, inflated, lofty, noble, sublime 2. animated, bright, cheerful, cheery, elated, excited, exhilarated, gleeful, in high spirits, overjoyed

elevation 1. altitude, height 2. acclivity, eminence, height, hill, hillock, mountain, rise, rising ground 3. exaltedness, grandeur, loftiness, nobility, nobleness, sublimity 4. advancement, aggrandizement, exaltation, preferment, promotion, upgrading

elicit bring forth, bring out, bring to light, call forth, cause, derive, draw out, educe, evoke, evolve, exact, extort, extract, give rise to, obtain, wrest

eligible acceptable, appropriate, desirable, fit, preferable, proper, qualified, suitable, suited, worthy

eliminate 1. cut out, dispose of, do away with, eradicate, exterminate, get rid of, remove, stamp out, take out 2. dispense with, disregard, drop, eject, exclude, expel, ignore, knock out, leave out, omit, put out, reject, throw out 3. *Sl.* annihilate, bump off (*Sl.*), kill, liquidate, murder, rub out (*U.S. sl.*), slay, terminate, waste (*U.S. sl.*)

elite 1. *n.* aristocracy, best, cream, crème de la crème, elect, flower, gentry, high society, nobility, pick, upper class 2. *adj.* aristocratic, best, choice, crack (*Sl.*), elect, exclusive, first-class, noble, pick, selected, upper-class

elocution articulation, declamation, delivery, diction, enunciation, oratory, pronunciation, public speaking, rhetoric, speech, speechmaking, utterance, voice production

elongate draw out, extend, lengthen, make longer, prolong, protract, stretch

elope abscond, bolt, decamp, disappear, escape, leave, run away, run off, slip away, steal away

eloquence expression, expressiveness, fluency, forcefulness, oratory, persuasiveness, rhetoric, way with words

eloquent 1. articulate, fluent, forceful, graceful, moving, persuasive, silver-tongued, stirring, well-expressed 2. expressive, meaningful, pregnant, revealing, suggestive, telling, vivid

elsewhere abroad, absent, away, hence (*Archaic*), in *or* to another place, not here, not present, somewhere else

elucidate annotate, clarify, clear up, explain, explicate, expound, gloss, illuminate, illustrate, interpret, make plain, shed *or* throw light upon, spell out, unfold

elucidation annotation, clarification, comment, commentary, explanation, explication, exposition, gloss, illumination, illustration, interpretation

elude 1. avoid, circumvent, dodge, duck (*Inf.*), escape, evade, flee, get away from, outrun, shirk, shun 2. baffle, be beyond (someone), con-

found, escape, foil, frustrate, puz~
zle, stump, thwart

elusive 1. difficult to catch, shifty,
slippery, tricky 2. baffling, fleeting,
indefinable, intangible, puzzling,
subtle, transient, transitory 3. am~
biguous, deceitful, deceptive, elu~
sory, equivocal, evasive, fallacious,
fraudulent, illusory, misleading,
unspecific

emaciated atrophied, attenuate,
attenuated, cadaverous, gaunt,
haggard, lank, 'lean, meagre,
pinched, scrawny, skeletal, thin,
wasted

emaciation atrophy, attenuation,
gauntness, haggardness, leanness,
meagreness, scrawniness, thin~
ness, wasting away

emanate 1. arise, come forth, de~
rive, emerge, flow, issue, originate,
proceed, spring, stem 2. discharge,
emit, exhale, give off, give out, is~
sue, radiate, send forth

emanation 1. arising, derivation,
emergence, flow, origination, pro~
ceeding 2. discharge, effluent, ef~
flux, effusion, emission, exhalation,
radiation

emancipate deliver, discharge,
disencumber, disenthral, enfran~
chise, free, liberate, manumit, re~
lease, set free, unchain, unfetter,
unshackle

emancipation deliverance, dis~
charge, enfranchisement, freedom,
liberation, liberty, manumission,
release

embalm 1. mummify, preserve 2.
Of memories cherish, consecrate,
conserve, enshrine, immortalize,
store, treasure 3. *Poetic* make fra~
grant, perfume, scent

embargo 1. *n.* ban, bar, barrier,
blockage, check, hindrance, im~
pediment, interdict, interdiction,
prohibition, proscription, restraint,
restriction, stoppage 2. *v.* ban, bar,
block, check, impede, interdict,
prohibit, proscribe, restrict, stop

embark 1. board ship, go aboard,
put on board, take on board, take
ship 2. *With* **on** *or* **upon** begin,
broach, commence, engage, enter,
initiate, launch, plunge into, set

about, set out, start, take up,
undertake

embarrass abash, chagrin, con~
fuse, discomfit, discompose, dis~
concert, discountenance, distress,
fluster, mortify, put out of counte~
nance, shame, show up (*Inf.*)

embarrassing awkward, blush-
making, compromising, discomfit~
ing, disconcerting, distressing, hu~
miliating, mortifying, sensitive,
shameful, shaming, touchy, tricky,
uncomfortable

embarrassment 1. awkwardness,
bashfulness, chagrin, confusion,
discomfiture, discomposure, dis~
tress, humiliation, mortification,
self-consciousness, shame, showing
up (*Inf.*) 2. bind (*Inf.*), difficulty,
mess, pickle (*Inf.*), predicament,
scrape (*Inf.*) 3. excess, overabun~
dance, superabundance, superflu~
ity, surfeit, surplus

embellish adorn, beautify, bedeck,
deck, decorate, dress up, elabo~
rate, embroider, enhance, enrich,
exaggerate, festoon, garnish, gild,
grace, ornament, varnish

embellishment adornment, deco~
ration, elaboration, embroidery,
enhancement, enrichment, exag~
geration, gilding, ornament, orna~
mentation

embezzle abstract, appropriate,
defalcate (*Law*), filch, have one's
hand in the till (*Inf.*), misapply,
misappropriate, misuse, peculate,
pilfer, purloin, steal

embezzlement abstraction, ap~
propriation, defalcation (*Law*),
filching, fraud, larceny, misappli~
cation, misappropriation, misuse,
peculation, pilferage, pilfering,
purloining, stealing, theft, thieving

embitter 1. alienate, anger, disaf~
fect, disillusion, envenom, make
bitter *or* resentful, poison, sour 2.
aggravate, exacerbate, exasperate,
worsen

emblazon 1. adorn, blazon, colour,
decorate, embellish, illuminate,
ornament, paint 2. extol, glorify,
laud (*Literary*), praise, proclaim,
publicize, publish, trumpet

emblem badge, crest, device, fig~

ure, image, insignia, mark, representation, sigil (*Rare*), sign, symbol, token, type

embodiment 1. bodying forth, example, exemplar, exemplification, expression, incarnation, incorporation, manifestation, personification, realization, reification, representation, symbol, type 2. bringing together, codification, collection, combination, comprehension, concentration, consolidation, inclusion, incorporation, integration, organization, systematization

embolden animate, cheer, encourage, fire, hearten, inflame, inspirit, invigorate, nerve, reassure, rouse, stimulate, stir, strengthen, vitalize

embrace v. 1. clasp, cuddle, encircle, enfold, grasp, hold, hug, seize, squeeze, take *or* hold in one's arms 2. accept, adopt, avail oneself of, espouse, grab, make use of, receive, seize, take up, welcome 3. comprehend, comprise, contain, cover, deal with, embody, enclose, encompass, include, involve, provide for, subsume, take in, take into account ~n. 4. clasp, clinch (*Sl.*), cuddle, hug, squeeze

embroil complicate, compromise, confound, confuse, disorder, disturb, encumber, enmesh, ensnare, entangle, implicate, incriminate, involve, mire, mix up, muddle, perplex, trouble

embryo beginning, germ, nucleus, root, rudiment

emend amend, correct, edit, improve, rectify, redact, revise

emendation amendment, correction, editing, improvement, rectification, redaction, revision

emerge 1. appear, arise, become visible, come forth, come into view, come out, come up, emanate, issue, proceed, rise, spring up, surface 2. become apparent, become known, come out, come to light, crop up, develop, materialize, transpire, turn up

emergence advent, apparition, appearance, arrival, coming, dawn, development, disclosure, emanation, issue, materialization, rise

emergency crisis, danger, difficulty, exigency, extremity, necessity, pass, pinch, plight, predicament, quandary, scrape (*Inf.*), strait

emigrate migrate, move, move abroad, remove

emigration departure, exodus, migration, removal

eminence 1. celebrity, dignity, distinction, esteem, fame, greatness, illustriousness, importance, notability, note, pre-eminence, prestige, prominence, rank, renown, reputation, repute, superiority 2. elevation, height, high ground, hill, hillock, knoll, rise, summit

eminent celebrated, conspicuous, distinguished, elevated, esteemed, exalted, famous, grand, great, high, high-ranking, illustrious, important, notable, noted, noteworthy, outstanding, paramount, pre-eminent, prestigious, prominent, renowned, signal, superior, well-known

eminently conspicuously, exceedingly, exceptionally, extremely, greatly, highly, notably, outstandingly, prominently, remarkably, signally, strikingly, surpassingly, well

emission diffusion, discharge, ejaculation, ejection, emanation, exhalation, exudation, issuance, issue, radiation, shedding, transmission, utterance, venting

emit breathe forth, cast out, diffuse, discharge, eject, emanate, exhale, exude, give off, give out, give vent to, issue, radiate, send forth, send out, shed, throw out, transmit, utter, vent

emolument benefit, compensation, earnings, fee, gain, hire, pay, payment, profits, recompense, remuneration, return, reward, salary, stipend, wages

emotion agitation, ardour, excitement, feeling, fervour, passion, perturbation, sensation, sentiment, vehemence, warmth

emotional 1. demonstrative, excitable, feeling, hot-blooded, passion~ ate, responsive, sensitive, senti~ mental, susceptible, temperamen~ tal, tender, warm 2. affecting, emotive, exciting, heart-warming, moving, pathetic, poignant, senti~ mental, stirring, tear-jerking (*Inf.*), thrilling, touching 3. ardent, en~ thusiastic, fervent, fervid, fiery, heated, impassioned, passionate, roused, stirred, zealous

emotive 1. argumentative, contro~ versial, delicate, sensitive, touchy 2. affecting, emotional, exciting, heart-warming, moving, pathetic, poignant, sentimental, stirring, tear-jerking (*Inf.*), thrilling, touch~ ing 3. ardent, emotional, enthusi~ astic, fervent, fervid, fiery, heated, impassioned, passionate, roused, stirred, zealous

emphasis accent, accentuation, attention, decidedness, force, im~ portance, impressiveness, insist~ ence, intensity, moment, positive~ ness, power, pre-eminence, prior~ ity, prominence, significance, strength, stress, underscoring, weight

emphasize accent, accentuate, dwell on, give priority to, highlight, insist on, lay stress on, play up, press home, put the accent on, stress, underline, underscore, weight

emphatic absolute, categorical, certain, decided, definite, direct, distinct, earnest, energetic, force~ ful, forcible, important, impressive, insistent, marked, momentous, positive, powerful, pronounced, resounding, significant, striking, strong, telling, unequivocal, un~ mistakable, vigorous

empire 1. commonwealth, domain, imperium (*Rare*), kingdom, realm 2. authority, command, control, dominion, government, power, rule, sovereignty, supremacy, sway

empirical, empiric experiential, experimental, observed, practical, pragmatic

emplacement 1. location, lodg~ ment, platform, position, site, situation, station 2. placement,

placing, positioning, putting in place, setting up, stationing

employ *v.* 1. commission, engage, enlist, hire, retain, take on 2. en~ gage, fill, keep busy, make use of, occupy, spend, take up, use up 3. apply, bring to bear, exercise, ex~ ert, make use of, ply, put to use, use, utilize ~*n.* 4. employment, en~ gagement, hire, service

employed active, busy, engaged, in a job, in employment, in work, oc~ cupied, working

employee hand, job-holder, staff member, wage-earner, worker, workman

employer boss (*Inf.*), business, company, establishment, firm, gaffer (*Inf., chiefly Brit.*), organi~ zation, outfit (*Inf.*), owner, patron, proprietor

employment 1. engagement, en~ listment, hire, retaining, taking on 2. application, exercise, exertion, use, utilization 3. avocation (*Ar~ chaic*), business, calling, craft, em~ ploy, job, line, métier, occupation, profession, pursuit, service, trade, vocation, work

emporium bazaar, market, mart, shop, store

empower allow, authorize, com~ mission, delegate, enable, entitle, license, permit, qualify, sanction, warrant

emptiness 1. bareness, blankness, desertedness, desolation, destitu~ tion, vacancy, vacuum, void, waste 2. aimlessness, banality, barren~ ness, frivolity, futility, hollowness, inanity, ineffectiveness, meaning~ lessness, purposelessness, sense~ lessness, silliness, unreality, unsat~ isfactoriness, unsubstantiality, vainness, valuelessness, vanity, worthlessness 3. cheapness, hol~ lowness, idleness, insincerity, triviality, trivialness 4. absentness, blankness, expressionlessness, un~ intelligence, vacancy, vacantness, vacuity, vacuousness 5. *Inf.* desire, hunger, ravening

empty *adj.* 1. bare, blank, clear, deserted, desolate, destitute, hol~ low, unfurnished, uninhabited, un~

occupied, untenanted, vacant, void, waste 2. aimless, banal, bootless, frivolous, fruitless, futile, hollow, inane, ineffective, meaningless, purposeless, senseless, silly, unreal, unsatisfactory, unsubstantial, vain, valueless, worthless 3. cheap, hollow, idle, insincere, trivial 4. absent, blank, expressionless, unintelligent, vacant, vacuous 5. *Inf.* famished, hungry, ravenous, starving (*Inf.*), unfed, unfilled ~*v.* 6. clear, consume, deplete, discharge, drain, dump, evacuate, exhaust, gut, pour out, unburden, unload, use up, vacate, void

empty-headed brainless, dizzy (*Inf.*), featherbrained, flighty, frivolous, giddy, harebrained, inane, scatterbrained, silly, skittish, vacuous

enable allow, authorize, capacitate, commission, empower, facilitate, fit, license, permit, prepare, qualify, sanction, warrant

enact 1. authorize, command, decree, establish, legislate, ordain, order, pass, proclaim, ratify, sanction 2. act, act out, appear as, depict, perform, personate, play, play the part of, portray, represent

enactment 1. authorization, command, commandment, decree, dictate, edict, law, legislation, order, ordinance, proclamation, ratification, regulation, statute 2. acting, depiction, performance, personation, play-acting, playing, portrayal, representation

enamour bewitch, captivate, charm, enchant, endear, enrapture, entrance, fascinate, infatuate

enamoured bewitched, captivated, charmed, crazy about (*Inf.*), enchanted, enraptured, entranced, fascinated, fond, infatuated, in love, nuts on or about (*Sl.*), smitten, swept off one's feet, taken, wild about (*Inf.*)

encampment base, bivouac, camp, camping ground, campsite, cantonment, quarters, tents

encapsulate, **incapsulate** abridge, compress, condense, digest, epitomize, précis, summarize, sum up

enchant beguile, bewitch, captivate, cast a spell on, charm, delight, enamour, enrapture, enthral, fascinate, hypnotize, mesmerize, spellbind

enchanter conjurer, magician, magus, necromancer, sorcerer, spellbinder, warlock, witch, wizard

enchanting alluring, appealing, attractive, bewitching, captivating, charming, delightful, endearing, entrancing, fascinating, lovely, pleasant, ravishing, winsome

enchantment 1. allure, allurement, beguilement, bliss, charm, delight, fascination, hypnotism, mesmerism, rapture, ravishment, transport 2. charm, conjuration, incantation, magic, necromancy, sorcery, spell, witchcraft, wizardry

enchantress 1. conjurer, lamia, magician, necromancer, sorceress, spellbinder, witch 2. charmer, *femme fatale*, seductress, siren, vamp (*Inf.*)

enclose, **inclose** 1. bound, circumscribe, cover, encase, encircle, encompass, environ, fence, hedge, hem in, pen, shut in, wall in, wrap 2. include, insert, put in, send with 3. comprehend, contain, embrace, hold, include, incorporate

encompass 1. circle, circumscribe, encircle, enclose, envelop, environ, girdle, hem in, ring, surround 2. bring about, cause, contrive, devise, effect, manage 3. admit, comprehend, comprise, contain, cover, embody, embrace, hold, include, incorporate, involve, subsume, take in

encounter *v.* 1. bump into (*Inf.*), chance upon, come upon, confront, experience, face, happen on or upon, meet, run across, run into (*Inf.*) 2. attack, clash with, combat, come into conflict with, contend, cross swords with, do battle with, engage, fight, grapple with, strive, struggle ~*n.* 3. brush, confrontation, meeting 4. action, battle, clash, collision, combat, conflict, contest, dispute, engagement, fight, run-in (*Inf.*), set to (*Inf.*), skirmish

encourage 1. animate, buoy up, cheer, comfort, console, embolden, hearten, incite, inspire, inspirit, rally, reassure, rouse, stimulate 2. abet, advance, advocate, aid, boost, egg on, favour, forward, foster, further, help, promote, spur, strengthen, succour, support, urge

encouragement advocacy, aid, boost, cheer, consolation, favour, help, incitement, inspiration, inspiritment, promotion, reassurance, stimulation, stimulus, succour, support, urging

encouraging bright, cheerful, cheering, comforting, good, heartening, hopeful, promising, reassuring, rosy, satisfactory, stimulating

encroach appropriate, arrogate, impinge, infringe, intrude, invade, make inroads, overstep, trench, trespass, usurp

encroachment appropriation, arrogation, impingement, incursion, infringement, inroad, intrusion, invasion, trespass, usurpation, violation

encumber burden, clog, cramp, embarrass, hamper, handicap, hinder, impede, incommode, inconvenience, make difficult, obstruct, oppress, overload, retard, saddle, slow down, trammel, weigh down

encumbrance burden, clog, difficulty, drag, embarrassment, handicap, hindrance, impediment, inconvenience, liability, load, millstone, obstacle, obstruction

end *n.* 1. bound, boundary, edge, extent, extreme, extremity, limit, point, terminus, tip 2. attainment, cessation, close, closure, completion, conclusion, consequence, consummation, culmination, denouement, ending, expiration, expiry, finale, finish, issue, outcome, resolution, result, stop, termination, upshot, wind-up 3. aim, aspiration, design, drift, goal, intent, intention, object, objective, point, purpose, reason 4. part, piece, portion, responsibility, share, side 5. bit, fragment, leftover, remainder, remnant, scrap, stub, tag end 6. annihilation, death, demise, destruction, dissolution, doom, extermination, extinction, ruin, ruination 7. **the end** *Sl.* beyond endurance, insufferable, intolerable, the final blow, the last straw, the limit (*Inf.*), the worst, too much (*Inf.*), unbearable, unendurable ~*v.* 8. bring to an end, cease, close, complete, conclude, culminate, dissolve, expire, finish, resolve, stop, terminate, wind up 9. abolish, annihilate, destroy, exterminate, extinguish, kill, put to death, ruin

endanger compromise, hazard, imperil, jeopardize, put at risk, put in danger, risk, threaten

endear attach, attract, bind, captivate, charm, engage, win

endearing adorable, attractive, captivating, charming, engaging, lovable, sweet, winning, winsome

endearment 1. affectionate utterance, loving word, sweet nothing 2. affection, attachment, fondness, love

endeavour 1. *n.* aim, attempt, crack (*Inf.*), effort, enterprise, essay, go, shot (*Inf.*), stab (*Inf.*), trial, try, undertaking, venture 2. *v.* aim, aspire, attempt, do one's best, essay, have a go (crack, shot, stab), labour, make an effort, strive, struggle, take pains, try, undertake

ending catastrophe, cessation, close, completion, conclusion, consummation, culmination, denouement, end, finale, finish, resolution, termination, wind-up

endless 1. boundless, ceaseless, constant, continual, eternal, everlasting, immortal, incessant, infinite, interminable, limitless, measureless, perpetual, unbounded, unbroken, undying, unending, uninterrupted, unlimited 2. interminable, monotonous, overlong 3. continuous, unbroken, undivided, whole

endorse, indorse 1. advocate, affirm, approve, authorize, back, champion, confirm, favour, ratify, recommend, sanction, subscribe to, support, sustain, vouch for, warrant 2. countersign, sign, superscribe, undersign

endorsement, indorsement 1. comment, countersignature, qualification, signature, superscription 2. advocacy, affirmation, approbation, approval, authorization, backing, championship, confirmation, favour, fiat, O.K. (*Inf.*), ratification, recommendation, sanction, seal of approval, subscription to, support, warrant

endow award, bequeath, bestow, confer, donate, endue, enrich, favour, finance, fund, furnish, give, grant, invest, leave, make over, provide, settle on, supply, will

endowment 1. award, benefaction, bequest, bestowal, boon, donation, fund, gift, grant, income, largess, legacy, presentation, property, provision, revenue 2. *Often plural* ability, aptitude, attribute, capability, capacity, faculty, flair, genius, gift, power, qualification, quality, talent

end up 1. become eventually, finish as, finish up, turn out to be 2. arrive finally, come to a halt, fetch up (*Inf.*), finish up, stop, wind up

endurable bearable, sufferable, supportable, sustainable, tolerable

endurance 1. bearing, fortitude, patience, perseverance, persistence, pertinacity, resignation, resolution, stamina, staying power, strength, submission, sufferance, tenacity, toleration 2. continuation, continuity, durability, duration, immutability, lastingness, longevity, permanence, stability

endure 1. bear, brave, cope with, experience, go through, stand, stick it out (*Inf.*), suffer, support, sustain, take it (*Inf.*), thole (*Scot.*), undergo, weather, withstand 2. abide, allow, bear, brook, countenance, permit, put up with, stand, stick (*Sl.*), stomach, submit to, suffer, swallow, take patiently, tolerate 3. abide, be durable, continue, hold, last, live, live on, persist, prevail, remain, stand, stay, survive, wear well

enduring abiding, continuing, durable, eternal, firm, immortal, imperishable, lasting, living, long-lasting, perennial, permanent, persistent, persisting, prevailing, remaining, steadfast, steady, surviving, unfaltering, unwavering

enemy adversary, antagonist, competitor, foe, opponent, rival, the opposition, the other side

energetic active, animated, brisk, dynamic, forceful, forcible, high-powered, indefatigable, lively, potent, powerful, spirited, strenuous, strong, tireless, vigorous, zippy (*Inf.*)

energy activity, animation, ardour, *brio*, drive, efficiency, élan, exertion, fire, force, forcefulness, get-up-and-go (*Inf.*), go (*Inf.*), intensity, life, liveliness, pluck, power, spirit, stamina, strength, strenuousness, verve, vigour, vim (*Sl.*), vitality, vivacity, zeal, zest, zip (*Inf.*)

enfold, infold clasp, embrace, enclose, encompass, envelop, enwrap, fold, hold, hug, shroud, swathe, wrap, wrap up

enforce administer, apply, carry out, coerce, compel, constrain, exact, execute, implement, impose, insist on, oblige, prosecute, put in force, put into effect, reinforce, require, urge

enforced compelled, compulsory, constrained, dictated, imposed, involuntary, necessary, ordained, prescribed, required, unavoidable, unwilling

enforcement 1. administration, application, carrying out, exaction, execution, implementation, imposition, prosecution, reinforcement 2. coercion, compulsion, constraint, insistence, obligation, pressure, requirement

enfranchise 1. give the vote to, grant suffrage to, grant the franchise to, grant voting rights to 2. emancipate, free, liberate, manumit, release, set free

enfranchisement 1. giving the vote, granting suffrage *or* the franchise, granting voting rights 2. emancipation, freedom, freeing,

liberating, liberation, manumis~
sion, release, setting free

engage 1. appoint, commission,
employ, enlist, enrol, hire, retain,
take on 2. bespeak, book, charter,
hire, lease, prearrange, rent, re~
serve, secure 3. absorb, busy, en~
gross, grip, involve, occupy, pre~
occupy, tie up 4. allure, arrest, at~
tach, attract, captivate, catch,
charm, draw, enamour, enchant,
fascinate, fix, gain, win 5. embark
on, enter into, join, partake, par~
ticipate, practise, set about, take
part, undertake 6. affiance, agree,
betroth (*Archaic*), bind, commit,
contract, covenant, guarantee, ob~
ligate, oblige, pledge, promise,
undertake, vouch, vow 7. *Military*
assail, attack, combat, come to
close quarters with, encounter, fall
on, fight with, give battle to, join
battle with, meet, take on 8. acti~
vate, apply, bring into operation,
energize, set going, switch on 9.
dovetail, interact, interconnect,
interlock, join, mesh

engaged 1. affianced, betrothed
(*Archaic*), pledged, promised, spo~
ken for 2. absorbed, busy, commit~
ted, employed, engrossed, in use,
involved, occupied, preoccupied,
tied up, unavailable

engagement 1. assurance, be~
trothal, bond, compact, contract,
oath, obligation, pact, pledge,
promise, troth (*Archaic*), under~
taking, vow, word 2. appointment,
arrangement, commitment, date,
meeting 3. commission, employ~
ment, gig (*Sl.*), job, post, situation,
stint, work 4. action, battle, com~
bat, conflict, confrontation, con~
test, encounter, fight

engaging agreeable, appealing,
attractive, captivating, charming,
enchanting, fascinating, fetching
(*Inf.*), likable, lovable, pleasant,
pleasing, winning, winsome

engender 1. beget, breed, bring
about, cause, create, excite, fo~
ment, generate, give rise to, hatch,
incite, induce, instigate, lead to,
make, occasion, precipitate, pro~
duce, provoke 2. beget, breed,

bring forth, father, generate, give
birth to, procreate, propagate, sire,
spawn

engine 1. machine, mechanism,
motor 2. agency, agent, apparatus,
appliance, contrivance, device,
implement, instrument, means,
tool, weapon

engineer 1. *n.* architect, contriver,
designer, deviser, director, inven~
tor, manager, manipulator, origi~
nator, planner, schemer 2. *v.* bring
about, cause, concoct, contrive,
control, create, devise, effect, en~
compass, finagle (*Inf.*), manage,
manoeuvre, mastermind, origi~
nate, plan, plot, scheme, wangle
(*Inf.*)

engrave 1. carve, chase, chisel, cut,
enchase (*Rare*), etch, grave (*Ar~
chaic*), inscribe 2. impress, im~
print, print 3. embed, fix, impress,
imprint, infix, ingrain, lodge

engraving 1. carving, chasing,
chiselling, cutting, dry point, en~
chasing (*Rare*), etching, inscribing,
inscription 2. block, carving, etch~
ing, inscription, plate, woodcut 3.
etching, impression, print

engross 1. absorb, arrest, engage,
engulf, hold, immerse, involve, oc~
cupy, preoccupy 2. corner, mo~
nopolize, sew up (*U.S.*)

engrossed absorbed, captivated,
caught up, deep, enthralled, fasci~
nated, gripped, immersed, intent,
intrigued, lost, preoccupied, rapt,
riveted

engrossing absorbing, captivating,
compelling, enthralling, fascinat~
ing, gripping, interesting, intrigu~
ing, riveting

enhance add to, augment, boost,
complement, elevate, embellish,
exalt, heighten, improve, increase,
intensify, lift, magnify, raise, re~
inforce, strengthen, swell

enigma conundrum, mystery,
problem, puzzle, riddle

enigmatic, enigmatical ambigu~
ous, cryptic, Delphic, doubtful,
equivocal, incomprehensible, in~
decipherable, inexplicable, inscru~
table, mysterious, obscure, per~
plexing, puzzling, recondite,

sphinxlike, uncertain, unfathom~
able, unintelligible

enjoin 1. advise, bid, call upon,
charge, command, counsel, de~
mand, direct, instruct, order, pre~
scribe, require, urge, warn 2. *Law*
ban, bar, disallow, forbid, interdict,
place an injunction on, preclude,
prohibit, proscribe, restrain

enjoy 1. appreciate, be entertained
by, be pleased with, delight in, like,
rejoice in, relish, revel in, take joy
in, take pleasure in *or* from 2. be
blessed *or* favoured with, experi~
ence, have, have the benefit of,
have the use of, own, possess, reap
the benefits of, use 3. **enjoy oneself**
have a ball (*Inf.*), have a good
time, have fun, make merry

enjoyable agreeable, amusing, de~
lectable, delicious, delightful, en~
tertaining, gratifying, pleasant,
pleasing, pleasurable, satisfying, to
one's liking

enjoyment 1. amusement, delec~
tation, delight, diversion, enter~
tainment, fun, gladness, gratifica~
tion, gusto, happiness, indulgence,
joy, pleasure, recreation, relish,
satisfaction, zest 2. advantage,
benefit, exercise, ownership, pos~
session, use

enlarge 1. add to, amplify, aug~
ment, blow up (*Inf.*), broaden, dif~
fuse, dilate, distend, elongate, ex~
pand, extend, grow, heighten, in~
crease, inflate, lengthen, magnify,
make *or* grow larger, multiply,
stretch, swell, wax, widen 2. am~
plify, descant, develop, dilate,
elaborate, expand, expatiate, give
details

enlighten advise, apprise, cause to
understand, civilize, counsel, edify,
educate, inform, instruct, make
aware, teach

enlightened aware, broad-minded,
civilized, cultivated, educated, in~
formed, knowledgeable, liberal,
literate, open-minded, reasonable,
refined, sophisticated

enlightenment awareness, broad-
mindedness, civilization, compre~
hension, cultivation, edification,
education, information, insight, in~

struction, knowledge, learning, lit~
eracy, open-mindedness, refine~
ment, sophistication, teaching,
understanding, wisdom

enlist engage, enrol, enter (into),
gather, join, join up, muster, ob~
tain, procure, recruit, register, se~
cure, sign up, volunteer

enliven animate, brighten, buoy up,
cheer, cheer up, excite, exhilarate,
fire, gladden, hearten, inspire, in~
spirit, invigorate, pep up, perk up,
quicken, rouse, spark, stimulate,
vitalize, vivify, wake up

enmity acrimony, animosity, ani~
mus, antagonism, antipathy, aver~
sion, bad blood, bitterness, hate,
hatred, hostility, ill will, malevo~
lence, malice, malignity, rancour,
spite, venom

ennoble aggrandize, dignify, el~
evate, enhance, exalt, glorify, hon~
our, magnify, raise

ennui boredom, dissatisfaction,
lassitude, listlessness, tedium, the
doldrums

enormity 1. atrociousness, atrocity,
depravity, disgrace, evilness, hei~
nousness, monstrousness, nefari~
ousness, outrageousness, turpitude,
viciousness, vileness, villainy,
wickedness 2. abomination, atroc~
ity, crime, disgrace, evil, horror,
monstrosity, outrage, villainy 3.
Inf. enormousness, greatness,
hugeness, immensity, magnitude,
massiveness, vastness

enormous 1. astronomic, Brob~
dingnagian, colossal, excessive,
gargantuan, gigantic, gross, huge,
immense, jumbo (*Inf.*), mammoth,
massive, monstrous, mountainous,
prodigious, titanic, tremendous,
vast 2. *Archaic* abominable, atro~
cious, depraved, disgraceful, evil,
heinous, monstrous, nefarious, odi~
ous, outrageous, vicious, vile, vil~
lainous, wicked

enough 1. *adj.* abundant, adequate,
ample, plenty, sufficient 2. *n.*
abundance, adequacy, ample sup~
ply, plenty, right amount, suffi~
ciency 3. *adv.* abundantly, ad~
equately, amply, fairly, moderate~

ly, passably, reasonably, satisfac~
torily, sufficiently, tolerably

enquire 1. ask, query, question, re~
quest information, seek informa~
tion 2. *Also* **inquire** conduct an in~
quiry, examine, explore, inspect,
investigate, look into, make in~
quiry, probe, scrutinize, search

enquiry 1. query, question 2. *Also*
inquiry examination, exploration,
inquest, inspection, investigation,
probe, research, scrutiny, search,
study, survey

enrage aggravate (*Inf.*), anger, ex~
asperate, incense, incite, inflame,
infuriate, irritate, madden, make
one's blood boil, make one see red
(*Inf.*), provoke

enraged aggravated (*Inf.*), an~
gered, angry, boiling mad, exas~
perated, fuming, furious, incensed,
inflamed, infuriated, irate, irritat~
ed, livid (*Inf.*), mad (*Inf.*), raging,
raging mad, wild

enrich 1. make rich, make wealthy
2. aggrandize, ameliorate, aug~
ment, cultivate, develop, endow,
enhance, improve, refine, sup~
plement 3. adorn, decorate, em~
bellish, grace, ornament

enrol 1. chronicle, inscribe, list,
note, record 2. accept, admit, en~
gage, enlist, join up, matriculate,
recruit, register, sign up *or* on,
take on

enrolment acceptance, admission,
engagement, enlistment, matricu~
lation, recruitment, registration

en route in transit, on *or* along the
way, on the road

ensemble *n.* 1. aggregate, assem~
blage, collection, entirety, set, sum,
total, totality, whole, whole thing 2.
costume, get-up (*Inf.*), outfit, suit 3.
band, cast, chorus, company,
group, supporting cast, troupe
~*adv.* 4. all at once, all together, as
a group, as a whole, at once, at the
same time, en masse, in concert

enshrine apotheosize, cherish,
consecrate, dedicate, embalm, ex~
alt, hallow, preserve, revere, sanc~
tify, treasure

enshroud cloak, cloud, conceal,
cover, enclose, enfold, envelop,

enwrap, hide, obscure, pall, shroud,
veil, wrap

ensign badge, banner, colours, flag,
jack, pennant, pennon, standard,
streamer

enslave bind, dominate, enchain,
enthral, reduce to slavery, subju~
gate, yoke

ensue arise, attend, be consequent
on, befall, come after, come next,
come to pass (*Archaic*), derive,
flow, follow, issue, proceed, result,
stem, succeed, supervene, turn out
or up

ensure, insure 1. certify, confirm,
effect, guarantee, make certain,
make sure, secure, warrant 2.
guard, make safe, protect, safe~
guard, secure

entail bring about, call for, cause,
demand, encompass, give rise to,
impose, involve, lead to, necessi~
tate, occasion, require, result in

entangle 1. catch, compromise,
embroil, enmesh, ensnare, entrap,
foul, implicate, involve, knot, mat,
mix up, ravel, snag, snare, tangle,
trammel, trap 2. bewilder, compli~
cate, confuse, jumble, mix up,
muddle, perplex, puzzle, snarl,
twist

entanglement 1. complication,
confusion, ensnarement, entrap~
ment, imbroglio (*Obsolete*), in~
volvement, jumble, knot, mesh,
mess, mix-up, muddle, snare, snarl-
up (*Inf.*), tangle, toils, trap 2. diffi~
culty, embarrassment, imbroglio,
involvement, liaison, predicament,
tie

enter 1. arrive, come *or* go in *or*
into, insert, introduce, make an
entrance, pass into, penetrate,
pierce 2. become a member of,
begin, commence, commit oneself
to, embark upon, enlist, enrol, join,
participate in, set about, set out on,
sign up, start, take part in, take up
3. inscribe, list, log, note, record,
register, set down, take down 4.
offer, present, proffer, put forward,
register, submit, tender

enterprise 1. adventure, effort, en~
deavour, essay, operation, plan,
programme, project, undertaking,

venture 2. activity, adventurous~
ness, alertness, audacity, boldness,
daring, dash, drive, eagerness, en~
ergy, enthusiasm, get-up-and-go
(*Inf.*), gumption (*Inf.*), initiative,
push (*Inf.*), readiness, resource,
resourcefulness, spirit, vigour, zeal
3. business, company, concern, es~
tablishment, firm, operation

enterprising active, adventurous,
alert, audacious, bold, daring,
dashing, eager, energetic, enthusi~
astic, go-ahead, intrepid, keen,
ready, resourceful, spirited, stir~
ring, up-and-coming, venturesome,
vigorous, zealous

entertain 1. amuse, charm, cheer,
delight, divert, occupy, please,
recreate (*Rare*), regale 2. accom~
modate, be host to, harbour, have
company, have guests *or* visitors,
lodge, put up, show hospitality to,
treat 3. cherish, cogitate on, con~
ceive, consider, contemplate, fos~
ter, harbour, hold, imagine, keep in
mind, maintain, muse over, pon~
der, support, think about, think
over

entertaining amusing, charming,
cheering, delightful, diverting,
funny, humorous, interesting,
pleasant, pleasing, pleasurable,
recreative (*Rare*), witty

entertainment amusement, cheer,
distraction, diversion, enjoyment,
fun, good time, leisure activity,
pastime, play, pleasure, recreation,
satisfaction, sport, treat

enthral beguile, captivate, charm,
enchant, enrapture, entrance, fas~
cinate, grip, hold spellbound, hyp~
notize, intrigue, mesmerize, rivet,
spellbind

enthralling beguiling, captivating,
charming, compelling, compulsive,
enchanting, entrancing, fascinat~
ing, gripping, hypnotizing, intrigu~
ing, mesmerizing, riveting, spell~
binding

enthusiasm 1. ardour, avidity, de~
votion, eagerness, earnestness, ex~
citement, fervour, frenzy, interest,
keenness, passion, relish, vehe~
mence, warmth, zeal, zest 2. craze,

fad (*Inf.*), hobby, hobbyhorse, in~
terest, mania, passion, rage

enthusiast admirer, aficionado,
buff (*Inf.*), devotee, fan, fanatic,
fiend (*Inf.*), follower, freak (*Sl.*),
lover, supporter, zealot

enthusiastic ardent, avid, devoted,
eager, earnest, ebullient, excited,
exuberant, fervent, fervid, forceful,
hearty, keen, lively, passionate,
spirited, unqualified, unstinting,
vehement, vigorous, warm, whole~
hearted, zealous

entice allure, attract, beguile, ca~
jole, coax, decoy, draw, inveigle,
lead on, lure, persuade, prevail on,
seduce, tempt, wheedle

entire 1. complete, full, total, whole
2. absolute, full, outright, thorough,
total, undiminished, unmitigated,
unreserved, unrestricted 3. intact,
perfect, sound, unbroken, undam~
aged, unmarked, unmarred, whole,
without a scratch 4. continuous,
integrated, unbroken, undivided,
unified

entirely 1. absolutely, altogether,
completely, fully, in every respect,
perfectly, thoroughly, totally, un~
reservedly, utterly, wholly, without
exception, without reservation 2.
exclusively, only, solely

entirety 1. absoluteness, complete~
ness, fullness, totality, undivided~
ness, unity, wholeness 2. aggre~
gate, sum, total, unity, whole

entitle 1. accredit, allow, authorize,
empower, enable, enfranchise, fit
for, license, make eligible, permit,
qualify for, warrant 2. call, char~
acterize, christen, denominate,
designate, dub, label, name, style,
term, title

entity 1. being, body, creature, ex~
istence, individual, object, organ~
ism, presence, quantity, substance,
thing 2. essence, essential nature,
quiddity (*Philosophy*), quintes~
sence, real nature

entourage 1. associates, attend~
ants, companions, company, cor~
tege, court, escort, followers, fol~
lowing, retainers, retinue, staff,
suite, train 2. ambience, environ~

ment, environs, milieu, surroundings

entrails bowels, guts, innards (*Inf.*),
insides (*Inf.*), intestines, offal, viscera

entrance[1] *n.* 1. access, avenue,
door, doorway, entry, gate, ingress,
inlet, opening, passage, portal, way
in 2. appearance, arrival, coming
in, entry, ingress, introduction 3.
access, admission, admittance, entrée, entry, ingress, permission to
enter 4. beginning, commencement, debut, initiation, introduction, outset, start

entrance[2] *v.* 1. bewitch, captivate,
charm, delight, enchant, enrap-
ture, enthral, fascinate, gladden,
ravish, spellbind, transport 2. hypnotize, mesmerize, put in a trance

entrant 1. beginner, convert, initiate, neophyte, newcomer, new
member, novice, probationer, tyro
2. candidate, competitor, contestant, entry, participant, player

entreaty appeal, earnest request,
exhortation, importunity, petition,
plea, prayer, request, solicitation,
suit, supplication

entrench, intrench 1. construct
defences, dig in, dig trenches, fortify 2. anchor, dig in, embed, ensconce, establish, fix, implant, ingrain, install, lodge, plant, root,
seat, set, settle 3. encroach, impinge, infringe, interlope, intrude,
make inroads, trespass

entrenched, intrenched deep-
rooted, deep-seated, firm, fixed,
indelible, ineradicable, ingrained,
rooted, set, unshakable, well-
established

entrust, intrust assign, authorize,
charge, commend, commit, confide, consign, delegate, deliver,
give custody of, hand over, invest,
trust, turn over

entry 1. appearance, coming in,
entering, entrance, initiation,
introduction 2. access, avenue,
door, doorway, entrance, gate, ingress, inlet, opening, passage,
passageway, portal, way in 3. access, admission, entrance, entrée,
free passage, permission to enter

4. account, item, jotting, listing,
memo, memorandum, minute,
note, record, registration 5. attempt, candidate, competitor, contestant, effort, entrant, participant,
player, submission

entwine, intwine braid, embrace,
encircle, entwist (*Archaic*), interlace, intertwine, interweave, knit,
plait, surround, twine, twist, weave,
wind

enumerate 1. cite, detail, itemize,
list, mention, name, quote, recapitulate, recite, recount, rehearse,
relate, specify, spell out, tell 2. add
up, calculate, compute, count,
number, reckon, sum up, tally, total

enunciate 1. articulate, enounce,
pronounce, say, sound, speak, utter, vocalize, voice 2. declare, proclaim, promulgate, pronounce,
propound, publish, state

envelop blanket, cloak, conceal,
cover, embrace, encase, encircle,
enclose, encompass, enfold, engulf,
enwrap, hide, obscure, sheathe,
shroud, surround, swaddle, swathe,
veil, wrap

envelope case, casing, coating,
cover, covering, jacket, sheath,
shell, skin, wrapper, wrapping

enviable advantageous, blessed,
covetable, desirable, favoured,
fortunate, lucky, much to be desired, privileged

envious begrudging, covetous,
green-eyed, green with envy,
grudging, jaundiced, jealous, malicious, resentful, spiteful

environ beset, besiege, encircle,
enclose, encompass, engird, envelop, gird, hem, invest (*Rare*),
ring, surround

environment atmosphere, background, conditions, context, domain, element, habitat, locale,
medium, milieu, scene, setting,
situation, surroundings, territory

environs district, locality, neighbourhood, outskirts, precincts,
purlieus, suburbs, surrounding
area, vicinity

envisage 1. conceive (of), conceptualize, contemplate, fancy, imag-

ine, picture, think up, visualize 2. anticipate, envision, foresee, predict, see

envision anticipate, conceive of, contemplate, envisage, foresee, predict, see, visualize

envoy agent, ambassador, courier, delegate, deputy, diplomat, emissary, intermediary, legate, messenger, minister, plenipotentiary, representative

envy 1. *n.* covetousness, enviousness, grudge, hatred, ill will, jealousy, malice, malignity, resentfulness, resentment, spite, the green-eyed monster (*Inf.*) 2. *v.* be envious (of), begrudge, be jealous (of), covet, grudge, resent

ephemeral brief, evanescent, fleeting, flitting, fugacious, fugitive, impermanent, momentary, passing, short, short-lived, temporary, transient, transitory

epicure 1. *bon vivant,* epicurean, gastronome, gourmet 2. glutton, gourmand, hedonist, sensualist, sybarite, voluptuary

epicurean 1. *adj.* gluttonous, gourmandizing, hedonistic, libertine, luscious, lush, luxurious, pleasure-seeking, self-indulgent, sensual, sybaritic, voluptuous 2. *n. bon vivant,* epicure, gastronome, gourmet

epidemic 1. *adj.* general, pandemic, prevailing, prevalent, rampant, rife, sweeping, wide-ranging, widespread 2. *n.* growth, outbreak, plague, rash, spread, upsurge, wave

epigram bon mot, quip, witticism

epilogue afterword, coda, concluding speech, conclusion, postscript

episode 1. adventure, affair, business, circumstance, event, experience, happening, incident, matter, occurrence 2. chapter, instalment, part, passage, scene, section

epistle communication, letter, message, missive, note

epithet appellation, description, designation, name, nickname, sobriquet, tag, title

epitome 1. archetype, embodi-

ment, essence, exemplar, personification, quintessence, representation, type, typical example 2. abbreviation, abridgment, abstract, compendium, condensation, conspectus, contraction, digest, précis, résumé, summary, syllabus, synopsis

epitomize 1. embody, exemplify, illustrate, incarnate, personify, represent, symbolize, typify 2. abbreviate, abridge, abstract, condense, contract, curtail, cut, encapsulate, précis, reduce, shorten, summarize, synopsize

epoch age, date, era, period, time

equable 1. agreeable, calm, composed, easy-going, even-tempered, imperturbable, level-headed, placid, serene, temperate, unexcitable, unflappable (*Inf.*), unruffled 2. consistent, constant, even, regular, smooth, stable, steady, temperate, tranquil, unchanging, uniform, unvarying

equal *adj.* 1. alike, commensurate, equivalent, identical, like, one and the same, proportionate, tantamount, the same, uniform 2. balanced, corresponding, egalitarian, even, evenly balanced, evenly matched, evenly proportioned, fifty-fifty (*Inf.*), level pegging (*Brit. inf.*), matched, regular, symmetrical, uniform, unvarying 3. able, adequate, capable, competent, fit, good enough, ready, strong enough, suitable, up to 4. egalitarian, equable, even-handed, fair, impartial, just, unbiased ~*n.* 5. brother, compeer, counterpart, equivalent, fellow, match, mate, parallel, peer, rival, twin ~*v.* 6. agree with, amount to, balance, be equal to, be even with, be level with, be tantamount to, come up to, correspond to, equalize, equate, even, level, match, parallel, rival, square with, tally with, tie with

equality balance, coequality, correspondence, egalitarianism, equal opportunity, equatability, equivalence, evenness, fairness, identity, likeness, parity, sameness, similarity, uniformity

equalize balance, equal, equate, even up, level, make equal, match, regularize, smooth, square, standardize

equate agree, balance, be commensurate, compare, correspond with *or* to, equalize, liken, make *or* be equal, match, offset, pair, parallel, square, tally, think of together

equation agreement, balancing, comparison, correspondence, equality, equalization, equating, equivalence, likeness, match, pairing, parallel

equestrian 1. *adj.* in the saddle, mounted, on horseback 2. *n.* cavalier (*Archaic*), horseman, knight, rider

equilibrium 1. balance, counterpoise, equipoise, evenness, rest, stability, steadiness, symmetry 2. calm, calmness, collectedness, composure, coolness, equanimity, poise, self-possession, serenity, stability, steadiness

equip accoutre, arm, array, attire, deck out, dress, endow, fit out, fit up, furnish, kit out, outfit, prepare, provide, rig, stock, supply

equipment accoutrements, apparatus, appurtenances, baggage, equipage, furnishings, furniture, gear, materiel, outfit, paraphernalia, rig, stuff, supplies, tackle, tools

equitable candid, disinterested, dispassionate, due, even-handed, fair, honest, impartial, just, nondiscriminatory, proper, proportionate, reasonable, right, rightful, unbiased, unprejudiced

equity disinterestedness, equitableness, even-handedness, fairmindedness, fairness, fair play, honesty, impartiality, integrity, justice, reasonableness, rectitude, righteousness, uprightness

equivalence agreement, alikeness, conformity, correspondence, equality, evenness, identity, interchangeableness, likeness, match, parallel, parity, sameness, similarity, synonymy

equivalent 1. *adj.* alike, commensurate, comparable, correspond-
ent, corresponding, equal, even, homologous, interchangeable, of a kind, same, similar, synonymous, tantamount 2. *n.* correspondent, counterpart, equal, match, opposite number, parallel, peer, twin

equivocal ambiguous, ambivalent, doubtful, dubious, evasive, indefinite, indeterminate, misleading, oblique, obscure, questionable, suspicious, uncertain, vague

era age, cycle, date, day *or* days, epoch, generation, period, stage, time

eradicate abolish, annihilate, deracinate, destroy, efface, eliminate, erase, expunge, exterminate, extinguish, extirpate, obliterate, remove, root out, stamp out, uproot, weed out, wipe out

eradication abolition, annihilation, deracination, destruction, effacement, elimination, erasure, expunction, extermination, extinction, extirpation, obliteration, removal

erase blot, cancel, delete, efface, expunge, obliterate, remove, rub out, scratch out, wipe out

erect *adj.* 1. elevated, firm, perpendicular, pricked-up, raised, rigid, standing, stiff, straight, upright, vertical ~*v.* 2. build, construct, elevate, lift, mount, pitch, put up, raise, rear, set up, stand up 3. create, establish, form, found, initiate, institute, organize, set up

erection 1. assembly, building, construction, creation, elevation, establishment, fabrication, manufacture 2. building, construction, edifice, pile, structure

erode abrade, consume, corrode, destroy, deteriorate, disintegrate, eat away, grind down, spoil, wear down *or* away

erosion abrasion, attrition, consumption, corrasion, corrosion, destruction, deterioration, disintegration, eating away, grinding down, spoiling, wear, wearing down *or* away

erotic amatory, aphrodisiac, carnal, erogenous, rousing, seductive, sensual, sexy (*Inf.*), stimulating, suggestive, titillating, voluptuous

err 1. be inaccurate, be incorrect, be in error, blunder, go astray, go wrong, make a mistake, misapprehend, miscalculate, misjudge, mistake, slip up (*Inf.*) 2. deviate, do wrong, fall, go astray, lapse, misbehave, offend, sin, transgress, trespass

errand charge, commission, job, message, mission, task

erratic 1. aberrant, abnormal, capricious, changeable, desultory, eccentric, fitful, inconsistent, irregular, shifting, unpredictable, unreliable, unstable, variable, wayward 2. directionless, meandering, planetary, wandering

erroneous amiss, fallacious, false, faulty, flawed, inaccurate, incorrect, inexact, invalid, mistaken, spurious, unfounded, unsound, untrue, wrong

error 1. bloomer (*Inf.*), blunder, boner (*Sl.*), boob (*Sl.*), delusion, erratum, fallacy, fault, flaw, howler (*Inf.*), inaccuracy, misapprehension, miscalculation, misconception, mistake, oversight, slip, solecism 2. delinquency, deviation, fault, lapse, misdeed, offence, sin, transgression, trespass, wrong, wrongdoing

erstwhile bygone, ex (*Inf.*), former, late, old, once, one-time, past, previous, quondam, sometime

erudite cultivated, cultured, educated, knowledgeable, learned, lettered, literate, scholarly, well-educated, well-read

erupt 1. be ejected, belch forth, blow up, break out, burst forth, burst into, burst out, discharge, explode, flare up, gush, pour forth, spew forth *or* out, spit out, spout, throw off, vent, vomit 2. *Medical* appear, break out

eruption 1. discharge, ejection, explosion, flare-up, outbreak, outburst, sally, venting 2. *Medical* inflammation, outbreak, rash

escalate amplify, ascend, be increased, enlarge, expand, extend, grow, heighten, increase, intensify, magnify, mount, raise, rise, step up

escapade adventure, antic, caper, fling, lark (*Inf.*), mischief, prank, romp, scrape (*Inf.*), spree, stunt, trick

escape v. 1. abscond, bolt, break free *or* out, decamp, do a bunk (*Sl.*), flee, fly, get away, make *or* effect one's escape, make one's getaway, run away *or* off, skip, slip away ~n. 2. bolt, break, break-out, decampment, flight, getaway ~v. 3. avoid, circumvent, dodge, duck, elude, evade, pass, shun, slip ~n. 4. avoidance, circumvention, elusion, evasion ~v. 5. discharge, drain, emanate, flow, gush, issue, leak, pour forth, seep, spurt ~n. 6. discharge, drain, effluence, efflux, emanation, emission, gush, leak, leakage, outflow, outpour, seepage, spurt ~v. 7. baffle, be beyond (someone), be forgotten by, elude, puzzle, stump ~n. 8. distraction, diversion, pastime, recreation, relief

escort n. 1. bodyguard, company, convoy, cortege, entourage, guard, protection, retinue, safeguard, train 2. attendant, beau, chaperon, companion, guide, partner, protector, squire (*Rare*) ~v. 3. accompany, chaperon, conduct, convoy, guard, guide, lead, partner, protect, shepherd, squire, usher

especial 1. chief, distinguished, exceptional, extraordinary, marked, notable, noteworthy, outstanding, principal, signal, special, uncommon, unusual 2. exclusive, express, individual, particular, peculiar, personal, private, singular, special, specific, unique

especially 1. chiefly, conspicuously, exceptionally, extraordinarily, mainly, markedly, notably, outstandingly, principally, remarkably, signally, specially, strikingly, supremely, uncommonly, unusually 2. exclusively, expressly, particularly, peculiarly, singularly, specifically, uniquely

espionage counter-intelligence,

intelligence, spying, undercover work

espousal 1. adoption, advocacy, backing, championing, championship, defence, embracing, maintenance, support, taking up 2. *Archaic* affiancing, betrothal, betrothing (*Archaic*), engagement, espousing (*Archaic*), marriage, nuptials, plighting, wedding

espouse 1. adopt, advocate, back, champion, defend, embrace, maintain, stand up for, support, take up 2. *Archaic* betroth (*Archaic*), marry, take as spouse, take to wife, wed

essay article, composition, discourse, disquisition, dissertation, paper, piece, tract

essence 1. being, core, crux, entity, heart, kernel, life, lifeblood, meaning, nature, pith, principle, quiddity, quintessence, significance, soul, spirit, substance 2. concentrate, distillate, elixir, extract, spirits, tincture 3. *Rare* cologne, fragrance, perfume, scent 4. **in essence** basically, essentially, fundamentally, in effect, in substance, in the main, materially, substantially, to all intents and purposes, virtually 5. **of the essence** crucial, essential, indispensable, of the utmost importance, vital, vitally important

essential *adj.* 1. crucial, important, indispensable, necessary, needed, requisite, vital 2. basic, cardinal, constitutional, elemental, elementary, fundamental, inherent, innate, intrinsic, key, main, principal 3. absolute, complete, ideal, perfect, quintessential 4. concentrated, distilled, extracted, rectified, refined, volatile ~*n.* 5. basic, fundamental, must, necessity, prerequisite, principle, requisite, rudiment, *sine qua non*, vital part

establish 1. base, constitute, create, decree, enact, ensconce, entrench, fix, form, found, ground, implant, inaugurate, install, institute, organize, plant, root, secure, settle, set up, start 2. authenticate, certify, confirm, corroborate,

demonstrate, prove, ratify, show, substantiate, validate, verify

establishment 1. creation, enactment, formation, foundation, founding, inauguration, installation, institution, organization, setting up 2. business, company, concern, corporation, enterprise, firm, house, institute, institution, organization, outfit (*Inf.*), setup (*Inf.*), structure, system 3. building, factory, house, office, plant, quarters 4. abode, domicile, dwelling, home, house, household, residence 5. **the Establishment** established order, institutionalized authority, ruling class, the powers that be, the system

estate 1. area, demesne, domain, holdings, lands, manor, property 2. *Property law* assets, belongings, effects, fortune, goods, possessions, property, wealth 3. caste, class, order, rank 4. condition, lot, period, place, position, quality, rank, situation, standing, state, station, status

esteem *v.* 1. admire, be fond of, cherish, honour, like, love, prize, regard highly, respect, revere, reverence, think highly of, treasure, value, venerate 2. *Formal* account, believe, calculate, consider, deem, estimate, hold, judge, rate, reckon, regard, think, view ~*n.* 3. admiration, consideration, credit, estimation, good opinion, honour, regard, respect, reverence, veneration

estimate *v.* 1. appraise, assess, calculate roughly, evaluate, gauge, guess, judge, number, reckon, value 2. assess, believe, conjecture, consider, form an opinion, guess, judge, rank, rate, reckon, surmise, think ~*n.* 3. appraisal, appraisement, approximate calculation, assessment, evaluation, guess, guesstimate (*Inf.*), judgment, reckoning, valuation 4. appraisal, appraisement, assessment, belief, conjecture, educated guess, estimation, judgment, opinion, surmise, thought(s)

estimation 1. appraisal, apprecia~

tion, assessment, belief, considera~
tion, considered opinion, estimate,
evaluation, judgment, opinion,
view 2. admiration, credit, esteem,
good opinion, honour, regard, re~
spect, reverence, veneration

estrange alienate, antagonize, dis~
affect, disunite, divide, drive apart,
lose *or* destroy the affection of,
make hostile, part, separate, set at
odds, withdraw, withhold

estrangement alienation, antago~
nization, breach, break-up, disaf~
fection, dissociation, disunity, divi~
sion, hostility, parting, separation,
split, withdrawal, withholding

estuary creek, firth, fjord, inlet,
mouth

et cetera and others, and so forth,
and so on, and the like, and the
rest, et al.

etch carve, corrode, cut, eat into,
engrave, furrow, impress, imprint,
incise, ingrain, inscribe, stamp

etching carving, engraving, im~
pression, imprint, inscription, print

eternal 1. abiding, ceaseless, con~
stant, deathless, endless, ever~
lasting, immortal, infinite, inter~
minable, never-ending, perennial,
perpetual, sempiternal (*Literary*),
timeless, unceasing, undying, un~
ending, unremitting, without end 2.
deathless, enduring, everlasting,
immortal, immutable, imperish~
able, indestructible, lasting, per~
manent

eternity 1. age, ages, endlessness,
for ever, immortality, infinitude,
infinity, perpetuity, timelessness,
time without end 2. *Theology*
heaven, paradise, the afterlife, the
hereafter, the next world

ethical conscientious, correct, de~
cent, fair, fitting, good, honest,
honourable, just, moral, principled,
proper, right, righteous, upright,
virtuous

ethics conscience, moral code,
morality, moral philosophy, moral
values, principles, rules of conduct,
standards

ethnic cultural, indigenous, nation~
al, native, racial, traditional

etiquette civility, code, conven~

tion, courtesy, customs, decorum,
formalities, good *or* proper behav~
iour, manners, politeness, poli~
tesse, propriety, protocol, rules,
usage

eulogy acclaim, acclamation, ac~
colade, applause, commendation,
compliment, encomium, exalta~
tion, glorification, laudation,
paean, panegyric, plaudit, praise,
tribute

euphoria bliss, ecstasy, elation, ex~
altation, exhilaration, exultation,
glee, high spirits, intoxication, joy,
joyousness, jubilation, rapture,
transport

evacuate 1. abandon, clear, de~
camp, depart, desert, forsake,
leave, move out, pull out, quit, re~
linquish, remove, vacate, withdraw
2. defecate, discharge, eject,
eliminate, empty, excrete, expel,
void

evade 1. avoid, circumvent, de~
cline, dodge, duck, elude, escape,
escape the clutches of, get away
from, shirk, shun, sidestep, steer
clear of 2. balk, circumvent, cop
out (*Sl.*), equivocate, fence, fend
off, fudge, hedge, parry, prevari~
cate, quibble, waffle (*Inf.*)

evaluate appraise, assay, assess,
calculate, estimate, gauge, judge,
rank, rate, reckon, size up (*Inf.*),
value, weigh

evaluation appraisal, assessment,
calculation, estimate, estimation,
judgment, opinion, rating, valua~
tion

evanescent brief, ephemeral, fad~
ing, fleeting, fugacious, fugitive,
impermanent, momentary, pass~
ing, short-lived, transient, transi~
tory, vanishing

evangelical, evangelistic cru~
sading, missionary, propagandiz~
ing, proselytizing, zealous

evaporate 1. dehydrate, desiccate,
dry, dry up, vaporize 2. demateri~
alize, disappear, dispel, disperse,
dissipate, dissolve, evanesce, fade,
fade away, melt, melt away, vanish

evaporation 1. dehydration, desic~
cation, drying, drying up, vapori~
zation 2. dematerialization, disap~

pearance, dispelling, dispersal, dissipation, dissolution, evanes~ cence, fading, fading away, melt~ ing, melting away, vanishing

evasion artifice, avoidance, cir~ cumvention, cop-out (*Sl.*), cunning, dodge, elusion, equivocation, es~ cape, evasiveness, excuse, fudging, obliqueness, pretext, prevarica~ tion, ruse, shift, shirking, shuffling, sophism, sophistry, subterfuge, trickery, waffle (*Inf.*)

evasive cagey (*Inf.*), casuistic, casuistical, cunning, deceitful, de~ ceptive, devious, dissembling, elu~ sive, elusory, equivocating, indi~ rect, misleading, oblique, prevari~ cating, shifty, shuffling, slippery, sophistical, tricky

eve 1. day before, night before, vigil 2. brink, edge, point, threshold, verge

even *adj.* 1. flat, flush, horizontal, level, parallel, plane, plumb, smooth, steady, straight, true, uni~ form 2. constant, metrical, regular, smooth, steady, unbroken, uniform, uninterrupted, unvarying, unwa~ vering 3. calm, composed, cool, equable, equanimous, even-tempered, imperturbable, peace~ ful, placid, serene, stable, steady, tranquil, undisturbed, unexcitable, unruffled, well-balanced 4. coequal, commensurate, comparable, drawn, equal, equalized, equally balanced, fifty-fifty (*Inf.*), identical, level, level pegging (*Brit. inf.*), like, matching, neck and neck, on a par, parallel, similar, square, the same, tied, uniform 5. balanced, disinter~ ested, dispassionate, equitable, fair, fair and square, impartial, just, unbiased, unprejudiced 6. **get even (with)** *Inf.* be revenged *or* revenge oneself, even the score, give tit for tat, pay back, recipro~ cate, repay, requite, return like for like, settle the score, take an eye for an eye, take vengeance ~*adv.* 7. all the more, much, still, yet 8. despite, disregarding, in spite of, notwithstanding 9. **even as** at the same time as, at the time that, during the time that, exactly as, just as, while, whilst 10. **even so** all

the same, be that as it may, despite (that), however, in spite of (that), nevertheless, nonetheless, not~ withstanding (that), still, yet ~*v.* 11. *Often followed by* **out** *or* **up** align, balance, become level, equal, equalize, flatten, level, match, regularize, smooth, square, stabilize, steady 12. **even the score** be revenged *or* revenge oneself, equalize, get even (*Inf.*), give tit for tat, pay (someone) back, recipro~ cate, repay, requite, return like for like, settle the score, take an eye for an eye, take vengeance

even-handed balanced, disinter~ ested, equitable, fair, fair and square, impartial, just, unbiased, unprejudiced

event 1. adventure, affair, business, circumstance, episode, experience, fact, happening, incident, matter, milestone, occasion, occurrence 2. conclusion, consequence, effect, end, issue, outcome, result, termi~ nation, upshot 3. bout, competition, contest, game, tournament 4. **at all events** at any rate, come what may, in any case, in any event, regardless, whatever happens

even-tempered calm, composed, cool, cool-headed, equable, imper~ turbable, level-headed, peaceful, placid, serene, steady, tranquil, unexcitable, unruffled

eventful active, busy, consequen~ tial, critical, crucial, decisive, ex~ citing, fateful, full, historic, impor~ tant, lively, memorable, momen~ tous, notable, noteworthy, re~ markable, significant

eventual concluding, consequent, ensuing, final, future, later, overall, prospective, resulting, ultimate

eventuality case, chance, contin~ gency, event, likelihood, possibil~ ity, probability

eventually after all, at the end of the day, finally, in the course of time, in the end, in the long run, one day, some day, some time, sooner or later, ultimately, when all is said and done

ever 1. at all, at any time (period, point), by any chance, in any case, on any occasion 2. always, at all times, constantly, continually, endlessly, eternally, everlastingly, evermore, for ever, incessantly, perpetually, relentlessly, to the end of time, unceasingly, unendingly

everlasting 1. abiding, deathless, endless, eternal, immortal, imperishable, indestructible, infinite, interminable, never-ending, perpetual, timeless, undying 2. ceaseless, constant, continual, continuous, endless, incessant, interminable, never-ending, unceasing, uninterrupted, unremitting

evermore always, eternally, ever, for ever, *in perpetuum*, to the end of time

every all, each, each one, the whole number

everybody all and sundry, each one, each person, everyone, every person, one and all, the whole world

everyday 1. daily, quotidian 2. accustomed, common, common or garden (*Inf.*), commonplace, conventional, customary, dull, familiar, frequent, habitual, informal, mundane, ordinary, routine, run-of-the-mill, stock, unexceptional, unimaginative, usual, wonted, workaday

everyone all and sundry, each one, each person, everybody, every person, one and all, the whole world

everything all, each thing, the aggregate, the entirety, the lot, the sum, the total, the whole caboodle (*Inf.*), the whole lot

everywhere all around, all over, far and wide *or* near, high and low, in each place, in every place, omnipresent, the world over, to *or* in all places, ubiquitous, ubiquitously

evict boot out (*Inf.*), chuck out (*Inf.*), dislodge, dispossess, eject, expel, kick out (*Inf.*), oust, put out, remove, show the door (to), throw on to the streets, throw out, turf out (*Inf.*), turn out

evidence 1. *n.* affirmation, attestation, averment, confirmation, corroboration, data, declaration, demonstration, deposition, grounds, indication, manifestation, mark, proof, sign, substantiation, testimony, token, witness 2. *v.* demonstrate, denote, display, evince, exhibit, indicate, manifest, prove, reveal, show, signify, testify to, witness

evident apparent, clear, conspicuous, incontestable, incontrovertible, indisputable, manifest, noticeable, obvious, palpable, patent, perceptible, plain, tangible, unmistakable, visible

evidently 1. clearly, doubtless, doubtlessly, incontestably, incontrovertibly, indisputably, manifestly, obviously, patently, plainly, undoubtedly, unmistakably, without question 2. apparently, it seems, it would seem, ostensibly, outwardly, seemingly, to all appearances

evil *adj.* 1. bad, base, corrupt, depraved, heinous, immoral, iniquitous, maleficent, malevolent, malicious, malignant, nefarious, reprobate, sinful, vicious, vile, villainous, wicked, wrong ~*n.* 2. badness, baseness, corruption, curse, depravity, heinousness, immorality, iniquity, maleficence, malignity, sin, sinfulness, turpitude, vice, viciousness, villainy, wickedness, wrong, wrongdoing ~*adj.* 3. baneful (*Archaic*), calamitous, catastrophic, deleterious, destructive, detrimental, dire, disastrous, harmful, hurtful, inauspicious, injurious, mischievous, painful, pernicious, ruinous, sorrowful, unfortunate, unlucky, woeful ~*n.* 4. affliction, calamity, catastrophe, disaster, harm, hurt, ill, injury, mischief, misery, misfortune, pain, ruin, sorrow, suffering, woe ~*adj.* 5. foul, mephitic, noxious, offensive, pestilential, putrid, unpleasant, vile

evoke 1. arouse, awaken, call, excite, give rise to, induce, recall, rekindle, stimulate, stir up, summon up 2. call forth, educe (*Rare*), elicit, produce, provoke 3. arouse, call, call forth, conjure up, invoke, raise, summon

evolution development, enlarge~ ment, evolvement, expansion, growth, increase, maturation, pro~ gress, progression, unfolding, un~ rolling, working out

evolve develop, disclose, educe, elaborate, enlarge, expand, grow, increase, mature, open, progress, unfold, unroll, work out

exact *adj.* 1. accurate, careful, cor~ rect, definite, explicit, express, faithful, faultless, identical, literal, methodical, orderly, particular, precise, right, specific, true, un~ equivocal, unerring, veracious, very 2. careful, exacting, meticu~ lous, painstaking, punctilious, rig~ orous, scrupulous, severe, strict ~*v.* 3. call for, claim, command, compel, demand, extort, extract, force, impose, insist upon, require, squeeze, wrest, wring

exacting demanding, difficult, hard, harsh, imperious, oppressive, painstaking, rigid, rigorous, severe, stern, strict, stringent, taxing, tough, unsparing

exactly *adv.* 1. accurately, careful~ ly, correctly, definitely, explicitly, faithfully, faultlessly, literally, me~ thodically, precisely, rigorously, scrupulously, severely, strictly, truly, truthfully, unequivocally, unerringly, veraciously 2. abso~ lutely, bang, explicitly, expressly, indeed, in every respect, just, par~ ticularly, precisely, quite, specifi~ cally 3. **not exactly** *Ironical* by no means, certainly not, hardly, in no manner, in no way, not at all, not by any means, not quite, not really ~*interj.* 4. absolutely, assuredly, as you say, certainly, indeed, just so, of course, precisely, quite, quite so, spot-on (*Inf.*), truly

exactness accuracy, carefulness, correctness, exactitude, faithful~ ness, faultlessness, nicety, orderli~ ness, painstakingness, preciseness, precision, promptitude, regularity, rigorousness, rigour, scrupulous~ ness, strictness, truth, unequivo~ calness, veracity

exaggerate amplify, embellish, embroider, emphasize, enlarge,

exalt, hyperbolize, inflate, lay it on thick (*Inf.*), magnify, overdo, over~ emphasize, overestimate, over~ state

exaggerated amplified, exalted, excessive, extravagant, highly col~ oured, hyperbolic, inflated, over~ blown, overdone, overestimated, overstated, pretentious, tall (*Inf.*)

exaggeration amplification, em~ bellishment, emphasis, enlarge~ ment, exaltation, excess, extrava~ gance, hyperbole, inflation, mag~ nification, overemphasis, overesti~ mation, overstatement, pretension, pretentiousness

exalt 1. advance, aggrandize, dig~ nify, elevate, ennoble, honour, promote, raise, upgrade 2. ac~ claim, apotheosize, applaud, bless, extol, glorify, idolize, laud, magnify (*Archaic*), pay homage to, pay tribute to, praise, reverence, set on a pedestal, worship 3. animate, arouse, electrify, elevate, excite, fire the imagination (of), heighten, inspire, inspirit, stimulate, uplift 4. delight, elate, exhilarate, fill with joy, thrill

exaltation 1. advancement, ag~ grandizement, dignity, elevation, eminence, ennoblement, grandeur, high rank, honour, loftiness, pres~ tige, promotion, rise, upgrading 2. acclaim, acclamation, apotheosis, applause, blessing, extolment, glo~ rification, glory, homage, idoliza~ tion, laudation, lionization, magni~ fication, panegyric, plaudits, praise, reverence, tribute, worship 3. animation, elevation, excite~ ment, inspiration, stimulation, up~ lift 4. bliss, delight, ecstasy, elation, exhilaration, exultation, joy, joy~ ousness, jubilation, rapture, trans~ port

exalted 1. august, dignified, elevat~ ed, eminent, grand, high, high- ranking, honoured, lofty, prestig~ ious 2. elevated, high-minded, ideal, intellectual, lofty, noble, sublime, superior, uplifting 3. *Inf.* elevated, exaggerated, excessive, inflated, overblown, pretentious 4. animated, blissful, ecstatic, elated, elevated, excited, exhilarated, exultant, in high spirits, in seventh heaven, inspired, inspirited, joyous, jubilant, on cloud nine (*Inf.*), rapturous, stimulated, transported, uplifted

examination analysis, assay, catechism, checkup, exploration, inquiry, inquisition, inspection, interrogation, investigation, observation, perusal, probe, questioning, quiz, research, review, scrutiny, search, study, survey, test, trial

examine 1. analyse, appraise, assay, check, check out, consider, explore, go over *or* through, inspect, investigate, look over, peruse, ponder, pore over, probe, review, scan, scrutinize, sift, study, survey, take stock of, test, vet, weigh **2.** catechize, cross-examine, grill (*Inf.*), inquire, interrogate, question, quiz

example 1. case, case in point, exemplification, illustration, instance, sample, specimen **2.** archetype, exemplar, ideal, illustration, model, paradigm, paragon, pattern, precedent, prototype, standard **3.** admonition, caution, lesson, warning **4. for example** as an illustration, by way of illustration, e.g., *exempli gratia*, for instance, to cite an instance, to illustrate

exasperate aggravate (*Inf.*), anger, annoy, bug (*Inf.*), embitter, enrage, exacerbate, excite, gall, get (*Inf.*), incense, inflame, infuriate, irk, irritate, madden, needle (*Inf.*), nettle, peeve (*Inf.*), pique, provoke, rankle, rile (*Inf.*), rouse, try the patience of, vex

exasperation aggravation (*Inf.*), anger, annoyance, exacerbation, fury, ire (*Literary*), irritation, passion, pique, provocation, rage, vexation, wrath

excavate burrow, cut, delve, dig, dig out, dig up, gouge, hollow, mine, quarry, scoop, trench, tunnel, uncover, unearth

excavation burrow, cavity, cut, cutting, dig, diggings, ditch, dugout, hole, hollow, mine, pit, quarry, shaft, trench, trough

exceed 1. beat, be superior to, better, cap (*Inf.*), eclipse, excel, go beyond, outdistance, outdo, outreach, outrun, outshine, outstrip, overtake, pass, surmount, surpass, top, transcend **2.** go beyond the bounds of, go over the limit of, go over the top, overstep

exceeding enormous, exceptional, excessive, extraordinary, great, huge, pre-eminent, superior, superlative, surpassing, vast

exceedingly enormously, especially, exceptionally, excessively, extraordinarily, extremely, greatly, highly, hugely, inordinately, superlatively, surpassingly, unusually, vastly, very

excel 1. beat, be superior, better, cap (*Inf.*), eclipse, exceed, go beyond, outdo, outrival, outshine, pass, surmount, surpass, top, transcend **2.** be good, be master of, be proficient, be skilful, be talented, predominate, shine, show talent, take precedence

excellence distinction, eminence, fineness, goodness, greatness, high quality, merit, perfection, pre-eminence, purity, superiority, supremacy, transcendence, virtue, worth

excellent A1 (*Inf.*), admirable, capital, champion, choice, distinguished, estimable, exemplary, exquisite, fine, first-class, first-rate, good, great, meritorious, notable, noted, outstanding, prime, select, sterling, superb, superior, superlative, tiptop, top-notch (*Inf.*), worthy

except 1. *prep. Also* **except for** apart from, bar, barring, besides, but, excepting, excluding, exclusive of, omitting, other than, save (*Archaic*), saving, with the exception of **2.** *v.* ban, bar, disallow, exclude, leave out, omit, pass over, reject, rule out

exception 1. debarment, disallowment, excepting, exclusion, leaving out, omission, passing over, rejection **2.** anomaly, departure, deviation, freak, inconsistency, irregularity, oddity, peculiarity, quirk, special case 3. **take exception** be offended, be resentful, demur, disagree, object, quibble, take offence, take umbrage

exceptional 1. aberrant, abnormal, anomalous, atypical, deviant, extraordinary, inconsistent, irregular, odd, peculiar, rare, singular, special, strange, uncommon, unusual 2. excellent, extraordinary, marvellous, outstanding, phenomenal, prodigious, remarkable, special, superior

excess *n.* 1. glut, leftover, overabundance, overdose, overflow, overload, plethora, remainder, superabundance, superfluity, surfeit, surplus, too much 2. debauchery, dissipation, dissoluteness, exorbitance, extravagance, immoderation, intemperance, overindulgence, prodigality, unrestraint ~*adj.* 3. extra, leftover, redundant, remaining, residual, spare, superfluous, surplus

excessive disproportionate, enormous, exaggerated, exorbitant, extravagant, extreme, immoderate, inordinate, intemperate, needless, overdone, overmuch, prodigal, profligate, superfluous, too much, unconscionable, undue, unreasonable

exchange *v.* 1. bandy, barter, change, commute, convert into, interchange, reciprocate, swap (*Inf.*), switch, trade, truck ~*n.* 2. barter, dealing, interchange, quid pro quo, reciprocity, substitution, swap (*Inf.*), switch, tit for tat, trade, traffic, truck 3. Bourse, market

excitable edgy, emotional, hasty, highly strung, hot-headed, hot-tempered, irascible, mercurial, nervous, passionate, quick-tempered, sensitive, susceptible, temperamental, testy, touchy, violent, volatile

excite agitate, animate, arouse, awaken, discompose, disturb, electrify, elicit, evoke, fire, foment, galvanize, incite, inflame, inspire, instigate, kindle, move, provoke,

quicken, rouse, stimulate, stir up, thrill, titillate, waken, whet

excited aflame, agitated, animated, aroused, awakened, discomposed, disturbed, enthusiastic, feverish, flurried, high (*Inf.*), hot and bothered (*Inf.*), moved, nervous, overwrought, roused, stimulated, stirred, thrilled, tumultuous, wild, worked up

excitement 1. action, activity, ado, adventure, agitation, animation, commotion, discomposure, elation, enthusiasm, ferment, fever, flurry, furore, heat, kicks (*Inf.*), passion, perturbation, thrill, tumult, warmth 2. impulse, incitement, instigation, motivation, motive, provocation, stimulation, stimulus, urge

exciting electrifying, exhilarating, inspiring, intoxicating, moving, provocative, rip-roaring (*Inf.*), rousing, sensational, stimulating, stirring, thrilling, titillating

exclaim call, call out, cry, cry out, declare, ejaculate, proclaim, shout, utter, vociferate, yell

exclamation call, cry, ejaculation, expletive, interjection, outcry, shout, utterance, vociferation, yell

exclude 1. ban, bar, blackball, debar, disallow, embargo, forbid, interdict, keep out, ostracize, prohibit, proscribe, refuse, shut out, veto 2. count out, eliminate, except, ignore, leave out, omit, pass over, preclude, reject, repudiate, rule out, set aside 3. bounce (*Sl.*), drive out, eject, evict, expel, force out, get rid of, oust, remove, throw out

exclusion 1. ban, bar, debarment, embargo, forbiddance, interdict, nonadmission, preclusion, prohibition, proscription, refusal, veto 2. elimination, exception, omission, rejection, repudiation 3. eviction, expulsion, removal

exclusive 1. absolute, complete, entire, full, only, private, single, sole, total, undivided, unique, unshared, whole 2. aristocratic, chic, choice, clannish, classy (*Sl.*), cliquish, closed, discriminative, el~

egant, fashionable, limited, narrow, posh (*Inf.*), private, restricted, restrictive, select, selfish, snobbish 3. confined, limited, peculiar, restricted, unique 4. debarring, except for, excepting, excluding, leaving aside, not counting, omitting, restricting, ruling out

excommunicate anathematize, ban, banish, cast out, denounce, eject, exclude, expel, proscribe, remove, repudiate, unchurch

excruciating acute, agonizing, burning, exquisite, extreme, harrowing, insufferable, intense, piercing, racking, searing, severe, tormenting, torturous, unbearable, unendurable, violent

excursion 1. airing, day trip, expedition, jaunt, journey, outing, pleasure trip, ramble, tour, trip 2. detour, deviation, digression, episode, excursus, wandering

excusable allowable, defensible, forgivable, justifiable, minor, pardonable, permissible, slight, understandable, venial, warrantable

excuse *v.* 1. absolve, acquit, bear with, exculpate, exonerate, extenuate, forgive, indulge, make allowances for, overlook, pardon, pass over, tolerate, turn a blind eye to, wink at 2. apologize for, condone, defend, explain, justify, mitigate, vindicate 3. absolve, discharge, exempt, free, let off, liberate, release, relieve, spare ~*n.* 4. apology, defence, explanation, grounds, justification, mitigation, plea, pretext, reason, vindication 5. cop-out (*Sl.*), disguise, evasion, expedient, makeshift, pretence, pretext, semblance, shift, subterfuge 6. *Inf.* apology, makeshift, mockery, substitute, travesty

execrate abhor, abominate, anathematize, condemn, curse, damn, denounce, deplore, despise, detest, excoriate, hate, imprecate, loathe, revile, vilify

execration abhorrence, abomination, anathema, condemnation, contempt, curse, damnation, detestation, excoriation, hate, hatred, imprecation, loathing, malediction, odium, vilification

execute 1. behead, electrocute, guillotine, hang, kill, put to death, shoot 2. accomplish, achieve, administer, bring off, carry out, complete, consummate, discharge, do, effect, enact, enforce, finish, fulfil, implement, perform, prosecute, put into effect, realize, render 3. *Law* deliver, seal, serve, sign, validate

execution 1. accomplishment, achievement, administration, carrying out, completion, consummation, discharge, effect, enactment, enforcement, implementation, operation, performance, prosecution, realization, rendering 2. capital punishment, hanging, killing 3. delivery, manner, mode, performance, rendition, style, technique 4. *Law* warrant, writ

executioner 1. hangman, headsman 2. assassin, hit man (*Sl.*), killer, murderer, slayer

executive *n.* 1. administrator, director, manager, official 2. administration, directorate, directors, government, hierarchy, leadership, management ~*adj.* 3. administrative, controlling, decision-making, directing, governing, managerial

exemplary 1. admirable, commendable, correct, estimable, excellent, good, honourable, ideal, laudable, meritorious, model, praiseworthy, punctilious, sterling 2. admonitory, cautionary, monitory, warning 3. characteristic, illustrative, representative, typical

exemplify demonstrate, depict, display, embody, evidence, exhibit, illustrate, instance, manifest, represent, serve as an example of, show

exempt 1. *v.* absolve, discharge, except, excuse, exonerate, free, grant immunity, let off, liberate, release, relieve, spare 2. *adj.* absolved, clear, discharged, excepted, excused, favoured, free, immune, liberated, not liable, not subject, privileged, released, spared

exemption absolution, discharge, dispensation, exception, exoneration, freedom, immunity, privilege, release

exercise v. 1. apply, bring to bear, employ, enjoy, exert, practise, put to use, use, utilize, wield 2. discipline, drill, habituate, inure, practise, train, work out 3. afflict, agitate, annoy, burden, distress, disturb, occupy, pain, perturb, preoccupy, trouble, try, vex, worry ~n. 4. action, activity, discipline, drill, drilling, effort, labour, toil, training, work, work-out 5. accomplishment, application, discharge, employment, enjoyment, exertion, fulfilment, implementation, practice, use, utilization 6. drill, lesson, practice, problem, schooling, schoolwork, task, work

exert 1. bring into play, bring to bear, employ, exercise, expend, make use of, put forth, use, utilize, wield 2. **exert oneself** apply oneself, do one's best, endeavour, labour, make an effort, spare no effort, strain, strive, struggle, toil, try hard, work

exertion action, application, attempt, effort, employment, endeavour, exercise, industry, labour, pains, strain, stretch, struggle, toil, travail (*Literary*), trial, use, utilization

exhaust 1. bankrupt, cripple, debilitate, disable, drain, enervate, enfeeble, fatigue, impoverish, prostrate, sap, tire, tire out, weaken, wear out 2. consume, deplete, dissipate, expend, finish, run through, spend, squander, use up, waste 3. drain, dry, empty, strain, void 4. be emitted, discharge, emanate, escape, issue

exhausted 1. all in (*Sl.*), beat (*Sl.*), crippled, dead (*Inf.*), dead beat (*Inf.*), dead tired, debilitated, disabled, dog-tired (*Inf.*), done in (*Inf.*), drained, enervated, enfeebled, fatigued, jaded, knackered (*Sl.*), out on one's feet, prostrated, ready to drop, sapped, spent, tired

out, wasted, weak, worn out 2. at an end, consumed, depleted, dissipated, done, expended, finished, gone, spent, squandered, used up, wasted 3. bare, drained, dry, empty, void

exhausting arduous, backbreaking, crippling, debilitating, difficult, draining, enervating, fatiguing, gruelling, hard, laborious, punishing, sapping, strenuous, taxing, testing, tiring

exhaustion 1. debilitation, enervation, fatigue, feebleness, lassitude, prostration, tiredness, weariness 2. consumption, depletion, emptying

exhaustive all-embracing, all-inclusive, all-out (*Inf.*), complete, comprehensive, encyclopedic, extensive, far-reaching, full, full-scale, in-depth, intensive, sweeping, thorough, thoroughgoing, total

exhibit 1. v. air, demonstrate, disclose, display, evidence, evince, expose, express, flaunt, indicate, make clear *or* plain, manifest, offer, parade, present, put on view, reveal, show 2. n. display, exhibition, illustration, model, show

exhibition airing, demonstration, display, exhibit, expo (*Inf.*), exposition, fair, manifestation, performance, presentation, representation, show, showing, spectacle

exhilarating breathtaking, cheering, enlivening, exalting, exciting, exhilarant, exhilarative, exhilaratory, gladdening, invigorating, stimulating, thrilling, vitalizing

exhort admonish, advise, beseech, bid, call upon, caution, counsel, encourage, enjoin, entreat, goad, incite, persuade, press, spur, urge, warn

exhortation admonition, advice, beseeching, bidding, caution, counsel, encouragement, enjoinder (*Rare*), entreaty, goading, incitement, lecture, persuasion, sermon, urging, warning

exhume dig up, disentomb, disinter, unbury, unearth

exigency, exigence 1. acuteness, constraint, criticalness, demandingness, difficulty, distress, emergency, imperativeness, necessity, needfulness, pressingness, pressure, stress, urgency 2. constraint, demand, necessity, need, requirement, wont 3. crisis, difficulty, emergency, extremity, fix (*Inf.*), hardship, jam (*Inf.*), juncture, pass, pickle (*Inf.*), pinch, plight, predicament, quandary, scrape (*Inf.*), strait

exile *n.* 1. banishment, deportation, expatriation, expulsion, ostracism, proscription, separation 2. deportee, émigré, expatriate, outcast, refugee ~*v.* 3. banish, deport, drive out, eject, expatriate, expel, ostracize, oust, proscribe

exist 1. abide, be, be extant, be living, be present, breathe, continue, endure, happen, last, live, obtain, occur, prevail, remain, stand, survive 2. eke out a living, get along *or* by, stay alive, subsist, survive

existence 1. actuality, animation, being, breath, continuance, continuation, duration, endurance, life, subsistence, survival 2. being, creature, entity, thing 3. creation, life, reality, the world

existent abiding, around, current, enduring, existing, extant, in existence, living, obtaining, present, prevailing, remaining, standing, surviving

exit *n.* 1. door, egress, gate, outlet, passage out, vent, way out 2. adieu, departure, evacuation, exodus, farewell, going, goodbye, leavetaking, retirement, retreat, withdrawal 3. death, decease, demise, expiry, passing away ~*v.* 4. bid farewell, depart, go away, go offstage (*Theatre*), go out, issue, leave, retire, retreat, say goodbye, take one's leave, withdraw

exodus departure, evacuation, exit, flight, going out, leaving, migration, retirement, retreat, withdrawal

exonerate 1. absolve, acquit, clear, discharge, dismiss, exculpate, excuse, justify, pardon, vindicate 2. discharge, dismiss, except, excuse,

exempt, free, let off, liberate, release, relieve

exorbitant enormous, excessive, extortionate, extravagant, extreme, immoderate, inordinate, outrageous, preposterous, unconscionable, undue, unreasonable, unwarranted

exorcise adjure, cast out, deliver (from), drive out, expel, purify

exorcism adjuration, casting out, deliverance, driving out, expulsion, purification

exotic 1. alien, external, extraneous, extrinsic, foreign, imported, introduced, naturalized, not native 2. bizarre, colourful, curious, different, extraordinary, fascinating, glamorous, mysterious, outlandish, peculiar, strange, striking, unfamiliar, unusual

expand 1. amplify, augment, bloat, blow up, broaden, develop, dilate, distend, enlarge, extend, fatten, fill out, grow, heighten, increase, inflate, lengthen, magnify, multiply, prolong, protract, swell, thicken, wax, widen 2. diffuse, open (out), outspread, spread (out), stretch (out), unfold, unfurl, unravel, unroll 3. amplify, develop, dilate, elaborate, embellish, enlarge, expatiate, expound, flesh out, go into detail

expanse area, breadth, extent, field, plain, range, space, stretch, sweep, tract

expansion amplification, augmentation, development, diffusion, dilatation, distension, enlargement, expanse, growth, increase, inflation, magnification, multiplication, opening out, spread, swelling, unfolding, unfurling

expansive 1. dilating, distending, elastic, enlargeable, expanding, extendable, inflatable, stretching, stretchy, swelling 2. all-embracing, broad, comprehensive, extensive, far-reaching, inclusive, thorough, voluminous, wide, wide-ranging, widespread 3. affable, communicative, easy, effusive, free, friendly, garrulous, genial, loquacious, open, outgoing, sociable, talkative, unreserved, warm

expatiate amplify, descant, develop, dilate, dwell on, elaborate, embellish, enlarge, expound, go into detail

expatriate 1. *adj.* banished, emigrant, émigré, exiled, refugee 2. *n.* emigrant, émigré, exile 3. *v.* banish, exile, expel, ostracize, proscribe

expect 1. assume, believe, calculate, conjecture, forecast, foresee, imagine, presume, reckon, suppose, surmise, think, trust 2. anticipate, await, bargain for, contemplate, envisage, hope for, look ahead to, look for, look forward to, predict, watch for 3. call for, count on, demand, insist on, look for, rely upon, require, want, wish

expectancy 1. anticipation, assumption, belief, conjecture, expectation, hope, looking forward, prediction, presumption, probability, supposition, surmise, suspense, waiting 2. likelihood, outlook, prospect

expectant 1. anticipating, anxious, apprehensive, awaiting, eager, expecting, hopeful, in suspense, ready, watchful 2. enceinte, expecting (*Inf.*), gravid, pregnant

expectation 1. assumption, assurance, belief, calculation, confidence, conjecture, forecast, likelihood, presumption, probability, supposition, surmise, trust 2. anticipation, apprehension, chance, expectancy, fear, hope, looking forward, outlook, possibility, prediction, promise, prospect, suspense 3. demand, insistence, reliance, requirement, trust, want, wish

expecting enceinte, expectant, gravid, in the family way (*Inf.*), pregnant, with child

expediency, expedience 1. advantageousness, advisability, appropriateness, aptness, benefit, convenience, desirability, effectiveness, fitness, helpfulness, judiciousness, meetness, practicality, pragmatism, profitability, properness, propriety, prudence, suitability, usefulness, utilitarianism, utility 2. contrivance, device, expedient, makeshift, manoeuvre, means, measure, method, resort, resource, scheme, shift, stopgap, stratagem, substitute

expedient 1. *adj.* advantageous, advisable, appropriate, beneficial, convenient, desirable, effective, fit, helpful, judicious, meet, opportune, politic, practical, pragmatic, profitable, proper, prudent, suitable, useful, utilitarian, worthwhile 2. *n.* contrivance, device, expediency, makeshift, manoeuvre, means, measure, method, resort, resource, scheme, shift, stopgap, stratagem, substitute

expedite accelerate, advance, assist, dispatch, facilitate, forward, hasten, hurry, precipitate, press, promote, quicken, rush, speed (up), urge

expedition 1. enterprise, excursion, exploration, journey, mission, quest, safari, tour, trek, trip, undertaking, voyage 2. company, crew, explorers, team, travellers, voyagers, wayfarers 3. alacrity, celerity, dispatch, expeditiousness, haste, hurry, promptness, quickness, rapidity, readiness, speed, swiftness

expel 1. belch, cast out, discharge, dislodge, drive out, eject, remove, spew, throw out 2. ban, banish, bar, blackball, discharge, dismiss, drum out, evict, exclude, exile, expatriate, oust, proscribe, send packing, throw out, turf out (*Inf.*)

expend consume, disburse, dissipate, employ, exhaust, fork out (*Sl.*), go through, lay out (*Inf.*), pay out, shell out (*Inf.*), spend, use (up)

expendable dispensable, inessential, nonessential, replaceable, unimportant

expenditure application, charge, consumption, cost, disbursement, expense, outgoings, outlay, output, payment, spending, use

expense charge, consumption, cost, disbursement, expenditure, loss, outlay, output, payment, sacrifice, spending, toll, use

expensive costly, dear, excessive,

exorbitant, extravagant, high-priced, inordinate, lavish, over-priced, rich, steep (*Inf.*), stiff

experience *n.* 1. contact, doing, evidence, exposure, familiarity, involvement, know-how (*Inf.*), knowledge, observation, participation, practice, proof, training, trial, understanding 2. adventure, affair, encounter, episode, event, happening, incident, occurrence, ordeal, test, trial ~*v.* 3. apprehend, become familiar with, behold, encounter, endure, face, feel, go through, have, know, live through, meet, observe, participate in, perceive, sample, sense, suffer, sustain, taste, try, undergo

experienced 1. accomplished, adept, capable, competent, expert, familiar, knowledgeable, master, practised, professional, qualified, seasoned, skilful, tested, trained, tried, veteran, well-versed 2. knowing, mature, sophisticated, wise, worldly, worldly-wise

experiment 1. *n.* assay, attempt, examination, experimentation, investigation, procedure, proof, research, test, trial, trial and error, trial run, venture 2. *v.* assay, examine, investigate, put to the test, research, sample, test, try, verify

experimental empirical, exploratory, pilot, preliminary, probationary, provisional, speculative, tentative, test, trial, trial-and-error

expert 1. *n.* ace (*Inf.*), adept, authority, connoisseur, dab hand (*Inf.*), master, past master, pro (*Inf.*), professional, specialist, virtuoso, wizard 2. *adj.* able, adept, adroit, apt, clever, deft, dexterous, experienced, facile, handy, knowledgeable, master, masterly, practised, professional, proficient, qualified, skilful, skilled, trained, virtuoso

expertise ableness, adroitness, aptness, cleverness, command, deftness, dexterity, expertness, facility, judgment, knack, know-how (*Inf.*), knowledge, masterliness, mastery, proficiency, skilfulness, skill

expertness ableness, adroitness, aptness, command, deftness, dexterity, expertise, facility, judgment, know-how (*Inf.*), knowledge, masterliness, mastery, proficiency, skilfulness, skill

expire 1. cease, close, come to an end, conclude, end, finish, lapse, run out, stop, terminate 2. breathe out, emit, exhale, expel 3. decease, depart, die, kick the bucket (*Inf.*), pass away *or* on, perish

explain 1. clarify, clear up, define, demonstrate, describe, disclose, elucidate, explicate (*Formal*), expound, illustrate, interpret, make clear *or* plain, resolve, solve, teach, unfold 2. account for, excuse, give an explanation for, give a reason for, justify

explanation 1. clarification, definition, demonstration, description, elucidation, explication, exposition, illustration, interpretation, resolution 2. account, answer, cause, excuse, justification, meaning, mitigation, motive, reason, sense, significance, vindication

explanatory demonstrative, descriptive, elucidatory, explicative, expository, illuminative, illustrative, interpretive, justifying

explicit absolute, categorical, certain, clear, definite, direct, distinct, exact, express, frank, open, outspoken, patent, plain, positive, precise, specific, stated, straightforward, unambiguous, unequivocal, unqualified, unreserved

explode 1. blow up, burst, detonate, discharge, erupt, go off, set off, shatter, shiver 2. belie, debunk, discredit, disprove, give the lie to, invalidate, refute, repudiate

exploit *n.* 1. accomplishment, achievement, adventure, attainment, deed, feat, stunt ~*v.* 2. abuse, impose upon, manipulate, milk, misuse, play on *or* upon, take advantage of 3. capitalize on, cash in on (*Sl.*), make capital out of, make use of, profit by *or* from, put to use, turn to account, use, use to advantage, utilize

exploration 1. analysis, examina-

tion, inquiry, inspection, investiga~
tion, probe, research, scrutiny,
search, study 2. expedition, recon~
naissance, survey, tour, travel, trip

exploratory analytic, experimen~
tal, fact-finding, investigative,
probing, searching, trial

explore 1. analyse, examine, in~
quire into, inspect, investigate,
look into, probe, prospect, re~
search, scrutinize, search 2. have
or take a look around, range over,
reconnoitre, scout, survey, tour,
travel, traverse

explosion 1. bang, blast, burst,
clap, crack, detonation, discharge,
outburst, report 2. eruption, fit,
outbreak, outburst, paroxysm

explosive 1. unstable, volatile 2.
fiery, stormy, touchy, vehement,
violent 3. charged, dangerous,
hazardous, overwrought, perilous,
tense, ugly

exponent 1. advocate, backer,
champion, defender, promoter,
propagandist, proponent, spokes~
man, spokeswoman, supporter,
upholder 2. commentator, demon~
strator, elucidator, expositor, ex~
pounder, illustrator, interpreter 3.
example, exemplar, illustration,
indication, model, sample, speci~
men, type 4. executant, interpret~
er, performer, player, presenter

expose 1. display, exhibit, mani~
fest, present, put on view, reveal,
show, uncover, unveil 2. air, be~
tray, bring to light, denounce, de~
tect, disclose, divulge, lay bare, let
out, make known, reveal, show up,
smoke out, uncover, unearth, un~
mask 3. endanger, hazard, imperil,
jeopardize, lay open, leave open,
make vulnerable, risk, subject 4.
With **to** acquaint with, bring into
contact with, familiarize with,
introduce to, make conversant
with

exposed 1. bare, exhibited, laid
bare, made manifest, made public,
on display, on show, on view, re~
vealed, shown, unconcealed, un~
covered, unveiled 2. open, open to
the elements, unprotected, unshel~
tered 3. in danger, in peril, laid

bare, laid open, left open, liable,
open, susceptible, vulnerable

exposition 1. account, commen~
tary, critique, description, elucida~
tion, exegesis, explanation, expli~
cation, illustration, interpretation,
presentation 2. demonstration,
display, exhibition, expo (*Inf.*), fair,
presentation, show

expostulate argue (with), dis~
suade, protest, reason (with), re~
monstrate (with)

exposure 1. baring, display, exhi~
bition, manifestation, presentation,
publicity, revelation, showing, un~
covering, unveiling 2. airing, be~
trayal, denunciation, detection,
disclosure, divulgence, divulging,
exposé, revelation, unmasking 3.
danger, hazard, jeopardy, risk,
vulnerability 4. acquaintance, con~
tact, conversancy, experience, fa~
miliarity, introduction, knowledge
5. aspect, frontage, location, out~
look, position, setting, view

expound describe, elucidate, ex~
plain, explicate (*Formal*), illus~
trate, interpret, set forth, spell out,
unfold

express *v.* 1. articulate, assert, as~
severate, communicate, couch,
declare, enunciate, phrase, pro~
nounce, put, put across, put into
words, say, speak, state, tell, utter,
verbalize, voice, word 2. bespeak,
convey, denote, depict, designate,
disclose, divulge, embody, evince,
exhibit, indicate, intimate, make
known, manifest, represent, re~
veal, show, signify, stand for, sym~
bolize, testify 3. extract, force out,
press out, squeeze out ~*adj.* 4. ac~
curate, categorical, certain, clear,
definite, direct, distinct, exact, ex~
plicit, outright, plain, pointed, pre~
cise, unambiguous 5. clearcut, es~
pecial, particular, singular, special
6. direct, fast, high-speed, nonstop,
quick, rapid, speedy, swift

expression 1. announcement, as~
sertion, asseveration, communica~
tion, declaration, enunciation,
mention, pronouncement, speak~
ing, statement, utterance, verbali~
zation, voicing 2. demonstration,

embodiment, exhibition, indica~
tion, manifestation, representation,
show, sign, symbol, token 3. air,
appearance, aspect, countenance,
face, look, mien (*Literary*) 4.
choice of words, delivery, diction,
emphasis, execution, intonation,
language, phraseology, phrasing,
speech, style, wording 5. idiom, lo~
cution, phrase, remark, set phrase,
term, turn of phrase, word

expressive 1. eloquent, emphatic,
energetic, forcible, lively, mobile,
moving, poignant, striking, strong,
sympathetic, telling, vivid 2. allu~
sive, demonstrative, indicative,
meaningful, pointed, pregnant, re~
vealing, significant, suggestive,
thoughtful

expressly 1. especially, exactly,
intentionally, on purpose, particu~
larly, precisely, purposely, spe~
cially, specifically 2. absolutely,
categorically, clearly, decidedly,
definitely, distinctly, explicitly, in
no uncertain terms, manifestly,
outright, plainly, pointedly, posi~
tively, unambiguously, unequivo~
cally, unmistakably

expropriate appropriate, arrogate,
assume, commandeer, confiscate,
impound, requisition, seize, take,
take over

expulsion banishment, debarment,
discharge, dislodgment, dismissal,
ejection, eviction, exclusion, exile,
expatriation, extrusion, proscrip~
tion, removal

expurgate blue-pencil, bowdlerize,
censor, clean up (*Inf.*), cut, purge,
purify

exquisite 1. beautiful, dainty, deli~
cate, elegant, fine, lovely, precious
2. attractive, beautiful, charming,
comely, lovely, pleasing, striking 3.
admirable, choice, consummate,
delicious, excellent, fine, flawless,
incomparable, matchless, out~
standing, peerless, perfect, rare,
select, splendid, superb, superla~
tive 4. appreciative, consummate,
cultivated, discerning, discrimi~
nating, fastidious, impeccable,
meticulous, polished, refined, se~
lective, sensitive 5. acute, excruci~

ating, intense, keen, piercing,
poignant, sharp

extempore *adv./adj.* ad lib, ex~
temporaneous, extemporary, free~
ly, impromptu, improvised, off~
hand, off the cuff (*Inf.*), off the top
of one's head, on the spot, sponta~
neously, unplanned, unpremedi~
tated, unprepared

extemporize ad-lib, improvise,
make up, play (it) by ear

extend 1. carry on, continue, drag
out, draw out, elongate, lengthen,
make longer, prolong, protract,
spin out, spread out, stretch, unfurl,
unroll 2. carry on, continue, go on,
last, take 3. amount to, attain, go as
far as, reach, spread 4. add to, am~
plify, augment, broaden, develop,
dilate, enhance, enlarge, expand,
increase, spread, supplement, wid~
en 5. advance, bestow, confer, give,
grant, hold out, impart, offer, pres~
ent, proffer, put forth, reach out,
stretch out, yield

extended 1. continued, drawn-out,
elongated, enlarged, lengthened,
long, prolonged, protracted, spread
(out), stretched out, unfolded, un~
furled, unrolled 2. broad, compre~
hensive, enlarged, expanded, ex~
tensive, far-reaching, large-scale,
sweeping, thorough, wide, wide~
spread 3. conferred, outstretched,
proffered, stretched out

extension 1. amplification, aug~
mentation, broadening, continu~
ation, delay, development, dilata~
tion, distension, elongation, en~
largement, expansion, extent, in~
crease, lengthening, postpone~
ment, prolongation, protraction,
spread, stretching, widening 2. ad~
dendum, addition, adjunct, annexe,
appendage, appendix, branch, ell,
supplement, wing

extensive all-inclusive, broad, ca~
pacious, commodious, compre~
hensive, expanded, extended, far-
flung, far-reaching, general, great,
huge, large, large-scale, lengthy,
long, pervasive, prevalent, pro~
tracted, spacious, sweeping, thor~
ough, universal, vast, voluminous,
wholesale, wide, widespread

extent 1. bounds, compass, play, range, reach, scope, sphere, sweep 2. amount, amplitude, area, breadth, bulk, degree, duration, expanse, expansion, length, magnitude, measure, quantity, size, stretch, term, time, volume, width

extenuating justifying, mitigating, moderating, qualifying, serving as an excuse

exterior n. 1. appearance, aspect, coating, covering, façade, face, finish, outside, shell, skin, surface ~adj. 2. external, outer, outermost, outside, outward, superficial, surface 3. alien, exotic, external, extraneous, extrinsic, foreign, outside

exterminate abolish, annihilate, destroy, eliminate, eradicate, extirpate

external 1. apparent, exterior, outer, outermost, outside, outward, superficial, surface, visible 2. alien, exotic, exterior, extramural, extraneous, extrinsic, foreign, independent, outside

extinct 1. dead, defunct, gone, lost, vanished 2. doused, extinguished, inactive, out, quenched, snuffed out 3. abolished, defunct, ended, obsolete, terminated, void

extinction abolition, annihilation, death, destruction, dying out, eradication, excision, extermination, extirpation, obliteration, oblivion

extinguish 1. blow out, douse, put out, quench, smother, snuff out, stifle 2. abolish, annihilate, destroy, eliminate, end, eradicate, erase, expunge, exterminate, extirpate, kill, obscure, remove, suppress, wipe out

extol acclaim, applaud, celebrate, commend, cry up, eulogize, exalt, glorify, laud, magnify (Archaic), panegyrize, pay tribute to, praise, sing the praises of

extort blackmail, bleed (Inf.), bully, coerce, exact, extract, force, squeeze, wrest, wring

extortion 1. blackmail, coercion, compulsion, demand, exaction, force, oppression, rapacity 2. enormity, exorbitance, expensiveness, overcharging

extortionate 1. excessive, exorbitant, extravagant, immoderate, inflated, inordinate, outrageous, preposterous, sky-high, unreasonable 2. blood-sucking (Inf.), exacting, grasping, hard, harsh, oppressive, rapacious, rigorous, severe, usurious

extra adj. 1. accessory, added, additional, ancillary, auxiliary, fresh, further, more, new, other, supplemental, supplementary 2. excess, extraneous, inessential, leftover, needless, redundant, reserve, spare, supererogatory, superfluous, supernumerary, surplus, unnecessary, unneeded, unused ~n. 3. accessory, addendum, addition, adjunct, affix, appendage, appurtenance, attachment, bonus, complement, extension, supernumerary, supplement ~adv. 4. especially, exceptionally, extraordinarily, extremely, particularly, remarkably, uncommonly, unusually

extract v. 1. draw, extirpate, pluck out, pull, pull out, remove, take out, uproot, withdraw 2. bring out, derive, draw, elicit, evoke, exact, gather, get, glean, obtain, reap, wrest, wring 3. deduce, derive, develop, educe, elicit, evolve 4. distil, draw out, express, obtain, press out, separate out, squeeze, take out 5. abstract, choose, cite, copy out, cull, cut out, quote, select ~n. 6. concentrate, decoction, distillate, distillation, essence, juice 7. abstract, citation, clipping, cutting, excerpt, passage, quotation, selection

extraction 1. drawing, extirpation, pulling, removal, taking out, uprooting, withdrawal 2. derivation, distillation, separation 3. ancestry, birth, blood, derivation, descent, family, lineage, origin, parentage, pedigree, race, stock

extraneous 1. accidental, additional, adventitious, extra, incidental, inessential, needless, nonessential, peripheral, redundant, superfluous, supplementary, unessential, unnecessary, unneeded 2. beside the point, immaterial, impertinent, inadmissible, inapplicable, inapposite, inappropriate, inapt, irrelevant, off the subject, unconnected, unrelated 3. adventitious, alien, exotic, external, extrinsic, foreign, out of place, strange

extraordinary amazing, bizarre, curious, exceptional, fantastic, marvellous, odd, outstanding, particular, peculiar, phenomenal, rare, remarkable, singular, special, strange, surprising, uncommon, unfamiliar, unheard-of, unique, unprecedented, unusual, unwonted, weird, wonderful

extravagance 1. improvidence, lavishness, overspending, prodigality, profligacy, profusion, squandering, waste, wastefulness 2. absurdity, dissipation, exaggeration, excess, exorbitance, folly, immoderation, outrageousness, preposterousness, recklessness, unreasonableness, unrestraint, wildness

extravagant 1. excessive, improvident, imprudent, lavish, prodigal, profligate, spendthrift, wasteful 2. absurd, exaggerated, excessive, exorbitant, fanciful, fantastic, foolish, immoderate, inordinate, outrageous, preposterous, reckless, unreasonable, unrestrained, wild 3. fancy, flamboyant, flashy, garish, gaudy, grandiose, ornate, ostentatious, pretentious, showy 4. costly, excessive, exorbitant, expensive, extortionate, inordinate, overpriced, steep (Inf.), unreasonable

extreme adj. 1. acute, great, greatest, high, highest, intense, maximum, severe, supreme, ultimate, utmost, uttermost, worst 2. downright, egregious, exaggerated, exceptional, excessive, extraordinary, extravagant, fanatical, immoderate, inordinate, intemperate, out-and-out, outrageous, radical, remarkable, sheer, uncommon, unconventional, unreasonable, unusual, utter, zealous 3. dire, Draconian, drastic, harsh, radical, rigid,

severe, stern, strict, unbending, uncompromising 4. faraway, far-off, farthest, final, last, most distant, outermost, remotest, terminal, ultimate, utmost, uttermost ~n. 5. acme, apex, apogee, boundary, climax, consummation, depth, edge, end, excess, extremity, height, limit, maximum, minimum, nadir, pinnacle, pole, termination, top, ultimate, zenith

extremely acutely, awfully (Inf.), exceedingly, exceptionally, excessively, extraordinarily, greatly, highly, inordinately, intensely, markedly, quite, severely, terribly, to or in the extreme, ultra, uncommonly, unusually, utterly, very

extremist die-hard, fanatic, radical, ultra, zealot

extremity 1. acme, apex, apogee, border, bound, boundary, brim, brink, edge, end, extreme, frontier, limit, margin, maximum, minimum, nadir, pinnacle, pole, rim, terminal, termination, terminus, tip, top, ultimate, verge, zenith 2. acuteness, climax, consummation, depth, excess, height 3. adversity, crisis, dire straits, disaster, emergency, exigency, hardship, pinch, plight, setback, trouble 4. Plural fingers and toes, hands and feet, limbs

extricate clear, deliver, disembarrass, disengage, disentangle, free, get out, get (someone) off the hook (Sl.), liberate, release, relieve, remove, rescue, withdraw, wriggle out of

exuberance 1. animation, buoyancy, cheerfulness, eagerness, ebullience, effervescence, energy, enthusiasm, excitement, exhilaration, high spirits, life, liveliness, spirit, sprightliness, vigour, vitality, vivacity, zest 2. effusiveness, exaggeration, excessiveness, fulsomeness, lavishness, prodigality, superfluity 3. abundance, copiousness, lavishness, lushness, luxuriance, plenitude, profusion, rankness, richness, superabundance, teemingness

exuberant 1. animated, buoyant,

cheerful, eager, ebullient, effer~ vescent, elated, energetic, enthu~ siastic, excited, exhilarated, high-spirited, in high spirits, lively, sparkling, spirited, sprightly, vig~ orous, vivacious, zestful 2. effusive, exaggerated, excessive, fulsome, lavish, overdone, prodigal, super~ fluous 3. abundant, copious, lavish, lush, luxuriant, overflowing, plen~ teous, plentiful, profuse, rank, rich, superabundant, teeming

exult 1. be delighted, be elated, be in high spirits, be joyful, be jubi~ lant, be overjoyed, celebrate, jubi~ late, jump for joy, make merry, rejoice 2. boast, brag, crow, gloat, glory (in), revel, take delight in, taunt, triumph, vaunt

exultant cock-a-hoop, delighted, elated, exulting, flushed, gleeful, joyful, joyous, jubilant, overjoyed, rejoicing, revelling, transported, triumphant

exultation 1. celebration, delight, elation, glee, high spirits, joy, joy~ ousness, jubilation, merriness, re~ joicing, transport 2. boasting, bragging, crowing, gloating, glory, glorying, revelling, triumph

eye n. 1. eyeball, optic (*Inf.*), orb (*Poetic*), peeper (*Sl.*) 2. apprecia~ tion, discernment, discrimination, judgment, perception, recognition, taste 3. *Often plural* belief, judg~ ment, mind, opinion, point of view, viewpoint 4. keep an *or* one's eye on guard, keep in view, keep tabs on (*Inf.*), keep under surveillance, look after, look out for, monitor, observe, pay attention to, regard, scrutinize, supervise, survey, watch, watch over 5. an eye for an eye justice, reprisal, requital, re~ taliation, retribution, revenge, vengeance 6. lay, clap *or* set eyes on behold, come across, encounter, meet, notice, observe, run into, see 7. see eye to eye accord, agree, back, be in unison, coincide, con~ cur, fall in, get on, go along, har~ monize, jibe (*Inf.*), subscribe to 8. up to one's eyes busy, caught up, engaged, flooded out, fully occu~ pied, inundated, overwhelmed, up to here, up to one's elbows, wrapped up in ~v. 9. contemplate, gaze at, glance at, have *or* take a look at, inspect, look at, peruse, regard, scan, scrutinize, stare at, study, survey, view, watch 10. eye up, give (someone) the (glad) eye, leer at, make eyes at, ogle

eyesight observation, perception, range of vision, sight, vision

eyesore atrocity, blemish, blight, blot, disfigurement, disgrace, hor~ ror, mess, monstrosity, sight (*Inf.*), ugliness

eyewitness bystander, looker-on, observer, onlooker, passer-by, spectator, viewer, watcher, wit~ ness

F

fable 1. allegory, apologue, legend, myth, parable, story, tale 2. fabrication, fairy story (*Inf.*), falsehood, fantasy, fib, fiction, figment, invention, lie, romance, tall story (*Inf.*), untruth, white lie, yarn (*Inf.*)

fabric 1. cloth, material, stuff, textile, web 2. constitution, construction, foundations, framework, infrastructure, make-up, organization, structure

fabricate 1. assemble, build, construct, erect, fashion, form, frame, make, manufacture, shape 2. coin, concoct, devise, fake, falsify, feign, forge, form, invent, make up, trump up

fabrication 1. assemblage, assembly, building, construction, erection, manufacture, production 2. cock-and-bull story (*Inf.*), concoction, fable, fairy story (*Inf.*), fake, falsehood, fiction, figment, forgery, invention, lie, myth, untruth

fabulous *n.* 1. amazing, astounding, breathtaking, fictitious, immense, inconceivable, incredible, legendary, phenomenal, unbelievable 2. *Inf.* fantastic (*Inf.*), marvellous, out-of-this-world (*Inf.*), spectacular, superb, wonderful 3. apocryphal, fantastic, fictitious, imaginary, invented, legendary, made-up, mythical, unreal

façade appearance, exterior, face, front, frontage, guise, mask, pretence, semblance, show, veneer

face *n.* 1. clock (*Sl.*), countenance, dial (*Sl.*), features, kisser (*Sl.*), lineaments, mug (*Sl.*), phiz *or* phizog (*Sl.*), physiognomy, visage 2. appearance, aspect, expression, frown, grimace, look, *moue*, pout, scowl, smirk 3. air, appearance, disguise, display, exterior, façade, front, mask, pretence, semblance, show 4. authority, dignity, honour, image, prestige, reputation, self-respect, standing, status 5. *Inf.* assurance, audacity, boldness, brass neck (*Inf.*), cheek (*Inf.*), confidence, effrontery, gall (*Inf.*), impudence, nerve, presumption, sauce (*Inf.*) 6. aspect, cover, exterior, facet, front, outside, right side, side, surface 7. **face to face** à deux, confronting, eyeball to eyeball, in confrontation, opposite, tête-à-tête, vis-à-vis 8. **fly in the face of** act in defiance of, defy, disobey, go against, oppose, rebel against, snap one's fingers at (*Inf.*) 9. **on the face of it** apparently, at first sight, seemingly, to all appearances, to the eye 10. **pull** (*or* **make**) **a long face** frown, grimace, knit one's brows, look black (disapproving, displeased, put out, stern), lower, pout, scowl, sulk 11. **show one's face** approach, be seen, come, put in *or* make an appearance, show up (*Inf.*), turn up 12. **to one's face** directly, in one's presence, openly, straight ~*v.* 13. be confronted by, brave, come up against, confront, cope with, deal with, defy, encounter, experience, meet, oppose 14. be opposite, front onto, give towards *or* onto, look onto, overlook 15. clad, coat, cover, dress, finish, level, line, overlay, sheathe, surface, veneer

facet angle, aspect, face, part, phase, plane, side, slant, surface

facetious amusing, comical, droll, flippant, frivolous, funny, humorous, jesting, jocose, jocular, merry, playful, pleasant, tongue in cheek, unserious, waggish, witty

face up to accept, acknowledge, come to terms with, confront, cope with, deal with, meet head-on

facile 1. adept, adroit, dexterous, easy, effortless, fluent, light, proficient, quick, ready, simple, skilful, smooth, uncomplicated 2. cursory, glib, hasty, shallow, slick, superficial

facilitate assist the progress of, ease, expedite, forward, further, help, make easy, promote, smooth the path of, speed up

facility 1. ability, adroitness, dexterity, ease, efficiency, effortlessness, expertness, fluency, knack, proficiency, quickness, readiness, skilfulness, skill, smoothness 2. *Often plural* advantage, aid, amenity, appliance, convenience, equipment, means, opportunity, resource

facing 1. *adj.* fronting, opposite, partnering 2. *n.* cladding, coating, façade, false front, front, overlay, plaster, reinforcement, revetment, stucco, surface, trimming, veneer

facsimile carbon, carbon copy, copy, duplicate, photocopy, Photostat (*Trademark*), print, replica, reproduction, transcript, Xerox (*Trademark*)

fact 1. act, deed, event, *fait accompli*, happening, incident, occurrence, performance 2. actuality, certainty, gospel (truth), naked truth, reality, truth 3. circumstance, detail, feature, item, particular, point, specific 4. **in fact** actually, indeed, in point of fact, in reality, in truth, really, truly

faction 1. bloc, cabal, camp, caucus, clique, coalition, combination, confederacy, contingent, division, gang, ginger group, group, junta, lobby, minority, party, pressure group, section, sector, set, splinter group 2. conflict, disagreement, discord, disharmony, dissension, disunity, division, divisiveness, friction, infighting, rebellion, sedition, strife, tumult, turbulence

factious conflicting, contentious, disputatious, dissident, divisive, insurrectionary, litigious, malcontent, mutinous, partisan, rebellious, refractory, rival, sectarian, seditious, troublemaking, tumultuous, turbulent, warring

factor 1. aspect, cause, circumstance, component, consideration, determinant, element, influence, item, part, point, thing 2. *Scot.* agent, deputy, estate manager, middleman, reeve, steward

factory manufactory (*Obsolete*), mill, plant, works

factotum Girl Friday, handyman, jack of all trades, Man Friday, man of all work, odd job man

facts data, details, gen (*Inf.*), info (*Inf.*), information, the lowdown (*Inf.*), the score (*Inf.*), the whole story

factual accurate, authentic, circumstantial, close, correct, credible, exact, faithful, genuine, literal, matter-of-fact, objective, precise, real, sure, true, true-to-life, unadorned, unbiased, veritable

faculties capabilities, intelligence, powers, reason, senses, wits

faculty 1. ability, adroitness, aptitude, bent, capability, capacity, cleverness, dexterity, facility, gift, knack, power, propensity, readiness, skill, talent, turn 2. branch of learning, department, discipline, profession, school, teaching staff (*Chiefly U.S.*) 3. authorization, licence, prerogative, privilege, right

fad affectation, craze, fancy, fashion, mania, mode, rage, trend, vogue, whim

fade 1. blanch, bleach, blench, dim, discolour, dull, grow dim, lose colour, lose lustre, pale, wash out 2. decline, die away, die out, dim, disappear, disperse, dissolve, droop, dwindle, ebb, etiolate, evanesce, fail, fall, flag, languish, melt away, perish, shrivel, vanish, vanish into thin air, wane, waste away, wilt, wither

faded bleached, dim, discoloured, dull, etiolated, indistinct, lustreless, pale, washed out

fading declining, decreasing, disappearing, dying, on the decline, vanishing

faeces bodily waste, droppings, dung, excrement, excreta, ordure, stools

fail 1. be defeated, be found lacking *or* wanting, be in vain, be unsuccessful, break down, come a cropper (*Inf.*), come to grief, come to naught, come to nothing, fall, fall short, fall short of, fall through, fizzle out (*Inf.*), flop (*Inf.*), founder, go astray, go down, go up in smoke (*Inf.*), meet with disaster, miscarry, misfire, miss, not make the grade (*Inf.*), run aground, turn out badly 2. abandon, break one's word, desert, disappoint, forget, forsake, let down, neglect, omit 3. be on one's last legs (*Inf.*), cease, conk out (*Inf.*), cut out, decline, die, disappear, droop, dwindle, fade, give out, give up, gutter, languish, peter out, sicken, sink, stop working, wane, weaken 4. become insolvent, close down, crash, fold (*Inf.*), go bankrupt, go broke (*Inf.*), go bust (*Inf.*), go into receivership, go out of business, go to the wall, go under, smash 5. **without fail** conscientiously, constantly, dependably, like clockwork, punctually, regularly, religiously, without exception

failing 1. *n.* blemish, blind spot, defect, deficiency, drawback, error, failure, fault, flaw, foible, frailty, imperfection, lapse, miscarriage, misfortune, shortcoming, weakness 2. *prep.* in default of, in the absence of, lacking

failure 1. abortion, breakdown, collapse, defeat, downfall, fiasco, frustration, lack of success, miscarriage, overthrow, wreck 2. black sheep, dead duck (*Inf.*), disappointment, dud (*Inf.*), flop (*Inf.*), incompetent, loser, ne'er-do-well, no-good, no-hoper (*Chiefly Aust.*), nonstarter, washout (*Inf.*) 3. default, deficiency, dereliction, neglect, negligence, nonobservance, nonperformance, nonsuccess, omission, remissness, shortcoming, stoppage 4. breakdown, decay, decline, deterioration, failing, loss 5. bankruptcy, crash, downfall, folding (*Inf.*), insolvency, ruin

faint *adj.* 1. bleached, delicate, dim, distant, dull, faded, faltering, feeble, hazy, hushed, ill-defined, indistinct, light, low, muffled, muted, soft, subdued, thin, vague, whispered 2. feeble, remote, slight, unenthusiastic, weak 3. dizzy, drooping, enervated, exhausted, faltering, fatigued, giddy, languid, lethargic, light-headed, muzzy, ver-

tiginous, weak, woozy (*Inf.*) 4. faint-hearted, lily-livered, spiritless, timid, timorous ~*v.* 5. black out, collapse, fade, fail, flake out (*Inf.*), keel over (*Inf.*), languish, lose consciousness, pass out, swoon (*Literary*), weaken ~*n.* 6. blackout, collapse, swoon (*Literary*), syncope (*Medical*), unconsciousness

faint-hearted diffident, half-hearted, irresolute, timid, timorous, weak

faintly 1. feebly, in a whisper, indistinctly, softly, weakly 2. a little, dimly, slightly, somewhat

fair[1] *adj.* 1. above board, according to the rules, clean, disinterested, dispassionate, equal, equitable, even-handed, honest, honourable, impartial, just, lawful, legitimate, objective, on the level (*Inf.*), proper, square, trustworthy, unbiased, unprejudiced, upright 2. blond, blonde, fair-haired, flaxen-haired, light, light-complexioned, towhaired, towheaded 3. adequate, all right, average, decent, mediocre, middling, moderate, not bad, O.K. (*Inf.*), passable, reasonable, respectable, satisfactory, so-so (*Inf.*), tolerable 4. beauteous, beautiful, bonny, comely, handsome, lovely, pretty, well-favoured 5. bright, clear, clement, cloudless, dry, favourable, fine, sunny, sunshiny, unclouded

fair[2] *n.* bazaar, carnival, expo (*Inf.*), exposition, festival, fête, gala, market, show

fair-and-square above board, correct, honest, just, on the level (*Inf.*), straight

fairly 1. adequately, moderately, pretty well, quite, rather, reasonably, somewhat, tolerably 2. deservedly, equitably, honestly, impartially, justly, objectively, properly, without fear or favour 3. absolutely, in a manner of speaking, positively, really, veritably

fair-minded disinterested, even-handed, impartial, just, open-minded, unbiased, unprejudiced

fairness decency, disinterestedness, equitableness, equity, impartiality, justice, legitimacy, rightful~ness, uprightness

fairy brownie, elf, hob, leprechaun, pixie, Robin Goodfellow, sprite

fairy tale *or* **fairy story** 1. folk tale, romance 2. cock-and-bull story (*Inf.*), fabrication, fantasy, fiction, invention, lie, tall story, untruth

faith 1. assurance, confidence, con~viction, credence, credit, depend~ence, reliance, trust 2. belief, church, communion, creed, de~nomination, dogma, persuasion, religion 3. allegiance, constancy, faithfulness, fealty, fidelity, loyalty, truth, truthfulness 4. *As in* keep faith, in good faith honour, pledge, promise, sincerity, vow, word, word of honour

faithful 1. attached, constant, de~pendable, devoted, loyal, reliable, staunch, steadfast, true, true-blue, trusty, truthful, unswerving, unwa~vering 2. accurate, close, exact, just, precise, strict, true 3. **the faithful** adherents, believers, brethren, communicants, congre~gation, followers, the elect

faithfulness 1. adherence, con~stancy, dependability, devotion, fealty, fidelity, loyalty, trust~worthiness 2. accuracy, closeness, exactness, justice, strictness, truth

faithless disloyal, doubting, false, false-hearted, fickle, inconstant, perfidious, recreant (*Archaic*), traitorous, treacherous, unbeliev~ing, unfaithful, unreliable, untrue, untrustworthy, untruthful

faithlessness betrayal, disloyalty, fickleness, inconstancy, infidelity, perfidy, treachery, unfaithfulness

fake 1. *v.* affect, assume, copy, counterfeit, fabricate, feign, forge, pretend, put on, sham, simulate 2. *n.* charlatan, copy, forgery, fraud, hoax, imitation, impostor, moun~tebank, phoney (*Sl.*), reproduction, sham 3. *adj.* affected, artificial, as~sumed, counterfeit, false, forged, imitation, mock, phoney (*Sl.*), pinchbeck, pseudo, reproduction, sham

fall *v.* 1. be precipitated, cascade, collapse, crash, descend, dive,

drop, drop down, go head over heels, keel over, nose-dive, pitch, plummet, plunge, settle, sink, stumble, subside, topple, trip, trip over, tumble 2. abate, become lower, decline, decrease, depreci~ate, diminish, dwindle, ebb, fall off, flag, go down, lessen, slump, sub~side 3. be overthrown, be taken, capitulate, give in *or* up, give way, go out of office, pass into enemy hands, resign, succumb, surrender, yield 4. be a casualty, be killed, be lost, be slain, die, meet one's end, perish 5. become, befall, chance, come about, come to pass, fall out, happen, occur, take place 6. **fall foul of** brush with, come into con~flict with, cross swords with, have trouble with, make an enemy of 7. **fall in love (with)** become at~tached to, become enamoured of, become fond of, become infatuated (with), be smitten by, conceive an affection for, fall (for), lose one's heart (to), take a fancy to 8. fall away, incline, incline downwards, slope 9. backslide, err, go astray, lapse, offend, sin, transgress, tres~pass, yield to temptation ~*n.* 10. descent, dive, drop, nose dive, plummet, plunge, slip, spill, tumble 11. cut, decline, decrease, diminu~tion, dip, drop, dwindling, falling off, lessening, lowering, reduction, slump 12. capitulation, collapse, death, defeat, destruction, down~fall, failure, overthrow, resigna~tion, ruin, surrender 13. declivity, descent, downgrade, incline, slant, slope 14. degradation, failure, lapse, sin, slip, transgression

fallacy casuistry, deceit, deception, delusion, error, falsehood, faulti~ness, flaw, illusion, inconsistency, misapprehension, misconception, mistake, sophism, sophistry, un~truth

fall apart break up, crumble, dis~band, disintegrate, disperse, dis~solve, fall to bits, go *or* come to pieces, lose cohesion, shatter

fall asleep doze off, drop off (*Inf.*), go to sleep, nod off (*Inf.*)

fall back on call upon, employ,

have recourse to, make use of, press into service, resort to

fall behind be in arrears, drop back, get left behind, lag, lose one's place, trail

fall down disappoint, fail, fail to make the grade, fall short, go wrong, prove unsuccessful

fallen *adj.* 1. collapsed, decayed, flat, on the ground, ruinous, sunken 2. disgraced, dishonoured, immoral, loose, lost, ruined, shamed, sinful, unchaste 3. dead, killed, lost, perished, slain, slaughtered

fall for 1. become infatuated with, desire, fall in love with, lose one's head over, succumb to the charms of 2. accept, be deceived (duped, fooled, taken in) by, give credence to, swallow (*Inf.*)

fallible erring, frail, ignorant, imperfect, mortal, prone to error, uncertain, weak

fall in cave in, collapse, come down about one's ears, sink

falling off *n.* deceleration, decline, decrease, deterioration, downward trend, drop, slackening, slowing down, slump, waning, worsening

fall in with accept, agree with, assent, concur with, cooperate with, go along with, support

fall out 1. altercate, argue, clash, differ, disagree, fight, quarrel, squabble 2. chance, come to pass, happen, occur, result, take place, turn out

fallow dormant, idle, inactive, inert, resting, uncultivated, undeveloped, unplanted, untilled, unused

fall short be deficient (lacking, wanting), fail, miss, prove inadequate

fall through come to nothing, fail, fizzle out (*Inf.*), miscarry

false 1. concocted, erroneous, faulty, fictitious, improper, inaccurate, incorrect, inexact, invalid, mistaken, unfounded, unreal, wrong 2. lying, mendacious, truthless, unreliable, unsound, untrue, untrustworthy, untruthful 3. artificial, bogus, counterfeit, ersatz, fake, feigned, forged, imitation, mock, pretended, sham, simulated,

spurious, synthetic 4. deceitful, deceiving, deceptive, delusive, fallacious, fraudulent, hypocritical, misleading, trumped up 5. dishonest, dishonourable, disloyal, double-dealing, duplicitous, faithless, false-hearted, hypocritical, perfidious, treacherous, treasonable, two-faced, unfaithful, untrustworthy 6. **play** (**someone**) **false** betray, cheat, deceive, double-cross, give the Judas kiss to, sell down the river (*Inf.*), stab in the back

falsehood 1. deceit, deception, dishonesty, dissimulation, inveracity (*Rare*), mendacity, perjury, prevarication, untruthfulness 2. fabrication, fib, fiction, lie, misstatement, story, untruth

falsification adulteration, deceit, dissimulation, distortion, forgery, misrepresentation, perversion, tampering with

falsify alter, belie, cook (*Sl.*), counterfeit, distort, doctor, fake, forge, garble, misrepresent, misstate, pervert, tamper with

falter break, hesitate, shake, speak haltingly, stammer, stumble, stutter, totter, tremble, vacillate, waver

faltering broken, hesitant, irresolute, stammering, tentative, timid, uncertain, weak

fame celebrity, credit, eminence, glory, honour, illustriousness, name, prominence, public esteem, renown, reputation, repute, stardom

familiar 1. accustomed, common, common or garden (*Inf.*), conventional, customary, domestic, everyday, frequent, household, mundane, ordinary, recognizable, repeated, routine, stock, well-known 2. **familiar with** abreast of, acquainted with, at home with, *au courant, au fait,* aware of, conscious of, conversant with, introduced, knowledgeable, no stranger to, on speaking terms with, versed in, well up in 3. amicable, chummy (*Inf.*), close, confidential, cordial, easy, free, free-and-easy, friendly, hail-fellow-well-met, informal, intimate, near, open, relaxed, uncer~ emonious, unconstrained, unre~ served 4. bold, disrespectful, for~ ward, impudent, intrusive, over~ free, presuming, presumptuous

familiarity 1. acquaintance, ac~ quaintanceship, awareness, ex~ perience, grasp, understanding 2. absence of reserve, closeness, ease, fellowship, freedom, friendli~ ness, friendship, informality, inti~ macy, naturalness, openness, so~ ciability, unceremoniousness 3. boldness, disrespect, forwardness, liberties, liberty, presumption

familiarize accustom, bring into common use, coach, get to know (about), habituate, instruct, inure, make conversant, make used to, prime, school, season, train

family 1. brood, children, descend~ ants, folk (*Inf.*), household, issue, kin, kindred, kinsmen, kith and kin, ménage, offspring, one's nearest and dearest, one's own flesh and blood, people, progeny, relations, relatives 2. ancestors, ancestry, birth, blood, clan, descent, dynasty, extraction, forebears, forefathers, genealogy, house, line, lineage, parentage, pedigree, race, sept, stemma, stirps, strain, tribe 3. class, classification, genre, group, kind, network, subdivision, system

family tree ancestry, extraction, genealogy, line, lineage, line of de~ scent, pedigree, stemma, stirps

famine dearth, destitution, hunger, scarcity, starvation

famous acclaimed, celebrated, conspicuous, distinguished, emi~ nent, excellent, far-famed, glori~ ous, honoured, illustrious, legend~ ary, lionized, much-publicized, no~ table, noted, prominent, remark~ able, renowned, signal, well-known

fan[1] *v.* 1. *Often fig.* add fuel to the flames, agitate, arouse, enkindle, excite, impassion, increase, pro~ voke, rouse, stimulate, stir up, whip up, work up 2. air-condition, air-cool, blow, cool, refresh, venti~ late, winnow (*Rare*) ~*n.* 3. air conditioner, blade, blower, propel~

ler, punkah (*In India*), vane, venti~ lator

fan[2] adherent, admirer, aficionado, buff (*Inf.*), devotee, enthusiast, fiend (*Inf.*), follower, freak (*Sl.*), lover, rooter (*U.S.*), supporter, zealot

fanatic *n.* activist, addict, bigot, devotee, enthusiast, extremist, militant, visionary, zealot

fanatical bigoted, burning, enthu~ siastic, extreme, fervent, frenzied, immoderate, mad, obsessive, overenthusiastic, passionate, rabid, visionary, wild, zealous

fanciful capricious, chimerical, cu~ rious, extravagant, fabulous, fairy~ tale, fantastic, ideal, imaginary, imaginative, mythical, poetic, ro~ mantic, unreal, visionary, whimsi~ cal, wild

fancy *v.* 1. be inclined to think, believe, conceive, conjecture, guess, imagine, infer, reckon, sup~ pose, surmise, think, think likely 2. be attracted to, crave, desire, dream of, hanker after, have a yen for, long for, relish, wish for, would like, yearn for 3. *Inf.* be attracted to, be captivated by, desire, favour, go for (*Inf.*), have an eye for, like, lust after, prefer, take a liking to, take to ~*n.* 4. caprice, desire, hu~ mour, idea, impulse, inclination, notion, thought, urge, whim 5. fondness, hankering, inclination, liking, partiality, predilection, preference, relish 6. conception, image, imagination, impression 7. chimera, daydream, delusion, dream, fantasy, nightmare, phan~ tasm, vision ~*adj.* 8. baroque, decorated, decorative, elaborate, elegant, embellished, extravagant, fanciful, intricate, ornamental, or~ namented, ornate 9. capricious, chimerical, delusive, fanciful, fan~ tastic, far-fetched, illusory, whim~ sical

fanfare ballyhoo, fanfaronade, flourish, trump (*Archaic*), trumpet call, tucket (*Archaic*)

fantastic 1. comical, eccentric, exotic, fanciful, freakish, gro~ tesque, imaginative, odd, outland~

ish, peculiar, phantasmagorical, quaint, queer, rococo, strange, un~ real, weird, whimsical **2.** ambi~ tious, chimerical, extravagant, far~ fetched, grandiose, illusory, ludi~ crous, ridiculous, unrealistic, vi~ sionary, wild **3.** absurd, capricious, implausible, incredible, irrational, mad, preposterous, unlikely **4.** *Inf.* enormous, extreme, great, over~ whelming, severe, tremendous **5.** *Inf.* excellent, first-rate, marvel~ lous, out of this world (*Inf.*), sensa~ tional, superb, wonderful

fantasy, phantasy 1. creativity, fancy, imagination, invention, originality **2.** apparition, day~ dream, delusion, dream, fancy, figment of the imagination, flight of fancy, hallucination, illusion, mirage, nightmare, pipe dream, reverie, vision

far *adv.* **1.** afar, a good way, a great distance, a long way, deep, miles **2.** considerably, decidedly, extreme~ ly, greatly, incomparably, much, very much **3. by far** by a long chalk (*Inf.*), by a long shot, by a long way, easily, far and away, im~ measurably, incomparably, to a great degree, very much **4. far and wide** broadly, everywhere, exten~ sively, far and near, here, there, and everywhere, widely, world~ wide **5. so far** thus far, to date, until now, up to now, up to the present ~*adj.* **6.** distant, faraway, far-flung, far-off, far-removed, long, outlying, out-of-the-way, remote, removed

faraway 1. beyond the horizon, distant, far, far-flung, far-off, far~ removed, outlying, remote **2.** ab~ sent, abstracted, distant, dreamy, lost

farce 1. broad comedy, buffoonery, burlesque, comedy, satire, slap~ stick **2.** absurdity, joke, mockery, nonsense, parody, ridiculousness, sham, travesty

farcical absurd, amusing, comic, custard-pie, derisory, diverting, droll, funny, laughable, ludicrous, nonsensical, preposterous, ridicu~ lous, risible, slapstick

fare *n.* **1.** charge, passage money, price, ticket money, transport cost **2.** passenger, pick-up (*Inf.*), travel~ ler **3.** commons, diet, eatables, food, meals, menu, provisions, ra~ tions, sustenance, table, victuals ~*v.* **4.** do, get along, get on, make out, manage, prosper **5.** *Used im~ personally* go, happen, proceed, turn out

farewell adieu, adieux *or* adieus, departure, goodbye, leave-taking, parting, sendoff (*Inf.*), valediction

far-fetched doubtful, dubious, fan~ tastic, hard to swallow (*Inf.*), im~ plausible, improbable, incredible, preposterous, strained, unbeliev~ able, unconvincing, unlikely, un~ natural, unrealistic

farm 1. *n.* acreage, acres, croft (*Scot.*), farmstead, grange, holding, homestead, land, plantation, ranch (*Chiefly North American*), small~ holding, station (*Aust. & New Zea~ land*) **2.** *v.* bring under cultivation, cultivate, operate, plant, practise husbandry, till the soil, work

farmer agriculturist, agronomist, husbandman, smallholder, yeoman

farming agriculture, agronomy, husbandry

far-reaching broad, extensive, im~ portant, momentous, pervasive, significant, sweeping, widespread

far-sighted acute, canny, cautious, discerning, far-seeing, judicious, politic, prescient, provident, pru~ dent, sage, shrewd, wise

fascinate absorb, allure, beguile, bewitch, captivate, charm, delight, enamour, enchant, engross, en~ rapture, enravish, enthral, en~ trance, hold spellbound, hypnotize, infatuate, intrigue, mesmerize, rivet, spellbind, transfix

fascinated absorbed, beguiled, be~ witched, captivated, charmed, en~ grossed, enthralled, entranced, hooked on, hypnotized, infatuated, smitten, spellbound, under a spell

fascinating alluring, bewitching, captivating, compelling, enchant~ ing, engaging, engrossing, enticing, gripping, intriguing, irresistible, ravishing, riveting, seductive

fascination allure, attraction, charm, enchantment, glamour, lure, magic, magnetism, pull, sor~ cery, spell

fashion *n.* 1. convention, craze, custom, fad, latest, latest style, look, mode, prevailing taste, rage, style, trend, usage, vogue 2. atti~ tude, demeanour, manner, method, mode, style, way 3. appearance, configuration, cut, figure, form, guise (*Archaic*), line, make, model, mould, pattern, shape 4. descrip~ tion, kind, sort, type 5. beau monde, fashionable society, high society, jet set 6. **after a fashion** in a manner of speaking, in a way, moderately, somehow, somehow or other, to a degree, to some ex~ tent ~*v.* 7. construct, contrive, create, design, forge, form, make, manufacture, mould, shape, work 8. accommodate, adapt, adjust, fit, suit, tailor

fashionable à la mode, all the go (*Inf.*), all the rage, chic, current, customary, genteel, in (*Inf.*), in vogue, latest, modern, modish, popular, prevailing, smart, stylish, trendsetting, trendy (*Inf.*), up-to-date, up-to-the-minute, usual, with it (*Inf.*)

fast *adj.* 1. accelerated, brisk, fleet, flying, hasty, hurried, mercurial, nippy (*Inf.*), quick, rapid, speedy, swift, winged ~*adv.* 2. apace, hastily, hell for leather, hurriedly, in haste, like a bat out of hell (*Inf.*), like a flash, like a shot (*Inf.*), post~ haste, presto, quickly, rapidly, speedily, swiftly, with all haste ~*adj.* 3. close, constant, fastened, firm, fixed, fortified, immovable, impregnable, lasting, loyal, per~ manent, secure, sound, staunch, steadfast, tight, unwavering ~*adv.* 4. deeply, firmly, fixedly, securely, soundly, tightly ~*adj.* 5. dissipated, dissolute, extravagant, gadabout, giddy, immoral, intemperate, li~ centious, loose, profligate, promis~ cuous, rakish, reckless, self-indulgent, wanton, wild ~*adv.* 6. extravagantly, intemperately, loosely, promiscuously, rakishly, recklessly, wildly 7. **pull a fast one**

bamboozle (*Inf.*), cheat, con (*Sl.*), deceive, defraud, hoodwink, put one over on (*Inf.*), swindle, take advantage of, take for a ride (*Inf.*), trick

fasten 1. affix, anchor, attach, bind, bolt, chain, connect, fix, grip, join, lace, link, lock, make fast, make firm, seal, secure, tie, unite 2. *Fig.* aim, bend, concentrate, direct, fix, focus, rivet

fat *adj.* 1. beefy (*Inf.*), broad in the beam (*Inf.*), corpulent, elephan~ tine, fleshy, gross, heavy, obese, overweight, plump, podgy, portly, roly-poly, rotund, solid, stout, tubby 2. adipose, fatty, greasy, oily, oleaginous, suety (*Sl.*) 3. affluent, cushy (*Sl.*), fertile, flourishing, fruitful, jammy (*Sl.*), lucrative, lush, pro~ ductive, profitable, prosperous, re~ munerative, rich, thriving ~*n.* 4. adipose tissue, blubber, bulk, cel~ lulite, corpulence, fatness, flab, flesh, obesity, overweight, paunch, weight problem

fatal 1. deadly, destructive, final, incurable, killing, lethal, malig~ nant, mortal, pernicious, terminal 2. baleful, baneful, calamitous, catastrophic, disastrous, lethal, ru~ inous 3. critical, crucial, decisive, destined, determining, doomed, fateful, final, foreordained, inevi~ table, predestined

fatality casualty, deadliness, death, disaster, fatal accident, lethalness, loss, mortality

fate 1. chance, destiny, divine will, fortune, kismet, nemesis, predesti~ nation, providence, weird (*Archa~ ic*) 2. cup, fortune, horoscope, lot, portion, stars 3. end, future, issue, outcome, upshot 4. death, destruc~ tion, doom, downfall, end, ruin

fated destined, doomed, foreor~ dained, ineluctable, inescapable, inevitable, marked down, predes~ tined, pre-elected, preordained, sure, written

fateful 1. critical, crucial, decisive, important, portentous, significant 2. deadly, destructive, disastrous, fatal, lethal, ominous, ruinous

father *n.* 1. begetter, dad (*Inf.*),

daddy (*Inf.*), governor (*Inf.*), old boy (*Inf.*), old man (*Inf.*), pa (*Inf.*), pater, paterfamilias, patriarch, pop (*Inf.*), sire 2. ancestor, forebear, forefather, predecessor, progenitor 3. architect, author, creator, founder, inventor, maker, originator, prime mover 4. city father, elder, leader, patriarch, patron, senator 5. abbé, confessor, curé, padre (*Inf.*), pastor, priest ~*v.* 6. beget, get, procreate, sire 7. create, engender, establish, found, institute, invent, originate

fatherland homeland, land of one's birth, land of one's fathers, motherland, native land, old country

fatherly affectionate, benevolent, benign, forbearing, indulgent, kind, kindly, paternal, patriarchal, protective, supportive, tender

fathom 1. divine, estimate, gauge, measure, penetrate, plumb, probe, sound 2. comprehend, get to the bottom of, grasp, interpret, understand

fatigue 1. *v.* drain, drain of energy, exhaust, fag (out) (*Inf.*), jade, overtire, take it out of (*Inf.*), tire, weaken, wear out, weary, whack (*Inf.*) 2. *n.* debility, ennui, heaviness, languor, lethargy, listlessness, overtiredness, tiredness

fatten 1. broaden, coarsen, expand, gain weight, grow fat, put on weight, spread, swell, thicken, thrive 2. *Often with* **up** bloat, build up, cram, distend, feed, feed up, nourish, overfeed, stuff

fatuous absurd, asinine, brainless, dense, dull, foolish, idiotic, inane, ludicrous, lunatic, mindless, moronic, puerile, silly, stupid, vacuous, weak-minded, witless

fault *n.* 1. blemish, defect, deficiency, drawback, failing, flaw, imperfection, infirmity, lack, shortcoming, snag, weakness, weak point 2. blunder, boob (*Sl.*), error, error of judgment, inaccuracy, indiscretion, lapse, mistake, negligence, offence, omission, oversight, slip, slip-up 3. accountability, culpability, liability, responsibility

4. delinquency, frailty, lapse, misconduct, misdeed, misdemeanour, offence, peccadillo, sin, transgression, trespass, wrong 5. **at fault** answerable, blamable, culpable, guilty, in the wrong, responsible, to blame 6. **find fault with** carp at, complain, criticize, pick holes in, pull to pieces, quibble, take to task 7. **to a fault** excessively, immoderately, in the extreme, needlessly, out of all proportion, overly (*U.S.*), overmuch, preposterously, ridiculously, unduly ~*v.* 8. blame, call to account, censure, criticize, find fault with, find lacking, hold (someone) accountable (responsible, to blame), impugn

fault-finding 1. *n.* carping, hairsplitting, nagging, niggling, nitpicking (*Inf.*) 2. *adj.* captious, carping, censorious, critical, hypercritical, pettifogging

faultless 1. accurate, classic, correct, exemplary, faithful, flawless, foolproof, impeccable, model, perfect, unblemished 2. above reproach, blameless, guiltless, immaculate, innocent, irreproachable, pure, sinless, spotless, stainless, unblemished, unspotted, unsullied

faulty bad, blemished, broken, damaged, defective, erroneous, fallacious, flawed, impaired, imperfect, imprecise, inaccurate, incorrect, invalid, malfunctioning, not working, out of order, unsound, weak, wrong

faux pas blunder, boob (*Sl.*), breach of etiquette, clanger (*Inf.*), gaffe, gaucherie, impropriety, indiscretion, solecism

favour *n.* 1. approbation, approval, backing, bias, championship, esteem, favouritism, friendliness, good opinion, good will, grace, kindness, kind regard, partiality, patronage, support 2. benefit, boon, courtesy, good turn, indulgence, kindness, obligement (*Scot. or Archaic*), service 3. **in favour of** all for (*Inf.*), backing, for, on the side of, pro, supporting, to the benefit of 4. gift, keepsake, love-token, memento, present, souvenir, token 5. badge, decoration, knot, ribbons, rosette ~v. 6. be partial to, esteem, have in one's good books, indulge, pamper, pull strings for (*Inf.*), reward, side with, smile upon, spoil, treat with partiality, value 7. advocate, approve, back, be in favour of, champion, choose, commend, countenance, encourage, fancy, incline towards, like, opt for, patronize, prefer, single out, support 8. abet, accommodate, advance, aid, assist, befriend, do a kindness to, facilitate, help, oblige, promote, succour 9. *Inf.* be the image *or* picture of, look like, resemble, take after 10. ease, extenuate, spare

favourable 1. advantageous, appropriate, auspicious, beneficial, convenient, encouraging, fair, fit, good, helpful, hopeful, opportune, promising, propitious, suitable, timely 2. affirmative, agreeable, amicable, approving, benign, encouraging, enthusiastic, friendly, kind, positive, reassuring, sympathetic, understanding, welcoming, well-disposed

favourably 1. advantageously, auspiciously, conveniently, fortunately, opportunely, profitably, to one's advantage, well 2. agreeably, approvingly, enthusiastically, genially, graciously, helpfully, in a kindly manner, positively, with approval (approbation, cordiality), without prejudice

favourite 1. *adj.* best-loved, choice, dearest, esteemed, preferred 2. *n.* beloved, blue-eyed boy (*Inf.*), choice, darling, dear, idol, pet, pick, preference, teacher's pet, the apple of one's eye

favouritism bias, jobs for the boys (*Inf.*), nepotism, one-sidedness, partiality, partisanship, preference, preferential treatment

fawn[1] *adj.* beige, buff, greyish-brown, neutral

fawn[2] *v. Often with* **on** *or* **upon** be obsequious, be servile, bow and scrape, court, crawl, creep, cringe, curry favour, dance attendance, flatter, grovel, ingratiate oneself, kneel, kowtow, lick (someone's) boots, pay court, toady, truckle

fawning abject, bootlicking (*Inf.*), bowing and scraping, crawling, cringing, deferential, flattering, grovelling, obsequious, prostrate, servile, slavish, sycophantic

fear *n.* 1. alarm, apprehensiveness, awe, blue funk (*Inf.*), consternation, cravenness, dismay, dread, fright, horror, panic, qualms, terror, timidity, tremors, trepidation 2. *bête noire*, bogey, bugbear, horror, nightmare, phobia, spectre 3. agitation, anxiety, apprehension, concern, disquietude, distress, doubt, foreboding(s), misgiving(s), solicitude, suspicion, unease, uneasiness, worry 4. awe, reverence, veneration, wonder ~v. 5. apprehend, be apprehensive (afraid, frightened, scared), be in a blue funk (*Inf.*), dare not, dread, have a horror of, have a phobia about, have butterflies in one's stomach (*Inf.*), have qualms, live in dread of, shake in one's shoes, shudder at, take fright, tremble at 6. anticipate, apprehend, be afraid, expect, foresee, suspect 7. *With* **for** be anxious (concerned, distressed) about, be disquieted over, feel concern for, tremble for, worry about 8. respect, revere, reverence, stand in awe of, venerate

fearful 1. afraid, alarmed, anxious, apprehensive, diffident, faint-hearted, frightened, hesitant, intimidated, jittery (*Inf.*), jumpy, nervous, nervy, panicky, pusillanimous, scared, shrinking, tense, timid, timorous, uneasy 2. appalling, atrocious, awful, dire, distressing, dreadful, frightful, ghastly, grievous, grim, gruesome, hair-raising, hideous, horrendous, horrible, horrific, monstrous, shocking, terrible, unspeakable

fearfully 1. apprehensively, diffidently, in fear and trembling, nervously, timidly, timorously, uneasily, with many misgivings *or* forebodings, with one's heart in one's mouth 2. awfully, exceedingly, excessively, frightfully, terribly, tremendously, very

fearless bold, brave, confident, courageous, daring, dauntless, doughty, gallant, game (*Inf.*), gutsy (*Sl.*), heroic, indomitable, intrepid, lion-hearted, plucky, unabashed, unafraid, undaunted, unflinching, valiant, valorous

fearlessness boldness, bravery, confidence, courage, dauntlessness, guts (*Inf.*), indomitability, intrepidity, lion-heartedness, nerve, pluckiness

fearsome alarming, appalling, awe-inspiring, awesome, awful, daunting, dismaying, formidable, frightening, hair-raising, horrendous, horrifying, menacing, unnerving

feasibility expediency, practicability, usefulness, viability, workability

feasible achievable, attainable, likely, possible, practicable, realizable, reasonable, viable, workable

feast *n.* 1. banquet, barbecue, beanfeast (*Brit. inf.*), beano (*Brit. sl.*), blowout (*Sl.*), carousal, carouse, dinner, entertainment, festive board, jollification, junket, repast, revels, slap-up meal (*Brit. inf.*), spread (*Inf.*), treat 2. celebration, festival, fête, gala day, holiday, holy day, saint's day 3. delight, enjoyment, gratification, pleasure, treat ~*v.* 4. eat one's fill, eat to one's heart's content, fare sumptuously, gorge, gormandize, indulge, overindulge, stuff, stuff one's face (*Sl.*), wine and dine 5. entertain, hold a reception for, kill the fatted calf for, regale, treat, wine and dine 6. delight, gladden, gratify, rejoice, thrill

feat accomplishment, achievement, act, attainment, deed, exploit, performance

feathers down, plumage, plumes

feathery downy, feathered, fluffy, plumate *or* plumose (*Bot. & Zool.*), plumed, plumy, wispy

feature *n.* 1. aspect, attribute, characteristic, facet, factor, hallmark, mark, peculiarity, point, property, quality, trait 2. attraction, crowd puller (*Inf.*), draw, highlight, innovation, main item, special, special attraction, speciality, specialty 3. article, column, comment, item, piece, report, story ~*v.* 4. accentuate, call attention to, emphasize, give prominence to, give the full works (*Sl.*), headline, play up, present, promote, set off, spotlight, star

features countenance, face, lineaments, physiognomy

feckless aimless, feeble, futile, hopeless, incompetent, ineffectual, irresponsible, shiftless, useless, weak, worthless

federate *v.* amalgamate, associate, combine, confederate, integrate, syndicate, unify, unite

federation alliance, amalgamation, association, *Bund*, coalition, combination, confederacy, copartnership, entente, federacy, league, syndicate, union

fed up (with) annoyed, blue, bored, brassed off (*Inf.*), browned-off (*Inf.*), depressed, discontented, dismal, dissatisfied, down, gloomy, glum, sick and tired of (*Inf.*), tired of, weary of

fee account, bill, charge, compensation, emolument, hire, honorarium, pay, payment, recompense, remuneration, reward, toll

feeble 1. debilitated, delicate, doddering, effete, enervated, enfeebled, etiolated, exhausted, failing, faint, frail, infirm, languid, powerless, puny, shilpit (*Scot.*), sickly, weak, weakened 2. flat, flimsy, inadequate, incompetent, indecisive, ineffective, ineffectual, inefficient, insignificant, insufficient, lame, paltry, poor, slight, tame, thin, unconvincing, weak

feeble-minded addle-pated, bone-headed (*Sl.*), deficient, dim-witted (*Inf.*), dull, dumb (*Inf.*), half-witted, idiotic, imbecilic, lacking, moronic, retarded, simple, slow on the uptake, slow-witted, soft in the head (*Inf.*), stupid, vacant, weak-minded

feebleness 1. debility, delicacy, effeteness, enervation, etiolation, exhaustion, frailness, frailty, incapacity, infirmity, lack of strength, languor, lassitude, sickliness, weakness 2. flimsiness, inadequa~ cy, incompetence, indecisiveness, ineffectualness, insignificance, in~ sufficiency, lameness, weakness

feed v. 1. cater for, nourish, provide for, provision, supply, sustain, vict~ ual, wine and dine 2. *Sometimes with on* devour, eat, exist on, fare, graze, live on, nurture, partake of, pasture, subsist, take nourishment 3. augment, bolster, encourage, foster, fuel, minister to, strengthen, supply ~n. 4. fodder, food, forage, pasturage, provender, silage 5. *Inf.* feast, meal, nosh (*Sl.*), nosh-up (*Brit. sl.*), repast, spread (*Inf.*), tuck-in (*Inf.*)

feel v. 1. caress, finger, fondle, handle, manipulate, maul, paw, run one's hands over, stroke, touch 2. be aware of, be sensible of, endure, enjoy, experience, go through, have, have a sensation of, know, notice, observe, perceive, suffer, take to heart, undergo 3. explore, fumble, grope, sound, test, try 4. be convinced, feel in one's bones, have a hunch, have the impres~ sion, intuit, sense 5. believe, be of the opinion that, consider, deem, hold, judge, think 6. appear, re~ semble, seem, strike one as 7. *With for* be moved by, be sorry for, bleed for, commiserate, compas~ sionate, condole with, empathize, feel compassion for, pity, sympa~ thize with 8. **feel like** could do with, desire, fancy, feel inclined, feel the need for, feel up to, have the inclination, want ~n. 9. finish, surface, texture, touch 10. air, am~ bience, atmosphere, feeling, im~ pression, quality, sense, vibes (*Inf.*)

feeler 1. antenna, tentacle, whisker 2. advance, approach, probe, trial balloon

feeling 1. feel, perception, sensa~ tion, sense, sense of touch, touch 2. apprehension, consciousness, hunch, idea, impression, inkling, notion, presentiment, sense, suspi~ cion 3. affection, ardour, emotion, fervour, fondness, heat, intensity, passion, sentiment, sentimentality, warmth 4. appreciation, compas~

sion, concern, empathy, pity, sen~ sibility, sensitivity, sympathy, understanding 5. inclination, in~ stinct, opinion, point of view, view 6. air, ambience, atmosphere, aura, feel, mood, quality 7. **bad feeling** anger, dislike, distrust, en~ mity, hostility, upset

feelings ego, emotions, self~ esteem, sensitivities, susceptibil~ ities

feline 1. catlike, leonine 2. graceful, sinuous, sleek, slinky, smooth, stealthy

fell v. cut, cut down, demolish, flat~ ten, floor, hew, knock down, level, prostrate, raze, strike down

fellow n. 1. bloke (*Inf.*), boy, chap (*Inf.*), character, customer (*Inf.*), guy (*Inf.*), individual, man, person 2. associate, colleague, companion, compeer, comrade, co-worker, equal, friend, member, partner, peer 3. brother, counterpart, dou~ ble, duplicate, match, mate, twin ~adj. 4. affiliated, akin, allied, as~ sociate, associated, co-, like, relat~ ed, similar

fellowship 1. amity, brotherhood, camaraderie, communion, com~ panionability, companionship, fa~ miliarity, fraternization, inter~ course, intimacy, kindliness, so~ ciability 2. association, brother~ hood, club, fraternity, guild, league, order, sisterhood, society, sodality

feminine 1. delicate, gentle, girlish, graceful, ladylike, modest, soft, tender, womanly 2. effeminate, ef~ fete, unmanly, unmasculine, weak, womanish

femme fatale charmer, Circe, en~ chantress, seductress, siren, vamp (*Inf.*)

fen bog, holm (*Dialect*), marsh, morass, moss (*Scot.*), quagmire, slough, swamp

fence n. 1. barbed wire, barricade, barrier, defence, guard, hedge, paling, palisade, railings, rampart, shield, stockade, wall 2. **on the fence** between two stools, irreso~ lute, uncertain, uncommitted, un~ decided, vacillating ~v. 3. *Often with in or off* bound, circumscribe, confine, coop, defend, encircle, enclose, fortify, guard, hedge, pen, protect, restrict, secure, separate, surround 4. beat about the bush, cavil, dodge, equivocate, evade, hedge, parry, prevaricate, quibble, shift, stonewall, tergiversate

fencing *Fig.* beating about the bush, double talk, equivocation, evasiveness, hedging, parrying, prevarication, quibbling, stone~ walling, tergiversation, weasel words (*Inf., chiefly U.S.*)

ferment *v.* 1. boil, brew, bubble, concoct, effervesce, foam, froth, heat, leaven, rise, seethe, work ~*n.* 2. bacteria, barm, fermentation agent, leaven, leavening, mother, mother-of-vinegar, yeast ~*v.* 3. *Fig.* agitate, boil, excite, fester, fo~ ment, heat, incite, inflame, pro~ voke, rouse, seethe, smoulder, stir up ~*n.* 4. *Fig.* agitation, brouhaha, commotion, disruption, excite~ ment, fever, frenzy, furore, glow, heat, hubbub, imbroglio, state of unrest, stew, stir, tumult, turbu~ lence, turmoil, unrest, uproar

ferocious 1. feral, fierce, preda~ tory, rapacious, ravening, savage, violent, wild 2. barbaric, barba~ rous, bloodthirsty, brutal, brutish, cruel, merciless, pitiless, relent~ less, ruthless, tigerish, vicious

ferocity barbarity, bloodthirstiness, brutality, cruelty, ferociousness, fierceness, inhumanity, rapacity, ruthlessness, savageness, savage~ ry, viciousness, wildness

ferret out bring to light, dig up, disclose, discover, drive out, elicit, get at, nose out, root out, run to earth, search out, smell out, trace, track down, unearth

ferry 1. *n.* ferryboat, packet, packet boat 2. *v.* carry, chauffeur, convey, run, ship, shuttle, transport

fertile abundant, fat, fecund, flow~ ering, flowing with milk and hon~ ey, fruit-bearing, fruitful, genera~ tive, luxuriant, plenteous, plentiful, productive, prolific, rich, teeming, yielding

fertility abundance, fecundity,

fruitfulness, luxuriance, produc~ tiveness, richness

fertilize 1. fecundate, fructify, im~ pregnate, inseminate, make fruit~ ful, make pregnant, pollinate 2. compost, dress, enrich, feed, ma~ nure, mulch, top-dress

fertilizer compost, dressing, dung, guano, manure, marl

fervent, fervid animated, ardent, devout, eager, earnest, ecstatic, emotional, enthusiastic, excited, fiery, heartfelt, impassioned, in~ tense, perfervid (*Literary*), vehe~ ment, warm, zealous

fervour animation, ardour, eager~ ness, earnestness, enthusiasm, ex~ citement, fervency, intensity, pas~ sion, vehemence, warmth, zeal

festival 1. anniversary, com~ memoration, feast, fête, fiesta, holiday, holy day, saint's day 2. carnival, celebration, entertain~ ment, festivities, fête, field day, gala, jubilee, treat

festive back-slapping, carnival, celebratory, cheery, Christmassy, convivial, festal, gala, gay, gleeful, happy, hearty, holiday, jolly, jovial, joyful, joyous, jubilant, light~ hearted, merry, mirthful, sportive

festivity 1. amusement, convivial~ ity, fun, gaiety, jollification, jovial~ ity, joyfulness, merriment, merry~ making, mirth, pleasure, revelry, sport 2. *Often plural* carousal, cel~ ebration, entertainment, festival, festive event, festive proceedings, fun and games, jollification, party

festoon 1. *n.* chaplet, garland, lei, swag, swathe, wreath 2. *v.* array, bedeck, beribbon, deck, decorate, drape, garland, hang, swathe, wreathe

fetch 1. bring, carry, conduct, con~ vey, deliver, escort, get, go for, lead, obtain, retrieve, transport 2. draw forth, elicit, give rise to, pro~ duce 3. bring in, earn, go for, make, realize, sell for, yield

fetching alluring, attractive, capti~ vating, charming, cute, enchant~ ing, enticing, fascinating, intrigu~ ing, sweet, taking, winsome

fête, fete 1. *n.* bazaar, fair, festival,

gala, garden party, sale of work 2. v. bring out the red carpet for (someone), entertain regally, hold a reception for (someone), honour, kill the fatted calf for (someone), lionize, make much of, treat, wine and dine

fetish 1. amulet, cult object, talisman 2. fixation, *idée fixe*, mania, obsession, thing (*Inf.*)

feud 1. *n.* argument, bad blood, bickering, broil, conflict, contention, disagreement, discord, dissension, enmity, estrangement, faction, falling out, grudge, hostility, quarrel, rivalry, strife, vendetta 2. *v.* be at daggers drawn, be at odds, bicker, brawl, clash, contend, dispute, duel, fall out, quarrel, row, squabble, war

fever *Fig.* agitation, delirium, ecstasy, excitement, ferment, fervour, flush, frenzy, heat, intensity, passion, restlessness, turmoil, unrest

feverish 1. burning, febrile, fevered, flushed, hectic, hot, inflamed, pyretic (*Medical*) 2. agitated, distracted, excited, frantic, frenetic, frenzied, impatient, obsessive, overwrought, restless

few *adj.* 1. hardly any, inconsiderable, infrequent, insufficient, meagre, negligible, not many, rare, scant, scanty, scarce, scarcely any, scattered, sparse, sporadic, thin 2. **few and far between** at great intervals, hard to come by, infrequent, in short supply, irregular, rare, scarce, scattered, seldom met with, uncommon, unusual, widely spaced ~*pron.* 3. handful, scarcely any, scattering, small number, some

fiancé, fiancée betrothed, intended, prospective spouse, wife- *or* husband-to-be

fiasco catastrophe, debacle, disaster, failure, flap (*Inf.*), mess, rout, ruin, washout (*Inf.*)

fib *n.* fiction, lie, prevarication, story, untruth, white lie, whopper (*Inf.*)

fibre 1. fibril, filament, pile, staple, strand, texture, thread 2. *Fig.* essence, nature, quality, spirit, substance 3. *Fig., as in* moral fibre resolution, stamina, strength, strength of character, toughness

fickle blowing hot and cold, capricious, changeable, faithless, fitful, flighty, inconstant, irresolute, mercurial, mutable, quicksilver, unfaithful, unpredictable, unstable, unsteady, vacillating, variable, volatile

fickleness capriciousness, fitfulness, flightiness, inconstancy, mutability, unfaithfulness, unpredictability, unsteadiness, volatility

fiction 1. fable, fantasy, legend, myth, novel, romance, story, storytelling, tale, work of imagination, yarn (*Inf.*) 2. cock and bull story (*Inf.*), concoction, fabrication, falsehood, fancy, fantasy, figment of the imagination, imagination, improvisation, invention, lie, tall story, untruth

fictional imaginary, invented, legendary, made-up, nonexistent, unreal

fictitious apocryphal, artificial, assumed, bogus, counterfeit, fabricated, false, fanciful, feigned, imaginary, imagined, improvised, invented, made-up, make-believe, mythical, spurious, unreal, untrue

fiddle *v.* 1. *Often with with* fidget, finger, interfere with, mess about *or* around, play, tamper with, tinker, toy, trifle 2. *Inf.* cheat, cook the books, diddle (*Inf.*), finagle (*Inf.*), fix, gerrymander, graft, manoeuvre, racketeer, swindle, wangle (*Inf.*) ~*n.* 3. violin 4. **fit as a fiddle** blooming, hale and hearty, healthy, in fine fettle, in good form, in good shape, in rude health, in the pink, sound, strong 5. *Inf.* fix, fraud, graft, piece of sharp practice, racket, swindle, wangle (*Inf.*)

fiddling futile, insignificant, pettifogging, petty, trifling, trivial

fidelity 1. allegiance, constancy, dependability, devotedness, devotion, faith, faithfulness, fealty, integrity, lealty (*Archaic or Scot.*), loyalty, staunchness, trueheartedness, trustworthiness 2.

accuracy, adherence, closeness, correspondence, exactitude, exactness, faithfulness, preciseness, precision, scrupulousness

fidget 1. *v.* be like a cat on hot bricks (*Inf.*), bustle, chafe, fiddle, fret, jiggle, jitter (*Inf.*), move restlessly, squirm, twitch, worry 2. *n. Usually* the fidgets fidgetiness, jitters (*Inf.*), nervousness, restlessness, unease, uneasiness

fidgety impatient, jerky, jittery (*Inf.*), jumpy, nervous, on edge, restive, restless, twitchy, uneasy

field *n.* 1. grassland, green, greensward (*Archaic*), lea (*Literary*), mead (*Archaic*), meadow, pasture 2. applicants, candidates, competition, competitors, contestants, entrants, possibilities, runners 3. area, bailiwick, bounds, confines, department, discipline, domain, environment, limits, line, metier, province, purview, range, scope, speciality, specialty, sphere of influence (activity, interest, study), territory ~*v.* 4. catch, pick up, retrieve, return, stop 5. *Fig.* deal with, deflect, handle, turn aside

fiend 1. demon, devil, evil spirit, hellhound 2. barbarian, beast, brute, degenerate, monster, ogre, savage 3. *Inf.* addict, enthusiast, fanatic, freak (*Sl.*), maniac

fiendish accursed, atrocious, black-hearted, cruel, demoniac, devilish, diabolical, hellish, implacable, infernal, inhuman, malevolent, malicious, malignant, monstrous, satanic, savage, ungodly, unspeakable, wicked

fierce 1. barbarous, brutal, cruel, dangerous, fell (*Archaic*), feral, ferocious, fiery, menacing, murderous, passionate, savage, threatening, tigerish, truculent, uncontrollable, untamed, vicious, wild 2. blustery, boisterous, furious, howling, powerful, raging, stormy, strong, tempestuous, tumultuous, uncontrollable, violent 3. cutthroat, intense, keen, relentless, strong

fiercely ferociously, frenziedly, furiously, in a frenzy, like cat and dog, menacingly, passionately, savagely, tempestuously, tigerishly, tooth and nail, uncontrolledly, viciously, with bared teeth, with no holds barred

fight *v.* 1. assault, battle, bear arms against, box, brawl, carry on war, clash, close, combat, come to blows, conflict, contend, cross swords, do battle, engage, engage in hostilities, exchange blows, feud, go to war, grapple, joust, scrap (*Inf.*), spar, struggle, take the field, take up arms against, tilt, tussle, wage war, war, wrestle 2. contest, defy, dispute, make a stand against, oppose, resist, stand up to, strive, struggle, withstand 3. argue, bicker, dispute, fall out (*Inf.*), squabble, wrangle 4. carry on, conduct, engage in, prosecute, wage 5. **fight shy of** avoid, duck out of (*Inf.*), keep aloof from, keep at arm's length, shun, steer clear of ~*n.* 6. action, affray (*Law*), altercation, battle, bout, brawl, brush, clash, combat, conflict, contest, dispute, dissension, dogfight, duel, encounter, engagement, exchange of blows, fracas, fray, free-for-all (*Inf.*), hostilities, joust, melee, passage of arms, riot, row, rumble (*U.S. sl.*), scrap (*Inf.*), scuffle, set-to (*Inf.*), skirmish, sparring match, struggle, tussle, war 7. *Fig.* belligerence, gameness, mettle, militancy, pluck, resistance, spirit, will to resist

fight back 1. defend oneself, give tit for tat, put up a fight, reply, resist, retaliate 2. bottle up, contain, control, curb, hold back, hold in check, restrain

fight down bottle up, control, curb, hold back, repress, restrain, suppress

fighter 1. fighting man, man-at-arms, soldier, warrior 2. boxer, bruiser (*Inf.*), prize fighter, pugilist 3. antagonist, battler, belligerent, combatant, contender, contestant, disputant, militant

fighting 1. *adj.* aggressive, argumentative, bellicose, belligerent, combative, contentious, disputatious, hawkish, martial, militant, pugnacious, sabre-rattling, trucu~ lent, warlike 2. *n.* battle, bloodshed, blows struck, combat, conflict, hostilities, warfare

fight off beat off, keep *or* hold at bay, repel, repress, repulse, resist, stave off, ward off

figure *n.* 1. character, cipher, digit, number, numeral, symbol 2. amount, cost, price, sum, total, value 3. form, outline, shadow, shape, silhouette 4. body, build, chassis (*Sl.*), frame, physique, pro~ portions, shape, torso 5. depiction, design, device, diagram, drawing, emblem, illustration, motif, pat~ tern, representation, sketch 6. ce~ lebrity, character, dignitary, force, leader, notability, notable, person~ age, personality, presence, some~ body, worthy ~*v.* 7. *Often with up* add, calculate, compute, count, reckon, sum, tally, tot up, work out 8. *Usually with in* act, appear, be conspicuous, be featured, be in~ cluded, be mentioned, contribute to, feature, have a place in, play a part 9. **it figures** it follows, it goes without saying, it is to be expected

figurehead cipher, dummy, front man (*Inf.*), leader in name only, man of straw, mouthpiece, name, nonentity, puppet, straw man (*Chiefly U.S.*), titular *or* nominal head, token

figure of speech conceit, image, trope, turn of phrase

figure out 1. calculate, compute, reckon, work out 2. comprehend, decipher, fathom, make head or tail of (*Inf.*), make out, resolve, see, understand

filament cilium (*Biol. & Zool.*), fi~ bre, fibril, pile, staple, strand, string, thread, wire

filch abstract, crib (*Inf.*), embezzle, half-inch (*Sl.*), lift (*Inf.*), misappro~ priate, nick (*Sl.*), pilfer, pinch (*Inf.*), purloin, rip off (*Sl.*), snaffle (*Inf.*), steal, swipe (*Sl.*), take, thieve, walk off with

file[1] *v.* abrade, burnish, furbish, polish, rasp, refine, rub, rub down, scrape, shape, smooth

file[2] *n.* 1. case, data, documents, dossier, folder, information, port~ folio ~*v.* 2. document, enter, pigeonhole, put in place, record, register, slot in ~*n.* 3. column, line, list, queue, row, string ~*v.* 4. march, parade, troop

filibuster *n.* 1. *Chiefly U.S., with reference to legislation* delay, hin~ drance, obstruction, postponement, procrastination ~*v.* 2. *Chiefly U.S., with reference to legislation* delay, hinder, obstruct, prevent, procras~ tinate, put off ~*n.* 3. adventurer, buccaneer, corsair, freebooter, pi~ rate, sea robber, sea rover, soldier of fortune

fill 1. brim over, cram, crowd, fur~ nish, glut, gorge, inflate, pack, per~ vade, replenish, sate, satiate, satis~ fy, stock, store, stuff, supply, swell 2. charge, imbue, impregnate, overspread, pervade, saturate, suffuse 3. block, bung, close, cork, plug, seal, stop 4. assign, carry out, discharge, engage, execute, fulfil, hold, occupy, officiate, perform, take up 5. **one's fill** all one wants, ample, a sufficiency, enough, plen~ ty, sufficient

fill in 1. answer, complete, fill out (*U.S.*), fill up 2. *Inf.* acquaint, ap~ prise, bring up to date, give the facts *or* background, inform, put wise (*Sl.*) 3. deputize, replace, rep~ resent, stand in, sub, substitute, take the place of

filling 1. *n.* contents, filler, innards (*Inf.*), inside, insides, padding, stuffing, wadding 2. *adj.* ample, heavy, satisfying, square, substan~ tial

film *n.* 1. coat, coating, covering, dusting, gauze, integument, layer, membrane, pellicle, scum, skin, tissue 2. blur, cloud, haze, haziness, mist, mistiness, opacity, veil 3. flick (*Sl.*), motion picture, movie (*U.S. inf.*) ~*v.* 4. photograph, shoot, take 5. *Often with over* blear, blur, cloud, dull, haze, mist, veil

filmy 1. chiffon, cobwebby, delicate, diaphanous, fine, finespun, flimsy, floaty, fragile, gauzy, gossamer, insubstantial, seethrough, sheer, transparent 2. bleared, bleary, blurred, blurry, cloudy, dim, hazy, membranous, milky, misty, opalescent, opaque, pearly

filter v. 1. clarify, filtrate, purify, refine, screen, sieve, sift, strain, winnow 2. *Often with through or out* dribble, escape, exude, leach, leak, ooze, penetrate, percolate, seep, trickle, well ~n. 3. gauze, membrane, mesh, riddle, sieve, strainer

filth 1. carrion, contamination, defilement, dirt, dung, excrement, excreta, faeces, filthiness, foul matter, foulness, garbage, grime, muck, nastiness, ordure, pollution, putrefaction, putrescence, refuse, sewage, slime, sludge, squalor, uncleanness 2. corruption, dirty-mindedness, impurity, indecency, obscenity, pornography, smut, vileness, vulgarity

filthy 1. dirty, faecal, feculent, foul, nasty, polluted, putrid, scummy, slimy, squalid, unclean, vile 2. begrimed, black, blackened, grimy, grubby, miry, mucky, muddy, mud-encrusted, smoky, sooty, unwashed 3. bawdy, coarse, corrupt, depraved, dirty-minded, foul, foul-mouthed, impure, indecent, lewd, licentious, obscene, pornographic, smutty, suggestive 4. base, contemptible, despicable, low, mean, offensive, scurvy, vicious, vile

final 1. closing, concluding, end, eventual, last, last-minute, latest, terminal, terminating, ultimate 2. absolute, conclusive, decided, decisive, definite, definitive, determinate, finished, incontrovertible, irrevocable, settled

finale climax, close, conclusion, crowning glory, culmination, dénouement, epilogue, finis, last act

finality certitude, conclusiveness, decidedness, decisiveness, definiteness, inevitableness, irrevocability, resolution, unavoidability

finalize agree, clinch (*Inf.*), complete, conclude, decide, settle, sew up (*Inf.*), tie up, work out, wrap up (*Inf.*)

finally 1. at last, at length, at long last, at the last, at the last moment, eventually, in the end, in the long run, lastly, ultimately, when all is said and done 2. in conclusion, in summary, to conclude 3. beyond the shadow of a doubt, completely, conclusively, convincingly, decisively, for all time, for ever, for good, inescapably, inexorably, irrevocably, once and for all, permanently

finance 1. n. accounts, banking, business, commerce, economics, financial affairs, investment, money, money management 2. v. back, bankroll (*U.S.*), float, fund, guarantee, pay for, provide security for, set up in business, subsidize, support, underwrite

finances affairs, assets, capital, cash, financial condition, funds, money, resources, wherewithal

financial budgeting, economic, fiscal, monetary, money, pecuniary

find v. 1. catch sight of, chance upon, come across, come up with, descry, discover, encounter, espy, expose, ferret out, hit upon, lay one's hand on, light upon, locate, meet, recognize, run to earth, spot, stumble upon, track down, turn up, uncover, unearth 2. achieve, acquire, attain, earn, gain, get, obtain, procure, win 3. get back, recover, regain, repossess, retrieve 4. arrive at, ascertain, become aware, detect, discover, experience, learn, note, notice, observe, perceive, realise, remark 5. be responsible for, bring, contribute, cough up (*Inf.*), furnish, provide, supply ~n. 6. acquisition, asset, bargain, catch, discovery, good buy

finding award, conclusion, decision, decree, judgment, pronouncement, recommendation, verdict

find out 1. detect, discover, learn, note, observe, perceive, realize 2. bring to light, catch, detect, disclose, expose, reveal, rumble (*Sl.*), suss out (*Sl.*), uncover, unmask

fine[1] *adj.* 1. accomplished, admirable, beautiful, choice, excellent, exceptional, exquisite, first-class, first-rate, great, magnificent, masterly, ornate, outstanding, rare, se-

lect, showy, skilful, splendid, su~
perior, supreme 2. balmy, bright,
clear, clement, cloudless, dry, fair,
pleasant, sunny 3. dainty, delicate,
elegant, expensive, exquisite,
fragile, quality 4. abstruse, acute,
critical, discriminating, fastidious,
hairsplitting, intelligent, keen,
minute, nice, precise, quick, re~
fined, sensitive, sharp, subtle,
tasteful, tenuous 5. delicate, di~
aphanous, fine-grained, flimsy,
gauzy, gossamer, light, lightweight,
powdered, powdery, pulverized,
sheer, slender, small, thin 6. clear,
pure, refined, solid, sterling, un~
adulterated, unalloyed, unpolluted
7. attractive, bonny, good-looking,
handsome, lovely, smart, striking,
stylish, well-favoured 8. accept~
able, agreeable, all right, conveni~
ent, good, O.K. (Inf.), satisfactory,
suitable 9. brilliant, cutting, honed,
keen, polished, razor-sharp, sharp

fine² 1. v. amerce (Archaic), mulct,
penalize, punish 2. n. amercement
(Archaic), damages, forfeit, penal~
ty, punishment

finery best bib and tucker (Inf.),
decorations, frippery, gear (Inf.),
gewgaws, glad rags (Sl.), orna~
ments, showiness, splendour, Sun~
day best, trappings, trinkets

finesse n. 1. adeptness, adroitness,
artfulness, cleverness, craft, deli~
cacy, diplomacy, discretion, know-
how (Inf.), polish, quickness,
savoir-faire, skill, sophistication,
subtlety, tact 2. artifice, bluff, feint,
manoeuvre, ruse, stratagem, trick,
wile ~v. 3. bluff, manipulate, ma~
noeuvre

finger v. 1. feel, fiddle with (Inf.),
handle, manipulate, maul, meddle
with, paw (Inf.), play about with,
touch, toy with 2. **put one's finger
on** bring to mind, discover, find
out, hit the nail on the head, hit
upon, identify, indicate, locate, pin
down, place, recall, remember

finish v. 1. accomplish, achieve,
bring to a close or conclusion, car~
ry through, cease, close, complete,
conclude, culminate, deal with,
discharge, do, end, execute, final~
ize, fulfil, get done, get out of the
way, make short work of, put the
finishing touch(es) to, round off,
settle, stop, terminate, wind up
(Inf.), wrap up (Inf.) 2. Sometimes
with up or off consume, deplete,
devour, dispatch, dispose of, drain,
drink, eat, empty, exhaust, expend,
spend, use, use up 3. Often with off
administer or give the coup de
grâce, annihilate, best, bring down,
defeat, destroy, dispose of, drive to
the wall, exterminate, get rid of,
kill, overcome, overpower, put an
end to, rout, ruin, worst ~n. 4. ces~
sation, close, closing, completion,
conclusion, culmination, dénoue~
ment, end, ending, finale, last
stage(s), termination, winding up
(Inf.), wind-up (Inf., chiefly U.S.) 5.
annihilation, bankruptcy, curtains
(Inf.), death, defeat, end, end of the
road, liquidation, ruin ~v. 6. elabo~
rate, perfect, polish, refine ~n. 7.
cultivation, culture, elaboration,
perfection, polish, refinement ~v.
8. coat, face, gild, lacquer, polish,
smooth off, stain, texture, veneer,
wax ~n. 9. appearance, grain, lus~
tre, patina, polish, shine, smooth~
ness, surface, texture

finished 1. accomplished, classic,
consummate, cultivated, elegant,
expert, flawless, impeccable, mas~
terly, perfected, polished, profes~
sional, proficient, refined, skilled,
smooth, urbane 2. accomplished,
achieved, closed, complete, com~
pleted, concluded, done, ended,
entire, final, finalized, full, in the
past, over, over and done with,
sewed up (Inf.), shut, terminated,
through, tied up, wrapped up (Inf.)
3. done, drained, empty, exhausted,
gone, played out (Inf.), spent, used
up 4. bankrupt, defeated, devastat~
ed, done for (Inf.), doomed, gone,
liquidated, lost, ruined, through,
undone, washed up (Inf., chiefly
U.S.), wiped out, wound up,
wrecked

finite bounded, circumscribed,
conditioned, delimited, demarcat~
ed, limited, restricted, subject to
limitations, terminable

fire n. 1. blaze, combustion, confla~

gration, flames, inferno 2. barrage, bombardment, cannonade, flak, fusillade, hail, salvo, shelling, snip~ ing, volley 3. *Fig.* animation, ar~ dour, brio, burning passion, dash, eagerness, élan, enthusiasm, ex~ citement, fervency, fervour, force, heat, impetuosity, intensity, life, light, lustre, passion, radiance, scintillation, sparkle, spirit, splen~ dour, verve, vigour, virtuosity, vi~ vacity 4. **hanging fire** delayed, in abeyance, pending, postponed, put back, put off, shelved, suspended, undecided 5. **on fire a.** ablaze, aflame, alight, blazing, burning, fiery, flaming, in flames **b.** ardent, eager, enthusiastic, excited, in~ spired, passionate ~*v.* 6. enkindle, ignite, kindle, light, put a match to, set ablaze, set aflame, set alight, set fire to, set on fire 7. detonate, discharge, eject, explode, hurl, launch, let off, loose, pull the trig~ ger, set off, shell, shoot, touch off 8. *Fig.* animate, arouse, electrify, en~ liven, excite, galvanize, impassion, incite, inflame, inspire, inspirit, ir~ ritate, quicken, rouse, stir 9. *Inf.* cashier, discharge, dismiss, give marching orders, make redundant, sack (*Sl.*), show the door

firebrand *Fig.* agitator, dema~ gogue, fomenter, incendiary, insti~ gator, rabble-rouser, soapbox ora~ tor, tub-thumper

fireworks 1. illuminations, pyro~ technics 2. *Fig.* fit of rage, hyster~ ics, paroxysms, rage, rows, storm, temper, trouble, uproar

firm[1] *adj.* 1. close-grained, compact, compressed, concentrated, con~ gealed, dense, hard, inelastic, in~ flexible, jelled, jellified, rigid, set, solid, solidified, stiff, unyielding 2. anchored, braced, cemented, em~ bedded, fast, fastened, fixed, im~ movable, motionless, riveted, ro~ bust, rooted, secure, secured, sta~ ble, stationary, steady, strong, sturdy, taut, tight, unfluctuating, unmoving, unshakable 3. adamant, constant, definite, fixed, inflexible, obdurate, resolute, resolved, set on, settled, staunch, steadfast, strict, true, unalterable, unbending, un~ faltering, unflinching, unshakable, unshaken, unswerving, unwaver~ ing, unyielding

firm[2] *n.* association, business, com~ pany, concern, conglomerate, cor~ poration, enterprise, house, or~ ganization, outfit (*Inf.*), partnership

firmly 1. enduringly, immovably, like a rock, motionlessly, securely, steadily, tightly, unflinchingly, un~ shakably 2. determinedly, reso~ lutely, staunchly, steadfastly, strictly, through thick and thin, unchangeably, unwaveringly, with a rod of iron, with decision

firmness 1. compactness, density, fixedness, hardness, inelasticity, inflexibility, resistance, rigidity, solidity, stiffness 2. immovability, soundness, stability, steadiness, strength, tautness, tensile strength, tension, tightness 3. constancy, fixedness, fixity of purpose, inflex~ ibility, obduracy, resolution, re~ solve, staunchness, steadfastness, strength of will, strictness

first *adj.* 1. chief, foremost, head, highest, leading, pre-eminent, prime, principal, ruling 2. earliest, initial, introductory, maiden, opening, original, premier, pri~ meval, primitive, primordial, pris~ tine 3. basic, cardinal, elementary, fundamental, key, primary, rudi~ mentary ~*adv.* 4. at the beginning, at the outset, before all else, beforehand, firstly, initially, in the first place, to begin with, to start with ~*n.* 5. *As in* **from the first** beginning, commencement, in~ ception, introduction, outset, start, starting point, word 'go' (*Inf.*)

firsthand direct, straight from the horse's mouth

first-rate admirable, A-one (*Inf.*), crack (*Sl.*), elite, excellent, excep~ tional, exclusive, first class, out~ standing, prime, second to none, superb, superlative, tiptop, top, topnotch (*Inf.*), tops (*Sl.*)

fish out extract, extricate, find, haul out, produce, pull out

fishy 1. *Inf.* doubtful, dubious, funny (*Inf.*), implausible, improbable, odd, queer, questionable, suspect,

suspicious, unlikely 2. blank, dead~
pan, dull, expressionless, glassy,
glassy-eyed, inexpressive, lack~
lustre, lifeless, vacant, wooden 3.
fishlike, piscatorial, piscatory, pis~
cine

fissure breach, break, chink,
cleavage, cleft, crack, cranny,
crevice, fault, fracture, gap, hole,
interstice, opening, rent, rift, rup~
ture, slit, split

fit[1] *adj.* 1. able, adapted, adequate,
appropriate, apt, becoming, ca~
pable, competent, convenient,
correct, deserving, equipped, ex~
pedient, fitted, fitting, good enough,
meet (*Archaic*), prepared, proper,
qualified, ready, right, seemly,
suitable, trained, well-suited, wor~
thy 2. able-bodied, hale, healthy, in
good condition, in good shape, in
good trim, robust, strapping, toned
up, trim, well ~*v.* 3. accord, agree,
be consonant, belong, concur, con~
form, correspond, dovetail, go,
interlock, join, match, meet, suit,
tally 4. *Often with out or up* ac~
commodate, accoutre, arm, equip,
fit out, kit out, outfit, prepare, pro~
vide, rig out 5. adapt, adjust, alter,
arrange, dispose, fashion, modify,
place, position, shape

fit[2] *n.* 1. attack, bout, convulsion,
paroxysm, seizure, spasm 2. ca~
price, fancy, humour, mood, whim
3. bout, burst, outbreak, outburst,
spell 4. **by fits and starts** errati~
cally, fitfully, intermittently, ir~
regularly, on and off, spasmodical~
ly, sporadically, unsystematically

fitful broken, desultory, disturbed,
erratic, flickering, fluctuating,
haphazard, impulsive, intermittent,
irregular, spasmodic, sporadic, un~
stable, variable

fitfully desultorily, erratically, in
fits and starts, in snatches, inter~
mittently, interruptedly, irregular~
ly, off and on, spasmodically, spo~
radically

fitness 1. adaptation, applicability,
appropriateness, aptness, compe~
tence, eligibility, pertinence, pre~
paredness, propriety, qualifica~
tions, readiness, seemliness, suit~

ability 2. good condition, good
health, health, robustness,
strength, vigour

fitted 1. adapted, cut out for,
equipped, fit, qualified, right, suit~
able, tailor-made 2. *Often with
with* accoutred, appointed, armed,
equipped, furnished, outfitted, pro~
vided, rigged out, set up, supplied
3. built-in, permanent

fitting 1. *adj.* appropriate, becom~
ing, *comme il faut*, correct, decent,
decorous, desirable, meet (*Archa~
ic*), proper, right, seemly, suitable
2. *n.* accessory, attachment, com~
ponent, connection, part, piece,
unit

fix *v.* 1. anchor, embed, establish,
implant, install, locate, place,
plant, position, root, set, settle 2.
attach, bind, cement, connect,
couple, fasten, glue, link, make
fast, pin, secure, stick, tie 3. agree
on, appoint, arrange, arrive at,
conclude, decide, define, deter~
mine, establish, limit, name, re~
solve, set, settle, specify 4. adjust,
correct, mend, patch up, put to
rights, regulate, repair, see to, sort
5. congeal, consolidate, harden, ri~
gidify, set, solidify, stiffen, thicken
6. direct, focus, level at, rivet 7. *Inf.*
bribe, fiddle, influence, manipu~
late, manoeuvre, pull strings (*Inf.*),
rig 8. *Sl.* cook (someone's) goose
(*Inf.*), get even with, get revenge
on, pay back, settle (someone's)
hash (*Inf.*), sort (someone) out
(*Inf.*), take retribution on, wreak
vengeance on ~*n.* 9. *Inf.* difficult
situation, difficulty, dilemma, em~
barrassment, hole (*Sl.*), jam (*Inf.*),
mess, pickle (*Inf.*), plight, predica~
ment, quandary, spot (*Inf.*), ticklish
situation

fixation complex, hang-up (*Inf.*),
idée fixe, infatuation, mania, ob~
session, preoccupation, thing (*Inf.*)

fixed 1. anchored, attached, estab~
lished, immovable, made fast, per~
manent, rigid, rooted, secure, set 2.
intent, level, resolute, steady, un~
bending, unblinking, undeviating,
unflinching, unwavering 3. agreed,
arranged, decided, definite, estab~

lished, planned, resolved, settled 4. going, in working order, mended, put right, repaired, sorted 5. *Inf.* framed, manipulated, packed, put-up, rigged

fix up 1. agree on, arrange, fix, organize, plan, settle, sort out 2. *Often with* with accommodate, arrange for, bring about, furnish, lay on, provide

fizz bubble, effervesce, fizzle, froth, hiss, sparkle, sputter

fizzle out abort, collapse, come to nothing, die away, end in disappointment, fail, fall through, fold (*Inf.*), miss the mark, peter out

fizzy bubbling, bubbly, carbonated, effervescent, gassy, sparkling

flabbergasted abashed, amazed, astonished, astounded, bowled over (*Inf.*), confounded, dazed, disconcerted, dumbfounded, nonplussed, overcome, overwhelmed, rendered speechless, speechless, staggered, struck dumb, stunned

flag[1] *v.* abate, decline, die, droop, ebb, fade, fail, faint, fall, fall off, feel the pace, languish, peter out, pine, sag, sink, slump, succumb, taper off, wane, weaken, weary, wilt

flag[2] *n.* 1. banderole, banner, colours, ensign, gonfalon, jack, pennant, pennon, standard, streamer ~*v.* 2. *Sometimes with* down hail, salute, signal, warn, wave 3. docket, indicate, label, mark, note, tab

flagging declining, decreasing, deteriorating, ebbing, fading, failing, faltering, giving up, sinking, slowing down, tiring, waning, weakening, wilting

flagrant arrant, atrocious, awful, barefaced, blatant, bold, brazen, crying, dreadful, egregious, enormous, flagitious, flaunting, glaring, heinous, immodest, infamous, notorious, open, ostentatious, out-and-out, outrageous, scandalous, shameless, undisguised

flagstone block, flag, paving stone, slab

flail *v.* beat, thrash, thresh, windmill

flair 1. ability, accomplishment, aptitude, faculty, feel, genius, gift,

knack, mastery, talent 2. chic, dash, discernment, elegance, panache, style, stylishness, taste

flake 1. *n.* disk, lamina, layer, peeling, scale, shaving, sliver, squama (*Biol.*), wafer 2. *v.* blister, chip, desquamate, peel (off), scale (off)

flamboyant 1. baroque, elaborate, extravagant, florid, ornate, ostentatious, rich, rococo, showy, theatrical 2. brilliant, colourful, dashing, dazzling, exciting, glamorous, swashbuckling

flame *v.* 1. blaze, burn, flare, flash, glare, glow, shine ~*n.* 2. blaze, brightness, fire, light 3. *Fig.* affection, ardour, enthusiasm, fervency, fervour, fire, intensity, keenness, passion, warmth 4. *Inf.* beau, beloved, boyfriend, girlfriend, heartthrob (*Brit.*), ladylove, lover, sweetheart

flameproof fire-resistant, incombustible, nonflammable, noninflammable

flaming 1. ablaze, afire, blazing, brilliant, burning, fiery, glowing, ignited, in flames, raging, red, redhot 2. angry, ardent, aroused, frenzied, hot, impassioned, intense, raging, scintillating, vehement, vivid

flank *n.* 1. ham, haunch, hip, loin, quarter, side, thigh 2. side, wing ~*v.* 3. border, bound, edge, fringe, line, screen, skirt, wall

flannel *Fig.* 1. *n.* baloney (*Inf.*), blarney, equivocation, flattery, hedging, prevarication, soft soap (*Inf.*), sweet talk (*U.S. inf.*), waffle (*Inf.*), weasel words (*Inf., chiefly U.S.*) 2. *v.* blarney, butter up, equivocate, flatter, hedge, prevaricate, pull the wool over (someone's) eyes, soft-soap (*Inf.*), sweet-talk (*U.S. inf.*), waffle

flap *v.* 1. agitate, beat, flail, flutter, shake, swing, swish, thrash, thresh, vibrate, wag, wave ~*n.* 2. bang, banging, beating, flutter, shaking, swinging, swish, waving ~*v.* 3. *Inf.* dither, fuss, panic ~*n.* 4. *Inf.* agitation, commotion, fluster, panic, state (*Inf.*), stew (*Inf.*), sweat (*Inf.*), tizzy (*Inf.*), twitter 5. apron, cover, fly, fold, lapel, lappet, overlap, skirt, tab, tail

flare v. 1. blaze, burn up, dazzle, flicker, flutter, glare, waver 2. *Often with* **out** broaden, spread out, widen ~n. 3. blaze, burst, dazzle, flame, flash, flicker, glare

flare up blaze, blow one's top (*Inf.*), boil over, break out, explode, fire up, fly off the handle (*Inf.*), lose control, lose one's cool (*Inf.*), lose one's temper, throw a tantrum

flash v. 1. blaze, coruscate, flare, flicker, glare, gleam, glint, glisten, glitter, light, scintillate, shimmer, sparkle, twinkle ~n. 2. blaze, burst, coruscation, dazzle, flare, flicker, gleam, ray, scintillation, shaft, shimmer, spark, sparkle, streak, twinkle ~v. 3. bolt, dart, dash, fly, race, shoot, speed, sprint, streak, sweep, whistle, zoom ~n. 4. instant, jiffy (*Inf.*), moment, second, shake, split second, trice, twinkling, twinkling of an eye, two shakes of a lamb's tail (*Inf.*) ~v. 5. display, exhibit, expose, flaunt, flourish, show ~n. 6. burst, demonstration, display, manifestation, outburst, show, sign, touch ~adj. 7. *Inf.* cheap, glamorous, ostentatious, tacky (*U.S. inf.*), tasteless, vulgar

flashy cheap, cheap and nasty, flamboyant, flaunting, garish, gaudy, glittery, glitzy, in poor taste, jazzy (*Inf.*), loud, meretricious, ostentatious, showy, snazzy (*Inf.*), tasteless, tawdry, tinselly

flat[1] adj. 1. even, horizontal, level, levelled, low, planar, plane, smooth, unbroken 2. laid low, lying full length, outstretched, prostrate, reclining, recumbent, supine 3. boring, dead, dull, flavourless, insipid, jejune, lacklustre, lifeless, monotonous, pointless, prosaic, spiritless, stale, tedious, uninteresting, vapid, watery, weak 4. absolute, categorical, direct, downright, explicit, final, fixed, out-and-out, peremptory, plain, positive, straight, unconditional, unequivocal, unmistakable, unqualified 5. blown out, burst, collapsed, deflat-

ed, empty, punctured ~n. 6. *Often plural* lowland, marsh, mud flat, plain, shallow, shoal, strand, swamp ~adv. 7. absolutely, categorically, completely, exactly, point blank, precisely, utterly 8. **flat out** all out, at full gallop, at full speed, at full tilt, for all one is worth, hell for leather, posthaste, under full steam

flat[2] apartment, rooms

flatly absolutely, categorically, completely, positively, unhesitatingly

flatness 1. evenness, horizontality, levelness, smoothness, uniformity 2. dullness, emptiness, insipidity, monotony, staleness, tedium, vapidity

flatten 1. compress, even out, iron out, level, plaster, raze, roll, smooth off, squash, trample 2. bowl over, crush, fell, floor, knock down, knock off one's feet, prostrate, subdue

flatter 1. blandish, butter up, cajole, compliment, court, fawn, flannel (*Inf.*), humour, inveigle, lay it on (thick) (*Sl.*), praise, puff, soft-soap (*Inf.*), sweet-talk (*U.S. inf.*), wheedle 2. become, do something for, enhance, set off, show to advantage, suit

flattering 1. becoming, effective, enhancing, kind, well-chosen 2. adulatory, complimentary, fawning, fulsome, gratifying, honeyed, honey-tongued, ingratiating, laudatory, sugary

flattery adulation, blandishment, blarney, cajolery, false praise, fawning, flannel (*Inf.*), fulsomeness, honeyed words, obsequiousness, servility, soft-soap (*Inf.*), sweet-talk (*U.S. inf.*), sycophancy, toadyism

flavour n. 1. aroma, essence, extract, flavouring, odour, piquancy, relish, savour, seasoning, smack, tang, taste, zest, zing (*Inf.*) 2. aspect, character, essence, feel, feeling, property, quality, soupçon, stamp, style, suggestion, tinge, tone, touch ~v. 3. ginger up, imbue, infuse, lace, leaven, season, spice

flavouring essence, extract, spirit, tincture, zest

flaw 1. blemish, defect, disfigure~ ment, failing, fault, imperfection, speck, spot, weakness, weak spot 2. breach, break, cleft, crack, crev~ ice, fissure, fracture, rent, rift, scission, split, tear

flawed blemished, broken, chipped, cracked, damaged, de~ fective, erroneous, faulty, imper~ fect, unsound

flawless 1. faultless, impeccable, perfect, spotless, unblemished, un~ sullied 2. intact, sound, unbroken, undamaged, whole

flee abscond, avoid, beat a hasty retreat, bolt, cut and run (*Inf.*), de~ camp, depart, escape, fly, get away, leave, make a quick exit, make off, make oneself scarce (*Inf.*), make one's escape, make one's getaway, run away, scarper (*Sl.*), shun, skedaddle (*Inf.*), split (*Sl.*), take flight, take off (*Inf.*), take to one's heels, vanish

fleece 1. *Fig.* bleed (*Inf.*), cheat, con (*Sl.*), defraud, despoil, diddle (*Inf.*), mulct, overcharge, plunder, rifle, rip off (*Sl.*), rob, rook (*Sl.*), soak (*Sl., chiefly U.S.*), steal, swin~ dle, take for a ride (*Inf.*), take to the cleaners (*Sl.*) 2. clip, shear

fleet *n.* argosy, armada, flotilla, na~ val force, navy, sea power, squad~ ron, task force, vessels, warships

fleeting brief, ephemeral, evanes~ cent, flitting, flying, fugacious, fu~ gitive, here today, gone tomorrow, momentary, passing, short, short- lived, temporary, transient, transi~ tory

flesh 1. beef (*Inf.*), body, brawn, fat, fatness, food, meat, tissue, weight 2. animality, body, carnality, flesh and blood, human nature, physi~ cality, physical nature, sensuality 3. homo sapiens, humankind, hu~ man race, living creatures, man, mankind, mortality, people, race, stock, world 4. **one's own flesh and blood** blood, family, kin, kindred,

kinsfolk, kith and kin, relations, relatives

flex *v.* angle, bend, contract, crook, curve, tighten

flexibility adaptability, adjustabil~ ity, complaisance, elasticity, give (*Inf.*), pliability, pliancy, resilience, springiness, tensility

flexible 1. bendable, ductile, elastic, limber, lithe, mouldable, plastic, pliable, pliant, springy, stretchy, supple, tensile, whippy, willowy, yielding 2. adaptable, adjustable, discretionary, open, variable 3. amenable, biddable, complaisant, compliant, docile, gentle, manage~ able, responsive, tractable

flick *v.* 1. dab, fillip, flip, hit, jab, peck, rap, strike, tap, touch 2. *With* **through** browse, flip, glance, skim, skip, thumb ~*n.* 3. fillip, flip, jab, peck, rap, tap, touch

flicker *v.* 1. flare, flash, glimmer, gutter, shimmer, sparkle, twinkle 2. flutter, quiver, vibrate, waver ~*n.* 3. flare, flash, gleam, glimmer, spark 4. atom, breath, drop, glim~ mer, iota, spark, trace, vestige

flickering fitful, guttering, twin~ kling, unsteady, wavering

flight[1] 1. flying, mounting, soaring, winging 2. *Of air travel* journey, trip, voyage 3. aerial navigation, aeronautics, air transport, avia~ tion, flying 4. cloud, flock, forma~ tion, squadron, swarm, unit, wing

flight[2] 1. departure, escape, exit, exodus, fleeing, getaway, retreat, running away 2. **put to flight** chase off, disperse, drive off, rout, scare off, scatter, send packing, stam~ pede 3. **take (to) flight** abscond, beat a retreat, bolt, decamp, do a bunk (*Sl.*), flee, light out (*Inf.*), make a hasty retreat, run away *or* off, withdraw hastily

flimsy 1. delicate, fragile, frail, gimcrack, insubstantial, makeshift, rickety, shaky, shallow, slight, superficial, unsubstantial 2. chif~ fon, gauzy, gossamer, light, sheer, thin, transparent 3. feeble, frivo~ lous, implausible, inadequate, poor, thin, transparent, trivial, uncon~ vincing, unsatisfactory, weak

flinch baulk, blench, cower, cringe, draw back, duck, flee, quail, recoil, retreat, shirk, shrink, shy away, start, swerve, wince, withdraw

fling v. 1. cast, catapult, chuck (*Inf.*), heave, hurl, jerk, let fly, lob (*Inf.*), pitch, precipitate, propel, send, shy, sling, throw, toss ~n. 2. cast, lob, pitch, shot, throw, toss 3. binge, bit of fun, good time, indulgence, spree 4. attempt, bash (*Inf.*), crack (*Inf.*), gamble, go, shot, stab, trial, try, venture, whirl (*Inf.*)

flip v./n. cast, flick, jerk, pitch, snap, spin, throw, toss, twist

flippancy cheek (*Inf.*), cheekiness, disrespectfulness, frivolity, impertinence, irreverence, levity, pertness, sauciness

flippant cheeky, disrespectful, flip (*Inf., chiefly U.S.*), frivolous, glib, impertinent, impudent, irreverent, offhand, pert, rude, saucy, superficial

flirt v. 1. chat up (*Inf.*), coquet, dally, lead on, make advances, make eyes at, philander 2. *Usually with with* consider, dabble in, entertain, expose oneself to, give a thought to, play with, toy with, trifle with ~n. 3. coquette, heart-breaker, philanderer, tease, trifler, wanton

flirtation coquetry, dalliance, intrigue, philandering, teasing, toying, trifling

flirtatious amorous, arch, come-hither, come-on (*Inf.*), coquettish, coy, enticing, flirty, provocative, sportive, teasing

flirting amorous play, chatting up (*Inf.*), coquetry, dalliance, sport

float v. 1. be *or* lie on the surface, be buoyant, displace water, hang, hover, poise, rest on water, stay afloat 2. bob, drift, glide, move gently, sail, slide, slip along 3. get going, launch, promote, push off, set up

floating 1. afloat, buoyant, buoyed up, nonsubmersible, ocean-going, sailing, swimming, unsinkable 2. fluctuating, free, migratory, movable, unattached, uncommitted, unfixed, variable, wandering

flock v. 1. collect, congregate, converge, crowd, gather, group, herd, huddle, mass, throng, troop ~n. 2. colony, drove, flight, gaggle, herd, skein 3. assembly, bevy, collection, company, congregation, convoy, crowd, gathering, group, herd, host, mass, multitude, throng

flog 1. beat, castigate, chastise, flagellate, flay, lash, scourge, thrash, trounce, whack, whip 2. drive, oppress, overexert, overtax, overwork, punish, push, strain, tax

flogging beating, caning, flagellation, hiding (*Inf.*), horsewhipping, lashing, scourging, thrashing, trouncing, whipping

flood v. 1. brim over, deluge, drown, immerse, inundate, overflow, pour over, submerge, swamp 2. engulf, flow, gush, overwhelm, rush, surge, swarm, sweep 3. choke, fill, glut, oversupply, saturate ~n. 4. deluge, downpour, flash flood, freshet, inundation, overflow, spate, tide, torrent 5. abundance, flow, glut, multitude, outpouring, profusion, rush, stream, torrent

floor 1. n. level, stage, storey, tier 2. v. *Fig.* baffle, beat, bewilder, bowl over (*Inf.*), bring up short, confound, conquer, defeat, discomfit, disconcert, dumbfound, knock down, nonplus, overthrow, perplex, prostrate, puzzle, stump, throw (*Inf.*)

flop v. 1. collapse, dangle, droop, drop, fall, hang limply, sag, slump, topple, tumble 2. *Inf.* bomb (*U.S. sl.*), close, come to nothing, fail, fall flat, fall short, fold (*Inf.*), founder, misfire ~n. 3. *Inf.* cockup (*Brit. sl.*), debacle, disaster, failure, fiasco, loser, nonstarter, washout (*Inf.*)

floral flower-patterned, flowery

florid 1. blowzy, flushed, high-coloured, high-complexioned, rubicund, ruddy 2. baroque, busy, embellished, euphuistic, figurative, flamboyant, flowery, fussy, grandiloquent, high-flown, ornate, overelaborate

flotsam debris, detritus, jetsam,

junk, odds and ends, sweepings, wreckage

flounder v. be in the dark, blunder, fumble, grope, muddle, plunge, struggle, stumble, thrash, toss, tumble, wallow

flourish v. 1. bear fruit, be in one's prime, be successful, be vigorous, bloom, blossom, boom, burgeon, develop, do well, flower, get ahead, get on, go great guns (*Sl.*), go up in the world, grow, grow fat, increase, prosper, succeed, thrive 2. brandish, display, flaunt, flutter, shake, sweep, swing, swish, twirl, vaunt, wag, wave, wield ~n. 3. brandishing, dash, display, fanfare, parade, shaking, show, showy gesture, twirling, wave 4. curlicue, decoration, embellishment, ornamentation, plume, sweep

flourishing blooming, burgeoning, doing well, going strong, in the pink, in top form, lush, luxuriant, mushrooming, on the up and up (*Inf.*), prospering, rampant, successful, thriving

flout defy, deride, gibe at, insult, jeer at, laugh in the face of, mock, outrage, ridicule, scoff at, scorn, scout (*Archaic*), show contempt for, sneer at, spurn, taunt, treat with disdain

flow v. 1. circulate, course, glide, gush, move, pour, purl, ripple, roll, run, rush, slide, surge, sweep, swirl, whirl 2. cascade, deluge, flood, inundate, overflow, pour, run, run out, spew, spill, spurt, squirt, stream, teem, well forth 3. arise, emanate, emerge, issue, pour, proceed, result, spring ~n. 4. course, current, drift, flood, flux, gush, outflow, outpouring, spate, stream, tide 5. abundance, deluge, effusion, emanation, outflow, outpouring, plenty, plethora, succession, train

flower n. 1. bloom, blossom, efflorescence 2. *Fig.* best, choicest part, cream, elite, freshness, greatest *or* finest point, height, pick, vigour ~v. 3. bloom, blossom, blow, burgeon, effloresce, flourish, mature, open, unfold

flowering adj. abloom, blooming,

blossoming, florescent, in bloom, in blossom, in flower, open, out, ready

flowery baroque, embellished, euphuistic, fancy, figurative, florid, high-flown, ornate, overwrought, rhetorical

flowing 1. falling, gushing, rolling, rushing, smooth, streaming, sweeping 2. continuous, cursive, easy, fluent, smooth, unbroken, uninterrupted 3. abounding, brimming over, flooded, full, overrun, prolific, rich, teeming

fluctuate alter, alternate, change, ebb and flow, go up and down, hesitate, oscillate, rise and fall, seesaw, shift, swing, undulate, vacillate, vary, veer, waver

fluctuation alternation, change, fickleness, inconstancy, instability, oscillation, shift, swing, unsteadiness, vacillation, variation, wavering

fluency articulateness, assurance, command, control, ease, facility, glibness, readiness, slickness, smoothness, volubility

fluent articulate, easy, effortless, facile, flowing, glib, natural, ready, smooth, smooth-spoken, voluble, well-versed

fluff 1. n. down, dust, dustball, fuzz, lint, nap, oose (*Scot.*), pile 2. v. *Inf.* bungle, cock up (*Sl.*), foul up (*Inf.*), make a mess off, mess up (*Inf.*), muddle, screw up (*Inf.*), spoil

fluid adj. 1. aqueous, flowing, in solution, liquefied, liquid, melted, molten, running, runny, watery 2. adaptable, adjustable, changeable, flexible, floating, fluctuating, indefinite, mercurial, mobile, mutable, protean, shifting 3. easy, elegant, feline, flowing, graceful, sinuous, smooth ~n. 4. liquid, liquor, solution

flurry n. 1. *Fig.* ado, agitation, bustle, commotion, disturbance, excitement, ferment, flap, fluster, flutter, furore, fuss, hurry, stir, todo, tumult, whirl 2. flaw, gust, squall 3. burst, outbreak, spell, spurt ~v. 4. agitate, bewilder, bother, bustle, confuse, disconcert, disturb, fluster, flutter, fuss, hassle

(*Inf.*), hurry, hustle, rattle (*Inf.*), ruffle, unsettle, upset

flush[1] *v.* 1. blush, burn, colour, colour up, crimson, flame, glow, go red, redden, suffuse ~*n.* 2. bloom, blush, colour, freshness, glow, redness, rosiness ~*v.* 3. cleanse, douche, drench, eject, expel, flood, hose down, rinse out, swab, syringe, wash out

flush[2] *adj.* 1. even, flat, level, plane, square, true 2. abundant, affluent, full, generous, lavish, liberal, overflowing, prodigal 3. *Inf.* in funds, in the money (*Inf.*), moneyed, rich, rolling (*Sl.*), wealthy, well-heeled, well-off, well-supplied ~*adv.* 4. even with, hard against, in contact with, level with, squarely, touching

flushed 1. blushing, burning, crimson, embarrassed, feverish, glowing, hot, red, rosy, rubicund, ruddy 2. *Often with* with ablaze, animated, aroused, elated, enthused, excited, exhilarated, high (*Inf.*), inspired, intoxicated, thrilled

fluster 1. *v.* agitate, bother, bustle, confound, confuse, disturb, excite, flurry, hassle (*Inf.*), heat, hurry, make nervous, perturb, rattle (*Inf.*), ruffle, throw off balance, upset 2. *n.* agitation, bustle, commotion, disturbance, dither, flap (*Inf.*), flurry, flutter, furore, perturbation, ruffle, state (*Inf.*), turmoil

flutter *v.* 1. agitate, bat, beat, flap, flicker, flit, flitter, fluctuate, hover, palpitate, quiver, ripple, ruffle, shiver, tremble, vibrate, waver ~*n.* 2. palpitation, quiver, quivering, shiver, shudder, tremble, tremor, twitching, vibration 3. agitation, commotion, confusion, dither, excitement, flurry, fluster, perturbation, state (*Inf.*), state of nervous excitement, tremble, tumult

fly *v.* 1. flit, flutter, hover, mount, sail, soar, take to the air, take wing, wing 2. aviate, be at the controls, control, manoeuvre, operate, pilot 3. display, flap, float, flutter, show, wave 4. elapse, flit, glide, pass, pass swiftly, roll on, run its course, slip away 5. be off like a shot (*Inf.*), bolt, career, dart, dash,

hare (*Inf.*), hasten, hurry, race, rush, scamper, scoot, shoot, speed, sprint, tear, whiz (*Inf.*), zoom 6. abscond, avoid, beat a retreat, clear out (*Inf.*), cut and run (*Inf.*), decamp, disappear, escape, flee, get away, hasten away, hightail (*Inf., chiefly U.S.*), light out (*Inf.*), make a getaway, make a quick exit, make one's escape, run, run for it, run from, show a clean pair of heels, shun, take flight, take off, take to one's heels 7. **fly in the ointment** difficulty, drawback, flaw, hitch, problem, rub, small problem, snag 8. **fly off the handle** blow one's top, explode, flip one's lid (*Sl.*), fly into a rage, have a tantrum, hit *or* go through the roof (*Inf.*), let fly (*Inf.*), lose one's cool (*Sl.*), lose one's temper 9. **let fly a.** burst forth, give free reign, keep nothing back, lash out, let (someone) have it, lose one's temper, tear into (*Inf.*), vent **b.** cast, chuck, fire, fling, heave, hurl, hurtle, launch, let off, lob (*Inf.*), shoot, sling, throw

fly at assail, assault, attack, fall upon, get stuck into (*Inf.*), go for, have a go at (*Inf.*), lay about, pitch into, rush at

fly-by-night *adj.* 1. cowboy (*Inf.*), dubious, questionable, shady, undependable, unreliable, untrustworthy 2. brief, here today, gone tomorrow, impermanent, shortlived

flying *adj.* 1. brief, fleeting, fugacious, hasty, hurried, rushed, shortlived, transitory 2. express, fast, fleet, mercurial, mobile, rapid, speedy, winged 3. airborne, flapping, floating, fluttering, gliding, hovering, in the air, soaring, streaming, volitant, waving, windborne, winging

foam 1. *n.* bubbles, froth, head, lather, spray, spume, suds 2. *v.* boil, bubble, effervesce, fizz, froth, lather

focus *n.* 1. bull's eye, centre, centre of activity, centre of attraction, core, cynosure, focal point, headquarters, heart, hub, meeting place, target 2. **in focus** clear, distinct, sharp-edged, sharply defined 3. **out of focus** blurred, fuzzy, ill-defined, indistinct, muzzy, unclear ~*v.* 4. aim, bring to bear, centre, concentrate, converge, direct, fix, join, meet, pinpoint, rivet, spotlight, zero in (*Inf.*), zoom in

foe adversary, antagonist, enemy, foeman (*Archaic*), opponent, rival

fog *n.* 1. gloom, miasma, mist, murk, murkiness, peasouper (*Inf.*), smog 2. *Fig.* blindness, confusion, daze, haze, mist, obscurity, perplexity, stupor, trance ~*v.* 3. becloud, bedim, befuddle, bewilder, blind, cloud, confuse, darken, daze, dim, muddle, obfuscate, obscure, perplex, stupefy 4. cloud, mist over *or* up, steam up

foggy 1. blurred, brumous (*Rare*), cloudy, dim, grey, hazy, indistinct, misty, murky, nebulous, obscure, smoggy, soupy, vaporous 2. *Fig.* befuddled, bewildered, clouded, cloudy, confused, dark, dazed, dim, indistinct, muddled, obscure, stupefied, stupid, unclear, vague

foil *v.* baffle, balk, check, checkmate, circumvent, counter, defeat, disappoint, elude, frustrate, nip in the bud, nullify, outwit, put a spoke in (someone's) wheel (*Brit.*), stop, thwart

foist fob off, get rid of, impose, insert, insinuate, interpolate, introduce, palm off, pass off, put over, sneak in, unload

fold *v.* 1. bend, crease, crumple, dog-ear, double, double over, gather, intertwine, overlap, pleat, tuck, turn under ~*n.* 2. bend, crease, double thickness, folded portion, furrow, knife-edge, layer, overlap, pleat, turn, wrinkle ~*v.* 3. do up, enclose, enfold, entwine, envelop, wrap, wrap up 4. *Inf.* be ruined, close, collapse, crash, fail, go bankrupt, go bust (*Inf.*), go to the wall, go under (*Inf.*), shut down

folder binder, envelope, file, portfolio

folk clan, ethnic group, family, kin, kindred, people, race, tribe

follow 1. come after, come next, step into the shoes of, succeed, supersede, supplant, take the place of 2. chase, dog, hound, hunt, pursue, run after, shadow, stalk, tail, track, trail 3. accompany, attend, bring up the rear, come *or* go with, come after, escort, tag along, tread on the heels of 4. act in accordance with, be guided by, comply, conform, give allegiance to, heed, mind, note, obey, observe, regard, watch 5. appreciate, catch, catch on (*Inf.*), comprehend, fathom, get, get the picture, grasp, keep up with, realize, see, take in, understand 6. arise, be consequent, develop, emanate, ensue, flow, issue, proceed, result, spring, supervene 7. adopt, copy, emulate, imitate, live up to, pattern oneself upon, take as example 8. be a devotee *or* supporter of, be devoted to, be interested in, cultivate, keep abreast of, support

follower 1. adherent, admirer, apostle, backer, believer, convert, devotee, disciple, fan, fancier, habitué, partisan, pupil, representative, supporter, votary, worshipper 2. attendant, companion, hanger-on, helper, henchman, lackey, minion, retainer (*History*), sidekick (*Sl.*)

following 1. *adj.* coming, consequent, consequential, ensuing, later, next, specified, subsequent, succeeding, successive 2. *n.* audience, circle, clientele, coterie, entourage, fans, patronage, public, retinue, suite, support, supporters, train

follow up 1. check out, find out about, investigate, look into, make inquiries, pursue 2. consolidate, continue, make sure, reinforce

folly absurdity, daftness, fatuity, foolishness, idiocy, imbecility, imprudence, indiscretion, irrationality, lunacy, madness, nonsense, preposterousness, rashness, recklessness, silliness, stupidity

fond 1. *With* **of** addicted to, attached to, enamoured of, have a liking (fancy, taste) for, have a soft spot for, hooked on, keen on, partial to, predisposed towards 2. adoring, affectionate, amorous, caring, devoted, doting, indulgent, loving, tender, warm 3. absurd, credulous, deluded, delusive, delusory, empty, foolish, indiscreet, naive, overoptimistic, vain

fondle caress, cuddle, dandle, pat, pet, stroke

fondly 1. affectionately, dearly, indulgently, lovingly, possessively, tenderly, with affection 2. credulously, foolishly, naively, stupidly, vainly

fondness 1. attachment, fancy, liking, love, partiality, penchant, predilection, preference, soft spot, susceptibility, taste, weakness 2. affection, attachment, devotion, kindness, love, tenderness

food 1. aliment, board, bread, chow (*Inf.*), comestibles, commons, cooking, cuisine, diet, eatables (*Sl.*), eats (*Sl.*), edibles, fare, foodstuffs, grub (*Sl.*), larder, meat, menu, nosh (*Sl.*), nourishment, nutriment, nutrition, pabulum (*Rare*), provender, provisions, rations, refreshment, scoff (*Sl.*), stores, subsistence, sustenance, table, tuck (*Inf.*), viands, victuals 2. *Cattle, etc.* feed, fodder, forage, provender

fool *n.* 1. ass, bird-brain (*Inf.*), blockhead, bonehead (*Sl.*), chump (*Inf.*), clodpate (*Archaic*), clot (*Inf.*), dimwit (*Inf.*), dolt, dope (*Sl.*), dunce, dunderhead, fat-head (*Inf.*), goose (*Inf.*), halfwit, idiot, ignoramus, illiterate, imbecile (*Inf.*), jackass, loon, mooncalf, moron, nincompoop, ninny, nit (*Inf.*), nitwit, numskull, sap (*Sl.*), silly, simpleton, twerp (*Inf.*), twit (*Inf.*) 2. butt, chump (*Inf.*), dupe, easy mark (*Sl.*), fall guy (*Inf., chiefly U.S.*), greenhorn (*Inf.*), gull (*Archaic*), laughing stock, mug (*Sl.*), stooge (*Sl.*), sucker (*Sl.*) 3. buffoon, clown, comic, harlequin, jester, merry-andrew, motley, pierrot, punchinello 4. **act** *or* **play the fool** act up, be silly, cavort, clown, cut capers, frolic, lark about (*Inf.*), mess about, play the goat, show off ~*v.* 5. bamboozle, beguile, bluff, cheat, con

(*Sl.*), deceive, delude, dupe, gull (*Archaic*), have (someone) on, hoax, hoodwink, kid (*Inf.*), make a fool of, mislead, play a trick on, put one over on (*Inf.*), take in, trick 6. act the fool, cut capers, feign, jest, joke, kid (*Inf.*), make believe, pretend, tease 7. *With* **with, around with** *or* **about with** fiddle, meddle, mess, monkey, play, tamper, toy, trifle

foolery antics, capers, carry-on (*Inf.*), childishness, clowning, folly, fooling, horseplay, larks, mischief, monkey tricks (*Inf.*), nonsense, practical jokes, pranks, shenanigans (*Inf.*), silliness, tomfoolery

foolhardy adventurous, bold, hot-headed, impetuous, imprudent, incautious, irresponsible, madcap, precipitate, rash, reckless, temerarious, venturesome, venturous

foolish 1. absurd, ill-advised, ill-considered, ill-judged, imprudent, incautious, indiscreet, injudicious, nonsensical, senseless, short-sighted, silly, unintelligent, unreasonable, unwise 2. brainless, crazy, daft (*Inf.*), doltish, fatuous, half-baked (*Inf.*), half-witted, hare-brained, idiotic, imbecilic, ludicrous, mad, moronic, potty (*Brit. inf.*), ridiculous, senseless, silly, simple, stupid, weak, witless

foolishly absurdly, idiotically, ill-advisedly, imprudently, incautiously, indiscreetly, injudiciously, like a fool, mistakenly, short-sightedly, stupidly, unwisely, without due consideration

foolishness 1. absurdity, folly, imprudence, inanity, indiscretion, irresponsibility, silliness, stupidity, weakness 2. bunk (*Inf.*), bunkum, carrying-on (*Inf.*), claptrap (*Inf.*), foolery, nonsense, rigmarole, rubbish

foolproof certain, guaranteed, infallible, never-failing, safe, sure-fire (*Inf.*), unassailable, unbreakable

footing 1. basis, establishment, foot-hold, foundation, ground, groundwork, installation, settlement 2. condition, grade, position, rank, relations, relationship, standing, state, status, terms

footling fiddling, fussy, hair~splitting, immaterial, insignificant, irrelevant, minor, niggly, petty, pointless, silly, time-wasting, tri~fling, trivial, unimportant

footstep 1. footfall, step, tread 2. footmark, footprint, trace, track

forage 1. n. Cattle, etc. feed, fodder, food, foodstuffs, provender 2. v. cast about, explore, hunt, look round, plunder, raid, ransack, rummage, scour, scrounge (Inf.), search, seek

forbear abstain, avoid, cease, de~cline, desist, eschew, hold back, keep from, omit, pause, refrain, resist the temptation to, restrain oneself, stop, withhold

forbearance 1. indulgence, lenien~cy, lenity, longanimity (Rare), long-suffering, mildness, modera~tion, patience, resignation, re~straint, self-control, temperance, tolerance 2. abstinence, avoidance, refraining

forbearing clement, easy, forgiv~ing, indulgent, lenient, long-suffering, merciful, mild, moder~ate, patient, tolerant

forbid ban, debar, disallow, ex~clude, hinder, inhibit, interdict, outlaw, preclude, prohibit, pro~scribe, rule out, veto

forbidden banned, outlawed, out of bounds, prohibited, proscribed, ta~boo, verboten, vetoed

forbidding 1. abhorrent, disagree~able, odious, offensive, off-putting (Inf.), repellent, repulsive 2. daunting, foreboding, frightening, grim, hostile, menacing, ominous, sinister, threatening, unfriendly

force n. 1. dynamism, energy, im~pact, impulse, life, might, momen~tum, muscle, potency, power, pressure, stimulus, strength, stress, vigour 2. arm-twisting (Inf.), coer~cion, compulsion, constraint, du~ress, enforcement, pressure, vio~lence 3. bite, cogency, effect, ef~fectiveness, efficacy, influence, persuasiveness, power, punch (Inf.), strength, validity, weight 4. drive, emphasis, fierceness, inten~sity, persistence, vehemence, vig~our 5. army, battalion, body, corps, detachment, division, host, legion, patrol, regiment, squad, squadron, troop, unit 6. **in force a.** binding, current, effective, in operation, on the statute book, operative, valid, working **b.** all together, in full strength, in great numbers ~v. 7. bring pressure to bear upon, co~erce, compel, constrain, drive, im~pel, impose, make, necessitate, ob~ligate, oblige, overcome, press, press-gang, pressure, pressurize, put the squeeze on (Inf.), strong-arm (Inf.), urge 8. blast, break open, prise, propel, push, thrust, use violence on, wrench, wrest 9. drag, exact, extort, wring

forced 1. compulsory, conscripted, enforced, involuntary, mandatory, obligatory, slave, unwilling 2. af~fected, artificial, contrived, false, insincere, laboured, stiff, strained, unnatural, wooden

forceful cogent, compelling, con~vincing, dynamic, effective, per~suasive, pithy, potent, powerful, telling, vigorous, weighty

forcible 1. active, cogent, compel~ling, effective, efficient, energetic, forceful, impressive, mighty, po~tent, powerful, strong, telling, val~id, weighty 2. aggressive, armed, coercive, compulsory, drastic, vio~lent

forcibly against one's will, by force, by main force, compulsorily, under compulsion, under protest, willy-nilly

forebear ancestor, father, fore~father, forerunner, predecessor, progenitor

forebode augur, betoken, fore~shadow, foreshow, foretell, foreto~ken, forewarn, indicate, portend, predict, presage, prognosticate, promise, warn of

foreboding 1. anxiety, apprehen~sion, apprehensiveness, chill, dread, fear, misgiving, premoni~tion, presentiment 2. augury, fore~shadowing, foretoken, omen, por~

tent, prediction, presage, prognostication, sign, token, warning

forecast 1. *v.* anticipate, augur, calculate, divine, estimate, foresee, foretell, plan, predict, prognosticate, prophesy **2.** *n.* anticipation, conjecture, foresight, forethought, guess, outlook, planning, prediction, prognosis, projection, prophecy

forefather ancestor, father, forebear, forerunner, predecessor, primogenitor, procreator, progenitor

foregoing above, antecedent, anterior, former, preceding, previous, prior

foreground centre, forefront, front, limelight, prominence

foreign 1. alien, borrowed, distant, exotic, external, imported, outlandish, outside, overseas, remote, strange, unfamiliar, unknown **2.** extraneous, extrinsic, incongruous, irrelevant, unassimilable, uncharacteristic, unrelated

foreigner alien, immigrant, incomer, newcomer, outlander, stranger

foremost chief, first, front, headmost, highest, inaugural, initial, leading, paramount, pre-eminent, primary, prime, principal, supreme

forerunner 1. ancestor, announcer, envoy, forebear, foregoer, harbinger, herald, precursor, predecessor, progenitor, prototype **2.** augury, foretoken, indication, omen, portent, premonition, prognostic, sign, token

foresee anticipate, divine, envisage, forebode, forecast, foretell, predict, prophesy

foreshadow adumbrate, augur, betoken, bode, forebode, imply, indicate, portend, predict, prefigure, presage, promise, prophesy, signal

foresight anticipation, care, caution, circumspection, farsightedness, forethought, precaution, premeditation, preparedness, prescience, prevision (*Rare*), provision, prudence

forestry arboriculture, dendrology

(*Bot.*), silviculture, woodcraft, woodmanship

foretell adumbrate, augur, bode, forebode, forecast, foreshadow, foreshow, forewarn, portend, predict, presage, prognosticate, prophesy, signify, soothsay

forethought anticipation, farsightedness, foresight, precaution, providence, provision, prudence

forever 1. always, evermore, for all time, for good and all (*Inf.*), for keeps, in perpetuity, till Doomsday, till the cows come home (*Inf.*), till the end of time, world without end **2.** all the time, constantly, continually, endlessly, eternally, everlastingly, incessantly, interminably, perpetually, unremittingly

forewarn admonish, advise, alert, apprise, caution, dissuade, give fair warning, put on guard, put on the qui vive, tip off

foreword introduction, preamble, preface, preliminary, prolegomenon, prologue

forfeit 1. *n.* amercement (*Obsolete*), damages, fine, forfeiture, loss, mulct, penalty **2.** *v.* be deprived of, be stripped of, give up, lose, relinquish, renounce, surrender

forfeiture confiscation, giving up, loss, relinquishment, sequestration (*Law*), surrender

forge *v.* **1.** construct, contrive, create, devise, fabricate, fashion, form, frame, hammer out, invent, make, mould, shape, work **2.** coin, copy, counterfeit, fake, falsify, feign, imitate

forger coiner, counterfeiter, falsifier

forgery 1. coining, counterfeiting, falsification, fraudulence, fraudulent imitation **2.** counterfeit, fake, falsification, imitation, phoney (*Inf.*), sham

forget 1. consign to oblivion, dismiss from one's mind, let bygones be bygones, let slip from the memory **2.** leave behind, lose sight of, omit, overlook

forgetful absent-minded, apt to

forget, careless, dreamy, heedless, inattentive, lax, neglectful, negligent, oblivious, unmindful

forgetfulness absent-mindedness, abstraction, carelessness, dreaminess, heedlessness, inattention, lapse of memory, laxness, oblivion, obliviousness, woolgathering

forgive absolve, accept (someone's) apology, acquit, bear no malice, condone, excuse, exonerate, let bygones be bygones, let off (*Inf.*), pardon, remit

forgiveness absolution, acquittal, amnesty, condonation, exoneration, mercy, overlooking, pardon, remission

forgiving clement, compassionate, forbearing, humane, lenient, magnanimous, merciful, mild, softhearted, tolerant

forgo, forego abandon, abjure, cede, do without, give up, leave alone *or* out, relinquish, renounce, resign, sacrifice, surrender, waive, yield

forgotten blotted out, buried, bygone, consigned to oblivion, gone (clean) out of one's mind, left behind *or* out, lost, obliterated, omitted, past, past recall, unremembered

fork *v.* bifurcate, branch, branch off, diverge, divide, go separate ways, part, split

forked angled, bifurcate(d), branched, branching, divided, pronged, split, tined, zigzag

forlorn abandoned, bereft, cheerless, comfortless, deserted, desolate, destitute, disconsolate, forgotten, forsaken, friendless, helpless, homeless, hopeless, lonely, lost, miserable, pathetic, pitiable, pitiful, unhappy, woebegone, wretched

form^1 *v.* 1. assemble, bring about, build, concoct, construct, contrive, create, devise, establish, fabricate, fashion, forge, found, invent, make, manufacture, model, mould, produce, put together, set up, shape 2. arrange, combine, design, dispose, draw up, frame, organize, pattern, plan, think up 3. accumulate, ap-

pear, become visible, come into being, crystallize, grow, materialize, rise, settle, show up, take shape 4. acquire, contract, cultivate, develop, get into (*Inf.*), pick up 5. compose, comprise, constitute, make, make up, serve as 6. bring up, discipline, educate, instruct, rear, school, teach, train

form^2 *n.* 1. appearance, cast, configuration, construction, cut, fashion, formation, model, mould, pattern, shape, structure 2. anatomy, being, body, build, figure, frame, outline, person, physique, shape, silhouette 3. arrangement, character, description, design, guise, kind, manifestation, manner, method, mode, order, practice, semblance, sort, species, stamp, style, system, type, variety, way 4. format, framework, harmony, order, orderliness, organization, plan, proportion, structure, symmetry 5. condition, fettle, fitness, good condition, good spirits, health, shape, trim 6. **off form** below par, not in the pink (*Inf.*), not up to the mark, out of condition, stale, under the weather (*Inf.*), unfit 7. behaviour, ceremony, conduct, convention, custom, done thing, etiquette, formality, manners, procedure, protocol, ritual, rule 8. application, document, paper, sheet 9. class, grade, rank

formal 1. approved, ceremonial, explicit, express, fixed, lawful, legal, methodical, official, prescribed, *pro forma,* regular, rigid, ritualistic, set, solemn, strict 2. affected, aloof, ceremonious, conventional, correct, exact, precise, prim, punctilious, reserved, starched, stiff, unbending

formality 1. ceremony, convention, conventionality, custom, form, gesture, matter of form, procedure, red tape, rite, ritual 2. ceremoniousness, correctness, decorum, etiquette, politesse, protocol, punctilio

formation 1. accumulation, compilation, composition, constitution, crystallization, development, establishment, evolution, forming, generation, genesis, manufacture, organization, production 2. arrangement, configuration, design, disposition, figure, grouping, pattern, rank, structure

formative 1. impressionable, malleable, mouldable, pliant, sensitive, susceptible 2. determinative, developmental, influential, moulding, shaping

former 1. antecedent, anterior, *ci-devant*, earlier, erstwhile, ex-, late, one-time, previous, prior, quondam, whilom (*Archaic*) 2. ancient, bygone, departed, long ago, long gone, of yore, old, old-time, past 3. above, aforementioned, aforesaid, first mentioned, foregoing, preceding

formerly aforetime (*Archaic*), already, at one time, before, heretofore, lately, once, previously

formidable 1. appalling, dangerous, daunting, dismaying, dreadful, fearful, frightful, horrible, intimidating, menacing, shocking, terrifying, threatening 2. arduous, challenging, colossal, difficult, mammoth, onerous, overwhelming, staggering, toilsome 3. awesome, great, impressive, indomitable, mighty, powerful, puissant, redoubtable, terrific, tremendous

formula 1. form of words, formulary, rite, ritual, rubric 2. blueprint, method, modus operandi, precept, prescription, principle, procedure, recipe, rule, way

formulate 1. codify, define, detail, express, frame, give form to, particularize, set down, specify, systematize 2. coin, develop, devise, evolve, forge, invent, map out, originate, plan, work out

forsake 1. abandon, cast off, desert, disown, jettison, jilt, leave, leave in the lurch, quit, repudiate, throw over 2. abdicate, forgo, forswear, give up, have done with, relinquish, renounce, set aside, surrender, turn one's back on, yield

forsaken abandoned, cast off, deserted, destitute, disowned, forlorn, friendless, ignored, isolated, jilted,

left behind, left in the lurch, lonely, marooned, outcast, solitary

fort 1. blockhouse, camp, castle, citadel, fastness, fortification, fortress, garrison, redoubt, station, stronghold 2. **hold the fort** carry on, keep things moving, keep things on an even keel, maintain the status quo, stand in, take over the reins

forte gift, long suit (*Inf.*), métier, speciality, strength, strong point, talent

forth ahead, away, forward, into the open, onward, out, out of concealment, outward

forthcoming 1. approaching, coming, expected, future, imminent, impending, prospective 2. accessible, at hand, available, in evidence, obtainable, on tap (*Inf.*), ready 3. chatty, communicative, expansive, free, informative, open, sociable, talkative, unreserved

forthright above-board, blunt, candid, direct, frank, open, outspoken, plain-spoken, straightforward, straight from the shoulder (*Inf.*)

forthwith at once, directly, immediately, instantly, quickly, right away, straightaway, *tout de suite*, without delay

fortification 1. bastion, bulwark, castle, citadel, defence, fastness, fort, fortress, keep, protection, stronghold 2. embattlement, reinforcement, strengthening

fortify 1. brace, buttress, embattle, garrison, protect, reinforce, secure, shore up, strengthen, support 2. brace, cheer, confirm, embolden, encourage, hearten, invigorate, reassure, stiffen, strengthen, sustain

fortitude backbone, braveness, courage, dauntlessness, determination, endurance, fearlessness, firmness, grit, guts (*Inf.*), hardihood, intrepidity, patience, perseverance, pluck, resolution, staying power, stoutheartedness, strength, strength of mind, valour

fortress castle, citadel, fastness, fort, redoubt, stronghold

fortunate 1. born with a silver

spoon in one's mouth, bright, fa~
voured, golden, happy, having a
charmed life, in luck, lucky, pros~
perous, rosy, sitting pretty (*Inf.*),
successful, well-off **2.** advanta~
geous, auspicious, convenient, en~
couraging, favourable, felicitous,
fortuitous, helpful, opportune,
profitable, promising, propitious,
providential, timely

fortunately by a happy chance, by
good luck, happily, luckily, provi~
dentially

fortune 1. affluence, gold mine,
opulence, possessions, property,
prosperity, riches, treasure, wealth
2. accident, chance, contingency,
destiny, fate, fortuity, hap (*Archa~
ic*), hazard, kismet, luck, provi~
dence **3.** *Often plural* adventures,
circumstances, destiny, doom, ex~
pectation, experience(s), history,
life, lot, portion, star, success **4.**
bomb (*Sl.*), bundle (*Sl.*), king's ran~
som, mint, packet (*Sl.*), pile (*Sl.*),
wealth

forward *adj.* **1.** advanced, advanc~
ing, early, forward-looking, on~
ward, precocious, premature, pro~
gressive, well-developed **2.** ad~
vance, first, fore, foremost, front,
head, leading **3.** assuming, bare~
faced, bold, brash, brass-necked
(*Inf.*), brazen, brazen-faced,
cheeky, confident, familiar, fresh
(*Inf.*), impertinent, impudent,
overassertive, overweening, pert,
presuming, presumptuous, pushy
(*Inf.*) ~*adv.* **4.** *Also* **forwards**
ahead, forth, on, onward **5.** in to
consideration, into prominence,
into the open, into view, out, to
light, to the fore, to the surface ~*v.*
6. advance, aid, assist, back, en~
courage, expedite, favour, foster,
further, hasten, help, hurry, pro~
mote, speed, support **7.** *Commerce*
dispatch, freight, post, route, send,
send on, ship, transmit

forward-looking dynamic, en~
lightened, enterprising, go-ahead,
go-getting (*Inf.*), liberal, modern,
progressive, reforming

forwardness boldness, brashness,
brazenness, cheek (*Inf.*), cheeki~
ness, impertinence, impudence,
overconfidence, pertness, pre~
sumption

foster 1. cultivate, encourage, feed,
foment, nurture, promote, stimu~
late, support, uphold **2.** bring up,
mother, nurse, raise, rear, take
care of **3.** accommodate, cherish,
entertain, harbour, nourish, sustain

foul *adj.* **1.** contaminated, dirty, dis~
gusting, fetid, filthy, impure, loath~
some, malodorous, mephitic, nasty,
nauseating, noisome, offensive,
polluted, putrid, rank, repulsive,
revolting, rotten, squalid, stinking,
sullied, tainted, unclean **2.** abusive,
blasphemous, blue, coarse, dirty,
filthy, foul-mouthed, gross, inde~
cent, lewd, low, obscene, profane,
scatological, scurrilous, smutty,
vulgar **3.** abhorrent, abominable,
base, despicable, detestable, dis~
graceful, dishonourable, egregious,
hateful, heinous, infamous, iniqui~
tous, nefarious, notorious, offen~
sive, scandalous, shameful, vicious,
vile, wicked **4.** crooked, dirty, dis~
honest, fraudulent, inequitable,
shady (*Inf.*), underhand, unfair,
unjust, unscrupulous, un~
sportsmanlike **5.** bad, blustery, dis~
agreeable, foggy, murky, rainy,
rough, stormy, wet, wild ~*v.* **6.** be~
grime, besmear, besmirch, con~
taminate, defile, dirty, pollute,
smear, soil, stain, sully, taint **7.**
block, catch, choke, clog, ensnare,
entangle, jam, snarl, twist

foul play chicanery, corruption,
crime, deception, dirty work,
double-dealing, duplicity, fraud,
perfidy, roguery, sharp practice,
skulduggery, treachery, villainy

found 1. bring into being, consti~
tute, construct, create, endow,
erect, establish, fix, inaugurate, in~
stitute, organize, originate, plant,
raise, settle, set up, start **2.** base,
bottom, build, ground, rest, root,
sustain

foundation 1. base, basis, bedrock,
bottom, footing, groundwork, sub~
structure, underpinning **2.** endow~
ment, establishment, inauguration,

institution, organization, setting up, settlement

founder[1] *n.* architect, author, beginner, benefactor, builder, constructor, designer, establisher, father, framer, generator, initiator, institutor, inventor, maker, organizer, originator, patriarch

founder[2] *v.* 1. be lost, go down, go to the bottom, sink, submerge 2. *Fig.* abort, break down, collapse, come to grief, come to nothing, fail, fall through, miscarry, misfire 3. collapse, fall, go lame, lurch, sprawl, stagger, stumble, trip

foundling orphan, outcast, stray, waif

fountain 1. font, fount, jet, reservoir, spout, spray, spring, well 2. *Fig.* beginning, cause, commencement, derivation, fountainhead, genesis, origin, rise, source, wellhead, wellspring

foxy artful, astute, canny, crafty, cunning, devious, guileful, knowing, sharp, shrewd, sly, tricky, wily

foyer antechamber, anteroom, entrance hall, lobby, reception area, vestibule

fracas affray (*Law*), aggro (*Sl.*), brawl, disturbance, donnybrook, fight, free-for-all (*Inf.*), melee, quarrel, riot, row, rumpus, scrimmage, scuffle, trouble, uproar

fractious awkward, captious, crabby, cross, fretful, froward, grouchy (*Inf.*), irritable, peevish, pettish, petulant, querulous, recalcitrant, refractory, testy, touchy, unruly

fracture 1. *n.* breach, break, cleft, crack, fissure, gap, opening, rent, rift, rupture, schism, split 2. *v.* break, crack, rupture, splinter, split

fragile breakable, brittle, dainty, delicate, feeble, fine, flimsy, frail, frangible, infirm, slight, weak

fragment 1. *n.* bit, chip, fraction, morsel, part, particle, piece, portion, remnant, scrap, shiver, sliver 2. *v.* break, break up, come apart, come to pieces, crumble, disintegrate, disunite, divide, shatter, shiver, splinter, split, split up

fragmentary bitty, broken, disconnected, discrete, disjointed, incoherent, incomplete, partial, piecemeal, scattered, scrappy, sketchy, unsystematic

fragrance aroma, balm, bouquet, fragrancy, perfume, redolence, scent, smell, sweet odour

fragrant ambrosial, aromatic, balmy, odoriferous, odorous, perfumed, redolent, sweet-scented, sweet-smelling

frail breakable, brittle, decrepit, delicate, feeble, flimsy, fragile, frangible, infirm, insubstantial, puny, slight, tender, unsound, vulnerable, weak, wispy

frailty 1. fallibility, feebleness, frailness, infirmity, peccability, puniness, susceptibility, weakness 2. blemish, defect, deficiency, failing, fault, flaw, foible, imperfection, peccadillo, shortcoming, vice, weak point

frame *v.* 1. assemble, build, constitute, construct, fabricate, fashion, forge, form, institute, invent, make, manufacture, model, mould, put together, set up 2. block out, compose, conceive, concoct, contrive, cook up, devise, draft, draw up, form, formulate, hatch, map out, plan, shape, sketch 3. case, enclose, mount, surround ~*n.* 4. casing, construction, fabric, form, framework, scheme, shell, structure, system 5. anatomy, body, build, carcass, morphology, physique, skeleton 6. mount, mounting, setting 7. **frame of mind** attitude, disposition, fettle, humour, mood, outlook, spirit, state, temper

frame-up fabrication, fit-up (*Sl.*), put-up job, trumped-up charge

framework core, fabric, foundation, frame, frame of reference, groundwork, plan, schema, shell, skeleton, structure, the bare bones

franchise authorization, charter, exemption, freedom, immunity, prerogative, privilege, right, suffrage, vote

frank artless, blunt, candid, direct, downright, forthright, free, honest, ingenuous, open, outright, outspo~

ken, plain, plain-spoken, sincere, straightforward, straight from the shoulder (*Inf.*), transparent, truthful, unconcealed, undisguised, unreserved, unrestricted

frankly 1. candidly, honestly, in truth, to be honest 2. bluntly, directly, freely, openly, plainly, straight (*Inf.*), without reserve

frankness absence of reserve, bluntness, candour, forthrightness, ingenuousness, openness, outspokenness, plain speaking, truthfulness

frantic at one's wits' end, berserk, beside oneself, distracted, distraught, fraught (*Inf.*), frenetic, frenzied, furious, hectic, mad, overwrought, raging, raving, wild

fraternity association, brotherhood, camaraderie, circle, clan, club, companionship, company, comradeship, fellowship, guild, kinship, league, set, sodality, union

fraternize associate, concur, consort, cooperate, go around with, hang out (*Inf.*), hobnob, keep company, mingle, mix, socialize, sympathize, unite

fraud 1. artifice, cheat, chicane, chicanery, craft, deceit, deception, double-dealing, duplicity, guile, hoax, humbug, imposture, sharp practice, spuriousness, stratagems, swindling, treachery, trickery 2. bluffer, charlatan, cheat, counterfeit, double-dealer, fake, forgery, hoax, hoaxer, impostor, mountebank, phoney (*Inf.*), pretender, quack, sham, swindler

fraudulent counterfeit, crafty, criminal, crooked (*Inf.*), deceitful, deceptive, dishonest, double-dealing, duplicitous, false, knavish, phoney (*Inf.*), sham, spurious, swindling, treacherous

fray v. become threadbare, chafe, fret, rub, wear, wear away, wear thin

frayed frazzled, out at elbows, ragged, tattered, threadbare, worn

freak n. 1. aberration, abnormality, abortion, anomaly, grotesque, malformation, monster, monstrosity, mutant, oddity, queer fish

(*Inf.*), *rara avis*, sport, teratism, weirdo or weirdie (*Inf.*) 2. caprice, crotchet, fad, fancy, folly, humour, irregularity, quirk, turn, twist, vagary, whim, whimsy 3. *Sl.* addict, aficionado, buff, devotee, enthusiast, fan, fanatic, fiend (*Inf.*), nut (*Sl.*) ~adj. 4. aberrant, abnormal, atypical, bizarre, erratic, exceptional, fluky (*Inf.*), fortuitous, odd, queer, unaccountable, unexpected, unforeseen, unparalleled, unpredictable, unusual

free adj. 1. complimentary, for free (*Inf.*), for nothing, free of charge, gratis, gratuitous, on the house, unpaid, without charge 2. at large, at liberty, footloose, independent, liberated, loose, off the hook (*Inf.*), on the loose, uncommitted, unconstrained, unengaged, unfettered, unrestrained 3. able, allowed, clear, disengaged, loose, open, permitted, unattached, unengaged, unhampered, unimpeded, unobstructed, unregulated, unrestricted, untrammelled 4. *With of* above, beyond, deficient in, devoid of, exempt from, immune to, lacking (in), not liable to, safe from, sans (*Archaic*), unaffected by, unencumbered by, untouched by, without 5. autarchic, autonomous, democratic, emancipated, independent, self-governing, self-ruling, sovereign 6. at leisure, available, empty, extra, idle, not tied down, spare, unemployed, uninhabited, unoccupied, unused, vacant 7. casual, easy, familiar, forward, frank, free and easy, informal, laid-back (*Inf.*), lax, liberal, loose, natural, open, relaxed, spontaneous, unbidden, unceremonious, unconstrained, unforced, uninhibited 8. big (*Inf.*), bounteous, bountiful, charitable, eager, generous, hospitable, lavish, liberal, munificent, open-handed, prodigal, unsparing, unstinting, willing 9. **free and easy** casual, easy-going, informal, laid-back (*Inf.*), lax, lenient, liberal, relaxed, tolerant, unceremonious ~adv. 10. at no cost, for love, gratis, without charge 11. abundantly, copiously, freely, idly, loosely ~v.

12. deliver, discharge, disenthrall, emancipate, let go, let out, liberate, loose, manumit, release, set at liberty, set free, turn loose, uncage, unchain, unfetter, unleash, untie 13. clear, cut loose, deliver, disengage, disentangle, exempt, extricate, ransom, redeem, relieve, rescue, rid, unburden, undo, unshackle

freedom 1. autonomy, deliverance, emancipation, home rule, independence, liberty, manumission, release, self-government 2. exemption, immunity, impunity, privilege 3. ability, carte blanche, discretion, elbowroom, facility, flexibility, free rein, latitude, leeway, licence, opportunity, play, power, range, scope 4. abandon, candour, directness, ease, familiarity, frankness, informality, ingenuousness, lack of restraint or reserve, openness, unconstraint 5. boldness, brazenness, disrespect, forwardness, impertinence, laxity, licence, overfamiliarity, presumption

free-for-all affray (*Law*), brawl, donnybrook, dust-up (*Inf.*), fight, fracas, melee, riot, row, shindy (*Sl.*)

free hand *n.* authority, carte blanche, discretion, freedom, latitude, liberty, scope

freely 1. of one's own accord, of one's own free will, spontaneously, voluntarily, willingly, without prompting 2. candidly, frankly, openly, plainly, unreservedly, without reserve 3. as you please, unchallenged, without let or hindrance, without restraint 4. abundantly, amply, bountifully, copiously, extravagantly, lavishly, liberally, like water, open-handedly, unstintingly, with a free hand 5. cleanly, easily, loosely, readily, smoothly

freethinker agnostic, deist, doubter, infidel, sceptic, unbeliever

freeze 1. benumb, chill, congeal, glaciate, harden, ice over or up, stiffen 2. fix, hold up, inhibit, peg, stop, suspend

freezing arctic, biting, bitter, chill, chilled, cutting, frost-bound, frosty, glacial, icy, numbing, penetrating, polar, raw, Siberian, wintry

freight *n.* 1. carriage, conveyance, shipment, transportation 2. bales, bulk, burden, cargo, consignment, contents, goods, haul, lading, load, merchandise, payload, tonnage

French Gallic

frenzied agitated, all het up (*Inf.*), convulsive, distracted, distraught, excited, feverish, frantic, frenetic, furious, hysterical, mad, maniacal, rabid, uncontrolled, wild

frenzy 1. aberration, agitation, delirium, derangement, distraction, fury, hysteria, insanity, lunacy, madness, mania, paroxysm, passion, rage, seizure, transport, turmoil 2. bout, burst, convulsion, fit, outburst, paroxysm, spasm

frequency constancy, frequentness, periodicity, prevalence, recurrence, repetition

frequent[1] *adj.* common, constant, continual, customary, everyday, familiar, habitual, incessant, numerous, persistent, recurrent, recurring, reiterated, repeated, usual

frequent[2] *v.* attend, be a regular customer of, be found at, hang out at (*Inf.*), haunt, patronize, resort, visit

frequently commonly, customarily, habitually, many a time, many times, much, not infrequently, oft (*Literary*), often, oftentimes (*Archaic*), over and over again, repeatedly, thick and fast, very often

fresh 1. different, latest, modern, modernistic, new, new-fangled, novel, original, recent, this season's, unconventional, unusual, up-to-date 2. added, additional, auxiliary, extra, further, more, other, renewed, supplementary 3. bracing, bright, brisk, clean, clear, cool, crisp, invigorating, pure, refreshing, spanking, sparkling, stiff, sweet, unpolluted 4. alert, bouncing, bright, bright eyed and bushy tailed (*Inf.*), chipper (*Inf., chiefly U.S.*), energetic, full of vim and vigour (*Inf.*), invigorated, keen, like a new man, lively, refreshed, rested, restored, revived, sprightly, spry, vigorous, vital 5. blooming, clear, fair, florid, glowing, good, hardy, healthy, rosy, ruddy, whole~ some 6. dewy, undimmed, unfaded, unwearied, unwithered, verdant, vivid, young 7. artless, callow, green, inexperienced, natural, new, raw, uncultivated, untrained, untried, youthful 8. crude, green, natural, raw, uncured, undried, un~ processed, unsalted 9. *Inf.* bold, brazen, cheeky, disrespectful, fa~ miliar, flip (*Inf., chiefly U.S.*), for~ ward, impudent, insolent, pert, presumptuous, saucy, smart-alecky (*Inf.*)

freshen 1. enliven, freshen up, liv~ en up, refresh, restore, revitalize, rouse, spruce up, titivate 2. air, pu~ rify, ventilate

freshness 1. innovativeness, in~ ventiveness, newness, novelty, originality 2. bloom, brightness, cleanness, clearness, dewiness, glow, shine, sparkle, vigour, wholesomeness

fret 1. affront, agonize, anguish, an~ noy, brood, chagrin, goad, grieve, harass, irritate, lose sleep over, provoke, ruffle, torment, upset *or* distress oneself, worry 2. agitate, bother, distress, disturb, gall, irk, nag, nettle, peeve (*Inf.*), pique, rankle with, rile, trouble, vex

fretful captious, complaining, cross, crotchety (*Inf.*), edgy, fractious, ir~ ritable, out of sorts, peevish, petu~ lant, querulous, short-tempered, splenetic, testy, touchy, uneasy

friction 1. abrasion, attrition, chaf~ ing, erosion, fretting, grating, irri~ tation, rasping, resistance, rubbing, scraping, wearing away 2. ani~ mosity, antagonism, bad blood, bad feeling, bickering, conflict, dis~ agreement, discontent, discord, disharmony, dispute, dissension, hostility, incompatibility, opposi~ tion, resentment, rivalry, wran~ gling

friend 1. Achates, alter ego, boon companion, bosom friend, buddy (*Inf.*), china (*Sl.*), chum (*Inf.*), companion, comrade, confidant, crony, familiar, intimate, mate (*Inf.*), pal, partner, playmate, soul mate 2. adherent, advocate, ally, associate, backer, benefactor, par~ tisan, patron, supporter, well- wisher

friendless abandoned, alienated, all alone, alone, cut off, deserted, estranged, forlorn, forsaken, iso~ lated, lonely, lonesome, ostracized, shunned, solitary, unattached, with no one to turn to, without a friend in the world, without ties

friendliness affability, amiability, companionability, congeniality, conviviality, geniality, kindliness, mateyness (*Brit. inf.*), neighbourli~ ness, open arms, sociability, warmth

friendly affable, affectionate, ami~ able, amicable, attached, attentive, auspicious, beneficial, benevolent, benign, chummy (*Inf.*), close, club~ by, companionable, comradely, conciliatory, confiding, convivial, cordial, familiar, favourable, fond, fraternal, genial, good, helpful, in~ timate, kind, kindly, matey (*Brit. inf.*), neighbourly, on good terms, on visiting terms, outgoing, peace~ able, propitious, receptive, socia~ ble, sympathetic, thick (*Inf.*), wel~ coming, well-disposed

friendship affection, affinity, alli~ ance, amity, attachment, benevo~ lence, closeness, concord, famili~ arity, fondness, friendliness, good- fellowship, good will, harmony, in~ timacy, love, rapport, regard

fright 1. alarm, apprehension, (blue) funk (*Inf.*), cold sweat, con~ sternation, dismay, dread, fear, fear and trembling, horror, panic, quaking, scare, shock, terror, the shivers, trepidation 2. *Inf.* eyesore, frump, mess (*Inf.*), scarecrow, sight (*Inf.*)

frighten affright (*Archaic*), alarm, appal, cow, daunt, dismay, freeze one's blood, intimidate, make one's blood run cold, make one's hair stand on end (*Inf.*), make (some~ one) jump out of his skin (*Inf.*), petrify, put the wind up (someone)

(*Inf.*), scare, scare (someone) stiff, scare the living daylights out of (someone) (*Inf.*), shock, startle, terrify, terrorize, throw into a fright, throw into a panic, unman, unnerve

frightened abashed, affrighted (*Archaic*), afraid, alarmed, cowed, dismayed, frozen, in a cold sweat, in a panic, in fear and trepidation, numb with fear, panicky, petrified, scared, scared stiff, startled, terrified, terrorized, terror-stricken, unnerved

frightening alarming, appalling, bloodcurdling, daunting, dismaying, dreadful, fearful, fearsome, hair-raising, horrifying, intimidating, menacing, scary (*Inf.*), shocking, spooky (*Inf.*), terrifying, unnerving

frightful 1. alarming, appalling, awful, dire, dread, dreadful, fearful, ghastly, grim, grisly, gruesome, harrowing, hideous, horrendous, horrible, horrid, lurid, macabre, petrifying, shocking, terrible, terrifying, traumatic, unnerving, unspeakable 2. annoying, awful, disagreeable, dreadful, extreme, great, insufferable, terrible, terrific, unpleasant

frigid 1. arctic, chill, cold, cool, frost-bound, frosty, frozen, gelid, glacial, hyperboreal, icy, Siberian, wintry 2. aloof, austere, coldhearted, forbidding, formal, icy, lifeless, passionless, passive, repellent, rigid, stiff, unapproachable, unbending, unfeeling, unloving, unresponsive

frigidity aloofness, austerity, chill, cold-heartedness, coldness, frostiness, iciness, impassivity, lack of response, lifelessness, passivity, touch-me-not attitude, unapproachability, unresponsiveness, wintriness

frills additions, affectation(s), bits and pieces, decoration(s), dressing up, embellishment(s), extras, fanciness, fandangles, finery, frilliness, frippery, fuss, gewgaws, jazz (*Sl.*), mannerisms, nonsense, ornamentation, ostentation, superfluities, tomfoolery, trimmings

fringe *n.* 1. binding, border, edging, hem, tassel, trimming 2. borderline, edge, limits, march, marches, margin, outskirts, perimeter, periphery ~*adj.* 3. unconventional, unofficial, unorthodox ~*v.* 4. border, edge, enclose, skirt, surround, trim

frisk 1. bounce, caper, cavort, curvet, dance, frolic, gambol, hop, jump, play, prance, rollick, romp, skip, sport, trip 2. *Inf.* check, inspect, run over, search, shake down (*U.S. sl.*)

frisky bouncy, coltish, frolicsome, full of beans (*Inf.*), full of joie de vivre, high-spirited, in high spirits, kittenish, lively, playful, rollicking, romping, spirited, sportive

fritter (away) dally away, dissipate, fool away, idle (away), misspend, run through, spend like water, squander, waste

frivolity childishness, flightiness, flippancy, flummery, folly, frivolousness, fun, gaiety, giddiness, jest, levity, light-heartedness, lightness, nonsense, puerility, shallowness, silliness, superficiality, trifling, triviality

frivolous 1. childish, dizzy, empty-headed, flighty, flip (*Inf.*), flippant, foolish, giddy, idle, ill-considered, juvenile, light-minded, nonserious, puerile, silly, superficial 2. extravagant, impractical, light, minor, niggling, paltry, peripheral, petty, pointless, shallow, trifling, trivial, unimportant

frizzle crisp, fry, hiss, roast, scorch, sizzle, sputter

frolic *v.* 1. caper, cavort, cut capers, frisk, gambol, lark, make merry, play, rollick, romp, sport ~*n.* 2. antic, escapade, gambado, gambol, game, lark, prank, revel, romp, spree 3. amusement, drollery, fun, fun and games, gaiety, high jinks, merriment, skylarking (*Inf.*), sport

frolicsome coltish, frisky, gay, kittenish, lively, merry, playful, rollicking, sportive, sprightly, wanton (*Archaic*)

front *n.* 1. anterior, exterior, fa~
çade, face, facing, foreground,
forepart, frontage, obverse 2. be~
ginning, fore, forefront, front line,
head, lead, top, van, vanguard 3.
air, appearance, aspect, bearing,
countenance, demeanour, expres~
sion, exterior, face, manner, mien,
show 4. blind, cover, cover-up, dis~
guise, façade, mask, pretext, show
5. **in front** ahead, before, first, in
advance, in the lead, in the van,
leading, preceding, to the fore
~*adj.* 6. first, foremost, head,
headmost, lead, leading, topmost
~*v.* 7. face (onto), look over *or*
onto, overlook

frontier borderland, borderline,
bound, boundary, confines, edge,
limit, marches, perimeter, verge

frost freeze, freeze-up, hoarfrost,
Jack Frost, rime

frosty 1. chilly, cold, frozen, hoar
(*Rare*), ice-capped, icicled, icy,
rimy, wintry 2. discouraging, frigid,
off-putting, standoffish, unenthusi~
astic, unfriendly, unwelcoming

froth 1. *n.* bubbles, effervescence,
foam, head, lather, scum, spume,
suds 2. *v.* bubble over, come to a
head, effervesce, fizz, foam, lather

frothy 1. foaming, foamy, spumes~
cent, spumous, spumy, sudsy 2. *Fig.*
empty, frilly, frivolous, light, petty,
slight, trifling, trivial, trumpery,
unnecessary, unsubstantial, vain

frown 1. give a dirty look, glare,
glower, knit one's brows, look dag~
gers, lower, scowl 2. *With* **on** *or*
upon disapprove of, discoun~
tenance, discourage, dislike, look
askance at, not take kindly to,
show disapproval *or* displeasure,
take a dim view of, view with dis~
favour

frowsty close, fuggy, fusty, ill-
smelling, musty, stale, stuffy

frozen 1. arctic, chilled, chilled to
the marrow, frigid, frosted, ice~
bound, ice-cold, ice-covered, ice~
numb 2. fixed, pegged (*of prices*),
petrified, rooted, stock-still,
stopped, suspended, turned to
stone

frugal abstemious, careful, cheese~
paring, economical, meagre, nig~
gardly, parsimonious, penny-wise,
provident, prudent, saving, spar~
ing, thrifty

fruit 1. crop, harvest, produce,
product, yield 2. advantage, ben~
efit, consequence, effect, outcome,
profit, result, return, reward

fruitful 1. fecund, fertile, fructifer~
ous 2. abundant, copious, flush,
plenteous, plentiful, productive,
profuse, prolific, rich, spawning 3.
advantageous, beneficial, effective,
gainful, productive, profitable, re~
warding, successful, useful, well-
spent, worthwhile

fruition actualization, attainment,
completion, consummation, enjoy~
ment, fulfilment, materialization,
maturation, maturity, perfection,
realization, ripeness

fruitless abortive, barren, bootless,
futile, idle, ineffectual, in vain,
pointless, profitless, to no avail, to
no effect, unavailing, unfruitful,
unproductive, unprofitable, unpro~
lific, unsuccessful, useless, vain

fruity 1. full, mellow, resonant, rich
2. *Inf.* bawdy, blue, hot, indecent,
indelicate, juicy, near the knuckle
(*Inf.*), racy, ripe, risqué, salacious,
sexy, smutty, spicy (*Inf.*), sugges~
tive, titillating, vulgar

frustrate 1. baffle, balk, block,
check, circumvent, confront,
counter, defeat, disappoint, foil,
forestall, inhibit, neutralize, nullify,
render null and void, stymie,
thwart 2. depress, discourage, dis~
hearten

frustrated carrying a chip on one's
shoulder (*Inf.*), disappointed, dis~
contented, discouraged, disheart~
ened, embittered, foiled, irked, re~
sentful

frustration 1. blocking, circum~
vention, contravention, curbing,
failure, foiling, nonfulfilment, non~
success, obstruction, thwarting 2.
annoyance, disappointment, dis~
satisfaction, grievance, irritation,
resentment, vexation

fuddled confused, drunk, inebriat~
ed, intoxicated, muddled, muzzy,

sozzled (*Inf.*), stupefied, tipsy, woozy (*Inf.*)

fuddy-duddy *n.* back number (*Inf.*), conservative, dodo (*Inf.*), fossil, museum piece, (old) fogy, square (*Inf.*), stick-in-the-mud (*Inf.*), stuffed shirt (*Inf.*)

fudge *v.* avoid, cook (*Sl.*), dodge, equivocate, evade, fake, falsify, hedge, misrepresent, patch up, shuffle, slant, stall

fuel 1. *n. Fig.* ammunition, encouragement, fodder, food, incitement, material, means, nourishment, provocation 2. *v.* charge, fan, feed, fire, incite, inflame, nourish, stoke up, sustain

fugitive 1. *n.* deserter, escapee, refugee, runagate (*Archaic*), runaway 2. *adj.* brief, ephemeral, evanescent, fleeing, fleeting, flitting, flying, fugacious, momentary, passing, short, short-lived, temporary, transient, transitory, unstable

fulfil accomplish, achieve, answer, bring to completion, carry out, complete, comply with, conclude, conform to, discharge, effect, execute, fill, finish, keep, meet, obey, observe, perfect, perform, realise, satisfy

fulfilment accomplishment, achievement, attainment, carrying out *or* through, completion, consummation, crowning, discharge, discharging, effecting, end, implementation, observance, perfection, realization

full 1. brimful, brimming, complete, entire, filled, gorged, intact, loaded, replete, sated, satiated, satisfied, saturated, stocked, sufficient 2. abundant, adequate, all-inclusive, ample, broad, comprehensive, copious, detailed, exhaustive, extensive, generous, maximum, plenary, plenteous, plentiful, thorough, unabridged 3. chock-a-block, chock-full, crammed, crowded, in use, jammed, occupied, packed, taken 4. clear, deep, distinct, loud, resonant, rich, rounded 5. baggy, balloonlike, buxom, capacious, curvaceous, large, loose, plump, puffy, rounded,

voluminous, voluptuous 6. **in full** completely, in its entirety, in total, *in toto*, without exception 7. **to the full** completely, entirely, fully, thoroughly, to the utmost, without reservation

full-blooded gutsy (*Sl.*), hearty, lusty, mettlesome, red-blooded, vigorous, virile

full-bodied fruity, full-flavoured, heady, heavy, mellow, redolent, rich, strong, well-matured

full-grown adult, developed, full-fledged, grown-up, in one's prime, marriageable, mature, nubile, of age, ripe

fullness 1. abundance, adequateness, ampleness, copiousness, fill, glut, plenty, profusion, repletion, satiety, saturation, sufficiency 2. broadness, completeness, comprehensiveness, entirety, extensiveness, plenitude, totality, vastness, wealth, wholeness 3. clearness, loudness, resonance, richness, strength 4. curvaceousness, dilation, distension, enlargement, roundness, swelling, tumescence, voluptuousness

full-scale all-encompassing, all-out, comprehensive, exhaustive, extensive, full-dress, in-depth, major, proper, sweeping, thorough, thoroughgoing, wide-ranging

fully 1. absolutely, altogether, completely, entirely, every inch, from first to last, heart and soul, in all respects, intimately, perfectly, positively, thoroughly, totally, utterly, wholly 2. abundantly, adequately, amply, comprehensively, enough, plentifully, satisfactorily, sufficiently 3. at least, quite, without (any) exaggeration, without a word of a lie (*Inf.*)

fully-fledged experienced, mature, professional, proficient, qualified, senior, time-served, trained

fulmination condemnation, denunciation, diatribe, invective, obloquy, philippic, reprobation, tirade

fulsome adulatory, cloying, excessive, extravagant, fawning, gross, immoderate, ingratiating, inordi

nate, insincere, nauseating, over~
done, saccharine, sickening,
smarmy (*Inf.*), sycophantic, unctu~
ous

fumble 1. bumble, feel around,
flounder, grope, paw (*Inf.*), scrab~
ble 2. botch, bungle, make a hash
of (*Inf.*), mess up, misfield, mis~
handle, mismanage, muff, spoil

fume *Fig.* 1. *v.* boil, chafe, champ
at the bit (*Inf.*), get hot under the
collar (*Inf.*), get steamed up about
(*Sl.*), rage, rant, rave, seethe,
smoulder, storm 2. *n.* agitation,
dither, fit, fret, fury, passion, rage,
stew (*Inf.*), storm

fumes effluvium, exhalation, ex~
haust, gas, haze, miasma, pollution,
reek, smog, smoke, stench, vapour

fumigate clean out *or* up, cleanse,
disinfect, purify, sanitize, sterilize

fuming all steamed up (*Sl.*), angry,
at boiling point (*Inf.*), enraged,
foaming at the mouth, in a rage,
incensed, raging, roused, seething,
up in arms

fun *n.* 1. amusement, cheer, dis~
traction, diversion, enjoyment, en~
tertainment, frolic, gaiety, good
time, high jinks, jollification, jollity,
joy, junketing, living it up, merri~
ment, merrymaking, mirth, pleas~
ure, recreation, romp, sport, treat,
whoopee (*Inf.*) 2. buffoonery,
clowning, foolery, game, horse~
play, jesting, jocularity, joking,
nonsense, play, playfulness, sky~
larking (*Inf.*), sport, teasing, tom~
foolery 3. **in** *or* **for fun** facetiously,
for a joke, for a laugh, in jest,
jokingly, light-heartedly, mischie~
vously, playfully, roguishly, teas~
ingly, tongue in cheek, with a
gleam *or* twinkle in one's eye, with
a straight face 4. **make fun of** de~
ride, hold up to ridicule, lampoon,
laugh at, make a fool of, make
game of, make sport of, make the
butt of, mock, parody, poke fun at,
rag, rib (*Inf.*), ridicule, satirize,
scoff at, send up (*Brit. inf.*), sneer
at, take ff, taunt ~*adj.* 5. amusing,
convivial, diverting, enjoyable, en~
tertaining, lively, witty

function *n.* 1. activity, business,
capacity, charge, concern, duty,
employment, exercise, job, mis~
sion, occupation, office, operation,
part, post, province, purpose, rai~
son d'être, responsibility, role,
situation, task ~*v.* 2. act, act the
part of, behave, be in commission,
be in operation *or* action, be in
running order, do duty, go, offici~
ate, operate, perform, run, serve,
serve one's turn, work ~*n.* 3. affair,
do (*Inf.*), gathering, reception, so~
cial occasion

functional hard-wearing, opera~
tive, practical, serviceable, useful,
utilitarian, utility, working

fund *n.* 1. capital, endowment,
foundation, kitty, pool, reserve,
stock, store, supply 2. hoard, mine,
repository, reserve, reservoir,
source, storehouse, treasury, vein
~*v.* 3. capitalize, endow, finance,
float, pay for, promote, stake, sub~
sidize, support

fundamental 1. *adj.* basic, cardi~
nal, central, constitutional, crucial,
elementary, essential, first, impor~
tant, indispensable, integral, in~
trinsic, key, necessary, organic,
primary, prime, principal, rudi~
mentary, underlying, vital 2. *n.*
axiom, basic, cornerstone, essen~
tial, first principle, law, principle,
rudiment, rule, *sine qua non*

fundamentally at bottom, at heart,
basically, essentially, intrinsically,
primarily, radically

funds 1. bread (*Sl.*), capital, cash,
dough (*Sl.*), finance, hard cash,
money, ready money, resources,
savings, the ready (*Inf.*), the
wherewithal 2. **in funds** flush
(*Inf.*), in the black, solvent, well-off,
well-supplied

funeral burial, inhumation, inter~
ment, obsequies

funnel *v.* channel, conduct, convey,
direct, filter, move, pass, pour

funny *adj.* 1. absurd, amusing, a
scream (card, caution) (*Inf.*),
comic, comical, diverting, droll,
entertaining, facetious, farcical,
hilarious, humorous, jocose, jocu~
lar, jolly, killing (*Inf.*), laughable,
ludicrous, rich, ridiculous, riotous,

risible, side-splitting, silly, slap~ stick, waggish, witty 2. curious, du~ bious, mysterious, odd, peculiar, perplexing, puzzling, queer, re~ markable, strange, suspicious, un~ usual, weird ~n. 3. *Inf.* crack (*Sl.*), jest, joke, play on words, pun, quip, wisecrack, witticism

furious 1. angry, beside oneself, boiling, enraged, frantic, frenzied, fuming, incensed, infuriated, in high dudgeon, livid (*Inf.*), mad, maddened, on the warpath (*Inf.*), raging, up in arms, wrathful, wroth (*Archaic*) 2. agitated, boisterous, fierce, impetuous, intense, savage, stormy, tempestuous, tumultuous, turbulent, ungovernable, unre~ strained, vehement, violent, wild

furnish 1. appoint, decorate, equip, fit (out, up), outfit, provide, provi~ sion, rig, stock, store, supply 2. af~ ford, bestow, endow, give, grant, offer, present, provide, reveal, supply

furniture appliances, appoint~ ments, chattels, effects, equip~ ment, fittings, furnishings, goods, household goods, movable proper~ ty, movables, possessions, things (*Inf.*)

furore 1. commotion, disturbance, excitement, flap (*Inf.*), frenzy, fury, hullabaloo, outburst, outcry, stir, to-do, uproar 2. craze, enthusiasm, mania, rage

further 1. *adj.* additional, extra, fresh, more, new, other, sup~ plementary 2. *adv.* additionally, also, as well as, besides, further~ more, in addition, moreover, on top of, over and above, to boot, what's more, yet 3. *v.* advance, aid, assist, champion, contribute to, encourage, expedite, facilitate, forward, foster, hasten, help, lend support to, patronize, plug (*Inf.*), promote, push, speed, succour, work for

furthest extreme, farthest, furthermost, most distant, outer~ most, outmost, remotest, ultimate, uttermost

furtive clandestine, cloaked, con~ spiratorial, covert, hidden, secret, secretive, skulking, slinking, sly, sneaking, sneaky, stealthy, surrep~ titious, underhand, under-the-table

fury 1. anger, frenzy, impetuosity, ire, madness, passion, rage, wrath 2. ferocity, fierceness, force, in~ tensity, power, savagery, severity, tempestuousness, turbulence, ve~ hemence, violence 3. bacchante, hag, hellcat, shrew, spitfire, ter~ magant, virago, vixen

fuss *n.* 1. ado, agitation, bother, bustle, commotion, confusion, ex~ citement, fidget, flap (*Inf.*), flurry, fluster, flutter, hurry, palaver, pother, stir, storm in a teacup (*Brit.*), to-do, upset, worry 2. alter~ cation, argument, bother, com~ plaint, difficulty, display, furore, hassle (*Inf.*), objection, row, squabble, trouble, unrest, upset ~v. 3. bustle, chafe, fidget, flap (*Inf.*), fret, fume, get in a stew (*Inf.*), get worked up, labour over, make a meal of (*Inf.*), make a thing of (*Inf.*), niggle, take pains, worry

fussy 1. choosy (*Inf.*), dainty, diffi~ cult, discriminating, exacting, fad~ dish, faddy, fastidious, finicky, hard to please, nit-picking (*Inf.*), old-maidish, old womanish, overpar~ ticular, particular, pernickety, squeamish 2. busy, cluttered, over~ decorated, overelaborate, over~ embellished, overworked, rococo

futile 1. abortive, barren, bootless, empty, forlorn, fruitless, hollow, ineffectual, in vain, nugatory, profitless, sterile, to no avail, un~ availing, unproductive, unprofit~ able, unsuccessful, useless, vain, valueless, worthless 2. idle, point~ less, trifling, trivial, unimportant

futility 1. emptiness, fruitlessness, hollowness, ineffectiveness, use~ lessness 2. pointlessness, triviality, unimportance, vanity

future 1. *n.* expectation, hereafter, outlook, prospect, time to come 2. *adj.* approaching, coming, des~ tined, eventual, expected, fated, forthcoming, impending, in the of~ fing, later, prospective, subse~ quent, to be, to come, ultimate, unborn

G

gad (about or around) gallivant,
ramble, range, roam, rove, run
around, stravaig (Scot., & northern
English dialect), stray, traipse
(Inf.), wander

gadabout gallivanter, pleasureseeker, rambler, rover, wanderer

gadget appliance, contraption
(Inf.), contrivance, device, gimmick, gizmo (Sl., chiefly U.S.), invention, novelty, thing, tool

gaffe bloomer (Inf.), blunder, boob
(Brit. sl.), boo-boo (Inf.), clanger
(Inf.), faux pas, gaucherie, howler,
indiscretion, mistake, slip, solecism

gaffer 1. granddad, greybeard, old
boy (Inf.), old fellow, old man, old-
timer (U.S.) 2. Inf. boss (Inf.), foreman, ganger, manager, overseer,
superintendent, supervisor

gag¹ v. 1. curb, muffle, muzzle, quiet, silence, stifle, still, stop up, suppress, throttle 2. Sl. disgorge,
heave, puke (Sl.), retch, spew,
throw up (Inf.), vomit 3. Sl. choke,
gasp, pant, struggle for breath

gag² crack (Sl.), funny (Inf.), hoax,
jest, joke, wisecrack (Inf.), witticism

gaiety 1. animation, blitheness,
blithesomeness (Literary), cheerfulness, effervescence, elation, exhilaration, glee, good humour, high
spirits, hilarity, joie de vivre, jollity, joviality, joyousness, light-
heartedness, liveliness, merriment,
mirth, sprightliness, vivacity 2.
celebration, conviviality, festivity,
fun, jollification, merrymaking,
revelry, revels 3. brightness, brilliance, colour, colourfulness,
gaudiness, glitter, show, showiness,
sparkle

gaily 1. blithely, cheerfully, gleefully, happily, joyfully, light-
heartedly, merrily 2. brightly, bril-
liantly, colourfully, flamboyantly,
flashily, gaudily, showily

gain v. 1. achieve, acquire, advance, attain, bag, build up, capture, collect, enlist, gather, get,
glean, harvest, improve, increase,
net, obtain, pick up, procure, profit,
realize, reap, secure, win, win over
2. acquire, bring in, clear, earn,
get, make, net, obtain, produce,
realize, win, yield 3. Usually with
on a. approach, catch up with,
close with, get nearer, narrow the
gap, overtake b. draw or pull away
from, get farther away, leave behind, outdistance, recede, widen
the gap 4. arrive at, attain, come
to, get to, reach 5. gain time delay,
procrastinate, stall, temporize, use
delaying tactics ~n. 6. accretion,
achievement, acquisition, advance,
advancement, advantage, attainment, benefit, dividend, earnings,
emolument, growth, headway, improvement, income, increase, increment, lucre, proceeds, produce,
profit, progress, return, rise, winnings, yield

gains booty, earnings, gainings,
pickings, prize, proceeds, profits,
revenue, takings, winnings

gainsay contradict, contravene,
controvert, deny, disaffirm, disagree with, dispute

gait bearing, carriage, pace, step,
stride, tread, walk

gala 1. n. carnival, celebration, festival, festivity, fête, jamboree,
pageant, party 2. adj. celebratory,
convivial, festal, festive, gay, jovial, joyful, merry

gale 1. blast, cyclone, hurricane,
squall, storm, tempest, tornado,
typhoon 2. Inf. burst, eruption, explosion, fit, howl, outbreak, outburst, peal, shout, shriek

gall¹ 1. Inf. brass (Inf.), brass neck
(Inf.), brazenness, cheek (Inf.), effrontery, impertinence, impudence, insolence, nerve (Inf.), sauciness 2. acrimony, animosity, animus, antipathy, bad blood, bile,
bitterness, enmity, hostility, ma-

levolence, malice, malignity, rancour, sourness, spite, spleen, venom

gall[2] n. 1. abrasion, chafe, excoriation, raw spot, scrape, sore, sore spot, wound 2. aggravation (Inf.), annoyance, bother, botheration (Inf.), exasperation, harassment, irritant, irritation, nuisance, pest, provocation, vexation ~v. 3. abrade, bark, chafe, excoriate, fret, graze, irritate, rub raw, scrape, skin 4. aggravate (Inf.), annoy, bother, exasperate, fret, harass, irk, irritate, nag, nettle, peeve (Inf.), pester, plague, provoke, rankle, rile (Inf.), rub up the wrong way, ruffle, vex

gallant adj. 1. bold, brave, courageous, daring, dashing, dauntless, doughty, fearless, game (Inf.), heroic, high-spirited, honourable, intrepid, lion-hearted, manful, manly, mettlesome, noble, plucky, valiant, valorous 2. attentive, chivalrous, courteous, courtly, gentlemanly, gracious, magnanimous, noble, polite 3. august, dignified, elegant, glorious, grand, imposing, lofty, magnificent, noble, splendid, stately ~n. 4. admirer, beau, boyfriend, escort, lover, paramour, suitor, wooer 5. beau, blade (Archaic), buck (Inf.), dandy, fop, ladies' man, lady-killer (Inf.), man about town, man of fashion 6. adventurer, cavalier, champion, daredevil, hero, knight, man of mettle, preux chevalier

gallantry 1. audacity, boldness, bravery, courage, courageousness, daring, dauntlessness, derring-do (Archaic), fearlessness, heroism, intrepidity, manliness, mettle, nerve, pluck, prowess, spirit, valiance, valour 2. attentiveness, chivalry, courteousness, courtesy, courtliness, elegance, gentlemanliness, graciousness, nobility, politeness

galling aggravating (Inf.), annoying, bitter, bothersome, exasperating, harassing, humiliating, irksome, irritating, nettlesome, plaguing, provoking, rankling, vexatious, vexing

gallop bolt, career, dart, dash, fly, hasten, hie (Archaic), hurry, race, run, rush, scud, shoot, speed, sprint, tear along, zoom

galore all over the place, aplenty, everywhere, in abundance, in great quantity, in numbers, in profusion, to spare

galvanize arouse, awaken, electrify, excite, fire, inspire, invigorate, jolt, move, provoke, quicken, shock, spur, startle, stimulate, stir, thrill, vitalize, wake

gamble v. 1. back, bet, game, have a flutter (Inf.), lay or make a bet, play, punt, stake, try one's luck, wager 2. back, chance, hazard, put one's faith or trust in, risk, speculate, stake, stick one's neck out (Inf.), take a chance, venture ~n. 3. chance, leap in the dark, lottery, risk, speculation, uncertainty, venture 4. bet, flutter (Inf.), punt, wager

gambol 1. v. caper, cavort, curvet, cut a caper, frisk, frolic, hop, jump, prance, rollick, skip 2. n. antic, caper, frolic, gambado, hop, jump, prance, skip, spring

game[1] n. 1. amusement, distraction, diversion, entertainment, frolic, fun, jest, joke, lark, merriment, pastime, play, recreation, romp, sport 2. competition, contest, event, match, meeting, round, tournament 3. adventure, business, enterprise, line, occupation, plan, proceeding, scheme, undertaking 4. chase, prey, quarry, wild animals 5. Inf. design, device, plan, plot, ploy, scheme, stratagem, strategy, tactic, trick 6. make (a) game of deride, make a fool of, make a laughing stock, make fun of, make sport of, mock, poke fun at, ridicule, send up (Brit. inf.)

game[2] adj. 1. bold, brave, courageous, dauntless, dogged, fearless, gallant, heroic, intrepid, persevering, persistent, plucky, resolute, spirited, unflinching, valiant, valorous 2. desirous, disposed, eager, inclined, interested, prepared, ready, willing

gamut area, catalogue, compass,

field, range, scale, scope, series, sweep

gang band, circle, clique, club, company, coterie, crew (*Inf.*), crowd, group, herd, horde, lot, mob, pack, party, ring, set, shift, squad, team, troupe

gangling, gangly angular, awk~ ward, lanky, loose-jointed, rangy, rawboned, skinny, spindly, tall

gangster bandit, brigand, crook (*Inf.*), desperado, gang member, hood (*U.S. sl.*), hoodlum (*Chiefly U.S.*), mobster (*U.S. sl.*), racketeer, robber, ruffian, thug, tough

gap 1. blank, breach, break, chink, cleft, crack, cranny, crevice, dis~ continuity, divide, hiatus, hole, interlude, intermission, interrup~ tion, interstice, interval, lacuna, lull, opening, pause, recess, rent, rift, space, vacuity, void 2. differ~ ence, disagreement, disparity, di~ vergence, inconsistency

gape 1. gawk, gawp (*Brit. sl.*), gog~ gle, stare, wonder 2. crack, open, split, yawn

gaping broad, cavernous, great, open, vast, wide, wide open, yawn~ ing

garbage 1. bits and pieces, debris, detritus, junk, litter, odds and ends, rubbish, scraps 2. dross, filth, muck, offal, refuse, rubbish, scour~ ings, slops, sweepings, swill, trash (*Chiefly U.S.*), waste

garble 1. confuse, jumble, mix up 2. corrupt, distort, doctor, falsify, misinterpret, misquote, misreport, misrepresent, misstate, mistrans~ late, mutilate, pervert, slant, tam~ per with, twist

garish brassy, brummagem, cheap, flash (*Inf.*), flashy, flaunting, gaudy, glaring, glittering, loud, meretri~ cious, raffish, showy, tasteless, tawdry, vulgar

garland 1. *n.* bays, chaplet, coronal, crown, festoon, honours, laurels, wreath 2. *v.* adorn, crown, deck, festoon, wreathe

garments apparel, array, articles of clothing, attire, clothes, clothing, costume, dress, duds (*Inf.*), garb, gear (*Sl.*), habiliment, habit, outfit,

raiment (*Archaic*), robes, togs, uniform, vestments, wear

garner 1. *v.* accumulate, amass, as~ semble, collect, deposit, gather, hoard, husband, lay in or up, put by, reserve, save, stockpile, store, stow away, treasure 2. *n. Literary* depository, granary, store, store~ house, vault

garnish 1. *v.* adorn, beautify, be~ deck, deck, decorate, embellish, enhance, grace, ornament, set off, trim 2. *n.* adornment, decoration, embellishment, enhancement, garniture, ornament, ornamenta~ tion, trim, trimming

garrison *n.* 1. armed force, com~ mand, detachment, troops, unit 2. base, camp, encampment, fort, fortification, fortress, post, station, stronghold ~*v.* 3. assign, mount, position, post, put on duty, station 4. defend, guard, man, occupy, protect, supply with troops

garrulous 1. babbling, chattering, chatty, effusive, gabby (*Inf.*), glib, gossiping, gushing, loquacious, mouthy, prating, prattling, talka~ tive, verbose, voluble 2. diffuse, gassy (*Sl.*), long-winded, prolix, prosy, verbose, windy, wordy

gash 1. *v.* cleave, cut, gouge, incise, lacerate, rend, slash, slit, split, tear, wound 2. *n.* cleft, cut, gouge, incision, laceration, rent, slash, slit, split, tear, wound

gasp 1. *v.* blow, catch one's breath, choke, fight for breath, gulp, pant, puff 2. *n.* blow, ejaculation, excla~ mation, gulp, pant, puff

gate access, barrier, door, door~ way, egress, entrance, exit, gate~ way, opening, passage, port (*Scot.*), portal

gather 1. accumulate, amass, as~ semble, bring or get together, col~ lect, congregate, convene, flock, forgather, garner, group, heap, hoard, marshal, mass, muster, pile up, round up, stack up, stockpile 2. assume, be led to believe, con~ clude, deduce, draw, hear, infer, learn, make, surmise, understand 3. clasp, draw, embrace, enfold, hold, hug 4. crop, cull, garner, glean, harvest, pick, pluck, reap, select 5. build, deepen, enlarge, expand, grow, heighten, increase, intensify, rise, swell, thicken, wax 6. fold, pleat, pucker, ruffle, shirr, tuck

gathering 1. assemblage, assembly, company, conclave, concourse, congregation, congress, convention, convocation, crowd, flock, get-together (*Inf.*), group, knot, meeting, muster, party, rally, throng, turnout 2. accumulation, acquisition, aggregate, collecting, collection, concentration, gain, heap, hoard, mass, pile, procuring, roundup, stock, stockpile 3. *Inf.* abscess, boil, carbuncle, pimple, pustule, sore, spot, tumour, ulcer

gauche awkward, clumsy, graceless, ignorant, ill-bred, ill-mannered, inelegant, inept, insensitive, lacking in social graces, maladroit, tactless, uncultured, unpolished, unsophisticated

gaudy bright, brilliant, brummagem, flash (*Inf.*), flashy, florid, garish, gay, glaring, loud, meretricious, ostentatious, raffish, showy, tasteless, tawdry, vulgar

gauge *v.* 1. ascertain, calculate, check, compute, count, determine, measure, weigh 2. adjudge, appraise, assess, estimate, evaluate, guess, judge, rate, reckon, value ~*n.* 3. basis, criterion, example, exemplar, guide, guideline, indicator, measure, meter, model, pattern, rule, sample, standard, test, touchstone, yardstick 4. bore, capacity, degree, depth, extent, height, magnitude, measure, scope, size, span, thickness, width

gaunt 1. angular, attenuated, bony, cadaverous, emaciated, haggard, lank, lean, meagre, pinched, rawboned, scraggy, scrawny, skeletal, skinny, spare, thin, wasted 2. bare, bleak, desolate, dismal, dreary, forbidding, forlorn, grim, harsh

gawky awkward, clownish, clumsy, gauche, loutish, lumbering, lumpish, maladroit, oafish, uncouth, ungainly

gay 1. animated, blithe, carefree, cheerful, debonair, glad, gleeful, happy, hilarious, insouciant, jolly, jovial, joyful, joyous, light-hearted, lively, merry, sparkling, sunny, vivacious 2. bright, brilliant, colourful, flamboyant, flashy, fresh, garish, gaudy, rich, showy, vivid 3. convivial, festive, frivolous, frolicsome, fun-loving, gamesome, merry, playful, pleasure-seeking, rakish, rollicking, sportive, waggish

gaze 1. *v.* contemplate, gape, look, look fixedly, regard, stare, view, watch, wonder 2. *n.* fixed look, look, stare

gazette journal, newspaper, newssheet, organ, paper, periodical

gear *n.* 1. cog, cogwheel, gearwheel, toothed wheel 2. cogs, gearing, machinery, mechanism, works 3. accessories, accoutrements, apparatus, equipment, harness, instruments, outfit, paraphernalia, rigging, supplies, tackle, tools, trappings 4. baggage, belongings, effects, kit, luggage, stuff, things 5. *Sl.* apparel, array, attire, clothes, clothing, costume, dress, garb, garments, habit, outfit, rigout (*Inf.*), togs, wear ~*v.* 6. adapt, adjust, equip, fit, rig, suit, tailor

gelatinous gluey, glutinous, gummy, jelly-like, mucilaginous, sticky, viscid, viscous

gelid arctic, chilly, cold, freezing, frigid, frosty, frozen, glacial, ice-cold, icy, polar

gem 1. jewel, precious stone, semiprecious stone, stone 2. flower, jewel, masterpiece, pearl, pick, prize, treasure

genealogy ancestry, blood line, derivation, descent, extraction, family tree, line, lineage, pedigree, progeniture, stemma, stirps, stock, strain

general 1. accepted, broad, common, extensive, popular, prevailing, prevalent, public, universal, widespread 2. accustomed, conventional, customary, everyday, habitual, normal, ordinary, regular, typical, usual 3. approximate, ill-defined, imprecise, inaccurate, indefinite, inexact, loose, undetailed, unspecific, vague 4. across-the-board, all-inclusive, blanket, broad, catholic, collective, comprehensive, encyclopedic, generic, indiscriminate, miscellaneous, panoramic, sweeping, total, universal

generality 1. abstract principle, generalization, loose statement, sweeping statement, vague notion 2. acceptedness, commonness, extensiveness, popularity, prevalence, universality 3. approximateness, impreciseness, indefiniteness, inexactness, lack of detail, looseness, vagueness 4. breadth, catholicity, comprehensiveness, miscellaneity, sweepingness, universality

generally 1. almost always, as a rule, by and large, conventionally, customarily, for the most part, habitually, in most cases, mainly, normally, on average, on the whole, ordinarily, regularly, typically, usually 2. commonly, extensively, popularly, publicly, universally, widely 3. approximately, broadly, chiefly, for the most part, in the main, largely, mainly, mostly, on the whole, predominantly, principally

generate beget, breed, bring about, cause, create, engender, form, give rise to, initiate, make, originate, procreate, produce, propagate, spawn, whip up

generation 1. begetting, breeding, creation, engenderment, formation, genesis, origination, procreation, production, propagation, reproduction 2. age group, breed, crop 3. age, day, days, epoch, era, period, time, times

generic all-encompassing, blanket, collective, common, comprehensive, general, inclusive, sweeping, universal, wide

generosity 1. beneficence, benevolence, bounteousness, bounty, charity, kindness, liberality, munificence, open-handedness 2. disinterestedness, goodness, high-mindedness, magnanimity, nobleness, unselfishness

generous 1. beneficent, benevolent, bounteous, bountiful, charitable, free, hospitable, kind, lavish, liberal, munificent, open-handed, princely, ungrudging, unstinting 2. big-hearted, disinterested, good, high-minded, lofty, magnanimous, noble, unselfish 3. abundant, ample, copious, full, lavish, liberal, overflowing, plentiful, rich, unstinting

genesis beginning, birth, commencement, creation, dawn, engendering, formation, generation, inception, origin, outset, propagation, root, source, start

genial affable, agreeable, amiable, cheerful, cheery, congenial, convivial, cordial, easygoing, enlivening, friendly, glad, good-natured, happy, hearty, jolly, jovial, joyous, kind, kindly, merry, pleasant, sunny, warm, warm-hearted

geniality affability, agreeableness, amiability, cheerfulness, cheeriness, congenialness, conviviality, cordiality, friendliness, gladness, good cheer, good nature, happiness, heartiness, jollity, joviality, joy, joyousness, kindliness, kindness, mirth, pleasantness, sunniness, warm-heartedness, warmth

genius 1. adept, brain (*Inf.*), expert, intellect (*Inf.*), maestro, master, master-hand, mastermind, virtuoso 2. ability, aptitude, bent, brilliance, capacity, creative power, endowment, faculty, flair, gift, inclination, knack, propensity, talent, turn

genteel aristocratic, civil, courteous, courtly, cultivated, cultured, elegant, fashionable, formal, gentlemanly, ladylike, mannerly, polished, polite, refined, respectable, stylish, urbane, well-bred, well-mannered

gentility 1. civility, courtesy, courtliness, cultivation, culture, decorum, elegance, etiquette, formality, good breeding, good manners, mannerliness, polish, politeness, propriety, refinement, respectability, urbanity 2. blue blood, gentle birth, good family, high birth, nobility, rank 3. aristocracy, elite, gentlefolk, gentry, nobility, nobles, ruling class, upper class

gentle 1. amiable, benign, bland, compassionate, dove-like, humane, kind, kindly, lenient, meek, merciful, mild, pacific, peaceful, placid, quiet, soft, sweet-tempered, tender 2. balmy, calm, clement, easy, light, low, mild, moderate, muted, placid, quiet, serene, slight, smooth, soft, soothing, temperate, tranquil, untroubled 3. easy, gradual, imperceptible, light, mild, moderate, slight, slow 4. biddable, broken, docile, manageable, placid, tame, tractable 5. *Archaic* aristocratic, courteous, cultured, elegant, genteel, gentlemanlike, gentlemanly, high-born, ladylike, noble, polished, polite, refined, upper-class, well-born, well-bred

gentlemanly civil, civilized, courteous, cultivated, gallant, genteel, gentlemanlike, honourable, mannerly, noble, obliging, polished, polite, refined, reputable, suave, urbane, well-bred, well-mannered

genuine 1. actual, authentic, bona fide, honest, legitimate, natural, original, pure, real, sound, sterling, true, unadulterated, unalloyed, veritable 2. artless, candid, earnest, frank, heartfelt, honest, sincere, unaffected, unfeigned

germ 1. bacterium, bug (*Inf.*), microbe, microorganism, virus 2. beginning, bud, cause, embryo, origin, root, rudiment, seed, source, spark 3. bud, egg, embryo, nucleus, ovule, ovum, seed, spore, sprout

germane akin, allied, apposite, appropriate, apropos, apt, cognate, connected, fitting, kindred, material, pertinent, proper, related, relevant, suitable, to the point *or* purpose

germinate bud, develop, generate, grow, originate, pullulate, shoot, sprout, swell, vegetate

gestation development, evolution, incubation, maturation, pregnancy, ripening

gesticulate gesture, indicate, make a sign, motion, sign, signal, wave

gesture 1. *n.* action, gesticulation, indication, motion, sign, signal 2. *v.* gesticulate, indicate, motion, sign, signal, wave

get 1. achieve, acquire, attain, bag, bring, come by, come into possession of, earn, fall heir to, fetch, gain, glean, inherit, make, net, obtain, pick up, procure, realize, reap, receive, secure, succeed to, win 2. be afflicted with, become infected with, be smitten by, catch, come down with, contract, fall victim to, take 3. arrest, capture, collar (*Inf.*), grab, lay hold of, seize, take, trap 4. become, come to be, grow, turn, wax 5. catch, comprehend, fathom, follow, hear, notice, perceive, see, take in, understand, work out 6. arrive, come, make it (*Inf.*), reach 7. arrange, contrive, fix, manage, succeed, wangle (*Inf.*) 8. coax, convince, induce, influence, persuade, prevail upon, sway, talk into, wheedle, win over 9. communicate with, contact, get in touch with, reach 10. *Inf.* affect, arouse, excite, have an effect on, impress, move, stimulate, stir, touch 11. *Inf.* annoy, bother, bug (*Inf.*), get (someone's) goat (*Sl.*), irk, irritate, pique, rub (someone) up the wrong way, upset, vex 12. baffle, confound, mystify, nonplus, perplex, puzzle, stump

get across 1. cross, ford, negotiate, pass over, traverse 2. bring home to, communicate, convey, get (something) through to, impart, make clear *or* understood, put over, transmit

get ahead 1. advance, be successful, do well, flourish, get on, make good, progress, prosper, succeed, thrive 2. excel, leave behind, outdo, outmanoeuvre, overtake, surpass

get along 1. agree, be compatible, be friendly, get on, harmonize, hit it off (*Inf.*) 2. cope, develop, fare, get by (*Inf.*), make out (*Inf.*), manage, progress, shift 3. be off, depart, go, go away, leave, move off

get at 1. acquire, attain, come to grips with, gain access to, get, get hold of, reach 2. hint, imply, intend, lead up to, mean, suggest 3. annoy, attack, blame, carp, criticize, find fault with, irritate, nag, pick on, taunt 4. bribe, buy off, corrupt, in~fluence, suborn, tamper with

getaway break, break-out, de~campment, escape, flight

get away break free, break out, decamp, depart, disappear, escape, flee, leave, make good one's es~cape

get back 1. recoup, recover, re~gain, repossess, retrieve 2. arrive home, come back *or* home, return, revert, revisit 3. *With* **at** be avenged, get even with, give tit for tat, retaliate, settle the score with, take vengeance on

get by 1. circumvent, get ahead of, go around, go past, overtake, pass, round 2. *Inf.* contrive, cope, exist, fare, get along, make both ends meet, manage, subsist, survive

get down 1. alight, bring down, climb down, descend, disembark, dismount, get off, lower, step down 2. bring down, depress, dishearten, dispirit

get in alight, appear, arrive, col~lect, come, embark, enter, include, infiltrate, insert, interpose, land, mount, penetrate

get off 1. alight, depart, descend, disembark, dismount, escape, exit, leave 2. detach, remove, shed, take off

get on 1. ascend, board, climb, em~bark, mount 2. advance, cope, fare, get along, make out (*Inf.*), manage, progress, prosper, succeed 3. agree, be compatible, be friendly, concur, get along, harmonize, hit it off (*Inf.*)

get out alight, break out, clear out (*Inf.*), decamp, escape, evacuate, extricate oneself, free oneself, leave, vacate, withdraw

get out of avoid, dodge, escape, evade, shirk

get over 1. cross, ford, get across, pass, pass over, surmount, traverse 2. come round, get better, mend, pull through, recover from, revive, survive 3. defeat, get the better of,

master, overcome, shake off 4. communicate, convey, get *or* put across, impart, make clear *or* understood

get round 1. bypass, circumvent, edge, evade, outmanoeuvre, skirt 2. *Inf.* cajole, coax, convert, per~suade, prevail upon, talk round, wheedle, win over

get together accumulate, assem~ble, collect, congregate, convene, converge, gather, join, meet, mus~ter, rally, unite

get up arise, ascend, climb, in~crease, mount, rise, scale, stand

ghastly ashen, cadaverous, death~like, deathly pale, dreadful, fright~ful, grim, grisly, gruesome, hid~eous, horrendous, horrible, horrid, livid, loathsome, pale, pallid, re~pellent, shocking, spectral, terri~ble, terrifying, wan

ghost 1. apparition, manes, phan~tasm, phantom, revenant, shade (*Literary*), soul, spectre, spirit, spook (*Inf.*), wraith 2. glimmer, hint, possibility, semblance, shad~ow, suggestion, trace

ghostly eerie, ghostlike, illusory, insubstantial, phantasmal, phan~tom, spectral, spooky (*Inf.*), super~natural, uncanny, unearthly, weird, wraithlike

giant 1. *n.* behemoth, colossus, Hercules, leviathan, monster, titan 2. *adj.* Brobdingnagian, colossal, elephantine, enormous, gargan~tuan, gigantic, huge, immense, jumbo (*Inf.*), large, mammoth, monstrous, prodigious, titanic, vast

gibberish babble, balderdash, blather, double talk, drivel, gabble, gobbledegook (*Inf.*), jabber, jargon, mumbo jumbo, nonsense, prattle, twaddle, yammer (*Inf.*)

gibe, jibe 1. *v.* deride, flout, jeer, make fun of, mock, poke fun at, ridicule, scoff, scorn, sneer, taunt, twit 2. *n.* crack (*Sl.*), cutting re~mark, derision, dig, jeer, mockery, ridicule, sarcasm, scoffing, sneer, taunt

giddiness dizziness, faintness, light-headedness, vertigo

giddy 1. dizzy, dizzying, faint, light-headed, reeling, unsteady, vertiginous 2. capricious, careless, changeable, changeful, erratic, fickle, flighty, frivolous, heedless, impulsive, inconstant, irresolute, irresponsible, reckless, scatterbrained, silly, thoughtless, unbalanced, unstable, unsteady, vacillating, volatile, wild

gift 1. benefaction, bequest, bonus, boon, bounty, contribution, donation, grant, gratuity, largess, legacy, offering, present 2. ability, aptitude, attribute, bent, capability, capacity, endowment, faculty, flair, genius, knack, power, talent, turn

gifted able, accomplished, adroit, brilliant, capable, clever, expert, ingenious, intelligent, masterly, skilled, talented

gigantic Brobdingnagian, colossal, Cyclopean, elephantine, enormous, gargantuan, giant, herculean, huge, immense, mammoth, monstrous, prodigious, stupendous, titanic, tremendous, vast

giggle v./n. cackle, chortle, chuckle, laugh, snigger, te-hee, titter, twitter

gild adorn, beautify, bedeck, brighten, coat, deck, dress up, embellish, embroider, enhance, enrich, garnish, grace, ornament

gimmick contrivance, device, dodge, gadget, gambit, gizmo (*Sl.*, *chiefly U.S.*), ploy, scheme, stratagem, stunt, trick

gingerly 1. *adv.* carefully, cautiously, charily, circumspectly, daintily, delicately, fastidiously, hesitantly, reluctantly, squeamishly, suspiciously, timidly, warily 2. *adj.* careful, cautious, chary, circumspect, dainty, delicate, fastidious, hesitant, reluctant, squeamish, suspicious, timid, wary

gird 1. belt, bind, girdle 2. blockade, encircle, enclose, encompass, enfold, engird, environ, hem in, pen, ring, surround 3. brace, fortify, make ready, prepare, ready, steel

girdle 1. *n.* band, belt, cincture, cummerbund, fillet, sash, waistband 2. *v.* bind, bound, encircle,

enclose, encompass, engird, environ, gird, hem, ring, surround

girl bird (*Sl.*), chick (*Sl.*), colleen (*Irish*), damsel (*Archaic*), daughter, female child, lass, lassie (*Inf.*), maid (*Archaic*), maiden (*Archaic*), miss, wench

girth bulk, circumference, measure, size

gist core, drift, essence, force, idea, import, marrow, meaning, nub, pith, point, quintessence, sense, significance, substance

give 1. accord, administer, allow, award, bestow, commit, confer, consign, contribute, deliver, donate, entrust, furnish, grant, hand over *or* out, make over, permit, present, provide, supply, vouchsafe 2. announce, be a source of, communicate, emit, impart, issue, notify, pronounce, publish, render, transmit, utter 3. demonstrate, display, evidence, indicate, manifest, offer, proffer, provide, set forth, show 4. allow, cede, concede, devote, grant, hand over, lend, relinquish, surrender, yield 5. cause, do, engender, lead, make, occasion, perform, produce 6. bend, break, collapse, fall, recede, retire, sink

give away betray, disclose, divulge, expose, inform on, leak, let out, let slip, reveal, uncover

give in admit defeat, capitulate, collapse, comply, concede, quit, submit, surrender, yield

given addicted, apt, disposed, inclined, liable, likely, prone

give off discharge, emit, exhale, exude, produce, release, send out, smell of, throw out, vent

give out 1. discharge, emit, exhale, exude, produce, release, send out, smell of, throw out, vent 2. announce, broadcast, communicate, disseminate, impart, make known, notify, publish, transmit, utter

give up abandon, capitulate, cease, cede, cut out, desist, despair, forswear, hand over, leave off, quit, relinquish, renounce, resign, stop, surrender, throw in the towel, waive

glad 1. blithesome (*Literary*), cheerful, chuffed (*Sl.*), contented, delighted, gay, gleeful, gratified, happy, jocund, jovial, joyful, overjoyed, pleased, willing 2. animated, cheerful, cheering, cheery, delightful, felicitous, gratifying, joyous, merry, pleasant, pleasing

gladden cheer, delight, elate, enliven, exhilarate, gratify, hearten, please, rejoice

gladly cheerfully, freely, gaily, gleefully, happily, jovially, joyfully, joyously, merrily, readily, willingly, with (a) good grace, with pleasure

gladness animation, blitheness, cheerfulness, delight, felicity, gaiety, glee, happiness, high spirits, hilarity, jollity, joy, joyousness, mirth, pleasure

glamorous alluring, attractive, beautiful, bewitching, captivating, charming, dazzling, elegant, enchanting, entrancing, exciting, fascinating, glittering, glossy, lovely, prestigious, smart

glamour allure, appeal, attraction, beauty, bewitchment, charm, enchantment, fascination, magnetism, prestige, ravishment, witchery

glance v. 1. gaze, glimpse, look, peek, peep, scan, view 2. flash, gleam, glimmer, glint, glisten, glitter, reflect, shimmer, shine, twinkle 3. bounce, brush, graze, rebound, ricochet, skim 4. With over, through, *etc.* browse, dip into, flip through, leaf through, riffle through, run over *or* through, scan, skim through, thumb through ~n. 5. brief look, dekko (*Sl.*), gander (*Inf.*), glimpse, look, peek, peep, quick look, squint, view 6. flash, gleam, glimmer, glint, reflection, sparkle, twinkle 7. allusion, passing mention, reference

glare v. 1. frown, give a dirty look, glower, look daggers, lower, scowl, stare angrily 2. blaze, dazzle, flame, flare ~n. 3. angry stare, black look, dirty look, frown, glower, lower, scowl 4. blaze, brilliance, dazzle, flame, flare, glow 5. flashiness, floridness, gaudiness, loudness, meretriciousness, showiness, tawdriness

glaring 1. audacious, blatant, conspicuous, egregious, flagrant, gross, manifest, obvious, open, outrageous, outstanding, overt, patent, rank, unconcealed, visible 2. blazing, bright, dazzling, flashy, florid, garish, glowing, loud

glassy 1. clear, glossy, icy, shiny, slick, slippery, smooth, transparent 2. blank, cold, dazed, dull, empty, expressionless, fixed, glazed, lifeless, vacant

glaze 1. v. burnish, coat, enamel, furbish, gloss, lacquer, polish, varnish 2. n. coat, enamel, finish, gloss, lacquer, lustre, patina, polish, shine, varnish

gleam n. 1. beam, flash, glimmer, glow, ray, sparkle 2. brightness, brilliance, coruscation, flash, gloss, lustre, sheen, splendour 3. flicker, glimmer, hint, inkling, ray, suggestion, trace ~v. 4. coruscate, flare, flash, glance, glimmer, glint, glisten, glitter, glow, scintillate, shimmer, shine, sparkle

glee cheerfulness, delight, elation, exhilaration, exuberance, exultation, fun, gaiety, gladness, hilarity, jocularity, jollity, joviality, joy, joyfulness, joyousness, liveliness, merriment, mirth, sprightliness, triumph, verve

gleeful cheerful, cock-a-hoop, delighted, elated, exuberant, exultant, gay, gratified, happy, jocund, jovial, joyful, joyous, jubilant, merry, mirthful, overjoyed, pleased, triumphant

glib artful, easy, fast-talking, fluent, garrulous, insincere, plausible, quick, ready, slick, slippery, smooth, smooth-tongued, suave, talkative, voluble

glide coast, drift, float, flow, fly, roll, run, sail, skate, skim, slide, slip, soar

glimmer v. 1. blink, flicker, gleam, glisten, glitter, glow, shimmer, shine, sparkle, twinkle ~n. 2. blink, flicker, gleam, glow, ray, shimmer, sparkle, twinkle 3. flicker, gleam, grain, hint, inkling, ray, suggestion, trace

glimpse 1. *n.* brief view, glance, look, peek, peep, quick look, sight, sighting, squint 2. *v.* catch sight of, descry, espy, sight, spot, spy, view

glint 1. *v.* flash, gleam, glimmer, glitter, shine, sparkle, twinkle 2. *n.* flash, gleam, glimmer, glitter, shine, sparkle, twinkle, twinkling

glisten coruscate, flash, glance, glare, gleam, glimmer, glint, glitter, scintillate, shimmer, shine, sparkle, twinkle

glitter *v.* 1. coruscate, flare, flash, glare, gleam, glimmer, glint, glisten, scintillate, shimmer, shine, sparkle, twinkle ~*n.* 2. beam, brightness, brilliance, flash, glare, gleam, lustre, radiance, scintillation, sheen, shimmer, shine, sparkle 3. display, gaudiness, glamour, pageantry, show, showiness, splendour, tinsel

gloat crow, exult, glory, relish, revel in, rub it in (*Inf.*), triumph, vaunt

global 1. international, pandemic, planetary, universal, world, worldwide 2. all-encompassing, all-inclusive, all-out, comprehensive, encyclopedic, exhaustive, general, thorough, total, unbounded, unlimited

globe ball, earth, orb, planet, round, sphere, world

globule bead, bubble, drop, droplet, particle, pearl, pellet

gloom 1. blackness, cloud, cloudiness, dark, darkness, dimness, dullness, dusk, duskiness, gloominess, murk, murkiness, obscurity, shade, shadow, twilight 2. blues, dejection, depression, desolation, despair, despondency, downheartedness, low spirits, melancholy, misery, sadness, sorrow, unhappiness, woe

gloomy 1. black, crepuscular, dark, dim, dismal, dreary, dull, dusky, murky, obscure, overcast, shadowy, sombre, Stygian, tenebrous 2. bad, black, cheerless, comfortless, depressing, disheartening, dispiriting, dreary, joyless, sad, saddening, sombre 3. blue, chapfallen, cheer-

less, crestfallen, dejected, despondent, dismal, dispirited, down, downcast, downhearted, down in the dumps (*Inf.*), down in the mouth, glum, in low spirits, melancholy, miserable, moody, morose, pessimistic, sad, saturnine, sullen

glorify 1. add lustre to, adorn, aggrandize, augment, dignify, elevate, enhance, ennoble, illuminate, immortalize, lift up, magnify, raise 2. adore, apotheosize, beatify, bless, canonize, deify, enshrine, exalt, honour, idolize, pay homage to, revere, sanctify, venerate, worship 3. celebrate, cry up (*Inf.*), eulogize, extol, hymn, laud, lionize, magnify, panegyrize, praise, sing *or* sound the praises of

glorious 1. celebrated, distinguished, elevated, eminent, excellent, famed, famous, grand, honoured, illustrious, magnificent, majestic, noble, noted, renowned, sublime, triumphant 2. beautiful, bright, brilliant, dazzling, divine, effulgent, gorgeous, radiant, resplendent, shining, splendid, superb 3. *Inf.* delightful, enjoyable, excellent, fine, great, heavenly (*Inf.*), marvellous, pleasurable, splendid, wonderful

glory *n.* 1. celebrity, dignity, distinction, eminence, exaltation, fame, honour, illustriousness, immortality, kudos, praise, prestige, renown 2. adoration, benediction, blessing, gratitude, homage, laudation, praise, thanksgiving, veneration, worship 3. grandeur, greatness, magnificence, majesty, nobility, pageantry, pomp, splendour, sublimity, triumph 4. beauty, brilliance, effulgence, gorgeousness, lustre, radiance, resplendence ~*v.* 5. boast, crow, exult, gloat, pride oneself, relish, revel, take delight, triumph

gloss[1] *n.* 1. brightness, brilliance, burnish, gleam, lustre, polish, sheen, shine, varnish, veneer 2. appearance, façade, front, mask, semblance, show, surface ~*v.* 3. burnish, finish, furbish, glaze, lacquer, polish, shine, varnish, veneer 4. camouflage, conceal, cover up, disguise, hide, mask, smooth over, veil, whitewash (*Inf.*)

gloss² 1. *n.* annotation, comment, commentary, elucidation, explanation, footnote, interpretation, note, scholium, translation 2. *v.* annotate, comment, construe, elucidate, explain, interpret, translate

glossy bright, brilliant, burnished, glassy, glazed, lustrous, polished, sheeny, shining, shiny, silken, silky, sleek, smooth

glow *n.* 1. burning, gleam, glimmer, incandescence, lambency, light, luminosity, phosphorescence 2. brightness, brilliance, effulgence, radiance, splendour, vividness 3. ardour, earnestness, enthusiasm, excitement, fervour, gusto, impetuosity, intensity, passion, vehemence, warmth 4. bloom, blush, flush, reddening, rosiness ~*v.* 5. brighten, burn, gleam, glimmer, redden, shine, smoulder 6. be suffused, blush, colour, fill, flush, radiate, thrill, tingle

glower 1. *v.* frown, give a dirty look, glare, look daggers, lower, scowl 2. *n.* angry stare, black look, dirty look, frown, glare, lower, scowl

glowing 1. aglow, beaming, bright, flaming, florid, flushed, lambent, luminous, red, rich, ruddy, suffused, vibrant, vivid, warm 2. adulatory, complimentary, ecstatic, enthusiastic, eulogistic, laudatory, panegyrical, rave (*Inf.*), rhapsodic

glue 1. *n.* adhesive, cement, gum, mucilage, paste 2. *v.* affix, agglutinate, cement, fix, gum, paste, seal, stick

glum chapfallen, churlish, crabbed, crestfallen, crusty, dejected, doleful, down, gloomy, gruff, grumpy, ill-humoured, low, moody, morose, pessimistic, saturnine, sour, sulky, sullen, surly

glut *n.* 1. excess, overabundance, oversupply, saturation, superabundance, superfluity, surfeit, surplus ~*v.* 2. cram, fill, gorge, overfeed, satiate, stuff 3. choke, clog, deluge, flood, inundate, overload, oversupply, saturate

glutton gannet (*Sl.*), gobbler, gorger, gormandizer, gourmand, pig (*Inf.*)

gluttony gormandizing, gourmandism, greed, greediness, pigishness, rapacity, voraciousness, voracity

gnarled contorted, knotted, knotty, knurled, leathery, rough, rugged, twisted, weather-beaten, wrinkled

gnaw 1. bite, chew, munch, nibble, worry 2. consume, devour, eat away *or* into, erode, fret, wear away *or* down 3. distress, fret, harry, haunt, nag, plague, prey on one's mind, trouble, worry

go *v.* 1. advance, decamp, depart, fare (*Archaic*), journey, leave, make for, move, move out, pass, proceed, repair, set off, travel, withdraw 2. function, move, operate, perform, run, work 3. connect, extend, fit, give access, lead, reach, run, span, spread, stretch 4. avail, concur, conduce, contribute, incline, lead to, serve, tend, work towards 5. develop, eventuate, fall out, fare, happen, proceed, result, turn out, work out 6. accord, agree, blend, chime, complement, correspond, fit, harmonize, jibe (*Inf.*), match, suit 7. die, expire, give up the ghost, pass away, perish 8. elapse, expire, flow, lapse, pass, slip away ~*n.* 9. attempt, bid, crack (*Inf.*), effort, essay, shot (*Inf.*), stab, try, turn, whack (*Inf.*), whirl (*Inf.*) 10. *Inf.* activity, animation, drive, energy, force, get-up-and-go (*Inf.*), life, oomph (*Inf.*), pep, spirit, verve, vigour, vitality, vivacity

goad 1. *n.* impetus, incentive, incitement, irritation, motivation, pressure, spur, stimulation, stimulus, urge 2. *v.* annoy, arouse, drive, egg on, exhort, harass, hound, impel, incite, instigate, irritate, lash, prick, prod, prompt, propel, spur, stimulate, sting, urge, worry

go-ahead 1. *n. Inf.* assent, authorization, consent, green light, leave, O.K. (*Inf.*), permission 2. *adj.* ambitious, enterprising, go-getting

(*Inf.*), pioneering, progressive, up-and-coming

go ahead advance, begin, continue, go forward, go on, proceed, progress

goal aim, ambition, design, destination, end, intention, limit, mark, object, objective, purpose, target

go along 1. acquiesce, agree, assent, concur, cooperate, follow 2. accompany, carry on, escort, join, keep up, move, pass, travel

go away decamp, depart, exit, leave, move out, recede, withdraw

go back 1. return, revert 2. change one's mind, desert, forsake, renege, repudiate, retract

gobble bolt, cram, devour, gorge, gulp, guzzle, stuff, swallow, wolf

go-between agent, broker, dealer, factor, intermediary, liaison, mediator, medium, middleman

go by 1. elapse, exceed, flow on, move onward, pass, proceed 2. adopt, be guided by, follow, heed, judge from, observe, take as guide

godforsaken abandoned, backward, bleak, deserted, desolate, dismal, dreary, forlorn, gloomy, lonely, neglected, remote, wretched

godless atheistic, depraved, evil, impious, irreligious, profane, ungodly, unprincipled, unrighteous, wicked

godlike celestial, deific, deiform, divine, heavenly, superhuman, transcendent

godly devout, god-fearing, good, holy, pious, religious, righteous, saintly

go down 1. be beaten, collapse, decline, decrease, drop, fall, founder, go under, lose, set, sink, submerge, submit, suffer defeat 2. be commemorated (recalled, recorded, remembered)

godsend blessing, boon, manna, stroke of luck, windfall

go far advance, be successful, do well, get ahead (*Inf.*), get on (*Inf.*), make a name for oneself, progress, succeed

go for 1. clutch at, fetch, obtain, reach, seek, stretch for 2. admire,

be attracted to, be fond of, choose, favour, hold with, like, prefer 3. assail, assault, attack, launch oneself at, rush upon, set about *or* upon, spring upon

go in (for) adopt, embrace, engage in, enter, espouse, practise, pursue, take up, undertake

go into 1. begin, develop, enter, participate in, undertake 2. analyse, consider, delve into, discuss, examine, inquire into, investigate, look into, probe, pursue, review, scrutinize, study

golden 1. blond *or* blonde, bright, brilliant, flaxen, resplendent, shining, yellow 2. best, blissful, delightful, flourishing, glorious, happy, joyful, joyous, precious, prosperous, rich, successful 3. advantageous, auspicious, excellent, favourable, opportune, promising, propitious, rosy, valuable

gone 1. elapsed, ended, finished, over, past 2. absent, astray, away, lacking, lost, missing, vanished 3. dead, deceased, defunct, departed, extinct, no more 4. consumed, done, finished, spent, used up

good *adj.* 1. acceptable, admirable, agreeable, capital, choice, commendable, excellent, fine, first-class, first-rate, great, pleasant, pleasing, positive, precious, satisfactory, splendid, super (*Inf.*), superior, tiptop, valuable, worthy 2. admirable, estimable, ethical, exemplary, honest, honourable, moral, praiseworthy, right, righteous, upright, virtuous, worthy 3. able, accomplished, adept, adroit, capable, clever, competent, dexterous, efficient, expert, first-rate, proficient, reliable, satisfactory, serviceable, skilled, sound, suitable, talented, thorough, trustworthy, useful 4. adequate, advantageous, auspicious, beneficial, convenient, favourable, fit, fitting, healthy, helpful, opportune, profitable, propitious, salubrious, salutary, suitable, useful, wholesome 5. eatable, fit to eat, sound, uncorrupted, untainted, whole 6. altruistic, approving, beneficent, benevolent, charitable, friendly, gracious, humane, kind, kind-hearted, kindly, merciful, obliging, well-disposed 7. authentic, bona fide, dependable, genuine, honest, legitimate, proper, real, reliable, sound, true, trustworthy, valid 8. decorous, dutiful, mannerly, obedient, orderly, polite, proper, seemly, well-behaved, well-mannered 9. agreeable, cheerful, congenial, convivial, enjoyable, gratifying, happy, pleasant, pleasing, pleasurable, satisfying 10. adequate, ample, complete, considerable, entire, extensive, full, large, long, sizable, solid, substantial, sufficient, whole 11. best, fancy, finest, newest, nicest, precious, smartest, special, valuable 12. *Of weather* balmy, bright, calm, clear, clement, cloudless, fair, halcyon, mild, sunny, sunshiny, tranquil ~n. 13. advantage, avail, behalf, benefit, gain, interest, profit, service, use, usefulness, welfare, wellbeing, worth 14. excellence, goodness, merit, morality, probity, rectitude, right, righteousness, uprightness, virtue, worth 15. **for good** finally, for ever, irrevocably, never to return, once and for all, permanently, *sine die*

goodbye adieu, farewell, leave-taking, parting

good-for-nothing 1. *n.* black sheep, idler, layabout, ne'er-do-well, profligate, rapscallion, scapegrace, waster, wastrel 2. *adj.* feckless, idle, irresponsible, useless, worthless

good-humoured affable, amiable, cheerful, congenial, genial, good-tempered, happy, pleasant

good-looking attractive, comely, fair, handsome, personable, pretty, well-favoured

goodly 1. ample, considerable, large, significant, sizable, substantial, tidy (*Inf.*) 2. agreeable, attractive, comely, desirable, elegant, fine, good-looking, graceful, handsome, personable, pleasant, pleasing, well-favoured

good-natured agreeable, benevo-

lent, friendly, good-hearted, helpful, kind, kindly, tolerant, warm-hearted, well-disposed, willing to please

goodness 1. excellence, merit, quality, superiority, value, worth 2. beneficence, benevolence, friendliness, generosity, good will, graciousness, humaneness, kind-heartedness, kindliness, kindness, mercy, obligingness 3. honesty, honour, integrity, merit, morality, probity, rectitude, righteousness, uprightness, virtue 4. advantage, benefit, nourishment, nutrition, salubriousness, wholesomeness

goods 1. appurtenances, belongings, chattels, effects, furnishings, furniture, gear, movables, paraphernalia, possessions, property, things, trappings 2. commodities, merchandise, stock, stuff, wares

good will amity, benevolence, favour, friendliness, friendship, heartiness, kindliness, zeal

go off 1. blow up, detonate, explode, fire 2. happen, occur, take place 3. decamp, depart, go away, leave, move out, part, quit 4. *Inf.* go bad, go stale, rot

go on 1. continue, endure, happen, last, occur, persist, proceed, stay 2. blether, carry on, chatter, prattle, ramble on, waffle, witter (on) (*Inf.*)

go out 1. depart, exit, leave 2. be extinguished, die out, expire, fade out

go over 1. examine, inspect, rehearse, reiterate, review, revise, study 2. peruse, read, scan, skim

gorge[1] *n.* canyon, cleft, clough (*Dialect*), defile, fissure, pass, ravine

gorge[2] *v.* bolt, cram, devour, feed, fill, glut, gobble, gormandize, gulp, guzzle, overeat, raven, sate, satiate, stuff, surfeit, swallow, wolf

gorgeous 1. beautiful, brilliant, dazzling, elegant, glittering, grand, luxuriant, magnificent, opulent, ravishing, resplendent, showy, splendid, stunning (*Inf.*), sumptuous, superb 2. *Inf.* attractive, bright, delightful, enjoyable, exquisite, fine, glorious, good, good-looking, lovely, pleasing

gory blood-soaked, bloodstained, bloodthirsty, bloody, ensanguined (*Literary*), murderous, sanguinary

gospel 1. certainty, fact, the last word, truth, verity 2. credo, creed, doctrine, message, news, revelation, tidings

gossamer *adj.* airy, delicate, diaphanous, fine, flimsy, gauzy, light, sheer, silky, thin, transparent

gossip *n.* 1. blether, chinwag (*Brit. inf.*), chitchat, clishmaclaver (*Scot.*), hearsay, idle talk, jaw (*Sl.*), newsmongering (*Old-fashioned*), prattle, scandal, small talk, tittle-tattle 2. babbler, blatherskite, blether, busybody, chatterbox (*Inf.*), chatterer, flibbertigibbet, gossipmonger, newsmonger (*Old-fashioned*), prattler, quidnunc, scandalmonger, tattler, telltale ~*v.* 3. blather, blether, chat, gabble, jaw (*Sl.*), prate, prattle, tattle

go through 1. bear, brave, endure, experience, suffer, tolerate, undergo, withstand 2. consume, exhaust, squander, use 3. check, examine, explore, hunt, look, search

go under default, die, drown, fail, fold (*Inf.*), founder, go down, sink, submerge, succumb

govern 1. administer, be in power, command, conduct, control, direct, guide, hold sway, lead, manage, order, oversee, pilot, reign, rule, steer, superintend, supervise 2. bridle, check, contain, control, curb, direct, discipline, get the better of, hold in check, inhibit, master, regulate, restrain, subdue, tame 3. decide, determine, guide, influence, rule, sway, underlie

government 1. administration, authority, dominion, execution, governance, law, polity, rule, sovereignty, state, statecraft 2. administration, executive, ministry, powers-that-be, regime 3. authority, command, control, direction, domination, guidance, management, regulation, restraint, superintendence, supervision, sway

governor administrator, boss (*Inf.*), chief, commander, comptroller, controller, director, executive, head, leader, manager, overseer, ruler, superintendent, supervisor

go with accompany, agree, blend, complement, concur, correspond, fit, harmonize, match, suit

go without abstain, be denied, be deprived of, deny oneself, do without, go short, lack, want

gown costume, dress, frock, garb, garment, habit, robe

grab bag, capture, catch, catch *or* take hold of, clutch, grasp, grip, latch on to, nab (*Inf.*), pluck, seize, snap up, snatch

grace *n.* 1. attractiveness, beauty, charm, comeliness, ease, elegance, finesse, gracefulness, loveliness, pleasantness, poise, polish, refinement, shapeliness, tastefulness 2. benefaction, beneficence, benevolence, favour, generosity, goodness, good will, kindliness, kindness 3. breeding, consideration, cultivation, decency, decorum, etiquette, mannerliness, manners, propriety, tact 4. charity, clemency, compassion, forgiveness, indulgence, leniency, lenity, mercy, pardon, quarter, reprieve 5. benediction, blessing, prayer, thanks, thanksgiving ~*v.* 6. adorn, beautify, bedeck, deck, decorate, dignify, distinguish, elevate, embellish, enhance, enrich, favour, garnish, glorify, honour, ornament, set off

graceful agile, beautiful, becoming, charming, comely, easy, elegant, fine, flowing, gracile (*Rare*), natural, pleasing, smooth, symmetrical, tasteful

gracious accommodating, affable, amiable, beneficent, benevolent, benign, benignant, charitable, chivalrous, civil, compassionate, considerate, cordial, courteous, courtly, friendly, hospitable, indulgent, kind, kindly, lenient, loving, merciful, mild, obliging, pleasing, polite, well-mannered

grade *n.* 1. brand, category, class, condition, degree, echelon, group, level, mark, notch, order, place, position, quality, rank, rung, size, stage, station, step 2. **make the grade** *Inf.* come through with flying colours, come up to scratch (*Inf.*), measure up, measure up to expectations, pass muster, prove acceptable, succeed, win through 3. acclivity, bank, declivity, gradient, hill, incline, rise, slope ~*v.* 4. arrange, brand, class, classify, evaluate, group, order, range, rank, rate, sort, value

gradient acclivity, bank, declivity, grade, hill, incline, rise, slope

gradual continuous, even, gentle, graduated, moderate, piecemeal, progressive, regular, slow, steady, successive, unhurried

gradually bit by bit, by degrees, drop by drop, evenly, gently, little by little, moderately, piece by piece, piecemeal, progressively, slowly, steadily, step by step, unhurriedly

graduate *v.* 1. calibrate, grade, mark off, measure out, proportion, regulate 2. arrange, classify, grade, group, order, range, rank, sort

graft 1. *n.* bud, implant, scion, shoot, splice, sprout 2. *v.* affix, implant, ingraft, insert, join, splice, transplant

grain 1. cereals, corn 2. grist, kernel, seed 3. atom, bit, crumb, fragment, granule, iota, jot, mite, modicum, molecule, morsel, mote, ounce, particle, piece, scintilla (*Rare*), scrap, scruple, spark, speck, suspicion, trace, whit 4. fibre, nap, pattern, surface, texture, weave 5. character, disposition, humour, inclination, make-up, temper

grand 1. ambitious, august, dignified, elevated, eminent, exalted, fine, glorious, grandiose, great, haughty, illustrious, imposing, impressive, large, lofty, lordly, luxurious, magnificent, majestic, monumental, noble, opulent, ostentatious, palatial, pompous, pretentious, princely, regal, splendid, stately, striking, sublime, sumptuous 2. admirable, excellent, fine, first-class, first-rate, great (*Inf.*),

marvellous (*Inf.*), outstanding, smashing (*Inf.*), splendid, super (*Inf.*), superb, terrific (*Inf.*), very good, wonderful 3. chief, head, highest, leading, main, preeminent, principal, supreme

grandeur augustness, dignity, greatness, importance, loftiness, magnificence, majesty, nobility, pomp, splendour, state, stateliness, sublimity

grandiose 1. affected, ambitious, bombastic, extravagant, flamboyant, high-flown, ostentatious, pompous, pretentious, showy 2. ambitious, grand, imposing, impressive, lofty, magnificent, majestic, monumental, stately

grant *v.* 1. accede to, accord, acknowledge, admit, agree to, allocate, allot, allow, assign, award, bestow, cede, concede, confer, consent to, donate, give, impart, permit, present, vouchsafe, yield 2. *Law* assign, convey, transfer, transmit ~*n.* 3. admission, allocation, allotment, allowance, award, benefaction, bequest, boon, bounty, concession, donation, endowment, gift, present, subsidy

granule atom, crumb, fragment, grain, iota, jot, molecule, particle, scrap, speck

graphic 1. clear, descriptive, detailed, explicit, expressive, forcible, illustrative, lively, lucid, picturesque, striking, telling, vivid, well-drawn 2. delineated, diagrammatic, drawn, illustrative, pictorial, representational, seen, visible, visual

grapple 1. catch, clasp, clutch, come to grips, fasten, grab, grasp, grip, hold, hug, lay *or* take hold, make fast, seize, wrestle 2. address oneself to, attack, battle, clash, combat, confront, contend, cope, deal with, do battle, encounter, engage, face, fight, struggle, tackle, take on, tussle, wrestle

grasp *v.* 1. catch, clasp, clinch, clutch, grab, grapple, grip, hold, lay *or* take hold of, seize, snatch 2. catch *or* get the drift of, catch on, comprehend, follow, get, realize, see, take in, understand ~n. 3. clasp, clutches, embrace, grip, hold, possession, tenure 4. capac~ ity, compass, control, extent, mas~ tery, power, range, reach, scope, sway, sweep 5. awareness, com~ prehension, ken, knowledge, mas~ tery, perception, realization, understanding

grasping acquisitive, avaricious, close-fisted, covetous, greedy, mean, miserly, niggardly, penny-pinching (*Inf.*), rapacious, selfish, stingy, tightfisted, usurious, venal

grate v. 1. mince, pulverize, shred, triturate 2. creak, grind, rasp, rub, scrape, scratch 3. annoy, chafe, exasperate, fret, gall, get one down, get on one's nerves (*Inf.*), irk, irritate, jar, nettle, peeve, ran~ kle, rub one up the wrong way, set one's teeth on edge, vex

grateful 1. appreciative, beholden, indebted, obliged, thankful 2. ac~ ceptable, agreeable, favourable, gratifying, nice, pleasing, refresh~ ing, restful, satisfactory, satisfying, welcome

gratify cater to, delight, favour, fulfil, give pleasure, gladden, hu~ mour, indulge, please, recompense, requite, satisfy, thrill

grating adj. annoying, disagree~ able, discordant, displeasing, grinding, harsh, irksome, irritating, jarring, offensive, rasping, raucous, scraping, squeaky, strident, un~ pleasant, vexatious

gratis for nothing, free, freely, free of charge, gratuitously, on the house, unpaid

gratitude appreciation, grateful~ ness, indebtedness, obligation, rec~ ognition, sense of obligation, thankfulness, thanks

gratuitous 1. complimentary, free, spontaneous, unasked-for, unpaid, unrewarded, voluntary 2. assumed, baseless, causeless, groundless, ir~ relevant, needless, superfluous, uncalled-for, unfounded, unjusti~ fied, unmerited, unnecessary, un~ provoked, unwarranted, wanton

gratuity baksheesh, benefaction, bonus, boon, bounty, donation, gift, largess, perquisite, *pourboire*, present, recompense, reward, tip

grave[1] n. burying place, crypt, last resting place, mausoleum, pit, sep~ ulchre, tomb, vault

grave[2] 1. dignified, dour, dull, ear~ nest, gloomy, grim-faced, heavy, leaden, long-faced, muted, quiet, sage (*Obsolete*), sedate, serious, sober, solemn, sombre, staid, sub~ dued, thoughtful, unsmiling 2. acute, critical, crucial, dangerous, exigent, hazardous, important, life-and-death, momentous, of great consequence, perilous, pressing, serious, severe, significant, threat~ ening, urgent, vital, weighty

graveyard boneyard (*Inf.*), burial ground, cemetery, charnel house, churchyard, God's acre (*Literary*), necropolis

gravitate 1. *With to or towards* be influenced (attracted, drawn, pulled), incline, lean, move, tend 2. be precipitated, descend, drop, fall, precipitate, settle, sink

gravity 1. acuteness, consequence, exigency, hazardousness, impor~ tance, moment, momentousness, perilousness, pressingness, seri~ ousness, severity, significance, ur~ gency, weightiness 2. demureness, dignity, earnestness, gloom, grim~ ness, reserve, sedateness, serious~ ness, sobriety, solemnity, thought~ fulness

graze v. 1. brush, glance off, kiss, rub, scrape, shave, skim, touch 2. abrade, bark, chafe, scrape, scratch, skin ~n. 3. abrasion, scrape, scratch

greasy 1. fatty, oily, slick, slimy, slippery 2. fawning, glib, grovel~ ling, ingratiating, oily, slick, smarmy (*Brit. inf.*), smooth, syco~ phantish, toadying, unctuous

great 1. big, bulky, colossal, enor~ mous, extensive, gigantic, huge, immense, large, mammoth, prodi~ gious, stupendous, tremendous, vast, voluminous 2. extended, lengthy, long, prolonged, protract~ ed 3. capital, chief, grand, leading, main, major, paramount, primary, principal, prominent, superior 4.

considerable, decided, excessive, extravagant, extreme, grievous, high, inordinate, prodigious, pronounced, strong 5. consequential, critical, crucial, grave, heavy, important, momentous, serious, significant, weighty 6. celebrated, distinguished, eminent, exalted, excellent, famed, famous, glorious, illustrious, notable, noteworthy, outstanding, prominent, remarkable, renowned, superlative, talented 7. august, chivalrous, dignified, distinguished, exalted, fine, glorious, grand, heroic, high-minded, idealistic, impressive, lofty, magnanimous, noble, princely, sublime 8. active, devoted, enthusiastic, keen, zealous 9. able, adept, adroit, crack (*Sl.*), expert, good, masterly, proficient, skilful, skilled 10. *Inf.* admirable, excellent, fantastic (*Inf.*), fine, first-rate, good, marvellous (*Inf.*), terrific (*Inf.*), tremendous (*Inf.*), wonderful 11. absolute, arrant, complete, consummate, downright, egregious, flagrant, out-and-out, perfect, positive, thoroughgoing, thundering (*Inf.*), total, unmitigated, unqualified, utter

greatly abundantly, by leaps and bounds, by much, considerably, enormously, exceedingly, extremely, highly, hugely, immensely, markedly, mightily, much, notably, powerfully, remarkably, tremendously, vastly, very much

greatness 1. bulk, enormity, hugeness, immensity, largeness, length, magnitude, mass, prodigiousness, size, vastness 2. amplitude, force, high degree, intensity, potency, power, strength 3. gravity, heaviness, import, importance, moment, momentousness, seriousness, significance, urgency, weight 4. celebrity, distinction, eminence, fame, glory, grandeur, illustriousness, lustre, note, renown 5. chivalry, dignity, disinterestedness, generosity, grandeur, heroism, high-mindedness, idealism, loftiness, majesty, nobility, nobleness, stateliness, sublimity

greed, greediness 1. edacity,

esurience, gluttony, gormandizing, hunger, insatiableness, ravenousness, voracity 2. acquisitiveness, avidity, covetousness, craving, cupidity, desire, eagerness, graspingness, longing, rapacity, selfishness

greedy 1. edacious, esurient, gluttonous, gormandizing, hoggish, hungry, insatiable, piggish, ravenous, voracious 2. acquisitive, avaricious, avid, covetous, craving, desirous, eager, grasping, hungry, impatient, rapacious, selfish

Greek 1. *n.* Hellene 2. *adj.* Hellenic

green *adj.* 1. blooming, budding, flourishing, fresh, grassy, leafy, new, undecayed, verdant, verdurous 2. fresh, immature, new, raw, recent, unripe 3. callow, credulous, gullible, immature, inexperienced, inexpert, ingenuous, innocent, naive, new, raw, unpolished, unpractised, unskilful, unsophisticated, untrained, unversed, wet behind the ears (*Inf.*) 4. covetous, envious, grudging, jealous, resentful 5. ill, nauseous, pale, sick, unhealthy, wan 6. immature, pliable, supple, tender, undried, unseasoned, young ~*n.* 7. common, grassplot, lawn, sward, turf

greet accost, address, compliment, hail, meet, nod to, receive, salute, tip one's hat to, welcome

greeting 1. address, hail, reception, salutation, salute, welcome 2. *Plural* best wishes, compliments, devoirs, good wishes, regards, respects, salutations

gregarious affable, companionable, convivial, cordial, friendly, outgoing, sociable, social

grey 1. ashen, bloodless, colourless, livid, pale, pallid, wan 2. cheerless, cloudy, dark, depressing, dim, dismal, drab, dreary, dull, foggy, gloomy, misty, murky, overcast, sunless 3. anonymous, characterless, colourless, dull, indistinct, neutral, unclear, unidentifiable 4. aged, ancient, elderly, experienced, hoary, mature, old, venerable

grief 1. affliction, agony, anguish,

bereavement, dejection, distress, grievance, heartache, heartbreak, misery, mournfulness, mourning, pain, regret, remorse, sadness, sorrow, suffering, trial, tribulation, trouble, woe 2. **come to grief** *Inf.* come unstuck, fail, meet with disaster, miscarry

grievance affliction, beef (*Sl.*), complaint, damage, distress, grief, gripe (*Inf.*), hardship, injury, injustice, resentment, sorrow, trial, tribulation, trouble, unhappiness, wrong

grieve 1. ache, bemoan, bewail, complain, deplore, lament, mourn, regret, rue, sorrow, suffer, wail, weep 2. afflict, agonize, break the heart of, crush, distress, hurt, injure, make one's heart bleed, pain, sadden, wound

grievous 1. afflicting, calamitous, damaging, distressing, dreadful, grave, harmful, heavy, hurtful, injurious, lamentable, oppressive, painful, severe, wounding 2. appalling, atrocious, deplorable, dreadful, egregious, flagrant, glaring, heinous, intolerable, lamentable, monstrous, offensive, outrageous, shameful, shocking, unbearable 3. agonized, grief-stricken, heartrending, mournful, pitiful, sorrowful, tragic

grim cruel, ferocious, fierce, forbidding, formidable, frightful, ghastly, grisly, gruesome, harsh, hideous, horrible, horrid, implacable, merciless, morose, relentless, resolute, ruthless, severe, shocking, sinister, stern, sullen, surly, terrible, unrelenting, unyielding

grimace 1. *n.* face, frown, mouth, scowl, sneer, wry face 2. *v.* frown, make a face *or* faces, mouth, scowl, sneer

grime dirt, filth, smut, soot

grimy begrimed, besmeared, besmirched, dirty, filthy, foul, grubby, smutty, soiled, sooty, unclean

grind *v.* 1. abrade, comminute, crush, granulate, grate, kibble, mill, pound, powder, pulverize, triturate 2. file, polish, sand, sharpen, smooth, whet 3. gnash,

grate, grit, scrape 4. *With down* afflict, harass, hold down, hound, oppress, persecute, plague, trouble, tyrannize (over) ~*n.* 5. *Inf.* chore, drudgery, hard work, labour, sweat (*Inf.*), task, toil

grip *n.* 1. clasp, handclasp (*U.S.*), purchase 2. clutches, comprehension, control, domination, grasp, hold, influence, keeping, mastery, perception, possession, power, tenure, understanding 3. **come** *or* **get to grips (with)** close with, confront, contend with, cope with, deal with, encounter, face up to, grapple with, grasp, handle, meet, tackle, take on, undertake ~*v.* 4. clasp, clutch, grasp, hold, latch on to, seize, take hold of 5. catch up, compel, engross, enthral, entrance, fascinate, hold, involve, mesmerize, rivet, spellbind

gripping compelling, compulsive, engrossing, enthralling, entrancing, exciting, fascinating, riveting, spellbinding, thrilling, unputdownable (*Inf.*)

grisly abominable, appalling, awful, dreadful, frightful, ghastly, grim, gruesome, hideous, horrible, horrid, macabre, shocking, sickening, terrible, terrifying

grit *n.* 1. dust, gravel, pebbles, sand 2. backbone, courage, determination, doggedness, fortitude, gameness, guts (*Inf.*), hardihood, mettle, nerve, perseverance, pluck, resolution, spirit, tenacity, toughness ~*v.* 3. clench, gnash, grate, grind

gritty 1. abrasive, dusty, grainy, granular, gravelly, rasping, rough, sandy 2. brave, courageous, determined, dogged, game, hardy, mettlesome, plucky, resolute, spirited, steadfast, tenacious, tough

groan *n.* 1. cry, moan, sigh, whine 2. *Inf.* beef (*Sl.*), complaint, gripe (*Inf.*), grouse, grumble, objection ~*v.* 3. cry, moan, sigh, whine 4. *Inf.* beef (*Sl.*), bemoan, bitch (*Sl.*), complain, gripe (*Inf.*), grouse, grumble, lament, object

groggy befuddled, confused, dazed, dizzy, faint, muzzy, punch-drunk, reeling, shaky, staggering, stunned, stupefied, unsteady, weak, wobbly, woozy (*Inf.*)

groom *n.* 1. currier (*Rare*), hostler *or* ostler (*Archaic*), stableboy, stableman ~*v.* 2. clean, dress, get up (*Inf.*), preen, primp, smarten up, spruce up, tidy, turn out 3. brush, clean, curry, rub down, tend 4. coach, drill, educate, make ready, nurture, prepare, prime, ready, train

groove channel, cut, cutting, flute, furrow, gutter, hollow, indentation, rebate, rut, score, trench

grope cast about, feel, finger, fish, flounder, fumble, grabble, scrabble, search

gross *adj.* 1. big, bulky, corpulent, dense, fat, great, heavy, hulking, large, lumpish, massive, obese, overweight, thick 2. aggregate, before deductions, before tax, entire, total, whole 3. coarse, crude, improper, impure, indecent, indelicate, lewd, low, obscene, offensive, ribald, rude, sensual, smutty, unseemly, vulgar 4. apparent, arrant, blatant, downright, egregious, flagrant, glaring, grievous, heinous, manifest, obvious, outrageous, plain, rank, serious, shameful, sheer, shocking, unmitigated, unqualified, utter 5. boorish, callous, coarse, crass, dull, ignorant, imperceptive, insensitive, tasteless, uncultured, undiscriminating, unfeeling, unrefined, unsophisticated ~*v.* 6. bring in, earn, make, rake in (*Inf.*), take

grotesque absurd, bizarre, deformed, distorted, extravagant, fanciful, fantastic, freakish, incongruous, ludicrous, malformed, misshapen, odd, outlandish, preposterous, ridiculous, strange, unnatural, weird, whimsical

ground *n.* 1. clod, dirt, dry land, dust, earth, field, land, loam, mould, sod, soil, terra firma, terrain, turf 2. *Often plural* area, country, district, domain, estate, fields, gardens, habitat, holding, land, property, realm, terrain, territory, tract 3. *Usually plural* account, argument, base, basis, call,

cause, excuse, factor, foundation, inducement, justification, motive, occasion, premise, pretext, rationale, reason 4. *Usually plural* deposit, dregs, grouts, lees, sediment, settlings 5. arena, field, park (*Inf.*), pitch, stadium ~*v.* 6. base, establish, fix, found, set, settle 7. acquaint with, coach, familiarize with, inform, initiate, instruct, prepare, teach, train, tutor

groundless baseless, chimerical, empty, false, idle, illusory, imaginary, unauthorized, uncalled-for, unfounded, unjustified, unprovoked, unsupported, unwarranted

groundwork base, basis, cornerstone, footing, foundation, fundamentals, preliminaries, preparation, spadework, underpinnings

group *n.* 1. aggregation, assemblage, association, band, batch, bunch, category, circle, class, clique, clump, cluster, collection, company, congregation, coterie, crowd, faction, formation, pack, gathering, organization, party, party, set, troop ~*v.* 2. arrange, assemble, associate, assort, bracket, class, classify, dispose, gather, marshal, order, organize, put together, range, sort 3. associate, band together, cluster, congregate, consort, fraternize, gather, get together

grouse 1. *v.* beef (*Sl.*), bellyache (*Sl.*), bitch (*Sl.*), carp, complain, find fault, gripe (*Inf.*), grouch (*Inf.*), grumble, moan, whine 2. *n.* beef (*Sl.*), complaint, grievance, gripe (*Inf.*), grouch (*Inf.*), grumble, moan, objection

grovel abase oneself, bootlick (*Inf.*), bow and scrape, cower, crawl, creep, cringe, crouch, demean oneself, fawn, flatter, humble oneself, kowtow, sneak, toady

grow 1. develop, enlarge, expand, extend, fill out, get bigger, get taller, heighten, increase, multiply, spread, stretch, swell, thicken, widen 2. develop, flourish, germinate, shoot, spring up, sprout, vegetate 3. arise, issue, originate, spring, stem 4. advance, expand, flourish, improve, progress, prosper, succeed, thrive 5. become, come to be, develop (into), get, turn, wax 6. breed, cultivate, farm, nurture, produce, propagate, raise

grown-up 1. *adj.* adult, fully-grown, mature, of age 2. *n.* adult, man, woman

growth 1. aggrandizement, augmentation, development, enlargement, evolution, expansion, extension, growing, heightening, increase, multiplication, proliferation, stretching, thickening, widening 2. crop, cultivation, development, germination, produce, production, shooting, sprouting, vegetation 3. advance, advancement, expansion, improvement, progress, prosperity, rise, success 4. *Medicine* excrescence, lump, tumour

grub *v.* 1. burrow, dig up, probe, pull up, root (*Inf.*), rootle (*Brit.*), search for, uproot 2. ferret, forage, hunt, rummage, scour, search, uncover, unearth 3. drudge, grind (*Inf.*), labour, plod, slave, slog, sweat, toil ~*n.* 4. caterpillar, larva, maggot 5. *Sl.* eats (*Sl.*), food, nosh (*Sl.*), rations, sustenance, victuals

grubby besmeared, dirty, filthy, frowzy, grimy, manky (*Scot. dialect*), mean, messy, mucky, scruffy, seedy, shabby, slovenly, smutty, soiled, sordid, squalid, unkempt, untidy, unwashed

grudge 1. *n.* animosity, animus, antipathy, aversion, bitterness, dislike, enmity, grievance, hard feelings, hate, ill will, malevolence, malice, pique, rancour, resentment, spite, venom 2. *v.* begrudge, be reluctant, complain, covet, envy, hold back, mind, resent, stint

gruelling arduous, backbreaking, brutal, crushing, demanding, difficult, exhausting, fatiguing, fierce, grinding, hard, harsh, laborious, punishing, severe, stiff, strenuous, taxing, tiring, trying

gruesome abominable, awful, fearful, ghastly, grim, grisly, hideous, horrendous, horrible, horrid, horrific, horrifying, loathsome, macabre, repugnant, repulsive, shocking, spine-chilling, terrible

gruff 1. bad-tempered, bearish, blunt, brusque, churlish, crabbed, crusty, curt, discourteous, grouchy (*Inf.*), grumpy, ill-humoured, ill-natured, impolite, rough, rude, sour, sullen, surly, uncivil, ungracious, unmannerly 2. croaking, guttural, harsh, hoarse, husky, low, rasping, rough, throaty

grumble *v.* 1. beef (*Sl.*), bellyache (*Sl.*), bitch (*Sl.*), carp, complain, find fault, gripe (*Inf.*), grouch (*Inf.*), grouse, moan, repine, whine 2. growl, gurgle, murmur, mutter, roar, rumble ~*n.* 3. beef (*Sl.*), complaint, grievance, gripe (*Inf.*), grouch (*Inf.*), grouse, moan, objection 4. growl, gurgle, murmur, muttering, roar, rumble

guarantee 1. *n.* assurance, bond, certainty, collateral, covenant, earnest, guaranty, pledge, promise, security, surety, undertaking, warranty, word, word of honour 2. *v.* answer for, assure, certify, ensure, insure, maintain, make certain, pledge, promise, protect, secure, stand behind, swear, vouch for, warrant

guard *v.* 1. cover, defend, escort, keep, mind, oversee, patrol, police, preserve, protect, safeguard, save, screen, secure, shelter, shield, supervise, tend, watch, watch over ~*n.* 2. custodian, defender, lookout, picket, protector, sentinel, sentry, warder, watch, watchman 3. convoy, escort, patrol 4. buffer, bulwark, bumper, defence, pad, protection, rampart, safeguard, screen, security, shield 5. attention, care, caution, heed, vigilance, wariness, watchfulness 6. **off (one's) guard** napping, unprepared, unready, unwary, with one's defences down 7. **on (one's) guard** alert, cautious, circumspect, on the alert, on the lookout, on the qui vive, prepared, ready, vigilant, wary, watchful

guarded cagey (*Inf.*), careful, cautious, circumspect, discreet, non~

committal, prudent, reserved, re~
strained, reticent, suspicious, wary

guardian attendant, champion, cu~
rator, custodian, defender, escort,
guard, keeper, preserver, protec~
tor, trustee, warden, warder

guerrilla freedom fighter, irregu~
lar, member of the underground *or*
resistance, partisan, underground
fighter

guess *v.* 1. conjecture, estimate,
fathom, hypothesize, penetrate,
predict, solve, speculate, work out
2. believe, conjecture, dare say,
deem, divine, fancy, hazard, imag~
ine, judge, reckon, suppose, sur~
mise, suspect, think ~*n.* 3. conjec~
ture, feeling, hypothesis, judgment,
notion, prediction, reckoning,
speculation, supposition, surmise,
suspicion, theory

guesswork conjecture, estimation,
presumption, speculation, supposi~
tion, surmise, suspicion, theory

guest boarder, caller, company,
lodger, visitant, visitor

guidance advice, auspices, con~
duct, control, counsel, counselling,
direction, government, help, in~
struction, intelligence, leadership,
management, teaching

guide *v.* 1. accompany, attend,
conduct, convoy, direct, escort,
lead, pilot, shepherd, show the
way, steer, usher 2. command,
control, direct, handle, manage,
manoeuvre, steer 3. advise, coun~
sel, educate, govern, influence, in~
struct, oversee, regulate, rule,
superintend, supervise, sway,
teach, train ~*n.* 4. adviser, attend~
ant, chaperon, cicerone, conduc~
tor, controller, counsellor, director,
escort, leader, mentor, monitor,
pilot, steersman, teacher, usher 5.
criterion, example, exemplar,
ideal, inspiration, lodestar, master,
model, paradigm, standard 6. bea~
con, clue, guiding light, key, land~
mark, lodestar, mark, marker,
pointer, sign, signal, signpost 7.
catalogue, directory, guidebook,
handbook, instructions, key,
manual, vade mecum

guild association, brotherhood,
club, company, corporation, fel~
lowship, fraternity, league, lodge,
order, organization, society, union

guile art, artfulness, artifice, clev~
erness, craft, craftiness, cunning,
deceit, deception, duplicity,
gamesmanship (*Inf.*), knavery,
ruse, sharp practice, slyness,
treachery, trickery, trickiness,
wiliness

guilt 1. blame, blameworthiness,
criminality, culpability, delinquen~
cy, guiltiness, iniquity, misconduct,
responsibility, sinfulness, wicked~
ness, wrong, wrongdoing 2. bad
conscience, contrition, disgrace,
dishonour, guiltiness, guilty con~
science, infamy, regret, remorse,
self-condemnation, self-reproach,
shame, stigma

guiltless blameless, clean (*Sl.*),
clear, immaculate, impeccable,
innocent, irreproachable, pure,
sinless, spotless, unimpeachable,
unsullied, untainted, untarnished

guilty 1. at fault, blameworthy,
convicted, criminal, culpable, de~
linquent, erring, evil, felonious, in~
iquitous, offending, reprehensible,
responsible, sinful, to blame, wick~
ed, wrong 2. ashamed, conscience-
stricken, contrite, hangdog, re~
gretful, remorseful, rueful, shame~
faced, sheepish, sorry

gulf 1. bay, bight, sea inlet 2. abyss,
breach, chasm, cleft, gap, opening,
rent, rift, separation, split, void,
whirlpool

gullibility credulity, innocence, na~
iveté, simplicity, trustingness

gullible born yesterday, credulous,
easily taken in, foolish, green, in~
nocent, naive, silly, simple, trust~
ing, unsceptical, unsophisticated,
unsuspecting

gully channel, ditch, gutter, water~
course

gulp *v.* 1. bolt, devour, gobble, guz~
zle, knock back (*Inf.*), quaff, swal~
low, swig (*Inf.*), swill, toss off, wolf
2. choke, gasp, stifle, swallow ~*n.*
3. draught, mouthful, swallow, swig
(*Inf.*)

gum 1. *n.* adhesive, cement, exu~
date, glue, mucilage, paste, resin 2.

v. affix, cement, clog, glue, paste, stick, stiffen

gumption ability, acumen, astuteness, cleverness, common sense, discernment, enterprise, get-up-and-go (*Inf.*), horse sense, initiative, mother wit, nous (*Brit. sl.*), resourcefulness, sagacity, savvy (*Sl.*), shrewdness, spirit, wit(s)

gunman assassin, bandit, bravo, desperado, gangster, gunslinger (*U.S. sl.*), hit man (*Sl.*), killer, mobster (*U.S. sl.*), murderer, terrorist, thug

gurgle 1. *v.* babble, bubble, burble, crow, lap, murmur, plash, purl, ripple, splash **2.** *n.* babble, murmur, purl, ripple

guru authority, guiding light, leader, maharishi, master, mentor, sage, swami, teacher, tutor

gush *v.* **1.** burst, cascade, flood, flow, jet, pour, run, rush, spout, spurt, stream **2.** babble, blather, chatter, effervesce, effuse, enthuse, jabber, overstate, spout ~*n.* **3.** burst, cascade, flood, flow, jet, outburst, outflow, rush, spout, spurt, stream, torrent **4.** babble, blather, chatter, effusion, exuberance

gust *n.* **1.** blast, blow, breeze, flurry, gale, puff, rush, squall **2.** burst, eruption, explosion, fit, gale, outburst, paroxysm, passion, storm, surge ~*v.* **3.** blast, blow, puff, squall

gusto appetite, appreciation, brio, delight, enjoyment, enthusiasm,

exhilaration, fervour, liking, pleasure, relish, savour, verve, zeal, zest

gut *n.* **1.** *Often plural* belly, bowels, entrails, innards (*Inf.*), insides (*Inf.*), intestines, inwards, paunch, stomach, viscera **2.** *Plural. Inf.* audacity, backbone, boldness, bottle (*Sl.*), courage, daring, forcefulness, grit, hardihood, mettle, nerve, pluck, spirit, spunk (*Inf.*), willpower ~*v.* **3.** clean, disembowel, draw, dress, eviscerate **4.** clean out, despoil, empty, pillage, plunder, ransack, ravage, rifle, sack, strip ~*adj.* **5.** *Inf.* basic, deep-seated, emotional, heartfelt, innate, instinctive, intuitive, involuntary, natural, spontaneous, un-thinking, visceral

gutter channel, conduit, ditch, drain, duct, pipe, sluice, trench, trough, tube

guttural deep, gravelly, gruff, hoarse, husky, low, rasping, rough, thick, throaty

guy 1. *n. Inf.* bloke (*Brit. inf.*), cat (*Sl.*), chap, fellow, lad, man, person, youth **2.** *v.* caricature, make (a) game of, make fun of, mock, poke fun at, rib (*Inf.*), ridicule, send up (*Brit inf.*), take off (*Inf.*)

guzzle bolt, carouse, cram, devour, drink, gobble, gorge, gormandize, knock back (*Inf.*), quaff, stuff (oneself), swill, tope, wolf

Gypsy, Gipsy Bohemian, nomad, rambler, roamer, Romany, rover, traveller, vagabond, vagrant, wanderer

H

habit *n.* 1. bent, custom, disposition, manner, mannerism, practice, proclivity, propensity, quirk, tendency, way 2. convention, custom, mode, practice, routine, rule, second nature, usage, wont 3. constitution, disposition, frame of mind, make-up, nature 4. addiction, dependence, fixation, obsession, weakness 5. apparel, dress, garb, garment, habiliment, riding dress ~*v.* 6. array, attire, clothe, dress, equip

habitation 1. abode, domicile, dwelling, dwelling house, home, house, living quarters, lodging, quarters, residence 2. inhabitance, inhabitancy, occupancy, occupation, tenancy

habitual 1. accustomed, common, customary, familiar, fixed, natural, normal, ordinary, regular, routine, standard, traditional, usual, wonted 2. chronic, confirmed, constant, established, frequent, hardened, ingrained, inveterate, persistent, recurrent

habituate acclimatize, accustom, break in, condition, discipline, familiarize, harden, inure, make used to, school, season, train

habitué constant customer, frequenter, frequent visitor, regular (*Inf.*), regular patron

hack¹ *v.* 1. chop, cut, gash, hew, kick, lacerate, mangle, mutilate, notch, slash ~*n.* 2. chop, cut, gash, notch, slash ~*v./n.* 3. *Inf.* bark, cough, rasp

hack² *adj.* 1. banal, mediocre, pedestrian, poor, stereotyped, tired, undistinguished, uninspired, unoriginal ~*n.* 2. Grub Street writer, literary hack, penny-a-liner, scribbler 3. drudge, plodder, slave 4. crock, hired horse, horse, jade, nag, poor old tired horse

hackles make one's hackles rise anger, annoy, bridle at, cause resentment, get one's dander up (*Sl.*), make one see red (*Inf.*)

hackneyed banal, clichéd, common, commonplace, overworked, pedestrian, played out (*Inf.*), run-of-the-mill, stale, stereotyped, stock, threadbare, timeworn, tired, trite, unoriginal, worn-out

hag beldam (*Archaic*), crone, fury, harridan, Jezebel, shrew, termagant, virago, vixen, witch

haggard careworn, drawn, emaciated, gaunt, ghastly, hollow-eyed, pinched, shrunken, thin, wan, wasted, wrinkled

haggle 1. bargain, barter, beat down, chaffer, dicker (*Chiefly U.S.*), higgle, palter 2. bicker, dispute, quarrel, squabble, wrangle

hail¹ *Fig.* 1. *n.* barrage, bombardment, pelting, rain, shower, storm, volley 2. *v.* barrage, batter, beat down upon, bombard, pelt, rain, rain down on, shower, storm, volley

hail² 1. acclaim, acknowledge, applaud, cheer, exalt, glorify, greet, honour, salute, welcome 2. accost, address, call, flag down, halloo, shout to, signal to, sing out, speak to, wave down 3. *With* **from** be a native of, be born in, come from, originate in

hair 1. head of hair, locks, mane, mop, shock, tresses 2. **by a hair** by a fraction of an inch, by a hair's-breadth, by a narrow margin, by a split second, by a whisker, by the skin of one's teeth 3. **get in one's hair** annoy, exasperate, harass, irritate, pester, plague 4. **let one's hair down** let it all hang out (*Inf.*), let off steam (*Inf.*), let oneself go, relax 5. **not turn a hair** keep one's cool (*Sl.*), keep one's hair on (*Brit. inf.*), not bat an eyelid, remain calm 6. **split hairs** cavil, find fault, overrefine, pettifog, quibble

hair-raising alarming, bloodcurdling, breathtaking, creepy, ex-

citing, frightening, horrifying, pet~
rifying, scary, shocking, spine-
chilling, startling, terrifying, thrill~
ing

hair's-breadth 1. *n.* fraction, hair,
jot, narrow margin, whisker 2. *adj.*
close, hazardous, narrow

hairsplitting *adj.* captious, carping,
cavilling, fault-finding, fine, finicky,
nice, niggling, nit-picking (*Inf.*),
overrefined, pettifogging, quib~
bling, subtle

hairy 1. bearded, bewhiskered,
bushy, fleecy, furry, hirsute, pi~
leous (*Biol.*), pilose (*Biol.*), shaggy,
stubbly, unshaven, woolly 2. *Sl.*
dangerous, difficult, hazardous,
perilous, risky, scaring

halcyon 1. calm, gentle, mild, pa~
cific, peaceful, placid, quiet, se~
rene, still, tranquil, undisturbed,
unruffled 2. *Fig.* carefree, flourish~
ing, golden, happy, palmy, pros~
perous

hale able-bodied, blooming, fit,
flourishing, healthy, hearty, in fine
fettle, in the pink, robust, sound,
strong, vigorous, well

half 1. *n.* bisection, division, equal
part, fifty per cent, fraction, hemi~
sphere, portion, section 2. *adj.* di~
vided, fractional, halved, incom~
plete, limited, moderate, partial 3.
adv. after a fashion, all but, barely,
inadequately, incompletely, in
part, partially, partly, pretty near~
ly, slightly 4. **by half** considerably,
excessively, very much

half-baked 1. brainless, crazy,
foolish, harebrained, senseless, sil~
ly, stupid 2. ill-conceived, ill-judged,
impractical, poorly planned, short-
sighted, unformed, unthought out
or through

half-hearted apathetic, cool, indif~
ferent, lacklustre, listless, luke~
warm, neutral, passive, perfunc~
tory, spiritless, tame, unenthusias~
tic, uninterested

halfway *adv.* 1. midway, to *or* in
the middle, to the midpoint 2. in~
completely, moderately, nearly,
partially, partly, rather 3. **meet
halfway** accommodate, come to
terms, compromise, concede, give

and take, strike a balance, trade
off ~*adj.* 4. central, equidistant,
intermediate, mid, middle, midway
5. imperfect, incomplete, moder~
ate, partial, part-way

halfwit dimwit (*Inf.*), dolt, dullard,
dunce, dunderhead, fool, idiot, im~
becile (*Inf.*), mental defective,
moron, nitwit, simpleton

half-witted addle-brained, barmy
(*Sl.*), batty (*Sl.*), crazy, doltish, dull,
dull-witted, feeble-minded, foolish,
idiotic, moronic, silly, simple,
simple-minded, stupid

hall 1. corridor, entrance hall, en~
try, foyer, hallway, lobby, passage,
passageway, vestibule 2. assembly
room, auditorium, chamber, con~
cert hall, meeting place

hallmark 1. authentication, device,
endorsement, mark, seal, sign,
stamp, symbol 2. badge, emblem,
indication, sure sign, telltale sign

hallucination aberration, appari~
tion, delusion, dream, fantasy, fig~
ment of the imagination, illusion,
mirage, phantasmagoria, vision

halo aura, aureole *or* aureola, co~
rona, halation (*Photog.*), nimbus,
radiance, ring of light

halt[1] *v.* 1. break off, call it a day,
cease, close down, come to an end,
desist, draw up, pull up, rest, stand
still, stop, wait 2. arrest, block,
bring to an end, check, curb, cut
short, end, hold back, impede, ob~
struct, stem, terminate ~*n.* 3. ar~
rest, break, close, end, impasse,
interruption, pause, stand, stand~
still, stop, stoppage, termination

halt[2] *v.* 1. be defective, falter, hob~
ble, limp, stumble 2. be unsure,
boggle, dither, haver, hesitate,
pause, stammer, swither (*Scot.
dialect*), think twice, waver ~*adj.*
3. *Archaic* crippled, lame, limping

halting awkward, faltering, hesi~
tant, imperfect, laboured, stam~
mering, stumbling, stuttering

halve 1. bisect, cut in half, divide
equally, reduce by fifty per cent,
share equally, split in two 2. **by
halves** imperfectly, incompletely,
scrappily, skimpily

hammer *v.* 1. bang, beat, drive, hit,

knock, strike, tap 2. beat out, fashion, forge, form, make, shape 3. *Often with into* din into, drive home, drub into, drum into, grind into, impress upon, instruct, repeat 4. *Often with away (at)* beaver away (*Brit. inf.*), drudge, grind, keep on, peg away (*Chiefly Brit.*), persevere, persist, plug away (*Inf.*), pound away, stick at, work 5. *Inf.* beat, clobber (*Sl.*), defeat, drub, slate (*Inf.*), thrash, trounce, worst

hammer out accomplish, bring about, come to a conclusion, complete, excogitate, finish, form a resolution, make a decision, negotiate, produce, settle, sort out, thrash out, work out

hamper *v.* bind, cramp, curb, embarrass, encumber, entangle, fetter, frustrate, hamstring, handicap, hinder, hold up, impede, interfere with, obstruct, prevent, restrain, restrict, slow down, thwart, trammel

hamstrung at a loss, crippled, disabled, helpless, *hors de combat*, incapacitated, paralysed

hand *n.* 1. fist, mitt (*Sl.*), palm, paw (*Inf.*) 2. agency, direction, influence, part, participation, share 3. aid, assistance, help, support 4. artificer, artisan, craftsman, employee, hired man, labourer, operative, worker, workman 5. calligraphy, chirography, handwriting, longhand, penmanship, script 6. clap, ovation, round of applause 7. ability, art, artistry, skill 8. **at** *or* **on hand** approaching, available, close, handy, imminent, near, nearby, on tap (*Inf.*), ready, within reach 9. **from hand to mouth** by necessity, improvidently, in poverty, insecurely, on the breadline (*Inf.*), precariously, uncertainly 10. **hand in glove** allied, in cahoots (*Inf.*), in league, in partnership 11. **hand over fist** by leaps and bounds, easily, steadily, swiftly 12. **in hand a.** in order, receiving attention, under control **b.** available for use, in reserve, put by, ready ~*v.* 13. deliver, hand over, pass 14. aid, assist, conduct, convey, give, guide, help, lead, present, transmit

handbook Baedeker, guide, guidebook, instruction book, manual, vade mecum

handcuff 1. *v.* fetter, manacle, shackle 2. *n. Plural* bracelets (*Sl.*), cuffs (*Inf.*), fetters, manacles, shackles

hand down *or* **on** bequeath, give, grant, pass on *or* down, transfer, will

handful few, small number, small quantity, smattering, sprinkling

handicap *n.* 1. barrier, block, disadvantage, drawback, encumbrance, hindrance, impediment, limitation, millstone, obstacle, restriction, shortcoming, stumbling block 2. advantage, edge, head start, odds, penalty, upper hand 3. defect, disability, impairment ~*v.* 4. burden, encumber, hamper, hamstring, hinder, hold back, impede, limit, place at a disadvantage, restrict, retard

handicraft art, artisanship, craft, craftsmanship, handiwork, skill, workmanship

handiwork 1. craft, handicraft, handwork 2. achievement, artefact, creation, design, invention, product, production, result

handle *n.* 1. grip, haft, handgrip, helve, hilt, knob, stock ~*v.* 2. feel, finger, fondle, grasp, hold, maul, paw (*Inf.*), pick up, poke, touch 3. control, direct, guide, manage, manipulate, manoeuvre, operate, steer, use, wield 4. administer, conduct, cope with, deal with, manage, supervise, take care of, treat 5. discourse, discuss, treat 6. carry, deal in, market, sell, stock, trade, traffic in

handling administration, approach, conduct, direction, management, manipulation, running, treatment

hand-out 1. alms, charity, dole 2. bulletin, circular, free sample, leaflet, literature (*Inf.*), press release

hand out deal out, disburse, dish out (*Inf.*), dispense, disseminate, distribute, give out, mete

hand over deliver, donate, fork out *or* up (*Sl.*), present, release, surrender, turn over, yield

hand-picked choice, chosen, elect, elite, recherché, select, selected

hands 1. authority, care, charge, command, control, custody, disposal, guardianship, keeping, possession, power, supervision 2. **hands down** easily, effortlessly, with no contest

handsome 1. admirable, attractive, becoming, comely, elegant, fine, good-looking, graceful, majestic, personable, stately, well-proportioned 2. abundant, ample, bountiful, considerable, generous, gracious, large, liberal, magnanimous, plentiful, sizable

handsomely abundantly, amply, bountifully, generously, liberally, magnanimously, munificently, plentifully, richly

handwriting calligraphy, chirography, fist, hand, longhand, penmanship, scrawl, script

handy 1. accessible, at *or* on hand, available, close, convenient, near, nearby, within reach 2. convenient, easy to use, helpful, manageable, neat, practical, serviceable, useful 3. adept, adroit, clever, deft, dexterous, expert, nimble, proficient, ready, skilful, skilled

hang 1. be pendent, dangle, depend, droop, incline, suspend 2. execute, gibbet, send to the gallows, string up (*Inf.*) 3. adhere, cling, hold, rest, stick 4. attach, cover, deck, decorate, drape, fasten, fix, furnish 5. be poised, drift, float, hover, remain, swing 6. bend downward, bend forward, bow, dangle, drop, incline, lean over, let droop, loll, lower, sag, trail 7. **hang fire** be slow, be suspended, delay, hang back, procrastinate, stall, stick, vacillate 8. **get the hang of** comprehend, get the knack *or* technique, grasp, understand

hang about *or* **around** 1. dally, linger, loiter, roam, tarry, waste time 2. associate with, frequent, haunt, resort

hang back be backward, be reluctant, demur, hesitate, hold back, recoil

hangdog *adj.* abject, browbeaten, cowed, cringing, defeated, downcast, furtive, guilty, shamefaced, sneaking, wretched

hanger-on dependant, follower, freeloader (*Sl., chiefly U.S.*), lackey, leech, minion, parasite, sponger (*Inf.*)

hanging *adj.* 1. dangling, drooping, flapping, flopping, floppy, loose, pendent, suspended, swinging, unattached, unsupported 2. undecided, unresolved, unsettled, up in the air (*Inf.*) 3. beetle, beetling, jutting, overhanging, projecting

hang on 1. carry on, continue, endure, go on, hold on, hold out, persevere, persist, remain 2. cling, clutch, grasp, grip, hold fast 3. be conditional upon, be contingent on, be dependent on, be determined by, depend on, hinge, rest, turn on 4. *Also* **hang onto, hang upon** be rapt, give ear, listen attentively 5. *Inf.* hold on, hold the line, remain, stop, wait

hangover aftereffects, crapulence, head (*Inf.*), morning after (*Inf.*)

hang over be imminent, impend, loom, menace, threaten

hang-up block, difficulty, inhibition, obsession, preoccupation, problem, thing (*Inf.*)

hank coil, length, loop, piece, roll, skein

hanker *With* **for** *or* **after** covet, crave, desire, hunger, itch, long, lust, pine, thirst, want, wish, yearn, yen (*Inf.*)

hankering craving, desire, hunger, itch, longing, pining, thirst, urge, wish, yearning, yen (*Inf.*)

haphazard 1. accidental, arbitrary, chance, fluky (*Inf.*), random 2. aimless, careless, casual, disorderly, disorganized, hit or miss (*Inf.*), indiscriminate, slapdash, slipshod, unmethodical, unsystematic

happen 1. appear, arise, come about, come off (*Inf.*), come to pass, crop up (*Inf.*), develop, ensue, eventuate, follow, materialize, occur, present itself, result, take place, transpire (*Inf.*) 2. become of, befall, betide 3. chance, fall out, have the fortune to be, supervene, turn out

happening accident, adventure, affair, case, chance, episode, event, experience, incident, occasion, occurrence, phenomenon, proceeding, scene

happily 1. agreeably, contentedly, delightedly, enthusiastically, freely, gladly, heartily, willingly, with pleasure 2. blithely, cheerfully, gaily, gleefully, joyfully, joyously, merrily 3. auspiciously, favourably, fortunately, luckily, opportunely, propitiously, providentially, seasonably 4. appropriately, aptly, felicitously, gracefully, successfully

happiness beatitude, blessedness, bliss, cheer, cheerfulness, cheeriness, contentment, delight, ecstasy, elation, enjoyment, exuberance, felicity, gaiety, gladness, high spirits, joy, jubilation, lightheartedness, merriment, pleasure, prosperity, satisfaction, wellbeing

happy 1. blessed, blest, blissful, blithe, cheerful, content, contented, delighted, ecstatic, elated, glad, gratified, jolly, joyful, joyous, jubilant, merry, overjoyed, over the moon (*Inf.*), pleased, sunny, thrilled, walking on air (*Inf.*) 2. advantageous, appropriate, apt, auspicious, befitting, convenient, enviable, favourable, felicitous, fortunate, lucky, opportune, promising, propitious, satisfactory, seasonable, successful, timely, well-timed

happy-go-lucky blithe, carefree, casual, devil-may-care, easy-going, heedless, improvident, insouciant, irresponsible, light-hearted, nonchalant, unconcerned, untroubled

harangue 1. *n.* address, declamation, diatribe, exhortation, lecture, oration, philippic, screed, speech, spiel (*Inf.*), tirade 2. *v.* address, declaim, exhort, hold forth, lecture, rant, spout (*Inf.*)

harass annoy, badger, bait, beleaguer, bother, chivvy (*Brit.*), devil (*Inf.*), disturb, exasperate, exhaust,

fatigue, harry, hassle (*Inf.*), hound, perplex, persecute, pester, plague, tease, tire, torment, trouble, vex, weary, worry

harassed careworn, distraught, harried, hassled (*Inf.*), plagued, strained, tormented, troubled, under pressure, under stress, vexed, worried

harassment aggravation (*Inf.*), annoyance, badgering, bedevilment, bother, hassle (*Inf.*), irritation, molestation, nuisance, persecution, pestering, torment, trouble, vexation

harbour *n.* 1. anchorage, destination, haven, port 2. asylum, covert, haven, refuge, retreat, sanctuary, sanctum, security, shelter ~*v.* 3. conceal, hide, lodge, protect, provide refuge, relieve, secrete, shelter, shield 4. believe, brood over, cherish, cling to, entertain, foster, hold, imagine, maintain, nurse, nurture, retain

hard *adj.* 1. compact, dense, firm, impenetrable, inflexible, rigid, rocklike, solid, stiff, stony, strong, tough, unyielding 2. arduous, backbreaking, burdensome, exacting, exhausting, fatiguing, formidable, Herculean, laborious, rigorous, strenuous, toilsome, tough, uphill, wearying 3. baffling, complex, complicated, difficult, intricate, involved, knotty, perplexing, puzzling, tangled, thorny, unfathomable 4. callous, cold, cruel, exacting, grim, hardhearted, harsh, implacable, obdurate, pitiless, ruthless, severe, stern, strict, stubborn, unfeeling, unjust, unkind, unrelenting, unsparing, unsympathetic 5. calamitous, dark, disagreeable, disastrous, distressing, grievous, grim, intolerable, painful, unpleasant 6. driving, fierce, forceful, heavy, powerful, strong, violent 7. *Of feelings or words* acrimonious, angry, antagonistic, bitter, hostile, rancorous, resentful 8. *Of truth or facts* actual, bare, cold, definite, indisputable, plain, undeniable, unvarnished, verified ~*adv.* 9. energetically, fiercely, forcefully, forcibly, heavily, intensely, powerfully, severely, sharply, strongly, vigorously, violently, with all one's might, with might and main 10. assiduously, determinedly, diligently, doggedly, earnestly, industriously, intently, persistently, steadily, strenuously, untiringly 11. agonizingly, badly, distressingly, harshly, laboriously, painfully, roughly, severely, with difficulty 12. bitterly, hardly, keenly, rancorously, reluctantly, resentfully, slowly, sorely

hard and fast binding, immutable, incontrovertible, inflexible, invariable, rigid, set, strict, stringent, unalterable

hard-bitten *or* **hard-boiled** case-hardened, cynical, down-to-earth, hard-headed, hard-nosed (*Sl.*), matter-of-fact, practical, realistic, shrewd, tough, unsentimental

hard-core 1. dedicated, die-hard, dyed-in-the-wool, extreme, intransigent, obstinate, rigid, staunch, steadfast 2. explicit, obscene

harden 1. anneal, bake, cake, freeze, set, solidify, stiffen 2. brace, buttress, fortify, gird, indurate, nerve, reinforce, steel, strengthen, toughen 3. accustom, brutalize, case-harden, habituate, inure, season, train

hardened 1. chronic, fixed, habitual, incorrigible, inveterate, irredeemable, reprobate, set, shameless 2. accustomed, habituated, inured, seasoned, toughened

hard-headed astute, cool, hard-boiled (*Inf.*), level-headed, practical, pragmatic, realistic, sensible, shrewd, tough, unsentimental

hardhearted callous, cold, cruel, hard, heartless, indifferent, inhuman, insensitive, intolerant, merciless, pitiless, stony, uncaring, unfeeling, unkind, unsympathetic

hard-hitting critical, no holds barred, pulling no punches, strongly worded, tough, unsparing, vigorous

hardiness boldness, courage, fortitude, intrepidity, resilience, resolution, robustness, ruggedness, sturdiness, toughness, valour

hardline definite, inflexible, intransigent, tough, uncompromising, undeviating, unyielding

hardly almost not, barely, by no means, faintly, infrequently, just, not at all, no quite, no way, only, only just, scarcely, with difficulty

hard-pressed harried, hotly pursued, in difficulties, pushed (*Inf.*), under attack, under pressure, up against it (*Inf.*), with one's back to the wall

hardship adversity, affliction, austerity, burden, calamity, destitution, difficulty, fatigue, grievance, labour, misery, misfortune, need, oppression, persecution, privation, suffering, toil, torment, trial, tribulation, trouble, want

hard up bankrupt, broke (*Inf.*), bust (*Inf.*), cleaned out (*Sl.*), impecunious, impoverished, in the red (*Inf.*), on one's uppers (*Inf.*), out of pocket, penniless, poor, short, short of cash *or* funds, skint (*Brit. sl.*)

hard-wearing durable, resilient, rugged, stout, strong, tough, well-made

hard-working assiduous, busy, conscientious, diligent, energetic, indefatigable, industrious, sedulous, zealous

hardy 1. firm, fit, hale, healthy, hearty, in fine fettle, lusty, robust, rugged, sound, stalwart, stout, strong, sturdy, tough, vigorous 2. bold, brave, courageous, daring, heroic, intrepid, manly, plucky, resolute, stouthearted, valiant, valorous 3. audacious, brazen, foolhardy, headstrong, impudent, rash, reckless

hark back look back, recall, recollect, regress, remember, revert, think back

harlot call girl, fallen woman, hussy, loose woman, pro (*Inf.*), prostitute, scrubber (*Sl.*), streetwalker, strumpet, tart (*Inf.*), tramp (*Sl.*), whore

harm *n.* 1. abuse, damage, detriment, disservice, hurt, ill, impairment, injury, loss, mischief, misfortune 2. evil, immorality, iniquity, sin, sinfulness, vice, wickedness, wrong ~*v.* 3. abuse, blemish, damage, hurt, ill-treat, ill-use, impair, injure, maltreat, mar, molest, ruin, spoil, wound

harmful baleful, baneful, damaging, deleterious, destructive, detrimental, disadvantageous, evil, hurtful, injurious, noxious, pernicious

harmless gentle, innocent, innocuous, innoxious, inoffensive, nontoxic, not dangerous, safe, unobjectionable

harmonious 1. agreeable, compatible, concordant, congruous, consonant, coordinated, correspondent, dulcet, euphonious, harmonic, harmonizing, matching, mellifluous, melodious, musical, sweetsounding, symphonious (*Literary*), tuneful 2. agreeable, amicable, compatible, concordant, congenial, cordial, *en rapport*, fraternal, friendly, in accord, in harmony, in unison, of one mind, sympathetic

harmonize accord, adapt, agree, arrange, attune, be in unison, be of one mind, blend, chime with, cohere, compose, coordinate, correspond, match, reconcile, suit, tally, tone in with

harmony 1. accord, agreement, amicability, amity, compatibility, concord, conformity, consensus, cooperation, friendship, good will, like-mindedness, peace, rapport, sympathy, unanimity, understanding, unity 2. balance, compatibility, concord, congruity, consistency, consonance, coordination, correspondence, fitness, parallelism, suitability, symmetry 3. euphony, melodiousness, melody, tune, tunefulness

harness *n.* 1. equipment, gear, tack, tackle, trappings 2. in harness active, at work, busy, in action, working ~*v.* 3. couple, hitch up, put in harness, saddle, yoke 4. apply, channel, control, employ, exploit, make productive, mobilize, render useful, turn to account, utilize

harp *With* on *or* upon dwell on, go on, labour, press, reiterate, renew, repeat

harrowing agonizing, alarming, chilling, distressing, disturbing, excruciating, frightening, heartbreaking, heart-rending, nerveracking, painful, racking, soaring, terrifying, tormenting, traumatic

harry 1. annoy, badger, bedevil, chivvy, disturb, fret, harass, hassle (*Inf.*), molest, persecute, pester, plague, tease, torment, trouble, vex, worry 2. depredate (*Rare*), despoil, devastate, pillage, plunder, raid, ravage, rob, sack

harsh 1. coarse, croaking, crude, discordant, dissonant, glaring, grating, guttural, jarring, rasping, raucous, rough, strident, unmelodious 2. abusive, austere, bitter, bleak, brutal, comfortless, cruel, dour, Draconian, grim, hard, pitiless, punitive, relentless, ruthless, severe, sharp, Spartan, stern, stringent, unfeeling, unkind, unpleasant, unrelenting

harshly brutally, cruelly, grimly, roughly, severely, sharply, sternly, strictly

harshness acerbity, acrimony, asperity, austerity, bitterness, brutality, churlishness, coarseness, crudity, hardness, ill-temper, rigour, roughness, severity, sourness, sternness

harvest *n.* 1. harvesting, harvesttime, ingathering, reaping 2. crop, produce, yield 3. *Fig.* consequence, effect, fruition, product, result, return ~*v.* 4. gather, mow, pick, pluck, reap 5. accumulate, acquire, amass, collect, garner

hash 1. confusion, hotchpotch, jumble, mess, mishmash, mix-up, muddle, shambles 2. make a hash of *Inf.* botch, bungle, jumble, mess up, mishandle, mismanage, mix, muddle

hassle *n.* 1. altercation, argument, bickering, disagreement, dispute, fight, quarrel, squabble, tussle, wrangle 2. bother, difficulty, inconvenience, problem, struggle, trial, trouble, upset ~*v.* 3. annoy, badger, bother, bug (*Inf.*), harass, harry, hound, pester

haste 1. alacrity, briskness, celerity, dispatch, expedition, fleetness, nimbleness, promptitude, quickness, rapidity, rapidness, speed, swiftness, urgency, velocity 2. bustle, hastiness, helter-skelter, hurry, hustle, impetuosity, precipitateness, rashness, recklessness, rush

hasten 1. bolt, dash, fly, haste, hurry (up), make haste, race, run, rush, scurry, scuttle, speed, sprint, step on it (*Inf.*), tear (along) 2. accelerate, advance, dispatch, expedite, goad, hurry (up), precipitate, press, push forward, quicken, speed (up), step up (*Inf.*), urge

hastily 1. apace, double-quick, fast, posthaste, promptly, quickly, rapidly, speedily, straightaway 2. heedlessly, hurriedly, impetuously, impulsively, on the spur of the moment, precipitately, rashly, recklessly, too quickly

hasty 1. brisk, eager, expeditious, fast, fleet, hurried, prompt, rapid, speedy, swift, urgent 2. brief, cursory, fleeting, passing, perfunctory, rushed, short, superficial 3. foolhardy, headlong, heedless, impetuous, impulsive, indiscreet, precipitate, rash, reckless, thoughtless, unduly quick 4. brusque, excited, fiery, hot-headed, hot-tempered, impatient, irascible, irritable, passionate, quick-tempered, snappy

hatch 1. breed, bring forth, brood, incubate 2. *Fig.* conceive, concoct, contrive, cook up (*Inf.*), design, devise, dream up (*Inf.*), plan, plot, project, scheme, think up

hatchet man assassin, bravo, calumniator, cutthroat, debunker, defamer, destroyer, detractor, gunman, hired assassin, hit man (*Sl.*), killer, murderer, smear campaigner, thug, traducer

hate v. 1. abhor, abominate, be hostile to, be repelled by, be sick of, despise, detest, dislike, execrate, have an aversion to, loathe, recoil from 2. be loath, be reluctant, be sorry, be unwilling, dislike, feel disinclined, have no stomach

for, shrink from ~n. 3. abhorrence, abomination, animosity, animus, antagonism, antipathy, aversion, detestation, dislike, enmity, execration, hatred, hostility, loathing, odium

hateful abhorrent, abominable, despicable, detestable, disgusting, execrable, forbidding, foul, heinous, horrible, loathsome, obnoxious, odious, offensive, repellent, repugnant, repulsive, revolting, vile

hatred abomination, animosity, animus, antagonism, antipathy, aversion, detestation, dislike, enmity, execration, hate, ill will, odium, repugnance, revulsion

haughty arrogant, assuming, conceited, contemptuous, disdainful, high, high and mighty (*Inf.*), hoity-toity (*Inf.*), imperious, lofty, overweening, proud, scornful, snobbish, snooty (*Inf.*), stuck-up (*Inf.*), supercilious, uppish (*Brit. inf.*)

haul v. 1. drag, draw, hale, heave, lug, pull, tow, trail, tug 2. carry, cart, convey, hump (*Brit. sl.*), move, transport ~n. 3. drag, heave, pull, tug 4. booty, catch, find, gain, harvest, loot, spoils, takings, yield

haunt v. 1. visit, walk 2. beset, come back, obsess, plague, possess, prey on, recur, stay with, torment, trouble, weigh on 3. frequent, hang around *or* about, repair, resort, visit ~n. 4. den, gathering place, hangout (*Inf.*), meeting place, rendezvous, resort, stamping ground

haunted 1. cursed, eerie, ghostly, jinxed, possessed, spooky (*Inf.*) 2. obsessed, plagued, preoccupied, tormented, troubled, worried

haunting disturbing, eerie, evocative, indelible, nostalgic, persistent, poignant, recurrent, recurring, unforgettable

have 1. hold, keep, obtain, occupy, own, possess, retain 2. accept, acquire, gain, get, obtain, procure, receive, secure, take 3. comprehend, comprise, contain, embody, include, take in 4. endure, enjoy, experience, feel, meet with, suffer, sustain, undergo 5. *Sl.* cheat, deceive, dupe, fool, outwit, swindle, take in (*Inf.*), trick 6. *Usually* **have to** be bound, be compelled, be forced, be obliged, have got to, must, ought, should 7. allow, consider, entertain, permit, put up with (*Inf.*), think about, tolerate 8. bear, beget, bring forth, bring into the world, deliver, give birth to 9. **have had it** *Inf.* be defeated, be exhausted, be finished, be out, be past it (*Inf.*)

haven 1. anchorage, harbour, port, roads (*Nautical*) 2. *Fig.* asylum, refuge, retreat, sanctuary, sanc~tum, shelter

have on 1. be clothed in, be dressed in, wear 2. be committed to, be engaged to, have on the agenda, have planned 3. *Of a person* deceive, kid (*Inf.*), play a joke on, tease, trick

havoc 1. carnage, damage, desola~tion, despoliation, destruction, devastation, rack and ruin, ravag~es, ruin, slaughter, waste, wreck 2. *Inf.* chaos, confusion, disorder, dis~ruption, mayhem, shambles 3. **play havoc (with)** bring into chaos, confuse, demolish, destroy, devas~tate, disorganize, disrupt, wreck

hawk *v.* 1. bark (*Inf.*), cry, market, peddle, sell, tout (*Inf.*), vend 2. *Of~ten with* about bandy about (*Inf.*), bruit about (*Archaic*), buzz, noise abroad, put about, retail, rumour

hazardous 1. dangerous, dicey (*Sl., chiefly Brit.*), difficult, fraught with danger, hairy (*Sl.*), insecure, peri~lous, precarious, risky, unsafe 2. chancy (*Inf.*), haphazard, precari~ous, uncertain, unpredictable

haze cloud, dimness, film, fog, mist, obscurity, smog, smokiness, steam, vapour

hazy 1. blurry, cloudy, dim, dull, faint, foggy, misty, nebulous, ob~scure, overcast, smoky, veiled 2. *Fig.* fuzzy, ill-defined, indefinite, indistinct, loose, muddled, muzzy, nebulous, uncertain, unclear, vague

head *n.* 1. conk (*Sl.*), cranium, crown, loaf (*Sl.*), noddle (*Inf., chiefly Brit.*), nut (*Sl.*), pate, skull 2.

boss (*Inf.*), captain, chief, chieftain, commander, director, headmaster, headmistress, head teacher, lead~er, manager, master, principal, superintendent, supervisor 3. apex, crest, crown, height, peak, pitch, summit, tip, top, vertex 4. first place, fore, forefront, front, van, vanguard 5. beginning, com~mencement, origin, rise, source, start 6. ability, aptitude, brain, brains (*Inf.*), capacity, faculty, flair, intellect, intelligence, men~tality, mind, talent, thought, understanding 7. branch, category, class, department, division, head~ing, section, subject, topic 8. cli~max, conclusion, crisis, culmina~tion, end, turning point 9. *Geog.* cape, foreland, headland, point, promontory 10. **go to one's head** dizzy, excite, intoxicate, make conceited, puff up 11. **head over heels** completely, intensely, thor~oughly, uncontrollably, utterly, wholeheartedly 12. **put (our, their, etc.) heads together** *Inf.* confab (*Inf.*), confabulate, confer, consult, deliberate, discuss, palaver, pow~wow, talk over ~*adj.* 13. arch, chief, first, foremost, front, highest, leading, main, pre-eminent, premier, prime, principal, su~preme, topmost ~*v.* 14. be *or* go first, cap, crown, lead, lead the way, precede, top 15. be in charge of, command, control, direct, gov~ern, guide, lead, manage, rule, run, supervise 16. *Often with* for aim, go to, make a beeline for, make for, point, set off for, set out, start towards, steer, turn

headache 1. cephalalgia (*Medical*), migraine, neuralgia 2. *Inf.* bane, bother, inconvenience, nuisance, problem, trouble, vexation, worry

headfirst 1. *adj./adv.* diving, head~long, head-on 2. *adv.* carelessly, hastily, head over heels, precipi~tately, rashly, recklessly

heading 1. caption, headline, name, rubric, title 2. category, class, division, section

headlong 1. *adj./adv.* headfirst, headforemost, head-on 2. *adj.* breakneck, dangerous, hasty, im~

petuous, impulsive, inconsiderate, precipitate, reckless, thoughtless 3. *adv.* hastily, heedlessly, helter-skelter, hurriedly, pell-mell, precipitately, rashly, thoughtlessly, wildly

head off 1. block off, cut off, deflect, divert, intercept, interpose, intervene 2. avert, fend off, forestall, parry, prevent, stop, ward off

headstrong contrary, foolhardy, froward, heedless, imprudent, impulsive, intractable, mulish, obstinate, perverse, pig-headed, rash, reckless, self-willed, stubborn, ungovernable, unruly, wilful

headway 1. advance, improvement, progress, progression, way 2. **make headway** advance, come *or* get on, cover ground, develop, gain, gain ground, make strides, progress

heady 1. inebriating, intoxicating, potent, spirituous, strong 2. exciting, exhilarating, intoxicating, overwhelming, stimulating, thrilling 3. hasty, impetuous, impulsive, inconsiderate, precipitate, rash, reckless, thoughtless

heal 1. cure, make well, mend, regenerate, remedy, restore, treat 2. alleviate, ameliorate, compose, conciliate, harmonize, patch up, reconcile, settle, soothe

healing 1. analeptic, curative, medicinal, remedial, restorative, restoring, sanative, therapeutic 2. assuaging, comforting, emollient, gentle, lenitive, mild, mitigative, palliative, soothing

health 1. fitness, good condition, haleness, healthiness, robustness, salubrity, soundness, strength, vigour, wellbeing 2. condition, constitution, fettle, form, shape, state, tone

healthy 1. active, blooming, fit, flourishing, hale, hale and hearty, hardy, hearty, in fine feather, in fine fettle, in fine form, in good condition, in good shape (*Inf.*), in the pink, physically fit, robust, sound, strong, sturdy, vigorous, well 2. beneficial, bracing, good for one, healthful, health-giving, hygienic, invigorating, nourishing, nutritious, salubrious, salutary, wholesome

heap *n.* 1. accumulation, aggregation, collection, hoard, lot, mass, mound, mountain, pile, stack, stockpile, store 2. *Often plural Inf.* abundance, a lot, great deal, lashings (*Brit. inf.*), load(s) (*Inf.*), lots (*Inf.*), mass, mint, ocean(s), oodles (*Inf.*), plenty, pot(s) (*Inf.*), quantities, stack(s), tons ~*v.* 3. accumulate, amass, augment, bank, collect, gather, hoard, increase, mound, pile, stack, stockpile, store 4. assign, bestow, burden, confer, load, shower upon

hear 1. attend, be all ears (*Inf.*), catch, eavesdrop, give attention, hark, hearken (*Archaic*), heed, listen in, listen to, overhear 2. ascertain, be informed, be told of, discover, find out, gather, get wind of (*Inf.*), hear tell (*Dialect*), learn, pick up, understand 3. *Law* examine, investigate, judge, try

hearing 1. audition, auditory, ear, perception 2. audience, audition, chance to speak, interview 3. auditory range, earshot, hearing distance, range, reach, sound 4. inquiry, investigation, review, trial

hearsay buzz, gossip, grapevine (*Inf.*), idle talk, mere talk, *on dit*, report, rumour, talk, talk of the town, tittle-tattle, word of mouth

heart 1. character, disposition, emotion, feeling, inclination, nature, sentiment, soul, sympathy, temperament 2. affection, benevolence, compassion, concern, humanity, love, pity, tenderness, understanding 3. boldness, bravery, courage, fortitude, guts (*Inf.*), mettle, mind, nerve, pluck, purpose, resolution, spirit, spunk (*Inf.*), will 4. central part, centre, core, crux, essence, hub, kernel, marrow, middle, nucleus, pith, quintessence, root 5. **at heart** *au fond*, basically, essentially, fundamentally, in essence, in reality, really, truly 6. **by heart** by memory, by rote, off pat, parrot-fashion (*Inf.*), pat, word for word 7. **eat one's**

heart out agonize, brood, grieve, mope, mourn, pine, regret, repine, sorrow 8. **from (the bottom of) one's heart** deeply, devoutly, fervently, heart and soul, heartily, sincerely, with all one's heart 9. **heart and soul** absolutely, completely, devotedly, entirely, gladly, wholeheartedly 10. **take heart** be comforted, be encouraged, be heartened, brighten up, buck up (*Inf.*), cheer up, perk up, revive

heartbreaking agonizing, bitter, desolating, disappointing, distressing, grievous, heart-rending, pitiful, poignant, sad, tragic

heartbroken brokenhearted, crestfallen, crushed, dejected, desolate, despondent, disappointed, disconsolate, disheartened, dispirited, downcast, grieved, heartsick, miserable

heartfelt ardent, cordial, deep, devout, earnest, fervent, genuine, hearty, honest, profound, sincere, unfeigned, warm, wholehearted

heartily 1. cordially, deeply, feelingly, genuinely, profoundly, sincerely, unfeignedly, warmly 2. eagerly, earnestly, enthusiastically, resolutely, vigorously, zealously 3. absolutely, completely, thoroughly, totally, very

heartless brutal, callous, cold, cold-blooded, cold-hearted, cruel, hard, hardhearted, harsh, inhuman, merciless, pitiless, uncaring, unfeeling, unkind

heart-rending affecting, distressing, harrowing, heartbreaking, moving, pathetic, piteous, pitiful, poignant, sad, tragic

heart-to-heart 1. *adj.* candid, intimate, open, personal, sincere, unreserved 2. *n.* cosy chat, tête-à-tête

heart-warming 1. gratifying, pleasing, rewarding, satisfying 2. affecting, cheering, encouraging, heartening, moving, touching, warming

hearty 1. affable, ardent, back-slapping, cordial, eager, ebullient, effusive, enthusiastic, friendly, generous, genial, jovial, unreserved, warm 2. earnest, genuine, heartfelt, honest, real, sincere, true, unfeigned, wholehearted 3. active, energetic, hale, hardy, healthy, robust, sound, strong, vigorous, well 4. ample, filling, nourishing, sizable, solid, square, substantial

heat *n.* 1. calefaction, fever, fieriness, high temperature, hotness, hot spell, sultriness, swelter, torridity, warmness, warmth 2. *Fig.* agitation, ardour, earnestness, excitement, fervour, fever, fury, impetuosity, intensity, passion, vehemence, violence, warmth, zeal ~*v.* 3. become warm, chafe, flush, glow, grow hot, make hot, reheat, warm up 4. animate, excite, impassion, inflame, inspirit, rouse, stimulate, stir, warm

heated angry, bitter, excited, fierce, fiery, frenzied, furious, impassioned, intense, passionate, raging, stormy, tempestuous, vehement, violent

heathen *n.* 1. idolater, idolatress, infidel, pagan, unbeliever 2. barbarian, philistine, savage ~*adj.* 3. godless, heathenish, idolatrous, infidel, irreligious, pagan 4. barbaric, philistine, savage, uncivilized, unenlightened

heave 1. drag (up), elevate, haul (up), heft (*Inf.*), hoist, lever, lift, pull (up), raise, tug 2. cast, fling, hurl, pitch, send, sling, throw, toss 3. breathe heavily, groan, puff, sigh, sob, suspire (*Archaic*), utter wearily 4. billow, breathe, dilate, exhale, expand, palpitate, pant, rise, surge, swell, throb 5. gag (*Sl.*), retch, spew, throw up (*Inf.*), vomit

heaven 1. abode of God, bliss, Elysium *or* Elysian fields (*Greek myth*), happy hunting ground (*Amerind legend*), hereafter, life everlasting, life to come, next world, nirvana (*Buddhism, Hinduism*), paradise, Valhalla (*Norse myth*), Zion (*Christianity*) 2. *Usually plural* empyrean (*Poetic*), ether, firmament, sky, welkin (*Archaic*) 3. *Fig.* bliss, dreamland, ecstasy, enchantment, felicity, happiness, paradise, rapture, seventh heaven, sheer bliss, transport, utopia

heavenly 1. *Inf.* alluring, beautiful, blissful, delightful, divine (*Inf.*), entrancing, exquisite, glorious, lovely, rapturous, ravishing, sublime, wonderful 2. angelic, beatific, blessed, blest, celestial, cherubic, divine, empyrean, extraterrestrial, godlike, holy, immortal, paradisaical, seraphic, superhuman, supernal (*Literary*), supernatural

heavily 1. awkwardly, clumsily, ponderously, weightily 2. laboriously, painfully, with difficulty 3. completely, decisively, roundly, thoroughly, utterly 4. dejectedly, dully, gloomily, sluggishly, woodenly 5. closely, compactly, densely, fast, hard, thick, thickly 6. deep, deeply, profoundly, sound, soundly 7. a great deal, considerably, copiously, excessively, frequently, to excess, very much

heaviness 1. gravity, heftiness, ponderousness, weight 2. arduousness, burdensomeness, grievousness, onerousness, oppressiveness, severity, weightiness 3. deadness, dullness, languor, lassitude, numbness, sluggishness, torpor 4. dejection, depression, despondency, gloom, gloominess, glumness, melancholy, sadness, seriousness

heavy 1. bulky, hefty, massive, ponderous, portly, weighty 2. burdensome, difficult, grievous, hard, harsh, intolerable, laborious, onerous, oppressive, severe, tedious, vexatious, wearisome 3. apathetic, drowsy, dull, inactive, indolent, inert, listless, slow, sluggish, stupid, torpid, wooden 4. crestfallen, dejected, depressed, despondent, disconsolate, downcast, gloomy, grieving, melancholy, sad, sorrowful 5. complex, deep, difficult, grave, profound, serious, solemn, weighty 6. abundant, considerable, copious, excessive, large, profuse 7. burdened, encumbered, laden, loaded, oppressed, weighted 8. boisterous, rough, stormy, tempestuous, turbulent, violent, wild 9. dull, gloomy, leaden, louring, lowering, overcast

heavy-handed 1. awkward, bungling, clumsy, graceless, hamfisted (*Inf.*), ham-handed (*Inf.*), inept, inexpert, like a bull in a china shop (*Inf.*), maladroit, unhandy 2. bungling, inconsiderate, insensitive, tactless, thoughtless 3. autocratic, domineering, harsh, oppressive, overbearing

heckle bait, barrack (*Inf.*), disrupt, interrupt, jeer, pester, shout down, taunt

hectic animated, boisterous, chaotic, excited, fevered, feverish, flurrying, flustering, frantic, frenetic, frenzied, furious, heated, riotous, rumbustious, tumultuous, turbulent, wild

hector bluster, boast, browbeat, bully, bullyrag, harass, huff and puff, intimidate, menace, provoke, ride roughshod over, roister, threaten, worry

hedge *n.* 1. hedgerow, quickset 2. barrier, boundary, screen, windbreak 3. compensation, counterbalance, guard, insurance cover, protection ~*v.* 4. border, edge, enclose, fence, surround 5. block, confine, hem in (about, around), hinder, obstruct, restrict 6. beg the question, be noncommittal, dodge, duck, equivocate, evade, prevaricate, pussyfoot (*Inf.*), quibble, sidestep, temporize, waffle (*Inf.*) 7. cover, fortify, guard, insure, protect, safeguard, shield

heed 1. *n.* attention, care, caution, consideration, ear, heedfulness, mind, note, notice, regard, respect, thought, watchfulness 2. *v.* attend, bear in mind, be guided by, consider, follow, give ear to, listen to, mark, mind, note, obey, observe, pay attention to, regard, take notice of, take to heart

heedful attentive, careful, cautious, chary, circumspect, mindful, observant, prudent, vigilant, wary, watchful

heedless careless, foolhardy, imprudent, inattentive, incautious, neglectful, negligent, oblivious, precipitate, rash, reckless,

thoughtless, unmindful, unobserv~
ant, unthinking

heel[1] *n.* **1.** crust, end, remainder,
rump, stub, stump **2.** *Sl.* black~
guard, bounder (*Brit. inf.*), cad
(*Brit inf.*), rotter (*Sl., chiefly Brit.*),
scoundrel, swine **3. down at heel**
dowdy, impoverished, out at el~
bows, run-down, seedy, shabby,
slipshod, slovenly, worn **4. take to
one's heels** escape, flee, run away
or off, show a clean pair of heels,
skedaddle (*Inf.*), take flight, va~
moose (*Sl., chiefly U.S.*) **5. well-
heeled** affluent, flush (*Inf.*), mon~
eyed, prosperous, rich, wealthy,
well-off, well-to-do

heel[2] cant, careen, incline, keel
over, lean over, list, tilt

hefty 1. beefy (*Inf.*), big, brawny,
burly, hulking, husky (*Inf.*), mas~
sive, muscular, robust, strapping,
strong **2.** forceful, heavy, powerful,
thumping (*Sl.*), vigorous **3.** ample,
awkward, bulky, colossal, cumber~
some, heavy, large, massive, pon~
derous, substantial, tremendous,
unwieldy, weighty

height 1. altitude, elevation, high~
ness, loftiness, stature, tallness **2.**
apex, apogee, crest, crown, eleva~
tion, hill, mountain, peak, pinnacle,
summit, top, vertex, zenith **3.**
acme, dignity, eminence, exalta~
tion, grandeur, loftiness, promi~
nence **4.** climax, culmination, ex~
tremity, limit, maximum, *ne plus
ultra*, ultimate, utmost degree,
uttermost

heighten 1. add to, aggravate, am~
plify, augment, enhance, improve,
increase, intensify, magnify,
sharpen, strengthen **2.** elevate, en~
hance, ennoble, exalt, magnify,
raise, uplift

heir beneficiary, heiress (*Fem.*),
inheritor, inheritress *or* inheritrix
(*Fem.*), next in line, scion, succes~
sor

hell 1. Abaddon, abode of the
damned, abyss, Acheron (*Greek
myth*), bottomless pit, fire and
brimstone, Gehenna (*New Testa~
ment, Judaism*), Hades (*Greek
myth*), hellfire, infernal regions,

inferno, lower world, nether world,
Tartarus (*Greek myth*), under~
world **2.** affliction, agony, anguish,
martyrdom, misery, nightmare,
ordeal, suffering, torment, trial,
wretchedness **3. hell for leather** at
the double, full-tilt, headlong, hot~
foot, hurriedly, like a bat out of hell
(*Inf.*), pell-mell, posthaste, quickly,
speedily, swiftly

hellish 1. damnable, damned, de~
moniacal, devilish, diabolical,
fiendish, infernal **2.** abominable,
accursed, atrocious, barbarous,
cruel, detestable, execrable, inhu~
man, monstrous, nefarious, vicious,
wicked

helm 1. *Nautical* rudder, steering
gear, tiller, wheel **2.** *Fig.* com~
mand, control, direction, leader~
ship, rule **3. at the helm** at the
wheel, directing, in charge, in
command, in control, in the driv~
ing seat, in the saddle

help *v.* **1.** abet, aid, assist, back,
befriend, cooperate, lend a hand,
promote, relieve, save, second,
serve, stand by, succour, support **2.**
alleviate, ameliorate, cure, ease,
facilitate, heal, improve, mitigate,
relieve, remedy, restore **3.** abstain,
avoid, control, eschew, forbear,
hinder, keep from, prevent, refrain
from, resist, shun, withstand ~*n.* **4.**
advice, aid, assistance, avail, ben~
efit, cooperation, guidance, helping
hand, service, support, use, utility
5. assistant, employee, hand, help~
er, worker **6.** balm, corrective,
cure, relief, remedy, restorative,
salve, succour

helper abettor, adjutant, aide, aid~
er, ally, assistant, attendant, aux~
iliary, coadjutor, collaborator, col~
league, deputy, helpmate, mate,
partner, right-hand man, second,
subsidiary, supporter

helpful 1. advantageous, beneficial,
constructive, favourable, fortunate,
practical, productive, profitable,
serviceable, timely, useful **2.** ac~
commodating, beneficent, benevo~
lent, caring, considerate, coopera~
tive, friendly, kind, neighbourly,
supportive, sympathetic

helping n. dollop (Inf.), piece, plateful, portion, ration, serving

helpless 1. abandoned, defence~ less, dependent, destitute, exposed, forlorn, unprotected, vulnerable 2. debilitated, disabled, feeble, impo~ tent, incapable, incompetent, in~ firm, paralysed, powerless, unfit, weak

helter-skelter 1. adv. carelessly, hastily, headlong, hurriedly, pell-mell, rashly, recklessly, wildly 2. adj. anyhow, confused, disordered, haphazard, higgledy-piggledy (Inf.), hit-or-miss, jumbled, mud~ dled, random, topsy-turvy

hem 1. n. border, edge, fringe, margin, trimming 2. v. Usually with in beset, border, circum~ scribe, confine, edge, enclose, en~ viron, hedge in, restrict, shut in, skirt, surround

hence ergo, for this reason, on that account, therefore, thus

henceforth from now on, from this day forward, hence, hereafter, hereinafter, in the future

henpecked browbeaten, bullied, cringing, dominated, led by the nose, meek, subject, subjugated, timid, treated like dirt

herald n. 1. bearer of tidings, crier, messenger 2. forerunner, harbin~ ger, indication, omen, precursor, sign, signal, token ~v. 3. advertise, announce, broadcast, proclaim, publicize, publish, trumpet 4. fore~ token, harbinger, indicate, pave the way, portend, precede, pres~ age, promise, show, usher in

herd n. 1. assemblage, collection, crowd, crush, drove, flock, horde, mass, mob, multitude, press, swarm, throng 2. mob, populace, rabble, riffraff, the hoi polloi, the masses, the plebs ~v. 3. assemble, associate, collect, congregate, flock, gather, huddle, muster, rally 4. drive, force, goad, guide, lead, shepherd, spur

hereafter 1. adv. after this, from now on, hence, henceforth, hence~ forward, in future 2. n. afterlife, future life, life after death, next world, the beyond

hereditary 1. family, genetic, in~ born, inbred, inheritable, trans~ missible 2. ancestral, bequeathed, handed down, inherited, patrimo~ nial, traditional, transmitted, willed

heredity congenital traits, consti~ tution, genetic make-up, genetics, inheritance

heresy apostasy, dissidence, error, heterodoxy, iconoclasm, impiety, revisionism, schism, unorthodoxy

heretic apostate, dissenter, dissi~ dent, nonconformist, renegade, re~ visionist, schismatic, sectarian, separatist

heretical freethinking, heterodox, iconoclastic, idolatrous, impious, revisionist, schismatic, unorthodox

heritage bequest, birthright, en~ dowment, estate, inheritance, legacy, lot, patrimony, portion, share, tradition

hermit anchoret, anchorite, er~ emite, monk, recluse, solitary, sty~ lite

hero 1. celebrity, champion, con~ queror, exemplar, great man, heart-throb (Brit.), idol, man of the hour, popular figure, star, super~ star, victor 2. lead actor, leading man, male lead, principal male character, protagonist

heroic 1. bold, brave, courageous, daring, dauntless, doughty, fear~ less, gallant, intrepid, lion-hearted, stouthearted, undaunted, valiant, valorous 2. classical, Homeric, legendary, mythological 3. classic, elevated, epic, exaggerated, ex~ travagant, grand, grandiose, high-flown, inflated

heroine 1. celebrity, goddess, ideal, woman of the hour 2. diva, female lead, lead actress, leading lady, prima donna, principal female character, protagonist

heroism boldness, bravery, cour~ age, courageousness, daring, fear~ lessness, fortitude, gallantry, in~ trepidity, prowess, spirit, valour

hero worship admiration, adora~ tion, adulation, idealization, idoli~ zation, putting on a pedestal, ven~ eration

hesitant diffident, doubtful, half-hearted, halting, hanging back, hesitating, irresolute, lacking confidence, reluctant, sceptical, shy, timid, uncertain, unsure, vacillating, wavering

hesitate 1. be uncertain, delay, dither, doubt, haver (*Brit.*), pause, shillyshally (*Inf.*), swither (*Scot. dialect*), vacillate, wait, waver 2. balk, be reluctant, be unwilling, boggle, demur, hang back, scruple, shrink from, think twice 3. falter, fumble, hem and haw, stammer, stumble, stutter

hesitation 1. delay, doubt, dubiety, hesitancy, indecision, irresolution, uncertainty, vacillation 2. demurral, misgiving(s), qualm(s), reluctance, scruple(s), unwillingness 3. faltering, fumbling, hemming and hawing, stammering, stumbling, stuttering

hew 1. axe, chop, cut, hack, lop, split 2. carve, fashion, form, make, model, sculpt, sculpture, shape, smooth

heyday bloom, flowering, pink, prime, prime of life, salad days

hiatus aperture, blank, breach, break, chasm, discontinuity, gap, interruption, interval, lacuna, lapse, opening, rift, space

hidden abstruse, clandestine, close, concealed, covered, covert, cryptic, dark, hermetic, hermetical, masked, mysterious, mystic, mystical, obscure, occult, recondite, secret, shrouded, ulterior, unrevealed, unseen, veiled

hide¹ 1. cache, conceal, go into hiding, go to ground, go underground, hole up, lie low, secrete, take cover 2. blot out, bury, camouflage, cloak, conceal, cover, disguise, eclipse, mask, obscure, screen, shelter, shroud, veil 3. hush up, keep secret, suppress, withhold

hide² fell, pelt, skin

hidebound brassbound, conventional, narrow, narrow-minded, rigid, set, set in one's ways, straitlaced, ultraconservative

hideous 1. ghastly, grim, grisly, grotesque, gruesome, monstrous, repulsive, revolting, ugly, unsightly 2. abominable, appalling, awful, detestable, disgusting, dreadful, horrendous, horrible, horrid, loathsome, macabre, odious, shocking, sickening, terrible, terrifying

hide-out den, hideaway, hiding place, lair, secret place, shelter

hiding *n.* beating, caning, drubbing, flogging, larruping (*Brit. dialect*), lathering (*Inf.*), licking (*Inf.*), spanking, tanning (*Sl.*), thrashing, walloping (*Inf.*), whaling, whipping

hierarchy grading, pecking order, ranking

hieroglyphic *adj.* enigmatical, figurative, indecipherable, obscure, runic, symbolical

high *adj.* 1. elevated, lofty, soaring, steep, tall, towering 2. excessive, extraordinary, extreme, great, intensified, sharp, strong 3. arch, chief, consequential, distinguished, eminent, exalted, important, influential, leading, powerful, prominent, ruling, significant, superior 4. arrogant, boastful, bragging, despotic, domineering, haughty, lofty, lordly, ostentatious, overbearing, proud, tyrannical, vainglorious 5. capital, extreme, grave, important, serious 6. boisterous, bouncy (*Inf.*), cheerful, elated, excited, exhilarated, exuberant, joyful, light-hearted, merry, strong, tumultuous, turbulent 7. *Inf.* delirious, euphoric, freaked out (*Inf.*), hyped up (*Sl.*), inebriated, intoxicated, on a trip (*Inf.*), spaced out (*Sl.*), stoned (*Sl.*), tripping (*Inf.*), turned on (*Sl.*) 8. costly, dear, exorbitant, expensive, high-priced, steep (*Inf.*), stiff 9. acute, high-pitched, penetrating, piercing, piping, sharp, shrill, soprano, strident, treble 10. extravagant, grand, lavish, luxurious, rich 11. gamy, niffy (*Sl.*), pongy (*Brit. sl.*), strong-flavoured, tainted, whiffy (*Inf.*) 12. high and dry abandoned, bereft, destitute, helpless, stranded 13. high and low all over, everywhere, exhaustively, far and wide, in every nook and cranny 14. high and mighty *Inf.*

arrogant, cavalier, conceited, dis~
dainful, haughty, imperious, over~
bearing, self-important, snobbish,
stuck-up (*Inf.*), superior ~*adv.* 15.
aloft, at great height, far up, way
up ~*n.* 16. apex, height, peak, rec~
ord level, summit, top 17. *Inf.* de~
lirium, ecstasy, euphoria, intoxica~
tion, trip (*Inf.*)

highbrow 1. *n.* aesthete, Brahmin
(*U.S.*), brain (*Inf.*), brainbox (*Sl.*),
egghead (*Inf.*), intellectual,
mastermind, savant, scholar 2. *adj.*
bookish, brainy (*Inf.*), cultivated,
cultured, deep, highbrowed, intel~
lectual, sophisticated

high-class A-one (*Inf.*), choice,
classy (*Sl.*), elite, exclusive, first-
rate, high-quality, posh (*Inf., chief~
ly Brit.*), select, superior, tip-top,
top-flight, tops (*Sl.*), U (*Brit. inf.*),
upper-class

high-flown elaborate, exaggerat~
ed, extravagant, florid, grandiose,
highfalutin (*Inf.*), inflated, lofty,
magniloquent, overblown, preten~
tious

high-handed arbitrary, autocratic,
bossy (*Inf.*), despotic, dictatorial,
domineering, imperious, inconsid~
erate, oppressive, overbearing,
peremptory, self-willed, tyrannical,
wilful

highland *n.* heights, hill country,
hills, mountainous region, plateau,
tableland, uplands

highlight 1. *n.* best part, climax,
feature, focal point, focus, high
point, high spot, main feature,
memorable part, peak 2. *v.* accent,
accentuate, bring to the fore, em~
phasize, feature, focus attention
on, give prominence to, play up,
set off, show up, spotlight, stress,
underline

highly 1. decidedly, eminently, ex~
ceptionally, extraordinarily, ex~
tremely, greatly, immensely, su~
premely, tremendously, vastly,
very, very much 2. appreciatively,
approvingly, enthusiastically, fa~
vourably, warmly, well

highly strung easily upset, edgy,
excitable, irascible, irritable,
nervous, nervy (*Brit. inf.*), neurot~

ic, restless, sensitive, stressed, taut,
temperamental, tense

high-minded elevated, ethical,
fair, good, honourable, idealistic,
magnanimous, moral, noble, prin~
cipled, pure, righteous, upright,
virtuous, worthy

high-powered aggressive, driving,
dynamic, effective, energetic, en~
terprising, forceful, go-ahead, go-
getting (*Inf.*), highly capable, vig~
orous

high-pressure *Of salesmanship*
aggressive, bludgeoning, coercive,
compelling, forceful, high-
powered, importunate, insistent,
intensive, persistent, persuasive,
pushy (*Inf.*)

high-sounding affected, artificial,
bombastic, extravagant, flamboy~
ant, florid, grandiloquent, grandi~
ose, high-flown, imposing, mag~
niloquent, ostentatious, overblown,
pompous, pretentious, stilted,
strained

high-speed brisk, express, fast,
hotted-up (*Inf.*), quick, rapid,
souped-up (*Inf.*), streamlined, swift

high-spirited animated, boister~
ous, bold, bouncy, daring, dashing,
ebullient, effervescent, energetic,
exuberant, frolicsome, full of life,
fun-loving, gallant, lively, mettle~
some, spirited, spunky (*Inf.*), vi~
brant, vital, vivacious

high spirits abandon, boisterous~
ness, exhilaration, exuberance,
good cheer, hilarity, *joie de vivre*,
rare good humour

hijack commandeer, expropriate,
seize, skyjack, take over

hike *v.* 1. back-pack, hoof it (*Sl.*),
leg it (*Inf.*), ramble, tramp, walk 2.
Usually with up hitch up, jack up,
lift, pull up, raise ~*n.* 3. journey on
foot, march, ramble, tramp, trek,
walk

hilarious amusing, comical, con~
vivial, entertaining, exhilarated,
funny, gay, happy, humorous, jolly,
jovial, joyful, joyous, merry, mirth~
ful, noisy, rollicking, side-splitting,
uproarious

hilarity amusement, boisterous~
ness, cheerfulness, conviviality,

exhilaration, exuberance, gaiety, glee, high spirits, jollification, jollity, joviality, joyousness, laughter, levity, merriment, mirth

hill 1. brae (*Scot.*), down (*Archaic*), elevation, eminence, fell, height, hillock, hilltop, knoll, mound, mount, prominence, tor 2. drift, heap, hummock, mound, pile, stack 3. acclivity, brae (*Scot.*), climb, gradient, incline, rise, slope

hillock barrow, hummock, knap (*Dialect*), knoll, monticule, mound, tump (*Western Brit. dialect*)

hilt 1. grip, haft, handgrip, handle, helve 2. **to the hilt** completely, entirely, fully, totally, wholly

hind after, back, caudal (*Anat.*), hinder, posterior, rear

hinder arrest, check, debar, delay, deter, encumber, frustrate, hamper, hamstring, handicap, hold up *or* back, impede, interrupt, obstruct, oppose, prevent, retard, slow down, stop, stymie, thwart, trammel

hindmost concluding, final, furthest, furthest behind, last, most remote, rearmost, terminal, trailing, ultimate

hindrance bar, barrier, check, deterrent, difficulty, drag, drawback, encumbrance, handicap, hitch, impediment, interruption, limitation, obstacle, obstruction, restraint, restriction, snag, stoppage, stumbling block, trammel

hinge v. be contingent, be subject to, depend, hang, pivot, rest, revolve around, turn

hint n. 1. allusion, clue, implication, indication, inkling, innuendo, insinuation, intimation, mention, reminder, suggestion, tip-off, word to the wise 2. advice, help, pointer, suggestion, tip, wrinkle (*Inf.*) 3. breath, dash, *soupçon*, speck, suggestion, suspicion, taste, tinge, touch, trace, undertone, whiff, whisper ~v. 4. allude, cue, imply, indicate, insinuate, intimate, let it be known, mention, prompt, suggest, tip off

hippie beatnik, bohemian, dropout, flower child

hire v. 1. appoint, commission, employ, engage, sign up, take on 2. charter, engage, lease, let, rent ~n. 3. charge, cost, fee, price, rent, rental

hiss n. 1. buzz, hissing, sibilance, sibilation 2. boo, catcall, contempt, derision, jeer, raspberry ~v. 3. rasp, shrill, sibilate, wheeze, whirr, whistle, whiz 4. blow a raspberry, boo, catcall, condemn, damn, decry, deride, hoot, jeer, mock, revile, ridicule

historian annalist, biographer, chronicler, historiographer, recorder

historic celebrated, consequential, epoch-making, extraordinary, famous, momentous, notable, outstanding, red-letter, remarkable, significant

historical actual, archival, attested, authentic, chronicled, documented, factual, real, verifiable

history 1. account, annals, autobiography, biography, chronicle, memoirs, narration, narrative, recapitulation, recital, record, relation, saga, story 2. ancient history, antiquity, bygone times, days of old, days of yore, olden days, the good old days, the old days, the past, yesterday, yesteryear

hit v. 1. bang, bash (*Inf.*), batter, beat, belt (*Sl.*), clip (*Sl.*), clobber (*Sl.*), clout (*Inf.*), cuff, flog, knock, lob, punch, slap, smack, smite (*Archaic*), sock (*Sl.*), strike, swat, thump, wallop (*Inf.*), whack 2. bang into, bump, clash with, collide with, crash against, meet head-on, run into, smash into 3. accomplish, achieve, arrive at, attain, gain, reach, secure, strike, touch 4. affect, damage, devastate, impinge on, influence, leave a mark on, make an impact *or* impression on, move, overwhelm, touch ~n. 5. blow, bump, clash, clout (*Inf.*), collision, cuff, impact, knock, rap, shot, slap, smack, stroke, swipe (*Inf.*), wallop (*Inf.*) 6. *Inf.* sellout, sensation, smash (*Inf.*), success, triumph, winner

hitch v. 1. attach, connect, couple,

fasten, harness, join, make fast, tether, tie, unite, yoke 2. *Often with up* hoick, jerk, pull, tug, yank 3. *Inf.* hitchhike, thumb a lift ~*n.* 4. catch, check, delay, difficulty, drawback, hindrance, hold-up, impediment, mishap, problem, snag, stoppage, trouble

hither close, closer, here, near, nearer, nigh (*Archaic*), over here, to this place

hitherto heretofore, previously, so far, thus far, till now, until now, up to now

hit off 1. capture, catch, impersonate, mimic, represent, take off (*Inf.*) 2. **hit it off** *Inf.* be on good terms, click (*Sl.*), get on (well) with, take to, warm to

hit on *or* **upon** arrive at, chance upon, come upon, discover, guess, invent, light upon, realize, strike upon, stumble on, think up

hit or miss aimless, casual, cursory, disorganized, haphazard, indiscriminate, perfunctory, random, undirected, uneven

hit out (at) assail, attack, castigate, condemn, denounce, inveigh against, lash out, rail against, strike out at

hoard 1. *n.* accumulation, cache, fund, heap, mass, pile, reserve, stockpile, store, supply, treasure-trove 2. *v.* accumulate, amass, buy up, cache, collect, deposit, garner, gather, hive, lay up, put away, put by, save, stash away (*Inf.*), stockpile, store, treasure

hoarder collector, magpie (*Brit.*), miser, niggard, saver, squirrel (*Inf.*)

hoarse croaky, discordant, grating, gravelly, growling, gruff, guttural, harsh, husky, rasping, raucous, rough, throaty

hoary 1. frosty, grey, grey-haired, grizzled, hoar, silvery, white, white-haired 2. aged, ancient, antiquated, antique, old, venerable

hoax 1. *n.* cheat, con (*Sl.*), deception, fast one (*Inf.*), fraud, imposture, joke, practical joke, prank, ruse, spoof (*Inf.*), swindle, trick 2. *v.* bamboozle (*Inf.*), befool, bluff,

con (*Sl.*), deceive, delude, dupe, fool, gammon (*Inf.*), gull, (*Archaic*), hoodwink, hornswoggle (*Sl.*), swindle, take in (*Inf.*), take (someone) for a ride (*Inf.*), trick

hobby diversion, favourite occupation, (leisure) activity, leisure pursuit, pastime, relaxation, sideline

hobnob associate, consort, fraternize, hang about, keep company, mingle, mix, socialize

hoi polloi admass, *canaille*, commonalty, riffraff, the (common) herd, the common people, the great unwashed (*Inf. and derogatory*), the lower orders, the masses, the plebs, the populace, the proles (*Derogatory sl., chiefly Brit.*), the proletariat, the rabble, the third estate

hoist 1. *v.* elevate, erect, heave, lift, raise, rear, upraise 2. *n.* crane, elevator, lift, tackle, winch

hold *v.* 1. have, keep, maintain, occupy, own, possess, retain 2. adhere, clasp, cleave, clinch, cling, clutch, cradle, embrace, enfold, grasp, grip, stick 3. arrest, bind, check, confine, curb, detain, imprison, restrain, stay, stop, suspend 4. assume, believe, consider, deem, entertain, esteem, judge, maintain, presume, reckon, regard, think, view 5. continue, endure, last, persevere, persist, remain, resist, stay, wear 6. assemble, call, carry on, celebrate, conduct, convene, have, officiate at, preside over, run, solemnize 7. bear, brace, carry, prop, shoulder, support, sustain, take 8. accommodate, comprise, contain, have a capacity for, seat, take 9. apply, be in force, be the case, exist, hold good, operate, remain true, remain valid, stand up 10. **hold one's own** do well, hold fast, hold out, keep one's head above water, keep pace, keep up, maintain one's position, stand firm, stand one's ground, stay put, stick to one's guns (*Inf.*) ~*n.* 11. clasp, clutch, grasp, grip 12. anchorage, foothold, footing, leverage, prop, purchase, stay, support, vantage 13. ascendancy, authority, clout

(*Inf.*), control, dominance, domin~
ion, influence, mastery, pull (*Inf.*),
sway

hold back 1. check, control, curb,
inhibit, repress, restrain, suppress
2. desist, forbear, keep back, ref~
use, withhold

holder 1. bearer, custodian, incum~
bent, keeper, occupant, owner,
possessor, proprietor, purchaser 2.
case, container, cover, housing,
receptacle, sheath

hold forth declaim, descant, dis~
course, go on (*Inf.*), harangue, lec~
ture, orate, preach, speak,
speechify, spiel (*Inf.*), spout (*Inf.*)

hold off 1. avoid, defer, delay, keep
from, postpone, put off, refrain 2.
fend off, keep off, rebuff, repel,
repulse, stave off

hold out 1. extend, give, offer,
present, proffer 2. carry on, con~
tinue, endure, hang on, last, per~
severe, persist, stand fast, with~
stand

hold over adjourn, defer, delay,
postpone, put off, suspend, waive

hold-up 1. bottleneck, delay, diffi~
culty, hitch, obstruction, setback,
snag, stoppage, traffic jam, trouble,
wait 2. burglary, mugging (*Inf.*),
robbery, stick-up (*Sl.*), theft

hold up 1. delay, detain, hinder,
impede, retard, set back, slow
down, stop 2. brace, buttress, jack
up, prop, shore up, support, sustain
3. mug (*Inf.*), rob, stick up (*Sl.*),
waylay 4. display, exhibit, flaunt,
present, show 5. bear up, endure,
last, survive, wear

hold with agree to *or* with, ap~
prove of, be in favour of, counte~
nance, subscribe to, support, take
kindly to

hole 1. aperture, breach, break,
crack, fissure, gap, opening, ori~
fice, outlet, perforation, puncture,
rent, split, tear, vent 2. cave, cav~
ern, cavity, chamber, depression,
excavation, hollow, pit, pocket,
scoop, shaft 3. burrow, covert, den,
earth, lair, nest, retreat, shelter 4.
Inf. dive (*Sl.*), dump (*Inf.*), hovel,
joint (*Sl.*), slum 5. *Inf.* cell, dun~
geon, oubliette, prison 6. defect,

discrepancy, error, fallacy, fault,
flaw, inconsistency, loophole 7. *Sl.*
dilemma, fix (*Inf.*), imbroglio, jam
(*Inf.*), mess, predicament, quanda~
ry, scrape (*Inf.*), tangle, (tight) spot
(*Inf.*) 8. **pick holes in** cavil, crab
(*Inf.*), criticize, denigrate, dispar~
age, disprove, find fault, niggle,
pull to pieces, run down, slate (*Inf.*)

holiday 1. break, leave, recess,
time off, vacation 2. anniversary,
bank holiday, celebration, feast,
festival, festivity, fête, gala, public
holiday, saint's day

holier-than-thou   goody-goody
(*Inf.*), pietistic, pietistical, priggish,
religiose,   sanctimonious,   self-
righteous,   self-satisfied,   smug,
unctuous

holiness blessedness, devoutness,
divinity, godliness, piety, purity,
religiousness, righteousness, sa~
credness, saintliness, sanctity,
spirituality, virtuousness

hollow *adj.* 1. empty, not solid, un~
filled, vacant, void 2. cavernous,
concave, deep-set, depressed, in~
dented, sunken 3. deep, dull, ex~
pressionless, flat, low, muffled,
muted, reverberant, rumbling, se~
pulchral, toneless 4. empty, fruit~
less, futile, meaningless, pointless,
Pyrrhic, specious, unavailing, use~
less, vain, worthless 5. empty,
famished,   hungry,   ravenous,
starved 6. artificial, cynical, de~
ceitful, faithless, false, flimsy,
hollow-hearted, hypocritical, in~
sincere,   treacherous,   unsound,
weak 7. **beat (someone) hollow**
Inf. defeat, hammer (*Inf.*), outdo,
overcome, rout, thrash, trounce,
worst ~*n.* 8. basin, bowl, cave,
cavern, cavity, concavity, crater,
cup, den, dent, depression, dimple,
excavation, hole, indentation, pit,
trough 9. bottom, dale, dell, dingle,
glen, valley ~*v.* 10. channel, dig,
dish,   excavate,   furrow,   gouge,
groove, pit, scoop

holocaust annihilation, carnage,
conflagration, destruction, devas~
tation, genocide, inferno, massa~
cre, mass murder

holy 1. devout, divine, faithful, god~

fearing, godly, hallowed, pious, pure, religious, righteous, saintly, sublime, virtuous 2. blessed, consecrated, dedicated, hallowed, sacred, sacrosanct, sanctified, venerable, venerated

home *n.* 1. abode, domicile, dwelling, dwelling place, habitation, house, residence 2. birthplace, family, fireside, hearth, homestead, home town, household 3. abode, element, environment, habitat, habitation, haunt, home ground, range, stamping ground, territory 4. **at home** a. available, in, present b. at ease, comfortable, familiar, relaxed c. entertaining, giving a party, having guests, receiving d. *As a noun* party, reception, soirée 5. **at home in, on,** *or* **with** conversant with, familiar with, knowledgeable, proficient, skilled, well-versed 6. **bring home to** drive home, emphasize, impress upon, make clear, press home ~*adj.* 7. central, domestic, familiar, family, household, inland, internal, local, national, native

homeland country of origin, fatherland, mother country, motherland, native land

homeless 1. *adj.* abandoned, destitute, displaced, dispossessed, down-and-out, exiled, forlorn, forsaken, outcast, unsettled 2. *n.* **the homeless** dossers (*Sl.*), squatters, vagrants

homelike cheerful, comfortable, cosy, easy, familiar, homy, informal, intimate, relaxing, snug

homely comfortable, comfy (*Inf.*), cosy, domestic, everyday, familiar, friendly, homelike, homespun, homy, informal, modest, natural, ordinary, plain, simple, unaffected, unassuming, unpretentious, welcoming

homespun artless, coarse, homely, home-made, inelegant, plain, rough, rude, rustic, unpolished, unsophisticated

homicidal deadly, death-dealing, lethal, maniacal, mortal, murderous

homicide 1. bloodshed, killing, manslaughter, murder, slaying 2. killer, murderer, slayer

homogeneity analogousness, comparability, consistency, correspondence, identicalness, oneness, sameness, similarity, uniformity

homogeneous akin, alike, analogous, cognate, comparable, consistent, identical, kindred, similar, uniform, unvarying

homosexual *adj.* bent (*Sl.*), camp (*Inf.*), gay (*Inf.*), homoerotic, lesbian, queer (*Inf.*), sapphic

honest 1. conscientious, decent, ethical, high-minded, honourable, law-abiding, reliable, reputable, scrupulous, trustworthy, trusty, truthful, upright, veracious, virtuous 2. above board, authentic, bona fide, genuine, honest to goodness, on the level (*Inf.*), on the up and up, proper, real, straight, true 3. equitable, fair, fair and square, impartial, just 4. candid, direct, forthright, frank, ingenuous, open, outright, plain, sincere, straightforward, undisguised, unfeigned

honestly 1. by fair means, cleanly, ethically, honourably, in good faith, lawfully, legally, legitimately, on the level (*Inf.*), with clean hands 2. candidly, frankly, in all sincerity, in plain English, plainly, straight (out), to one's face, truthfully

honesty 1. faithfulness, fidelity, honour, incorruptibility, integrity, morality, probity, rectitude, reputability, scrupulousness, straightness, trustworthiness, truthfulness, uprightness, veracity, virtue 2. bluntness, candour, equity, even-handedness, fairness, frankness, genuineness, openness, outspokenness, plainness, sincerity, straightforwardness

honorary complimentary, ex officio, formal, *honoris causa,* in name *or* title only, nominal, titular, unofficial, unpaid

honour *n.* 1. credit, dignity, distinction, elevation, esteem, fame, glory, high standing, prestige, rank, renown, reputation, repute 2. acclaim, accolade, adoration, commendation, deference, homage, kudos, praise, recognition, regard, respect, reverence, tribute, veneration **3.** decency, fairness, goodness, honesty, integrity, morality, principles, probity, rectitude, righteousness, trustworthiness, uprightness **4.** compliment, credit, favour, pleasure, privilege, source of pride *or* satisfaction **5.** chastity, innocence, modesty, purity, virginity, virtue ~*v.* **6.** admire, adore, appreciate, esteem, exalt, glorify, hallow, prize, respect, revere, reverence, value, venerate, worship **7.** be as good as (*Inf.*), be faithful to, be true to, carry out, discharge, fulfil, keep, live up to, observe **8.** acclaim, celebrate, commemorate, commend, compliment, decorate, dignify, exalt, glorify, laud, lionize, praise **9.** accept, acknowledge, cash, clear, credit, pass, pay, take

honourable 1. ethical, fair, highminded, honest, just, moral, principled, true, trustworthy, trusty, upright, upstanding, virtuous **2.** distinguished, eminent, great, illustrious, noble, notable, noted, prestigious, renowned, venerable **3.** creditable, estimable, proper, reputable, respectable, respected, right, righteous, virtuous

honours adornments, awards, decorations, dignities, distinctions, laurels, titles

hoodwink bamboozle (*Inf.*), befool, cheat, con (*Sl.*), cozen, delude, dupe, fool, gull (*Archaic*), hoax, impose, lead up the garden path (*Inf.*), mislead, pull a fast one on (*Inf.*), rook (*Sl.*), swindle, trick

hook *n.* **1.** catch, clasp, fastener, hasp, holder, link, lock, peg **2.** noose, snare, springe, trap **3. by hook or by crook** by any means, by fair means or foul, somehow, somehow or other, someway **4. hook, line, and sinker** *Inf.* completely, entirely, thoroughly, through and through, totally, utterly, wholly **5. off the hook** *Sl.* acquitted, cleared, exonerated, in the clear, let off, under no obligation, vindicated ~*v.* **6.** catch, clasp, fasten, fix, hasp, secure **7.** catch,

enmesh, ensnare, entrap, snare, trap

hooligan delinquent, hoodlum (*Chiefly U.S.*), rowdy, ruffian, tough, vandal, yob *or* yobbo (*Brit. sl.*)

hoop band, circlet, girdle, loop, ring, wheel

hoot *n.* **1.** call, cry, toot **2.** boo, catcall, hiss, jeer, yell **3.** *Inf.* card (*Inf.*), caution (*Inf.*), laugh (*Inf.*), scream (*Inf.*) ~*v.* **4.** boo, catcall, condemn, decry, denounce, execrate, hiss, howl down, jeer, yell at **5.** cry, scream, shout, shriek, toot, whoop, yell

hop 1. *v.* bound, caper, dance, jump, leap, skip, spring, vault **2.** *n.* bounce, bound, jump, leap, skip, spring, step, vault

hope 1. *n.* ambition, anticipation, assumption, belief, confidence, desire, dream, expectancy, expectation, faith, longing **2.** *v.* anticipate, aspire, await, believe, contemplate, count on, desire, expect, foresee, long, look forward to, rely, trust

hopeful 1. anticipating, assured, buoyant, confident, expectant, looking forward to, optimistic, sanguine **2.** auspicious, bright, cheerful, encouraging, heartening, promising, propitious, reassuring, rosy

hopefully 1. confidently, expectantly, optimistically, sanguinely **2.** *Inf.* all being well, conceivably, expectedly, feasibly, probably

hopeless 1. defeatist, dejected, demoralized, despairing, desperate, despondent, disconsolate, downhearted, forlorn, in despair, pessimistic, woebegone **2.** helpless, incurable, irremediable, irreparable, irreversible, lost, past remedy, remediless **3.** forlorn, futile, impossible, impracticable, pointless, unachievable, unattainable, useless, vain **4.** *Inf.* inadequate, incompetent, ineffectual, inferior, no good, poor, useless (*Inf.*)

horde band, crew, crowd, drove, gang, host, mob, multitude, pack, press, swarm, throng, troop

horizon 1. field of vision, skyline, vista 2. compass, ken, perspective, prospect, purview, range, realm, scope, sphere, stretch

horrible 1. abhorrent, abominable, appalling, awful, dreadful, fearful, frightful, ghastly, grim, grisly, gruesome, heinous, hideous, horrid, loathsome, repulsive, revolting, shameful, shocking, terrible, terrifying 2. *Inf.* awful, beastly (*Inf.*), cruel, disagreeable, dreadful, ghastly (*Inf.*), mean, nasty, terrible, unkind, unpleasant

horrid 1. awful, disagreeable, disgusting, dreadful, horrible, nasty, offensive, terrible, unpleasant 2. abominable, alarming, appalling, formidable, frightening, hairraising, harrowing, hideous, horrific, odious, repulsive, revolting, shocking, terrifying, terrorizing 3. *Inf.* beastly (*Inf.*), cruel, mean, nasty, unkind

horrify 1. affright, alarm, frighten, intimidate, petrify, scare, terrify, terrorize 2. appal, disgust, dismay, outrage, shock, sicken

horror 1. alarm, apprehension, awe, consternation, dismay, dread, fear, fright, panic, terror 2. abhorrence, abomination, antipathy, aversion, detestation, disgust, hatred, loathing, repugnance, revulsion

horror-struck *or* **horror-stricken** aghast, appalled, awe-struck, frightened to death, horrified, petrified, scared out of one's wits, shocked

horseman cavalier, cavalryman, dragoon, equestrian, horse-soldier, rider

horseplay buffoonery, clowning, fooling around, high jinks, pranks, romping, rough-and-tumble, roughhousing (*Sl.*), skylarking (*Inf.*)

horse sense common sense, gumption (*Inf.*), judgment, mother wit, nous (*Inf.*), practicality

hospitable 1. amicable, bountiful, cordial, friendly, generous, genial, gracious, kind, liberal, sociable, welcoming 2. accessible, amenable, open-minded, receptive, responsive, tolerant

hospitality cheer, conviviality, cordiality, friendliness, heartiness, hospitableness, neighbourliness, sociability, warmth, welcome

host[1] *n.* 1. entertainer, innkeeper, landlord, master of ceremonies, proprietor 2. anchor man, compere (*Brit.*), presenter ~*v.* 3. compere (*Brit.*), introduce, present

host[2] army, array, drove, horde, legion, multitude, myriad, swarm, throng

hostage captive, gage, pawn, pledge, prisoner, security, surety

hostile 1. antagonistic, anti (*Inf.*), bellicose, belligerent, contrary, ill-disposed, inimical, malevolent, opposed, opposite, rancorous, unkind, warlike 2. adverse, alien, inhospitable, unfriendly, unpropitious, unsympathetic, unwelcoming

hostilities conflict, fighting, state of war, war, warfare

hostility abhorrence, animosity, animus, antagonism, antipathy, aversion, detestation, enmity, hatred, ill will, malevolence, malice, opposition, resentment, unfriendliness

hot 1. blistering, boiling, burning, fiery, flaming, heated, piping hot, roasting, scalding, scorching, searing, steaming, sultry, sweltering, torrid, warm 2. acrid, biting, peppery, piquant, pungent, sharp, spicy 3. *Fig.* animated, ardent, excited, fervent, fervid, fierce, fiery, impetuous, inflamed, intense, irascible, lustful, passionate, raging, stormy, touchy, vehement, violent 4. fresh, just out, latest, new, recent, up to the minute 5. approved, favoured, in demand, in vogue, popular, sought-after 6. close, following closely, in hot pursuit, near

hot air blather, blether, bombast, bosh (*Inf.*), bunkum, claptrap (*Inf.*), empty talk, gas (*Sl.*), guff (*Sl.*), rant, tall talk (*Inf.*), verbiage, wind

hotbed breeding ground, den, forcing house, nest, nursery, seedbed

hot-blooded ardent, excitable, fervent, fiery, heated, impulsive,

passionate, rash, spirited, tem~
peramental, wild

hotchpotch conglomeration, far~
rago, gallimaufry, hash, jumble,
medley, *mélange*, mess, miscella~
ny, mishmash, mixture, olio, olla
podrida, potpourri

hotfoot hastily, helter-skelter, hur~
riedly, pell-mell, posthaste, quickly,
speedily

hothead daredevil, desperado,
hotspur, madcap, tearaway

hot-headed fiery, foolhardy, hasty,
hot-tempered, impetuous, precipi~
tate, quick-tempered, rash, reck~
less, unruly, volatile

hound *v.* 1. chase, drive, give
chase, hunt, hunt down, pursue 2.
badger, goad, harass, harry, impel,
persecute, pester, prod, provoke

house *n.* 1. abode, building, domi~
cile, dwelling, edifice, habitation,
home, homestead, residence 2.
family, household, ménage 3. an~
cestry, clan, dynasty, family tree,
kindred, line, lineage, race, tribe 4.
business, company, concern, es~
tablishment, firm, organization,
outfit (*Inf.*), partnership 5. Com~
mons, legislative body, parliament
6. hotel, inn, public house, tavern 7.
on the house for nothing, free,
gratis, without expense ~*v.* 8. ac~
commodate, billet, board, domicile,
harbour, lodge, put up, quarter,
take in 9. contain, cover, keep,
protect, sheathe, shelter, store

household 1. *n.* family, home,
house, ménage 2. *adj.* domestic,
domiciliary, family, ordinary, plain

householder homeowner, occu~
pant, resident, tenant

housekeeping home economy,
homemaking (*U.S.*), housecraft,
household management, housewif~
ery

housing 1. accommodation, dwell~
ings, homes, houses 2. case, casing,
container, cover, covering, enclo~
sure, sheath

hovel cabin, den, hole, hut, shack,
shanty, shed

hover 1. be suspended, drift, float,
flutter, fly, hang, poise 2. hang
about, linger, wait nearby 3. alter~

nate, dither, falter, fluctuate, haver
(*Brit.*), oscillate, pause, seesaw,
swither (*Scot. dialect*), vacillate,
waver

however after all, anyhow, be that
as it may, but, nevertheless, none~
theless, notwithstanding, on the
other hand, still, though, yet

howl 1. *n.* bay, bellow, clamour,
cry, groan, hoot, outcry, roar,
scream, shriek, ululation, wail,
yelp, yowl 2. *v.* bellow, cry, cry out,
lament, quest (*used of hounds*),
roar, scream, shout, shriek, ululate,
wail, weep, yell, yelp

howler bloomer (*Brit. inf.*), blun~
der, boner (*Sl.*), bull (*Sl.*), clanger
(*Inf.*), error, malapropism, mis~
take, schoolboy howler

hub centre, core, focal point, focus,
heart, middle, nerve centre, pivot

huddle *n.* 1. confusion, crowd, dis~
order, heap, jumble, mass, mess,
muddle 2. *Inf.* confab (*Inf.*), con~
ference, discussion, meeting ~*v.* 3.
cluster, converge, crowd, flock,
gather, press, throng 4. crouch,
cuddle, curl up, hunch up, make
oneself small, nestle, snuggle

hue 1. colour, dye, shade, tincture,
tinge, tint, tone 2. aspect, cast,
complexion, light

hue and cry brouhaha, clamour,
furore, hullabaloo, much ado, out~
cry, ruction (*Inf.*), rumpus, uproar

hug *v.* 1. clasp, cuddle, embrace,
enfold, hold close, squeeze, take in
one's arms 2. cling to, follow
closely, keep close, stay near 3.
cherish, cling, hold onto, nurse, re~
tain ~*n.* 4. bear hug, clasp, clinch
(*Sl.*), embrace, squeeze

huge Brobdingnagian, bulky, co~
lossal, enormous, extensive, gar~
gantuan, giant, gigantic, great, im~
mense, jumbo (*Inf.*), large, mam~
moth, massive, monumental,
mountainous, prodigious, stupen~
dous, titanic, tremendous, vast

hulk 1. derelict, frame, hull, shell,
shipwreck, wreck 2. lout, lubber,
lump (*Inf.*), oaf

hull *n.* 1. body, casing, covering,
frame, framework, skeleton 2.
husk, peel, pod, rind, shell, shuck,

skin ~v. 3. husk, peel, shell, shuck, skin, trim

hum 1. bombinate *or* bombilate (*Literary*), buzz, croon, drone, mumble, murmur, purr, sing, throb, thrum, vibrate, whir 2. be active, be busy, bustle, buzz, move, pulsate, pulse, stir, vibrate

human *adj.* 1. anthropoid, fleshly, manlike, mortal 2. approachable, compassionate, considerate, fallible, forgivable, humane, kind, kindly, natural, understandable, understanding, vulnerable ~n. 3. body, child, creature, human being, individual, man, mortal, person, soul, wight (*Archaic*), woman

humane benevolent, benign, charitable, clement, compassionate, forbearing, forgiving, gentle, good, good-natured, kind, kindhearted, kindly, lenient, merciful, mild, sympathetic, tender, understanding

humanitarian 1. *adj.* altruistic, beneficent, benevolent, charitable, compassionate, humane, philanthropic, public-spirited 2. *n.* altruist, benefactor, Good Samaritan, philanthropist

humanitarianism beneficence, benevolence, charity, generosity, good will, humanism, philanthropy

humanities classical studies, classics, liberal arts, literae humaniores

humanity 1. flesh, Homo sapiens, humankind, human race, man, mankind, men, mortality, people 2. human nature, humanness, mortality 3. benevolence, benignity, brotherly love, charity, compassion, fellow feeling, kindheartedness, kindness, mercy, philanthropy, sympathy, tenderness, tolerance, understanding

humanize civilize, cultivate, educate, enlighten, improve, mellow, polish, reclaim, refine, soften, tame

humble *adj.* 1. meek, modest, self-effacing, submissive, unassuming, unostentatious, unpretentious 2. common, commonplace, insignificant, low, low-born, lowly, mean,

modest, obscure, ordinary, plebeian, poor, simple, undistinguished, unimportant, unpretentious 3. courteous, deferential, obliging, obsequious, polite, respectful, servile, subservient ~v. 4. abase, abash, break, bring down, chagrin, chasten, crush, debase, degrade, demean, disgrace, humiliate, lower, mortify, put down (*Sl.*), reduce, shame, sink, subdue, take down a peg (*Inf.*) 5. **humble oneself** abase oneself, eat crow (*U.S. inf.*), eat humble pie, go on bended knee, grovel, swallow one's pride

humbug *n.* 1. bluff, cheat, deceit, deception, dodge, feint, fraud, hoax, imposition, imposture, ruse, sham, swindle, trick, trickery, wile 2. charlatan, cheat, con man (*Sl.*), faker, fraud, impostor, phoney (*Sl.*), quack, swindler, trickster 3. baloney (*Inf.*), cant, charlatanry, claptrap (*Inf.*), eyewash (*Inf.*), gammon (*Brit. inf.*), hypocrisy, nonsense, quackery, rubbish ~v. 4. bamboozle (*Inf.*), befool, beguile, cheat, cozen, deceive, delude, dupe, fool, gull (*Archaic*), hoax, hoodwink, impose, mislead, swindle, take in (*Inf.*), trick

humdrum boring, commonplace, dreary, dull, monotonous, mundane, ordinary, repetitious, routine, tedious, tiresome, uneventful, uninteresting, unvaried, wearisome

humid clammy, damp, dank, moist, muggy, steamy, sticky, sultry, watery, wet

humidity clamminess, damp, dampness, dankness, dew, humidness, moistness, moisture, mugginess, sogginess, wetness

humiliate abase, abash, bring low, chagrin, chasten, crush, debase, degrade, discomfit, disgrace, embarrass, humble, make (someone) eat humble pie, mortify, put down (*Sl.*), shame, subdue, take down a peg (*Inf.*)

humiliating crushing, degrading, disgracing, embarrassing, hum~

bling, ignominious, mortifying, shaming

humiliation abasement, affront, chagrin, condescension, degradation, disgrace, dishonour, embarrassment, humbling, ignominy, indignity, loss of face, mortification, put-down, resignation, self-abasement, shame, submission, submissiveness

humility diffidence, humbleness, lack of pride, lowliness, meekness, modesty, self-abasement, servility, submissiveness, unpretentiousness

humorist comedian, comic, droll, eccentric, funny man, jester, joker, wag, wit

humorous amusing, comic, comical, entertaining, facetious, farcical, funny, hilarious, jocose, jocular, laughable, ludicrous, merry, playful, pleasant, side-splitting, waggish, whimsical, witty

humour n. 1. amusement, comedy, drollery, facetiousness, fun, funniness, jocularity, ludicrousness, wit 2. comedy, farce, gags (Sl.), jesting, jests, jokes, joking, pleasantry, wisecracks (Inf.), wit, witticisms, wittiness 3. disposition, frame of mind, mood, spirits, temper 4. bent, bias, fancy, freak, mood, propensity, quirk, vagary, whim ~v. 5. accommodate, cosset, favour, flatter, go along with, gratify, indulge, mollify, pamper, spoil

hump n. 1. bulge, bump, knob, mound, projection, protrusion, protuberance, swelling 2. **the hump** Brit. inf. megrims (Rare), the blues, the doldrums, the dumps (Inf.), the grumps (Inf.), the mopes, the sulks ~v. 3. arch, curve, form a hump, hunch, lift, tense 4. Sl. carry, heave, hoist, lug, shoulder

hunch 1. n. feeling, idea, impression, inkling, intuition, premonition, presentiment, suspicion 2. v. arch, bend, crouch, curve, draw in, huddle, hump, squat, stoop, tense

hunchback crookback (Rare), crouch-back (Archaic), humpback, kyphosis (Pathol.), Quasimodo

hunger n. 1. appetite, emptiness, esurience, famine, hungriness,

ravenousness, starvation, voracity 2. appetence, appetite, craving, desire, greediness, itch, lust, yearning, yen (Inf.) ~v. 3. crave, desire, hanker, itch, long, pine, starve, thirst, want, wish, yearn

hungry 1. empty, famished, famishing, hollow, peckish (Inf., chiefly Brit.), ravenous, sharp-set, starved, starving, voracious 2. athirst, avid, covetous, craving, desirous, eager, greedy, keen, yearning

hunk block, chunk, gobbet, lump, mass, piece, slab, wedge, wodge (Brit. inf.)

hunt v. 1. chase, gun for, hound, pursue, stalk, track, trail 2. ferret about, forage, go in quest of, look, look high and low, rummage through, scour, search, seek, try to find ~n. 3. chase, hunting, investigation, pursuit, quest, search

hunted careworn, desperate, distraught, gaunt, haggard, harassed, harried, persecuted, stricken, terror-stricken, tormented, worn

hurdle n. 1. barricade, barrier, fence, hedge, wall 2. barrier, complication, difficulty, handicap, hindrance, impediment, obstacle, obstruction, snag, stumbling block

hurl cast, chuck (Inf.), fire, fling, heave, launch, let fly, pitch, project, propel, send, shy, sling, throw, toss

hurly-burly bedlam, brouhaha, chaos, commotion, confusion, disorder, furore, hubbub, pandemonium, tumult, turbulence, turmoil, uproar

hurricane cyclone, gale, storm, tempest, tornado, twister (U.S. inf.), typhoon, willy-willy (Aust.), windstorm

hurried breakneck, brief, cursory, hasty, hectic, perfunctory, precipitate, quick, rushed, short, slapdash, speedy, superficial, swift

hurry v. 1. dash, fly, get a move on (Inf.), lose no time, make haste, rush, scoot, scurry, step on it (Inf.) 2. accelerate, expedite, goad, hasten, hustle, push on, quicken, speed (up), urge ~n. 3. bustle, celerity, commotion, dispatch, expedition, flurry, haste, precipitation, promptitude, quickness, rush, speed, urgency

hurt v. 1. bruise, damage, disable, harm, impair, injure, mar, spoil, wound 2. ache, be sore, be tender, burn, pain, smart, sting, throb 3. afflict, aggrieve, annoy, cut to the quick, distress, grieve, pain, sadden, sting, upset, wound ~n. 4. discomfort, distress, pain, pang, soreness, suffering 5. bruise, sore, wound 6. damage, detriment, disadvantage, harm, injury, loss, mischief, wrong ~adj. 7. bruised, cut, damaged, grazed, harmed, injured, scarred, scraped, scratched, wounded 8. aggrieved, crushed, injured, miffed (Inf.), offended, pained, piqued, rueful, sad, wounded

hurtful cruel, cutting, damaging, destructive, detrimental, disadvantageous, distressing, harmful, injurious, malicious, mean, mischievous, nasty, pernicious, prejudicial, spiteful, unkind, upsetting, wounding

husband v. budget, conserve, economize, hoard, manage thriftily, save, store, use sparingly

husbandry agriculture, agronomy, cultivation, farming, land management, tillage

hush v. 1. mute, muzzle, quieten, shush, silence, still, suppress 2. allay, appease, calm, compose, mollify, soothe ~n. 3. calm, peace, peacefulness, quiet, silence, still (Poetic), stillness, tranquillity

husk bark, chaff, covering, glume, hull, rind, shuck

husky 1. croaking, croaky, gruff, guttural, harsh, hoarse, rasping, raucous, rough, throaty 2. Inf. beefy (Inf.), brawny, burly, hefty, muscular, powerful, rugged, stocky, strapping, thickset

hustle bustle, crowd, elbow, force, haste, hasten, hurry, impel, jog, jostle, push, rush, shove, thrust

hut cabin, den, hovel, lean-to, refuge, shanty, shed, shelter

hybrid n. amalgam, composite, compound, cross, crossbreed, half-blood, half-breed, mixture, mongrel, mule

hygiene cleanliness, hygienics, sanitary measures, sanitation

hygienic aseptic, clean, disinfected, germ-free, healthy, pure, salutary, sanitary, sterile

hype ballyhoo (Inf.), brouhaha, build-up, plugging (Inf.), publicity, puffing, racket, razz-matazz (Sl.)

hypnotic mesmeric, mesmerizing, narcotic, opiate, sleep-inducing, somniferous, soothing, soporific, spellbinding

hypnotize 1. mesmerize, put in a trance, put to sleep 2. entrance, fascinate, magnetize, spellbind

hypocrisy cant, deceit, deceitfulness, deception, dissembling, duplicity, falsity, imposture, insincerity, pharisaism, phariseeism, phoneyness (Sl.), pretence, sanctimoniousness, speciousness, two-facedness

hypocrite charlatan, deceiver, dissembler, fraud, Holy Willie, impostor, pharisee, phoney (Sl.), pretender, whited sepulchre

hypocritical canting, deceitful, deceptive, dissembling, duplicitous, false, fraudulent, hollow, insincere, Janus-faced, pharisaical, phoney (Sl.), sanctimonious, specious, spurious, two-faced

hypothesis assumption, postulate, premise, premiss, proposition, supposition, theory, thesis

hypothetical academic, assumed, conjectural, imaginary, putative, speculative, supposed, theoretical

hysteria agitation, delirium, frenzy, hysterics, madness, panic, unreason

hysterical 1. berserk, beside oneself, convulsive, crazed, distracted, distraught, frantic, frenzied, mad, overwrought, raving, uncontrollable 2. Inf. comical, farcical, hilarious, screaming, side-splitting, uproarious, wildly funny

I

ice-cold arctic, biting, bitter, chilled to the bone *or* marrow, freezing, frozen, glacial, icy, raw, refrigerated, shivering

icy 1. arctic, biting, bitter, chill, chilling, chilly, cold, freezing, frostbound, frosty, frozen over, ice-cold, raw 2. glacial, glassy, like a sheet of glass, rimy, slippery, slippy (*Inf.*) 3. *Fig.* aloof, cold, distant, forbidding, frigid, frosty, glacial, hostile, indifferent, steely, stony, unfriendly, unwelcoming

idea 1. abstraction, concept, conception, conclusion, fancy, impression, judgment, perception, thought, understanding 2. belief, conviction, doctrine, interpretation, notion, opinion, teaching, view, viewpoint 3. approximation, clue, estimate, guess, hint, impression, inkling, intimation, notion, suspicion 4. aim, end, import, intention, meaning, object, objective, plan, purpose, *raison d'être*, reason, sense, significance 5. design, hypothesis, plan, recommendation, scheme, solution, suggestion, theory 6. archetype, essence, form, pattern

ideal *n.* 1. archetype, criterion, epitome, example, exemplar, last word, model, nonpareil, paradigm, paragon, pattern, perfection, prototype, standard, standard of perfection 2. *Often plural* moral value, principle, standard ~*adj.* 3. archetypal, classic, complete, consummate, model, optimal, perfect, quintessential, supreme 4. abstract, conceptual, hypothetical, intellectual, mental, theoretical, transcendental 5. fanciful, imaginary, impractical, ivory-tower, unattainable, unreal, Utopian, visionary

idealist *n.* romantic, Utopian, visionary

idealistic impracticable, optimistic, perfectionist, quixotic, romantic, starry-eyed, Utopian, visionary

ideally all things being equal, if one had one's way, in a perfect world, under the best of circumstances

identical alike, corresponding, duplicate, equal, equivalent, indistinguishable, interchangeable, like, matching, selfsame, the same, twin

identification 1. cataloguing, classifying, establishment of identity, labelling, naming, pinpointing, recognition 2. association, connection, empathy, fellow feeling, involvement, rapport, relationship, sympathy 3. credentials, ID, letters of introduction, papers

identify 1. catalogue, classify, diagnose, label, make out, name, pick out, pinpoint, place, put one's finger on (*Inf.*), recognize, single out, spot, tag 2. *Often with* with ally, associate, empathize, feel for, put in the same category, put oneself in the place *or* shoes of, relate to, respond to, see through another's eyes, think of in connection (with)

identity 1. distinctiveness, existence, individuality, oneness, particularity, personality, self, selfhood, singularity, uniqueness 2. accord, correspondence, empathy, rapport, sameness, unanimity, unity

idiocy abject stupidity, asininity, fatuity, fatuousness, foolishness, imbecility, inanity, insanity, lunacy, senselessness, tomfoolery

idiom 1. expression, locution, phrase, set phrase, turn of phrase 2. jargon, language, mode of expression, parlance, style, talk, usage, vernacular

idiomatic dialectal, native, vernacular

idiosyncrasy affectation, characteristic, eccentricity, habit, mannerism, oddity, peculiarity, personal trait, quirk, singularity, trick

idiot ass, blockhead, booby, cretin, dimwit (*Inf.*), dunderhead, fool, halfwit, imbecile, mooncalf, moron, nincompoop, nitwit, simpleton

idiotic asinine, crazy, daft (*Inf.*), dumb (*Inf.*), fatuous, foolhardy, foolish, halfwitted, harebrained, imbecile, imbecilic, inane, insane, lunatic, moronic, senseless, stupid, unintelligent

idle *adj.* 1. dead, empty, gathering dust, inactive, jobless, mothballed, out of action *or* operation, out of work, redundant, stationary, ticking over, unemployed, unoccupied, unused, vacant 2. indolent, lackadaisical, lazy, shiftless, slothful, sluggish 3. frivolous, insignificant, irrelevant, nugatory, superficial, trivial, unhelpful, unnecessary 4. abortive, bootless, fruitless, futile, groundless, ineffective, of no avail, otiose, pointless, unavailing, unproductive, unsuccessful, useless, vain, worthless ~*v.* 5. *Often followed by* away dally, dawdle, fool, fritter, kill time, laze, loiter, lounge, potter, waste, while 6. coast, drift, mark time, shirk, sit back and do nothing, skive (*Brit. sl.*), slack, slow down, take it easy (*Inf.*), vegetate

idleness 1. inaction, inactivity, leisure, time on one's hands, unemployment 2. hibernation, inertia, laziness, shiftlessness, sloth, sluggishness, torpor, trifling 3. dilly-dallying (*Inf.*), lazing, loafing, pottering, skiving (*Brit. sl.*), time-wasting, trifling

idling *adj.* dawdling, drifting, loafing, pottering, resting, resting on one's oars, taking it easy (*Inf.*), ticking over

idol 1. deity, god, graven image, image, pagan symbol 2. *Fig.* beloved, darling, favourite, hero, pet, pin-up (*Sl.*), superstar

idolater 1. heathen, idol-worshipper, pagan 2. admirer, adorer, devotee, idolizer, votary, worshipper

idolatry adoration, adulation, apotheosis, deification, exaltation, glorification, hero worship, idolizing

idolize admire, adore, apotheosize, bow down before, deify, dote upon, exalt, glorify, hero-worship, look up to, love, revere, reverence, venerate, worship, worship to excess

if 1. *conj.* admitting, allowing, assuming, granting, in case, on condition that, on the assumption that, provided, providing, supposing, though, whenever, wherever, whether 2. *n.* condition, doubt, hesitation, stipulation, uncertainty

ignite burn, burst into flames, catch fire, fire, flare up, inflame, kindle, light, put a match to (*Inf.*), set alight, set fire to, take fire, touch off

ignominious abject, despicable, discreditable, disgraceful, dishonourable, disreputable, humiliating, indecorous, inglorious, mortifying, scandalous, shameful, sorry, undignified

ignominy bad odour, contempt, discredit, disgrace, dishonour, disrepute, humiliation, infamy, mortification, obloquy, odium, opprobrium, reproach, shame, stigma

ignorance 1. greenness, inexperience, innocence, nescience (*Literary*), oblivion, unawareness, unconsciousness, unfamiliarity 2. benightedness, blindness, illiteracy, lack of education, mental darkness, unenlightenment, unintelligence

ignorant 1. benighted, blind to, inexperienced, innocent, in the dark about, oblivious, unaware, unconscious, unenlightened, uninformed, uninitiated, unknowing, unschooled, unwitting 2. green, illiterate, naive, unaware, uncultivated, uneducated, unknowledgeable, unlearned, unlettered, unread, untaught, untrained, untutored 3. crass, crude, gross, half-baked (*Inf.*), insensitive, rude, shallow, superficial, uncomprehending, unscholarly

ignore be oblivious to, bury one's head in the sand, cold-shoulder, cut

(*Inf.*), disregard, give the cold shoulder to, neglect, overlook, pass over, pay no attention to, reject, send (someone) to Coventry, shut one's eyes to, take no notice of, turn a blind eye to, turn a deaf ear to, turn one's back on

ill *adj.* 1. ailing, dicky (*Sl.*), diseased, funny (*Inf.*), indisposed, infirm, laid up (*Inf.*), not up to snuff (*Inf.*), off-colour, on the sick list (*Inf.*), out of sorts (*Inf.*), poorly (*Inf.*), queasy, queer, seedy (*Inf.*), sick, under the weather (*Inf.*), unhealthy, unwell, valetudinarian 2. bad, damaging, deleterious, detrimental, evil, foul, harmful, iniquitous, injurious, ru- inous, unfortunate, unlucky, vile, wicked, wrong 3. acrimonious, ad- verse, antagonistic, cantankerous, cross, harsh, hateful, hostile, hurt- ful, inimical, malevolent, mali- cious, sullen, surly, unfriendly, un- kind 4. disturbing, foreboding, in- auspicious, ominous, sinister, threatening, unfavourable, un- healthy, unlucky, unpromising, un- propitious, unwholesome ~*n.* 5. af- fliction, harm, hurt, injury, misery, misfortune, pain, trial, tribulation, trouble, unpleasantness, woe 6. ailment, complaint, disease, disor- der, illness, indisposition, infirmity, malady, malaise, sickness 7. abuse, badness, cruelty, damage, deprav- ity, destruction, evil, ill usage, malice, mischief, suffering, wick- edness ~*adv.* 8. badly, hard, inaus- piciously, poorly, unfavourably, unfortunately, unluckily 9. barely, by no means, hardly, insufficiently, scantily 10. *As in* **ill-gotten** crimi- nally, dishonestly, foully, fraudu- lently, illegally, illegitimately, il- licitly, unlawfully, unscrupulously

ill-advised foolhardy, foolish, ill- considered, ill-judged, impolitic, imprudent, inappropriate, incau- tious, indiscreet, injudicious, mis- guided, overhasty, rash, reckless, short-sighted, thoughtless, un- seemly, unwise, wrong-headed

ill-assorted incompatible, incon- gruous, inharmonious, mis- matched, uncongenial, unsuited

ill at ease anxious, awkward, dis- quieted, disturbed, edgy, faltering, fidgety, hesitant, nervous, on edge, on pins and needles (*Inf.*), on tenterhooks, out of place, restless, self-conscious, strange, tense, un- comfortable, uneasy, unquiet, un- relaxed, unsettled, unsure

ill-bred bad-mannered, boorish, churlish, coarse, crass, discour- teous, ill-mannered, impolite, in- delicate, rude, uncivil, uncivilized, uncouth, ungallant, ungentlemanly, unladylike, unmannerly, unrefined, vulgar

ill-defined blurred, dim, fuzzy, in- distinct, nebulous, shadowy, un- clear, vague, woolly

ill-disposed against, antagonistic, anti (*Inf.*), antipathetic, averse, disobliging, down on (*Inf.*), hostile, inimical, opposed, uncooperative, unfriendly, unwelcoming

illegal actionable (*Law*), banned, black-market, bootleg, criminal, felonious, forbidden, illicit, lawless, outlawed, prohibited, proscribed, unauthorized, unconstitutional, un- der the counter, unlawful, unli- censed, unofficial, wrongful

illegality crime, criminality, felony, illegitimacy, illicitness, lawless- ness, unlawfulness, wrong, wrong- ness

illegible crabbed, faint, hard to make out, hieroglyphic, indeci- pherable, obscure, scrawled, un- decipherable, unreadable

illegitimate 1. illegal, illicit, im- proper, unauthorized, unconstitu- tional, unlawful, unsanctioned 2. baseborn (*Archaic*), bastard, born on the wrong side of the blanket, born out of wedlock, fatherless, misbegotten (*Literary*), natural, spurious (*Rare*) 3. illogical, incor- rect, invalid, spurious, unsound

ill-fated blighted, doomed, hapless, ill-omened, ill-starred, luckless, star-crossed, unfortunate, unhappy, unlucky

ill feeling animosity, animus, an- tagonism, bad blood, bitterness, disgruntlement, dissatisfaction, dudgeon (*Archaic*), enmity, frus- tration, hard feelings, hostility, ill will, indignation, offence, rancour, resentment

ill-founded baseless, empty, groundless, idle, unjustified, unproven, unreliable, unsubstantiated, unsupported

ill-humoured acrimonious, bad-tempered, crabbed, crabby, cross, disagreeable, grumpy, huffy, impatient, irascible, irritable, like a bear with a sore head (*Inf.*), mardy (*Dialect*), moody, morose, out of sorts, out of temper, petulant, sharp, snappish, snappy, sulky, sullen, tart, testy, thin-skinned, touchy, waspish

illicit 1. black-market, bootleg, contraband, criminal, felonious, illegal, illegitimate, prohibited, unauthorized, unlawful, unlicensed 2. clandestine, forbidden, furtive, guilty, immoral, improper, wrong

illiteracy benightedness, ignorance, illiterateness, lack of education

illiterate benighted, ignorant, uncultured, uneducated, unlettered, untaught, untutored

ill-judged foolish, ill-advised, ill-considered, injudicious, misguided, overhasty, rash, short-sighted, unwise, wrong-headed

ill-mannered badly behaved, boorish, churlish, coarse, discourteous, ill-behaved, ill-bred, impolite, insolent, loutish, rude, uncivil, uncouth, unmannerly

ill-natured bad-tempered, catty (*Inf.*), churlish, crabbed, cross, cross-grained, disagreeable, disobliging, malevolent, malicious, mean, nasty, perverse, petulant, spiteful, sulky, sullen, surly, unfriendly, unkind, unpleasant

illness affliction, ailment, attack, complaint, disability, disease, disorder, ill health, indisposition, infirmity, malady, malaise, poor health, sickness

illogical absurd, fallacious, faulty, inconclusive, inconsistent, incorrect, invalid, irrational, meaningless, senseless, sophistical, specious, spurious, unreasonable, unscientific, unsound

ill-starred doomed, ill-fated, ill-omened, inauspicious, star-crossed, unfortunate, unhappy, unlucky

ill temper annoyance, bad temper, crossness, curtness, impatience, irascibility, irritability, petulance, sharpness, spitefulness, tetchiness

ill-tempered annoyed, bad-tempered, choleric, cross, curt, grumpy, ill-humoured, impatient, irascible, irritable, sharp, spiteful, testy, tetchy, touchy

ill-timed awkward, inappropriate, inconvenient, inept, inopportune, unseasonable, untimely, unwelcome

ill-treat abuse, damage, handle roughly, harass, harm, harry, ill-use, injure, knock about, maltreat, mishandle, misuse, oppress, wrong

ill-treatment abuse, damage, harm, ill-use, injury, mistreatment, misuse, rough handling

illuminate 1. brighten, illumine (*Literary*), irradiate, light, light up 2. clarify, clear up, elucidate, enlighten, explain, give insight into, instruct, make clear, shed light on 3. adorn, decorate, illustrate, ornament

illuminating enlightening, explanatory, helpful, informative, instructive, revealing

illumination 1. beam, brightening, brightness, light, lighting, lighting up, lights, radiance, ray 2. awareness, clarification, edification, enlightenment, insight, inspiration, instruction, perception, revelation, understanding

illusion 1. chimera, daydream, fantasy, figment of the imagination, hallucination, ignis fatuus, mirage, mockery, phantasm, semblance, will-o'-the-wisp 2. deception, delusion, error, fallacy, false impression, fancy, misapprehension, misconception

illusory *or* **illusive** apparent, Barmecide, beguiling, chimerical, deceitful, deceptive, delusive, fallacious, false, hallucinatory, misleading, mistaken, seeming, sham, unreal, untrue

illustrate 1. bring home, clarify, demonstrate, elucidate, emphasize, exemplify, exhibit, explain, instance, interpret, make clear, make plain, point up, show 2. adorn, decorate, depict, draw, ornament, picture, sketch

illustrated decorated, embellished, graphic, illuminated, pictorial, picture, pictured, with illustrations

illustration 1. analogy, case, case in point, clarification, demonstration, elucidation, example, exemplification, explanation, instance, interpretation, specimen 2. adornment, decoration, figure, picture, plate, sketch

illustrious brilliant, celebrated, distinguished, eminent, exalted, famed, famous, glorious, great, noble, notable, noted, prominent, remarkable, renowned, resplendent, signal, splendid

ill will acrimony, animosity, animus, antagonism, antipathy, aversion, bad blood, dislike, enmity, envy, grudge, hard feelings, hatred, hostility, malevolence, malice, no love lost, rancour, resentment, spite, unfriendliness, venom

image 1. appearance, effigy, figure, icon, idol, likeness, picture, portrait, reflection, representation, statue 2. chip off the old block (*Inf.*), counterpart, (dead) ringer (*Sl.*), Doppelgänger, double, facsimile, replica, similitude, spit (*Inf.*), spitting image *or* spit and image (*Inf.*) 3. conceit, concept, conception, figure, idea, impression, mental picture, perception, trope

imaginable believable, comprehensible, conceivable, credible, likely, plausible, possible, supposable, thinkable, under the sun, within the bounds of possibility

imaginary assumed, chimerical, dreamlike, fancied, fanciful, fictional, fictitious, hallucinatory, hypothetical, ideal, illusive, illusory, imagined, invented, legendary, made-up, mythological, nonexistent, phantasmal, shadowy, supposed, suppositious, supposititious, unreal, unsubstantial, visionary

imagination 1. creativity, enterprise, fancy, ingenuity, insight, inspiration, invention, inventiveness, originality, resourcefulness, vision, wit, wittiness 2. chimera, conception, idea, ideality, illusion, image, invention, notion, supposition, unreality

imaginative clever, creative, dreamy, enterprising, fanciful, fantastic, ingenious, inspired, inventive, original, poetical, visionary, vivid, whimsical

imagine 1. conceive, conceptualize, conjure up, create, devise, dream up (*Inf.*), envisage, fantasize, form a mental picture of, frame, invent, picture, plan, project, scheme, see in the mind's eye, think of, think up, visualize 2. apprehend, assume, believe, conjecture, deduce, deem, fancy, gather, guess, infer, realize, suppose, surmise, suspect, take for granted, take it, think

imbecile 1. *n.* bungler, cretin, dolt, dotard, fool, halfwit, idiot, moron, thickhead 2. *adj.* asinine, fatuous, feeble-minded, foolish, idiotic, imbecilic, inane, ludicrous, moronic, simple, stupid, thick, witless

imbecility asininity, childishness, cretinism, fatuity, foolishness, idiocy, inanity, incompetency, stupidity

imbibe 1. consume, drink, knock back (*Inf.*), quaff, sink (*Inf.*), suck, swallow, swig (*Inf.*) 2. *Literary* absorb, acquire, assimilate, gain, gather, ingest, receive, take in

imitate affect, ape, burlesque, caricature, copy, counterfeit, do (*Inf.*), do an impression of, duplicate, echo, emulate, follow, follow in the footsteps of, follow suit, impersonate, mimic, mirror, mock, parody, personate, repeat, send up (*Brit. inf.*), simulate, spoof (*Inf.*), take a leaf out of (someone's) book, take off (*Inf.*), travesty

imitation *n.* 1. aping, copy, counterfeit, counterfeiting, duplication, echoing, likeness, mimicry, resemblance, simulation 2. fake, forgery, impersonation, impression, mockery, parody, reflection, replica, reproduction, sham, substitution, takeoff (*Inf.*), travesty ~*adj.* 3. artificial, dummy, ersatz, man-made, mock, phoney (*Inf.*), pseudo (*Inf.*), repro, reproduction, sham, simulated, synthetic

imitative copied, copycat (*Inf.*), copying, derivative, echoic, mimetic, mimicking, mock, onomatopoeic, parrotlike, plagiarized, pseudo (*Inf.*), put-on, second-hand, simulated, unoriginal

imitator aper, copier, copycat (*Inf.*), echo, epigone (*Rare*), follower, impersonator, impressionist, mimic, parrot, shadow

immaculate 1. clean, impeccable, neat, neat as a new pin, spick-and-span, spruce, trim, unexceptionable 2. above reproach, faultless, flawless, guiltless, incorrupt, innocent, perfect, pure, sinless, spotless, stainless, unblemished, uncontaminated, undefiled, unpolluted, unsullied, untarnished, virtuous

immaterial 1. a matter of indifference, extraneous, impertinent, inapposite, inconsequential, inconsiderable, inessential, insignificant, irrelevant, of little account, of no consequence, of no importance, trifling, trivial, unimportant, unnecessary 2. airy, disembodied, ethereal, ghostly, incorporeal, metaphysical, spiritual, unembodied, unsubstantial

immature 1. adolescent, crude, green, imperfect, premature, raw, undeveloped, unfinished, unfledged, unformed, unripe, unseasonable, untimely, young 2. babyish, callow, childish, inexperienced, infantile, jejune, juvenile, puerile, wet behind the ears (*Inf.*)

immaturity 1. crudeness, crudity, greenness, imperfection, rawness, unpreparedness, unripeness 2. babyishness, callowness, childishness, inexperience, juvenility, puerility

immeasurable bottomless, boundless, endless, illimitable, immense, incalculable, inestimable, inexhaustible, infinite, limitless, measureless, unbounded, unfathomable, unlimited, vast

immediate 1. instant, instantaneous 2. adjacent, close, contiguous, direct, near, nearest, next, primary, proximate, recent 3. actual, current, existing, extant, on hand, present, pressing, up to date, urgent

immediately 1. at once, before you could say Jack Robinson (*Inf.*), directly, forthwith, instantly, now, promptly, pronto (*Inf.*), right away, right now, straight away, this instant, this very minute, *tout de suite*, unhesitatingly, without delay, without hesitation 2. at first hand, closely, directly, nearly

immemorial age-old, ancient, archaic, fixed, long-standing, of yore, olden (*Archaic*), rooted, time-honoured, traditional

immense Brobdingnagian, colossal, elephantine, enormous, extensive, giant, gigantic, great, huge, illimitable, immeasurable, infinite, interminable, jumbo (*Inf.*), large, mammoth, massive, monstrous, monumental, prodigious, stupendous, titanic, tremendous, vast

immensity bulk, enormity, expanse, extent, greatness, hugeness, infinity, magnitude, massiveness, scope, size, sweep, vastness

immersion 1. baptism, bathe, dip, dipping, dousing, ducking, dunking, plunging, submerging 2. *Fig.* absorption, concentration, involvement, preoccupation

immigrant incomer, newcomer, settler

imminent at hand, brewing, close, coming, fast-approaching, forthcoming, gathering, impending, in the air, in the offing, looming, menacing, near, nigh (*Archaic*), on the horizon, on the way, threatening

immobile at a standstill, at rest, fixed, frozen, immobilized, immotile, immovable, like a statue, motionless, rigid, riveted, rooted, stable, static, stationary, stiff, still, stock-still, stolid, unmoving

immobility absence of movement,

firmness, fixity, immovability, in~ertness, motionlessness, stability, steadiness, stillness

immobilize bring to a standstill, cripple, disable, freeze, halt, lay up (*Inf.*), paralyse, put out of action, render inoperative, stop, transfix

immoderate egregious, enormous, exaggerated, excessive, exorbi~tant, extravagant, extreme, inor~dinate, intemperate, over the odds (*Inf.*), profligate, steep (*Inf.*), uncalled-for, unconscionable, un~controlled, undue, unjustified, un~reasonable, unrestrained, unwar~ranted, wanton

immodesty 1. bawdiness, coarse~ness, impurity, indecorousness, in~delicacy, lewdness, obscenity 2. audacity, boldness, brass neck (*Sl.*), forwardness, gall (*Inf.*), impu~dence, shamelessness, temerity

immoral abandoned, bad, corrupt, debauched, degenerate, depraved, dishonest, dissolute, evil, impure, indecent, iniquitous, lewd, licen~tious, nefarious, obscene, of easy virtue, pornographic, profligate, reprobate, sinful, unchaste, un~ethical, unprincipled, vicious, vile, wicked, wrong

immorality badness, corruption, debauchery, depravity, dissolute~ness, evil, iniquity, licentiousness, profligacy, sin, turpitude, vice, wickedness, wrong

immortal *adj.* 1. abiding, constant, death-defying, deathless, endless, enduring, eternal, everlasting, im~perishable, incorruptible, inde~structible, lasting, perennial, per~petual, sempiternal (*Literary*), timeless, undying, unfading ~*n.* 2. god, goddess, Olympian 3. genius, great (*Usually plural*), hero, para~gon

immortality 1. deathlessness, end~lessness, eternity, everlasting life, incorruptibility, indestructibility, perpetuity, timelessness 2. celeb~rity, fame, glorification, glorious~ness, glory, greatness, renown

immortalize apotheosize, cel~ebrate, commemorate, enshrine, eternalize, eternize, exalt, glorify, memorialize, perpetuate, solem~nize

immovable 1. fast, firm, fixed, im~mutable, jammed, rooted, secure, set, stable, stationary, stuck, un~budgeable 2. adamant, constant, impassive, inflexible, obdurate, resolute, steadfast, stony-hearted, unchangeable, unimpressionable, unshakable, unshaken, unwaver~ing, unyielding

immune clear, exempt, free, in~susceptible, invulnerable, let off (*Inf.*), not affected, not liable, not subject, proof (against), protected, resistant, safe, unaffected

immunity 1. amnesty, charter, ex~emption, exoneration, franchise, freedom, indemnity, invulnerabil~ity, liberty, licence, prerogative, privilege, release, right 2. immu~nization, protection, resistance

immunize inoculate, protect, safe~guard, vaccinate

imp brat, demon, devil, gamin, minx, rascal, rogue, scamp, sprite, urchin

impact *n.* 1. bang, blow, bump, col~lision, concussion, contact, crash, force, jolt, knock, shock, smash, stroke, thump 2. brunt, burden, consequences, effect, full force, impression, influence, meaning, power, repercussions, significance, thrust, weight ~*v.* 3. clash, collide, crash, crush, hit, strike

impair blunt, damage, debilitate, decrease, deteriorate, diminish, enervate, enfeeble, harm, hinder, injure, lessen, mar, reduce, spoil, undermine, vitiate, weaken, wors~en

impaired damaged, defective, faulty, flawed, imperfect, unsound

impart 1. communicate, convey, disclose, discover, divulge, make known, pass on, relate, reveal, tell 2. accord, afford, bestow, confer, contribute, give, grant, lend, offer, yield

impartial detached, disinterested, equal, equitable, even-handed, fair, just, neutral, nondiscriminating, nonpartisan, objective, open-minded, unbiased, unprejudiced, without fear or favour

impartiality detachment, disinterest, disinterestedness, dispassion, equality, equity, even-handedness, fairness, lack of bias, neutrality, nonpartisanship, objectivity, open-mindedness

impassable blocked, closed, impenetrable, obstructed, pathless, trackless, unnavigable

impasse blind alley (*Inf.*), dead end, deadlock, stalemate, standoff, standstill

impassioned animated, ardent, blazing, excited, fervent, fervid, fiery, furious, glowing, heated, inflamed, inspired, intense, passionate, rousing, stirring, vehement, violent, vivid, warm, worked up

impatience 1. haste, hastiness, heat, impetuosity, intolerance, irritability, irritableness, quick temper, rashness, shortness, snappiness, vehemence, violence 2. agitation, anxiety, avidity, disquietude, eagerness, edginess, fretfulness, nervousness, restiveness, restlessness, uneasiness

impatient 1. abrupt, brusque, curt, demanding, edgy, hasty, hot-tempered, indignant, intolerant, irritable, quick-tempered, snappy, sudden, testy, vehement, violent 2. agog, athirst, chafing, eager, fretful, headlong, impetuous, like a cat on hot bricks (*Inf.*), restless, straining at the leash

impeach 1. accuse, arraign, blame, censure, charge, criminate (*Rare*), denounce, indict, tax 2. call into question, cast aspersions on, cast doubt on, challenge, disparage, impugn, question

impeachment accusation, arraignment, indictment

impeccable above suspicion, exact, exquisite, faultless, flawless, immaculate, incorrupt, innocent, irreproachable, perfect, precise, pure, sinless, stainless, unblemished, unerring, unimpeachable

impecunious broke (*Inf.*), cleaned out (*Sl.*), destitute, indigent, insol-

vent, penniless, poverty-stricken, skint (*Sl.*), stony (*Sl.*), strapped (*Sl.*)

impede bar, block, brake, check, clog, curb, delay, disrupt, hamper, hinder, hold up, obstruct, restrain, retard, slow (down), stop, throw a spanner in the works (*Inf.*), thwart

impediment bar, barrier, block, check, clog, curb, defect, difficulty, encumbrance, hindrance, obstacle, obstruction, snag, stumbling block

impedimenta accoutrements, baggage, belongings, effects, equipment, gear, junk (*Inf.*), luggage, movables, odds and ends, paraphernalia, possessions, stuff, things, trappings, traps

impel actuate, compel, constrain, drive, force, goad, incite, induce, influence, inspire, instigate, motivate, move, oblige, power, prod, prompt, propel, push, require, spur, stimulate, urge

impending approaching, brewing, coming, forthcoming, gathering, hovering, imminent, in the offing, looming, menacing, near, nearing, on the horizon, threatening

impenetrable 1. dense, hermetic, impassable, impermeable, impervious, inviolable, solid, thick, unpiercable 2. arcane, baffling, cabbalistic, dark, enigmatic, enigmatical, hidden, incomprehensible, indiscernible, inexplicable, inscrutable, mysterious, obscure, unfathomable, unintelligible

imperative 1. compulsory, crucial, essential, exigent, indispensable, insistent, obligatory, pressing, urgent, vital 2. authoritative, autocratic, commanding, dictatorial, domineering, high-handed, imperious, lordly, magisterial, peremptory

imperceptible faint, fine, gradual, impalpable, inappreciable, inaudible, indiscernible, indistinguishable, infinitesimal, insensible, invisible, microscopic, minute, shadowy, slight, small, subtle, tiny, undetectable, unnoticeable

imperceptibly by a hair's-breadth, inappreciably, indiscernibly, invisibly, little by little, slowly, subtly, unnoticeably, unobtrusively, unseen

imperfect broken, damaged, defective, deficient, faulty, flawed, immature, impaired, incomplete, inexact, limited, partial, patchy, rudimentary, sketchy, undeveloped, unfinished

imperfection blemish, defect, deficiency, failing, fallibility, fault, flaw, foible, frailty, inadequacy, incompleteness, infirmity, insufficiency, peccadillo, shortcoming, stain, taint, weakness, weak point

imperial 1. kingly, majestic, princely, queenly, regal, royal, sovereign 2. august, exalted, grand, great, high, imperious, lofty, magnificent, noble, superior, supreme

imperil endanger, expose, hazard, jeopardize, risk

imperishable abiding, enduring, eternal, everlasting, immortal, indestructible, perennial, permanent, perpetual, undying, unfading, unforgettable

impersonal bureaucratic, businesslike, cold, detached, dispassionate, formal, inhuman, neutral, remote

impersonate act, ape, do (*Inf.*), do an impression of, enact, imitate, masquerade as, mimic, pass oneself off as, personate, pose as (*Inf.*), take off (*Inf.*)

impersonation caricature, imitation, impression, mimicry, parody, takeoff (*Inf.*)

impertinence assurance, audacity, backchat (*Inf.*), boldness, brass neck (*Sl.*), brazenness, cheek (*Inf.*), disrespect, effrontery, forwardness, impudence, incivility, insolence, nerve (*Inf.*), pertness, presumption, rudeness, sauce (*Inf.*)

impertinent 1. bold, brazen, cheeky (*Inf.*), discourteous, disrespectful, flip (*Inf.*), forward, fresh (*Inf.*), impolite, impudent, insolent, interfering, pert, presumptuous, rude, saucy (*Inf.*), uncivil, unmannerly 2. inapplicable, inappropriate, incongruous, irrelevant

imperturbable calm, collected, complacent, composed, cool, equanimous, nerveless, sedate, self-possessed, stoical, tranquil, undisturbed, unexcitable, unflappable (*Inf.*), unmoved, unruffled

impervious 1. hermetic, impassable, impenetrable, impermeable, imperviable, invulnerable, resistant, sealed 2. closed to, immune, invulnerable, proof against, unaffected by, unmoved by, unreceptive, unswayable, untouched by

impetuosity haste, hastiness, impulsiveness, precipitancy, precipitateness, rashness, vehemence, violence

impetuous ardent, eager, fierce, furious, hasty, headlong, impassioned, impulsive, passionate, precipitate, rash, spontaneous, spur-of-the-moment, unbridled, unplanned, unpremeditated, unreflecting, unrestrained, unthinking, vehement, violent

impetuously helter-skelter, impulsively, in the heat of the moment, on the spur of the moment, passionately, rashly, recklessly, spontaneously, unthinkingly, vehemently, without thinking

impetus 1. catalyst, goad, impulse, impulsion, incentive, motivation, push, spur, stimulus 2. energy, force, momentum, power

impiety godlessness, iniquity, irreligion, irreverence, profaneness, profanity, sacrilege, sinfulness, ungodliness, unholiness, unrighteousness, wickedness

impinge 1. encroach, invade, make inroads, obtrude, trespass, violate 2. affect, bear upon, have a bearing on, influence, infringe, relate to, touch, touch upon 3. clash, collide, dash, strike

impious blasphemous, godless, iniquitous, irreligious, irreverent, profane, sacrilegious, sinful, ungodly, unholy, unrighteous, wicked

impish devilish, elfin, mischievous, prankish, puckish, rascally, roguish, sportive, waggish

implacability implacableness, inexorability, inflexibility, intractability, mercilessness, pitilessness, relentlessness, ruthlessness, un~ forgivingness, vengefulness

implacable cruel, inexorable, in~ flexible, intractable, merciless, pitiless, rancorous, relentless, re~ morseless, ruthless, unappeasable, unbending, uncompromising, un~ forgiving, unrelenting, unyielding

implant 1. inculcate, infix, infuse, inseminate, instil, sow 2. embed, fix, graft, ingraft, insert, place, plant, root, sow

implement 1. *n.* agent, apparatus, appliance, device, gadget, instru~ ment, tool, utensil 2. *v.* bring about, carry out, complete, effect, en~ force, execute, fulfil, perform, put into action *or* effect, realize

implementation accomplishment, carrying out, discharge, effecting, enforcement, execution, fulfilment, performance, performing, realiza~ tion

implicate associate, compromise, concern, embroil, entangle, imply, include, incriminate, inculcate, in~ volve, mire, tie up with

implicated incriminated, involved, suspected, under suspicion

implication 1. association, con~ nection, entanglement, incrimina~ tion, involvement 2. conclusion, inference, innuendo, meaning, overtone, presumption, ramifica~ tion, significance, signification, suggestion

implicit 1. contained, implied, in~ ferred, inherent, latent, tacit, taken for granted, undeclared, under~ stood, unspoken 2. absolute, con~ stant, entire, firm, fixed, full, steadfast, total, unhesitating, un~ qualified, unreserved, unshakable, unshaken, wholehearted

implicitly absolutely, completely, firmly, unconditionally, unhesitat~ ingly, unreservedly, utterly, with~ out reservation

implied hinted at, implicit, indirect, inherent, insinuated, suggested, tacit, undeclared, unexpressed, unspoken, unstated

implore beg, beseech, conjure, crave, entreat, go on bended knee

to, importune, plead with, pray, solicit, supplicate

imply 1. connote, give (someone) to understand, hint, insinuate, inti~ mate, signify, suggest 2. betoken, denote, entail, evidence, import, include, indicate, involve, mean, point to, presuppose

impolite bad-mannered, boorish, churlish, discourteous, disrespect~ ful, ill-bred, ill-mannered, indeco~ rous, indelicate, insolent, loutish, rough, rude, uncivil, ungallant, un~ gentlemanly, ungracious, unlady~ like, unmannerly, unrefined

impoliteness bad manners, boor~ ishness, churlishness, discourtesy, disrespect, incivility, indelicacy, insolence, rudeness, unmannerli~ ness

import *n.* 1. bearing, drift, gist, im~ plication, intention, meaning, message, purport, sense, signifi~ cance, thrust 2. consequence, im~ portance, magnitude, moment, significance, substance, weight ~*v.* 3. bring in, introduce, land

importance 1. concern, conse~ quence, import, interest, moment, momentousness, significance, sub~ stance, value, weight 2. distinction, eminence, esteem, influence, mark, pre-eminence, prestige, prominence, standing, status, use~ fulness, worth

important 1. far-reaching, grave, large, material, meaningful, mo~ mentous, of substance, primary, salient, serious, signal, significant, substantial, urgent, weighty 2. eminent, foremost, high-level, high-ranking, influential, leading, notable, noteworthy, of note, out~ standing, powerful, pre-eminent, prominent, seminal 3. *Usually with* **to** basic, essential, of concern *or* interest, relevant, valuable, valued

importunate burning, clamant, clamorous, demanding, dogged, earnest, exigent, insistent, persis~ tent, pertinacious, pressing, solici~ tous, troublesome, urgent

impose 1. decree, establish, exact, fix, institute, introduce, lay, levy, ordain, place, promulgate, put, set

2. appoint, charge with, dictate, enforce, enjoin, inflict, prescribe, saddle (someone) with 3. *With on or upon* butt in, encroach, foist, force oneself, gate-crash (*Inf.*), horn in (*Inf.*), intrude, obtrude, presume, take liberties, trespass 4. *With on or upon* a. abuse, exploit, play on, take advantage of, use b. con (*Inf.*), deceive, dupe, hood~ wink, pull the wool over (some~ body's) eyes, trick

imposing august, commanding, dignified, effective, grand, impres~ sive, majestic, stately, striking

imposition 1. application, decree, introduction, laying on, levying, promulgation 2. cheek (*Inf.*), en~ croachment, intrusion, liberty, presumption 3. artifice, cheating, con (*Inf.*), deception, dissimulation, fraud, hoax, imposture, stratagem, trickery 4. burden, charge, con~ straint, duty, levy, tax

impossibility hopelessness, im~ practicability, inability, inconceiv~ ability

impossible 1. beyond one, beyond the bounds of possibility, hopeless, impracticable, inconceivable, not to be thought of, out of the ques~ tion, unachievable, unattainable, unobtainable, unthinkable 2. ab~ surd, inadmissible, insoluble, intol~ erable, ludicrous, outrageous, pre~ posterous, unacceptable, unan~ swerable, ungovernable, unrea~ sonable, unsuitable, unworkable

impostor charlatan, cheat, deceiv~ er, fake, fraud, hypocrite, imper~ sonator, knave (*Archaic*), phoney (*Sl.*), pretender, quack, rogue, sham, trickster

impotence disability, enervation, feebleness, frailty, helplessness, inability, inadequacy, incapacity, incompetence, ineffectiveness, in~ efficacy, inefficiency, infirmity, paralysis, powerlessness, useless~ ness, weakness

impotent disabled, emasculate, enervated, feeble, frail, helpless, incapable, incapacitated, incom~ petent, ineffective, infirm, nerve~

less, paralysed, powerless, unable, unmanned, weak

impoverish 1. bankrupt, beggar, break, ruin 2. deplete, diminish, drain, exhaust, pauperize, reduce, sap, use up, wear out

impoverished 1. bankrupt, desti~ tute, distressed, impecunious, indi~ gent, in reduced *or* straitened cir~ cumstances, necessitous, needy, on one's uppers, penurious, poverty- stricken, ruined, straitened 2. bar~ ren, denuded, depleted, drained, empty, exhausted, played out, re~ duced, spent, sterile, worn out

impracticability futility, hopeless~ ness, impossibility, impracticality, unsuitableness, unworkability, uselessness

impracticable 1. impossible, out of the question, unachievable, unat~ tainable, unfeasible, unworkable 2. awkward, impractical, inappli~ cable, inconvenient, unserviceable, unsuitable, useless

impractical 1. impossible, imprac~ ticable, inoperable, nonviable, un~ realistic, unserviceable, unwork~ able, visionary, wild 2. idealistic, romantic, starry-eyed, unbusiness~ like, unrealistic, visionary

impracticality hopelessness, im~ possibility, inapplicability, roman~ ticism, unworkability

imprecise ambiguous, blurred round the edges, careless, equivo~ cal, estimated, fluctuating, hazy, ill- defined, inaccurate, indefinite, in~ determinate, inexact, inexplicit, loose, rough, sloppy (*Inf.*), vague, wide of the mark, woolly

impregnable immovable, impen~ etrable, indestructible, invincible, invulnerable, secure, strong, unas~ sailable, unbeatable, unconquer~ able, unshakable

impregnate 1. fill, imbrue (*Rare*), imbue, infuse, percolate, perme~ ate, pervade, saturate, soak, steep, suffuse 2. fecundate, fertilize, fruc~ tify, get with child, inseminate, make pregnant

impress 1. affect, excite, grab (*Sl.*), influence, inspire, make an im~ pression, move, stir, strike, sway, touch 2. *Often with on or upon* bring home to, emphasize, fix, inculcate, instil into, stress 3. emboss, engrave, imprint, indent, mark, print, stamp

impression 1. effect, feeling, impact, influence, reaction, sway 2. make an impression arouse comment, be conspicuous, cause a stir, excite notice, find favour, make a hit (*Inf.*), make an impact, stand out 3. belief, concept, conviction, fancy, feeling, funny feeling (*Inf.*), hunch, idea, memory, notion, opinion, recollection, sense, suspicion 4. brand, dent, hollow, impress, imprint, indentation, mark, outline, stamp, stamping 5. edition, imprinting, issue, printing 6. imitation, impersonation, parody, send-up (*Brit. inf.*), takeoff (*Inf.*)

impressionable feeling, gullible, ingenuous, open, receptive, responsive, sensitive, suggestible, susceptible, vulnerable

impressive affecting, exciting, forcible, moving, powerful, stirring, touching

imprint 1. *n.* impression, indentation, mark, print, sign, stamp 2. *v.* engrave, establish, etch, fix, impress, print, stamp

imprison confine, constrain, detain, immure, incarcerate, intern, jail, lock up, put away, put under lock and key, send down (*Inf.*), send to prison

imprisoned behind bars, captive, confined, immured, incarcerated, in irons, in jail, inside (*Sl.*), interned, jailed, locked up, put away, under lock and key

imprisonment confinement, custody, detention, durance (*Archaic*), duress, incarceration, internment, porridge (*Sl.*)

improbability doubt, doubtfulness, dubiety, uncertainty, unlikelihood

improbable doubtful, dubious, fanciful, far-fetched, implausible, questionable, unbelievable, uncertain, unconvincing, unlikely, weak

impromptu 1. *adj.* ad-lib, extemporaneous, extempore, extemporized, improvised, offhand, off the cuff (*Inf.*), spontaneous, unpremeditated, unprepared, unrehearsed, unscripted, unstudied 2. *adv.* ad lib, off the cuff (*Inf.*), off the top of one's head (*Inf.*), on the spur of the moment, spontaneously, without preparation

improper 1. impolite, indecent, indecorous, indelicate, off-colour, risqué, smutty, suggestive, unbecoming, unfitting, unseemly, untoward, vulgar 2. ill-timed, inapplicable, inapposite, inappropriate, inapt, incongruous, infelicitous, inopportune, malapropos, out of place, uncalled-for, unfit, unseasonable, unsuitable, unsuited, unwarranted 3. abnormal, erroneous, false, inaccurate, incorrect, irregular, wrong

impropriety 1. bad taste, immodesty, incongruity, indecency, indecorum, unsuitability, vulgarity 2. blunder, faux pas, gaffe, gaucherie, mistake, slip, solecism

improve 1. advance, ameliorate, amend, augment, better, correct, help, mend, polish, rectify, touch up, upgrade 2. develop, enhance, gain strength, increase, look up (*Inf.*), make strides, perk up, pick up, progress, rally, reform, rise, take a turn for the better (*Inf.*), take on a new lease of life (*Inf.*) 3. convalesce, gain ground, gain strength, grow better, make progress, mend, recover, recuperate, turn the corner

improvement 1. advancement, amelioration, amendment, augmentation, betterment, correction, gain, rectification 2. advance, development, enhancement, furtherance, increase, progress, rally, recovery, reformation, rise, upswing

improvisation ad-lib, ad-libbing, expedient, extemporizing, impromptu, invention, makeshift, spontaneity

improvise 1. ad-lib, coin, extemporize, invent, play it by ear (*Inf.*), speak off the cuff (*Inf.*) 2. concoct, contrive, devise, make do, throw together

improvised ad-lib, extemporaneous, extempore, extemporized, makeshift, off the cuff (*Inf.*), spontaneous, spur-of-the-moment, unprepared, unrehearsed

imprudent careless, foolhardy, foolish, heedless, ill-advised, ill-considered, ill-judged, impolitic, improvident, incautious, inconsiderate, indiscreet, injudicious, irresponsible, overhasty, rash, reckless, temerarious, unthinking, unwise

impudence assurance, audacity, backchat (*Inf.*), boldness, brass neck (*Sl.*), bumptiousness, cheek (*Inf.*), effrontery, face (*Inf.*), impertinence, insolence, lip (*Sl.*), nerve (*Inf.*), pertness, presumption, rudeness, sauciness, shamelessness

impudent audacious, bold, bold-faced, brazen, bumptious, cheeky (*Inf.*), cocky (*Inf.*), forward, fresh (*Inf.*), immodest, impertinent, insolent, pert, presumptuous, rude, saucy (*Inf.*), shameless

impulse 1. catalyst, force, impetus, momentum, movement, pressure, push, stimulus, surge, thrust 2. *Fig.* caprice, drive, feeling, incitement, inclination, influence, instinct, motive, notion, passion, resolve, urge, whim, wish

impulsive devil-may-care, emotional, hasty, headlong, impetuous, instinctive, intuitive, passionate, precipitate, quick, rash, spontaneous, unconsidered, unpredictable, unpremeditated

impunity dispensation, exemption, freedom, immunity, liberty, licence, nonliability, permission, security

impure 1. admixed, adulterated, alloyed, debased, mixed, unrefined 2. contaminated, defiled, dirty, filthy, foul, infected, polluted, sullied, tainted, unclean, unwholesome, vitiated 3. carnal, coarse, corrupt, gross, immodest, immoral, indecent, indelicate, lascivious, lewd, licentious, lustful, obscene, prurient, ribald, salacious, smutty, unchaste, unclean

impurity 1. admixture, adultera-

tion, mixture 2. befoulment, contamination, defilement, dirtiness, filth, foulness, infection, pollution, taint, uncleanness 3. *Often plural* bits, contaminant, dirt, dross, foreign body, foreign matter, grime, marks, pollutant, scum, spots, stains 4. carnality, coarseness, corruption, grossness, immodesty, immorality, indecency, lasciviousness, lewdness, licentiousness, obscenity, prurience, salaciousness, smuttiness, unchastity, vulgarity

imputation accusation, ascription, aspersion, attribution, blame, censure, charge, insinuation, reproach, slander, slur

impute accredit, ascribe, assign, attribute, credit, lay at the door of, refer, set down to

inability disability, disqualification, impotence, inadequacy, incapability, incapacity, incompetence, ineptitude, powerlessness

inaccessible impassable, out of reach, out of the way, remote, unapproachable, unattainable, un-get-at-able (*Inf.*), unreachable

inaccuracy 1. erroneousness, imprecision, incorrectness, inexactness, unfaithfulness, unreliability 2. blunder, corrigendum, defect, erratum, error, fault, howler (*Inf.*), literal (*Printing*), miscalculation, mistake, slip, typo (*Inf., printing*)

inaccurate careless, defective, discrepant, erroneous, faulty, imprecise, incorrect, in error, inexact, mistaken, out, unfaithful, unreliable, unsound, wide of the mark, wild, wrong

inaccurately carelessly, clumsily, imprecisely, inexactly, unfaithfully, unreliably

inaction dormancy, idleness, immobility, inactivity, inertia, rest, torpidity, torpor

inactive 1. abeyant, dormant, idle, immobile, inert, inoperative, jobless, kicking one's heels, latent, mothballed, out of service, out of work, unemployed, unoccupied, unused 2. dull, indolent, lazy, lethargic, low-key (*Inf.*), passive, quiet, sedentary, slothful, slow, sluggish, somnolent, torpid

inactivity 1. dormancy, hibernation, immobility, inaction, passivity, unemployment 2. dilatoriness, *dolce far niente*, dullness, heaviness, indolence, inertia, inertness, lassitude, laziness, lethargy, quiescence, sloth, sluggishness, stagnation, torpor, vegetation

inadequacy 1. dearth, deficiency, inadequateness, incompleteness, insufficiency, meagreness, paucity, poverty, scantiness, shortage, skimpiness 2. defectiveness, faultiness, inability, inaptness, incapacity, incompetence, incompetency, ineffectiveness, inefficacy, unfitness, unsuitableness 3. defect, failing, imperfection, lack, shortage, shortcoming, weakness

inadequate 1. defective, deficient, faulty, imperfect, incommensurate, incomplete, insubstantial, insufficient, meagre, niggardly, scanty, short, sketchy, skimpy, sparse 2. found wanting, inapt, incapable, incompetent, not up to scratch (*Inf.*), unequal, unfitted, unqualified

inadequately imperfectly, insufficiently, meagrely, poorly, scantily, sketchily, skimpily, sparsely, thinly

inadmissible immaterial, improper, inappropriate, incompetent, irrelevant, unacceptable, unallowable, unqualified, unreasonable

inadvertently 1. carelessly, heedlessly, in an unguarded moment, negligently, thoughtlessly, unguardedly, unthinkingly 2. accidentally, by accident, by mistake, involuntarily, mistakenly, unintentionally, unwittingly

inadvisable ill-advised, impolitic, imprudent, inexpedient, injudicious, unwise

inane asinine, daft (*Inf.*), devoid of intelligence, empty, fatuous, frivolous, futile, idiotic, imbecilic, mindless, puerile, senseless, silly, stupid, trifling, unintelligent, vacuous, vain, vapid, worthless

inanimate cold, dead, defunct, extinct, inactive, inert, insensate, insentient, lifeless, quiescent, soulless, spiritless

inapplicable inapposite, inappropriate, inapt, irrelevant, unsuitable, unsuited

inappropriate disproportionate, ill-fitted, ill-suited, ill-timed, improper, incongruous, malapropos, out of place, tasteless, unbecoming, unbefitting, unfit, unfitting, unseemly, unsuitable, untimely

inapt 1. ill-fitted, ill-suited, inapposite, inappropriate, infelicitous, unsuitable, unsuited 2. awkward, clumsy, dull, gauche, incompetent, inept, inexpert, maladroit, slow, stupid

inarticulate 1. blurred, incoherent, incomprehensible, indistinct, muffled, mumbled, unclear, unintelligible 2. dumb, mute, silent, speechless, tongue-tied, unspoken, unuttered, unvoiced, voiceless, wordless 3. faltering, halting, hesitant, poorly spoken

inattention absent-mindedness, carelessness, daydreaming, disregard, forgetfulness, heedlessness, inadvertence, inattentiveness, indifference, neglect, preoccupation, thoughtlessness, woolgathering

inattentive absent-minded, careless, distracted, distrait, dreamy, heedless, inadvertent, neglectful, negligent, preoccupied, regardless, remiss, thoughtless, unheeding, unmindful, unobservant, vague

inaudible indistinct, low, mumbling, out of earshot, stifled, unheard

inaugural dedicatory, first, initial, introductory, maiden, opening

inaugurate 1. begin, commence, get under way, initiate, institute, introduce, kick off (*Inf.*), launch, originate, set in motion, set up, usher in 2. induct, install, instate, invest 3. commission, dedicate, open, ordain

inauguration 1. initiation, institution, launch, launching, opening, setting up 2. induction, installation, investiture

inauspicious bad, black, discouraging, ill-omened, ominous, unfa~

vourable, unfortunate, unlucky, unpromising, unpropitious, unto~ward

inborn congenital, connate, heredi~tary, inbred, ingrained, inherent, inherited, innate, instinctive, intui~tive, native, natural

inbred constitutional, deep-seated, ingrained, inherent, innate, native, natural

incalculable boundless, countless, enormous, immense, incomput~able, inestimable, infinite, innu~merable, limitless, measureless, numberless, uncountable, untold, vast, without number

incantation abracadabra, chant, charm, conjuration, formula, hex (*U.S. dialect*), invocation, spell

incapable 1. feeble, inadequate, incompetent, ineffective, inept, in~expert, insufficient, not equal to, not up to, unfit, unfitted, unquali~fied, weak 2. helpless, impotent, powerless, unable, unfit 3. *With of* impervious, not admitting of, not susceptible to, resistant

incapacitate cripple, disable, dis~qualify, immobilize, lay up (*Inf.*), paralyse, prostrate, put out of ac~tion (*Inf.*), scupper (*Brit. sl.*), unfit (*Rare*)

incapacitated disqualified, *hors de combat*, immobilized, indisposed, laid up (*Inf.*), out of action (*Inf.*), unfit

incapacity disqualification, feeble~ness, impotence, inability, inad~equacy, incapability, incompeten~cy, ineffectiveness, powerlessness, unfitness, weakness

incarcerate commit, confine, coop up, detain, gaol, immure, impound, imprison, intern, jail, lock up, put under lock and key, restrain, re~strict, send down (*Brit.*), throw in jail

incarnate 1. in bodily form, in hu~man form, in the flesh, made flesh 2. embodied, personified, typified

incarnation avatar, bodily form, embodiment, exemplification, im~personation, manifestation, per~sonification, type

incautious careless, hasty, heed~less, ill-advised, ill-judged, im~provident, imprudent, impulsive, inconsiderate, indiscreet, injudi~cious, negligent, precipitate, rash, reckless, thoughtless, unguarded, unthinking, unwary

incautiously imprudently, impul~sively, indiscreetly, precipitately, rashly, recklessly, thoughtlessly, unthinkingly

incendiary *adj.* 1. dissentious, in~flammatory, provocative, rabble-rousing, seditious, subversive ~*n.* 2. arsonist, firebug (*Inf.*), fire rais~er, pyromaniac 3. agitator, dema~gogue, firebrand, insurgent, rabble-rouser, revolutionary

incense[1] *v.* anger, enrage, exas~perate, excite, get one's hackles up, inflame, infuriate, irritate, madden, make one's blood boil (*Inf.*), make one see red (*Inf.*), make one's hackles rise, provoke, raise one's hackles, rile (*Inf.*)

incense[2] *n.* aroma, balm, bouquet, fragrance, perfume, redolence, scent

incensed angry, enraged, exas~perated, fuming, furious, indignant, infuriated, irate, ireful (*Literary*), mad (*Inf.*), maddened, on the war~path (*Inf.*), steamed up (*Sl.*), up in arms, wrathful

incentive bait, carrot (*Inf.*), en~couragement, enticement, goad, impetus, impulse, inducement, lure, motivation, motive, spur, stimulant, stimulus

inception beginning, birth, com~mencement, dawn, inauguration, initiation, kickoff (*Inf.*), origin, outset, rise, start

incessant ceaseless, constant, continual, continuous, endless, eternal, everlasting, interminable, never-ending, nonstop, perpetual, persistent, relentless, unbroken, unceasing, unending, unrelenting, unremitting

incessantly all the time, cease~lessly, constantly, continually, endlessly, eternally, everlastingly, interminably, nonstop, perpetually, persistently, without a break

incident 1. adventure, circum~

stance, episode, event, fact, happening, matter, occasion, occurrence 2. brush, clash, commotion, confrontation, contretemps, disturbance, mishap, scene, skirmish

incidental 1. accidental, casual, chance, fortuitous, odd, random 2. *With* to accompanying, attendant, by-the-way, concomitant, contingent, contributory, related 3. ancillary, minor, nonessential, occasional, secondary, subordinate, subsidiary

incidentally 1. accidentally, by chance, casually, fortuitously 2. by the bye, by the way, in passing, parenthetically

incidentals contingencies, extras, minutiae, odds and ends

incinerate burn up, carbonize, char, consume by fire, cremate, reduce to ashes

incipient beginning, commencing, developing, embryonic, inceptive, inchoate, nascent, originating, starting

incise carve, chisel, cut (into), engrave, etch

incision cut, gash, notch, opening, slash, slit

incisive 1. acute, keen, penetrating, perspicacious, piercing, trenchant 2. acid, biting, caustic, cutting, mordant, sarcastic, sardonic, satirical, severe, sharp

incisiveness 1. keenness, penetration, perspicacity, sharpness, trenchancy 2. acidity, pungency, sarcasm

incite agitate for *or* against, animate, drive, egg on, encourage, excite, foment, goad, impel, inflame, instigate, prompt, provoke, put up to, rouse, set on, spur, stimulate, stir up, urge, whip up

incitement agitation, encouragement, goad, impetus, impulse, inducement, instigation, motivation, motive, prompting, provocation, spur, stimulus

incivility bad manners, boorishness, discourteousness, discourtesy, disrespect, ill-breeding, impoliteness, rudeness, unmannerliness

inclemency 1. bitterness, boisterousness, rawness, rigour, roughness, severity, storminess 2. callousness, cruelty, harshness, mercilessness, severity, tyranny, unfeelingness

inclement 1. bitter, boisterous, foul, harsh, intemperate, rigorous, rough, severe, stormy, tempestuous 2. callous, cruel, draconian, harsh, intemperate, merciless, pitiless, rigorous, severe, tyrannical, unfeeling, unmerciful

inclination 1. affection, aptitude, bent, bias, desire, disposition, fancy, fondness, leaning, liking, partiality, penchant, predilection, predisposition, prejudice, proclivity, proneness, propensity, stomach, taste, tendency, turn, turn of mind, wish 2. bending, bow, bowing, nod 3. angle, bend, bending, deviation, gradient, incline, leaning, pitch, slant, slope, tilt

incline *v.* 1. be disposed *or* predisposed, bias, influence, persuade, predispose, prejudice, sway, tend, turn 2. bend, bow, lower, nod, stoop 3. bend, bevel, cant, deviate, diverge, lean, slant, slope, tend, tilt, tip, veer ~*n.* 4. acclivity, ascent, declivity, descent, dip, grade, gradient, ramp, rise, slope

inclined apt, disposed, given, liable, likely, minded, of a mind (*Inf.*), predisposed, prone, willing

inclose *see* ENCLOSE

include 1. comprehend, comprise, contain, cover, embody, embrace, encompass, incorporate, involve, subsume, take in, take into account 2. add, allow for, build in, count, enter, insert, introduce, number among

including as well as, containing, counting, inclusive of, plus, together with, with

inclusion addition, incorporation, insertion

inclusive across-the-board, all-embracing, all in, all together, blanket, catch-all (*Chiefly U.S.*), comprehensive, full, general, *in toto*, overall, sweeping, umbrella, without exception

incognito disguised, in disguise, under an assumed name, unknown, unrecognized

incoherence disconnectedness, disjointedness, inarticulateness, unintelligibility

incoherent confused, disconnected, disjointed, disordered, inarticulate, inconsistent, jumbled, loose, muddled, rambling, stammering, stuttering, unconnected, uncoordinated, unintelligible, wandering, wild

incombustible fireproof, flameproof, noncombustible, nonflammable, noninflammable

income earnings, gains, interest, means, pay, proceeds, profits, receipts, revenue, salary, takings, wages

incoming approaching, arriving, entering, homeward, landing, new, returning, succeeding

incomparable beyond compare, inimitable, matchless, paramount, peerless, superlative, supreme, transcendent, unequalled, unmatched, unparalleled, unrivalled

incomparably beyond compare, by far, easily, eminently, far and away, immeasurably

incompatibility antagonism, conflict, discrepancy, disparateness, incongruity, inconsistency, irreconcilability, uncongeniality

incompatible antagonistic, antipathetic, conflicting, contradictory, discordant, discrepant, disparate, ill-assorted, incongruous, inconsistent, inconsonant, irreconcilable, mismatched, uncongenial, unsuitable, unsuited

incompetence inability, inadequacy, incapability, incapacity, incompetency, ineffectiveness, ineptitude, ineptness, insufficiency, skill-lessness, unfitness, uselessness

incompetent bungling, floundering, incapable, incapacitated, ineffectual, inept, inexpert, insufficient, skill-less, unable, unfit, unfitted, unskilful, useless

incomplete broken, defective, deficient, fragmentary, imperfect, insufficient, lacking, partial, short, unaccomplished, undeveloped, undone, unexecuted, unfinished, wanting

incomprehensible above one's head, all Greek to (*Inf.*), baffling, beyond comprehension, beyond one's grasp, enigmatic, impenetrable, inconceivable, inscrutable, mysterious, obscure, opaque, perplexing, puzzling, unfathomable, unimaginable, unintelligible, unthinkable

inconceivable beyond belief, impossible, incomprehensible, incredible, mind-boggling (*Sl.*), not to be thought of, out of the question, staggering (*Inf.*), unbelievable, unheard-of, unimaginable, unknowable, unthinkable

inconclusive ambiguous, indecisive, indeterminate, open, uncertain, unconvincing, undecided, unsettled, up in the air (*Inf.*), vague

incongruity conflict, discrepancy, disparity, inappropriateness, inaptness, incompatibility, inconsistency, inharmoniousness, unsuitability

incongruous absurd, conflicting, contradictory, contrary, disconsonant, discordant, extraneous, improper, inappropriate, inapt, incoherent, incompatible, inconsistent, out of keeping, out of place, unbecoming, unsuitable, unsuited

inconsiderable exiguous, inconsequential, insignificant, light, minor, negligible, petty, slight, small, small-time (*Inf.*), trifling, trivial, unimportant

inconsiderate careless, indelicate, insensitive, intolerant, rude, self-centred, selfish, tactless, thoughtless, uncharitable, ungracious, unkind, unthinking

inconsistency 1. contrariety, disagreement, discrepancy, disparity, divergence, incompatibility, incongruity, inconsonance, paradox, variance 2. fickleness, instability, unpredictability, unreliability, unsteadiness

inconsistent 1. at odds, at variance, conflicting, contradictory, contrary, discordant, discrepant, incoherent, incompatible, in conflict, incongruous, irreconcilable, out of step 2. capricious, changeable, erratic, fickle, inconstant, irregular, unpredictable, unstable, unsteady, vagarious (*Rare*), variable

inconsistently contradictorily, differently, eccentrically, erratically, inequably, randomly, unequally, unfairly, unpredictably, variably

inconsolable brokenhearted, desolate, despairing, heartbroken, heartsick, prostrate with grief, sick at heart

inconspicuous camouflaged, hidden, insignificant, modest, muted, ordinary, plain, quiet, retiring, unassuming, unnoticeable, unobtrusive, unostentatious

incontestable beyond doubt, beyond question, certain, incontrovertible, indisputable, indubitable, irrefutable, self-evident, sure, undeniable, unquestionable

incontinent 1. unbridled, unchecked, uncontrollable, uncontrolled, ungovernable, ungoverned, unrestrained 2. debauched, lascivious, lecherous, lewd, loose, lustful, profligate, promiscuous, unchaste, wanton

incontrovertible beyond dispute, certain, established, incontestable, indisputable, indubitable, irrefutable, positive, sure, undeniable, unquestionable, unshakable

inconvenience *n.* 1. annoyance, awkwardness, bother, difficulty, disadvantage, disruption, disturbance, drawback, fuss, hindrance, nuisance, trouble, uneasiness, upset, vexation 2. awkwardness, cumbersomeness, unfitness, unhandiness, unsuitableness, untimeliness, unwieldiness ~*v.* 3. bother, discommode, disrupt, disturb, give (someone) bother *or* trouble, irk, make (someone) go out of his way, put out, put to trouble, trouble, upset

inconvenient 1. annoying, awkward, bothersome, disadvanta-

geous, disturbing, embarrassing, inopportune, tiresome, troublesome, unseasonable, unsuitable, untimely, vexatious 2. awkward, cumbersome, difficult, unhandy, unmanageable, unwieldy

incorporate absorb, amalgamate, assimilate, blend, coalesce, combine, consolidate, embody, fuse, include, integrate, merge, mix, subsume, unite

incorrect erroneous, false, faulty, flawed, improper, inaccurate, inappropriate, inexact, mistaken, out, specious, unfitting, unsuitable, untrue, wide of the mark (*Inf.*), wrong

incorrectness erroneousness, error, fallacy, faultiness, impreciseness, imprecision, impropriety, inaccuracy, inexactness, speciousness, unsoundness, unsuitability, wrongness

incorrigible hardened, hopeless, incurable, intractable, inveterate, irredeemable, unreformed

incorruptibility honesty, honour, integrity, justness, uprightness

incorruptible 1. above suspicion, honest, honourable, just, straight, trustworthy, unbribable, upright 2. everlasting, imperishable, undecaying

increase *v.* 1. add to, advance, aggrandize, amplify, augment, boost, build up, develop, dilate, enhance, enlarge, escalate, expand, extend, grow, heighten, inflate, intensify, magnify, mount, multiply, proliferate, prolong, raise, snowball, spread, step up (*Inf.*), strengthen, swell, wax ~*n.* 2. addition, augmentation, boost, development, enlargement, escalation, expansion, extension, gain, growth, increment, intensification, rise, upsurge, upturn 3. on the increase developing, escalating, expanding, growing, increasing, multiplying, on the rise, proliferating, spreading

increasingly more and more, progressively, to an increasing extent

incredible 1. absurd, beyond belief, far-fetched, implausible, impossible, improbable, inconceivable, preposterous, unbelievable, unimaginable, unthinkable 2. *Inf.* ace (*Inf.*), amazing, astonishing, astounding, awe-inspiring, extraordinary, far-out (*Sl.*), great, marvellous, prodigious, superhuman, wonderful

incredulity disbelief, distrust, doubt, scepticism, unbelief

incredulous disbelieving, distrustful, doubtful, doubting, dubious, mistrustful, sceptical, suspicious, unbelieving, unconvinced

increment accretion, accrual, accrument, addition, advancement, augmentation, enlargement, gain, increase, step (up)

incriminate accuse, arraign, blacken the name of, blame, charge, impeach, implicate, inculpate, indict, involve, point the finger at (*Inf.*), stigmatize

incumbent binding, compulsory, mandatory, necessary, obligatory

incur arouse, bring (upon oneself), contract, draw, earn, expose oneself to, gain, induce, lay oneself open to, meet with, provoke

incurable *adj.* 1. dyed-in-the-wool, hopeless, incorrigible, inveterate 2. fatal, inoperable, irrecoverable, irremediable, remediless, terminal

indebted beholden, grateful, in debt, obligated, obliged, under an obligation

indecency bawdiness, coarseness, crudity, foulness, grossness, immodesty, impropriety, impurity, indecorum, indelicacy, lewdness, licentiousness, obscenity, outrageousness, pornography, smut, smuttiness, unseemliness, vileness, vulgarity

indecent 1. blue, coarse, crude, dirty, filthy, foul, gross, immodest, improper, impure, indelicate, lewd, licentious, pornographic, salacious, scatological, smutty, vile 2. ill-bred, improper, in bad taste, indecorous, offensive, outrageous, tasteless, unbecoming, unseemly, vulgar

indecipherable crabbed, illegible, indistinguishable, unintelligible, unreadable

indecision ambivalence, doubt, hesitancy, hesitation, indecisiveness, irresolution, shilly-shallying (*Inf.*), uncertainty, vacillation, wavering

indecisive 1. doubtful, faltering, hesitating, in two minds (*Inf.*), irresolute, pussyfooting (*Inf.*), tentative, uncertain, undecided, undetermined, vacillating, wavering 2. inconclusive, indefinite, indeterminate, unclear, undecided

indeed actually, certainly, doubtlessly, in point of fact, in truth, positively, really, strictly, to be sure, truly, undeniably, undoubtedly, verily (*Archaic*), veritably

indefensible faulty, inexcusable, insupportable, unforgivable, unjustifiable, unpardonable, untenable, unwarrantable, wrong

indefinable dim, hazy, impalpable, indescribable, indistinct, inexpressible, nameless, obscure, unrealized, vague

indefinite ambiguous, confused, doubtful, equivocal, evasive, general, ill-defined, imprecise, indeterminate, indistinct, inexact, loose, obscure, uncertain, unclear, undefined, undetermined, unfixed, unknown, unlimited, unsettled, vague

indefinitely continually, endlessly, for ever, *sine die*

indelible enduring, indestructible, ineffaceable, ineradicable, inexpungible, inextirpable, ingrained, lasting, permanent

indelicacy bad taste, coarseness, crudity, grossness, immodesty, impropriety, indecency, obscenity, offensiveness, rudeness, smuttiness, suggestiveness, tastelessness, vulgarity

indelicate blue, coarse, crude, embarrassing, gross, immodest, improper, indecent, indecorous, low, near the knuckle (*Inf.*), obscene, off-colour, offensive, risqué, rude, suggestive, tasteless, unbecoming, unseemly, untoward, vulgar

indemnify 1. endorse, guarantee, insure, protect, secure, underwrite 2. compensate, pay, reimburse, remunerate, repair, repay, requite, satisfy

indemnity 1. guarantee, insurance, protection, security 2. compensation, redress, reimbursement, remuneration, reparation, requital, restitution, satisfaction 3. *Law* exemption, immunity, impunity, privilege

indent v. 1. ask for, order, request, requisition 2. cut, dint, mark, nick, notch, pink, scallop, score, serrate

independence autarchy, autonomy, freedom, home rule, liberty, self-determination, self-government, self-reliance, self-rule, self-sufficiency, separation, sovereignty

independent 1. absolute, free, liberated, separate, unconnected, unconstrained, uncontrolled, unrelated 2. autarchic, autarchical, autonomous, decontrolled, nonaligned, self-determining, self-governing, separated, sovereign 3. bold, individualistic, liberated, self-contained, self-reliant, self-sufficient, self-supporting, unaided, unconventional

independently alone, autonomously, by oneself, individually, on one's own, separately, solo, unaided

indescribable beggaring description, beyond description, beyond words, incommunicable, indefinable, ineffable, inexpressible, unutterable

indestructible abiding, durable, enduring, everlasting, immortal, imperishable, incorruptible, indelible, indissoluble, lasting, nonperishable, permanent, unbreakable, unfading

indeterminate imprecise, inconclusive, indefinite, inexact, uncertain, undefined, undetermined, unfixed, unspecified, unstipulated, vague

index 1. clue, guide, indication, mark, sign, symptom, token 2. director, forefinger, hand, indicator, needle, pointer

indicate 1. add up to (*Inf.*), bespeak, be symptomatic of, betoken, denote, evince, imply, manifest, point to, reveal, show, signify, suggest 2. designate, point out, point to, specify 3. display, express, mark, read, record, register, show

indication clue, evidence, explanation, forewarning, hint, index, inkling, intimation, manifestation, mark, note, omen, portent, sign, signal, suggestion, symptom, warning

indicative exhibitive, indicatory, indicial, pointing to, significant, suggestive, symptomatic

indicator display, gauge, guide, index, mark, marker, meter, pointer, sign, signal, signpost, symbol

indictment accusation, allegation, charge, impeachment, prosecution, summons

indifference 1. absence of feeling, aloofness, apathy, callousness, carelessness, coldness, coolness, detachment, disregard, heedlessness, inattention, lack of interest, negligence, stoicalness, unconcern 2. disinterestedness, dispassion, equity, impartiality, neutrality, objectivity 3. insignificance, irrelevance, triviality, unimportance

indifferent 1. aloof, apathetic, callous, careless, cold, cool, detached, distant, heedless, impervious, inattentive, regardless, uncaring, unconcerned, unimpressed, uninterested, unmoved, unresponsive, unsympathetic 2. immaterial, insignificant, of no consequence, unimportant 3. average, fair, mediocre, middling, moderate, ordinary, passable, perfunctory, so-so (*Inf.*), undistinguished, uninspired 4. disinterested, dispassionate, equitable, impartial, neutral, nonaligned, nonpartisan, objective, unbiased, uninvolved, unprejudiced

indigestion dyspepsia, dyspepsy, upset stomach

indignant angry, annoyed, disgruntled, exasperated, fuming (*Inf.*), furious, heated, huffy (*Inf.*), in a huff, incensed, in high dudgeon, irate, livid (*Inf.*), mad (*Inf.*), miffed (*Inf.*), narked (*Sl.*), peeved (*Inf.*), provoked, resentful, riled, scornful, seeing red (*Inf.*), sore (*Inf.*), up in arms (*Inf.*), wrathful

indignation anger, exasperation, fury, ire (*Literary*), pique, rage, resentment, righteous anger, scorn, umbrage, wrath

indignity abuse, affront, contumely, dishonour, disrespect, humiliation, injury, insult, obloquy, opprobrium, outrage, reproach, slap in the face (*Inf.*), slight, snub

indirect 1. backhanded, circuitous, circumlocutory, crooked, devious, long-drawn-out, meandering, oblique, periphrastic, rambling, roundabout, tortuous, wandering, winding, zigzag 2. ancillary, collateral, contingent, incidental, secondary, subsidiary, unintended

indirectly by implication, circumlocutorily, in a roundabout way, obliquely, periphrastically, secondhand

indiscernible hidden, impalpable, imperceptible, indistinct, indistinguishable, invisible, unapparent, undiscernible

indiscreet foolish, hasty, heedless, ill-advised, ill-considered, illjudged, impolitic, imprudent, incautious, injudicious, naive, rash, reckless, tactless, undiplomatic, unthinking, unwise

indiscretion error, faux pas, folly, foolishness, gaffe, gaucherie, imprudence, mistake, rashness, recklessness, slip, slip of the tongue, tactlessness

indiscriminate 1. aimless, careless, desultory, general, hit or miss (*Inf.*), random, sweeping, uncritical, undiscriminating, unmethodical, unselective, unsystematic, wholesale 2. chaotic, confused, haphazard, higgledy-piggledy (*Inf.*), jumbled, mingled, miscellaneous, mixed, mongrel, motley, promiscuous, undistinguishable

indispensable crucial, essential, imperative, key, necessary, needed, needful, requisite, vital

indisposed 1. ailing, confined to bed, ill, laid up (*Inf.*), on the sick list (*Inf.*), poorly (*Inf.*), sick, unwell

2. averse, disinclined, loath, reluctant, unwilling

indisposition 1. ailment, ill health, illness, sickness 2. aversion, disinclination, dislike, distaste, hesitancy, reluctance, unwillingness

indisputable absolute, beyond doubt, certain, evident, incontestable, incontrovertible, indubitable, irrefutable, positive, sure, unassailable, undeniable, unquestionable

indissoluble abiding, binding, enduring, eternal, fixed, imperishable, incorruptible, indestructible, inseparable, lasting, permanent, solid, unbreakable

indistinct ambiguous, bleary, blurred, confused, dim, doubtful, faint, fuzzy, hazy, ill-defined, indefinite, indeterminate, indiscernible, indistinguishable, misty, muffled, obscure, out of focus, shadowy, unclear, undefined, unintelligible, vague, weak

indistinguishable 1. alike, identical, like as two peas in a pod (*Inf.*), (the) same, twin 2. imperceptible, indiscernible, invisible, obscure

individual 1. *adj.* characteristic, discrete, distinct, distinctive, exclusive, identical, idiosyncratic, own, particular, peculiar, personal, personalized, proper, respective, separate, several, single, singular, special, specific, unique 2. *n.* being, body (*Inf.*), character, creature, mortal, party, person, personage, soul, type, unit

individualism egocentricity, egoism, freethinking, independence, originality, self-direction, self-interest, self-reliance

individualist freethinker, independent, loner, lone wolf, maverick, nonconformist, original

individuality character, discreteness, distinction, distinctiveness, originality, peculiarity, personality, separateness, singularity, uniqueness

individually apart, independently, one at a time, one by one, personally, separately, severally, singly

indoctrinate brainwash, drill,

ground, imbue, initiate, instruct, school, teach, train

indoctrination brainwashing, drilling, grounding, inculcation, instruction, schooling, training

indolent fainéant, idle, inactive, inert, lackadaisical, languid, lazy, lethargic, listless, lumpish, slack, slothful, slow, sluggish, torpid, workshy

indomitable invincible, resolute, staunch, steadfast, unbeatable, unconquerable, unflinching, untameable, unyielding

indubitable certain, evident, incontestable, incontrovertible, indisputable, irrefutable, obvious, sure, unarguable, undeniable, undoubted, unquestionable, veritable

induce 1. actuate, convince, draw, encourage, get, impel, incite, influence, instigate, move, persuade, press, prevail upon, prompt, talk into 2. bring about, cause, effect, engender, generate, give rise to, lead to, occasion, produce, set in motion

inducement attraction, bait, carrot (*Inf.*), cause, come-on (*Inf.*), consideration, encouragement, impulse, incentive, incitement, influence, lure, motive, reward, spur, stimulus, urge

indulge 1. cater to, give way to, gratify, pander to, regale, satiate, satisfy, treat oneself to, yield to 2. *With* in bask in, give free rein to, give oneself up to, luxuriate in, revel in, wallow in 3. baby, coddle, cosset, favour, foster, give in to, go along with, humour, mollycoddle, pamper, pet, spoil

indulgence 1. excess, fondness, immoderation, intemperance, intemperateness, kindness, leniency, pampering, partiality, permissiveness, profligacy, profligateness, spoiling 2. appeasement, fulfilment, gratification, satiation, satisfaction 3. extravagance, favour, luxury, privilege, treat 4. courtesy, forbearance, good will, patience, tolerance, understanding

indulgent compliant, easy-going, favourable, fond, forbearing, gentle, gratifying, kind, kindly, lenient, liberal, mild, permissive, tender, tolerant, understanding

industrialist baron, big businessman, boss, capitalist, captain of industry, financier, magnate, manufacturer, producer, tycoon

industrious active, assiduous, busy, conscientious, diligent, energetic, hard-working, laborious, persevering, persistent, productive, purposeful, sedulous, steady, tireless, zealous

industriously assiduously, conscientiously, diligently, doggedly, hard, like a Trojan, nose to the grindstone (*Inf.*), perseveringly, sedulously, steadily, without slacking

industry 1. business, commerce, commercial enterprise, manufacturing, production, trade 2. activity, application, assiduity, determination, diligence, effort, labour, perseverance, persistence, tirelessness, toil, vigour, zeal

inebriated befuddled, blind drunk, blotto (*Sl.*), drunk, fou *or* fu' (*Scot.*), half-cut (*Inf.*), half seas over (*Inf.*), high (*Inf.*), high as a kite (*Inf.*), inebriate, in one's cups, intoxicated, legless (*Inf.*), merry, paralytic (*Inf.*), pie-eyed (*Sl.*), plastered (*Sl.*), smashed (*Sl.*), sozzled (*Inf.*), stoned (*Sl.*), the worse for drink, three sheets in the wind (*Inf.*), tight (*Inf.*), tipsy, under the influence (*Inf.*), under the weather (*Inf.*)

ineffective barren, bootless, feeble, fruitless, futile, idle, impotent, inadequate, ineffectual, inefficacious, inefficient, unavailing, unproductive, useless, vain, weak, worthless

ineffectual abortive, bootless, emasculate, feeble, fruitless, futile, idle, impotent, inadequate, incompetent, ineffective, inefficacious, inefficient, inept, lame, powerless, unavailing, useless, vain, weak

inefficiency carelessness, disorganization, incompetence, muddle, slackness

inefficient disorganized, feeble, incapable, incompetent, ineffectual, inefficacious, inept, inexpert, slipshod, sloppy, wasteful, weak

ineligible disqualified, incompetent (*Law*), objectionable, ruled out, unacceptable, undesirable, unequipped, unfit, unfitted, unqualified, unsuitable

inept 1. awkward, bumbling, bungling, cack-handed (*Inf.*), clumsy, gauche, incompetent, inexpert, maladroit, unhandy, unskilful, unworkmanlike 2. absurd, improper, inappropriate, inapt, infelicitous, malapropos, meaningless, out of place, pointless, ridiculous, unfit, unsuitable

ineptitude 1. clumsiness, gaucheness, incapacity, incompetence, inexpertness, unfitness, unhandiness 2. absurdity, inappropriateness, pointlessness, uselessness

inequality bias, difference, disparity, disproportion, diversity, imparity, irregularity, lack of balance, preferentiality, prejudice, unevenness

inequitable biased, discriminatory, one-sided, partial, partisan, preferential, prejudiced, unfair, unjust

inert dead, dormant, dull, idle, immobile, inactive, inanimate, indolent, lazy, leaden, lifeless, motionless, passive, quiescent, slack, slothful, sluggish, slumberous (*Chiefly poetic*), static, still, torpid, unmoving, unreactive, unresponsive

inertia apathy, deadness, disinclination to move, drowsiness, dullness, idleness, immobility, inactivity, indolence, languor, lassitude, laziness, lethargy, listlessness, passivity, sloth, sluggishness, stillness, stupor, torpor, unresponsiveness

inescapable certain, destined, fated, ineluctable, ineludible (*Rare*), inevitable, inexorable, sure, unavoidable

inestimable beyond price, immeasurable, incalculable, invaluable, precious, priceless, prodigious

inevitable assured, certain, decreed, destined, fixed, ineluctable,

inescapable, inexorable, necessary, ordained, settled, sure, unavoidable, unpreventable

inevitably as a necessary consequence, as a result, automatically, certainly, necessarily, of necessity, perforce, surely, unavoidably, willy-nilly

inexcusable indefensible, inexpiable, outrageous, unforgivable, unjustifiable, unpardonable, unwarrantable

inexhaustible 1. bottomless, boundless, endless, illimitable, infinite, limitless, measureless, never-ending, unbounded 2. indefatigable, tireless, undaunted, unfailing, unflagging, untiring, unwearied, unwearying

inexorable adamant, cruel, hard, harsh, immovable, implacable, ineluctable, inescapable, inflexible, merciless, obdurate, pitiless, relentless, remorseless, severe, unappeasable, unbending, unrelenting, unyielding

inexorably implacably, inevitably, irresistibly, relentlessly, remorselessly, unrelentingly

inexpensive bargain, budget, cheap, economical, low-cost, low-priced, modest, reasonable

inexperience callowness, greenness, ignorance, newness, rawness, unexpertness, unfamiliarity

inexperienced amateur, callow, fresh, green, immature, new, raw, unaccustomed, unacquainted, unfamiliar, unfledged, unpractised, unschooled, unseasoned, unskilled, untrained, untried, unused, unversed, wet behind the ears (*Inf.*)

inexpert amateurish, awkward, bungling, cack-handed (*Inf.*), clumsy, inept, maladroit, skill-less, unhandy, unpractised, unprofessional, unskilful, unskilled, unworkmanlike

inexplicable baffling, beyond comprehension, enigmatic, incomprehensible, inscrutable, insoluble, mysterious, mystifying, strange, unaccountable, unfathomable, unintelligible

inexpressible incommunicable,

indefinable, indescribable, ineffable, unspeakable, unutterable

inexpressive bland, blank, cold, dead, deadpan, emotionless, empty, expressionless, impassive, inanimate, inscrutable, lifeless, stony, vacant

inextinguishable enduring, eternal, immortal, imperishable, indestructible, irrepressible, undying, unquenchable, unsuppressible

inextricably indissolubly, indistinguishably, inseparably, intricately, irretrievably, totally

infallibility 1. faultlessness, impeccability, irrefutability, omniscience, perfection, supremacy, unerringness 2. dependability, reliability, safety, sureness, trustworthiness

infallible 1. faultless, impeccable, omniscient, perfect, unerring, unimpeachable 2. certain, dependable, foolproof, reliable, sure, sure-fire (*Inf.*), trustworthy, unbeatable, unfailing

infamous abominable, atrocious, base, detestable, disgraceful, dishonourable, disreputable, egregious, flagitious, hateful, heinous, ignominious, ill-famed, iniquitous, loathsome, monstrous, nefarious, notorious, odious, opprobrious, outrageous, scandalous, scurvy, shameful, shocking, vile, villainous, wicked

infancy 1. babyhood, early childhood 2. beginnings, cradle, dawn, early stages, emergence, inception, origins, outset, start

infant 1. *n.* babe, baby, bairn (*Scot.*), child, little one, neonate, newborn child, suckling, toddler, tot, wean (*Scot.*) 2. *adj.* baby, dawning, developing, early, emergent, growing, immature, initial, nascent, newborn, unfledged, young

infantile babyish, childish, immature, puerile, tender, weak, young

infatuate befool, beguile, besot, bewitch, captivate, delude, enchant, enrapture, enravish, fascinate, make a fool of, mislead, obsess, stupefy, sweep one off one's feet, turn (someone's) head

infatuated beguiled, besotted, bewitched, captivated, carried away, crazy about (*Inf.*), enamoured, enraptured, fascinated, head over heels in love with, inflamed, intoxicated, obsessed, possessed, smitten (*Inf.*), spellbound, swept off one's feet, under the spell of

infatuation crush (*Inf.*), fixation, folly, foolishness, madness, obsession, passion, thing (*Inf.*)

infect affect, blight, contaminate, corrupt, defile, influence, poison, pollute, spread to *or* among, taint, touch, vitiate

infection contagion, contamination, corruption, defilement, poison, pollution, septicity, virus

infectious catching, communicable, contagious, contaminating, corrupting, defiling, infective, pestilential, poisoning, polluting, spreading, transmittable, virulent, vitiating

infer conclude, conjecture, deduce, derive, gather, presume, read between the lines, surmise, understand

inference assumption, conclusion, conjecture, consequence, corollary, deduction, illation (*Rare*), presumption, reading, surmise

inferior *adj.* 1. junior, lesser, lower, menial, minor, secondary, subordinate, subsidiary, under, underneath 2. bad, imperfect, indifferent, low-grade, mean, mediocre, poor, poorer, second-class, second-rate, shoddy, substandard, worse ~*n.* 3. junior, menial, subordinate, underling

inferiority 1. badness, deficiency, imperfection, inadequacy, insignificance, meanness, mediocrity, shoddiness, unimportance, worthlessness 2. abasement, inferior status *or* standing, lowliness, subordination, subservience

infernal 1. chthonian, Hadean, hellish, lower, nether, Plutonian, Stygian, Tartarean (*Literary*), underworld 2. accursed, damnable, damned, demonic, devilish, dia-

bolical, fiendish, hellish, malevo~
lent, malicious, satanic

infertile barren, infecund, nonpro~
ductive, sterile, unfruitful, unpro~
ductive

infertility barrenness, infecundity,
sterility, unfruitfulness, unproduc~
tiveness

infest beset, flood, invade, overrun,
penetrate, ravage, swarm, throng

infested alive, beset, crawling,
lousy, overrun, pervaded, plagued,
ravaged, ridden, swarming, teem~
ing

infiltrate creep in, filter through,
insinuate oneself, penetrate, per~
colate, permeate, pervade, sneak
in (*Inf.*), work *or* worm one's way
into

infinite absolute, all-embracing,
bottomless, boundless, enormous,
eternal, everlasting, illimitable,
immeasurable, immense, inesti~
mable, inexhaustible, intermi~
nable, limitless, measureless,
never-ending, numberless, perpet~
ual, stupendous, total, unbounded,
uncounted, untold, vast, wide,
without end, without number

infinitesimal atomic, inappre~
ciable, insignificant, microscopic,
minuscule, minute, negligible, tee~
ny, tiny, unnoticeable, wee

infinity boundlessness, endlessness,
eternity, immensity, infinitude,
perpetuity, vastness

infirm 1. ailing, debilitated, decrep~
it, doddering, doddery, enfeebled,
failing, feeble, frail, lame, weak 2.
faltering, indecisive, insecure, ir~
resolute, shaky, unsound, unstable,
vacillating, wavering, weak, wob~
bly

infirmity 1. debility, decrepitude,
deficiency, feebleness, frailty, ill
health, imperfection, sickliness,
vulnerability 2. ailment, defect,
disorder, failing, fault, malady,
sickness, weakness

inflame 1. agitate, anger, arouse,
embitter, enrage, exasperate, ex~
cite, fire, foment, heat, ignite, im~
passion, incense, infuriate, intoxi~
cate, kindle, madden, provoke, rile,
rouse, stimulate 2. aggravate, ex~

acerbate, exasperate, fan, in~
crease, intensify, worsen

inflamed angry, chafing, festering,
fevered, heated, hot, infected, red,
septic, sore, swollen

inflammable combustible, flam~
mable, incendiary

inflammation burning, heat, pain~
fulness, rash, redness, sore, sore~
ness, tenderness

inflammatory anarchic, dema~
gogic, explosive, fiery, incendiary,
inflaming, instigative, insurgent,
intemperate, provocative, rabble-
rousing, rabid, riotous, seditious

inflate aerate, aggrandize, amplify,
balloon, bloat, blow up, boost, di~
late, distend, enlarge, escalate, ex~
aggerate, expand, increase, puff up
or out, pump up, swell

inflated bombastic, exaggerated,
grandiloquent, ostentatious, over~
blown, swollen

inflation aggrandizement, blowing
up, distension, enhancement, en~
largement, escalation, expansion,
extension, increase, intensification,
puffiness, rise, spread, swelling,
tumefaction

inflection 1. accentuation, bend,
bow, crook, curvature, intonation,
modulation 2. *Gram.* conjugation,
declension 3. angle, arc, arch

inflexibility 1. hardness, immova~
bility, inelasticity, rigidity, stiff~
ness, stringency 2. fixity, intransi~
gence, obduracy, obstinacy, steeli~
ness

inflexible 1. adamant, brassbound,
dyed-in-the-wool, firm, fixed, hard
and fast, immovable, immutable,
implacable, inexorable, intrac~
table, iron, obdurate, obstinate, re~
lentless, resolute, rigorous, set, set
in one's ways, steadfast, steely,
strict, stringent, stubborn, una~
daptable, unbending, unchange~
able, uncompromising, unyielding
2. hard, hardened, inelastic, non~
flexible, rigid, stiff, taut

inflict administer, apply, deliver,
exact, impose, levy, mete *or* deal
out, visit, wreak

infliction 1. administration, exac~
tion, imposition, perpetration,

wreaking 2. affliction, penalty, punishment, trouble, visitation, worry

influence n. 1. agency, ascendancy, authority, control, credit, direction, domination, effect, guidance, magnetism, mastery, power, pressure, rule, spell, sway, weight 2. clout (*Inf.*), connections, good offices, hold, importance, leverage, power, prestige, pull (*Inf.*), weight ~v. 3. act *or* work upon, affect, arouse, bias, control, count, direct, dispose, guide, impel, impress, incite, incline, induce, instigate, lead to believe, manipulate, modify, move, persuade, predispose, prompt, rouse, sway 4. bring pressure to bear upon, carry weight with, make oneself felt, pull strings (*Inf.*)

influential authoritative, controlling, effective, efficacious, forcible, guiding, important, instrumental, leading, meaningful, momentous, moving, persuasive, potent, powerful, significant, telling, weighty

influx arrival, convergence, flow, incursion, inflow, inrush, inundation, invasion, rush

inform 1. acquaint, advise, apprise, communicate, enlighten, give (someone) to understand, instruct, leak to, let know, make conversant (with), notify, put (someone) in the picture (*Inf.*), send word to, teach, tell, tip off 2. *Often with* against *or* on betray, blab, blow the whistle on (*U.S. inf.*), clype (*Scot.*), denounce, grass (*Brit. sl.*), incriminate, inculpate, nark (*Brit. sl.*), peach (*Sl.*), rat, snitch (*Sl.*), squeal (*Sl.*), tell on (*Inf.*) 3. animate, characterize, illuminate, imbue, inspire, permeate, suffuse, typify

informal casual, colloquial, easy, familiar, natural, relaxed, simple, unceremonious, unconstrained, unofficial

informality casualness, ease, familiarity, lack of ceremony, naturalness, relaxation, simplicity

information advice, counsel, data, dope (*Sl.*), facts, gen (*Brit. inf.*), info (*Inf.*), inside story, instruction, intelligence, knowledge, lowdown (*Inf.*), material, message, news, notice, report, tidings, word

informative chatty, communicative, edifying, educational, enlightening, forthcoming, gossipy, illuminating, instructive, newsy, revealing

informed abreast, acquainted, *au courant, au fait*, briefed, conversant, enlightened, erudite, expert, familiar, genned up (*Brit. inf.*), in the know (*Inf.*), knowledgeable, learned, posted, primed, reliable, up, up to date, versed, well-read

informer accuser, betrayer, grass (*Brit. sl.*), Judas, nark (*Brit. sl.*), sneak, squealer (*Sl.*), stool pigeon

infrequent few and far between, occasional, rare, sporadic, uncommon, unusual

infringe 1. break, contravene, disobey, transgress, violate 2. *With on or upon* encroach, intrude, trespass

infringement breach, contravention, infraction, noncompliance, nonobservance, transgression, trespass, violation

infuriate anger, be like a red rag to a bull, enrage, exasperate, get one's back up (*Inf.*), get one's goat (*Sl.*), incense, irritate, madden, make one's blood boil, make one see red (*Inf.*), make one's hackles rise, provoke, raise one's hackles, rile

infuriating aggravating (*Inf.*), annoying, exasperating, galling, irritating, maddening, mortifying, pestilential, provoking, vexatious

ingenious adroit, bright, brilliant, clever, crafty, creative, dexterous, fertile, inventive, masterly, original, ready, resourceful, shrewd, skilful, subtle

ingenuity adroitness, cleverness, faculty, flair, genius, gift, ingeniousness, inventiveness, knack, originality, resourcefulness, sharpness, shrewdness, skill, turn

ingenuous artless, candid, childlike, frank, guileless, honest, innocent, naive, open, plain, simple, sincere, trustful, trusting, unreserved, unsophisticated, unstudied

ingenuousness artlessness, candour, frankness, guilelessness, innocence, naivety, openness, trustingness, unsuspiciousness

inglorious discreditable, disgraceful, dishonourable, disreputable, failed, humiliating, ignoble, ignominious, infamous, obscure, shameful, unheroic, unknown, unsuccessful, unsung

ingratiate be a yes man, blandish, crawl, curry favour, fawn, flatter, get in with (Inf.), get on the right side of, grovel, insinuate oneself, lick (someone's) boots, play up to, rub (someone) up the right way (Inf.), seek the favour (of someone), suck up to (Inf.), toady, worm oneself into (someone's) favour

ingratiating bootlicking (Inf.), crawling, fawning, flattering, humble, obsequious, servile, sycophantic, timeserving, toadying, unctuous

ingratitude thanklessness, unappreciativeness, ungratefulness

ingredient component, constituent, element, part

inhabit abide, dwell, live, lodge, make one's home, occupy, people, populate, possess, reside, take up residence in, tenant

inhabitant aborigine, citizen, denizen, dweller, indigene, indweller, inmate, native, occupant, occupier, resident, tenant

inhabited colonized, developed, held, occupied, peopled, populated, settled, tenanted

inhale breathe in, draw in, gasp, respire, suck in

inherent basic, congenital, connate, essential, hereditary, inborn, inbred, inbuilt, ingrained, inherited, innate, instinctive, intrinsic, native, natural

inherit accede to, be bequeathed, be left, come into, fall heir to, succeed to

inheritance bequest, birthright, heritage, legacy, patrimony

inhibit arrest, bar, bridle, check, constrain, cramp (someone's) style (Inf.), curb, debar, discourage, forbid, frustrate, hinder, hold back or in, impede, obstruct, prevent, prohibit, restrain, stop

inhibited constrained, frustrated, guarded, repressed, reserved, reticent, self-conscious, shy, subdued, uptight (Inf.), withdrawn

inhibition bar, check, embargo, hang-up (Sl.), hindrance, interdict, mental blockage, obstacle, prohibition, reserve, restraint, restriction, reticence, self-consciousness, shyness

inhospitable 1. cool, uncongenial, unfriendly, ungenerous, unkind, unreceptive, unsociable, unwelcoming, xenophobic 2. bare, barren, bleak, desolate, empty, forbidding, hostile, lonely, sterile, unfavourable, uninhabitable

inhuman animal, barbaric, barbarous, bestial, brutal, cold-blooded, cruel, diabolical, fiendish, heartless, merciless, pitiless, remorseless, ruthless, savage, unfeeling, vicious

inhumane brutal, cruel, heartless, pitiless, uncompassionate, unfeeling, unkind, unsympathetic

inhumanity atrocity, barbarism, brutality, brutishness, coldbloodedness, cold-heartedness, cruelty, hardheartedness, heartlessness, pitilessness, ruthlessness, unkindness, viciousness

inimical adverse, antagonistic, antipathetic, contrary, destructive, disaffected, harmful, hostile, hurtful, ill-disposed, injurious, noxious, opposed, oppugnant (Rare), pernicious, repugnant, unfavourable, unfriendly, unwelcoming

inimitable consummate, incomparable, matchless, nonpareil, peerless, supreme, unequalled, unexampled, unique, unmatched, unparalleled, unrivalled, unsurpassable

iniquitous abominable, accursed, atrocious, base, criminal, evil, heinous, immoral, infamous, nefarious, reprehensible, reprobate, sinful, unjust, unrighteous, vicious, wicked

iniquity abomination, baseness, crime, evil, evildoing, heinousness, infamy, injustice, misdeed, offence, sin, sinfulness, unrighteousness, wickedness, wrong, wrongdoing

initial *adj.* beginning, commencing, early, first, inaugural, inceptive, inchoate, incipient, introductory, opening, primary

initially at *or* in the beginning, at first, at the outset, at the start, first, firstly, in the early stages, originally, primarily, to begin with

initiate *v.* 1. begin, break the ice, commence, get under way, inaugurate, institute, kick off (*Inf.*), launch, lay the foundations of, open, originate, pioneer, set going, set in motion, set the ball rolling, start 2. coach, familiarize with, indoctrinate, induct, instate, instruct, introduce, invest, teach, train ~*n.* 3. beginner, convert, entrant, learner, member, novice, probationer, proselyte, tyro

initiation admission, commencement, debut, enrolment, entrance, inauguration, inception, induction, installation, instatement, introduction, investiture

initiative 1. advantage, beginning, commencement, first move, first step, lead 2. ambition, drive, dynamism, enterprise, get-up-and-go (*Inf.*), inventiveness, leadership, originality, push (*Inf.*), resource, resourcefulness

inject 1. inoculate, jab (*Inf.*), shoot (*Inf.*), vaccinate 2. bring in, infuse, insert, instil, interject, introduce

injection 1. inoculation, jab (*Inf.*), shot (*Inf.*), vaccination, vaccine 2. dose, infusion, insertion, interjection, introduction

injudicious foolish, hasty, ill-advised, ill-judged, ill-timed, impolitic, imprudent, incautious, inconsiderate, indiscreet, inexpedient, rash, unthinking, unwise

injunction admonition, command, dictate, exhortation, instruction, mandate, order, precept, ruling

injure abuse, blemish, blight, break, damage, deface, disable, harm, hurt, impair, maltreat, mar, ruin, spoil, tarnish, undermine, vitiate, weaken, wound, wrong

injured 1. broken, disabled, hurt, lamed, undermined, weakened, wounded 2. cut to the quick, disgruntled, displeased, hurt, long-suffering, put out, reproachful, stung, unhappy, upset, wounded 3. abused, blackened, blemished, defamed, ill-treated, maligned, maltreated, offended, tarnished, vilified, wronged

injury abuse, damage, detriment, disservice, evil, grievance, harm, hurt, ill, injustice, mischief, ruin, wound, wrong

injustice bias, discrimination, favouritism, inequality, inequity, iniquity, one-sidedness, oppression, partiality, partisanship, prejudice, unfairness, unjustness, unlawfulness, wrong

inkling clue, conception, faintest *or* foggiest idea, glimmering, hint, idea, indication, intimation, notion, suggestion, suspicion, whisper

inland *adj.* domestic, interior, internal, upcountry

inlet arm (of the sea), bay, bight, cove, creek, entrance, firth *or* frith (*Scot.*), ingress, passage, sea loch (*Scot.*)

inmost *or* **innermost** basic, buried, central, deep, deepest, essential, intimate, personal, private, secret

innate congenital, connate, constitutional, essential, inborn, inbred, indigenous, ingrained, inherent, inherited, instinctive, intrinsic, intuitive, native, natural

inner 1. central, essential, inside, interior, internal, intestinal, inward, middle 2. esoteric, hidden, intimate, personal, private, repressed, secret, unrevealed 3. emotional, mental, psychological, spiritual

innkeeper host, hostess, hotelier, landlady, landlord, mine host, publican

innocence 1. blamelessness, chastity, clean hands, guiltlessness, incorruptibility, probity, purity, righteousness, sinlessness, stainlessness, uprightness, virginity, virtue 2. harmlessness, innocuous~

ness, innoxiousness, inoffensive~
ness 3. artlessness, credulousness,
freshness, guilelessness, gullibility,
inexperience, ingenuousness, na~
iveté, simplicity, unsophistication,
unworldliness 4. ignorance, lack of
knowledge, nescience (*Literary*),
unawareness, unfamiliarity

innocent *adj.* 1. blameless, clear,
faultless, guiltless, honest, in the
clear, not guilty, uninvolved, unof~
fending 2. chaste, immaculate, im~
peccable, incorrupt, pristine, pure,
righteous, sinless, spotless, stain~
less, unblemished, unsullied, up~
right, virgin, virginal 3. *With of*
clear of, empty of, free from, igno~
rant, lacking, nescient, unac~
quainted with, unaware, unfamiliar
with, untouched by 4. harmless,
innocuous, inoffensive, unmali~
cious, unobjectionable, well-
intentioned, well-meant 5. artless,
childlike, credulous, frank, guile~
less, gullible, ingenuous, naive,
open, simple, unsuspicious, un~
worldly, wet behind the ears (*Inf.*)
~*n.* 6. babe (in arms) (*Inf.*), child,
greenhorn (*Inf.*), ingénue (*fem.*)

innovation alteration, change, de~
parture, introduction, modernism,
modernization, newness, novelty,
variation

innuendo aspersion, hint, implica~
tion, imputation, insinuation, inti~
mation, overtone, suggestion,
whisper

innumerable beyond number,
countless, incalculable, infinite,
many, multitudinous, myriad,
numberless, numerous, unnum~
bered, untold

inoffensive harmless, humble, in~
nocent, innocuous, innoxious, mild,
neutral, nonprovocative, peace~
able, quiet, retiring, unobjection~
able, unobtrusive, unoffending

inoperative broken, broken-down,
defective, *hors de combat*, ineffec~
tive, ineffectual, inefficacious, in~
valid, nonactive, null and void, out
of action, out of commission, out of
order, out of service, unservice~
able, unworkable, useless

inopportune ill-chosen, ill-timed,

inappropriate, inauspicious, incon~
venient, malapropos, mistimed,
unfavourable, unfortunate, unpro~
pitious, unseasonable, unsuitable,
untimely

inordinate disproportionate, ex~
cessive, exorbitant, extravagant,
immoderate, intemperate, prepos~
terous, unconscionable, undue, un~
reasonable, unrestrained, unwar~
ranted

inorganic artificial, chemical, man-
made, mineral

inquest inquiry, inquisition, inves~
tigation, probe

inquire 1. examine, explore, in~
spect, investigate, look into, make
inquiries, probe, scrutinize, search
2. *Also* **enquire** ask, query, ques~
tion, request information, seek in~
formation

inquiring analytical, curious,
doubtful, inquisitive, interested, in~
vestigative, outward-looking,
probing, questioning, searching,
wondering

inquiry 1. examination, explora~
tion, inquest, interrogation, inves~
tigation, probe, research, scrutiny,
search, study, survey 2. *Also* en~
quiry query, question

inquisition cross-examination, ex~
amination, grilling (*Inf.*), inquest,
inquiry, investigation, question,
quizzing, third degree (*Inf.*)

inquisitive curious, inquiring, in~
trusive, nosy (*Inf.*), nosy-parkering
(*Inf.*), peering, probing, prying,
questioning, scrutinizing, snooping
(*Inf.*), snoopy (*Inf.*)

inroad 1. advance, encroachment,
foray, incursion, intrusion, inva~
sion, irruption, onslaught, raid 2.
make inroads upon consume, eat
away, eat up *or* into, encroach
upon, use up

insane 1. crazed, crazy, demented,
deranged, mad, mentally disor~
dered, mentally ill, *non compos
mentis*, of unsound mind, out of
one's mind, unhinged 2. barmy
(*Sl.*), batty (*Sl.*), bonkers (*Sl.*),
cracked (*Sl.*), crackers (*Sl.*),
cuckoo (*Inf.*), loony (*Sl.*), loopy
(*Inf.*), mental (*Sl.*), nuts (*Sl.*), nutty

(*Sl.*), off one's chump (*Inf.*), off one's head (*Inf.*), off one's nut (*Inf.*), off one's rocker (*Inf.*), round the bend (*Inf.*), round the twist (*Inf.*), screwy (*Inf.*) 3. bizarre, daft (*Inf.*), fatuous, foolish, idiotic, impractical, irrational, irresponsible, lunatic (*Inf.*), preposterous, senseless, stupid

insanitary contaminated, dirtied, dirty, disease-ridden, feculent, filthy, impure, infected, infested, insalubrious, noxious, polluted, unclean, unhealthy, unhygienic

insanity 1. aberration, craziness, delirium, dementia, frenzy, madness, mental derangement, mental disorder, mental illness 2. folly, irresponsibility, lunacy, preposterousness, senselessness, stupidity

insatiable gluttonous, greedy, insatiate, intemperate, quenchless, rapacious, ravenous, unappeasable, unquenchable, voracious

inscribe 1. carve, cut, engrave, etch, impress, imprint 2. engross, enlist, enrol, enter, record, register, write 3. address, dedicate

inscription dedication, engraving, label, legend, lettering, saying, words

inscrutable 1. blank, deadpan, enigmatic, impenetrable, poker-faced (*Inf.*), sphinxlike, unreadable 2. hidden, incomprehensible, inexplicable, mysterious, undiscoverable, unexplainable, unfathomable, unintelligible

insecure 1. afraid, anxious, uncertain, unconfident, unsure 2. dangerous, defenceless, exposed, hazardous, ill-protected, open to attack, perilous, unguarded, unprotected, unsafe, unshielded, vulnerable 3. built upon sand, flimsy, frail, insubstantial, loose, on thin ice, precarious, rickety, rocky, shaky, unreliable, unsound, unstable, unsteady, weak, wobbly

insecurity 1. anxiety, fear, uncertainty, unsureness, worry 2. danger, defencelessness, hazard, peril, risk, uncertainty, vulnerability, weakness 3. dubiety, frailness, instability, precariousness, shaki-

ness, uncertainty, unreliability, unsteadiness, weakness

insensibility 1. apathy, callousness, dullness, indifference, insensitivity, lethargy, thoughtlessness, torpor 2. inertness, numbness, unconsciousness

insensible 1. anaesthetized, benumbed, dull, inert, insensate, numbed, senseless, stupid, torpid 2. apathetic, callous, cold, deaf, hardhearted, impassive, impervious, indifferent, oblivious, unaffected, unaware, unconscious, unfeeling, unmindful, unmoved, unresponsive, unsusceptible, untouched 3. imperceivable, imperceptible, minuscule, negligible, unnoticeable

insensitive 1. callous, crass, hardened, imperceptive, indifferent, obtuse, tactless, thick-skinned, tough, uncaring, unconcerned, unfeeling, unresponsive, unsusceptible 2. *With* to dead to, immune to, impervious to, nonreactive, proof against, unaffected by, unmoved by

inseparable 1. conjoined, inalienable, indissoluble, indivisible, inseverable 2. bosom, close, devoted, intimate

insert embed, enter, implant, infix, interject, interpolate, interpose, introduce, place, pop in (*Inf.*), put, set, stick in, tuck in, work in

insertion addition, implant, inclusion, insert, inset, interpolation, introduction, supplement

inside *n.* 1. contents, inner part, interior 2. *Often plural. Inf.* belly, bowels, entrails, gut, guts, innards (*Inf.*), internal organs, stomach, viscera, vitals ~*adv.* 3. indoors, under cover, within ~*adj.* 4. inner, innermost, interior, internal, intramural, inward 5. classified, confidential, esoteric, exclusive, internal, limited, private, restricted, secret

insidious artful, crafty, crooked, cunning, deceitful, deceptive, designing, disingenuous, duplicitous, guileful, intriguing, Machiavellian, slick, sly, smooth, sneaking, stealthy, subtle, surreptitious, treacherous, tricky, wily

insight acumen, awareness, comprehension, discernment, intuition, intuitiveness, judgment, observation, penetration, perception, perspicacity, understanding, vision

insignia badge, crest, decoration, distinguishing mark, earmark, emblem, ensign, symbol

insignificance immateriality, inconsequence, irrelevance, meaninglessness, negligibility, paltriness, pettiness, triviality, unimportance, worthlessness

insignificant flimsy, immaterial, inconsequential, inconsiderable, irrelevant, meagre, meaningless, minor, negligible, nondescript, nonessential, not worth mentioning, nugatory, of no account (consequence, moment), paltry, petty, scanty, trifling, trivial, unimportant, unsubstantial

insincere deceitful, deceptive, devious, dishonest, disingenuous, dissembling, dissimulating, double-dealing, duplicitous, evasive, faithless, false, hollow, hypocritical, Janus-faced, lying, mendacious, perfidious, pretended, two-faced, unfaithful, untrue, untruthful

insincerity deceitfulness, deviousness, dishonesty, disingenuousness, dissimulation, duplicity, faithlessness, hypocrisy, lip service, mendacity, perfidy, pretence, untruthfulness

insinuate 1. allude, hint, imply, indicate, intimate, suggest 2. infiltrate, infuse, inject, instil, introduce 3. curry favour, get in with (*Inf.*), ingratiate, worm *or* work one's way in

insinuation 1. allusion, aspersion, hint, implication, innuendo, slur, suggestion 2. infiltration, infusion, ingratiating, injection, instillation, introduction

insipid 1. anaemic, banal, bland, characterless, colourless, drab, dry, dull, flat, jejune, lifeless, limp, pointless, prosaic, prosy, spiritless, stale, stupid, tame, tedious, trite, unimaginative, uninteresting, vap-

id, weak, wearisome, wishy-washy (*Inf.*) 2. bland, flavourless, savourless, tasteless, unappetizing, watered down, watery, wishy-washy (*Inf.*)

insipidity, insipidness 1. banality, colourlessness, dullness, flatness, lack of imagination, pointlessness, staleness, tameness, tediousness, triteness, uninterestingness, vapidity 2. blandness, flavourlessness, lack of flavour, tastelessness

insist 1. be firm, brook no refusal, demand, lay down the law, not take no for an answer, persist, press (someone), require, stand firm, stand one's ground, take *or* make a stand, urge 2. assert, asseverate, aver, claim, contend, hold, maintain, reiterate, repeat, swear, urge, vow

insistence assertion, contention, demands, emphasis, importunity, insistency, persistence, pressing, reiteration, stress, urging

insistent demanding, dogged, emphatic, exigent, forceful, importunate, incessant, peremptory, persevering, persistent, pressing, unrelenting, urgent

insolence abuse, audacity, backchat (*Inf.*), boldness, cheek (*Inf.*), chutzpah (*U.S. inf.*), contemptuousness, contumely, disrespect, effrontery, gall (*Inf.*), impertinence, impudence, incivility, insubordination, offensiveness, pertness, rudeness, sauce (*Inf.*), uncivility

insolent abusive, bold, brazen-faced, contemptuous, fresh (*Inf.*), impertinent, impudent, insubordinate, insulting, pert, rude, saucy, uncivil

insoluble baffling, impenetrable, indecipherable, inexplicable, mysterious, mystifying, obscure, unaccountable, unfathomable, unsolvable

insolvency bankruptcy, failure, liquidation, ruin

insolvent bankrupt, broke (*Inf.*), failed, gone bust (*Inf.*), gone to the wall (*Inf.*), in queer street (*Inf.*), in receivership, in the hands of the receivers, on the rocks (*Inf.*), ruined

insomnia sleeplessness, wakeful~ness

inspect check, examine, give (something *or* someone) the once-over (*Inf.*), go over *or* through, in~vestigate, look over, oversee, scan, scrutinize, search, superintend, supervise, survey, vet

inspection check, checkup, ex~amination, investigation, look-over, once-over (*Inf.*), review, scan, scrutiny, search, superintendence, supervision, surveillance, survey

inspector censor, checker, critic, examiner, investigator, overseer, scrutineer, scrutinizer, superin~tendent, supervisor

inspiration 1. arousal, awakening, encouragement, influence, muse, spur, stimulus 2. afflatus, creativ~ity, elevation, enthusiasm, exalta~tion, genius, illumination, insight, revelation, stimulation

inspire 1. animate, be responsible for, encourage, enliven, fire *or* touch the imagination of, galva~nize, hearten, imbue, influence, in~fuse, inspirit, instil, spark off, spur, stimulate 2. arouse, enkindle, ex~cite, give rise to, produce, quicken, stir

inspired 1. brilliant, dazzling, en~thralling, exciting, impressive, memorable, of genius, outstanding, superlative, thrilling, wonderful 2. *Of a guess* instinctive, instinctual, intuitive 3. aroused, elated, en~thused, exalted, exhilarated, gal~vanized, possessed, stimulated, stirred up, uplifted

inspiring affecting, encouraging, exciting, exhilarating, heartening, moving, rousing, stimulating, stir~ring, uplifting

instability capriciousness, change~ableness, disequilibrium, fickle~ness, fitfulness, fluctuation, fluidity, frailty, imbalance, impermanence, inconstancy, insecurity, irresolu~tion, mutability, oscillation, pre~cariousness, restlessness, shaki~ness, transience, unpredictability,

unsteadiness, vacillation, variabil~ity, volatility, wavering, weakness

install, instal 1. fix, lay, lodge, place, position, put in, set up, sta~tion 2. establish, inaugurate, in~duct, instate, institute, introduce, invest, set up 3. ensconce, position, settle

installation 1. establishment, fit~ting, instalment, placing, position~ing, setting up 2. inauguration, in~duction, instatement, investiture 3. equipment, machinery, plant, sys~tem 4. *Military* base, establish~ment, post, station

instalment chapter, division, epi~sode, part, portion, repayment, section

instance *n.* 1. case, case in point, example, illustration, occasion, occurrence, precedent, situation, time 2. application, behest, de~mand, entreaty, importunity, im~pulse, incitement, insistence, insti~gation, pressure, prompting, re~quest, solicitation, urging ~*v.* 3. adduce, cite, mention, name, quote, specify

instant *n.* 1. flash, jiffy (*Inf.*), mo~ment, second, shake (*Inf.*), split second, tick (*Brit. inf.*), trice, twin~kling, twinkling of an eye (*Inf.*), two shakes of a lamb's tail (*Inf.*) 2. **on the instant** forthwith, immedi~ately, instantly, now, right away, without delay 3. juncture, moment, occasion, point, time ~*adj.* 4. di~rect, immediate, instantaneous, on-the-spot, prompt, quick, split-second, urgent 5. convenience, fast, precooked, ready-mixed 6. burning, exigent, imperative, im~portunate, pressing, urgent

instantaneous direct, immediate, instant, on-the-spot

instantaneously at once, forth~with, immediately, in a fraction of a second, instantly, in the same breath, in the twinkling of an eye (*Inf.*), like greased lightning (*Inf.*), on the instant, on the spot, promptly, quick as lightning, straight away, then and there

instantly at once, directly, forth~with, immediately, instantaneous~

ly, instanter (*Law*), now, on the spot, pronto (*Inf.*), right away, right now, straight away, there and then, this minute, *tout de suite*, without delay

instead 1. alternatively, in lieu, in preference, on second thoughts, preferably, rather 2. *With* **of** as an alternative *or* equivalent to, in lieu of, in place of, rather than

instigate actuate, bring about, encourage, foment, impel, incite, influence, initiate, kindle, move, persuade, prompt, provoke, rouse, set on, spur, start, stimulate, stir up, urge, whip up

instigation behest, bidding, encouragement, incentive, incitement, prompting, urging

instigator agitator, firebrand, fomenter, goad, incendiary, inciter, leader, mischief-maker, motivator, prime mover, ringleader, spur, troublemaker

instil, instill engender, engraft, imbue, implant, impress, inculcate, infix, infuse, insinuate, introduce

instinct aptitude, faculty, feeling, gift, gut feeling (*Inf.*), gut reaction (*Inf.*), impulse, intuition, knack, natural inclination, predisposition, proclivity, sixth sense, talent, tendency, urge

instinctive automatic, inborn, inherent, innate, instinctual, intuitional, intuitive, involuntary, mechanical, native, natural, reflex, spontaneous, unlearned, unpremeditated, unthinking, visceral

instinctively automatically, by instinct, intuitively, involuntarily, naturally, without thinking

institute[1] *v.* appoint, begin, bring into being, commence, constitute, enact, establish, fix, found, induct, initiate, install, introduce, invest, launch, ordain, organize, originate, pioneer, put into operation, set in motion, settle, set up, start

institute[2] *n.* 1. academy, association, college, conservatory, foundation, guild, institution, school, seat of learning, seminary, society 2. custom, decree, doctrine, dogma, edict, law, maxim, precedent,

precept, principle, regulation, rule, tenet

institution 1. constitution, creation, enactment, establishment, formation, foundation, initiation, introduction, investiture, investment, organization 2. academy, college, establishment, foundation, hospital, institute, school, seminary, society, university 3. convention, custom, fixture, law, practice, ritual, rule, tradition

institutional 1. accepted, bureaucratic, conventional, established, establishment (*Inf.*), formal, organized, orthodox, societal 2. cheerless, clinical, cold, drab, dreary, dull, forbidding, formal, impersonal, monotonous, regimented, routine, uniform, unwelcoming

instruct 1. bid, charge, command, direct, enjoin, order, tell 2. coach, discipline, drill, educate, enlighten, ground, guide, inform, school, teach, train, tutor 3. acquaint, advise, apprise, brief, counsel, inform, notify, tell

instruction 1. apprenticeship, coaching, discipline, drilling, education, enlightenment, grounding, guidance, information, lesson(s), preparation, schooling, teaching, training, tuition, tutelage 2. briefing, command, direction, directive, injunction, mandate, order, ruling

instructions advice, directions, guidance, information, key, orders, recommendations, rules

instructive cautionary, didactic, edifying, educational, enlightening, helpful, illuminating, informative, instructional, revealing, useful

instructor adviser, coach, demonstrator, exponent, guide, master, mentor, mistress, pedagogue, preceptor (*Rare*), schoolmaster, schoolmistress, teacher, trainer, tutor

instrument 1. apparatus, appliance, contraption (*Inf.*), contrivance, device, gadget, implement, mechanism, tool, utensil 2. agency, agent, channel, factor, force, means, mechanism, medium, organ, vehicle 3. *Inf.* cat's-paw, dupe, pawn, puppet, tool

instrumental active, assisting, auxiliary, conducive, contributory, helpful, helping, influential, involved, of help *or* service, subsidiary, useful

insubordinate contumacious, defiant, disobedient, disorderly, fractious, insurgent, mutinous, rebellious, recalcitrant, refractory, riotous, seditious, turbulent, undisciplined, ungovernable, unruly

insubordination defiance, disobedience, indiscipline, insurrection, mutinousness, mutiny, rebellion, recalcitrance, revolt, riotousness, sedition, ungovernability

insufferable detestable, dreadful, enough to test the patience of a saint, enough to try the patience of Job, impossible, insupportable, intolerable, more than flesh and blood can stand, outrageous, past bearing, too much, unbearable, unendurable, unspeakable

insufficient deficient, inadequate, incapable, incommensurate, incompetent, lacking, short, unfitted, unqualified

insular *Fig.* blinkered, circumscribed, closed, contracted, cut off, illiberal, inward-looking, isolated, limited, narrow, narrow-minded, parish-pump, parochial, petty, prejudiced, provincial

insulate *Fig.* close off, cocoon, cushion, cut off, isolate, protect, sequester, shield, wrap up in cotton wool

insult 1. *n.* abuse, affront, aspersion, contumely, indignity, insolence, offence, outrage, rudeness, slap in the face (*Inf.*), slight, snub 2. *v.* abuse, affront, call names, give offence to, injure, miscall (*Dialect*), offend, outrage, revile, slag (*Sl.*), slander, slight, snub

insulting abusive, affronting, contemptuous, degrading, disparaging, insolent, offensive, rude, scurrilous, slighting

insuperable impassable, insurmountable, invincible, unconquerable

insupportable 1. insufferable, intolerable, past bearing, unbearable, unendurable 2. indefensible, unjustifiable, untenable

insurance assurance, cover, coverage, guarantee, indemnification, indemnity, protection, provision, safeguard, security, something to fall back on (*Inf.*), warranty

insure assure, cover, guarantee, indemnify, underwrite, warrant

insurgent 1. *n.* insurrectionist, mutineer, rebel, resister, revolter, revolutionary, revolutionist, rioter 2. *adj.* disobedient, insubordinate, insurrectionary, mutinous, rebellious, revolting, revolutionary, riotous, seditious

insurmountable hopeless, impassable, impossible, insuperable, invincible, overwhelming, unconquerable

insurrection coup, insurgency, mutiny, putsch, rebellion, revolt, revolution, riot, rising, sedition, uprising

intact all in one piece, complete, entire, perfect, scatheless, sound, together, unbroken, undamaged, undefiled, unharmed, unhurt, unimpaired, uninjured, unscathed, untouched, unviolated, virgin, whole

integral 1. basic, component, constituent, elemental, essential, fundamental, indispensable, intrinsic, necessary, requisite 2. complete, entire, full, intact, undivided, whole

integrate accommodate, amalgamate, assimilate, blend, coalesce, combine, fuse, harmonize, incorporate, intermix, join, knit, merge, mesh, unite

integration amalgamation, assimilation, blending, combining, commingling, fusing, harmony, incorporation, mixing, unification

integrity 1. candour, goodness, honesty, honour, incorruptibility, principle, probity, purity, rectitude, righteousness, uprightness, virtue 2. coherence, cohesion, completeness, soundness, unity, wholeness

intellect 1. brains (*Inf.*), intelligence, judgment, mind, reason, sense, understanding 2. *Inf.* brain (*Inf.*), egghead (*Inf.*), genius, intellectual, intelligence, mind, thinker

intellectual 1. *adj.* bookish, cerebral, highbrow, intelligent, mental, rational, scholarly, studious, thoughtful 2. *n.* academic, egghead (*Inf.*), highbrow, thinker

intelligence 1. acumen, alertness, aptitude, brain power, brains (*Inf.*), brightness, capacity, cleverness, comprehension, discernment, grey matter (*Inf.*), intellect, mind, nous (*Brit. sl.*), penetration, perception, quickness, reason, understanding 2. advice, data, disclosure, facts, findings, gen (*Inf.*), information, knowledge, low-down (*Inf.*), news, notice, notification, report, rumour, tidings, tip-off, word

intelligent acute, alert, apt, brainy (*Inf.*), bright, clever, discerning, enlightened, instructed, knowing, penetrating, perspicacious, quick, quick-witted, rational, sharp, smart, thinking, well-informed

intelligentsia eggheads (*Inf.*), highbrows, illuminati, intellectuals, literati, masterminds, the learned

intelligibility clarity, clearness, comprehensibility, distinctness, explicitness, lucidity, plainness, precision, simplicity

intelligible clear, comprehensible, distinct, lucid, open, plain, understandable

intemperate excessive, extravagant, extreme, immoderate, incontinent, inordinate, intoxicated, passionate, prodigal, profligate, self-indulgent, severe, tempestuous, unbridled, uncontrollable, ungovernable, unrestrained, violent, wild

intend 1. aim, be resolved *or* determined, contemplate, determine, have in mind *or* view, mean, meditate, plan, propose, purpose, scheme 2. *Often with* for aim, consign, design, destine, earmark, mark out, mean, set apart

intense 1. acute, agonizing, close, concentrated, deep, excessive, exquisite, extreme, fierce, forceful, great, harsh, intensive, powerful, profound, protracted, severe, strained 2. ardent, burning, consuming, eager, earnest, energetic, fanatical, fervent, fervid, fierce, forcible, heightened, impassioned, keen, passionate, speaking, vehement

intensely deeply, extremely, fiercely, passionately, profoundly, strongly

intensify add fuel to the flames (*Inf.*), add to, aggravate, boost, concentrate, deepen, emphasize, enhance, escalate, exacerbate, heighten, increase, magnify, quicken, redouble, reinforce, set off, sharpen, step up (*Inf.*), strengthen, whet

intensity ardour, concentration, depth, earnestness, emotion, energy, excess, extremity, fanaticism, fervency, fervour, fierceness, fire, force, intenseness, keenness, passion, potency, power, severity, strain, strength, tension, vehemence, vigour

intensive all-out, comprehensive, concentrated, demanding, exhaustive, in-depth, thorough, thoroughgoing

intent *adj.* 1. absorbed, alert, attentive, committed, concentrated, determined, eager, earnest, engrossed, fixed, industrious, intense, occupied, piercing, preoccupied, rapt, resolute, resolved, steadfast, steady, watchful, wrapped up 2. bent, hellbent (*Inf.*), set ~*n.* 3. aim, design, end, goal, intention, meaning, object, objective, plan, purpose 4. **to all intents and purposes** as good as, practically, virtually

intention aim, design, end, end in view, goal, idea, intent, meaning, object, objective, point, purpose, scope, target, view

intentional calculated, deliberate, designed, done on purpose, intended, meant, planned, prearranged, preconcerted, premeditated, purposed, studied, wilful

intentionally by design, deliberately, designedly, on purpose, wilfully

intently attentively, closely, fixedly, hard, keenly, searchingly, steadily, watchfully

inter bury, entomb, inhume, inurn, lay to rest, sepulchre

intercede advocate, arbitrate, interpose, intervene, mediate, plead, speak

intercept arrest, block, catch, check, cut off, deflect, head off, interrupt, obstruct, seize, stop, take

intercession advocacy, entreaty, good offices, intervention, mediation, plea, pleading, prayer, solicitation, supplication

interchange 1. *v.* alternate, bandy, barter, exchange, reciprocate, swap (*Inf.*), switch, trade 2. *n.* alternation, crossfire, exchange, give and take, intersection, junction, reciprocation

interchangeable commutable, equivalent, exchangeable, identical, reciprocal, synonymous, the same, transposable

intercourse 1. association, commerce, communication, communion, connection, contact, converse, correspondence, dealings, intercommunication, trade, traffic, truck 2. carnal knowledge, coition, coitus, congress, copulation, intimacy, sex (*Inf.*), sexual act, sexual intercourse, sexual relations

interest *n.* 1. affection, attention, attentiveness, attraction, concern, curiosity, notice, regard, suspicion, sympathy 2. concern, consequence, importance, moment, note, relevance, significance, weight 3. activity, diversion, hobby, leisure activity, pastime, preoccupation, pursuit, relaxation 4. advantage, benefit, gain, good, profit 5. **in the interest of** for the sake of, on behalf of, on the part of, profitable to, to the advantage of 6. authority, claim, commitment, influence, investment, involvement, participation, portion, right, share, stake 7. *Often plural* affair, business, care, concern, matter ~*v.* 8. amuse, arouse one's curiosity, attract, divert, engross, fascinate, hold the attention of, intrigue, move, touch 9. affect, concern, engage, involve

interested 1. affected, attentive, attracted, curious, drawn, excited, fascinated, intent, keen, moved, responsive, stimulated 2. biased, concerned, implicated, involved, partial, partisan, predisposed, prejudiced

interesting absorbing, amusing, appealing, attractive, compelling, curious, engaging, engrossing, entertaining, gripping, intriguing, pleasing, provocative, stimulating, suspicious, thought-provoking, unusual

interfere 1. butt in, get involved, intermeddle, intervene, intrude, meddle, poke one's nose in (*Inf.*), stick one's oar in (*Inf.*), tamper 2. *Often with* with be a drag upon (*Sl.*), block, clash, collide, conflict, cramp, frustrate, get in the way of, hamper, handicap, hinder, impede, inhibit, obstruct, trammel

interference 1. intermeddling, intervention, intrusion, meddlesomeness, meddling, prying 2. clashing, collision, conflict, impedance, obstruction, opposition

interim 1. *adj.* acting, caretaker, improvised, intervening, makeshift, pro tem, provisional, stopgap, temporary 2. *n.* interregnum, interval, meantime, meanwhile

interior *adj.* 1. inner, inside, internal, inward 2. *Geog.* central, inland, remote, upcountry 3. *Politics* domestic, home 4. hidden, inner, intimate, mental, personal, private, secret, spiritual ~*n.* 5. bosom, centre, contents, core, heart, innards (*Inf.*), inside 6. *Geog.* centre, heartland, upcountry

interjection cry, ejaculation, exclamation, interpolation, interposition

interloper gate-crasher (*Inf.*), intermeddler, intruder, meddler, trespasser, uninvited guest, unwanted visitor

interlude break, breathing space, delay, episode, halt, hiatus, intermission, interval, pause, respite, rest, spell, stop, stoppage, wait

intermediary n. agent, broker, entrepreneur, go-between, mediator, middleman

intermediate halfway, in-between (Inf.), intermediary, interposed, intervening, mean, mid, middle, midway, transitional

interment burial, burying, funeral, inhumation, sepulture

interminable boundless, ceaseless, dragging, endless, everlasting, immeasurable, infinite, limitless, long, long-drawn-out, long-winded, never-ending, perpetual, protracted, unbounded, unlimited, wearisome

intermingle amalgamate, blend, combine, commingle, commix, fuse, interlace, intermix, interweave, merge, mix

intermission break, cessation, entr'acte, interlude, interruption, interval, let-up (Inf.), lull, pause, recess, respite, rest, stop, stoppage, suspense, suspension

intermittent broken, discontinuous, fitful, irregular, occasional, periodic, punctuated, recurrent, recurring, spasmodic, sporadic, stop-go (Inf.)

intern confine, detain, hold, hold in custody

internal 1. inner, inside, interior, intimate, private, subjective 2. civic, domestic, home, in-house, intramural

international cosmopolitan, ecumenical (Rare), global, intercontinental, universal, worldwide

interpolate add, insert, intercalate, introduce

interpolation addition, aside, insert, insertion, intercalation, interjection, introduction

interpose 1. come or place between, intercede, interfere, intermediate, intervene, intrude, step in 2. insert, interject, interrupt (with), introduce, put forth

interpret adapt, clarify, construe, decipher, decode, define, elucidate, explain, explicate, expound, make sense of, paraphrase, read, render, solve, spell out, take, throw light on, translate, understand

interpretation analysis, clarification, construction, diagnosis, elucidation, exegesis, explanation, explication, exposition, meaning, performance, portrayal, reading, rendering, rendition, sense, signification, translation, understanding, version

interpreter annotator, commentator, exponent, scholiast, translator

interrogate ask, catechize, cross-examine, cross-question, enquire, examine, give (someone) the third degree (Inf.), grill (Inf.), inquire, investigate, pump, put the screws on (Inf.), question, quiz

interrogation cross-examination, cross-questioning, enquiry, examination, grilling (Inf.), inquiry, inquisition, probing, questioning, third degree (Inf.)

interrogative curious, inquiring, inquisitive, inquisitorial, questioning, quizzical

interrupt barge in (Inf.), break, break in, break off, break (someone's) train of thought, butt in, check, cut, cut off, cut short, delay, disconnect, discontinue, disjoin, disturb, disunite, divide, heckle, hinder, hold up, interfere (with), intrude, lay aside, obstruct, punctuate, separate, sever, stay, stop, suspend

interrupted broken, cut off, disconnected, discontinuous, disturbed, incomplete, intermittent, uneven

interruption break, cessation, disconnection, discontinuance, disruption, dissolution, disturbance, disuniting, division, halt, hiatus, hindrance, hitch, impediment, intrusion, obstacle, obstruction, pause, separation, severance, stop, stoppage, suspension

intersect bisect, crisscross, cross, cut, cut across, divide, meet

intersection crossing, crossroads, interchange, junction

interval break, delay, distance, gap, hiatus, interim, interlude, intermission, meantime, meanwhile, opening, pause, period, playtime, rest, season, space, spell, term, time, wait

intervene 1. arbitrate, intercede, interfere, interpose oneself, intrude, involve oneself, mediate, step in (*Inf.*), take a hand (*Inf.*) 2. befall, come to pass, ensue, happen, occur, succeed, supervene, take place

intervention agency, intercession, interference, interposition, intrusion, mediation

interview 1. *n.* audience, conference, consultation, dialogue, evaluation, meeting, oral (examination), press conference, talk 2. *v.* examine, interrogate, question, sound out, talk to

interviewer examiner, interlocutor, interrogator, investigator, questioner, reporter

interwoven blended, connected, entwined, inmixed, interconnected, interlaced, interlocked, intermingled, knit

intestinal abdominal, coeliac, duodenal, gut (*Inf.*), inner, stomachic, visceral

intestines bowels, entrails, guts, innards (*Inf.*), insides (*Inf.*), internal organs, viscera, vitals

intimacy closeness, confidence, confidentiality, familiarity, fraternization, understanding

intimate[1] *adj.* 1. bosom, cherished, close, confidential, dear, friendly, near, nearest and dearest, thick (*Inf.*), warm 2. confidential, personal, private, privy, secret 3. deep, detailed, exhaustive, experienced, first-hand, immediate, in-depth, penetrating, personal, profound, thorough 4. comfy (*Inf.*), cosy, friendly, informal, snug, tête-à-tête, warm ~*n.* 5. bosom friend, buddy (*Inf.*), china (*Brit. sl.*), chum (*Inf.*), close friend, comrade, confidant, confidante, (constant) companion, crony, familiar, friend, mate (*Inf.*), mucker (*Brit. sl.*), pal

intimate[2] *v.* allude, announce, communicate, declare, drop a hint, give (someone) to understand, hint, impart, imply, indicate, insinuate, let it be known, make

known, remind, state, suggest, tip (someone) the wink (*Brit. inf.*), warn

intimately 1. affectionately, closely, confidentially, confidingly, familiarly, personally, tenderly, very well, warmly 2. fully, in detail, inside out, thoroughly, through and through, to the core, very well

intimation 1. allusion, hint, indication, inkling, insinuation, reminder, suggestion, warning 2. announcement, communication, declaration, notice

intimidate affright (*Archaic*), alarm, appal, browbeat, bully, coerce, cow, daunt, dishearten, dismay, dispirit, frighten, lean on (*Inf.*), overawe, scare, scare off (*Inf.*), subdue, terrify, terrorize, threaten, twist someone's arm (*Inf.*)

intimidation arm-twisting (*Inf.*), browbeating, bullying, coercion, fear, menaces, pressure, terror, terrorization, threat(s)

intolerable beyond bearing, excruciating, impossible, insufferable, insupportable, more than flesh and blood can stand, not to be borne, painful, unbearable, unendurable

intolerance bigotry, chauvinism, discrimination, dogmatism, fanaticism, illiberality, impatience, jingoism, narrow-mindedness, narrowness, prejudice, racialism, racism, xenophobia

intolerant bigoted, chauvinistic, dictatorial, dogmatic, fanatical, illiberal, impatient, narrow, narrow-minded, one-sided, prejudiced, racialist, racist, small-minded, uncharitable, xenophobic

intone chant, croon, intonate, recite, sing

intoxicate 1. addle, befuddle, fuddle, go to one's head, inebriate, put (someone) under the table (*Inf.*), stupefy 2. *Fig.* elate, excite, exhilarate, inflame, make one's head spin, stimulate

intoxicated 1. blotto (*Sl.*), canned (*Sl.*), cut (*Brit. sl.*), drunk, drunken, fuddled, half seas over (*Brit. inf.*), high (*Inf.*), inebriated, in one's cups (*Inf.*), lit up (*Sl.*), plastered (*Sl.*), smashed (*Sl.*), sozzled (*Inf.*), stewed (*Sl.*), stiff (*Sl.*), stoned (*Sl.*), the worse for drink, three sheets in the wind (*Inf.*), tight (*Inf.*), tipsy, under the influence 2. *Fig.* dizzy, elated, enraptured, euphoric, excited, ex~ hilarated, high (*Inf.*), infatuated, sent (*Sl.*), stimulated

intoxicating 1. alcoholic, inebriant, intoxicant, spirituous, strong 2. *Fig.* exciting, exhilarating, heady, stimulating, thrilling

intoxication 1. drunkenness, in~ ebriation, inebriety, insobriety, tipsiness 2. *Fig.* delirium, elation, euphoria, exaltation, excitement, exhilaration, infatuation

intransigent hardline, immovable, intractable, obdurate, obstinate, stubborn, tenacious, tough, un~ bending, unbudgeable, uncompro~ mising, unyielding

intrepid audacious, bold, brave, courageous, daring, dauntless, doughty, fearless, gallant, game (*Inf.*), heroic, lion-hearted, nerve~ less, plucky, resolute, stalwart, stouthearted, unafraid, undaunted, unflinching, valiant, valorous

intricacy complexity, complica~ tion, convolutions, elaborateness, entanglement, intricateness, invo~ lution, involvement, knottiness, obscurity

intricate baroque, Byzantine, com~ plex, complicated, convoluted, daedal (*Literary*), difficult, elabo~ rate, fancy, involved, knotty, laby~ rinthine, obscure, perplexing, ro~ coco, sophisticated, tangled, tortu~ ous

intrigue *v.* 1. arouse the curiosity of, attract, charm, fascinate, inter~ est, pique, rivet, tickle one's fancy, titillate 2. connive, conspire, machinate, manoeuvre, plot, scheme ~*n.* 3. cabal, chicanery, collusion, conspiracy, double-dealing, knavery, machination, manipulation, manoeuvre, plot, ruse, scheme, sharp practice, stratagem, trickery, wile 4. affair, amour, intimacy, liaison, romance

intriguing beguiling, compelling, diverting, exciting, fascinating, in~ teresting, tantalizing, titillating

intrinsic basic, built-in, central, congenital, constitutional, el~ emental, essential, fundamental, genuine, inborn, inbred, inherent, native, natural, real, true, underly~ ing

introduce 1. acquaint, do the hon~ ours, familiarize, make known, make the introduction, present 2. begin, bring in, commence, estab~ lish, found, inaugurate, initiate, in~ stitute, launch, organize, pioneer, set up, start, usher in 3. advance, air, bring up, broach, moot, offer, propose, put forward, recommend, set forth, submit, suggest, ventilate 4. announce, lead into, lead off, open, preface 5. add, inject, insert, interpolate, interpose, put in, throw in (*Inf.*)

introduction 1. baptism, debut, es~ tablishment, first acquaintance, inauguration, induction, initiation, institution, launch, pioneering, presentation 2. commencement, exordium, foreword, intro (*Inf.*), lead-in, opening, opening passage, opening remarks, overture, pre~ amble, preface, preliminaries, prelude, proem, prolegomena, prolegomenon, prologue 3. addi~ tion, insertion, interpolation

introductory early, elementary, first, inaugural, initial, initiatory, opening, precursory, prefatory, preliminary, preparatory, starting

introspective brooding, contem~ plative, inner-directed, introverted, inward-looking, meditative, pen~ sive, subjective

introverted indrawn, inner-directed, introspective, inward-looking, self-centred, self-contained, withdrawn

intrude butt in, encroach, infringe, interfere, interrupt, meddle, ob~ trude, push in, thrust oneself in *or* forward, trespass, violate

intruder burglar, gate-crasher (*Inf.*), infiltrator, interloper, invad~ er, prowler, raider, snooper (*Inf.*), squatter, thief, trespasser

intrusion encroachment, infringement, interference, interruption, invasion, trespass, violation

intrusive disturbing, forward, impertinent, importunate, interfering, invasive, meddlesome, nosy (*Inf.*), officious, presumptuous, pushy (*Inf.*), uncalled-for, unwanted

intuition discernment, hunch, insight, instinct, perception, presentiment, sixth sense

intuitive innate, instinctive, instinctual, involuntary, spontaneous, unreflecting, untaught

inundate deluge, drown, engulf, flood, glut, immerse, overflow, overrun, overwhelm, submerge, swamp

invade 1. assail, assault, attack, burst in, descend upon, encroach, infringe, make inroads, occupy, raid, violate 2. infect, infest, overrun, overspread, penetrate, permeate, pervade, swarm over

invader aggressor, alien, attacker, looter, plunderer, raider, trespasser

invalid¹ 1. *adj.* ailing, bedridden, disabled, feeble, frail, ill, infirm, poorly (*Inf.*), sick, sickly, valetudinarian, weak 2. *n.* convalescent, patient, valetudinarian

invalid² *adj.* baseless, fallacious, false, ill-founded, illogical, inoperative, irrational, not binding, nugatory, null, null and void, unfounded, unscientific, unsound, untrue, void, worthless

invalidate abrogate, annul, cancel, nullify, overrule, overthrow, quash, render null and void, rescind, undermine, undo, weaken

invaluable beyond price, costly, inestimable, precious, priceless, valuable

invariable changeless, consistent, constant, fixed, immutable, inflexible, regular, rigid, set, unalterable, unchangeable, unchanging, unfailing, uniform, unvarying, unwavering

invariably always, consistently, customarily, day in, day out, ever, every time, habitually, inevitably, on every occasion, perpetually, regularly, unfailingly, without exception

invasion 1. aggression, assault, attack, foray, incursion, inroad, irruption, offensive, onslaught, raid 2. breach, encroachment, infiltration, infraction, infringement, intrusion, overstepping, usurpation, violation

invective abuse, berating, billingsgate, castigation, censure, contumely, denunciation, diatribe, obloquy, philippic(s), reproach, revilement, sarcasm, tirade, tonguelashing, vilification, vituperation

invent 1. coin, come up with (*Inf.*), conceive, contrive, create, design, devise, discover, dream up (*Inf.*), formulate, imagine, improvise, originate, think up 2. concoct, cook up (*Inf.*), fabricate, feign, forge, make up, trump up

invention 1. brainchild (*Inf.*), contraption, contrivance, creation, design, development, device, discovery, gadget 2. coinage, creativeness, creativity, genius, imagination, ingenuity, inspiration, inventiveness, originality, resourcefulness 3. deceit, fabrication, fake, falsehood, fantasy, fib (*Inf.*), fiction, figment or product of (someone's) imagination, forgery, lie, prevarication, sham, story, tall story (*Inf.*), untruth, yarn

inventive creative, fertile, gifted, imaginative, ingenious, innovative, inspired, original, resourceful

inventor architect, author, coiner, creator, designer, father, framer, maker, originator

inventory *n.* account, catalogue, file, list, record, register, roll, roster, schedule, stock book

inverse *adj.* contrary, converse, inverted, opposite, reverse, reversed, transposed

inversion antipode, antithesis, contraposition, contrariety, contrary, opposite, reversal, transposal, transposition

invert capsize, introvert, intussuscept (*Pathol.*), invaginate (*Pathol.*), overset, overturn, reverse, transpose, turn inside out, turn turtle, turn upside down, upset, upturn

invest 1. advance, devote, lay out, put in, sink, spend 2. endow, endue, provide, supply 3. authorize, charge, empower, license, sanction, vest 4. adopt, consecrate, enthrone, establish, inaugurate, induct, install, ordain 5. *Mil.* beleaguer, beset, besiege, enclose, lay siege to, surround 6. *Archaic* array, bedeck, bedizen (*Archaic*), clothe, deck, drape, dress, robe

investigate consider, enquire into, examine, explore, go into, inquire into, inspect, look into, make enquiries, probe, put to the test, scrutinize, search, sift, study

investigation analysis, enquiry, examination, exploration, fact finding, hearing, inquest, inquiry, inspection, probe, research, review, scrutiny, search, study, survey

investigator dick (*Sl.*), examiner, gumshoe (*U.S. sl.*), inquirer, (private) detective, private eye (*Inf.*), researcher, reviewer, sleuth or sleuthhound (*Inf.*)

investiture admission, enthronement, inauguration, induction, installation, instatement, investing, investment, ordination

investment 1. asset, investing, speculation, transaction, venture 2. ante (*Inf.*), contribution, stake 3. *Mil.* beleaguering, besieging, blockading, siege, surrounding

inveterate chronic, confirmed, deep-dyed, deep-rooted, deep-seated, dyed-in-the-wool, entrenched, established, habitual, hard-core, hardened, incorrigible, incurable, ineradicable, ingrained, long-standing, obstinate

invidious discriminatory, envious (*Obsolete*), hateful, obnoxious, odious, offensive, repugnant, slighting, undesirable

invigorate animate, brace, buck up (*Inf.*), energize, enliven, exhilarate, fortify, freshen (up), galvanize, harden, liven up, nerve, pep up, perk up, put new heart into, quick-

en, refresh, rejuvenate, revitalize, stimulate, strengthen

invincible impregnable, indestructible, indomitable, inseparable, insuperable, invulnerable, unassailable, unbeatable, unconquerable, unsurmountable, unyielding

inviolable hallowed, holy, inalienable, sacred, sacrosanct, unalterable

inviolate entire, intact, pure, sacred, stainless, unbroken, undefiled, undisturbed, unhurt, unpolluted, unstained, unsullied, untouched, virgin, whole

invisible 1. imperceptible, indiscernible, out of sight, unperceivable, unseen 2. concealed, disguised, hidden, inappreciable, inconspicuous, infinitesimal, microscopic

invitation 1. asking, begging, bidding, call, invite (*Inf.*), request, solicitation, summons, supplication 2. allurement, challenge, come-on (*Inf.*), coquetry, enticement, glad eye (*Inf.*), incitement, inducement, open door, overture, provocation, temptation

invite 1. ask, beg, bid, call, request, request the pleasure of (someone's) company, solicit, summon 2. allure, ask for (*Inf.*), attract, bring on, court, draw, encourage, entice, lead, leave the door open to, provoke, solicit, tempt, welcome

inviting alluring, appealing, attractive, beguiling, captivating, delightful, engaging, enticing, fascinating, intriguing, magnetic, mouthwatering, pleasing, seductive, tempting, warm, welcoming, winning

invocation appeal, beseeching, entreaty, petition, prayer, supplication

invoke 1. adjure, appeal to, beg, beseech, call upon, conjure, entreat, implore, petition, pray, solicit, supplicate 2. apply, call in, have recourse to, implement, initiate, put into effect, resort to, use

involuntary 1. compulsory, forced, obligatory, reluctant, unwilling 2.

automatic, blind, conditioned, in~
stinctual, instinctive, reflex, spon~
taneous, unconscious, uncon~
trolled, unintentional, unthinking

involve 1. entail, imply, mean, ne~
cessitate, presuppose, require 2.
affect, associate, compromise,
concern, connect, draw in, impli~
cate, incriminate, inculpate, mix
up (*Inf.*), touch 3. comprehend,
comprise, contain, cover, em~
brace, include, incorporate, num~
ber among, take in 4. absorb, bind,
commit, engage, engross, grip,
hold, preoccupy, rivet, wrap up 5.
complicate, embroil, enmesh, en~
tangle, link, mire, mix up, snarl up,
tangle

involved 1. Byzantine, complex,
complicated, confusing, convolut~
ed, difficult, elaborate, intricate,
knotty, labyrinthine, sophisticated,
tangled, tortuous 2. caught (up),
concerned, implicated, in on (*Inf.*),
mixed up in *or* with, occupied,
participating, taking part

involvement 1. association, com~
mitment, concern, connection,
dedication, interest, participation,
responsibility 2. complexity, com~
plication, difficulty, embarrass~
ment, entanglement, imbroglio,
intricacy, problem, ramification

invulnerable impenetrable, inde~
structible, insusceptible, invincible,
proof against, safe, secure, unas~
sailable

inward *adj.* 1. entering, inbound,
incoming, inflowing, ingoing, in~
pouring, penetrating 2. confiden~
tial, hidden, inmost, inner, inner~
most, inside, interior, internal,
personal, private, privy, secret

inwardly at heart, deep down, in
one's head, in one's inmost heart,
inside, privately, secretly, to one~
self, within

Irish Hibernian

irksome annoying, boring, bother~
some, burdensome, disagreeable,
exasperating, irritating, tedious,
tiresome, troublesome, uninterest~
ing, unwelcome, vexatious, vexing,
wearisome

iron *adj.* 1. chalybeate, ferric, fer~

rous, irony 2. *Fig.* adamant, cruel,
hard, heavy, immovable, implac~
able, indomitable, inflexible, obdu~
rate, rigid, robust, steel, steely,
strong, tough, unbending, unyield~
ing

ironic, ironical 1. double-edged,
mocking, sarcastic, sardonic, sa~
tirical, scoffing, sneering, wry 2.
incongruous, paradoxical

iron out clear up, eliminate, eradi~
cate, erase, expedite, get rid of,
harmonize, put right, reconcile,
resolve, settle, simplify, smooth
over, sort out, straighten out, un~
ravel

irons bonds, chains, fetters, gyves
(*Archaic*), manacles, shackles

irony 1. mockery, sarcasm, satire 2.
contrariness, incongruity, paradox

irrational 1. absurd, crazy, foolish,
illogical, injudicious, nonsensical,
preposterous, silly, unreasonable,
unreasoning, unsound, unthinking,
unwise 2. aberrant, brainless, cra~
zy, demented, insane, mindless,
muddle-headed, raving, senseless,
unstable, wild

irrationality absurdity, brainless~
ness, illogicality, insanity, lack of
judgment, lunacy, madness, pre~
posterousness, senselessness, un~
reasonableness, unsoundness

irreconcilable 1. hardline, implac~
able, inexorable, inflexible, intran~
sigent, unappeasable, uncompro~
mising 2. clashing, conflicting, dia~
metrically opposed, incompatible,
incongruous, inconsistent, opposed

irrecoverable gone for ever, irre~
claimable, irredeemable, irre~
mediable, irreparable, irretriev~
able, lost, unregainable, unsal~
vageable, unsavable

irrefutable apodeictic, apodictic,
beyond question, certain, incon~
testable, incontrovertible, indis~
putable, indubitable, invincible, ir~
refragable, irresistible, sure, unan~
swerable, unassailable, undeniable,
unquestionable

irregular *adj.* 1. desultory, discon~
nected, eccentric, erratic, fitful,
fluctuating, fragmentary, haphaz~
ard, intermittent, nonuniform, oc~

casional, out of order, patchy, ran~
dom, shifting, spasmodic, sporadic,
uncertain, unmethodical, unpunc~
tual, unsteady, unsystematic, vari~
able, wavering 2. abnormal,
anomalous, capricious, disorderly,
eccentric, exceptional, extraordi~
nary, immoderate, improper, in~
appropriate, inordinate, odd, pecu~
liar, queer, quirky, unconventional,
unofficial, unorthodox, unsuitable,
unusual 3. asymmetrical, broken,
bumpy, craggy, crooked, elliptic,
elliptical, holey, jagged, lopsided,
lumpy, pitted, ragged, rough, ser~
rated, unequal, uneven, unsym~
metrical ~n. 4. guerrilla, partisan,
volunteer

irregularity 1. asymmetry, bumpi~
ness, crookedness, jaggedness,
lack of symmetry, lopsidedness,
lumpiness, patchiness, raggedness,
roughness, unevenness 2. aberra~
tion, abnormality, anomaly,
breach, deviation, eccentricity,
freak, malfunction, malpractice,
oddity, peculiarity, singularity, un~
conventionality, unorthodoxy 3.
confusion, desultoriness, disorder~
liness, disorganization, haphazard~
ness, lack of method, randomness,
uncertainty, unpunctuality, un~
steadiness

irrelevance, irrelevancy inappo~
siteness, inappropriateness, inapt~
ness, inconsequence, non sequitur

irrelevant beside the point, extra~
neous, immaterial, impertinent,
inapplicable, inapposite, inappro~
priate, inapt, inconsequent, neither
here nor there, unconnected, un~
related

irreparable beyond repair, incur~
able, irrecoverable, irremediable,
irreplaceable, irretrievable, irre~
versible

irreplaceable indispensable, in~
valuable, priceless, unique, vital

irrepressible boisterous, bubbling
over, buoyant, ebullient, efferves~
cent, insuppressible, uncontain~
able, uncontrollable, unmanage~
able, unquenchable, unrestrain~
able, unstoppable

irreproachable beyond reproach,

blameless, faultless, guiltless, im~
peccable, inculpable, innocent, ir~
reprehensible, irreprovable, per~
fect, pure, unblemished, unim~
peachable

irresistible 1. compelling, impera~
tive, overmastering, overpowering,
overwhelming, potent, urgent 2.
ineluctable, inescapable, inevi~
table, inexorable, unavoidable 3.
alluring, beckoning, enchanting,
fascinating, ravishing, seductive,
tempting

irresolute doubtful, fickle, half~
hearted, hesitant, hesitating, inde~
cisive, infirm, in two minds, tenta~
tive, undecided, undetermined, un~
settled, unstable, unsteady, vacil~
lating, wavering, weak

irrespective of apart from, de~
spite, discounting, in spite of, not~
withstanding, regardless of, with~
out reference to, without regard to

irresponsible careless, feather~
brained, flighty, giddy, hare~
brained, harum-scarum, ill~
considered, immature, reckless,
scatter-brained, shiftless, thought~
less, undependable, unreliable, un~
trustworthy, wild

irreverence cheek (*Inf.*), cheeki~
ness (*Inf.*), derision, disrespect,
flippancy, impertinence, impu~
dence, lack of respect, mockery,
sauce (*Inf.*)

irreverent cheeky (*Inf.*), contemp~
tuous, derisive, disrespectful, flip
(*Inf.*), flippant, iconoclastic, im~
pertinent, impious, impudent,
mocking, saucy, tongue-in-cheek

irreversible final, incurable, ir~
reparable, irrevocable, unalterable

irrevocable changeless, fated,
fixed, immutable, invariable, irre~
mediable, irretrievable, irrevers~
ible, predestined, predetermined,
settled, unalterable, unchangeable,
unreversible

irrigate flood, inundate, moisten,
water, wet

irritability bad temper, ill humour,
impatience, irascibility, peevish~
ness, petulance, prickliness, testi~
ness, tetchiness, touchiness

irritable bad-tempered, cantanker~

lous, envious, green, green-eyed, grudging, intolerant, invidious, resentful, rival 2. anxious, apprehensive, attentive, guarded, mistrustful, protective, solicitous, suspicious, vigilant, wary, watchful, zealous

jealousy covetousness, distrust, envy, heart-burning, ill-will, mistrust, possessiveness, resentment, spite, suspicion

jeer 1. *v.* banter, barrack, cock a snook at (*Brit.*), contemn, deride, flout, gibe, heckle, hector, knock (*Sl.*), mock, ridicule, scoff, sneer, taunt 2. *n.* abuse, aspersion, catcall, derision, gibe, hiss, hoot, obloquy, ridicule, scoff, sneer, taunt

jeopardize chance, endanger, expose, gamble, hazard, imperil, risk, stake, venture

jeopardy danger, endangerment, exposure, hazard, insecurity, liability, peril, precariousness, risk, venture, vulnerability

jeremiad complaint, groan, keen, lament, lamentation, moan, plaint, wail

jerk *v./n.* jolt, lurch, pull, throw, thrust, tug, tweak, twitch, wrench, yank

jerky bouncy, bumpy, convulsive, fitful, jolting, jumpy, rough, shaky, spasmodic, tremulous, twitchy, uncontrolled

jerry-built cheap, defective, faulty, flimsy, ramshackle, rickety, shabby, slipshod, thrown together, unsubstantial

jest 1. *n.* banter, bon mot, crack (*Sl.*), fun, gag (*Sl.*), hoax, jape, joke, play, pleasantry, prank, quip, sally, sport, wisecrack (*Inf.*), witticism 2. *v.* banter, chaff, deride, gibe, jeer, joke, kid (*Inf.*), mock, quip, scoff, sneer, tease

jester 1. comedian, comic, humorist, joker, quipster, wag, wit 2. buffoon, clown, fool, harlequin, madcap, mummer, pantaloon, prankster, zany

jet¹ black, coal-black, ebony, inky, pitch-black, raven, sable

jet² *n.* 1. flow, fountain, gush, spout, spray, spring, stream 2. atomizer,

nose, nozzle, rose, spout, sprayer, sprinkler ~*v.* 3. flow, gush, issue, rush, shoot, spew, spout, squirt, stream, surge 4. fly, soar, zoom

jettison abandon, discard, dump, eject, expel, heave, scrap, throw overboard, unload

jetty breakwater, dock, groyne, mole, pier, quay, wharf

jewel 1. brilliant, gemstone, ornament, precious stone, rock (*Sl.*), sparkler (*Inf.*), trinket 2. charm, find, gem, humdinger (*Sl.*), masterpiece, paragon, pearl, prize, rarity, treasure (*Fig.*), wonder

jewellery finery, gems, jewels, ornaments, precious stones, regalia, treasure, trinkets

Jezebel harlot, harridan, hussy, jade, virago, wanton, witch

jib balk, recoil, refuse, retreat, shrink, stop short

jig *v.* bob, bounce, caper, jiggle, jounce, prance, shake, skip, twitch, wiggle, wobble

jingle *v.* 1. chime, clatter, clink, jangle, rattle, ring, tinkle, tintinnabulate ~*n.* 2. clang, clangour, clink, rattle, reverberation, ringing, tinkle 3. chorus, ditty, doggerel, limerick, melody, song, tune

jinx 1. *n.* black magic, curse, evil eye, hex (*U.S.*), nemesis, plague, voodoo 2. *v.* bewitch, curse, hex (*U.S.*)

jitters anxiety, fidgets, nerves, nervousness, tenseness, the shakes (*Inf.*), the willies (*Inf.*)

jittery agitated, anxious, fidgety, jumpy, nervous, quivering, shaky, trembling

job 1. affair, assignment, charge, chore, concern, contribution, duty, enterprise, errand, function, pursuit, responsibility, role, stint, task, undertaking, venture, work 2. activity, business, calling, capacity, career, craft, employment, function, livelihood, métier, occupation, office, position, post, profession, situation, trade, vocation 3. allotment, assignment, batch, commission, consignment, contract, lot, output, piece, portion, product, share

jobless idle, inactive, out of work, unemployed, unoccupied

jockey 1. bamboozle, cheat, con (*Sl.*), deceive, dupe, fool, hoax, hoodwink, trick 2. cajole, engineer, finagle (*Inf.*), ingratiate, insinuate, manage, manipulate, manoeuvre, negotiate, trim, wheedle

jocular amusing, comical, droll, facetious, frolicsome, funny, humorous, jesting, jocose, jocund, joking, jolly, jovial, playful, roguish, sportive, teasing, waggish, whimsical, witty

jog 1. activate, arouse, nudge, prod, prompt, push, remind, shake, stimulate, stir, suggest 2. bounce, jar, jerk, jiggle, joggle, jolt, jostle, jounce, rock, run, shake 3. canter, dogtrot, lope, run, trot 4. lumber, plod, traipse (*Inf.*), tramp, trudge

joie de vivre ebullience, enjoyment, enthusiasm, gaiety, gusto, joy, joyfulness, pleasure, relish, zest

join 1. accompany, add, adhere, annex, append, attack, cement, combine, connect, couple, fasten, knit, link, marry, splice, tie, unite, yoke 2. affiliate with, associate with, enlist, enrol, enter, sign up 3. adjoin, border, border on, butt, conjoin, extend, meet, reach, touch, verge on

joint *n.* 1. articulation, connection, hinge, intersection, junction, juncture, knot, nexus, node, seam, union ~*adj.* 2. collective, combined, communal, concerted, consolidated, cooperative, joined, mutual, shared, united ~*v.* 3. connect, couple, fasten, fit, join, unite 4. carve, cut up, dismember, dissect, divide, segment, sever, sunder

jointly as one, collectively, in common, in conjunction, in league, in partnership, mutually, together, unitedly

joke *n.* 1. frolic, fun, gag (*Sl.*), jape, jest, lark, play, pun, quip, quirk, sally, sport, whimsy, wisecrack (*Inf.*), witticism, yarn 2. buffoon, butt, clown, laughing stock, simpleton, target ~*v.* 3. banter, chaff, deride, frolic, gambol, jest, kid (*Inf.*), mock, quip, ridicule, taunt, tease

joker buffoon, clown, comedian, comic, humorist, jester, kidder (*Inf.*), prankster, trickster, wag, wit

jolly blithesome, carefree, cheerful, convivial, festive, frolicsome, funny, gay, gladsome, hilarious, jocund, jovial, joyful, joyous, jubilant, merry, mirthful, playful, sportive, sprightly

jolt *v.* 1. jar, jerk, jog, jostle, knock, push, shake, shove 2. astonish, discompose, disturb, perturb, stagger, startle, stun, surprise, upset ~*n.* 3. bump, jar, jerk, jog, jump, lurch, quiver, shake, start 4. blow, bolt from the blue, bombshell, reversal, setback, shock, surprise, thunderbolt

jostle bump, butt, crowd, elbow, hustle, jog, joggle, jolt, press, push, scramble, shake, shove, squeeze, throng, thrust

journal 1. chronicle, daily, gazette, magazine, monthly, newspaper, paper, periodical, record, register, review, tabloid, weekly 2. chronicle, commonplace book, daybook, diary, log, record

journalist broadcaster, columnist, commentator, contributor, correspondent, hack, newsman, newspaperman, pressman, reporter, scribe (*Inf.*), stringer

journey 1. *n.* excursion, expedition, jaunt, odyssey, outing, passage, peregrination, pilgrimage, progress, ramble, tour, travel, trek, trip, voyage 2. *v.* fare, fly, go, peregrinate, proceed, ramble, range, roam, rove, tour, travel, traverse, trek, voyage, wander, wend

jovial airy, animated, blithe, buoyant, cheery, convivial, cordial, gay, glad, happy, hilarious, jocose, jocund, jolly, jubilant, merry, mirthful

joy 1. bliss, delight, ecstasy, elation, exaltation, exultation, felicity, festivity, gaiety, gladness, glee, hilarity, pleasure, rapture, ravishment, satisfaction, transport 2. charm, delight, gem, jewel, pride, prize, treasure, treat, wonder

joyful blithesome, delighted, elated,

enraptured, glad, gladsome, gratified, happy, jocund, jolly, jovial, jubilant, light-hearted, merry, pleased, satisfied

joyless cheerless, dejected, depressed, dismal, dispirited, downcast, dreary, gloomy, miserable, sad, unhappy

joyous cheerful, festive, heartening, joyful, merry, rapturous

jubilant elated, enraptured, euphoric, excited, exuberant, exultant, glad, joyous, overjoyed, rejoicing, rhapsodic, thrilled, triumphal, triumphant

jubilation celebration, ecstasy, elation, excitement, exultation, festivity, jamboree, joy, jubilee, triumph

jubilee carnival, celebration, festival, festivity, fête, gala, holiday

judge n. 1. adjudicator, arbiter, arbitrator, moderator, referee, umpire 2. appraiser, arbiter, assessor, authority, connoisseur, critic, evaluator, expert 3. beak (*Brit. sl.*), justice, magistrate ~v. 4. adjudge, adjudicate, arbitrate, ascertain, conclude, decide, determine, discern, distinguish, mediate, referee, umpire 5. appraise, appreciate, assess, consider, criticize, esteem, estimate, evaluate, examine, rate, review, value 6. adjudge, condemn, decree, doom, find, pass sentence, pronounce sentence, rule, sentence, sit, try

judgment 1. acumen, common sense, discernment, discrimination, intelligence, penetration, percipience, perspicacity, prudence, sagacity, sense, shrewdness, taste, understanding, wisdom 2. arbitration, award, conclusion, decision, decree, determination, finding, order, result, ruling, sentence, verdict 3. appraisal, assessment, belief, conviction, deduction, diagnosis, estimate, finding, opinion, valuation, view 4. damnation, doom, fate, misfortune, punishment, retribution

judicial 1. judiciary, juridical, legal, official 2. discriminating, distin-

guished, impartial, judgelike, magisterial, magistral

judicious acute, astute, careful, cautious, circumspect, considered, diplomatic, discerning, discreet, discriminating, enlightened, expedient, informed, politic, prudent, rational, reasonable, sagacious, sage, sane, sapient, sensible, shrewd, skilful, sober, sound, thoughtful, well-advised, well-judged, wise

jug carafe, container, crock, ewer, jar, pitcher, urn, vessel

juggle alter, change, disguise, doctor (*Inf.*), falsify, fix (*Inf.*), manipulate, manoeuvre, misrepresent, modify, tamper with

juice extract, fluid, liquid, liquor, nectar, sap, secretion, serum

juicy 1. lush, moist, sappy, succulent, watery 2. colourful, interesting, provocative, racy, risqué, sensational, spicy, suggestive, vivid

jumble 1. v. confound, confuse, disarrange, dishevel, disorder, disorganize, entangle, mistake, mix, muddle, shuffle, tangle 2. n. chaos, clutter, confusion, disarrangement, disarray, disorder, farrago, gallimaufry, hodgepodge, hotchpotch, litter, medley, *mélange*, mess, miscellany, mishmash, mixture, muddle

jumbo giant, gigantic, huge, immense, large, oversized

jump v. 1. bounce, bound, caper, clear, gambol, hop, hurdle, leap, skip, spring, vault 2. flinch, jerk, recoil, start, wince 3. avoid, digress, evade, miss, omit, overshoot, skip, switch 4. advance, ascend, boost, escalate, gain, hike, increase, mount, rise, surge ~n. 5. bound, buck, caper, hop, leap, skip, spring, vault 6. barricade, barrier, fence, hurdle, impediment, obstacle, rail 7. breach, break, gap, hiatus, interruption, lacuna, space 8. advance, augmentation, boost, increase, increment, rise, upsurge, upturn 9. jar, jerk, jolt, lurch, shock, start, swerve, twitch, wrench

jumper pullover, sweater, woolly

jumpy agitated, anxious, apprehensive, fidgety, jittery, nervous, on edge, restless, shaky, tense, timorous

junction alliance, combination, connection, coupling, joint, juncture, linking, seam, union

juncture 1. conjuncture, contingency, crisis, crux, emergency, exigency, moment, occasion, point, predicament, strait, time 2. bond, connection, convergence, edge, intersection, junction, link, seam, weld

junior inferior, lesser, lower, minor, secondary, subordinate, younger

junk clutter, debris, leavings, litter, oddments, odds and ends, refuse, rubbish, rummage, scrap, trash, waste

jurisdiction 1. authority, command, control, dominion, influence, power, prerogative, rule, say, sway 2. area, bounds, circuit, compass, district, dominion, field, orbit, province, range, scope, sphere, zone

just _adj._ 1. blameless, conscientious, decent, equitable, fair, fairminded, good, honest, honourable, impartial, lawful, pure, right, righteous, unbiased, upright, virtuous 2. accurate, correct, exact, faithful, normal, precise, proper, regular, sound, true 3. appropriate, apt, condign, deserved, due, fitting, justified, legitimate, merited, proper, reasonable, rightful, suitable, well-deserved ~_adv._ 4. absolutely, completely, entirely, exactly, perfectly, precisely 5. hardly, lately, only now, recently, scarcely 6. at most, but, merely, no more than, nothing but, only, simply, solely

just about all but, almost, around, close to, nearly, not quite, practically, well-nigh

justice 1. equity, fairness, honesty, impartiality, integrity, justness, law, legality, legitimacy, reasonableness, rectitude, right 2. amends, compensation, correction, penalty, recompense, redress, reparation 3. judge, magistrate

justifiable acceptable, defensible, excusable, fit, lawful, legitimate, proper, reasonable, right, sound, tenable, understandable, valid, vindicable, warrantable, well-founded

justification 1. absolution, apology, approval, defence, exculpation, excuse, exoneration, explanation, extenuation, plea, rationalization, vindication 2. basis, defence, grounds, plea, reason, warrant

justify absolve, acquit, approve, confirm, defend, establish, exculpate, excuse, exonerate, explain, legalize, legitimize, maintain, substantiate, support, sustain, uphold, validate, vindicate, warrant

justly accurately, correctly, equally, equitably, fairly, honestly, impartially, lawfully, properly

jut bulge, extend, impend, overhang, poke, project, protrude, stick out

juvenile 1. _n._ adolescent, boy, child, girl, infant, minor, youth 2. _adj._ babyish, boyish, callow, childish, girlish, immature, inexperienced, infantile, jejune, puerile, undeveloped, unsophisticated, young, youthful

juxtaposition adjacency, closeness, contact, contiguity, nearness, propinquity, proximity, vicinity

K

keen 1. ardent, avid, devoted to, eager, earnest, ebullient, enthusiastic, fervid, fierce, fond of, impassioned, intense, zealous 2. acid, acute, biting, caustic, cutting, edged, finely honed, incisive, penetrating, piercing, pointed, razorlike, sardonic, satirical, sharp, tart, trenchant 3. astute, brilliant, canny, clever, discerning, discriminating, perceptive, perspicacious, quick, sagacious, sapient, sensitive, shrewd, wise

keenness 1. ardour, avidity, avidness, diligence, eagerness, earnestness, ebullience, enthusiasm, fervour, impatience, intensity, passion, zeal, zest 2. acerbity, harshness, incisiveness, mordancy, penetration, pungency, rigour, severity, sharpness, sternness, trenchancy, unkindness, virulence 3. astuteness, canniness, cleverness, discernment, insight, sagacity, sapience, sensitivity, shrewdness, wisdom

keep v. 1. conserve, control, hold, maintain, possess, preserve, retain 2. accumulate, amass, carry, deal in, deposit, furnish, garner, heap, hold, pile, place, stack, stock, store, trade in 3. care for, defend, guard, look after, maintain, manage, mind, operate, protect, safeguard, shelter, shield, tend, watch over 4. board, feed, foster, maintain, nourish, nurture, provide for, provision, subsidize, support, sustain, victual 5. accompany, associate with, consort with, fraternize with 6. arrest, block, check, constrain, control, curb, delay, detain, deter, hamper, hamstring, hinder, hold, hold back, impede, inhibit, keep back, limit, obstruct, prevent, restrain, retard, shackle, stall, withhold 7. adhere to, celebrate, commemorate, comply with, fulfil, hold, honour, obey, observe, perform, respect, ritualize, solemnize ~n. 8. board, food, livelihood, living, mainte-

nance, means, nourishment, subsistence, support 9. castle, citadel, donjon, dungeon, fastness, stronghold, tower

keep at be steadfast, carry on, complete, continue, drudge, endure, finish, grind, labour, last, maintain, persevere, persist, remain, slave, stay, stick, toil

keep back 1. check, constrain, control, curb, delay, hold back, limit, prohibit, restrain, restrict, retard, withhold 2. censor, conceal, hide, reserve, suppress, withhold

keeper attendant, caretaker, curator, custodian, defender, gaoler, governor, guard, guardian, jailer, overseer, preserver, steward, superintendent, warden, warder

keeping 1. aegis, auspices, care, charge, custody, guardianship, keep, maintenance, patronage, possession, protection, safekeeping, trust 2. accord, agreement, balance, compliance, conformity, congruity, consistency, correspondence, harmony, observance, proportion

keep on carry on, continue, endure, last, persevere, persist, prolong, remain

keepsake emblem, favour, memento, relic, remembrance, reminder, souvenir, symbol, token

keep up balance, compete, contend, continue, emulate, keep pace, maintain, match, persevere, preserve, rival, sustain, vie

keg barrel, cask, drum, firkin, hogshead, tun, vat

kernel core, essence, germ, gist, grain, marrow, nub, pith, seed, substance

key n. 1. latchkey, opener 2. *Fig.* answer, clue, cue, explanation, guide, indicator, interpretation, lead, means, pointer, sign, solution, translation ~*adj.* 3. basic, chief, crucial, decisive, essential, fundamental, important, leading, main, major, pivotal, principal

keynote centre, core, essence, gist, heart, kernel, marrow, pith, sub~ stance, theme

kick v. 1. boot, punt 2. *Fig.* com~ plain, gripe (*Inf.*), grumble, object, oppose, protest, rebel, resist, spurn 3. *Inf.* abandon, desist from, give up, leave off, quit, stop ~n. 4. force, intensity, pep, power, punch, pun~ gency, snap (*Inf.*), sparkle, strength, tang, verve, vitality, zest 5. buzz (*Sl.*), enjoyment, excite~ ment, fun, gratification, pleasure, stimulation, thrill

kickoff n. beginning, commence~ ment, opening, outset, start

kick off v. begin, commence, get under way, initiate, open, start

kick out discharge, dismiss, eject, evict, expel, get rid of, oust, reject, remove, sack, toss out

kid 1. n. baby, bairn, boy, child, girl, infant, lad, little one, stripling, teenager, tot, youngster, youth 2. v. bamboozle, beguile, cozen, delude, fool, gull (*Archaic*), hoax, hood~ wink, jest, joke, mock, plague, pre~ tend, rag (*Sl.*), ridicule, tease, trick

kidnap abduct, capture, hijack, hold to ransom, remove, seize, skyjack, steal

kill 1. annihilate, assassinate, bump off (*Sl.*), butcher, destroy, dispatch, do away with, do in (*Sl.*), eradicate, execute, exterminate, extirpate, knock off (*Sl.*), liquidate, massacre, murder, neutralize, obliterate, slaughter, slay, take (someone's) life, waste (*Sl.*) 2. *Fig.* cancel, cease, deaden, defeat, extinguish, halt, quash, quell, ruin, scotch, smother, stifle, still, stop, suppress, veto

killer assassin, butcher, cutthroat, destroyer, executioner, extermi~ nator, gunman, hit man (*Sl.*), liqui~ dator, murderer, slaughterer, slayer

killing n. 1. bloodshed, carnage, ex~ ecution, extermination, fatality, homicide, manslaughter, massa~ cre, murder, slaughter, slaying 2. *Inf.* bomb (*Sl.*), bonanza, cleanup

(*Inf.*), coup, gain, profit, success, windfall ~adj. 3. deadly, death~ dealing, deathly, fatal, lethal, mor~ tal, murderous 4. *Inf.* debilitating, enervating, exhausting, fatiguing, punishing, tiring 5. *Inf.* absurd, amusing, comical, hilarious, ludi~ crous, uproarious

kill-joy dampener, damper, spoil~ sport, wet blanket (*Inf.*)

kin n. 1. affinity, blood, connection, consanguinity, extraction, kinship, lineage, relationship, stock 2. con~ nections, family, kindred, kinsfolk, kinsmen, kith, people, relations, relatives ~adj. 3. akin, allied, close, cognate, consanguine, consan~ guineous, kindred, near, related

kind[1] n. 1. brand, breed, class, family, genus, ilk, race, set, sort, species, variety 2. character, de~ scription, essence, habit, manner, mould, nature, persuasion, sort, style, temperament, type

kind[2] adj. affectionate, amiable, amicable, beneficent, benevolent, benign, bounteous, charitable, clement, compassionate, congen~ ial, considerate, cordial, courteous, friendly, generous, gentle, good, gracious, humane, indulgent, kind~ hearted, kindly, lenient, loving, mild, neighbourly, obliging, phil~ anthropic, propitious, sympathetic, tender-hearted, thoughtful, under~ standing

kind-hearted altruistic, amicable, compassionate, considerate, gen~ erous, good-natured, gracious, helpful, humane, kind, sympathet~ ic, tender-hearted

kindle 1. fire, ignite, inflame, light, set fire to 2. *Fig.* agitate, animate, arouse, awaken, bestir, enkindle, exasperate, excite, foment, incite, induce, inflame, inspire, provoke, rouse, sharpen, stimulate, stir, thrill

kindliness amiability, beneficence, benevolence, benignity, charity, compassion, friendliness, gentle~ ness, humanity, kind-heartedness, kindness, sympathy

kindly 1. adj. beneficial, benevolent, benign, compassionate, cordial, favourable, genial, gentle, good-natured, hearty, helpful, kind, mild, pleasant, polite, sympathetic, warm 2. *adv.* agreeably, cordially, graciously, politely, tenderly, thoughtfully

kindness 1. affection, amiability, beneficence, benevolence, charity, clemency, compassion, decency, fellow-feeling, generosity, gentleness, goodness, good will, grace, hospitality, humanity, indulgence, kindliness, magnanimity, patience, philanthropy, tenderness, tolerance, understanding 2. aid, assistance, benefaction, bounty, favour, generosity, good deed, help, service

kindred *n.* 1. affinity, consanguinity, relationship 2. connections, family, flesh, kin, kinsfolk, kinsmen, lineage, relations, relatives ~*adj.* 3. affiliated, akin, allied, cognate, congenial, corresponding, kin, like, matching, related, similar

king crowned head, emperor, majesty, monarch, overlord, prince, ruler, sovereign

kingdom 1. dominion, dynasty, empire, monarchy, realm, reign, sovereignty 2. commonwealth, county, division, nation, province, state, territory, tract 3. area, domain, field, province, sphere, territory

kink 1. bend, coil, corkscrew, crimp, entanglement, frizz, knot, tangle, twist, wrinkle 2. cramp, crick, pang, pinch, spasm, stab, tweak, twinge 3. complication, defect, difficulty, flaw, hitch, imperfection, knot, tangle 4. crotchet, eccentricity, fetish, foible, idiosyncrasy, quirk, singularity, vagary, whim

kinky 1. bizarre, eccentric, odd, outlandish, peculiar, queer, quirky, strange, unconventional, weird 2. degenerated, depraved, deviant, licentious, perverted, unnatural, warped 3. coiled, crimped, curled, curly, frizzled, frizzy, tangled, twisted

kinship 1. blood relationship, consanguinity, kin, relation, ties of

blood 2. affinity, alliance, association, bearing, connection, correspondence, relationship, similarity

kinsman blood relative, fellow clansman, fellow tribesman, relation, relative

kiosk bookstall, booth, counter, newsstand, stall, stand

kiss *v.* 1. buss (*Archaic*), canoodle (*Inf.*), greet, neck (*Inf.*), osculate, peck (*Inf.*), salute, smooch (*Inf.*) 2. brush, caress, glance, graze, scrape, touch ~*n.* 3. buss (*Archaic*), osculation, peck (*Inf.*), smacker (*Sl.*)

kit accoutrements, apparatus, effects, equipment, gear, impedimenta, implements, instruments, outfit, paraphernalia, provisions, rig, supplies, tackle, tools, trappings, utensils

kitchen cookhouse, galley, kitchenette

knack ability, adroitness, aptitude, bent, capacity, dexterity, expertise, expertness, facility, flair, forte, genius, gift, handiness, ingenuity, propensity, quickness, skilfulness, skill, talent, trick

knave blackguard, bounder (*Inf.*), cheat, rapscallion, rascal, reprobate, rogue, rotter (*Sl.*), scallywag (*Inf.*), scamp, scapegrace, scoundrel, swindler, varlet (*Archaic*), villain

knavery chicanery, corruption, deceit, deception, dishonesty, double-dealing, duplicity, fraud, imposture, rascality, roguery, trickery, villainy

knead blend, form, manipulate, massage, mould, press, rub, shape, squeeze, stroke, work

kneel bow, bow down, curtsey, genuflect, get down on one's knees, kowtow, make obeisance, stoop

knell 1. *v.* announce, chime, herald, peal, resound, ring, sound, toll 2. *n.* chime, peal, ringing, sound, toll

knickers bloomers, briefs, drawers, panties, smalls, underwear

knick-knack bagatelle, bauble, bibelot, bric-a-brac, gewgaw, gimcrack, kickshaw, plaything, trifle, trinket

knife 1. *n.* blade, cutter, cutting tool 2. *v.* cut, impale, lacerate, pierce, slash, stab, wound

knit 1. affix, ally, bind, connect, contract, fasten, heal, interlace, intertwine, join, link, loop, mend, secure, tie, unite, weave 2. crease, furrow, knot, wrinkle

knob boss, bulk, bump, bunch, door-handle, knot, knurl, lump, nub, projection, protrusion, protuber~ance, snag, stud, swell, swelling, tumour

knock *v.* 1. buffet, clap, cuff, hit, punch, rap, slap, smack, smite (*Ar~chaic*), strike, thump, thwack ~*n.* 2. blow, box, clip, clout, cuff, ham-mering, rap, slap, smack, thump ~*v.* 3. *Inf.* abuse, belittle, carp, cavil, censure, condemn, criticize, deprecate, disparage, find fault, lambaste, run down, slam (*Sl.*) ~*n.* 4. blame, censure, condemnation, criticism, defeat, failure, rebuff, rejection, reversal, setback, stric~ture

knock about *or* **around** 1. ramble, range, roam, rove, traipse, travel, wander 2. abuse, batter, beat up (*Inf.*), bruise, buffet, damage, hit, hurt, maltreat, manhandle, maul, mistreat, strike, wound

knock down batter, clout (*Inf.*), demolish, destroy, fell, floor, level, pound, raze, smash, wallop (*Inf.*), wreck

knock off 1. clock off, clock out, complete, conclude, finish, stop work, terminate 2. filch, nick (*Sl.*), pilfer, pinch, purloin, rob, steal, thieve 3. assassinate, bump off (*Sl.*), do away with, do in (*Sl.*), kill, liquidate, murder, slay, waste (*Sl.*)

knockout 1. *coup de grâce*, kayo (*Sl.*), K.O. (*Sl.*) 2. hit, sensation, smash, smash-hit, stunner (*Inf.*), success, triumph, winner

knot *v.* 1. bind, complicate, entan~gle, knit, loop, secure, tether, tie, weave ~*n.* 2. bond, bow, braid, connection, joint, ligature, loop, rosette, tie 3. aggregation, bunch, clump, cluster, collection, heap, mass, pile, tuft 4. assemblage, band, circle, clique, company,

crew (*Inf.*), crowd, gang, group, mob, pack, set, squad

know 1. apprehend, comprehend, experience, fathom, feel certain, ken (*Scot.*), learn, notice, perceive, realize, recognize, see, undergo, understand 2. associate with, be acquainted with, be familiar with, fraternize with, have dealings with, have knowledge of, recognize 3. differentiate, discern, distinguish, identify, make out, perceive, rec~ognize, see, tell

know-how ability, adroitness, ap~titude, capability, dexterity, ex~perience, expertise, faculty, flair, ingenuity, knack, knowledge, pro~ficiency, savoir-faire, skill, talent

knowing 1. astute, clever, compe~tent, discerning, experienced, ex~pert, intelligent, qualified, skilful, well-informed 2. acute, cunning, eloquent, expressive, meaningful, perceptive, sagacious, shrewd, sig~nificant 3. aware, conscious, delib~erate, intended, intentional

knowingly consciously, deliber~ately, intentionally, on purpose, purposely, wilfully, wittingly

knowledge 1. education, enlight~enment, erudition, instruction, in~telligence, learning, scholarship, schooling, science, tuition, wisdom 2. ability, apprehension, cognition, comprehension, consciousness, discernment, grasp, judgment, recognition, understanding 3. ac~quaintance, cognizance, familiar~ity, information, intimacy, notice

knowledgeable 1. acquainted, *au courant*, *au fait*, aware, cognizant, conscious, conversant, experi~enced, familiar, in the know (*Inf.*), understanding, well-informed 2. educated, erudite, intelligent, learned, lettered, scholarly

known acknowledged, admitted, avowed, celebrated, common, confessed, familiar, famous, mani~fest, noted, obvious, patent, plain, popular, published, recognized, well-known

knuckle under *v.* accede, acqui~esce, capitulate, give in, give way, submit, succumb, surrender, yield

L

label *n.* 1. docket (*Chiefly Brit.*), marker, sticker, tag, tally, ticket 2. characterization, classification, description, epithet 3. brand, company, mark, trademark ~*v.* 4. docket (*Chiefly Brit.*), mark, stamp, sticker, tag, tally 5. brand, call, characterize, class, classify, define, describe, designate, identify, name

labour *n.* 1. industry, toil, work 2. employees, hands, labourers, workers, work force, workmen 3. donkey-work, drudgery, effort, exertion, grind (*Inf.*), industry, pains, painstaking, sweat (*Inf.*), toil, travail 4. chore, job, task, undertaking 5. childbirth, contractions, delivery, labour pains, pains, parturition, throes, travail ~*v.* 6. drudge, endeavour, grind (*Inf.*), peg along *or* away (*Chiefly Brit.*), plod, plug along *or* away (*Inf.*), slave, strive, struggle, sweat (*Inf.*), toil, travail, work 7. *Usually with* **under** be a victim of, be burdened by, be disadvantaged, suffer 8. dwell on, elaborate, overdo, overemphasize, strain 9. *Of a ship* heave, pitch, roll, toss

laboured 1. awkward, difficult, forced, heavy, stiff, strained 2. affected, contrived, overdone, overwrought, ponderous, studied, unnatural

labourer blue-collar worker, drudge, hand, labouring man, manual worker, navvy (*Brit. inf.*), unskilled worker, worker, working man, workman

labyrinth coil, complexity, complication, convolution, entanglement, intricacy, jungle, knotty problem, maze, perplexity, puzzle, riddle, snarl, tangle, windings

lace *n.* 1. filigree, netting, openwork, tatting 2. bootlace, cord, shoelace, string, thong, tie ~*v.* 3. attach, bind, close, do up, fasten, intertwine, interweave, thread, tie, twine 4. add to, fortify, mix in, spike

lacerate 1. claw, cut, gash, jag, maim, mangle, rend, rip, slash, tear, wound 2. *Fig.* afflict, distress, harrow, rend, torment, torture, wound

lachrymose crying, dolorous, lugubrious, mournful, sad, tearful, weeping, weepy (*Inf.*), woeful

lack 1. *n.* absence, dearth, deficiency, deprivation, destitution, insufficiency, need, privation, scantiness, scarcity, shortage, shortcoming, shortness, want 2. *v.* be deficient in, be short of, be without, miss, need, require, want

lackadaisical 1. apathetic, dull, enervated, half-hearted, indifferent, languid, languorous, lethargic, limp, listless, spiritless 2. abstracted, dreamy, idle, indolent, inert, lazy

lackey 1. creature, fawner, flatterer, flunky, hanger-on, instrument, menial, minion, parasite, pawn, sycophant, toady, tool, yes man 2. attendant, flunky, footman, manservant, valet

lacking defective, deficient, flawed, impaired, inadequate, minus (*Inf.*), missing, needing, sans (*Archaic*), wanting, without

lacklustre boring, dim, drab, dry, dull, flat, leaden, lifeless, lustreless, muted, prosaic, sombre, unimaginative, uninspired, vapid

laconic brief, compact, concise, crisp, curt, pithy, sententious, short, succinct, terse, to the point

lad boy, chap (*Inf.*), fellow, guy (*Inf.*), juvenile, kid, laddie (*Scot.*), schoolboy, shaver (*Inf.*), stripling, youngster, youth

laden burdened, charged, encumbered, fraught, full, hampered, loaded, oppressed, taxed, weighed down, weighted

lady-killer Casanova, Don Juan, heartbreaker, ladies' man, liber~

tine, Lothario, philanderer, rake, roué, wolf (*Inf.*), womanizer

ladylike courtly, cultured, decorous, elegant, genteel, modest, polite, proper, refined, respectable, well-bred

lag 1. be behind, dawdle, delay, drag (behind), drag one's feet, hang back, idle, linger, loiter, saunter, straggle, tarry, trail 2. decrease, diminish, ebb, fail, fall off, flag, lose strength, slacken, wane

laggard dawdler, idler, lingerer, loafer, loiterer, lounger, saunterer, slowcoach (*Brit. inf.*), sluggard, snail, straggler

laid-back at ease, casual, easygoing, free and easy, relaxed, unflappable (*Inf.*), unhurried

laid up bedridden, disabled, housebound, ill, immobilized, incapacitated, injured, on the sick list, out of action (*Inf.*), sick

lair 1. burrow, den, earth, form, hole, nest, resting place 2. *Inf.* den, hide-out, refuge, retreat, sanctuary

laissez faire n. free enterprise, free trade, individualism, live and let live, nonintervention

lame 1. crippled, defective, disabled, game, halt (*Archaic*), handicapped, hobbling, limping 2. *Fig.* feeble, flimsy, inadequate, insufficient, poor, thin, unconvincing, unsatisfactory, weak

lament *v.* 1. bemoan, bewail, complain, deplore, grieve, mourn, regret, sorrow, wail, weep ~*n.* 2. complaint, keening, lamentation, moan, moaning, plaint, ululation, wail, wailing 3. coronach (*Scot., Irish*), dirge, elegy, monody, requiem, threnody

lamentable 1. deplorable, distressing, grievous, mournful, regrettable, sorrowful, tragic, unfortunate, woeful 2. low, meagre, mean, miserable, pitiful, poor, unsatisfactory, wretched

lamentation dirge, grief, grieving, keening, lament, moan, mourning, plaint, sobbing, sorrow, ululation, wailing, weeping

lampoon 1. *n.* burlesque, caricature, parody, pasquinade, satire,

send-up (*Brit. inf.*), skit, squib, takeoff (*Inf.*) 2. *v.* burlesque, caricature, make fun of, mock, parody, pasquinade, ridicule, satirize, send up (*Brit. inf.*), squib, take off (*Inf.*)

land *n.* 1. dry land, earth, ground, terra firma 2. dirt, ground, loam, soil 3. countryside, farming, farmland, rural districts 4. acres, estate, grounds, property, real property, realty 5. country, district, fatherland, motherland, nation, province, region, territory, tract ~*v.* 6. alight, arrive, berth, come to rest, debark, disembark, dock, touch down 7. *Sometimes with up* arrive, bring, carry, cause, end up, lead, turn up, wind up 8. *Inf.* acquire, gain, get, obtain, secure, win

landlord 1. host, hotelier, hotelkeeper, innkeeper 2. freeholder, lessor, owner, proprietor

landmark 1. feature, monument 2. crisis, milestone, turning point, watershed 3. benchmark, boundary, cairn, milepost, signpost

landscape countryside, outlook, panorama, prospect, scene, scenery, view, vista

landslide 1. *n.* avalanche, landslip, rockfall 2. *adj.* decisive, overwhelming, runaway

language 1. communication, conversation, discourse, expression, interchange, parlance, speech, talk, utterance, verbalization, vocalization 2. argot, cant, dialect, idiom, jargon, lingo (*Inf.*), lingua franca, patois, speech, terminology, tongue, vernacular, vocabulary 3. diction, expression, phraseology, phrasing, style, wording

languid 1. drooping, faint, feeble, languorous, limp, pining, sickly, weak, weary 2. indifferent, lackadaisical, languorous, lazy, listless, spiritless, unenthusiastic, uninterested 3. dull, heavy, inactive, inert, lethargic, sluggish, torpid

languish 1. decline, droop, fade, fail, faint, flag, sicken, waste, weaken, wilt, wither 2. *Often with for* desire, hanker, hunger, long, pine, sigh, want, yearn 3. be abandoned, be disregarded, be neglected, rot, suffer, waste away 4. brood, despond, grieve, repine, sorrow

languishing 1. declining, deteriorating, drooping, droopy, fading, failing, flagging, sickening, sinking, wasting away, weak, weakening, wilting, withering 2. dreamy, longing, lovelorn, lovesick, melancholic, nostalgic, pensive, pining, soulful, tender, wistful, woebegone, yearning

lank 1. dull, lifeless, limp, long, lustreless, straggling 2. attenuated, emaciated, gaunt, lanky, lean, rawboned, scraggy, scrawny, skinny, slender, slim, spare, thin

lanky angular, bony, gangling, gaunt, loose-jointed, rangy, rawboned, scraggy, scrawny, spare, tall, thin, weedy (*Inf.*)

lap[1] 1. *n.* circle, circuit, course, distance, loop, orbit, round, tour 2. *v.* cover, enfold, envelop, fold, swaddle, swathe, turn, twist, wrap

lap[2] 1. gurgle, plash, purl, ripple, slap, splash, swish, wash 2. drink, lick, sip, sup

lapse *n.* 1. error, failing, fault, indiscretion, mistake, negligence, omission, oversight, slip 2. break, gap, intermission, interruption, interval, lull, passage, pause 3. backsliding, decline, descent, deterioration, drop, fall, relapse ~*v.* 4. decline, degenerate, deteriorate, drop, fail, fall, sink, slide, slip 5. become obsolete, become void, end, expire, run out, stop, terminate

lapsed 1. discontinued, ended, expired, finished, invalid, out of date, run out, unrenewed 2. backsliding, lacking faith, nonpractising

large 1. big, bulky, colossal, considerable, enormous, giant, gigantic, goodly, great, huge, immense, jumbo (*Inf.*), king-size, man-size, massive, monumental, sizable, substantial, tidy (*Inf.*), vast 2. abundant, ample, broad, capacious, comprehensive, copious, extensive, full, generous, grand, grandiose, liberal, plentiful, roomy, spacious, sweeping, wide 3. **at large** *a.* at liberty, free, on the loose, on the run, roaming, unconfined **b.** as a whole, chiefly, generally, in general, in the main, mainly **c.** at length, considerably, exhaustively, greatly, in full detail

largely as a rule, by and large, chiefly, considerably, extensively, generally, mainly, mostly, predominantly, primarily, principally, to a great extent, widely

large-scale broad, extensive, far-reaching, global, sweeping, vast, wholesale, wide, wide-ranging

largess 1. alms-giving, benefaction, bounty, charity, generosity, liberality, munificence, open-handedness, philanthropy 2. bequest, bounty, donation, endowment, gift, grant, present

lark 1. *n.* antic, caper, escapade, fling, frolic, fun, gambol, game, jape, mischief, prank, revel, rollick, romp, skylark, spree 2. *v.* caper, cavort, cut capers, frolic, gambol, have fun, make mischief, play, rollick, romp, sport

lash[1] *n.* 1. blow, hit, stripe, stroke, swipe (*Inf.*) ~*v.* 2. beat, birch, chastise, flagellate, flog, horsewhip, lam (*Sl.*), scourge, thrash, whip 3. beat, buffet, dash, drum, hammer, hit, knock, larrup (*Dialect*), pound, smack, strike 4. attack, belabour, berate, castigate, censure, criticize, flay, lambaste, lampoon, ridicule, satirize, scold, tear into (*Inf.*), upbraid

lash[2] bind, fasten, join, make fast, rope, secure, strap, tie

lass bird (*Sl.*), chick (*Sl.*), colleen (*Irish*), damsel, girl, lassie (*Scot.*), maid, maiden, miss, schoolgirl, young woman

last[1] *adj.* 1. aftermost, at the end, hindmost, rearmost 2. latest, most recent 3. closing, concluding, extreme, final, furthest, remotest, terminal, ultimate, utmost ~*adv.* 4. after, behind, bringing up the rear, in *or* at the end, in the rear ~*n.* 5. close, completion, conclusion, end, ending, finale, finish, termination 6. **at last** at length, eventually, finally, in conclusion, in the end, ultimately

last[2] *v.* abide, carry on, continue, endure, hold on, hold out, keep, keep on, persist, remain, stand up, survive, wear

last-ditch all-out (*Inf.*), desperate, final, frantic, heroic, straining, struggling

lasting abiding, continuing, deep-rooted, durable, enduring, indelible, lifelong, long-standing, long-term, perennial, permanent, perpetual, unceasing, undying, unending

lastly after all, all in all, at last, finally, in conclusion, in the end, to conclude, to sum up, ultimately

last word, the 1. final say, finis, summation, ultimatum 2. best, cream, *crème de la crème*, crown, epitome, *ne plus ultra*, perfection, quintessence, ultimate 3. *dernier cri*, fashion, latest, newest, rage, vogue

latch 1. *n.* bar, bolt, catch, clamp, fastening, hasp, hook, lock, sneck (*Dialect*) 2. *v.* bar, bolt, fasten, lock, make fast, secure, sneck (*Dialect*)

late *adj.* 1. behind, behindhand, belated, delayed, last-minute, overdue, slow, tardy, unpunctual 2. advanced, fresh, modern, new, recent 3. dead, deceased, defunct, departed, ex-, former, old, past, preceding, previous ~*adv.* 4. at the last minute, behindhand, behind time, belatedly, dilatorily, slowly, tardily, unpunctually

lately in recent times, just now, latterly, not long ago, of late, recently

lateness advanced hour, belatedness, delay, late date, retardation, tardiness, unpunctuality

later *adv.* after, afterwards, by and by, in a while, in time, later on, next, subsequently, thereafter

lateral edgeways, flanking, side, sideward, sideways

latest *adj.* current, fashionable, in, modern, most recent, newest, now, up-to-date, up-to-the-minute, with it (*Inf.*)

lather *n.* 1. bubbles, foam, froth, soap, soapsuds, suds 2. *Inf.* dither, fever, flap (*Inf.*), fluster, fuss, pother, state (*Inf.*), stew (*Inf.*), sweat, tizzy (*Inf.*), twitter ~*v.* 3. foam, froth, soap 4. *Inf.* beat, cane, drub, flog, lambaste, strike, thrash, whip

lathery bubbly, foamy, frothy, soapy, sudsy

latitude 1. breadth, compass, extent, range, reach, room, scope, space, span, spread, sweep, width 2. elbowroom, freedom, indulgence, laxity, leeway, liberty, licence, play, unrestrictedness

latter closing, concluding, last, last-mentioned, later, latest, modern, recent, second

latterly hitherto, lately, of late, recently

lattice fretwork, grating, grid, grille, latticework, mesh, network, openwork, reticulation, tracery, trellis, web

laudable admirable, commendable, creditable, estimable, excellent, meritorious, of note, praiseworthy, worthy

laudatory acclamatory, adulatory, approbatory, approving, commendatory, complimentary, eulogistic, panegyrical

laugh *v.* 1. be convulsed (*Inf.*), be in stitches, chortle, chuckle, crease up (*Inf.*), giggle, guffaw, roar with laughter, snigger, split one's sides, titter 2. **laugh at** belittle, deride, jeer, lampoon, make a mock of, make fun of, mock, ridicule, scoff at, take the mickey (out of) (*Inf.*), taunt ~*n.* 3. belly laugh (*Inf.*), chortle, chuckle, giggle, guffaw, roar *or* shriek of laughter, snigger, titter 4. *Inf.* card (*Inf.*), caution (*Inf.*), clown, comedian, comic, entertainer, hoot (*Inf.*), humorist, joke, lark, scream (*Inf.*), wag, wit

laughable 1. absurd, derisive, derisory, ludicrous, nonsensical, preposterous, ridiculous, worthy of scorn 2. amusing, comical, diverting, droll, farcical, funny, hilarious, humorous, mirthful, risible

laughing stock Aunt Sally (*Brit.*), butt, everybody's fool, fair game, figure of fun, target, victim

laugh off brush aside, dismiss, disregard, ignore, minimize, pooh-pooh, shrug off

laughter 1. cachinnation, chortling, chuckling, giggling, guffawing, laughing, tittering 2. amusement, glee, hilarity, merriment, mirth

launch 1. cast, discharge, dispatch, fire, project, propel, send off, set afloat, set in motion, throw 2. begin, commence, embark upon, inaugurate, initiate, instigate, introduce, open, start

laurels acclaim, awards, bays, commendation, credit, distinction, fame, glory, honour, kudos, praise, prestige, recognition, renown, reward

lavatory bathroom, bog (*Brit. sl.*), can (*U.S. sl.*), cloakroom (*Brit.*), Gents, head(s) (*Nautical sl.*), john (*U.S. sl.*), Ladies, latrine, loo (*Brit. inf.*), powder room, (public) convenience, toilet, washroom, water closet, W.C.

lavish *adj.* 1. abundant, copious, exuberant, lush, luxuriant, opulent, plentiful, profuse, prolific, sumptuous 2. bountiful, effusive, free, generous, liberal, munificent, openhanded, unstinting 3. exaggerated, excessive, extravagant, immoderate, improvident, intemperate, prodigal, thriftless, unreasonable, unrestrained, wasteful, wild ~*v.* 4. deluge, dissipate, expend, heap, pour, shower, spend, squander, waste

law 1. charter, code, constitution, jurisprudence 2. act, code, command, commandment, covenant, decree, edict, enactment, order, ordinance, rule, statute 3. axiom, canon, criterion, formula, precept, principle, regulation, standard 4. **lay down the law** dictate, dogmatize, emphasize, pontificate

law-abiding compliant, dutiful, good, honest, honourable, lawful, obedient, orderly, peaceable, peaceful

lawbreaker convict, criminal, crook (*Inf.*), culprit, delinquent, felon (*Formerly criminal law*), miscreant, offender, sinner, transgressor, trespasser, violater, wrongdoer

lawful allowable, authorized, constitutional, just, legal, legalized, legitimate, licit, permissible, proper, rightful, valid, warranted

lawless anarchic, chaotic, disorderly, insubordinate, insurgent, mutinous, rebellious, reckless, riotous, seditious, ungoverned, unrestrained, unruly, wild

lawsuit action, argument, case, cause, contest, dispute, litigation, proceedings, prosecution, suit, trial

lawyer advocate, attorney, barrister, counsel, counsellor, legal adviser, solicitor

lax 1. careless, casual, easy-going, lenient, neglectful, negligent, overindulgent, remiss, slack, slipshod 2. broad, general, imprecise, inaccurate, indefinite, inexact, nonspecific, shapeless, vague 3. flabby, flaccid, loose, slack, soft, yielding

lay^1 1. deposit, establish, leave, place, plant, posit, put, set, set down, settle, spread 2. arrange, dispose, locate, organize, position, set out 3. bear, deposit, produce 4. advance, bring forward, lodge, offer, present, put forward, submit 5. allocate, allot, ascribe, assign, attribute, charge, impute 6. concoct, contrive, design, devise, hatch, plan, plot, prepare, work out 7. apply, assess, burden, charge, encumber, impose, saddle, tax 8. bet, gamble, give odds, hazard, risk, stake, wager 9. allay, alleviate, appease, assuage, calm, quiet, relieve, soothe, still, suppress 10. **lay bare** disclose, divulge, explain, expose, reveal, show, unveil 11. **lay hands on** a. acquire, get, get hold of, grab, grasp, seize b. assault, attack, beat up, lay into, set on c. discover, find, unearth d. *Christianity* bless, confirm, consecrate, ordain 12. **lay hold of** get, get hold of, grab, grasp, grip, seize, snatch

lay^2 1. laic, laical, nonclerical, secular 2. amateur, inexpert, nonprofessional, nonspecialist

layabout beachcomber, good-for-nothing, idler, laggard, loafer, lounger, ne'er-do-well, shirker, skiver (*Brit. sl.*), slubberdegullion (*Archaic*), vagrant, wastrel

lay aside abandon, cast aside, dismiss, postpone, put aside, put off, reject, shelve

lay down 1. discard, drop, give, give up, relinquish, surrender, yield 2. affirm, assume, establish, formulate, ordain, postulate, prescribe, stipulate

layer 1. bed, ply, row, seam, stratum, thickness, tier 2. blanket, coat, coating, cover, covering, film, mantle, sheet

lay in accumulate, amass, build up, collect, hoard, stockpile, stock up, store (up)

lay into assail, attack, belabour, hit out at, lambaste, let fly at, pitch into, set about

layman amateur, lay person, nonprofessional, outsider

lay-off discharge, dismissal, unemployment

lay off 1. discharge, dismiss, drop, let go, make redundant, oust, pay off 2. *Inf.* cease, desist, give it a rest (*Inf.*), give over (*Inf.*), give up, leave alone, leave off, let up, quit, stop

lay on 1. cater (for), furnish, give, provide, supply 2. **lay it on** *Sl.* butter up, exaggerate, flatter, overdo it, overpraise, soft-soap

layout arrangement, design, draft, formation, geography, outline, plan

lay out 1. arrange, design, display, exhibit, plan, spread out 2. *Inf.* disburse, expend, fork out (*Sl.*), invest, pay, shell out (*Inf.*), spend 3. *Inf.* kayo (*Sl.*), knock for six (*Inf.*), knock out, knock unconscious, KO (*Sl.*)

laziness dilatoriness, donothingness, faineance, faineancy, idleness, inactivity, indolence, lackadaisicalness, slackness, sloth, slothfulness, slowness, sluggishness, tardiness

lazy 1. idle, inactive, indolent, inert, remiss, shiftless, slack, slothful, slow, workshy 2. drowsy, languid, languorous, lethargic, sleepy, slow-moving, sluggish, somnolent, torpid

leach drain, extract, filter, filtrate, lixiviate (*Chem.*), percolate, seep, strain

lead *v.* 1. conduct, escort, guide, pilot, precede, show the way, steer, usher 2. cause, dispose, draw, incline, induce, influence, persuade, prevail, prompt 3. command, direct, govern, head, manage, preside over, supervise 4. be ahead (of), blaze a trail, come first, exceed, excel, outdo, outstrip, surpass, transcend 5. experience, have, live, pass, spend, undergo 6. bring on, cause, conduce, contribute, produce, result in, serve, tend ~*n.* 7. advance, advantage, edge, first place, margin, precedence, primacy, priority, start, supremacy, van, vanguard 8. direction, example, guidance, leadership, model 9. clue, guide, hint, indication, suggestion, tip, trace 10. leading role, principal, protagonist, star part, title role ~*adj.* 11. chief, first, foremost, head, leading, main, most important, premier, primary, prime, principal

leader bellwether, boss (*Inf.*), captain, chief, chieftain, commander, conductor, counsellor, director, guide, head, number one, principal, ringleader, ruler, superior

leadership 1. administration, direction, directorship, domination, guidance, management, running, superintendency 2. authority, command, control, influence, initiative, pre-eminence, supremacy, sway

leading chief, dominant, first, foremost, governing, greatest, highest, main, number one, outstanding, pre-eminent, primary, principal, ruling, superior

lead on beguile, deceive, draw on, entice, inveigle, lure, seduce, string along (*Inf.*), tempt

lead up to approach, intimate, introduce, make advances, make overtures, pave the way, prepare for, prepare the way, work round to

leaf *n.* **1.** blade, bract, flag, foliole, frond, needle, pad **2.** folio, page, sheet **3. turn over a new leaf** amend, begin anew, change, change one's ways, improve, reform ~*v.* **4.** bud, green, put out leaves, turn green **5.** browse, flip, glance, riffle, skim, thumb (through)

leaflet advert (*Brit. inf.*), bill, booklet, brochure, circular, handbill, pamphlet

league *n.* **1.** alliance, association, band, coalition, combination, combine, compact, confederacy, confederation, consortium, federation, fellowship, fraternity, group, guild, partnership, union **2.** ability group, category, class, level **3. in league (with)** allied, collaborating, hand in glove, in cahoots (*Inf.*), leagued ~*v.* **4.** ally, amalgamate, associate, band, collaborate, combine, confederate, join forces, unite

leak *n.* **1.** aperture, chink, crack, crevice, fissure, hole, opening, puncture **2.** drip, leakage, leaking, oozing, percolation, seepage **3.** disclosure, divulgence ~*v.* **4.** discharge, drip, escape, exude, ooze, pass, percolate, seep, spill, trickle **5.** disclose, divulge, give away, let slip, let the cat out of the bag, make known, make public, pass on, reveal, spill the beans (*Inf.*), tell

leaky cracked, holey, leaking, not watertight, perforated, porous, punctured, split, waterlogged

lean[1] *v.* **1.** be supported, prop, recline, repose, rest **2.** bend, incline, slant, slope, tilt, tip **3.** be disposed to, be prone to, favour, gravitate towards, have a propensity, prefer, tend **4.** confide, count on, depend, have faith in, rely, trust

lean[2] *adj.* **1.** angular, bony, emaciated, gaunt, lank, rangy, scraggy, scrawny, skinny, slender, slim, spare, thin, unfatty, wiry **2.** bare, barren, inadequate, infertile, meagre, pitiful, poor, scanty, sparse, unfruitful, unproductive

leaning aptitude, bent, bias, disposition, inclination, liking, partiality, penchant, predilection, proclivity, proneness, propensity, taste, tendency

leap *v.* **1.** bounce, bound, caper, cavort, frisk, gambol, hop, jump, skip, spring **2.** *Fig.* arrive at, come to, form hastily, hasten, hurry, jump, reach, rush **3.** clear, jump (over), vault **4.** advance, become prominent, escalate, gain attention, increase, rocket, soar, surge ~*n.* **5.** bound, caper, frisk, hop, jump, skip, spring, vault **6.** escalation, increase, rise, surge, upsurge, upswing

learn 1. acquire, attain, become able, grasp, imbibe, master, pick up **2.** commit to memory, con (*Archaic*), get off pat, get (something) word-perfect, learn by heart, memorize **3.** ascertain, detect, determine, discern, discover, find out, gain, gather, hear, understand

learned academic, cultured, erudite, experienced, expert, highbrow, intellectual, lettered, literate, scholarly, skilled, versed, well-informed, well-read

learner apprentice, beginner, disciple, neophyte, novice, pupil, scholar, student, trainee, tyro

learning acquirements, attainments, culture, education, erudition, information, knowledge, letters, literature, lore, research, scholarship, schooling, study, tuition, wisdom

lease *v.* charter, hire, let, loan, rent

leash *n.* **1.** lead, rein, tether **2.** check, control, curb, hold, restraint ~*v.* **3.** fasten, secure, tether, tie up **4.** check, control, curb, hold back, restrain, suppress

least feeblest, fewest, last, lowest, meanest, minimum, minutest, poorest, slightest, smallest, tiniest

leathery coriaceous, durable, hard, hardened, leatherlike, leathern (*Archaic*), rough, rugged, tough, wrinkled

leave[1] *v.* **1.** abandon, decamp, depart, desert, disappear, do a bunk (*Brit. sl.*), exit, flit (*Inf.*), forsake, go, go away, move, pull out, quit, relinquish, retire, set out, take off

(*Inf.*), withdraw 2. forget, lay down, leave behind, mislay 3. cause, deposit, generate, produce, result in 4. abandon, cease, desert, desist, drop, evacuate, forbear, give up, refrain, relinquish, renounce, stop, surrender 5. allot, assign, cede, commit, consign, entrust, give over, refer 6. bequeath, demise, devise (*Law*), hand down, transmit, will

leave[2] *n.* 1. allowance, authorization, concession, consent, dispensation, freedom, liberty, permission, sanction 2. furlough, holiday, leave of absence, sabbatical, time off, vacation 3. adieu, departure, farewell, goodbye, leave-taking, parting, retirement, withdrawal

leaven *n.* 1. barm, ferment, leavening, yeast 2. *Fig.* catalyst, influence, inspiration ~*v.* 3. ferment, lighten, raise, work 4. *Fig.* elevate, imbue, inspire, permeate, pervade, quicken, stimulate, suffuse

leave off abstain, break off, cease, desist, discontinue, end, give over (*Inf.*), give up, halt, knock off (*Inf.*), refrain, stop

leave out bar, cast aside, count out, disregard, except, exclude, ignore, neglect, omit, overlook, reject

leavings bits, dregs, fragments, leftovers, orts (*Archaic or dialect*), pieces, refuse, remains, remnants, residue, scraps, spoil, sweepings, waste

lecherous carnal, concupiscent, goatish (*Archaic*), lascivious, lewd, libidinous, licentious, lubricous, lustful, prurient, randy (*Sl., chiefly Brit.*), raunchy (*U.S. Sl.*), ruttish, salacious, unchaste, wanton

lechery carnality, concupiscence, debauchery, lasciviousness, lecherousness, leching (*Inf.*), lewdness, libertinism, libidinousness, licentiousness, lubricity, lust, lustfulness, profligacy, prurience, rakishness, randiness (*Sl., chiefly Brit.*), salaciousness, sensuality, wantonness, womanizing

lecture *n.* 1. address, discourse, disquisition, harangue, instruction, lesson, speech, talk ~*v.* 2. address,

discourse, expound, give a talk, harangue, hold forth, speak, talk, teach ~*n.* 3. castigation, censure, chiding, dressing-down (*Inf.*), going-over (*Inf.*), rebuke, reprimand, reproof, scolding, talking-to (*Inf.*), telling off (*Inf.*), wigging (*Brit. sl.*) ~*v.* 4. admonish, berate, carpet (*Inf.*), castigate, censure, chide, rate, reprimand, reprove, scold, tell off (*Inf.*)

ledge mantle, projection, ridge, shelf, sill, step

leer *n./v.* eye, gloat, goggle, grin, ogle, smirk, squint, stare, wink

lees deposit, dregs, grounds, precipitate, refuse, sediment, settlings

leeway elbowroom, latitude, margin, play, room, scope, space

left *adj.* 1. larboard (*Nautical*), left-hand, port, sinistral 2. *Of politics* leftist, left-wing, liberal, progressive, radical, socialist

left-handed 1. awkward, cack-handed (*Inf.*), careless, clumsy, fumbling, gauche, maladroit 2. ambiguous, backhanded, double-edged, enigmatic, equivocal, indirect, ironic, sardonic

leftover *n.* 1. legacy, remainder, residue, surplus, survivor 2. *Plural* leavings, oddments, odds and ends, remains, remnants, scraps ~*adj.* 3. excess, extra, remaining, surplus, uneaten, unused, unwanted

leg 1. limb, lower limb, member, pin (*Inf.*), stump (*Inf.*) 2. brace, prop, support, upright 3. lap, part, portion, section, segment, stage, stretch 4. **a leg up** assistance, boost, help, helping hand, push, support 5. **not have a leg to stand on** *Inf.* be defenceless, be full of holes, be illogical, be invalid, be undermined, be vulnerable, lack support 6. **on one's (its) last legs** about to break down, about to collapse, at death's door, dying, exhausted, failing, giving up the ghost, worn out 7. **pull someone's leg** *Inf.* chaff, deceive, fool, make fun of, tease, trick 8. **shake a leg** *Sl.* a. get a move on (*Inf.*), get cracking (*Inf.*), hasten, hurry, look lively (*Inf.*), rush, stir one's stumps b.

dance, hoof it (*Sl.*), trip the light fantastic 9. **stretch one's legs** exercise, go for a walk, move about, promenade, stroll, take a walk, take the air 10. **leg it** *Inf.* go on foot, hotfoot, hurry, run, skedaddle (*Inf.*), walk

legacy 1. bequest, devise (*Law*), estate, gift, heirloom, inheritance 2. birthright, endowment, heritage, inheritance, patrimony, throwback, tradition

legal 1. allowable, allowed, authorized, constitutional, lawful, legalized, legitimate, licit, permissible, proper, rightful, sanctioned, valid 2. forensic, judicial, juridical

legality accordance with the law, admissibleness, lawfulness, legitimacy, permissibility, rightfulness, validity

legalize allow, approve, authorize, decriminalize, legitimate, legitimatize, license, permit, sanction, validate

legation consulate, delegation, diplomatic mission, embassy, envoys, ministry, representation

legend 1. fable, fiction, folk tale, myth, narrative, saga, story, tale 2. celebrity, luminary, marvel, phenomenon, prodigy, spectacle, wonder 3. caption, device, inscription, motto 4. cipher, code, key, table of symbols

legendary 1. apocryphal, fabled, fabulous, fanciful, fictitious, mythical, romantic, storied, traditional 2. celebrated, famed, famous, illustrious, immortal, renowned, wellknown

legibility clarity, decipherability, ease of reading, legibleness, neatness, plainness, readability, readableness

legible clear, decipherable, distinct, easily read, easy to read, neat, plain, readable

legion *n.* 1. army, brigade, company, division, force, troop 2. drove, horde, host, mass, multitude, myriad, number, throng ~*adj.* 3. countless, multitudinous, myriad, numberless, numerous, very many

legislate codify, constitute, enact,

establish, make laws, ordain, pass laws, prescribe, put in force

legislation 1. codification, enactment, lawmaking, prescription, regulation 2. act, bill, charter, law, measure, regulation, ruling, statute

legislative *adj.* congressional, judicial, juridical, jurisdictive, lawgiving, lawmaking, ordaining, parliamentary

legislator lawgiver, lawmaker, parliamentarian

legislature assembly, chamber, congress, diet, house, lawmaking body, parliament, senate

legitimate *adj.* 1. acknowledged, authentic, authorized, genuine, lawful, legal, legit (*Sl.*), licit, proper, real, rightful, sanctioned, statutory, true 2. admissible, correct, just, justifiable, logical, reasonable, sensible, valid, warranted, wellfounded ~*v.* 3. authorize, legalize, legitimatize, legitimize, permit, pronounce lawful, sanction

legitimatize, legitimize authorize, legalize, legitimate, permit, pronounce lawful, sanction

leisure 1. breathing space, ease, freedom, free time, holiday, liberty, opportunity, pause, quiet, recreation, relaxation, respite, rest, retirement, spare moments, spare time, time off, vacation 2. **at leisure a.** available, free, not booked up, on holiday, unengaged, unoccupied **b.** *Also* **at one's leisure** at an unhurried pace, at one's convenience, deliberately, in one's own (good) time, unhurriedly, when it suits one, when one gets round to it (*Inf.*), without hurry

leisurely 1. *adj.* comfortable, easy, gentle, laid-back (*Inf.*), lazy, relaxed, restful, slow, unhurried 2. *adv.* at one's convenience, at one's leisure, comfortably, deliberately, easily, indolently, lazily, lingeringly, slowly, unhurriedly, without haste

lend 1. accommodate one with, advance, loan 2. add, afford, bestow, confer, contribute, furnish, give, grant, impart, present, provide, supply 3. **lend an ear** give ear, hearken (*Archaic*), heed, listen, take notice **4. lend a hand** aid, assist, give a (helping) hand, help, help out **5. lend itself to** be adaptable, be appropriate, be serviceable, fit, present opportunities of, suit **6. lend oneself to** agree, consent, cooperate, countenance, espouse, support

length 1. *Of linear extent* distance, extent, longitude, measure, reach, span **2.** *Of time* duration, period, space, span, stretch, term **3.** measure, piece, portion, section, segment **4.** elongation, extensiveness, lengthiness, protractedness **5. at length a.** completely, fully, in depth, in detail, thoroughly, to the full **b.** for ages, for a long time, for hours, interminably **c.** at last, at long last, eventually, finally, in the end

lengthen continue, draw out, elongate, expand, extend, increase, make longer, prolong, protract, spin out, stretch

lengthy diffuse, drawn-out, extended, interminable, lengthened, long, long-drawn-out, long-winded, overlong, prolix, prolonged, protracted, tedious, verbose, very long

leniency, lenience clemency, compassion, forbearance, gentleness, indulgence, lenity, mercy, mildness, moderation, tenderness, tolerance

lenient clement, compassionate, forbearing, forgiving, gentle, indulgent, kind, merciful, mild, sparing, tender, tolerant

lesbian 1. *n.* butch (*Sl.*), dyke (*Sl.*), sapphist, tribade **2.** *adj.* butch (*Sl.*), gay (*Inf.*), homosexual, sapphic, tribadic

less *adj.* **1.** shorter, slighter, smaller **2.** inferior, minor, secondary, subordinate ~*adv.* **3.** barely, little, meagrely, to a smaller extent ~*prep.* **4.** excepting, lacking, minus, subtracting, without

lessen abate, abridge, contract, curtail, decrease, de-escalate, degrade, die down, diminish, dwindle, ease, erode, grow less, impair, lighten, lower, minimize, moder-

ate, narrow, reduce, shrink, slacken, slow down, weaken, wind down

lessening abatement, contraction, curtailment, decline, decrease, de-escalation, diminution, dwindling, ebbing, erosion, let-up (*Inf.*), minimization, moderation, petering out, reduction, shrinkage, slackening, slowing down, waning, weakening

lesser inferior, less important, lower, minor, secondary, slighter, subordinate, under-

lesson 1. class, coaching, instruction, period, schooling, teaching, tutoring **2.** assignment, drill, exercise, homework, lecture, practice, reading, recitation, task **3.** deterrent, example, exemplar, message, model, moral, precept **4.** admonition, censure, chiding, punishment, rebuke, reprimand, reproof, scolding, warning

let[1] *v.* **1.** allow, authorize, give leave, give permission, give the go-ahead (green light, O.K.) (*Inf.*), grant, permit, sanction, suffer (*Archaic*), tolerate, warrant **2.** hire, lease, rent **3.** allow, cause, enable, grant, make, permit

let[2] *n.* constraint, hindrance, impediment, interference, obstacle, obstruction, prohibition, restriction

letdown anticlimax, bitter pill, blow, comedown (*Inf.*), disappointment, disgruntlement, disillusionment, frustration, setback, washout (*Inf.*)

let down disappoint, disenchant, disillusion, dissatisfy, fail, fall short, leave in the lurch, leave stranded

lethal baleful, dangerous, deadly, deathly, destructive, devastating, fatal, mortal, murderous, noxious, pernicious, poisonous, virulent

lethargic apathetic, comatose, debilitated, drowsy, dull, enervated, heavy, inactive, indifferent, inert, languid, lazy, listless, sleepy, slothful, slow, sluggish, somnolent, stupefied, torpid

lethargy apathy, drowsiness, dullness, hebetude (*Rare*), inaction, indifference, inertia, languor, lassitude, listlessness, sleepiness, sloth, slowness, sluggishness, stupor, torpidity, torpor

let in admit, allow to enter, give access to, greet, include, incorporate, receive, take in, welcome

let off 1. detonate, discharge, emit, explode, exude, fire, give off, leak, release **2.** absolve, discharge, dispense, excuse, exempt, exonerate, forgive, pardon, release, spare

let out 1. emit, give vent to, produce **2.** discharge, free, let go, liberate, release **3.** betray, disclose, leak, let fall, let slip, make known, reveal

letter 1. character, sign, symbol **2.** acknowledgment, answer, billet (*Archaic*), communication, dispatch, epistle, line, message, missive, note, reply **3. to the letter** accurately, exactly, literally, precisely, strictly, word for word

letters belles-lettres, culture, erudition, humanities, learning, literature, scholarship

let-up abatement, break, cessation, interval, lessening, lull, pause, recess, remission, respite, slackening

let up abate, decrease, diminish, ease (up), moderate, slacken, stop, subside

level *adj.* **1.** consistent, even, flat, horizontal, plain, plane, smooth, uniform **2.** aligned, balanced, commensurate, comparable, equivalent, even, flush, in line, neck and neck, on a line, on a par, proportionate **3.** calm, equable, even, even-tempered, stable, steady ~*v.* **4.** even off *or* out, flatten, make flat, plane, smooth **5.** bulldoze, demolish, destroy, devastate, equalize, flatten, knock down, lay low, pull down, raze, smooth, tear down, wreck **6.** aim, beam, direct, focus, point, train **7.** *Inf.* be above board, be frank, be honest, be open, be straightforward, be up front (*Sl.*), come clean (*Inf.*), keep nothing back ~*n.* **8.** altitude, elevation, height, vertical position **9.** achievement, degree, grade, position, rank, stage, standard, standing, status **10.** bed, floor, layer, storey, stratum, zone **11.** flat surface,

horizontal, plain, plane **12. on the level** *Inf.* above board, fair, genuine, honest, open, sincere, square, straight, straightforward, up front (*Sl.*)

level-headed balanced, calm, collected, composed, cool, dependable, even-tempered, reasonable, sane, self-possessed, sensible, steady, together (*Sl., chiefly U.S.*), unflappable (*Inf.*)

lever 1. *n.* bar, crowbar, handle, handspike, jemmy **2.** *v.* force, jemmy, move, prise, pry (*U.S.*), purchase, raise

leverage ascendancy, authority, clout (*Inf.*), influence, pull (*Inf.*), purchasing power, rank, weight

levity buoyancy, facetiousness, fickleness, flightiness, flippancy, frivolity, giddiness, light-heartedness, light-mindedness, silliness, skittishness, triviality

levy *v.* **1.** charge, collect, demand, exact, gather, impose, tax **2.** call, call up, conscript, mobilize, muster, press, raise, summon ~*n.* **3.** assessment, collection, exaction, gathering, imposition **4.** assessment, duty, excise, fee, imposition, impost, tariff, tax, toll

lewd bawdy, blue, dirty, impure, indecent, lascivious, libidinous, licentious, loose, lustful, obscene, pornographic, profligate, salacious, smutty, unchaste, vile, vulgar, wanton, wicked

lewdness bawdiness, carnality, crudity, debauchery, depravity, impurity, indecency, lasciviousness, lechery, licentiousness, lubricity, obscenity, pornography, profligacy, salaciousness, smut, smuttiness, unchastity, vulgarity, wantonness

liability 1. accountability, answerability, culpability, duty, obligation, onus, responsibility **2.** arrear, debit, debt, indebtedness, obligation **3.** burden, disadvantage, drag, drawback, encumbrance, handicap, hindrance, impediment, inconvenience, millstone, minus (*Inf.*), nuisance **4.** likelihood, probability, proneness, susceptibility, tendency

liable 1. accountable, amenable, answerable, bound, chargeable, obligated, responsible 2. exposed, open, subject, susceptible, vulnerable 3. apt, disposed, inclined, likely, prone, tending 4. **render oneself liable to** expose oneself to, incur, lay oneself open to, run the risk of

liaison 1. communication, connection, contact, go-between, hook-up, interchange, intermediary 2. affair, amour, entanglement, illicit romance, intrigue, love affair, romance

liar fabricator, falsifier, fibber, perjurer, prevaricator, storyteller (*Inf.*)

libel 1. *n.* aspersion, calumny, defamation, denigration, obloquy, slander, smear, vituperation 2. *v.* blacken, calumniate, defame, derogate, drag (someone's) name through the mud, malign, revile, slander, slur, smear, traduce, vilify

libellous aspersive, calumniatory, calumnious, defamatory, derogatory, false, injurious, malicious, maligning, scurrilous, slanderous, traducing, untrue, vilifying, vituperative

liberal 1. advanced, humanistic, latitudinarian, libertarian, progressive, radical, reformist 2. altruistic, beneficent, bounteous, bountiful, charitable, free-handed, generous, kind, open-handed, openhearted, unstinting 3. advanced, broad-minded, catholic, enlightened, high-minded, humanitarian, indulgent, magnanimous, permissive, tolerant, unbiased, unbigoted, unprejudiced 4. abundant, ample, bountiful, copious, handsome, lavish, munificent, plentiful, profuse, rich 5. broad, flexible, free, general, inexact, lenient, loose, not close, not literal, not strict

liberality 1. altruism, beneficence, benevolence, bounty, charity, free-handedness, generosity, kindness, largess, munificence, openhandedness, philanthropy 2. breadth, broad-mindedness, candour, catholicity, impartiality, latitude, liberalism, libertarianism, magnanimity, permissiveness, progressivism, toleration

liberalize ameliorate, broaden, ease, expand, extend, loosen, mitigate, moderate, modify, relax, slacken, soften, stretch

liberate deliver, discharge, disenthral, emancipate, free, let loose, let out, manumit, redeem, release, rescue, set free

liberation deliverance, emancipation, enfranchisement, freedom, freeing, liberating, liberty, manumission, redemption, release, unfettering, unshackling

liberator deliverer, emancipator, freer, manumitter, redeemer, rescuer, saviour

libertine 1. *n.* debauchee, lecher, loose liver, profligate, rake, reprobate, roué, seducer, sensualist, voluptuary, womanizer 2. *adj.* abandoned, corrupt, debauched, decadent, degenerate, depraved, dissolute, immoral, licentious, profligate, rakish, reprobate, voluptuous, wanton

liberty 1. autonomy, emancipation, freedom, immunity, independence, liberation, release, self-determination, sovereignty 2. authorization, carte blanche, dispensation, exemption, franchise, freedom, leave, licence, permission, prerogative, privilege, right, sanction 3. *Often plural* disrespect, familiarity, forwardness, impertinence, impropriety, impudence, insolence, overfamiliarity, presumption, presumptuousness 4. **at liberty** free, not confined, on the loose, unlimited, unoccupied, unrestricted

libidinous carnal, concupiscent, debauched, impure, incontinent, lascivious, lecherous, lickerish (*Archaic*), loose, lustful, prurient, randy (*Sl., chiefly Brit.*), ruttish, salacious, sensual, unchaste, wanton, wicked

licence *n.* 1. authority, authorization, carte blanche, certificate, charter, dispensation, entitlement, exemption, immunity, leave, liberty, permission, permit, privilege, right, warrant 2. freedom, independence, latitude, liberty, self-determination 3. abandon, anarchy, disorder, excess, immoderation, impropriety, indulgence, irresponsibility, lawlessness, laxity, profligacy, unruliness

license *v.* accredit, allow, authorize, certify, commission, empower, permit, sanction, warrant

licentious abandoned, debauched, disorderly, dissolute, immoral, impure, lascivious, lax, lewd, libertine, libidinous, lubricous, lustful, profligate, promiscuous, sensual, uncontrollable, uncontrolled, uncurbed, unruly, wanton

licentiousness abandon, debauchery, dissipation, dissoluteness, lechery, lewdness, libertinism, libidinousness, lubricity, lust, lustfulness, profligacy, promiscuity, prurience, salaciousness, salacity, wantonness

lick *v.* 1. brush, lap, taste, tongue, touch, wash 2. *Of flames* dart, flick, flicker, ignite, kindle, play over, ripple, touch 3. *Inf.* a. defeat, overcome, rout, trounce, vanquish, wipe the floor with (*Inf.*) b. beat, flog, slap, spank, strike, thrash, wallop (*Inf.*) c. beat, best, excel, outdo, outstrip, surpass, top ~*n.* 4. bit, brush, dab, little, sample, speck, stroke, taste, touch 5. *Inf.* clip (*Inf.*), pace, rate, speed

licking 1. beating, drubbing, flogging, hiding (*Inf.*), spanking, tanning (*Sl.*), thrashing, whipping 2. beating, defeat, drubbing, trouncing

lie¹ 1. *v.* dissimulate, equivocate, fabricate, falsify, fib, forswear oneself, invent, misrepresent, perjure, prevaricate, tell a lie, tell untruths 2. *n.* deceit, fabrication, falsehood, falsification, falsity, fib, fiction, invention, mendacity, prevarication, untruth, white lie

lie² *v.* 1. be prone, be prostrate, be recumbent, be supine, couch, loll, lounge, recline, repose, rest, sprawl, stretch out 2. be, be buried, be found, be interred, be located,

belong, be placed, be situated, exist, extend, remain 3. *Usually with* **on** *or* **upon** burden, oppress, press, rest, weigh 4. *Usually with* **in** be present, consist, dwell, exist, inhere, pertain 5. **lie low** conceal oneself, go to earth, go underground, hide, hide away, hide out, hole up, keep a low profile, keep out of sight, lurk, skulk, take cover

life 1. animation, being, breath, entity, growth, sentience, viability, vitality 2. being, career, continuance, course, duration, existence, lifetime, span, time 3. human, human being, individual, mortal, person, soul 4. autobiography, biography, career, confessions, history, life story, memoirs, story 5. behaviour, conduct, life style, way of life 6. the human condition, the times, the world, this mortal coil, trials and tribulations, vicissitudes 7. activity, animation, brio, energy, get-up-and-go (*Inf.*), go (*Inf.*), high spirits, liveliness, oomph (*Inf.*), sparkle, spirit, verve, vigour, vitality, vivacity, zest 8. animating spirit, *élan vital*, essence, heart, lifeblood, soul, spirit, vital spark 9. creatures, living beings, living things, organisms, wildlife 10. **come to life** awaken, become animate, revive, rouse, show signs of life 11. **for dear life** *Inf.* desperately, for all one is worth, intensely, quickly, urgently, vigorously

lifeless 1. cold, dead, deceased, defunct, extinct, inanimate, inert 2. bare, barren, desert, empty, sterile, uninhabited, unproductive, waste 3. cold, colourless, dull, flat, heavy, hollow, lacklustre, lethargic, listless, passive, pointless, slow, sluggish, spent, spiritless, static, stiff, torpid, wooden 4. comatose, dead to the world, in a faint, inert, insensate, insensible, out cold, out for six, unconscious

lifelike authentic, exact, faithful, graphic, natural, photographic, real, realistic, true-to-life, undistorted, vivid

lifelong constant, deep-rooted, enduring, for all one's life, for life, lasting, lifetime, long-lasting, long-standing, perennial, permanent, persistent

lifetime all one's born days, career, course, day(s), existence, life span, one's natural life, period, span, time

lift v. 1. bear aloft, buoy up, draw up, elevate, heft (Inf.), hoist, pick up, raise, raise high, rear, upheave, uplift, upraise 2. advance, ameliorate, boost, dignify, elevate, enhance, exalt, improve, promote, raise, upgrade 3. annul, cancel, countermand, end, relax, remove, rescind, revoke, stop, terminate 4. ascend, be dispelled, climb, disappear, disperse, dissipate, mount, rise, vanish 5. Inf. appropriate, copy, crib (Inf.), half-inch (Brit. sl.), nick (Sl., chiefly Brit.), pilfer, pinch (Inf.), pirate, plagiarize, pocket, purloin, steal, take, thieve ~n. 6. car ride, drive, ride, run, transport 7. boost, encouragement, fillip, pick-me-up, reassurance, shot in the arm (Inf.), uplift 8. elevator (Chiefly U.S.)

light¹ n. 1. blaze, brightness, brilliance, effulgence, flash, glare, gleam, glint, glow, illumination, incandescence, lambency, luminescence, luminosity, lustre, phosphorescence, radiance, ray, refulgence, scintillation, shine, sparkle 2. beacon, bulb, candle, flare, lamp, lantern, lighthouse, star, taper, torch, windowpane 3. broad day, cockcrow, dawn, daybreak, daylight, daytime, morn (Poetic), morning, sun, sunbeam, sunrise, sunshine 4. Fig. angle, approach, aspect, attitude, context, interpretation, point of view, slant, vantage point, viewpoint 5. awareness, comprehension, elucidation, explanation, illustration, information, insight, knowledge, understanding 6. example, exemplar, guiding light, model, paragon, shining example 7. flame, lighter, match 8. **bring to light** disclose, discover, expose, reveal, show, uncover, unearth, unveil 9. **come to light** appear, be disclosed, be discovered, be revealed, come out, transpire, turn up 10. **in (the) light of** bearing

in mind, because of, considering, in view of, taking into account, with knowledge of 11. **shed** or **throw light on** clarify, clear up, elucidate, explain, simplify ~adj. 12. aglow, bright, brilliant, glowing, illuminated, luminous, lustrous, shining, sunny, well-lighted, well-lit 13. bleached, blond, faded, fair, lighthued, light-toned, pale, pastel ~v. 14. fire, ignite, inflame, kindle, set a match to 15. brighten, clarify, floodlight, flood with light, illuminate, illumine, irradiate, lighten, light up, put on, switch on, turn on 16. animate, brighten, cheer, irradiate, lighten

light² adj. 1. airy, buoyant, delicate, easy, flimsy, imponderous, insubstantial, lightsome, lightweight, portable, slight, underweight 2. faint, gentle, indistinct, mild, moderate, slight, soft, weak 3. inconsequential, inconsiderable, insignificant, minute, scanty, slight, small, thin, tiny, trifling, trivial, unsubstantial, wee 4. cushy (Sl.), easy, effortless, manageable, moderate, simple, undemanding, unexacting, untaxing 5. agile, airy, graceful, light-footed, lithe, nimble, sprightly, sylphlike 6. amusing, diverting, entertaining, frivolous, funny, gay, humorous, lighthearted, pleasing, superficial, trifling, trivial, witty 7. airy, animated, blithe, carefree, cheerful, cheery, fickle, frivolous, gay, lively, merry, sunny 8. dizzy, giddy, light-headed, reeling, unsteady, volatile 9. digestible, frugal, modest, not heavy, not rich, restricted, small 10. crumbly, friable, loose, porous, sandy, spongy ~v. 11. alight, land, perch, settle 12. With **on** or **upon** chance, come across, discover, encounter, find, happen upon, hit upon, stumble on

lighten¹ become light, brighten, flash, gleam, illuminate, irradiate, light up, make bright, shine

lighten² 1. disburden, ease, make lighter, reduce in weight, unload 2. alleviate, ameliorate, assuage, ease, facilitate, lessen, mitigate, reduce, relieve 3. brighten, buoy

up, cheer, elate, encourage, glad~
den, hearten, inspire, lift, perk up,
revive

light-fingered crafty, crooked
(*Inf.*), dishonest, furtive, pilfering,
pinching (*Inf.*), shifty, sly, stealing,
thieving, underhand

light-headed 1. bird-brained (*Inf.*),
featherbrained, fickle, flighty, flip~
pant, foolish, frivolous, giddy, in~
ane, rattlebrained (*Inf.*), shallow,
silly, superficial, trifling **2.** deliri~
ous, dizzy, faint, giddy, hazy, ver~
tiginous, woozy (*Inf.*)

light-hearted blithe, blithesome
(*Literary*), bright, carefree, cheer~
ful, effervescent, frolicsome, gay,
glad, gleeful, happy-go-lucky, in~
souciant, jocund, jolly, jovial, joy~
ful, joyous, merry, playful, sunny,
untroubled, upbeat (*Inf.*)

lightless caliginous (*Archaic*),
dark, dim, dusky, gloomy, inky, jet
black, murky, pitch-black, pitch-
dark, pitchy, Stygian, sunless, ten~
ebrous, unilluminated, unlighted,
unlit

lightly 1. airily, delicately, faintly,
gently, gingerly, slightly, softly,
timidly **2.** moderately, sparingly,
sparsely, thinly **3.** easily, effort~
lessly, readily, simply **4.** breezily,
carelessly, flippantly, frivolously,
heedlessly, indifferently, slighting~
ly, thoughtlessly

lightweight *adj.* inconsequential,
insignificant, of no account, paltry,
petty, slight, trifling, trivial, unim~
portant, worthless

likable, likeable agreeable, ami~
able, appealing, attractive, charm~
ing, engaging, friendly, genial,
nice, pleasant, pleasing, sympa~
thetic, winning, winsome

like¹ 1. *adj.* akin, alike, allied,
analogous, approximating, cog~
nate, corresponding, equivalent,
identical, parallel, relating, re~
sembling, same, similar **2.** *n.*
counterpart, equal, fellow, match,
parallel, twin

like² v. 1. adore (*Inf.*), be fond of, be
keen on, be partial to, delight in,
dig (*Sl.*), enjoy, go for (*Sl.*), love,
relish, revel in **2.** admire, appreci~

ate, approve, cherish, esteem, hold
dear, prize, take a shine to (*Inf.*),
take to **3.** care to, choose, choose
to, desire, fancy, feel inclined, pre~
fer, select, want, wish ~*n.* 4. Usu~
ally plural cup of tea (*Inf.*), favour~
ite, liking, partiality, predilection,
preference

likelihood chance, good chance,
liability, likeliness, possibility,
probability, prospect, reasonable~
ness, strong possibility

likely *adj.* **1.** anticipated, apt, dis~
posed, expected, in a fair way, in~
clined, liable, on the cards, pos~
sible, probable, prone, tending, to
be expected **2.** be or seem likely
be in the running for, bid fair, in~
cline towards, promise, stand a
good chance, suggest, tend **3.** be~
lievable, credible, feasible, plau~
sible, reasonable, verisimilar **4.**
acceptable, agreeable, appropri~
ate, befitting, fit, pleasing, proper,
qualified, suitable **5.** fair, favourite,
hopeful, odds-on, promising, up-
and-coming ~*adv.* **6.** doubtlessly, in
all probability, like as not (*Inf.*),
like enough (*Inf.*), no doubt, pre~
sumably, probably

liken compare, equate, juxtapose,
match, parallel, relate, set beside

likeness 1. affinity, correspond~
ence, resemblance, similarity, si~
militude **2.** copy, counterpart, de~
lineation, depiction, effigy, fac~
simile, image, model, photograph,
picture, portrait, replica, repre~
sentation, reproduction, study **3.**
appearance, form, guise, sem~
blance

liking affection, affinity, apprecia~
tion, attraction, bent, bias, desire,
fondness, inclination, love, partial~
ity, penchant, predilection, prefer~
ence, proneness, propensity, soft
spot, stomach, taste, tendency,
weakness

limb 1. appendage, arm, extension,
extremity, leg, member, part, wing
2. bough, branch, offshoot, projec~
tion, spur

limelight attention, celebrity,
fame, glare of publicity, promi~
nence, public eye, publicity, public

notice, recognition, stardom, the spotlight

limit *n.* 1. bound, breaking point, cutoff point, deadline, end, end point, furthest bound, greatest extent, termination, the bitter end, ultimate, utmost 2. *Often plural* border, boundary, confines, edge, end, extent, frontier, perimeter, periphery, precinct 3. ceiling, check, curb, limitation, maximum, obstruction, restraint, restriction 4. **the limit** *Inf.* enough, it (*Inf.*), the end, the last straw ~*v.* 5. bound, check, circumscribe, confine, curb, delimit, demarcate, fix, hem in, hinder, ration, restrain, restrict, specify

limitation block, check, condition, constraint, control, curb, disadvantage, drawback, impediment, obstruction, qualification, reservation, restraint, restriction, snag

limited 1. bounded, checked, circumscribed, confined, constrained, controlled, curbed, defined, finite, fixed, hampered, hemmed in, restricted 2. cramped, diminished, inadequate, insufficient, minimal, narrow, reduced, restricted, short, unsatisfactory

limitless boundless, countless, endless, illimitable, immeasurable, immense, inexhaustible, infinite, measureless, never-ending, numberless, unbounded, uncalculable, undefined, unending, unlimited, untold, vast

limp[1] 1. *v.* falter, halt (*Archaic*), hobble, hop, shamble, shuffle 2. *n.* hobble, lameness

limp[2] *adj.* 1. drooping, flabby, flaccid, flexible, floppy, lax, limber, loose, pliable, relaxed, slack, soft 2. debilitated, enervated, exhausted, lethargic, spent, tired, weak, worn out

line[1] *n.* 1. band, bar, channel, dash, groove, mark, rule, score, scratch, streak, stripe, stroke, underline 2. crease, crow's foot, furrow, mark, wrinkle 3. border, borderline, boundary, demarcation, edge, frontier, limit, mark 4. configuration, contour, features, figure, outline, profile, silhouette 5. cable, cord, filament, rope, strand, string, thread, wire 6. axis, course, direction, path, route, track, trajectory 7. approach, avenue, belief, course, course of action, ideology, method, policy, position, practice, procedure, scheme, system 8. activity, area, business, calling, department, employment, field, forte, interest, job, occupation, profession, province, pursuit, specialization, trade, vocation 9. column, crocodile (*Brit.*), file, procession, queue, rank, row, sequence, series 10. ancestry, breed, family, lineage, race, stock, strain, succession 11. card, letter, message, note, postcard, report, word 12. clue, hint, indication, information, lead 13. *Military* disposition, firing line, formation, front, front line, position, trenches 14. **draw the line** lay down the law, object, prohibit, put one's foot down, restrict, set a limit 15. **in line a.** in alignment, in a row, plumb, straight, true **b.** in accord, in agreement, in conformity, in harmony, in step 16. **in line for** a candidate for, being considered for, due for, in the running for, next in succession to, on the short list for ~*v.* 17. crease, cut, draw, furrow, inscribe, mark, rule, score, trace, underline 18. border, bound, edge, fringe, rank, rim, skirt, verge

line[2] *v.* ceil, cover, face, fill, interline

lineaments configuration, countenance, face, features, line, outline, phiz *or* phizog (*Sl., chiefly Brit.*), physiognomy, trait, visage

lined 1. feint, ruled 2. furrowed, wizened, worn, wrinkled

lines 1. appearance, configuration, contour, cut, outline, shape, style 2. convention, example, model, pattern, plan, principle, procedure 3. part, script, words

line-up arrangement, array, row, selection, team

line up 1. fall in, form ranks, queue up 2. assemble, come up with, lay on, obtain, organize, prepare, procure, produce, secure 3. align, arrange, array, marshal, order, range, regiment, straighten

linger 1. hang around, loiter, remain, stay, stop, tarry, wait 2. dally, dawdle, delay, idle, lag, procrastinate, take one's time 3. cling to life, die slowly, hang on, last, survive 4. abide, continue, endure, persist, remain, stay

lingering dragging, long-drawn-out, persistent, protracted, remaining, slow

link *n.* 1. component, constituent, division, element, member, part, piece 2. association, attachment, bond, connection, joint, knot, relationship, tie, tie-up, vinculum ~*v.* 3. attach, bind, connect, couple, fasten, join, tie, unite, yoke 4. associate, bracket, connect, identify, relate

lion *Fig.* 1. brave man, champion, conqueror, fighter, hero, warrior 2. big name, celebrity, idol, luminary, notable, prodigy, star, superstar, V.I.P., wonder 3. **beard the lion in his den** brave, confront, court destruction, defy danger, face, stand up to, tempt providence

lip 1. brim, brink, edge, margin, rim 2. *Sl.* backchat (*Inf.*), cheek (*Inf.*), effrontery, impertinence, insolence, rudeness, sauce (*Inf.*) 3. *Music* control, embouchure 4. **smack or lick one's lips** anticipate, delight in, drool over, enjoy, gloat over, relish, savour, slaver over

liquid *n.* 1. fluid, juice, liquor, solution ~*adj.* 2. aqueous, flowing, fluid, liquefied, melted, molten, running, runny, thawed, wet 3. bright, brilliant, clear, limpid, shining, translucent, transparent 4. dulcet, fluent, mellifluent, mellifluous, melting, smooth, soft, sweet 5. *Of assets* convertible, negotiable

liquidate 1. clear, discharge, honour, pay, pay off, settle, square 2. abolish, annul, cancel, dissolve, terminate 3. cash, convert to cash, realize, sell off, sell up 4. annihilate, bump off (*Sl.*), destroy, dispatch, do away with, do in (*Sl.*), eliminate, exterminate, finish off, get rid of, kill, murder, remove,

rub out (*U.S. sl.*), silence, wipe out (*Inf.*)

liquor 1. alcohol, booze (*Inf.*), drink, grog, hard stuff (*Inf.*), hooch (*Sl., chiefly U.S.*), intoxicant, juice (*Inf.*), spirits, strong drink 2. broth, extract, gravy, infusion, juice, liquid, stock

list[1] 1. *n.* catalogue, directory, file, index, inventory, invoice, leet (*Scot.*), listing, record, register, roll, schedule, series, syllabus, tabulation, tally 2. *v.* bill, book, catalogue, enrol, enter, enumerate, file, index, itemize, note, record, register, schedule, set down, tabulate, write down

list[2] 1. *v.* cant, careen, heel, heel over, incline, lean, tilt, tip 2. *n.* cant, leaning, slant, tilt

listen 1. attend, be all ears, be attentive, give ear, hang on (someone's) words, hark, hear, hearken (*Archaic*), keep one's ears open, lend an ear, pin back one's ears (*Inf.*), prick up one's ears 2. concentrate, do as one is told, give heed to, heed, mind, obey, observe, pay attention, take notice

listless apathetic, enervated, heavy, impassive, inattentive, indifferent, indolent, inert, languid, languishing, lethargic, lifeless, limp, lymphatic, mopish, sluggish, spiritless, supine, torpid, vacant

literacy ability, articulacy, articulateness, cultivation, education, knowledge, learning, proficiency, scholarship

literal 1. accurate, close, exact, faithful, strict, verbatim, word for word 2. boring, colourless, down-to-earth, dull, factual, matter-of-fact, prosaic, prosy, unimaginative, uninspired 3. actual, bona fide, genuine, gospel, plain, real, simple, true, unexaggerated, unvarnished

literally actually, exactly, faithfully, plainly, precisely, really, simply, strictly, to the letter, truly, verbatim, word for word

literary bookish, erudite, formal, learned, lettered, literate, scholarly, well-read

literate cultivated, cultured, edu-

cated, erudite, informed, knowl~
edgeable, learned, lettered, schol~
arly, well-informed, well-read

literature 1. belles-lettres, letters,
lore, writings, written works 2.
brochure, information, leaflet,
pamphlet

lithe flexible, limber, lissom, loose-
jointed, loose-limbed, pliable, pli~
ant, supple

litigant claimant, contestant, dis~
putant, litigator, party, plaintiff

litigate contest at law, file a suit, go
to court, go to law, institute legal
proceedings, press charges, pros~
ecute, sue

litigation action, case, contending,
disputing, lawsuit, process, pros~
ecution

litigious argumentative, belliger~
ent, contentious, disputatious,
quarrelsome

litter n. 1. debris, detritus, frag~
ments, muck, refuse, rubbish,
shreds 2. clutter, confusion, disar~
ray, disorder, jumble, mess, scat~
ter, untidiness 3. brood, family,
offspring, progeny, young 4. bed~
ding, couch, floor cover, mulch,
straw-bed 5. palanquin, stretcher
~v. 6. clutter, derange, disarrange,
disorder, mess up, scatter, strew

little adj. 1. diminutive, dwarf, elfin,
infinitesimal, Lilliputian, mini,
miniature, minute, petite, pygmy,
short, slender, small, tiny, wee 2.
babyish, immature, infant, junior,
undeveloped, young 3. hardly any,
insufficient, meagre, scant,
skimpy, small, sparse 4. brief,
fleeting, hasty, passing, short,
short-lived 5. inconsiderable, in~
significant, minor, negligible, pal~
try, trifling, trivial, unimportant 6.
base, cheap, illiberal, mean,
narrow-minded, petty, small-
minded ~adv. 7. barely, hardly, not
much, not quite, only just 8. hardly
ever, not often, rarely, scarcely,
seldom 9. **little by little** bit by bit,
by degrees, gradually, impercep~
tibly, piecemeal, progressively,
slowly, step by step ~n. 10. bit, dab,
dash, fragment, hint, modicum,
particle, pinch, small amount,

snippet, speck, spot, taste, touch,
trace, trifle

live[1] v. 1. be, be alive, breathe,
draw breath, exist, have life 2. be
permanent, be remembered, last,
persist, prevail, remain alive 3.
Sometimes with in abide, dwell,
hang out (*Inf.*), inhabit, lodge, oc~
cupy, reside, settle, stay (*Chiefly
Scot.*) 4. abide, continue, earn a
living, endure, fare, feed, get along,
lead, make ends meet, pass, re~
main, subsist, support oneself, sur~
vive 5. be happy, enjoy life, flour~
ish, luxuriate, make the most of
life, prosper, thrive 6. **live it up** *Inf.*
celebrate, enjoy oneself, have a
ball (*Inf.*), have fun, make whoo~
pee (*Inf.*), paint the town red, push
the boat out (*Brit. inf.*), revel

live[2] adj. 1. alive, animate, breath~
ing, existent, living, quick (*Archa~
ic*), vital 2. active, burning, contro~
versial, current, hot, pertinent,
pressing, prevalent, topical, unset~
tled, vital 3. *Inf.* active, alert, brisk,
dynamic, earnest, energetic, lively,
vigorous, vivid, wide-awake 4. ac~
tive, alight, blazing, burning, con~
nected, glowing, hot, ignited,
smouldering, switched on

livelihood employment, job, living,
maintenance, means, (means of)
support, occupation, (source of)
income, subsistence, sustenance,
work

liveliness activity, animation,
boisterousness, briskness, dyna~
mism, energy, gaiety, quickness,
smartness, spirit, sprightliness, vi~
tality, vivacity

lively 1. active, agile, alert, brisk,
chipper (*Inf.*), chirpy, energetic,
full of pep (*Inf.*), keen, nimble,
perky, quick, sprightly, spry, vig~
orous 2. animated, blithe, blithe~
some, cheerful, frisky, frolicsome,
gay, merry, sparkling, spirited, vi~
vacious 3. astir, bustling, busy,
buzzing, crowded, eventful, mov~
ing, stirring 4. bright, colourful,
exciting, forceful, invigorating,
racy, refreshing, stimulating, vivid

liven animate, brighten, buck up
(*Inf.*), enliven, hot up (*Inf.*), pep up,

perk up, put life into, rouse, stir, vitalize, vivify

liverish 1. bilious, queasy, sick 2. crotchety (*Inf.*), crusty, disagree~ able, fratchy (*Inf.*), grumpy, ill-humoured, irascible, irritable, peevish, snappy, splenetic

livery attire, clothing, costume, dress, garb, raiment (*Poetic*), re~ galia, suit, uniform, vestments

live wire ball of fire (*Inf.*), dynamo, go-getter (*Inf.*), hustler (*U.S.*), life and soul of the party, self-starter

livid 1. angry, black-and-blue, bruised, contused, discoloured, purple 2. ashen, blanched, blood~ less, doughy, greyish, leaden, pale, pallid, pasty, wan, waxen 3. *Inf.* angry, beside oneself, boiling, en~ raged, exasperated, fuming, furi~ ous, incensed, indignant, infuriat~ ed, mad (*Inf.*), outraged

living *adj.* 1. active, alive, animated, breathing, existing, in the land of the living (*Inf.*), lively, quick (*Ar~ chaic*), strong, vigorous, vital 2. active, contemporary, continuing, current, developing, extant, in use, ongoing, operative, persisting ~*n.* 3. animation, being, existence, ex~ isting, life, subsistence 4. life style, mode of living, way of life 5. job, livelihood, maintenance, (means of) support, occupation, (source of) income, subsistence, sustenance, work 6. *Church of England* ben~ efice 7. **the living** flesh and blood, the quick (*Archaic*)

load *n.* 1. bale, cargo, consignment, freight, lading, shipment 2. afflic~ tion, burden, encumbrance, incu~ bus, millstone, onus, oppression, pressure, trouble, weight, worry ~*v.* 3. cram, fill, freight, heap, lade, pack, pile, stack, stuff 4. burden, encumber, hamper, oppress, sad~ dle with, trouble, weigh down, worry 5. *Of firearms* charge, make ready, prepare to fire, prime 6. **load the dice** fix, rig, set up

loaded 1. burdened, charged, freighted, full, laden, weighted 2. biased, distorted, weighted 3. art~ ful, insidious, manipulative, preju~ dicial, tricky 4. at the ready,

charged, primed, ready to shoot *or* fire 5. *Sl.* affluent, flush (*Inf.*), moneyed, rich, rolling (*Sl.*), wealthy, well-heeled (*Sl.*), well off, well-to-do

loaf *n.* 1. block, cake, cube, lump, slab 2. *Sl.* block (*Inf.*), chump (*Brit. sl.*), gumption (*Inf.*), head, noddle (*Inf., chiefly Brit.*), nous (*Brit. sl.*), sense

loan 1. *n.* accommodation, advance, allowance, credit, mortgage, touch (*Sl.*) 2. *v.* accommodate, advance, allow, credit, lend, let out

loath, loth against, averse, back~ ward, counter, disinclined, indis~ posed, opposed, reluctant, resist~ ing, unwilling

loathing abhorrence, abomination, antipathy, aversion, detestation, disgust, execration, hatred, horror, odium, repugnance, repulsion, re~ vulsion

loathsome abhorrent, abominable, detestable, disgusting, execrable, hateful, horrible, nasty, nauseating, obnoxious, odious, offensive, re~ pugnant, repulsive, revolting, vile

lobby *n.* 1. corridor, entrance hall, foyer, hall, hallway, passage, passageway, porch, vestibule 2. pressure group ~*v.* 3. bring pres~ sure to bear, campaign for, exert influence, influence, persuade, press for, pressure, promote, pull strings (*Brit. inf.*), push for, solicit votes, urge

local *adj.* 1. community, district, neighbourhood, parish, provincial, regional 2. confined, limited, nar~ row, parish, parochial, provincial, pump, restricted, small-town ~*n.* 3. character (*Inf.*), inhabitant, local yokel (*Disparaging*), native, resi~ dent

locality 1. area, district, neck of the woods (*Inf.*), neighbourhood, re~ gion, vicinity 2. locale, location, place, position, scene, setting, site, spot

localize 1. circumscribe, concen~ trate, confine, contain, delimit, de~ limitate, limit, restrain, restrict 2. ascribe, assign, narrow down, pin~ point, specify

locate 1. come across, detect, dis~
cover, find, lay one's hands on, pin
down, pinpoint, run to earth, track
down, unearth 2. establish, fix,
place, put, seat, set, settle, situate

location bearings, locale, locus,
place, point, position, site, situa~
tion, spot, venue, whereabouts

lock[1] n. 1. bolt, clasp, fastening,
padlock ~v. 2. bolt, close, fasten,
latch, seal, secure, shut, sneck
(*Dialect*) 3. clench, engage, entan~
gle, entwine, join, link, mesh, unite
4. clasp, clutch, embrace, encircle,
enclose, grapple, grasp, hug, press

lock[2] curl, ringlet, strand, tress, tuft

lock out ban, bar, debar, exclude,
keep out, refuse admittance to,
shut out

lockup cell, cooler (*Sl.*), gaol, jail,
jug (*Sl.*), police cell

lock up cage, confine, detain, im~
prison, incarcerate, jail, put behind
bars, shut up

lodge n. 1. cabin, chalet, cottage,
gatehouse, house, hunting lodge,
hut, shelter 2. assemblage, asso~
ciation, branch, chapter, club,
group, society 3. den, haunt, lair,
retreat ~v. 4. accommodate, billet,
board, entertain, harbour, put up,
quarter, room, shelter, sojourn,
stay, stop 5. become fixed, catch,
come to rest, imbed, implant, stick
6. deposit, file, lay, place, put, put
on record, register, set, submit

lodger boarder, guest, paying guest,
P.G., resident, roomer, tenant

lodging *Often plural* abode, ac~
commodation, apartments, board~
ing, digs (*Brit. inf.*), dwelling, habi~
tation, quarters, residence, rooms,
shelter

lofty 1. elevated, high, raised, sky-
high, soaring, tall, towering 2. dig~
nified, distinguished, elevated, ex~
alted, grand, illustrious, imposing,
majestic, noble, renowned, stately,
sublime, superior 3. arrogant, con~
descending, disdainful, haughty,
high and mighty (*Inf.*), lordly, pat~
ronizing, proud, snooty (*Inf.*),
supercilious, toffee-nosed (*Brit. sl.*)

log n. 1. block, bole, chunk, piece of
timber, stump, trunk ~v. 2. chop,

cut, fell, hew ~n. 3. account, chart,
daybook, journal, listing, logbook,
record, tally ~v. 4. book, chart,
make a note of, note, record, reg~
ister, report, set down, tally

loggerhead **at loggerheads** at
daggers drawn, at each other's
throats, at enmity, at odds, es~
tranged, feuding, in dispute, op~
posed, quarrelling

logic 1. argumentation, deduction,
dialectics, ratiocination, science of
reasoning, syllogistic reasoning 2.
good reason, good sense, reason,
sense, sound judgment 3. chain of
thought, coherence, connection,
link, rationale, relationship

logical 1. clear, cogent, coherent,
consistent, deducible, pertinent,
rational, reasonable, relevant,
sound, valid, well-organized 2. ju~
dicious, most likely, necessary, ob~
vious, plausible, reasonable, sen~
sible, wise

loiter dally, dawdle, delay, dilly-
dally (*Inf.*), hang about *or* around,
idle, lag, linger, loaf, loll, saunter,
skulk, stroll

loll 1. flop, lean, loaf, lounge, re~
cline, relax, slouch, slump, sprawl
2. dangle, droop, drop, flap, flop,
hang, hang loosely, sag

lone by oneself, deserted, isolated,
lonesome, one, only, separate,
separated, single, sole, solitary,
unaccompanied

loneliness aloneness, deserted~
ness, desolation, dreariness, for~
lornness, isolation, lonesomeness,
seclusion, solitariness, solitude

lonely 1. abandoned, destitute, es~
tranged, forlorn, forsaken, friend~
less, lonesome, outcast 2. alone,
apart, by oneself, companionless,
isolated, lone, single, solitary,
withdrawn 3. deserted, desolate,
isolated, off the beaten track (*Inf.*),
out-of-the-way, remote, secluded,
sequestered, solitary, unfrequent~
ed, uninhabited

long[1] *adj.* 1. elongated, expanded,
extended, extensive, far-reaching,
lengthy, spread out, stretched 2.
dragging, interminable, late,
lengthy, lingering, long-drawn-out,

prolonged, protracted, slow, sus~
tained, tardy

long² v. covet, crave, desire, dream
of, hanker, hunger, itch, lust, pine,
want, wish, yearn

longing 1. n. ambition, aspiration,
coveting, craving, desire, hanker~
ing, hungering, itch, thirst, urge,
wish, yearning, yen (*Inf.*) **2.** adj.
anxious, ardent, avid, craving, de~
sirous, eager, hungry, languishing,
pining, wishful, wistful, yearning

long-lived enduring, full of years,
longevous, long-lasting, old as Me~
thuselah

long-standing abiding, enduring,
established, fixed, hallowed by
time, long-established, long-lasting,
long-lived, time-honoured

long-suffering easygoing, for~
bearing, forgiving, patient, re~
signed, stoical, tolerant, uncom~
plaining

long-winded diffuse, discursive,
garrulous, lengthy, long-drawn-out,
overlong, prolix, prolonged, ram~
bling, repetitious, tedious, verbose,
wordy

look v. **1.** behold (*Archaic*), consid~
er, contemplate, examine, eye,
feast one's eyes upon, gaze, glance,
inspect, observe, peep, regard,
scan, scrutinize, see, study, survey,
take a gander at (*Inf.*), view, watch
2. appear, display, evidence, ex~
hibit, look like, make clear, mani~
fest, present, seem, seem to be,
show, strike one as **3.** face, front,
front on, give onto, overlook **4.** an~
ticipate, await, expect, hope, reck~
on on **5.** forage, hunt, search, seek
6. gape, gawk, gawp (*Brit. sl.*),
glower, goggle, rubberneck (*Sl.*),
ogle, stare **7. look like** be the im~
age of, favour, make one think of,
put one in mind of, remind one of,
resemble, take after ~n. **8.** exami~
nation, eyeful (*Inf.*), gaze, glance,
glimpse, inspection, look-see (*Sl.*),
observation, once-over (*Inf.*), peek,
review, sight, squint (*Inf.*), survey,
view **9.** air, appearance, aspect,
bearing, cast, complexion, counte~
nance, demeanour, effect, expres~

sion, face, fashion, guise, manner,
mien (*Literary*), semblance

look after attend to, care for,
guard, keep an eye on, mind,
nurse, protect, sit with, supervise,
take care of, take charge of, tend,
watch

look down on *or* **upon** contemn,
despise, disdain, hold in contempt,
look down one's nose at (*Inf.*), mis~
prize, scorn, sneer, spurn, treat
with contempt, turn one's nose up
(at) (*Inf.*)

look forward to anticipate, await,
count on, count the days until, ex~
pect, hope for, long for, look for,
wait for

look into check out, delve into, ex~
amine, explore, follow up, go into,
inquire about, inspect, investigate,
look over, make enquiries, probe,
research, scrutinize, study

lookout 1. guard, qui vive, readi~
ness, vigil, watch **2.** guard, sentinel,
sentry, vedette (*Military*), watch~
man **3.** beacon, citadel, observa~
tion post, post, tower, watchtower
4. *Inf.* business, concern, funeral
(*Inf.*), pigeon (*Brit. inf.*), worry **5.**
chances, future, likelihood, out~
look, prospect, view

look out be alert, be careful, be on
guard, be on the qui vive, be vigi~
lant, beware, keep an eye out, keep
one's eyes open (peeled, skinned),
pay attention, watch out

look over cast an eye over, check,
examine, flick through, inspect,
look through, monitor, peruse,
scan, view

look up 1. find, hunt for, research,
search for, seek out, track down **2.**
ameliorate, come along, get better,
improve, perk up, pick up, pro~
gress, shape up, show improve~
ment **3.** *With* **to** admire, defer to,
esteem, have a high opinion of,
honour, regard highly, respect, re~
vere **4.** call (on), drop in on (*Inf.*),
go to see, look in on, pay a visit to,
visit

loom 1. appear, become visible, be
imminent, bulk, emerge, hover,
impend, menace, take shape,
threaten **2.** dominate, hang over,

mount, overhang, overshadow, overtop, rise, soar, tower

loop 1. *n.* bend, circle, coil, convo~ lution, curl, curve, eyelet, hoop, kink, loophole, noose, ring, spiral, twirl, twist, whorl 2. *v.* bend, braid, circle, coil, connect, curl, curve round, encircle, fold, join, knot, roll, spiral, turn, twist, wind round

loophole 1. aperture, knothole, opening, slot 2. *Fig.* avoidance, es~ cape, evasion, excuse, let-out, means of escape, plea, pretence, pretext, subterfuge

loose *adj.* 1. floating, free, insecure, movable, released, unattached, unbound, unconfined, unfastened, unfettered, unrestricted, un~ secured, untied, wobbly 2. baggy, easy, hanging, loosened, not fitting, not tight, relaxed, slack, slackened, sloppy 3. diffuse, disconnected, disordered, ill-defined, imprecise, inaccurate, indefinite, indistinct, inexact, rambling, random, vague 4. abandoned, debauched, disrepu~ table, dissipated, dissolute, fast, immoral, lewd, libertine, licen~ tious, profligate, promiscuous, un~ chaste, wanton 5. careless, heed~ less, imprudent, lax, negligent, rash, thoughtless, unmindful ~*v.* 6. detach, disconnect, disengage, ease, free, let go, liberate, loosen, release, set free, slacken, unbind, undo, unfasten, unleash, unloose, untie

loosen 1. detach, let out, separate, slacken, unbind, undo, unloose, un~ stick, untie, work free, work loose 2. deliver, free, let go, liberate, re~ lease, set free 3. *Often with* **up** ease up *or* off, go easy (*Inf.*), less~ en, let up, mitigate, moderate, re~ lax, soften, weaken

loot 1. *n.* booty, goods, haul, plun~ der, prize, spoils, swag (*Sl.*) 2. *v.* despoil, pillage, plunder, raid, ran~ sack, ravage, rifle, rob, sack

lopsided askew, asymmetrical, awry, cockeyed, crooked, dispro~ portionate, off balance, one-sided, out of shape, out of true, squint, tilting, unbalanced, unequal, un~ even, warped

lord 1. commander, governor, king, leader, liege, master, monarch, overlord, potentate, prince, ruler, seigneur, sovereign, superior 2. earl, noble, nobleman, peer, vis~ count 3. **lord it over** act big (*Sl.*), be overbearing, boss around (*Inf.*), domineer, order around, play the lord, pull rank, put on airs, swag~ ger

Lord, Our *or* **The** Christ, God, Jeho~ vah, Jesus Christ, the Almighty

lordly 1. arrogant, condescending, despotic, dictatorial, disdainful, domineering, haughty, high and mighty (*Inf.*), high-handed, hoity- toity (*Inf.*), imperious, lofty, over~ bearing, patronizing, proud, stuck- up (*Inf.*), supercilious, toffee-nosed (*Sl., chiefly Brit.*), tyrannical 2. aristocratic, dignified, exalted, gracious, grand, imperial, lofty, majestic, noble, princely, regal, stately

lore 1. beliefs, doctrine, experience, folk-wisdom, mythos, saws, say~ ings, teaching, traditional wisdom, traditions, wisdom 2. erudition, knowhow (*Inf.*), knowledge, learn~ ing, letters, scholarship

lose 1. be deprived of, displace, drop, fail to keep, forget, mislay, misplace, miss, suffer loss 2. ca~ pitulate, default, fail, fall short, forfeit, lose out on (*Inf.*), miss, pass up (*Inf.*), yield 3. be defeated, be the loser, be worsted, come a cropper (*Inf.*), come to grief, get the worst of, lose out, suffer defeat, take a licking (*Inf.*) 4. consume, deplete, dissipate, drain, exhaust, expend, lavish, misspend, squan~ der, use up, waste 5. confuse, miss, stray from, wander from 6. lap, leave behind, outdistance, outrun, outstrip, overtake, pass 7. dodge, duck, elude, escape, evade, give someone the slip, shake off, slip away, throw off

loser also-ran, dud (*Inf.*), failure, flop (*Inf.*), lemon (*Sl.*), no-hoper (*Austral. sl.*), underdog, washout (*Inf.*)

loss 1. bereavement, deprivation, disappearance, failure, forfeiture, losing, misfortune, mislaying, privation, squandering, waste 2. cost, damage, defeat, destruction, detriment, disadvantage, harm, hurt, impairment, injury, ruin 3. *Plural* casualties, dead, death toll, fatalities, number killed (captured, injured, missing, wounded) 4. *Sometimes plural* debit, debt, deficiency, deficit, depletion, losings, shrinkage 5. at a loss at one's wits' end, baffled, bewildered, confused, helpless, nonplussed, perplexed, puzzled, stuck (*Inf.*), stumped

lost 1. disappeared, forfeited, mislaid, misplaced, missed, missing, strayed, vanished, wayward 2. adrift, astray, at sea, disoriented, off-course, off-track 3. baffled, bewildered, clueless (*Sl.*), confused, helpless, ignorant, mystified, perplexed, puzzled 4. abolished, annihilated, demolished, destroyed, devastated, eradicated, exterminated, obliterated, perished, ruined, wasted, wiped out, wrecked 5. absent, absorbed, abstracted, distracted, dreamy, engrossed, entranced, preoccupied, rapt, spellbound, taken up 6. consumed, dissipated, frittered away, misapplied, misdirected, misspent, misused, squandered, wasted 7. bygone, dead, extinct, forgotten, gone, lapsed, obsolete, out-of-date, past, unremembered 8. abandoned, corrupt, damned, depraved, dissolute, fallen, irreclaimable, licentious, profligate, unchaste, wanton

lot 1. assortment, batch, bunch (*Inf.*), collection, consignment, crowd, group, quantity, set 2. accident, chance, destiny, doom, fate, fortune, hazard, plight, portion 3. allowance, cut (*Inf.*), parcel, part, percentage, piece, portion, quota, ration, share 4. a lot *or* lots abundance, a great deal, heap(s), large amount, load(s) (*Inf.*), masses (*Inf.*), numbers, ocean(s), oodles (*Inf.*), piles, plenty, quantities, reams (*Inf.*), scores, stack(s) 5. draw lots choose, cut for aces, cut straws (*Inf.*), decide, pick, select, spin a coin, toss up 6. throw in one's lot with ally *or* align oneself

with, join, join forces with, join fortunes with, make common cause with, support

lotion balm, cream, embrocation, liniment, salve, solution

lottery 1. draw, raffle, sweepstake 2. chance, gamble, hazard, risk, toss-up (*Inf.*), venture

loud 1. blaring, blatant, boisterous, booming, clamorous, deafening, ear-piercing, ear-splitting, forte (*Music*), high-sounding, noisy, obstreperous, piercing, resounding, rowdy, sonorous, stentorian, strident, strong, thundering, tumultuous, turbulent, vehement, vociferous 2. *Fig.* brassy, flamboyant, flashy, garish, gaudy, glaring, lurid, ostentatious, showy, tasteless, tawdry, vulgar 3. brash, brazen, coarse, crass, crude, loud-mouthed (*Inf.*), offensive, raucous, vulgar

loudly at full volume, at the top of one's voice, clamorously, deafeningly, fortissimo (*Music*), lustily, noisily, shrilly, uproariously, vehemently, vigorously, vociferously

lounge v. 1. laze, lie about, loaf, loiter, loll, recline, relax, saunter, sprawl, take it easy (*Inf.*) 2. dawdle, fritter time away, idle, kill time, pass time idly, potter, waste time

lout bear, boor, bumpkin, churl, clod, clumsy idiot, dolt, gawk, lubber, lummox (*Inf.*), oaf, yahoo, yob *or* yobbo (*Brit. sl.*)

lovable adorable, amiable, attractive, captivating, charming, cuddly, delightful, enchanting, endearing, engaging, fetching (*Inf.*), likable, lovely, pleasing, sweet, winning, winsome

love v. 1. adore, adulate, be attached to, be in love with, cherish, dote on, have affection for, hold dear, idolize, prize, think the world of, treasure, worship 2. appreciate, delight in, desire, enjoy, fancy, have a weakness for, like, relish, savour, take pleasure in 3. canoodle (*Sl.*), caress, cuddle, embrace, fondle, kiss, neck (*Inf.*), pet ~n. 4. adoration, adulation, affection, amity, ardour, attachment, devo~

tion, fondness, friendship, infatua~
tion, liking, passion, rapture, re~
gard, tenderness, warmth 5. de~
light, devotion, enjoyment, fond~
ness, inclination, liking, partiality,
relish, soft spot, taste, weakness 6.
angel, beloved, darling, dear,
dearest, dear one, inamorata, in~
amorato, loved one, lover, sweet,
sweetheart, truelove 7. **for love** for
nothing, freely, free of charge,
gratis, pleasurably, without pay~
ment 8. **for love or money** by any
means, ever, under any conditions
9. **in love** besotted, charmed, en~
amoured, enraptured, infatuated,
smitten 10. **fall in love (with)** be~
stow one's affections on, be taken
with, fall for, lose one's heart (to),
take a shine to (*Inf.*)

love affair 1. affair, *affaire de
coeur*, amour, intrigue, liaison, re~
lationship, romance 2. apprecia~
tion, devotion, enthusiasm, love,
mania, passion

lovely 1. admirable, adorable, ami~
able, attractive, beautiful, charm~
ing, comely, exquisite, graceful,
handsome, pretty, sweet, winning
2. agreeable, captivating, delight~
ful, enchanting, engaging, enjoy~
able, gratifying, nice, pleasant,
pleasing

lover admirer, beau, beloved, boy~
friend, fancy man (*Sl.*), fancy
woman (Sl.), fiancé, fiancée, flame
(*Inf.*), girlfriend, inamorata, in~
amorato, mistress, paramour, suit~
or, swain (*Archaic*), sweetheart

loving affectionate, amorous, ar~
dent, cordial, dear, demonstrative,
devoted, doting, fond, friendly,
kind, solicitous, tender, warm,
warm-hearted

low 1. little, short, small, squat,
stunted 2. deep, depressed, ground-
level, low-lying, shallow, subsided,
sunken 3. depleted, insignificant,
little, meagre, paltry, reduced,
scant, small, sparse, trifling 4. de~
ficient, inadequate, inferior, low-
grade, mediocre, poor, puny,
second-rate, shoddy, substandard,
worthless 5. coarse, common,
crude, disgraceful, dishonourable,
disreputable, gross, ill-bred, ob~
scene, rough, rude, unbecoming,
undignified, unrefined, vulgar 6.
humble, lowborn, lowly, meek, ob~
scure, plain, plebeian, poor, simple,
unpretentious 7. blue, brassed off
(*Inf.*), dejected, depressed, de~
spondent, disheartened, down,
downcast, down in the dumps
(*Inf.*), fed up, forlorn, gloomy,
glum, miserable, morose, sad, un~
happy 8. debilitated, dying, ex~
hausted, feeble, frail, ill, prostrate,
reduced, sinking, stricken, weak 9.
gentle, hushed, muffled, muted,
quiet, soft, subdued, whispered 10.
cheap, economical, inexpensive,
moderate, modest, reasonable 11.
abject, base, contemptible, das~
tardly, degraded, depraved, des~
picable, ignoble, mean, menial,
nasty, scurvy, servile, sordid, un~
worthy, vile, vulgar

lowdown dope (*Sl.*), gen (*Brit. inf.*),
info (*Inf.*), information, inside sto~
ry, intelligence

lower[1] *adj.* 1. inferior, junior, less~
er, low-level, minor, secondary,
second-class, smaller, subordinate,
under 2. curtailed, decreased, di~
minished, lessened, pared down,
reduced ~*v.* 3. depress, drop, fall,
let down, make lower, sink, sub~
merge, take down 4. abase, belittle,
condescend, debase, degrade,
deign, demean, devalue, disgrace,
downgrade, humble, humiliate,
stoop 5. abate, curtail, cut, de~
crease, diminish, lessen, minimize,
moderate, prune, reduce, slash 6.
soften, tone down

lower[2], **lour** 1. be brewing, black~
en, cloud up *or* over, darken, loom,
menace, threaten 2. frown, give a
dirty look, glare, glower, look dag~
gers, look sullen, scowl

low-grade bad, inferior, not good
enough, not up to snuff (*Inf.*), poor,
second-rate, substandard

low-key low-pitched, muffled,
muted, played down, quiet, re~
strained, subdued, toned down,
understated

lowly 1. ignoble, inferior, lowborn,
mean, obscure, plebeian, proletar~

ian, subordinate 2. docile, dutiful, gentle, humble, meek, mild, modest, submissive, unassuming 3. average, common, homespun, modest, ordinary, plain, poor, simple, unpretentious

low-spirited apathetic, blue, brassed off (*Inf.*), dejected, depressed, despondent, down, downhearted, down in the dumps (*Inf.*), fed up, gloomy, heavy-hearted, low, miserable, moody, sad, unhappy

loyal attached, constant, dependable, devoted, dutiful, faithful, patriotic, staunch, steadfast, tried and true, true, true-blue, true-hearted, trustworthy, trusty, unswerving, unwavering

loyalty allegiance, constancy, dependability, devotion, faithfulness, fealty, fidelity, patriotism, reliability, staunchness, steadfastness, true-heartedness, trueness, trustiness, trustworthiness

lubricate grease, make slippery, make smooth, oil, oil the wheels, smear, smooth the way

lucid 1. clear, clear-cut, comprehensible, crystal clear, distinct, evident, explicit, intelligible, limpid, obvious, pellucid, plain, transparent 2. beaming, bright, brilliant, effulgent, gleaming, luminous, radiant, resplendent, shining 3. clear, crystalline, diaphanous, glassy, limpid, pellucid, pure, translucent, transparent 4. all there, clearheaded, *compos mentis*, in one's right mind, rational, reasonable, sane, sensible, sober, sound

luck 1. accident, chance, destiny, fate, fortuity, fortune, hap (*Archaic*), hazard 2. advantage, blessing, break (*Inf.*), fluke, godsend, good fortune, good luck, prosperity, serendipity, stroke, success, windfall

luckily 1. favourably, fortunately, happily, opportunely, propitiously, providentially 2. as it chanced, as luck would have it, by chance, fortuitously

luckless calamitous, cursed, disastrous, doomed, hapless, hopeless, ill-fated, ill-starred, jinxed, star-crossed, unfortunate, unhappy, unlucky, unpropitious, unsuccessful

lucky 1. advantageous, blessed, charmed, favoured, fortunate, prosperous, serendipitous, successful 2. adventitious, auspicious, fortuitous, opportune, propitious, providential, timely

lucrative advantageous, fat, fruitful, gainful, high-income, money-making, paying, productive, profitable, remunerative, well-paid

lucre gain, mammon, money, pelf, profit, riches, spoils, wealth

ludicrous absurd, burlesque, comic, comical, crazy, droll, farcical, funny, incongruous, laughable, nonsensical, odd, outlandish, preposterous, ridiculous, silly, zany

luggage baggage, bags, cases, gear, impedimenta, paraphernalia, suitcases, things, trunks

lugubrious dirgelike, dismal, doleful, dreary, funereal, gloomy, melancholy, morose, mournful, sad, serious, sombre, sorrowful, woebegone, woeful

lukewarm 1. blood-warm, tepid, warm 2. *Fig.* apathetic, cold, cool, half-hearted, indifferent, laodicean, phlegmatic, unconcerned, unenthusiastic, uninterested, unresponsive

lull *v.* 1. allay, calm, compose, hush, lullaby, pacify, quell, quiet, rock to sleep, soothe, still, subdue, tranquillize 2. abate, cease, decrease, diminish, dwindle, ease off, let up, moderate, quieten down, slacken, subside, wane ~*n.* 3. calm, calmness, hush, let-up (*Inf.*), pause, quiet, respite, silence, stillness, tranquillity

lullaby berceuse, cradlesong

lumber¹ 1. *n.* castoffs, clutter, discards, jumble, junk, refuse, rubbish, trash, trumpery, white elephants 2. *v. Brit. sl.* burden, encumber, impose upon, land, load, saddle

lumber² *v.* clump, lump along, plod, shamble, shuffle, stump, trudge, trundle, waddle

lumbering awkward, blundering, bovine, bumbling, clumsy, elephantine, heavy, heavy-footed, hulking, lubberly, overgrown, pon~ derous, ungainly, unwieldy

luminous bright, brilliant, glowing, illuminated, lighted, lit, lumines~ cent, lustrous, radiant, resplendent, shining, vivid

lump n. 1. ball, bunch, cake, chunk, clod, cluster, dab, gob, gobbet, group, hunk, mass, nugget, piece, spot, wedge 2. bulge, bump, growth, protrusion, protuberance, swelling, tumescence, tumour ~v. 3. agglutinate, aggregate, batch, bunch, coalesce, collect, combine, conglomerate, consolidate, group, mass, pool, unite

lunacy 1. dementia, derangement, idiocy, insanity, madness, mania, psychosis 2. absurdity, craziness, folly, foolhardiness, foolishness, idiocy, imbecility, madness, sense~ lessness, stupidity, tomfoolery

lunatic 1. adj. barmy (Sl.), bonkers (Sl.), crackbrained, crazy, daft, de~ mented, deranged, insane, irra~ tional, mad, maniacal, nuts (Sl.), psychotic, unhinged 2. n. loony (Sl.), madman, maniac, nut (Sl.), nutcase (Sl.), nutter (Sl.), psycho~ path

lunge 1. n. charge, cut, jab, pass, pounce, spring, stab, swing, swipe, thrust 2. v. bound, charge, cut, dash, dive, fall upon, hit at, jab, leap, pitch into, plunge, poke, pounce, set upon, stab, strike at, thrust

lure 1. v. allure, attract, beckon, decoy, draw, ensnare, entice, in~ veigle, invite, lead on, seduce, tempt 2. n. allurement, attraction, bait, carrot (Inf.), come-on (Inf.), decoy, enticement, inducement, magnet, siren song, temptation

lurk conceal oneself, crouch, go furtively, hide, lie in wait, move with stealth, prowl, skulk, slink, sneak, snoop

luscious appetizing, delectable, delicious, honeyed, juicy, mouth~ watering, palatable, rich, savoury,

scrumptious (Inf.), succulent, sweet, toothsome, yummy (Sl.)

lush abundant, dense, flourishing, green, lavish, overgrown, prolific, rank, teeming, verdant

lust n. 1. carnality, concupiscence, lasciviousness, lechery, lewdness, libido, licentiousness, pruriency, randiness (Sl., chiefly Brit.), sala~ ciousness, sensuality, wantonness 2. appetence, appetite, avidity, covetousness, craving, cupidity, desire, greed, longing, passion, thirst ~v. 3. be consumed with de~ sire for, covet, crave, desire, hun~ ger for or after, lech after (Inf.), need, slaver over, want, yearn

lustre 1. burnish, gleam, glint, glit~ ter, gloss, glow, sheen, shimmer, shine, sparkle 2. brightness, bril~ liance, dazzle, lambency, lumi~ nousness, radiance, resplendence 3. distinction, fame, glory, honour, illustriousness, prestige, renown

lusty brawny, energetic, hale, healthy, hearty, in fine fettle, pow~ erful, red-blooded (Inf.), robust, rugged, stalwart, stout, strapping, strong, sturdy, vigorous, virile

luxurious comfortable, costly, de luxe, expensive, lavish, magnifi~ cent, opulent, plush (Inf.), rich, ritzy (Sl.), splendid, sumptuous, well-appointed

luxury 1. affluence, hedonism, opu~ lence, richness, splendour, sump~ tuousness, voluptuousness 2. bliss, comfort, delight, enjoyment, grati~ fication, indulgence, pleasure, sat~ isfaction, wellbeing 3. extra, ex~ travagance, frill, indulgence, non~ essential, treat

lying 1. n. deceit, dishonesty, dis~ simulation, double-dealing, duplic~ ity, fabrication, falsity, fibbing, guile, mendacity, perjury, prevari~ cation, untruthfulness 2. adj. de~ ceitful, dishonest, dissembling, double-dealing, false, guileful, mendacious, perfidious, treacher~ ous, two-faced, untruthful

M

macabre cadaverous, deathlike, deathly, dreadful, eerie, frightening, frightful, ghastly, ghostly, ghoulish, grim, grisly, gruesome, hideous, horrid, morbid, unearthly, weird

machine 1. apparatus, appliance, contraption, contrivance, device, engine, instrument, mechanism, tool 2. agency, machinery, organization, party, setup (*Inf.*), structure, system 3. *Fig.* agent, automaton, mechanical man, puppet, robot, zombie

machinery 1. apparatus, equipment, gear, instruments, mechanism, tackle, tools, works 2. agency, channels, machine, organization, procedure, structure, system

mad 1. aberrant, bananas (*Sl.*), barmy (*Sl.*), batty (*Sl.*), bonkers (*Sl.*), crackers (*Sl.*), crazed, crazy (*Inf.*), cuckoo (*Inf.*), delirious, demented, deranged, distracted, frantic, frenzied, insane, loony (*Sl.*), loopy (*Inf.*), lunatic, mental (*Sl.*), *non compos mentis*, nuts (*Sl.*), nutty (*Sl.*), off one's chump (*Sl.*), off one's head, off one's nut (*Sl.*), off one's rocker (*Sl.*), off one's trolley (*Sl.*), of unsound mind, out of one's mind, psychotic, rabid, raving, round the bend (*Brit. sl.*), round the twist (*Brit. sl.*), screwy (*Inf.*), unbalanced, unhinged, unstable 2. absurd, daft (*Inf.*), foolhardy, foolish, imprudent, irrational, ludicrous, nonsensical, preposterous, senseless, unreasonable, unsafe, unsound, wild 3. *Inf.* angry, berserk, enraged, exasperated, fuming, furious, in a wax (*Inf.*), incensed, infuriated, irate, irritated, livid (*Inf.*), raging, resentful, seeing red (*Inf.*), wild, wrathful 4. ardent, avid, crazy, daft (*Inf.*), devoted, dotty (*Brit. sl.*), enamoured, enthusiastic, fanatical, fond, hooked (*Sl.*), impassioned, infatuated, in love with, keen, nuts (*Sl.*), wild, zealous

madden annoy, craze, derange, drive one crazy (off one's head, out of one's mind, round the bend (*Brit. sl.*), round the twist (*Brit. sl.*), to distraction), enrage, exasperate, get one's hackles up, incense, inflame, infuriate, irritate, make one's blood boil, make one see red (*Inf.*), make one's hackles rise, provoke, raise one's hackles, unhinge, upset, vex

made-up fabricated, false, fictional, imaginary, invented, make-believe, mythical, specious, trumped-up, unreal, untrue

madly 1. crazily, deliriously, dementedly, distractedly, frantically, frenziedly, hysterically, insanely, rabidly 2. absurdly, foolishly, irrationally, ludicrously, nonsensically, senselessly, unreasonably, wildly 3. energetically, excitedly, furiously, hastily, hurriedly, like mad, quickly, rapidly, recklessly, speedily, violently, wildly 4. *Inf.* desperately, devotedly, exceedingly, excessively, extremely, intensely, passionately, to distraction

madman *or* **madwoman** loony (*Sl.*), lunatic, maniac, mental case (*Sl.*), nut (*Sl.*), nutcase (*Sl.*), nutter (*Sl.*), psycho (*Sl.*), psychopath, psychotic

madness 1. aberration, craziness, delusion, dementia, derangement, distraction, insanity, lunacy, mania, mental illness, psychopathy, psychosis 2. absurdity, daftness (*Inf.*), folly, foolhardiness, foolishness, nonsense, preposterousness, wildness 3. anger, exasperation, frenzy, fury, ire, rage, raving, wildness, wrath 4. ardour, craze, enthusiasm, fanaticism, fondness, infatuation, keenness, passion, rage, zeal 5. abandon, agitation, excitement, frenzy, furore, intoxication, riot, unrestraint, uproar

magazine 1. journal, pamphlet, paper, periodical 2. ammunition dump, arsenal, depot, powder-room (*Obsolete*), store, storehouse, warehouse

magic *n.* **1.** black art, enchantment, necromancy, occultism, sorcery, sortilege, spell, theurgy, witch-craft, wizardry **2.** conjuring, hocus-pocus, illusion, jiggery-pokery (*Inf.*, *chiefly Brit.*), jugglery, leger-demain, prestidigitation, sleight of hand, trickery **3.** allurement, charm, enchantment, fascination, glamour, magnetism, power ~*adj.* **4.** *Also* **magical** bewitching, char-ismatic, charming, enchanting, entrancing, fascinating, magnetic, marvellous, miraculous, sorcerous, spellbinding

magician 1. archimage (*Rare*), conjurer, conjuror, enchanter, en-chantress, illusionist, necroman-cer, sorcerer, thaumaturge (*Rare*), theurgist, warlock, witch, wizard **2.** genius, marvel, miracle-worker, spellbinder, virtuoso, wizard, wonder-worker

magisterial arrogant, assertive, authoritative, bossy (*Inf.*), com-manding, dictatorial, domineering, high-handed, imperious, lordly, masterful, overbearing, peremp-tory

magistrate bailie (*Scot.*), J.P., judge, justice, justice of the peace, provost (*Scot.*)

magnanimity altruism, benefi-cence, big-heartedness, bountiful-ness, charitableness, generosity, high-mindedness, largess, munifi-cence, nobility, open-handedness, selflessness, unselfishness

magnanimous beneficent, big, big-hearted, bountiful, charitable, free, generous, great-hearted, hand-some, high-minded, kind, kindly, munificent, noble, open-handed, selfless, ungrudging, unselfish, un-stinting

magnate 1. baron, big cheese (*Sl.*), big noise (*Sl.*), big shot (*Sl.*), big wheel (*Sl.*), bigwig (*Sl.*), captain of industry, chief, fat cat (*Sl.*), leader, mogul, Mr. Big (*Sl.*), nabob (*Inf.*), notable, plutocrat, tycoon, V.I.P. **2.** aristocrat, baron, bashaw, gran-

dee, magnifico, merchant, noble, notable, personage, prince

magnetic alluring, attractive, cap-tivating, charismatic, charming, enchanting, entrancing, fascinat-ing, hypnotic, irresistible, mes-merizing, seductive

magnetism allure, appeal, attrac-tion, attractiveness, captivating-ness, charisma, charm, draw, drawing power, enchantment, fas-cination, hypnotism, magic, mes-merism, power, pull, seductive-ness, spell

magnification aggrandizement, amplification, augmentation, blow-up (*Inf.*), boost, build-up, deepen-ing, dilation, enhancement, en-largement, exaggeration, expan-sion, heightening, increase, infla-tion, intensification

magnificence brilliance, glory, gorgeousness, grandeur, luxuri-ousness, luxury, majesty, nobility, opulence, pomp, resplendence, splendour, stateliness, sublimity, sumptuousness

magnificent august, brilliant, el-egant, elevated, exalted, excellent, fine, glorious, gorgeous, grand, grandiose, imposing, impressive, lavish, luxurious, majestic, noble, opulent, outstanding, princely, re-gal, resplendent, rich, splendid, stately, sublime, sumptuous, su-perb, superior, transcendent

magnify 1. aggrandize, amplify, augment, blow up (*Inf.*), boost, build up, deepen, dilate, enlarge, expand, heighten, increase, inten-sify **2.** aggravate, blow up, blow up out of all proportion, dramatize, enhance, exaggerate, inflate, make a mountain out of a molehill, over-do, overemphasize, overestimate, overplay, overrate, overstate

magnitude 1. consequence, emi-nence, grandeur, greatness, im-portance, mark, moment, note, significance, weight **2.** amount, amplitude, bigness, bulk, capacity, dimensions, enormity, expanse, extent, hugeness, immensity, in-tensity, largeness, mass, measure, proportions, quantity, size, space, strength, vastness, volume

maid 1. damsel, girl, lass, lassie (*Inf.*), maiden, miss, nymph (*Poetic*), wench 2. abigail (*Archaic*), handmaiden (*Archaic*), housemaid, maid-servant, servant, serving-maid

maiden n. 1. damsel, girl, lass, lassie (*Inf.*), maid, miss, nymph, virgin, wench ~adj. 2. chaste, intact, pure, undefiled, unmarried, unwed, virgin, virginal 3. first, inaugural, initial, initiatory, introductory 4. fresh, new, unbroached, untapped, untried, unused

maidenly chaste, decent, decorous, demure, gentle, girlish, modest, pure, reserved, undefiled, unsullied, vestal, virginal, virtuous

mail n. 1. correspondence, letters, packages, parcels, post 2. post, postal service, postal system ~v. 3. dispatch, forward, post, send, send by mail or post

maim cripple, disable, hamstring, hurt, impair, incapacitate, injure, lame, mangle, mar, mutilate, put out of action, wound

main adj. 1. capital, cardinal, central, chief, critical, crucial, essential, foremost, head, leading, necessary, outstanding, paramount, particular, predominant, pre-eminent, premier, primary, prime, principal, special, supreme, vital 2. absolute, brute, direct, downright, entire, mere, pure, sheer, undisguised, utmost, utter ~n. 3. cable, channel, conduit, duct, line, pipe 4. effort, force, might, potency, power, puissance, strength 5. **in** (*or* **for**) **the main** for the most part, generally, in general, mainly, mostly, on the whole

mainly above all, chiefly, first and foremost, for the most part, generally, in general, in the main, largely, mostly, most of all, on the whole, overall, predominantly, primarily, principally, substantially, to the greatest extent, usually

mainstay anchor, backbone, bulwark, buttress, chief support, linchpin, pillar, prop

maintain 1. care for, carry on, conserve, continue, finance, keep, keep up, prolong, look after, nurture, perpetuate, preserve, provide, retain, supply, support, sustain, take care of, uphold 2. affirm, allege, assert, asseverate, aver, avow, claim, contend, declare, hold, insist, profess, state 3. advocate, argue for, back, champion, defend, fight for, justify, plead for, stand by, take up the cudgels for, uphold, vindicate

maintenance 1. care, carrying-on, conservation, continuance, continuation, keeping, nurture, perpetuation, preservation, prolongation, provision, repairs, retainment, supply, support, sustainment, sustention, upkeep 2. aliment, alimony, allowance, food, keep, livelihood, living, subsistence, support, sustenance, upkeep

majestic august, awesome, dignified, elevated, exalted, grand, grandiose, imperial, imposing, impressive, kingly, lofty, magnificent, monumental, noble, pompous, princely, regal, royal, splendid, stately, sublime, superb

majesty augustness, awesomeness, dignity, exaltedness, glory, grandeur, imposingness, impressiveness, kingliness, loftiness, magnificence, nobility, pomp, queenliness, royalty, splendour, state, stateliness, sublimity

major 1. better, bigger, chief, elder, greater, higher, larger, leading, main, most, senior, superior, supreme, uppermost 2. critical, crucial, grave, great, important, notable, outstanding, pre-eminent, radical, serious, significant, vital, weighty

majority 1. best part, bulk, greater number, mass, more, most, plurality, preponderance, superiority 2. adulthood, manhood, maturity, seniority, womanhood

make v. 1. assemble, build, compose, constitute, construct, create, fabricate, fashion, forge, form, frame, manufacture, mould, originate, produce, put together, shape, synthesize 2. accomplish, beget, bring about, cause, create, effect, engender, generate, give rise to, lead to, occasion, produce 3. cause, coerce, compel, constrain, dra~ goon, drive, force, impel, induce, oblige, press, pressurize, prevail upon, require 4. appoint, assign, create, designate, elect, install, in~ vest, nominate, ordain 5. draw up, enact, establish, fix, form, frame, pass 6. add up to, amount to, com~ pose, constitute, embody, form, represent 7. act, carry out, do, ef~ fect, engage in, execute, perform, practise, prosecute 8. calculate, estimate, gauge, judge, reckon, suppose, think 9. acquire, clear, earn, gain, get, net, obtain, realize, secure, take in, win 10. arrive at, arrive in time for, attain, catch, get to, meet, reach 11. **make it** *Inf.* arrive (*Inf.*), be successful, come through, get on, get somewhere, prosper, pull through, succeed, survive ~*n.* 12. brand, build, char~ acter, composition, constitution, construction, cut, designation, form, kind, make-up, mark, model, shape, sort, structure, style, type, variety 13. cast of mind, character, disposition, frame of mind, hu~ mour, kidney, make-up, nature, stamp, temper, temperament

make away 1. abscond, beat a hasty retreat, clear out (*Inf.*), cut and run (*Inf.*), decamp, depart, flee, fly, make off, run away *or* off, run for it (*Inf.*), scoot, skedaddle (*Inf.*), take to one's heels 2. *With* **with** abduct, carry off, filch, kid~ nap, knock off (*Sl.*), make off with, nab (*Inf.*), nick (*Sl.*), pilfer, pinch (*Inf.*), purloin, steal, swipe (*Sl.*) 3. *With* **with** bump off (*Sl.*), destroy, dispose of, do away with, do in (*Sl.*), eliminate, get rid of, kill, murder

make-believe 1. *n.* charade, dream, fantasy, imagination, play~ acting, pretence, unreality 2. *adj.* dream, fantasized, fantasy, imagi~ nary, imagined, made-up, mock, pretend, pretended, sham, unreal

make believe act as if *or* though, dream, enact, fantasize, imagine, play, play-act, pretend

make do cope, get along *or* by, improvise, manage, muddle through, scrape along *or* by

make for 1. aim for, be bound for, head for *or* towards, proceed to~ wards, steer (a course) for 2. as~ sail, assault, attack, fall on, fly at, go for, have a go at (*Inf.*), lunge at, set upon 3. be conducive to, con~ duce to, contribute to, facilitate, favour, promote

make off 1. abscond, beat a hasty retreat, bolt, clear out (*Inf.*), cut and run (*Inf.*), decamp, flee, fly, make away, run away *or* off, run for it (*Inf.*), take to one's heels 2. *With* **with** abduct, carry off, filch, kidnap, knock off (*Sl.*), make away with, nab (*Inf.*), nick (*Sl.*), pilfer, pinch (*Inf.*), purloin, run away *or* off with, steal, swipe (*Sl.*)

make out 1. descry, detect, dis~ cern, discover, distinguish, espy, perceive, recognize, see 2. com~ prehend, decipher, fathom, follow, grasp, perceive, realize, see, understand, work out 3. complete, draw up, fill in *or* out, inscribe, write (out) 4. demonstrate, de~ scribe, prove, represent, show 5. assert, claim, let on, make as if *or* though, pretend 6. fare, get on, manage, prosper, succeed, thrive

maker author, builder, constructor, director, fabricator, framer, manufacturer, producer

Maker Creator, God

makeshift 1. *adj.* expedient, jury (*Chiefly nautical*), make-do, provi~ sional, rough and ready, stopgap, substitute, temporary 2. *n.* expedi~ ent, shift, stopgap, substitute

make-up 1. cosmetics, face (*Inf.*), greasepaint (*Theatre*), maquillage, paint (*Inf.*), powder, war paint (*Inf., humorous*) 2. arrangement, assembly, composition, configura~ tion, constitution, construction, form, format, formation, organiza~ tion, structure 3. build, cast of mind, character, constitution, dis~ position, figure, frame of mind, make, nature, stamp, temper, temperament

make up 1. compose, comprise,

constitute, form 2. coin, compose, concoct, construct, cook up (*Inf.*), create, devise, dream up, fabricate, formulate, frame, hatch, invent, originate, trump up, write 3. complete, fill, meet, supply 4. *With for* atone, balance, compensate, make amends, offset, recompense, redeem, redress, requite 5. bury the hatchet, call it quits, come to terms, compose, forgive and forget, make peace, mend, reconcile, settle, shake hands 6. **make up one's mind** choose, come to a decision, decide, determine, make a decision, reach a decision, resolve, settle 7. **make up to** *Inf.* chat up (*Inf.*), court, curry favour with, flirt with, make overtures to, woo

makings 1. beginnings, capability, capacity, ingredients, materials, potentiality, potential(s), qualities 2. earnings, income, proceeds, profits, returns, revenue, takings

maladjusted alienated, disturbed, estranged, hung-up (*Sl.*), neurotic, unstable

maladministration blundering, bungling, corruption, dishonesty, incompetence, inefficiency, malfeasance (*Law*), malpractice, misgovernment, mismanagement, misrule

malady affliction, ailment, complaint, disease, disorder, ill, illness, indisposition, infirmity, sickness

malcontent 1. *adj.* disaffected, discontented, disgruntled, disgusted, dissatisfied, dissentious, factious, ill-disposed, rebellious, resentful, restive, unhappy, unsatisfied 2. *n.* agitator, complainer, fault-finder, grouch (*Inf.*), grouser, grumbler, mischief-maker, rebel, troublemaker

male manful, manlike, manly, masculine, virile

malefactor convict, criminal, crook (*Inf.*), culprit, delinquent, evildoer, felon, lawbreaker, miscreant, offender, outlaw, transgressor, villain, wrongdoer

malevolence hate, hatred, ill will, malice, maliciousness, malignity,

rancour, spite, spitefulness, vengefulness, vindictiveness

malevolent baleful, evil-minded, hateful (*Archaic*), hostile, ill-natured, malicious, malign, malignant, pernicious, rancorous, spiteful, vengeful, vicious, vindictive

malformation crookedness, deformity, distortion, misshape, misshapeness

malfunction 1. *v.* break down, develop a fault, fail, go wrong 2. *n.* breakdown, defect, failure, fault, flaw, impairment

malice animosity, animus, bad blood, bitterness, enmity, evil intent, hate, hatred, ill will, malevolence, maliciousness, malignity, rancour, spite, spitefulness, spleen, vengefulness, venom, vindictiveness

malicious baleful, bitchy (*Sl.*), bitter, catty (*Inf.*), evil-minded, hateful, ill-disposed, ill-natured, injurious, malevolent, malignant, mischievous, pernicious, rancorous, resentful, spiteful, vengeful, vicious

malign 1. *adj.* bad, baleful, baneful, deleterious, destructive, evil, harmful, hostile, hurtful, injurious, malevolent, malignant, pernicious, vicious, wicked 2. *v.* abuse, blacken (someone's name), calumniate, defame, denigrate, derogate, disparage, do a hatchet job on (*Inf.*), harm, injure, libel, revile, run down, slander, smear, speak ill of, traduce, vilify

malignant 1. baleful, bitter, destructive, harmful, hostile, hurtful, inimical, injurious, malevolent, malicious, malign, of evil intent, pernicious, spiteful, vicious 2. *Medical* cancerous, dangerous, deadly, evil, fatal, irremediable, metastatic, uncontrollable, virulent

malpractice 1. abuse, dereliction, misbehaviour, misconduct, mismanagement, negligence 2. abuse, misdeed, offence, transgression

maltreat abuse, bully, damage, handle roughly, harm, hurt, ill-treat, injure, mistreat

mammoth Brobdingnagian, colossal, enormous, gargantuan, giant, gigantic, huge, immense, jumbo (*Inf.*), massive, mighty, monumental, mountainous, prodigious, stupendous, titanic, vast

man *n.* 1. bloke (*Brit. inf.*), chap (*Inf.*), gentleman, guy (*Inf.*), male 2. adult, being, body, human, human being, individual, one, person, personage, somebody, soul 3. Homo sapiens, humanity, humankind, human race, mankind, mortals, people 4. attendant, employee, follower, hand, hireling, manservant, retainer, servant, soldier, subject, subordinate, valet, vassal, worker, workman 5. beau, boyfriend, husband, lover, partner, spouse 6. **to a man** bar none, every one, one and all, unanimously, without exception ~*v.* 7. crew, fill, furnish with men, garrison, occupy, people, staff

manacle 1. *n.* bond, chain, fetter, gyve (*Archaic*), handcuff, iron, shackle, tie 2. *v.* bind, chain, check, clap *or* put in irons, confine, constrain, curb, fetter, hamper, handcuff, inhibit, put in chains, restrain, shackle, tie one's hands

manage 1. administer, be in charge (of), command, concert, conduct, direct, govern, manipulate, oversee, preside over, rule, run, superintend, supervise 2. accomplish, arrange, bring about *or* off, contrive, cope with, deal with, effect, engineer, succeed 3. control, dominate, govern, guide, handle, influence, manipulate, operate, pilot, ply, steer, train, use, wield 4. carry on, cope, fare, get along, get by, get on, make do, make out, muddle through, shift, survive

manageable amenable, compliant, controllable, convenient, docile, easy, governable, handy, submissive, tamable, tractable, wieldy

management 1. administration, board, bosses (*Inf.*), directorate, directors, employers, executive(s) 2. administration, care, charge, command, conduct, control, governance, government, guidance, handling, manipulation, operation, rule, running, superintendence, supervision

manager administrator, boss (*Inf.*), comptroller, conductor, controller, director, executive, gaffer (*Inf.*), governor, head, organizer, overseer, proprietor, superintendent, supervisor

mandate authority, authorization, bidding, charge, command, commission, decree, directive, edict, fiat, injunction, instruction, order, precept, sanction, warrant

mandatory binding, compulsory, obligatory, required, requisite

manful bold, brave, courageous, daring, determined, gallant, hardy, heroic, indomitable, intrepid, manly, noble, powerful, resolute, stalwart, stout, stout-hearted, strong, valiant, vigorous

manfully boldly, bravely, courageously, desperately, determinedly, gallantly, hard, heroically, intrepidly, like a Trojan, like one possessed, like the devil, nobly, powerfully, resolutely, stalwartly, stoutly, strongly, to the best of one's ability, valiantly, vigorously, with might and main

mangle butcher, cripple, crush, cut, deform, destroy, disfigure, distort, hack, lacerate, maim, mar, maul, mutilate, rend, ruin, spoil, tear, wreck

mangy dirty, mean, moth-eaten, scabby (*Inf.*), scruffy, seedy, shabby, shoddy, squalid

manhandle 1. handle roughly, knock about, maul, paw (*Inf.*), pull, push, rough up 2. carry, haul, heave, hump (*Brit. sl.*), lift, manoeuvre, pull, push, shove, tug

manhood bravery, courage, determination, firmness, fortitude, hardihood, manfulness, manliness, masculinity, maturity, mettle, resolution, spirit, strength, valour, virility

mania 1. aberration, craziness, delirium, dementia, derangement, disorder, frenzy, insanity, lunacy, madness 2. cacoethes, craving, craze, desire, enthusiasm, fad (*Inf.*), fetish, fixation, obsession, partiality, passion, preoccupation, rage, thing (*Inf.*)

maniac 1. loony (*Sl.*), lunatic, mad~ man, madwoman, nutcase (*Sl.*), nutter (*Brit. sl.*), psycho (*Sl.*), psychopath 2. enthusiast, fan, fa~ natic, fiend (*Inf.*), freak (*Sl.*)

manifest 1. *adj.* apparent, clear, conspicuous, distinct, evident, glaring, noticeable, obvious, open, palpable, patent, plain, unmistak~ able, visible 2. *v.* declare, demon~ strate, display, establish, evince, exhibit, expose, express, make plain, prove, reveal, set forth, show

manifestation appearance, dem~ onstration, disclosure, display, ex~ hibition, exposure, expression, in~ dication, instance, mark, materi~ alization, revelation, show, sign, symptom, token

manifold abundant, assorted, copi~ ous, diverse, diversified, many, multifarious, multifold, multiple, multiplied, multitudinous, numer~ ous, varied, various

manipulate 1. employ, handle, op~ erate, ply, use, wield, work 2. con~ duct, control, direct, engineer, guide, influence, manoeuvre, ne~ gotiate, steer

mankind Homo sapiens, humanity, humankind, human race, man, people

manliness boldness, bravery, courage, fearlessness, firmness, hardihood, heroism, independence, intrepidity, manfulness, manhood, masculinity, mettle, resolution, stoutheartedness, valour, vigour, virility

manly bold, brave, courageous, daring, dauntless, fearless, gallant, hardy, heroic, male, manful, mas~ culine, muscular, noble, powerful, red-blooded (*Inf.*), resolute, robust, stout-hearted, strapping, strong, valiant, valorous, vigorous, virile, well-built

man-made artificial, ersatz, manufactured, plastic (*Sl.*), syn~ thetic

manner 1. air, appearance, aspect, bearing, behaviour, comportment, conduct, demeanour, deportment, look, mien (*Literary*), presence, tone 2. approach, custom, fashion, form, genre, habit, line, means, method, mode, practice, pro~ cedure, process, routine, style, tack, tenor, usage, way, wont 3. brand, breed, category, form, kind, nature, sort, type, variety

mannered affected, artificial, posed, pretentious, pseudo (*Inf.*), put-on, stilted

mannerism characteristic, foible, habit, idiosyncrasy, peculiarity, quirk, trait, trick

mannerly civil, civilized, courteous, decorous, genteel, gentlemanly, gracious, ladylike, polished, polite, refined, respectful, well-behaved, well-bred, well-mannered

manners 1. bearing, behaviour, breeding, carriage, comportment, conduct, demeanour, deportment 2. ceremony, courtesy, decorum, etiquette, formalities, good form, polish, politeness, politesse, pro~ prieties, protocol, refinement, so~ cial graces, the done thing

manoeuvre *n.* 1. action, artifice, dodge, intrigue, machination, move, movement, plan, plot, ploy, ruse, scheme, stratagem, subter~ fuge, tactic, trick 2. deployment, evolution, exercise, movement, operation ~*v.* 3. contrive, devise, engineer, intrigue, machinate, manage, manipulate, plan, plot, pull strings, scheme, wangle (*Inf.*) 4. deploy, exercise, move 5. direct, drive, guide, handle, navigate, ne~ gotiate, pilot, steer

mansion abode, dwelling, habita~ tion, hall, manor, residence, seat, villa

mantle *n.* 1. *Archaic* cape, cloak, hood, shawl, wrap 2. blanket, canopy, cloud, cover, covering, curtain, envelope, pall, screen, shroud, veil ~*v.* 3. blanket, cloak, cloud, cover, disguise, envelop, hide, mask, overspread, screen, shroud, veil, wrap

manual 1. *adj.* done by hand, hand-operated, human, physical 2. *n.* bi~ ble, enchiridion (*Rare*), guide, guidebook, handbook, instructions, workbook

manufacture v. 1. assemble, build, compose, construct, create, fabri~ cate, forge, form, make, mass-produce, mould, process, produce, put together, shape, turn out 2. concoct, cook up (*Inf.*), devise, fabricate, hatch, invent, make up, think up, trump up ~n. 3. assem~ bly, construction, creation, fabri~ cation, making, mass-production, produce, production

manufacturer builder, construc~ tor, creator, fabricator, factory-owner, industrialist, maker, pro~ ducer

manure compost, droppings, dung, muck, ordure

many adj. 1. abundant, copious, countless, divers (*Archaic*), fre~ quent, innumerable, manifold, multifarious, multifold, multitudi~ nous, myriad, numerous, profuse, sundry, umpteen (*Inf.*), varied, various ~n. 2. a horde, a lot, a mass, a multitude, a thousand and one, heaps (*Inf.*), large numbers, lots (*Inf.*), piles (*Inf.*), plenty, scores, tons (*Inf.*), umpteen (*Inf.*) 3. the many crowd, hoi polloi, ma~ jority, masses, multitude, people, rank and file

mar blemish, blight, blot, damage, deface, detract from, disfigure, harm, hurt, impair, injure, maim, mangle, mutilate, ruin, scar, spoil, stain, sully, taint, tarnish, vitiate

maraud despoil, forage, foray, har~ ry, loot, pillage, plunder, raid, ran~ sack, ravage, reive (*Dialect*), sack

marauder bandit, brigand, bucca~ neer, cateran (*Scot.*), corsair, free~ booter, mosstrooper, outlaw, pil~ lager, pirate, plunderer, raider, ravager, reiver (*Dialect*), robber

march v. 1. file, footslog, pace, pa~ rade, stalk, stride, strut, tramp, tread, walk ~n. 2. route-march, tramp, trek, walk 3. demo (*Inf.*), demonstration, parade, pro~ cession 4. gait, pace, step, stride 5. advance, development, evolution, progress, progression 6. on the march advancing, afoot, astir, en

route, marching, on one's way, on the way, proceeding, progressing, under way

marches borderland, borders, boundaries, confines, frontiers, limits, marchlands

margin 1. border, bound, boundary, brim, brink, confine, edge, limit, perimeter, periphery, rim, side, verge 2. allowance, compass, elbowroom, extra, latitude, leeway, play, room, scope, space, surplus

marginal 1. bordering, borderline, on the edge, peripheral 2. insig~ nificant, low, minimal, minor, neg~ ligible, slight, small

marijuana bhang, cannabis, char~ as, dope (*Sl.*), ganja, grass (*Sl.*), hash (*Sl.*), hashish, hemp, kif, leaf (*Sl.*), mary jane (*U.S. sl.*), pot (*Sl.*), smoke (*Inf.*), stuff (*Sl.*), tea (*U.S. sl.*), weed (*Sl.*)

marine maritime, nautical, naval, ocean-going, oceanic, pelagic, saltwater, sea, seafaring, seagoing, thalassic

mariner bluejacket, gob (*Inf.*), hand, Jack Tar, matelot (*Brit. sl.*), navigator, sailor, salt, sea dog, seafarer, seafaring man, seaman, tar

marital conjugal, connubial, mar~ ried, matrimonial, nuptial, spousal, wedded

maritime 1. marine, nautical, na~ val, oceanic, sea, seafaring 2. coastal, littoral, seaside

mark n. 1. blemish, blot, blotch, bruise, dent, impression, line, nick, pock, scar, scratch, smudge, splotch, spot, stain, streak 2. badge, blaze, brand, characteristic, de~ vice, earmark, emblem, evidence, feature, hallmark, impression, in~ cision, index, indication, label, note, print, proof, seal, sign, stamp, symbol, symptom, token 3. criteri~ on, level, measure, norm, standard, yardstick 4. aim, end, goal, object, objective, purpose, target 5. con~ sequence, dignity, distinction, emi~ nence, fame, importance, influ~ ence, notability, note, notice, pres~ tige, quality, regard, standing 6. footmark, footprint, sign, trace, track, trail, vestige 7. **make one's mark** achieve recognition, be a success, find a place in the sun, get on in the world, make a success of oneself, make good, make it (*Inf.*), make something of oneself, prosper, succeed ~v. 8. blemish, blot, blotch, brand, bruise, dent, impress, imprint, nick, scar, scratch, smudge, splotch, stain, streak 9. brand, characterize, identify, label, stamp 10. betoken, denote, distinguish, evince, exemplify, illustrate, show 11. attend, hearken (*Archaic*), mind, note, notice, observe, pay attention, pay heed, regard, remark, watch 12. appraise, assess, correct, evaluate, grade

marked apparent, clear, considerable, conspicuous, decided, distinct, evident, manifest, notable, noted, noticeable, obvious, outstanding, patent, prominent, pronounced, remarkable, salient, signal, striking

markedly clearly, considerably, conspicuously, decidedly, distinctly, evidently, greatly, manifestly, notably, noticeably, obviously, outstandingly, patently, remarkably, signally, strikingly, to a great extent

market 1. *n.* bazaar, fair, mart 2. *v.* offer for sale, retail, sell, vend

marketable in demand, merchantable, salable, sought after, vendible, wanted

marksman, -woman crack shot (*Inf.*), deadeye (*Inf., chiefly U.S.*), dead shot (*Inf.*), good shot, sharpshooter

maroon abandon, cast ashore, cast away, desert, leave, leave high and dry (*Inf.*), strand

marriage 1. espousal, match, matrimony, nuptial rites, nuptials, wedding, wedding ceremony, wedlock 2. alliance, amalgamation, association, confederation, coupling, link, merger, union

married 1. hitched (*Inf.*), joined, one, spliced (*Inf.*), united, wed, wedded 2. conjugal, connubial, husbandly, marital, matrimonial, nuptial, spousal, wifely

marrow core, cream, essence, gist, heart, kernel, pith, quick, quintessence, soul, spirit, substance

marry 1. become man and wife, espouse, get hitched (*Inf.*), get spliced (*Inf.*), take the plunge (*Inf.*), take to wife, tie the knot (*Inf.*), walk down the aisle (*Inf.*), wed, wive (*Archaic*) 2. ally, bond, join, knit, link, match, merge, splice, tie, unify, unite, yoke

marsh bog, fen, morass, moss (*Scot., & northern English dialect*), quagmire, slough, swamp

marshal 1. align, arrange, array, assemble, collect, deploy, dispose, draw up, gather, group, line up, muster, order, organize, rank 2. conduct, escort, guide, lead, shepherd, usher

marshy boggy, fenny, miry, quaggy, spongy, swampy, waterlogged, wet

martial bellicose, belligerent, brave, heroic, military, soldierly, warlike

martinet disciplinarian, drillmaster, stickler

martyrdom agony, anguish, ordeal, persecution, suffering, torment, torture

marvel 1. *v.* be amazed, be awed, be filled with surprise, gape, gaze, goggle, wonder 2. *n.* genius, miracle, phenomenon, portent, prodigy, whiz (*Inf.*), wonder

marvellous 1. amazing, astonishing, astounding, breathtaking, extraordinary, miraculous, phenomenal, prodigious, remarkable, singular, spectacular, stupendous, wondrous 2. difficult *or* hard to believe, fabulous, fantastic, implausible, improbable, incredible, surprising, unbelievable, unlikely 3. *Inf.* colossal, excellent, fabulous (*Inf.*), fantastic (*Inf.*), glorious, great (*Inf.*), magnificent, sensational, smashing (*Inf.*), splendid, stupendous, super (*Inf.*), superb, terrific (*Inf.*), wonderful

masculine 1. male, manful, manlike, manly, mannish, virile 2. bold, brave, gallant, hardy, muscular, powerful, red-blooded (*Inf.*), resolute, robust, stout-hearted, strapping, strong, vigorous, well-built

mask n. **1.** domino, false face, visor, vizard (*Archaic*) **2.** blind, camouflage, cloak, concealment, cover, cover-up, disguise, façade, front, guise, screen, semblance, show, veil, veneer ~v. **3.** camouflage, cloak, conceal, cover, disguise, hide, obscure, screen, veil

mass n. **1.** block, chunk, concretion, hunk, lump, piece **2.** aggregate, body, collection, entirety, sum, sum total, totality, whole **3.** accumulation, aggregation, assemblage, batch, bunch, collection, combination, conglomeration, heap, load, lot, pile, quantity, stack **4.** assemblage, band, body, bunch (*Inf.*), crowd, group, horde, host, lot, mob, number, throng, troop **5.** body, bulk, greater part, lion's share, majority, preponderance **6.** bulk, dimension, greatness, magnitude, size **7. the masses** commonalty, common people, crowd, hoi polloi, multitude ~adj. **8.** extensive, general, indiscriminate, large-scale, pandemic, popular, wholesale, widespread ~v. **9.** accumulate, amass, assemble, collect, congregate, forgather, gather, mob, muster, rally, swarm, throng

massacre **1.** n. annihilation, blood bath, butchery, carnage, extermination, killing, mass slaughter, murder, slaughter **2.** v. annihilate, butcher, cut to pieces, exterminate, kill, mow down, murder, slaughter, slay, wipe out

massage **1.** n. kneading, manipulation, rubbing, rub-down **2.** v. knead, manipulate, rub, rub down

massive big, bulky, colossal, enormous, extensive, gargantuan, gigantic, great, heavy, hefty, huge, hulking, immense, imposing, impressive, mammoth, monster, monumental, ponderous, solid, substantial, titanic, vast, weighty, whacking (*Inf.*), whopping (*Inf.*)

master n. **1.** boss (*Inf.*), captain, chief, commander, controller, director, employer, governor, head, lord, manager, overlord, overseer, owner, principal, ruler, skipper (*Inf.*), superintendent **2.** ace (*Inf.*), adept, dab hand (*Brit. inf.*), doyen, expert, genius, maestro, past master, pro (*Inf.*), virtuoso, wizard **3.** guide, guru, instructor, pedagogue, preceptor, schoolmaster, spiritual leader, swami, teacher, tutor ~adj. **4.** adept, crack (*Inf.*), expert, masterly, proficient, skilful, skilled **5.** chief, controlling, foremost, grand, great, leading, main, predominant, prime, principal ~v. **6.** acquire, become proficient in, get the hang of (*Inf.*), grasp, learn **7.** bridle, check, conquer, curb, defeat, overcome, overpower, quash, quell, subdue, subjugate, suppress, tame, triumph over, vanquish **8.** command, control, direct, dominate, govern, manage, regulate, rule

masterful **1.** adept, adroit, clever, consummate, crack (*Inf.*), deft, dexterous, excellent, expert, exquisite, fine, finished, first-rate, masterly, skilful, skilled, superior, superlative, supreme **2.** arrogant, authoritative, bossy (*Inf.*), despotic, dictatorial, domineering, highhanded, imperious, magisterial, overbearing, overweening, peremptory, self-willed, tyrannical

masterly adept, adroit, clever, consummate, crack (*Inf.*), dexterous, excellent, expert, exquisite, fine, finished, first-rate, masterful, skilful, skilled, superior, superlative, supreme

mastermind **1.** v. be the brains behind (*Inf.*), conceive, devise, direct, manage, organize, plan **2.** n. architect, authority, brain(s) (*Inf.*), director, engineer, genius, intellect, manager, organizer, planner, virtuoso

masterpiece chef d'oeuvre, classic, jewel, magnum opus, master work, *pièce de résistance*, *tour de force*

mastery **1.** command, comprehension, familiarity, grasp, knowledge, understanding **2.** ability, acquirement, attainment, cleverness, deftness, dexterity, expertise, finesse, know-how (*Inf.*), proficiency, prowess, skill, virtuosity 3. ascendancy, authority, command, conquest, control, domination, dominion, pre-eminence, rule, superiority, supremacy, sway, triumph, upper hand, victory, whip hand

match n. 1. bout, competition, contest, game, test, trial 2. competitor, counterpart, equal, equivalent, peer, rival 3. companion, complement, counterpart, equal, equivalent, fellow, mate, tally 4. copy, dead ringer (*Sl.*), double, duplicate, equal, lookalike, replica, ringer (*Sl.*), spit (*Inf.*), spit and image (*Inf.*), spitting image (*Inf.*), twin 5. affiliation, alliance, combination, couple, duet, marriage, pair, pairing, partnership, union ~v. 6. ally, combine, couple, join, link, marry, mate, pair, unite, yoke 7. accompany, accord, adapt, agree, blend, coordinate, correspond, fit, go with, harmonize, suit, tally, tone with 8. compare, compete, contend, emulate, equal, measure up to, oppose, pit against, rival, vie

matching analogous, comparable, coordinating, corresponding, double, duplicate, equal, equivalent, identical, like, paired, parallel, same, toning, twin

matchless consummate, exquisite, incomparable, inimitable, peerless, perfect, superlative, supreme, unequalled, unique, unmatched, unparalleled, unrivalled

mate n. 1. better half (*Humorous*), husband, partner, spouse, wife 2. *Inf.* buddy (*Inf.*), china (*Brit. sl.*), chum (*Inf.*), comrade, crony, friend, pal (*Inf.*) 3. associate, colleague, companion, compeer, coworker, fellow-worker 4. assistant, helper, subordinate 5. companion, double, fellow, match, twin ~v. 6. breed, copulate, couple, pair 7. marry, match, wed 8. couple, join, match, pair, yoke

material n. 1. body, constituents, element, matter, stuff, substance 2. data, evidence, facts, information, notes, work 3. cloth, fabric, stuff ~*adj.* 4. bodily, concrete, corporeal, fleshly, nonspiritual, palpable, physical, substantial, tangible, worldly 5. consequential, essential, grave, important, indispensable, key, meaningful, momentous, serious, significant, vital, weighty 6. applicable, apposite, apropos, germane, pertinent, relevant

materialize appear, come about, come into being, come to pass, happen, occur, take place, take shape, turn up

materially considerably, essentially, gravely, greatly, much, seriously, significantly, substantially

maternal motherly

maternity motherhood, motherliness

matrimonial conjugal, connubial, hymeneal, marital, married, nuptial, spousal, wedded, wedding

matrimony marital rites, marriage, nuptials, wedding ceremony, wedlock

matrix forge, mould, origin, source, womb

matted knotted, tangled, tousled, uncombed

matter n. 1. body, material, stuff, substance 2. affair, business, concern, episode, event, incident, issue, occurrence, proceeding, question, situation, subject, thing, topic, transaction 3. amount, quantity, sum 4. argument, context, purport, sense, subject, substance, text, thesis 5. consequence, import, importance, moment, note, significance, weight 6. complication, difficulty, distress, problem, trouble, upset, worry 7. *Medical* discharge, purulence, pus, secretion ~v. 8. be important, be of consequence, carry weight, count, have influence, make a difference, mean something, signify

matter-of-fact deadpan, down-to-earth, dry, dull, emotionless, flat, lifeless, mundane, plain, prosaic, sober, unembellished, unimaginative, unsentimental, unvarnished

mature 1. *adj.* adult, complete, fit, full-blown, fully fledged, full-grown, grown, grown-up, matured, mel~

low, of age, perfect, prepared, ready, ripe, ripened, seasoned 2. *v.* age, become adult, bloom, come of age, develop, grow up, maturate, mellow, perfect, reach adulthood, ripen, season

maturity adulthood, completion, experience, full bloom, full growth, fullness, majority, manhood, maturation, matureness, perfection, ripeness, wisdom, womanhood

maudlin lachrymose, mawkish, mushy (*Inf.*), overemotional, sentimental, slushy (*Inf.*), soppy (*Brit. inf.*), tearful, weepy (*Inf.*)

maul 1. abuse, handle roughly, illtreat, manhandle, molest, paw 2. batter, beat, beat up (*Inf.*), claw, knock about, lacerate, mangle, pummel, rough up, thrash

maunder 1. dawdle, dilly-dally (*Inf.*), drift, idle, loaf, meander, mooch (*Sl.*), potter, ramble, straggle, stray, traipse (*Inf.*) 2. babble, blather, blether, chatter, gabble, prattle, rabbit (*Brit. sl.*), ramble, rattle on, witter (*Inf.*)

mawkish 1. emotional, feeble, gushy (*Inf.*), maudlin, mushy (*Inf.*), schmaltzy (*Sl.*), sentimental, slushy (*Inf.*), soppy (*Brit. inf.*) 2. disgusting, flat, foul, insipid, jejune, loathsome, nauseous, offensive, stale, vapid

maxim adage, aphorism, apophthegm, axiom, byword, gnome, motto, proverb, rule, saw, saying

maximum 1. *n.* apogee, ceiling, crest, extremity, height, most, peak, pinnacle, summit, top, upper limit, utmost, uttermost, zenith 2. *adj.* greatest, highest, maximal, most, paramount, supreme, topmost, utmost

maybe it could be, mayhap (*Archaic*), peradventure (*Archaic*), perchance (*Archaic*), perhaps, possibly

mayhem chaos, commotion, confusion, destruction, disorder, fracas, havoc, trouble, violence

maze 1. convolutions, intricacy, labyrinth, meander 2. *Fig.* bewilderment, confusion, imbroglio,

mesh, perplexity, puzzle, snarl, tangle, uncertainty, web

meadow field, grassland, lea (*Poetic*), ley, pasture

meagre 1. deficient, exiguous, inadequate, insubstantial, little, paltry, poor, puny, scanty, scrimpy, short, skimpy, slender, slight, small, spare, sparse 2. bony, emaciated, gaunt, hungry, lank, lean, scraggy, scrawny, skinny, starved, thin, underfed 3. barren, infertile, poor, unfruitful, unproductive, weak

mean¹ *v.* 1. betoken, connote, convey, denote, drive at, express, hint at, imply, indicate, purport, represent, say, signify, spell, stand for, suggest, symbolize 2. aim, aspire, contemplate, design, desire, have in mind, intend, plan, propose, purpose, set out, want, wish 3. design, destine, fate, fit, make, match, predestine, preordain, suit 4. bring about, cause, engender, entail, give rise to, involve, lead to, necessitate, produce, result in 5. adumbrate, augur, betoken, foreshadow, foretell, herald, portend, presage, promise

mean² *adj.* 1. beggarly, close, mercenary, mingy (*Brit. inf.*), miserly, near (*Inf.*), niggardly, parsimonious, penny-pinching, penurious, selfish, stingy, tight, tight-fisted, ungenerous 2. bad-tempered, cantankerous, churlish, disagreeable, hostile, ill-tempered, malicious, nasty, rude, sour, unfriendly, unpleasant 3. abject, base, callous, contemptible, degenerate, degraded, despicable, disgraceful, dishonourable, hard-hearted, ignoble, low-minded, narrow-minded, petty, scurvy, shabby, shameful, sordid, vile, wretched 4. beggarly, contemptible, down-at-heel, insignificant, miserable, paltry, petty, poor, run-down, scruffy, seedy, shabby, sordid, squalid, tawdry, wretched 5. base, baseborn (*Archaic*), common, humble, ignoble, inferior, low, lowborn, lowly, menial, modest, obscure, ordinary, plebeian, proletarian, servile, undistinguished, vulgar

mean³ 1. *n.* average, balance, compromise, happy medium, median, middle, middle course *or* way, mid-point, norm 2. *adj.* average, intermediate, medial, median, medium, middle, middling, normal, standard

meander 1. *v.* ramble, snake, stravaig (*Scot.*), stray, stroll, turn, wander, wind, zigzag 2. *n.* bend, coil, curve, loop, turn, twist, zigzag

meaning *n.* 1. connotation, denotation, drift, explanation, gist, implication, import, interpretation, message, purport, sense, significance, signification, substance, upshot, value 2. aim, design, end, goal, idea, intention, object, plan, point, purpose, trend 3. effect, efficacy, force, point, thrust, use, usefulness, validity, value, worth ~*adj.* 4. eloquent, expressive, meaningful, pointed, pregnant, speaking, suggestive

meaningful 1. important, material, purposeful, relevant, serious, significant, useful, valid, worthwhile 2. eloquent, expressive, meaning, pointed, pregnant, speaking, suggestive

meaningless aimless, empty, futile, hollow, inane, inconsequential, insignificant, insubstantial, nonsensical, nugatory, pointless, purposeless, senseless, trifling, trivial, useless, vain, valueless, worthless

meanness 1. minginess (*Brit. inf.*), miserliness, niggardliness, parsimony, penuriousness, selfishness, stinginess, tight-fistedness 2. bad temper, cantankerousness, churlishness, disagreeableness, hostility, ill temper, malice, maliciousness, nastiness, rudeness, sourness, unfriendliness, unpleasantness 3. abjectness, baseness, degeneracy, degradation, despicableness, disgracefulness, dishonourableness, low-mindedness, narrow-mindedness, pettiness, scurviness, shabbiness, shamefulness, sordidness, vileness, wretchedness 4. beggarliness, contemptibleness, insignificance, paltriness, pettiness, poorness, scruffiness, seedi-

ness, shabbiness, sordidness, squalor, tawdriness, wretchedness 5. baseness, humbleness, lowliness, obscurity, servility

means 1. agency, avenue, channel, course, expedient, instrument, measure, medium, method, mode, process, way 2. affluence, capital, estate, fortune, funds, income, money, property, resources, riches, substance, wealth, wherewithal 3. **by all means** absolutely, certainly, definitely, doubtlessly, of course, positively, surely 4. **by means of** by dint of, by way of, through, using, utilizing, via, with the aid of 5. **by no means** absolutely not, definitely not, in no way, not at all, not in the least, not in the slightest, not the least bit, on no account

meantime at the same time, concurrently, for now, for the duration, for the moment, for then, in the interim, in the interval, in the intervening time, in the meantime, in the meanwhile, simultaneously

meanwhile at the same time, concurrently, for now, for the duration, for the moment, for then, in the interim, in the interval, in the intervening time, in the meantime, in the meanwhile, simultaneously

measurable assessable, computable, determinable, gaugeable, material, mensurable, perceptible, quantifiable, quantitative, significant

measure *n.* 1. allotment, allowance, amount, amplitude, capacity, degree, extent, magnitude, portion, proportion, quantity, quota, range, ration, reach, scope, share, size 2. gauge, metre, rule, scale, yardstick 3. method, standard, system 4. criterion, example, model, norm, standard, test, touchstone, yardstick 5. bounds, control, limit, limitation, moderation, restraint 6. act, action, course, deed, expedient, manoeuvre, means, procedure, proceeding, step 7. act, bill, enactment, law, resolution, statute 8. beat, cadence, foot, metre, rhythm, verse 9. **for good measure** as a bonus, besides, in addition, into the bargain, to boot ~v. 10. appraise, assess, calculate, calibrate, compute, determine, estimate, evaluate, gauge, judge, mark out, quantify, rate, size, sound, survey, value, weigh 11. adapt, adjust, calculate, choose, fit, judge, tailor

measurement 1. appraisal, assessment, calculation, calibration, computation, estimation, evaluation, judgment, mensuration, metage, survey, valuation 2. amount, amplitude, area, capacity, depth, dimension, extent, height, length, magnitude, size, volume, weight, width

measure out allot, apportion, assign, deal out, dispense, distribute, divide, dole out, issue, mete out, parcel out, pour out, share out

measure up (to) be adequate, be capable, be equal to, be fit, be suitable, be suited, come up to scratch (*Inf.*), come up to standard, compare, cut the mustard (*U.S. sl.*), equal, fit *or* fill the bill, fulfil the expectations, make the grade (*Inf.*), match, meet, rival

meat 1. aliment, cheer, chow (*Inf.*), comestibles, eats (*Sl.*), fare, flesh, food, grub (*Inf.*), nourishment, nutriment, provender, provisions, rations, subsistence, sustenance, viands, victuals 2. core, essence, gist, heart, kernel, marrow, nub, nucleus, pith, point, substance

mechanical 1. automated, automatic, machine-driven 2. automatic, cold, cursory, dead, emotionless, habitual, impersonal, instinctive, involuntary, lacklustre, lifeless, machine-like, matter-of-fact, perfunctory, routine, spiritless, unconscious, unfeeling, unthinking

mechanism 1. apparatus, appliance, contrivance, device, instrument, machine, structure, system, tool 2. action, components, gears, innards (*Inf.*), machinery, motor, workings, works 3. agency, execution, functioning, means, medium, method, operation, performance, procedure, process, system, technique, workings

meddle butt in, interfere, intermeddle, interpose, intervene, intrude, pry, put one's oar in, stick one's nose in (*Inf.*), tamper

mediate act as middleman, arbitrate, bring to an agreement, bring to terms, conciliate, intercede, interpose, intervene, make peace between, moderate, reconcile, referee, resolve, restore harmony, settle, step in (*Inf.*), umpire

mediator advocate, arbiter, arbitrator, go-between, honest broker, interceder, intermediary, judge, middleman, moderator, negotiator, peacemaker, referee, umpire

medicinal analeptic, curative, healing, medical, remedial, restorative, roborant, sanatory, therapeutic

medicine cure, drug, medicament, medication, physic, remedy

medieval 1. Gothic 2. *Inf.* antediluvian, antiquated, antique, archaic, old-fashioned, primitive, unenlightened

mediocre average, commonplace, fair to middling (*Inf.*), indifferent, inferior, insignificant, mean, medium, middling, ordinary, passable, pedestrian, run-of-the-mill, secondrate, so-so (*Inf.*), tolerable, undistinguished, uninspired

mediocrity 1. commonplaceness, indifference, inferiority, insignificance, ordinariness, poorness, unimportance 2. cipher, lightweight (*Inf.*), nobody, nonentity, secondrater

meditate 1. be in a brown study, cogitate, consider, contemplate, deliberate, muse, ponder, reflect, ruminate, study, think 2. consider, contemplate, design, devise, have in mind, intend, mull over, plan, purpose, scheme, think over

meditation brown study, cerebration, cogitation, concentration, contemplation, musing, pondering, reflection, reverie, ruminating, rumination, study, thought

medium *adj.* 1. average, fair, intermediate, mean, medial, median, mediocre, middle, middling, midway ~n. 2. average, centre, compromise, mean, middle, middle course (ground, path, way), midpoint 3. agency, avenue, channel, form, instrument, instrumentality, means, mode, organ, vehicle, way 4. atmosphere, conditions, element, environment, habitat, influences, milieu, setting, surroundings 5. spiritist, spiritualist

medley assortment, confusion, farrago, gallimaufry, hodgepodge, hotchpotch, jumble, *mélange*, miscellany, mishmash, mixed bag (*Inf.*), mixture, olio, omniumgatherum, pastiche, patchwork, potpourri, salmagundi

meek 1. deferential, docile, forbearing, gentle, humble, longsuffering, mild, modest, patient, peaceful, soft, submissive, unassuming, unpretentious, yielding 2. acquiescent, compliant, resigned, spineless, spiritless, tame, timid, unresisting, weak, weak-kneed (*Inf.*)

meekness 1. deference, docility, forbearance, gentleness, humbleness, humility, long-suffering, lowliness, mildness, modesty, patience, peacefulness, resignation, softness, submission, submissiveness 2. acquiescence, compliance, resignation, spinelessness, spiritlessness, tameness, timidity, weakness

meet 1. bump into, chance on, come across, confront, contact, encounter, find, happen on, run across, run into 2. abut, adjoin, come together, connect, converge, cross, intersect, join, link up, touch, unite 3. answer, carry out, come up to, comply, cope with, discharge, equal, fulfil, gratify, handle, match, measure up, perform, satisfy 4. assemble, collect, come together, congregate, convene, forgather, gather, muster, rally 5. bear, encounter, endure, experience, face, go through, suffer, undergo

meeting 1. assignation, confrontation, encounter, engagement, introduction, rendezvous, tryst (*Archaic*) 2. assembly, audience, company, conclave, conference, congregation, convention, convocation, gathering, get-together (*Inf.*), meet, rally, reunion, session 3. concourse, confluence, conjunction, convergence, crossing, intersection, junction, union

melancholy 1. *n.* blues, dejection, depression, despondency, gloom, gloominess, low spirits, pensiveness, sadness, sorrow, unhappiness, woe 2. *adj.* blue, dejected, depressed, despondent, disconsolate, dismal, dispirited, doleful, down, downcast, downhearted, down in the dumps (*Inf.*), down in the mouth, gloomy, glum, heavyhearted, joyless, low, low-spirited, lugubrious, melancholic, miserable, moody, mournful, pensive, sad, sombre, sorrowful, unhappy, woebegone, woeful

mellow *adj.* 1. delicate, fullflavoured, juicy, mature, perfect, rich, ripe, soft, sweet, well-matured 2. dulcet, full, mellifluous, melodious, rich, rounded, smooth, sweet, tuneful, well-tuned 3. cheerful, cordial, elevated, expansive, genial, half-tipsy, happy, jolly, jovial, merry (*Brit. inf.*), relaxed ~*v.* 4. develop, improve, mature, perfect, ripen, season, soften, sweeten

melodious concordant, dulcet, euphonious, harmonious, melodic, musical, silvery, sweet-sounding, sweet-toned, tuneful

melodramatic blood-and-thunder, extravagant, hammy (*Inf.*), histrionic, overdramatic, overemotional, sensational, stagy, theatrical

melody 1. air, descant, music, refrain, song, strain, theme, tune 2. euphony, harmony, melodiousness, music, musicality, tunefulness

melt 1. deliquesce, diffuse, dissolve, flux, fuse, liquefy, soften, thaw 2. *Often with away* disappear, disperse, dissolve, evanesce, evaporate, fade, vanish 3. disarm, mollify, relax, soften, touch

member 1. associate, fellow, representative 2. appendage, arm, component, constituent, element, extremity, leg, limb, organ, part, portion

membership 1. associates, body, fellows, members 2. belonging, enrolment, fellowship, participation

memoir account, biography, essay, journal, life, monograph, narrative, record, register

memoirs 1. autobiography, diary, experiences, journals, life, life story, memories, recollections, reminiscences 2. annals, chronicles, records, transactions

memorable catchy, celebrated, distinguished, extraordinary, famous, historic, illustrious, important, impressive, momentous, notable, noteworthy, remarkable, signal, significant, striking, unforgettable

memorial adj. 1. commemorative, monumental ~n. 2. cairn, memento, monument, plaque, record, remembrance, souvenir 3. address, memorandum, petition, statement

memorize commit to memory, con (Archaic), get by heart, learn, learn by heart, learn by rote, remember

memory 1. recall, recollection, remembrance, reminiscence, retention 2. commemoration, honour, remembrance 3. celebrity, fame, glory, name, renown, reputation, repute

menace v. 1. alarm, bode ill, browbeat, bully, frighten, impend, intimidate, loom, lour, lower, terrorize, threaten, utter threats to ~n. 2. commination, intimidation, scare, threat, warning 3. danger, hazard, jeopardy, peril 4. Inf. annoyance, nuisance, pest, plague, troublemaker

menacing alarming, dangerous, frightening, intimidating, intimidatory, looming, louring, lowering, minacious, minatory, ominous, threatening

mend v. 1. cure, darn, fix, heal, patch, rectify, refit, reform, remedy, renew, renovate, repair, restore, retouch 2. ameliorate, amend, better, correct, emend, improve, rectify, reform, revise 3. convalesce, get better, heal, recover, recuperate ~n. 4. darn, patch, repair, stitch 5. on the mend convalescent, convalescing, getting better, improving, recovering, recuperating

mendacious deceitful, deceptive, dishonest, duplicitous, fallacious, false, fraudulent, insincere, lying, perfidious, perjured, untrue, untruthful

menial adj. 1. boring, dull, humdrum, low-status, routine, unskilled 2. abject, base, degrading, demeaning, fawning, grovelling, humble, ignoble, ignominious, low, lowly, mean, obsequious, servile, slavish, sorry, subservient, sycophantic, vile ~n. 3. attendant, dogsbody (Inf.), domestic, drudge, flunky, labourer, lackey, serf, servant, skivvy (Brit.), slave, underling

menstruation catamenia (Physiology), courses (Physiology), flow (Inf.), menses, menstrual cycle, monthly (Inf.), period, the curse (Inf.)

mental 1. cerebral, intellectual 2. deranged, disturbed, insane, lunatic, mad, mentally ill, psychiatric, psychotic, unbalanced, unstable

mentality 1. brainpower, brains, comprehension, grey matter (Inf.), intellect, intelligence quotient, I.Q., mental age, mind, rationality, understanding, wit 2. attitude, cast of mind, character, disposition, frame of mind, make-up, outlook, personality, psychology, turn of mind, way of thinking

mentally in one's head, intellectually, in the mind, inwardly, psychologically, rationally, subjectively

mention v. 1. acknowledge, adduce, allude to, bring up, broach, call attention to, cite, communicate, declare, disclose, divulge, hint at, impart, intimate, make known, name, point out, recount, refer to, report, reveal, speak about or of, state, tell, touch upon 2. **not to mention** as well as, besides, not counting, to say nothing of ~n. 3. acknowledgment, citation, recognition, tribute 4. allusion, announcement, indication, notification, observation, reference, remark

mentor adviser, coach, counsellor, guide, guru, instructor, teacher, tutor

menu bill of fare, carte du jour, tariff (*Chiefly Brit.*)

mercantile commercial, marketable, trade, trading

mercenary adj. 1. acquisitive, avaricious, bribable, covetous, grasping, greedy, money-grubbing (*Inf.*), sordid, venal 2. bought, hired, paid, venal ~n. 3. condottiere (*Hist.*), free companion (*Hist.*), freelance (*Hist.*), hireling, soldier of fortune

merchandise 1. n. commodities, goods, produce, products, staples, stock, stock in trade, truck, vendibles, wares 2. v. buy and sell, deal in, distribute, do business in, market, retail, sell, trade, traffic in, vend

merchant broker, dealer, retailer, salesman, seller, shopkeeper, trader, tradesman, trafficker, vendor, wholesaler

merciful beneficent, benignant, clement, compassionate, forbearing, forgiving, generous, gracious, humane, kind, lenient, liberal, mild, pitying, soft, sparing, sympathetic, tender-hearted

merciless barbarous, callous, cruel, fell (*Archaic*), hard, hardhearted, harsh, heartless, implacable, inexorable, inhumane, pitiless, relentless, ruthless, severe, unappeasable, unfeeling, unforgiving, unmerciful, unpitying, unsparing, unsympathetic

mercy 1. benevolence, charity, clemency, compassion, favour, forbearance, forgiveness, grace, kindness, leniency, pity, quarter 2. benison (*Archaic*), blessing, boon, godsend, piece of luck, relief 3. **at the mercy of** defenceless against, exposed to, in the clutches of, in the power of, naked before, open to, prey to, subject to, threatened

by, unprotected against, vulnerable to

mere adj. absolute, bare, common, complete, entire, nothing more than, plain, pure, pure and simple, sheer, simple, stark, unadulterated, unmitigated, unmixed, utter

merge amalgamate, be swallowed up by, become lost in, blend, coalesce, combine, consolidate, converge, fuse, incorporate, intermix, join, meet, meld, melt into, mingle, mix, tone with, unite

merger amalgamation, coalition, combination, consolidation, fusion, incorporation, union

merit n. 1. advantage, asset, excellence, good, goodness, integrity, quality, strong point, talent, value, virtue, worth, worthiness 2. claim, credit, desert, due, right ~v. 3. be entitled to, be worthy of, deserve, earn, have a claim to, have a right to, have coming to one, incur, rate, warrant

meritorious admirable, commendable, creditable, deserving, excellent, exemplary, good, honourable, laudable, praiseworthy, right, righteous, virtuous, worthy

merriment amusement, conviviality, festivity, frolic, fun, gaiety, glee, hilarity, jocularity, jollity, joviality, laughter, levity, liveliness, merry-making, mirth, revelry, sport

merry 1. blithe, blithesome, carefree, cheerful, convivial, festive, frolicsome, fun-loving, gay, glad, gleeful, happy, jocund, jolly, joyful, joyous, light-hearted, mirthful, rollicking, sportive, vivacious 2. amusing, comic, comical, facetious, funny, hilarious, humorous, jocular, mirthful 3. *Brit. inf.* elevated (*Inf.*), happy, mellow, squiffy (*Brit. inf.*), tiddly (*Brit. sl.*), tipsy 4. **make merry** carouse, celebrate, enjoy oneself, feast, frolic, have a good time, have fun, make whoopee (*Inf.*), revel

mesh n. 1. net, netting, network, plexus, reticulation, tracery, web 2. entanglement, snare, tangle, toils, trap, web ~v. 3. catch, enmesh, ensnare, entangle, net, snare, tangle, trap 4. combine, come together, connect, coordinate, dovetail, engage, fit together, harmonize, interlock, knit

mesmerize captivate, enthral, entrance, fascinate, grip, hold spellbound, hypnotize, magnetize, spellbind

mess *n.* 1. botch, chaos, clutter, confusion, dirtiness, disarray, disorder, disorganization, hash (*Inf.*), jumble, litter, mishmash, shambles, turmoil, untidiness 2. difficulty, dilemma, fine kettle of fish (*Inf.*), fix (*Inf.*), imbroglio, jam (*Inf.*), mix-up, muddle, perplexity, pickle (*Inf.*), plight, predicament, stew (*Inf.*) ~*v.* 3. *Often with up* befoul, besmirch, botch, bungle, clutter, dirty, disarrange, dishevel, foul, litter, make a hash of (*Inf.*), muck up (*Brit. sl.*), muddle, pollute, scramble 4. *Often with with* fiddle (*Inf.*), interfere, meddle, play, tamper, tinker

mess about *or* **around** 1. amuse oneself, dabble, footle (*Inf.*), muck about (*Inf.*), play about *or* around, potter, trifle 2. fiddle (*Inf.*), interfere, meddle, play, tamper, tinker, toy

message 1. bulletin, communication, communiqué, dispatch, intimation, letter, memorandum, missive, note, notice, tidings, word 2. idea, import, meaning, moral, point, purport, theme 3. commission, errand, job, mission, task 4. **get the message** catch on (*Inf.*), comprehend, get it (*Inf.*), get the point, see, take the hint, understand

messenger agent, bearer, carrier, courier, delivery boy, emissary, envoy, errand-boy, go-between, harbinger, herald, runner

messy chaotic, cluttered, confused, dirty, dishevelled, disordered, disorganized, grubby, littered, muddled, shambolic (*Inf.*), sloppy (*Inf.*), slovenly, unkempt, untidy

metaphor allegory, analogy, emblem, figure of speech, image, symbol, trope

metaphorical allegorical, emblematic, emblematical, figurative, symbolic, tropical (*Rhetoric*)

metaphysical 1. basic, esoteric, essential, eternal, fundamental, general, ideal, intellectual, philosophical, profound, speculative, spiritual, subjective, universal 2. abstract, abstruse, deep, highflown, oversubtle, recondite, theoretical, transcendental 3. immaterial, impalpable, incorporeal, intangible, spiritual, supernatural, unreal, unsubstantial

mete *v.* administer, allot, apportion, assign, deal, dispense, distribute, divide, dole, measure, parcel, portion, ration, share

meteoric brief, brilliant, dazzling, ephemeral, fast, flashing, fleeting, momentary, overnight, rapid, spectacular, speedy, sudden, swift, transient

method 1. approach, arrangement, course, fashion, form, manner, mode, modus operandi, plan, practice, procedure, process, programme, routine, rule, scheme, style, system, technique, way 2. design, form, order, orderliness, organization, pattern, planning, purpose, regularity, structure, system

methodical businesslike, deliberate, disciplined, efficient, meticulous, neat, ordered, orderly, organized, painstaking, planned, precise, regular, structured, systematic, tidy, well-regulated

meticulous detailed, exact, fastidious, fussy, microscopic, painstaking, particular, perfectionist, precise, punctilious, scrupulous, strict, thorough

métier 1. calling, craft, line, occupation, profession, pursuit, trade, vocation 2. forte, long suit (*Inf.*), speciality, specialty, strong point, strong suit

metropolis capital, city

microbe bacillus, bacterium, bug (*Inf.*), germ, microorganism, virus

microscopic imperceptible, infinitesimal, invisible, minuscule, minute, negligible, tiny

midday noon, noonday, noontide, noontime, twelve noon, twelve o'clock

middle *adj.* 1. central, halfway, inner, inside, intermediate, intervening, mean, medial, median, medium, mid ~*n.* 2. centre, focus, halfway point, heart, inside, mean, midpoint, midsection, midst, thick 3. midriff, midsection, waist

middleman broker, distributor, entrepreneur, go-between, intermediary

middling adequate, all right, average, fair, indifferent, mediocre, medium, moderate, modest, O.K. (*Inf.*), okay (*Inf.*), ordinary, passable, run-of-the-mill, so-so (*Inf.*), tolerable, unexceptional, unremarkable

midget 1. *n.* dwarf, gnome, homuncule, homunculus, manikin, pygmy, shrimp (*Inf.*), Tom Thumb 2. *adj.* baby, dwarf, Lilliputian, little, miniature, pocket, pygmy, small, tiny

midnight dead of night, middle of the night, the witching hour, twelve o'clock (at night)

midst 1. bosom, centre, core, depths, heart, hub, interior, middle, thick 2. **in the midst of** among, during, enveloped by, in the middle of, in the thick of, surrounded by

midway betwixt and between, halfway, in the middle

might 1. ability, capability, capacity, clout (*Sl.*), efficacy, efficiency, energy, force, potency, power, prowess, puissance, strength, sway, valour, vigour 2. (**with**) **might and main** as hard as one can, as hard as possible, forcefully, full blast, full force, lustily, manfully, mightily, vigorously, with all one's might *or* strength

mighty 1. doughty, forceful, hardy, indomitable, lusty, manful, potent, powerful, puissant, robust, stalwart, stout, strapping, strong, sturdy, vigorous 2. bulky, colossal, enormous, gigantic, grand, great, huge, immense, large, massive, monumental, prodigious, stupendous, titanic, towering, tremendous, vast

migrant 1. *n.* drifter, emigrant, gypsy, immigrant, itinerant, nomad, rover, tinker, transient, vagrant, wanderer 2. *adj.* drifting, gypsy, immigrant, itinerant, migratory, nomadic, roving, shifting, transient, travelling, vagrant, wandering

migrate drift, emigrate, journey, move, roam, rove, shift, travel, trek, voyage, wander

migration emigration, journey, movement, roving, shift, travel, trek, voyage, wandering

migratory gypsy, itinerant, migrant, nomadic, peripatetic, roving, shifting, transient, travelling, unsettled, vagrant, wandering

mild 1. amiable, balmy, bland, calm, clement, compassionate, docile, easy, easy-going, equable, forbearing, forgiving, gentle, indulgent, kind, meek, mellow, merciful, moderate, pacific, peaceable, placid, pleasant, serene, smooth, soft, temperate, tender, tranquil, warm 2. demulcent, emollient, lenitive, mollifying, soothing

mildness blandness, calmness, clemency, docility, forbearance, gentleness, indulgence, kindness, leniency, lenity, meekness, mellowness, moderation, placidity, smoothness, softness, temperateness, tenderness, tranquillity, warmth

milieu background, element, environment, locale, location, *mise en scène*, scene, setting, sphere, surroundings

militant *adj.* 1. active, aggressive, assertive, combative, vigorous 2. belligerent, combating, contending, embattled, fighting, in arms, warring ~*n.* 3. activist, partisan 4. belligerent, combatant, fighter, warrior

military 1. *adj.* armed, martial, soldierlike, soldierly, warlike 2. *n.* armed forces, army, forces, services

militia fencibles (*History*), National Guard (*U.S.*), reserve(s), Territorial Army (*Brit.*), trainband (*History*), yeomanry (*History*)

milk *v.* 1. drain, draw off, express, extract, let out, press, siphon, tap 2. bleed, drain, exploit, extract, impose on, pump, take advantage of, use, wring

milk-and-water feeble, innocuous, insipid, jejune, vapid, weak, wishy-washy (*Inf.*)

mill *n.* 1. factory, foundry, plant, shop, works 2. crusher, grinder 3. **run of the mill** average, commonplace, everyday, fair, middling, ordinary, routine, unexceptional, unremarkable ~*v.* 4. comminute, crush, granulate, grate, grind, pound, powder, press, pulverize 5. crowd, seethe, swarm, throng

millstone 1. grindstone, quernstone 2. affliction, burden, dead weight, drag, encumbrance, load, weight

mime 1. *n.* dumb show, gesture, mummery, pantomime 2. *v.* act out, gesture, pantomime, represent, simulate

mimic *v.* 1. ape, caricature, imitate, impersonate, parody, take off (*Inf.*) 2. echo, look like, mirror, resemble, simulate, take on the appearance of ~*n.* 3. caricaturist, copycat (*Inf.*), imitator, impersonator, impressionist, parodist, parrot ~*adj.* 4. echoic, imitation, imitative, make-believe, mimetic, mock, sham, simulated

mince 1. chop, crumble, cut, grind, hash 2. diminish, euphemize, extenuate, hold back, moderate, palliate, soften, spare, tone down, weaken 3. attitudinize, give oneself airs, ponce (*Sl.*), pose, posture

mincing affected, dainty, effeminate, foppish, lah-di-dah (*Inf.*), nice, niminy-piminy, poncy (*Sl.*), precious, pretentious, sissy

mind *n.* 1. brain(s) (*Inf.*), grey matter (*Inf.*), intellect, intelligence, mentality, ratiocination, reason, sense, spirit, understanding, wits 2. memory, recollection, remembrance 3. brain, head, imagination, psyche 4. brain (*Inf.*), genius, intellect, intellectual, thinker 5. attitude, belief, feeling, judgment, opinion, outlook, point of view, sentiment, thoughts, view, way of thinking 6. bent, desire, disposition, fancy, inclination, intention, leaning, notion, purpose, tendency, urge, will, wish 7. attention, concentration, thinking, thoughts 8. judgment, marbles (*Inf.*), mental balance, rationality, reason, sanity, senses, wits 9. **in** *or* **of two minds** dithering, hesitant, shillyshallying (*Inf.*), swithering (*Scot.*), uncertain, undecided, unsure, vacillating, wavering 10. **make up one's mind** choose, come to a decision, decide, determine, reach a decision, resolve 11. **bear** *or* **keep in mind** be cognizant of, be mindful of, remember, take note of ~*v.* 12. be affronted, be bothered, care, disapprove, dislike, look askance at, object, resent, take offence 13. adhere to, attend, comply with, follow, heed, listen to, mark, note, notice, obey, observe, pay attention, pay heed to, regard, respect, take heed, watch 14. be sure, ensure, make certain 15. attend to, guard, have charge of, keep an eye on, look after, take care of, tend, watch 16. be careful, be cautious, be on (one's) guard, be wary, take care, watch 17. **never mind** disregard, do not concern yourself, don't bother, don't give (it) a second thought, forget (it), it does not matter, it's none of your business, it's nothing to do with you, pay no attention

mindful alert, alive to, attentive, aware, careful, chary, cognizant, conscious, heedful, regardful, respectful, sensible, thoughtful, wary, watchful

mindless 1. asinine, brutish, careless, foolish, forgetful, gratuitous, heedless, idiotic, imbecilic, inattentive, moronic, neglectful, negligent, oblivious, obtuse, stupid, thoughtless, unintelligent, unmindful, unthinking, witless 2. automatic, brainless, mechanical

mind out be careful, be on one's guard, beware, keep one's eyes open, look out, pay attention, take care, watch

mine *n.* 1. coalfield, colliery, de~ posit, excavation, lode, pit, shaft, vein 2. abundance, fund, hoard, re~ serve, source, stock, store, supply, treasury, wealth 3. sap, trench, tunnel ~*v.* 4. delve, dig for, dig up, excavate, extract, hew, quarry, unearth 5. lay mines in *or* under, sow with mines 6. sap, subvert, tunnel, undermine, weaken

miner coalminer, collier (*Brit.*), pitman (*Brit.*)

mingle 1. alloy, blend, coalesce, combine, commingle, compound, intermingle, intermix, interweave, join, marry, merge, mix, unite 2. associate, circulate, consort, frat~ ernize, hang about *or* around, hang out (*Inf.*), hobnob, rub shoulders (*Inf.*), socialize

miniature *adj.* baby, diminutive, dwarf, Lilliputian, little, midget, mini, minuscule, minute, pocket, pygmy, reduced, scaled-down, small, tiny, toy, wee

minimal least, least possible, lit~ tlest, minimum, nominal, slightest, smallest, token

minimize 1. abbreviate, attenuate, curtail, decrease, diminish, minia~ turize, prune, reduce, shrink 2. be~ little, decry, deprecate, depreciate, discount, disparage, make light *or* little of, play down, underestimate, underrate

minimum 1. *n.* bottom, depth, least, lowest, nadir, slightest 2. *adj.* least, least possible, littlest, lowest, minimal, slightest, smallest

minion bootlicker (*Inf.*), creature, darling, dependant, favourite, flat~ terer, flunky, follower, hanger-on, henchman, hireling, lackey, lick~ spittle, myrmidon, parasite, pet, sycophant, toady, underling, yes man

minister *n.* 1. churchman, clergy~ man, cleric, divine, ecclesiastic, parson, pastor, preacher, priest, vicar 2. administrator, ambassa~ dor, cabinet member, delegate, diplomat, envoy, executive, office-holder, official, plenipotentiary 3.

agent, aide, assistant, lieutenant, servant, subordinate, underling ~*v.* 4. accommodate, administer, an~ swer, attend, be solicitous of, cater to, pander to, serve, take care of, tend

ministry 1. administration, cabinet, council, government, holy orders, the church, the priesthood, the pulpit 2. bureau, department, office

minor inconsequential, inconsider~ able, inferior, insignificant, junior, lesser, light, negligible, paltry, pet~ ty, secondary, slight, small, small~ er, subordinate, trifling, trivial, un~ important, younger

minstrel bard, harper, jongleur, musician, singer, troubadour

mint *n.* 1. bomb (*Brit. sl.*), bundle (*Sl.*), fortune, heap (*Inf.*), King's ransom, million, packet (*Sl.*), pile (*Inf.*) ~*adj.* 2. brand-new, excel~ lent, first-class, fresh, perfect, un~ blemished, undamaged, untar~ nished ~*v.* 3. cast, coin, make, produce, punch, stamp, strike 4. coin, construct, devise, fabricate, fashion, forge, invent, make up, produce, think up

minute[1] *n.* 1. sixtieth of an hour, sixty seconds 2. flash, instant, jiffy (*Inf.*), moment, second, shake (*Inf.*), tick (*Inf.*), trice 3. any min~ ute any moment, any second, any time, at any time, before long, very soon 4. up to the minute all the rage, in, latest, modish, (most) fashionable, newest, now (*Inf.*), smart, stylish, trendiest, trendy, up to date, vogue, with it (*Inf.*)

minute[2] *adj.* 1. diminutive, fine, in~ finitesimal, Lilliputian, little, microscopic, miniature, minuscule, slender, small, tiny 2. inconsider~ able, negligible, paltry, petty, pica~ yune (*U.S.*), piddling (*Inf.*), puny, slight, trifling, trivial, unimportant 3. close, critical, detailed, exact, exhaustive, meticulous, pains~ taking, precise, punctilious

minutely closely, critically, exact~ ly, exhaustively, in detail, meticu~ lously, painstakingly, precisely, with a fine-tooth comb

minutes memorandum, notes,

proceedings, record(s), transac~
tions, transcript

minutiae details, finer points, ni~
ceties, particulars, subtleties, tri~
fles, trivia

minx baggage (*Inf.*), coquette, flirt,
hoyden, hussy, jade, tomboy, wan~
ton

miracle marvel, phenomenon,
prodigy, thaumaturgy, wonder

miraculous amazing, astonishing,
astounding, extraordinary, incred~
ible, inexplicable, magical, mar~
vellous, phenomenal, preternatu~
ral, prodigious, superhuman,
supernatural, thaumaturgic, unac~
countable, unbelievable, wonder~
ful, wondrous

mirage hallucination, illusion, opti~
cal illusion, phantasm

mire *n.* 1. bog, marsh, morass,
quagmire, swamp 2. dirt, muck,
mud, ooze, slime 3. **in the mire**
encumbered, entangled, in diffi~
culties, in trouble ~*v.* 4. bog down,
flounder, sink, stick in the mud 5.
begrime, besmirch, bespatter,
cake, dirty, muddy, soil 6. catch up,
enmesh, entangle, involve

mirror *n.* 1. glass, looking-glass, re~
flector, speculum 2. copy, double,
image, likeness, reflection, replica,
representation, twin ~*v.* 3. copy,
depict, echo, emulate, follow, re~
flect, represent, show

mirth amusement, cheerfulness,
festivity, frolic, fun, gaiety, glad~
ness, glee, hilarity, jocularity, jol~
lity, joviality, joyousness, laughter,
levity, merriment, merrymaking,
pleasure, rejoicing, revelry, sport

mirthful amused, amusing, blithe,
cheerful, cheery, festive, frolic~
some, funny, gay, glad, gladsome
(*Archaic*), happy, hilarious, jocund,
jolly, jovial, laughable, light-
hearted, merry, playful, sportive,
uproarious, vivacious

misadventure accident, bad break
(*Inf.*), bad luck, calamity, catastro~
phe, debacle, disaster, failure, ill
fortune, ill luck, mischance, mis~
fortune, mishap, reverse, setback

misanthrope cynic, egoist, egotist,
mankind-hater, misanthropist

misapprehend get the wrong idea
or impression, misconceive, mis~
construe, misinterpret, misread,
mistake, misunderstand

misapprehension delusion, error,
fallacy, false belief, false impres~
sion, misconception, misconstruc~
tion, misinterpretation, misread~
ing, mistake, misunderstanding,
wrong idea *or* impression

misappropriate defalcate (*Law*),
embezzle, misapply, misspend,
misuse, peculate, pocket, steal,
swindle

misbehave act up (*Inf.*), be bad, be
insubordinate, be naughty, carry
on (*Inf.*), get up to mischief, muck
about (*Brit. sl.*)

misbehaviour acting up (*Inf.*), bad
behaviour, impropriety, incivility,
indiscipline, insubordination, mis~
conduct, misdeeds, misdemeanour,
monkey business (*Inf.*), naughti~
ness, rudeness, shenanigans (*Inf.*)

misbelief delusion, error, fallacy,
false belief, heresy, unorthodoxy

miscalculate blunder, calculate
wrongly, err, get (it) wrong (*Inf.*),
go wrong, make a mistake, mis~
judge, overestimate, overrate, slip
up, underestimate, underrate

miscarriage 1. miss (*Inf.*), sponta~
neous abortion 2. botch (*Inf.*),
breakdown, error, failure, misad~
venture, mischance, misfire, mis~
hap, mismanagement, nonsuccess,
perversion, thwarting, undoing

miscarry 1. abort 2. come to grief,
come to nothing, fail, fall through,
gang agley (*Scot.*), go amiss, go
astray, go awry, go wrong, misfire

miscellaneous assorted, confused,
diverse, diversified, farraginous,
heterogeneous, indiscriminate,
jumbled, many, mingled, mixed,
motley, multifarious, multiform,
promiscuous, sundry, varied, vari~
ous

miscellany anthology, assortment,
collection, diversity, farrago, galli~
maufry, hotchpotch, jumble, med~
ley, *mélange*, mixed bag, mixture,
omnium-gatherum, potpourri, sal~
magundi, variety

mischance accident, bad break

(*Inf.*), bad luck, calamity, contre~
temps, disaster, ill chance, ill for~
tune, ill luck, infelicity, misadven~
ture, misfortune, mishap

mischief 1. devilment, impishness,
misbehaviour, monkey business
(*Inf.*), naughtiness, pranks, ro~
guery, roguishness, shenanigans
(*Inf.*), trouble, waywardness 2.
devil, imp, monkey, nuisance, pest,
rascal, rogue, scallywag (*Inf.*),
scamp, tyke (*Inf.*), villain 3. dam~
age, detriment, disadvantage, dis~
ruption, evil, harm, hurt, injury,
misfortune, trouble

mischievous 1. arch, bad, badly
behaved, exasperating, frolicsome,
impish, naughty, playful, puckish,
rascally, roguish, sportive, teasing,
troublesome, vexatious, wayward
2. bad, damaging, deleterious, de~
structive, detrimental, evil, harm~
ful, hurtful, injurious, malicious,
malignant, pernicious, sinful,
spiteful, troublesome, vicious,
wicked

misconception delusion, error,
fallacy, misapprehension, miscon~
struction, mistaken belief, mis~
understanding, wrong end of the
stick (*Inf.*), wrong idea

misconduct 1. *n.* delinquency,
dereliction, immorality, impropri~
ety, malfeasance (*Law*), malprac~
tice, malversation (*Rare*), misbe~
haviour, misdemeanour, misman~
agement, naughtiness, rudeness,
transgression, unethical behaviour,
wrongdoing 2. *v.* behave badly,
botch (up), bungle, err, make a
mess of, misdirect, mismanage, sin

misdemeanour fault, infringe~
ment, misbehaviour, misconduct,
misdeed, offence, peccadillo,
transgression, trespass

miser cheapskate (*Inf.*), churl, cur~
mudgeon, hunks (*Rare*), niggard,
penny-pincher (*Inf.*), screw (*Sl.*),
Scrooge, skinflint, tightwad (*U.S.
sl.*)

miserable 1. afflicted, brokenhearted, crestfallen, dejected, de~
pressed, desolate, despondent, dis~
consolate, distressed, doleful,
down, downcast, down in the

mouth (*Inf.*), forlorn, gloomy,
heartbroken, melancholy, mourn~
ful, sorrowful, unhappy, woebe~
gone, wretched 2. destitute, im~
poverished, indigent, meagre,
needy, penniless, poor, poverty-
stricken, scanty 3. abject, bad,
contemptible, deplorable, despic~
able, detestable, disgraceful, lam~
entable, low, mean, pathetic, pit~
eous, pitiable, scurvy, shabby,
shameful, sordid, sorry, squalid,
vile, worthless, wretched

miserly avaricious, beggarly, close,
close-fisted, covetous, grasping, il~
liberal, mean, mingy (*Brit. inf.*),
near, niggardly, parsimonious,
penny-pinching (*Inf.*), penurious,
sordid, stingy, tightfisted, ungener~
ous

misery 1. agony, anguish, depres~
sion, desolation, despair, discom~
fort, distress, gloom, grief, hard~
ship, melancholy, sadness, sorrow,
suffering, torment, torture, unhap~
piness, woe, wretchedness 2. af~
fliction, bitter pill (*Inf.*), burden,
calamity, catastrophe, curse, dis~
aster, load, misfortune, ordeal,
sorrow, trial, tribulation, trouble,
woe 3. destitution, indigence, need,
penury, poverty, privation, sordid~
ness, squalor, want, wretchedness
4. *Brit. inf.* grouch (*Inf.*), killjoy,
moaner, pessimist, prophet of
doom, sourpuss (*Inf.*), spoilsport,
wet blanket (*Inf.*)

misfire fail, fail to go off, fall
through, go phut (*Inf.*), go wrong,
miscarry

misfit eccentric, fish out of water
(*Inf.*), nonconformist, square peg
(in a round hole) (*Inf.*)

misfortune 1. bad luck, evil for~
tune, hard luck, ill luck, infelicity 2.
accident, adversity, affliction,
blow, calamity, disaster, evil
chance, failure, hardship, harm,
loss, misadventure, mischance,
misery, mishap, reverse, setback,
stroke of bad luck, tragedy, trial,
tribulation, trouble

misgiving anxiety, apprehension,
distrust, doubt, hesitation, qualm,

reservation, scruple, suspicion, un~ certainty, unease, worry

misguided deluded, erroneous, foolish, ill-advised, imprudent, in~ judicious, labouring under a delu~ sion *or* misapprehension, misled, misplaced, mistaken, uncalled-for, unreasonable, unwarranted, un~ wise

mishandle botch, bungle, make a hash of (*Inf.*), make a mess of, mess up (*Inf.*), mismanage, muff, screw (up) (*Inf.*)

mishap accident, adversity, bad luck, calamity, contretemps, dis~ aster, evil chance, evil fortune, hard luck, ill fortune, ill luck, infe~ licity, misadventure, mischance, misfortune

misinform deceive, give (some~ one) a bum steer (*Sl.*), give (some~ one) duff gen (*Brit. inf.*), misdirect, misguide, mislead

misinterpret distort, falsify, get wrong, misapprehend, miscon~ ceive, misconstrue, misjudge, mis~ read, misrepresent, mistake, mis~ understand, pervert

misjudge be wrong about, get the wrong idea about, miscalculate, overestimate, overrate, underesti~ mate, underrate

mislay be unable to find, be unable to put *or* lay one's hand on, forget the whereabouts of, lose, lose track of, misplace, miss

mislead beguile, bluff, deceive, de~ lude, fool, give (someone) a bum steer (*Sl.*), hoodwink, lead astray, misdirect, misguide, misinform, pull the wool over (someone's) eyes (*Inf.*), take in (*Inf.*)

misleading ambiguous, casuistical, confusing, deceitful, deceptive, de~ lusive, delusory, disingenuous, evasive, false, sophistical, specious, spurious, tricky (*Inf.*), unstraight~ forward

mismanage be incompetent, be inefficient, botch, bungle, make a hash of (*Inf.*), make a mess of, maladminister, mess up, miscon~ duct, misdirect, misgovern, mis~ handle

misplace 1. be unable to find, be

unable to put *or* lay one's hand on, forget the whereabouts of, lose, lose track of, misfile, mislay, miss, put in the wrong place 2. place unwisely, place wrongly

misprint corrigendum, erratum, literal, mistake, printing error, typo (*Inf.*), typographical error

misquote distort, falsify, garble, mangle, misreport, misrepresent, misstate, muddle, pervert, quote *or* take out of context, twist

misrepresent belie, disguise, dis~ tort, falsify, garble, misinterpret, misstate, pervert, twist

misrule 1. bad government, mal~ administration, misgovernment, mismanagement 2. anarchy, cha~ os, confusion, disorder, lawless~ ness, tumult, turmoil

miss[1] *v.* 1. avoid, be late for, blun~ der, err, escape, evade, fail, fail to grasp, fail to notice, forego, lack, leave out, let go, let slip, lose, mis~ carry, mistake, omit, overlook, pass over, pass up, skip, slip, trip 2. feel the loss of, long for, need, pine for, want, wish, yearn for ~*n.* 3. blunder, error, failure, fault, loss, mistake, omission, oversight, want

miss[2] damsel, girl, lass, lassie (*Inf.*), maid, maiden, schoolgirl, spinster, young lady

misshapen contorted, crippled, crooked, deformed, distorted, gro~ tesque, ill-made, ill-proportioned, malformed, twisted, ugly, ungainly, unshapely, unsightly, warped, wry

missile projectile, rocket, weapon

missing absent, astray, gone, lack~ ing, left behind, left out, lost, mis~ laid, misplaced, not present, no~ where to be found, unaccounted-for, wanting

mission 1. aim, assignment, busi~ ness, calling, charge, commission, duty, errand, goal, job, office, op~ eration, purpose, pursuit, quest, task, trust, undertaking, vocation, work 2. commission, delegation, deputation, embassy, legation, ministry, task force

missionary apostle, converter, evangelist, preacher, propagandist, proselytizer

missive communication, dispatch, epistle, letter, memorandum, mes~ sage, note, report

misspent dissipated, idle, impru~ dent, misapplied, prodigal, profit~ less, squandered, thrown away, wasted

mist 1. *n.* cloud, condensation, dew, drizzle, film, fog, haar (*Eastern Brit.*), haze, smog, smur *or* smir (*Scot.*), spray, steam, vapour 2. *v.* becloud, befog, blur, cloud, film, fog, obscure, steam (up)

mistake *n.* 1. bloomer (*Brit. inf.*), blunder, boob (*Brit. sl.*), boo-boo (*Inf.*), clanger (*Inf.*), erratum, er~ ror, error of judgment, false move, fault, faux pas, gaffe, goof (*Inf.*), howler (*Inf.*), inaccuracy, miscal~ culation, misconception, misstep, misunderstanding, oversight, slip, slip-up (*Inf.*), solecism ~*v.* 2. get wrong, misapprehend, miscon~ ceive, misconstrue, misinterpret, misjudge, misread, misunderstand 3. accept as, confound, confuse with, misinterpret as, mix up with, take for 4. be wide of *or* be off the mark, be wrong, blunder, drop a clanger (*Inf.*), err, goof (*Inf.*), mis~ calculate, misjudge, put one's foot in it (*Inf.*), slip up (*Inf.*)

mistaken barking up the wrong tree (*Inf.*), erroneous, fallacious, false, faulty, inaccurate, inappro~ priate, incorrect, in the wrong, la~ bouring under a misapprehension, misguided, misinformed, mislead, off target, off the mark, unfounded, unsound, wide of the mark, wrong

mistakenly by mistake, erro~ neously, fallaciously, falsely, inac~ curately, inappropriately, incor~ rectly, in error, misguidedly, wrongly

mistimed badly timed, ill-timed, inconvenient, inopportune, unsea~ sonable, unsynchronized, untimely

mistreat abuse, brutalize, handle roughly, harm, ill-treat, ill-use, in~ jure, knock about (*Inf.*), maltreat, manhandle, maul, misuse, molest, rough up, wrong

mistress concubine, doxy (*Archa~ ic*), fancy woman (*Sl.*), girlfriend,

inamorata, kept woman, ladylove (*Rare*), lover, paramour

mistrust 1. *v.* apprehend, beware, be wary of, distrust, doubt, fear, have doubts about, suspect 2. *n.* apprehension, distrust, doubt, du~ biety, fear, misgiving, scepticism, suspicion, uncertainty, wariness

mistrustful apprehensive, cau~ tious, chary, cynical, distrustful, doubtful, dubious, fearful, hesitant, leery (*Sl.*), sceptical, suspicious, uncertain, wary

misty bleary, blurred, cloudy, dark, dim, foggy, fuzzy, hazy, indistinct, murky, nebulous, obscure, opaque, overcast, unclear, vague

misunderstand get (it) wrong, get the wrong end of the stick (*Inf.*), get the wrong idea (about), misap~ prehend, misconceive, miscon~ strue, mishear, misinterpret, mis~ judge, misread, miss the point (of), mistake

misunderstanding 1. error, false impression, misapprehension, misconception, misconstruction, misinterpretation, misjudgment, misreading, mistake, mix-up, wrong idea 2. argument, breach, conflict, difference, difficulty, dis~ agreement, discord, dissension, falling-out (*Inf.*), quarrel, rift, rup~ ture, squabble, variance

misunderstood misconstrued, misheard, misinterpreted, mis~ judged, misread, unappreciated, unrecognized

misuse *n.* 1. abuse, barbarism, catachresis, corruption, desecra~ tion, dissipation, malapropism, misapplication, misemployment, misusage, perversion, profanation, solecism, squandering, waste 2. abuse, cruel treatment, exploita~ tion, harm, ill-treatment, ill-usage, inhumane treatment, injury, mal~ treatment, manhandling, mis~ treatment, rough handling ~*v.* 3. abuse, corrupt, desecrate, dissi~ pate, misapply, misemploy, per~ vert, profane, prostitute, squander, waste 4. abuse, brutalize, exploit, handle roughly, harm, ill-treat, ill-use, injure, maltreat, manhandle, maul, mistreat, molest, wrong

mitigate abate, allay, appease, as~ suage, blunt, calm, check, dimin~ ish, dull, ease, extenuate, lessen, lighten, moderate, modify, mollify, pacify, palliate, placate, quiet, re~ duce the force of, remit, soften, soothe, subdue, take the edge off, temper, tone down, tranquillize, weaken

mitigation abatement, allaying, alleviation, assuagement, diminu~ tion, easement, extenuation, mod~ eration, mollification, palliation, relief, remission

mix v. **1.** alloy, amalgamate, asso~ ciate, blend, coalesce, combine, commingle, commix, compound, cross, fuse, incorporate, intermin~ gle, interweave, join, jumble, merge, mingle, put together, unite **2.** associate, come together, con~ sort, fraternize, hang out (*Inf.*), hobnob, join, mingle, socialize ~n. **3.** alloy, amalgam, assortment, blend, combination, compound, fu~ sion, medley, mixture

mixed **1.** alloyed, amalgamated, blended, combined, composite, compound, fused, incorporated, joint, mingled, united **2.** assorted, cosmopolitan, diverse, diversified, heterogeneous, miscellaneous, motley, varied **3.** crossbred, hy~ brid, interbred, interdenomina~ tional, mongrel **4.** ambivalent, equivocal, indecisive, uncertain

mixed-up bewildered, confused, distraught, disturbed, maladjusted, muddled, perplexed, puzzled, upset

mixture admixture, alloy, amal~ gam, amalgamation, association, assortment, blend, brew, combine, composite, compound, concoction, conglomeration, cross, fusion, hotchpotch, jumble, medley, *mélange*, miscellany, mix, pot~ pourri, salmagundi, union, variety

mix-up confusion, disorder, fankle (*Scot.*), jumble, mess, mistake, misunderstanding, muddle, snarl~ up (*Brit. inf.*), tangle

mix up **1.** blend, combine, commix, mix **2.** confound, confuse, muddle

3. bewilder, confuse, disturb, flus~ ter, muddle, perplex, puzzle, throw into confusion, upset **4.** embroil, entangle, implicate, involve

moan n. **1.** groan, lament, lamenta~ tion, sigh, sob, sough, wail, whine **2.** *Inf.* beef (*Sl.*), bitch (*Sl.*), com~ plaint, gripe (*Inf.*), grouse, grum~ ble, whine, whinge ~v. **3.** bemoan, bewail, deplore, grieve, groan, keen, lament, mourn, sigh, sob, sough, whine **4.** *Inf.* beef (*Sl.*), bitch (*Sl.*), carp, complain, gripe (*Inf.*), groan, grouse, grumble, moan and groan, whine, whinge

mob n. **1.** assemblage, body, collec~ tion, crowd, drove, flock, gang, gathering, herd, horde, host, mass, multitude, pack, press, swarm, throng **2.** class, company, crew (*Inf.*), gang, group, lot, set, troop **3.** canaille, commonalty, great un~ washed (*Inf.*), hoi polloi, masses, rabble, riffraff, scum ~v. **4.** crowd around, jostle, overrun, set upon, surround, swarm around **5.** cram into, crowd, crowd into, fill, fill to overflowing, jam, pack

mobile **1.** ambulatory, itinerant, lo~ comotive, migrant, motile, mov~ able, moving, peripatetic, portable, travelling, wandering **2.** animated, changeable, ever-changing, ex~ pressive

mobilize activate, animate, call to arms, call up, get *or* make ready, marshal, muster, organize, pre~ pare, put in motion, rally, ready

mock v. **1.** chaff, deride, flout, in~ sult, jeer, laugh at, laugh to scorn, make fun of, poke fun at, ridicule, scoff, scorn, show contempt for, sneer, take the mickey (out of) (*Inf.*), taunt, tease **2.** ape, bur~ lesque, caricature, counterfeit, imitate, lampoon, mimic, parody, satirize, send up (*Brit. inf.*), take off (*Inf.*), travesty **3.** belie, cheat, deceive, delude, disappoint, dupe, elude, fool, let down, mislead **4.** defeat, defy, disappoint, foil, frus~ trate, thwart ~n. **5.** banter, deri~ sion, gibe, jeering, mockery, ridi~ cule, scorn, sneer, sneering **6.** Aunt Sally (*Brit.*), butt, dupe, fool, jest, laughing stock, sport, travesty 7. counterfeit, fake, forgery, fraud, imitation, phoney (*Sl.*), sham ~*adj.* 8. artificial, bogus, counterfeit, dummy, ersatz, fake, faked, false, feigned, forged, fraudulent, imitation, phoney (*Sl.*), pretended, pseudo (*Inf.*), sham, spurious

mockery 1. contempt, contumely, derision, disdain, disrespect, gibes, insults, jeering, ridicule, scoffing, scorn 2. burlesque, caricature, deception, farce, imitation, lampoon, laughing stock, mimicry, parody, ·pretence, send-up (*Brit. sl.*), sham, spoof (*Inf.*), take-off (*Inf.*), travesty 3. apology, disappointment, farce, joke, letdown

mocking contemptuous, contumelious, derisive, derisory, disdainful, disrespectful, insulting, irreverent, sarcastic, sardonic, satiric, satirical, scoffing, scornful, taunting

model *n.* 1. copy, dummy, facsimile, image, imitation, miniature, mock-up, replica, representation 2. archetype, design, epitome, example, exemplar, gauge, ideal, lodestar, mould, original, paradigm, paragon, pattern, prototype, standard, type 3. poser, sitter, subject 4. mannequin 5. configuration, design, form, kind, mark, mode, style, type, variety, version ~*v.* 6. base, carve, cast, design, fashion, form, mould, pattern, plan, sculpt, shape 7. display, show off, sport (*Inf.*), wear ~*adj.* 8. copy, dummy, facsimile, imitation, miniature 9. archetypal, exemplary, ideal, illustrative, paradigmatic, perfect, standard, typical

moderate *adj.* 1. calm, controlled, cool, deliberate, equable, gentle, judicious, limited, middle-of-the-road, mild, modest, peaceable, reasonable, restrained, sober, steady, temperate 2. average, fair, fairish, fair to middling (*Inf.*), indifferent, mediocre, medium, middling, ordinary, passable, so-so (*Inf.*), unexceptional ~*v.* 3. abate, allay, appease, assuage, calm, control, curb, decrease, diminish, lessen, mitigate, modulate, pacify,

play down, quiet, regulate, repress, restrain, soften, soft pedal (*Inf.*), subdue, tame, temper, tone down 4. arbitrate, chair, judge, mediate, preside, referee, take the chair

moderately fairly, gently, in moderation, passably, quite, rather, reasonably, slightly, somewhat, to a degree, tolerably, to some extent, within limits, within reason

moderation 1. calmness, composure, coolness, equanimity, fairness, judiciousness, justice, justness, mildness, moderateness, reasonableness, restraint, sedateness, temperance 2. **in moderation** moderately, within limits, within reason

modern contemporary, current, fresh, late, latest, neoteric (*Rare*), new, newfangled, novel, present, present-day, recent, twentieth-century, up-to-date, up-to-the-minute, with-it (*Inf.*)

modernize bring into the twentieth century, bring up to date, rejuvenate, remake, remodel, renew, renovate, revamp, update

modest 1. bashful, blushing, coy, demure, diffident, discreet, humble, meek, quiet, reserved, reticent, retiring, self-conscious, self-effacing, shy, simple, unassuming, unpretentious 2. fair, limited, middling, moderate, ordinary, small, unexceptional

modesty bashfulness, coyness, decency, demureness, diffidence, discreetness, humbleness, humility, lack of pretension, meekness, propriety, quietness, reserve, reticence, self-effacement, shyness, simplicity, timidity, unobtrusiveness, unpretentiousness

modification adjustment, alteration, change, modulation, mutation, qualification, refinement, reformation, restriction, revision, variation

modify 1. adapt, adjust, alter, change, convert, recast, redo, refashion, reform, remodel, reorganize, reshape, revise, rework, transform, vary 2. abate, lessen, limit, lower, moderate, qualify, reduce, restrain, restrict, soften, temper, tone down

mogul baron, bashaw, big cheese (*Sl.*), big gun (*Sl.*), big noise (*Brit. sl.*), big shot (*Sl.*), big wheel (*Sl.*), lord, magnate, nabob (*Inf.*), notable, personage, potentate, tycoon, V.I.P.

moist clammy, damp, dampish, dank, dewy, dripping, drizzly, humid, not dry, rainy, soggy, wet, wettish

moisten bedew, damp, dampen, humidify, lick, moisturize, soak, water, wet

moisture damp, dampness, dankness, dew, humidity, liquid, perspiration, sweat, water, wateriness, wetness

molecule atom, iota, jot, mite, mote, particle, speck

molest 1. abuse, afflict, annoy, badger, beset, bother, bug (*Inf.*), disturb, harass, harry, hector, irritate, persecute, pester, plague, tease, torment, upset, vex, worry 2. abuse, accost, assail, attack, harm, hurt, illtreat, injure, interfere with, maltreat, manhandle

moment 1. flash, instant, jiffy (*Inf.*), minute, no time, second, shake (*Inf.*), split second, tick (*Brit. inf.*), trice, twinkling, two shakes (*Inf.*), two shakes of a lamb's tail (*Inf.*) 2. hour, instant, juncture, point, point in time, stage, time 3. concern, consequence, gravity, import, importance, seriousness, significance, substance, value, weight, weightiness, worth

momentarily briefly, for a moment (little while, minute, second, short time, short while), for an instant, temporarily

momentary brief, ephemeral, evanescent, fleeting, flying, fugitive, hasty, passing, quick, short, short-lived, temporary, transitory

momentous consequential, critical, crucial, decisive, earth-shaking (*Inf.*), fateful, grave, historic, important, of moment, pivotal, serious, significant, vital, weighty

momentum drive, energy, force, impetus, power, propulsion, push, strength, thrust

monarch crowned head, emperor, empress, king, potentate, prince, princess, queen, ruler, sovereign

monarchy 1. absolutism, autocracy, despotism, kingship, monocracy, royalism, sovereignty 2. empire, kingdom, principality, realm

monastery abbey, cloister, convent, friary, house, nunnery, priory, religious community

monastic ascetic, austere, celibate, cenobitic, cloistered, cloistral, coenobitic, contemplative, conventual, eremitic, hermit-like, monachal, monkish, recluse, reclusive, secluded, sequestered, withdrawn

monetary budgetary, capital, cash, financial, fiscal, pecuniary

money 1. banknotes, bread (*Sl.*), capital, cash, coin, currency, dough (*Sl.*), filthy lucre (*Facetious*), funds, gelt (*Sl.*), green (*Sl.*), hard cash, legal tender, lolly (*Brit. sl.*), loot (*Inf.*), mazuma (*Sl., chiefly U.S.*), moolah (*Sl.*), pelf (*Contemptuous*), readies (*Inf.*), riches, specie, spondulix (*Sl.*), the ready (*Inf.*), the wherewithal, wealth 2. in the money affluent, flush (*Inf.*), in clover (*Inf.*), loaded (*Sl.*), on Easy Street (*Inf.*), prosperous, rich, rolling (*Sl.*), wealthy, well-heeled (*Sl.*), well-off, well-to-do

moneymaking adj. gainful, going, lucrative, paying, profitable, remunerative, successful, thriving

mongrel 1. n. bigener (*Biol.*), cross, crossbreed, half-breed, hybrid, mixed breed 2. adj. bastard, crossbred, half-breed, hybrid, of mixed breed

monitor 1. n. guide, invigilator, overseer, prefect (*Brit.*), supervisor, watchdog 2. v. check, follow, keep an eye on, keep track of, observe, oversee, record, scan, supervise, survey, watch

monk brother, friar (*loosely*), monastic, religious

monkey n. 1. primate, simian 2. devil, imp, mischief maker, rascal, rogue, scamp 3. *Sl.* ass, butt, dupe, fool, laughing stock 4. **make a monkey of** make a fool of, make (someone) a laughing stock, make fun of, make (someone) look fool~ ish (ridiculous, silly), play a trick on, ridicule ~*v.* 5. fiddle, fool, interfere, meddle, mess, play, tamper, tinker, trifle

monkey business 1. carry-on (*Inf.*), clowning, mischief, monkey tricks, pranks, shenanigans (*Inf.*), skylarking (*Inf.*), tomfoolery 2. chicanery, dishonesty, funny busi~ ness, hanky-panky (*Inf.*), skuldug~ gery (*Inf.*), trickery

monolithic colossal, giant, gigan~ tic, huge, immovable, impen~ etrable, imposing, intractable, massive, monumental, solid, sub~ stantial, undifferentiated, undivid~ ed, unitary

monologue harangue, lecture, sermon, soliloquy, speech

monopolize control, corner, cor~ ner the market in, dominate, en~ gross, exercise *or* have a monopo~ ly of, hog (*Sl.*), keep to oneself, take over, take up

monotonous all the same, boring, colourless, droning, dull, flat, hum~ drum, plodding, repetitious, re~ petitive, samey (*Inf.*), soporific, te~ dious, tiresome, toneless, un~ changing, uniform, uninflected, unvaried, wearisome

monotony boredom, colourless~ ness, dullness, flatness, humdrum~ ness, monotonousness, repetitive~ ness, repetitiousness, routine, sameness, tediousness, tedium, tiresomeness, uniformity, weari~ someness

monster *n.* 1. barbarian, beast, bogeyman, brute, demon, devil, fiend, ogre, savage, villain 2. abor~ tion, freak, lusus naturae, mis~ creation, monstrosity, mutant, teratism 3. behemoth, Brobding~ nagian, colossus, giant, leviathan, mammoth, titan ~*adj.* 4. Brob~ dingnagian, colossal, enormous, gargantuan, giant, gigantic, huge, immense, jumbo (*Inf.*), mammoth, massive, monstrous, stupendous, titanic, tremendous

monstrosity 1. abortion, eyesore, freak, horror, lusus naturae, mis~ creation, monster, mutant, ogre, teratism 2. abnormality, atrocity, dreadfulness, evil, frightfulness, heinousness, hellishness, hideous~ ness, horror, loathsomeness, ob~ scenity

monstrous 1. abnormality, dreadful, enormous, fiendish, freakish, frightful, grotesque, gruesome, hellish, hideous, horrendous, hor~ rible, miscreated, obscene, tera~ toid, terrible, unnatural 2. atro~ cious, cruel, devilish, diabolical, disgraceful, egregious, evil, fiend~ ish, foul, heinous, horrifying, infa~ mous, inhuman, intolerable, loath~ some, odious, outrageous, satanic, scandalous, shocking, vicious, vil~ lainous 3. colossal, elephantine, enormous, gargantuan, giant, gi~ gantic, great, huge, immense, mammoth, massive, prodigious, stupendous, titanic, towering, tre~ mendous, vast

month four weeks, moon, thirty days

monument 1. cairn, cenotaph, commemoration, gravestone, headstone, marker, mausoleum, memorial, obelisk, pillar, shrine, statue, tombstone 2. memento, record, remembrance, reminder, testament, token, witness

monumental 1. awe-inspiring, awesome, classic, enduring, enor~ mous, epoch-making, historic, im~ mortal, important, lasting, majes~ tic, memorable, outstanding, pro~ digious, significant, stupendous, unforgettable 2. commemorative, cyclopean, funerary, memorial, monolithic, statuary 3. *Inf.* cata~ strophic, colossal, egregious, gi~ gantic, great, horrible, immense, indefensible, massive, staggering, terrible, tremendous, unforgivable, whopping (*Inf.*)

mood 1. disposition, frame of mind, humour, spirit, state of mind, tem~ per, tenor, vein 2. bad temper, blues, depression, doldrums, dumps (*Inf.*), fit of pique, grumps (*Inf.*), low spirits, melancholy, sulk, the sulks 3. **in the mood** disposed (to~ wards), eager, favourable, inclined, interested, in the (right) frame of mind, keen, minded, willing

moody 1. angry, broody, cantan~ kerous, crabbed, crabby, crest~ fallen, cross, crotchety (*Inf.*), crusty, curt, dismal, doleful, dour, downcast, down in the dumps (*Inf.*), down in the mouth (*Inf.*), frowning, gloomy, glum, huffish, huffy, ill-humoured, ill-tempered, in a huff, in the doldrums, intro~ spective, irascible, irritable, lugu~ brious, melancholy, miserable, mopish, mopy, morose, offended, out of sorts (*Inf.*), pensive, petu~ lant, piqued, sad, saturnine, short-tempered, splenetic, sulky, sullen, temperamental, testy, touchy, waspish, wounded 2. capricious, changeable, erratic, faddish, fickle, fitful, flighty, impulsive, inconstant, mercurial, temperamental, unpre~ dictable, unstable, unsteady, vola~ tile

moon *n.* 1. satellite 2. **once in a blue moon** almost never, hardly ever, rarely, very seldom ~*v.* 3. daydream, idle, languish, mooch (*Sl.*), mope, waste time

moor[1] fell (*Brit.*), heath, moorland, muir (*Scot.*)

moor[2] anchor, berth, dock, fasten, fix, lash, make fast, secure, tie up

moot 1. *adj.* arguable, at issue, con~ testable, controversial, debatable, disputable, doubtful, open, open to debate, undecided, unresolved, un~ settled 2. *v.* bring up, broach, introduce, propose, put forward, suggest, ventilate

mop *n.* 1. sponge, squeegee, swab 2. mane, shock, tangle, thatch ~*v.* 3. clean, soak up, sponge, swab, wash, wipe

mop up 1. clean up, mop, soak up, sponge, swab, wash, wipe 2. *Mili~ tary* account for, clean out, clear, eliminate, finish off, neutralize, pacify, round up, secure

moral *adj.* 1. ethical 2. blameless, chaste, decent, ethical, good, high-minded, honest, honourable, in~ corruptible, innocent, just, merito~

rious, noble, principled, proper, pure, right, righteous, upright, up~ standing, virtuous ~*n.* 3. lesson, meaning, message, point, signifi~ cance 4. adage, aphorism, apo~ phthegm, epigram, gnome, maxim, motto, proverb, saw, saying

morale confidence, esprit de corps, heart, mettle, self-esteem, spirit, temper

morality 1. chastity, decency, ethi~ cality, ethicalness, goodness, hon~ esty, integrity, justice, principle, rectitude, righteousness, rightness, uprightness, virtue 2. conduct, eth~ ics, habits, ideals, manners, moral code, morals, mores, philosophy, principles, standards

morals behaviour, conduct, ethics, habits, integrity, manners, moral~ ity, mores, principles, scruples, standards

moratorium freeze, halt, post~ ponement, respite, standstill, stay, suspension

morbid 1. brooding, ghoulish, gloomy, grim, melancholy, pessi~ mistic, sick, sombre, unhealthy, unwholesome 2. dreadful, ghastly, grisly, gruesome, hideous, horrid, macabre 3. ailing, deadly, diseased, infected, malignant, pathological, sick, sickly, unhealthy, unsound

more 1. *adj.* added, additional, ex~ tra, fresh, further, new, other, spare, supplementary 2. *adv.* bet~ ter, further, longer, to a greater extent

moreover additionally, also, as well, besides, further, furthermore, in addition, into the bargain, like~ wise, to boot, too, what is more, withal (*Literary*)

morgue mortuary

moribund 1. at death's door, breathing one's last, doomed, dy~ ing, fading fast, failing, (having) one foot in the grave, *in extremis*, near death, near the end, on one's deathbed, on one's last legs 2. at a standstill, declining, forceless, ob~ solescent, on its last legs, on the way out, stagnant, stagnating, standing still, waning, weak

morning a.m., break of day, dawn,

daybreak, forenoon, morn (*Poet~ ic*), morrow (*Archaic*), sunrise

moron ass, blockhead, bonehead (*Sl.*), cretin, dimwit (*Inf.*), dolt, dope (*Sl.*), dummy (*Sl.*), dunce, dunderhead, fool, halfwit, idiot, imbecile, mental defective, muttonhead (*Sl.*), numskull, sim~ pleton, thickhead

morose blue, churlish, crabbed, crabby, cross, crusty, depressed, dour, down, down in the dumps (*Inf.*), gloomy, glum, grouchy (*Inf.*), gruff, ill-humoured, ill-natured, ill-tempered, in a bad mood, low, melancholy, moody, mournful, perverse, pessimistic, saturnine, sour, sulky, sullen, surly, taciturn

morsel bit, bite, crumb, fraction, fragment, grain, mouthful, nibble, part, piece, scrap, segment, slice, snack, soupçon, taste, titbit

mortal *adj.* 1. corporeal, earthly, ephemeral, human, impermanent, passing, sublunary, temporal, transient, worldly 2. deadly, death-dealing, destructive, fatal, killing, lethal, murderous, terminal 3. bit~ ter, deadly, implacable, irreconcil~ able, out-and-out, remorseless, sworn, to the death, unrelenting 4. agonizing, awful, dire, enormous, extreme, grave, great, intense, se~ vere, terrible ~*n.* 5. being, body, earthling, human, human being, individual, man, person, woman

mortality 1. ephemerality, human~ ity, impermanence, temporality, transience 2. bloodshed, carnage, death, destruction, fatality, killing, loss of life

mortification 1. abasement, an~ noyance, chagrin, discomfiture, dissatisfaction, embarrassment, humiliation, loss of face, shame, vexation 2. abasement, chastening, control, denial, discipline, subjuga~ tion 3. *Medical* corruption, fester~ ing, gangrene, necrosis, putres~ cence

mortified 1. abashed, affronted, annoyed, ashamed, chagrined, chastened, confounded, crushed, deflated, discomfited, displeased, embarrassed, given a showing up (*Inf.*), humbled, humiliated, made to eat humble pie (*Inf.*), put down, put out (*Inf.*), put to shame, ren~ dered speechless, shamed, vexed 2. abased, chastened, conquered, controlled, crushed, disciplined, subdued 3. *Of flesh* decayed, gan~ grenous, necrotic, rotted

mortify 1. abase, abash, affront, annoy, chagrin, chasten, confound, crush, deflate, disappoint, discom~ fit, displease, embarrass, humble, humiliate, make (someone) eat humble pie (*Inf.*), put down, put to shame, shame, take (someone) down a peg (*Inf.*), vex 2. abase, chasten, control, deny, discipline, subdue 3. *Of flesh* become gangre~ nous, corrupt, deaden, die, fester, gangrene, necrose, putrefy

mortuary funeral parlour, morgue

mostly above all, almost entirely, as a rule, chiefly, customarily, for the most part, generally, largely, mainly, most often, on the whole, particularly, predominantly, prin~ cipally, usually

moth-eaten antiquated, decayed, decrepit, dilapidated, obsolete, outdated, outworn, ragged, seedy, shabby, stale, tattered, threadbare, worn-out

mother *n.* 1. dam, ma (*Inf.*), mater, mom (*U.S. inf.*), mum (*Brit. inf.*), mummy (*Brit. inf.*), old lady (*Inf.*), old woman (*Inf.*) ~*adj.* 2. connate, inborn, innate, native, natural ~*v.* 3. bear, bring forth, give birth to, produce 4. care for, cherish, nurse, nurture, protect, raise, rear, tend 5. baby, fuss over, indulge, pamper, spoil

motherly affectionate, caring, comforting, fond, gentle, kind, lov~ ing, maternal, protective, shelter~ ing, tender, warm

mother wit brains, common sense, gumption (*Brit. inf.*), horse sense, judgment, native intelligence, sav~ vy (*Sl.*)

motion *n.* 1. action, change, flow, kinesics, locomotion, mobility, motility, move, movement, pas~ sage, passing, progress, travel 2. gesticulation, gesture, sign, signal,

wave 3. proposal, proposition, rec~
ommendation, submission, sugges~
tion 4. **in motion** afoot, functioning,
going, in progress, moving, on the
go (Inf.), on the move (Inf.), op~
erational, travelling, under way,
working ~v. 5. beckon, direct, ges~
ticulate, gesture, nod, signal, wave

motionless at a standstill, at rest,
calm, fixed, frozen, halted, immo~
bile, inanimate, inert, lifeless,
paralysed, standing, static, station~
ary, still, stock-still, transfixed, un~
moved, unmoving

motivate actuate, arouse, bring,
cause, draw, drive, give incentive
to, impel, induce, inspire, inspirit,
instigate, lead, move, persuade,
prompt, provoke, set on, stimulate,
stir, trigger

motivation 1. ambition, desire,
drive, hunger, inspiration, interest,
wish 2. impulse, incentive, incite~
ment, inducement, inspiration, in~
stigation, motive, persuasion, rea~
son, spur, stimulus

motive 1. n. cause, design,
ground(s), incentive, incitement,
inducement, influence, inspiration,
intention, mainspring, motivation,
object, occasion, purpose, ration~
ale, reason, spur, stimulus, thinking
2. adj. activating, driving, impel~
ling, motivating, moving, opera~
tive, prompting

motley 1. assorted, disparate, dis~
similar, diversified, heterogeneous,
mingled, miscellaneous, mixed,
unlike, varied 2. chequered, multi~
coloured, particoloured, polychro~
matic, polychrome, polychromous,
rainbow, variegated

mottled blotchy, brindled, cheq~
uered, dappled, flecked, freckled,
marbled, piebald, pied, speckled,
spotted, stippled, streaked, tabby,
variegated

motto adage, byword, cry, formula,
gnome, maxim, precept, proverb,
rule, saw, saying, slogan, watch~
word

mould¹ n. 1. cast, die, form, matrix,
pattern, shape 2. brand, build, con~
figuration, construction, cut, de~
sign, fashion, form, format, frame,

kind, line, make, pattern, shape,
structure, style 3. calibre, charac~
ter, ilk, kidney, kind, nature, qual~
ity, sort, stamp, type ~v. 4. carve,
cast, construct, create, fashion,
forge, form, make, model, sculpt,
shape, stamp, work 5. affect, con~
trol, direct, form, influence, make,
shape

mould² blight, fungus, mildew,
mouldiness, mustiness

mouldy bad, blighted, decaying,
fusty, mildewed, musty, rotten,
rotting, spoiled, stale

mound 1. bing (Scot.), drift, heap,
pile, stack 2. bank, dune, embank~
ment, hill, hillock, knoll, rise 3. Ar~
chaeology barrow, tumulus 4. bul~
wark, earthwork, motte (History),
rampart

mount v. 1. ascend, clamber up,
climb, escalade, go up, make one's
way up, scale 2. bestride, climb
onto, climb up on, get astride, get
(up) on, jump on 3. arise, ascend,
rise, soar, tower 4. accumulate,
build, escalate, grow, increase, in~
tensify, multiply, pile up, swell 5.
display, frame, set, set off 6. exhib~
it, get up (Inf.), prepare, produce,
put on, stage 7. Military deliver,
launch, prepare, ready, set in mo~
tion, stage 8. emplace, fit, install,
place, position, put in place, set up
~n. 9. backing, base, fixture, foil,
frame, mounting, setting, stand,
support 10. horse, steed (Literary)

mountain 1. alp, ben (Scot.),
elevation, eminence, fell (Brit.),
height, mount, peak 2. abundance,
heap, mass, mound, pile, stack, ton

mountainous 1. alpine, high, high~
land, rocky, soaring, steep, tower~
ing, upland 2. daunting, enormous,
gigantic, great, huge, hulking, im~
mense, mammoth, mighty, monu~
mental, ponderous, prodigious

mourn bemoan, bewail, deplore,
grieve, keen, lament, miss, rue,
sorrow, wail, wear black, weep

mournful 1. afflicting, calamitous,
deplorable, distressing, grievous,
lamentable, melancholy, painful,
piteous, plaintive, sad, sorrowful,
tragic, unhappy, woeful 2. broken~

hearted, cheerless, desolate, disconsolate, downcast, funereal, gloomy, grief-stricken, grieving, heartbroken, heavy, heavy-hearted, joyless, lugubrious, melancholy, rueful, sad, sombre, unhappy, woeful

mourning 1. bereavement, grief, grieving, keening, lamentation, weeping, woe 2. black, sackcloth and ashes, weeds, widow's weeds

mouth *n.* 1. chops (*Sl.*), gob (*Sl.*), jaws, lips, maw, trap (*Sl.*), yap (*Sl.*) 2. *Inf.* boasting, braggadocio, bragging, empty talk, gas (*Sl.*), hot air (*Sl.*), idle talk 3. *Inf.* backchat (*Inf.*), cheek (*Inf.*), impudence, insolence, lip (*Sl.*), rudeness, sauce (*Inf.*) 4. aperture, cavity, crevice, door, entrance, gateway, inlet, lips, opening, orifice, rim 5. face, grimace, *moue*, pout, wry face 6. **down in** *or* **at the mouth** blue, crestfallen, dejected, depressed, disheartened, dispirited, down, downcast, down in the dumps (*Inf.*), in low spirits, melancholy, sad, unhappy

mouthful bit, bite, drop, forkful, little, morsel, sample, sip, spoonful, sup, swallow, taste

mouthpiece 1. agent, delegate, representative, spokesman, spokeswoman 2. journal, organ, periodical, publication

movable detachable, mobile, not fixed, portable, portative, transferable, transportable

move *v.* 1. advance, budge, change position, drift, go, march, proceed, progress, shift, stir, walk 2. carry, change, shift, switch, transfer, transport, transpose 3. change residence, flit (*Scot., & northern English dialect*), go away, leave, migrate, move house, quit, relocate, remove 4. activate, drive, impel, motivate, operate, propel, push, set going, shift, shove, start, turn 5. actuate, affect, agitate, cause, excite, give rise to, impel, impress, incite, induce, influence, inspire, instigate, lead, make an impression on, motivate, persuade, prompt, rouse, stimulate, touch,

urge 6. advocate, propose, put forward, recommend, suggest, urge ~*n.* 7. act, action, deed, manoeuvre, measure, motion, movement, ploy, shift, step, stratagem, stroke, turn 8. change of address, flit (*Scot., & northern English dialect*), flitting (*Scot., & northern English dialect*), migration, relocation, removal, shift, transfer 9. **get a move on** get cracking (*Inf.*), get going (*Inf.*), hurry (up), make haste, speed up, step on it (*Inf.*), stir oneself 10. **on the move** *Inf.* **a.** in transit, journeying, moving, on the road (*Inf.*), on the run, on the wing, travelling, under way, voyaging **b.** active, advancing, astir, going forward, moving, progressing, stirring, succeeding

movement 1. act, action, activity, advance, agitation, change, development, displacement, exercise, flow, gesture, manoeuvre, motion, move, moving, operation, progress, progression, shift, steps, stir, stirring, transfer 2. campaign, crusade, drive, faction, front, group, grouping, organization, party 3. current, drift, flow, swing, tendency, trend 4. action, innards (*Inf.*), machinery, mechanism, workings, works 5. *Music* division, part, passage, section 6. beat, cadence, measure, metre, pace, rhythm, swing, tempo

moving 1. affecting, arousing, emotional, emotive, exciting, impelling, impressive, inspiring, pathetic, persuasive, poignant, stirring, touching 2. mobile, motile, movable, portable, running, unfixed 3. dynamic, impelling, inspirational, motivating, propelling, stimulating, stimulative

mow crop, cut, scythe, shear, trim

mow down butcher, cut down, cut to pieces, massacre, shoot down, slaughter

much 1. *adj.* abundant, a lot of, ample, considerable, copious, great, plenteous, plenty of, sizeable, substantial 2. *adv.* a great deal, a lot, considerably, decidedly, exceedingly, frequently, greatly, indeed, often, regularly 3. *n.* a good deal, a great deal, a lot, an appreciable amount, heaps (*Inf.*), loads (*Inf.*), lots (*Inf.*), plenty

muck 1. dung, manure, ordure 2. dirt, filth, gunge (*Inf.*), gunk (*Inf.*), mire, mud, ooze, scum, sewage, slime, sludge 3. **make a muck of** *Sl.* botch, bungle, make a mess of, mar, mess up, muff, ruin, screw up (*Inf.*), spoil

muck up botch, bungle, make a mess of, make a muck of (*Sl.*), mar, mess up, muff, ruin, screw up (*Inf.*), spoil

mud clay, dirt, mire, ooze, silt, sludge

muddle *v.* 1. confuse, disarrange, disorder, disorganize, jumble, make a mess of, mess, mix up, scramble, spoil, tangle 2. befuddle, bewilder, confound, confuse, daze, disorient, perplex, stupefy ~*n.* 3. chaos, clutter, confusion, daze, disarray, disorder, disorganization, fankle (*Scot.*), jumble, mess, mix-up, perplexity, plight, predicament, tangle

muddled 1. chaotic, confused, disarrayed, disordered, disorganized, higgledy-piggledy (*Inf.*), jumbled, messy, mixed-up, scrambled, tangled 2. at sea, befuddled, bewildered, confused, dazed, disoriented, perplexed, stupefied, vague 3. confused, incoherent, loose, muddleheaded, unclear, woolly

muddy *adj.* 1. bespattered, boggy, clarty (*Scot., & northern English dialect*), dirty, grimy, marshy, miry, mucky, mud-caked, quaggy, soiled, swampy 2. blurred, dingy, dull, flat, lustreless, smoky, unclear, washed-out 3. cloudy, dirty, foul, impure, opaque, turbid 4. confused, fuzzy, hazy, indistinct, muddled, unclear, vague, woolly ~*v.* 5. begrime, bespatter, cloud, dirty, smear, smirch, soil

muffle 1. cloak, conceal, cover, disguise, envelop, hood, mask, shroud, swaddle, swathe, wrap up 2. deaden, dull, gag, hush, muzzle, quieten, silence, soften, stifle, suppress

muffled dim, dull, faint, indistinct, muted, stifled, strangled, subdued, suppressed

mug[1] beaker, cup, flagon, jug, pot, tankard, toby jug

mug[2] chump (*Inf.*) gull (*Archaic*), easy *or* soft touch (*Sl.*), fool, innocent, mark (*Sl.*), muggins (*Brit. sl.*), simpleton, sucker (*Sl.*)

muggy clammy, close, damp, humid, moist, oppressive, sticky, stuffy, sultry

mug up bone up (*Inf. chiefly U.S.*), burn the midnight oil (*Inf.*), cram (*Inf.*), get up (*Inf.*), study, swot (*Brit. inf.*)

mull consider, contemplate, deliberate, examine, meditate, muse on, ponder, reflect on, review, ruminate, study, think about, think over, turn over in one's mind, weigh

multifarious different, diverse, diversified, legion, manifold, many, miscellaneous, multiform, multiple, multitudinous, numerous, sundry, varied, variegated

multiple collective, manifold, many, multitudinous, numerous, several, sundry, various

multiply accumulate, augment, breed, build up, expand, extend, increase, proliferate, propagate, reproduce, spread

multitude 1. army, assemblage, assembly, collection, concourse, congregation, crowd, great number, horde, host, legion, lot, lots (*Inf.*), mass, mob, myriad, sea, swarm, throng 2. commonalty, common people, herd, hoi polloi, mob, populace, proletariat, public, rabble

munch champ, chew, chomp, crunch, masticate, scrunch

mundane 1. banal, commonplace, day-to-day, everyday, humdrum, ordinary, prosaic, routine, workaday 2. earthly, fleshly, human, material, mortal, secular, sublunary, temporal, terrestrial, worldly

municipal borough, city, civic, community, public, town, urban

municipality borough, burgh (*Scot.*), city, district, town, township, urban community

munificence beneficence, benevolence, big-heartedness, bounteousness, bounty, generosity, generousness, largess, liberality, magnanimousness, open-handedness, philanthropy

munificent beneficent, benevolent, big-hearted, bounteous, bountiful, free-handed, generous, lavish, liberal, magnanimous, open-handed, philanthropical, princely, rich, unstinting

murder n. 1. assassination, bloodshed, butchery, carnage, homicide, killing, manslaughter, massacre, slaying 2. *Inf.* agony, an ordeal, a trial, danger, difficulty, hell (*Inf.*), misery, trouble ~v. 3. assassinate, bump off (*Inf.*), butcher, destroy, dispatch, do in (*Inf.*), do to death, eliminate (*Sl.*), hit (*U.S. sl.*), kill, massacre, rub out (*U.S. sl.*), slaughter, slay, take the life of, waste (*U.S. sl.*) 4. abuse, butcher, destroy, mangle, mar, misuse, ruin, spoil 5. *Inf.* beat decisively, defeat utterly, drub, hammer (*Inf.*), make mincemeat of (*Inf.*), slaughter, thrash

murderer assassin, butcher, cutthroat, hit man (*Sl.*), homicide, killer, slaughterer, slayer

murderous 1. barbarous, bloodthirsty, bloody, brutal, cruel, deadly, death-dealing, destructive, devastating, fatal, fell (*Archaic*), ferocious, internecine, lethal, sanguinary, savage, slaughterous, withering 2. *Inf.* arduous, dangerous, difficult, exhausting, harrowing, hellish (*Inf.*), killing (*Inf.*), sapping, strenuous, unpleasant

murky cheerless, cloudy, dark, dim, dismal, dreary, dull, dusky, foggy, gloomy, grey, impenetrable, misty, nebulous, obscure, overcast

murmur n. 1. babble, buzzing, drone, humming, mumble, muttering, purr, rumble, susurrus (*Literary*), undertone, whisper, whispering ~v. 2. babble, buzz, drone, hum, mumble, mutter, purr, rumble, speak in an undertone, whisper ~n. 3. beef (*Sl.*), complaint, gripe (*Inf.*), grouse, grumble, moan

(*Inf.*), word ~v. 4. beef (*Sl.*), carp, cavil, complain, gripe (*Inf.*), grouse, grumble, moan (*Inf.*)

muscle n. 1. muscle tissue, sinew, tendon, thew 2. brawn, clout (*Sl.*), force, forcefulness, might, potency, power, stamina, strength, sturdiness, weight ~v. 3. **muscle in** *Inf.* butt in, elbow one's way in, force one's way in, impose oneself

muscular athletic, beefy (*Inf.*), brawny, husky (*Inf.*), lusty, powerful, powerfully built, robust, sinewy, stalwart, strapping, strong, sturdy, vigorous, well-knit

muse be in a brown study, be lost in thought, brood, cogitate, consider, contemplate, deliberate, dream, meditate, mull over, ponder, reflect, ruminate, speculate, think, think over, weigh

mushroom v. boom, burgeon, expand, flourish, grow rapidly, increase, luxuriate, proliferate, shoot up, spread, spring up, sprout

musical dulcet, euphonious, harmonious, lilting, lyrical, melodic, melodious, sweet-sounding, tuneful

musing n. absent-mindedness, abstraction, brown study, cerebration, cogitation, contemplation, day-dreaming, dreaming, introspection, meditation, reflection, reverie, rumination, thinking, woolgathering

must n. duty, essential, fundamental, imperative, necessary thing, necessity, obligation, prerequisite, requirement, requisite, *sine qua non*

muster v. 1. assemble, call together, call up, collect, come together, congregate, convene, convoke, enrol, gather, group, marshal, meet, mobilize, rally, round up, summon ~n. 2. assemblage, assembly, collection, concourse, congregation, convention, convocation, gathering, meeting, mobilization, rally, roundup 3. **pass muster** be or come up to scratch, be acceptable, fill the bill (*Inf.*), make the grade, measure up, qualify

musty 1. airless, dank, decayed, frowsty, fusty, mildewed, mildewy, mouldy, old, smelly, stale, stuffy 2. ancient, antediluvian, antiquated, banal, clichéd, dull, hackneyed, hoary, moth-eaten, obsolete, old-fashioned, stale, threadbare, trite, worn-out

mutability alteration, change, evolution, metamorphosis, transition, variation, vicissitude

mutable adaptable, alterable, changeable, changing, fickle, flexible, inconsistent, inconstant, irresolute, uncertain, undependable, unreliable, unsettled, unstable, unsteady, vacillating, variable, volatile, wavering

mute 1. *adj.* aphasiac, aphasic, aphonic, dumb, mum, silent, speechless, unexpressed, unspeaking, unspoken, voiceless, wordless 2. *v.* dampen, deaden, lower, moderate, muffle, soften, soft-pedal, subdue, tone down, turn down

mutilate 1. amputate, butcher, cripple, cut to pieces, cut up, damage, disable, disfigure, dismember, hack, injure, lacerate, lame, maim, mangle 2. adulterate, bowdlerize, butcher, censor, cut, damage, distort, expurgate, hack, mar, spoil

mutinous bolshie (*Brit. inf.*), contumacious, disobedient, insubordinate, insurgent, rebellious, refractory, revolutionary, riotous, seditious, subversive, turbulent, ungovernable, unmanageable, unruly

mutiny 1. *n.* defiance, disobedience, insubordination, insurrection, rebellion, refusal to obey orders, resistance, revolt, revolution, riot, rising, strike, uprising 2. *v.* insubordinate, defy authority, disobey, rebel, refuse to obey orders, resist, revolt, rise up, strike

mutter complain, grouch, grouse, grumble, mumble, murmur, rumble

mutual common, communal, correlative, interactive, interchangeable, interchanged, joint, reciprocal, reciprocated, requited, returned, shared

muzzle *n.* 1. jaws, mouth, nose, snout 2. gag, guard ~*v.* 3. censor, choke, curb, gag (*Inf.*), restrain, silence, stifle, suppress

myopic near-sighted, short-sighted

myriad 1. *adj.* a thousand and one, countless, immeasurable, incalculable, innumerable, multitudinous, untold 2. *n.* a million, army, a thousand, flood, horde, host, millions, mountain, multitude, scores, sea, swarm, thousands

mysterious abstruse, arcane, baffling, concealed, covert, cryptic, curious, dark, enigmatic, furtive, hidden, impenetrable, incomprehensible, inexplicable, inscrutable, insoluble, mystical, mystifying, obscure, perplexing, puzzling, recondite, secret, secretive, sphinxlike, strange, uncanny, unfathomable, unknown, veiled, weird

mystery conundrum, enigma, problem, puzzle, question, riddle, secrecy, secret

mystic, mystical abstruse, arcane, cabalistic, cryptic, enigmatical, esoteric, hidden, inscrutable, metaphysical, mysterious, nonrational, occult, otherworldly, paranormal, preternatural, supernatural, transcendental

mystify baffle, bamboozle (*Inf.*), beat (*Sl.*), befog, bewilder, confound, confuse, elude, escape, perplex, puzzle, stump

myth 1. allegory, fable, fairy story, fiction, folk tale, legend, parable, saga, story, tradition 2. delusion, fancy, fantasy, figment, illusion, imagination, superstition, tall story

mythical 1. allegorical, chimerical, fabled, fabulous, fairy-tale, legendary, mythological, storied 2. fabricated, fanciful, fantasy, fictitious, imaginary, invented, made-up, make-believe, nonexistent, pretended, unreal, untrue

mythology folklore, folk tales, legend, lore, mythos, myths, stories, tradition

N

nadir bottom, depths, lowest point, minimum, rock bottom, zero

nag¹ 1. *v.* annoy, badger, berate, chivvy, goad, harass, harry, henpeck, irritate, pester, plague, provoke, scold, torment, upbraid, vex, worry 2. *n.* harpy, scold, shrew, tartar, termagant, virago

nag² hack, horse, jade, plug (*U.S.*)

nagging continuous, critical, distressing, irritating, painful, persistent, scolding, shrewish, worrying

nail *v.* attach, beat, fasten, fix, hammer, join, pin, secure, tack

naive 1. artless, candid, childlike, confiding, frank, guileless, ingenuous, innocent, jejune, natural, open, simple, trusting, unaffected, unpretentious, unsophisticated, unworldly 2. callow, credulous, gullible, green (*Inf.*), unsuspicious

naiveté 1. artlessness, candour, frankness, guilelessness, inexperience, ingenuousness, innocence, naturalness, openness, simplicity 2. callowness, credulity, gullibility

naked 1. bare, denuded, disrobed, divested, exposed, in one's birthday suit (*Inf.*), in the altogether (*Inf.*), in the buff (*Inf.*), nude, starkers (*Inf.*), stripped, unclothed, unconcealed, uncovered, undraped, undressed 2. blatant, evident, manifest, open, overt, patent, plain, simple, stark, unadorned, undisguised, unexaggerated, unmistakable, unqualified, unvarnished 3. defenceless, helpless, insecure, unarmed, unguarded, unprotected, vulnerable

nakedness 1. baldness, bareness, nudity, undress 2. openness, plainness, simplicity, starkness

namby-pamby anaemic, colourless, feeble, insipid, mawkish, prim, prissy (*Inf.*), sentimental, spineless, vapid, weak, wishywashy (*Inf.*)

name *n.* 1. appellation, cognomen, denomination, designation, epithet, handle (*Sl.*), moniker (*Inf.*), nickname, sobriquet, term, title 2. distinction, eminence, esteem, fame, honour, note, praise, renown, repute 3. character, credit, reputation ~*v.* 4. baptize, call, christen, denominate, dub, entitle, label, style, term 5. appoint, choose, cite, classify, commission, designate, identify, mention, nominate, select, specify

named 1. baptized, called, christened, denominated, dubbed, entitled, known as, labelled, styled, termed 2. appointed, chosen, cited, classified, commissioned, designated, identified, mentioned, nominated, picked, selected, singled out, specified

nameless 1. anonymous, innominate, undesignated, unnamed, untitled 2. incognito, obscure, undistinguished, unheard-of, unknown, unsung 3. abominable, horrible, indescribable, ineffable, inexpressible, unmentionable, unspeakable, unutterable

namely i.e., specifically, that is to say, to wit, viz.

nap¹ 1. *v.* catnap, doze, drop off (*Inf.*), drowse, nod, nod off (*Inf.*), rest, sleep, snooze (*Inf.*) 2. *n.* catnap, forty winks (*Inf.*), rest, shuteye (*Sl.*), siesta, sleep

nap² down, fibre, grain, pile, shag, weave

narcissism egotism, self-admiration, self-love, vanity

narcotic 1. *n.* anaesthetic, analgesic, anodyne, drug, opiate, painkiller, sedative, tranquillizer 2. *adj.* analgesic, calming, dulling, hypnotic, Lethean, numbing, painkilling, sedative, somnolent, soporific, stupefacient, stupefactive, stupefying

narrate chronicle, describe, detail, recite, recount, rehearse, relate, repeat, report, set forth, tell, unfold

narration description, explanation,

reading, recital, rehearsal, rela~
tion, storytelling, telling, voice~
over (*in film*)

narrative account, chronicle, de~
tail, history, report, statement,
story, tale

narrator annalist, author, bard,
chronicler, commentator, racon~
teur, reciter, relater, reporter,
storyteller, writer

narrow *adj.* 1. circumscribed, close,
confined, constricted, contracted,
cramped, incapacious, limited,
meagre, near, pinched, restricted,
scanty, straitened, tight 2. biased,
bigoted, dogmatic, illiberal, intol~
erant, narrow-minded, partial,
prejudiced, reactionary, small-
minded 3. attenuated, fine, slender,
slim, spare, tapering, thin 4. exclu~
sive, select 5. *Inf.* avaricious, close
(*Inf.*), mean, mercenary, niggard~
ly, ungenerous ~*v.* 6. circum~
scribe, constrict, diminish, limit,
reduce, simplify, straiten, tighten

narrowly 1. barely, by a whisker *or*
hair's-breadth, just, only just,
scarcely 2. carefully, closely,
painstakingly, scrutinizingly

narrow-minded biased, bigoted,
conservative, hidebound, illiberal,
insular, intolerant, opinionated,
parochial, petty, prejudiced, pro~
vincial, reactionary, short-sighted,
small-minded, strait-laced

narrows channel, gulf, passage,
sound, straits

nastiness 1. defilement, dirtiness,
filth, filthiness, foulness, impurity,
pollution, squalor, uncleanliness 2.
indecency, licentiousness, obscen~
ity, pollution, porn (*Inf.*), pornog~
raphy, ribaldry, smuttiness 3. dis~
agreeableness, malice, meanness,
offensiveness, spitefulness, un~
pleasantness

nasty 1. dirty, disagreeable, dis~
gusting, filthy, foul, horrible, loath~
some, malodorous, mephitic, nau~
seating, noisome, objectionable,
obnoxious, odious, offensive, pol~
luted, repellent, repugnant, sick~
ening, unappetizing, unpleasant,
vile 2. blue, foul, gross, impure,
indecent, lascivious, lewd, licen~

tious, obscene, pornographic, rib~
ald, smutty 3. abusive, annoying,
bad-tempered, despicable, dis~
agreeable, distasteful, malicious,
mean, spiteful, unpleasant, vicious,
vile 4. bad, critical, dangerous,
painful, serious, severe

nation commonwealth, community,
country, people, population, race,
realm, society, state, tribe

national *adj.* 1. civil, countrywide,
governmental, nationwide, public,
state, widespread 2. domestic, in~
ternal, social ~*n.* 3. citizen, inhab~
itant, native, resident, subject

nationalism allegiance, chauvin~
ism, fealty, jingoism, loyalty, na~
tionality, patriotism

nationality birth, ethnic group, na~
tion, race

nationwide countrywide, general,
national, overall, widespread

native *adj.* 1. built-in, congenital,
endemic, hereditary, inborn, in~
bred, indigenous, ingrained, inher~
ent, inherited, innate, instinctive,
intrinsic, inveterate, natal, natural
2. genuine, original, real 3. domes~
tic, home, home-grown, home-
made, indigenous, local, mother,
vernacular 4. aboriginal, autoch~
thonous ~*n.* 5. aborigine, autoch~
thon, citizen, countryman, dweller,
inhabitant, national, resident

natter 1. *v.* blather, blether, chat~
ter, gabble, gossip, jabber, jaw (*Sl.*),
palaver, prate, prattle, talk, talk
idly, witter (*Inf.*) 2. *n.* blather,
blether, chat, chinwag (*Brit. inf.*),
chitchat, confabulation, conversa~
tion, gab (*Inf.*), gabble, gossip, jab~
ber, jaw (*Sl.*), palaver, prattle, talk

natty chic, dapper, elegant, fash~
ionable, neat, smart, snazzy (*Inf.*),
spruce, stylish, trim, well-dressed,
well-turned-out

natural 1. common, everyday, le~
gitimate, logical, normal, ordinary,
regular, typical, usual 2. charac~
teristic, congenital, essential, in~
born, indigenous, inherent, innate,
instinctive, intuitive, natal, native
3. artless, candid, frank, genuine,
ingenuous, open, real, simple,
spontaneous, unaffected, unpre~

tentious, unsophisticated, unstud~
ied 4. organic, plain, pure, un~
bleached, unmixed, unpolished,
unrefined, whole

naturalism factualism, realism,
verisimilitude

naturalist 1. biologist, botanist,
ecologist, zoologist 2. factualist,
realist

naturalize acclimate, acclimatize,
acculturate, accustom, adapt,
adopt, domesticate, enfranchise,
familiarize, grant citizenship, ha~
bituate

naturally 1. *adv.* as anticipated,
customarily, genuinely, informally,
normally, simply, spontaneously,
typically, unaffectedly, unpreten~
tiously 2. *interj.* absolutely, as a
matter of course, certainly, of
course

nature 1. attributes, character,
complexion, constitution, essence,
features, make-up, quality, traits 2.
category, description, kind, sort,
species, style, type, variety 3. cos~
mos, creation, earth, environment,
universe, world 4. disposition, hu~
mour, mood, outlook, temper,
temperament 5. country, country~
side, landscape, natural history,
scenery

naturist nudist

naughty 1. annoying, bad, dis~
obedient, exasperating, fractious,
impish, misbehaved, mischievous,
perverse, playful, refractory, ro~
guish, sinful, teasing, wayward,
wicked, worthless 2. bawdy, blue,
improper, lewd, obscene, off-
colour, ribald, risqué, smutty, vul~
gar

nausea 1. biliousness, qualm(s),
queasiness, retching, sickness,
squeamishness, vomiting 2. abhor~
rence, aversion, disgust, loathing,
repugnance, revulsion

nauseate disgust, horrify, offend,
repel, repulse, revolt, sicken

nautical marine, maritime, naval,
oceanic, seafaring, seagoing,
yachting

naval marine, maritime, nautical,
oceanic

navel 1. bellybutton (*Inf.*), ompha~

los (*Literary*), umbilicus 2. central
point, centre, hub, middle

navigable 1. clear, negotiable,
passable, traversable, unobstruct~
ed 2. controllable, dirigible, sail~
able, steerable

navigate con (*Nautical*), cross,
cruise, direct, drive, guide, handle,
journey, manoeuvre, pilot, plan,
plot, sail, skipper, steer, voyage

navigation cruising, helmsman~
ship, pilotage, sailing, seamanship,
steering, voyaging

navigator mariner, pilot, seaman

navvy labourer

navy argosy (*Archaic*), armada,
fleet, flotilla, warships

near *adj.* 1. adjacent, adjoining,
alongside, at close quarters, be~
side, bordering, close, close by,
contiguous, nearby, neighbouring,
nigh, touching 2. approaching,
forthcoming, imminent, impend~
ing, in the offing, looming, near-at-
hand, next, on the cards (*Inf.*) 3.
akin, allied, attached, connected,
dear, familiar, intimate, related 4.
Inf. close-fisted, mean, miserly,
niggardly, parsimonious, stingy,
tightfisted, ungenerous

nearby 1. *adj.* adjacent, adjoining,
convenient, handy, neighbouring 2.
adv. at close quarters, close at
hand, not far away, within reach

nearly *adv.* about, all but, almost,
approaching, approximately, as
good as, closely, just about, not
quite, practically, roughly, virtual~
ly, well-nigh

nearness 1. accessibility, avail~
ability, closeness, contiguity,
handiness, juxtaposition, propin~
quity, proximity, vicinity 2. im~
mediacy, imminence 3. dearness,
familiarity, intimacy 4. *Inf.* mean~
ness, niggardliness, parsimony,
stinginess

near-sighted myopic, short-
sighted

near thing close shave (*Inf.*), nar~
row escape, near miss

neat 1. accurate, dainty, fastidious,
methodical, nice, orderly, ship~
shape, smart, spick-and-span,
spruce, straight, systematic, tidy,

trim, uncluttered 2. adept, adroit, agile, apt, clever, deft, dexterous, efficient, effortless, elegant, expert, graceful, handy, nimble, practised, precise, skilful, stylish, well-judged 3. *Of alcoholic drinks* pure, straight, undiluted, unmixed

neatly 1. accurately, daintily, fastidiously, methodically, nicely, smartly, sprucely, systematically, tidily 2. adeptly, adroitly, agilely, aptly, cleverly, deftly, dexterously, efficiently, effortlessly, elegantly, expertly, gracefully, handily, nimbly, precisely, skilfully, stylishly

neatness 1. accuracy, daintiness, fastidiousness, methodicalness, niceness, nicety, orderliness, smartness, spruceness, straightness, tidiness, trimness 2. adeptness, adroitness, agility, aptness, cleverness, deftness, dexterity, efficiency, effortlessness, elegance, expertness, grace, gracefulness, handiness, nimbleness, preciseness, precision, skilfulness, skill, style, stylishness

nebulous ambiguous, amorphous, cloudy, confused, dim, hazy, imprecise, indefinite, indeterminate, indistinct, misty, murky, obscure, shadowy, shapeless, uncertain, unclear, unformed, vague

necessarily accordingly, automatically, axiomatically, by definition, certainly, compulsorily, consequently, incontrovertibly, ineluctably, inevitably, inexorably, irresistibly, naturally, *nolens volens*, of course, of necessity, perforce, undoubtedly, willy-nilly

necessary 1. compulsory, *de rigueur*, essential, imperative, indispensable, mandatory, needed, needful, obligatory, required, requisite, vital 2. certain, fated, inescapable, inevitable, inexorable, unavoidable

necessitate call for, coerce, compel, constrain, demand, force, impel, make necessary, oblige, require

necessities essentials, fundamentals, indispensables

necessity 1. demand, exigency, indispensability, need, needfulness, requirement 2. desideratum, essential, fundamental, necessary, need, prerequisite, requirement, requisite, *sine qua non*, want 3. destitution, extremity, indigence, need, penury, poverty, privation 4. compulsion, destiny, fate, inevitability, inexorableness, obligation

need *v.* 1. call for, demand, have occasion to *or* for, lack, miss, necessitate, require, want ~*n.* 2. longing, requisite, want, wish 3. deprivation, destitution, distress, extremity, impecuniousness, inadequacy, indigence, insufficiency, lack, neediness, paucity, penury, poverty, privation, shortage 4. emergency, exigency, necessity, obligation, urgency, want 5. demand, desideratum, essential, requirement, requisite

needed called for, desired, lacked, necessary, required, wanted

needful essential, indispensable, necessary, needed, required, requisite, stipulated, vital

needle *v.* aggravate (*Inf.*), annoy, bait, goad, harass, irk, irritate, nag, nettle, pester, prick, prod, provoke, rile, ruffle, spur, sting, taunt

needless causeless, dispensable, excessive, expendable, gratuitous, groundless, nonessential, pointless, redundant, superfluous, uncalled-for, undesired, unnecessary, unwanted, useless

needlework embroidery, fancywork, needlecraft, sewing, stitching, tailoring

needy deprived, destitute, disadvantaged, impecunious, impoverished, indigent, on the breadline (*Inf.*), penniless, poor, poverty-stricken, underprivileged

nefarious abominable, atrocious, base, criminal, depraved, detestable, dreadful, evil, execrable, foul, heinous, horrible, infamous, infernal, iniquitous, monstrous, odious, opprobrious, shameful, sinful, vicious, vile, villainous, wicked

negate 1. abrogate, annul, cancel, countermand, invalidate, neutralize, nullify, repeal, rescind, retract, reverse, revoke, void, wipe out 2. contradict, deny, disallow, disprove, gainsay, oppose, refute

negation 1. antithesis, antonym, contradiction, contrary, converse, counterpart, denial, disavowal, disclaimer, inverse, opposite, rejection, renunciation, reverse 2. opposition, proscription, refusal, repudiation, veto 3. cancellation, neutralization, nullification 4. blank, nonexistence, nothingness, nullity, vacuity, void

negative *adj.* 1. contradictory, contrary, denying, dissenting, opposing, recusant, refusing, rejecting, resisting 2. annulling, counteractive, invalidating, neutralizing, nullifying 3. antagonistic, colourless, contrary, cynical, gloomy, jaundiced, neutral, pessimistic, uncooperative, unenthusiastic, uninterested, unwilling, weak ~*n.* 4. contradiction, denial, refusal

negativeness, negativity 1. contradiction, contradictoriness, contrariness, denial, dissent, opposition, recusancy, refusal, rejection, resistance 2. antagonism, colourlessness, contrariness, cynicism, gloom, neutrality, pessimism, uncooperativeness, uninterestedness, unwillingness, weakness

neglect *v.* 1. contemn, disdain, disregard, ignore, leave alone, overlook, pass by, rebuff, scorn, slight, spurn 2. be remiss, evade, forget, let slide, omit, pass over, procrastinate, shirk, skimp ~*n.* 3. disdain, disregard, disrespect, heedlessness, inattention, indifference, slight, unconcern 4. carelessness, default, dereliction, failure, forgetfulness, laxity, laxness, neglectfulness, negligence, oversight, remissness, slackness, slovenliness

neglected 1. abandoned, derelict, overgrown 2. disregarded, unappreciated, underestimated, undervalued

negligence carelessness, default, dereliction, disregard, failure, forgetfulness, heedlessness, inadvertence, inattention, inattentiveness, indifference, laxity, laxness, neglect, omission, oversight, remissness, shortcoming, slackness, thoughtlessness

negligent careless, cursory, disregardful, forgetful, heedless, inadvertent, inattentive, indifferent, neglectful, nonchalant, offhand, regardless, remiss, slack, thoughtless, unmindful, unthinking

negligible imperceptible, inconsequential, insignificant, minor, minute, petty, small, trifling, trivial, unimportant

negotiable debatable, discussable, discussible, transactional, transferable, variable

negotiate 1. adjudicate, arbitrate, arrange, bargain, conciliate, confer, consult, contract, deal, debate, discuss, handle, manage, mediate, parley, settle, transact, work out 2. clear, cross, get over, get past, get round, pass, pass through, surmount

negotiation arbitration, bargaining, debate, diplomacy, discussion, mediation, transaction

neighbourhood community, confines, district, environs, locale, locality, precincts, proximity, purlieus, quarter, region, surroundings, vicinity

neighbouring abutting, adjacent, adjoining, bordering, connecting, contiguous, near, nearby, nearest, next, surrounding

nerve *n.* 1. bottle (*Brit. sl.*), bravery, coolness, courage, daring, determination, endurance, energy, fearlessness, firmness, force, fortitude, gameness, grit (*Inf.*), guts (*Inf.*), hardihood, intrepidity, mettle, might, pluck, resolution, spirit, spunk (*Inf.*), steadfastness, vigour, will 2. *Inf.* audacity, boldness, brass (*Inf.*), brazenness, cheek (*Inf.*), effrontery, gall, impertinence, impudence, insolence, sauce (*Inf.*), temerity ~*v.* 3. brace, embolden, encourage, fortify, hearten, invigorate, steel, strengthen

nerve-racking annoying, difficult, distressing, frightening, harassing, harrowing, maddening, stressful, tense, trying, worrying

nerves anxiety, fretfulness, imbal~ance, nervousness, strain, stress, tension

nervous agitated, anxious, appre~hensive, edgy, excitable, fearful, fidgety, flustered, hesitant, highly strung, hysterical, jittery (*Inf.*), jumpy, nervy (*Inf.*), neurotic, on edge, ruffled, shaky, tense, timid, timorous, uneasy, uptight (*Inf.*), weak, worried

nervous breakdown breakdown, collapse, crack-up (*Inf.*), nervous disorder, neurasthenia (*Obsolete*)

nervousness agitation, anxiety, disquiet, excitability, fluster, per~turbation, tension, timidity, touchi~ness, tremulousness, worry

nest 1. den, haunt, hideaway, ref~uge, resort, retreat, snuggery 2. breeding-ground, den, hotbed

nest egg cache, deposit, fund(s), reserve, savings, store

nestle cuddle, curl up, huddle, nuz~zle, snuggle

nestling 1. chick, fledgling 2. babe, babe in arms, baby, infant, suck~ling

net¹ 1. *n.* lacework, lattice, mesh, netting, network, openwork, re~ticulum, tracery, web 2. *v.* bag, capture, catch, enmesh, ensnare, entangle, nab (*Inf.*), trap

net², **nett** *adj.* 1. after taxes, clear, final, take-home 2. closing, conclu~sive, final ~*v.* 3. accumulate, bring in, clear, earn, gain, make, realize, reap

nether basal, below, beneath, bot~tom, inferior, lower, under, under~ground

nether world Avernus, Hades, hell, infernal regions, nether regions, underworld

nettle annoy, chafe, exasperate, fret, goad, harass, incense, irritate, pique, provoke, ruffle, sting, tease, vex

nettled aggrieved, angry, annoyed, chafed, cross, exasperated, galled, goaded, harassed, huffy, incensed, irritable, irritated, peeved, peev~ish, piqued, provoked, put out, riled, ruffled, stung, teased, touchy, vexed

network arrangement, channels, circuitry, complex, convolution, grid, grill, interconnections, laby~rinth, maze, mesh, net, nexus, or~ganization, plexus, structure, sys~tem, tracks, web

neurosis abnormality, affliction, derangement, deviation, instabil~ity, maladjustment, mental dis~turbance, mental illness, obsession, phobia, psychological *or* emotional disorder

neurotic abnormal, anxious, com~pulsive, deviant, disordered, dis~traught, disturbed, maladjusted, manic, nervous, obsessive, over~wrought, unhealthy, unstable

neuter *v.* castrate, doctor (*Inf.*), dress, emasculate, fix (*Inf.*), geld, spay

neutral 1. disinterested, dispas~sionate, even-handed, impartial, indifferent, nonaligned, nonbellig~erent, noncombatant, noncommit~tal, nonpartisan, sitting on the fence, unaligned, unbiased, un~committed, undecided, uninvolved, unprejudiced 2. achromatic, col~ourless, dull, expressionless, inde~terminate, indistinct, indistin~guishable, intermediate, toneless, undefined

neutrality detachment, disinter~estedness, impartiality, nonalign~ment, noninterference, noninter~ventionism, noninvolvement, non~partisanship

neutralize cancel, compensate for, counteract, counterbalance, frus~trate, invalidate, negate, nullify, offset, undo

never-ending boundless, cease~less, constant, continual, continu~ous, eternal, everlasting, incessant, interminable, nonstop, perpetual, persistent, relentless, unbroken, unceasing, unchanging, uninter~rupted, unremitting

nevertheless but, even so, how~ever, nonetheless, notwithstanding, regardless, still, yet

new 1. advanced, contemporary, current, different, fresh, latest, modern, modernistic, modish, newfangled, novel, original, recent, topical, ultramodern, unfamiliar, unknown, unused, unusual, up-to-date, virgin 2. added, extra, more, supplementary 3. altered, changed, improved, modernized, redesigned, renewed, restored

newcomer alien, arrival, beginner, foreigner, immigrant, incomer, novice, outsider, settler, stranger

newfangled contemporary, fashionable, gimmicky, modern, new, new-fashioned, novel, recent

newly anew, freshly, just, lately, latterly, recently

news account, advice, bulletin, communiqué, disclosure, dispatch, exposé, gossip, hearsay, information, intelligence, leak, news flash, release, report, revelation, rumour, scandal, statement, story, tidings, word

next adj. 1. consequent, ensuing, following, later, subsequent, succeeding 2. adjacent, adjoining, closest, nearest, neighbouring ~adv. 3. afterwards, closely, following, later, subsequently, thereafter

next world afterlife, afterworld, heaven, hereafter, nirvana, paradise

nibble 1. n. bite, crumb, morsel, peck, snack, soupçon, taste, titbit 2. v. bite, eat, gnaw, munch, nip, peck, pick at

nice 1. agreeable, amiable, attractive, charming, commendable, courteous, delightful, friendly, good, kind, likable, pleasant, pleasurable, polite, prepossessing, refined, well-mannered 2. dainty, fine, neat, tidy, trim 3. accurate, careful, critical, delicate, discriminating, exact, exacting, fastidious, fine, meticulous, precise, rigorous, scrupulous, strict, subtle 4. cultured, genteel, refined, respectable, virtuous, well-bred

nicely 1. acceptably, agreeably, amiably, attractively, charmingly, commendably, courteously, delightfully, kindly, likably, pleasantly, pleasingly, pleasurably, politely, prepossessingly, well 2. daintily, finely, neatly, tidily, trimly 3. ac-

curately, carefully, critically, delicately, exactingly, exactly, fastidiously, finely, meticulously, precisely, rigorously, scrupulously, strictly, subtly 4. genteelly, respectably, virtuously

niceness 1. agreeableness, amiability, attractiveness, charm, courtesy, delightfulness, friendliness, good manners, goodness, kindness, likableness, pleasantness, pleasurableness, politeness, refinement 2. daintiness, fineness, neatness, tidiness, trimness 3. accuracy, care, carefulness, criticalness, delicacy, discrimination, exactingness, exactitude, exactness, fastidiousness, fineness, meticulosity, meticulousness, preciseness, precision, rigorousness, rigour, scrupulosity, scrupulousness, strictness, subtleness, subtlety 4. gentility, good breeding, refinement, respectability, virtue

nicety 1. accuracy, exactness, fastidiousness, finesse, meticulousness, minuteness, precision 2. daintiness, delicacy, discrimination, distinction, nuance, refinement, subtlety

niche 1. alcove, corner, hollow, nook, opening, recess 2. calling, pigeonhole (Inf.), place, position, slot (Inf.), vocation

nick chip, cut, damage, dent, mark, notch, scar, score, scratch, snick

nickname diminutive, epithet, familiar name, handle (Sl.), label, pet name, moniker (Inf.), sobriquet

niggard cheapskate (Inf.), cheeseparer, churl, miser, penny-pincher (Inf.), screw (Sl.), Scrooge, skinflint

niggardliness 1. avarice, avariciousness, closeness, covetousness, frugality, grudgingness, meanness, mercenariness, miserliness, nearness (Inf.), parsimony, penuriousness, sordidness, sparingness, stinginess, thrift, tightfistedness, ungenerousness 2. beggarliness, inadequacy, insufficiency, meagreness, meanness, miserableness, paltriness, scantiness, skimpiness, smallness, wretchedness

niggardly 1. avaricious, close, covetous, frugal, grudging, mean, mercenary, miserly, near (*Inf.*), parsimonious, penurious, Scrooge-like, sordid, sparing, stinging, stingy, tightfisted, ungenerous 2. beggarly, inadequate, insufficient, meagre, mean, miserable, paltry, scanty, skimpy, small, wretched

niggle 1. carp, cavil, criticize, find fault, fuss 2. annoy, irritate, rankle, worry

niggling 1. cavilling, finicky, fussy, insignificant, minor, nit-picking (*Inf.*), pettifogging, petty, piddling (*Inf.*), quibbling, trifling, unimportant 2. gnawing, irritating, persistent, troubling, worrying

night dark, darkness, dead of night, hours of darkness, night-time, night watches

night and day all the time, ceaselessly, constantly, continually, continuously, day in, day out, endlessly, incessantly, interminably, unremittingly

nightfall crepuscule, dusk, eve (*Archaic*), evening, eventide, gloaming, sundown, sunset, twilight, vespers

nightly *adv./adj.* 1. each night, every night, night after night, nights (*Inf.*) ~*adv.* 2. after dark, at night, by night, in the night, nights (*Inf.*), nocturnally ~*adj.* 3. night-time, nocturnal

nightmare 1. bad dream, hallucination, incubus, succubus 2. horror, ordeal, torment, trial, tribulation

nil duck, love, naught, *nihil*, none, nothing, zero

nimble active, agile, alert, brisk, deft, dexterous, lively, nippy (*Brit. inf.*), proficient, prompt, quick, quick-witted, ready, smart, sprightly, spry, swift

nimbly actively, acutely, agilely, alertly, briskly, deftly, dexterously, easily, fast, fleetly, proficiently, promptly, quickly, quick-wittedly, readily, sharply, smartly, speedily, spryly, swiftly

nimbus ambience, atmosphere, aura, aureole, cloud, corona, glow, halo, irradiation

nincompoop blockhead, dimwit

(*Inf.*), dolt, dunce, fool, idiot, ninny, nitwit, noodle, numskull, simpleton

nip[1] *v.* 1. bite, catch, clip, compress, grip, nibble, pinch, snag, snap, snip, squeeze, tweak, twitch 2. check, frustrate, thwart

nip[2] *n.* dram, draught, drop, finger, mouthful, peg (*Brit.*), portion, shot (*Inf.*), sip, snifter (*Inf.*), *soupçon*, sup, swallow, taste

nipper 1. claw, pincer 2. *Inf.* baby, boy, child, girl, infant, kid (*Inf.*), little one, tot

nipple breast, dug, mamilla, pap, papilla, teat, tit, udder

nippy 1. biting, chilly, nipping, sharp, stinging 2. *Brit. inf.* active, agile, fast, nimble, quick, spry

nit-picking captious, carping, cavilling, finicky, fussy, hairsplitting, pedantic, pettifogging, quibbling

nitty-gritty basics, brass tacks (*Inf.*), core, crux, essence, essentials, facts, fundamentals, gist, heart of the matter, reality, substance

nitwit dimwit (*Inf.*), dummy (*Sl.*), fool, halfwit, nincompoop, ninny, simpleton

nob big shot (*Sl.*), bigwig (*Sl.*), fat cat (*U.S. sl.*), nabob (*Inf.*), toff (*Brit. sl.*)

nobble 1. disable, handicap, incapacitate, weaken 2. bribe, get at, influence, intimidate, outwit, win over 3. filch, knock off (*Sl.*), nick (*Sl.*), pilfer, pinch (*Inf.*), purloin, snitch (*Sl.*), steal, swipe (*Sl.*) 4. get hold of, grab, take

nobility 1. aristocracy, elite, high society, lords, nobles, patricians, peerage, ruling class, upper class 2. dignity, eminence, excellence, grandeur, greatness, illustriousness, loftiness, magnificence, majesty, nobleness, stateliness, sublimity, superiority, worthiness 3. honour, incorruptibility, integrity, uprightness, virtue

noble *n.* 1. aristocrat, lord, nobleman, peer ~*adj.* 2. aristocratic, blue-blooded, gentle (*Archaic*), highborn, lordly, patrician, titled 3. august, dignified, distinguished, elevated, eminent, excellent, grand, great, imposing, impressive, lofty, splendid, stately **4.** generous, hon~ ourable, magnanimous, upright, virtuous, worthy

nobody 1. no-one **2.** cipher, light~ weight (*Inf.*), menial, nonentity, nothing (*Inf.*)

nocturnal night, nightly, night~ time, of the night

nod *v.* **1.** acknowledge, bob, bow, dip, duck, gesture, indicate, salute, signal **2.** agree, assent, concur, show agreement **3.** be sleepy, doze, droop, drowse, nap, sleep, slump ~*n.* **4.** acknowledgment, beck, ges~ ture, greeting, indication, salute, sign, signal

no go futile, hopeless, impossible, not on (*Inf.*), vain

noise 1. *n.* babble, blare, clamour, clatter, commotion, cry, din, fra~ cas, hubbub, outcry, pandemo~ nium, racket, row, sound, talk, tu~ mult, uproar **2.** *v.* advertise, bruit (*Archaic*), circulate, gossip, publi~ cize, repeat, report, rumour

noiseless hushed, inaudible, mute, muted, quiet, silent, soundless, still

noisy boisterous, cacophonous, chattering, clamorous, deafening, ear-splitting, loud, obstreperous, piercing, riotous, strident, tumul~ tuous, turbulent, uproarious, vocif~ erous

nomad drifter, itinerant, migrant, rambler, rover, vagabond, wan~ derer

nomadic itinerant, migrant, mi~ gratory, pastoral, peripatetic, roaming, roving, travelling, va~ grant, wandering

nom de plume alias, assumed name, nom de guerre, pen name, pseudonym

nomenclature classification, codi~ fication, locution, phraseology, taxonomy, terminology, vocabu~ lary

nominal 1. formal, ostensible, pre~ tended, professed, puppet, pur~ ported, self-styled, so-called, *soi- disant*, supposed, theoretical, titu~ lar **2.** inconsiderable, insignificant, minimal, small, symbolic, token, trifling, trivial

nominate appoint, assign, choose, commission, designate, elect, el~ evate, empower, name, present, propose, recommend, select, sub~ mit, suggest, term

nomination appointment, choice, designation, election, proposal, recommendation, selection, sug~ gestion

nominee aspirant, candidate, con~ testant, entrant, favourite, protégé, runner

nonaligned impartial, neutral, un~ committed, undecided

nonchalance calm, composure, cool (*Sl.*), equanimity, imperturb~ ability, indifference, sang-froid, self-possession, unconcern

nonchalant airy, apathetic, blasé, calm, careless, casual, collected, cool, detached, dispassionate, in~ different, insouciant, offhand, un~ concerned, unemotional, unper~ turbed

noncombatant civilian, neutral, nonbelligerent

noncommittal ambiguous, careful, cautious, circumspect, discreet, equivocal, evasive, guarded, in~ definite, neutral, politic, reserved, tactful, temporizing, tentative, un~ revealing, vague, wary

non compos mentis crazy, de~ ranged, insane, mentally ill, of un~ sound mind

nonconformist dissenter, dissen~ tient, eccentric, heretic, iconoclast, individualist, maverick, protester, radical, rebel

nondescript characterless, com~ mon or garden (*Inf.*), common~ place, dull, featureless, indetermi~ nate, mousy, ordinary, unclassifi~ able, unclassified, undistinguished, unexceptional, uninspiring, unin~ teresting, unmemorable, unre~ markable, vague

none nil, nobody, no-one, no part, not a bit, not any, nothing, not one, zero

nonentity cipher, lightweight (*Inf.*), mediocrity, nobody, small fry, unimportant person

nonessential dispensable, exces~ sive, expendable, extraneous, in~

essential, peripheral, superfluous, unimportant, unnecessary

nonetheless despite that, even so, however, in spite of that, never~ theless, yet

nonexistent chimerical, fancied, fictional, hallucinatory, hypotheti~ cal, illusory, imaginary, imagined, insubstantial, legendary, missing, mythical, unreal

nonsense absurdity, balderdash, blather, bombast, bunk (*Inf.*), claptrap (*Inf.*), double Dutch (*Brit. inf.*), drivel, fatuity, folly, foolish~ ness, gibberish, inanity, jest, ludi~ crousness, ridiculousness, rot, rub~ bish, senselessness, silliness, stuff, stupidity, trash, twaddle, waffle (*Brit. inf.*)

nonstop 1. *adj.* ceaseless, constant, continuous, direct, endless, inces~ sant, interminable, relentless, steady, unbroken, unending, unfal~ tering, uninterrupted, unremitting 2. *adv.* ceaselessly, constantly, continuously, directly, endlessly, incessantly, interminably, relent~ lessly, steadily, unbrokenly, un~ endingly, unfalteringly, uninter~ ruptedly, unremittingly, without stopping

nook alcove, cavity, corner, cran~ ny, crevice, cubbyhole, hide-out, inglenook (*Brit.*), niche, opening, recess, retreat

noon high noon, midday, noonday, noontide, noontime, twelve noon

norm average, benchmark, criteri~ on, mean, measure, model, pat~ tern, rule, standard, type, yardstick

normal 1. accustomed, acknowl~ edged, average, common, conven~ tional, habitual, natural, ordinary, popular, regular, routine, run-of- the-mill, standard, typical, usual 2. rational, reasonable, sane, well- adjusted

normality 1. accustomedness, av~ erageness, commonness, com~ monplaceness, conventionality, habitualness, naturalness, ordi~ nariness, popularity, regularity, routineness, typicality, usualness 2. adjustment, balance, rationality, reason, sanity

normally as a rule, commonly, ha~ bitually, ordinarily, regularly, typi~ cally, usually

north 1. *adj.* Arctic, boreal, nor~ therly, northern, polar 2. *adv.* nor~ therly, northward(s)

nose *v.* 1. detect, scent, search (for), smell, sniff 2. ease forward, nudge, nuzzle, push, shove 3. med~ dle, pry, snoop (*Inf.*)

nose dive dive, drop, plummet, plunge

nosegay bouquet, posy

nostalgia homesickness, longing, pining, regret, regretfulness, re~ membrance, reminiscence, wist~ fulness, yearning

nostalgic homesick, longing, re~ gretful, sentimental, wistful

nostrum cure, cure-all, drug, elixir, medicine, panacea, patent medi~ cine, potion, quack medicine, rem~ edy, sovereign cure, specific, treatment

nosy, nosey curious, eavesdrop~ ping, inquisitive, interfering, intru~ sive, meddlesome, prying, snoop~ ing (*Inf.*)

notability 1. celebrity, distinction, eminence, esteem, fame, renown 2. celebrity, dignitary, notable, personage, V.I.P., worthy

notable 1. *adj.* celebrated, con~ spicuous, distinguished, eminent, evident, extraordinary, famous, manifest, marked, memorable, noteworthy, noticeable, notorious, outstanding, pre-eminent, pro~ nounced, rare, remarkable, re~ nowned, striking, uncommon, un~ usual, well-known 2. *n.* celebrity, dignitary, notability, personage, V.I.P., worthy

notably conspicuously, distinctly, especially, markedly, noticeably, outstandingly, particularly, re~ markably, signally, strikingly, un~ commonly

notation 1. characters, code, script, signs, symbols, system 2. jotting, notating, note, noting, record

notch *n.* 1. cleft, cut, incision, in~ dentation, mark, nick, score 2. *Inf.* cut (*Inf.*), degree, grade, level, step

~*v.* 3. cut, indent, mark, nick, score, scratch

notch up achieve, gain, make, register, score

note *n.* 1. annotation, comment, communication, epistle, gloss, jotting, letter, memo, memorandum, message, minute, record, remark, reminder 2. indication, mark, sign, symbol, token 3. heed, notice, observation, regard 4. celebrity, character, consequence, distinction, eminence, fame, prestige, renown, reputation ~*v.* 5. denote, designate, indicate, mark, mention, notice, observe, perceive, record, register, remark, see

notebook commonplace book, diary, exercise book, jotter, journal, memorandum book, notepad, record book

noted acclaimed, celebrated, conspicuous, distinguished, eminent, famous, illustrious, notable, notorious, prominent, recognized, renowned, well-known

notes impressions, jottings, outline, record, report, sketch

noteworthy exceptional, extraordinary, important, notable, outstanding, remarkable, significant, unusual

nothing bagatelle, cipher, emptiness, naught, nobody, nonentity, nonexistence, nothingness, nought, nullity, trifle, void, zero

nothingness 1. nihility, nonbeing, nonexistence, nullity, oblivion 2. insignificance, unimportance, worthlessness

notice *v.* 1. detect, discern, distinguish, heed, mark, mind, note, observe, perceive, remark, see, spot ~*n.* 2. cognizance, consideration, heed, note, observation, regard 3. advice, announcement, communication, instruction, intelligence, intimation, news, notification, order, warning 4. advertisement, comment, criticism, poster, review, sign 5. attention, civility, respect

noticeable appreciable, clear, conspicuous, distinct, evident, manifest, observable, obvious, perceptible, plain, striking, unmistakable

notification advice, alert, announcement, declaration, information, intelligence, message, notice, notifying, publication, statement, telling, warning

notify acquaint, advise, alert, announce, apprise, declare, inform, publish, tell, warn

notion 1. apprehension, belief, concept, conception, idea, impression, inkling, judgment, knowledge, opinion, sentiment, understanding, view 2. caprice, desire, fancy, impulse, inclination, whim, wish

notional abstract, conceptual, fanciful, hypothetical, ideal, imaginary, speculative, theoretical, unreal, visionary

notoriety dishonour, disrepute, infamy, obloquy, opprobrium, scandal

notorious 1. dishonourable, disreputable, infamous, opprobrious, scandalous 2. blatant, flagrant, glaring, obvious, open, overt, patent, undisputed

notoriously 1. dishonourably, disreputably, infamously, opprobriously, scandalously 2. blatantly, flagrantly, glaringly, notably, obviously, openly, overtly, particularly, patently, spectacularly, undisputedly

notwithstanding although, despite, however, nevertheless, nonetheless, though, yet

nought naught, nil, nothing, nothingness, zero

nourish 1. attend, feed, furnish, nurse, nurture, supply, sustain, tend 2. comfort, cultivate, encourage, foster, maintain, promote, support

nourishing alimentative, beneficial, healthful, health-giving, nutritious, nutritive, wholesome

nourishment aliment, diet, food, nutriment, nutrition, sustenance, viands, victuals

nouveau riche arriviste, new-rich, parvenu, upstart

novel 1. *adj.* different, fresh, innovative, new, original, rare, singu-

lar, strange, uncommon, unfamil~
iar, unusual 2. *n.* fiction, narrative,
romance, story, tale

novelty 1. freshness, innovation,
newness, oddity, originality,
strangeness, surprise, unfamiliar~
ity, uniqueness 2. bagatelle, bauble,
curiosity, gadget, gewgaw, gim~
crack, gimmick, knick-knack, me~
mento, souvenir, trifle, trinket

novice amateur, apprentice, be~
ginner, convert, learner, neophyte,
newcomer, novitiate, probationer,
proselyte, pupil, tyro

now 1. at once, immediately, in~
stanter (*Law*), instantly, presently
(*Scot. & U.S.*), promptly, straight~
away 2. any more, at the moment,
nowadays, these days 3. **now and
then** *or* **again** at times, from time
to time, infrequently, intermittent~
ly, occasionally, on and off, once in
a while, on occasion, sometimes,
sporadically

nowadays any more, at the mo~
ment, in this day and age, now,
these days, today

nucleus basis, centre, core, focus,
heart, kernel, nub; pivot

nude *au naturel*, bare, disrobed,
exposed, in one's birthday suit
(*Inf.*), in the altogether (*Inf.*), in
the buff (*Inf.*), naked, starkers
(*Inf.*), stark-naked, stripped, un~
clad, unclothed, uncovered, un~
draped, undressed

nudge *v.* bump, dig, elbow, jog,
poke, prod, push, shove, touch

nudity bareness, nakedness, un~
dress

nugget chunk, clump, hunk, lump,
mass, piece

nuisance annoyance, bore, bother,
inconvenience, infliction, irrita~
tion, offence, pest, plague, prob~
lem, trouble, vexation

null characterless, ineffectual, in~
operative, invalid, nonexistent, null
and void, powerless, useless, vain,
valueless, void, worthless

nullify abolish, abrogate, annul,
bring to naught, cancel, counter~
act, countervail, invalidate, negate,
neutralize, quash, render null and

void, repeal, rescind, revoke, veto,
void

numb 1. *adj.* benumbed, dead,
deadened, frozen, immobilized, in~
sensible, insensitive, paralysed,
stupefied, torpid, unfeeling 2. *v.*
benumb, deaden, dull, freeze, im~
mobilize, paralyse, stun, stupefy

number *n.* 1. character, count, dig~
it, figure, integer, numeral, sum,
total, unit 2. aggregate, amount,
collection, company, crowd, horde,
many, multitude, quantity, throng
3. copy, edition, imprint, issue,
printing ~*v.* 4. account, add, cal~
culate, compute, count, enumerate,
include, reckon, tell, total

numbered categorized, contained,
counted, designated, fixed, includ~
ed, limited, limited in number,
specified, totalled

numberless countless, endless, in~
finite, innumerable, multitudinous,
myriad, unnumbered, untold

numbness deadness, dullness, in~
sensibility, insensitivity, paralysis,
stupefaction, torpor, unfeelingness

numeral character, cipher, digit,
figure, integer, number, symbol

numerous abundant, copious,
many, plentiful, profuse, several

nunnery abbey, cloister, convent,
house, monastery

nurse *v.* 1. care for, look after,
minister to, tend, treat 2. breast~
feed, feed, nourish, nurture, suckle,
wet-nurse 3. *Fig.* cherish, cultivate,
encourage, foster, harbour, keep
alive, preserve, promote, succour,
support

nurture *n.* 1. diet, food, nourish~
ment 2. development, discipline,
education, instruction, rearing,
training, upbringing ~*v.* 3. feed,
nourish, nurse, support, sustain,
tend 4. bring up, cultivate, develop,
discipline, educate, instruct, rear,
school, train

nutrition food, nourishment, nutri~
ment, sustenance

nutritious alimental, alimentative,
beneficial, healthful, health-giving,
invigorating, nourishing, nutritive,
strengthening, wholesome

O

oaf blockhead, bonehead (*Sl.*), booby, brute, clod, dolt, dullard, dummy (*Sl.*), dunce, fool, galoot (*Sl.*), gawk, goon, gorilla (*Inf.*), halfwit, idiot, imbecile, lout, lummox (*Inf.*), moron, nincompoop, sap (*Sl.*), simpleton

oafish blockish, Boeotian, boneheaded (*Sl.*), bovine, brutish, dense, dim, dim-witted (*Inf.*), doltish, dull, dumb (*Inf., chiefly U.S.*), heavy, loutish, lubberly, lumbering, moronic, obtuse, slow on the uptake (*Inf.*), stupid, thick

oasis *Fig.* haven, island, refuge, resting place, retreat, sanctuary, sanctum

oath 1. affirmation, avowal, bond, pledge, promise, sworn statement, vow, word 2. blasphemy, curse, cuss (*Inf.*), expletive, imprecation, malediction, profanity, strong language, swearword

obdurate adamant, callous, dogged, firm, fixed, hard, hard-hearted, harsh, immovable, implacable, indurate (*Rare*), inexorable, inflexible, iron, mulish, obstinate, perverse, pig-headed, proof against persuasion, relentless, stiff-necked, stubborn, unbending, unfeeling, unimpressible, unrelenting, unshakable, unyielding

obedience accordance, acquiescence, agreement, compliance, conformability, deference, docility, dutifulness, duty, observance, respect, reverence, submission, submissiveness, subservience, tractability

obedient acquiescent, amenable, biddable, compliant, deferential, docile, duteous, dutiful, law-abiding, observant, regardful, respectful, submissive, subservient, tractable, under control, well-trained, yielding

obelisk column, monolith, monument, needle, pillar, shaft

obese corpulent, Falstaffian, fat, fleshy, gross, heavy, outsize, overweight, paunchy, plump, podgy, portly, roly-poly, rotund, stout, tubby, well-upholstered (*Inf.*)

obesity bulk, corpulence, *embonpoint*, fatness, fleshiness, grossness, overweight, portliness, stoutness, tubbiness, weight problem

obey 1. abide by, act upon, adhere to, be ruled by, carry out, comply, conform, discharge, do what is expected, embrace, execute, follow, fulfil, heed, keep, mind, observe, perform, respond, serve 2. bow to, come to heel, do what one is told, get into line, give in, give way, knuckle under (*Inf.*), submit, surrender (to), take orders from, toe the line, yield

object[1] *n.* 1. article, body, entity, fact, item, phenomenon, reality, thing 2. aim, butt, focus, recipient, target, victim 3. design, end, end in view, end purpose, goal, idea, intent, intention, motive, objective, point, purpose, reason

object[2] *v.* argue against, demur, expostulate, oppose, protest, raise objections, take exception

objection cavil, censure, counter-argument, demur, doubt, exception, niggle (*Inf.*), opposition, protest, remonstrance, scruple

objectionable abhorrent, deplorable, disagreeable, dislikable, displeasing, distasteful, exceptionable, indecorous, insufferable, intolerable, noxious, obnoxious, offensive, regrettable, repugnant, unacceptable, undesirable, unpleasant, unseemly, unsociable

objective 1. *adj.* detached, disinterested, dispassionate, equitable, even-handed, fair, impartial, impersonal, judicial, just, open-minded, unbiased, uncoloured, unemotional, uninvolved, unprejudiced 2. *n.* aim, ambition, aspiration, design, end, end in view, goal, intention, mark, object, purpose, target

objectively disinterestedly, dispassionately, even-handedly, impartially, with an open mind, with objectivity *or* impartiality, without fear or favour

objectivity detachment, disinterest, disinterestedness, dispassion, equitableness, impartiality, impersonality

obligation 1. accountability, accountableness, burden, charge, compulsion, duty, liability, must, onus, requirement, responsibility, trust 2. agreement, bond, commitment, contract, debt, engagement, promise, understanding 3. **under an obligation** beholden, dutybound, grateful, honour-bound, indebted, in (someone's) debt, obligated, obliged, owing a favour, thankful

obligatory binding, coercive, compulsory, *de rigueur*, enforced, essential, imperative, mandatory, necessary, required, requisite, unavoidable

oblige 1. bind, coerce, compel, constrain, force, impel, make, necessitate, obligate, require 2. accommodate, benefit, do (someone) a favour *or* a kindness, favour, gratify, indulge, please, put oneself out for, serve

obliged 1. appreciative, beholden, grateful, gratified, indebted, in (someone's) debt, thankful 2. bound, compelled, forced, required, under an obligation, under compulsion, without any option

obliging accommodating, agreeable, amiable, civil, complaisant, considerate, cooperative, courteous, eager to please, friendly, good-natured, helpful, kind, polite, willing

oblique 1. angled, aslant, at an angle, inclined, slanted, slanting, sloped, sloping, tilted 2. backhanded, circuitous, circumlocutory, evasive, implied, indirect, roundabout, sidelong

obliquely 1. aslant, aslope, at an angle, diagonally, slantwise 2. circuitously, evasively, in a roundabout manner *or* way, indirectly, not in so many words

obliterate annihilate, blot out, cancel, delete, destroy, destroy root and branch, efface, eradicate, erase, expunge, extirpate, root out, wipe off the face of the earth, wipe out

obliteration annihilation, deletion, effacement, elimination, eradication, erasure, expunction, extirpation, wiping (blotting, rooting, sponging) out

oblivion 1. abeyance, disregard, forgetfulness, insensibility, neglect, obliviousness, unawareness, unconsciousness, (waters of) Lethe 2. blackness, darkness, eclipse, extinction, limbo, nothingness, obscurity, void

oblivious blind, careless, deaf, disregardful, forgetful, heedless, ignorant, inattentive, insensible, neglectful, negligent, regardless, unaware, unconcerned, unconscious, unmindful, unobservant

obnoxious abhorrent, abominable, detestable, disagreeable, disgusting, dislikable, foul, hateable, hateful, horrid, insufferable, loathsome, nasty, nauseating, objectionable, odious, offensive, repellent, reprehensible, repugnant, repulsive, revolting, sickening, unpleasant

obscene 1. bawdy, blue, coarse, dirty, disgusting, Fescennine (*Rare*), filthy, foul, gross, immodest, immoral, improper, impure, indecent, lewd, licentious, loose, offensive, pornographic, prurient, ribald, salacious, scabrous, shameless, smutty, suggestive, unchaste, unwholesome 2. *Fig.* atrocious, evil, heinous, loathsome, outrageous, shocking, sickening, vile, wicked

obscenity 1. bawdiness, blueness, coarseness, dirtiness, filthiness, foulness, grossness, immodesty, impurity, lewdness, licentiousness, pornography, prurience, salacity, smuttiness, suggestiveness, vileness 2. four-letter word, impropriety, indecency, indelicacy, profanity, smut, swearword, vulgarism 3. abomination, affront, atrocity, blight, evil, offence, outrage, vileness, wrong

obscure *adj.* 1. abstruse, ambiguous, arcane, concealed, confusing, cryptic, deep, doubtful, enigmatic, esoteric, hazy, hidden, incomprehensible, indefinite, intricate, involved, mysterious, occult, opaque, recondite, unclear, vague 2. blurred, clouded, cloudy, dim, dusky, faint, gloomy, indistinct, murky, obfuscated, shadowy, shady, sombre, tenebrous, unlit, veiled 3. humble, inconspicuous, inglorious, little-known, lowly, minor, nameless, out-of-the-way, remote, undistinguished, unheard-of, unhonoured, unimportant, unknown, unnoted, unseen, unsung ~*v.* 4. conceal, cover, disguise, hide, muddy, obfuscate, screen, throw a veil over, veil 5. adumbrate, bedim, befog, block, block out, blur, cloak, cloud, darken, dim, dull, eclipse, mask, overshadow, shade, shroud

obscurity 1. abstruseness, ambiguity, complexity, impenetrableness, incomprehensibility, intricacy, reconditeness, vagueness 2. darkness, dimness, dusk, duskiness, gloom, haze, haziness, indistinctness, murkiness, shadowiness, shadows 3. inconspicuousness, ingloriousness, insignificance, lowliness, namelessness, nonrecognition, unimportance

observable apparent, appreciable, clear, detectable, discernible, evident, noticeable, obvious, open, patent, perceivable, perceptible, recognizable, visible

observance 1. adherence to, attention, carrying out, celebration, compliance, discharge, fulfilment, heeding, honouring, notice, observation, performance 2. ceremonial, ceremony, custom, fashion, form, formality, practice, rite, ritual, service, tradition

observant alert, attentive, eagle-eyed, heedful, mindful, obedient, perceptive, quick, sharp-eyed,

submissive, vigilant, watchful, wide-awake

observation 1. attention, cognition, consideration, examination, experience, information, inspection, knowledge, monitoring, notice, review, scrutiny, study, surveillance, watching 2. annotation, comment, finding, note, obiter dictum, opinion, pronouncement, reflection, remark, thought, utterance

observe 1. detect, discern, discover, espy, note, notice, perceive, see, spot, witness 2. contemplate, keep an eye on (*Inf.*), keep under observation, look at, monitor, pay attention to, regard, scrutinize, study, survey, view, watch 3. animadvert, comment, declare, mention, note, opine, remark, say, state 4. abide by, adhere to, comply, conform to, follow, fulfil, heed, honour, keep, mind, obey, perform, respect 5. celebrate, commemorate, keep, remember, solemnize

observer beholder, bystander, commentator, eyewitness, looker-on, onlooker, spectator, spotter, viewer, watcher, witness

obsess bedevil, be on one's mind, be uppermost in one's thoughts, consume, dominate, engross, grip, haunt, monopolize, plague, possess, preoccupy, prey on one's mind, rule, torment

obsessed beset, dominated, gripped, hag-ridden, haunted, hung up on (*Sl., chiefly U.S.*), immersed in, infatuated, in the grip of, preoccupied, troubled

obsession bee in one's bonnet (*Inf.*), complex, enthusiasm, fetish, fixation, hang-up (*Inf.*), idée fixe, infatuation, mania, phobia, preoccupation, ruling passion, thing (*Inf.*)

obsessive besetting, compulsive, consuming, fixed, gripping, haunting, tormenting, unforgettable

obsolescent ageing, declining, dying out, not with it (*Inf.*), on the decline, on the wane, on the way out, past its prime, waning

obsolete anachronistic, ancient, antediluvian, antiquated, antique, archaic, bygone, dated, *démodé*, discarded, disused, extinct, musty, old, old-fashioned, old hat, out, outmoded, out of date, out of fashion, out of the ark (*Inf.*), outworn, passé, superannuated, *vieux jeu*

obstacle bar, barrier, check, difficulty, hindrance, hitch, hurdle, impediment, interference, interruption, obstruction, snag, stumbling block

obstinacy doggedness, firmness, inflexibility, intransigence, mulishness, obduracy, perseverance, persistence, pertinacity, pigheadedness, resoluteness, stubbornness, tenacity, wilfulness

obstinate contumacious, determined, dogged, firm, headstrong, immovable, inflexible, intractable, intransigent, mulish, opinionated, persistent, pertinacious, perverse, pig-headed, recalcitrant, refractory, self-willed, steadfast, strongminded, stubborn, tenacious, unyielding, wilful

obstreperous boisterous, clamorous, disorderly, loud, noisy, out of control, out of hand, rackety, rambunctious (*Inf.*), rampaging, raucous, restive, riotous, rip-roaring (*Inf.*), roistering, roisterous, rough, rowdy, stroppy (*Brit. sl.*), tempestuous, tumultuous, turbulent, uncontrolled, undisciplined, unmanageable, unruly, uproarious, vociferous, wild

obstruct arrest, bar, barricade, block, bring to a standstill, check, choke, clog, cumber, curb, cut off, frustrate, get in the way of, hamper, hamstring, hide, hinder, hold up, impede, inhibit, interfere with, interrupt, mask, obscure, prevent, restrict, retard, shield, shut off, slow down, stop, thwart, trammel

obstruction bar, barricade, barrier, blockage, check, difficulty, hindrance, impediment, snag, stop, stoppage, trammel

obstructive awkward, blocking, delaying, hindering, inhibiting, preventative, restrictive, stalling, uncooperative, unhelpful

obtain 1. achieve, acquire, attain,

come by, earn, gain, get, get hold of, get one's hands on, procure, secure 2. be in force, be prevalent, be the case, exist, hold, prevail, stand

obtainable achievable, at hand, attainable, available, on tap (*Inf.*), procurable, ready, realizable, to be had

obtrusive 1. forward, importunate, interfering, intrusive, meddling, nosy, officious, prying, pushy (*Inf.*) 2. noticeable, obvious, prominent, protruding, protuberant, sticking out

obvious apparent, clear, clear as a bell, conspicuous, distinct, evident, indisputable, manifest, much in evidence, noticeable, open, overt, palpable, patent, perceptible, plain, plain as the nose on your face (*Inf.*), pronounced, recognizable, right under one's nose (*Inf.*), self-evident, self-explanatory, staring one in the face (*Inf.*), sticking out a mile (*Inf.*), straightforward, transparent, unconcealed, undeniable, undisguised, unmistakable, unsubtle, visible

obviously certainly, clearly, distinctly, manifestly, of course, palpably, patently, plainly, undeniably, unmistakably, unquestionably, without doubt

occasion *n.* 1. chance, convenience, incident, moment, occurrence, opening, opportunity, time 2. affair, celebration, event, experience, occurrence 3. call, cause, excuse, ground(s), inducement, influence, justification, motive, prompting, provocation, reason ~*v.* 4. bring about, cause, create, effect, elicit, engender, evoke, generate, give rise to, induce, influence, inspire, lead to, move, originate, persuade, produce, prompt, provoke

occasional casual, desultory, incidental, infrequent, intermittent, irregular, odd, rare, sporadic, uncommon

occasionally at intervals, at times, (every) now and then, every so often, from time to time, irregularly, now and again, off and on, on and off, once in a while, on occasion, periodically, sometimes

occupant addressee, denizen, holder, incumbent, indweller, inhabitant, inmate, lessee, occupier, resident, tenant, user

occupation 1. activity, business, calling, craft, employment, job, line (of work), post, profession, pursuit, trade, vocation, walk of life, work 2. control, holding, occupancy, possession, residence, tenancy, tenure, use 3. conquest, foreign rule, invasion, seizure, subjugation

occupied 1. busy, employed, engaged, hard at it (*Inf.*), tied up (*Inf.*), working 2. engaged, full, in use, taken, unavailable 3. full, inhabited, lived-in, peopled, settled, tenanted

occupy 1. *Often passive* absorb, amuse, busy, divert, employ, engage, engross, entertain, hold the attention of, immerse, interest, involve, keep busy *or* occupied, monopolize, preoccupy, take up, tie up 2. be established in, be in residence in, dwell in, ensconce oneself in, establish oneself in, inhabit, live in, own, possess, reside in, stay in (*Scot.*), tenant 3. cover, fill, hold, permeate, pervade, take up, use, utilize 4. capture, garrison, hold, invade, keep, overrun, seize, take over, take possession of

occur 1. arise, befall, betide, chance, come about, come off (*Inf.*), come to pass (*Archaic*), crop up (*Inf.*), eventuate, happen, materialize, result, take place, turn up (*Inf.*) 2. appear, be found, be met with, be present, develop, exist, manifest itself, obtain, show itself 3. *With to* come to mind, come to one, cross one's mind, dawn on, enter one's head, spring to mind, strike one, suggest (offer, present) itself

occurrence 1. adventure, affair, circumstance, episode, event, happening, incident, instance, proceeding, transaction 2. appearance, development, existence, manifestation, materialization

odd 1. abnormal, atypical, bizarre, curious, deviant, different, eccentric, exceptional, extraordinary, fantastic, freak, freakish, freaky (*Sl.*), funny, irregular, kinky (*Sl.*), outlandish, out of the ordinary, peculiar, quaint, queer, rare, remarkable, singular, strange, uncanny, uncommon, unconventional, unusual, weird, whimsical 2. casual, fragmentary, incidental, irregular, miscellaneous, occasional, periodic, random, seasonal, sundry, varied, various 3. leftover, lone, remaining, single, solitary, spare, surplus, unconsumed, uneven, unmatched, unpaired

oddity 1. abnormality, anomaly, eccentricity, freak, idiosyncrasy, irregularity, kink (*Sl.*), peculiarity, phenomenon, quirk, rarity 2. card (*Inf.*), crank (*Inf.*), fish out of water, maverick, misfit, oddball (*Inf., chiefly U.S.*), odd bird (*Inf.*), odd fish (*Brit. inf.*), rara avis, screwball (*U.S. sl.*), weirdie *or* weirdo (*Inf.*) 3. abnormality, bizarreness, eccentricity, extraordinariness, freakishness, incongruity, oddness, outlandishness, peculiarity, queerness, singularity, strangeness, unconventionality, unnaturalness

odds 1. advantage, allowance, edge, lead, superiority 2. balance, chances, likelihood, probability 3. *Brit.* difference, disparity, dissimilarity, distinction 4. **at odds** at daggers drawn, at loggerheads, at sixes and sevens, at variance, in conflict, in disagreement, in opposition to, not in keeping, on bad terms, out of line

odds and ends bits, bits and pieces, debris, leavings, litter, oddments, remnants, rubbish, scraps, sundry *or* miscellaneous items

odious abhorrent, abominable, detestable, disgusting, execrable, foul, hateful, horrible, horrid, loathsome, obnoxious, offensive, repellent, repugnant, repulsive, revolting, unpleasant, vile

odour 1. aroma, bouquet, essence,

fragrance, perfume, redolence, scent, smell, stench, stink 2. air, atmosphere, aura, emanation, flavour, quality, spirit

off adj. 1. absent, cancelled, finished, gone, inoperative, postponed, unavailable 2. bad, below par, disappointing, disheartening, displeasing, low-quality, mortifying, poor, quiet, slack, substandard, unrewarding, unsatisfactory 3. bad, decomposed, high, mouldy, rancid, rotten, sour, turned ~adv. 4. apart, aside, away, elsewhere, out

off and on (every) now and again, every once in a while, from time to time, intermittently, now and then, occasionally, on and off, sometimes, sporadically

offbeat bizarre, Bohemian, eccentric, far-out (Sl.), freaky (Sl.), idiosyncratic, kinky (Sl.), novel, oddball (Chiefly U.S. inf.), outré, strange, uncommon, unconventional, unorthodox, unusual, way-out (Inf.), weird

off colour ill, not up to par, off form, out of sorts, peaky, poorly (Inf.), queasy, run down, sick, under the weather (Inf.), unwell, washed out

offence 1. breach of conduct, crime, delinquency, fault, lapse, misdeed, misdemeanour, peccadillo, sin, transgression, trespass, wrong, wrongdoing 2. affront, displeasure, harm, hurt, indignity, injury, injustice, insult, outrage, putdown (Sl.), slight, snub 3. anger, annoyance, displeasure, hard feelings, huff, indignation, ire (Literary), needle (Sl.), pique, resentment, umbrage, wounded feelings, wrath 4. **take offence** be disgruntled, be offended, get riled, go into a huff, resent, take the huff, take the needle (Brit. sl.), take umbrage

offend 1. affront, annoy, disgruntle, displease, fret, gall, give offence, hurt (someone's) feelings, insult, irritate, miff (Inf.), outrage, pain, pique, provoke, put (someone's) back up (Inf.), rile, slight, snub, tread on (someone's) toes (Inf.), upset, vex, wound 2. be disagree-

able to, disgust, make (someone) sick, nauseate, repel, repulse, sicken, turn (someone) off (Sl.)

offended affronted, disgruntled, displeased, huffy, in a huff, miffed (Inf.), outraged, pained, piqued, put out (Inf.), resentful, smarting, stung, upset

offender criminal, culprit, delinquent, lawbreaker, malefactor, miscreant, sinner, transgressor, wrongdoer

offensive adj. 1. abusive, annoying, detestable, discourteous, displeasing, disrespectful, embarrassing, impertinent, insolent, insulting, irritating, objectionable, rude, uncivil, unmannerly 2. abominable, detestable, disagreeable, disgusting, grisly, loathsome, nasty, nauseating, noisome, obnoxious, odious, repellent, revolting, sickening, unpalatable, unpleasant, unsavoury, vile 3. aggressive, attacking, invading ~n. 4. attack, drive, onslaught, push (Inf.) 5. **on the offensive** advancing, aggressive, attacking, invading, invasive, on the warpath (Inf.)

offer v. 1. bid, extend, give, hold out, proffer, put on the market, put under the hammer, put up for sale, tender 2. afford, furnish, make available, place at (someone's) disposal, present, provide, show 3. advance, extend, move, propose, put forth, put forward, submit, suggest 4. be at (someone's) service, come forward, offer one's services, volunteer ~n. 5. attempt, bid, endeavour, essay, overture, proposal, proposition, submission, suggestion, tender

offering contribution, donation, gift, oblation (in religious contexts), present, sacrifice, subscription, widow's mite

offhand 1. adj. abrupt, aloof, brusque, careless, casual, cavalier, couldn't-care-less, curt, glib, informal, offhanded, perfunctory, take-it-or-leave-it (Inf.), unceremonious, unconcerned, uninterested 2. adv. ad lib, extempore, just like that (Inf.), off the cuff (Inf.), off the top

of one's head (*Inf.*), without prepa~
ration

office 1. appointment, business, ca~
pacity, charge, commission, duty,
employment, function, obligation,
occupation, place, post, respon~
sibility, role, service, situation, sta~
tion, trust, work **2.** *Plural* advoca~
cy, aegis, aid, auspices, backing,
favour, help, intercession, inter~
vention, mediation, patronage,
recommendation, referral, sup~
port, word

officer agent, appointee, bureau~
crat, dignitary, executive, func~
tionary, office-holder, official, pub~
lic servant, representative

official 1. *adj.* accredited, authen~
tic, authoritative, authorized, bona
fide, certified, endorsed, ex ca~
thedra, ex officio, formal, legiti~
mate, licensed, proper, sanctioned,
straight from the horse's mouth
(*Inf.*) **2.** *n.* agent, bureaucrat, ex~
ecutive, functionary, office bearer,
officer, representative

officiate chair, conduct, emcee
(*Inf.*), manage, oversee, preside,
serve, superintend

officious bustling, dictatorial, for~
ward, impertinent, inquisitive,
interfering, intrusive, meddlesome,
meddling, mischievous, obtrusive,
opinionated, overbusy, overzeal~
ous, pragmatical (*Rare*), pushy
(*Inf.*), self-important

offing in the offing close at hand,
coming up, hovering, imminent, in
prospect, in the immediate future,
in the wings, on the horizon, on the
way

off-load disburden, discharge,
dump, get rid of, jettison, shift, take
off, transfer, unburden, unload, un~
ship

off-putting daunting, discomfiting,
disconcerting, discouraging, dis~
maying, dispiriting, disturbing,
formidable, frustrating, intimidat~
ing, unnerving, unsettling, upset~
ting

offset 1. *v.* balance out, cancel out,
compensate for, counteract,
counterbalance, counterpoise,
countervail, make up for, neutral~

ize **2.** *n.* balance, compensation,
counterbalance, counterweight,
equipoise

offshoot adjunct, appendage,
branch, by-product, development,
limb, outgrowth, spin-off, sprout

offspring child, children, descend~
ant, descendants, family, fry, heir,
heirs, issue, kids (*Inf.*), progeny,
scion, seed, spawn, successor, suc~
cessors, young

often again and again, frequently,
generally, many a time, much, oft
(*Poetic*), oftentimes (*Archaic*),
ofttimes (*Archaic*), over and over
again, repeatedly, time after time,
time and again

ogre bogey, bogeyman, bugbear,
demon, devil, giant, monster,
spectre

oil *v.* grease, lubricate

ointment balm, cerate, cream,
embrocation, emollient, liniment,
lotion, salve, unguent

O.K., okay 1. *adj.* acceptable, ac~
curate, adequate, all right, ap~
proved, convenient, correct, fair,
fine, good, in order, middling, not
bad (*Inf.*), passable, permitted,
satisfactory, so-so (*Inf.*), tolerable
2. *n.* agreement, approbation, ap~
proval, assent, authorization, con~
sent, endorsement, go-ahead (*Inf.*),
green light, permission, sanction,
say-so (*Inf.*), seal of approval **3.** *v.*
agree to, approve, authorize, con~
sent to, endorse, give one's consent
to, give the go-ahead to (*Inf.*), give
the green light to, give the thumbs
up to, pass, rubber-stamp (*Inf.*),
sanction, say yes to **4.** *interj.*
agreed, all right, right, very good,
very well, yes

old 1. advanced in years, aged, an~
cient, decrepit, elderly, full of
years, getting on (*Inf.*), grey, grey-
haired, grizzled, hoary, mature,
over the hill (*Inf.*), past one's
prime, patriarchal, senescent, se~
nile, venerable **2.** antediluvian,
antiquated, antique, cast-off,
crumbling, dated, decayed, done,
hackneyed, obsolete, old-fashioned,
outdated, outmoded, out of date,
passé, stale, superannuated, time~

worn, unfashionable, unoriginal, worn-out 3. aboriginal, antique, ar~ chaic, bygone, early, immemorial, of old, of yore, olden (*Archaic*), original, primeval, primitive, pri~ mordial, pristine, remote 4. age-old, experienced, familiar, hard~ ened, long-established, of long standing, practised, skilled, time-honoured, traditional, versed, vet~ eran, vintage 5. earlier, erstwhile, ex-, former, one-time, previous, quondam

old age advancing years, age, agedness, Anno Domini (*Inf.*), autumn *or* evening of one's life, declining years, dotage, senes~ cence, senility

old-fashioned ancient, antiquated, archaic, behind the times, corny (*Sl.*), dated, dead, *démodé*, fusty, musty, not with it (*Inf.*), obsoles~ cent, obsolete, oldfangled, (old-) fogyish, old hat, old-time, outdated, outmoded, out of date, out of style, out of the ark (*Inf.*), passé, past, square (*Inf.*), superannuated, un~ fashionable

old man elder, elder statesman, fa~ ther, gaffer, grandfather, grey~ beard, O.A.P. (*Brit.*), old codger (*Inf.*), old stager, oldster (*Inf.*), old-timer (*U.S.*), patriarch, senior citi~ zen

old-time ancient, antique, bygone, former, old-fashioned, past, vintage

old-world archaic, ceremonious, chivalrous, courtly, gallant, old-fashioned, picturesque, quaint, traditional

omen augury, foreboding, foreto~ ken, indication, portent, premoni~ tion, presage, prognostic, prognos~ tication, sign, straw in the wind, warning, writing on the wall

ominous baleful, dark, fateful, foreboding, inauspicious, menac~ ing, minatory, portentous, pre~ monitory, sinister, threatening, unpromising, unpropitious

omission default, exclusion, fail~ ure, forgetfulness, gap, lack, leav~ ing out, neglect, noninclusion, oversight

omit disregard, drop, eliminate,

exclude, fail, forget, give (some~ thing) a miss (*Inf.*), leave out, leave (something) undone, let (something) slide, miss (out), ne~ glect, overlook, pass over, skip

omnipotence divine right, invin~ cibility, mastery, sovereignty, su~ premacy, supreme power, undis~ puted sway

omnipotent all-powerful, almighty, supreme

on and off discontinuously, (every) now and again, fitfully, from time to time, intermittently, now and then, off and on, on occasion, sometimes, spasmodically

once 1. at one time, formerly, in the old days, in the past, in times gone by, in times past, long ago, once upon a time, previously 2. **at once a.** directly, forthwith, im~ mediately, instantly, now, right away, straight away, straightway (*Archaic*), this (very) minute, without delay, without hesitation **b.** at *or* in one go (*Inf.*), at the same time, simultaneously, together 3. **once and for all** conclusively, de~ cisively, finally, for all time, for good, for the last time, perma~ nently, positively, with finality 4. **once in a while** at intervals, at times, every now and then, from time to time, now and again, occa~ sionally, once in a blue moon (*Inf.*), on occasion, sometimes

one-horse backwoods, inferior, minor, obscure, petty, quiet, sleepy, slow, small, small-time (*Inf.*), tinpot (*Brit. inf.*), unimpor~ tant

onerous backbreaking, burden~ some, crushing, demanding, diffi~ cult, exacting, exhausting, exigent, formidable, grave, hard, heavy, la~ borious, oppressive, responsible, taxing, weighty

one-sided biased, coloured, dis~ criminatory, inequitable, lopsided, partial, partisan, prejudiced, un~ equal, unfair, unjust

one-time erstwhile, ex-, former, late, previous, quondam, sometime

onlooker bystander, eyewitness,

looker-on, observer, spectator, viewer, watcher, witness

only 1. *adv.* at most, barely, exclusively, just, merely, purely, simply **2.** *adj.* exclusive, individual, lone, one and only, single, sole, solitary, unique

onomatopoeic echoic, imitative, onomatopoetic

onslaught assault, attack, blitz, charge, offensive, onrush, onset

onus burden, liability, load, obligation, responsibility, task

ooze 1. *v.* bleed, discharge, drain, dribble, drip, drop, emit, escape, exude, filter, leach, leak, overflow with, percolate, seep, strain, sweat, weep **2.** *n.* alluvium, mire, muck, mud, silt, slime, sludge

opaque 1. clouded, cloudy, dim, dull, filmy, hazy, impenetrable, lustreless, muddied, muddy, murky, obfuscated, turbid **2.** abstruse, baffling, cryptic, difficult, enigmatic, incomprehensible, obscure, unclear, unfathomable, unintelligible

open *adj.* **1.** agape, ajar, expanded, extended, gaping, revealed, spread out, unbarred, unclosed, uncovered, unfastened, unfolded, unfurled, unlocked, unobstructed, unsealed, yawning **2.** airy, bare, clear, exposed, extensive, free, navigable, not built-up, passable, rolling, spacious, sweeping, uncluttered, uncrowded, unenclosed, unfenced, unsheltered, wide, wideopen **3.** accessible, available, free, general, nondiscriminatory, public, unconditional, unengaged, unoccupied, unqualified, unrestricted, vacant **4.** apparent, avowed, barefaced, blatant, clear, conspicuous, downright, evident, flagrant, frank, manifest, noticeable, obvious, overt, plain, unconcealed, undisguised, visible **5.** arguable, debatable, moot, undecided, unresolved, unsettled, up in the air, yet to be decided **6.** disinterested, free, impartial, objective, receptive, unbiased, uncommitted, unprejudiced **7.** *With* to an easy target for, at the mercy of, defenceless against, dis-

posed, exposed, liable, susceptible, vulnerable **8.** artless, candid, fair, frank, guileless, honest, ingenuous, innocent, natural, sincere, transparent, unreserved **9.** filigree, fretted, holey, honeycombed, lacy, loose, openwork, porous, spongy **10.** bounteous, bountiful, generous, liberal, munificent **11.** exposed, undefended, unfortified, unprotected ~*v.* **12.** begin, begin business, commence, get *or* start the ball rolling, inaugurate, initiate, kick off (*Inf.*), launch, put up one's plate, set in motion, set up shop, start **13.** clear, crack, throw wide, unbar, unblock, unclose, uncork, uncover, undo, unfasten, unlock, unseal, untie, unwrap **14.** expand, spread (out), unfold, unfurl, unroll **15.** come apart, crack, rupture, separate, split **16.** disclose, divulge, exhibit, explain, lay bare, pour out, show, uncover

open-air alfresco, outdoor

open-handed bountiful, free, generous, lavish, liberal, munificent, unstinting

opening *n.* **1.** aperture, breach, break, chink, cleft, crack, fissure, gap, hole, interstice, orifice, perforation, rent, rupture, slot, space, split, vent **2.** break (*Inf.*), chance, look-in (*Inf.*), occasion, opportunity, place, vacancy **3.** beginning, birth, commencement, dawn, inauguration, inception, initiation, kickoff (*Inf.*), launch, launching, onset, outset, start ~*adj.* **4.** beginning, commencing, early, first, inaugural, initial, initiatory, introductory, maiden, primary

openly 1. candidly, face to face, forthrightly, frankly, plainly, straight from the shoulder (*Inf.*), unhesitatingly, unreservedly **2.** blatantly, brazenly, flagrantly, in full view, in public, publicly, shamelessly, unabashedly, unashamedly, wantonly, without pretence

open-minded broad, broadminded, catholic, dispassionate, enlightened, free, impartial, liberal, reasonable, receptive, tolerant, unbiased, undogmatic, unprejudiced

operate 1. act, be in action, function, go, perform, run, work 2. be in charge of, handle, manage, manoeuvre, use, work 3. perform surgery

operation 1. action, affair, course, exercise, motion, movement, performance, procedure, process, use, working 2. **in operation** effective, functioning, going, in action, in force, operative 3. activity, agency, effect, effort, force, influence, instrumentality, manipulation 4. affair, business, deal, enterprise, proceeding, transaction, undertaking 5. assault, campaign, exercise, manoeuvre 6. surgery

operational functional, going, in working order, operative, prepared, ready, usable, viable, workable, working

operative adj. 1. active, current, effective, efficient, functional, functioning, in force, in operation, operational, serviceable, standing, workable 2. crucial, important, indicative, influential, key, relevant, significant ~n. 3. artisan, employee, hand, labourer, machinist, mechanic, worker

operator 1. conductor, driver, handler, mechanic, operative, practitioner, skilled employee, technician, worker 2. administrator, contractor, dealer, director, manager, speculator, trader 3. Inf. Machiavellian, machinator, manipulator, mover, punter, shyster (Sl., chiefly U.S.), smart aleck (Inf.), wheeler-dealer (Inf.), wirepuller, worker

opinion 1. assessment, belief, conception, conjecture, estimation, feeling, idea, impression, judgment, mind, notion, persuasion, point of view, sentiment, theory, view 2. **be of the opinion** be convinced, believe, be under the impression, conclude, consider, hold, judge, reckon, suppose, surmise, think 3. **matter of opinion** debatable point, matter of judgment,

moot point, open question, open to debate, up to the individual

opinionated adamant, biased, bigoted, bull-headed, cocksure, dictatorial, doctrinaire, dogmatic, inflexible, obdurate, obstinate, overbearing, pig-headed, prejudiced, self-assertive, single-minded, stubborn, uncompromising

opponent adversary, antagonist, challenger, competitor, contestant, disputant, dissentient, enemy, foe, opposer, rival, the opposition

opportune advantageous, appropriate, apt, auspicious, convenient, favourable, felicitous, fit, fitting, fortunate, happy, lucky, proper, propitious, seasonable, suitable, timely, well-timed

opportunism expediency, exploitation, Machiavellianism, making hay while the sun shines (Inf.), pragmatism, realism, Realpolitik, striking while the iron is hot (Inf.), trimming, unscrupulousness

opportunity break (Inf.), chance, convenience, hour, look-in (Inf.), moment, occasion, opening, scope, time

oppose 1. bar, check, combat, confront, contradict, counter, counterattack, defy, face, fight, fly in the face of, hinder, obstruct, prevent, resist, speak against, stand up to, take a stand against, take issue with, take on, thwart, withstand 2. compare, contrast, counterbalance, match, pit or set against, play off

opposed against, antagonistic, anti (Inf.), antipathetic, antithetical, at daggers drawn, clashing, conflicting, contrary, dissentient, hostile, incompatible, inimical, in opposition, opposing, opposite

opposing antagonistic, antipathetic, clashing, combatant, conflicting, contrary, enemy, hostile, incompatible, irreconcilable, opposed, opposite, rival, warring

opposite adj. 1. corresponding, facing, fronting 2. adverse, antagonistic, antithetical, conflicting, contradictory, contrary, contrasted, diametrically opposed, differ-

ent, differing, diverse, hostile, in~
consistent, inimical, irreconcilable,
opposed, reverse, unlike ~*n.* 3. an~
tithesis, contradiction, contrary,
converse, inverse, reverse, the
other extreme, the other side of
the coin (*Inf.*)

opposition 1. antagonism, compe~
tition, contrariety, counteraction,
disapproval, hostility, obstruction,
obstructiveness, prevention, resis~
tance, unfriendliness 2. antagonist,
competition, foe, opponent, other
side, rival

oppress 1. afflict, burden, depress,
dispirit, harass, lie *or* weigh heavy
upon, sadden, take the heart out of,
torment, vex 2. abuse, crush, har~
ry, maltreat, overpower, over~
whelm, persecute, rule with an
iron hand, subdue, subjugate, sup~
press, trample underfoot, tyran~
nize over, wrong

oppressed abused, browbeaten,
burdened, disadvantaged, down~
trodden, enslaved, harassed, hen~
pecked, maltreated, misused,
prostrate, slave, subject, troubled,
tyrannized, underprivileged

oppression abuse, brutality, ca~
lamity, cruelty, hardship, harsh~
ness, injury, injustice, iron hand,
maltreatment, misery, persecu~
tion, severity, subjection, suffering,
tyranny

oppressive 1. brutal, burdensome,
cruel, despotic, grinding, harsh,
heavy, inhuman, onerous, over~
bearing, overwhelming, repres~
sive, severe, tyrannical, unjust 2.
airless, close, heavy, muggy, over~
powering, stifling, stuffy, suffocat~
ing, sultry, torrid

oppressor autocrat, bully, despot,
harrier, intimidator, iron hand,
persecutor, scourge, slave-driver,
taskmaster, tormentor, tyrant

opt (for) choose, decide (on), elect,
exercise one's discretion (in favour
of), go for (*Inf.*), make a selection,
plump for, prefer

optimistic 1. disposed to take a
favourable view, idealistic, seen
through rose-coloured spectacles,
Utopian 2. assured, bright, buoy~

ant, buoyed up, cheerful, confident,
encouraged, expectant, hopeful,
positive, sanguine

optimum *adj.* A1 (*Inf.*), best,
choicest, flawless, highest, ideal,
most favourable *or* advantageous,
optimal, peak, perfect, superlative

option alternative, choice, election,
preference, selection

optional discretionary, elective,
extra, noncompulsory, open, pos~
sible, up to the individual, volun~
tary

opulence 1. affluence, easy cir~
cumstances, easy street (*Inf.*), for~
tune, lavishness, luxuriance, luxu~
ry, plenty, prosperity, riches, rich~
ness, sumptuousness, wealth 2.
abundance, copiousness, cornuco~
pia, fullness, profusion, richness,
superabundance

opulent 1. affluent, lavish, luxuri~
ous, moneyed, prosperous, rich,
sumptuous, wealthy, well-heeled
(*Sl.*), well-off, well-to-do 2. abun~
dant, copious, lavish, luxuriant,
plentiful, profuse, prolific

oracle 1. augur, Cassandra, proph~
et, seer, sibyl, soothsayer 2. an~
swer, augury, divination, divine ut~
terance, prediction, prognostica~
tion, prophecy, revelation, vision 3.
adviser, authority, guru, high
priest, horse's mouth, mastermind,
mentor, pundit, source, wizard

oral spoken, verbal, viva voce, vo~
cal

oration address, declamation, dis~
course, harangue, homily, lecture,
speech, spiel (*Inf.*)

orator Cicero, declaimer, lecturer,
public speaker, rhetorician,
speaker, spellbinder, spieler (*Inf.*)

oratorical bombastic, Ciceronian,
declamatory, eloquent, grandilo~
quent, high-flown, magniloquent,
rhetorical, silver-tongued, sono~
rous

oratory declamation, elocution,
eloquence, grandiloquence, public
speaking, rhetoric, speechifying,
speech-making, spieling (*Inf.*)

orb ball, circle, globe, ring, round,
sphere

orbit *n.* 1. circle, circumgyration,

course, cycle, ellipse, path, revolu~
tion, rotation, track, trajectory 2.
Fig. ambit, compass, course, do~
main, influence, range, reach,
scope, sphere, sphere of influence,
sweep ~*v.* 3. circle, circumnavi~
gate, encircle, revolve around

orchestrate 1. arrange, score 2.
arrange, concert, coordinate, inte~
grate, organize, present, put to~
gether, set up, stage-manage

ordain 1. anoint, appoint, call, con~
secrate, destine, elect, frock, in~
vest, nominate 2. fate, foreordain,
intend, predestine, predetermine
3. decree, dictate, enact, enjoin,
fix, lay down, legislate, order, pre~
scribe, pronounce, rule, set, will

ordeal affliction, agony, anguish,
nightmare, suffering, test, torture,
trial, tribulation(s), trouble(s)

order *n.* 1. arrangement, harmony,
method, neatness, orderliness, or~
ganization, pattern, plan, propri~
ety, regularity, symmetry, system,
tidiness 2. arrangement, array,
categorization, classification, codi~
fication, disposal, disposition,
grouping, layout, line, line-up, or~
dering, placement, progression,
sequence, series, setup (*Inf.*),
structure, succession 3. in order a.
arranged, in sequence, neat, or~
derly, shipshape, tidy b. accept~
able, appropriate, called for, cor~
rect, fitting, O.K. (*Inf.*), right, suit~
able 4. out of order a. broken,
broken-down, bust (*Sl.*), gone hay~
wire (*Inf.*), gone phut (*Inf.*), in dis~
repair, inoperative, kaput (*Inf.*),
nonfunctional, not working, on the
blink (*Sl.*), out of commission, U/S
(*Inf.*), wonky (*Brit. sl*) b. improper,
indecorous, not cricket (*Inf.*), not
done, not on (*Inf.*), out of place, out
of turn, uncalled-for, wrong 5.
calm, control, discipline, law, law
and order, peace, quiet, tranquil~
lity 6. caste, class, degree, grade,
hierarchy, pecking order (*Inf.*),
position, rank, status 7. breed, cast,
class, family, genre, genus, ilk,
kind, sort, species, subclass, taxo~
nomic group, tribe, type 8. behest,
command, decree, dictate, direc~
tion, directive, injunction, instruc~

tion, law, mandate, ordinance,
precept, regulation, rule, say-so
(*Inf.*), stipulation 9. application,
booking, commission, request,
requisition, reservation 10. asso~
ciation, brotherhood, community,
company, fraternity, guild, league,
lodge, organization, sect, sister~
hood, society, sodality, union ~*v.*
11. adjure, bid, charge, command,
decree, direct, enact, enjoin, in~
struct, ordain, prescribe, require
12. apply for, authorize, book, call
for, contract for, engage, pre~
scribe, request, reserve, send away
for 13. adjust, align, arrange, cata~
logue, class, classify, conduct, con~
trol, dispose, group, lay out, man~
age, marshal, neaten, organize, put
to rights, regulate, set in order,
sort out, systematize, tabulate, tidy

orderly *adj.* 1. businesslike, in
apple-pie order (*Inf.*), in order,
methodical, neat, regular, scientif~
ic, shipshape, systematic, sys~
tematized, tidy, trim, well-
organized, well-regulated 2. con~
trolled, decorous, disciplined, law-
abiding, nonviolent, peaceable,
quiet, restrained, well-behaved

ordinarily as a rule, commonly,
customarily, generally, habitually,
in general, in the general run (of
things), in the usual way, normally,
usually

ordinary 1. accustomed, common,
customary, established, everyday,
habitual, humdrum, normal, pre~
vailing, quotidian, regular, routine,
settled, standard, stock, typical,
usual, wonted 2. common or gar~
den (*Inf.*), conventional, familiar,
homespun, household, humble,
modest, plain, prosaic, run-of-the-
mill, simple, unmemorable, unpre~
tentious, unremarkable, workaday
3. average, commonplace, fair, in~
different, inferior, mean, medio~
cre, pedestrian, second-rate, ste~
reotyped, undistinguished, unex~
ceptional, uninspired, unremark~
able 4. out of the ordinary atypi~
cal, distinguished, exceptional, ex~
citing, extraordinary, high-calibre,
imaginative, important, impres~
sive, inspired, noteworthy, out~

standing, rare, remarkable, significant, special, striking, superior, uncommon, unusual

organ 1. device, implement, instrument, tool 2. element, member, part, process, structure, unit 3. agency, channel, forum, journal, means, medium, mouthpiece, newspaper, paper, periodical, publication, vehicle, voice

organism animal, being, body, creature, entity, living thing, structure

organization 1. assembling, assembly, construction, coordination, disposal, formation, forming, formulation, making, management, methodology, organizing, planning, regulation, running, standardization, structuring 2. arrangement, chemistry, composition, configuration, conformation, constitution, design, format, framework, grouping, make-up, method, organism, pattern, plan, structure, system, unity, whole 3. association, body, combine, company, concern, confederation, consortium, corporation, federation, group, institution, league, outfit (*Inf.*), syndicate

organize arrange, be responsible for, catalogue, classify, codify, constitute, construct, coordinate, dispose, establish, form, frame, get going (*Inf.*), get together (*Sl.*), group, lay the foundations of, lick into shape, look after, marshal, pigeonhole, put in order, put together, run, see to (*Inf.*), set up, shape, straighten out, systematize, tabulate, take care of

orgy 1. bacchanal, bacchanalia, debauch, revel, revelry, Saturnalia 2. binge (*Inf.*), bout, excess, indulgence, overindulgence, splurge, spree, surfeit

orientation 1. bearings, coordination, direction, location, position, sense of direction 2. acclimatization, adaptation, adjustment, assimilation, breaking in, familiarization, introduction, settling in

orifice aperture, cleft, hole, mouth, opening, perforation, pore, rent, vent

origin 1. base, basis, cause, derivation, *fons et origo*, font (*Poetic*), fountain, fountainhead, occasion, provenance, root, roots, source, spring, wellspring 2. beginning, birth, commencement, creation, dawning, early stages, emergence, foundation, genesis, inauguration, inception, launch, origination, outset, start 3. ancestry, beginnings, birth, descent, extraction, family, heritage, lineage, parentage, pedigree, stirps, stock

original *adj.* 1. aboriginal, autochthonous, commencing, earliest, early, embryonic, first, infant, initial, introductory, opening, primary, primitive, primordial, pristine, rudimentary, starting 2. creative, fertile, fresh, imaginative, ingenious, innovative, innovatory, inventive, new, novel, resourceful, seminal, unconventional, unprecedented, untried, unusual 3. archetypal, authentic, first, first-hand, genuine, master, primary, prototypical ~*n.* 4. archetype, master, model, paradigm, pattern, precedent, prototype, standard, type 5. anomaly, card (*Inf.*), case (*Inf.*), character, eccentric, nonconformist, oddity, queer fish (*Brit. inf.*), weirdo (*Inf.*)

originality boldness, break with tradition, cleverness, creativeness, creative spirit, creativity, daring, freshness, imagination, imaginativeness, individuality, ingenuity, innovation, innovativeness, inventiveness, new ideas, newness, novelty, resourcefulness, unconventionality, unorthodoxy

originally at first, at the outset, at the start, by origin (birth, derivation), first, initially, in the beginning, in the first place, to begin with

originate 1. arise, be born, begin, come, derive, emanate, emerge, flow, issue, proceed, result, rise, spring, start, stem 2. bring about, conceive, create, develop, discover, evolve, form, formulate, generate, give birth to, inaugurate, initiate, institute, introduce, invent, launch, pioneer, produce, set in motion, set up

originator architect, author, creator, father, founder, generator, innovator, inventor, maker, mother, pioneer, prime mover

ornament n. 1. accessory, adornment, bauble, decoration, embellishment, frill, furbelow, garnish, gewgaw, knick-knack, trimming, trinket 2. flower, honour, jewel, leading light, pride, treasure ~v. 3. adorn, beautify, bedizen (*Archaic*), brighten, deck, decorate, dress up, embellish, festoon, garnish, gild, grace, prettify, prink, trim

ornamental attractive, beautifying, decorative, embellishing, for show, showy

ornamentation adornment, decoration, elaboration, embellishment, embroidery, frills, ornateness

ornate aureate, baroque, beautiful, bedecked, busy, convoluted, decorated, elaborate, elegant, fancy, florid, flowery, fussy, high-wrought, ornamented, overelaborate, rococo

orthodox accepted, approved, conformist, conventional, correct, customary, doctrinal, established, official, received, sound, traditional, true, well-established

orthodoxy authenticity, authoritativeness, authority, conformism, conformity, conventionality, devotion, devoutness, faithfulness, inflexibility, received wisdom, soundness, traditionalism

oscillate fluctuate, seesaw, sway, swing, vacillate, vary, vibrate, waver

oscillation fluctuation, instability, seesawing, swing, vacillation, variation, wavering

ossify fossilize, freeze, harden, indurate (*Rare*), petrify, solidify, stiffen

ostensible alleged, apparent, avowed, exhibited, manifest, outward, plausible, pretended, professed, purported, seeming, so-called, specious, superficial, supposed

ostensibly apparently, for the os-

tensible purpose of, on the face of it, on the surface, professedly, seemingly, supposedly, to all intents and purposes

ostentation affectation, boasting, display, exhibitionism, flamboyance, flashiness, flaunting, flourish, pageantry, parade, pomp, pretension, pretentiousness, show, showiness, showing off (*Inf.*), swank (*Inf.*), vaunting, window-dressing

ostentatious boastful, conspicuous, crass, dashing, extravagant, flamboyant, flash (*Inf.*), flashy, flaunted, gaudy, loud, obtrusive, pompous, pretentious, showy, swanky (*Inf.*), vain, vulgar

ostracize avoid, banish, blackball, blacklist, boycott, cast out, cold-shoulder, exclude, excommunicate, exile, expatriate, expel, give (someone) the cold shoulder, reject, send to Coventry, shun

other adj. 1. added, additional, alternative, auxiliary, extra, further, more, spare, supplementary 2. contrasting, different, dissimilar, distinct, diverse, remaining, separate, unrelated, variant

otherwise adv. 1. if not, or else, or then 2. any other way, contrarily, differently

ounce atom, crumb, drop, grain, iota, particle, scrap, shred, speck, trace, whit

out adj. 1. impossible, not allowed, not on (*Inf.*), ruled out, unacceptable 2. abroad, absent, away, elsewhere, gone, not at home, outside 3. antiquated, behind the times, dated, old, dead, *démodé*, old-fashioned, old hat, passé, square (*Inf.*), unfashionable 4. at an end, cold, dead, doused, ended, exhausted, expired, extinguished, finished, used up

out-and-out absolute, complete, consummate, downright, dyed-in-the-wool, outright, perfect, thoroughgoing, total, unmitigated, unqualified, utter

outbreak burst, epidemic, eruption, explosion, flare-up, flash, outburst, rash, spasm, upsurge

outburst access, attack, discharge,

eruption, explosion, fit of temper, flare-up, gush, outbreak, outpour~ ing, paroxysm, spasm, storm, surge

outcast *n.* castaway, derelict, dis~ placed person, exile, leper, pariah, *persona non grata*, refugee, repro~ bate, untouchable, vagabond, wretch

outclass be a cut above (*Inf.*), beat, eclipse, exceed, excel, leave *or* put in the shade, leave standing (*Inf.*), outdistance, outdo, outrank, out~ shine, outstrip, overshadow, sur~ pass

outcome aftereffect, aftermath, conclusion, consequence, end, end result, issue, payoff (*Inf.*), result, upshot

outcry clamour, commotion, com~ plaint, cry, exclamation, howl, hue and cry, hullaballoo, noise, out~ burst, protest, scream, screech, uproar, yell

outdated antiquated, antique, ar~ chaic, behind the times (*Inf.*), *démodé*, obsolete, old-fashioned, outmoded, out of date, out of style, passé, unfashionable

outdistance leave behind, leave standing (*Inf.*), lose, outrun, out~ strip, shake off

outdo beat, be one up on, best, eclipse, exceed, excel, get the bet~ ter of, go one better than (*Inf.*), outclass, outdistance, outfox, out~ jockey, outmanoeuvre, outshine, outsmart (*Inf.*), overcome, surpass, top, transcend

outdoor alfresco, open-air, out-of-door(s), outside

outer exposed, exterior, external, outlying, outside, outward, periph~ eral, remote, superficial, surface

outfit *n.* 1. accoutrements, clothes, costume, ensemble, garb, gear, get-up (*Inf.*), kit, rigout (*Inf.*), suit, togs (*Inf.*), trappings 2. *Inf.* clique, company, corps, coterie, crew, firm, *galère*, group, organization, set, setup (*Inf.*), squad, team, unit ~*v.* 3. accoutre, appoint, equip, fit out, furnish, kit out, provision, stock, supply, turn out

outfitter clothier, costumier, cou~ turier, dressmaker, haberdasher (*U.S.*), modiste, tailor

outflow discharge, drainage, ebb, effluence, efflux, effusion, emana~ tion, emergence, gush, jet, outfall, outpouring, rush, spout

outgoing 1. departing, ex-, former, last, leaving, past, retiring, with~ drawing 2. approachable, commu~ nicative, cordial, demonstrative, easy, expansive, extrovert, friend~ ly, genial, gregarious, informal, open, sociable, sympathetic, unre~ served, warm

outgoings costs, expenditure, ex~ penses, outlay, overheads

outing excursion, expedition, jaunt, pleasure trip, spin (*Inf.*), trip

outlandish alien, barbarous, bi~ zarre, eccentric, exotic, fantastic, far-out (*Sl.*), foreign, freakish, gro~ tesque, *outré*, preposterous, queer, strange, unheard-of, weird

outlaw 1. *n.* bandit, brigand, des~ perado, fugitive, highwayman, marauder, outcast, pariah, robber 2. *v.* ban, banish, bar, condemn, disallow, embargo, exclude, forbid, interdict, make illegal, prohibit, proscribe, put a price on (some~ one's) head

outlay *n.* cost, disbursement, ex~ penditure, expenses, investment, outgoings, spending

outlet 1. avenue, channel, duct, egress, exit, means of expression, opening, orifice, release, safety valve, vent, way out 2. market, shop, store

outline *n.* 1. draft, drawing, frame, framework, layout, lineament(s), plan, rough, skeleton, sketch, trac~ ing 2. bare facts, main features, recapitulation, résumé, rough idea, rundown, summary, synopsis, thumbnail sketch 3. configuration, contour, delineation, figure, form, profile, shape, silhouette ~*v.* 4. ad~ umbrate, delineate, draft, plan, rough out, sketch (in), summarize, trace

outlive come through, endure be~ yond, live through, outlast, survive

outlook 1. angle, attitude, frame of mind, perspective, point of view, slant, standpoint, viewpoint, views 2. expectations, forecast, future, prospect 3. aspect, panorama, prospect, scene, view, vista

outlying backwoods, distant, far-flung, outer, out-of-the-way, peripheral, provincial, remote

outmoded anachronistic, antediluvian, antiquated, antique, archaic, behind the times (*Inf.*), bygone, dated, *démodé*, fossilized, obsolescent, obsolete, olden (*Archaic*), oldfangled, old-fashioned, old-time, out, out of date, out of style, outworn, passé, square (*Inf.*), superannuated, superseded, unfashionable, unusable

out of date antiquated, archaic, dated, discarded, elapsed, expired, extinct, invalid, lapsed, obsolete, old-fashioned, outmoded, outworn, passé, stale, superannuated, superseded, unfashionable

out-of-the-way 1. distant, far-flung, inaccessible, isolated, lonely, obscure, off the beaten track, outlying, remote, secluded, unfrequented 2. abnormal, curious, exceptional, extraordinary, odd, outlandish, out of the ordinary, peculiar, strange, uncommon, unusual

out of work idle, jobless, laid off, on the dole (*Brit.*), out of a job, redundant, unemployed

outpouring cascade, debouchment, deluge, effluence, efflux, effusion, emanation, flow, flux, outflow, spate, spurt, stream, torrent

output achievement, manufacture, outturn (*Rare*), product, production, productivity, yield

outrage n. 1. atrocity, barbarism, enormity, evil, inhumanity 2. abuse, affront, desecration, indignity, injury, insult, offence, profanation, rape, ravishing, shock, violation, violence 3. anger, fury, hurt, indignation, resentment, shock, wrath ~v. 4. affront, incense, infuriate, madden, make one's blood boil, offend, scandalize, shock 5. abuse, defile, desecrate, injure, insult, maltreat, rape, ravage, ravish, violate

outrageous 1. abominable, atrocious, barbaric, beastly, egregious, flagrant, heinous, horrible, infamous, inhuman, iniquitous, nefarious, scandalous, shocking, unspeakable, villainous, violent, wicked 2. disgraceful, excessive, exorbitant, extravagant, immoderate, offensive, preposterous, scandalous, shocking, steep (*Inf.*), unreasonable

outright adj. 1. absolute, arrant, complete, consummate, downright, out-and-out, perfect, pure, thorough, thoroughgoing, total, unconditional, undeniable, unmitigated, unqualified, utter, wholesale 2. definite, direct, flat, straightforward, unequivocal, unqualified ~adv. 3. absolutely, completely, explicitly, openly, overtly, straightforwardly, thoroughly, to the full, without hesitation, without restraint 4. at once, cleanly, immediately, instantaneously, instantly, on the spot, straight away, there and then, without more ado

outset beginning, commencement, early days, inauguration, inception, kickoff (*Inf.*), onset, opening, start, starting point

outshine be head and shoulders above, be superior to, eclipse, leave *or* put in the shade, outclass, outdo, outstrip, overshadow, surpass, top, transcend, upstage

outside adj. 1. exterior, external, extramural, extraneous, extreme, out, outdoor, outer, outermost, outward, surface 2. distant, faint, marginal, negligible, remote, slight, slim, small, unlikely ~n. 3. exterior, façade, face, front, skin, surface, topside

outsider alien, foreigner, incomer, interloper, intruder, newcomer, nonmember, odd man out, outlander, stranger

outskirts borders, boundary, edge, environs, faubourgs, periphery, purlieus, suburbia, suburbs, vicinity

outspoken abrupt, blunt, candid, direct, explicit, forthright, frank, free, free-spoken, open, plain-spoken, round, unceremonious,

undissembling, unequivocal, unre~
served

outstanding 1. celebrated, distin~
guished, eminent, excellent, ex~
ceptional, great, important, im~
pressive, meritorious, pre-eminent,
special, superior, superlative, well-
known 2. arresting, conspicuous,
eye-catching, marked, memorable,
notable, noteworthy, prominent,
salient, signal, striking 3. due, on~
going, open, owing, payable, pend~
ing, remaining, uncollected, un~
paid, unresolved, unsettled

outward adj. apparent, evident,
exterior, external, noticeable, ob~
servable, obvious, ostensible, outer,
outside, perceptible, superficial,
surface, visible

outwardly apparently, as far as
one can see, externally, officially,
on the face of it, on the surface,
ostensibly, professedly, seemingly,
superficially, to all appearances, to
all intents and purposes, to the eye

outweigh cancel (out), compen~
sate for, eclipse, make up for, out~
balance, overcome, override, pre~
dominate, preponderate, prevail
over, take precedence over, tip the
scales

outwit cheat, circumvent, deceive,
defraud, dupe, get the better of,
gull (Archaic), make a fool or
monkey of, outfox, outjockey, out~
manoeuvre, outsmart (Inf.), out~
think, put one over on (Inf.), run
rings round (Inf.), swindle, take in
(Inf.)

outworn abandoned, antiquated,
behind the times (Inf.), defunct,
discredited, disused, exhausted,
hackneyed, obsolete, outdated,
outmoded, out of date, overused,
rejected, stale, superannuated,
threadbare, tired, worn-out

oval adj. egg-shaped, ellipsoidal, el~
liptical, ovate, oviform, ovoid

ovation acclaim, acclamation, ap~
plause, cheering, cheers, clapping,
laudation, plaudits, tribute

over adj. 1. accomplished, ancient
history (Inf.), at an end, by, by~
gone, closed, completed, conclud~
ed, done (with), ended, finished,
gone, past, settled, up (Inf.)
~adj./adv. 2. beyond, extra, in ad~
dition, in excess, left over, remain~
ing, superfluous, surplus, unused
~prep. 3. above, on, on top of, su~
perior to, upon 4. above, exceed~
ing, in excess of, more than ~adv.
5. above, aloft, on high, overhead 6.
over and above added to, as well
as, besides, in addition to, let alone,
not to mention, on top of, plus 7.
over and over (again) ad nau~
seam, again and again, frequently,
often, repeatedly, time and again

overact exaggerate, ham or ham
up (Inf.), overdo, overplay

overall 1. adj. all-embracing, blan~
ket, complete, comprehensive,
general, global, inclusive, long-
range, long-term, total, umbrella 2.
adv. generally speaking, in gener~
al, in (the) large, in the long term,
on the whole

overawe abash, alarm, browbeat,
cow, daunt, frighten, intimidate,
scare, terrify

overbalance capsize, keel over,
lose one's balance, lose one's foot~
ing, overset, overturn, slip, take a
tumble, tip over, topple over, tum~
ble, turn turtle, upset

overbearing arrogant, autocratic,
bossy (Inf.), cavalier, despotic,
dictatorial, dogmatic, domineering,
haughty, high-handed, imperious,
lordly, magisterial, officious, op~
pressive, overweening, peremp~
tory, supercilious, superior, tyran~
nical

overcast clouded, clouded over,
cloudy, darkened, dismal, dreary,
dull, grey, hazy, leaden, lowering,
murky, sombre, sunless, threaten~
ing

overcharge 1. cheat, clip (Sl.), did~
dle (Inf.), do (Sl.), fleece, rip off
(Sl.), rook (Sl.), short-change, sting
(Inf.), surcharge 2. burden, op~
press, overburden, overload, over~
task, overtax, strain, surfeit 3. Lit~
erary embellish, embroider, exag~
gerate, hyperbolize, lay it on thick
(Inf.), overstate

overcome 1. v. beat, best, be victo~
rious, come out on top (Inf.), con~

quer, crush, defeat, get the better of, lick (*Inf.*), master, overpower, overthrow, overwhelm, prevail, render incapable (helpless, pow~erless), rise above, subdue, subju~gate, surmount, survive, triumph over, vanquish, weather, worst **2.** *adj.* affected, at a loss for words, bowled over (*Inf.*), overwhelmed, speechless, swept off one's feet, unable to continue, visibly moved

overconfident brash, cocksure, foolhardy, hubristic, overweening, presumptuous, riding for a fall (*Inf.*), uppish (*Brit. inf.*)

overcritical captious, carping, cavilling, fault-finding, hair~splitting, hard to please, hyper~critical, nit-picking (*Inf.*), overpar~ticular, pernickety (*Inf.*)

overcrowded choked, congested, crammed full, jam-packed, like the Black Hole of Calcutta, overloaded, overpopulated, packed (out), swarming

overdo 1. be intemperate, bela~bour, carry too far, do to death (*Inf.*), exaggerate, gild the lily, go overboard (*Inf.*), go to extremes, lay it on thick (*Inf.*), not know when to stop, overindulge, over~play, overreach, overstate, over~use, overwork, run riot **2. overdo it** bite off more than one can chew, burn the candle at both ends (*Inf.*), drive oneself, fatigue, go too far, have too many irons in the fire, overburden, overload, overtax one's strength, overtire, overwork, strain *or* overstrain oneself, wear oneself out

overdone 1. beyond all bounds, ex~aggerated, excessive, fulsome, im~moderate, inordinate, overelabo~rate, preposterous, too much, un~due, unnecessary **2.** burnt, burnt to a cinder, charred, dried up, over~cooked, spoiled

overdue behindhand, behind schedule, behind time, belated, late, long delayed, not before time (*Inf.*), owing, tardy, unpunctual

overeat binge (*Inf.*), eat like a horse (*Inf.*), gorge, gormandize, guzzle, make a pig of oneself (*Inf.*),

overindulge, pack away (*Sl.*), pig away (*Sl.*), stuff, stuff oneself

overemphasize belabour, blow up out of all proportion, lay too much stress on, make a big thing of (*Inf.*), make a mountain out of a molehill (*Inf.*), make something out of nothing, make too much of, overdramatize, overstress

overflow *v.* **1.** bubble (brim, fall, pour, run, slop, well) over, dis~charge, pour out, run with, shower, spill, spray, surge **2.** cover, deluge, drown, flood, inundate, soak, sub~merge, swamp ~*n.* **3.** discharge, flash flood, flood, flooding, inunda~tion, overabundance, spill, spilling over, surplus

overflowing abounding, bountiful, brimful, copious, plentiful, profuse, rife, superabundant, swarming, teeming, thronged

overhang *v.* beetle, bulge, cast a shadow, extend, impend, jut, loom, project, protrude, stick out, threat~en

overhaul *v.* **1.** check, do up (*Inf.*), examine, inspect, recondition, re~examine, repair, restore, service, survey ~*n.* **2.** check, checkup, ex~amination, going-over (*Inf.*), in~spection, reconditioning, service ~*v.* **3.** catch up with, draw level with, get ahead of, overtake, pass

overhead 1. *adv.* above, aloft, atop, in the sky, on high, skyward, up above, upward **2.** *adj.* aerial, over~hanging, roof, upper

overheads burden, oncosts, oper~ating cost(s), running cost(s)

overheated agitated, fiery, flam~ing, impassioned, inflamed, over~excited, roused

overindulge be immoderate *or* in~temperate, drink *or* eat too much, have a binge (*Inf.*), live it up (*Inf.*), make a pig of oneself (*Inf.*), overdo it

overindulgence excess, immod~eration, intemperance, overeating, surfeit

overjoyed delighted, deliriously happy, elated, euphoric, happy as a lark, in raptures, joyful, jubilant, on cloud nine (*Inf.*), only too happy, over the moon (*Inf.*), rapturous, thrilled, tickled pink, transported

overlay 1. *v.* adorn, blanket, cover, inlay, laminate, ornament, over~ spread, superimpose, veneer 2. *n.* adornment, appliqué, covering, decoration, ornamentation, veneer

overload burden, encumber, op~ press, overburden, overcharge, overtax, saddle (with), strain, weigh down

overlook 1. disregard, fail to notice, forget, ignore, leave out of consid~ eration, leave undone, miss, ne~ glect, omit, pass, slight, slip up on 2. blink at, condone, disregard, ex~ cuse, forgive, let bygones be by~ gones, let one off with, let pass, let ride, make allowances for, pardon, turn a blind eye to, wink at 3. afford a view of, command a view of, front on to, give upon, have a view of, look over *or* out on

overly exceedingly, excessively, immoderately, inordinately, over, too, unduly, very much

overpower beat, conquer, crush, defeat, get the upper hand over, immobilize, knock out, master, overcome, overthrow, overwhelm, quell, subdue, subjugate, vanquish

overpowering compelling, ex~ treme, forceful, invincible, irrefu~ table, irresistible, nauseating, overwhelming, powerful, sicken~ ing, strong, suffocating, telling, un~ bearable, uncontrollable

overrate assess too highly, exag~ gerate, make too much of, over~ estimate, overpraise, overprize, oversell, overvalue, rate too high~ ly, think *or* expect too much of, think too highly of

override annul, cancel, counter~ mand, disregard, ignore, nullify, outweigh, overrule, quash, reverse, ride roughshod over, set aside, supersede, take no account of, trample underfoot, upset, vanquish

overriding cardinal, compelling, determining, dominant, final, ma~ jor, number one, overruling, para~ mount, pivotal, predominant, pre~ vailing, primary, prime, ruling, su~ preme, ultimate

overrule 1. alter, annul, cancel, countermand, disallow, invalidate, make null and void, outvote, over~ ride, overturn, recall, repeal, re~ scind, reverse, revoke, rule against, set aside, veto 2. bend to one's will, control, direct, domi~ nate, govern, influence, prevail over, sway

overrun 1. cut to pieces, invade, massacre, occupy, overwhelm, put to flight, rout, swamp 2. choke, in~ fest, inundate, overflow, overgrow, permeate, ravage, spread like wildfire, spread over, surge over, swarm over 3. exceed, go beyond, overshoot, run over *or* on

overseer boss (*Inf.*), chief, fore~ man, gaffer (*Inf.*), manager, mas~ ter, super (*Inf.*), superintendent, superior, supervisor

overshadow 1. dominate, dwarf, eclipse, excel, leave *or* put in the shade, outshine, outweigh, render insignificant by comparison, rise above, steal the limelight from, surpass, take precedence over, throw into the shade, tower above 2. adumbrate, becloud, bedim, cloud, darken, dim, obfuscate, ob~ scure, veil 3. blight, cast a gloom upon, mar, ruin, spoil, take the edge off, take the pleasure *or* en~ joyment out of, temper

oversight 1. blunder, carelessness, delinquency, error, fault, inatten~ tion, lapse, laxity, mistake, neglect, omission, slip 2. administration, care, charge, control, custody, di~ rection, handling, inspection, keeping, management, superin~ tendence, supervision, surveillance

overt apparent, manifest, observ~ able, obvious, open, patent, plain, public, unconcealed, undisguised, visible

overtake 1. catch up with, do bet~ ter than, draw level with, get past, leave behind, outdistance, outdo, outstrip, overhaul, pass 2. befall, catch unprepared, come upon, en~ gulf, happen, hit, overwhelm, strike, take by surprise

overthrow *v.* 1. abolish, beat, bring down, conquer, crush, defeat, de~

pose, dethrone, do away with, master, oust, overcome, over~ power, overwhelm, subdue, subju~ gate, topple, unseat, vanquish 2. bring to ruin, demolish, destroy, knock down, level, overturn, put an end to, raze, ruin, subvert, upend, upset ~n. 3. defeat, deposition, de~ struction, dethronement, discomfi~ ture, disestablishment, displace~ ment, dispossession, downfall, end, fall, ousting, prostration, rout, ruin, subjugation, subversion, suppres~ sion, undoing, unseating

overtone association, connotation, flavour, hint, implication, innuen~ do, intimation, nuance, sense, sug~ gestion, undercurrent

overture 1. *Often plural* advance, approach, conciliatory move, invi~ tation, offer, opening move, propo~ sal, proposition, signal, tender 2. *Music* introduction, opening, prel~ ude

overturn 1. capsize, keel over, knock over *or* down, overbalance, reverse, spill, tip over, topple, tumble, upend, upset, upturn 2. abolish, annul, bring down, countermand, depose, destroy, in~ validate, overthrow, repeal, re~ scind, reverse, set aside, unseat

overweight *adj.* ample, bulky, chubby, chunky, corpulent, fat, fleshy, gross, heavy, hefty, huge, massive, obese, on the plump side, outsize, plump, podgy, portly, stout, tubby (*Inf.*), well-padded (*Inf.*), well-upholstered (*Inf.*)

overwhelm 1. bury, crush, deluge, engulf, flood, inundate, snow under, submerge, swamp 2. bowl over (*Inf.*), confuse, devastate, knock (someone) for six (*Inf.*), overcome, overpower, prostrate, render speechless, stagger 3. crush, cut to pieces, destroy, massacre, over~ power, overrun, rout

overwhelming breathtaking, crushing, devastating, invincible, irresistible, overpowering, shat~ tering, stunning, towering, uncon~ trollable, vast, vastly superior

overwork be a slave-driver *or* hard

taskmaster to, burden, burn the midnight oil, drive into the ground, exhaust, exploit, fatigue, oppress, overstrain, overtax, overuse, pros~ trate, strain, sweat (*Inf.*), wear out, weary, work one's fingers to the bone

overwrought 1. agitated, beside oneself, distracted, excited, frantic, in a state (tizzy, twitter) (*Inf.*), keyed up, on edge, overexcited, overworked, stirred, strung up (*Inf.*), tense, uptight (*Inf.*), worked up (*Inf.*), wound up (*Inf.*) 2. ba~ roque, busy, contrived, florid, flowery, fussy, overdone, over~ elaborate, overembellished, over~ ornate, rococo

owe be beholden, be in arrears, be in debt, be obligated *or* indebt~ ed, be under an obligation to

owing *adj.* due, outstanding, over~ due, owed, payable, unpaid, unset~ tled

owing to *prep.* as a result of, be~ cause of, on account of

own *adj.* 1. individual, particular, personal, private 2. on one's own alone, by oneself, by one's own ef~ forts, independently, isolated, left to one's own devices, off one's own bat, on one's tod (*Brit. sl.*), singly, (standing) on one's own two feet, unaided, unassisted 3. hold one's own compete, keep going, keep one's end up, keep one's head above water, maintain one's posi~ tion ~v. 4. be in possession of, be responsible for, enjoy, have, hold, keep, possess, retain 5. own up (to) admit, come clean (about) (*Inf.*), confess, make a clean breast of, tell the truth (about) 6. acknowl~ edge, admit, allow, allow to be val~ id, avow, concede, confess, dis~ close, go along with (*Inf.*), grant, recognize

owner holder, landlord, lord, mas~ ter, mistress, possessor, proprietor, proprietress, proprietrix

ownership dominion, possession, proprietary rights, proprietorship, right of possession, title

P

pace *n.* 1. gait, measure, step, stride, tread, walk 2. clip (*Inf.*), lick (*Inf.*), momentum, motion, movement, progress, rate, speed, tempo, time, velocity ~*v.* 3. march, patrol, pound, stride, walk back and forth, walk up and down 4. count, determine, mark out, measure, step

pacific 1. appeasing, conciliatory, diplomatic, irenic, pacificatory, peacemaking, placatory, propitiatory 2. dovelike, dovish, friendly, gentle, mild, nonbelligerent, nonviolent, pacifist, peaceable, peace-loving 3. at peace, calm, halcyon, peaceful, placid, quiet, serene, smooth, still, tranquil, unruffled

pacifist conchie (*Inf.*), conscientious objector, dove, passive resister, peace lover, peacemonger, peacenik (*Inf.*), satyagrahi

pack *n.* 1. back pack, bale, bundle, burden, fardel (*Archaic*), kit, kitbag, knapsack, load, package, packet, parcel, rucksack, truss 2. assemblage, band, bunch, collection, company, crew, crowd, deck, drove, flock, gang, group, herd, lot, mob, set, troop ~*v.* 3. batch, bundle, burden, load, package, packet, store, stow 4. charge, compact, compress, cram, crowd, fill, jam, mob, press, ram, stuff, tamp, throng, wedge 5. *With* off bundle out, dismiss, hustle out, send away, send packing (*Inf.*), send someone about his business

package *n.* 1. box, carton, container, packet, parcel 2. amalgamation, combination, entity, unit, whole ~*v.* 3. batch, box, pack, packet, parcel (up), wrap, wrap up

packed brimful, chock-a-block, chock-full, congested, cram-full, crammed, crowded, filled, full, hoatching (*Scot.*), jammed, jam-packed, loaded *or* full to the gunwales, overflowing, overloaded, packed like sardines, seething, swarming

packet 1. bag, carton, container, package, parcel, poke (*Dialect*), wrapper, wrapping 2. *Sl.* a bob or two (*Brit. inf.*), bomb (*Brit. sl.*), bundle (*Sl.*), fortune, king's ransom (*Inf.*), lot(s), mint, pile (*Inf.*), pot(s) (*Inf.*), pretty penny (*Inf.*), tidy sum (*Inf.*)

pack in 1. attract, cram, draw, fill to capacity, squeeze in 2. *Brit. inf.* cease, chuck (*Inf.*), desist, give up *or* over, jack in, leave off, stop

pack up 1. put away, store, tidy up 2. *Inf.* call it a day (*Inf.*), finish, give up, pack in (*Brit. inf.*) 3. break down, conk out (*Inf.*), fail, give out, stall, stop

pact agreement, alliance, arrangement, bargain, bond, compact, concord, concordat, contract, convention, covenant, deal, league, protocol, treaty, understanding

pad *n.* 1. buffer, cushion, protection, stiffening, stuffing, wad 2. block, jotter, notepad, tablet, writing pad 3. foot, paw, sole 4. *Sl.* apartment, flat, hang-out (*Inf.*), home, place, quarters, room ~*v.* 5. cushion, fill, line, pack, protect, shape, stuff 6. *Often with* out amplify, augment, eke, elaborate, fill out, flesh out, inflate, lengthen, protract, spin out, stretch

padding 1. filling, packing, stuffing, wadding 2. hot air (*Inf.*), prolixity, verbiage, verbosity, waffle (*Inf.*), wordiness

paddle[1] 1. *n.* oar, scull, sweep 2. *v.* oar, propel, pull, row, scull

paddle[2] dabble, plash, slop, splash (about), stir, wade

pagan 1. *n.* Gentile, heathen, idolater, infidel, polytheist, unbeliever 2. *adj.* Gentile, heathen, heathenish, idolatrous, infidel, irreligious, polytheistic

page[1] *n.* 1. folio, leaf, sheet, side 2. chapter, episode, epoch, era, event, incident, period, phase, point, stage, time ~v. 3. foliate, number, paginate

page[2] 1. *n.* attendant, bellboy (*U.S.*), footboy, pageboy, servant, squire 2. *v.* announce, call, call out, preconize, seek, send for, summon

pageant display, extravaganza, parade, procession, ritual, show, spectacle, tableau

pageantry display, drama, extravagance, glamour, glitter, grandeur, magnificence, parade, pomp, show, showiness, spectacle, splash (*Inf.*), splendour, state, theatricality

pain *n.* 1. ache, cramp, discomfort, hurt, irritation, pang, smarting, soreness, spasm, suffering, tenderness, throb, throe (*Rare*), trouble, twinge 2. affliction, agony, anguish, bitterness, distress, grief, heartache, misery, suffering, torment, torture, tribulation, woe, wretchedness 3. *Inf.* aggravation, annoyance, bore, bother, drag (*Sl.*), headache (*Inf.*), irritation, nuisance, pain in the neck (*Inf.*), pest, vexation ~v. 4. ail, chafe, discomfort, harm, hurt, inflame, injure, smart, sting, throb 5. afflict, aggrieve, agonize, cut to the quick, disquiet, distress, grieve, hurt, sadden, torment, torture, vex, worry, wound 6. *Inf.* annoy, exasperate, gall, harass, irritate, rile, vex

pained aggrieved, anguished, distressed, hurt, injured, miffed (*Inf.*), offended, reproachful, stung, unhappy, upset, worried, wounded

painful 1. afflictive, disagreeable, distasteful, distressing, grievous, saddening, unpleasant 2. aching, agonizing, excruciating, harrowing, hurting, inflamed, raw, smarting, sore, tender, throbbing 3. arduous, difficult, hard, laborious, severe, tedious, troublesome, trying, vexatious 4. *Inf.* awful, dire, dreadful, excruciating, extremely bad, terrible

painfully alarmingly, clearly, deplorably, distressingly, dreadfully, excessively, markedly, sadly, unfortunately, woefully

painkiller anaesthetic, analgesic,

anodyne, drug, palliative, remedy, sedative

painless easy, effortless, fast, no trouble, pain-free, quick, simple, trouble-free

pains 1. assiduousness, bother, care, diligence, effort, industry, labour, special attention, trouble 2. birth-pangs, childbirth, contractions, labour

painstaking assiduous, careful, conscientious, diligent, earnest, exacting, hard-working, industrious, meticulous, persevering, punctilious, scrupulous, sedulous, strenuous, thorough, thoroughgoing

paint *n.* 1. colour, colouring, dye, emulsion, pigment, stain, tint 2. *Inf.* cosmetics, face (*Inf.*), greasepaint, make-up, *maquillage*, war paint (*Inf.*) ~v. 3. catch a likeness, delineate, depict, draw, figure, picture, portray, represent, sketch 4. apply, coat, colour, cover, daub, decorate, slap on (*Inf.*) 5. bring to life, capture, conjure up a vision, depict, describe, evoke, make one see, portray, put graphically, recount, tell vividly 6. paint the town red *Inf.* celebrate, go on a binge (*Inf.*), go on a spree, go on the town, live it up (*Inf.*), make merry, make whoopee (*Inf.*), revel

pair 1. *n.* brace, combination, couple, doublet, duo, match, matched set, span, twins, two of a kind, twosome, yoke 2. *v.* bracket, couple, join, marry, match, match up, mate, pair off, put together, team, twin, wed, yoke

palatable 1. appetizing, delectable, delicious, luscious, mouthwatering, savoury, tasty, toothsome 2. acceptable, agreeable, attractive, enjoyable, fair, pleasant, satisfactory

palate 1. appetite, heart, stomach, taste 2. appreciation, enjoyment, gusto, liking, relish, zest

palatial de luxe, grand, grandiose, illustrious, imposing, luxurious, magnificent, majestic, opulent, plush (*Inf.*), regal, spacious, splendid, stately, sumptuous

pale *adj.* 1. anaemic, ashen, ashy, bleached, bloodless, colourless, faded, light, pallid, pasty, sallow, wan, washed-out, white, whitish 2. dim, faint, feeble, inadequate, poor, thin, weak ~*v.* 3. become pale, blanch, go white, lose colour, whiten 4. decrease, dim, diminish, dull, fade, grow dull, lessen, lose lustre

pall *v.* become dull *or* tedious, bore, cloy, glut, jade, satiate, sicken, surfeit, tire, weary

palm[1] 1. hand, mitt (*Sl.*), paw (*Inf.*) 2. **in the palm of one's hand** at one's mercy, in one's clutches (control, power) 3. **grease someone's palm** *Sl.* bribe, buy, corrupt, fix (*Inf.*), give a backhander (*Sl.*), induce, influence, pay off (*Inf.*), square, suborn

palm[2] *Fig.* bays, crown, fame, glory, honour, laurels, merit, prize, success, triumph, trophy, victory

palm off 1. *With on or* with fob off, foist off, pass off 2. *With on* foist on, force upon, impose upon, take advantage of, thrust upon, unload upon

palmy flourishing, fortunate, glorious, golden, halcyon, happy, joyous, luxurious, prosperous, thriving, triumphant

palpable 1. apparent, blatant, clear, conspicuous, evident, manifest, obvious, open, patent, plain, unmistakable, visible 2. concrete, material, real, solid, substantial, tangible, touchable

palpitate beat, flutter, pitapat, pitter-patter, pound, pulsate, pulse, quiver, shiver, throb, tremble, vibrate

palsied arthritic, atonic (*Pathol.*), crippled, debilitated, disabled, helpless, paralysed, paralytic, rheumatic, sclerotic, shaking, shaky, spastic, trembling

palter 1. be evasive, deceive, double-talk, equivocate, fudge, hedge, mislead, prevaricate, shuffle, tergiversate, trifle 2. bargain, barter, chaffer, dicker (*Chiefly U.S.*), haggle, higgle

paltry base, beggarly, contemptible, derisory, despicable, inconsiderable, insignificant, low, meagre, mean, Mickey Mouse (*Sl.*), minor, miserable, petty, picayune (*U.S.*), piddling (*Inf.*), pitiful, poor, puny, slight, small, sorry, trifling, trivial, twopenny-halfpenny (*Brit. inf.*), unimportant, worthless, wretched

pamper baby, cater to one's every whim, coddle, cosset, fondle, gratify, humour, indulge, mollycoddle, pet, spoil

pamphlet booklet, brochure, circular, folder, leaflet, tract

pan[1] *n.* 1. container, pot, saucepan, vessel ~*v.* 2. look for, search for, separate, sift out, wash 3. *Inf.* censure, criticize, flay, hammer (*Brit.*), knock (*Inf.*), roast (*Inf.*), rubbish (*Inf.*), slam (*Sl.*), slate (*Inf.*), throw brickbats at (*Inf.*)

pan[2] *v.* follow, move, scan, sweep, swing, track, traverse

panacea catholicon, cure-all, elixir, nostrum, sovereign remedy, universal cure

panache a flourish, *brio*, dash, élan, flair, flamboyance, spirit, style, swagger, verve

pandemonium babel, bedlam, chaos, clamour, commotion, confusion, din, hubbub, hue and cry, hullabaloo, racket, ruckus (*Inf.*), ruction (*Inf.*), rumpus, tumult, turmoil, uproar

pang ache, agony, anguish, discomfort, distress, gripe, pain, prick, spasm, stab, sting, stitch, throe (*Rare*), twinge, wrench

panic *n.* 1. agitation, alarm, consternation, dismay, fear, fright, horror, hysteria, scare, terror ~*v.* 2. become hysterical, be terror-stricken, go to pieces (*Inf.*), lose one's bottle (*Sl.*), lose one's nerve, overreact 3. alarm, put the wind up (someone) (*Inf.*), scare, startle, terrify, unnerve

panicky afraid, agitated, distressed, fearful, frantic, frenzied, frightened, hysterical, in a flap (*Inf.*), in a tizzy (*Inf.*), jittery (*Inf.*), nervous, windy (*Sl.*), worked up, worried

panic-stricken *or* **panic-struck** aghast, agitated, alarmed, ap-

palled, fearful, frenzied, frightened, frightened out of one's wits, frightened to death, horrified, horror-stricken, hysterical, in a cold sweat (*Inf.*), panicky, petrified, scared, scared stiff, startled, terrified, terror-stricken, unnerved

panoply array, attire, dress, garb, get-up (*Inf.*), insignia, raiment (*Archaic*), regalia, show, trappings, turnout

panorama 1. bird's-eye view, prospect, scenery, scenic view, view, vista 2. overall picture, overview, perspective, survey

panoramic all-embracing, bird's-eye, comprehensive, extensive, far-reaching, general, inclusive, overall, scenic, sweeping, wide

pant *v.* 1. blow, breathe, gasp, heave, huff, palpitate, puff, throb, wheeze 2. *Fig.* ache, covet, crave, desire, hanker after, hunger, long, pine, set one's heart on, sigh, thirst, want, yearn ~*n.* 3. gasp, huff, puff, wheeze

pants 1. *Brit.* boxer shorts, briefs, drawers, knickers, panties, underpants, Y-fronts 2. *U.S.* slacks, trousers

pap 1. baby food, mash, mush, pulp 2. drivel, rubbish, trash, trivia

paper *n.* 1. *Often plural* certificate, deed, documents, instrument, record 2. *Plural* archive, diaries, documents, dossier, file, letters, records 3. daily, gazette, journal, news, newspaper, organ, rag (*Inf.*) 4. analysis, article, assignment, composition, critique, dissertation, essay, examination, monograph, report, script, study, thesis, treatise 5. **on paper** ideally, in the abstract, in theory, theoretically ~*adj.* 6. cardboard, disposable, flimsy, insubstantial, paper-thin, papery, thin ~*v.* 7. cover with paper, hang, line, paste up, wallpaper

papery flimsy, fragile, frail, insubstantial, light, lightweight, paperlike, paper-thin, thin

par *n.* 1. average, level, mean, median, norm, standard, usual 2. balance, equal footing, equality, equilibrium, equivalence, parity 3.

above par excellent, exceptional, first-rate (*Inf.*), outstanding, superior 4. **below par** a. below average, inferior, lacking, not up to scratch (*Inf.*), poor, second-rate, substandard, wanting b. not oneself, off colour (*Chiefly Brit.*), off form, poorly (*Inf.*), sick, under the weather (*Inf.*), unfit, unhealthy 5. **par for the course** average, expected, ordinary, predictable, standard, typical, usual 6. **on a par** equal, much the same, the same, well-matched 7. **up to par** acceptable, adequate, good enough, passable, satisfactory, up to scratch (*Inf.*), up to the mark

parable allegory, exemplum, fable, lesson, moral tale, story

parade *n.* 1. array, cavalcade, ceremony, column, march, pageant, procession, review, spectacle, train 2. array, display, exhibition, flaunting, ostentation, pomp, show, spectacle, vaunting ~*v.* 3. defile, march, process 4. air, brandish, display, exhibit, flaunt, make a show of, show, show off (*Inf.*), strut, swagger, vaunt

paradise 1. City of God, divine abode, Elysian fields, garden of delights (*Islam*), heaven, heavenly kingdom, Olympus (*Poetic*), Promised Land, Zion 2. Eden, Garden of Eden 3. bliss, delight, felicity, heaven, seventh heaven, utopia

paradox absurdity, ambiguity, anomaly, contradiction, enigma, inconsistency, mystery, oddity, puzzle

paradoxical absurd, ambiguous, baffling, confounding, contradictory, enigmatic, equivocal, illogical, impossible, improbable, inconsistent, puzzling, riddling

paragon apotheosis, archetype, criterion, cynosure, epitome, exemplar, ideal, jewel, masterpiece, model, nonesuch (*Archaic*), nonpareil, paradigm, pattern, prototype, quintessence, standard

paragraph clause, item, notice, part, passage, portion, section, subdivision

parallel *adj.* 1. aligned, alongside,

coextensive, equidistant, side by side 2. akin, analogous, complementary, correspondent, corresponding, like, matching, resembling, similar, uniform ~n. 3. analogue, complement, corollary, counterpart, duplicate, equal, equivalent, likeness, match, twin 4. analogy, comparison, correlation, correspondence, likeness, parallelism, resemblance, similarity ~v. 5. agree, be alike, chime with, compare, complement, conform, correlate, correspond, equal, keep pace (with), match

paralyse 1. cripple, debilitate, disable, incapacitate, lame 2. anaesthetize, arrest, benumb, freeze, halt, immobilize, numb, petrify, stop dead, stun, stupefy, transfix

paralysis 1. immobility, palsy, paresis (*Pathol.*) 2. arrest, breakdown, halt, shutdown, stagnation, standstill, stoppage

paralytic *adj.* 1. crippled, disabled, immobile, immobilized, incapacitated, lame, numb, palsied, paralysed 2. *Inf.* canned (*Sl.*), drunk, inebriated, intoxicated, legless (*Inf.*), pie-eyed (*Sl.*), plastered (*Sl.*), sloshed (*Sl.*), smashed (*Sl.*), stewed (*Sl.*), stoned (*Sl.*)

parameter constant, criterion, framework, guideline, limit, limitation, restriction, specification

paramount capital, cardinal, chief, dominant, eminent, first, foremost, main, outstanding, predominant, pre-eminent, primary, prime, principal, superior, supreme

paraphernalia accoutrements, apparatus, appurtenances, baggage, belongings, clobber (*Brit. sl.*), effects, equipage, equipment, gear, impedimenta, material, stuff, tackle, things, trappings

paraphrase 1. *n.* interpretation, rehash, rendering, rendition, rephrasing, restatement, rewording, translation, version 2. *v.* express in other words *or* one's own words, interpret, rehash, render, rephrase, restate, reword

parasite bloodsucker (*Inf.*), cadger, drone (*Brit.*), hanger-on, leech,

scrounger (*Inf.*), sponge (*Inf.*), sponger (*Inf.*)

parasitic, parasitical bloodsucking (*Inf.*), cadging, leechlike, scrounging (*Inf.*), sponging (*Inf.*)

parcel *n.* 1. bundle, carton, pack, package, packet 2. band, batch, bunch, collection, company, crew, crowd, gang, group, lot, pack 3. piece of land, plot, property, tract ~v. 4. *Often with up* do up, pack, package, tie up, wrap 5. *Often with out* allocate, allot, apportion, carve up, deal out, dispense, distribute, divide, dole out, mete out, portion, share out, split up

parch blister, burn, dehydrate, desiccate, dry up, evaporate, make thirsty, scorch, sear, shrivel, wither

parched arid, dehydrated, dried out *or* up, drouthy (*Scot.*), dry, scorched, shrivelled, thirsty, waterless, withered

parching *adj.* baking, blistering, burning, dry, drying, hot, roasting (*Inf.*), scorching, searing, sweltering, withering

pardon 1. *v.* absolve, acquit, amnesty, condone, exculpate, excuse, exonerate, forgive, free, let off (*Inf.*), liberate, overlook, release, remit, reprieve 2. *n.* absolution, acquittal, allowance, amnesty, condonation, discharge, excuse, exoneration, forgiveness, grace, indulgence, mercy, release, remission, reprieve

pardonable allowable, condonable, excusable, forgivable, minor, not serious, permissible, understandable, venial

parent 1. begetter, father, guardian, mother, procreator, progenitor, sire 2. architect, author, cause, creator, forerunner, origin, originator, prototype, root, source, wellspring

parentage ancestry, birth, derivation, descent, extraction, family, line, lineage, origin, paternity, pedigree, race, stirps, stock

pariah exile, leper, outcast, outlaw, undesirable, unperson, untouchable

parish church, churchgoers, community, congregation, flock, fold, parishioners

parity 1. consistency, equality, equal terms, equivalence, par, parallelism, quits (*Inf.*), uniformity, unity **2.** affinity, agreement, analogy, conformity, congruity, correspondence, likeness, resemblance, sameness, similarity, similitude

park 1. *n.* estate, garden, grounds, parkland, pleasure garden, recreation ground, woodland **2.** *v.* leave, manoeuvre, position, station

parley 1. *n.* colloquy, confab (*Inf.*), conference, council, dialogue, discussion, meeting, palaver, powwow, talk(s) **2.** *v.* confabulate, confer, deliberate, discuss, negotiate, palaver, powwow, speak, talk

parliament 1. assembly, congress, convocation, council, diet, legislature, senate, talking shop (*Inf.*) **2. Parliament** Houses of Parliament, Mother of Parliaments, the House, the House of Commons and the House of Lords, Westminster

parliamentary congressional, deliberative, governmental, lawgiving, lawmaking, legislative

parlour best room, drawing room, front room, lounge, reception room, sitting room

parlous chancy (*Inf.*), dangerous, desperate, difficult, dire, hairy (*Sl.*), hazardous, perilous, risky

parochial insular, inward-looking, limited, narrow, narrow-minded, parish-pump, petty, provincial, restricted, small-minded

parody *n.* **1.** burlesque, caricature, imitation, lampoon, satire, send-up (*Brit. inf.*), skit, spoof (*Inf.*), takeoff (*Inf.*) **2.** apology, caricature, farce, mockery, travesty ~*v.* **3.** burlesque, caricature, do a takeoff of (*Inf.*), lampoon, mimic, poke fun at, satirize, send up (*Brit. inf.*), spoof (*Inf.*), take off (*Inf.*), travesty

paroxysm attack, convulsion, eruption, fit, flare-up (*Inf.*), outburst, seizure, spasm

parrot *n.* **1.** *Fig.* copycat (*Inf.*), imitator, (little) echo, mimic **2. parrot-fashion** *Inf.* by rote, mechanically, mindlessly ~*v.* **3.** copy, echo, imitate, mimic, reiterate, repeat

parry 1. block, deflect, fend off, hold at bay, rebuff, repel, repulse, stave off, ward off **2.** avoid, circumvent, dodge, duck (*Inf.*), evade, fence, fight shy of, shun, sidestep

parsimonious cheeseparing, close, close-fisted, frugal, grasping, mean, mingy (*Brit. inf.*), miserable, miserly, near (*Inf.*), niggardly, penny-pinching (*Inf.*), penurious, saving, scrimpy, skinflinty, sparing, stingy, stinting, tightfisted

parsimony frugality, meanness, minginess (*Brit. inf.*), miserliness, nearness (*Inf.*), niggardliness, penny-pinching (*Inf.*), stinginess, tightness

parson churchman, clergyman, cleric, divine, ecclesiastic, incumbent, man of God, man of the cloth, minister, pastor, preacher, priest, rector, reverend (*Inf.*), vicar

part *n.* **1.** bit, fraction, fragment, lot, particle, piece, portion, scrap, section, sector, segment, share, slice **2.** branch, component, constituent, department, division, element, ingredient, limb, member, module, organ, piece, unit **3.** behalf, cause, concern, faction, interest, party, side **4.** bit, business, capacity, charge, duty, function, involvement, office, place, responsibility, role, say, share, task, work **5.** *Theat.* character, lines, role **6.** *Often plural* airt (*Scot.*), area, district, neck of the woods (*Inf.*), neighbourhood, quarter, region, territory, vicinity **7. for the most part** chiefly, generally, in the main, largely, mainly, mostly, on the whole, principally **8. in good part** cheerfully, cordially, goodnaturedly, well, without offence **9. in part** a little, in some measure, partially, partly, slightly, somewhat, to a certain extent, to some degree **10. on the part of** for the sake of, in support of, in the name of, on behalf of **11. take part in** associate oneself with, be instrumental in, be involved in, have a

hand in, join in, partake in, par~
ticipate in, play a part in, put one's
twopence-worth in, take a hand in
~v. 12. break, cleave, come apart,
detach, disconnect, disjoin, dis~
mantle, disunite, divide, rend,
separate, sever, split, tear 13.
break up, depart, go, go away, go
(their) separate ways, leave, part
company, quit, say goodbye, sepa~
rate, split up, take one's leave,
withdraw 14. part with abandon,
discard, forgo, give up, let go of,
relinquish, renounce, sacrifice,
surrender, yield

partake 1. With in engage, enter
into, participate, share, take part
2. With of consume, eat, receive,
share, take 3. With of evince,
evoke, have the quality of, show,
suggest

partial 1. fragmentary, imperfect,
incomplete, limited, uncompleted,
unfinished 2. biased, discrimina~
tory, influenced, interested, one-
sided, partisan, predisposed,
prejudiced, tendentious, unfair,
unjust 3. be partial to be fond of,
be keen on, be taken with, care for,
have a liking (soft spot, weakness)
for

partiality 1. bias, favouritism, par~
tisanship, predisposition, prefer~
ence, prejudice 2. affinity, fond~
ness, inclination, liking, love, pen~
chant, predilection, predisposition,
preference, proclivity, taste,
weakness

partially fractionally, halfway, in~
completely, in part, moderately,
not wholly, partly, piecemeal,
somewhat, to a certain extent or
degree

participant associate, contributor,
member, partaker, participator,
party, shareholder

participate be a participant, be a
party to, engage in, enter into, get
in on the act, have a hand in, join
in, partake, perform, share, take
part

participation assistance, contribu~
tion, involvement, joining in, par~
taking, partnership, sharing in,
taking part

particle atom, bit, crumb, grain,
iota, jot, mite, molecule, mote,
piece, scrap, shred, speck, tittle,
whit

particular adj. 1. distinct, exact,
express, peculiar, precise, special,
specific 2. especial, exceptional,
marked, notable, noteworthy, re~
markable, singular, uncommon,
unusual 3. blow-by-blow, circum~
stantial, detailed, itemized, minute,
painstaking, precise, selective,
thorough 4. choosy (Inf.), critical,
dainty, demanding, discriminating,
exacting, fastidious, finicky, fussy,
meticulous, nice (Rare), overnice,
pernickety (Inf.), picky (Inf.) ~n. 5.
Usually plural circumstance, de~
tail, fact, feature, item, specifica~
tion 6. in particular distinctly, es~
pecially, exactly, expressly, par~
ticularly, specifically

particularly 1. decidedly, especial~
ly, exceptionally, markedly, no~
tably, outstandingly, peculiarly,
singularly, surprisingly, uncom~
monly, unusually 2. distinctly, es~
pecially, explicitly, expressly, in
particular, specifically

parting n. 1. adieu, departure,
farewell, going, goodbye, leave-
taking, valediction 2. breaking, de~
tachment, divergence, division,
partition, rift, rupture, separation,
split ~adj. 3. departing, farewell,
final, last, valedictory

partisan n. 1. adherent, backer,
champion, devotee, disciple, fol~
lower, stalwart, supporter, uphold~
er, votary ~adj. 2. biased, faction~
al, interested, one-sided, partial,
prejudiced, sectarian, tendentious
~n. 3. guerrilla, irregular, resis~
tance fighter, underground fighter
~adj. 4. guerrilla, irregular, resis~
tance, underground

partition n. 1. dividing, division,
segregation, separation, sever~
ance, splitting 2. barrier, divider,
room divider, screen, wall 3. allot~
ment, apportionment, distribution,
portion, rationing out, share ~v. 4.
apportion, cut up, divide, parcel
out, portion, section, segment,
separate, share, split up, subdivide

5. divide, fence off, screen, separate, wall off

partly halfway, incompletely, in part, in some measure, not fully, partially, relatively, slightly, somewhat, to a certain degree *or* extent, up to a certain point

partner 1. accomplice, ally, associate, bedfellow, collaborator, colleague, companion, comrade, confederate, copartner, helper, mate, participant, team-mate 2. bedfellow, consort, helpmate, husband, mate, spouse, wife

partnership 1. companionship, connection, cooperation, copartnership, fellowship, interest, participation, sharing 2. alliance, association, combine, company, conglomerate, cooperative, corporation, firm, house, society, union

parts 1. ability, accomplishments, attributes, calibre, capabilities, endowments, faculties, genius, gifts, intellect, intelligence, talents 2. bits and pieces, components, spare parts, spares

party 1. at-home, bash (*Inf.*), celebration, do (*Inf.*), festivity, function, gathering, get-together (*Inf.*), knees-up (*Brit. inf.*), rave-up (*Brit. sl.*), reception, shindig (*Sl.*), social, social gathering, soirée 2. band, body, bunch (*Inf.*), company, crew, detachment (*Military*), gang, gathering, group, squad, team, unit 3. alliance, association, cabal, clique, coalition, combination, confederacy, coterie, faction, grouping, league, set, side 4. individual, person, somebody, someone 5. *Law* contractor (*Law*), defendant, litigant, participant, plaintiff

pass¹ *v.* 1. depart, elapse, flow, go, go by *or* past, lapse, leave, move, move onwards, proceed, roll, run 2. beat, exceed, excel, go beyond, outdistance, outdo, outstrip, surmount, surpass, transcend 3. answer, come up to scratch (*Inf.*), do, get through, graduate, pass muster, qualify, succeed, suffice, suit 4. beguile, devote, employ, experience, fill, occupy, spend, suffer, undergo, while away 5. befall, come up, de-

velop, fall out, happen, occur, take place 6. convey, deliver, exchange, give, hand, kick, let have, reach, send, throw, transfer, transmit 7. accept, adopt, approve, authorize, decree, enact, establish, legislate, ordain, ratify, sanction, validate 8. declare, deliver, express, pronounce, utter 9. disregard, ignore, miss, neglect, not heed, omit, overlook, skip (*Inf.*) 10. defecate, discharge, eliminate, empty, evacuate, excrete, expel, void 11. blow over, cease, die, disappear, dissolve, dwindle, ebb, end, evaporate, expire, fade, go, melt away, terminate, vanish, wane 12. *With* for *or* as be accepted as, be mistaken for, be regarded as, be taken for, impersonate, serve as

pass² *n.* 1. canyon, col, defile, gap, gorge, ravine 2. authorization, identification, licence, passport, permission, permit, safe-conduct, ticket, warrant 3. *Inf.* advances, approach, overture, play (*Inf.*), proposition, suggestion 4. condition, juncture, pinch, plight, predicament, situation, stage, state, state of affairs, straits 5. feint, jab, lunge, push, swing, thrust

passable 1. acceptable, adequate, admissible, allowable, all right, average, fair, fair enough, mediocre, middling, moderate, not too bad, ordinary, presentable, so-so (*Inf.*), tolerable, unexceptional 2. clear, crossable, navigable, open, traversable, unobstructed

passage 1. avenue, channel, course, lane, opening, path, road, route, thoroughfare, way 2. corridor, doorway, entrance, entrance hall, exit, hall, hallway, lobby, passageway, vestibule 3. clause, excerpt, extract, paragraph, piece, quotation, reading, section, sentence, text, verse 4. crossing, journey, tour, trek, trip, voyage 5. advance, change, conversion, flow, motion, movement, passing, progress, progression, transit, transition 6. allowance, authorization, freedom, permission, right, safe-conduct, visa, warrant 7. acceptance, enactment, establishment, legalization, legislation, passing, ratification

pass away croak (*Sl.*), decease, depart (this life), die, expire, pass on, pass over, peg out (*Inf.*), shuffle off this mortal coil, snuff it (*Inf.*)

pass by 1. go past, leave, move past, pass 2. disregard, miss, neglect, not choose, overlook, pass over

passenger fare, hitchhiker, pillion rider, rider, traveller

passer-by bystander, onlooker, witness

passing *adj.* 1. brief, ephemeral, fleeting, momentary, short, short-lived, temporary, transient, transitory 2. casual, cursory, glancing, hasty, quick, shallow, short, slight, superficial ~*n.* 3. death, decease, demise, end, finish, loss, termination 4. **in passing** accidentally, by the bye, by the way, en passant, incidentally, on the way

passion 1. animation, ardour, eagerness, emotion, excitement, feeling, fervour, fire, heat, intensity, joy, rapture, spirit, transport, warmth, zeal, zest 2. adoration, affection, ardour, attachment, concupiscence, desire, fondness, infatuation, itch, keenness, love, lust 3. bug (*Inf.*), craving, craze, enthusiasm, fancy, fascination, idol, infatuation, mania, obsession 4. anger, fit, flare-up (*Inf.*), frenzy, fury, indignation, ire, outburst, paroxysm, rage, resentment, storm, vehemence, wrath

passionate 1. amorous, ardent, aroused, desirous, erotic, hot, loving, lustful, sensual, sexy (*Inf.*), wanton 2. animated, ardent, eager, emotional, enthusiastic, excited, fervent, fervid, fierce, frenzied, heartfelt, impassioned, impetuous, impulsive, intense, strong, vehement, warm, wild, zealous 3. choleric, excitable, fiery, hot-headed, hot-tempered, irascible, irritable, peppery, quick-tempered, stormy, tempestuous, violent

passive acquiescent, compliant, docile, enduring, inactive, inert, lifeless, long-suffering, nonviolent, patient, quiescent, receptive, resigned, submissive, unassertive, uninvolved, unresisting

pass off 1. counterfeit, fake, feign, make a pretence of, palm off 2. come to an end, die away, disappear, fade out, vanish 3. emit, evaporate, give off, send forth, vaporize 4. be completed, go off, happen, occur, take place, turn out 5. dismiss, disregard, ignore, pass by, wink at

pass out 1. *Inf.* become unconscious, black out (*Inf.*), drop, faint, flake out (*Inf.*), keel over (*Inf.*), lose consciousness, swoon (*Literary*) 2. deal out, distribute, dole out, hand out

pass over disregard, forget, ignore, not dwell on, omit, overlook, pass by, take no notice of

pass up decline, forgo, give (something) a miss (*Inf.*), ignore, let go, let slip, miss, neglect, refuse, reject

password countersign, key word, open sesame, signal, watchword

past *adj.* 1. accomplished, completed, done, elapsed, ended, extinct, finished, forgotten, gone, over, over and done with, spent 2. ancient, bygone, early, erstwhile, foregoing, former, late, long-ago, olden, preceding, previous, prior, quondam, recent ~*n.* 3. **the past** antiquity, days gone by, days of yore, former times, good old days, history, long ago, olden days, old times, times past, yesteryear (*Literary*) 4. background, experience, history, life, past life ~*adv.* 5. across, beyond, by, on, over ~*prep.* 6. after, beyond, farther than, later than, outside, over, subsequent to

paste 1. *n.* adhesive, cement, glue, gum, mucilage 2. *v.* cement, fasten, fix, glue, gum, stick

pastel *adj.* delicate, light, muted, pale, soft, soft-hued

pastiche blend, farrago, gallimaufry, hotchpotch, medley, *mélange*, miscellany, mixture, motley

pastime activity, amusement, distraction, diversion, entertainment,

game, hobby, leisure, play, recrea~
tion, relaxation, sport

past master ace (*Inf.*), artist, dab
hand (*Brit. inf.*), expert, old hand,
virtuoso, wizard

pastor churchman, clergyman, di~
vine, ecclesiastic, minister, parson,
priest, rector, vicar

pastoral *adj.* 1. Arcadian, bucolic,
country, georgic (*Literary*), idyllic,
rural, rustic, simple 2. clerical, ec~
clesiastical, ministerial, priestly

pasture grass, grassland, grazing,
grazing land, lea (*Poetic*), mead~
ow, pasturage, shieling (*Scot.*)

pat *v.* 1. caress, dab, fondle, pet,
slap, stroke, tap, touch ~*n.* 2. clap,
dab, light blow, slap, stroke, tap 3.
cake, dab, lump, portion, small
piece

patch *n.* 1. piece of material, re~
inforcement 2. bit, scrap, shred,
small piece, spot, stretch 3. area,
ground, land, plot, tract ~*v.* 4. cov~
er, fix, mend, reinforce, repair,
sew up 5. *With up* bury the hatch~
et, conciliate, make friends, pla~
cate, restore, settle, settle differ~
ences, smooth

patchwork confusion, hash, hotch~
potch, jumble, medley, mishmash,
mixture, pastiche

patchy bitty, erratic, fitful, irregu~
lar, random, sketchy, spotty, un~
even, variable, varying

patent 1. *adj.* apparent, blatant,
clear, conspicuous, downright, evi~
dent, flagrant, glaring, indisput~
able, manifest, obvious, open, pal~
pable, transparent, unconcealed,
unequivocal, unmistakable 2. *n.*
copyright, invention, licence

paternal 1. benevolent, concerned,
fatherlike, fatherly, protective, so~
licitous, vigilant 2. patrilineal, pat~
rimonial

paternity 1. fatherhood, fathership
2. descent, extraction, family, line~
age, parentage 3. authorship, deri~
vation, origin, source

path 1. footpath, footway, pathway,
towpath, track, trail, walkway
(*Chiefly U.S.*) 2. avenue, course,
direction, passage, procedure,
road, route, track, walk, way

pathetic 1. affecting, distressing,
heartbreaking,   heart-rending,
melting, moving, pitiable, plain~
tive, poignant, sad, tender, touch~
ing 2. deplorable, feeble, inad~
equate, lamentable, meagre, mis~
erable, paltry, petty, pitiful, poor,
puny, sorry, wet (*Brit. inf.*), woeful
3. *Sl.* crummy (*Sl.*), rubbishy,
trashy,   uninteresting,   useless,
worthless

pathfinder discoverer, explorer,
guide, pioneer, scout, trailblazer

pathless impassable, impen~
etrable, trackless, uncharted, un~
explored, untrodden, waste, wild

pathos pitiableness, pitifulness,
plaintiveness, poignancy, sadness

patience 1. calmness, composure,
cool (*Sl.*), equanimity, even tem~
per, forbearance, imperturbability,
restraint, serenity, sufferance, tol~
erance, toleration 2. constancy,
diligence, endurance, fortitude,
long-suffering, perseverance, per~
sistence,   resignation,   stoicism,
submission

patient *adj.* 1. calm, composed, en~
during, long-suffering, persevering,
persistent, philosophical, quiet, re~
signed, self-possessed, serene, stoi~
cal, submissive, uncomplaining,
untiring 2. accommodating, even-
tempered, forbearing, forgiving,
indulgent, lenient, mild, tolerant,
understanding ~*n.* 3. case, invalid,
sick person, sufferer

patriot chauvinist, flag-waver
(*Inf.*), jingo, lover of one's country,
loyalist, nationalist

patriotic chauvinistic, flag-waving
(*Inf.*), jingoistic, loyal, nationalistic

patriotism flag-waving (*Inf.*), jin~
goism, love of one's country, loyal~
ty, nationalism

patrol *n.* 1. guarding, policing, pro~
tecting, rounds, safeguarding, vigi~
lance, watching 2. garrison, guard,
patrolman, sentinel, watch, watch~
man ~*v.* 3. cruise, guard, inspect,
keep guard, keep watch, make the
rounds, police, pound, range, safe~
guard, walk the beat

patron 1. advocate, angel (*Inf.*),
backer, benefactor, champion, de~

fender, friend, guardian, helper, philanthropist, protector, sponsor, supporter 2. buyer, client, customer, frequenter, habitué, shopper

patronage 1. aid, assistance, backing, benefaction, championship, encouragement, help, promotion, sponsorship, support 2. business, clientele, commerce, custom, trade, trading, traffic 3. condescension, deigning, disdain, patronizing, stooping

patronize 1. be lofty with, look down on, talk down to, treat as inferior, treat condescendingly, treat like a child 2. assist, back, befriend, foster, fund, help, maintain, promote, sponsor, subscribe to, support 3. be a customer *or* client of, buy from, deal with, do business with, frequent, shop at, trade with

patronizing condescending, contemptuous, disdainful, gracious, haughty, lofty, snobbish, stooping, supercilious, superior, toffee-nosed (*Sl.*)

patter[1] *v.* 1. scurry, scuttle, skip, tiptoe, trip, walk lightly 2. beat, pat, pelt, pitapat, pitter-patter, rat-a-tat, spatter, tap ~*n.* 3. pattering, pitapat, pitter-patter, tapping

patter[2] *n.* 1. line, monologue, pitch, spiel (*Inf.*) 2. chatter, gabble, jabber, nattering, prattle, yak (*Sl.*) 3. argot, cant, jargon, lingo (*Inf.*), patois, slang, vernacular ~*v.* 4. babble, blab, chatter, hold forth, jabber, prate, rattle off, rattle on, spiel (*Inf.*), spout (*Inf.*), tattle

pattern *n.* 1. arrangement, decoration, decorative design, design, device, figure, motif, ornament 2. arrangement, method, order, orderliness, plan, sequence, system 3. kind, shape, sort, style, type, variety 4. design, diagram, guide, instructions, original, plan, stencil, template 5. archetype, criterion, cynosure, example, exemplar, guide, model, norm, original, paradigm, paragon, prototype, sample, specimen, standard ~*v.* 6. copy, emulate, follow, form, imitate,

model, mould, order, shape, style 7. decorate, design, trim

paucity dearth, deficiency, fewness, insufficiency, lack, meagreness, paltriness, poverty, rarity, scantiness, scarcity, shortage, slenderness, slightness, smallness, sparseness, sparsity

paunch abdomen, beer-belly (*Sl.*), belly, corporation (*Brit. inf.*), pot, potbelly

pauper bankrupt, beggar, downand-out, have-not, indigent, insolvent, mendicant, poor person

pause 1. *v.* break, cease, delay, deliberate, desist, discontinue, halt, have a breather (*Inf.*), hesitate, interrupt, rest, stop briefly, take a break, wait, waver 2. *n.* break, breather (*Inf.*), caesura, cessation, delay, discontinuance, gap, halt, hesitation, interlude, intermission, interruption, interval, let-up (*Inf.*), lull, respite, rest, stay, stoppage, wait

pave asphalt, concrete, cover, flag, floor, macadamize, surface, tar, tile

paw *v.* grab, handle roughly, manhandle, maul, molest

pawn[1] 1. *v.* deposit, gage (*Archaic*), hazard, hock (*Inf., chiefly U.S.*), mortgage, pledge, pop (*Inf.*), stake, wager 2. *n.* assurance, bond, collateral, gage, guarantee, guaranty, pledge, security

pawn[2] *n.* cat's-paw, creature, dupe, instrument, plaything, puppet, stooge (*Sl.*), tool, toy

pay *v.* 1. clear, compensate, cough up (*Inf.*), discharge, foot, give, honour, liquidate, meet, offer, recompense, reimburse, remit, remunerate, render, requite, reward, settle, square up 2. be advantageous, benefit, be worthwhile, repay, serve 3. bestow, extend, give, grant, present, proffer, render 4. *Often with* **for** answer for, atone, be punished, compensate, get one's deserts, make amends, suffer, suffer the consequences 5. bring in, produce, profit, return, yield 6. be profitable, be remunerative, make a return, make money, provide a living 7. avenge oneself for, get even with (*Inf.*), get revenge on, pay back, punish, reciprocate, repay, requite, settle a score ~*n.* 8. allowance, compensation, earnings, emoluments, fee, hire, income, payment, recompense, reimbursement, remuneration, reward, salary, stipend, takings, wages

payable due, mature, obligatory, outstanding, owed, owing, receivable, to be paid

pay back 1. get even with (*Inf.*), get one's own back, reciprocate, recompense, retaliate, settle a score 2. refund, reimburse, repay, return, settle up, square

payment 1. defrayal, discharge, outlay, paying, remittance, settlement 2. advance, deposit, instalment, portion, premium, remittance 3. fee, hire, remuneration, reward, wage

pay off 1. discharge, dismiss, fire, lay off, let go, sack (*Inf.*) 2. clear, discharge, liquidate, pay in full, settle, square 3. be effective (profitable, successful), succeed, work 4. get even with (*Inf.*), pay back, retaliate, settle a score 5. *Inf.* bribe, buy off, corrupt, get at, grease the palm of (*Sl.*), oil (*Inf.*), suborn

pay out 1. cough up (*Inf.*), disburse, expend, fork out *or* over *or* up (*Sl.*), lay out (*Inf.*), shell out (*Inf.*), spend 2. get even with (*Inf.*), pay back, retaliate, settle a score

peace 1. accord, agreement, amity, concord, harmony 2. armistice, cessation of hostilities, conciliation, pacification, treaty, truce 3. calm, composure, contentment, placidity, relaxation, repose, serenity 4. calm, calmness, hush, peacefulness, quiet, quietude, repose, rest, silence, stillness, tranquillity

peaceable 1. amiable, amicable, conciliatory, dovish, friendly, gentle, inoffensive, mild, nonbelligerent, pacific, peaceful, peace-loving, placid, unwarlike 2. balmy, calm,

peaceful, quiet, restful, serene, still, tranquil, undisturbed

peaceful 1. amicable, at peace, free from strife, friendly, harmonious, nonviolent, on friendly *or* good terms, without hostility 2. calm, gentle, placid, quiet, restful, serene, still, tranquil, undisturbed, unruffled, untroubled 3. conciliatory, irenic, pacific, peaceable, peace-loving, placatory, unwarlike

peacemaker appeaser, arbitrator, conciliator, mediator, pacifier, peacemonger

peak *n.* 1. aiguille, apex, brow, crest, pinnacle, point, summit, tip, top 2. acme, apogee, climax, crown, culmination, high point, maximum point, *ne plus ultra*, zenith ~*v.* 3. be at its height, climax, come to a head, culminate, reach its highest point, reach the zenith

peal 1. *n.* blast, carillon, chime, clamour, clang, clap, crash, resounding, reverberation, ring, ringing, roar, rumble, sound, tintinnabulation 2. *v.* chime, crack, crash, resonate, resound, reverberate, ring, roar, roll, rumble, sound, tintinnabulate, toll

peasant 1. churl (*Archaic*), countryman, hind (*Archaic*), rustic, son of the soil, swain (*Archaic*) 2. *Inf.* boor, churl, country bumpkin, lout, provincial, yokel

peccadillo error, indiscretion, infraction, lapse, misdeed, misdemeanour, petty offence, slip, trifling fault

peck *v./n.* bite, dig, hit, jab, kiss, nibble, pick, poke, prick, strike, tap

peculiar 1. abnormal, bizarre, curious, eccentric, exceptional, extraordinary, far-out (*Sl.*), freakish, funny, odd, offbeat, outlandish, out-of-the-way, quaint, queer, singular, strange, uncommon, unconventional, unusual, weird 2. appropriate, characteristic, distinct, distinctive, distinguishing, endemic, idiosyncratic, individual, local, particular, personal, private, restricted, special, specific, unique

peculiarity 1. abnormality, bizarreness, eccentricity, foible, freakishness, idiosyncrasy, mannerism, oddity, odd trait, queerness, quirk 2. attribute, characteristic, distinctiveness, feature, mark, particularity, property, quality, singularity, speciality, trait

pedagogue dogmatist, dominie (*Scot.*), educator, instructor, master, mistress, pedant, schoolmaster, schoolmistress, teacher

pedantic abstruse, academic, bookish, didactic, donnish, erudite, formal, fussy, hairsplitting, nitpicking (*Inf.*), overnice, particular, pedagogic, pompous, precise, priggish, punctilious, scholastic, schoolmasterly, sententious, stilted

pedantry bookishness, finicality, hairsplitting, overnicety, pedagogism, pettifoggery, pomposity, punctiliousness, quibbling, sophistry, stuffiness

peddle flog (*Sl.*), hawk, huckster, market, push (*Inf.*), sell, sell door to door, trade, vend

pedestal 1. base, dado (*Architect.*), foot, foundation, mounting, pier, plinth, socle, stand, support 2. **put on a pedestal** apotheosize, deify, dignify, ennoble, exalt, glorify, idealize, worship

pedestrian 1. *n.* footslogger, foottraveller, walker 2. *adj.* banal, boring, commonplace, dull, flat, humdrum, mediocre, mundane, ordinary, plodding, prosaic, run-of-the-mill, unimaginative, uninspired, uninteresting

pedigree 1. *n.* ancestry, blood, breed, derivation, descent, extraction, family, family tree, genealogy, heritage, line, lineage, race, stemma, stirps, stock 2. *adj.* full-blooded, purebred, thoroughbred

peek 1. *v.* glance, keek (*Scot.*), look, peep, peer, snatch a glimpse, sneak a look, spy, squinny, take *or* have a gander (*Inf.*), take a look 2. *n.* blink, gander (*Inf.*), glance, glim (*Scot.*), glimpse, keek (*Scot.*), look, look-see (*Sl.*), peep

peel 1. *v.* decorticate, desquamate, flake off, pare, scale, skin, strip off

2. *n.* epicarp, exocarp, peeling, rind, skin

peep *v.* 1. keek (*Scot.*), look from hiding, look surreptitiously, peek, peer, sneak a look, spy, steal a look 2. appear briefly, emerge, peer out, show partially ~*n.* 3. gander (*Inf.*), glim (*Scot.*), glimpse, keek (*Scot.*), look, look-see (*Sl.*), peek

peephole aperture, chink, crack, crevice, fissure, hole, keyhole, opening, pinhole, slit, spyhole

peer[1] *n.* 1. aristocrat, baron, count, duke, earl, lord, marquess, marquis, noble, nobleman, viscount 2. coequal, compeer, equal, fellow, like, match

peer[2] *v.* 1. gaze, inspect, peep, scan, scrutinize, snoop, spy, squinny, squint 2. appear, become visible, emerge, peep out

peerage aristocracy, lords and ladies, nobility, peers, titled classes

peerless beyond compare, excellent, incomparable, matchless, nonpareil, outstanding, second to none, superlative, unequalled, unique, unmatched, unparalleled, unrivalled, unsurpassed

peevish acrimonious, cantankerous, captious, childish, churlish, crabbed, cross, crotchety (*Inf.*), crusty, fractious, fretful, grumpy, ill-natured, ill-tempered, irritable, pettish, petulant, querulous, ratty (*Brit. sl.*), short-tempered, snappy, splenetic, sulky, sullen, surly, testy, touchy, waspish, whingeing (*Inf.*)

peg *v.* 1. attach, fasten, fix, join, make fast, secure 2. *With* **along** *or* **away** apply oneself to, beaver away (*Brit. inf.*), keep at it, keep going, keep on, persist, plod along, plug away at (*Inf.*), stick to it, work at, work away 3. *Of prices, etc.* control, fix, freeze, limit, set

pelt *v.* 1. assail, batter, beat, belabour, bombard, cast, hurl, pepper, pummel, shower, sling, strike, thrash, throw, wallop (*Inf.*) 2. belt (*Sl.*), career, charge, dash, hurry, run fast, rush, shoot, speed, tear, whiz (*Inf.*) 3. bucket down (*Inf.*), pour, rain cats and dogs (*Inf.*), rain hard, teem

pen[1] *v.* commit to paper, compose, draft, draw up, jot down, write

pen[2] 1. *n.* cage, coop, enclosure, fold, hutch, sty 2. *v.* cage, confine, coop up, enclose, fence in, hedge, hem in, hurdle, mew (up), shut up *or* in

penal corrective, disciplinary, penalizing, punitive, retributive

penalize award a penalty against (*Sport*), correct, discipline, handicap, impose a penalty on, inflict a handicap on, punish, put at a disadvantage

penalty disadvantage, fine, forfeit, forfeiture, handicap, mulct, price, punishment, retribution

penance 1. atonement, mortification, penalty, punishment, reparation, sackcloth and ashes 2. **do penance** accept punishment, atone, make amends, make reparation, mortify oneself, show contrition, suffer

penchant affinity, bent, bias, disposition, fondness, inclination, leaning, liking, partiality, predilection, predisposition, proclivity, proneness, propensity, taste, tendency, turn

pending awaiting, forthcoming, hanging fire, imminent, impending, in the balance, in the offing, undecided, undetermined, unsettled, up in the air

penetrate 1. bore, enter, go through, perforate, pierce, prick, probe, stab 2. diffuse, enter, get in, infiltrate, permeate, pervade, seep, suffuse 3. *Fig.* affect, become clear, be understood, come across, get through to, impress, touch 4. *Fig.* comprehend, decipher, discern, fathom, figure out (*Inf.*), get to the bottom of, grasp, understand, unravel, work out

penetrating 1. biting, carrying, harsh, intrusive, pervasive, piercing, pungent, sharp, shrill, stinging, strong 2. *Fig.* acute, astute, critical, discerning, discriminating, incisive, intelligent, keen, perceptive, perspicacious, profound, quick, sagacious, searching, sharp, sharp-witted, shrewd

penetration 1. entrance, entry, incision, inroad, invasion, perforation, piercing, puncturing 2. acuteness, astuteness, discernment, insight, keenness, perception, perspicacity, sharpness, shrewdness, wit

penitence compunction, contrition, regret, remorse, repentance, ruefulness, self-reproach, shame, sorrow

penitent *adj.* abject, apologetic, atoning, conscience-stricken, contrite, regretful, remorseful, repentant, rueful, sorrowful, sorry

penmanship calligraphy, chirography, fist (*Inf.*), hand, handwriting, longhand, script, writing

pen name allonym, nom de plume, pseudonym

pennant banderole, banner, burgee (*Nautical*), ensign, flag, jack, pennon, streamer

penniless bankrupt, broke (*Inf.*), cleaned out (*Sl.*), destitute, impecunious, impoverished, indigent, moneyless, necessitous, needy, on one's uppers, penurious, poor, poverty-stricken, ruined, skint (*Brit. sl.*), stony-broke (*Brit. sl.*), strapped (*U.S. sl.*), without a penny to one's name

pension allowance, annuity, benefit, superannuation

pensioner O.A.P., retired person, senior citizen

pensive blue (*Inf.*), cogitative, contemplative, dreamy, grave, in a brown study (*Inf.*), meditative, melancholy, mournful, musing, preoccupied, reflective, ruminative, sad, serious, sober, solemn, sorrowful, thoughtful, wistful

pent-up bottled up, bridled, checked, constrained, curbed, held back, inhibited, repressed, smothered, stifled, suppressed

penury 1. beggary, destitution, indigence, need, pauperism, poverty, privation, straitened circumstances, want 2. dearth, deficiency, lack, paucity, scantiness, scarcity, shortage, sparseness

people *n.* 1. human beings, humanity, humans, mankind, men and

pepper *v.* 1. flavour, season, spice 2. bespeckle, dot, fleck, spatter, speck, sprinkle, stipple, stud 3. bombard, pelt, riddle, scatter, shower

peppery 1. fiery, highly seasoned, hot, piquant, pungent, spicy 2. choleric, hot-tempered, irascible, irritable, quick-tempered, snappish, testy, touchy, waspish 3. astringent, biting, caustic, incisive, sarcastic, sharp, stinging, trenchant

women, mortals, persons 2. citizens, clan, community, family, folk, inhabitants, nation, population, public, race, tribe 3. commonalty, crowd, general public, grass roots, hoi polloi, masses, mob, multitude, plebs (*Brit. sl.*), populace, rabble, rank and file, the herd ~*v.* 4. colonize, inhabit, occupy, populate, settle

perceive 1. be aware of, behold, descry, discern, discover, distinguish, espy, make out, note, notice, observe, recognize, remark, see, spot 2. appreciate, apprehend, comprehend, conclude, deduce, feel, gather, get (*Inf.*), grasp, know, learn, realize, see, sense, understand

perceptible apparent, appreciable, clear, conspicuous, detectable, discernible, distinct, evident, noticeable, observable, obvious, palpable, perceivable, recognizable, tangible, visible

perception apprehension, awareness, conception, consciousness, discernment, feeling, grasp, idea, impression, insight, notion, observation, recognition, sensation, sense, taste, understanding

perceptive acute, alert, astute, aware, discerning, insightful, intuitive, observant, penetrating, percipient, perspicacious, quick, responsive, sensitive, sharp

perch 1. *n.* branch, pole, post, resting place, roost 2. *v.* alight, balance, land, rest, roost, settle, sit on

perchance by chance, for all one knows, haply (*Archaic*), maybe, mayhap (*Archaic*), peradventure

(*Archaic*), perhaps, possibly, probably

percipient alert, alive, astute, aware, discerning, discriminating, intelligent, penetrating, perceptive, perspicacious, quick-witted, sharp, wide-awake

percolate drain, drip, exude, filter, filtrate, leach, ooze, penetrate, perk (*of coffee, inf.*), permeate, pervade, seep, strain, transfuse

percussion blow, brunt, bump, clash, collision, concussion, crash, impact, jolt, knock, shock, smash, thump

peremptory 1. absolute, binding, categorical, commanding, compelling, decisive, final, imperative, incontrovertible, irrefutable, obligatory, undeniable 2. arbitrary, assertive, authoritative, autocratic, bossy (*Inf.*), dictatorial, dogmatic, domineering, high-handed, imperious, intolerant, overbearing

perennial 1. abiding, chronic, constant, continual, continuing, enduring, incessant, inveterate, lasting, lifelong, persistent, recurrent, unchanging 2. ceaseless, deathless, eternal, everlasting, immortal, imperishable, never-ending, permanent, perpetual, unceasing, undying, unfailing, uninterrupted

perfect *adj.* 1. absolute, complete, completed, consummate, entire, finished, full, out-and-out, sheer, unadulterated, unalloyed, unmitigated, utter, whole 2. blameless, excellent, faultless, flawless, ideal, immaculate, impeccable, pure, splendid, spotless, sublime, superb, superlative, supreme, unblemished, unmarred, untarnished 3. accurate, close, correct, exact, faithful, precise, right, spot-on (*Brit. inf.*), strict, true, unerring 4. accomplished, adept, experienced, expert, finished, masterly, polished, practised, skilful, skilled ~*v.* 5. accomplish, achieve, carry out, complete, consummate, effect, finish, fulfil, perform, realize 6. ameliorate, cultivate, develop, elaborate, hone, improve, polish, refine

perfection 1. accomplishment, achievement, achieving, completion, consummation, evolution, fulfilment, realization 2. completeness, exactness, excellence, exquisiteness, faultlessness, integrity, maturity, perfectness, precision, purity, sublimity, superiority, wholeness 3. acme, crown, ideal, paragon

perfectionist formalist, precisian, precisionist, purist, stickler

perfectly 1. absolutely, altogether, completely, consummately, entirely, fully, quite, thoroughly, totally, utterly, wholly 2. admirably, exquisitely, faultlessly, flawlessly, ideally, impeccably, superbly, superlatively, supremely, to perfection, wonderfully

perfidious corrupt, deceitful, dishonest, disloyal, double-dealing, double-faced, faithless, false, recreant (*Archaic*), traitorous, treacherous, treasonous, two-faced, unfaithful, untrustworthy

perfidy betrayal, deceit, disloyalty, double-dealing, duplicity, faithlessness, falsity, infidelity, perfidiousness, treachery, treason

perforate bore, drill, hole, honeycomb, penetrate, pierce, punch, puncture

perform 1. accomplish, achieve, act, bring about, carry out, complete, comply with, discharge, do, effect, execute, fulfil, function, observe, pull off, satisfy, transact, work 2. act, appear as, depict, enact, play, present, produce, put on, render, represent, stage

performance 1. accomplishment, achievement, act, carrying out, completion, conduct, consummation, discharge, execution, exploit, feat, fulfilment, work 2. acting, appearance, exhibition, gig (*Inf.*), interpretation, play, portrayal, presentation, production, representation, show 3. action, conduct, efficiency, functioning, operation, practice, running, working 4. *Inf.* act, behaviour, bother, business, carry-on (*Brit. inf.*), fuss, pother, rigmarole, to-do

performer actor, actress, artiste, play-actor, player, Thespian, trouper

perfume aroma, attar, balminess, bouquet, cologne, essence, fragrance, incense, odour, redolence, scent, smell, sweetness

perfunctory automatic, careless, cursory, heedless, inattentive, indifferent, mechanical, negligent, offhand, routine, sketchy, slipshod, slovenly, stereotyped, superficial, unconcerned, unthinking, wooden

perhaps as the case may be, conceivably, feasibly, for all one knows, it may be, maybe, perchance (*Archaic*), possibly

peril danger, exposure, hazard, insecurity, jeopardy, menace, pitfall, risk, uncertainty, vulnerability

perilous chancy (*Inf.*), dangerous, exposed, fraught with danger, hairy (*Sl.*), hazardous, parlous (*Archaic*), precarious, risky, threatening, unsafe, unsure, vulnerable

perimeter ambit, border, borderline, boundary, bounds, circumference, confines, edge, limit, margin, periphery

period 1. interval, season, space, span, spell, stretch, term, time, while 2. aeon, age, course, cycle, date, days, epoch, era, generation, season, stage, term, time, years

periodical *n.* journal, magazine, monthly, organ, paper, publication, quarterly, review, serial, weekly

perish 1. be killed, be lost, decease, die, expire, lose one's life, pass away 2. be destroyed, collapse, decline, disappear, fall, go under, vanish 3. decay, decompose, disintegrate, moulder, rot, waste, wither

perishable decaying, decomposable, destructible, easily spoilt, liable to rot, short-lived, unstable

perjure (oneself) bear false witness, commit perjury, forswear, give false testimony, lie under oath, swear falsely

perjury bearing false witness, false oath, false statement, false swearing, forswearing, giving false testimony, lying under oath, oath

breaking, violation of an oath, wil~
ful falsehood

permanence constancy, continu~
ance, continuity, dependability,
durability, duration, endurance, fi~
nality, fixedness, fixity, immortal~
ity, indestructibility, lastingness,
perdurability (*Rare*), permanency,
perpetuity, stability, survival

permanent abiding, constant, du~
rable, enduring, everlasting, fixed,
immutable, imperishable, inde~
structible, invariable, lasting, long-
lasting, perennial, perpetual, per~
sistent, stable, steadfast, unchang~
ing, unfading

permeate charge, diffuse through~
out, fill, filter through, imbue, im~
pregnate, infiltrate, pass through,
penetrate, percolate, pervade,
saturate, seep through, soak
through, spread throughout

permissible acceptable, admis~
sible, allowable, all right, author~
ized, kosher (*Inf.*), lawful, legal, le~
git (*Sl.*), legitimate, licit, O.K. (*Inf.*),
permitted, proper, sanctioned

permission allowance, approval,
assent, authorization, consent, dis~
pensation, freedom, go-ahead
(*Inf.*), green light, leave, liberty,
licence, permit, sanction, suffer~
ance, tolerance

permissive acquiescent, easy-
going, forbearing, free, indulgent,
latitudinarian, lax, lenient, liberal,
open-minded, tolerant

permit 1. *v.* admit, agree, allow,
authorize, consent, empower, en~
able, endorse, endure, give leave
or permission, grant, let, license,
sanction, suffer, tolerate, warrant
2. *n.* authorization, liberty, licence,
pass, passport, permission, sanc~
tion, warrant

permutation alteration, change,
shift, transformation, transmuta~
tion, transposition

pernicious bad, baleful, baneful
(*Archaic*), damaging, dangerous,
deadly, deleterious, destructive,
detrimental, evil, fatal, harmful,
hurtful, injurious, maleficent, ma~
levolent, malicious, malign, malig~
nant, noisome, noxious, offensive,

pestilent, poisonous, ruinous, ven~
omous, wicked

pernickety 1. careful, carping, dif~
ficult to please, exacting, fastidi~
ous, finicky, fussy, hairsplitting,
nice, nit-picking (*Inf.*), overprecise,
painstaking, particular, punctilious
2. detailed, exacting, fiddly, fine,
tricky

peroration closing remarks, con~
clusion, recapitulation, recapping
(*Inf.*), reiteration, summing-up

perpendicular at right angles to,
on end, plumb, straight, upright,
vertical

perpetrate be responsible for,
bring about, carry out, commit, do,
effect, enact, execute, inflict, per~
form, wreak

perpetual 1. abiding, endless, en~
during, eternal, everlasting, im~
mortal, infinite, lasting, never-
ending, perennial, permanent,
sempiternal (*Literary*), unchang~
ing, undying, unending 2. cease~
less, constant, continual, continu~
ous, endless, incessant, intermi~
nable, never-ending, perennial,
persistent, recurrent, repeated,
unceasing, unfailing, uninterrupt~
ed, unremitting

perpetuate continue, eternalize,
immortalize, keep alive, keep go~
ing, keep up, maintain, preserve,
sustain

perplex 1. baffle, befuddle, beset,
bewilder, confound, confuse,
dumbfound, mix up, muddle, mys~
tify, nonplus, puzzle, stump 2.
complicate, encumber, entangle,
involve, jumble, mix up, snarl up,
tangle, thicken

perplexing baffling, bewildering,
complex, complicated, confusing,
difficult, enigmatic, hard, inexpli~
cable, intricate, involved, knotty,
labyrinthine, mysterious, mystify~
ing, paradoxical, puzzling, strange,
taxing, thorny, unaccountable,
weird

perplexity 1. bafflement, bewil~
derment, confusion, incomprehen~
sion, mystification, puzzlement,
stupefaction 2. complexity, diffi~
culty, inextricability, intricacy, in~

volvement, obscurity 3. difficulty, dilemma, enigma, fix (*Inf.*), knotty problem, mystery, paradox, puzzle, snarl

perquisite benefit, bonus, dividend, extra, fringe benefit, perk (*Inf.*), plus

persecute 1. afflict, distress, dragoon, harass, hound, hunt, ill-treat, injure, maltreat, martyr, molest, oppress, pursue, torment, torture, victimize 2. annoy, badger, bait, bother, pester, tease, vex, worry

perseverance constancy, dedication, determination, diligence, doggedness, endurance, indefatigability, persistence, pertinacity, purposefulness, resolution, sedulity, stamina, steadfastness, tenacity

persevere be determined *or* resolved, carry on, continue, endure, go on, hang on, hold fast, hold on (*Inf.*), keep going, keep on *or* at, maintain, persist, plug away (*Inf.*), pursue, remain, stand firm, stick at *or* to

persist 1. be resolute, continue, hold on (*Inf.*), insist, persevere, stand firm 2. abide, carry on, continue, endure, keep up, last, linger, remain

persistence constancy, determination, diligence, doggedness, endurance, grit, indefatigability, perseverance, pertinacity, pluck, resolution, stamina, steadfastness, tenacity, tirelessness

persistent 1. assiduous, determined, dogged, enduring, fixed, immovable, indefatigable, obdurate, obstinate, persevering, pertinacious, resolute, steadfast, steady, stubborn, tenacious, tireless, unflagging 2. constant, continual, continuous, endless, incessant, interminable, never-ending, perpetual, relentless, repeated, unrelenting, unremitting

person 1. being, body, human, human being, individual, living soul, soul 2. **in person** bodily, in the flesh, oneself, personally

personable affable, agreeable, amiable, attractive, charming, good-looking, handsome, likable, nice, pleasant, pleasing, presentable, winning

personage big noise (*Brit. sl.*), big shot (*Sl.*), celebrity, dignitary, luminary, notable, personality, public figure, somebody, V.I.P., well-known person, worthy

personal 1. exclusive, individual, intimate, own, particular, peculiar, private, privy, special 2. bodily, corporal, corporeal, exterior, material, physical 3. derogatory, disparaging, insulting, nasty, offensive, pejorative, slighting

personality 1. character, disposition, identity, individuality, makeup, nature, psyche, temper, temperament, traits 2. attraction, attractiveness, character, charisma, charm, dynamism, likableness, magnetism, pleasantness 3. celebrity, famous name, household name, notable, personage, star, well-known face, well-known person

personally 1. alone, by oneself, independently, in person, in the flesh, on one's own, solely 2. for oneself, for one's part, from one's own viewpoint, in one's own view 3. individualistically, individually, privately, specially, subjectively

personate act, depict, do (*Inf.*), enact, feign, imitate, impersonate, play-act, portray, represent

personification embodiment, image, incarnation, likeness, portrayal, recreation, representation, semblance

personify body forth, embody, epitomize, exemplify, express, image (*Rare*), incarnate, mirror, represent, symbolize, typify

personnel employees, helpers, human resources, liveware, members, men and women, people, staff, workers, work force

perspective 1. angle, attitude, broad view, context, frame of reference, objectivity, outlook, overview, proportion, relation, relative importance, relativity, way of looking 2. outlook, panorama, prospect, scene, view, vista

perspicacious acute, alert, astute, aware, clear-sighted, clever, discerning, keen, observant, penetrating, perceptive, percipient, sagacious, sharp, sharp-witted, shrewd

perspicacity acumen, acuteness, discernment, discrimination, insight, keenness, penetration, perceptiveness, percipience, perspicaciousness, perspicuity, sagaciousness, sagacity, sharpness, shrewdness, wit

perspiration exudation, moisture, sweat, wetness

perspire be damp, be wet, drip, exude, glow, pour with sweat, secrete, sweat, swelter

persuade 1.actuate, advise, allure, bring round (*Inf.*), coax, counsel, entice, impel, incite, induce, influence, inveigle, prevail upon, prompt, sway, talk into, urge, win over 2. cause to believe, convert, convince, satisfy

persuasion 1.blandishment, cajolery, conversion, enticement, exhortation, inducement, influencing, inveiglement, wheedling 2.cogency, force, persuasiveness, potency, power, pull (*Inf.*) 3. belief, certitude, conviction, credo, creed, faith, firm belief, fixed opinion, opinion, tenet, views 4.camp, cult, denomination, faction, party, school, school of thought, sect, side

persuasive cogent, compelling, convincing, credible, effective, eloquent, forceful, impelling, impressive, inducing, influential, logical, moving, plausible, sound, telling, touching, valid, weighty, winning

pertain appertain, apply, be appropriate, bear on, befit, belong, be part of, be relevant, concern, refer, regard, relate

pertinacious bull-headed, determined, dogged, headstrong, inflexible, intractable, mulish, obdurate, obstinate, persevering, persistent, perverse, pig-headed, relentless, resolute, self-willed, strong-willed, stubborn, tenacious, unyielding, wilful

pertinent admissible, *ad rem*, applicable, apposite, appropriate, apropos, apt, fit, fitting, germane, material, pat, proper, relevant, suitable, to the point, to the purpose

pertness audacity, brashness, brass (*Inf.*), bumptiousness, cheek (*Inf.*), cheekiness, cockiness, effrontery, forwardness, impertinence, impudence, insolence, presumption, rudeness, sauciness

perturb 1. agitate, alarm, bother, discompose, disconcert, discountenance, disquiet, disturb, fluster, ruffle, trouble, unsettle, upset, vex, worry 2. confuse, disarrange, disorder, muddle, unsettle

perturbed agitated, alarmed, anxious, disconcerted, disquieted, disturbed, fearful, flurried, flustered, ill at ease, nervous, restless, shaken, troubled, uncomfortable, uneasy, upset, worried

perusal browse, check, examination, inspection, look through, read, scrutiny, study

peruse browse, check, examine, inspect, look through, read, run one's eye over, scan, scrutinize, study

pervade affect, charge, diffuse, extend, fill, imbue, infuse, overspread, penetrate, percolate, permeate, spread through, suffuse

pervasive common, extensive, general, inescapable, omnipresent, permeating, pervading, prevalent, rife, ubiquitous, universal, widespread

perverse 1. abnormal, contradictory, contrary, delinquent, depraved, deviant, disobedient, froward, improper, incorrect, miscreant, rebellious, refractory, troublesome, unhealthy, unmanageable, unreasonable 2.contrary, contumacious, cross-grained, dogged, headstrong, intractable, intransigent, obdurate, wilful, wrongheaded 3.contrary, mulish, obstinate, pig-headed, stubborn, unyielding, wayward 4. cantankerous, churlish, crabbed, cross, fractious, ill-natured, ill-tempered, peevish, petulant, spiteful, stroppy (*Brit. sl.*), surly

perversion 1. aberration, abnormality, debauchery, depravity, deviation, immorality, kink (*Brit. sl.*), kinkiness (*Sl.*), unnaturalness, vice, vitiation, wickedness 2. corruption, distortion, falsification, misinterpretation, misrepresentation, misuse, twisting

perversity contradictiveness, contradictoriness, contrariness, contumacy, frowardness, intransigence, obduracy, refractoriness, waywardness, wrong-headedness

pervert *v.* 1. abuse, distort, falsify, garble, misconstrue, misinterpret, misrepresent, misuse, twist, warp 2. corrupt, debase, debauch, degrade, deprave, desecrate, initiate, lead astray, subvert ~*n.* 3. debauchee, degenerate, deviant, weirdo (*Sl.*)

perverted aberrant, abnormal, corrupt, debased, debauched, depraved, deviant, distorted, evil, immoral, impaired, kinky (*Sl.*), misguided, sick, twisted, unhealthy, unnatural, vicious, vitiated, warped, wicked

pessimism cynicism, dejection, depression, despair, despondency, distrust, gloom, gloominess, gloomy outlook, glumness, hopelessness, melancholy

pessimist cynic, defeatist, doomster, gloom merchant (*Inf.*), killjoy, melancholic, misanthrope, prophet of doom, wet blanket (*Inf.*), worrier

pessimistic bleak, cynical, dark, dejected, depressed, despairing, despondent, distrustful, downhearted, fatalistic, foreboding, gloomy, glum, hopeless, melancholy, misanthropic, morose, resigned, sad

pest 1. annoyance, bane, bore, bother, irritation, nuisance, pain (*Inf.*), pain in the neck (*Inf.*), thorn in one's flesh, trial, vexation 2. bane, blight, bug, curse, epidemic, infection, pestilence, plague, scourge

pester annoy, badger, bedevil, bother, bug (*Inf.*), chivvy, disturb, drive one up the wall (*Sl.*), fret, get at, get on someone's nerves, harass, harry, hassle (*Inf.*), irk, nag, pick on, plague, ride (*Inf.*), torment, worry

pestilence 1. Black Death, epidemic, pandemic, plague, visitation 2. affliction, bane, blight, cancer, canker, curse, scourge

pestilential 1. annoying, dangerous, deleterious, destructive, detrimental, evil, foul, harmful, hazardous, injurious, pernicious, ruinous, troublesome 2. catching, contagious, contaminated, deadly, disease-ridden, infectious, malignant, noxious, pestiferous, poisonous, venomous

pet[1] *n.* 1. apple of one's eye, blue-eyed boy (*Inf.*), darling, favourite, idol, jewel, treasure ~*adj.* 2. cherished, dearest, dear to one's heart, favoured, favourite, particular, preferred, special 3. domesticated, house, house-broken, house-trained (*Brit.*), tame, trained ~*v.* 4. baby, coddle, cosset, mollycoddle, pamper, spoil 5. caress, fondle, pat, stroke 6. *Inf.* canoodle (*Sl.*), cuddle, kiss, neck (*Inf.*), smooch (*Sl.*), snog (*Brit. sl.*)

pet[2] bad mood, huff, ill temper, miff (*Inf.*), paddy (*Brit. inf.*), paddywhack (*Brit. inf.*), pique, pout, sulk, sulks, tantrum, temper

peter out come to nothing, die out, dwindle, ebb, evaporate, fade, fail, give out, run dry, run out, stop, taper off, wane

petition 1. *n.* address, appeal, application, entreaty, invocation, memorial, plea, prayer, request, round robin, solicitation, suit, supplication 2. *v.* adjure, appeal, ask, beg, beseech, call upon, crave, entreat, plead, pray, press, solicit, sue, supplicate, urge

petrified 1. fossilized, ossified, rocklike 2. aghast, appalled, dazed, dumbfounded, frozen, horrified, numb, scared stiff, shocked, speechless, stunned, stupefied, terrified, terror-stricken

petrify 1. calcify, fossilize, harden,

set, solidify, turn to stone 2. amaze, appal, astonish, astound, confound, dumbfound, horrify, immobilize, paralyse, stun, stupefy, terrify, transfix

petty 1. contemptible, inconsiderable, inessential, inferior, insignificant, little, measly (*Inf.*), negligible, paltry, piddling (*Inf.*), slight, small, trifling, trivial, unimportant 2. cheap, grudging, mean, meanminded, shabby, small-minded, spiteful, stingy, ungenerous 3. inferior, junior, lesser, lower, minor, secondary, subordinate

petulance bad temper, crabbiness, ill humour, irritability, peevishness, pettishness, pique, pouts, querulousness, spleen, sulkiness, sullenness, waspishness

petulant bad-tempered, captious, cavilling, crabbed, cross, crusty, fault-finding, fretful, ill-humoured, impatient, irritable, moody, peevish, perverse, pouting, querulous, snappish, sour, sulky, sullen, ungracious, waspish

phantom 1. apparition, eidolon, ghost, phantasm, revenant, shade (*Literary*), spectre, spirit, spook (*Inf.*), wraith 2. chimera, figment, figment of the imagination, hallucination, illusion, vision

pharisee canter, dissembler, dissimulator, fraud, humbug, hypocrite, phoney (*Sl.*), pietist, whited sepulchre

phase aspect, chapter, condition, development, juncture, period, point, position, stage, state, step, time

phase out close, deactivate, dispose of gradually, ease off, eliminate, pull out, remove, replace, run down, taper off, terminate, wind down, wind up (*Inf.*), withdraw

phenomenal exceptional, extraordinary, fantastic, marvellous, miraculous, outstanding, prodigious, remarkable, sensational, singular, uncommon, unique, unparalleled, unusual, wondrous

phenomenon 1. circumstance, episode, event, fact, happening, incident, occurrence 2. exception, marvel, miracle, nonpareil, prodigy, rarity, sensation, sight, spectacle, wonder

philander coquet, court, dally, flirt, fool around (*Inf.*), toy, trifle, womanize (*Inf.*)

philanderer Casanova, dallier, Don Juan, flirt, gallant, gay dog, ladies' man, lady-killer (*Inf.*), Lothario, playboy, stud (*Sl.*), trifler, wolf (*Inf.*), womanizer (*Inf.*)

philanthropic alms-giving, altruistic, beneficent, benevolent, benignant, charitable, eleemosynary, gracious, humane, humanitarian, kind, kind-hearted, munificent, public-spirited

philanthropist alms-giver, altruist, benefactor, contributor, donor, giver, humanitarian, patron

philanthropy alms-giving, altruism, beneficence, benevolence, benignity, bounty, brotherly love, charitableness, charity, generosity, humanitarianism, kind-heartedness, liberality, munificence, open-handedness, patronage, public-spiritedness

philistine 1. *n.* barbarian, boor, bourgeois, Goth, ignoramus, lout, lowbrow, vulgarian, yahoo 2. *adj.* anti-intellectual, boorish, bourgeois, crass, ignorant, lowbrow, tasteless, uncultivated, uncultured, uneducated, unrefined

philosopher dialectician, logician, metaphysician, sage, seeker after truth, theorist, thinker, wise man

philosophical, philosophic 1. abstract, erudite, learned, logical, rational, sagacious, theoretical, thoughtful, wise 2. calm, collected, composed, cool, impassive, imperturbable, patient, resigned, serene, stoical, tranquil, unruffled

philosophy 1. aesthetics, knowledge, logic, metaphysics, rationalism, reason, reasoning, thinking, thought, wisdom 2. attitude to life, basic idea, beliefs, convictions, doctrine, ideology, principle, tenets, thinking, values, viewpoint, *Weltanschauung*, world-view 3. composure, coolness, dispassion, equanimity, resignation, restraint, self-possession, serenity, stoicism

phlegmatic apathetic, bovine, cold, dull, frigid, heavy, impassive, indifferent, lethargic, listless, lymphatic, matter-of-fact, placid, sluggish, stoical, stolid, undemonstrative, unemotional, unfeeling

phobia aversion, detestation, dislike, distaste, dread, fear, hatred, horror, irrational fear, loathing, obsession, overwhelming anxiety, repulsion, revulsion, terror, thing (*Inf.*)

phone n. 1. blower (*Inf.*), telephone 2. bell (*Brit. sl.*), buzz (*Inf.*), call, ring, tinkle (*Brit. inf.*) ~v. 3. buzz (*Inf.*), call, get on the blower (*Inf.*), give someone a bell (*Brit. sl.*), give someone a buzz (*Inf.*), give someone a call, give someone a ring, give someone a tinkle (*Brit. inf.*), make a call, ring, ring up, telephone

phoney 1. adj. affected, assumed, bogus, counterfeit, fake, false, forged, imitation, pseudo (*Inf.*), put-on, sham, spurious, trick 2. n. counterfeit, fake, faker, forgery, fraud, humbug, impostor, pretender, pseud (*Sl.*), sham

photograph 1. n. image, likeness, photo (*Inf.*), picture, print, shot, slide, snap (*Inf.*), snapshot, transparency 2. v. capture on film, film, get a shot of, record, shoot, snap (*Inf.*), take, take a picture of, take (someone's) picture

photographic accurate, cinematic, detailed, exact, faithful, filmic, graphic, lifelike, minute, natural, pictorial, precise, realistic, retentive, visual, vivid

phrase 1. n. expression, group of words, idiom, locution, motto, remark, saying, tag, utterance, way of speaking 2. v. couch, express, formulate, frame, present, put, put into words, say, term, utter, voice, word

phraseology choice of words, diction, expression, idiom, language, parlance, phrase, phrasing, speech, style, syntax, wording

physical 1. bodily, carnal, corporal, corporeal, earthly, fleshly, incarnate, mortal, somatic, unspiritual 2. material, natural, palpable, real, sensible, solid, substantial, tangible, visible

physician doc (*Inf.*), doctor, doctor of medicine, general practitioner, G.P., healer, M.D., medic (*Inf.*), medical practitioner, medico (*Inf.*), sawbones (*Sl.*), specialist

physique body, build, constitution, figure, form, frame, make-up, shape, structure

pick v. 1. choose, decide upon, elect, fix upon, hand-pick, mark out, opt for, select, settle upon, sift out, single out, sort out 2. collect, cull, cut, gather, harvest, pluck, pull 3. have no appetite, nibble, peck at, play or toy with, push the food round the plate 4. foment, incite, instigate, provoke, start 5. break into, break open, crack, force, jemmy, open, prise open 6. **pick one's way** be tentative, find or make one's way, move cautiously, tread carefully, work through ~n. 7. choice, choosing, decision, option, preference, selection 8. choicest, crème de la crème, elect, elite, flower, pride, prize, the best, the cream, the tops (*Sl.*)

picket n. 1. pale, paling, palisade, peg, post, stake, stanchion, upright 2. demonstrator, picketer, protester 3. guard, lookout, patrol, scout, sentinel, sentry, spotter, vedette (*Military*), watch ~v. 4. blockade, boycott, demonstrate 5. corral (*U.S.*), enclose, fence, hedge in, palisade, pen in, rail in, shut in, wall in

pickle n. 1. Inf. bind (*Inf.*), difficulty, dilemma, fix (*Inf.*), hot water (*Inf.*), jam (*Inf.*), predicament, quandary, scrape (*Inf.*), spot (*Inf.*), tight spot 2. Brit. inf. little horror, mischief, mischief maker, monkey, naughty child, rascal ~v. 3. cure, keep, marinade, preserve, steep

pick-me-up bracer (*Inf.*), drink, pick-up (*Sl.*), refreshment, restorative, roborant, shot in the arm (*Inf.*), stimulant, tonic

pick on badger, bait, blame, bully, goad, hector, tease, torment

pick out 1. choose, cull, hand-pick, select, separate the sheep from the goats, single out, sort out 2. discriminate, distinguish, make distinct, make out, notice, perceive, recognize, tell apart

pick-up n. 1. acceleration, response, revving (Inf.), speed-up 2. change for the better, gain, improvement, rally, recovery, revival, strengthening, upswing, upturn

pick up v. 1. gather, grasp, hoist, lift, raise, take up, uplift 2. buy, come across, find, garner, happen upon, obtain, purchase, score (Sl.) 3. gain, gain ground, get better, improve, make a comeback (Inf.), mend, perk up, rally, recover, take a turn for the better 4. call for, collect, get, give someone a lift, go to get, uplift (Scot.) 5. acquire, get the hang of (Inf.), learn, master 6. Sl. apprehend, arrest, bust (Inf.), collar (Inf.), do (Sl.), nab (Inf.), nick (Brit. sl.), pinch (Inf.), pull in (Brit. sl.), run in (Sl.), take into custody

picnic 1. excursion, fête champêtre, outdoor meal, outing 2. Inf. child's play (Inf.), cinch (Sl.), piece of cake (Brit. inf.), pushover (Sl.), snap (Inf.), walkover (Inf.)

pictorial expressive, graphic, illustrated, picturesque, representational, scenic, striking, vivid

picture n. 1. delineation, drawing, effigy, engraving, illustration, image, likeness, painting, photograph, portrait, portrayal, print, representation, similitude, sketch 2. account, depiction, description, image, impression, re-creation, report 3. carbon copy, copy, dead ringer (Sl.), double, duplicate, image, likeness, living image, look-alike, replica, ringer (Sl.), spit (Inf.), spit and image (Inf.), spitting image (Inf.), twin 4. archetype, embodiment, epitome, essence, living example, perfect example, personification 5. film, flick (Sl.), motion picture, movie (U.S. inf.) ~v. 6. conceive of, envision, image,

see, see in the mind's eye, visualize 7. delineate, depict, describe, draw, illustrate, paint, photograph, portray, render, represent, show, sketch

picturesque attractive, beautiful, charming, colourful, graphic, pretty, quaint, scenic, striking, vivid

piddling derisory, fiddling, insignificant, little, measly (Inf.), Mickey Mouse (Sl.), paltry, petty, piffling, puny, trifling, trivial, unimportant, useless, worthless

piebald black and white, brindled, dappled, flecked, mottled, pied, speckled, spotted

piece n. 1. allotment, bit, chunk, division, fraction, fragment, length, morsel, mouthful, part, portion, quantity, scrap, section, segment, share, shred, slice 2. case, example, instance, occurrence, sample, specimen, stroke 3. article, bit (Sl.), composition, creation, item, production, study, work, work of art 4. **go to pieces** break down, crack up (Inf.), crumble, disintegrate, fall apart, lose control, lose one's head 5. **in pieces** broken, bust (Inf.), damaged, disintegrated, in bits, in smithereens, ruined, shattered, smashed 6. **of a piece** alike, analogous, consistent, identical, of the same kind, similar, the same, uniform ~v. 7. Often with **together** assemble, compose, fix, join, mend, patch, repair, restore, unite

pièce de résistance chef-d'oeuvre, jewel, masterpiece, masterwork, showpiece

piecemeal 1. adv. at intervals, bit by bit, by degrees, by fits and starts, fitfully, intermittently, little by little, partially, slowly 2. adj. fragmentary, intermittent, interrupted, partial, patchy, spotty, unsystematic

pier n. 1. jetty, landing place, promenade, quay, wharf 2. buttress, column, pile, piling, pillar, post, support, upright

pierce 1. bore, drill, enter, penetrate, perforate, prick, probe, puncture, run through, spike, stab, stick into, transfix 2. comprehend, discern, discover, fathom, grasp, realize, see, understand 3. *Fig.* affect, cut, cut to the quick, excite, hurt, move, pain, rouse, sting, stir, strike, thrill, touch, wound

piercing 1. *Usually of sound* earsplitting, high-pitched, loud, penetrating, sharp, shattering, shrill 2. alert, aware, keen, penetrating, perceptive, perspicacious, probing, quick-witted, searching, sharp, shrewd 3. *Usually of weather* arctic, biting, bitter, cold, freezing, frosty, keen, nipping, nippy, numbing, raw, wintry 4. acute, agonizing, excruciating, exquisite, fierce, intense, painful, powerful, racking, severe, sharp, shooting, stabbing

piety devotion, devoutness, dutifulness, duty, faith, godliness, grace, holiness, piousness, religion, reverence, sanctity, veneration

pig 1. boar, grunter, hog, piggy, piglet, porker, shoat, sow, swine 2. *Inf.* animal, beast, boor, brute, glutton, greedy guts (*Sl.*), guzzler, hog (*Inf.*), slob (*Sl.*), sloven, swine

pigeon 1. bird, culver (*Archaic*), cushat, dove, squab 2. *Sl.* dupe, fall guy (*Inf.*), gull (*Archaic*), mug (*Sl.*), sitting duck, sucker (*Sl.*), victim 3. *Brit. inf.* baby (*Sl.*), business, concern, lookout (*Inf.*), responsibility, worry

pigeonhole *n.* 1. compartment, cubbyhole, cubicle, locker, niche, place, section 2. *Inf.* category, class, classification, slot (*Inf.*) ~*v.* 3. defer, file, postpone, put off, shelve 4. catalogue, characterize, classify, codify, compartmentalize, label, slot (*Inf.*), sort

pig-headed bull-headed, contrary, cross-grained, dense, froward, inflexible, mulish, obstinate, perverse, self-willed, stiff-necked, stubborn, stupid, unyielding, wilful, wrong-headed

pigment colorant, colour, colouring, colouring matter, dye, dyestuff, paint, stain, tincture, tint

pile[1] *n.* 1. accumulation, assemblage, assortment, collection, heap, hoard, mass, mound, mountain, stack, stockpile 2. *Inf.* bomb (*Brit. sl.*), fortune, mint, money, packet (*Sl.*), pot, tidy sum (*Inf.*), wealth 3. *Often plural. Inf.* a lot, great deal, ocean, oodles (*Inf.*), quantity, stacks 4. building, edifice, erection, structure ~*v.* 5. accumulate, amass, assemble, collect, gather, heap, hoard, load up, mass, stack, store 6. charge, crowd, crush, flock, flood, jam, pack, rush, stream

pile[2] beam, column, foundation, pier, piling, pillar, post, support, upright

pile[3] down, fibre, filament, fur, hair, nap, plush, shag, surface

piles haemorrhoids

pile-up accident, collision, crash, multiple collision, smash, smash-up (*Inf.*)

pilfer appropriate, embezzle, filch, knock off (*Sl.*), lift (*Inf.*), nick (*Brit. sl.*), pinch (*Inf.*), purloin, rifle, rob, snaffle (*Brit. inf.*), snitch (*Sl.*), steal, swipe (*Sl.*), take, thieve, walk off with

pilgrim crusader, hajji, palmer, traveller, wanderer, wayfarer

pilgrimage crusade, excursion, expedition, hajj, journey, mission, tour, trip

pill 1. bolus, capsule, pellet, pilule, tablet 2. the pill oral contraceptive 3. *Sl.* bore, drag (*Sl.*), nuisance, pain (*Inf.*), pain in the neck (*Inf.*), pest, trial

pillage *v.* 1. depredate (*Rare*), despoil, freeboot, loot, maraud, plunder, raid, ransack, ravage, reive (*Dialect*), rifle, rob, sack, spoil (*Archaic*), spoliate, strip ~*n.* 2. depredation, devastation, marauding, plunder, rapine, robbery, sack, spoliation 3. booty, loot, plunder, spoils

pillar 1. column, pier, pilaster, piling, post, prop, shaft, stanchion, support, upright 2. leader, leading light (*Inf.*), mainstay, rock, supporter, tower of strength, upholder, worthy

pillory *v.* brand, cast a slur on, denounce, expose to ridicule, heap *or* pour scorn on, hold up to shame, lash, show up, stigmatize

pilot 1. *n.* airman, aviator, captain, conductor, coxswain, director, flier, guide, helmsman, leader, navigator, steersman 2. *v.* conduct, control, direct, drive, fly, guide, handle, lead, manage, navigate, operate, shepherd, steer 3. *adj.* experimental, model, test, trial

pimple boil, papule (*Pathol.*), plook (*Scot.*), pustule, spot, swelling

pin *v.* 1. affix, attach, fasten, fix, join, secure 2. fix, hold down, hold fast, immobilize, pinion, press, restrain

pinch *v.* 1. compress, grasp, nip, press, squeeze, tweak 2. chafe, confine, cramp, crush, hurt, pain 3. afflict, be stingy, distress, economize, oppress, pinch pennies, press, scrimp, skimp, spare, stint 4. *Inf.* filch, knock off (*Sl.*), lift (*Inf.*), nick (*Brit. sl.*), pilfer, purloin, rob, snaffle (*Brit. inf.*), snatch, snitch (*Sl.*), steal, swipe (*Sl.*) 5. *Inf.* apprehend, arrest, bust (*Inf.*), collar (*Inf.*), do (*Sl.*), nab (*Inf.*), nick (*Brit. sl.*), pick up (*Sl.*), pull in (*Brit. sl.*), run in (*Sl.*), take into custody ~*n.* 6. nip, squeeze, tweak 7. bit, dash, jot, mite, small quantity, *soupçon*, speck, taste 8. crisis, difficulty, emergency, exigency, hardship, necessity, oppression, pass, plight, predicament, pressure, strait, stress

pinched careworn, drawn, gaunt, haggard, peaky, starved, thin, worn

pin down 1. compel, constrain, force, make, press, pressurize 2. designate, determine, home in on, identify, locate, name, pinpoint, specify 3. bind, confine, constrain, fix, hold, hold down, immobilize, nail down, tie down

pine 1. *Often with* for ache, carry a torch for, covet, crave, desire, hanker, hunger for, long, lust after, sigh, thirst for, wish, yearn 2. decay, decline, droop, dwindle, fade, flag, languish, peak, sicken, sink, waste, weaken, wilt, wither

pinion *v.* bind, chain, confine, fasten, fetter, immobilize, manacle, pin down, shackle, tie

pink 1. *n.* acme, best, height, peak, perfection, summit 2. *adj.* flesh, flushed, reddish, rose, roseate, rosy, salmon

pinnacle 1. acme, apex, apogee, crest, crown, eminence, height, meridian, peak, summit, top, vertex, zenith 2. belfry, cone, needle, obelisk, pyramid, spire, steeple

pinpoint define, distinguish, get a fix on, home in on, identify, locate, spot

pint ale, beer, jar (*Brit. inf.*), jug (*Brit. inf.*)

pioneer *n.* 1. colonist, colonizer, explorer, frontiersman, settler 2. developer, founder, founding father, innovator, leader, trailblazer ~*v.* 3. create, develop, discover, establish, initiate, instigate, institute, invent, launch, lay the groundwork, map out, open up, originate, prepare, show the way, start, take the lead

pious 1. dedicated, devoted, devout, God-fearing, godly, holy, religious, reverent, righteous, saintly, spiritual 2. goody-goody, holier-than-thou, hypocritical, pietistic, religiose, sanctimonious, self-righteous, unctuous

pipe *n.* 1. conduit, conveyor, duct, hose, line, main, passage, pipeline, tube 2. briar, clay, meerschaum 3. fife, horn, tooter, whistle, wind instrument ~*v.* 4. cheep, peep, play, sing, sound, tootle, trill, tweet, twitter, warble, whistle 5. bring in, channel, conduct, convey, siphon, supply, transmit

pipe down belt up (*Sl.*), be quiet, hold one's tongue, hush, quieten down, shush, shut one's mouth, shut up (*Inf.*), silence

pipeline 1. conduit, conveyor, duct, line, passage, pipe, tube 2. **in the pipeline** brewing, coming, getting ready, in process, in production, on the way, under way

piquant 1. biting, highly-seasoned, peppery, pungent, savoury, sharp, spicy, stinging, tangy, tart, with a kick (*Inf.*), zesty 2. interesting, lively, provocative, racy, salty, scintillating, sparkling, spirited, stimulating

pique n. 1. annoyance, displeasure, grudge, huff, hurt feelings, irrita~ tion, miff (*Inf.*), offence, resent~ ment, umbrage, vexation, wounded pride ~v. 2. affront, annoy, dis~ please, gall, get (*Inf.*), incense, irk, irritate, miff (*Inf.*), mortify, nettle, offend, peeve (*Inf.*), provoke, put out, put someone's nose out of joint (*Inf.*), rile, sting, vex, wound 3. arouse, excite, galvanize, goad, kindle, provoke, rouse, spur, stimulate, stir, whet 4. *With* on *or* upon *Of oneself* congratulate, flat~ ter, plume, preen, pride

piracy buccaneering, freebooting, hijacking, infringement, plagia~ rism, rapine, robbery at sea, steal~ ing, theft

pirate n. 1. buccaneer, corsair, fili~ buster, freebooter, marauder, raider, rover, sea robber, sea rov~ er, sea wolf 2. cribber (*Inf.*), in~ fringer, plagiarist, plagiarizer ~v. 3. appropriate, borrow, copy, crib (*Inf.*), lift (*Inf.*), plagiarize, poach, reproduce, steal

pit n. 1. abyss, cavity, chasm, coal mine, crater, dent, depression, dimple, excavation, gulf, hole, hol~ low, indentation, mine, pockmark, pothole, trench ~v. 2. *Often with* against match, oppose, put in op~ position, set against 3. dent, dint, gouge, hole, indent, mark, nick, notch, pockmark, scar

pitch v. 1. bung (*Brit. sl.*), cast, chuck (*Inf.*), fling, heave, hurl, launch, lob (*Inf.*), sling, throw, toss 2. erect, fix, locate, place, plant, put up, raise, settle, set up, station 3. flounder, lurch, make heavy weather, plunge, roll, toss, wallow, welter 4. dive, drop, fall headlong, stagger, topple, tumble ~n. 5. an~ gle, cant, dip, gradient, incline, slope, steepness, tilt 6. degree, height, highest point, level, point, summit 7. harmonic, modulation, sound, timbre, tone 8. line, patter, sales talk, spiel (*Inf.*) 9. field of

play, ground, park (*Brit. inf.*), sports field

pitch-black dark, ebony, inky, jet, jet-black, pitch-dark, raven, sable, unlit

pitch in 1. chip in (*Inf.*), contribute, cooperate, do one's bit, help, join in, lend a hand, participate 2. be~ gin, fall to, get busy, get cracking (*Inf.*), plunge into, set about, set to, tackle

piteous affecting, deplorable, dis~ tressing, doleful, grievous, heart~ breaking, heart-rending, lamen~ table, miserable, mournful, mov~ ing, pathetic, pitiable, pitiful, plaintive, poignant, sad, sorrowful, woeful, wretched

pitfall 1. catch, danger, difficulty, drawback, hazard, peril, snag, trap 2. deadfall, downfall, pit, snare, trap

pith 1. core, crux, essence, gist, heart, heart of the matter, kernel, marrow, meat, nub, point, quintes~ sence, salient point, the long and the short of it 2. consequence, depth, force, import, importance, matter, moment, power, signifi~ cance, strength, substance, value, weight

pithy brief, cogent, compact, con~ cise, epigrammatic, expressive, finely honed, forceful, laconic, meaningful, pointed, short, suc~ cinct, terse, to the point, trenchant

pitiful 1. deplorable, distressing, grievous, heartbreaking, heart~ rending, lamentable, miserable, pathetic, piteous, pitiable, sad, woeful, wretched 2. abject, base, beggarly, contemptible, despic~ able, inadequate, insignificant, low, mean, miserable, paltry, scurvy, shabby, sorry, vile, worthless

pitiless brutal, callous, cold-blooded, cold-hearted, cruel, hard-hearted, harsh, heartless, implac~ able, inexorable, inhuman, merci~ less, relentless, ruthless, uncaring, unfeeling, unmerciful, unsympa~ thetic

pittance allowance, chicken feed (*Sl.*), drop, mite, modicum, peanuts

(*Sl.*), portion, ration, slave wages, trifle

pity *n.* 1. charity, clemency, com~ miseration, compassion, condo~ lence, fellow feeling, forbearance, kindness, mercy, sympathy, ten~ derness, understanding 2. crime (*Inf.*), crying shame, misfortune, regret, sad thing, shame, sin 3. take pity on feel compassion for, forgive, have mercy on, melt, par~ don, put out of one's misery, relent, reprieve, show mercy, spare ~*v.* 4. bleed for, commiserate with, con~ dole with, feel for, feel sorry for, grieve for, have compassion for, sympathize with, weep for

pivot *n.* 1. axis, axle, fulcrum, spin~ dle, swivel 2. centre, focal point, heart, hinge, hub, kingpin ~*v.* 3. revolve, rotate, spin, swivel, turn, twirl 4. be contingent, depend, hang, hinge, rely, revolve round, turn

pixie brownie, elf, fairy, sprite

placard advertisement, *affiche*, bill, poster, public notice, sticker

placate appease, assuage, calm, conciliate, humour, mollify, pacify, propitiate, satisfy, soothe, win over

place *n.* 1. area, location, locus, point, position, site, situation, spot, station, venue, whereabouts 2. city, district, hamlet, locale, locality, neighbourhood, quarter, region, town, vicinity, village 3. grade, po~ sition, rank, station, status 4. ap~ pointment, berth (*Inf.*), billet (*Inf.*), employment, job, position, post 5. abode, apartment, domicile, dwelling, flat, home, house, manor, mansion, pad (*Sl.*), property, resi~ dence, seat 6. accommodation, room, space, stead 7. affair, charge, concern, duty, function, prerogative, responsibility, right, role 8. in place of as an alternative to, as a substitute for, in exchange for, in lieu of, instead of, taking the place of 9. put (someone) in his place bring down, cut down to size, humble, humiliate, make (some~ one) eat humble pie, make (some~ one) swallow his pride, mortify, take down a peg (*Inf.*) 10. take

place befall, betide, come about, come to pass (*Archaic*), go on, happen, occur, transpire (*Inf.*) ~*v.* 11. bung (*Inf.*), deposit, dispose, es~ tablish, fix, install, lay, locate, plant, position, put, rest, set, settle, situate, stand, station, stick (*Inf.*) 12. arrange, class, classify, grade, group, order, rank, sort 13. associ~ ate, identify, know, put one's finger on, recognize, remember, set in context 14. allocate, appoint, as~ sign, charge, commission, entrust, give

placid calm, collected, composed, cool, equable, even, even~ tempered, gentle, halcyon, imper~ turbable, mild, peaceful, quiet, self~ possessed, serene, still, tranquil, undisturbed, unexcitable, un~ moved, unruffled, untroubled

plagiarize appropriate, borrow, crib (*Inf.*), infringe, lift (*Inf.*), pi~ rate, steal, thieve

plague *n.* 1. contagion, disease, epidemic, infection, pandemic, pestilence 2. *Fig.* affliction, bane, blight, calamity, cancer, curse, evil, scourge, torment, trial 3. *Inf.* aggravation (*Inf.*), annoyance, bother, irritant, nuisance, pain (*Inf.*), pest, problem, thorn in one's flesh, vexation ~*v.* 4. afflict, annoy, badger, bedevil, bother, disturb, fret, harass, harry, hassle (*Inf.*), haunt, molest, pain, persecute, pester, tease, torment, torture, trouble, vex

plain *adj.* 1. apparent, clear, com~ prehensible, distinct, evident, leg~ ible, lucid, manifest, obvious, pa~ tent, transparent, unambiguous, understandable, unmistakable, visible 2. artless, blunt, candid, di~ rect, downright, forthright, frank, guileless, honest, ingenuous, open, outspoken, sincere, straight~ forward 3. common, common~ place, everyday, frugal, homely, lowly, modest, ordinary, simple, unaffected, unpretentious, worka~ day 4. austere, bare, basic, dis~ creet, modest, muted, pure, re~ strained, severe, simple, Spartan, stark, unadorned, unembellished, unornamented, unpatterned, un~

varnished 5. ill-favoured, not beautiful, not striking, ordinary, ugly, unalluring, unattractive, unlovely, unprepossessing 6. even, flat, level, plane, smooth ~*n.* 7. flatland, grassland, lowland, open country, plateau, prairie, steppe, tableland

plain-spoken blunt, candid, direct, downright, explicit, forthright, frank, open, outright, outspoken, straightforward, unequivocal

plaintive disconsolate, doleful, grief-stricken, grievous, heart-rending, melancholy, mournful, pathetic, piteous, pitiful, rueful, sad, sorrowful, wistful, woebegone, woeful

plan *n.* 1. contrivance, design, device, idea, method, plot, procedure, programme, project, proposal, proposition, scenario, scheme, strategy, suggestion, system 2. blueprint, chart, delineation, diagram, drawing, illustration, layout, map, representation, scale drawing, sketch ~*v.* 3. arrange, concoct, contrive, design, devise, draft, formulate, frame, invent, organize, outline, plot, prepare, represent, scheme, think out 4. aim, contemplate, envisage, foresee, intend, mean, propose, purpose

plane *n.* 1. flat surface, level surface 2. condition, degree, footing, level, position, stratum 3. aeroplane, aircraft, jet ~*adj.* 4. even, flat, flush, horizontal, level, plain, regular, smooth, uniform ~*v.* 5. glide, sail, skate, skim, volplane

plant *n.* 1. bush, flower, herb, shrub, vegetable, weed 2. factory, foundry, mill, shop, works, yard 3. apparatus, equipment, gear, machinery ~*v.* 4. implant, put in the ground, scatter, seed, set out, sow, transplant 5. establish, fix, found, imbed, insert, institute, lodge, root, set, settle

plaque badge, brooch, cartouche, medal, medallion, panel, plate, slab, tablet

plaster *n.* 1. gypsum, mortar, plaster of Paris, stucco 2. adhesive plaster, bandage, dressing, Elastoplast (*Trademark*), sticking plaster

~*v.* 3. bedaub, besmear, coat, cover, daub, overlay, smear, spread

plastic *adj.* 1. compliant, docile, easily influenced, impressionable, malleable, manageable, pliable, receptive, responsive, tractable 2. ductile, fictile, flexible, mouldable, pliable, pliant, soft, supple 3. *Sl.* artificial, false, meretricious, phoney (*Inf.*), pseudo (*Inf.*), sham, specious, spurious, superficial, synthetic

plate *n.* 1. dish, platter, trencher (*Archaic*) 2. course, dish, helping, portion, serving 3. layer, panel, sheet, slab 4. illustration, lithograph, print ~*v.* 5. anodize, coat, cover, electroplate, face, gild, laminate, nickel, overlay, platinize, silver

plateau 1. highland, mesa, table, tableland, upland 2. level, levelling off, stability, stage

platform 1. dais, podium, rostrum, stage, stand 2. manifesto, objective(s), party line, policy, principle, programme, tenet(s)

platitude 1. banality, bromide, cliché, commonplace, hackneyed saying, inanity, stereotype, trite remark, truism 2. banality, dullness, inanity, insipidity, triteness, triviality, vapidity, verbiage

platitudinous banal, clichéd, commonplace, corny (*Sl.*), hack, hackneyed, overworked, set, stale, stereotyped, stock, tired, trite, truistic, vapid, well-worn

platoon company, group, outfit (*Inf.*), patrol, squad, squadron, team

platter charger, dish, plate, salver, tray, trencher (*Archaic*)

plausible believable, colourable, conceivable, credible, fair-spoken, glib, likely, persuasive, possible, probable, reasonable, smooth, smooth-talking, smooth-tongued, specious, tenable

play *v.* 1. amuse oneself, caper, engage in games, entertain oneself, frisk, frolic, gambol, have fun, revel, romp, sport, trifle 2. be in a team, challenge, compete, contend against, participate, rival, take on, take part, vie with 3. act, act the part of, execute, impersonate, perform, personate, portray, represent, take the part of 4. bet, chance, gamble, hazard, punt (*Brit.*), risk, speculate, take, wager 5. **play ball** *Inf.* collaborate, cooperate, go along, play along, reciprocate, respond, show willing 6. **play by ear** ad lib, extemporize, improvise, rise to the occasion, take it as it comes 7. **play for time** delay, drag one's feet (*Inf.*), filibuster, hang fire, procrastinate, stall, temporize 8. **play the fool** act the goat (*Inf.*), clown, clown around, horse around (*Inf.*), lark (about) (*Inf.*), mess about, monkey around, skylark (*Inf.*) 9. **play the game** *Inf.* conform, follow the rules, go along with, keep in step, play by the rules, play fair, toe the line ~*n.* 10. comedy, drama, dramatic piece, entertainment, farce, masque, performance, piece, radio play, show, stage show, television drama, tragedy 11. amusement, caper, diversion, entertainment, frolic, fun, gambol, game, jest, pastime, prank, recreation, romp, sport 12. gambling, gaming 13. action, activity, elbowroom, exercise, give (*Inf.*), latitude, leeway, margin, motion, movement, operation, range, room, scope, space, sweep, swing 14. action, activity, employment, function, operation, transaction, working 15. foolery, fun, humour, jest, joking, lark (*Inf.*), prank, sport, teasing

play around dally, fool around, mess around, philander, take lightly, trifle, womanize

playboy gay dog, ladies' man, ladykiller (*Inf.*), lover boy (*Sl.*), man about town, philanderer, pleasure seeker, rake, roué, socialite, womanizer

play down gloss over, make light of, make little of, minimize, set no store by, soft-pedal (*Inf.*), underplay, underrate

player 1. competitor, contestant, participant, sportsman, sportswoman, team member 2. actor, actress, entertainer, performer,

Thespian, trouper 3. artist, instrumentalist, musician, music maker, performer, virtuoso

playful 1. cheerful, coltish, frisky, frolicsome, gay, impish, joyous, kittenish, larkish (*Inf.*), lively, merry, mischievous, puckish, rollicking, spirited, sportive, sprightly, vivacious 2. arch, coy, flirtatious, good-natured, humorous, jesting, jokey, joking, roguish, teasing, tongue-in-cheek, waggish

playmate chum (*Inf.*), companion, comrade, friend, neighbour, pal (*Inf.*), playfellow

play on *or* **upon** abuse, capitalize on, exploit, impose on, milk, profit by, take advantage of, trade on, turn to account, utilize

plaything amusement, bauble, game, gewgaw, gimcrack, pastime, toy, trifle, trinket

play up 1. accentuate, bring to the fore, call attention to, emphasize, highlight, magnify, point up, stress, turn the spotlight on, underline 2. *Brit. inf.* be painful, be sore, bother, give one gyp (*Brit. sl.*), give one trouble, hurt, pain, trouble 3. *Brit. inf.* be awkward, be bolshie (*Brit. inf.*), be cussed (*Inf.*), be disobedient, be stroppy (*Brit. sl.*), give trouble, misbehave 4. *Brit. inf.* be on the blink (*Sl.*), be wonky (*Brit. sl.*), malfunction, not work properly 5. **play up to** *Inf.* bootlick (*Inf.*), butter up, curry favour, fawn, flatter, get in with, ingratiate oneself, suck up to (*Inf.*), toady

play with 1. amuse oneself with, flirt with, string along, toy with, trifle with 2. fiddle with, fidget with, fool around, interfere with, jiggle, mess about, waggle, wiggle

playwright dramatist, dramaturge, dramaturgist

plea 1. appeal, begging, entreaty, intercession, overture, petition, prayer, request, suit, supplication 2. *Law* action, allegation, cause, suit 3. apology, claim, defence, excuse, explanation, extenuation, justification, pretext, vindication

plead 1. appeal (to), ask, beg, beseech, crave, entreat, implore, im~

portune, petition, request, solicit, supplicate 2. adduce, allege, argue, assert, maintain, put forward, use as an excuse

pleasant 1. acceptable, agreeable, amusing, delectable, delightful, enjoyable, fine, gratifying, lovely, nice, pleasing, pleasurable, refreshing, satisfying, welcome 2. affable, agreeable, amiable, charming, cheerful, cheery, congenial, engaging, friendly, genial, good-humoured, likable, nice

pleasantry badinage, banter, bon mot, good-natured remark, jest, joke, quip, sally, witticism

please 1. amuse, charm, cheer, content, delight, entertain, give pleasure to, gladden, gratify, humour, indulge, rejoice, satisfy, suit, tickle, tickle pink 2. be inclined, choose, desire, like, opt, prefer, see fit, want, will, wish

pleased chuffed (*Brit. sl.*), contented, delighted, euphoric, glad, gratified, happy, in high spirits, over the moon (*Inf.*), pleased as punch (*Inf.*), satisfied, thrilled, tickled, tickled pink

pleasing agreeable, amiable, amusing, attractive, charming, delightful, engaging, enjoyable, entertaining, gratifying, likable, pleasurable, polite, satisfying, winning

pleasure 1. amusement, bliss, comfort, contentment, delectation, delight, diversion, ease, enjoyment, gladness, gratification, happiness, joy, recreation, satisfaction, solace 2. choice, command, desire, inclination, mind, option, preference, purpose, will, wish

plebeian 1. *adj.* base, coarse, common, ignoble, low, lowborn, lower-class, mean, non-U (*Brit. inf.*), proletarian, uncultivated, unrefined, vulgar, working-class 2. *n.* commoner, common man, man in the street, peasant, pleb (*Brit. sl.*), prole (*Sl.*), proletarian

pledge *n.* 1. assurance, covenant, oath, promise, undertaking, vow, warrant, word, word of honour 2. bail, bond, collateral, deposit, ear-

nest, gage, guarantee, pawn, security, surety 3. health, toast ~*v.* 4. contract, engage, give one's oath (word, word of honour), promise, swear, undertake, vouch, vow 5. bind, engage, gage (*Archaic*), guarantee, mortgage, plight 6. drink the health of, drink to, toast

plentiful 1. abundant, ample, bounteous (*Literary*), bountiful, complete, copious, generous, inexhaustible, infinite, lavish, liberal, overflowing, plenteous, profuse 2. bumper, fertile, fruitful, luxuriant, plenteous, productive, prolific

plenty 1. abundance, enough, fund, good deal, great deal, heap(s) (*Inf.*), lots (*Inf.*), mass, masses, mine, mountain(s), oodles (*Inf.*), pile(s) (*Inf.*), plethora, quantities, quantity, stack(s), store, sufficiency, volume 2. abundance, affluence, copiousness, fertility, fruitfulness, luxury, opulence, plenitude, plenteousness, plentifulness, profusion, prosperity, wealth

plethora excess, glut, overabundance, profusion, superabundance, superfluity, surfeit, surplus

pliable 1. bendable, bendy, ductile, flexible, limber, lithe, malleable, plastic, pliant, supple 2. adaptable, compliant, docile, easily led, impressionable, influenceable, manageable, persuadable, pliant, receptive, responsive, susceptible, tractable, yielding

pliant 1. bendable, bendy, ductile, flexible, lithe, plastic, pliable, supple 2. adaptable, biddable, compliant, easily led, impressionable, influenceable, manageable, persuadable, pliable, susceptible, tractable, yielding

plight *n.* case, circumstances, condition, difficulty, dilemma, extremity, hole (*Sl.*), jam (*Inf.*), perplexity, pickle (*Inf.*), predicament, scrape (*Inf.*), situation, spot (*Inf.*), state, straits, trouble

plod 1. clump, drag, lumber, slog, stomp (*Inf.*), tramp, tread, trudge 2. drudge, grind (*Inf.*), grub, labour, peg away, persevere, plough

plot¹ n. 1. cabal, conspiracy, covin (*Law*), intrigue, machination, plan, scheme, stratagem 2. action, narrative, outline, scenario, story, story line, subject, theme, thread ~v. 3. cabal, collude, conspire, contrive, hatch, intrigue, machinate, manoeuvre, plan, scheme 4. calculate, chart, compute, draft, draw, locate, map, mark, outline 5. brew, conceive, concoct, contrive, cook up (*Inf.*), design, devise, frame, hatch, imagine, lay, project

plot² n. allotment, area, ground, lot, parcel, patch, tract

plough v. 1. break ground, cultivate, dig, furrow, ridge, till, turn over 2. *Usually with* through cut, drive, flounder, forge, plod, plunge, press, push, stagger, surge, wade 3. *With* into bulldoze, career, crash, hurtle, plunge, shove, smash

pluck¹ n. backbone, boldness, bottle (*Brit. sl.*), bravery, courage, determination, grit, guts (*Inf.*), hardihood, heart, intrepidity, mettle, nerve, resolution, spirit, spunk (*Inf.*)

pluck² v. 1. collect, draw, gather, harvest, pick, pull out *or* off 2. catch, clutch, jerk, pull at, snatch, tug, tweak, yank 3. finger, pick, plunk, strum, thrum, twang

plucky bold, brave, courageous, daring, doughty, game, gritty, gutsy (*Sl.*), hardy, heroic, intrepid, mettlesome, spirited, spunky (*Inf.*), undaunted, unflinching, valiant

plug n. 1. bung, cork, spigot, stopper, stopple 2. cake, chew, pigtail, quid, twist, wad 3. *Inf.* advert (*Brit. inf.*), advertisement, good word, hype (*Sl.*), mention, publicity, puff, push ~v. 4. block, bung, choke, close, cork, cover, fill, pack, seal, stop, stopper, stopple, stop up, stuff 5. *Inf.* advertise, build up, hype (*Sl.*), mention, promote, publicize, puff, push, write up 6. *Sl.* gun down, pick off, pop, pot, put a bullet in, shoot 7. *With* along *or* away *Inf.* drudge, grind (*Inf.*), labour, peg away, plod, slog, toil

through, plug away (*Inf.*), slog, soldier on, toil

plum *Fig.* 1. n. bonus, cream, find, pick, prize, treasure 2. adj. best, choice, first-class, prize

plumb n. 1. lead, plumb bob, plummet, weight ~adv. 2. perpendicularly, up and down, vertically 3. bang, exactly, precisely, slap, spot-on (*Brit. inf.*) ~v. 4. delve, explore, fathom, gauge, go into, measure, penetrate, probe, search, sound, unravel

plume 1. n. aigrette, crest, feather, pinion, quill 2. v. *With* on *or* upon congratulate oneself, pat oneself on the back, pique oneself, preen oneself, pride oneself

plump adj. beefy (*Inf.*), burly, buxom, chubby, corpulent, dumpy, fat, fleshy, full, obese, podgy, portly, roly-poly, rotund, round, stout, tubby, well-covered, well-upholstered (*Inf.*)

plunder 1. v. despoil, devastate, loot, pillage, raid, ransack, ravage, rifle, rob, sack, spoil, steal, strip 2. n. booty, ill-gotten gains, loot, pillage, prey, prize, rapine, spoils, swag (*Sl.*)

plunge v. 1. cast, descend, dip, dive, douse, drop, fall, go down, immerse, jump, nose-dive, pitch, plummet, sink, submerge, swoop, throw, tumble 2. career, charge, dash, hurtle, lurch, rush, tear ~n. 3. descent, dive, drop, fall, immersion, jump, submersion, swoop

plus 1. prep. added to, and, coupled with, with, with the addition of 2. adj. added, additional, extra, positive, supplementary 3. n. *Inf.* advantage, asset, benefit, bonus, extra, gain, good point, perk (*Inf.*), surplus

plutocrat capitalist, Croesus, Dives, fat cat (*Sl.*), magnate, millionaire, moneybags (*Sl.*), rich man, tycoon

ply 1. carry on, exercise, follow, practise, pursue, work at 2. employ, handle, manipulate, swing, utilize, wield 3. assail, beset, besiege, bombard, harass, importune, press, urge

poach appropriate, encroach, hunt *or* fish illegally, infringe, intrude, plunder, rob, steal, steal game, trespass

pocket *n.* 1. bag, compartment, hollow, pouch, receptacle, sack ~*adj.* 2. abridged, compact, concise, little, miniature, pint-size(d) (*Inf.*), portable, potted (*Inf.*), small ~*v.* 3. appropriate, filch, help oneself to, lift (*Inf.*), pilfer, purloin, snaffle (*Brit. inf.*), steal, take 4. accept, bear, brook, endure, put up with (*Inf.*), stomach, swallow, take, tolerate

pod *n./v.* hull, husk, shell, shuck

podgy chubby, chunky, dumpy, fat, fleshy, plump, roly-poly, rotund, short and fat, squat, stout, stubby, stumpy, tubby

podium dais, platform, rostrum, stage

poem lyric, ode, rhyme, song, sonnet, verse

poet bard, lyricist, maker (*Archaic*), rhymer, versifier

poetic elegiac, lyric, lyrical, metrical, rhythmical, songlike

poetry metrical composition, poems, poesy (*Archaic*), rhyme, rhyming, verse

poignancy 1. emotion, emotionalism, evocativeness, feeling, pathos, piteousness, plaintiveness, sadness, sentiment, tenderness 2. bitterness, intensity, keenness, piquancy, pungency, sharpness

poignant 1. affecting, agonizing, bitter, distressing, heartbreaking, heart-rending, intense, moving, painful, pathetic, sad, touching, upsetting 2. acute, biting, caustic, keen, penetrating, piercing, pointed, sarcastic, severe 3. acrid, piquant, pungent, sharp, stinging, tangy

point *n.* 1. dot, full stop, mark, period, speck, stop 2. location, place, position, site, spot, stage, station 3. apex, end, nib, prong, sharp end, spike, spur, summit, tine, tip, top 4. bill, cape, foreland, head, headland, ness (*Archaic*), promontory 5. circumstance, condition, degree, extent, position, stage 6. instant, juncture, moment, time, very minute 7. aim, design, end, goal, intent,

intention, motive, object, objective, purpose, reason, use, usefulness, utility 8. burden, core, crux, drift, essence, gist, heart, import, main idea, marrow, matter, meaning, nub, pith, proposition, question, subject, text, theme, thrust 9. aspect, detail, facet, feature, instance, item, nicety, particular 10. aspect, attribute, characteristic, peculiarity, property, quality, respect, side, trait 11. score, tally, unit 12. **beside the point** immaterial, incidental, inconsequential, irrelevant, not to the purpose, off the subject, out of the way, pointless, unimportant, without connection 13. **to the point** applicable, appropriate, apropos, apt, brief, fitting, germane, pertinent, pithy, pointed, relevant, short, suitable, terse ~*v.* 14. bespeak, call attention to, denote, designate, direct, indicate, show, signify 15. aim, bring to bear, direct, level, train 16. barb, edge, sharpen, taper, whet

point-blank 1. *adj.* abrupt, blunt, categorical, direct, downright, explicit, express, plain, straight-from-the-shoulder, unreserved 2. *adv.* bluntly, brusquely, candidly, directly, explicitly, forthrightly, frankly, openly, plainly, straight, straightforwardly

pointed acicular, acuminate, acute, barbed, cuspidate, edged, mucronate, sharp 2. accurate, acute, biting, cutting, incisive, keen, penetrating, pertinent, sharp, telling, trenchant

pointer 1. guide, hand, indicator, needle 2. advice, caution, hint, information, recommendation, suggestion, tip, warning

pointless absurd, aimless, fruitless, futile, inane, ineffectual, irrelevant, meaningless, nonsensical, senseless, silly, stupid, unavailing, unproductive, unprofitable, useless, vague, vain, worthless

point out allude to, bring up, call attention to, identify, indicate, mention, remind, reveal, show, specify

poise 1. *n.* aplomb, assurance, calmness, composure, cool (*Sl.*), coolness, dignity, elegance, equanimity, equilibrium, grace, presence, presence of mind, sang-froid, savoir-faire, self-possession, serenity 2. *v.* balance, float, hang, hang in midair, hang suspended, hold, hover, position, support, suspend

poised 1. calm, collected, composed, dignified, graceful, nonchalant, self-confident, self-possessed, serene, suave, together (*Inf.*), unruffled, urbane 2. all set, in the wings, on the brink, prepared, ready, standing by, waiting

poison *n.* 1. bane, toxin, venom 2. bane, blight, cancer, canker, contagion, contamination, corruption, malignancy, miasma, virus ~*v.* 3. adulterate, contaminate, envenom, give (someone) poison, infect, kill, murder, pollute 4. corrupt, defile, deprave, pervert, subvert, taint, undermine, vitiate, warp ~*adj.* 5. deadly, lethal, poisonous, toxic, venomous

poisonous 1. baneful (*Archaic*), deadly, fatal, lethal, mephitic, mortal, noxious, toxic, venomous, virulent 2. baleful, baneful (*Archaic*), corruptive, evil, malicious, noxious, pernicious, pestiferous, pestilential, vicious

poke *v.* 1. butt, dig, elbow, hit, jab, nudge, prod, punch, push, shove, stab, stick, thrust 2. butt in, interfere, intrude, meddle, nose, peek, poke one's nose into (*Inf.*), pry, snoop (*Inf.*), tamper 3. **poke fun at** chaff, jeer, make a mock of, make fun of, mock, rib (*Inf.*), ridicule, send up (*Brit. inf.*), take the mickey (*Inf.*), tease ~*n.* 4. butt, dig, hit, jab, nudge, prod, punch, thrust

poky confined, cramped, incommodious, narrow, small, tiny

polar 1. Antarctic, Arctic, cold, extreme, freezing, frozen, furthest, glacial, icy, terminal 2. beaconlike, cardinal, guiding, leading, pivotal 3. antagonistic, antipodal, antithetical, contradictory, contrary, diametric, opposed, opposite

pole[1] bar, mast, post, rod, shaft, spar, staff, standard, stick

pole[2] 1. antipode, extremity, limit, terminus 2. **poles apart** at opposite ends of the earth, at opposite extremes, incompatible, irreconcilable, miles apart, widely separated, worlds apart

police *n.* 1. boys in blue (*Inf.*), constabulary, fuzz (*Sl.*), law enforcement agency, police force, the law (*Inf.*), the Old Bill (*Sl.*) ~*v.* 2. control, guard, keep in order, keep the peace, patrol, protect, regulate, watch 3. *Fig.* check, monitor, observe, oversee, supervise

policeman bobby (*Inf.*), bogey (*Sl.*), constable, cop (*Sl.*), copper (*Sl.*), fuzz (*Sl.*), gendarme (*Sl.*), officer, peeler (*Obsolete Brit. sl.*), pig (*Sl.*), rozzer (*Sl.*)

policy 1. action, approach, code, course, custom, guideline, line, plan, practice, procedure, programme, protocol, rule, scheme, stratagem, theory 2. discretion, good sense, prudence, sagacity, shrewdness, wisdom

polish *v.* 1. brighten, buff, burnish, clean, furbish, rub, shine, smooth, wax 2. brush up, correct, cultivate, emend, enhance, finish, improve, perfect, refine, touch up ~*n.* 3. brightness, brilliance, finish, glaze, gloss, lustre, sheen, smoothness, sparkle, veneer 4. varnish, wax 5. *Fig.* class (*Inf.*), elegance, finesse, finish, grace, politesse, refinement, style, suavity, urbanity

polished 1. bright, burnished, furbished, glassy, gleaming, glossy, shining, slippery, smooth 2. *Fig.* accomplished, civilized, courtly, cultivated, elegant, finished, genteel, polite, refined, sophisticated, urbane, well-bred 3. adept, expert, faultless, fine, flawless, impeccable, masterly, outstanding, professional, skilful, superlative

polish off 1. consume, down, eat up, finish, put away, shift (*Inf.*), swill, wolf 2. bump off (*Inf.*), dispose of, do away with, do in (*Sl.*), eliminate, get rid of, kill, liquidate, murder

polite 1. affable, civil, complaisant, courteous, deferential, gracious, mannerly, obliging, respectful, well-behaved, well-mannered 2. civilized, courtly, cultured, elegant, genteel, polished, refined, urbane, well-bred

politic 1. artful, astute, canny, crafty, cunning, designing, ingen~ ious, intriguing, Machiavellian, scheming, shrewd, sly, subtle, un~ scrupulous 2. advisable, diplomat~ ic, discreet, expedient, in one's best interests, judicious, prudent, sagacious, sensible, tactful, wise

politician legislator, Member of Parliament, M.P., office bearer, politico (*Inf., chiefly U.S.*), public servant, statesman

politics 1. affairs of state, civics, government, government policy, political science, polity, statecraft, statesmanship 2. Machiavellian~ ism, machination, power struggle, *Realpolitik*

poll *n.* 1. figures, returns, tally, vote, voting 2. ballot, canvass, census, count, Gallup Poll, (public) opinion poll, sampling, survey ~*v.* 3. regis~ ter, tally 4. ballot, canvass, inter~ view, question, sample, survey

pollute 1. adulterate, befoul, con~ taminate, dirty, foul, infect, make filthy, mar, poison, soil, spoil, stain, taint 2. besmirch, corrupt, debase, debauch, defile, deprave, des~ ecrate, dishonour, profane, sully, violate

pollution adulteration, contamina~ tion, corruption, defilement, dirty~ ing, foulness, impurity, taint, un~ cleanness, vitiation

pomp 1. ceremony, flourish, gran~ deur, magnificence, pageant, pag~ eantry, parade, solemnity, splen~ dour, state 2. display, grandiosity, ostentation, pomposity, show, vainglory

pompous 1. affected, arrogant, bloated, grandiose, imperious, magisterial, ostentatious, over~ bearing, pontifical, portentous, pretentious, puffed up, self- important, showy, supercilious, vainglorious 2. boastful, bombastic,

flatulent, fustian, grandiloquent, high-flown, inflated, magniloquent, orotund, overblown, turgid, windy

pond dew pond, duck pond, fish pond, lochan (*Scot.*), millpond, pool, small lake, tarn

ponder brood, cerebrate, cogitate, consider, contemplate, deliberate, examine, excogitate, give thought to, meditate, mull over, muse, puz~ zle over, reflect, ruminate, study, think, weigh

ponderous 1. bulky, cumbersome, cumbrous, heavy, hefty, huge, massive, unwieldy, weighty 2. awkward, clumsy, elephantine, graceless, heavy-footed, laborious, lumbering 3. dreary, dull, heavy, laboured, lifeless, long-winded, pe~ dantic, pedestrian, plodding, prolix, stilted, stodgy, tedious, verbose

pontificate declaim, dogmatize, expound, hold forth, lay down the law, pontify, preach, pronounce, sound off

pooh-pooh belittle, brush aside, deride, disdain, dismiss, disregard, make little of, play down, scoff, scorn, slight, sneer, sniff at, spurn, turn up one's nose at (*Inf.*)

pool[1] 1. lake, mere, pond, puddle, splash, tarn 2. swimming bath, swimming pool

pool[2] *n.* 1. collective, combine, consortium, group, syndicate, team, trust 2. bank, funds, jackpot, kitty, pot, stakes ~*v.* 3. amalgam~ ate, combine, join forces, league, merge, put together, share

poor 1. badly off, broke (*Inf.*), desti~ tute, hard up (*Inf.*), impecunious, impoverished, indigent, in need, in want, necessitous, needy, on one's beam-ends, on one's uppers, on the rocks, penniless, penurious, poverty-stricken, skint (*Brit. sl.*), stony-broke (*Brit. sl.*) 2. deficient, exiguous, inadequate, incomplete, insufficient, lacking, meagre, mis~ erable, niggardly, pitiable, re~ duced, scanty, skimpy, slight, sparse, straitened 3. below par, faulty, feeble, inferior, low-grade, mediocre, rotten (*Inf.*), rubbishy, second-rate, shabby, shoddy, sorry, substandard, unsatisfactory, valueless, weak, worthless 4. bad, bare, barren, depleted, exhausted, fruitless, impoverished, infertile, sterile, unfruitful, unproductive 5. hapless, ill-fated, luckless, miserable, pathetic, pitiable, unfortunate, unhappy, unlucky, wretched 6. humble, insignificant, lowly, mean, modest, paltry, plain, trivial

poorly 1. *adv.* badly, crudely, inadequately, incompetently, inexpertly, inferiorly, insufficiently, meanly, shabbily, unsatisfactorily, unsuccessfully 2. *adj. Inf.* ailing, below par, ill, indisposed, off colour, out of sorts, rotten (*Inf.*), seedy (*Inf.*), sick, under the weather (*Inf.*), unwell

pop *v.* 1. bang, burst, crack, explode, go off, report, snap 2. *Often with in, out, etc. Inf.* appear, call, come *or* go suddenly, drop in (*Inf.*), leave quickly, nip in (*Brit. inf.*), nip out (*Brit. inf.*), visit 3. *Esp. of eyes* bulge, protrude, stick out 4. insert, push, put, shove, slip, stick, thrust, tuck ~*n.* 5. bang, burst, crack, explosion, noise, report 6. *Inf.* fizzy drink, lemonade, soda water, soft drink

pope Bishop of Rome, Holy Father, pontiff, Vicar of Christ

populace commonalty, crowd, general public, hoi polloi, inhabitants, masses, mob, multitude, people, rabble, throng

popular 1. accepted, approved, celebrated, famous, fashionable, favoured, favourite, in, in demand, in favour, liked, sought-after, well-liked 2. common, conventional, current, general, prevailing, prevalent, public, standard, stock, ubiquitous, universal, widespread

popularity acceptance, acclaim, adoration, approval, celebrity, currency, esteem, fame, favour, idolization, lionization, recognition, regard, renown, reputation, repute, vogue

popularize disseminate, familiarize, give currency to, give mass appeal, make available to all, simplify, spread, universalize

popularly commonly, conventionally, customarily, generally, ordinarily, regularly, traditionally, universally, usually, widely

populate colonize, inhabit, live in, occupy, people, settle

population citizenry, community, denizens, folk, inhabitants, natives, people, populace, residents, society

populous crowded, heavily populated, overpopulated, packed, populated, swarming, teeming, thronged

pore[1] *v.* brood, contemplate, dwell on, examine, go over, peruse, ponder, read, scrutinize, study

pore[2] *n.* hole, opening, orifice, outlet, stoma

pornographic blue, dirty, filthy, indecent, lewd, obscene, offensive, prurient, salacious, smutty

pornography dirt, erotica, filth, indecency, obscenity, porn (*Inf.*), porno (*Inf.*), smut

porous absorbent, absorptive, penetrable, permeable, pervious, spongy

port *Nautical* anchorage, harbour, haven, roads, roadstead, seaport

portable compact, convenient, easily carried, handy, light, lightweight, manageable, movable, portative

portend adumbrate, augur, bespeak, betoken, bode, foreshadow, foretell, foretoken, forewarn, harbinger, herald, indicate, omen, point to, predict, presage, prognosticate, promise, threaten, warn of

portent augury, foreboding, foreshadowing, forewarning, harbinger, indication, omen, premonition, presage, presentiment, prognostic, prognostication, sign, threat, warning

portentous 1. alarming, crucial, fateful, important, menacing, minatory, momentous, ominous, significant, sinister, threatening 2. amazing, astounding, awe-inspiring, extraordinary, miraculous, phenomenal, prodigious, remarkable 3. bloated, elephantine, heavy, pompous, ponderous, pontifical, self-important, solemn

porter[1] baggage attendant, bearer, carrier

porter[2] caretaker, concierge, doorman, gatekeeper, janitor

portion *n.* 1. bit, fraction, fragment, morsel, part, piece, scrap, section, segment 2. allocation, allotment, allowance, division, lot, measure, parcel, quantity, quota, ration, share 3. helping, piece, serving 4. cup, destiny, fate, fortune, lot, luck ~*v.* 5. allocate, allot, apportion, assign, deal, distribute, divide, divvy up (*Inf.*), dole out, parcel out, partition, share out

portrait 1. image, likeness, painting, photograph, picture, portraiture, representation, sketch 2. account, characterization, depiction, description, portrayal, profile, thumbnail sketch, vignette

portray 1. delineate, depict, draw, figure, illustrate, limn, paint, picture, render, represent, sketch 2. characterize, depict, describe, paint a mental picture of, put in words 3. act the part of, play, represent

portrayal characterization, delineation, depiction, description, impersonation, interpretation, performance, picture, rendering, representation

pose *v.* 1. arrange, model, position, sit, sit for 2. *Often with* **as** feign, impersonate, masquerade as, pass oneself off as, pretend to be, profess to be, sham 3. affect, attitudinize, posture, put on airs, show off (*Inf.*), strike an attitude 4. advance, posit, present, propound, put, put forward, set, state, submit ~*n.* 5. attitude, bearing, mien (*Literary*), position, posture, stance 6. act, affectation, air, attitudinizing, façade, front, mannerism, masquerade, posturing, pretence, role

poser brain-teaser (*Inf.*), conundrum, enigma, knotty point, problem, puzzle, question, riddle, tough one, vexed question

position *n.* 1. area, bearings, locale, locality, location, place, point, post, reference, site, situation, spot, station, whereabouts 2. arrangement, attitude, disposition, pose, posture, stance 3. angle, attitude, belief, opinion, outlook, point of view, slant, stance, stand, standpoint, view, viewpoint 4. circumstances, condition, pass, plight, predicament, situation, state, strait(s) 5. caste, class, consequence, importance, place, prestige, rank, reputation, standing, station, stature, status 6. berth (*Inf.*), billet (*Inf.*), capacity, duty, employment, function, job, occupation, office, place, post, role, situation ~*v.* 7. arrange, array, dispose, fix, lay out, locate, place, put, set, settle, stand, stick (*Inf.*)

positive 1. absolute, actual, affirmative, categorical, certain, clear, clear-cut, conclusive, concrete, decisive, definite, direct, explicit, express, firm, incontrovertible, indisputable, real, unequivocal, unmistakable 2. assured, certain, confident, convinced, sure 3. assertive, cocksure, decided, dogmatic, emphatic, firm, forceful, opinionated, peremptory, resolute, stubborn 4. beneficial, constructive, effective, efficacious, forward-looking, helpful, practical, productive, progressive, useful 5. *Inf.* absolute, complete, consummate, out-and-out, perfect, rank, thorough, thoroughgoing, unmitigated, utter

positively absolutely, assuredly, categorically, certainly, definitely, emphatically, firmly, surely, undeniably, unequivocally, unmistakably, unquestionably, with certainty, without qualification

possess 1. be blessed with, be born with, be endowed with, enjoy, have, have to one's name, hold, own 2. acquire, control, dominate, hold, occupy, seize, take over, take possession of 3. bewitch, consume, control, dominate, enchant, fixate, influence, mesmerize, obsess, put under a spell

possessed bedevilled, berserk, bewitched, consumed, crazed, cursed, demented, enchanted, frenetic, frenzied, hag-ridden, haunted, maddened, obsessed, raving, under a spell

possession 1. control, custody, hold, occupancy, occupation, own~ership, proprietorship, tenure, title 2. *Plural* assets, belongings, chat~tels, effects, estate, goods and chattels, property, things, wealth 3. colony, dominion, protectorate, province, territory

possessive acquisitive, control~ling, covetous, dominating, domi~neering, grasping, jealous, over~protective, selfish

possibility 1. feasibility, likelihood, plausibility, potentiality, practi~cability, workableness 2. chance, hazard, hope, liability, likelihood, odds, probability, prospect, risk 3. *Often plural* capabilities, potential, potentiality, promise, prospects, talent

possible 1. conceivable, credible, hypothetical, imaginable, likely, potential 2. attainable, doable, fea~sible, on (*Inf.*), practicable, realiz~able, viable, within reach, work~able 3. hopeful, likely, potential, probable, promising

possibly 1. God willing, haply (*Ar~chaic*), maybe, mayhap (*Archaic*), peradventure (*Archaic*), per~chance (*Archaic*), perhaps 2. at all, by any chance, by any means, in any way

post[1] 1. *n.* column, newel, pale, palisade, picket, pillar, pole, shaft, stake, standard, stock, support, up~right 2. *v.* advertise, affix, an~nounce, display, make known, pin up, proclaim, promulgate, publi~cize, publish, put up, stick up

post[2] *n.* 1. appointment, assign~ment, berth (*Inf.*), billet (*Inf.*), em~ployment, job, office, place, posi~tion, situation 2. beat, place, posi~tion, station ~*v.* 3. assign, establish, locate, place, position, put, situate, station

post[3] *n.* 1. collection, delivery, mail, postal service ~*v.* 2. dis~patch, mail, send, transmit 3. ad~vise, brief, fill in on, inform, notify, report to

poster advertisement, *affiche*, an~nouncement, bill, notice, placard, public notice, sticker

posterity 1. children, descendants, family, heirs, issue, offspring, progeny, scions, seed 2. future, fu~ture generations, succeeding gen~erations

postmortem *n.* analysis, autopsy, dissection, examination, necropsy

postpone adjourn, defer, delay, hold over, put back, put off, shelve, suspend, table

postponement adjournment, de~ferment, deferral, delay, morato~rium, respite, stay, suspension

postscript addition, afterthought, afterword, appendix, P.S., sup~plement

postulate advance, assume, hy~pothesize, posit, predicate, presup~pose, propose, put forward, sup~pose, take for granted, theorize

posture *n.* 1. attitude, bearing, car~riage, disposition, mien (*Literary*), pose, position, set, stance 2. cir~cumstance, condition, mode, phase, position, situation, state 3. attitude, disposition, feeling, frame of mind, inclination, mood, outlook, point of view, stance, standpoint ~*v.* 4. affect, attitudinize, do for effect, make a show, pose, put on airs, show off (*Inf.*), try to attract attention

potent 1. efficacious, forceful, mighty, powerful, puissant, strong, vigorous 2. cogent, compelling, convincing, effective, forceful, im~pressive, persuasive, telling 3. authoritative, commanding, domi~nant, dynamic, influential, power~ful

potential 1. *adj.* budding, dormant, embryonic, future, hidden, inher~ent, latent, likely, possible, prom~ising, undeveloped, unrealized 2. *n.* ability, aptitude, capability, capac~ity, possibility, potentiality, power, the makings, what it takes (*Inf.*), wherewithal

potion brew, concoction, cup, dose, draught, elixir, mixture, philtre, tonic

potter dabble, fiddle (*Inf.*), footle

(*Inf.*), fribble, fritter, mess about, poke along, tinker

pottery ceramics, earthenware, stoneware, terra cotta

pouch bag, container, pocket, poke (*Dialect*), purse, sack

pounce 1. *v.* ambush, attack, bound onto, dash at, drop, fall upon, jump, leap at, snatch, spring, strike, swoop, take by surprise, take unawares 2. *n.* assault, attack, bound, jump, leap, spring, swoop

pound[1] 1. batter, beat, belabour, clobber (*Sl.*), hammer, pelt, pummel, strike, thrash, thump 2. bray (*Dialect*), bruise, comminute, crush, powder, pulverize, triturate 3. din into, drub into, drum into, hammer into 4. *With* out bang, beat, hammer, thump 5. clomp, march, stomp (*Inf.*), thunder, tramp 6. beat, palpitate, pitapat, pulsate, pulse, throb

pound[2] *n.* compound, enclosure, pen, yard

pour 1. decant, let flow, spill, splash 2. course, emit, flow, gush, run, rush, spew, spout, stream 3. bucket down (*Inf.*), come down in torrents, rain, rain cats and dogs (*Inf.*), rain hard *or* heavily, sheet, teem 4. crowd, stream, swarm, teem, throng

pout 1. *v.* glower, look petulant, look sullen, lower, make a *moue*, mope, pull a long face, purse one's lips, sulk, turn down the corners of one's mouth 2. *n.* glower, long face, *moue*, sullen look

poverty 1. beggary, destitution, distress, hand-to-mouth existence, hardship, indigence, insolvency, necessitousness, necessity, need, pauperism, pennilessness, penury, privation, want 2. dearth, deficiency, insufficiency, lack, paucity, scarcity, shortage 3. aridity, bareness, barrenness, deficiency, infertility, meagreness, poorness, sterility, unfruitfulness

poverty-stricken bankrupt, beggared, broke (*Inf.*), destitute, distressed, impecunious, impoverished, indigent, needy, on one's beam-ends, on one's uppers, penniless, penurious, poor, skint (*Brit. sl.*), stony-broke (*Brit. sl.*)

powder *n.* 1. dust, fine grains, loose particles, pounce, talc ~*v.* 2. crush, granulate, grind, pestle, pound, pulverize 3. cover, dredge, dust, scatter, sprinkle, strew

power 1. ability, capability, capacity, competence, competency, faculty, potential 2. brawn, energy, force, forcefulness, intensity, might, muscle, potency, strength, vigour, weight 3. ascendancy, authority, command, control, dominance, domination, dominion, influence, mastery, rule, sovereignty, supremacy, sway 4. authority, authorization, licence, prerogative, privilege, right, warrant

powerful 1. energetic, mighty, potent, robust, stalwart, strapping, strong, sturdy, vigorous 2. authoritative, commanding, controlling, dominant, influential, prevailing, puissant, sovereign, supreme 3. cogent, compelling, convincing, effective, effectual, forceful, forcible, impressive, persuasive, telling, weighty

powerfully forcefully, forcibly, hard, mightily, strongly, vigorously, with might and main

powerless 1. debilitated, disabled, etiolated, feeble, frail, helpless, impotent, incapable, incapacitated, ineffectual, infirm, paralysed, prostrate, weak 2. defenceless, dependent, disenfranchised, disfranchised, ineffective, subject, tied, unarmed, vulnerable

practicability advantage, feasibility, operability, possibility, practicality, use, usefulness, value, viability, workability

practicable achievable, attainable, doable, feasible, performable, possible, viable, within the realm of possibility, workable

practical 1. applied, efficient, empirical, experimental, factual, functional, pragmatic, realistic, utilitarian 2. businesslike, down-to-earth, everyday, hard-headed, matter-of-fact, mundane, ordinary, realistic, sensible, workaday 3. doable, feasible, practicable, serviceable, sound, useful, workable 4. accomplished, efficient, experienced, proficient, qualified, seasoned, skilled, trained, veteran, working

practically 1. all but, almost, basically, close to, essentially, fundamentally, in effect, just about, nearly, to all intents and purposes, very nearly, virtually, well-nigh 2. clearly, matter-of-factly, rationally, realistically, reasonably, sensibly, unsentimentally, with common sense

practice 1. custom, habit, method, mode, praxis, routine, rule, system, tradition, usage, use, usual procedure, way, wont 2. discipline, drill, exercise, preparation, rehearsal, repetition, study, training, work-out 3. action, application, effect, exercise, experience, operation, use 4. business, career, profession, vocation, work

practise 1. discipline, drill, exercise, go over, go through, polish, prepare, rehearse, repeat, study, train, warm up, work out 2. apply, carry out, do, follow, live up to, observe, perform, put into practice 3. carry on, engage in, ply, pursue, specialize in, undertake, work at

practised able, accomplished, experienced, expert, proficient, qualified, seasoned, skilled, trained, versed

pragmatic businesslike, down-to-earth, efficient, hard-headed, matter-of-fact, practical, realistic, sensible, utilitarian

praise n. 1. acclaim, acclamation, accolade, applause, approbation, approval, cheering, commendation, compliment, congratulation, encomium, eulogy, good word, kudos, laudation, ovation, panegyric, plaudit, tribute 2. adoration, devotion, glory, homage, thanks, worship ~v. 3. acclaim, admire, applaud, approve, cheer, compliment, congratulate, cry up, eulogize, extol, honour, laud, pay tribute to, sing the praises of 4. adore,

bless, exalt, give thanks to, glorify, magnify (*Archaic*), pay homage to, worship

praiseworthy admirable, commendable, creditable, estimable, excellent, exemplary, fine, honourable, laudable, meritorious, worthy

prance 1. bound, caper, cavort, dance, frisk, gambol, jump, leap, romp, skip, spring 2. parade, show off (*Inf.*), stalk, strut, swagger, swank (*Inf.*)

prank antic, caper, escapade, frolic, jape, lark (*Inf.*), practical joke, skylarking (*Inf.*), trick

prattle babble, blather, blether, chatter, clack, drivel, gabble, jabber, patter, rattle on, run on, twitter, witter (*Inf.*)

pray 1. offer a prayer, recite the rosary, say one's prayers 2. adjure, ask, beg, beseech, call upon, crave, cry for, entreat, implore, importune, invoke, petition, plead, request, solicit, sue, supplicate, urge

prayer 1. communion, devotion, invocation, litany, orison, supplication 2. appeal, entreaty, petition, plea, request, suit, supplication

preach 1. address, deliver a sermon, evangelize, exhort, orate 2. admonish, advocate, exhort, harangue, lecture, moralize, sermonize, urge

preacher clergyman, evangelist, minister, missionary, parson, revivalist

preamble exordium, foreword, introduction, opening statement *or* remarks, overture, preface, prelude, proem, prolegomenon

precarious chancy (*Inf.*), dangerous, dicey (*Sl.*), dodgy (*Brit. inf.*), doubtful, dubious, hairy (*Sl.*), hazardous, insecure, perilous, risky, shaky, slippery, touch and go, tricky, uncertain, unreliable, unsafe, unsettled, unstable, unsteady, unsure

precaution 1. insurance, preventative measure, protection, provision, safeguard, safety measure 2. anticipation, care, caution, circumspection, foresight, forethought, providence, prudence, wariness

precede antecede, antedate, come first, forerun, go ahead of, go before, head, herald, introduce, lead, pave the way, preface, take precedence, usher

precedence antecedence, lead, pre-eminence, preference, primacy, priority, rank, seniority, superiority, supremacy

precedent n. antecedent, authority, criterion, example, exemplar, instance, model, paradigm, pattern, previous example, prototype, standard

preceding above, aforementioned, aforesaid, anterior, earlier, foregoing, former, past, previous, prior

precept 1. behest, canon, command, commandment, decree, direction, instruction, law, mandate, order, ordinance, principle, regulation, rule, statute 2. axiom, byword, guideline, maxim, motto, principle, rule, saying

precinct 1. bound, boundary, confine, enclosure, limit 2. area, district, quarter, section, sector, zone

precincts borders, bounds, confines, district, environs, limits, milieu, neighbourhood, purlieus, region, surrounding area

precious 1. adored, beloved, cherished, darling, dear, dearest, favourite, idolized, loved, prized, treasured, valued 2. choice, costly, dear, expensive, exquisite, fine, high-priced, inestimable, invaluable, priceless, prized, rare, recherché, valuable 3. affected, alembicated, artificial, chichi, fastidious, overnice, overrefined, twee (*Brit. inf.*)

precipice bluff, brink, cliff, cliff face, crag, height, rock face, sheer drop, steep

precipitate v. 1. accelerate, advance, bring on, dispatch, expedite, further, hasten, hurry, press, push forward, quicken, speed up, trigger 2. cast, discharge, fling, hurl, launch, let fly, send forth, throw ~adj. 3. breakneck, headlong, plunging, rapid, rushing, swift, vio-

lent 4. frantic, harum-scarum, hasty, heedless, hurried, ill-advised, impetuous, impulsive, indiscreet, madcap, precipitous, rash, reckless 5. abrupt, brief, quick, sudden, unexpected, without warning

precipitous 1. abrupt, dizzy, falling sharply, high, perpendicular, sheer, steep 2. abrupt, careless, harum-scarum, hasty, heedless, hurried, ill-advised, precipitate, rash, reckless, sudden

precise 1. absolute, accurate, actual, clear-cut, correct, definite, exact, explicit, express, fixed, literal, particular, specific, strict, unequivocal 2. careful, ceremonious, exact, fastidious, finicky, formal, inflexible, meticulous, nice, particular, prim, punctilious, puritanical, rigid, scrupulous, stiff, strict

precisely absolutely, accurately, bang, correctly, exactly, just, just so, literally, neither more nor less, plumb (*Inf.*), slap (*Inf.*), smack (*Inf.*), square, squarely, strictly

precision accuracy, care, correctness, definiteness, exactitude, exactness, fidelity, meticulousness, nicety, particularity, preciseness, rigour

preclude check, debar, exclude, forestall, hinder, inhibit, make impossible, make impracticable, obviate, prevent, prohibit, put a stop to, restrain, rule out, stop

precocious advanced, ahead, bright, developed, forward, quick, smart

preconception bias, notion, preconceived idea *or* notion, predisposition, prejudice, prepossession, presumption, presupposition

precondition essential, must, necessity, prerequisite, requirement, *sine qua non*

precursor 1. forerunner, harbinger, herald, messenger, usher, vanguard 2. antecedent, forebear, forerunner, originator, pioneer, predecessor

precursory antecedent, introductory, preceding, prefatory, preliminary, preparatory, previous, prior

predatory 1. carnivorous, hunting, predacious, rapacious, raptorial, ravening 2. despoiling, greedy, marauding, pillaging, plundering, rapacious, ravaging, thieving, voracious, vulturine, vulturous

predecessor 1. antecedent, forerunner, precursor, previous (former, prior) job holder 2. ancestor, antecedent, forebear, forefather

predestination destiny, doom, election (*Theology*), fate, foreordainment, foreordination, lot, necessity, predetermination

predestine doom, fate, foreordain, mean, predestinate, predetermine, pre-elect, preordain

predetermined agreed, arranged in advance, cut and dried (*Inf.*), decided beforehand, fixed, prearranged, preplanned, set, settled, set up

predicament corner, dilemma, emergency, fix (*Inf.*), hole (*Sl.*), jam (*Inf.*), mess, pickle (*Inf.*), pinch, plight, quandary, scrape (*Inf.*), situation, spot (*Inf.*), state

predicate 1. affirm, assert, aver, avouch, avow, contend, declare, maintain, proclaim, state 2. connote, imply, indicate, intimate, signify, suggest 3. *With* on *or* upon base, build, establish, found, ground, postulate, rest

predict augur, divine, forebode, forecast, foresee, foretell, portend, presage, prognosticate, prophesy, soothsay

predictable anticipated, calculable, certain, expected, foreseeable, foreseen, likely, reliable, sure, sure-fire (*Inf.*)

prediction augury, divination, forecast, prognosis, prognostication, prophecy, soothsaying

predilection bias, fancy, fondness, inclination, leaning, liking, love, partiality, penchant, predisposition, preference, proclivity, proneness, propensity, taste, tendency, weakness

predispose affect, bias, dispose, incline, induce, influence, lead, make (one) of a mind to, prejudice, prepare, prime, prompt, sway

predisposed agreeable, amenable, given to, inclined, liable, minded, prone, ready, subject, susceptible, willing

predisposition bent, bias, disposition, inclination, likelihood, penchant, potentiality, predilection, proclivity, proneness, propensity, susceptibility, tendency, willingness

predominance ascendancy, control, dominance, dominion, edge, greater number, hold, leadership, mastery, paramountcy, preponderance, supremacy, sway, upper hand, weight

predominant ascendant, capital, chief, controlling, dominant, important, leading, main, paramount, preponderant, prevailing, prevalent, primary, prime, principal, prominent, ruling, sovereign, superior, supreme

predominate be most noticeable, carry weight, get the upper hand, hold sway, outweigh, overrule, overshadow, preponderate, prevail, reign, rule, tell

pre-eminence distinction, excellence, paramountcy, predominance, prestige, prominence, renown, superiority, supremacy, transcendence

pre-eminent chief, consummate, distinguished, excellent, foremost, incomparable, matchless, outstanding, paramount, peerless, predominant, renowned, superior, supreme, transcendent, unequalled, unrivalled, unsurpassed

pre-eminently above all, by far, conspicuously, eminently, emphatically, exceptionally, far and away, incomparably, inimitably, matchlessly, notably, *par excellence*, particularly, second to none, signally, singularly, strikingly, superlatively, supremely

pre-empt acquire, anticipate, appropriate, arrogate, assume, seize, take over, usurp

preen 1. *Of birds* clean, plume 2. array, deck out, doll up (*Sl.*), dress up, prettify, primp, prink, spruce up, titivate, trim 3. **preen oneself (on)** congratulate oneself, pique oneself, plume oneself, pride oneself

preface 1. *n.* exordium, foreword, introduction, preamble, preliminary, prelude, proem, prolegomenon, prologue 2. *v.* begin, introduce, launch, lead up to, open, precede, prefix

prefer 1. adopt, be partial to, choose, desire, elect, fancy, favour, go for, incline towards, like better, opt for, pick, plump for, select, single out, wish, would rather, would sooner 2. file, lodge, place, present, press, put forward 3. advance, aggrandize, elevate, move up, promote, raise, upgrade

preferable best, better, choice, chosen, favoured, more desirable, more eligible, superior, worthier

preferably as a matter of choice, by choice, first, in *or* for preference, much rather, much sooner, rather, sooner, willingly

preference 1. choice, desire, election, favourite, first choice, option, partiality, pick, predilection, selection, top of the list 2. advantage, favoured treatment, favouritism, first place, precedence, pride of place, priority

preferential advantageous, better, favoured, partial, partisan, privileged, special, superior

preferment advancement, dignity, elevation, exaltation, promotion, rise, upgrading

pregnancy gestation, gravidity

pregnant 1. big *or* heavy with child, enceinte, expectant, expecting (*Inf.*), gravid, in the club (*Brit. sl.*), in the family way (*Inf.*), in the pudding club (*Sl.*), preggers (*Brit. inf.*), with child 2. charged, eloquent, expressive, loaded, meaningful, pointed, significant, suggestive, telling, weighty 3. creative, imaginative, inventive, original, seminal 4. abounding in, abundant, fecund, fertile, fraught, fruitful, full, productive, prolific, replete, rich in, teeming

prehistoric 1. earliest, early, primeval, primitive, primordial 2. ancient, antediluvian, antiquated, archaic, out of date, out of the ark (*Inf.*)

prejudge anticipate, forejudge, jump to conclusions, make a hasty assessment, presume, presuppose

prejudice *n.* 1. bias, jaundiced eye, partiality, preconceived notion, preconception, prejudgment, warp 2. bigotry, chauvinism, discrimination, injustice, intolerance, narrow-mindedness, racism, sexism, unfairness 3. damage, detriment, disadvantage, harm, hurt, impairment, loss, mischief ~*v.* 4. bias, colour, distort, influence, jaundice, poison, predispose, prepossess, slant, sway, warp 5. damage, harm, hinder, hurt, impair, injure, mar, spoil, undermine

prejudiced biased, bigoted, conditioned, discriminatory, influenced, intolerant, jaundiced, narrow-minded, one-sided, opinionated, partial, partisan, prepossessed, unfair

prejudicial counterproductive, damaging, deleterious, detrimental, disadvantageous, harmful, hurtful, inimical, injurious, undermining, unfavourable

preliminary 1. *adj.* exploratory, first, initial, initiatory, introductory, opening, pilot, precursory, prefatory, preparatory, prior, qualifying, test, trial 2. *n.* beginning, first round, foundation, groundwork, initiation, introduction, opening, preamble, preface, prelims, prelude, preparation, start

prelude beginning, commencement, curtain-raiser, exordium, foreword, intro (*Inf.*), introduction, overture, preamble, preface, preliminary, preparation, proem, prolegomenon, prologue, start

premature 1. abortive, early, embryonic, forward, green, immature, incomplete, predeveloped, raw, undeveloped, unfledged, unripe, unseasonable, untimely 2. *Fig.* hasty, ill-considered, ill-timed, impulsive, inopportune, overhasty, precipitate, previous (*Inf.*), rash, too soon, untimely

prematurely 1. before one's time, too early, too soon, untimely 2. at half-cock, half-cocked, overhastily, precipitately, rashly, too hastily, too soon

premeditated aforethought, calculated, conscious, considered, contrived, deliberate, intended, intentional, planned, prepense, studied, wilful

premeditation deliberation, design, determination, forethought, intention, malice aforethought, planning, plotting, prearrangement, predetermination, purpose

premier *n.* 1. chancellor, head of government, P.M., prime minister ~*adj.* 2. arch, chief, first, foremost, head, highest, leading, main, primary, prime, principal, top 3. earliest, first, inaugural, initial, original

premiere debut, first night, first performance, first showing, opening

premises building, establishment, place, property, site

premiss, premise argument, assertion, assumption, ground, hypothesis, postulate, postulation, presupposition, proposition, supposition, thesis

premium 1. bonus, boon, bounty, fee, percentage (*Inf.*), perk (*Brit. inf.*), perquisite, prize, recompense, remuneration, reward 2. appreciation, regard, stock, store, value 3. **at a premium** beyond one's means, costly, expensive, hard to come by, in great demand, in short supply, like gold dust, not to be had for love or money, rare, scarce, valuable

premonition apprehension, feeling, feeling in one's bones, foreboding, forewarning, funny feeling (*Inf.*), hunch, idea, intuition, misgiving, omen, portent, presage, presentiment, sign, suspicion, warning

preoccupation 1. absence of mind, absent-mindedness, absorption, abstraction, brown study, day-

dreaming, engrossment, immersion, inattentiveness, musing, oblivion, pensiveness, preposses-sion, reverie, woolgathering 2. bee in one's bonnet, concern, fixation, hang-up (*Inf.*), hobbyhorse, *idée fixe*, obsession, pet subject

preoccupied absent-minded, absorbed, abstracted, caught up in, distracted, distrait, engrossed, faraway, heedless, immersed, in a brown study, intent, lost in, lost in thought, oblivious, rapt, taken up, unaware, wrapped up

preparation 1. development, getting ready, groundwork, preparing, putting in order 2. alertness, anticipation, expectation, foresight, precaution, preparedness, provision, readiness, safeguard 3. *Often plural* arrangement, measure, plan, provision 4. composition, compound, concoction, medicine, mixture, tincture 5. homework, prep (*Inf.*), revision, schoolwork, study, swotting (*Inf.*)

preparatory 1. basic, elementary, introductory, opening, prefatory, preliminary, preparative, primary 2. **preparatory to** before, in advance of, in anticipation of, in preparation for, prior to

prepare 1. adapt, adjust, anticipate, arrange, coach, dispose, form, groom, make provision, make ready, plan, practise, prime, put in order, train, warm up 2. brace, fortify, gird, ready, steel, strengthen 3. assemble, concoct, construct, contrive, draw up, fashion, fix up, get up (*Inf.*), make, produce, put together, turn out 4. accoutre, equip, fit, fit out, furnish, outfit, provide, supply

prepared 1. all set, arranged, fit, in order, in readiness, planned, primed, ready, set 2. able, disposed, inclined, minded, of a mind, predisposed, willing

preparedness alertness, fitness, order, preparation, readiness

preponderance ascendancy, bulk, dominance, domination, dominion, extensiveness, greater numbers, greater part, lion's share, mass, power, predominance, prevalence, superiority, supremacy, sway, weight

preponderant ascendant, domi~ nant, extensive, foremost, greater, important, larger, paramount, predominant, prevailing, preva~ lent, significant

prepossessed biased, inclined, partial, partisan, predisposed, prejudiced

prepossessing alluring, amiable, appealing, attractive, beautiful, bewitching, captivating, charming, engaging, fair, fascinating, fetch~ ing, good-looking, handsome, invit~ ing, likable, lovable, magnetic, pleasing, striking, taking, winning

preposterous absurd, asinine, bi~ zarre, crazy, excessive, exorbitant, extravagant, extreme, foolish, im~ possible, incredible, insane, irra~ tional, laughable, ludicrous, mon~ strous, nonsensical, out of the question, outrageous, ridiculous, senseless, shocking, unreasonable, unthinkable

prerequisite 1. *adj.* called for, es~ sential, imperative, indispensable, mandatory, necessary, needful, obligatory, of the essence, re~ quired, requisite, vital **2.** *n.* condi~ tion, essential, imperative, must, necessity, precondition, qualifica~ tion, requirement, requisite, *sine qua non*

prerogative advantage, authority, birthright, choice, claim, droit, due, exemption, immunity, liberty, per~ quisite, privilege, right, sanction, title

prescribe appoint, assign, com~ mand, decree, define, dictate, di~ rect, enjoin, fix, impose, lay down, ordain, order, require, rule, set, specify, stipulate

prescription 1. direction, formula, instruction, recipe **2.** drug, medi~ cine, mixture, preparation, remedy

presence 1. attendance, being, companionship, company, exist~ ence, habitation, inhabitance, oc~ cupancy, residence **2.** closeness, immediate circle, nearness, neighbourhood, propinquity, prox~ imity, vicinity **3.** air, appearance, aspect, aura, bearing, carriage, comportment, demeanour, ease, mien (*Literary*), personality, poise, self-assurance **4.** apparition, ghost, manifestation, revenant, shade (*Literary*), spectre, spirit, super~ natural being, wraith

presence of mind alertness, aplomb, calmness, composure, cool (*Sl.*), coolness, imperturbabil~ ity, level-headedness, phlegm, quickness, sang-froid, self- assurance, self-command, self- possession, wits

present[1] *adj.* **1.** contemporary, current, existent, existing, extant, immediate, instant, present-day **2.** accounted for, at hand, available, here, in attendance, near, nearby, ready, there, to hand ~*n.* **3.** here and now, now, present moment, the time being, this day and age, today **4. at present** at the moment, just now, now, nowadays, right now **5. for the present** for a while, for the moment, for the time being, in the meantime, not for long, provi~ sionally, temporarily

present[2] *v.* **1.** acquaint with, intro~ duce, made known **2.** demonstrate, display, exhibit, give, mount, put before the public, put on, show, stage **3.** adduce, advance, declare, expound, extend, hold out, intro~ duce, offer, pose, produce, proffer, put forward, raise, recount, relate, state, submit, suggest, tender **4.** award, bestow, confer, donate, en~ trust, furnish, give, grant, hand over, offer, proffer, put at (some~ one's) disposal ~*n.* **5.** benefaction, boon, bounty, donation, endow~ ment, favour, gift, grant, gratuity, largess, offering, prezzie (*Inf.*)

presentable acceptable, becom~ ing, decent, fit to be seen, good enough, not bad (*Inf.*), O.K. (*Inf.*), passable, proper, respectable, sat~ isfactory, suitable, tolerable

presentation 1. award, bestowal, conferral, donation, giving, inves~ titure, offering **2.** appearance, ar~ rangement, delivery, exposition, production, rendition, staging, sub~

mission 3. demonstration, display, exhibition, performance, production, representation, show 4. coming out, debut, introduction, launch, launching, reception

presentiment anticipation, apprehension, expectation, fear, feeling, foreboding, forecast, forethought, hunch, intuition, misgiving, premonition, presage

presently anon (*Archaic*), before long, by and by, in a minute, in a moment, in a short while, pretty soon (*Inf.*), shortly, soon

preservation conservation, defence, keeping, maintenance, perpetuation, protection, safeguarding, safekeeping, safety, salvation, security, storage, support, upholding

preserve *v.* 1. care for, conserve, defend, guard, keep, protect, safeguard, save, secure, shelter, shield 2. continue, keep, keep up, maintain, perpetuate, retain, sustain, uphold 3. conserve, keep, put up, save, store ~*n.* 4. area, domain, field, realm, specialism, sphere 5. *Often plural* confection, confiture, conserve, jam, jelly, marmalade, sweetmeat 6. game reserve, reservation, reserve, sanctuary

preside administer, be at the head of, be in authority, chair, conduct, control, direct, govern, head, lead, manage, officiate, run, supervise

press *v.* 1. bear down on, compress, condense, crush, depress, force down, jam, mash, push, reduce, squeeze, stuff 2. calender, finish, flatten, iron, mangle, put the creases in, smooth, steam 3. clasp, crush, embrace, encircle, enfold, fold in one's arms, hold close, hug, squeeze 4. compel, constrain, demand, enforce, enjoin, force, insist on 5. beg, entreat, exhort, implore, importune, petition, plead, pressurize, sue, supplicate, urge 6. afflict, assail, beset, besiege, disquiet, harass, plague, torment, trouble, vex, worry 7. **be pressed** be hard put, be pushed (hurried, rushed), be short of 8. cluster, crowd, flock, gather, hasten, herd, hurry, mill,

push, rush, seethe, surge, swarm, throng ~*n.* 9. **the press a.** Fleet Street, fourth estate, journalism, news media, newspapers, the papers **b.** columnists, correspondents, gentlemen of the press, journalists, newsmen, photographers, pressmen, reporters 10. bunch, crowd, crush, flock, herd, horde, host, mob, multitude, pack, push (*Inf.*), swarm, throng 11. bustle, demand, hassle (*Inf.*), hurry, pressure, strain, stress, urgency

pressing burning, constraining, crucial, exigent, high-priority, imperative, important, importunate, serious, urgent, vital

pressure 1. compressing, compression, crushing, force, heaviness, squeezing, weight 2. coercion, compulsion, constraint, force, influence, obligation, power, sway 3. adversity, affliction, burden, demands, difficulty, distress, exigency, hassle (*Inf.*), heat, hurry, load, press, strain, stress, urgency

prestige authority, cachet, celebrity, credit, distinction, eminence, esteem, fame, honour, importance, influence, kudos, regard, renown, reputation, standing, stature, status, weight

presumably apparently, doubtless, doubtlessly, in all likelihood, in all probability, it would seem, likely, most likely, on the face of it, probably, seemingly

presume 1. assume, believe, conjecture, infer, posit, postulate, presuppose, suppose, surmise, take for granted, take it, think 2. dare, go so far, have the audacity, make bold, make so bold, take the liberty, undertake, venture 3. bank on, count on, depend, rely, trust

presumption 1. assurance, audacity, boldness, brass (*Inf.*), brass neck (*Inf.*), cheek (*Inf.*), effrontery, forwardness, gall (*Inf.*), impudence, insolence, nerve (*Inf.*), presumptuousness, temerity 2. anticipation, assumption, belief, conjecture, guess, hypothesis, opinion, premiss, presupposition, supposition, surmise 3. basis, chance, grounds, likelihood, plausibility, probability, reason

presumptuous arrogant, audacious, bigheaded (*Inf.*), bold, conceited, foolhardy, forward, insolent, overconfident, overfamiliar, overweening, presuming, pushy (*Inf.*), rash, too big for one's boots, uppish (*Brit. inf.*)

presuppose accept, assume, consider, imply, posit, postulate, presume, suppose, take as read, take for granted, take it

presupposition assumption, belief, hypothesis, preconceived idea, preconception, premiss, presumption, supposition, theory

pretence 1. acting, charade, deceit, deception, fabrication, fakery, faking, falsehood, feigning, invention, make-believe, sham, simulation, subterfuge, trickery 2. affectation, appearance, artifice, display, façade, posing, posturing, pretentiousness, show, veneer 3. claim, cloak, colour, cover, excuse, façade, garb, guise, mask, masquerade, pretext, ruse, semblance, show, veil, wile

pretend 1. affect, allege, assume, counterfeit, dissemble, dissimulate, fake, falsify, feign, impersonate, make out, pass oneself off as, profess, put on, sham, simulate 2. act, imagine, make believe, make up, play, play the part of, suppose 3. allege, aspire, claim, lay claim, profess, purport

pretended alleged, avowed, bogus, counterfeit, fake, false, feigned, fictitious, imaginary, ostensible, phoney (*Sl.*), pretend (*Inf.*), professed, pseudo (*Inf.*), purported, sham, so-called, spurious

pretender aspirant, claimant, claimer

pretension 1. aspiration, assertion, assumption, claim, demand, pretence, profession 2. affectation, airs, conceit, hypocrisy, ostentation, pomposity, pretentiousness, self-importance, show, showiness, snobbery, snobbishness, vainglory, vanity

pretentious affected, assuming, bombastic, conceited, exaggerated, extravagant, flaunting, grandiloquent, grandiose, highfalutin (*Inf.*), high-flown, high-sounding, hollow, inflated, magniloquent, mannered, ostentatious, overambitious, pompous, puffed up, showy, snobbish, specious, vainglorious

pretext affectation, alleged reason, appearance, cloak, cover, device, excuse, guise, mask, ploy, pretence, red herring, ruse, semblance, show, simulation, veil

pretty *adj.* 1. appealing, attractive, beautiful, bonny, charming, comely, cute, fair, good-looking, graceful, lovely, personable 2. bijou, dainty, delicate, elegant, fine, neat, nice, pleasing, tasteful, trim ~*adv.* 3. *Inf.* fairly, kind of (*Inf.*), moderately, quite, rather, reasonably, somewhat

prevail 1. be victorious, carry the day, gain mastery, overcome, overrule, prove superior, succeed, triumph, win 2. abound, be current (prevalent, widespread), exist generally, obtain, predominate, preponderate 3. *Often with* **on** *or* **upon** bring round, convince, dispose, incline, induce, influence, persuade, prompt, sway, talk into, win over

prevailing 1. common, current, customary, established, fashionable, general, in style, in vogue, ordinary, popular, prevalent, set, usual, widespread 2. dominant, influential, main, operative, predominating, preponderating, principal, ruling

prevalence 1. acceptance, commonness, common occurrence, currency, frequency, pervasiveness, popularity, profusion, regularity, ubiquity, universality 2. ascendancy, hold, mastery, predominance, preponderance, primacy, rule, sway

prevalent 1. accepted, common, commonplace, current, customary, established, everyday, extensive, frequent, general, habitual, popular, rampant, rife, ubiquitous, universal, usual, widespread 2. ascendant, compelling, dominant, governing, powerful, predominant, prevailing, successful, superior

prevaricate beat about the bush, beg the question, cavil, deceive, dodge, equivocate, evade, give a false colour to, hedge, lie, palter, quibble, shift, shuffle, stretch the truth, tergiversate

prevarication cavilling, deceit, deception, equivocation, evasion, falsehood, falsification, lie, misrepresentation, pretence, quibbling, tergiversation, untruth

prevent anticipate, avert, avoid, balk, bar, block, check, counteract, defend against, foil, forestall, frustrate, hamper, head off, hinder, impede, inhibit, intercept, nip in the bud, obstruct, obviate, preclude, restrain, stave off, stop, thwart, ward off

prevention 1. anticipation, avoidance, deterrence, elimination, forestalling, obviation, precaution, preclusion, prophylaxis, safeguard, thwarting 2. bar, check, deterrence, frustration, hindrance, impediment, interruption, obstacle, obstruction, stoppage

preventive, preventative adj. 1. hampering, hindering, impeding, obstructive 2. counteractive, deterrent, inhibitory, precautionary, prophylactic, protective, shielding ~n. 3. block, hindrance, impediment, obstacle, obstruction 4. deterrent, neutralizer, prevention, prophylactic, protection, protective, remedy, safeguard, shield

previous 1. antecedent, anterior, earlier, erstwhile, ex-, foregoing, former, one-time, past, preceding, prior, quondam, sometime 2. Inf. ahead of oneself, precipitate, premature, too early, too soon, untimely

previously at one time, a while ago, before, beforehand, earlier, formerly, heretofore, hitherto, in advance, in anticipation, in days or years gone by, in the past, once, then, until now

prey n. 1. game, kill, quarry 2. dupe, fall guy (Inf.), mark, mug (Sl.), tar-

get, victim ~v. 3. devour, eat, feed upon, hunt, live off, seize 4. blackmail, bleed (Inf.), bully, exploit, intimidate, take advantage of, terrorize, victimize 5. burden, distress, hang over, haunt, oppress, trouble, weigh down, weigh heavily, worry

price n. 1. amount, asking price, assessment, bill, charge, cost, damage (Inf.), estimate, expenditure, expense, face value, fee, figure, outlay, payment, rate, valuation, value, worth 2. consequences, cost, penalty, sacrifice, toll 3. bounty, compensation, premium, recompense, reward 4. **at any price** anyhow, cost what it may, expense no object, no matter what the cost, regardless, whatever the cost 5. **beyond price** inestimable, invaluable, of incalculable value, precious, priceless, treasured, without price ~v. 6. assess, cost, estimate, evaluate, put a price on, rate, value

priceless 1. beyond price, cherished, costly, dear, expensive, incalculable, incomparable, inestimable, invaluable, irreplaceable, precious, prized, rare, rich, treasured, worth a king's ransom 2. Inf. absurd, a hoot (Brit. inf.), amusing, a scream (Inf.), comic, droll, funny, hilarious, killing (Inf.), rib-tickling, ridiculous, riotous, side-splitting

prick v. 1. bore, jab, lance, perforate, pierce, pink, punch, puncture, stab 2. bite, itch, prickle, smart, sting, tingle 3. cut, distress, grieve, move, pain, stab, touch, trouble, wound 4. Usually with **up** point, raise, rise, stand erect ~n. 5. cut, gash, hole, perforation, pinhole, puncture, wound 6. gnawing, pang, prickle, smart, spasm, sting, twinge

prickle n. 1. barb, needle, point, spike, spine, spur, thorn 2. chill, formication, goose flesh, paraesthesia (Medical), pins and needles (Inf.), smart, tickle, tingle, tingling ~v. 3. itch, smart, sting, tingle, twitch 4. jab, nick, prick, stick

prickly 1. barbed, brambly, briery,

bristly, spiny, thorny 2. crawling, itchy, pricking, prickling, scratchy, sharp, smarting, stinging, tingling 3. bad-tempered, cantankerous, edgy, fractious, grumpy, irritable, peevish, pettish, petulant, ratty (*Brit. sl.*), shirty (*Sl.*), snappish, stroppy (*Brit. sl.*), tetchy, touchy, waspish 4. complicated, difficult, intricate, involved, knotty, thorny, ticklish, tricky, troublesome, trying

pride *n.* 1. *amour-propre*, dignity, honour, self-esteem, self-respect, self-worth 2. arrogance, big-headedness (*Inf.*), conceit, egotism, haughtiness, hauteur, hubris, lofti-ness, *morgue*, presumption, pre-tension, pretentiousness, self-importance, self-love, smugness, snobbery, superciliousness, vain-glory, vanity 3. boast, gem, jewel, pride and joy, prize, treasure 4. delight, gratification, joy, pleasure, satisfaction 5. best, choice, cream, elite, flower, glory, pick ~*v.* 6. be proud of, boast, brag, congratulate oneself, crow, exult, flatter oneself, glory in, pique, plume, preen, revel in, take pride, vaunt

priest churchman, clergyman, cleric, curate, divine, ecclesiastic, father, father confessor, holy man, man of God, man of the cloth, minister, padre (*Inf.*), vicar

priestly canonical, clerical, eccle-siastic, hieratic, pastoral, priest-like, sacerdotal

prig goody-goody (*Inf.*), Holy Joe (*Inf.*), Holy Willie (*Inf.*), Mrs Grun-dy, old maid (*Inf.*), pedant, prude, puritan, stuffed shirt (*Inf.*)

priggish goody-goody (*Inf.*), holier-than-thou, narrow-minded, pedan-tic, prim, prudish, puritanical, self-righteous, self-satisfied, smug, starchy (*Inf.*), stiff, stuffy

prim demure, fastidious, formal, fussy, old-maidish (*Inf.*), particular, precise, priggish, prissy (*Inf.*), proper, prudish, puritanical, schoolmarmish (*Brit. inf.*), starchy (*Inf.*), stiff, strait-laced

prima donna diva, leading lady, star

primarily 1. above all, basically,

chiefly, especially, essentially, for the most part, fundamentally, gen-erally, mainly, mostly, on the whole, principally 2. at first, at *or* from the start, first and foremost, initially, in the beginning, in the first place, originally

primary 1. best, capital, cardinal, chief, dominant, first, greatest, highest, leading, main, paramount, prime, principal, top 2. aboriginal, earliest, initial, original, primal, primeval, primitive, primordial, pristine 3. basic, beginning, el-emental, essential, fundamental, radical, ultimate, underlying 4. el-ementary, introductory, rudimen-tary, simple

prime *adj.* 1. best, capital, choice, excellent, first-class, first-rate, grade A, highest, quality, select, selected, superior, top 2. basic, earliest, fundamental, original, primary, underlying 3. chief, lead-ing, main, predominant, pre-eminent, primary, principal, rul-ing, senior ~*n.* 4. best days, bloom, flower, full flowering, height, hey-day, maturity, peak, perfection, zenith 5. beginning, morning, opening, spring, start ~*v.* 6. break in, coach, fit, get ready, groom, make ready, prepare, train 7. brief, clue up, fill in (*Inf.*), gen up (*Brit. inf.*), give someone the lowdown (*Inf.*), inform, notify, tell

primeval, primaeval ancient, earliest, early, first, old, original, prehistoric, primal, primitive, pri-mordial, pristine

primitive 1. earliest, early, el-ementary, first, original, primary, primeval, primordial, pristine 2. barbarian, barbaric, crude, rough, rude, rudimentary, savage, simple, uncivilized, uncultivated, undevel-oped, unrefined 3. childlike, naive, simple, undeveloped, unsophisti-cated, untrained, untutored

prince lord, monarch, potentate, ruler, sovereign

princely 1. bounteous, bountiful, generous, gracious, lavish, liberal, magnanimous, munificent, open-handed, rich 2. august, dignified, grand, high-born, imperial, imposing, lofty, magnificent, majestic, noble, regal, royal, sovereign, stately

principal *adj.* 1. capital, cardinal, chief, controlling, dominant, essential, first, foremost, highest, key, leading, main, most important, paramount, pre-eminent, primary, prime, strongest ~*n.* 2. boss (*Inf.*), chief, director, head, leader, master, ruler, superintendent 3. dean, director, head (*Inf.*), headmaster, headmistress, head teacher, master, rector 4. assets, capital, capital funds, money 5. first violin, lead, leader, star

principally above all, chiefly, especially, first and foremost, for the most part, in the main, mainly, mostly, particularly, predominantly, primarily

principle 1. assumption, axiom, canon, criterion, dictum, doctrine, dogma, ethic, formula, fundamental, golden rule, law, maxim, moral law, precept, proposition, rule, standard, truth, verity 2. attitude, belief, code, credo, ethic, morality, opinion, tenet 3. conscience, integrity, morals, probity, rectitude, scruples, sense of duty, sense of honour, uprightness. **in principle** ideally, in essence, in theory, theoretically

print *v.* 1. engrave, go to press, impress, imprint, issue, mark, publish, put to bed (*Inf.*), run off, stamp ~*n.* 2. book, magazine, newspaper, newsprint, periodical, printed matter, publication, typescript 3. **in print** a. in black and white, on paper, on the streets, out, printed, published b. available, current, in the shops, obtainable, on the market, on the shelves 4. **out of print** no longer published, o.p., unavailable, unobtainable 5. copy, engraving, photo (*Inf.*), photograph, picture, reproduction 6. characters, face, font (*Chiefly U.S.*), fount, lettering, letters, type, typeface

priority first concern, greater importance, precedence, pre-

eminence, preference, prerogative, rank, right of way, seniority, superiority, supremacy, the lead

priory abbey, cloister, convent, monastery, nunnery, religious house

prison can (*Sl.*), choky (*Sl.*), clink (*Sl.*), confinement, cooler (*Sl.*), dungeon, gaol, glasshouse (*Military inf.*), jail, jug (*Sl.*), lockup, penal institution, penitentiary (*U.S.*), quod (*Sl.*), stir (*Sl.*)

prisoner 1. con (*Sl.*), convict, jailbird, lag (*Sl.*) 2. captive, detainee, hostage, internee

privacy 1. isolation, privateness, retirement, retreat, seclusion, separateness, sequestration, solitude 2. clandestineness, concealment, confidentiality, secrecy

private *adj.* 1. clandestine, closet, confidential, hush-hush (*Inf.*), in camera, inside, off the record, privy (*Archaic*), secret, unofficial 2. exclusive, individual, intimate, own, particular, personal, reserved, special 3. independent, nonpublic 4. concealed, isolated, not overlooked, retired, secluded, secret, separate, sequestered, solitary, withdrawn 5. **in private** behind closed doors, confidentially, in camera, in secret, personally, privately ~*n.* 6. enlisted man (*U.S.*), private soldier, squaddy (*Inf.*), tommy (*Brit. inf.*), Tommy Atkins (*Brit. inf.*)

privilege advantage, benefit, birthright, claim, concession, due, entitlement, franchise, freedom, immunity, liberty, prerogative, right, sanction

privileged 1. advantaged, elite, entitled, favoured, honoured, indulged, powerful, ruling, special 2. allowed, empowered, exempt, free, granted, licensed, sanctioned, vested 3. *Of information* confidential, exceptional, inside, not for publication, off the record, privy, special

prize¹ *n.* 1. accolade, award, honour, premium, reward, trophy 2. haul, jackpot, purse, stakes, windfall, winnings 3. aim, ambition,

conquest, desire, gain, goal, hope 4.
booty, capture, loot, pickings, pil~
lage, plunder, spoil(s), trophy ~adj.
5. award-winning, best, champion,
first-rate, outstanding, top, top~
notch (Inf.), winning

prize² v. appreciate, cherish, es~
teem, hold dear, regard highly, set
store by, treasure, value

probability chance(s), expectation,
liability, likelihood, likeliness, odds,
presumption, prospect

probable apparent, credible, fea~
sible, likely, most likely, odds-on,
on the cards, ostensible, plausible,
possible, presumable, presumed,
reasonable, seeming

probably as likely as not, doubtless,
in all likelihood, in all probability,
likely, maybe, most likely, per~
chance (Archaic), perhaps, pos~
sibly, presumably

probation apprenticeship, exami~
nation, initiation, novitiate, test,
trial, trial period

probe v. 1. examine, explore, go
into, investigate, look into, query,
scrutinize, search, sift, sound, test,
verify 2. explore, feel around,
poke, prod ~n. 3. detection, ex~
amination, exploration, inquest,
inquiry, investigation, research,
scrutiny, study

problem n. 1. can of worms (Inf.),
complication, difficulty, dilemma,
disagreement, dispute, disputed
point, doubt, hard nut to crack
(Inf.), point at issue, predicament,
quandary, trouble 2. brain-teaser
(Inf.), conundrum, enigma, poser,
puzzle, question, riddle ~adj. 3. de~
linquent, difficult, intractable, un~
controllable, unmanageable, unru~
ly

problematic chancy (Inf.), debat~
able, doubtful, dubious, enigmatic,
moot, open to doubt, problemati~
cal, puzzling, questionable, tricky,
uncertain, unsettled

procedure action, conduct, course,
custom, form, formula, method,
modus operandi, operation, per~
formance, plan of action, policy,
practice, process, routine, scheme,
step, strategy, system, transaction

proceed 1. advance, carry on, con~
tinue, get going, get on with, get
under way with, go ahead, go on,
make a start, move on, press on,
progress, set in motion 2. arise,
come, derive, emanate, ensue,
flow, follow, issue, originate, result,
spring, stem

proceeding 1. act, action, course of
action, deed, measure, move, oc~
currence, procedure, process, step,
undertaking, venture 2. Plural ac~
count, affairs, annals, archives,
business, dealings, doings, matters,
minutes, records, report, transac~
tions

proceeds earnings, gain, income,
produce, products, profit, receipts,
returns, revenue, takings, yield

process n. 1. action, course, course
of action, manner, means, meas~
ure, method, mode, operation,
performance, practice, procedure,
proceeding, system, transaction 2.
advance, course, development,
evolution, formation, growth,
movement, progress, progression,
stage, step, unfolding 3. Law ac~
tion, case, suit, trial ~v. 4. deal
with, dispose of, fulfil, handle, take
care of 5. alter, convert, prepare,
refine, transform, treat

procession 1. cavalcade, column,
cortege, file, march, motorcade,
parade, train 2. course, cycle, run,
sequence, series, string, succes~
sion, train

proclaim advertise, affirm, an~
nounce, blaze (abroad), blazon
(abroad), circulate, declare, enun~
ciate, give out, herald, indicate,
make known, profess, promulgate,
publish, shout from the housetops
(Inf.), show, trumpet

proclamation announcement,
declaration, decree, edict, mani~
festo, notice, notification, promul~
gation, pronouncement, pronun~
ciamento, publication

procrastinate adjourn, be dilatory,
dally, defer, delay, drag one's feet
(Inf.), gain time, play a waiting
game, play for time, postpone,
prolong, protract, put off, retard,
stall, temporize

procure acquire, appropriate, buy, come by, earn, effect, find, gain, get, get hold of, lay hands on, manage to get, obtain, pick up, purchase, secure, win

prod *v.* 1. dig, drive, elbow, jab, nudge, poke, prick, propel, push, shove 2. egg on, goad, impel, incite, motivate, move, prompt, rouse, spur, stimulate, stir up, urge ~*n.* 3. boost, dig, elbow, jab, nudge, poke, push, shove 4. goad, poker, spur, stick 5. boost, cue, prompt, reminder, signal, stimulus

prodigal *adj.* 1. excessive, extravagant, immoderate, improvident, intemperate, profligate, reckless, spendthrift, squandering, wanton, wasteful 2. bounteous, bountiful, copious, exuberant, lavish, luxuriant, profuse, sumptuous, superabundant, teeming ~*n.* 3. big spender, profligate, spendthrift, squanderer, wastrel

prodigality 1. abandon, dissipation, excess, extravagance, immoderation, intemperance, profligacy, recklessness, squandering, wantonness, waste, wastefulness 2. abundance, amplitude, bounteousness, bounty, copiousness, cornucopia, exuberance, horn of plenty, lavishness, luxuriance, plenteousness, plenty, profusion, richness, sumptuousness

prodigious 1. colossal, enormous, giant, gigantic, huge, immeasurable, immense, inordinate, mammoth, massive, monstrous, monumental, stupendous, tremendous, vast 2. abnormal, amazing, astounding, exceptional, extraordinary, fabulous, fantastic (*Inf.*), flabbergasting (*Inf.*), impressive, marvellous, miraculous, phenomenal, remarkable, staggering, startling, striking, stupendous, unusual, wonderful

prodigy 1. child genius, genius, mastermind, talent, whiz (*Inf.*), whiz kid (*Inf.*), wizard, wonder child, wunderkind 2. marvel, miracle, one in a million, phenomenon, rare bird (*Inf.*), sensation, wonder 3. abnormality, curiosity, freak, grotesque, monster, monstrosity, mutation, spectacle

produce *v.* 1. compose, construct, create, develop, fabricate, invent, make, manufacture, originate, put together, turn out 2. afford, bear, beget, breed, bring forth, deliver, engender, furnish, give, render, supply, yield 3. bring about, cause, effect, generate, give rise to, make for, occasion, provoke, set off 4. advance, bring forward, bring to light, demonstrate, exhibit, offer, present, put forward, set forth, show 5. direct, do, exhibit, mount, present, put before the public, put on, show, stage 6. *Geometry* extend, lengthen, prolong, protract ~*n.* 7. crop, fruit and vegetables, greengrocery, harvest, product, yield

producer 1. director, impresario, *régisseur* 2. farmer, grower, maker, manufacturer

product 1. artefact, commodity, concoction, creation, goods, invention, merchandise, produce, production, work 2. consequence, effect, fruit, issue, legacy, offshoot, outcome, result, returns, spin-off, upshot, yield

production 1. assembly, construction, creation, fabrication, formation, making, manufacture, manufacturing, origination, preparation, producing 2. direction, management, presentation, staging

productive 1. creative, dynamic, energetic, fecund, fertile, fruitful, generative, inventive, plentiful, producing, prolific, rich, teeming, vigorous 2. advantageous, beneficial, constructive, effective, fruitful, gainful, gratifying, profitable, rewarding, useful, valuable, worthwhile

productivity abundance, mass production, output, production, productive capacity, productiveness, work rate, yield

profane *adj.* 1. disrespectful, godless, heathen, idolatrous, impious, impure, irreligious, irreverent, pagan, sacrilegious, sinful, ungodly, wicked 2. lay, secular, temporal, unconsecrated, unhallowed, unholy, unsanctified, worldly 3. abusive, blasphemous, coarse, crude, filthy, foul, obscene, vulgar ~*v.* 4. abuse, commit sacrilege, contaminate, debase, defile, desecrate, misuse, pervert, pollute, prostitute, violate, vitiate

profanity abuse, blasphemy, curse, cursing, execration, foul language, four-letter word, impiety, imprecation, irreverence, malediction, obscenity, profaneness, sacrilege, swearing, swearword

profess 1. acknowledge, admit, affirm, announce, assert, asseverate, aver, avow, certify, confess, confirm, declare, maintain, own, proclaim, state, vouch 2. act as if, allege, call oneself, claim, dissemble, fake, feign, let on, make out, pretend, purport, sham

professed 1. avowed, certified, confirmed, declared, proclaimed, self-acknowledged, self-confessed 2. alleged, apparent, ostensible, pretended, purported, self-styled, so-called, *soi-disant*, supposed, would-be

professedly 1. allegedly, apparently, by one's own account, falsely, ostensibly, purportedly, supposedly, under the pretext of 2. admittedly, avowedly, by open declaration, confessedly

profession 1. business, calling, career, employment, line, line of work, métier, occupation, office, position, sphere, vocation, walk of life 2. acknowledgment, affirmation, assertion, attestation, avowal, claim, confession, declaration, statement, testimony, vow

professional 1. *adj.* ace (*Inf.*), adept, competent, crack (*Sl.*), efficient, experienced, expert, finished, masterly, polished, practised, proficient, qualified, skilled, slick, trained 2. *n.* adept, authority, dab hand (*Brit. inf.*), expert, maestro, master, past master, pro (*Inf.*), specialist, virtuoso, wizard

professor don (*Brit.*), fellow (*Brit.*), head of faculty, prof (*Inf.*)

proficiency ability, accomplishment, aptitude, competence, dexterity, expertise, expertness, facility, knack, know-how (*Inf.*), mastery, skilfulness, skill, talent

proficient able, accomplished, adept, apt, capable, clever, competent, conversant, efficient, experienced, expert, gifted, masterly, qualified, skilful, skilled, talented, trained, versed

profile *n.* 1. contour, drawing, figure, form, outline, portrait, shape, side view, silhouette, sketch 2. biography, characterization, character sketch, sketch, thumbnail sketch, vignette 3. analysis, chart, diagram, examination, graph, review, study, survey, table

profit *n.* 1. *Often plural* bottom line, earnings, emoluments, gain, percentage (*Inf.*), proceeds, receipts, return, revenue, surplus, takings, winnings, yield 2. advancement, advantage, avail, benefit, gain, good, interest, use, value ~*v.* 3. aid, avail, benefit, be of advantage to, better, contribute, gain, help, improve, promote, serve, stand in good stead 4. capitalize on, cash in on (*Sl.*), exploit, learn from, make capital of, make good use of, make the most of, put to good use, reap the benefit of, take advantage of, turn to advantage *or* account, use, utilize 5. clean up (*Inf.*), clear, earn, gain, make a good thing of (*Inf.*), make a killing (*Inf.*), make money

profitable 1. commercial, cost-effective, fruitful, gainful, lucrative, money-making, paying, remunerative, rewarding, worthwhile 2. advantageous, beneficial, fruitful, productive, rewarding, serviceable, useful, valuable, worthwhile

profiteer 1. *n.* exploiter, racketeer 2. *v.* exploit, fleece, make a quick buck (*Sl.*), make someone pay through the nose, overcharge, racketeer, sting (*Inf.*)

profligate *adj.* 1. abandoned, corrupt, debauched, degenerate, depraved, dissipated, dissolute, immoral, iniquitous, libertine, licen-

tious, loose, promiscuous, shame~
less, unprincipled, vicious, vitiated,
wanton, wicked, wild 2. extrava~
gant, immoderate, improvident,
prodigal, reckless, spendthrift,
squandering, wasteful ~n. 3.
debauchee, degenerate, dissipater,
libertine, rake, reprobate, roué 4.
prodigal, spendthrift, squanderer,
waster, wastrel

profound 1. abstruse, deep, dis~
cerning, erudite, learned, pen~
etrating, philosophical, recondite,
sagacious, sage, serious, skilled,
subtle, thoughtful, weighty, wise 2.
abysmal, bottomless, cavernous,
deep, fathomless, yawning 3. ab~
ject, acute, deeply felt, extreme,
great, heartfelt, heartrending,
hearty, intense, keen, sincere 4.
absolute, complete, consummate,
exhaustive, extensive, extreme,
far-reaching, intense, out-and-out,
pronounced, thoroughgoing, total,
utter

profoundly abjectly, acutely,
deeply, extremely, from the bot~
tom of one's heart, greatly, hearti~
ly, intensely, keenly, seriously, sin~
cerely, thoroughly, very

profuse 1. abundant, ample, boun~
tiful, copious, luxuriant, overflow~
ing, plentiful, prolific, teeming 2.
excessive, extravagant, exuberant,
fulsome, generous, immoderate,
lavish, liberal, open-handed, prodi~
gal, unstinting

profusion abundance, bounty, co~
piousness, cornucopia, excess, ex~
travagance, exuberance, glut, lav~
ishness, luxuriance, multitude,
oversupply, plenitude, plethora,
prodigality, quantity, riot, super~
abundance, superfluity, surplus,
wealth

progeny breed, children, descend~
ants, family, issue, lineage, off~
spring, posterity, race, scions,
seed, stock, young

programme n. 1. agenda, curricu~
lum, line-up, list, listing, list of
players, order of events, order of
the day, plan, schedule, syllabus 2.
broadcast, performance, presen~
tation, production, show 3. design,

order of the day, plan, plan of ac~
tion, procedure, project, scheme
~v. 4. arrange, bill, book, design,
engage, formulate, itemize, lay on,
line up, list, map out, plan, prear~
range, schedule, work out

progress n. 1. advance, course,
movement, onward course, pas~
sage, progression, way 2. advance,
advancement, amelioration, bet~
terment, breakthrough, develop~
ment, gain, gaining ground,
growth, headway, improvement,
increase, progression, promotion,
step forward 3. **in progress** being
done, going on, happening, occur~
ring, proceeding, taking place, un~
der way ~v. 4. advance, come on,
continue, cover ground, forge
ahead, gain ground, gather way,
get on, go forward, make headway,
make one's way, make strides,
move on, proceed, travel 5. ad~
vance, ameliorate, better, blossom,
develop, gain, grow, improve, in~
crease, mature

progression 1. advance, advance~
ment, furtherance, gain, headway,
movement forward, progress 2.
chain, course, cycle, order, se~
quence, series, string, succession

progressive 1. accelerating, ad~
vancing, continuing, continuous,
developing, escalating, growing,
increasing, intensifying, ongoing 2.
advanced, avant-garde, dynamic,
enlightened, enterprising, forward-
looking, go-ahead, liberal, modern,
radical, reformist, revolutionary,
up-and-coming

prohibit 1. ban, debar, disallow,
forbid, interdict, outlaw, proscribe,
veto 2. constrain, hamper, hinder,
impede, make impossible, ob~
struct, preclude, prevent, restrict,
rule out, stop

prohibited banned, barred, forbid~
den, not allowed, proscribed, ta~
boo, *verboten*, vetoed

prohibition 1. constraint, exclu~
sion, forbiddance, interdiction, ne~
gation, obstruction, prevention,
restriction 2. ban, bar, disallow~
ance, embargo, injunction, inter~
dict, proscription, veto

prohibitive 1. forbidding, prohibiting, proscriptive, repressive, restraining, restrictive, suppressive 2. *Esp. of prices* beyond one's means, excessive, exorbitant, extortionate, high-priced, preposterous, sky-high, steep (*Inf.*)

project *n.* 1. activity, assignment, design, enterprise, job, occupation, plan, programme, proposal, scheme, task, undertaking, venture, work ~*v.* 2. contemplate, contrive, design, devise, draft, frame, map out, outline, plan, propose, purpose, scheme 3. cast, discharge, fling, hurl, launch, make carry, propel, shoot, throw, transmit 4. beetle, bulge, extend, jut, overhang, protrude, stand out, stick out 5. calculate, estimate, extrapolate, forecast, gauge, predetermine, predict, reckon

projectile bullet, missile, rocket, shell

projection 1. bulge, eaves, jut, ledge, overhang, protrusion, protuberance, ridge, shelf, sill 2. blueprint, diagram, map, outline, plan, representation 3. calculation, computation, estimate, estimation, extrapolation, forecast, prediction, reckoning

proletarian 1. *adj.* cloth-cap (*Inf.*), common, plebeian, working-class 2. *n.* commoner, Joe Bloggs (*Brit. inf.*), man of the people, pleb (*Sl.*), plebeian, prole (*Sl.*), worker

proletariat commonalty, commoners, hoi polloi, labouring classes, lower classes, lower orders, plebs, proles (*Sl.*), the common people, the great unwashed (*Derogatory*), the herd, the masses, the rabble, wage-earners, working class

prolific abundant, bountiful, copious, fecund, fertile, fruitful, generative, luxuriant, productive, profuse, rank, rich, teeming

prologue exordium, foreword, introduction, preamble, preface, preliminary, prelude, proem

prolong carry on, continue, delay, drag out, draw out, extend, lengthen, make longer, perpetuate, protract, spin out, stretch

promenade *n.* 1. boulevard, esplanade, parade, prom, public walk, walkway 2. airing, constitutional, saunter, stroll, turn, walk ~*v.* 3. perambulate, saunter, stretch one's legs, stroll, take a walk, walk 4. flaunt, parade, strut, swagger

prominence 1. cliff, crag, crest, elevation, headland, height, high point, hummock, mound, pinnacle, projection, promontory, rise, rising ground, spur 2. bulge, jutting, projection, protrusion, protuberance, swelling 3. conspicuousness, markedness, outstandingness, precedence, salience, specialness, top billing, weight 4. celebrity, distinction, eminence, fame, greatness, importance, name, notability, pre-eminence, prestige, rank, reputation, standing

prominent 1. bulging, jutting, projecting, protruding, protrusive, protuberant, standing out 2. conspicuous, easily seen, eye-catching, in the foreground, noticeable, obtrusive, obvious, outstanding, pronounced, remarkable, salient, striking, to the fore, unmistakable 3. celebrated, chief, distinguished, eminent, famous, foremost, important, leading, main, noted, outstanding, popular, pre-eminent, renowned, respected, top, well-known, well-thought-of

promiscuous 1. abandoned, debauched, dissipated, dissolute, fast, immoral, lax, libertine, licentious, loose, of easy virtue, profligate, unbridled, unchaste, wanton, wild 2. chaotic, confused, disordered, diverse, heterogeneous, illassorted, indiscriminate, intermingled, intermixed, jumbled, mingled, miscellaneous, mixed, motley 3. careless, casual, haphazard, heedless, indifferent, indiscriminate, irregular, irresponsible, random, slovenly, uncontrolled, uncritical, undiscriminating, unfastidious, unselective

promise *v.* 1. assure, contract, cross one's heart, engage, give an undertaking, give one's word, guarantee, pledge, plight, stipulate, swear, take an oath, undertake, vouch, vow, warrant 2. augur, be~ speak, betoken, bid fair, denote, give hope of, hint at, hold a prob~ ability, hold out hopes of, indicate, lead one to expect, look like, seem likely to, show signs of, suggest ~n. 3. assurance, bond, commitment, compact, covenant, engagement, guarantee, oath, pledge, undertak~ ing, vow, word, word of honour 4. ability, aptitude, capability, capac~ ity, flair, potential, talent

promising 1. auspicious, bright, encouraging, favourable, full of promise, hopeful, likely, propitious, reassuring, rosy 2. able, gifted, likely, rising, talented, up-and-coming

promote 1. advance, aid, assist, back, boost, contribute to, develop, encourage, forward, foster, fur~ ther, help, nurture, stimulate, sup~ port 2. aggrandize, dignify, elevate, exalt, honour, kick upstairs (*Inf.*), prefer, raise, upgrade 3. advocate, call attention to, champion, en~ dorse, espouse, popularize, push for, recommend, speak for, spon~ sor, support, urge, work for 4. ad~ vertise, beat the drum for (*Inf.*), hype (*Sl.*), plug (*Inf.*), publicize, puff, push, sell

promotion 1. advancement, ag~ grandizement, elevation, ennoble~ ment, exaltation, honour, move up, preferment, rise, upgrading 2. ad~ vancement, advocacy, backing, boosting, cultivation, development, encouragement, espousal, further~ ance, progress, support 3. adver~ tising, advertising campaign, bal~ lyhoo (*Inf.*), hard sell, hype (*Sl.*), media hype (*Sl.*), plugging (*Inf.*), propaganda, publicity, puffery (*Inf.*), pushing

prompt *adj.* 1. early, immediate, instant, instantaneous, on time, punctual, quick, rapid, speedy, swift, timely, unhesitating 2. alert, brisk, eager, efficient, expeditious, quick, ready, responsive, smart, willing ~*adv.* 3. *Inf.* exactly, on the dot, promptly, punctually, sharp ~*v.* 4. cause, impel, incite, induce, inspire, instigate, motivate, move,

provoke, spur, stimulate, urge 5. assist, cue, help out, jog the memory, prod, refresh the memo~ ry, remind 6. call forth, cause, elicit, evoke, give rise to, occasion, provoke ~*n.* 7. cue, help, hint, jog, jolt, prod, reminder, spur, stimulus

prompter 1. autocue, idiot board (*Sl.*), Teleprompter (*Trademark*) 2. agitator, catalyst, gadfly, inspir~ er, instigator, moving spirit, prime mover

prompting assistance, encourage~ ment, hint, incitement, influence, jogging, persuasion, pressing, pressure, prodding, pushing, re~ minder, reminding, suggestion, urging

promptly at once, by return, di~ rectly, immediately, instantly, on the dot, on time, pronto (*Inf.*), punctually, quickly, speedily, swiftly, unhesitatingly

promptness alacrity, alertness, briskness, dispatch, eagerness, haste, promptitude, punctuality, quickness, readiness, speed, swift~ ness, willingness

promulgate advertise, announce, broadcast, circulate, communi~ cate, declare, decree, disseminate, issue, make known, make public, notify, proclaim, promote, publish, spread

prone 1. face down, flat, horizontal, lying down, procumbent, prostrate, recumbent, supine 2. apt, bent, disposed, given, inclined, liable, likely, predisposed, subject, sus~ ceptible, tending

prong point, projection, spike, tine, tip

pronounce 1. accent, articulate, enunciate, say, sound, speak, stress, utter, vocalize, voice 2. af~ firm, announce, assert, declare, decree, deliver, judge, proclaim

pronounced broad, clear, con~ spicuous, decided, definite, distinct, evident, marked, noticeable, obvi~ ous, striking, strong, unmistakable

pronouncement announcement, declaration, decree, dictum, edict, judgment, manifesto, notification,

proclamation, promulgation, pro~
nunciamento, statement

pronunciation accent, accentua~
tion, articulation, diction, elocu~
tion, enunciation, inflection, into~
nation, speech, stress

proof *n.* 1. attestation, authentica~
tion, certification, confirmation,
corroboration, demonstration, evi~
dence, substantiation, testimony,
verification 2. *As in* put to the
proof assay, examination, experi~
ment, ordeal, scrutiny, test, trial 3.
Printing galley, galley proof, page
proof, pull, slip, trial impression,
trial print ~*adj.* 4. impenetrable,
impervious, repellent, resistant,
strong, tight, treated 5. be proof
against hold out against, resist,
stand firm against, stand up to,
withstand

prop *v.* 1. bolster, brace, buttress,
hold up, maintain, shore, stay, sup~
port, sustain, truss, uphold 2. lean,
rest, set, stand ~*n.* 3. brace, but~
tress, mainstay, stanchion, stay,
support, truss

propaganda advertising, agitprop,
ballyhoo (*Inf.*), brainwashing, dis~
information, hype (*Sl.*), informa~
tion, newspeak, promotion, public~
ity

propagate 1. beget, breed, engen~
der, generate, increase, multiply,
procreate, produce, proliferate,
reproduce 2. broadcast, circulate,
diffuse, disseminate, make known,
proclaim, promote, promulgate,
publicize, publish, spread, transmit

propagation 1. breeding, genera~
tion, increase, multiplication, pro~
creation, proliferation, reproduc~
tion 2. circulation, communication,
diffusion, dissemination, distribu~
tion, promotion, promulgation,
spread, spreading, transmission

propel drive, force, impel, launch,
push, send, set in motion, shoot,
shove, start, thrust

propensity aptness, bent, bias, dis~
position, inclination, leaning, lia~
bility, penchant, predisposition,
proclivity, proneness, susceptibil~
ity, tendency, weakness

proper 1. appropriate, apt, becom~

ing, befitting, fit, fitting, legitimate,
meet (*Archaic*), right, suitable,
suited 2. *comme il faut*, decent,
decorous, *de rigueur*, genteel,
gentlemanly, ladylike, mannerly,
polite, punctilious, refined, re~
spectable, seemly 3. accepted, ac~
curate, conventional, correct, es~
tablished, exact, formal, orthodox,
precise, right 4. characteristic, in~
dividual, own, particular, peculiar,
personal, respective, special, spe~
cific

property 1. assets, belongings,
building(s), capital, chattels, ef~
fects, estate, goods, holdings,
house(s), means, possessions, re~
sources, riches, wealth 2. acres,
estate, freehold, holding, land, real
estate, real property, realty, title 3.
ability, attribute, characteristic,
feature, hallmark, idiosyncrasy,
mark, peculiarity, quality, trait,
virtue

prophecy augury, divination, fore~
cast, foretelling, prediction, prog~
nosis, prognostication, revelation,
second sight, soothsaying, vatici~
nation (*Rare*)

prophesy augur, divine, forecast,
foresee, foretell, forewarn, predict,
presage, prognosticate, soothsay,
vaticinate (*Rare*)

prophet augur, Cassandra, clair~
voyant, diviner, forecaster, oracle,
prognosticator, prophesier, seer,
sibyl, soothsayer

prophetic augural, divinatory, fa~
tidic (*Rare*), foreshadowing, man~
tic, oracular, predictive, presaging,
prescient, prognostic, sibylline,
vatic (*Rare*)

propitious 1. advantageous, auspi~
cious, bright, encouraging, favour~
able, fortunate, full of promise,
happy, lucky, opportune, promis~
ing, prosperous, rosy, timely 2. be~
nevolent, benign, favourably in~
clined, friendly, gracious, kind,
well-disposed

proportion 1. distribution, ratio,
relationship, relative amount 2.
agreement, balance, congruity,
correspondence, harmony, sym~
metry 3. amount, cut (*Inf.*), divi~

sion, fraction, measure, part, percentage, quota, segment, share 4. *Plural* amplitude, breadth, bulk, capacity, dimensions, expanse, extent, magnitude, measurements, range, scope, size, volume

proportional, proportionate balanced, commensurate, comparable, compatible, consistent, correspondent, corresponding, equitable, equivalent, even, in proportion, just

proposal bid, design, motion, offer, overture, plan, presentation, proffer, programme, project, proposition, recommendation, scheme, suggestion, tender, terms

propose 1. advance, come up with, present, proffer, propound, put forward, submit, suggest, tender 2. introduce, invite, name, nominate, present, put up, recommend 3. aim, design, have every intention, have in mind, intend, mean, plan, purpose, scheme 4. ask for someone's hand (in marriage), offer marriage, pay suit, pop the question (*Inf.*)

proposition 1. *n.* motion, plan, programme, project, proposal, recommendation, scheme, suggestion 2. *v.* accost, make an improper suggestion, make an indecent proposal, solicit

propound advance, advocate, contend, lay down, postulate, present, propose, put forward, set forth, submit, suggest

proprietor, proprietress deed holder, freeholder, landlady, landlord, landowner, owner, possessor, titleholder

propriety 1. appropriateness, aptness, becomingness, correctness, fitness, rightness, seemliness, suitableness 2. breeding, courtesy, decency, decorum, delicacy, etiquette, good form, good manners, manners, modesty, politeness, protocol, punctilio, rectitude, refinement, respectability, seemliness 3. **the proprieties** accepted conduct, amenities, civilities, etiquette, niceties, rules of conduct,

social code, social conventions, social graces, the done thing

propulsion drive, impetus, impulse, impulsion, momentum, motive power, power, pressure, propelling force, push, thrust

prosaic banal, boring, commonplace, dry, dull, everyday, flat, hackneyed, humdrum, matter-of-fact, mundane, ordinary, pedestrian, routine, stale, tame, trite, unimaginative, uninspiring, vapid, workaday

proscribe 1. ban, boycott, censure, condemn, damn, denounce, doom, embargo, forbid, interdict, prohibit, reject 2. attaint (*Archaic*), banish, blackball, deport, exclude, excommunicate, exile, expatriate, expel, ostracize, outlaw

prosecute 1. *Law* arraign, bring action against, bring suit against, bring to trial, do (*Sl.*), indict, litigate, prefer charges, put in the dock, put on trial, seek redress, sue, summon, take to court, try 2. carry on, conduct, direct, discharge, engage in, manage, perform, practise, work at 3. carry through, continue, follow through, persevere, persist, pursue, see through

prospect *n.* 1. anticipation, calculation, contemplation, expectation, future, hope, odds, opening, outlook, plan, presumption, probability, promise, proposal, thought 2. landscape, outlook, panorama, perspective, scene, sight, spectacle, view, vision, vista 3. **in prospect** in sight, in store, in the offing, in the wind, in view, on the cards, on the horizon, planned, projected 4. *Sometimes plural* chance, likelihood, possibility ~*v.* 5. explore, go after, look for, search, seek, survey

prospective about to be, anticipated, approaching, awaited, coming, destined, eventual, expected, forthcoming, future, hoped-for, imminent, intended, likely, looked-for, possible, potential, soon-to-be, -to-be, to come

prospectus announcement, catalogue, conspectus, list, outline,

plan, programme, scheme, sylla~
bus, synopsis

prosper advance, be fortunate,
bloom, do well, fare well, flourish,
flower, get on, grow rich, make
good, make it (*Inf.*), progress, suc~
ceed, thrive

prosperity affluence, boom, ease,
fortune, good fortune, good times,
life of luxury, life of Riley (*Inf.*),
luxury, plenty, prosperousness,
riches, success, the good life,
wealth, well-being

prosperous 1. blooming, booming,
doing well, flourishing, fortunate,
lucky, on the up and up (*Brit.*),
palmy, prospering, successful,
thriving 2. affluent, in clover (*Inf.*),
in the money (*Inf.*), moneyed, opu~
lent, rich, wealthy, well-heeled
(*Sl.*), well-off, well-to-do 3. advan~
tageous, auspicious, bright, fa~
vourable, good, profitable, promis~
ing, propitious, timely

prostitute 1. *n.* bawd (*Archaic*),
brass (*Sl.*), call girl, camp follower,
cocotte, courtesan, fallen woman,
fille de joie, harlot, hooker (*U.S.
sl.*), hustler (*Sl.*), loose woman,
moll (*Sl.*), pro (*Sl.*), streetwalker,
strumpet, tart (*Inf.*), trollop, white
slave, whore 2. *v.* cheapen, debase,
degrade, demean, devalue, misap~
ply, pervert, profane

prostitution harlotry, harlot's
trade, Mrs. Warren's profession,
streetwalking, the game (*Sl.*), the
oldest profession, vice, whoredom

prostrate *adj.* 1. abject, bowed low,
flat, horizontal, kowtowing, pro~
cumbent, prone 2. at a low ebb,
dejected, depressed, desolate,
drained, exhausted, fagged out
(*Inf.*), fallen, inconsolable, over~
come, spent, worn out 3. brought to
one's knees, defenceless, disarmed,
helpless, impotent, overwhelmed,
paralysed, powerless, reduced ~*v.*
4. *Of oneself* abase, bend the knee
to, bow before, bow down to, cast
oneself before, cringe, fall at
(someone's) feet, fall on one's
knees before, grovel, kneel, kow~
tow, submit 5. bring low, crush,
depress, disarm, lay low, over~

come, overthrow, overturn, over~
whelm, paralyse, reduce, ruin 6.
drain, exhaust, fag out (*Inf.*), fa~
tigue, sap, tire, wear out, weary

protagonist 1. central character,
hero, heroine, lead, leading char~
acter, principal 2. advocate,
champion, exponent, leader,
mainstay, moving spirit, prime
mover, standard-bearer, supporter

protean changeable, ever~
changing, many-sided, mercurial,
multiform, mutable, polymor~
phous, variable, versatile, volatile

protect care for, chaperon, cover,
cover up for, defend, foster, give
sanctuary, guard, harbour, keep,
keep safe, look after, mount *or*
stand guard over, preserve, safe~
guard, save, screen, secure, shel~
ter, shield, support, take under
one's wing, watch over

protection 1. aegis, care, charge,
custody, defence, guardianship,
guarding, preservation, protecting,
safeguard, safekeeping, safety, se~
curity 2. armour, barrier, buffer,
bulwark, cover, guard, refuge,
safeguard, screen, shelter, shield

protective careful, covering, de~
fensive, fatherly, insulating, jeal~
ous, maternal, motherly, paternal,
possessive, protecting, safeguard~
ing, sheltering, shielding, vigilant,
warm, watchful

protector advocate, benefactor,
bodyguard, champion, counsel, de~
fender, guard, guardian, guardian
angel, knight in shining armour,
patron, safeguard, tower of
strength

protégé, protégée charge, de~
pendant, discovery, pupil, student,
ward

protest *n.* 1. complaint, declara~
tion, demur, demurral, disapprov~
al, dissent, formal complaint, ob~
jection, outcry, protestation, rem~
onstrance ~*v.* 2. complain, cry out,
demonstrate, demur, disagree, dis~
approve, expostulate, express dis~
approval, kick (against) (*Inf.*), ob~
ject, oppose, remonstrate, say no
to, take exception 3. affirm, argue,
assert, asseverate, attest, avow,

contend, declare, insist, maintain, profess, testify, vow

protestation 1. complaint, disagreement, dissent, expostulation, objection, outcry, protest, remonstrance, remonstration 2. affirmation, asseveration, avowal, declaration, oath, pledge, profession, vow

protester agitator, demonstrator, dissenter, dissident, protest marcher, rebel

protocol 1. code of behaviour, conventions, courtesies, customs, decorum, etiquette, formalities, good form, manners, politesse, propriety, rules of conduct 2. agreement, compact, concordat, contract, convention, covenant, pact, treaty

prototype archetype, example, first, mock-up, model, norm, original, paradigm, pattern, precedent, standard, type

protract continue, drag on or out, draw out, extend, keep going, lengthen, prolong, spin out, stretch out

protracted dragged out, drawn-out, extended, interminable, lengthy, long, long-drawn-out, never-ending, overlong, prolonged, spun out, time-consuming

protrude bulge, come through, extend, jut, obtrude, point, pop (of eyes), project, shoot out, stand out, start (from), stick out

protrusion bulge, bump, jut, lump, outgrowth, projection, protuberance, swelling

protuberance bulge, bump, excrescence, knob, lump, outgrowth, process, projection, prominence, protrusion, swelling, tumour

proud 1. appreciative, content, contented, glad, gratified, honoured, pleased, satisfied, self-respecting, well-pleased 2. arrogant, boastful, conceited, disdainful, egotistical, haughty, high and mighty (Inf.), imperious, lordly, narcissistic, orgulous (Archaic), overbearing, presumptuous, self-important, self-satisfied, snobbish, snooty (Inf.), stuck-up (Inf.), supercilious, toffee-nosed (Sl.), vain

3. exalted, glorious, gratifying, illustrious, memorable, pleasing, red-letter, rewarding, satisfying 4. august, distinguished, eminent, grand, great, illustrious, imposing, magnificent, majestic, noble, splendid, stately

prove 1. ascertain, attest, authenticate, bear out, confirm, corroborate, demonstrate, determine, establish, evidence, evince, justify, show, show clearly, substantiate, verify 2. analyse, assay, check, examine, experiment, put to the test, put to trial, test, try 3. be found to be, come out, end up, result, turn out

proverb adage, aphorism, apophthegm, byword, dictum, gnome, maxim, saw, saying

proverbial accepted, acknowledged, archetypal, axiomatic, conventional, current, customary, famed, famous, legendary, notorious, self-evident, time-honoured, traditional, typical, unquestioned, well-known

provide 1. accommodate, cater, contribute, equip, furnish, outfit, provision, stock up, supply 2. add, afford, bring, give, impart, lend, present, produce, render, serve, yield 3. With for or against anticipate, arrange for, forearm, get ready, make arrangements, make plans, plan ahead, plan for, prepare for, take measures, take precautions 4. With for care for, keep, look after, maintain, support, sustain, take care of 5. determine, lay down, require, specify, state, stipulate

providence 1. destiny, divine intervention, fate, fortune, God's will, predestination 2. care, caution, discretion, far-sightedness, foresight, forethought, perspicacity, presence of mind, prudence

provident canny, careful, cautious, discreet, economical, equipped, far-seeing, far-sighted, forearmed, foresighted, frugal, prudent, sagacious, shrewd, thrifty, vigilant, well-prepared, wise

providential fortuitous, fortunate,

happy, heaven-sent, lucky, oppor~
tune, timely, welcome

provider 1. benefactor, donor, giv~
er, source, supplier 2. bread~
winner, earner, mainstay, sup~
porter, wage earner

providing, provided *conj.* as long
as, contingent upon, given, if and
only if, in case, in the event, on
condition, on the assumption, sub~
ject to, upon these terms, with the
proviso, with the understanding

province 1. colony, county, depart~
ment, dependency, district, divi~
sion, domain, region, section, ter~
ritory, tract, zone 2. *Fig.* area,
business, capacity, charge, con~
cern, duty, employment, field,
function, line, orbit, part, pigeon
(*Brit. inf.*), post, responsibility,
role, sphere

provincial *adj.* 1. country, home-
grown, homespun, local, rural,
rustic 2. insular, inward-looking,
limited, narrow, narrow-minded,
parish-pump, parochial, small-
minded, small-town (*U.S.*), unin~
formed, unsophisticated, up~
country ~*n.* 3. country cousin, rus~
tic, yokel

provision 1. accoutrement, cater~
ing, equipping, fitting out, furnish~
ing, providing, supplying, victual~
ling 2. arrangement, plan, prear~
rangement, precaution, prepara~
tion 3. *Fig.* agreement, clause,
condition, demand, proviso, re~
quirement, specification, stipula~
tion, term

provisional conditional, contin~
gent, interim, limited, pro tem,
provisory, qualified, stopgap, tem~
porary, tentative, transitional

provisions comestibles, eatables,
eats (*Sl.*), edibles, fare, food, foodstuff, groceries, grub (*Sl.*), proven~
der, rations, stores, supplies, suste~
nance, viands, victuals

proviso clause, condition, limita~
tion, provision, qualification, re~
quirement, reservation, restric~
tion, rider, stipulation, strings

provocation 1. *casus belli*, cause,
grounds, incitement, inducement,
instigation, justification, motiva~

tion, reason, stimulus 2. affront,
annoyance, challenge, dare, griev~
ance, indignity, injury, insult, of~
fence, red rag, taunt, vexation

provocative 1. aggravating (*Inf.*),
annoying, challenging, disturbing,
galling, goading, incensing, insult~
ing, offensive, outrageous, provok~
ing, stimulating 2. alluring, arous~
ing, erotic, exciting, inviting, se~
ductive, sexy (*Inf.*), stimulating,
suggestive, tantalizing, tempting

provoke 1. affront, aggravate (*Inf.*),
anger, annoy, chafe, enrage, exas~
perate, gall, get on one's nerves,
incense, infuriate, insult, irk, irri~
tate, madden, make one's blood
boil, offend, pique, put out, rile, try
one's patience, vex 2. bring about,
bring on *or* down, call forth, cause,
draw forth, elicit, evoke, excite,
fire, generate, give rise to, incite,
induce, inflame, inspire, instigate,
kindle, lead to, motivate, move,
occasion, precipitate, produce,
promote, prompt, rouse, stimulate,
stir

prow bow(s), fore, forepart, front,
head, nose, sharp end (*Jocular*),
stem

prowess 1. ability, accomplish~
ment, adeptness, adroitness, apti~
tude, attainment, command, dex~
terity, excellence, expertise, ex~
pertness, facility, genius, mastery,
skill, talent 2. boldness, bravery,
courage, daring, dauntlessness,
doughtiness, fearlessness, gallant~
ry, hardihood, heroism, intrepidity,
mettle, valiance, valour

prowl cruise, hunt, lurk, move
stealthily, nose around, patrol,
range, roam, rove, scavenge,
skulk, slink, sneak, stalk, steal

proximity adjacency, closeness,
contiguity, juxtaposition, nearness,
neighbourhood, propinquity, vicin~
ity

proxy agent, attorney, delegate,
deputy, factor, representative,
substitute, surrogate

prude Grundy, old maid (*Inf.*), prig,
puritan, schoolmarm (*Brit. inf.*)

prudence 1. canniness, care, cau~
tion, circumspection, common

sense, discretion, good sense, heedfulness, judgment, judiciousness, sagacity, vigilance, wariness, wisdom 2. careful budgeting, economizing, economy, far-sightedness, foresight, forethought, frugality, good management, husbandry, planning, precaution, preparedness, providence, saving, thrift

prudent 1. canny, careful, cautious, circumspect, discerning, discreet, judicious, politic, sagacious, sage, sensible, shrewd, vigilant, wary, wise 2. canny, careful, economical, far-sighted, frugal, provident, sparing, thrifty

prudery Grundyism, old-maidishness (*Inf.*), overmodesty, priggishness, primness, prudishness, puritanicalness, squeamishness, starchiness (*Inf.*), strictness, stuffiness

prudish demure, narrow-minded, old-maidish (*Inf.*), overmodest, overnice, priggish, prim, prissy (*Inf.*), proper, puritanical, schoolmarmish (*Brit. inf.*), squeamish, starchy (*Inf.*), strait-laced, stuffy, Victorian

prune clip, cut, cut back, dock, lop, pare down, reduce, shape, shorten, snip, trim

pry be a busybody, be inquisitive, be nosy (*Inf.*), ferret about, interfere, intrude, meddle, nose into, peep, peer, poke, poke one's nose in *or* into (*Inf.*), snoop (*Inf.*)

prying curious, eavesdropping, impertinent, inquisitive, interfering, intrusive, meddlesome, meddling, nosy (*Inf.*), snooping (*Inf.*), snoopy (*Inf.*), spying

psalm chant, hymn, paean, song of praise

pseudo *adj.* artificial, bogus, counterfeit, ersatz, fake, false, imitation, mock, not genuine, phoney (*Sl.*), pretended, quasi-, sham, spurious

pseudonym alias, assumed name, false name, incognito, nom de guerre, nom de plume, pen name, professional name, stage name

psyche anima, essential nature, individuality, inner man, innermost self, mind, personality, pneuma (*Philos.*), self, soul, spirit, subconscious, true being

psychiatrist analyst, headshrinker (*Sl.*), psychoanalyser, psychoanalyst, psychologist, psychotherapist, shrink (*Sl.*), therapist

psychic 1. clairvoyant, extrasensory, mystic, occult, preternatural, supernatural, telekinetic, telepathic 2. mental, psychogenic, psychological, spiritual

psychological 1. cerebral, cognitive, intellectual, mental 2. all in the mind, emotional, imaginary, irrational, psychosomatic, subconscious, subjective, unconscious, unreal

psychology 1. behaviourism, science of mind, study of personality 2. *Inf.* attitude, mental make-up, mental processes, thought processes, way of thinking, what makes one tick

psychopath insane person, lunatic, madman, maniac, mental case, nutcase (*Sl.*), nutter (*Brit. sl.*), psychotic, sociopath

psychotic *adj.* certifiable, demented, deranged, insane, lunatic, mad, mental, *non compos mentis*, off one's chump (head, rocker, trolley) (*Sl.*), psychopathic, unbalanced

pub *or* **public house** alehouse (*Archaic*), bar, boozer (*Inf.*), inn, local (*Brit. inf.*), roadhouse, tavern

puberty adolescence, awkward age, juvenescence, pubescence, teenage, teens, young adulthood

public *adj.* 1. civic, civil, common, general, national, popular, social, state, universal, widespread 2. accessible, communal, community, free to all, not private, open, open to the public, unrestricted 3. acknowledged, exposed, in circulation, known, notorious, obvious, open, overt, patent, plain, published, recognized 4. important, prominent, respected, well-known ~*n.* 5. citizens, commonalty, community, country, electorate, everyone, hoi polloi, masses, multitude, nation, people, populace, population, society, voters **6.** audience, buyers, clientele, follow~ ers, following, patrons, supporters, those interested, trade **7. in public coram populo,** for all to see, in full view, openly, publicly

publication 1. advertisement, air~ ing, announcement, appearance, broadcasting, declaration, disclo~ sure, dissemination, notification, proclamation, promulgation, pub~ lishing, reporting **2.** book, booklet, brochure, handbill, issue, leaflet, magazine, newspaper, pamphlet, periodical

publicity advertising, attention, ballyhoo (*Sl.*), boost, build-up, hype (*Sl.*), plug (*Inf.*), press, promotion, public notice, puff, puffery (*Inf.*)

publicize advertise, beat the drum for (*Inf.*), bring to public notice, broadcast, give publicity to, hype (*Sl.*), make known, play up, plug (*Inf.*), promote, puff, push, spot~ light, spread about, write up

public-spirited altruistic, chari~ table, community-minded, gener~ ous, humanitarian, philanthropic, unselfish

publish 1. bring out, issue, print, produce, put out **2.** advertise, an~ nounce, broadcast, circulate, com~ municate, declare, disclose, dis~ tribute, divulge, impart, leak, pro~ claim, promulgate, publicize, re~ veal, spread

pudding afters (*Brit. inf.*), dessert, last course, pud (*Inf.*), second course, sweet

puerile babyish, childish, foolish, immature, inane, infantile, irre~ sponsible, jejune, juvenile, naive, petty, ridiculous, silly, trivial, weak

puff *n.* **1.** blast, breath, draught, emanation, flurry, gust, whiff **2.** drag (*Inf.*), pull, smoke **3.** bulge, bunching, swelling **4.** advertise~ ment, commendation, favourable mention, good word, plug (*Inf.*), sales talk ~*v.* **5.** blow, breathe, ex~ hale, gasp, gulp, pant, wheeze **6.** drag (*Sl.*), draw, inhale, pull at *or* on, smoke, suck **7.** *Usually with* **up** bloat, dilate, distend, expand, in~ flate, swell **8.** hype (*Sl.*), over~

praise, plug (*Inf.*), praise, promote, publicize, push

puffed 1. done in (*Inf.*), exhausted, gasping, out of breath, panting, short of breath, spent, winded **2. puffed up** bigheaded (*Inf.*), full of oneself, high and mighty (*Inf.*), proud, swollen-headed, too big for one's boots

puffy bloated, distended, enlarged, inflamed, inflated, puffed up, swol~ len

pugilist boxer, bruiser (*Inf.*), fight~ er, prizefighter, pug (*Sl.*)

pugnacious aggressive, antago~ nistic, argumentative, bellicose, belligerent, choleric, combative, contentious, disputatious, hot-tempered, irascible, irritable, petulant, quarrelsome

pull *v.* **1.** drag, draw, haul, jerk, tow, trail, tug, yank **2.** cull, draw out, extract, gather, pick, pluck, re~ move, take out, uproot, weed **3.** dislocate, rend, rip, sprain, strain, stretch, tear, wrench **4.** *Inf.* attract, draw, entice *or* lure, magnetize **5. pull apart** *or* **to pieces** attack, criticize, find fault, flay, lay into, pan (*Inf.*), pick holes in, run down, slam (*Sl.*), slate (*Inf.*) **6. pull one~ self together** buck up (*Inf.*), get a grip on oneself, get over it, regain composure, snap out of it (*Inf.*) **7. pull strings** *Brit. inf.* influ~ ence, pull wires (*U.S.*), use one's influence **8. pull someone's leg** *Inf.* chaff, have (someone) on, joke, make fun of, poke fun at, rag, rib (*Inf.*), tease, twit ~*n.* **9.** jerk, tug, twitch, yank **10.** attraction, draw~ ing power, effort, exertion, force, forcefulness, influence, lure, mag~ netism, power **11.** *Inf.* advantage, clout (*Inf.*), influence, leverage, muscle, weight **12.** drag (*Inf.*), in~ halation, puff

pull down bulldoze, demolish, de~ stroy, raze, remove

pull off 1. detach, doff, remove, rip off, tear off, wrench off **2.** accom~ plish, bring off, carry out, manage, score a success, secure one's ob~ ject, succeed

pull out abandon, depart, evacuate,

leave, quit, rat on, retreat, stop participating, withdraw

pull through come through, get better, get over, pull round, rally, recover, survive, weather

pull up 1. dig out, lift, raise, uproot 2. brake, come to a halt, halt, reach a standstill, stop 3. admonish, carpet (*Inf.*), castigate, dress down (*Inf.*), rebuke, reprimand, reprove, take to task, tell off (*Inf.*), tick off (*Inf.*)

pulp *n.* 1. flesh, marrow, soft part 2. mash, mush, pap, paste, pomace, semiliquid, semisolid, triturate ~*v.* 3. crush, mash, pulverize, squash, triturate ~*adj.* 4. cheap, lurid, mushy (*Inf.*), rubbishy, sensational, trashy

pulse 1. *n.* beat, beating, oscillation, pulsation, rhythm, stroke, throb, throbbing, vibration 2. *v.* beat, pulsate, throb, tick, vibrate

pump *v.* 1. *With* out bail out, drain, draw off, drive out, empty, force out, siphon 2. *With* up blow up, dilate, inflate 3. drive, force, inject, pour, push, send, supply 4. cross-examine, give (someone) the third degree, grill (*Inf.*), interrogate, probe, question closely, quiz, worm out of

pun double entendre, equivoque, paronomasia (*Rhetoric*), play on words, quip, witticism

punch[1] *v.* 1. bash (*Inf.*), biff (*Sl.*), bop (*Inf.*), box, clout (*Inf.*), hit, plug (*Sl.*), pummel, slam, slug, smash, sock (*Sl.*), strike, wallop (*Inf.*) ~*n.* 2. bash (*Inf.*), biff (*Sl.*), blow, bop (*Inf.*), clout (*Inf.*), hit, jab, knock, plug (*Sl.*), sock (*Sl.*), thump, wallop (*Inf.*) 3. *Inf.* bite, drive, effectiveness, force, forcefulness, impact, point, verve, vigour

punch[2] *v.* bore, cut, drill, perforate, pierce, pink, prick, puncture, stamp

punch-drunk befuddled, confused, dazed, groggy (*Inf.*), in a daze, knocked silly, punchy (*Inf.*), reeling, slaphappy (*Inf.*), staggering, stupefied, unsteady, woozy (*Inf.*)

punctilio 1. exactitude, finickiness, meticulousness, particularity, precision, punctiliousness, scrupulousness, strictness 2. convention, delicacy, distinction, fine point, formality, nicety, particular, refinement

punctilious careful, ceremonious, conscientious, exact, finicky, formal, fussy, meticulous, nice, particular, precise, proper, scrupulous, strict

punctual early, exact, in good time, on the dot, on time, precise, prompt, punctilious, seasonable, strict, timely

punctuality promptitude, promptness, readiness, regularity

punctuate 1. break, interject, interrupt, intersperse, pepper, sprinkle 2. accentuate, emphasize, lay stress on, mark, point up, stress, underline

puncture *n.* 1. break, cut, damage, hole, leak, nick, opening, perforation, rupture, slit 2. flat, flat tyre ~*v.* 3. bore, cut, nick, penetrate, perforate, pierce, prick, rupture 4. deflate, go down, go flat 5. deflate, discourage, disillusion, flatten, humble, take down a peg (*Inf.*)

pundit buff (*Inf.*), maestro, one of the cognoscenti, (self-appointed) authority *or* expert

pungent 1. acid, acrid, aromatic, bitter, highly flavoured, hot, peppery, piquant, seasoned, sharp, sour, spicy, stinging, strong, tangy, tart 2. acrimonious, acute, barbed, biting, caustic, cutting, incisive, keen, mordant, penetrating, piercing, poignant, pointed, sarcastic, scathing, sharp, stinging, stringent, telling, trenchant

punish 1. beat, castigate, chasten, chastise, correct, discipline, flog, give a lesson to, give (someone) the works (*Sl.*), lash, penalize, rap someone's knuckles, scourge, sentence, slap someone's wrist, whip 2. abuse, batter, give (someone) a going over (*Inf.*), harm, hurt, injure, knock about, maltreat, manhandle, misuse, oppress, rough up

punishable blameworthy, chargeable, convictable, criminal, culpable, indictable

punishing arduous, backbreaking, burdensome, demanding, exhaust~ ing, grinding, gruelling, hard, strenuous, taxing, tiring, uphill, wearing

punishment 1. chastening, chas~ tisement, comeuppance (*Sl.*), cor~ rection, discipline, just deserts, penalty, penance, punitive meas~ ures, retribution, sanction, what for (*Inf.*) **2.** *Inf.* abuse, beating, hard work, maltreatment, man~ handling, pain, rough treatment, slave labour, torture, victimization

punitive in reprisal, in retaliation, punitory, retaliative, retaliatory, revengeful, vindictive

punt *v.* **1.** back, bet, gamble, lay, stake, wager ~*n.* **2.** bet, gamble, stake, wager **3.** backer, better, gambler, punter

punter *n.* **1.** backer, better, gam~ bler, punt **2.** *Inf.* bloke (*Brit. inf.*), fellow, guy (*Inf.*), man in the street, person **3.** *Inf.* client, customer

puny 1. diminutive, dwarfish, fee~ ble, frail, little, pint-sized (*Inf.*), pygmy, sickly, stunted, tiny, underfed, undersized, undeveloped, weak, weakly **2.** inconsequential, inferior, insignificant, minor, pal~ try, petty, piddling (*Inf.*), trifling, trivial, worthless

pup or **puppy** *Fig.* braggart, cub, jackanapes, popinjay, whelp, whippersnapper, young dog

pupil beginner, catechumen, disci~ ple, learner, neophyte, novice, scholar, schoolboy, schoolgirl, stu~ dent, tyro

puppet 1. doll, marionette **2.** *Fig.* cat's-paw, creature, dupe, figure~ head, gull (*Archaic*), instrument, mouthpiece, pawn, stooge, tool

purchasable 1. bribable, corrupt, corruptible, dishonest, having one's price, unscrupulous, venal **2.** available, for sale, in stock, ob~ tainable, on sale, on the market, to be had

purchase *v.* **1.** acquire, buy, come by, gain, get, get hold of, invest in, make a purchase, obtain, pay for, pick up, procure, secure, shop for **2.** achieve, attain, earn, gain, real~ ize, win ~*n.* **3.** acquisition, asset, buy, gain, investment, possession, property **4.** advantage, edge, foot~ hold, footing, grasp, grip, hold, in~ fluence, lever, leverage, support, toehold

pure 1. authentic, clear, flawless, genuine, natural, neat, perfect, real, simple, straight, true, unal~ loyed, unmixed **2.** clean, disinfect~ ed, germ-free, immaculate, pas~ teurized, sanitary, spotless, sterile, sterilized, unadulterated, unblem~ ished, uncontaminated, unpolluted, untainted, wholesome **3.** blameless, chaste, guileless, honest, immacu~ late, innocent, maidenly, modest, true, uncorrupted, undefiled, un~ spotted, unstained, unsullied, up~ right, virgin, virginal, virtuous **4.** absolute, complete, mere, sheer, thorough, unmitigated, unqualified, utter **5.** abstract, academic, philo~ sophical, speculative, theoretical

purely absolutely, completely, en~ tirely, exclusively, just, merely, only, plainly, simply, solely, totally, wholly

purge *v.* **1.** clean out, dismiss, do away with, eject, eradicate, expel, exterminate, get rid of, kill, liqui~ date, oust, remove, rid of, rout out, sweep out, wipe out **2.** absolve, cleanse, clear, exonerate, expiate, forgive, pardon, purify, wash ~*n.* **3.** cleanup, crushing, ejection, elimi~ nation, eradication, expulsion, liq~ uidation, reign of terror, removal, suppression, witch hunt **4.** aperient (*Medical*), cathartic, dose of salts, emetic, enema, laxative, physic (*Rare*), purgative (*Medical*)

purify 1. clarify, clean, cleanse, de~ contaminate, disinfect, filter, fu~ migate, refine, sanitize, wash **2.** absolve, cleanse, exculpate, exon~ erate, lustrate, redeem, sanctify, shrive

purist classicist, formalist, pedant, precisian, stickler

puritan 1. *n.* fanatic, moralist, pi~ etist, prude, rigorist, zealot **2.** *adj.* ascetic, austere, hidebound, intol~ erant, moralistic, narrow, narrow-minded, prudish, puritanical, severe, strait-laced, strict

puritanical ascetic, austere, bigoted, disapproving, fanatical, forbidding, narrow, narrow-minded, prim, proper, prudish, puritan, rigid, severe, stiff, strait-laced, strict, stuffy

purpose n. 1. aim, design, function, idea, intention, object, point, principle, reason 2. aim, ambition, aspiration, design, desire, end, goal, hope, intention, object, objective, plan, project, scheme, target, view, wish 3. constancy, determination, firmness, persistence, resolution, resolve, single-mindedness, steadfastness, tenacity, will 4. advantage, avail, benefit, effect, gain, good, outcome, profit, result, return, use, utility 5. **on purpose** by design, deliberately, designedly, intentionally, knowingly, purposely, wilfully, wittingly ~v. 6. aim, aspire, commit oneself, contemplate, decide, design, determine, have a mind to, intend, make up one's mind, mean, meditate, plan, propose, resolve, set one's sights on, think to, work towards

purposeless aimless, empty, goalless, motiveless, needless, pointless, senseless, uncalled-for, unnecessary, useless, vacuous, wanton

purposely by design, calculatedly, consciously, deliberately, designedly, expressly, intentionally, knowingly, on purpose, wilfully, with intent

purse n. 1. money-bag, pouch, wallet 2. coffers, exchequer, funds, means, money, resources, treasury, wealth, wherewithal 3. award, gift, present, prize, reward ~v. 4. close, contract, press together, pucker, tighten, wrinkle

pursue 1. accompany, attend, chase, dog, follow, give chase to, go after, harass, harry, haunt, hound, hunt, hunt down, plague, run after, shadow, stalk, tail, track 2. aim for, aspire to, desire, have as one's goal, purpose, seek, strive for, try for, work towards 3. adhere to, carry on, continue, cultivate, hold to, keep on, maintain, persevere in, persist in, proceed, see through 4. apply oneself, carry on, conduct, engage in, perform, ply, practise, prosecute, tackle, wage, work at 5. chase after, court, make up to (Inf.), pay attention to, pay court to, set one's cap at, woo

pursuit 1. chase, hunt, hunting, inquiry, quest, search, seeking, tracking, trail, trailing 2. activity, hobby, interest, line, occupation, pastime, pleasure, vocation

purview 1. ambit, compass, confine(s), extent, field, limit, orbit, province, range, reach, scope, sphere 2. comprehension, ken, overview, understanding

push v. 1. depress, drive, poke, press, propel, ram, shove, thrust 2. elbow, jostle, make or force one's way, move, shoulder, shove, squeeze, thrust 3. egg on, encourage, expedite, hurry, impel, incite, persuade, press, prod, speed (up), spur, urge 4. advertise, boost, cry up, hype (Sl.), make known, plug (Inf.), promote, propagandize, publicize, puff 5. browbeat, coerce, constrain, dragoon, encourage, exert influence on, influence, oblige ~n. 6. butt, jolt, nudge, poke, prod, shove, thrust 7. Inf. ambition, determination, drive, dynamism, energy, enterprise, get-up-and-go (Inf.), go (Inf.), gumption (Inf.), initiative, vigour, vitality 8. Inf. advance, assault, attack, charge, effort, offensive, onset, thrust 9. **the push** Sl. discharge, dismissal, marching orders (Inf.), one's books (Inf.), one's cards, the boot (Sl.), the sack (Inf.)

pushed Often with **for** hurried, in difficulty, pressed, rushed, short of, tight, under pressure, up against it (Inf.)

pushing 1. ambitious, determined, driving, dynamic, enterprising, go-ahead, on the go, purposeful, resourceful 2. assertive, bold, brash, bumptious, forward, impertinent, intrusive, presumptuous, pushy (Inf.), self-assertive

pushover 1. child's play (*Inf.*), cinch (*Sl.*), doddle (*Brit. sl.*), picnic (*Inf.*), piece of cake (*Brit. inf.*), walkover (*Inf.*) 2. chump (*Inf.*), easy *or* soft mark, easy game (*Inf.*), mug (*Sl.*), soft touch (*Inf.*), stooge (*Sl.*), sucker (*Sl.*), walkover (*Inf.*)

pussyfoot 1. creep, prowl, slink, steal, tip-toe, tread warily 2. beat about the bush, be noncommittal, equivocate, hedge, hum and haw, prevaricate, sit on the fence, tergiversate

pustule abscess, blister, boil, fester, gathering, pimple, ulcer

put 1. bring, deposit, establish, fix, lay, place, position, rest, set, settle, situate 2. commit, condemn, consign, doom, enjoin, impose, inflict, levy, subject 3. assign, constrain, employ, force, induce, make, oblige, require, set, subject to 4. express, phrase, pose, set, state, utter, word 5. advance, bring forward, forward, offer, posit, present, propose, set before, submit, tender 6. cast, fling, heave, hurl, lob, pitch, throw, toss

put across *or* **over** communicate, convey, explain, get across, get through, make clear, make oneself understood, spell out

put aside *or* **by** 1. cache, deposit, keep in reserve, lay by, salt away, save, squirrel away, stockpile, store, stow away 2. bury, discount, disregard, forget, ignore

putative alleged, assumed, commonly believed, imputed, presumed, presumptive, reported, reputed, supposed

put away 1. put back, replace, return to (its) place, tidy away 2. deposit, keep, lay in, put by, save, set aside, store away 3. certify, commit, confine, institutionalize, lock up 4. consume, devour, eat up, gobble, gulp down, wolf down 5. destroy, do away with, put down, put out of its misery, put to sleep

put down 1. enter, inscribe, log, record, set down, take down, transcribe, write down 2. crush, quash, quell, repress, silence, stamp out,

suppress 3. *With* **to** ascribe, attribute, impute, set down 4. destroy, do away with, put away, put out of its misery, put to sleep 5. *Sl.* condemn, crush, deflate, dismiss, disparage, humiliate, mortify, reject, shame, slight, snub

put forward advance, introduce, move, nominate, present, press, proffer, propose, recommend, submit, suggest, tender

put off 1. defer, delay, hold over, postpone, put back, reschedule 2. abash, confuse, discomfit, disconcert, dismay, distress, nonplus, perturb, rattle (*Inf.*), throw (*Inf.*), unsettle 3. discourage, dishearten, dissuade

put on 1. change into, don, dress, get dressed in, slip into 2. affect, assume, fake, feign, make believe, play-act, pretend, sham, simulate 3. do, mount, present, produce, show, stage 4. add, gain, increase by 5. back, bet, lay, place, wager

put out 1. anger, annoy, confound, disturb, exasperate, harass, irk, irritate, nettle, perturb, provoke, vex 2. blow out, douse, extinguish, quench, smother, snuff out, stamp out 3. bother, discomfit, discommode, discompose, disconcert, discountenance, disturb, embarrass, impose upon, incommode, inconvenience, put on the spot, trouble, upset 4. bring out, broadcast, circulate, issue, make known, make public, publish, release

putrefy corrupt, decay, decompose, deteriorate, go bad, rot, spoil, stink, taint

putrescent decaying, decomposing, going bad, rotting, stinking

putrid bad, contaminated, corrupt, decayed, decomposed, fetid, foul, off, putrefied, rancid, rank, reeking, rotten, rotting, spoiled, stinking, tainted

put through accomplish, achieve, bring off, carry through, conclude, do, effect, execute, manage, pull off, realize

put up 1. build, construct, erect, fabricate, raise 2. accommodate, board, entertain, give one lodging, house, lodge, take in 3. float, nomi~ nate, offer, present, propose, put forward, recommend, submit 4. advance, give, invest, pay, pledge, provide, supply 5. **put up to** egg on, encourage, goad, incite, instigate, prompt, put the idea into one's head, urge 6. **put up with** *Inf.* abide, bear, brook, endure, lump (*Inf.*), pocket, stand, stand for, stomach, suffer, swallow, take, tol~ erate

put-upon abused, beset, exploited, harried, imposed upon, inconven~ ienced, overworked, put-out, sad~ dled, taken advantage of, taken for a fool, taken for granted, troubled

puzzle *v.* 1. baffle, beat (*Sl.*), bewil~ der, confound, confuse, flummox, mystify, nonplus, perplex, stump 2. ask oneself, brood, cudgel *or* rack one's brains, mull over, muse, pon~ der, study, think about, think hard, wonder 3. *Usually with* **out** clear up, crack, crack the code, deci~ pher, figure out, find the key, get it, get the answer, resolve, see, solve, sort out, think through, unravel, work out ~*n.* 4. brain-teaser (*Inf.*), conundrum, enigma, labyrinth, maze, mystery, paradox, poser, problem, question, question mark, riddle 5. bafflement, bewilder~ ment, confusion, difficulty, dilem~ ma, perplexity, quandary, uncer~ tainty

puzzled at a loss, at sea, baffled, beaten, bewildered, clueless, con~ fused, doubtful, flummoxed, in a fog, lost, mixed up, mystified, non~ plussed, perplexed, stuck, stumped, without a clue

puzzlement bafflement, bewilder~ ment, confusion, disorientation, doubt, doubtfulness, mystification, perplexity, questioning, surprise, uncertainty, wonder

puzzling abstruse, ambiguous, baf~ fling, bewildering, beyond one, en~ igmatic, full of surprises, hard, in~ comprehensible, inexplicable, in~ volved, knotty, labyrinthine, mis~ leading, mystifying, perplexing, unaccountable, unclear, unfath~ omable

pygmy *n.* 1. dwarf, homunculus, Lilliputian, manikin, midget, shrimp (*Inf.*), Tom Thumb 2. ci~ pher, lightweight (*Inf.*), medioc~ rity, nobody, nonentity, pipsqueak (*Inf.*), small fry ~*adj.* 3. baby, di~ minutive, dwarf, dwarfish, elfin, Lilliputian, midget, miniature, mi~ nuscule, pocket, pygmean, small, stunted, tiny, undersized, wee

Q

quack 1. *n.* charlatan, fake, fraud, humbug, impostor, mountebank, phoney (*Sl.*), pretender, quacksalver (*Archaic*) 2. *adj.* counterfeit, fake, fraudulent, phoney (*Sl.*), pretended, sham

quagmire 1. bog, fen, marsh, mire, morass, quicksand, slough, swamp 2. difficulty, dilemma, entanglement, fix (*Inf.*), imbroglio, impasse, jam (*Inf.*), muddle, pass, pickle (*Inf.*), pinch, plight, predicament, quandary, scrape (*Inf.*)

quail blanch, blench, cower, cringe, droop, faint, falter, flinch, have cold feet (*Inf.*), quake, recoil, shake, shrink, shudder, tremble

quaint 1. bizarre, curious, droll, eccentric, fanciful, fantastic, odd, old-fashioned, original, peculiar, queer, singular, strange, unusual, whimsical 2. antiquated, antique, artful, charming, gothic, ingenious, old-fashioned, old-world, picturesque

quake convulse, move, pulsate, quail, quiver, rock, shake, shiver, shudder, throb, totter, tremble, vibrate, waver, wobble

qualification 1. ability, accomplishment, aptitude, attribute, capability, capacity, eligibility, endowment(s), fitness, quality, skill, suitability, suitableness 2. allowance, caveat, condition, criterion, exception, exemption, limitation, modification, objection, prerequisite, proviso, requirement, reservation, restriction, stipulation

qualified 1. able, accomplished, adept, capable, certificated, competent, efficient, equipped, experienced, expert, fit, knowledgeable, licensed, practised, proficient, skilful, talented, trained 2. bounded, circumscribed, conditional, confined, contingent, equivocal, guarded, limited, modified, provisional, reserved, restricted

qualify 1. capacitate, certify, commission, condition, empower, endow, equip, fit, ground, permit, prepare, ready, sanction, train 2. abate, adapt, assuage, circumscribe, diminish, ease, lessen, limit, mitigate, moderate, modify, modulate, reduce, regulate, restrain, restrict, soften, temper, vary 3. characterize, describe, designate, distinguish, modify, name

quality 1. aspect, attribute, characteristic, condition, feature, mark, peculiarity, property, trait 2. character, constitution, description, essence, kind, make, nature, sort 3. calibre, distinction, excellence, grade, merit, position, preeminence, rank, standing, status, superiority, value, worth 4. *Obsolete* aristocracy, gentry, nobility, ruling class, upper class

qualm 1. anxiety, apprehension, compunction, disquiet, doubt, hesitation, misgiving, regret, reluctance, remorse, scruple, twinge *or* pang of conscience, uncertainty, uneasiness 2. agony, attack, nausea, pang, queasiness, sickness, spasm, throe (*Rare*), twinge

quandary bewilderment, cleft stick, delicate situation, difficulty, dilemma, doubt, embarrassment, impasse, perplexity, plight, predicament, puzzle, strait, uncertainty

quantity 1. aggregate, allotment, amount, lot, number, part, portion, quota, sum, total 2. bulk, capacity, expanse, extent, greatness, length, magnitude, mass, measure, size, volume

quarrel *n.* 1. affray, altercation, argument, brawl, breach, broil, commotion, contention, controversy, difference (of opinion), disagreement, discord, disputation, dispute, dissension, dissidence, disturbance, feud, fight, fracas, fray, misunderstanding, row, scrap (*Inf.*), spat, squabble, strife, tiff, tumult, vendetta, wrangle ~v. 2. altercate, argue, bicker, brawl, clash, differ, disagree, dispute, fall out (*Inf.*), fight, row, spar, squabble, wrangle 3. carp, cavil, complain, decry, disapprove, find fault, object to, take exception to

quarrelsome argumentative, belligerent, cat-and-dog (*Inf.*), choleric, combative, contentious, cross, disputatious, fractious, ill-tempered, irascible, irritable, peevish, petulant, pugnacious, querulous

quarry aim, game, goal, objective, prey, prize, victim

quarter n. 1. area, direction, district, locality, location, neighbourhood, part, place, point, position, province, region, side, spot, station, territory, zone 2. clemency, compassion, favour, forgiveness, leniency, mercy, pity ~v. 3. accommodate, billet, board, house, install, lodge, place, post, put up, station

quarters abode, accommodation, barracks, billet, cantonment (*Military*), chambers, digs (*Inf.*), domicile, dwelling, habitation, lodging, lodgings, post, residence, rooms, shelter, station

quash 1. beat, crush, destroy, extinguish, extirpate, overthrow, put down, quell, quench, repress, squash, subdue, suppress 2. annul, cancel, declare null and void, invalidate, nullify, overrule, overthrow, rescind, reverse, revoke, set aside, void

quasi- 1. almost, apparently, partly, seemingly, supposedly 2. apparent, fake, mock, near, nominal, pretended, pseudo-, seeming, semi-, sham, so-called, synthetic, virtual, would-be

quaver 1. v. flicker, flutter, oscillate, pulsate, quake, quiver, shake, shudder, thrill, tremble, trill, twitter, vibrate, waver 2. n. break, quiver, shake, sob, throb, tremble, trembling, tremor, trill, vibration, warble

queen 1. consort, monarch, ruler, sovereign 2. diva, doyenne, ideal, idol, mistress, model, perfection, prima donna, star

queer adj. 1. abnormal, anomalous, atypical, curious, disquieting, droll, eerie, erratic, extraordinary, funny, odd, outlandish, *outré*, peculiar, remarkable, singular, strange, uncanny, uncommon, unconventional, unnatural, unorthodox, unusual, weird 2. doubtful, dubious, fishy (*Inf.*), irregular, mysterious, puzzling, questionable, shady (*Inf.*), suspicious 3. dizzy, faint, giddy, light-headed, queasy, reeling, uneasy 4. crazy, demented, eccentric, idiosyncratic, irrational, mad, odd, touched, unbalanced, unhinged ~v. 5. botch, endanger, harm, impair, imperil, injure, jeopardize, mar, ruin, spoil, thwart, wreck

quell 1. conquer, crush, defeat, extinguish, overcome, overpower, put down, quash, squelch, stamp out, stifle, subdue, suppress, vanquish 2. allay, alleviate, appease, assuage, calm, compose, deaden, dull, mitigate, moderate, mollify, pacify, quiet, silence, soothe

quench 1. check, crush, destroy, douse, end, extinguish, put out, smother, snuff out, squelch, stifle, suppress 2. allay, appease, cool, sate, satiate, satisfy, slake

querulous cantankerous, captious, carping, censorious, complaining, critical, cross, discontented, dissatisfied, fault-finding, fretful, grouchy (*Inf.*), grumbling, hard to please, irascible, irritable, murmuring, peevish, petulant, plaintive, sour, testy, touchy, waspish, whining

query v. 1. ask, enquire, question 2. challenge, disbelieve, dispute, distrust, doubt, mistrust, suspect ~n. 3. demand, doubt, hesitation, inquiry, objection, problem, question, reservation, scepticism, suspicion

quest n. adventure, crusade, enterprise, expedition, exploration, hunt, journey, mission, pilgrimage, pursuit, search, voyage

question v. 1. ask, catechize, cross-examine, enquire, examine, grill (*Inf.*), interrogate, interview, investigate, probe, pump (*Inf.*), quiz, sound out 2. call into question, cast doubt upon, challenge, controvert, disbelieve, dispute, distrust, doubt, impugn, mistrust, oppose, query, suspect ~*n.* 3. examination, inquiry, interrogation, investigation 4. argument, confusion, contention, controversy, debate, difficulty, dispute, doubt, dubiety, misgiving, problem, query, uncertainty 5. issue, motion, point, point at issue, proposal, proposition, subject, theme, topic 6. **in question** at issue, in doubt, open to debate, under discussion 7. **out of the question** impossible, inconceivable, not to be thought of, unthinkable

questionable arguable, controversial, controvertible, debatable, disputable, doubtful, dubious, dubitable, equivocal, fishy (*Inf.*), moot, paradoxical, problematical, shady (*Inf.*), suspect, suspicious, uncertain, unproven, unreliable

queue chain, concatenation, file, line, order, progression, sequence, series, string, succession, train

quibble 1. *v.* carp, cavil, equivocate, evade, pretend, prevaricate, shift, split hairs 2. *n.* artifice, cavil, complaint, criticism, duplicity, equivocation, evasion, nicety, niggle, objection, pretence, prevarication, protest, quirk, shift, sophism, subterfuge, subtlety

quick 1. active, brief, brisk, cursory, expeditious, express, fast, fleet, hasty, headlong, hurried, perfunctory, prompt, rapid, speedy, sudden, swift 2. agile, alert, animated, energetic, flying, keen, lively, nimble, spirited, sprightly, spry, vivacious, winged 3. able, acute, adept, adroit, all there (*Inf.*), apt, astute, bright, clever, deft, dexterous, discerning, intelligent, nimble-witted, perceptive, quick on the uptake (*Inf.*), quick-witted, receptive, sharp, shrewd, skilful, smart 4. abrupt, curt, excitable, hasty, impatient, irascible, irritable, passionate, petulant, testy, touchy 5. *Archaic* alive, animate, existing, live, living, viable

quicken 1. accelerate, dispatch, expedite, hasten, hurry, impel, precipitate, speed 2. activate, animate, arouse, energize, excite, galvanize, incite, inspire, invigorate, kindle, refresh, reinvigorate, resuscitate, revitalize, revive, rouse, stimulate, strengthen, vitalize, vivify

quickly abruptly, at a rate of knots (*Inf.*), at *or* on the double, at speed, briskly, expeditiously, fast, hastily, hell for leather, hurriedly, immediately, instantly, posthaste, promptly, quick, rapidly, soon, speedily, swiftly, with all speed

quick-tempered choleric, excitable, fiery, hot-tempered, impatient, impulsive, irascible, irritable, petulant, quarrelsome, shrewish, splenetic, testy, waspish

quick-witted alert, astute, clever, keen, perceptive, sharp, shrewd, smart

quiescent calm, dormant, in abeyance, inactive, latent, motionless, peaceful, placid, quiet, resting, serene, silent, smooth, still, tranquil, unagitated, undisturbed, unmoving, unruffled

quiet *adj.* 1. dumb, hushed, inaudible, low, low-pitched, noiseless, peaceful, silent, soft, soundless 2. calm, contented, gentle, mild, motionless, pacific, peaceful, placid, restful, serene, smooth, tranquil, untroubled 3. isolated, private, retired, secluded, secret, sequestered, undisturbed, unfrequented 4. conservative, modest, plain, restrained, simple, sober, subdued, unassuming, unobtrusive, unpretentious 5. collected, docile, eventempered, gentle, imperturbable, meek, mild, phlegmatic, reserved, retiring, sedate, shy, unexcitable ~*n.* 6. calmness, ease, peace, quietness, repose, rest, serenity, silence, stillness, tranquillity

quieten *v.* allay, alleviate, appease, assuage, blunt, calm, compose, deaden, dull, hush, lull, mitigate, mollify, muffle, mute, palliate, quell, quiet, shush (*Inf.*), silence, soothe, stifle, still, stop, subdue, tranquillize

quietly 1. confidentially, dumbly, in a low voice *or* whisper, in an undertone, inaudibly, in hushed tones, in silence, mutely, noiselessly, privately, secretly, silently, softly, without talking 2. calmly, contentedly, dispassionately, meekly, mildly, patiently, placidly, serenely, undemonstratively 3. coyly, demurely, diffidently, humbly, modestly, unassumingly, unobtrusively, unostentatiously, unpretentiously

quietness calm, calmness, hush, peace, placidity, quiescence, quiet, quietude, repose, rest, serenity, silence, still, stillness, tranquillity

quilt bedspread, comforter (*U.S.*), counterpane, coverlet, duvet, eiderdown

quip *n.* badinage, *bon mot*, gibe, jest, joke, pleasantry, repartee, retort, riposte, sally, wisecrack (*Inf.*), witticism

quirk aberration, caprice, characteristic, eccentricity, fancy, fetish, foible, habit, *idée fixe*, idiosyncrasy, kink, mannerism, oddity, peculiarity, singularity, trait, vagary, whim

quisling betrayer, collaborator, fifth columnist, Judas, renegade, traitor, turncoat

quit *v.* 1. abandon, abdicate, decamp, depart, desert, exit, forsake, go, leave, pull out, relinquish, renounce, resign, retire, surrender, take off (*Inf.*), withdraw 2. abandon, cease, conclude, discontinue, drop, end, give up, halt, stop, suspend ~*adj.* 3. absolved, acquitted, clear, discharged, exculpated, exempt, exonerated, free, released, rid of

quite 1. absolutely, completely, considerably, entirely, fully, in all respects, largely, perfectly, precisely, totally, wholly, without reservation 2. fairly, moderately, rather, reasonably, relatively, somewhat, to a certain extent, to some degree 3. in fact, in reality, in truth, really, truly

quiver 1. *v.* agitate, convulse, oscillate, palpitate, pulsate, quake, quaver, shake, shiver, shudder, tremble, vibrate 2. *n.* convulsion, oscillation, palpitation, pulsation, shake, shiver, shudder, spasm, throb, tic, tremble, tremor, vibration

quiz 1. *n.* examination, investigation, questioning, test 2. *v.* ask, catechize, examine, grill (*Inf.*), interrogate, investigate, pump (*Inf.*), question

quota allocation, allowance, assignment, cut (*Inf.*), part, portion, proportion, ration, share, slice, whack (*Inf.*)

quotation 1. citation, cutting, excerpt, extract, passage, quote (*Inf.*), reference, selection 2. *Commerce* bid price, charge, cost, estimate, figure, price, quote (*Inf.*), rate, tender

quote adduce, attest, cite, detail, extract, instance, name, paraphrase, proclaim, recall, recite, recollect, refer to, repeat, retell

R

rabble 1. *canaille*, crowd, herd, horde, mob, swarm, throng 2. *Derogatory canaille*, commonalty, commoners, common people, crowd, dregs, hoi polloi, lower classes, masses, peasantry, populace, proletariat, riffraff, scum, the great unwashed (*Inf.*), trash

rabid 1. hydrophobic, mad 2. berserk, crazed, frantic, frenzied, furious, infuriated, mad, maniacal, raging, violent, wild 3. bigoted, extreme, fanatical, fervent, intemperate, intolerant, irrational, narrow-minded, zealous

race[1] 1. *n.* chase, competition, contention, contest, dash, pursuit, rivalry 2. *v.* career, compete, contest, dart, dash, fly, gallop, hare (*Brit. inf.*), hasten, hurry, run, run like mad (*Inf.*), speed, tear, zoom

race[2] blood, breed, clan, ethnic group, family, folk, house, issue, kin, kindred, line, lineage, nation, offspring, people, progeny, seed (*Archaic*), stock, tribe, type

racial ethnic, ethnological, folk, genealogical, genetic, national, tribal

rack *n.* 1. frame, framework, stand, structure 2. affliction, agony, anguish, misery, pain, pang, persecution, suffering, torment, torture ~*v.* 3. afflict, agonize, crucify, distress, excruciate, harass, harrow, oppress, pain, torment, torture 4. force, pull, shake, strain, stress, stretch, tear, wrench

racket 1. babel, ballyhoo (*Inf.*), clamour, commotion, din, disturbance, fuss, hubbub, hullabaloo, noise, outcry, pandemonium, row, shouting, tumult, uproar 2. criminal activity, fraud, illegal enterprise, scheme 3. *Sl.* business, game (*Inf.*), line, occupation

racy 1. animated, buoyant, energetic, entertaining, exciting, exhilarating, heady, lively, sparkling, spirited, stimulating, vigorous, zestful 2. distinctive, piquant, pungent, rich, sharp, spicy, strong, tangy, tart, tasty 3. bawdy, blue, broad, immodest, indecent, indelicate, naughty, near the knuckle (*Inf.*), off colour, risqué, smutty, spicy (*Inf.*), suggestive

radiance 1. brightness, brilliance, effulgence, glare, gleam, glitter, glow, incandescence, light, luminosity, lustre, resplendence, shine 2. delight, gaiety, happiness, joy, pleasure, rapture, warmth

radiant 1. beaming, bright, brilliant, effulgent, gleaming, glittering, glorious, glowing, incandescent, luminous, lustrous, resplendent, shining, sparkling, sunny 2. beaming, beatific, blissful, delighted, ecstatic, gay, glowing, happy, joyful, joyous, rapturous

radiate 1. diffuse, disseminate, emanate, emit, give off *or* out, gleam, glitter, pour, scatter, send out, shed, shine, spread 2. branch out, diverge, issue, spread out

radiation emanation, emission, rays

radical *adj.* 1. basic, constitutional, deep-seated, essential, fundamental, innate, native, natural, organic, profound, thoroughgoing 2. complete, entire, excessive, extreme, extremist, fanatical, revolutionary, severe, sweeping, thorough, violent ~*n.* 3. extremist, fanatic, militant, revolutionary

raffle draw, lottery, sweep, sweepstake

ragbag 1. confusion, hotchpotch, jumble, medley, miscellany, mixture, omnium-gatherum, potpourri 2. *Inf.* frump, scarecrow (*Inf.*), scruff (*Inf.*), slattern, sloven, slut, trollop

rage *n.* 1. agitation, anger, frenzy, fury, high dudgeon, ire, madness, mania, obsession, passion, rampage, raving, vehemence, violence, wrath 2. craze, enthusiasm, fad (*Inf.*), fashion, latest thing, mode, style, vogue ~v. 3. be beside one~ self, be furious, blow one's top, blow up (*Inf.*), chafe, foam at the mouth, fret, fume, rant and rave, rave, seethe, storm, throw a fit (*Inf.*) 4. be at its height, be uncon~ trollable, rampage, storm, surge

ragged 1. contemptible, down at heel, frayed, in holes, in rags, in tatters, mean, poor, rent, scraggy, shabby, shaggy, tattered, tatty, threadbare, torn, unkempt, worn~ out 2. crude, jagged, notched, poor, rough, rugged, serrated, uneven, unfinished 3. broken, desultory, disorganized, fragmented, irregu~ lar, uneven

raging beside oneself, boiling mad (*Inf.*), doing one's nut (*Brit. sl.*), enraged, fit to be tied (*Sl.*), fizzing (*Scot.*), foaming at the mouth, frenzied, fuming, furious, incensed, infuriated, mad, raving, seething

rags 1. castoffs, old clothes, tat~ tered clothing, tatters 2. **in rags** down at heel, out at elbow, ragged, seedy, shabby, tattered

raid 1. *n.* attack, break-in, descent, foray, hit-and-run attack, incursion, inroad, invasion, irruption, onset, sally, seizure, sortie, surprise at~ tack 2. *v.* assault, attack, break into, descend on, fall upon, forage (*Military*), foray, invade, pillage, plunder, reive (*Dialect*), rifle, sack, sally forth, swoop down upon

raider attacker, forager (*Military*), invader, marauder, plunderer, reiver (*Dialect*), robber, thief

railing balustrade, barrier, fence, paling, rails

rain *n.* 1. cloudburst, deluge, down~ pour, drizzle, fall, precipitation, raindrops, rainfall, showers 2. del~ uge, flood, hail, shower, spate, stream, torrent, volley ~v. 3. bucket down (*Inf.*), come down in buckets (*Inf.*), drizzle, fall, pour, rain cats and dogs (*Inf.*), shower, teem 4. deposit, drop, fall, shower, sprinkle 5. bestow, lavish, pour, shower

rainy damp, drizzly, showery, wet

raise 1. build, construct, elevate, erect, exalt, heave, hoist, lift, move

up, promote, put up, rear, set up~ right, uplift 2. advance, aggravate, amplify, augment, boost, enhance, enlarge, escalate, exaggerate, heighten, hike (up) (*Inf.*), increase, inflate, intensify, jack up, magnify, put up, reinforce, strengthen 3. ad~ vance, aggrandize, elevate, exalt, prefer, promote, upgrade 4. acti~ vate, arouse, awaken, cause, evoke, excite, foment, foster, in~ cite, instigate, kindle, motivate, provoke, set on foot, stir up, sum~ mon up, whip up 5. bring about, cause, create, engender, give rise to, occasion, originate, produce, provoke, start 6. advance, bring up, broach, introduce, moot, put for~ ward, suggest 7. assemble, collect, form, gather, get, levy, mass, mo~ bilize, muster, obtain, rally, recruit 8. breed, bring up, cultivate, devel~ op, grow, nurture, produce, propa~ gate, rear 9. abandon, end, give up, lift, relieve, relinquish, remove, terminate

rake[1] *v.* 1. collect, gather, remove, scrape up 2. break up, harrow, hoe, scour, scrape, scratch 3. *With up or together* assemble, collect, dig up, dredge up, gather, scrape to~ gether 4. comb, examine, hunt, ransack, scan, scour, scrutinize, search 5. graze, scrape, scratch 6. enfilade, pepper, sweep

rake[2] *n.* debauchee, dissolute man, lecher, libertine, playboy, profli~ gate, rakehell (*Archaic*), roué, sensualist, voluptuary

rakish breezy, dapper, dashing, debonair, devil-may-care, flashy, jaunty, natty (*Inf.*), raffish, smart, snazzy (*Inf.*), sporty

rally *v.* 1. bring *or* come to order, reassemble, re-form, regroup, re~ organize, unite ~n. 2. regrouping, reorganization, reunion, stand ~v. 3. assemble, bond together, bring *or* come together, collect, convene, gather, get together, marshal, mo~ bilize, muster, organize, round up, summon, unite ~n. 4. assembly, conference, congregation, con~ vention, convocation, gathering, mass meeting, meeting, muster ~v. 5. come round, get better, get one's second wind, improve, perk up, pick up, pull through, recover, recuperate, regain one's strength, revive, take a turn for the better ~n. 6. comeback (Inf.), improvement, recovery, recuperation, renewal, resurgence, revival, turn for the better

ram v. 1. butt, collide with, crash, dash, drive, force, hit, impact, run into, slam, smash, strike 2. beat, cram, crowd, drum, force, hammer, jam, pack, pound, stuff, tamp, thrust

ramble v. 1. amble, drift, perambulate, peregrinate, range, roam, rove, saunter, straggle, stravaig (Scot.), stray, stroll, traipse (Inf.), walk, wander 2. meander, snake, twist and turn, wind, zigzag 3. babble, chatter, digress, expatiate, maunder, rabbit on (Brit. sl.), rattle on, wander, witter on (Inf.) ~n. 4. excursion, hike, perambulation, peregrination, roaming, roving, saunter, stroll, tour, traipse (Inf.), trip, walk

rambler drifter, hiker, roamer, rover, stroller, walker, wanderer, wayfarer

rambling 1. circuitous, desultory, diffuse, digressive, disconnected, discursive, disjointed, incoherent, irregular, long-winded, periphrastic, prolix, wordy 2. irregular, sprawling, spreading, straggling, trailing

ramification 1. branch, development, divarication, division, excrescence, extension, forking, offshoot, outgrowth, subdivision 2. complication, consequence, development, result, sequel, upshot

ramp grade, gradient, incline, inclined plane, rise, slope

rampage v. 1. go berserk, rage, run amuck, run riot, run wild, storm, tear ~n. 2. destruction, frenzy, fury, rage, storm, tempest, tumult, uproar, violence 3. **on the rampage** amuck, berserk, destructive, out of control, raging, rampant, riotous, violent, wild

rampant 1. aggressive, dominant, excessive, flagrant, on the rampage, out of control, out of hand, outrageous, raging, rampaging, riotous, unbridled, uncontrollable, ungovernable, unrestrained, vehement, violent, wanton, wild 2. epidemic, exuberant, luxuriant, prevalent, profuse, rank, rife, spreading like wildfire, unchecked, uncontrolled, unrestrained, widespread 3. Heraldry erect, rearing, standing, upright

rampart barricade, bastion, breastwork, bulwark, defence, earthwork, embankment, fence, fort, fortification, guard, parapet, security, stronghold, wall

ramshackle broken-down, crumbling, decrepit, derelict, dilapidated, flimsy, jerry-built, rickety, shaky, tottering, tumbledown, unsafe, unsteady

rancid bad, fetid, foul, frowsty, fusty, musty, off, putrid, rank, rotten, sour, stale, strong-smelling, tainted

random 1. accidental, adventitious, aimless, arbitrary, casual, chance, desultory, fortuitous, haphazard, hit or miss, incidental, indiscriminate, purposeless, spot, stray, unplanned, unpremeditated 2. **at random** accidentally, adventitiously, aimlessly, arbitrarily, by chance, casually, haphazardly, indiscriminately, irregularly, purposelessly, randomly, unsystematically, willy-nilly

range n. 1. amplitude, area, bounds, compass, confines, distance, domain, extent, field, latitude, limits, orbit, parameters (Inf.), province, purview, radius, reach, scope, span, sphere, sweep 2. chain, file, line, rank, row, sequence, series, string, tier 3. assortment, class, collection, gamut, kind, lot, order, selection, series, sort, variety ~v. 4. align, arrange, array, dispose, draw up, line up, order 5. arrange, bracket, catalogue, categorize, class, classify, file, grade, group, pigeonhole, rank 6. aim, align, direct, level, point, train 7. cruise, explore, ramble, roam, rove, straggle, stray, stroll, sweep, traverse, wander 8. extend, fluctuate, go, reach, run, stretch, vary between

rank[1] *n.* 1. caste, class, classification, degree, dignity, division, echelon, grade, level, nobility, order, position, quality, sort, standing, station, status, stratum, type 2. column, file, formation, group, line, range, row, series, tier ~*v.* 3. align, arrange, array, class, classify, dispose, grade, line up, locate, marshal, order, position, range, sort

rank[2] 1. abundant, dense, exuberant, flourishing, lush, luxuriant, productive, profuse, strong-growing, vigorous 2. bad, disagreeable, disgusting, fetid, foul, fusty, gamy, mephitic, musty, noisome, noxious, off, offensive, pungent, putrid, rancid, revolting, stale, stinking, strong-smelling 3. absolute, arrant, blatant, complete, downright, egregious, excessive, extravagant, flagrant, glaring, gross, rampant, sheer, thorough, total, undisguised, unmitigated, utter 4. abusive, atrocious, coarse, crass, filthy, foul, gross, indecent, nasty, obscene, outrageous, scurrilous, shocking, vulgar

rank and file 1. lower ranks, men, other ranks, private soldiers, soldiers, troops 2. body, general public, majority, mass, masses

rankle anger, annoy, chafe, embitter, fester, gall, get one's goat (*Inf.*), irk, irritate, rile

ransack 1. comb, explore, go through, rake, rummage, scour, search, turn inside out 2. despoil, gut, loot, pillage, plunder, raid, ravage, rifle, sack, strip

ransom *n.* 1. deliverance, liberation, redemption, release, rescue 2. money, payment, payoff, price ~*v.* 3. buy (someone) out (*Inf.*), buy the freedom of, deliver, liberate, obtain *or* pay for the release of, redeem, release, rescue, set free

rant 1. *v.* bellow, bluster, cry, declaim, rave, roar, shout, spout (*Inf.*), vociferate, yell 2. *n.* bluster, bombast, diatribe, fanfaronade (*Rare*), harangue, philippic, rhetoric, tirade, vociferation

rapacious avaricious, extortionate, grasping, greedy, insatiable, marauding, plundering, predatory, preying, ravenous, usurious, voracious, wolfish

rapacity avarice, avidity, cupidity, graspingness, greed, greediness, insatiableness, predatoriness, rapaciousness, ravenousness, usury, voraciousness, voracity, wolfishness

rape *n.* 1. outrage, ravishment, sexual assault, violation 2. depredation, despoilment, despoliation, pillage, plundering, rapine, sack, spoliation 3. abuse, defilement, desecration, maltreatment, perversion, violation ~*v.* 4. outrage, ravish, sexually assault, violate 5. despoil, loot, pillage, plunder, ransack, sack, spoliate

rapid brisk, expeditious, express, fast, fleet, flying, hasty, hurried, precipitate, prompt, quick, speedy, swift

rapidity alacrity, briskness, celerity, dispatch, expedition, fleetness, haste, hurry, precipitateness, promptitude, promptness, quickness, rush, speed, speediness, swiftness, velocity

rapidly at speed, briskly, expeditiously, fast, hastily, hurriedly, in a hurry, in a rush, in haste, like a shot, precipitately, promptly, quickly, speedily, swiftly, with dispatch

rapport affinity, bond, empathy, harmony, interrelationship, link, relationship, sympathy, understanding

rapt 1. absorbed, carried away, engrossed, enthralled, entranced, fascinated, gripped, held, intent, preoccupied, spellbound 2. bewitched, blissful, captivated, charmed, delighted, ecstatic, enchanted, enraptured, rapturous, ravished, transported

rapture beatitude, bliss, cloud nine (*Inf.*), delectation, delight, ecstasy, enthusiasm, euphoria, exaltation, felicity, happiness, joy, ravishment, rhapsody, seventh heaven, spell, transport

rapturous blissful, delighted, ec~ static, enthusiastic, euphoric, ex~ alted, happy, in seventh heaven, joyful, joyous, on cloud nine (*Inf.*), overjoyed, over the moon (*Inf.*), ravished, rhapsodic, transported

rare 1. exceptional, few, infrequent, out of the ordinary, recherché, scarce, singular, sparse, sporadic, strange, thin on the ground, un~ common, unusual **2.** admirable, choice, excellent, exquisite, ex~ treme, fine, great, incomparable, peerless, superb, superlative **3.** in~ valuable, precious, priceless, rich

rarely 1. almost never, hardly, hardly ever, infrequently, little, once in a blue moon, once in a while, only now and then, on rare occasions, scarcely ever, seldom **2.** exceptionally, extraordinarily, finely, notably, remarkably, singu~ larly, uncommonly, unusually

rarity 1. curio, curiosity, find, gem, one-off, pearl, treasure **2.** infre~ quency, scarcity, shortage, singu~ larity, sparseness, strangeness, uncommonness, unusualness **3.** choiceness, excellence, exquisite~ ness, fineness, incomparability, in~ comparableness, peerlessness, quality, superbness **4.** invaluable~ ness, preciousness, pricelessness, richness, value, worth

rascal blackguard, caitiff (*Archa~ ic*), devil, disgrace, good-for-nothing, imp, knave (*Archaic*), miscreant, ne'er-do-well, rake, rapscallion, reprobate, rogue, scallywag (*Inf.*), scamp, scoundrel, varmint (*Inf.*), villain, wastrel, wretch

rash[1] adventurous, audacious, brash, careless, foolhardy, hare-brained, harum-scarum, hasty, headlong, headstrong, heedless, helter-skelter, hot-headed, ill-advised, ill-considered, impetuous, imprudent, impulsive, incautious, indiscreet, injudicious, madcap, precipitate, premature, reckless, thoughtless, unguarded, unthink~ ing, unwary, venturesome

rash[2] **1.** eruption, outbreak **2.** epi~ demic, flood, outbreak, plague, se~ ries, spate, succession, wave

rashness adventurousness, audac~ ity, brashness, carelessness, fool-hardiness, hastiness, heedlessness, indiscretion, precipitation, reck~ lessness, temerity, thoughtlessness

rate *n.* **1.** degree, percentage, pro~ portion, ratio, relation, scale, standard **2.** charge, cost, dues, duty, fee, figure, hire, price, tariff, tax, toll **3.** gait, measure, pace, speed, tempo, time, velocity **4.** class, classification, degree, grade, position, quality, rank, rating, sta~ tus, value, worth **5.** at any rate anyhow, anyway, at all events, in any case, nevertheless ~*v.* **6.** ad~ judge, appraise, assess, class, clas~ sify, consider, count, esteem, esti~ mate, evaluate, grade, measure, rank, reckon, regard, value, weigh **7.** be entitled to, be worthy of, de~ serve, merit **8.** *Sl.* admire, esteem, respect, think highly of, value

rather 1. a bit, a little, fairly, kind of (*Inf.*), moderately, pretty (*Inf.*), quite, relatively, slightly, some~ what, sort of (*Inf.*), to some degree, to some extent **2.** a good bit, no~ ticeably, significantly, very **3.** in~ stead, more readily, more willing~ ly, preferably, sooner

ratify affirm, approve, authenti~ cate, authorize, bear out, bind, certify, confirm, consent to, cor~ roborate, endorse, establish, sanc~ tion, sign, uphold, validate

rating class, classification, degree, designation, estimate, evaluation, grade, order, placing, position, rank, rate, standing, status

ratio arrangement, correlation, correspondence, equation, frac~ tion, percentage, proportion, rate, relation, relationship

ration *n.* **1.** allotment, allowance, dole, helping, measure, part, por~ tion, provision, quota, share **2.** *Plu~ ral* commons (*Brit.*), food, proven~ der, provisions, stores, supplies ~*v.* **3.** *With* out allocate, allot, appor~ tion, deal, distribute, dole, give out, issue, measure out, mete, parcel out 4. budget, conserve, control, limit, restrict, save

rational 1. enlightened, intelligent, judicious, logical, lucid, realistic, reasonable, sagacious, sane, sensible, sound, wise 2. cerebral, cognitive, ratiocinative, reasoning, thinking 3. all there (*Inf.*), balanced, *compos mentis*, in one's right mind, lucid, normal, of sound mind, sane

rationale exposition, grounds, logic, motivation, philosophy, principle, *raison d'être*, reasons, theory

rationalize 1. account for, excuse, explain away, extenuate, justify, make allowance for, make excuses for, vindicate 2. apply logic to, elucidate, reason out, resolve, think through 3. make cuts, make more efficient, streamline, trim

rattle *v.* 1. bang, clatter, jangle 2. bounce, jar, jiggle, jolt, jounce, shake, vibrate 3. *With* on blether, cackle, chatter, gabble, gibber, jabber, prate, prattle, rabbit on (*Brit. sl.*), run on, witter (*Inf.*), yak (away) (*Sl.*) 4. *Inf.* discomfit, discompose, disconcert, discountenance, disturb, faze (*U.S. inf.*), frighten, perturb, put (someone) off his stride, put (someone) out of countenance, scare, shake, upset 5. *With* off list, recite, reel off, rehearse, run through, spiel off (*Inf.*)

raucous grating, harsh, hoarse, husky, loud, noisy, rasping, rough, strident

ravage 1. *v.* demolish, desolate, despoil, destroy, devastate, gut, lay waste, leave in ruins, loot, pillage, plunder, ransack, raze, ruin, sack, shatter, spoil, wreak havoc on, wreck 2. *n. Often plural* damage, demolition, depredation, desolation, destruction, devastation, havoc, pillage, plunder, rapine, ruin, ruination, spoliation, waste

rave *v.* 1. babble, be delirious, fume, go mad, rage, rant, roar, run amuck, splutter, storm, talk wildly, thunder 2. *With* about *Inf.* be delighted by, be mad about (*Inf.*), be wild about (*Inf.*), cry up, enthuse, gush, praise, rhapsodize ~*n.* 3. *Inf.*

acclaim, applause, encomium, praise 4. *Also* **rave-up** *Brit. sl.* affair, bash (*Inf.*), blow-out (*Sl.*), celebration, do (*Inf.*), party 5. *Brit. sl.* craze, fad, fashion, vogue ~*adj.* 6. *Inf.* ecstatic, enthusiastic, excellent, favourable, laudatory

ravenous 1. famished, starved, starving, very hungry 2. avaricious, covetous, devouring, ferocious, gluttonous, grasping, greedy, insatiable, insatiate, predatory, rapacious, ravening, voracious, wolfish

ravine canyon, clough (*Dialect*), defile, flume, gap (*U.S.*), gorge, gulch (*U.S.*), gully, linn (*Scot.*), pass

raving berserk, crazed, crazy, delirious, frantic, frenzied, furious, hysterical, insane, irrational, mad, out of one's mind, rabid, raging, wild

raw 1. bloody (*of meat*), fresh, natural, uncooked, undressed, unprepared 2. basic, coarse, crude, green, natural, organic, rough, unfinished, unprocessed, unrefined, unripe, untreated 3. abraded, chafed, grazed, open, scratched, sensitive, skinned, sore, tender 4. callow, green, ignorant, immature, inexperienced, new, undisciplined, unpractised, unseasoned, unskilled, untrained, untried 5. bare, blunt, brutal, candid, frank, naked, plain, realistic, unembellished, unvarnished 6. biting, bitter, bleak, chill, chilly, cold, damp, freezing, harsh, piercing, unpleasant, wet

ray 1. bar, beam, flash, gleam, shaft 2. flicker, glimmer, hint, indication, scintilla, spark, trace

raze 1. bulldoze, demolish, destroy, flatten, knock down, level, pull down, remove, ruin, tear down, throw down 2. delete, efface, erase, expunge, extinguish, extirpate, obliterate, rub out, scratch out, strike out, wipe out

reach *v.* 1. arrive at, attain, get as far as, get to, land at, make 2. contact, extend to, get (a) hold of, go as far as, grasp, stretch to, touch 3. amount to, arrive at, attain, climb to, come to, drop, fall, move, rise, sink 4. *Inf.* hand, hold out, pass, stretch 5. communicate with, contact, establish contact with, find, get, get hold of, get in touch with, get through to, make contact with ~*n.* 6. ambit, capacity, command, compass, distance, extension, extent, grasp, influence, jurisdiction, mastery, power, range, scope, spread, stretch, sweep

react 1. acknowledge, answer, reply, respond 2. act, behave, conduct oneself, function, operate, proceed, work

reaction 1. acknowledgment, answer, feedback, reply, response 2. compensation, counteraction, counterbalance, counterpoise, recoil 3. conservatism, counterrevolution, obscurantism, the right

reactionary 1. *adj.* blimpish, conservative, counter-revolutionary, obscurantist, rightist 2. *n.* Colonel Blimp, conservative, counter-revolutionary, die-hard, obscurantist, rightist, right-winger

read 1. glance at, look at, peruse, pore over, refer to, run one's eye over, scan, study 2. announce, declaim, deliver, recite, speak, utter 3. comprehend, construe, decipher, discover, interpret, perceive the meaning of, see, understand 4. display, indicate, record, register, show

readily 1. cheerfully, eagerly, freely, gladly, promptly, quickly, voluntarily, willingly, with good grace, with pleasure 2. at once, easily, effortlessly, in no time, quickly, right away, smoothly, speedily, straight away, unhesitatingly, without delay, without demur, without difficulty, without hesitation

readiness 1. fitness, maturity, preparation, preparedness, ripeness 2. aptness, eagerness, gameness (*Inf.*), inclination, keenness, willingness 3. adroitness, dexterity, ease, facility, handiness, promptitude, promptness, quickness, rapidity, skill 4. **in readiness** all set, at *or* on hand, at the ready, fit,

prepared, primed, ready, set, waiting, waiting in the wings

reading 1. examination, inspection, perusal, review, scrutiny, study 2. homily, lecture, lesson, performance, recital, rendering, rendition, sermon 3. conception, construction, grasp, impression, interpretation, treatment, understanding, version 4. book-learning, edification, education, erudition, knowledge, learning, scholarship

ready *adj.* 1. all set, arranged, completed, fit, in readiness, organized, prepared, primed, ripe, set 2. agreeable, apt, disposed, eager, game (*Inf.*), glad, happy, inclined, keen, minded, predisposed, prone, willing 3. acute, adroit, alert, apt, astute, bright, clever, deft, dexterous, expert, handy, intelligent, keen, perceptive, prompt, quick, quick-witted, rapid, resourceful, sharp, skilful, smart 4. about, close, in danger of, liable, likely, on the brink of, on the point of, on the verge of 5. accessible, at *or* on hand, at one's fingertips, at the ready, available, close to hand, convenient, handy, near, on call, on tap (*Inf.*), present ~*n.* 6. **at the ready** in readiness, poised, prepared, ready for action, waiting ~*v.* 7. arrange, equip, fit out, get ready, make ready, order, organize, prepare, set

real absolute, actual, authentic, bona fide, certain, essential, existent, factual, genuine, heartfelt, honest, intrinsic, legitimate, positive, right, rightful, sincere, true, unaffected, unfeigned, valid, veritable

realistic 1. businesslike, commonsense, down-to-earth, hard-headed, level-headed, matter-of-fact, practical, pragmatic, rational, real, sensible, sober, unromantic, unsentimental 2. authentic, faithful, genuine, graphic, lifelike, natural, naturalistic, representational, true, true to life, truthful

reality 1. actuality, authenticity, certainty, corporeality, fact, genuineness, materiality, realism, truth, validity, verisimilitude, verity 2. **in reality** actually, as a matter of fact, in actuality, in fact, in point of fact, in truth, really

realization 1. appreciation, apprehension, awareness, cognizance, comprehension, conception, consciousness, grasp, imagination, perception, recognition, understanding 2. accomplishment, achievement, carrying-out, completion, consummation, effectuation, fulfilment

realize 1. appreciate, apprehend, be cognizant of, become aware of, become conscious of, catch on (*Inf.*), comprehend, conceive, grasp, imagine, recognize, take in, twig (*Brit. inf.*), understand 2. accomplish, actualize, bring about, bring off, bring to fruition, carry out *or* through, complete, consummate, do, effect, effectuate, fulfil, make concrete, make happen, perform, reify 3. acquire, bring *or* take in, clear, earn, gain, get, go for, make, net, obtain, produce, sell for

really absolutely, actually, assuredly, categorically, certainly, genuinely, in actuality, indeed, in fact, in reality, positively, surely, truly, undoubtedly, verily, without a doubt

reap acquire, bring in, collect, cut, derive, gain, garner, gather, get, harvest, obtain, win

rear[1] 1. *n.* back, back end, end, rearguard, stern, tail, tail end 2. *adj.* aft, after (*Nautical*), back, following, hind, hindmost, last

rear[2] *v.* 1. breed, bring up, care for, cultivate, educate, foster, grow, nurse, nurture, raise, train 2. elevate, hoist, hold up, lift, raise, set upright 3. build, construct, erect, fabricate, put up 4. loom, rise, soar, tower

reason *n.* 1. apprehension, brains, comprehension, intellect, judgment, logic, mentality, mind, ratiocination, rationality, reasoning, sanity, sense(s), sound mind, soundness, understanding 2. aim, basis, cause, design, end, goal,

grounds, impetus, incentive, inducement, intention, motive, object, occasion, purpose, target, warrant, why and wherefore (*Inf.*) 3. apologia, apology, argument, case, defence, excuse, explanation, exposition, ground, justification, rationale, vindication 4. bounds, limits, moderation, propriety, reasonableness, sense, sensibleness, wisdom 5. **in** *or* **within reason** in moderation, proper, reasonable, sensible, warrantable, within bounds, within limits ~*v.* 6. conclude, deduce, draw conclusions, infer, make out, ratiocinate, resolve, solve, syllogize, think, work out 7. **With** with argue, bring round (*Inf.*), debate, dispute, dissuade, expostulate, move, persuade, prevail upon, remonstrate, show (someone) the error of his ways, talk into *or* out of, urge, win over

reasonable 1. advisable, arguable, believable, credible, intelligent, judicious, justifiable, logical, plausible, practical, rational, reasoned, sane, sensible, sober, sound, tenable, well-advised, well thought-out, wise 2. acceptable, average, equitable, fair, fit, honest, inexpensive, just, moderate, modest, O.K. (*Inf.*), proper, right, tolerable, within reason

reasoned clear, judicious, logical, sensible, systematic, well expressed, well presented, well thought-out

reasoning 1. analysis, cogitation, deduction, logic, ratiocination, reason, thinking, thought 2. argument, case, exposition, hypothesis, interpretation, proof, train of thought

reassure bolster, buoy up, cheer up, comfort, encourage, hearten, inspirit, put *or* set one's mind at rest, relieve (someone) of anxiety, restore confidence to

rebel *v.* 1. man the barricades, mutiny, resist, revolt, rise up, take to the streets, take up arms 2. come out against, defy, disobey, dissent, refuse to obey 3. flinch, recoil, show repugnance, shrink, shy away ~*n.* 4. insurgent, insurrectionary, mutineer, resistance fighter, revolutionary, revolutionist, secessionist 5. apostate, dissenter, heretic, nonconformist, schismatic ~*adj.* 6. insubordinate, insurgent, insurrectionary, mutinous, rebellious, revolutionary

rebellion 1. insurgence, insurgency, insurrection, mutiny, resistance, revolt, revolution, rising, uprising 2. apostasy, defiance, disobedience, dissent, heresy, insubordination, nonconformity, schism

rebellious 1. contumacious, defiant, disaffected, disloyal, disobedient, disorderly, insubordinate, insurgent, insurrectionary, intractable, mutinous, rebel, recalcitrant, revolutionary, seditious, turbulent, ungovernable, unruly 2. difficult, incorrigible, obstinate, recalcitrant, refractory, resistant, unmanageable

rebirth new beginning, regeneration, reincarnation, renaissance, renascence, renewal, restoration, resurgence, resurrection, revitalization, revival

rebound *v.* 1. bounce, recoil, resound, return, ricochet, spring back 2. backfire, boomerang, misfire, recoil ~*n.* 3. bounce, comeback, kickback, repercussion, return, ricochet

rebuff 1. *v.* brush off (*Sl.*), check, cold-shoulder, cut, decline, deny, discourage, put off, refuse, reject, repulse, resist, slight, snub, spurn, turn down 2. *n.* brushoff (*Sl.*), check, cold shoulder, defeat, denial, discouragement, opposition, refusal, rejection, repulse, slight, snub, thumbs down

rebuke 1. *v.* admonish, bawl out (*Inf.*), berate, blame, carpet (*Inf.*), castigate, censure, chide, dress down (*Inf.*), haul (someone) over the coals (*Inf.*), lecture, reprehend, reprimand, reproach, reprove, scold, take to task, tear (someone) off a strip (*Inf.*), tell off (*Inf.*), tick off (*Inf.*), upbraid 2. *n.* admonition, blame, castigation, censure, dressing down (*Inf.*), lecture, reprimand, reproach, reproof, reproval, row, telling-off (*Inf.*), ticking-off (*Inf.*), tongue-lashing, wigging (*Brit. sl.*)

recalcitrant contrary, contumacious, defiant, disobedient, insubordinate, intractable, obstinate, refractory, stubborn, uncontrollable, ungovernable, unmanageable, unruly, unwilling, wayward, wilful

recall *v.* 1. bring *or* call to mind, call *or* summon up, evoke, look *or* think back to, mind (*Dialect*), recollect, remember, reminisce about 2. abjure, annul, call back, call in, cancel, countermand, nullify, repeal, rescind, retract, revoke, take back, withdraw ~*n.* 3. annulment, cancellation, nullification, recision, repeal, rescindment, rescission, retraction, revocation, withdrawal 4. memory, recollection, remembrance

recant abjure, apostatize, deny, disavow, disclaim, disown, forswear, recall, renounce, repudiate, retract, revoke, take back, unsay, withdraw

recapitulate epitomize, go over again, outline, recap (*Inf.*), recount, reiterate, repeat, restate, review, run over, run through again, summarize, sum up

recede 1. abate, draw back, ebb, fall back, go back, regress, retire, retreat, retrogress, return, subside, withdraw 2. decline, diminish, dwindle, fade, lessen, shrink, sink, wane

receipt 1. acknowledgment, counterfoil, proof of purchase, sales slip, stub, voucher 2. acceptance, delivery, receiving, reception, recipience 3. *Plural* gains, gate, income, proceeds, profits, return, takings

receive 1. accept, accept delivery of, acquire, be given, be in receipt of, collect, derive, get, obtain, pick up, take 2. apprehend, be informed of, be told, gather, hear, perceive 3. bear, be subjected to, encounter, experience, go through, meet with, suffer, sustain, undergo 4. accom-

modate, admit, be at home to, en~
tertain, greet, meet, take in, wel~
come

recent contemporary, current,
fresh, late, latter, latter-day, mod~
ern, new, novel, present-day, up-to-
date, young

recently currently, freshly, lately,
newly, not long ago, of late

receptacle container, holder, re~
pository

reception 1. acceptance, admis~
sion, receipt, receiving, recipience
2. acknowledgment, greeting, re~
action, recognition, response,
treatment, welcome 3. do (*Inf.*),
entertainment, function, levee,
party, soirée

receptive 1. alert, bright, percep~
tive, quick on the uptake (*Inf.*),
responsive, sensitive 2. accessible,
amenable, approachable, favour~
able, friendly, hospitable, interest~
ed, open, open-minded, open to
suggestions, susceptible, sympa~
thetic, welcoming

recess 1. alcove, bay, cavity, cor~
ner, depression, hollow, indenta~
tion, niche, nook, oriel 2. *Plural*
bowels, depths, heart, innards
(*Inf.*), innermost parts, penetralia,
reaches, retreats, secret places 3.
break, cessation of business, clo~
sure, holiday, intermission, inter~
val, respite, rest, vacation

recession decline, depression,
downturn, slump

recipe 1. directions, ingredients,
instructions, receipt (*Obsolete*) 2.
formula, method, modus operandi,
prescription, procedure, process,
programme, technique

reciprocal alternate, complemen~
tary, correlative, corresponding,
equivalent, exchanged, give-and-
take, interchangeable, interde~
pendent, mutual, reciprocative,
reciprocatory

reciprocate 1. barter, exchange,
feel in return, interchange, reply,
requite, respond, return, return the
compliment, swap, trade 2. be
equivalent, correspond, equal,
match

recital account, description, detail~

ing, enumeration, narration, nar~
rative, performance, reading, re~
capitulation, recitation, rehearsal,
relation, rendering, repetition,
statement, story, tale, telling

recitation lecture, narration, pas~
sage, performance, piece, reading,
recital, rendering, telling

recite declaim, deliver, describe,
detail, do one's party piece (*Inf.*),
enumerate, itemize, narrate, per~
form, recapitulate, recount, re~
hearse, relate, repeat, speak, tell

reckless careless, daredevil, devil-
may-care, foolhardy, harebrained,
harum-scarum, hasty, headlong,
heedless, ill-advised, imprudent,
inattentive, incautious, indiscreet,
irresponsible, madcap, mindless,
negligent, overventuresome, pre~
cipitate, rash, regardless, thought~
less, wild

reckon 1. add up, calculate, com~
pute, count, enumerate, figure,
number, tally, total 2. account, ap~
praise, consider, count, deem, es~
teem, estimate, evaluate, gauge,
hold, judge, look upon, rate, regard,
think of 3. assume, believe, be of
the opinion, conjecture, expect,
fancy, guess (*Inf.*), imagine, sup~
pose, surmise, think 4. *With* with
cope, deal, face, handle, settle ac~
counts, treat 5. *With* with antici~
pate, bargain for, bear in mind, be
prepared for, expect, foresee, plan
for, take cognizance of, take into
account 6. *With* on *or* upon bank,
calculate, count, depend, hope for,
rely, take for granted, trust in 7. to
be reckoned with consequential,
considerable, important, influen~
tial, powerful, significant, strong,
weighty

reckoning 1. adding, addition, cal~
culation, computation, count,
counting, estimate, summation,
working 2. account, bill, charge,
due, score, settlement 3. doom,
judgment, last judgment, retribu~
tion

reclaim get *or* take back, recap~
ture, recover, redeem, reform, re~
gain, regenerate, reinstate, rescue,
restore, retrieve, salvage

recline be recumbent, lay (something) down, lean, lie (down), loll, lounge, repose, rest, sprawl, stretch out

recluse 1. *n.* anchoress, anchorite, ascetic, eremite, hermit, monk, solitary 2. *adj.* cloistered, isolated, reclusive, retiring, secluded, sequestered, solitary, withdrawn

recognition 1. detection, discovery, identification, recall, recollection, remembrance 2. acceptance, acknowledgment, admission, allowance, appreciation, avowal, awareness, cognizance, concession, confession, notice, perception, realization, respect, understanding 3. acknowledgment, appreciation, approval, gratitude, greeting, honour, salute

recognize 1. identify, know, know again, make out, notice, place, recall, recollect, remember, spot 2. accept, acknowledge, admit, allow, appreciate, avow, be aware of, concede, confess, grant, own, perceive, realize, respect, see, understand 3. acknowledge, appreciate, approve, greet, honour, salute

recoil *v.* 1. jerk back, kick, react, rebound, resile, spring back 2. balk at, draw back, falter, flinch, quail, shrink, shy away 3. backfire, boomerang, go wrong, misfire, rebound ~*n.* 4. backlash, kick, reaction, rebound, repercussion

recollect call to mind, mind (*Dialect*), place, recall, remember, reminisce, summon up

recollection impression, memory, mental image, recall, remembrance, reminiscence

recommend 1. advance, advise, advocate, counsel, enjoin, exhort, propose, put forward, suggest, urge 2. approve, commend, endorse, praise, put in a good word for, speak well of, vouch for 3. make attractive (acceptable, appealing, interesting)

recommendation 1. advice, counsel, proposal, suggestion, urging 2. advocacy, approbation, approval, blessing, commendation, endorsement, favourable mention, good word, plug (*Inf.*), praise, reference, sanction, testimonial

reconcile 1. accept, accommodate, get used, make the best of, put up with (*Inf.*), resign, submit, yield 2. appease, bring to terms, conciliate, make peace between, pacify, placate, propitiate, re-establish friendly relations between, restore harmony between, reunite 3. adjust, compose, harmonize, patch up, put to rights, rectify, resolve, settle, square

reconciliation 1. appeasement, conciliation, détente, pacification, propitiation, *rapprochement*, reconcilement, reunion, understanding 2. accommodation, adjustment, compromise, harmony, rectification, settlement

recondite abstruse, arcane, cabbalistic, concealed, dark, deep, difficult, esoteric, hidden, involved, mysterious, mystical, obscure, occult, profound, secret

recondition do up (*Inf.*), fix up (*Inf., chiefly U.S.*), overhaul, remodel, renew, renovate, repair, restore, revamp

reconnaissance exploration, inspection, investigation, observation, patrol, recce (*Sl.*), reconnoitring, scan, scouting, scrutiny, survey

reconnoitre explore, get the lie of the land, inspect, investigate, make a reconnaissance (of), observe, patrol, recce (*Sl.*), scan, scout, scrutinize, see how the land lies, spy out, survey

reconsider change one's mind, have second thoughts, reassess, re-evaluate, re-examine, rethink, review, revise, take another look at, think again, think better of, think over, think twice

reconstruct 1. reassemble, rebuild, recreate, re-establish, reform, regenerate, remake, remodel, renovate, reorganize, restore 2. build up, build up a picture of, deduce, piece together

record *n.* 1. account, annals, archives, chronicle, diary, document, entry, file, journal, log, memoir, memorandum, memorial, minute, register, report 2. documentation, evidence, memorial, remem~ brance, testimony, trace, witness 3. background, career, curriculum vitae, history, performance, track record (*Inf.*) 4. album, disc, EP, forty-five, gramophone record, LP, platter (*U.S. sl.*), recording, re~ lease, single 5. **off the record** con~ fidential, confidentially, in confi~ dence, in private, not for publica~ tion, private, sub rosa, under the rose, unofficial, unofficially ~*v.* 6. chalk up (*Inf.*), chronicle, docu~ ment, enrol, enter, inscribe, log, minute, note, preserve, put down, put on file, put on record, register, report, set down, take down, tran~ scribe, write down 7. contain, give evidence on, indicate, read, regis~ ter, say, show 8. cut, lay down (*Sl.*), make a recording of, put on wax (*Inf.*), tape, tape-record, video, video-tape, wax (*Inf.*)

recorder annalist, archivist, chronicler, clerk, diarist, historian, registrar, scorekeeper, scorer, scribe

recording cut (*Inf.*), disc, gramo~ phone record, record, tape, video

recount delineate, depict, describe, detail, enumerate, give an account of, narrate, portray, recite, re~ hearse, relate, repeat, report, tell, tell the story of

recourse alternative, appeal, choice, expedient, option, refuge, remedy, resort, resource, way out

recover 1. find again, get back, make good, recapture, reclaim, recoup, redeem, regain, repair, repossess, restore, retake, re~ trieve, take back, win back 2. bounce back, come round, conva~ lesce, feel oneself again, get back on one's feet, get better, get well, heal, improve, mend, pick up, pull through, rally, recuperate, regain one's health *or* strength, revive, take a turn for the better

recovery 1. convalescence, heal~ ing, improvement, mending, rally, recuperation, return to health, re~ vival, turn for the better 2. amelio~ ration, betterment, improvement, rally, rehabilitation, restoration, revival, upturn 3. recapture, recla~ mation, redemption, repair, repos~ session, restoration, retrieval

recreation amusement, distraction, diversion, enjoyment, entertain~ ment, exercise, fun, hobby, leisure activity, pastime, play, pleasure, refreshment, relaxation, relief, sport

recrimination bickering, counter~ attack, countercharge, mutual ac~ cusation, name-calling, quarrel, retaliation, retort, squabbling

recruit *v.* 1. draft, enlist, enrol, im~ press, levy, mobilize, muster, raise, strengthen 2. engage, enrol, gath~ er, obtain, procure, proselytize, round up, take on, win (over) 3. augment, build up, refresh, re~ inforce, renew, replenish, restore, strengthen, supply ~*n.* 4. appren~ tice, beginner, convert, greenhorn (*Inf.*), helper, initiate, learner, neophyte, novice, proselyte, rookie (*Inf.*), trainee, tyro

rectify 1. adjust, amend, correct, emend, fix, improve, make good, mend, put right, redress, reform, remedy, repair, right, square 2. *Chem.* distil, purify, refine, sepa~ rate

rectitude 1. correctness, decency, equity, goodness, honesty, honour, incorruptibility, integrity, justice, morality, principle, probity, right~ eousness, scrupulousness, upright~ ness, virtue 2. accuracy, correct~ ness, exactness, justice, precision, rightness, soundness, verity

recuperate convalesce, get back on one's feet, get better, improve, mend, pick up, recover, regain one's health

recur 1. come again, come and go, come back, happen again, persist, reappear, repeat, return, revert 2. be remembered, come back, haunt one's thoughts, return to mind, run through one's mind

recurrent continued, cyclical, fre~ quent, habitual, periodic, recur~ ring, regular, repeated, repetitive

recycle reclaim, reprocess, reuse, salvage, save

red *adj.* 1. cardinal, carmine, cherry, coral, crimson, gules (*Heraldry*), maroon, pink, rose, ruby, scarlet, vermeil, vermilion, wine 2. bay, carroty, chestnut, flame-coloured, flaming, foxy, reddish, sandy, titian 3. blushing, embarrassed, florid, flushed, rubicund, shamefaced, suffused 4. blooming, glowing, healthy, roseate, rosy, ruddy 5. bloodshot, inflamed, red-rimmed 6. bloodstained, bloody, ensanguined (*Literary*), gory, sanguine ~*n.* 7. colour, redness 8. **in the red** *Inf.* bankrupt, in arrears, in debt, in deficit, insolvent, on the rocks, overdrawn, owing money, showing a loss 9. **see red** *Inf.* be *or* get very angry, be beside oneself with rage (*Inf.*), become enraged, blow one's top, boil, go mad (*Inf.*), go off one's head (*Sl.*), lose one's rag (*Sl.*), lose one's temper, seethe

redden blush, colour (up), crimson, flush, go red, suffuse

redeem 1. buy back, reclaim, recover, recover possession of, regain, repossess, repurchase, retrieve, win back 2. cash (in), change, exchange, trade in 3. abide by, acquit, adhere to, be faithful to, carry out, discharge, fulfil, hold to, keep, keep faith with, make good, meet, perform, satisfy 4. absolve, rehabilitate, reinstate, restore to favour 5. atone for, compensate for, defray, make amends for, make good, make up for, offset, outweigh, redress, save 6. buy the freedom of, deliver, emancipate, extricate, free, liberate, pay the ransom of, ransom, rescue, save, set free

redemption 1. reclamation, recovery, repossession, repurchase, retrieval 2. discharge, exchange, fulfilment, performance, quid pro quo, trade-in 3. amends, atonement, compensation, expiation, reparation 4. deliverance, emancipation, liberation, ransom, release, rescue, salvation

redress *v.* 1. compensate for, make amends (reparation, restitution) for, make up for, pay for, put right, recompense for 2. adjust, amend, balance, correct, ease, even up, mend, put right, rectify, reform, regulate, relieve, remedy, repair, restore the balance, square ~*n.* 3. aid, assistance, correction, cure, ease, help, justice, rectification, relief, remedy, satisfaction 4. amends, atonement, compensation, payment, quittance, recompense, reparation, requital, restitution

reduce 1. abate, abridge, contract, curtail, cut down, debase, decrease, depress, dilute, diminish, impair, lessen, lower, moderate, shorten, slow down, tone down, truncate, turn down, weaken, wind down 2. bankrupt, break, impoverish, pauperize, ruin 3. bring, bring to the point of, conquer, drive, force, master, overpower, subdue, vanquish 4. be *or* go on a diet, diet, lose weight, shed weight, slenderize (*Chiefly U.S.*), slim, trim 5. bring down the price of, cheapen, cut, discount, lower, mark down, slash 6. break, bring low, degrade, demote, downgrade, humble, humiliate, lower in rank, lower the status of, take down a peg (*Inf.*)

redundant 1. *de trop*, excessive, extra, inessential, inordinate, supererogatory, superfluous, supernumerary, surplus, unnecessary, unwanted 2. diffuse, padded, periphrastic, pleonastic, prolix, repetitious, tautological, verbose, wordy

reek *v.* 1. hum (*Sl.*), pong (*Brit. inf.*), smell, smell to high heaven, stink 2. be characterized by, be permeated by, be redolent of 3. *Dialect* fume, give off smoke *or* fumes, smoke, steam ~*n.* 4. effluvium, fetor, mephitis, odour, pong (*Brit. inf.*), smell, stench, stink 5. *Dialect* exhalation, fumes, smoke, steam, vapour

reel 1. falter, lurch, pitch, rock, roll, stagger, stumble, sway, totter, waver, wobble 2. go round and round, revolve, spin, swim, swirl, twirl, whirl

refer 1. advert, allude, bring up, cite, hint, invoke, make mention of, make reference, mention, speak of, touch on 2. direct, guide, point, recommend, send 3. apply, consult, go, have recourse to, look up, seek information from, turn to 4. apply, be directed to, belong, be relevant to, concern, pertain, relate 5. accredit, ascribe, assign, attribute, credit, impute, put down to 6. commit, consign, deliver, hand over, pass on, submit, transfer, turn over

referee 1. *n.* adjudicator, arbiter, arbitrator, judge, ref (*Inf.*), umpire 2. *v.* adjudicate, arbitrate, judge, umpire

reference 1. allusion, citation, mention, note, quotation, remark 2. applicability, bearing, concern, connection, consideration, regard, relation, respect 3. certification, character, credentials, endorsement, good word, recommendation, testimonial

referendum plebiscite, popular vote, public vote

refine 1. clarify, cleanse, distil, filter, process, purify, rarefy 2. civilize, cultivate, elevate, hone, improve, perfect, polish, temper

refined 1. civil, civilized, courtly, cultivated, cultured, elegant, genteel, gentlemanly, gracious, ladylike, polished, polite, sophisticated, urbane, well-bred, well-mannered 2. cultured, delicate, discerning, discriminating, exact, fastidious, fine, nice, precise, punctilious, sensitive, sublime, subtle 3. clarified, clean, distilled, filtered, processed, pure, purified

refinement 1. clarification, cleansing, distillation, filtering, processing, purification, rarefaction, rectification 2. fine point, fine tuning, nicety, nuance, subtlety 3. civility, civilization, courtesy, courtliness, cultivation, culture, delicacy, discrimination, elegance, fastidiousness, fineness, finesse, finish, gentility, good breeding,

good manners, grace, graciousness, polish, politeness, politesse, precision, sophistication, style, taste, urbanity

reflect 1. echo, give back, imitate, mirror, reproduce, return, throw back 2. bear out, bespeak, communicate, demonstrate, display, evince, exhibit, express, indicate, manifest, reveal, show 3. cogitate, consider, contemplate, deliberate, meditate, mull over, muse, ponder, ruminate, think, wonder

reflection 1. counterpart, echo, image, mirror image 2. cerebration, cogitation, consideration, contemplation, deliberation, idea, impression, meditation, musing, observation, opinion, pondering, rumination, study, thinking, thought, view 3. aspersion, censure, criticism, derogation, imputation, reproach, slur

reform *v.* 1. ameliorate, amend, better, correct, emend, improve, mend, rebuild, reclaim, reconstitute, reconstruct, rectify, regenerate, rehabilitate, remodel, renovate, reorganize, repair, restore, revolutionize 2. get back on the straight and narrow (*Inf.*), go straight (*Inf.*), mend one's ways, turn over a new leaf ~*n.* 3. amelioration, amendment, betterment, correction, improvement, rectification, rehabilitation, renovation

refrain *v.* abstain, avoid, cease, desist, do without, eschew, forbear, give up, leave off, renounce, stop

refresh 1. brace, breathe new life into, cheer, cool, enliven, freshen, inspirit, reanimate, reinvigorate, rejuvenate, revitalize, revive, revivify, stimulate 2. brush up (*Inf.*), jog, prod, prompt, renew, stimulate 3. renew, renovate, repair, replenish, restore, top up

refreshing bracing, cooling, different, fresh, inspiriting, invigorating, new, novel, original, revivifying, stimulating, thirst-quenching

refreshment 1. enlivenment, freshening, reanimation, renewal, renovation, repair, restoration, re~

vival, stimulation 2. *Plural* drinks, food and drink, snacks, titbits

refrigerate chill, cool, freeze, keep cold

refuge asylum, bolt hole, harbour, haven, hide-out, protection, resort, retreat, sanctuary, security, shelter

refugee displaced person, émigré, escapee, exile, fugitive, runaway

refund 1. *v.* give back, make good, pay back, reimburse, repay, restore, return 2. *n.* reimbursement, repayment, return

refurbish clean up, do up (*Inf.*), fix up (*Inf., chiefly U.S.*), mend, overhaul, re-equip, refit, remodel, renovate, repair, restore, revamp, set to rights, spruce up

refusal 1. defiance, denial, knockback (*Sl.*), negation, no, rebuff, rejection, repudiation, thumbs down 2. choice, consideration, opportunity, option

refuse *v.* decline, deny, reject, repel, repudiate, say no, spurn, turn down, withhold

refute confute, counter, discredit, disprove, give the lie to, negate, overthrow, prove false, rebut, silence

regain 1. get back, recapture, recoup, recover, redeem, repossess, retake, retrieve, take back, win back 2. get back to, reach again, reattain, return to

regard *v.* 1. behold, eye, gaze at, look closely at, mark, notice, observe, remark, scrutinize, view, watch 2. account, adjudge, believe, consider, deem, esteem, estimate, hold, imagine, judge, look upon, rate, see, suppose, think, treat, value, view 3. apply to, be relevant to, concern, have a bearing on, have to do with, interest, pertain to, relate to 4. attend, heed, listen to, mind, note, pay attention to, respect, take into consideration, take notice of ~*n.* 5. attention, heed, mind, notice 6. account, affection, attachment, care, concern, consideration, deference, esteem, honour, love, note, reputation, repute, respect, store, sympathy,

thought 7. aspect, detail, feature, item, matter, particular, point, respect 8. gaze, glance, look, scrutiny, stare 9. bearing, concern, connection, reference, relation, relevance 10. *Plural* best wishes, compliments, devoirs, good wishes, greetings, respects, salutations

regarding about, apropos, as regards, as to, concerning, in *or* with regard to, in re, in respect of, in the matter of, on the subject of, re, respecting, with reference to

regardless 1. *adj.* disregarding, heedless, inattentive, inconsiderate, indifferent, neglectful, negligent, rash, reckless, remiss, unconcerned, unmindful 2. *adv.* anyway, come what may, despite everything, for all that, in any case, in spite of everything, nevertheless, no matter what, nonetheless

regenerate breathe new life into, change, inspirit, invigorate, reawaken, reconstruct, re-establish, reinvigorate, rejuvenate, renew, renovate, reproduce, restore, revive, revivify, uplift

regime administration, establishment, government, leadership, management, reign, rule, system

regiment *v.* bully, control, discipline, order, organize, regulate, systematize

region 1. area, country, district, division, expanse, land, locality, part, place, province, quarter, section, sector, territory, tract, zone 2. domain, field, province, realm, sphere, world 3. area, locality, neighbourhood, range, scope, vicinity

regional district, local, parochial, provincial, sectional, zonal

register *n.* 1. annals, archives, catalogue, chronicle, diary, file, ledger, list, log, memorandum, record, roll, roster, schedule ~*v.* 2. catalogue, check in, chronicle, enlist, enrol, enter, inscribe, list, note, record, set down, sign on *or* up, take down 3. be shown, bespeak, betray, display, exhibit, express, indicate, manifest, mark, read, record, reflect, reveal, say, show 4. *Inf.* come home, dawn on, get through, have an effect, impress, make an impression, sink in, tell

regress backslide, degenerate, deteriorate, ebb, fall away *or* off, fall back, go back, lapse, lose ground, recede, relapse, retreat, retrogress, return, revert, wane

regret 1. *v.* bemoan, be upset, bewail, deplore, feel remorse for, feel sorry for, grieve, lament, miss, mourn, repent, rue, weep over 2. *n.* bitterness, compunction, contrition, disappointment, grief, lamentation, pang of conscience, penitence, remorse, repentance, ruefulness, self-reproach, sorrow

regrettable deplorable, disappointing, distressing, ill-advised, lamentable, pitiable, sad, shameful, unfortunate, unhappy, woeful, wrong

regular 1. common, commonplace, customary, daily, everyday, habitual, normal, ordinary, routine, typical, unvarying, usual 2. consistent, constant, established, even, fixed, ordered, periodic, rhythmic, set, stated, steady, systematic, uniform 3. dependable, efficient, formal, methodical, orderly, standardized, steady, systematic 4. balanced, even, flat, level, smooth, straight, symmetrical, uniform 5. approved, bona fide, classic, correct, established, formal, official, orthodox, prevailing, proper, sanctioned, standard, time-honoured, traditional

regulate adjust, administer, arrange, balance, conduct, control, direct, fit, govern, guide, handle, manage, moderate, modulate, monitor, order, organize, oversee, rule, run, settle, superintend, supervise, systematize, tune

regulation *n.* 1. adjustment, administration, arrangement, control, direction, governance, government, management, modulation, supervision, tuning 2. commandment, decree, dictate, direction, edict, law, order, ordinance, precept, procedure, requirement,

rule, standing order, statute ~*adj.* 3. customary, mandatory, normal, official, prescribed, required, standard, usual

rehabilitate 1. adjust, redeem, reform, reintegrate, save 2. clear, convert, fix up, make good, mend, rebuild, recondition, reconstitute, reconstruct, re-establish, reinstate, reinvigorate, renew, renovate, restore

rehearsal 1. drill, going-over, practice, practice session, preparation, reading, rehearsing, run-through 2. account, catalogue, description, enumeration, list, narration, recital, recounting, relation, telling

rehearse 1. act, drill, go over, practise, prepare, ready, recite, repeat, run through, study, train, try out 2. delineate, depict, describe, detail, enumerate, go over, list, narrate, recite, recount, relate, review, run through, spell out, tell, trot out (*Inf.*)

reign *n.* 1. ascendancy, command, control, dominion, empire, hegemony, influence, monarchy, power, rule, sovereignty, supremacy, sway ~*v.* 2. administer, be in power, command, govern, hold sway, influence, occupy *or* sit on the throne, rule, wear the crown, wield the sceptre 3. be rampant, be rife, be supreme, hold sway, obtain, predominate, prevail

rein *n.* 1. brake, bridle, check, control, curb, harness, hold, restraint, restriction 2. give (a) free rein (to) free, give a free hand, give carte blanche, give (someone) his head, give way to, indulge, let go, remove restraints ~*v.* 3. bridle, check, control, curb, halt, hold, hold back, limit, restrain, restrict, slow down

reincarnation metempsychosis, rebirth, transmigration of souls

reinforce augment, bolster, buttress, emphasize, fortify, harden, increase, prop, shore up, stiffen, strengthen, stress, supplement, support, toughen, underline

reinforcement 1. addition, amplification, augmentation, enlargement, fortification, increase, strengthening, supplement 2. brace, buttress, prop, shore, stay, support 3. *Plural* additional *or* fresh troops, auxiliaries, reserves, support

reinstate bring back, recall, re~establish, rehabilitate, replace, re~store, return

reject 1. *v.* cast aside, decline, deny, despise, disallow, discard, eliminate, exclude, jettison, jilt, rebuff, refuse, renounce, repel, re~pudiate, repulse, say no to, scrap, spurn, throw away *or* out, turn down, veto 2. *n.* castoff, discard, failure, flotsam, second

rejection brushoff (*Sl.*), denial, dis~missal, elimination, exclusion, re~buff, refusal, renunciation, repu~diation, thumbs down, veto

rejoice be glad (happy, overjoyed), celebrate, delight, exult, glory, joy, jump for joy, make merry, revel, triumph

rejoicing celebration, cheer, de~light, elation, exultation, festivity, gaiety, gladness, happiness, joy, jubilation, merrymaking, revelry, triumph

relapse *v.* 1. backslide, degenerate, fail, fall back, lapse, regress, retrogress, revert, slip back, weaken 2. deteriorate, fade, fail, sicken, sink, weaken, worsen ~*n.* 3. backsliding, fall from grace, lapse, recidivism, regression, retrogression, reversion 4. de~terioration, recurrence, setback, turn for the worse, weakening, worsening

relate 1. chronicle, describe, detail, give an account of, impart, nar~rate, present, recite, recount, re~hearse, report, set forth, tell 2. ally, associate, connect, coordinate, correlate, couple, join, link 3. ap~pertain, apply, bear upon, be rel~evant to, concern, have reference to, have to do with, pertain, refer

related 1. accompanying, affiliated, agnate, akin, allied, associated, cognate, concomitant, connected, correlated, interconnected, joint, linked 2. agnate, akin, cognate, consanguineous, kin, kindred

relation 1. affiliation, affinity, con~sanguinity, kindred, kinship, pro~pinquity, relationship 2. kin, kins~man, kinswoman, relative 3. appli~cation, bearing, bond, comparison, connection, correlation, interde~pendence, link, pertinence, refer~ence, regard, similarity, tie-in 4. account, description, narration, narrative, recital, recountal, re~port, story, tale

relations 1. affairs, associations, communications, connections, contact, dealings, interaction, intercourse, liaison, meetings, rapport, relationship, terms 2. clan, family, kin, kindred, kinsmen, relatives, tribe

relationship affair, association, bond, communications, conjunc~tion, connection, correlation, ex~change, kinship, liaison, link, par~allel, proportion, rapport, ratio, similarity, tie-up

relative *adj.* 1. allied, associated, comparative, connected, contin~gent, corresponding, dependent, proportionate, reciprocal, related, respective 2. applicable, apposite, appropriate, appurtenant, apropos, germane, pertinent, relevant 3. *With to* corresponding to, in pro~portion to, proportional to ~*n.* 4. connection, kinsman, kinswoman, member of one's *or* the family, relation

relatively comparatively, in *or* by comparison, rather, somewhat, to some extent

relax 1. abate, diminish, ease, ebb, lessen, let up, loosen, lower, miti~gate, moderate, reduce, relieve, slacken, weaken 2. be *or* feel at ease, calm, laze, let oneself go (*Inf.*), let one's hair down (*Inf.*), loosen up, put one's feet up, rest, soften, take it easy (*Inf.*), take one's ease, tranquillize, unbend, unwind

relaxation 1. amusement, enjoy~ment, entertainment, fun, leisure, pleasure, recreation, refreshment, rest 2. abatement, diminution, eas~

ing, lessening, let-up (*Inf.*), mod~
eration, reduction, slackening,
weakening

relay *n.* 1. relief, shift, turn 2. com~
munication, dispatch, message,
transmission ~*v.* 3. broadcast,
carry, communicate, hand on, pass
on, send, spread, transmit

release *v.* 1. deliver, discharge,
disengage, drop, emancipate, ex~
tricate, free, let go, let out, liber~
ate, loose, manumit, set free, turn
loose, unchain, undo, unfasten, un~
fetter, unloose, unshackle, untie 2.
absolve, acquit, dispense, excuse,
exempt, exonerate, let go, let off 3.
break, circulate, disseminate, dis~
tribute, issue, launch, make known,
make public, present, publish, put
out, unveil ~*n.* 4. acquittal, deliv~
erance, delivery, discharge,
emancipation, freedom, liberation,
liberty, manumission, relief 5. ab~
solution, acquittance, dispensation,
exemption, exoneration, let-off
(*Inf.*) 6. announcement, issue, of~
fering, proclamation, publication

relent 1. acquiesce, be merciful,
capitulate, change one's mind,
come round, forbear, give in, give
quarter, give way, have pity, melt,
show mercy, soften, unbend, yield
2. die down, drop, ease, fall, let up,
relax, slacken, slow, weaken

relentless 1. cruel, fierce, grim,
hard, harsh, implacable, inexo~
rable, inflexible, merciless, pitiless,
remorseless, ruthless, uncompro~
mising, undeviating, unforgiving,
unrelenting, unstoppable, unyield~
ing 2. incessant, nonstop, persis~
tent, punishing, sustained, unabat~
ed, unbroken, unfaltering, unflag~
ging, unrelenting, unrelieved, un~
remitting, unstoppable

relevant admissible, *ad rem*, appli~
cable, apposite, appropriate, ap~
purtenant, apt, fitting, germane,
material, pertinent, proper, relat~
ed, relative, significant, suited, to
the point, to the purpose

reliable certain, dependable, faith~
ful, honest, predictable, regular,
responsible, safe, sound, stable,
sure, tried and true, true, trust~
worthy, trusty, unfailing, upright

relic fragment, keepsake, memen~
to, remembrance, remnant, scrap,
souvenir, survival, token, trace,
vestige

relief 1. abatement, alleviation, as~
suagement, balm, comfort, cure,
deliverance, ease, easement, miti~
gation, palliation, release, remedy,
solace 2. aid, assistance, help, suc~
cour, support, sustenance 3. break,
breather (*Inf.*), diversion, let-up
(*Inf.*), refreshment, relaxation, re~
mission, respite, rest

relieve 1. abate, alleviate, appease,
assuage, calm, comfort, console,
cure, diminish, dull, ease, mitigate,
mollify, palliate, relax, salve, sof~
ten, solace, soothe 2. aid, assist,
bring aid to, help, succour, support,
sustain 3. give (someone) a break
or rest, stand in for, substitute for,
take over from, take the place of 4.
deliver, discharge, disembarrass,
disencumber, exempt, free, re~
lease, unburden 5. break, brighten,
interrupt, let up on (*Inf.*), lighten,
slacken, vary

religious 1. churchgoing, devotion~
al, devout, divine, doctrinal, faith~
ful, god-fearing, godly, holy, pious,
pure, reverent, righteous, sacred,
scriptural, sectarian, spiritual,
theological 2. conscientious, exact,
faithful, fastidious, meticulous,
punctilious, rigid, rigorous, scru~
pulous, unerring, unswerving

relish *v.* 1. appreciate, delight in,
enjoy, fancy, like, look forward to,
luxuriate in, prefer, revel in, sa~
vour, taste ~*n.* 2. appetite, appre~
ciation, enjoyment, fancy, fond~
ness, gusto, liking, love, partiality,
penchant, predilection, stomach,
taste, zest 3. appetizer, condiment,
sauce, seasoning 4. flavour, pi~
quancy, savour, smack, spice, tang,
taste, trace

reluctance aversion, backward~
ness, disinclination, dislike, disrel~
ish, distaste, hesitancy, indisposi~
tion, loathing, repugnance, unwill~
ingness

reluctant averse, backward, disin~

clined, grudging, hesitant, indis~
posed, loath, recalcitrant, slow,
unenthusiastic, unwilling

rely bank, be confident of, be sure
of, bet, count, depend, have confi~
dence in, lean, reckon, repose trust
in, swear by, trust

remain abide, be left, cling, con~
tinue, delay, dwell, endure, go on,
last, linger, persist, prevail, rest,
stand, stay, stay behind, stay put
(*Inf.*), survive, tarry, wait

remainder balance, dregs, excess,
leavings, relic, remains, remnant,
residue, residuum, rest, surplus,
trace, vestige(s)

remaining abiding, extant, lasting,
left, lingering, outstanding, per~
sisting, residual, surviving, unfin~
ished

remains 1. balance, crumbs, de~
bris, detritus, dregs, fragments,
leavings, leftovers, oddments, odds
and ends, pieces, relics, remainder,
remnants, residue, rest, scraps,
traces, vestiges 2. body, cadaver,
carcass, corpse

remark *v.* 1. animadvert, comment,
declare, mention, observe, pass
comment, reflect, say, state 2.
espy, heed, make out, mark, note,
notice, observe, perceive, regard,
see, take note *or* notice of ~*n.* 3.
assertion, comment, declaration,
observation, opinion, reflection,
statement, thought, utterance,
word 4. acknowledgment, atten~
tion, comment, consideration,
heed, mention, notice, observation,
recognition, regard, thought

remarkable conspicuous, distin~
guished, extraordinary, famous,
impressive, miraculous, notable,
noteworthy, odd, outstanding, phe~
nomenal, pre-eminent, prominent,
rare, signal, singular, strange,
striking, surprising, uncommon,
unusual, wonderful

remedy *n.* 1. antidote, counterac~
tive, cure, medicament, medicine,
nostrum, panacea, physic (*Rare*),
relief, restorative, specific, thera~
py, treatment 2. antidote, correc~
tive, countermeasure, panacea,
redress, relief, solution ~*v.* 3. alle~

viate, assuage, control, cure, ease,
heal, help, mitigate, palliate, re~
lieve, restore, soothe, treat 4.
ameliorate, correct, fix, put right,
rectify, redress, reform, relieve,
repair, set to rights, solve

remember bear in mind, call to
mind, call up, commemorate, keep
in mind, look back (on), recall,
recognize, recollect, reminisce,
retain, summon up, think back

remind awaken memories of, bring
back to, bring to mind, call to
mind, call up, jog one's memory,
make (someone) remember,
prompt, put in mind, refresh one's
memory

reminiscence anecdote, memoir,
memory, recall, recollection, re~
flection, remembrance, retrospec~
tion, review

reminiscent evocative, redolent,
remindful, similar, suggestive

remiss careless, culpable, delin~
quent, derelict, dilatory, forgetful,
heedless, inattentive, indifferent,
lackadaisical, lax, neglectful, neg~
ligent, regardless, slack, slipshod,
sloppy (*Inf.*), slothful, slow, tardy,
thoughtless, unmindful

remission 1. absolution, acquittal,
amnesty, discharge, excuse, ex~
emption, exoneration, forgiveness,
indulgence, pardon, release, re~
prieve 2. abatement, abeyance, al~
leviation, amelioration, decrease,
diminution, ebb, lessening, let-up
(*Inf.*), lull, moderation, reduction,
relaxation, respite, suspension

remit *v.* 1. dispatch, forward, mail,
post, send, transmit 2. cancel, de~
sist, forbear, halt, repeal, rescind,
stop 3. abate, alleviate, decrease,
diminish, dwindle, ease up, fall
away, mitigate, moderate, reduce,
relax, sink, slacken, soften, wane,
weaken 4. defer, delay, postpone,
put off, shelve, suspend ~*n.* 5.
authorization, brief, guidelines, in~
structions, orders, terms of refer~
ence

remittance allowance, considera~
tion, fee, payment

remnant balance, bit, end, frag~
ment, hangover, leftovers, piece,

remainder, remains, residue, re~ siduum, rest, rump, scrap, shred, survival, trace, vestige

remonstrate argue, challenge, complain, dispute, dissent, expos~ tulate, object, protest, take excep~ tion, take issue

remorse anguish, bad or guilty conscience, compassion, com~ punction, contrition, grief, guilt, pangs of conscience, penitence, pity, regret, repentance, rueful~ ness, self-reproach, shame, sorrow

remorseful apologetic, ashamed, chastened, conscience-stricken, contrite, guilt-ridden, guilty, peni~ tent, regretful, repentant, rueful, sad, self-reproachful, sorrowful, sorry

remorseless 1. inexorable, relent~ less, unrelenting, unremitting, un~ stoppable 2. callous, cruel, hard, hardhearted, harsh, implacable, inhumane, merciless, pitiless, ruthless, savage, uncompassionate, unforgiving, unmerciful

remote 1. backwoods, distant, far, faraway, far-off, godforsaken, in~ accessible, isolated, lonely, off the beaten track, outlying, out-of-the-way, secluded 2. alien, extraneous, extrinsic, foreign, immaterial, ir~ relevant, outside, removed, uncon~ nected, unrelated 3. doubtful, dubi~ ous, faint, implausible, inconsider~ able, meagre, negligible, outside, poor, slender, slight, slim, small, unlikely 4. abstracted, aloof, cold, detached, distant, faraway, indif~ ferent, introspective, introverted, removed, reserved, standoffish, unapproachable, uncommunica~ tive, uninterested, uninvolved, withdrawn

removal 1. abstraction, dislodg~ ment, dismissal, displacement, dispossession, ejection, elimina~ tion, eradication, erasure, expul~ sion, expunction, extraction, purg~ ing, stripping, subtraction, taking off, uprooting, withdrawal 2. de~ parture, flitting (Scot., & northern English dialect), move, relocation, transfer

remove 1. abolish, abstract, ampu~ tate, carry off or away, delete, de~ pose, detach, dethrone, discharge, dislodge, dismiss, displace, do away with, doff, efface, eject, eliminate, erase, expel, expunge, extract, get rid of, move, oust, purge, relegate, shed, strike out, take away, take off, take out, throw out, transfer, transport, unseat, wipe out, withdraw 2. depart, flit (Scot., & northern English dialect), move, move away, quit, relocate, shift, transfer, transport, vacate 3. Fig. assassinate, bump off (Sl.), dispose of, do away with, do in (Sl.), eliminate, execute, get rid of, kill, liquidate, murder

remuneration compensation, earnings, emolument, fee, income, indemnity, pay, payment, profit, recompense, reimbursement, reparation, repayment, retainer, return, reward, salary, stipend, wages

remunerative gainful, lucrative, moneymaking, paying, profitable, recompensing, rewarding, rich, worthwhile

renaissance, renascence awak~ ening, new birth, new dawn, re~ appearance, reawakening, rebirth, re-emergence, regeneration, re~ newal, restoration, resurgence, resurrection, revival

render 1. contribute, deliver, fur~ nish, give, make available, pay, present, provide, show, submit, supply, tender, turn over, yield 2. display, evince, exhibit, manifest, show 3. exchange, give, return, swap, trade 4. cause to become, leave, make 5. act, depict, do, give, interpret, perform, play, portray, present, represent 6. construe, ex~ plain, interpret, put, reproduce, restate, transcribe, translate 7. cede, deliver, give, give up, hand over, relinquish, surrender, turn over, yield 8. give back, make res~ titution, pay back, repay, restore, return

renew begin again, breathe new life into, bring up to date, continue, extend, fix up (Inf., chiefly U.S.), mend, modernize, overhaul, pro~

long, reaffirm, recommence, rec~
reate, re-establish, refit, refresh,
refurbish, regenerate, rejuvenate,
renovate, reopen, repair, repeat,
replace, replenish, restate, restock,
restore, resume, revitalize, trans~
form

renounce abandon, abdicate, ab~
jure, abnegate, abstain from, cast
off, decline, deny, discard, dis~
claim, disown, eschew, forgo, for~
sake, forswear, give up, leave off,
quit, recant, reject, relinquish, re~
pudiate, resign, spurn, swear off,
throw off, waive, wash one's hands
of

renovate do up (*Inf.*), fix up (*Inf.,
chiefly U.S.*), modernize, overhaul,
recondition, reconstitute, recreate,
refit, reform, refurbish, rehabili~
tate, remodel, renew, repair, re~
store, revamp

renowned acclaimed, celebrated,
distinguished, eminent, esteemed,
famed, famous, illustrious, notable,
noted, well-known

rent[1] 1. *n.* fee, hire, lease, payment,
rental, tariff 2. *v.* charter, hire,
lease, let

rent[2] 1. breach, break, chink,
crack, flaw, gash, hole, opening,
perforation, rip, slash, slit, split,
tear 2. breach, break, cleavage,
discord, dissension, disunity, divi~
sion, faction, rift, rupture, schism,
split

renunciation abandonment, abdi~
cation, abjuration, abnegation, ab~
stention, denial, disavowal, dis~
claimer, eschewal, forswearing,
giving up, rejection, relinquish~
ment, repudiation, resignation,
spurning, surrender, waiver

repair[1] *v.* 1. compensate for, fix,
heal, make good, make up for,
mend, patch, patch up, put back
together, put right, recover, recti~
fy, redress, renew, renovate, re~
store, restore to working order,
retrieve, square ~*n.* 2. adjustment,
darn, mend, overhaul, patch, res~
toration 3. condition, fettle, form,
nick (*Inf.*), shape (*Inf.*), state

repair[2] 1. betake oneself, go, head
for, leave for, move, remove, re~

tire, set off for, withdraw 2. have
recourse, resort, turn

reparation amends, atonement,
compensation, damages, indem~
nity, propitiation, recompense, re~
dress, renewal, repair, requital,
restitution, satisfaction

repartee badinage, banter, bon
mot, persiflage, pleasantry, rail~
lery, riposte, sally, wit, witticism,
wittiness, wordplay

repay 1. compensate, make resti~
tution, pay back, recompense, re~
fund, reimburse, remunerate, re~
quite, restore, return, reward, set~
tle up with, square 2. avenge, even
or settle the score with, get back at
(*Inf.*), get even with (*Inf.*), get one's
own back on (*Inf.*), make reprisal,
reciprocate, retaliate, return the
compliment, revenge

repeal 1. *v.* abolish, abrogate, an~
nul, cancel, countermand, declare
null and void, invalidate, nullify,
recall, rescind, reverse, revoke, set
aside, withdraw 2. *n.* abolition, ab~
rogation, annulment, cancellation,
invalidation, nullification, rescind~
ing, rescindment, rescission, revo~
cation, withdrawal

repeat 1. *v.* duplicate, echo, iterate,
quote, recapitulate, recite, redo,
rehearse, reiterate, relate, renew,
replay, reproduce, rerun, reshow,
restate, retell 2. *n.* duplicate, echo,
recapitulation, reiteration, repeti~
tion, replay, reproduction, rerun,
reshowing

repeatedly again and again, fre~
quently, many a time and oft,
many times, often, over and over,
time after time, time and (time)
again

repel 1. beat off, check, confront,
decline, drive off, fight, hold off,
keep at arm's length, oppose, par~
ry, put to flight, rebuff, refuse, re~
ject, repulse, resist, ward off 2. dis~
gust, give one the creeps (*Inf.*),
make one shudder, make one sick,
nauseate, offend, put one off, re~
volt, sicken, turn one off (*Inf.*), turn
one's stomach

repellent 1. abhorrent, abomi~
nable, discouraging, disgusting,

distasteful, hateful, horrid, loath~
some, nauseating, noxious, obnox~
ious, odious, offensive, off-putting
(*Brit. inf.*), repugnant, repulsive,
revolting, sickening 2. imper~
meable, proof, repelling, resistant

repent atone, be ashamed, be con~
trite, be sorry, deplore, feel re~
morse, lament, regret, relent, re~
proach oneself, rue, see the error
of one's ways, show penitence,
sorrow

repentance compunction, contri~
tion, grief, guilt, penitence, regret,
remorse, sackcloth and ashes, self-
reproach, sorriness, sorrow

repentant apologetic, ashamed,
chastened, contrite, penitent, re~
gretful, remorseful, rueful, self-
reproachful, sorry

repercussion backlash, conse~
quence, echo, rebound, recoil, re~
sult, reverberation, side effect

repetition duplication, echo, itera~
tion, reappearance, recapitulation,
recital, recurrence, redundancy,
rehearsal, reiteration, relation, re~
newal, repeat, repetitiousness,
replication, restatement, return,
tautology

repetitive boring, dull, mechanical,
monotonous, recurrent, samey
(*Inf.*), tedious, unchanging, unvar~
ied

repine brood, complain, fret,
grieve, grumble, lament, languish,
moan, mope, murmur, sulk

replace follow, oust, put back, re-
establish, reinstate, restore, stand
in lieu of, substitute, succeed,
supersede, supplant, supply, take
over from, take the place of

replacement double, fill-in, proxy,
stand-in, substitute, successor, sur~
rogate, understudy

replenish fill, furnish, make up,
provide, refill, reload, renew, re~
place, restock, restore, stock, sup~
ply, top up

replete abounding, brimful, brim~
ming, charged, chock-full,
crammed, filled, full, full to burst~
ing, full up, glutted, gorged,
jammed, jam-packed, sated, sati~

ated, stuffed, teeming, well-
provided, well-stocked

reply 1. *v.* acknowledge, answer,
come back, counter, echo, make
answer, react, reciprocate, rejoin,
respond, retaliate, retort, return,
riposte, write back 2. *n.* acknowl~
edgment, answer, comeback (*Inf.*),
counter, echo, reaction, recipro~
cation, rejoinder, response, re~
taliation, retort, return, riposte

report *n.* 1. account, announce~
ment, article, communication,
communiqué, declaration, de~
scription, detail, dispatch, infor~
mation, message, narrative, news,
note, paper, piece, recital, record,
relation, statement, story, sum~
mary, tale, tidings, version, word,
write-up 2. gossip, hearsay, ru~
mour, talk 3. character, esteem,
fame, regard, reputation, repute 4.
bang, blast, boom, crack, crash,
detonation, discharge, explosion,
noise, reverberation, sound ~*v.* 5.
air, announce, bring word, broad~
cast, circulate, communicate, cov~
er, declare, describe, detail, docu~
ment, give an account of, inform
of, mention, narrate, note, notify,
pass on, proclaim, publish, recite,
record, recount, relate, relay,
state, tell, write up 6. appear, ar~
rive, be present, clock in *or* on,
come, present oneself, show up
(*Inf.*), turn up

reporter announcer, correspond~
ent, hack (*Derogatory*), journalist,
newscaster, newshound (*Inf.*),
newspaperman, newspaper~
woman, pressman, writer

repose *n.* 1. ease, inactivity, peace,
quiet, quietness, quietude, relaxa~
tion, respite, rest, restfulness,
sleep, slumber, stillness, tranquil~
lity 2. aplomb, calmness, compo~
sure, dignity, equanimity, peace of
mind, poise, self-possession, seren~
ity, tranquillity ~*v.* 3. lay down, lie,
lie down, lie upon, recline, relax,
rest, rest upon, sleep, slumber,
take it easy (*Inf.*), take one's ease

reprehensible bad, blameworthy,
censurable, condemnable, cul~
pable, delinquent, discreditable,

disgraceful, errant, erring, ignoble, objectionable, opprobrious, remiss, shameful, unworthy

represent 1. act for, be, betoken, correspond to, equal, equate with, express, mean, serve as, speak for, stand for, substitute for, symbolize 2. embody, epitomize, exemplify, personify, symbolize, typify 3. delineate, denote, depict, describe, designate, evoke, express, illustrate, outline, picture, portray, render, reproduce, show, sketch 4. describe as, make out to be, pass off as, pose as, pretend to be 5. act, appear as, assume the role of, enact, exhibit, perform, play the part of, produce, put on, show, stage

representation 1. account, delineation, depiction, description, illustration, image, likeness, model, narration, narrative, picture, portrait, portrayal, relation, resemblance, sketch 2. body of representatives, committee, delegates, delegation, embassy 3. exhibition, performance, play, production, show, sight, spectacle 4. *Often plural* account, argument, explanation, exposition, expostulation, remonstrance, statement

representative *n.* 1. agent, commercial traveller, rep, salesman, traveller 2. archetype, embodiment, epitome, exemplar, personification, type, typical example 3. agent, commissioner, councillor, delegate, depute (*Scot.*), deputy, member, member of parliament, M.P., proxy, spokesman, spokeswoman ~*adj.* 4. archetypal, characteristic, emblematic, evocative, exemplary, illustrative, symbolic, typical 5. chosen, delegated, elected, elective

repress bottle up, chasten, check, control, crush, curb, hold back, hold in, inhibit, keep in check, master, muffle, overcome, overpower, quash, quell, restrain, silence, smother, stifle, subdue, subjugate, suppress, swallow

repression authoritarianism, censorship, coercion, constraint, control, despotism, domination, inhibition, restraint, subjugation, suppression, tyranny

repressive absolute, authoritarian, coercive, despotic, dictatorial, harsh, oppressive, severe, tough, tyrannical

reprieve *v.* 1. grant a stay of execution to, let off the hook (*Sl.*), pardon, postpone *or* remit the punishment of 2. abate, allay, alleviate, mitigate, palliate, relieve, respite ~*n.* 3. abeyance, amnesty, deferment, pardon, postponement, remission, stay of execution, suspension 4. abatement, alleviation, let-up (*Inf.*), mitigation, palliation, relief, respite

reprimand 1. *n.* admonition, blame, castigation, censure, dressing-down (*Inf.*), flea in one's ear (*Inf.*), lecture, rebuke, reprehension, reproach, reproof, row, talking-to (*Inf.*), telling-off (*Inf.*), ticking-off (*Inf.*), tongue-lashing, wigging (*Brit. sl.*) 2. *v.* admonish, blame, castigate, censure, check, chide, dress down (*Inf.*), give (someone) a row (*Inf.*), haul over the coals (*Inf.*), lecture, rap over the knuckles (*Inf.*), rebuke, reprehend, reproach, reprove, scold, send one away with a flea in one's ear (*Inf.*), take to task, tell off (*Inf.*), tick off (*Inf.*), tongue-lash, upbraid

reprisal an eye for an eye, counterstroke, requital, retaliation, retribution, revenge, vengeance

reproach 1. *v.* abuse, blame, censure, chide, condemn, criticize, defame, discredit, disparage, find fault with, rebuke, reprehend, reprimand, reprove, scold, take to task, upbraid 2. *n.* abuse, blame, blemish, censure, condemnation, contempt, disapproval, discredit, disgrace, dishonour, disrepute, ignominy, indignity, obloquy, odium, opprobrium, scorn, shame, slight, slur, stain, stigma

reproachful abusive, admonitory, castigatory, censorious, condemnatory, contemptuous, critical, disappointed, disapproving, faultfinding, reproving, scolding, upbraiding

reproduce 1. copy, duplicate, echo, emulate, imitate, match, mirror, parallel, print, recreate, repeat, replicate, represent, transcribe 2. breed, generate, multiply, procreate, produce young, proliferate, propagate, spawn

reproduction 1. breeding, generation, increase, multiplication, procreation, proliferation, propagation 2. copy, duplicate, facsimile, imitation, picture, print, replica

reproof admonition, blame, castigation, censure, chiding, condemnation, criticism, dressing-down (*Inf.*), rebuke, reprehension, reprimand, reproach, reproval, scolding, ticking-off (*Inf.*), tongue-lashing, upbraiding

reprove abuse, admonish, berate, blame, censure, check, chide, condemn, rebuke, reprehend, reprimand, scold, take to task, tell off (*Inf.*), tick off (*Inf.*), upbraid

repudiate abandon, abjure, cast off, cut off, deny, desert, disavow, discard, disclaim, disown, forsake, reject, renounce, rescind, retract, reverse, revoke, turn one's back on, wash one's hands of

repugnant 1. abhorrent, abominable, disgusting, distasteful, foul, hateful, horrid, loathsome, nauseating, objectionable, obnoxious, odious, offensive, repellent, revolting, sickening, vile 2. adverse, antagonistic, antipathetic, averse, contradictory, hostile, incompatible, inconsistent, inimical, opposed

repulsive abhorrent, abominable, disagreeable, disgusting, distasteful, forbidding, foul, hateful, hideous, horrid, loathsome, nauseating, objectionable, obnoxious, odious, offensive, repellent, revolting, sickening, ugly, unpleasant, vile

reputable creditable, estimable, excellent, good, honourable, honoured, legitimate, of good repute, reliable, respectable, trustworthy, upright, well-thought-of, worthy

reputation character, credit, distinction, esteem, estimation, fame,

honour, name, opinion, renown, repute, standing, stature

repute celebrity, distinction, esteem, estimation, fame, name, renown, reputation, standing, stature

reputed accounted, alleged, believed, considered, deemed, estimated, held, ostensible, putative, reckoned, regarded, rumoured, said, seeming, supposed, thought

reputedly allegedly, apparently, ostensibly, seemingly, supposedly

request 1. *v.* appeal for, apply for, ask (for), beg, beseech, call for, demand, desire, entreat, petition, pray, put in for, requisition, seek, solicit, sue for, supplicate 2. *n.* appeal, application, asking, begging, call, demand, desire, entreaty, petition, prayer, requisition, solicitation, suit, supplication

require 1. crave, depend upon, desire, have need of, lack, miss, need, stand in need of, want, wish 2. ask, beg, beseech, bid, call upon, command, compel, constrain, demand, direct, enjoin, exact, insist upon, instruct, oblige, order, request 3. call for, demand, involve, necessitate, take

required called for, compulsory, demanded, essential, mandatory, necessary, needed, obligatory, prescribed, recommended, requisite, set, unavoidable, vital

requirement demand, desideratum, essential, lack, must, necessity, need, precondition, prerequisite, qualification, requisite, *sine qua non*, specification, stipulation, want

requisite 1. *adj.* called for, essential, indispensable, mandatory, necessary, needed, needful, obligatory, prerequisite, required, vital 2. *n.* condition, desideratum, essential, must, necessity, need, precondition, prerequisite, requirement, *sine qua non*

requisition *n.* 1. application, call, demand, request, summons 2. appropriation, commandeering, occupation, seizure, takeover ~*v.* 3. apply for, call for, demand, put in for, request 4. appropriate, com~

mandeer, occupy, seize, take over, take possession of

rescue 1. v. deliver, extricate, free, get out, liberate, recover, redeem, release, salvage, save, save the life of, set free 2. n. deliverance, extrication, liberation, recovery, redemption, release, relief, salvage, salvation, saving

research 1. n. analysis, delving, examination, experimentation, exploration, fact-finding, groundwork, inquiry, investigation, probe, scrutiny, study v. analyse, consult the archives, do tests, examine, experiment, explore, investigate, look into, make inquiries, probe, scrutinize, study

resemblance affinity, analogy, closeness, comparability, comparison, conformity, correspondence, counterpart, facsimile, image, kinship, likeness, parallel, parity, sameness, semblance, similarity, similitude

resemble bear a resemblance to, be like, be similar to, duplicate, echo, favour (*Inf.*), look like, mirror, parallel, put one in mind of, remind one of, take after

resent be angry about, bear a grudge about, begrudge, be in a huff about, be offended by, dislike, feel bitter about, grudge, harbour a grudge against, have hard feelings about, object to, take amiss, take as an insult, take exception to, take offence at, take umbrage at

resentful aggrieved, angry, bitter, embittered, exasperated, grudging, huffish, huffy, hurt, in a huff, incensed, indignant, in high dudgeon, irate, jealous, miffed (*Inf.*), offended, peeved (*Inf.*), piqued, put out, revengeful, unforgiving, wounded

resentment anger, animosity, bitterness, displeasure, fury, grudge, huff, hurt, ill feeling, ill will, indignation, ire, irritation, malice, pique, rage, rancour, umbrage, vexation, wrath

reservation 1. condition, demur, doubt, hesitancy, proviso, qualification, scepticism, scruple, stipulation 2. enclave, homeland, preserve, reserve, sanctuary, territory, tract

reserve v. 1. conserve, hang on to, hoard, hold, husband, keep, keep back, lay up, preserve, put by, retain, save, set aside, stockpile, store, withhold 2. bespeak, book, engage, prearrange, pre-engage, retain, secure 3. defer, delay, keep back, postpone, put off, withhold ~n. 4. backlog, cache, capital, fund, hoard, reservoir, savings, stock, stockpile, store, supply 5. park, preserve, reservation, sanctuary, tract 6. aloofness, constraint, coolness, formality, modesty, reluctance, reservation, restraint, reticence, secretiveness, shyness, silence, taciturnity ~adj. 7. alternate, auxiliary, extra, secondary, spare, substitute

reserved 1. booked, engaged, held, kept, restricted, retained, set aside, spoken for, taken 2. aloof, cautious, close-mouthed, cold, cool, demure, formal, modest, prim, restrained, reticent, retiring, secretive, shy, silent, standoffish, taciturn, unapproachable, uncommunicative, undemonstrative, unforthcoming, unresponsive, unsociable 3. bound, destined, fated, intended, meant, predestined

reservoir 1. basin, lake, pond, tank 2. container, holder, receptacle, repository, store, tank 3. accumulation, fund, pool, reserves, source, stock, stockpile, store, supply

reside 1. abide, dwell, hang out (*Inf.*), have one's home, inhabit, live, lodge, remain, settle, sojourn, stay 2. abide, be intrinsic to, be vested, consist, dwell, exist, inhere, lie, rest with

residence 1. abode, domicile, dwelling, habitation, home, house, household, lodging, pad (*Sl.*), place, quarters 2. hall, manor, mansion, palace, seat, villa 3. occupancy, occupation, sojourn, stay, tenancy

resident 1. n. citizen, denizen, indweller, inhabitant, local, lodger, occupant, tenant 2. adj. dwelling, inhabiting, living, local, neighbourhood, settled

residue balance, dregs, excess, extra, leftovers, remainder, remains, remnant, residuum, rest, surplus

resign 1. abandon, abdicate, cede, forgo, forsake, give in one's notice, give up, hand over, leave, quit, relinquish, renounce, surrender, turn over, vacate, yield 2. **resign oneself** accept, acquiesce, bow, give in, give up, reconcile, submit, yield

resignation 1. abandonment, abdication, departure, leaving, notice, relinquishment, renunciation, retirement, surrender 2. acceptance, acquiescence, compliance, endurance, forbearing, fortitude, nonresistance, passivity, patience, submission, sufferance

resigned acquiescent, compliant, long-suffering, patient, stoical, subdued, submissive, unprotesting, unresisting

resilient 1. bouncy, elastic, flexible, plastic, pliable, rubbery, springy, supple, whippy 2. bouncy, buoyant, hardy, irrepressible, quick to recover, strong, tough

resist 1. battle, be proof against, check, combat, confront, contend with, counteract, countervail, curb, defy, dispute, fight back, hinder, hold out against, oppose, put up a fight (against), refuse, repel, stand up to, struggle against, thwart, weather, withstand 2. abstain from, avoid, forbear, forgo, keep from, leave alone, prevent oneself from, refrain from, refuse, turn down

resistance battle, combat, contention, counteraction, defiance, fight, fighting, hindrance, impediment, intransigence, obstruction, opposition, refusal, struggle

resistant 1. hard, impervious, insusceptible, proof against, strong, tough, unaffected by, unyielding 2. antagonistic, combative, defiant, dissident, hostile, intractable, intransigent, opposed, recalcitrant, unwilling

resolute bold, constant, determined, dogged, firm, fixed, inflexible, obstinate, persevering, purposeful, relentless, set, staunch, steadfast, strong-willed, stubborn, tenacious, unbending, undaunted, unflinching, unshakable, unshaken, unwavering

resolution 1. boldness, constancy, courage, dedication, determination, doggedness, earnestness, energy, firmness, fortitude, obstinacy, perseverance, purpose, relentlessness, resoluteness, resolve, sincerity, staunchness, staying power, steadfastness, stubbornness, tenacity, willpower 2. aim, decision, declaration, determination, intent, intention, judgment, motion, purpose, resolve, verdict 3. answer, end, finding, outcome, settlement, solution, solving, sorting out, unravelling, upshot, working out

resolve v. 1. agree, conclude, decide, design, determine, fix, intend, make up one's mind, purpose, settle, undertake 2. answer, clear up, crack, elucidate, fathom, find the solution to, work out 3. banish, clear up, dispel, explain, remove 4. analyse, anatomize, break down, clear, disentangle, disintegrate, dissect, dissolve, liquefy, melt, reduce, separate, solve, split up, unravel 5. alter, change, convert, metamorphose, transform, transmute ~n. 6. conclusion, decision, design, intention, objective, project, purpose, resolution, undertaking 7. boldness, courage, determination, earnestness, firmness, resoluteness, resolution, steadfastness, willpower

resort v. 1. avail oneself of, bring into play, employ, exercise, fall back on, have recourse to, look to, make use of, turn to, use, utilize 2. frequent, go, haunt, head for, repair, visit ~n. 3. haunt, holiday centre, refuge, retreat, spot, tourist centre, watering place (*Brit.*) 4. alternative, chance, course, expedient, hope, possibility, recourse, reference

resound echo, fill the air, re-echo, resonate, reverberate, ring

resounding booming, echoing, full, powerful, resonant, reverberating, rich, ringing, sonorous, sounding, vibrant

resource 1. ability, capability, cleverness, ingenuity, initiative, inventiveness, quick-wittedness, resourcefulness, talent 2. hoard, reserve, source, stockpile, supply 3. appliance, contrivance, course, device, expedient, means, resort

resourceful able, bright, capable, clever, creative, imaginative, ingenious, inventive, quick-witted, sharp, talented

resources assets, capital, funds, holdings, materials, means, money, property, reserves, riches, supplies, wealth, wherewithal

respect n. 1. admiration, appreciation, approbation, consideration, deference, esteem, estimation, honour, recognition, regard, reverence, veneration 2. aspect, characteristic, detail, facet, feature, matter, particular, point, sense, way 3. bearing, connection, reference, regard, relation 4. Plural compliments, devoirs, good wishes, greetings, regards, salutations ~v. 5. admire, adore, appreciate, defer to, esteem, have a good or high opinion of, honour, look up to, recognize, regard, revere, reverence, set store by, show consideration for, think highly of, value, venerate 6. abide by, adhere to, attend, comply with, follow, heed, honour, notice, obey, observe, pay attention to, regard, show consideration for

respectable 1. admirable, decent, decorous, dignified, estimable, good, honest, honourable, proper, reputable, respected, upright, venerable, worthy 2. ample, appreciable, considerable, decent, fair, fairly good, goodly, presentable, reasonable, sizable, substantial, tidy (*Inf.*), tolerable

respective corresponding, individual, own, particular, personal, relevant, separate, several, specific, various

respite 1. break, breather (*Inf.*), breathing space, cessation, halt, hiatus, intermission, interruption,

interval, let-up (*Inf.*), lull, pause, recess, relaxation, relief, rest 2. adjournment, delay, moratorium, postponement, reprieve, stay, suspension

respond acknowledge, act in response, answer, come back, counter, react, reciprocate, rejoin, reply, retort, return

response acknowledgment, answer, comeback (*Inf.*), counterblast, feedback, reaction, rejoinder, reply, retort, return, riposte

responsibility 1. accountability, amenability, answerability, care, charge, duty, liability, obligation, onus, trust 2. authority, importance, power 3. blame, burden, culpability, fault, guilt 4. conscientiousness, dependability, levelheadedness, maturity, rationality, reliability, sensibleness, soberness, stability, trustworthiness

responsible 1. at the helm, carrying the can (*Inf.*), in authority, in charge, in control 2. accountable, amenable, answerable, bound, chargeable, duty-bound, liable, subject, under obligation 3. authoritative, decision-making, executive, high, important 4. at fault, culpable, guilty, to blame 5. adult, conscientious, dependable, level-headed, mature, rational, reliable, sensible, sober, sound, stable, trustworthy

responsive alive, awake, aware, forthcoming, impressionable, open, perceptive, quick to react, reactive, receptive, sensitive, sharp, susceptible, sympathetic

rest[1] n. 1. calm, doze, forty winks (*Inf.*), idleness, inactivity, leisure, lie-down, motionlessness, nap, refreshment, relaxation, relief, repose, siesta, sleep, slumber, snooze (*Inf.*), somnolence, standstill, stillness, tranquillity 2. at rest asleep, at a standstill, at peace, calm, dead, motionless, peaceful, resting, sleeping, still, stopped, tranquil, unmoving 3. break, breather (*Inf.*), breathing space, cessation, halt, holiday, interlude, intermission, interval, lull, pause, stop, time off, vacation 4. haven, lodging, refuge, retreat, shelter 5. base, holder, prop, shelf, stand, support, trestle ~v. 6. be at ease, be calm, doze, have a snooze (*Inf.*), have forty winks (*Inf.*), idle, laze, lie down, lie still, nap, put one's feet up, refresh oneself, relax, sit down, sleep, slumber, snooze (*Inf.*), take a nap, take it easy (*Inf.*), take one's ease 7. be supported, lay, lean, lie, prop, recline, repose, sit, stand, stretch out 8. break off, cease, come to a standstill, desist, discontinue, halt, have a break, knock off (*Inf.*), stay, stop, take a breather (*Inf.*) 9. base, be based, be founded, depend, found, hang, hinge, lie, rely, reside, turn

rest² 1. *n.* balance, excess, left~ overs, others, remainder, remains, remnants, residue, residuum, rump, surplus 2. *v.* be left, continue being, go on being, keep, remain, stay

restful calm, calming, comfortable, languid, pacific, peaceful, placid, quiet, relaxed, relaxing, serene, sleepy, soothing, tranquil, tran~ quillizing, undisturbed, unhurried

restive agitated, edgy, fidgety, fractious, fretful, ill at ease, impa~ tient, jittery (*Inf.*), jumpy, nervous, on edge, recalcitrant, refractory, restless, uneasy, unquiet, unruly

restless 1. active, bustling, changeable, footloose, hurried, in~ constant, irresolute, moving, no~ madic, roving, transient, turbulent, unsettled, unstable, unsteady, wandering 2. agitated, anxious, disturbed, edgy, fidgeting, fidgety, fitful, fretful, ill at ease, jumpy, nervous, on edge, restive, sleep~ less, tossing and turning, troubled, uneasy, unquiet, unruly, unsettled, worried

restlessness 1. activity, bustle, hurry, hurry-scurry, inconstancy, instability, movement, transience, turbulence, turmoil, unrest, unset~ tledness 2. agitation, ants in one's pants (*Sl.*), anxiety, disquiet, dis~ turbance, edginess, fitfulness, fret~ fulness, heebie-jeebies (*Sl.*), inqui~

etude, insomnia, jitters (*Inf.*), jumpiness, nervousness, restive~ ness, uneasiness, worriedness

restoration 1. reconstruction, re~ covery, refreshment, refurbishing, rehabilitation, rejuvenation, re~ newal, renovation, repair, revitali~ zation, revival 2. recovery, re~ establishment, reinstallation, re~ instatement, replacement, restitu~ tion, return

restore 1. fix, mend, rebuild, re~ condition, reconstruct, recover, refurbish, rehabilitate, renew, renovate, repair, retouch, set to rights, touch up 2. bring back to health, build up, reanimate, re~ fresh, rejuvenate, revitalize, re~ vive, revivify, strengthen 3. bring back, give back, hand back, reco~ ver, re-establish, reinstate, replace, return, send back 4. reconstitute, re-enforce, reimpose, reinstate, reintroduce

restrain 1. bridle, check, confine, constrain, contain, control, curb, curtail, debar, govern, hamper, handicap, harness, hinder, hold, hold back, inhibit, keep, keep un~ der control, limit, muzzle, prevent, repress, restrict, subdue, suppress 2. arrest, bind, chain, confine, de~ tain, fetter, hold, imprison, jail, lock up, manacle, pinion, tie up

restrained 1. calm, controlled, mild, moderate, muted, reason~ able, reticent, self-controlled, soft, steady, temperate, undemonstra~ tive 2. discreet, quiet, subdued, tasteful, unobtrusive

restraint 1. coercion, command, compulsion, confines, constraint, control, curtailment, grip, hin~ drance, hold, inhibition, limitation, moderation, prevention, restric~ tion, self-control, self-discipline, self-possession, self-restraint, sup~ pression 2. arrest, bondage, bonds, captivity, chains, confinement, de~ tention, fetters, imprisonment, manacles, pinions, straitjacket 3. ban, bridle, check, curb, embargo, interdict, limit, limitation, rein, ta~ boo

restrict bound, circumscribe, con~

fine, contain, cramp, demarcate, hamper, handicap, hem in, impede, inhibit, keep within bounds or limits, limit, regulate, restrain

restriction check, condition, confinement, constraint, containment, control, curb, demarcation, handicap, inhibition, limitation, regulation, restraint, rule, stipulation

result n. 1. conclusion, consequence, decision, development, effect, end, event, fruit, issue, outcome, product, reaction, sequel, termination, upshot ~v. 2. appear, arise, derive, develop, emanate, ensue, eventuate, flow, follow, happen, issue, spring, stem, turn out 3. With in culminate, end, finish, terminate, wind up (Inf.)

resume 1. begin again, carry on, continue, go on, proceed, recommence, reinstitute, reopen, restart, take up or pick up where one left off 2. assume again, occupy again, reoccupy, take back, take up again

resumption carrying on, continuation, fresh outbreak, new beginning, re-establishment, renewal, reopening, restart, resurgence

resurrect breathe new life into, bring back, raise from the dead, reintroduce, renew, restore to life, revive

resurrection comeback (Inf.), raising or rising from the dead, reappearance, rebirth, renaissance, renascence, renewal, restoration, resurgence, resuscitation, return, return from the dead, revival

resuscitate breathe new life into, bring round, bring to life, give artificial respiration to, give the kiss of life (Inf.), quicken, reanimate, renew, rescue, restore, resurrect, revitalize, revive, revivify, save

retain 1. absorb, contain, detain, grasp, grip, hang or hold onto, hold, hold back, hold fast, keep, keep possession of, maintain, preserve, reserve, restrain, save 2. bear in mind, impress on the memory, keep in mind, memorize, recall, recollect, remember 3.

commission, employ, engage, hire, pay, reserve

retainer 1. attendant, dependant, domestic, flunky, footman, lackey, servant, supporter, valet, vassal 2. advance, deposit, fee

retaliate even the score, exact retribution, get back at (Inf.), get even with (Inf.), get one's own back (Inf.), give as good as one gets (Inf.), give one a taste of one's own medicine, give tit for tat, make reprisal, pay one back in one's own coin, reciprocate, return like for like, strike back, take an eye for an eye, take revenge, wreak vengeance

retaliation an eye for an eye, a taste of one's own medicine, counterblow, counterstroke, reciprocation, repayment, reprisal, requital, retribution, revenge, tit for tat, vengeance

retard arrest, brake, check, clog, decelerate, defer, delay, detain, encumber, handicap, hinder, hold back or up, impede, obstruct, set back, slow down, stall

reticence quietness, reserve, restraint, secretiveness, silence, taciturnity, uncommunicativeness, unforthcomingness

reticent close-mouthed, mum, quiet, reserved, restrained, secretive, silent, taciturn, tight-lipped, uncommunicative, unforthcoming, unspeaking

retire 1. be pensioned off, (be) put out to grass (Inf.), give up work, stop working 2. absent oneself, betake oneself, depart, exit, go away, leave, remove, withdraw 3. go to bed, go to one's room, go to sleep, hit the sack (Sl.), kip down (Brit. sl.), turn in (Inf.) 4. decamp, ebb, fall back, give ground, give way, pull back, pull out, recede, retreat, withdraw

retirement loneliness, obscurity, privacy, retreat, seclusion, solitude, withdrawal

retiring bashful, coy, demure, diffident, humble, meek, modest, quiet, reclusive, reserved, reticent, self-effacing, shrinking, shy, timid, timorous, unassertive, unassuming

retract 1. draw in, pull back, pull in, reel in, sheathe **2.** abjure, cancel, deny, disavow, disclaim, disown, recall, recant, renounce, repeal, repudiate, rescind, reverse, revoke, take back, unsay, withdraw **3.** back out of, go back on, renege on

retreat *v.* **1.** back away, depart, draw back, ebb, fall back, give ground, go back, leave, pull back, recede, recoil, retire, shrink, turn tail, withdraw ~*n.* **2.** departure, ebb, evacuation, flight, retirement, withdrawal **3.** asylum, den, haunt, haven, hideaway, privacy, refuge, resort, retirement, sanctuary, seclusion, shelter

retrench curtail, cut, cut back, decrease, diminish, economize, husband, lessen, limit, make economies, pare, prune, reduce, save, tighten one's belt, trim

retrenchment contraction, costcutting, curtailment, cut, cutback, economy, pruning, reduction, rundown, tightening one's belt

retribution an eye for an eye, compensation, justice, Nemesis, punishment, reckoning, recompense, redress, repayment, reprisal, requital, retaliation, revenge, reward, satisfaction, vengeance

retrieve fetch back, get back, recall, recapture, recoup, recover, redeem, regain, repair, repossess, rescue, restore, salvage, save, win back

retrospect afterthought, hindsight, recollection, re-examination, remembrance, reminiscence, review, survey

return *v.* **1.** come back, come round again, go back, reappear, rebound, recoil, recur, repair, retreat, revert, turn back **2.** carry back, convey, give back, put back, reestablish, reinstate, remit, render, replace, restore, send, send back, take back, transmit **3.** give back, pay back, reciprocate, recompense, refund, reimburse, repay, requite **4.** bring in, earn, make, net, repay, yield **5.** answer, come back (with), communicate, rejoin, reply, respond, retort **6.** choose, elect, pick, vote in **7.** announce, arrive at, bring in, come to, deliver, render, report, submit ~*n.* **8.** homecoming, reappearance, rebound, recoil, recrudescence, recurrence, retreat, reversion **9.** re-establishment, reinstatement, replacement, restoration **10.** advantage, benefit, gain, income, interest, proceeds, profit, revenue, takings, yield **11.** compensation, reciprocation, recompense, reimbursement, reparation, repayment, requital, retaliation, reward **12.** account, form, list, report, statement, summary **13.** answer, comeback (*Inf.*), rejoinder, reply, response, retort, riposte

reveal 1. announce, betray, broadcast, communicate, disclose, divulge, give away, give out, impart, leak, let on, let out, let slip, make known, make public, proclaim, publish, tell **2.** bare, bring to light, display, exhibit, expose to view, lay bare, manifest, open, show, uncover, unearth, unmask, unveil

revel *v.* **1.** *With* **in** bask, crow, delight, gloat, indulge, joy, lap up, luxuriate, rejoice, relish, savour, take pleasure, thrive on, wallow **2.** carouse, celebrate, go on a spree, live it up (*Inf.*), make merry, paint the town red (*Inf.*), push the boat out (*Brit. inf.*), rave (*Brit. sl.*), roister, whoop it up (*Inf.*) ~*n.* **3.** *Often plural* bacchanal, carousal, carouse, celebration, debauch, festivity, gala, jollification, merrymaking, party, saturnalia, spree

revelation announcement, betrayal, broadcasting, communication, disclosure, discovery, display, exhibition, exposé, exposition, exposure, giveaway, leak, manifestation, news, proclamation, publication, telling, uncovering, unearthing, unveiling

reveller carouser, celebrator, merrymaker, partygoer, pleasureseeker, roisterer

revelry carousal, carouse, celebration, debauch, debauchery, festiv-

ity, fun, jollification, jollity, merry~
making, party, roistering, saturna~
lia, spree

revenge 1. *n.* an eye for an eye,
reprisal, requital, retaliation, ret~
ribution, satisfaction, vengeance,
vindictiveness 2. *v.* avenge, even
the score for, get one's own back
for (*Inf.*), make reprisal for, repay,
requite, retaliate, take an eye for
an eye for, take revenge for, vindi~
cate

revenue gain, income, interest,
proceeds, profits, receipts, returns,
rewards, takings, yield

reverberate echo, rebound, recoil,
re-echo, resound, ring, vibrate

revere adore, be in awe of, defer to,
exalt, have a high opinion of, hon~
our, look up to, put on a pedestal,
respect, reverence, think highly of,
venerate, worship

reverence 1. *n.* admiration, adora~
tion, awe, deference, devotion,
high esteem, homage, honour, re~
spect, veneration, worship 2. *v.* ad~
mire, adore, be in awe of, hold in
awe, honour, pay homage to, re~
spect, revere, venerate, worship

reverent adoring, awed, decorous,
deferential, devout, humble, loving,
meek, pious, respectful, reveren~
tial, solemn, submissive

reverse *v.* 1. invert, transpose, turn
back, turn over, turn round, turn
upside down, upend 2. alter, annul,
cancel, change, countermand, de~
clare null and void, invalidate, ne~
gate, overrule, overset, overthrow,
overturn, quash, repeal, rescind,
retract, revoke, set aside, undo,
upset 3. back, backtrack, back up,
go backwards, move backwards,
retreat ~*n.* 4. antithesis, contra~
diction, contrary, converse, in~
verse, opposite 5. back, flip side,
other side, rear, underside, verso,
wrong side 6. adversity, affliction,
blow, check, defeat, disappoint~
ment, failure, hardship, misadven~
ture, misfortune, mishap, repulse,
reversal, setback, trial, vicissitude
~*adj.* 7. back to front, backward,
contrary, converse, inverse, in~
verted, opposite

revert backslide, come back, go
back, hark back, lapse, recur, re~
gress, relapse, resume, return,
take up where one left off

review *v.* 1. go over again, look at
again, reassess, recapitulate, re~
consider, re-evaluate, re-examine,
rethink, revise, run over, take an~
other look at, think over 2. call to
mind, look back on, recall, recol~
lect, reflect on, remember, sum~
mon up 3. assess, criticize, discuss,
evaluate, examine, give one's
opinion of, inspect, judge, read
through, scrutinize, study, weigh,
write a critique of ~*n.* 4. analysis,
examination, report, scrutiny,
study, survey 5. commentary,
critical assessment, criticism, cri~
tique, evaluation, judgment, notice,
study 6. journal, magazine, peri~
odical 7. another look, fresh look,
reassessment, recapitulation, re~
consideration, re-evaluation, re~
examination, rethink, retrospect,
revision, second look 8. *Military*
display, inspection, march past,
parade, procession

reviewer arbiter, commentator,
connoisseur, critic, essayist, judge

revise 1. alter, amend, change,
correct, edit, emend, modify, re~
consider, redo, re-examine, re~
vamp, review, rework, rewrite,
update 2. go over, memorize, re~
read, run through, study, swot up
(*Brit. inf.*)

revision 1. alteration, amendment,
change, correction, editing, emen~
dation, modification, re~
examination, review, rewriting,
updating 2. homework, memoriz~
ing, rereading, studying, swotting
(*Brit. inf.*)

revival awakening, quickening, re~
animation, reawakening, rebirth,
recrudescence, renaissance, re~
nascence, renewal, restoration,
resurgence, resurrection, resusci~
tation, revitalization, revivification

revive animate, awaken, breathe
new life into, bring back to life,
bring round, cheer, come round,
comfort, invigorate, quicken, rally,
reanimate, recover, refresh, re~

kindle, renew, renovate, restore, resuscitate, revitalize, rouse, spring up again

revoke abolish, abrogate, annul, call back, cancel, countermand, declare null and void, disclaim, invalidate, negate, nullify, quash, recall, recant, renounce, repeal, repudiate, rescind, retract, reverse, set aside, take aside, withdraw

revolt n. 1. defection, insurgency, insurrection, mutiny, putsch, rebellion, revolution, rising, sedition, uprising ~v. 2. defect, mutiny, rebel, resist, rise, take to the streets, take up arms (against) 3. disgust, give one the creeps (Sl.), make one's flesh creep, nauseate, offend, repel, repulse, shock, sicken, turn off (Inf.), turn one's stomach

revolting abhorrent, abominable, appalling, disgusting, distasteful, foul, horrible, horrid, loathsome, nasty, nauseating, nauseous, noisome, obnoxious, obscene, offensive, repellent, repugnant, repulsive, shocking, sickening

revolution n. 1. coup, coup d'état, insurgency, mutiny, putsch, rebellion, revolt, rising, uprising 2. drastic or radical change, innovation, metamorphosis, reformation, sea change, shift, transformation, upheaval 3. circle, circuit, cycle, gyration, lap, orbit, rotation, round, spin, turn, wheel, whirl

revolutionary n. 1. insurgent, insurrectionary, insurrectionist, mutineer, rebel, revolutionist ~adj. 2. extremist, insurgent, insurrectionary, mutinous, radical, rebel, seditious, subversive 3. avant-garde, different, drastic, experimental, fundamental, innovative, new, novel, progressive, radical, thoroughgoing

revolve 1. circle, go round, gyrate, orbit, rotate, spin, turn, twist, wheel, whirl 2. consider, deliberate, meditate, mull over, ponder, reflect, ruminate, study, think about, think over, turn over (in one's mind)

revulsion abhorrence, abomination, aversion, detestation, disgust, distaste, loathing, recoil, repugnance, repulsion

reward n. 1. benefit, bonus, bounty, compensation, gain, honour, merit, payment, premium, prize, profit, recompense, remuneration, repayment, requital, return, wages 2. comeuppance (Sl.), desert, just deserts, punishment, requital, retribution ~v. 3. compensate, honour, make it worth one's while, pay, recompense, remunerate, repay, requite

rewarding advantageous, beneficial, edifying, enriching, fruitful, fulfilling, gainful, gratifying, pleasing, productive, profitable, remunerative, satisfying, valuable, worthwhile

rhetoric 1. eloquence, oratory 2. bombast, fustian, grandiloquence, hot air (Inf.), hyperbole, magniloquence, pomposity, rant, verbosity, wordiness

rhetorical 1. bombastic, declamatory, flamboyant, flashy, florid, flowery, grandiloquent, high-flown, high-sounding, hyperbolic, magniloquent, oratorical, pompous, pretentious, showy, silver-tongued, verbose, windy 2. linguistic, oratorical, stylistic, verbal

rhyme n. 1. ode, poem, poetry, song, verse 2. **rhyme or reason** logic, meaning, method, plan, sense ~v. 3. chime, harmonize, sound like

rhythm accent, beat, cadence, flow, lilt, measure (Prosody), metre, movement, pattern, periodicity, pulse, swing, tempo, time

rhythmic, rhythmical cadenced, flowing, harmonious, lilting, melodious, metrical, musical, periodic, pulsating, throbbing

ribald bawdy, blue, broad, coarse, earthy, filthy, gross, indecent, licentious, naughty, near the knuckle (Inf.), obscene, off colour, Rabelaisian, racy, risqué, rude, scurrilous, smutty, vulgar

rich 1. affluent, filthy rich (Inf.), flush (Inf.), loaded (Sl.), made of money (Inf.), moneyed, opulent, propertied, prosperous, rolling

(*Sl.*), stinking rich (*Inf.*), wealthy, well-heeled (*Sl.*), well-off, well-to-do 2. abounding, full, productive, well-endowed, well-provided, well-stocked, well-supplied 3. abounding, abundant, ample, copious, exuberant, fecund, fertile, fruitful, full, lush, luxurious, plenteous, plentiful, productive, prolific 4. beyond price, costly, elaborate, elegant, expensive, exquisite, fine, gorgeous, lavish, palatial, precious, priceless, splendid, sumptuous, superb, valuable 5. creamy, delicious, fatty, flavoursome, full-bodied, heavy, highly-flavoured, juicy, luscious, savoury, spicy, succulent, sweet, tasty 6. bright, deep, gay, intense, strong, vibrant, vivid, warm 7. deep, dulcet, full, mellifluous, mellow, resonant 8. amusing, comical, funny, hilarious, humorous, laughable, ludicrous, ridiculous, risible, side-splitting

riches abundance, affluence, assets, fortune, gold, money, opulence, plenty, property, resources, richness, substance, treasure, wealth

richly 1. elaborately, elegantly, expensively, exquisitely, gorgeously, lavishly, luxuriously, opulently, palatially, splendidly, sumptuously 2. amply, appropriately, fully, in full measure, properly, suitably, thoroughly, well

rid 1. clear, deliver, disabuse, disburden, disembarrass, disencumber, free, make free, purge, relieve, unburden 2. **get rid of** dispense with, dispose of, do away with, dump, eject, eliminate, expel, jettison, remove, shake off, throw away *or* out, unload, weed out

riddle brain-teaser (*Inf.*), Chinese puzzle, conundrum, enigma, mystery, poser, problem, puzzle, rebus

ride *v.* 1. control, handle, manage, sit on 2. be borne (carried, supported), float, go, journey, move, progress, sit, travel 3. dominate, enslave, grip, haunt, oppress, tyrannize over ~*n.* 4. drive, jaunt, journey, lift, outing, spin (*Inf.*), trip, whirl (*Inf.*)

ridicule 1. *n.* banter, chaff, derision, gibe, irony, jeer, laughter, mockery, raillery, sarcasm, satire, scorn, sneer, taunting 2. *v.* banter, caricature, chaff, deride, humiliate, jeer, lampoon, laugh at, laugh out of court, laugh to scorn, make a fool of, make fun of, make one a laughing stock, mock, parody, poke fun at, pooh-pooh, satirize, scoff, send up (*Brit. inf.*), sneer, take the mickey out of (*Inf.*), taunt

ridiculous absurd, comical, contemptible, derisory, farcical, foolish, funny, hilarious, incredible, laughable, ludicrous, nonsensical, outrageous, preposterous, risible, silly, stupid, unbelievable

rifle *v.* burgle, despoil, go through, gut, loot, pillage, plunder, ransack, rob, rummage, sack, strip

rift 1. breach, break, chink, cleavage, cleft, crack, cranny, crevice, fault, fissure, flaw, fracture, gap, opening, space, split 2. alienation, breach, difference, disagreement, division, estrangement, falling out (*Inf.*), quarrel, schism, separation, split

rig *v.* 1. accoutre, equip, fit out, furnish, kit out, outfit, provision, supply, turn out 2. arrange, doctor, engineer, fake, falsify, fiddle with (*Inf.*), fix (*Inf.*), gerrymander, juggle, manipulate, tamper with, trump up ~*n.* 3. accoutrements, apparatus, equipage, equipment, fitments, fittings, fixtures, gear, machinery, outfit, tackle

right *adj.* 1. equitable, ethical, fair, good, honest, honourable, just, lawful, moral, proper, righteous, true, upright, virtuous 2. accurate, admissible, authentic, correct, exact, factual, genuine, precise, satisfactory, sound, spot-on (*Brit. inf.*), true, unerring, valid, veracious 3. advantageous, appropriate, becoming, *comme il faut*, convenient, deserved, desirable, done, due, favourable, fit, fitting, ideal, opportune, proper, propitious, rightful, seemly, suitable 4. all there (*Inf.*), balanced, *compos mentis*, fine, fit, healthy, in good health, in the pink, lucid, normal, rational, reasonable, sane, sound, unimpaired, up to par, well 5. conservative, reactionary, Tory 6. absolute, complete, out-and-out, real, thorough, thorough-going, utter ~*adv.* 7. accurately, aright, correctly, exactly, factually, genuinely, precisely, truly 8. appropriately, aptly, befittingly, fittingly, properly, satisfactorily, suitably 9. directly, immediately, instantly, promptly, quickly, straight, straightaway, without delay 10. bang, exactly, precisely, slap-bang (*Inf.*), squarely 11. absolutely, all the way, altogether, completely, entirely, perfectly, quite, thoroughly, totally, utterly, wholly 12. ethically, fairly, honestly, honourably, justly, morally, properly, righteously, virtuously 13. advantageously, beneficially, favourably, for the better, fortunately, to advantage, well ~*n.* 14. authority, business, claim, due, freedom, interest, liberty, licence, permission, power, prerogative, privilege, title 15. equity, good, goodness, honour, integrity, justice, lawfulness, legality, morality, propriety, reason, rectitude, righteousness, truth, uprightness, virtue 16. **by rights** equitably, in fairness, justly, properly 17. **to rights** arranged, in order, straight, tidy ~*v.* 18. compensate for, correct, fix, put right, rectify, redress, repair, settle, set upright, sort out, straighten, vindicate

right away at once, directly, forthwith, immediately, instantly, now, promptly, right off, straightaway, straight off (*Inf.*), this instant, without delay, without hesitation

righteous blameless, equitable, ethical, fair, good, honest, honourable, just, law-abiding, moral, pure, upright, virtuous

righteousness blamelessness, equity, ethicalness, faithfulness, goodness, honesty, honour, integrity, justice, morality, probity, purity, rectitude, uprightness, virtue

rigid adamant, austere, exact, fixed, harsh, inflexible, intransigent, invariable, rigorous, set, severe, stern, stiff, strict, stringent, unalterable, unbending, uncompromising, undeviating, unrelenting, unyielding

rigorous 1. austere, challenging, demanding, exacting, firm, hard, harsh, inflexible, rigid, severe, stern, strict, stringent, tough 2. accurate, conscientious, exact, meticulous, nice, painstaking, precise, punctilious, scrupulous, thorough 3. bad, bleak, extreme, harsh, inclement, inhospitable, severe

rigour 1. asperity, austerity, firmness, hardness, hardship, harshness, inflexibility, ordeal, privation, rigidity, sternness, strictness, stringency, suffering, trial 2. accuracy, conscientiousness, exactitude, exactness, meticulousness, preciseness, precision, punctiliousness, thoroughness

rig-out apparel, clobber (*Brit. sl.*), clothing, costume, dress, garb, gear (*Sl.*), get-up (*Inf.*), habit, outfit, raiment, togs

rig out 1. accoutre, equip, fit, furnish, kit out, outfit, set up 2. array, attire, clothe, costume, dress, kit out

rig up arrange, assemble, build, cobble together, construct, erect, fix up, improvise, put together, put up, set up, throw together

rim border, brim, brink, circumference, edge, lip, margin, verge

rind crust, epicarp, husk, integument, outer layer, peel, skin

ring[1] *n.* 1. band, circle, circuit, halo, hoop, loop, round 2. arena, circus, enclosure, rink 3. association, band, cabal, cartel, cell, circle, clique, combine, coterie, crew (*Inf.*), gang, group, junto, knot, mob, organization, syndicate ~*v.* 4. circumscribe, encircle, enclose, encompass, gird, girdle, hem in, seal off, surround

ring[2] *v.* 1. chime, clang, peal, resonate, resound, reverberate, sound, toll 2. buzz (*Inf.*), call, phone, telephone ~*n.* 3. chime, knell, peal 4. buzz (*Inf.*), call, phone call

rinse 1. *v.* bathe, clean, cleanse, dip,

splash, wash, wash out, wet 2. *n.* bath, dip, splash, wash, wetting

riot *n.* 1. anarchy, commotion, con~ fusion, disorder, disturbance, donnybrook, fray, lawlessness, mob violence, quarrel, row, street fighting, strife, tumult, turbulence, turmoil, uproar 2. boisterousness, carousal, excess, festivity, frolic, high jinks, jollification, merry~ making, revelry, romp 3. display, extravaganza, flourish, show, splash 4. **run riot a.** be out of con~ trol, break *or* cut loose, go wild, let oneself go, raise hell, rampage, throw off all restraint **b.** grow like weeds, grow profusely, luxuriate, spread like wildfire ~*v.* 5. fight in the streets, go on the rampage, raise an uproar, rampage, run riot, take to the streets 6. carouse, cut loose, frolic, go on a binge *or* spree, make merry, paint the town red (*Inf.*), revel, roister, romp

riotous 1. anarchic, disorderly, in~ subordinate, lawless, mutinous, rampageous, rebellious, refrac~ tory, rowdy, tumultuous, ungov~ ernable, unruly, uproarious, violent 2. boisterous, loud, luxurious, noisy, orgiastic, rambunctious (*Inf.*), roisterous, rollicking, saturnalian, side-splitting, unrestrained, up~ roarious, wanton, wild

ripe 1. fully developed, fully grown, mature, mellow, ready, ripened, seasoned 2. accomplished, com~ plete, finished, in readiness, per~ fect, prepared, ready 3. auspicious, favourable, ideal, opportune, right, suitable, timely

ripen burgeon, come of age, come to fruition, develop, get ready, grow ripe, make ripe, mature, prepare, season

riposte 1. *n.* answer, comeback (*Inf.*), rejoinder, repartee, reply, response, retort, return, sally 2. *v.* answer, come back, reciprocate, rejoin, reply, respond, retort, re~ turn

rise *v.* 1. arise, get out of bed, get to one's feet, get up, rise and shine, stand up, surface 2. arise, ascend, climb, enlarge, go up, grow, im~ prove, increase, intensify, levitate, lift, mount, move up, soar, swell, wax 3. advance, be promoted, climb the ladder, get on, get some~ where, go places (*Inf.*), progress, prosper, work one's way up 4. ap~ pear, become apparent, crop up, emanate, emerge, eventuate, flow, happen, issue, occur, originate, spring, turn up 5. mount the barri~ cades, mutiny, rebel, resist, revolt, take up arms 6. ascend, climb, get steeper, go uphill, mount, slope upwards ~*n.* 7. advance, ascent, climb, improvement, increase, up~ surge, upswing, upturn, upward turn 8. advancement, aggrandize~ ment, climb, progress, promotion 9. acclivity, ascent, elevation, hill~ ock, incline, rising ground, upward slope 10. increment, pay increase, raise (*U.S.*) 11. **give rise to** bring about, bring on, cause, effect, pro~ duce, provoke, result in

risk 1. *n.* chance, danger, gamble, hazard, jeopardy, peril, possibility, speculation, uncertainty, venture 2. *v.* chance, dare, endanger, ex~ pose to danger, gamble, hazard, imperil, jeopardize, put in jeop~ ardy, take a chance on, venture

risky chancy (*Inf.*), dangerous, dicey (*Sl.*), dodgy (*Brit. inf.*), fraught with danger, hazardous, perilous, precarious, touch-and-go, tricky, uncertain, unsafe

rite act, ceremonial, ceremony, communion, custom, form, for~ mality, liturgy, mystery, obser~ vance, ordinance, practice, pro~ cedure, ritual, sacrament, service, solemnity, usage

ritual *n.* 1. ceremonial, ceremony, communion, liturgy, mystery, ob~ servance, rite, sacrament, service, solemnity 2. convention, custom, form, formality, habit, ordinance, practice, prescription, procedure, protocol, red tape, routine, stereo~ type, usage ~*adj.* 3. ceremonial, ceremonious, conventional, cus~ tomary, formal, habitual, pre~ scribed, procedural, routine, ste~ reotyped

rival *n.* 1. adversary, antagonist,

challenger, competitor, contender, contestant, emulator, opponent 2. compeer, equal, equivalent, fellow, match, peer ~adj. 3. competing, competitive, conflicting, emulating, opposed, opposing ~v. 4. be a match for, bear comparison with, come up to, compare with, compete, contend, emulate, equal, match, measure up to, oppose, seek to displace, vie with

rivalry antagonism, competition, competitiveness, conflict, contention, contest, duel, emulation, opposition, struggle, vying

road 1. avenue, course, direction, highway, lane, motorway, path, pathway, roadway, route, street, thoroughfare, track, way 2. *Nautical* anchorage, roadstead

roam drift, meander, peregrinate, prowl, ramble, range, rove, stravaig (*Scot.*), stray, stroll, travel, walk, wander

roar v. 1. bawl, bay, bellow, clamour, crash, cry, howl, rumble, shout, thunder, vociferate, yell 2. guffaw, hoot, laugh heartily, split one's sides (*Inf.*) ~n. 3. bellow, clamour, crash, cry, howl, outcry, rumble, shout, thunder, yell 4. belly laugh (*Inf.*), guffaw, hoot

rob bereave, burgle, cheat, con (*Sl.*), defraud, deprive, despoil, dispossess, do out of (*Inf.*), gyp (*Sl.*), hold up, loot, pillage, plunder, raid, ransack, rifle, rip off (*Inf.*), sack, strip, swindle

robber bandit, brigand, burglar, cheat, con man (*Inf.*), fraud, highwayman, looter, pirate, plunderer, raider, stealer, swindler, thief

robbery burglary, depredation, embezzlement, filching, fraud, hold-up, larceny, pillage, plunder, raid, rapine, rip-off (*Inf.*), spoliation, stealing, stick-up (*U.S. sl.*), swindle, theft, thievery

robe n. 1. costume, gown, habit, vestment 2. bathrobe, dressing gown, housecoat, peignoir, wrapper ~v. 3. apparel (*Archaic*), attire, clothe, drape, dress, garb

robot android, automaton, machine, mechanical man

robust 1. able-bodied, athletic, brawny, fit, hale, hardy, healthy, hearty, husky (*Inf.*), in fine fettle, in good health, lusty, muscular, powerful, rude, rugged, sinewy, sound, staunch, stout, strapping, strong, sturdy, tough, vigorous, well 2. boisterous, coarse, earthy, indecorous, raw, roisterous, rollicking, rough, rude, unsubtle 3. common-sensical, down-to-earth, hard-headed, practical, pragmatic, realistic, sensible, straightforward

rock[1] 1. boulder, stone 2. anchor, bulwark, cornerstone, foundation, mainstay, protection, support, tower of strength

rock[2] 1. lurch, pitch, reel, roll, sway, swing, toss, wobble 2. astonish, astound, daze, dumbfound, jar, set one back on one's heels (*Inf.*), shake, shock, stagger, stun, surprise

rocky 1. boulder-strewn, craggy, pebbly, rough, rugged, stony 2. adamant, firm, flinty, hard, rocklike, rugged, solid, steady, tough, unyielding

rod bar, baton, birch, cane, dowel, mace, pole, sceptre, shaft, staff, stick, switch, wand

rogue blackguard, charlatan, cheat, con man (*Inf.*), crook (*Inf.*), deceiver, devil, fraud, knave (*Archaic*), mountebank, ne'er-do-well, rapscallion, rascal, reprobate, scamp, scoundrel, sharper, swindler, villain

role 1. character, impersonation, part, portrayal, representation 2. capacity, duty, function, job, part, position, post, task

roll v. 1. elapse, flow, go past, go round, gyrate, pass, pivot, reel, revolve, rock, rotate, run, spin, swivel, trundle, turn, twirl, undulate, wheel, whirl 2. bind, coil, curl, enfold, entwine, envelop, furl, swathe, twist, wind, wrap 3. even, flatten, level, press, smooth, spread 4. boom, drum, echo, grumble, resound, reverberate, roar, rumble, thunder 5. billow, lurch, reel, rock, sway, swing, toss, tumble, wallow, welter 6. lumber, lurch, reel, stag~ ger, swagger, sway, waddle ~*n.* 7. cycle, gyration, reel, revolution, rotation, run, spin, turn, twirl, un~ dulation, wheel, whirl 8. ball, bob~ bin, cylinder, reel, scroll, spool 9. annals, catalogue, census, chroni~ cle, directory, index, inventory, list, record, register, roster, sched~ ule, scroll, table 10. billowing, lurching, pitching, rocking, rolling, swell, tossing, undulation, wallow~ ing, waves 11. boom, drumming, growl, grumble, resonance, rever~ beration, roar, rumble, thunder

rollicking *adj.* boisterous, carefree, cavorting, devil-may-care, exuber~ ant, frisky, frolicsome, hearty, jaunty, jovial, joyous, lively, merry, playful, rip-roaring (*Inf.*), romping, spirited, sportive, sprightly, swashbuckling

roly-poly buxom, chubby, fat, overweight, plump, podgy, pudgy, rotund, rounded, tubby

romance *n.* 1. affair, *affaire* (*du coeur*), affair of the heart, amour, attachment, intrigue, liaison, love affair, passion, relationship 2. ad~ venture, charm, colour, excite~ ment, exoticness, fascination, glamour, mystery, nostalgia, senti~ ment 3. fairy tale, fantasy, fiction, idyll, legend, love story, melodra~ ma, novel, story, tale, tear-jerker (*Inf.*) 4. absurdity, exaggeration, fabrication, fairy tale, falsehood, fiction, flight of fancy, invention, lie, tall story (*Inf.*), trumped-up story ~*v.* 5. exaggerate, fantasize, let one's imagination run away with one, lie, make up stories, stretch the truth, tell stories

romantic *adj.* 1. amorous, fond, lovey-dovey, loving, mushy (*Inf.*), passionate, sentimental, sloppy (*Inf.*), soppy (*Brit. inf.*), tender 2. charming, colourful, exciting, ex~ otic, fascinating, glamorous, mys~ terious, nostalgic, picturesque 3. dreamy, high-flown, idealistic, im~ practical, quixotic, starry-eyed, unrealistic, utopian, visionary, whimsical 4. chimerical, exagger~ ated, extravagant, fabulous, fairy-

tale, fanciful, fantastic, fictitious, idyllic, imaginary, imaginative, improbable, legendary, made-up, unrealistic, wild ~*n.* 5. Don Quix~ ote, dreamer, idealist, romancer, sentimentalist, utopian, visionary

rook bilk, cheat, clip (*Sl.*), defraud, diddle (*Inf.*), do (*Sl.*), fleece, gyp (*Sl.*), mulct, overcharge, rip off (*Sl.*), sting (*Inf.*), swindle

room 1. allowance, area, capacity, compass, elbowroom, expanse, ex~ tent, latitude, leeway, margin, play, range, scope, space, territory, vol~ ume 2. apartment, chamber, office 3. chance, occasion, opportunity, scope

roomy ample, broad, capacious, commodious, extensive, generous, large, sizable, spacious, wide

root *n.* 1. radicle, radix, rhizome, stem, tuber 2. base, beginnings, bottom, cause, core, crux, deriva~ tion, essence, foundation, fountain~ head, fundamental, germ, heart, mainspring, nub, nucleus, occasion, origin, seat, seed, source, starting point 3. *Plural* birthplace, cradle, family, heritage, home, origins, sense of belonging 4. **root and branch** completely, entirely, final~ ly, radically, thoroughly, totally, to the last man, utterly, wholly, with~ out exception ~*v.* 5. anchor, be~ come established, become settled, embed, entrench, establish, fasten, fix, ground, implant, moor, set, stick, take root

rooted confirmed, deep, deeply felt, deep-seated, entrenched, estab~ lished, firm, fixed, ingrained, radi~ cal, rigid

root out 1. *Also* **root up** abolish, cut out, destroy, dig up by the roots, do away with, efface, eliminate, eradicate, erase, exterminate, ex~ tirpate, get rid of, remove, tear out by the roots, uproot, weed out 2. bring to light, dig out, discover, dredge up, produce, turn up, un~ earth

rope *n.* 1. cable, cord, hawser, line, strand 2. **the rope** capital punish~ ment, halter, hanging, lynching, noose 3. **know the ropes** be an old

hand, be experienced, be knowl~
edgeable, know all the ins and outs,
know one's way around, know the
score (*Inf.*), know what's what ~*v.*
4. bind, fasten, hitch, lash, lasso,
moor, pinion, tether, tie

rope in drag in, engage, enlist, in~
veigle, involve, persuade, talk into

roster agenda, catalogue, inven~
tory, list, listing, register, roll, rota,
schedule, scroll, table

rostrum dais, platform, podium,
stage

rosy 1. pink, red, roseate, rose-
coloured 2. blooming, blushing,
fresh, glowing, healthy-looking,
reddish, roseate, rubicund, ruddy 3.
auspicious, bright, cheerful, en~
couraging, favourable, hopeful,
optimistic, promising, reassuring,
roseate, rose-coloured, sunny

rot *v.* 1. corrode, corrupt, crumble,
decay, decompose, degenerate,
deteriorate, disintegrate, fester, go
bad, moulder, perish, putrefy, spoil,
taint 2. decline, degenerate, de~
teriorate, languish, waste away,
wither away ~*n.* 3. blight, canker,
corrosion, corruption, decay, de~
composition, deterioration, disin~
tegration, mould, putrefaction, pu~
trescence 4. balderdash, bosh
(*Inf.*), bunk (*Inf.*), bunkum, clap~
trap (*Inf.*), codswallop (*Brit. sl.*),
drivel, flapdoodle (*Sl.*), guff (*Sl.*),
hogwash, moonshine, nonsense,
poppycock (*Inf.*), rubbish, stuff and
nonsense, tommyrot, tosh (*Inf.*),
twaddle

rotary gyratory, revolving, rotating,
rotational, rotatory, spinning,
turning

rotate 1. go round, gyrate, pirou~
ette, pivot, reel, revolve, spin,
swivel, turn, wheel 2. alternate,
follow in sequence, interchange,
switch, take turns

rotation 1. gyration, orbit, pirou~
ette, reel, revolution, spin, spin~
ning, turn, turning, wheel 2. alter~
nation, cycle, interchanging, se~
quence, succession, switching

rotten 1. bad, corroded, corrupt,
crumbling, decayed, decaying, de~
composed, decomposing, disinte~

grating, festering, fetid, foul,
mouldering, mouldy, perished, pu~
trescent, putrid, rank, sour, stink~
ing, tainted, unsound 2. bent (*Sl.*),
corrupt, crooked (*Inf.*), deceitful,
degenerate, dishonest, dishonour~
able, disloyal, faithless, immoral,
mercenary, perfidious, treacher~
ous, untrustworthy, venal, vicious
3. *Inf.* base, contemptible, despic~
able, dirty, disagreeable, filthy,
mean, nasty, scurrilous, unpleas~
ant, vile, wicked 4. *Inf.* bad, de~
plorable, disappointing, regret~
table, unfortunate, unlucky 5. *Inf.*
crummy (*Sl.*), ill-considered, ill
thought-out, inadequate, inferior,
lousy (*Sl.*), low-grade, poor, punk,
ropy (*Inf.*), sorry, substandard, un~
acceptable, unsatisfactory 6. *Inf.*
bad, below par, ill, off colour,
poorly (*Inf.*), ropy (*Inf.*), rough
(*Inf.*), sick, under the weather
(*Inf.*), unwell

rotter bad lot, blackguard, blighter
(*Brit. inf.*), bounder (*Inf.*), cad
(*Brit. inf.*), cur, louse (*Sl.*), rat (*Sl.*),
stinker (*Sl.*), swine

rotund 1. bulbous, globular, orbicu~
lar, round, rounded, spherical 2.
chubby, corpulent, fat, fleshy,
heavy, obese, plump, podgy, portly,
roly-poly, rounded, stout, tubby 3.
full, grandiloquent, magniloquent,
orotund, resonant, rich, round, so~
norous

rough *adj.* 1. broken, bumpy, crag~
gy, irregular, jagged, rocky, rug~
ged, stony, uneven 2. bristly, bushy,
coarse, dishevelled, disordered,
fuzzy, hairy, shaggy, tangled, tou~
sled, uncut, unshaven, unshorn 3.
agitated, boisterous, choppy, in~
clement, squally, stormy, tempes~
tuous, turbulent, wild 4. bearish,
bluff, blunt, brusque, churlish,
coarse, curt, discourteous, ill-bred,
ill-mannered, impolite, inconsider~
ate, indelicate, loutish, rude, un~
ceremonious, uncivil, uncouth, un~
cultured, ungracious, unmannerly,
unpolished, unrefined, untutored 5.
boisterous, cruel, curt, drastic, ex~
treme, hard, harsh, nasty, rowdy,
severe, sharp, tough, unfeeling,
unjust, unpleasant, violent 6. *Inf.*

below par, ill, not a hundred per cent (*Inf.*), off colour, poorly (*Inf.*), ropy (*Inf.*), rotten (*Inf.*), sick, under the weather (*Inf.*), unwell, upset 7. cacophonous, discordant, grating, gruff, harsh, husky, inharmonious, jarring, rasping, raucous, unmusi~ cal 8. arduous, austere, hard, rug~ ged, spartan, tough, uncomfort~ able, unpleasant, unrefined 9. ba~ sic, crude, cursory, formless, hasty, imperfect, incomplete, quick, raw, rough-and-ready, rough-hewn, ru~ dimentary, shapeless, sketchy, un~ finished, unpolished, unrefined, untutored 10. crude, raw, rough-hewn, uncut, undressed, unhewn, unpolished, unprocessed, un~ wrought 11. amorphous, approxi~ mate, estimated, foggy, general, hazy, imprecise, inexact, sketchy, vague ~*n.* 12. draft, mock-up, out~ line, preliminary sketch, sugges~ tion 13. *Inf.* bruiser, bully boy, roughneck (*Sl.*), rowdy, ruffian, thug, tough ~*v.* 14. **rough out** ad~ umbrate, block out, delineate, draft, outline, plan, sketch, suggest 15. **rough up** bash up (*Sl.*), batter, beat up, do over (*Sl.*), knock about, maltreat, manhandle, mistreat, thrash

rough-and-tumble 1. *n.* affray (*Law*), brawl, donnybrook, dust-up, (*Inf.*), fight, fracas, melee, punch-up (*Brit. sl.*), roughhouse (*Sl.*), scrap (*Inf.*), scuffle, struggle 2. *adj.* boisterous, disorderly, haphazard, indisciplined, irregular, rough, rowdy, scrambled, scrambling

round *adj.* 1. annular, ball-shaped, bowed, bulbous, circular, curved, curvilinear, cylindrical, discoid, disc-shaped, globular, orbicular, ring-shaped, rotund, rounded, spherical 2. complete, entire, full, solid, unbroken, undivided, whole 3. ample, bounteous, bountiful, considerable, generous, great, large, liberal, substantial 4. ample, fleshy, full, full-fleshed, plump, roly-poly, rotund, rounded 5. full, mellifluous, orotund, resonant, rich, rotund, sonorous 6. blunt, candid, direct, frank, outspoken, plain, straightforward, unmodified

~*n.* 7. ball, band, circle, disc, globe, orb, ring, sphere 8. bout, cycle, se~ quence, series, session, succession 9. division, lap, level, period, ses~ sion, stage, turn 10. ambit, beat, circuit, compass, course, routine, schedule, series, tour, turn 11. bul~ let, cartridge, discharge, shell, shot ~*v.* 12. bypass, circle, circumnavi~ gate, encircle, flank, go round, skirt, turn

roundabout *adj.* circuitous, cir~ cumlocutory, devious, discursive, evasive, indirect, meandering, oblique, periphrastic, tortuous

round off bring to a close, cap, close, complete, conclude, crown, finish off, put the finishing touch to, settle

round up assemble, bring together, collect, drive, gather, group, herd, marshal, muster, rally

rouse 1. arouse, awaken, call, get up, rise, wake, wake up 2. agitate, anger, animate, arouse, bestir, dis~ turb, excite, exhilarate, galvanize, get going, incite, inflame, instigate, move, provoke, startle, stimulate, stir, whip up

rousing brisk, electrifying, excit~ ing, exhilarating, inflammatory, inspiring, lively, moving, spirited, stimulating, stirring, vigorous

rout 1. *n.* beating, debacle, defeat, disorderly retreat, drubbing, head~ long flight, hiding (*Inf.*), licking (*Inf.*), overthrow, overwhelming defeat, ruin, shambles, thrashing 2. *v.* beat, chase, conquer, crush, cut to pieces, defeat, destroy, dispel, drive off, drub, lick (*Inf.*), over~ power, overthrow, put to flight, put to rout, scatter, thrash, throw back in confusion, worst

route 1. *n.* avenue, beat, circuit, course, direction, itinerary, jour~ ney, passage, path, road, round, run, way 2. *v.* convey, direct, dis~ patch, forward, send, steer

routine *n.* 1. custom, formula, grind (*Inf.*), groove, method, order, pat~ tern, practice, procedure, pro~ gramme, usage, way, wont 2. *Inf.* act, bit (*Inf.*), line, performance, piece, spiel (*Inf.*) ~*adj.* 3. conven~

tional, customary, everyday, familiar, habitual, normal, ordinary, standard, typical, usual, wonted, workaday 4. boring, clichéd, dull, hackneyed, humdrum, predictable, run-of-the-mill, tedious, tiresome, unimaginative, uninspired, unoriginal

row[1] bank, column, file, line, queue, range, rank, sequence, series, string, tier

row[2] *n.* 1. altercation, brawl, commotion, controversy, dispute, disturbance, falling-out (*Inf.*), fracas, fray, fuss, noise, quarrel, racket, ruckus (*Inf.*), ruction (*Inf.*), rumpus, scrap (*Inf.*), shouting match (*Inf.*), slanging match (*Brit.*), squabble, tiff, trouble, tumult, uproar 2. castigation, dressing-down (*Inf.*), flea in one's ear (*Inf.*), lecture, reprimand, reproof, rollicking (*Brit. inf.*), talking-to (*Inf.*), telling-off (*Inf.*), ticking-off (*Inf.*), tongue-lashing ~*v.* 3. argue, brawl, dispute, fight, scrap (*Inf.*), squabble, wrangle

rowdy 1. *adj.* boisterous, disorderly, loud, loutish, noisy, obstreperous, rough, unruly, uproarious, wild 2. *n.* brawler, hooligan, lout, rough (*Inf.*), ruffian, tearaway (*Brit.*), tough, troublemaker, yahoo

royal 1. imperial, kinglike, kingly, monarchical, princely, queenly, regal, sovereign 2. august, grand, impressive, magnificent, majestic, splendid, stately, superb, superior

rub *v.* 1. abrade, caress, chafe, clean, fray, grate, knead, massage, polish, scour, scrape, shine, smooth, stroke, wipe 2. apply, put, smear, spread 3. **rub up the wrong way** anger, annoy, bug (*Inf.*), get one's goat (*Inf.*), get under one's skin (*Inf.*), irk, irritate, peeve (*Inf.*), vex ~*n.* 4. caress, kneading, massage, polish, shine, stroke, wipe 5. catch, difficulty, drawback, hindrance, hitch, impediment, obstacle, problem, snag, trouble

rubbish 1. debris, dregs, dross, flotsam and jetsam, garbage, junk, litter, lumber, offal, offscourings, refuse, scrap, trash, waste 2. balderdash, bosh (*Inf.*), bunkum, claptrap (*Inf.*), codswallop (*Brit. sl.*), drivel, flapdoodle (*Sl.*), gibberish, guff (*Sl.*), havers (*Scot.*), hogwash, moonshine, nonsense, piffle (*Inf.*), poppycock (*Inf.*), rot, stuff and nonsense, tommyrot, tosh (*Inf.*), twaddle

rub out cancel, delete, efface, erase, expunge, obliterate, remove, wipe out

ruddy 1. blooming, blushing, florid, flushed, fresh, glowing, healthy, red, reddish, rosy, rosy-cheeked, rubicund, sanguine, sunburnt 2. crimson, pink, red, reddish, roseate, ruby, scarlet

rude 1. abrupt, abusive, blunt, brusque, cheeky, churlish, curt, discourteous, disrespectful, ill-mannered, impertinent, impolite, impudent, inconsiderate, insolent, insulting, offhand, peremptory, short, uncivil, unmannerly 2. barbarous, boorish, brutish, coarse, crude, graceless, gross, ignorant, illiterate, loutish, low, oafish, obscene, rough, savage, scurrilous, uncivilised, uncouth, uncultured, uneducated, ungracious, unpolished, unrefined, untutored, vulgar 3. artless, crude, inartistic, inelegant, makeshift, primitive, raw, rough, rough-hewn, roughly-made, simple 4. abrupt, harsh, sharp, startling, sudden, unpleasant, violent

rudimentary basic, early, elementary, embryonic, fundamental, immature, initial, introductory, primary, primitive, undeveloped, vestigial

rudiments basics, beginnings, elements, essentials, first principles, foundation, fundamentals

rueful conscience-stricken, contrite, dismal, doleful, grievous, lugubrious, melancholy, mournful, penitent, pitiable, pitiful, plaintive, regretful, remorseful, repentant, sad, self-reproachful, sorrowful, sorry, woebegone, woeful

ruffian bruiser (*Inf.*), brute, bully, bully boy, hoodlum, hooligan, miscreant, rascal, rogue, rough (*Inf.*), roughneck (*Sl.*), rowdy, scoundrel, thug, tough, villain, wretch

ruffle 1. derange, disarrange, discompose, dishevel, disorder, mess up, rumple, tousle, wrinkle 2. agitate, annoy, confuse, disconcert, disquiet, disturb, fluster, harass, irritate, nettle, peeve (*Inf.*), perturb, put out, rattle (*Inf.*), shake up (*Inf.*), stir, torment, trouble, unsettle, upset, vex, worry

rugged 1. broken, bumpy, craggy, difficult, irregular, jagged, ragged, rocky, rough, stark, uneven 2. furrowed, leathery, lined, rough-hewn, strong-featured, weather-beaten, weathered, worn, wrinkled 3. austere, crabbed, dour, gruff, hard, harsh, rough, rude, severe, sour, stern, surly 4. barbarous, blunt, churlish, crude, graceless, rude, uncouth, uncultured, unpolished, unrefined 5. arduous, demanding, difficult, exacting, hard, harsh, laborious, rigorous, stern, strenuous, taxing, tough, trying, uncompromising 6. beefy (*Inf.*), brawny, burly, hale, hardy, husky (*Inf.*), muscular, robust, strong, sturdy, tough, vigorous, well-built

ruin *n.* 1. bankruptcy, breakdown, collapse, crackup (*Inf.*), crash, damage, decay, defeat, destitution, destruction, devastation, disintegration, disrepair, dissolution, downfall, failure, fall, havoc, insolvency, nemesis, overthrow, ruination, subversion, the end, undoing, Waterloo, wreck, wreckage ~*v.* 2. bankrupt, break, bring down, bring to nothing, bring to ruin, crush, defeat, demolish, destroy, devastate, impoverish, lay in ruins, lay waste, overthrow, overturn, overwhelm, pauperize, raze, shatter, smash, wreak havoc upon, wreck 3. botch, damage, disfigure, injure, make a mess of, mangle, mar, mess up, spoil

ruinous 1. baleful, baneful (*Archaic*), calamitous, catastrophic, crippling, deadly, deleterious, destructive, devastating, dire, disastrous, extravagant, fatal, immoderate, injurious, murderous, noxious, pernicious, shattering, wasteful,

withering 2. broken-down, decrepit, derelict, dilapidated, in ruins, ramshackle, ruined

rule *n.* 1. axiom, canon, criterion, decree, direction, guide, guideline, law, maxim, order, ordinance, precept, principle, regulation, ruling, standard, tenet 2. administration, ascendancy, authority, command, control, direction, domination, dominion, empire, government, influence, jurisdiction, leadership, mastery, power, regime, reign, supremacy, sway 3. condition, convention, custom, form, habit, order *or* way of things, practice, procedure, routine, wont 4. course, formula, method, policy, procedure, way 5. **as a rule** customarily, for the most part, generally, mainly, normally, on the whole, ordinarily, usually ~*v.* 6. administer, be in authority, be in power, be number one (*Inf.*), command, control, direct, dominate, govern, guide, hold sway, lead, manage, preside over, regulate, reign, wear the crown 7. adjudge, adjudicate, decide, decree, determine, establish, find, judge, lay down, pronounce, resolve, settle 8. be customary (pre-eminent, prevalent, superior), hold sway, obtain, predominate, preponderate, prevail

rule out ban, debar, dismiss, eliminate, exclude, forbid, leave out, obviate, preclude, prevent, prohibit, proscribe, reject

ruler 1. commander, controller, crowned head, emperor, empress, governor, head of state, king, leader, lord, monarch, potentate, prince, princess, queen, sovereign 2. measure, rule, straight edge, yardstick

ruling *n.* 1. adjudication, decision, decree, finding, judgment, pronouncement, resolution, verdict ~*adj.* 2. commanding, controlling, dominant, governing, leading, regnant, reigning, upper 3. chief, current, dominant, main, predominant, pre-eminent, preponderant, prevailing, prevalent, principal, regnant, supreme

ruminate brood, chew over, cogi~
tate, consider, contemplate, delib~
erate, meditate, mull over, muse,
ponder, reflect, revolve, think, turn
over in one's mind

rumour 1. *n.* bruit (*Archaic or U.S.*),
buzz, canard, gossip, hearsay,
news, report, story, talk, tidings,
whisper, word **2.** *v.* bruit (*Archaic
or U.S.*), circulate, gossip, noise
abroad, pass around, publish, put
about, report, say, tell, whisper

run *v.* **1.** bolt, career, dart, dash,
gallop, hare (*Brit. inf.*), hasten, hie,
hotfoot, hurry, jog, leg it (*Inf.*),
lope, race, rush, scamper, scram~
ble, scud, scurry, speed, sprint **2.**
abscond, beat a retreat, beat it
(*Sl.*), bolt, clear out, cut and run
(*Inf.*), decamp, depart, escape, flee,
leg it (*Inf.*), make a run for it,
make off, scarper (*Brit. sl.*), show a
clean pair of heels, skedaddle
(*Inf.*), take flight, take off (*Inf.*),
take to one's heels **3.** course, glide,
go, move, pass, roll, skim, slide **4.**
bear, carry, convey, drive, give a
lift to, manoeuvre, operate, propel,
transport **5.** go, operate, ply **6.**
function, go, operate, perform,
tick, work **7.** administer, be in
charge of, boss (*Inf.*), carry on,
conduct, control, coordinate, di~
rect, head, lead, look after, man~
age, mastermind, operate, oversee,
own, regulate, superintend, super~
vise, take care of **8.** continue, ex~
tend, go, last, lie, proceed, range,
reach, stretch **9.** cascade, dis~
charge, flow, go, gush, issue, leak,
move, pour, proceed, spill, spout,
stream **10.** dissolve, fuse, go soft,
liquefy, melt, turn to liquid **11.** be
diffused, bleed, lose colour, mix,
spread **12.** come apart, come un~
done, ladder, tear, unravel **13.** be
current, circulate, climb, creep, go
round, spread, trail **14.** display,
feature, print, publish **15.** be a
candidate, challenge, compete,
contend, put oneself up for, stand,
take part **16.** bootleg, deal in, ship,
smuggle, sneak, traffic in **17. run
for it** abscond, bolt, cut and run
(*Inf.*), do a bunk (*Brit. inf.*), escape,
flee, fly, make a break for it, make

off, scarper (*Brit. sl.*), scram (*Inf.*),
show a clean pair of heels, ske~
daddle (*Inf.*), take flight, take off
~*n.* **18.** dash, gallop, jog, race, rush,
sprint, spurt **19.** drive, excursion,
jaunt, journey, joy ride (*Inf.*), lift,
outing, ride, round, spin (*Inf.*), trip
20. chain, course, cycle, passage,
period, round, season, sequence,
series, spell, streak, stretch, string
21. category, class, kind, order,
sort, type, variety **22.** application,
demand, pressure, rush **23.** ladder,
rip, snag, tear **24.** course, current,
direction, drift, flow, motion,
movement, passage, path, pro~
gress, stream, tendency, tenor,
tide, trend, way **25.** coop, enclo~
sure, pen **26. in the long run** at the
end of the day, eventually, in the
end, in the final analysis, in time,
ultimately, when all is said and
done **27. on the run a.** at liberty,
escaping, fugitive, in flight, on the
lam (*U.S. sl.*), on the loose **b.** de~
feated, falling back, fleeing, in
flight, in retreat, retreating, run~
ning away **c.** at speed, hastily, hur~
riedly, hurrying, in a hurry, in a
rush, in haste

run across bump into, chance
upon, come across, come upon,
encounter, meet, meet with, run
into

runaway *n.* **1.** absconder, deserter,
escapee, escaper, fugitive, refugee,
truant ~*adj.* **2.** escaped, fleeing,
fugitive, loose, out of control, un~
controlled, wild **3.** easily won, easy,
effortless

run away 1. abscond, beat it (*Sl.*),
bolt, clear out, cut and run (*Inf.*),
decamp, do a bunk (*Brit. inf.*), es~
cape, flee, make a run for it, run
off, scarper (*Brit. sl.*), scram (*Inf.*),
show a clean pair of heels, ske~
daddle (*Inf.*), take flight, take off,
take to one's heels **2.** *With* **a.**
abduct, abscond, elope **b.** abscond,
make off, pinch (*Inf.*), run off,
snatch, steal **c.** romp home, walk it
(*Inf.*), win by a mile (*Inf.*), win
easily, win hands down

rundown briefing, outline, précis,
recap (*Inf.*), résumé, review, run~

through, sketch, summary, synopsis

run-down 1. below par, debilitated, drained, enervated, exhausted, fatigued, out of condition, peaky, tried, under the weather (*Inf.*), unhealthy, weak, weary, worn-out 2. broken-down, decrepit, dilapidated, dingy, ramshackle, seedy, shabby, tumble-down, worn-out

run down 1. curtail, cut, cut back, decrease, drop, pare down, reduce, trim 2. debilitate, exhaust, sap the strength of, tire, undermine the health of, weaken 3. belittle, criticize adversely, decry, defame, denigrate, disparage, knock (*Inf.*), revile, speak ill of, vilify 4. hit, knock down, knock over, run into, run over, strike

run in 1. break in gently, run gently 2. *Sl.* apprehend, arrest, bust (*Inf.*), collar (*Inf.*), jail, nab (*Inf.*), pinch (*Inf.*), pull in (*Brit. sl.*), take into custody, take to jail, throw in jail

run into 1. bump into, collide with, crash into, dash against, hit, ram, strike 2. be beset by, be confronted by, bump into, chance upon, come across, come upon, encounter, meet, meet with, run across

runner 1. athlete, harrier, jogger, miler, sprinter 2. courier, dispatch bearer, errand boy, messenger 3. offshoot, shoot, sprig, sprout, stem, stolon (*Bot.*), tendril

running *adj.* 1. constant, continuous, incessant, in succession, on the trot (*Inf.*), perpetual, together, unbroken, unceasing, uninterrupted 2. flowing, moving, streaming ~*n.* 3. administration, charge, conduct, control, coordination, direction, leadership, management, organization, regulation, superintendency, supervision 4. functioning, maintenance, operation, performance, working 5. competition, contention, contest

run off 1. bolt, clear out, cut and run (*Inf.*), decamp, escape, flee, make off, run away, scarper (*Brit. sl.*), show a clean pair of heels, skedaddle (*Inf.*), take flight, take to

one's heels 2. churn out (*Inf.*), duplicate, print, produce 3. bleed, drain, flow away, siphon, tap 4. *With with a.* lift (*Inf.*), make off, pinch (*Inf.*), purloin, run away, steal, swipe (*Sl.*) b. abscond, elope, run away

run-of-the-mill average, common, commonplace, fair, mediocre, middling, modest, ordinary, passable, tolerable, undistinguished, unexceptional, unexciting, unimpressive

run out 1. be exhausted, cease, close, come to a close, dry up, end, expire, fail, finish, give out, peter out, terminate 2. *With of* be cleaned out, be out of, exhaust one's supply of, have no more of, have none left, have no remaining 3. *With on Inf.* abandon, desert, forsake, leave high and dry, leave holding the baby, leave in the lurch, rat, run away from

run over 1. hit, knock down, knock over, run down, strike 2. brim over, overflow, spill, spill over 3. check, examine, go over, go through, rehearse, reiterate, review, run through, survey

run through 1. pierce, spit, stab, stick, transfix 2. blow (*Sl.*), dissipate, exhaust, fritter away, spend like water, squander, throw away, waste 3. go over, practise, read, rehearse, run over 4. check, examine, go through, look over, review, run over, survey

rupture *n.* 1. breach, break, burst, cleavage, cleft, crack, fissure, fracture, rent, split, tear 2. altercation, breach, break, bust-up (*Inf.*), contention, disagreement, disruption, dissolution, estrangement, falling-out (*Inf.*), feud, hostility, quarrel, rift, schism, split 3. *Medical* hernia ~*v.* 4. break, burst, cleave, crack, fracture, puncture, rend, separate, sever, split, tear 5. break off, cause a breach, come between, disrupt, dissever, divide, split

rural agrarian, agricultural, Arcadian, bucolic, countrified, country, pastoral, rustic, sylvan, upcountry

ruse artifice, blind, deception, device, dodge, hoax, imposture, manoeuvre, ploy, sham, stratagem, subterfuge, trick, wile

rush v. 1. accelerate, bolt, career, dart, dash, dispatch, expedite, fly, hasten, hotfoot, hurry, hustle, lose no time, make haste, make short work of, press, push, quicken, race, run, scramble, scurry, shoot, speed, speed up, sprint, tear ~n. 2. charge, dash, dispatch, expedition, haste, hurry, race, scramble, speed, surge, swiftness, urgency ~v. 3. attack, capture, charge, overcome, storm, take by storm ~n. 4. assault, charge, onslaught, push, storm, surge ~adj. 5. brisk, cursory, emergency, expeditious, fast, hasty, hurried, prompt, quick, rapid, swift, urgent

rust n. 1. corrosion, oxidation ~v. 2. corrode, oxidize ~n. 3. blight, mildew, mould, must, rot ~v. 4. atrophy, decay, decline, deteriorate, go stale, stagnate, tarnish

rustic adj. 1. Arcadian, bucolic, countrified, country, pastoral, rural, sylvan, upcountry 2. artless, homely, homespun, plain, simple, unaffected, unpolished, unrefined, unsophisticated 3. awkward, boorish, churlish, cloddish, clodhopping (Inf.), clownish, coarse, crude, graceless, loutish, lumpish, maladroit, rough, uncouth, uncultured, unmannerly ~n. 4. boor, bumpkin, clod, clodhopper (Inf.), clown, country boy, country cousin, countryman, countrywoman, hillbilly, Hodge, peasant, son of the soil, swain (Archaic), yokel

rustle 1. v. crackle, crepitate, crinkle, susurrate (Literary), swish, whish, whisper, whoosh 2. n. crackle, crepitation, crinkling, susurration or susurrus (Literary), rustling, whisper

rusty 1. corroded, oxidized, rust-covered, rusted 2. chestnut, coppery, reddish, reddish-brown, russet, rust-coloured 3. cracked, creaking, croaking, croaky, hoarse 4. ancient, antiquated, antique, dated, old-fashioned, outmoded, out of date, passé 5. deficient, impaired, not what it was, out of practice, sluggish, stale, unpractised, weak

rut n. 1. furrow, gouge, groove, indentation, pothole, score, track, trough, wheelmark 2. dead end, groove, habit, humdrum existence, pattern, routine, system ~v. 3. cut, furrow, gouge, groove, hole, indent, mark, score

ruthless adamant, barbarous, brutal, callous, cruel, ferocious, fierce, hard, hard-hearted, harsh, heartless, inexorable, inhuman, merciless, pitiless, relentless, remorseless, savage, severe, stern, unfeeling, unmerciful, unpitying, unrelenting, without pity

S

sabotage 1. *v.* cripple, damage, destroy, disable, disrupt, incapacitate, sap the foundations of, subvert, throw a spanner in the works (*Inf.*), undermine, vandalize, wreck 2. *n.* damage, destruction, disruption, subversion, treachery, treason, wrecking

sack¹ 1. *v.* axe (*Inf.*), discharge, dismiss, fire (*Inf.*), give (someone) his cards, give (someone) his marching orders, give (someone) the boot (*Sl.*), kick out (*Inf.*) 2. *n.* **the sack** discharge, dismissal, termination of employment, the axe (*Inf.*), the boot (*Sl.*), the chop (*Brit. sl.*), the push (*Sl.*)

sack² 1. *v.* demolish, depredate (*Rare*), despoil, destroy, devastate, lay waste, loot, maraud, pillage, plunder, raid, ravage, rifle, rob, ruin, spoil, strip 2. *n.* depredation, despoliation, destruction, devastation, looting, pillage, plunder, plundering, rape, rapine, ravage, ruin, waste

sackcloth and ashes compunction, contrition, grief, hair shirt, mortification, mourning, penitence, remorse, repentance

sacred 1. blessed, consecrated, divine, hallowed, holy, revered, sanctified, venerable 2. inviolable, inviolate, invulnerable, protected, sacrosanct, secure 3. holy, religious, solemn

sacrifice 1. *v.* forego, forfeit, give up, immolate, let go, lose, offer, offer up, surrender 2. *n.* burnt offering, destruction, hecatomb, immolation, loss, oblation, renunciation, surrender

sacrilege blasphemy, desecration, heresy, impiety, irreverence, mockery, profanation, profaneness, profanity, violation

sad 1. blue, cheerless, dejected, depressed, disconsolate, dismal, doleful, down, downcast, down in the dumps (*Inf.*), down in the

mouth (*Inf.*), gloomy, glum, grief-stricken, grieved, heavy-hearted, low, low-spirited, lugubrious, melancholy, mournful, pensive, sick at heart, sombre, triste (*Archaic*), unhappy, wistful, woebegone 2. calamitous, dark, depressing, disastrous, dismal, grievous, heart-rending, lachrymose, moving, pathetic, pitiable, pitiful, poignant, sorry, tearful, tragic, upsetting 3. bad, deplorable, dismal, distressing, grave, lamentable, miserable, regrettable, serious, shabby, sorry, to be deplored, unfortunate, unhappy, unsatisfactory, wretched

sadden bring tears to one's eyes, cast a gloom upon, cast down, dash, deject, depress, desolate, dispirit, distress, grieve, make blue, make one's heart bleed, upset

saddle *v.* burden, charge, encumber, load, lumber (*Brit. inf.*), task, tax

sadistic barbarous, brutal, cruel, fiendish, perverse, perverted, ruthless, vicious

sadness bleakness, cheerlessness, dejection, depression, despondency, dolefulness, dolour (*Poetic*), gloominess, grief, heavy heart, melancholy, misery, mournfulness, poignancy, sorrow, sorrowfulness, the blues, the dumps (*Inf.*), unhappiness

safe 1. free from harm, guarded, impregnable, in safety, intact, O.K. or okay (*Inf.*), out of danger, out of harm's way, protected, safe and sound, secure, undamaged, unharmed, unhurt, unscathed 2. harmless, innocuous, nonpoisonous, nontoxic, pure, tame, unpolluted, wholesome 3. cautious, circumspect, conservative, dependable, discreet, on the safe side, prudent, realistic, reliable, sure, tried and true, trustworthy, unadventurous 4. certain, impregnable, risk-free, riskless, secure, sound

~n. 5. coffer, deposit box, repository, safe-deposit box, strongbox, vault

safeguard 1. v. defend, guard, look after, preserve, protect, screen, shield, watch over 2. n. aegis, armour, bulwark, convoy, defence, escort, guard, protection, security, shield, surety

safely in one piece, in safety, safe and sound, securely, with impunity, without risk, with safety

safety assurance, cover, immunity, impregnability, protection, refuge, sanctuary, security, shelter

sage 1. adj. acute, canny, discerning, intelligent, judicious, learned, perspicacious, politic, prudent, sagacious, sapient, sensible, wise 2. n. authority, elder, expert, guru, man of learning, master, Nestor, philosopher, pundit, savant, Solomon, Solon, wise man

sail v. 1. cast or weigh anchor, embark, get under way, hoist the blue peter, put to sea, set sail 2. captain, cruise, go by water, navigate, pilot, ride the waves, skipper, steer, voyage 3. drift, float, fly, glide, scud, shoot, skim, skirr, soar, sweep, wing 4. Inf. With in or into assault, attack, begin, belabour, fall upon, get going, get to work on, lambaste, set about, tear into (Inf.)

sailor hearty (Inf.), Jack Tar, lascar, leatherneck (Sl.), marine, mariner, matelot (Sl.), navigator, salt, sea dog, seafarer, seafaring man, seaman, tar (Inf.)

saintly angelic, beatific, blameless, blessed, devout, full of good works, god-fearing, godly, holy, pious, religious, righteous, sainted, saintlike, sinless, virtuous, worthy

sake 1. account, advantage, behalf, benefit, consideration, gain, good, interest, profit, regard, respect, welfare, wellbeing 2. aim, cause, end, motive, objective, principle, purpose, reason

salary earnings, emolument, income, pay, remuneration, stipend

sale 1. deal, disposal, marketing, selling, transaction, vending 2. buyers, consumers, customers, demand, market, outlet, purchasers 3. **for sale** available, in stock, obtainable, on offer, on sale, on the market

salient arresting, conspicuous, important, jutting, marked, noticeable, outstanding, projecting, prominent, pronounced, protruding, remarkable, signal, striking

sallow anaemic, bilious, jaundiced-looking, pale, pallid, pasty, sickly, unhealthy, wan, yellowish

sally v. 1. erupt, go forth, issue, rush, set out, surge ~n. 2. Military foray, incursion, offensive, raid, sortie, thrust 3. Fig. bon mot, crack (Inf.), jest, joke, quip, retort, riposte, smart remark, wisecrack (Inf.), witticism 4. escapade, excursion, frolic, jaunt, trip

salt n. 1. flavour, relish, savour, seasoning, taste 2. **with a grain** or **pinch of salt** cynically, disbelievingly, doubtfully, sceptically, suspiciously, with reservations 3. Fig. Attic wit, bite, dry humour, liveliness, piquancy, punch, pungency, sarcasm, sharpness, wit, zest, zip (Inf.) 4. mariner, sailor, sea dog, seaman, tar (Inf.) ~adj. 5. brackish, briny, saline, salted, salty

salty 1. brackish, briny, over-salted, saline, salt, salted 2. colourful, humorous, lively, piquant, pungent, racy, sharp, snappy (Inf.), spicy, tangy, tart, witty, zestful

salubrious beneficial, good for one, healthful, health-giving, healthy, invigorating, salutary, wholesome

salutary 1. advantageous, beneficial, good, good for one, helpful, practical, profitable, timely, useful, valuable 2. healthful, healthy, salubrious

salutation address, greeting, obeisance, salute, welcome

salute v. 1. accost, acknowledge, address, doff one's cap to, greet, hail, kiss, pay one's respects to, salaam, welcome 2. acknowledge, honour, pay tribute or homage to, present arms, recognize, take one's hat off to (Inf.) ~n. 3. address, greeting, kiss, obeisance, recognition, salaam, salutation, tribute

salvage v. glean, recover, redeem, rescue, restore, retrieve, save

salvation deliverance, escape, lifeline, preservation, redemption, rescue, restoration, saving

same *adj.* 1. aforementioned, aforesaid, selfsame, very 2. alike, corresponding, duplicate, equal, equivalent, identical, indistin~ guishable, interchangeable, syn~ onymous, twin 3. changeless, con~ sistent, constant, invariable, unal~ tered, unchanged, unfailing, uni~ form, unvarying 4. all the same a. after all, anyhow, be that as it may, in any event, just the same, never~ theless, nonetheless, still b. imma~ terial, not worth mentioning, of no consequence, unimportant

sameness identicalness, identity, indistinguishability, lack of variety, likeness, monotony, oneness, pre~ dictability, repetition, resem~ blance, similarity, standardization, tedium, uniformity

sample 1. *n.* cross section, exam~ ple, exemplification, illustration, indication, instance, model, pat~ tern, representative, sign, speci~ men 2. *v.* experience, inspect, par~ take of, taste, test, try 3. *adj.* illus~ trative, pilot, representative, specimen, test, trial

sanctify absolve, anoint, bless, cleanse, consecrate, hallow, purify, set apart

sanctimonious canting, false, goody-goody (*Inf.*), holier-than~ thou, hypocritical, pharisaical, pi (*Brit. sl.*), pietistic, pious, self- righteous, self-satisfied, smug, Tartuffian *or* Tartufian, too good to be true, unctuous

sanction *n.* 1. allowance, approba~ tion, approval, authority, authori~ zation, backing, confirmation, countenance, endorsement, O.K. *or* okay (*Inf.*), ratification, stamp *or* seal of approval, support 2. *Often plural* ban, boycott, coercive measures, embargo, penalty ~*v.* 3. allow, approve, authorize, back, countenance, endorse, lend one's

name to, permit, support, vouch for 4. confirm, ratify, warrant

sanctity 1. devotion, godliness, goodness, grace, holiness, piety, purity, religiousness, righteous~ ness, sanctitude, spirituality 2. in~ violability, sacredness, solemnity

sanctuary 1. altar, church, Holy of Holies, sanctum, shrine, temple 2. asylum, haven, protection, refuge, retreat, shelter 3. conservation area, national park, nature re~ serve, reserve

sane 1. all there (*Inf.*), *compos mentis*, in one's right mind, in pos~ session of all one's faculties, lucid, mentally sound, normal, of sound mind, rational 2. balanced, judi~ cious, level-headed, moderate, reasonable, sensible, sober, sound

sanguine 1. animated, assured, buoyant, cheerful, confident, hopeful, in good heart, lively, opti~ mistic, spirited 2. florid, red, rubi~ cund, ruddy

sanitary clean, germ-free, healthy, hygienic, salubrious, unpolluted, wholesome

sanity 1. mental health, normality, rationality, reason, right mind (*Inf.*), saneness, stability 2. com~ mon sense, good sense, judicious~ ness, level-headedness, rationality, sense, soundness of judgment

sap[1] *n.* 1. animating force, essence, lifeblood, vital fluid 2. *Inf.* charlie (*Brit. inf.*), chump (*Inf.*), drip (*Inf.*), fool, gull (*Archaic*), idiot, jerk (*Sl.*), muggins (*Brit. sl.*), nincompoop, ninny, nitwit, noddy, noodle, Sim~ ple Simon, simpleton, twit (*Inf.*), weakling, wet (*Inf.*)

sap[2] *v.* bleed, deplete, devitalize, drain, enervate, erode, exhaust, rob, undermine, weaken, wear down

sarcasm bitterness, causticness, contempt, cynicism, derision, iro~ ny, mockery, mordancy, satire, scorn, sneering

sarcastic acerbic, acrimonious, backhanded, biting, caustic, con~ temptuous, cutting, cynical, deri~ sive, disparaging, ironical, mock~ ing, mordant, sardonic, sarky (*Brit.*

inf.), satirical, sharp, sneering, taunting

sardonic bitter, cynical, derisive, dry, ironical, jeering, malevolent, malicious, malignant, mocking, mordant, sarcastic, wry

Satan Apollyon, Beelzebub, Lord of the Flies, Lucifer, Mephistopheles, Old Nick, Prince of Darkness, The Devil, The Evil One

satanic accursed, black, demoniac, demoniacal, demonic, devilish, diabolic, evil, fiendish, hellish, infernal, inhuman, iniquitous, malevolent, malignant, wicked

satellite *n.* 1. communications satellite, moon, sputnik 2. *Fig.* attendant, dependant, follower, hanger-on, lackey, minion, parasite, retainer, sidekick (*Sl.*), sycophant, vassal ~*adj.* 3. *Fig.* client, dependent, puppet, subordinate, tributary, vassal

satiate 1. cloy, glut, gorge, jade, nauseate, overfill, stuff 2. sate, satisfy, slake, surfeit

satire burlesque, caricature, irony, lampoon, parody, pasquinade, raillery, ridicule, sarcasm, send-up (*Brit. inf.*), skit, spoof (*Inf.*), takeoff (*Inf.*), travesty, wit

satirical, satiric biting, bitter, burlesque, caustic, censorious, cutting, cynical, incisive, ironical, mocking, mordant, pungent, Rabelaisian, sarcastic, sardonic, taunting

satirize abuse, burlesque, censure, criticize, deride, hold up to ridicule, lampoon, lash, parody, ridicule, send up (*Brit. inf.*), take off (*Inf.*), travesty

satisfaction 1. comfort, complacency, content, contentedness, contentment, ease, enjoyment, gratification, happiness, peace of mind, pleasure, pride, repletion, satiety, well-being 2. achievement, appeasing, assuaging, fulfilment, gratification, resolution, settlement 3. amends, atonement, compensation, damages, indemnification, justice, recompense, redress, reimbursement, remuneration,

reparation, requital, restitution, settlement, vindication

satisfactory acceptable, adequate, all right, average, competent, fair, good enough, passable, sufficient, suitable, up to standard, up to the mark

satisfied at ease, complacent, content, contented, convinced, easy in one's mind, happy, like the cat that swallowed the canary (*Inf.*), pacified, positive, smug, sure

satisfy 1. appease, assuage, content, fill, gratify, indulge, mollify, pacify, please, quench, sate, satiate, slake, surfeit 2. answer, be enough (adequate, sufficient), come up to expectations, do, fill the bill (*Inf.*), fulfil, meet, qualify, serve, serve the purpose, suffice 3. assure, convince, dispel (someone's) doubts, persuade, put (someone's) mind at rest, quiet, reassure 4. answer, comply with, discharge, fulfil, meet, pay (off), settle, square up 5. atone, compensate, indemnify, make good, make reparation for, recompense, remunerate, requite, reward

satisfying cheering, convincing, filling, gratifying, pleasing, pleasurable, satisfactory

saturate douse, drench, drouk (*Scot.*), imbue, impregnate, ret (*used of flax, etc.*), soak, souse, steep, suffuse, waterlog, wet through

saturated drenched, dripping, droukit (*Scot.*), soaked, soaked to the skin, soaking (wet), sodden, sopping (wet), wet through, wringing wet

sauce *n.* backchat (*Inf.*), brass (*Inf.*), cheek (*Inf.*), cheekiness, disrespectfulness, impertinence, impudence, insolence, lip (*Sl.*), nerve (*Inf.*), rudeness

sauciness backchat (*Inf.*), brass (*Inf.*), brazenness, cheek (*Inf.*), flippancy, impertinence, impudence, insolence, lip (*Sl.*), pertness, rudeness, sauce (*Inf.*)

saucy 1. cheeky (*Inf.*), disrespectful, flip (*Inf.*), flippant, forward, fresh (*Inf.*), impertinent, impudent, insolent, pert, presumptuous, rude, smart-alecky (*Inf.*) 2. dashing, gay, jaunty, natty (*Inf.*), perky, rakish, sporty

saunter 1. *v.* amble, dally, linger, loiter, meander, mosey (*Inf.*), ramble, roam, rove, stravaig (*Scot. & Northern English dialect*), stroll, take a stroll, tarry, wander 2. *n.* airing, amble, constitutional, promenade, ramble, stroll, turn, walk

savage *adj.* 1. feral, rough, rugged, uncivilized, uncultivated, undo~ mesticated, untamed, wild 2. bar~ barous, beastly, bestial, blood~ thirsty, bloody, brutal, brutish, cruel, devilish, diabolical, fero~ cious, fierce, harsh, inhuman, merciless, murderous, pitiless, ravening, ruthless, sadistic, vicious 3. in a state of nature, nonliterate, primitive, rude, unspoilt ~n. 4. autochthon, barbarian, heathen, indigene, native, primitive 5. bar~ barian, bear, boor, roughneck (*Sl.*), yahoo, yobbo (*Brit. sl.*) 6. beast, brute, fiend, monster ~v. 7. attack, lacerate, mangle, maul, tear into (*Inf.*)

savagery barbarity, bestiality, bloodthirstiness, brutality, cruelty, ferocity, fierceness, inhumanity, ruthlessness, sadism, viciousness

save 1. bail (someone) out, come to (someone's) rescue, deliver, free, liberate, recover, redeem, rescue, salvage, set free 2. be frugal, be thrifty, collect, economize, gather, hide away, hoard, hold, husband, keep, keep up one's sleeve (*Inf.*), lay by, put aside for a rainy day, put by, reserve, retrench, salt away, set aside, store, tighten one's belt (*Inf.*), treasure up 3. conserve, guard, keep safe, look after, pre~ serve, protect, safeguard, screen, shield, take care of 4. hinder, obvi~ ate, prevent, rule out, spare

saving 1. *adj.* compensatory, ex~ tenuating, qualifying, redeeming 2. *n.* bargain, discount, economy, re~ duction

savings fund, nest egg, provision for a rainy day, reserves, re~ sources, store

saviour defender, deliverer, friend in need, Good Samaritan, guardian, knight in shining armour, libera~ tor, preserver, protector, rescuer, salvation

Saviour Our *or* **The** Christ, Jesus, Messiah, Redeemer

savoir-faire accomplishment, ad~ dress, diplomacy, discretion, fi~ nesse, poise, social graces, social know-how (*Inf.*), tact, urbanity

savour *n.* 1. flavour, piquancy, rel~ ish, smack, smell, tang, taste 2. distinctive quality, excitement, flavour, interest, salt, spice, zest ~v. 3. *Often with* **of** bear the hall~ marks, be indicative, be sugges~ tive, partake, show signs, smack, suggest, verge on 4. appreciate, delight in, enjoy, enjoy to the full, gloat over, like, luxuriate in, par~ take, relish, revel in, smack one's lips over

savoury 1. agreeable, appetizing, dainty, delectable, delicious, full-flavoured, good, luscious, mouth~ watering, palatable, piquant, rich, scrumptious (*Inf.*), spicy, tangy, tasty, toothsome 2. decent, edify~ ing, honest, reputable, respectable, wholesome

saw adage, aphorism, apophthegm, axiom, byword, dictum, gnome, maxim, proverb, saying

saw-toothed crenate (*Bot., Zool.*), dentate, denticulate (*Biol.*), notched, serrate, serrated

say *v.* 1. add, affirm, announce, as~ sert, come out with (*Inf.*), declare, give voice *or* utterance to, main~ tain, mention, pronounce, put into words, remark, speak, state, utter, voice 2. answer, disclose, divulge, give as one's opinion, make known, reply, respond, reveal, tell 3. al~ lege, bruit (*Archaic or U.S.*), claim, noise abroad, put about, report, rumour, suggest 4. deliver, do, orate, perform, read, recite, re~ hearse, render, repeat 5. assume, conjecture, dare say, estimate, guess, hazard a guess, imagine, judge, presume, suppose, surmise

6. communicate, convey, express, give the impression that, imply 7. go without saying be accepted, be a matter of course, be obvious, be self-evident, be taken as read, be taken for granted, be understood 8. to say the least at the very least, to put it mildly, without any exaggeration ~n. 9. crack (*Inf.*), turn (chance, opportunity) to speak, voice, vote 10. authority, clout (*Inf.*), influence, power, sway, weight

saying adage, aphorism, apophthegm, axiom, byword, dictum, gnome, maxim, proverb, saw

scale[1] *n.* 1. calibration, degrees, gamut, gradation, graduated system, graduation, hierarchy, ladder, pecking order (*Inf.*), progression, ranking, register, seniority system, sequence, series, spectrum, spread, steps 2. proportion, ratio 3. degree, extent, range, reach, scope, way ~v. 4. ascend, clamber, climb, escalade, mount, surmount 5. adjust, proportion, prorate (*Chiefly U.S.*), regulate

scale[2] *n.* flake, lamina, layer, plate, squama (*Biol.*)

scaly flaky, furfuraceous (*Medical*), scabrous, scurfy, squamous *or* squamose (*Biol.*), squamulose

scamp devil, imp, knave (*Archaic*), mischief-maker, monkey, prankster, rascal, rogue, scallywag (*Inf.*), scapegrace, tyke (*Inf.*), wretch

scamper dart, dash, fly, hasten, hie (*Archaic*), hurry, romp, run, scoot, scurry, scuttle, sprint

scan check, con (*Archaic*), examine, glance over, investigate, look one up and down, look through, run one's eye over, run over, scour, scrutinize, search, size up (*Inf.*), skim, survey, sweep, take stock of

scandal 1. crime, crying shame (*Inf.*), disgrace, embarrassment, offence, sin, wrongdoing 2. calumny, defamation, detraction, discredit, disgrace, dishonour, ignominy, infamy, obloquy, offence 3. abuse, aspersion, backbiting, dirt, dirty linen (*Inf.*), gossip, rumours,

skeleton in the cupboard, slander, talk, tattle

scandalize affront, appal, cause a few raised eyebrows (*Inf.*), disgust, horrify, offend, outrage, shock

scandalous 1. atrocious, disgraceful, disreputable, highly improper, infamous, monstrous, odious, opprobrious, outrageous, shameful, shocking, unseemly 2. defamatory, gossiping, libellous, scurrilous, slanderous, untrue

scant bare, barely sufficient, deficient, inadequate, insufficient, limited, little, minimal, sparse

scanty bare, deficient, exiguous, inadequate, insufficient, meagre, narrow, poor, restricted, scant, short, skimpy, slender, sparing, sparse, thin

scapegoat fall guy (*Inf.*), whipping boy

scar 1. *n.* blemish, cicatrix, injury, mark, wound 2. *v.* brand, damage, disfigure, mark, traumatize

scarce at a premium, deficient, few, few and far between, infrequent, in short supply, insufficient, rare, seldom met with, uncommon, unusual, wanting

scarcely 1. barely, hardly, only just, scarce (*Archaic*) 2. by no means, definitely not, hardly, not at all, on no account, under no circumstances

scarcity dearth, deficiency, infrequency, insufficiency, lack, paucity, poverty, rareness, shortage, undersupply, want

scare 1. *v.* affright (*Archaic*), alarm, daunt, dismay, frighten, give (someone) a fright, give (someone) a turn (*Inf.*), intimidate, panic, put the wind up (someone) (*Inf.*), shock, startle, terrify, terrorize 2. *n.* alarm, alert, fright, panic, shock, start, terror

scared fearful, frightened, panicky, panic-stricken, petrified, shaken, startled, terrified

scathing belittling, biting, brutal, caustic, critical, cutting, harsh, mordant, sarcastic, scornful, searing, trenchant, withering

scatter 1. broadcast, diffuse, disseminate, fling, litter, shower, sow, spread, sprinkle, strew 2. disband, dispel, disperse, dissipate, disunite, put to flight, separate

scatterbrain bird-brain (*Inf.*), butterfly, featherbrain, flibberti~ gibbet, grasshopper mind, madcap

scattering few, handful, scatter, smatter, smattering, sprinkling

scenario master plan, outline, ré~ sumé, rundown, scheme, sequence of events, sketch, story line, sum~ mary, synopsis

scene 1. display, exhibition, pag~ eant, picture, representation, show, sight, spectacle, tableau 2. area, locality, place, position, set~ ting, site, situation, spot, where~ abouts 3. backdrop, background, location, *mise en scène*, set, setting 4. act, division, episode, incident, part, stage 5. carry-on (*Brit. inf.*), commotion, confrontation, display of emotion, exhibition, fuss, per~ formance, row, tantrum, to-do, up~ set 6. landscape, panorama, pros~ pect, view, vista 7. *Inf.* arena, busi~ ness, environment, field of interest, milieu, world

scenery 1. landscape, surround~ ings, terrain, view, vista 2. *Theatre* backdrop, décor, flats, *mise en scène*, set, setting, stage set

scent *n.* 1. aroma, bouquet, fra~ grance, odour, perfume, redolence, smell 2. spoor, track, trail ~*v.* 3. be on the track *or* trail of, detect, discern, get wind of, nose out, rec~ ognize, sense, smell, sniff, sniff out

scented aromatic, fragrant, per~ fumed, sweet-smelling

sceptic agnostic, cynic, disbeliev~ er, doubter, doubting Thomas, Pyrrhonist, scoffer

sceptical cynical, disbelieving, doubtful, doubting, dubious, hesi~ tating, incredulous, mistrustful, questioning, quizzical, scoffing, un~ believing, unconvinced

scepticism cynicism, disbelief, doubt, incredulity, Pyrrhonism, suspicion

schedule 1. *n.* agenda, calendar, catalogue, inventory, itinerary, list, list of appointments, plan, pro~

gramme, timetable 2. *v.* appoint, arrange, be due, book, organize, plan, programme, time

scheme *n.* 1. contrivance, course of action, design, device, plan, pro~ gramme, project, proposal, strat~ egy, system, tactics, theory 2. ar~ rangement, blueprint, chart, codi~ fication, diagram, disposition, draft, layout, outline, pattern, schedule, schema, system 3. con~ spiracy, dodge, game (*Inf.*), in~ trigue, machinations, manoeuvre, plot, ploy, ruse, shift, stratagem, subterfuge ~*v.* 4. contrive, design, devise, frame, imagine, lay plans, plan, project, work out 5. collude, conspire, intrigue, machinate, ma~ noeuvre, plot, wheel and deal (*Inf.*)

scheming artful, calculating, con~ niving, cunning, deceitful, design~ ing, duplicitous, foxy, Machiavel~ lian, slippery, sly, tricky, under~ hand, wily

schism breach, break, discord, dis~ union, division, rift, rupture, sepa~ ration, splintering, split

scholar 1. academic, bookworm, egghead (*Inf.*), intellectual, man of letters, savant 2. disciple, learner, pupil, schoolboy, schoolgirl, stu~ dent

scholarly academic, bookish, eru~ dite, intellectual, learned, lettered

scholarship 1. accomplishments, attainments, book-learning, edu~ cation, erudition, knowledge, learning, lore 2. bursary, exhibi~ tion, fellowship

scholastic 1. academic, bookish, learned, lettered, literary, scholar~ ly 2. pedagogic, pedantic, precise

school *n.* 1. academy, alma mater, college, department, discipline, faculty, institute, institution, semi~ nary 2. adherents, circle, class, clique, denomination, devotees, disciples, faction, followers, fol~ lowing, group, pupils, sect, set 3. creed, faith, outlook, persuasion, school of thought, stamp, way of life ~*v.* 4. coach, discipline, drill, educate, indoctrinate, instruct, prepare, prime, train, tutor, verse

schooling 1. book-learning, educa~

tion, formal education, teaching, tuition 2. coaching, drill, ground~ ing, guidance, instruction, prepa~ ration, training

schoolteacher dominie (*Scot.*), in~ structor, pedagogue, schoolmarm (*Inf.*), schoolmaster, school~ mistress

science 1. body of knowledge, branch of knowledge, discipline 2. art, skill, technique

scientific accurate, controlled, ex~ act, mathematical, precise, sys~ tematic

scintillate coruscate, flash, give off sparks, gleam, glint, glisten, glitter, sparkle, twinkle

scintillating animated, bright, brilliant, dazzling, ebullient, excit~ ing, glittering, lively, sparkling, stimulating, witty

scoff belittle, deride, despise, flout, gibe, jeer, knock (*Inf.*), laugh at, make light of, make sport of, mock, poke fun at, pooh-pooh, re~ vile, ridicule, scorn, scout (*Archa~ ic*), sneer, taunt, twit

scold 1. *v.* bawl out (*Inf.*), berate, blame, bring (someone) to book, castigate, censure, chide, find fault with, give (someone) a dressing-down (row, talking-to) (*Inf.*), go on at (*Inf.*), haul (someone) over the coals (*Inf.*), have (someone) on the carpet (*Inf.*), lecture, nag, rate, re~ buke, remonstrate with, repri~ mand, reproach, reprove, take (someone) to task, tell off (*Inf.*), tick off (*Inf.*), upbraid, vituperate 2. *n.* nag, shrew, termagant (*Rare*), Xanthippe

scolding dressing-down (*Inf.*), (good) talking-to (*Inf.*), lecture, piece of one's mind (*Inf.*), rebuke, row, telling-off (*Inf.*), ticking-off (*Inf.*), tongue-lashing, wigging (*Brit. sl.*)

scoop *n.* 1. dipper, ladle, spoon 2. exclusive, exposé, inside story, revelation, sensation ~*v.* 3. *Often with up* clear away, gather up, lift, pick up, remove, sweep up *or* away, take up 4. bail, dig, dip, empty, excavate, gouge, hollow, ladle, scrape, shovel

scope area, capacity, compass, confines, elbowroom, extent, field of reference, freedom, latitude, liberty, opportunity, orbit, outlook, purview, range, reach, room, space, span, sphere

scorch blacken, blister, burn, char, parch, roast, sear, shrivel, singe, wither

scorching baking, boiling, broiling, burning, fiery, flaming, red-hot, roasting, searing, sizzling, swelter~ ing, torrid, tropical, unbearably hot

score *n.* 1. grade, mark, outcome, points, record, result, total 2. **the score** *Inf.* the facts, the reality, the setup (*Inf.*), the situation, the truth 3. *Plural* a flock, a great number, an army, a throng, crowds, droves, hosts, hundreds, legions, lots, masses, millions, multitudes, myri~ ads, swarms, very many 4. ac~ count, basis, cause, ground, grounds, reason 5. a bone to pick, grievance, grudge, injury, injustice, wrong 6. **pay off old scores** avenge, get even with (*Inf.*), get one's own back (*Inf.*), give an eye for an eye, give like for like *or* tit for tat, give (someone) a taste of his own medicine, pay (someone) back (in his own coin), repay, re~ quite, retaliate 7. account, amount due, bill, charge, debt, obligation, reckoning, tab (*U.S. inf.*), tally, to~ tal 8. achieve, amass, chalk up (*Inf.*), gain, make, notch up (*Inf.*), win 9. count, keep a tally of, keep count, record, register, tally 10. crosshatch, cut, deface, gouge, graze, indent, mar, mark, nick, notch, scrape, scratch, slash 11. *With out or through* cancel, cross out, delete, obliterate, put a line through, strike out 12. *Music* adapt, arrange, orchestrate, set 13. gain an advantage, go down well with (someone), impress, make a hit (*Inf.*), make an impact *or* impres~ sion, make a point, put oneself across, triumph

score off be one up on (*Inf.*), get the better of, have the laugh on, humiliate, make a fool of, make (someone) look silly, worst

scorn 1. *n.* contempt, contemptu~ousness, contumely, derision, de~spite, disdain, disparagement, mockery, sarcasm, scornfulness, slight, sneer 2. *v.* be above, consid~er beneath one, contemn, curl one's lip at, deride, disdain, flout, hold in contempt, look down on, make fun of, reject, scoff at, scout (*Archaic*), slight, sneer at, spurn, turn up one's nose at (*Inf.*)

scornful contemptuous, contumeli~ous, defiant, derisive, disdainful, haughty, insolent, insulting, jeer~ing, mocking, sarcastic, sardonic, scathing, scoffing, slighting, sneer~ing, supercilious, withering

scornfully contemptuously, dis~dainfully, dismissively, scathingly, slightingly, with a sneer, with con~tempt, with disdain, witheringly, with lip curled

Scots Caledonian, Scottish

scoundrel blackguard, caitiff (*Ar~chaic*), cheat, dastard (*Archaic*), good-for-nothing, heel (*Sl.*), incor~rigible, knave (*Archaic*), miscre~ant, ne'er-do-well, rascal, repro~bate, rogue, rotter (*Sl.*), scamp, scapegrace, vagabond, villain, wretch

scour[1] abrade, buff, burnish, clean, cleanse, flush, furbish, polish, purge, rub, scrub, wash, whiten

scour[2] beat, comb, forage, go over with a fine-tooth comb, hunt, look high and low, rake, ransack, search

scourge *n.* 1. affliction, bane, curse, infliction, misfortune, penalty, pest, plague, punishment, terror, torment, visitation 2. cat, cat-o'-nine-tails, lash, strap, switch, thong, whip ~*v.* 3. beat, belt, cane, castigate, chastise, discipline, flog, horsewhip, lash, lather (*Inf.*), leather, punish, take a strap to, tan (someone's) hide (*Sl.*), thrash, trounce, wallop (*Inf.*), whale, whip 4. afflict, curse, excoriate, harass, plague, terrorize, torment

scout *v.* 1. case (*Sl.*), check out, investigate, make a reconnais~sance, observe, probe, reconnoitre, see how the land lies, spy, spy out,

survey, watch 2. *Often with* out, up, *or* around cast around for, fer~ret out, hunt for, look for, rustle up, search for, search out, seek, track down ~*n.* 3. advance guard, escort, lookout, outrider, precursor, rec~onnoitrer, vanguard 4. recruiter, talent scout

scowl 1. *v.* frown, glower, look daggers at, lower 2. *n.* black look, dirty look, frown, glower

scramble *v.* 1. clamber, climb, crawl, move with difficulty, push, scrabble, struggle, swarm 2. con~tend, hasten, jockey for position, jostle, look lively *or* snappy (*Inf.*), make haste, push, run, rush, strive, vie ~*n.* 3. climb, trek 4. commo~tion, competition, confusion, free-for-all (*Inf.*), hassle (*Inf.*), hustle, melee, muddle, race, rat race, rush, struggle, tussle

scrap[1] *n.* 1. atom, bit, bite, crumb, fragment, grain, iota, mite, modi~cum, morsel, mouthful, part, parti~cle, piece, portion, sliver, snatch, snippet, trace 2. junk, off cuts, waste 3. **on the scrap heap** dis~carded, ditched (*Sl.*), jettisoned, put out to grass (*Inf.*), redundant, writ~ten off 4. *Plural* bits, leavings, left~overs, remains, scrapings ~*v.* 5. abandon, break up, demolish, dis~card, dispense with, ditch (*Sl.*), drop, get rid of, jettison, junk (*Inf.*), shed, throw away *or* out, throw on the scrapheap, toss out, write off

scrap[2] 1. *n.* argument, battle, brawl, disagreement, dispute, dust-up (*Inf.*), fight, quarrel, row, scuf~fle, set-to (*Inf.*), squabble, tiff, wrangle 2. *v.* argue, bicker, come to blows, fall out (*Inf.*), fight, have a shouting match (*Inf.*), have words, row, squabble, wrangle

scrape *v.* 1. abrade, bark, graze, rub, scratch, scuff, skin 2. grate, grind, rasp, scratch, screech, set one's teeth on edge, squeak 3. clean, erase, file, remove, rub, scour 4. pinch, save, scrimp, skimp, stint 5. **scrape by, in, through** barely make it, cut it fine (*Inf.*), get by (*Inf.*), have a close shave (*Inf.*), struggle ~*n.* 6. *Inf.*

awkward *or* embarrassing situation, difficulty, dilemma, distress, fix (*Inf.*), mess, plight, predicament, pretty pickle (*Inf.*), tight spot (*Inf.*), trouble

scrappy bitty, disjointed, fragmentary, incomplete, perfunctory, sketchy, thrown together

scratch v. 1. claw, cut, damage, etch, grate, graze, incise, lacerate, make a mark on, mark, rub, score, scrape 2. annul, cancel, delete, eliminate, erase, pull out, stand down, strike off, withdraw ~n. 3. blemish, claw mark, gash, graze, laceration, mark, scrape 4. **up to scratch** acceptable, adequate, capable, competent, satisfactory, sufficient, up to snuff (*Inf.*), up to standard ~adj. 5. haphazard, hastily prepared, impromptu, improvised, rough, rough-and-ready

scrawl doodle, scrabble, scratch, scribble, squiggle

scream v. 1. bawl, cry, holler (*Inf.*), screech, shriek, shrill, sing out, squeal, yell 2. *Fig.* be conspicuous, clash, jar, shriek ~n. 3. howl, outcry, screech, shriek, wail, yell, yelp 4. *Inf.* card (*Inf.*), caution (*Inf.*), character (*Inf.*), comedian, comic, entertainer, hoot (*Brit. inf.*), joker, laugh, riot (*Sl.*), sensation, wit

screen v. 1. cloak, conceal, cover, hide, mask, shade, shroud, shut out, veil 2. defend, guard, protect, safeguard, shelter, shield 3. cull, evaluate, examine, filter, gauge, grade, process, riddle, scan, sieve, sift, sort, vet 4. broadcast, present, put on, show ~n. 5. awning, canopy, cloak, concealment, cover, guard, hedge, mantle, shade, shelter, shield, shroud 6. mesh, net, partition, room divider

screw v. 1. tighten, turn, twist, work in 2. contort, contract, crumple, distort, pucker, wrinkle 3. *Inf.* bring pressure to bear on, coerce, constrain, force, hold a knife to (someone's) throat, oppress, pressurize, put the screws on (*Inf.*), squeeze 4. *Inf. Often with* out of bleed, extort, extract, wrest, wring

scribble v. dash off, doodle, jot, pen, scratch, scrawl, write

scribe amanuensis, clerk, copyist, notary (*Archaic*), penman (*Rare*), scrivener (*Archaic*), secretary, writer

script 1. calligraphy, hand, handwriting, letters, longhand, penmanship, writing 2. book, copy, dialogue, libretto, lines, manuscript, text, words

Scripture Holy Bible, Holy Scripture, Holy Writ, The Bible, The Book of Books, The Good Book, The Gospels, The Scriptures, The Word, The Word of God

scroll inventory, list, parchment, roll

Scrooge meanie (*Inf.*), miser, money-grubber (*Inf.*), niggard, penny-pincher (*Inf.*), skinflint, tightwad (*U.S. sl.*)

scrounge beg, bum (*Inf., chiefly U.S.*), cadge, forage for, freeload (*U.S. sl.*), hunt around (for), sorn (*Scot.*), sponge (*Inf.*), wheedle

scrounger cadger, freeloader (*U.S. sl.*), parasite, sorner (*Scot.*), sponger (*Inf.*)

scrub v. 1. clean, cleanse, rub, scour 2. *Inf.* abandon, abolish, call off, cancel, delete, discontinue, do away with, drop, forget about, give up

scruffy disreputable, draggletailed (*Archaic*), frowzy, ill-groomed, mangy, messy, ragged, run-down, scrubby (*Brit. inf.*), seedy, shabby, slatternly, slovenly, sluttish, squalid, tattered, ungroomed, unkempt, untidy

scrupulous careful, conscientious, exact, fastidious, honourable, meticulous, minute, moral, nice, painstaking, precise, principled, punctilious, rigorous, strict, upright

scrutinize analyse, dissect, examine, explore, inquire into, inspect, investigate, peruse, pore over, probe, scan, search, sift, study

scrutiny analysis, close study, examination, exploration, inquiry, inspection, investigation, perusal, search, sifting, study

scuffle 1. v. clash, come to blows,

contend, exchange blows, fight, grapple, jostle, struggle, tussle 2. *n.* affray (*Law*), brawl, commotion, disturbance, fight, fray, ruck (*Sl.*), ruckus (*Inf.*), ruction (*Inf.*), rumpus, scrap (*Inf.*), set-to (*Inf.*), tussle

sculpture *v.* carve, chisel, cut, fashion, form, hew, model, mould, sculp, sculpt, shape

scum 1. algae, crust, dross, film, froth, impurities, offscourings, scruff 2. *Fig. canaille*, dregs of society, lowest of the low, rabble, ragtag and bobtail, riffraff, rubbish, trash (*Chiefly U.S.*)

scurrilous abusive, coarse, defamatory, foul, foul-mouthed, gross, indecent, infamous, insulting, low, obscene, offensive, Rabelaisian, ribald, salacious, scabrous, scandalous, slanderous, vituperative, vulgar

scurry 1. *v.* dart, dash, fly, hurry, race, scamper, scoot, scud, scuttle, skim, sprint, whisk 2. *n.* bustle, flurry, scampering, whirl

scuttle bustle, hare (*Brit. inf.*), hasten, hurry, run, rush, scamper, scoot, scramble, scud, scurry, scutter (*Brit. inf.*)

sea *n.* 1. main, ocean, the briny (*Inf.*), the deep, the drink (*Inf.*), the waves 2. *Fig.* abundance, expanse, mass, multitude, plethora, profusion, sheet, vast number 3. **at sea** adrift, astray, at a loss, at sixes and sevens, baffled, bewildered, confused, disoriented, lost, mystified, puzzled, upset ~*adj.* 4. aquatic, briny, marine, maritime, ocean, ocean-going, oceanic, pelagic, salt, saltwater, seagoing

seafaring marine, maritime, nautical, naval, oceanic

seal *v.* 1. close, cork, enclose, fasten, make airtight, plug, secure, shut, stop, stopper, stop up, waterproof 2. assure, attest, authenticate, confirm, establish, ratify, stamp, validate 3. clinch, conclude, consummate, finalize, settle, shake hands on (*Inf.*) 4. *With* off board up, fence off, isolate, put out of bounds, quarantine, segregate ~*n.* 5. assurance, attestation, authenti-

cation, confirmation, imprimatur, insignia, notification, ratification, stamp

seam *n.* 1. closure, joint, suture (*Surgery*) 2. layer, lode, stratum, vein 3. furrow, line, ridge, scar, wrinkle

search *v.* 1. cast around, check, comb, examine, explore, ferret, frisk (*Inf.*), go over with a fine-tooth comb, inquire, inspect, investigate, leave no stone unturned, look, look high and low, probe, pry, ransack, rifle through, rummage through, scour, scrutinize, seek, sift, turn inside out, turn upside down ~*n.* 2. examination, exploration, going-over (*Inf.*), hunt, inquiry, inspection, investigation, pursuit, quest, researches, rummage, scrutiny 3. **in search of** hunting for, in need of, in pursuit of, looking for, making enquiries concerning, on the lookout for, on the track of, seeking

searching *adj.* close, intent, keen, minute, penetrating, piercing, probing, quizzical, severe, sharp, thorough

seasickness *mal de mer*

season *n.* 1. division, interval, juncture, occasion, opportunity, period, spell, term, time, time of year ~*v.* 2. colour, enliven, flavour, lace, leaven, pep up, salt, salt and pepper, spice 3. acclimatize, accustom, anneal, discipline, habituate, harden, inure, mature, prepare, toughen, train 4. mitigate, moderate, qualify, temper

seasonable appropriate, convenient, fit, opportune, providential, suitable, timely, welcome, well-timed

seasoned battle-scarred, experienced, hardened, long-serving, mature, old, practised, time-served, veteran, weathered, well-versed

seasoning condiment, dressing, flavouring, relish, salt and pepper, sauce, spice

seat *n.* 1. bench, chair, pew, settle, stall, stool 2. axis, capital, centre, cradle, headquarters, heart, hub, location, place, site, situation, source, station 3. base, bed, bottom, cause, footing, foundation, ground, groundwork 4. abode, ancestral hall, house, mansion, residence 5. chair, constituency, incumbency, membership, place ~v. 6. accommodate, cater for, contain, have room *or* capacity for, hold, sit, take 7. deposit, fix, install, locate, place, set, settle, sit

seating accommodation, chairs, places, room, seats

secede apostatize, break with, disaffiliate, leave, pull out, quit, resign, retire, separate, split from, withdraw

secluded cloistered, cut off, isolated, lonely, off the beaten track, out-of-the-way, private, reclusive, remote, retired, sequestered, sheltered, solitary, tucked away, unfrequented

seclusion concealment, hiding, isolation, privacy, remoteness, retirement, retreat, shelter, solitude

second¹ adj. 1. following, next, subsequent, succeeding 2. additional, alternative, extra, further, other, repeated 3. inferior, lesser, lower, secondary, subordinate, supporting 4. double, duplicate, reproduction, twin ~n. 5. assistant, backer, helper, supporter ~v. 6. advance, aid, approve, assist, back, encourage, endorse, forward, further, give moral support to, go along with, help, promote, support

second² n. flash, instant, jiffy (*Inf.*), minute, moment, sec (*Inf.*), split second, tick (*Brit. inf.*), trice, twinkling, twinkling of an eye, two shakes of a lamb's tail (*Inf.*)

secondary 1. derivative, derived, indirect, resultant, resulting, second-hand 2. consequential, contingent, inferior, lesser, lower, minor, second-rate, subordinate, unimportant 3. auxiliary, backup, extra, relief, reserve, second, subsidiary, supporting

second class adj. déclassé, indifferent, inferior, mediocre, outclassed, second-best, second-rate, undistinguished, uninspiring

second-hand 1. adj. handed down, hand-me-down (*Inf.*), nearly new, reach-me-down (*Inf.*), used 2. adv. at second-hand, indirectly, on the grapevine (*Inf.*)

second in command depute (*Scot.*), deputy, number two, right-hand man, successor designate

secondly in the second place, next, second

second-rate cheap, cheap and nasty (*Inf.*), commonplace, inferior, low-grade, low-quality, mediocre, poor, rubbishy, shoddy, substandard, tacky (*Inf.*), tawdry

secrecy 1. concealment, confidentiality, huggermugger (*Rare*), mystery, privacy, retirement, seclusion, silence, solitude, surreptitiousness 2. clandestineness, covertness, furtiveness, secretiveness, stealth

secret adj. 1. backstairs, camouflaged, cloak-and-dagger, close, closet (*Inf.*), concealed, conspiratorial, covered, covert, disguised, furtive, hidden, hole-and-corner (*Inf.*), hush-hush (*Inf.*), reticent, shrouded, undercover, underground, under wraps, undisclosed, unknown, unpublished, unrevealed, unseen 2. abstruse, arcane, cabbalistic, clandestine, classified, cryptic, esoteric, mysterious, occult, recondite 3. hidden, out-of-the-way, private, retired, secluded, unfrequented, unknown 4. close, deep, discreet, reticent, secretive, sly, stealthy, underhand ~n. 5. code, confidence, enigma, formula, key, mystery, recipe, skeleton in the cupboard 6. **in secret** behind closed doors, by stealth, huggermugger (*Archaic*), in camera, incognito, secretly, slyly, surreptitiously

secretive cagey (*Inf.*), clamlike, close, cryptic, deep, enigmatic, playing one's cards close to one's chest, reserved, reticent, tight-lipped, uncommunicative, unforthcoming, withdrawn

secretly behind closed doors, behind (someone's) back, clandestinely, confidentially, covertly, furtively, in camera, in confidence, in one's heart, in one's inmost thoughts, in secret, on the q.t. (*Inf.*), on the sly, privately, quietly, stealthily, surreptitiously, unobserved

sect camp, denomination, division, faction, group, party, school, school of thought, splinter group, wing

sectarian 1. *adj.* bigoted, clannish, cliquish, doctrinaire, dogmatic, exclusive, factional, fanatic, fanatical, hidebound, insular, limited, narrow-minded, parochial, partisan, rigid **2.** *n.* adherent, bigot, disciple, dogmatist, extremist, fanatic, partisan, true believer, zealot

section *n.* **1.** component, cross section, division, fraction, fragment, instalment, part, passage, piece, portion, sample, segment, slice, subdivision **2.** *Chiefly U.S.* area, department, district, region, sector, zone

sector area, category, district, division, part, quarter, region, stratum, subdivision, zone

secular civil, earthly, laic, laical, lay, nonspiritual, profane, state, temporal, worldly

secure *adj.* **1.** immune, impregnable, out of harm's way, protected, safe, sheltered, shielded, unassailable, undamaged, unharmed **2.** dependable, fast, fastened, firm, fixed, fortified, immovable, stable, steady, tight **3.** assured, certain, confident, easy, reassured, sure **4.** absolute, conclusive, definite, in the bag (*Inf.*), reliable, solid, steadfast, tried and true, wellfounded ~*v.* **5.** acquire, come by, gain, get, get hold of, land (*Inf.*), make sure of, obtain, pick up, procure, win possession of **6.** attach, batten down, bolt, chain, fasten, fix, lash, lock, lock up, make fast, moor, padlock, rivet, tie up **7.** assure, ensure, guarantee, insure

security 1. asylum, care, cover, custody, immunity, preservation, protection, refuge, retreat, safekeeping, safety, sanctuary **2.** defence, guards, precautions, protection, safeguards, safety measures, surveillance **3.** assurance, certainty, confidence, conviction, ease of mind, freedom from doubt, positiveness, reliance, sureness **4.** collateral, gage, guarantee, hostage, insurance, pawn, pledge, surety

sedate calm, collected, composed, cool, decorous, deliberate, demure, dignified, earnest, grave, imperturbable, middle-aged, placid, proper, quiet, seemly, serene, serious, slow-moving, sober, solemn, staid, tranquil, unflappable (*Inf.*), unruffled

sedative 1. *adj.* allaying, anodyne, calmative, calming, lenitive, relaxing, sleep-inducing, soothing, soporific, tranquillizing **2.** *n.* anodyne, calmative, downer *or* down (*Sl.*), narcotic, opiate, sleeping pill, tranquillizer

sedentary desk, desk-bound, inactive, motionless, seated, sitting, torpid

sediment deposit, dregs, grounds, lees, precipitate, residuum, settlings

sedition agitation, disloyalty, incitement to riot, rabble-rousing, subversion, treason

seditious disloyal, dissident, insubordinate, mutinous, rebellious, refractory, revolutionary, subversive, treasonable

seduce 1. betray, corrupt, debauch, deflower, deprave, dishonour, ruin (*Archaic*) **2.** allure, attract, beguile, deceive, decoy, ensnare, entice, inveigle, lead astray, lure, mislead, tempt

seduction 1. corruption, defloration, ruin (*Archaic*) **2.** allure, enticement, lure, snare, temptation

seductive alluring, attractive, beguiling, bewitching, captivating, come-hither (*Inf.*), enticing, flirtatious, inviting, irresistible, provocative, ravishing, sexy (*Inf.*), siren, specious, tempting

seductress Circe, enchantress, *femme fatale*, Lorelei, siren, temptress, vamp (*Inf.*)

see *v.* **1.** behold, catch a glimpse of, catch sight of, descry, discern, distinguish, espy, get a load of (*Sl.*), glimpse, heed, identify, lay *or* clap eyes on (*Inf.*), look, make out, mark, note, notice, observe, perceive, recognize, regard, sight, spot, view, witness **2.** appreciate, catch on (*Inf.*), comprehend, fathom, feel, follow, get, get the drift of, get the hang of (*Inf.*), grasp, know, make out, realize, take in, understand **3.** ascertain, determine, discover, find out, investigate, learn, make enquiries, refer to **4.** ensure, guarantee, make certain, make sure, mind, see to it, take care **5.** consider, decide, deliberate, give some thought to, judge, make up one's mind, mull over, reflect, think over **6.** confer with, consult, encounter, interview, meet, receive, run into, speak to, visit **7.** accompany, attend, escort, lead, show, usher, walk **8.** consort *or* associate with, court, date (*Inf.*, chiefly U.S.*), go out with, go steady with (*Inf.*), keep company with, walk out with (*Obsolete*) **9.** anticipate, divine, envisage, foresee, foretell, imagine, picture, visualize

see about 1. attend to, consider, deal with, give some thought to, look after, see to, take care of **2.** investigate, look into, make enquiries

seed 1. egg, egg cell, embryo, germ, grain, kernel, ovule, ovum, spore **2.** beginning, germ, inkling, nucleus, source, start, suspicion **3.** *Fig.* children, descendants, heirs, issue, offspring, progeny, race, scions, spawn, successors **4. go** *or* **run to seed** decay, decline, degenerate, deteriorate, go downhill (*Inf.*), go to pieces, go to pot, go to rack and ruin, go to waste, let oneself go

seedy 1. crummy (*Sl.*), decaying, dilapidated, down at heel, faded, grubby, mangy, manky (*Scot. dialect*), old, run-down, scruffy (*Brit. inf.*), shabby, sleazy, slovenly, squalid, tatty, unkempt, worn **2.** *Inf.* ailing, ill, off colour, out of sorts, poorly (*Inf.*), sickly, under the weather (*Inf.*), unwell

seeing *conj.* as, inasmuch as, in view of the fact that, since

seek 1. be after, follow, go gunning for, go in pursuit (quest, search) of, hunt, inquire, look for, pursue, search for **2.** aim, aspire to, attempt, endeavour, essay, have a go (*Inf.*), strive, try **3.** ask, beg, entreat, inquire, invite, petition, request, solicit

seem appear, assume, give the impression, have the *or* every appearance of, look, look as if, look to be, pretend, sound like, strike one as being

seemly appropriate, becoming, befitting, *comme il faut*, decent, decorous, fit, fitting, in good taste, meet (*Archaic*), nice, proper, suitable, suited, the done thing

see over inspect, look round, see round, tour

seer augur, predictor, prophet, sibyl, soothsayer

seesaw *v.* alternate, fluctuate, go from one extreme to the other, oscillate, pitch, swing, teeter

seethe 1. boil, bubble, churn, ferment, fizz, foam, froth **2.** be in a state (*Inf.*), be livid (furious, incensed), breathe fire and slaughter, foam at the mouth, fume, get hot under the collar (*Inf.*), rage, simmer, storm **3.** be alive with, swarm, teem

see through 1. be undeceived by, be wise to, fathom, get to the bottom of, have (someone's) number (*Inf.*), not fall for, penetrate **2. see (something** *or* **someone) through** help out, keep at, persevere (with), persist, see out, stay to the bitter end, stick by, stick out (*Inf.*), support

see to arrange, attend to, be responsible for, do, look after, manage, organize, sort out, take care of, take charge of

segment bit, compartment, division, part, piece, portion, section, slice, wedge

segregate discriminate against, dissociate, isolate, separate, set apart, single out

segregation apartheid (*in South Africa*), discrimination, isolation, separation

seize 1. clutch, collar (*Inf.*), fasten, grab, grasp, grip, lay hands on, snatch, take 2. apprehend, catch, get, grasp 3. abduct, annex, appropriate, arrest, capture, commandeer, confiscate, hijack, impound, take by storm, take captive, take possession of

seizure 1. abduction, annexation, apprehension, arrest, capture, commandeering, confiscation, grabbing, taking 2. attack, convulsion, fit, paroxysm, spasm

seldom hardly ever, infrequently, not often, occasionally, once in a blue moon (*Inf.*), rarely, scarcely ever

select *v.* 1. choose, opt for, pick, prefer, single out, sort out ~*adj.* 2. choice, excellent, first-class, first-rate, hand-picked, picked, posh (*Inf.*), preferable, prime, rare, recherché, selected, special, superior, topnotch (*Inf.*) 3. cliquish, elite, exclusive, limited, privileged

selection 1. choice, choosing, option, pick, preference 2. anthology, assortment, choice, collection, line-up, medley, miscellany, potpourri, range, variety

selective careful, discerning, discriminating, discriminatory, eclectic, particular

self-assurance assertiveness, confidence, positiveness, self-confidence

self-centred egotistic, inward looking, narcissistic, self-absorbed, selfish, self-seeking, wrapped up in oneself

self-confidence aplomb, confidence, high morale, nerve, poise, self-assurance, self-reliance, self-respect

self-confident assured, fearless, poised, secure, self-assured, self-reliant, sure of oneself

self-conscious affected, awkward, bashful, diffident, embarrassed, ill at ease, insecure, nervous, out of countenance, shamefaced, sheepish, uncomfortable

self-control restraint, self-discipline, self-mastery, self-restraint, strength of mind *or* will, willpower

self-esteem amour-propre, confidence, faith in oneself, pride, self-assurance, self-regard, self-respect, vanity

self-evident axiomatic, clear, incontrovertible, inescapable, manifestly *or* patently true, obvious, undeniable, written all over (something)

self-government autonomy, home rule, independence, self-determination, self-rule, sovereignty

self-important arrogant, conceited, overbearing, pompous, presumptuous, pushy (*Inf.*), strutting, swaggering, swollen-headed

self-indulgence dissipation, excess, extravagance, incontinence, intemperance, self-gratification, sensualism

selfish egoistic, egoistical, egotistic, egotistical, greedy, looking out for number one (*Inf.*), mean, mercenary, narrow, self-centred, self-interested, self-seeking, ungenerous

selfless altruistic, generous, magnanimous, self-denying, self-sacrificing, ungrudging, unselfish

self-possessed collected, confident, cool, cool as a cucumber (*Inf.*), poised, self-assured, sure of oneself, together (*Sl.*), unruffled

self-reliant able to stand on one's own two feet (*Inf.*), capable, independent, self-sufficient

self-respect amour-propre, dignity, faith in oneself, morale, one's own image, pride, self-esteem

self-righteous complacent, goody-goody (*Inf.*), holier-than-thou, hypocritical, pharisaic, pi (*Brit. sl.*), pietistic, pious, priggish, sanctimonious, self-satisfied, smug, superior, too good to be true

self-sacrifice altruism, generosity, self-abnegation, self-denial, selflessness

self-satisfaction complacency, contentment, ease of mind, flush of success, glow of achievement, pride, self-approbation, self-approval, smugness

self-satisfied complacent, flushed with success, like a cat that has swallowed the cream *or* the canary, pleased with oneself, proud of oneself, puffed up, self-congratulatory, smug, well-pleased

self-seeking *adj.* acquisitive, calculating, careerist, fortune-hunting, gold-digging, looking out for number one (*Inf.*), mercenary, on the make (*Sl.*), opportunistic, out for what one can get, self-interested, selfish, self-serving

sell 1. barter, dispose of, exchange, put up for sale, trade 2. be in the business of, deal in, handle, hawk, market, merchandise, peddle, retail, stock, trade in, traffic in, vend 3. gain acceptance for, promote, put across 4. *Inf. With* **on** convert to, convince of, get (someone) hooked on (*Inf.*), persuade of, talk (someone) into, win (someone) over to 5. betray, deliver up, give up, sell down the river (*Inf.*), sell out (*Inf.*), surrender

seller agent, dealer, merchant, rep, representative, retailer, salesman, saleswoman, shopkeeper, tradesman, traveller, vendor

selling 1. business, commercial transactions, dealing, trading, traffic 2. marketing, merchandising, promotion, salesmanship

sell out 1. be out of stock of, dispose of, get rid of, run out of, sell up 2. *Inf.* betray, break faith with, double-cross (*Inf.*), fail, give away, play false, rat on, sell down the river (*Inf.*), stab in the back

send 1. communicate, consign, convey, direct, dispatch, forward, remit, transmit 2. cast, deliver, fire, fling, hurl, let fly, propel, shoot 3. *With* **off, out,** *etc.* broadcast, discharge, emit, exude, give off, radiate 4. *Sl.* charm, delight, electrify, enrapture, enthrall, excite, intoxicate, move, please, ravish, stir, thrill, titillate, turn (someone) on (*Sl.*) 5. **send (someone) packing** discharge, dismiss, give (someone) the bird (*Inf.*), give (someone) the

brushoff (*Sl.*), send away, send (someone) about his *or* her business, send (someone) away with a flea in his *or* her ear (*Inf.*)

send for call for, order, request, summon

sendoff departure, farewell, going-away party, leave-taking, start, valediction

senile decrepit, doddering, doting, failing, imbecile, in one's dotage, in one's second childhood

senior *adj.* elder, higher ranking, major (*Brit.*), older, superior

seniority eldership, longer service, precedence, priority, rank, superiority

sensation 1. awareness, consciousness, feeling, impression, perception, sense, tingle 2. agitation, commotion, crowd puller (*Inf.*), excitement, furore, hit (*Inf.*), scandal, stir, surprise, thrill, wow (*Sl., chiefly U.S.*)

sensational 1. amazing, astounding, breathtaking, dramatic, electrifying, exciting, hair-raising, horrifying, lurid, melodramatic, revealing, scandalous, sensationalistic, shocking, spectacular, staggering, startling, thrilling, yellow (*of the press*) 2. *Inf.* excellent, exceptional, fabulous (*Inf.*), first class, impressive, marvellous, mind-blowing (*Inf.*), out of this world (*Inf.*), smashing (*Inf.*), superb

sense *n.* 1. faculty, feeling, sensation, sensibility 2. appreciation, atmosphere, aura, awareness, consciousness, feel, impression, intuition, perception, premonition, presentiment, sentiment 3. definition, denotation, drift, gist, implication, import, interpretation, meaning, message, nuance, purport, significance, signification, substance 4. *Sometimes plural* brains (*Inf.*), clear-headedness, cleverness, common sense, discernment, discrimination, gumption (*Brit. inf.*), intelligence, judgment, mother wit, nous (*Brit. sl.*), quickness, reason, sagacity, sanity, sharpness, tact, understanding, wisdom, wit(s) 5.

advantage, good, logic, point, pur~pose, reason, use, value, worth ~v. 6. appreciate, apprehend, be aware of, discern, divine, feel, get the impression, grasp, have a feel~ing in one's bones (*Inf.*), have a funny feeling (*Inf.*), have a hunch, just know, notice, observe, per~ceive, pick up, realize, suspect, understand

senseless 1. absurd, asinine, crazy, daft (*Inf.*), fatuous, foolish, half~witted, idiotic, illogical, imbecilic, inane, incongruous, inconsistent, irrational, ludicrous, mad, mean~ingless, mindless, moronic, non~sensical, pointless, ridiculous, silly, simple, stupid, unintelligent, un~reasonable, unwise 2. anaesthe~tized, cold, deadened, insensate, insensible, numb, numbed, out, out cold, stunned, unconscious, unfeel~ing

sensibility 1. responsiveness, sen~sitiveness, sensitivity, susceptibil~ity 2. *Often plural* emotions, feel~ings, moral sense, sentiments, sus~ceptibilities 3. appreciation, awareness, delicacy, discernment, insight, intuition, perceptiveness, taste

sensible 1. canny, discreet, dis~criminating, down-to-earth, far~sighted, intelligent, judicious, matter-of-fact, practical, prudent, rational, realistic, reasonable, sa~gacious, sage, sane, shrewd, sober, sound, well-reasoned, well-thought-out, wise 2. *Usually with of* ac~quainted with, alive to, aware, conscious, convinced, mindful, ob~servant, sensitive to, understand~ing 3. appreciable, considerable, discernable, noticeable, palpable, perceptible, significant, tangible, visible

sensitive 1. acute, delicate, easily affected, fine, impressionable, keen, perceptive, precise, reactive, responsive, sentient, susceptible 2. delicate, easily upset (hurt, offend~ed), irritable, temperamental, ten~der, thin-skinned, touchy, umbra~geous (*Rare*)

sensitivity delicacy, reactiveness, reactivity, receptiveness, respon~siveness, sensitiveness, suscep~tibility

sensual 1. animal, bodily, carnal, epicurean, fleshly, luxurious, physical, unspiritual, voluptuous 2. erotic, lascivious, lecherous, lewd, libidinous, licentious, lustful, randy (*Sl.*), raunchy (*U.S. sl.*), sexual, sexy (*Inf.*), unchaste

sensuality animalism, carnality, eroticism, lasciviousness, lecher~ousness, lewdness, libidinousness, licentiousness, prurience, sala~ciousness, sexiness (*Inf.*), voluptu~ousness

sensuous epicurean, gratifying, hedonistic, lush, pleasurable, rich, sensory, sumptuous, sybaritic

sentence 1. *n.* condemnation, de~cision, decree, doom, judgment, order, pronouncement, ruling, verdict 2. *v.* condemn, doom, mete out justice to, pass judgment on, penalize

sententious 1. aphoristic, axio~matic, brief, compact, concise, epigrammatic, gnomic, laconic, pithy, pointed, short, succinct, terse 2. canting, judgmental, mor~alistic, pompous, ponderous, preachifying (*Inf.*), sanctimonious

sentiment 1. emotion, sensibility, soft-heartedness, tender feeling, tenderness 2. *Often plural* attitude, belief, feeling, idea, judgment, opinion, persuasion, saying, thought, view, way of thinking 3. emotionalism, mawkishness, over~emotionalism, romanticism, senti~mentality, slush (*Inf.*)

sentimental corny (*Sl.*), dewy-eyed, drippy (*Inf.*), emotional, gushy (*Inf.*), impressionable, maudlin, mawkish, mushy (*Inf.*), nostalgic, overemotional, pathetic, romantic, schmaltzy (*Sl.*), simper~ing, sloppy (*Inf.*), slushy (*Inf.*), soft-hearted, tearful, tear-jerking (*Inf.*), tender, touching, weepy (*Inf.*)

sentimentality bathos, corniness (*Sl.*), emotionalism, gush (*Inf.*), mawkishness, mush (*Inf.*), nostal~gia, play on the emotions, roman~ticism, schmaltz (*Sl.*), sloppiness

(*Inf.*), slush (*Inf.*), sob stuff (*Inf.*), tenderness

separable detachable, distinguishable, divisible, scissile, severable

separate *v.* 1. break off, cleave, come apart, come away, come between, detach, disconnect, disentangle, disjoin, divide, keep apart, remove, sever, split, sunder, uncouple 2. discriminate between, isolate, put on one side, segregate, single out, sort out 3. bifurcate, break up, disunite, diverge, divorce, estrange, go different ways, part, part company, set at variance *or* at odds, split up ~*adj.* 4. detached, disconnected, discrete, disjointed, divided, divorced, isolated, unattached, unconnected 5. alone, apart, autonomous, distinct, independent, individual, particular, single, solitary

separated apart, broken up, disassociated, disconnected, disunited, divided, living apart, parted, put asunder, separate, split up, sundered

separately alone, apart, independently, individually, one at a time, one by one, personally, severally, singly

separation 1. break, detachment, disconnection, disengagement, disjunction, dissociation, disunion, division, gap, segregation, severance 2. break-up, divorce, estrangement, farewell, leave-taking, parting, rift, split, split-up

septic festering, infected, poisoned, pussy, putrefactive, putrefying, putrid, toxic

sepulchre burial place, grave, tomb, vault

sequel conclusion, consequence, continuation, development, end, follow-up, issue, outcome, payoff (*Inf.*), result, upshot

sequence arrangement, chain, course, cycle, order, procession, progression, series, succession

sequestered cloistered, isolated, lonely, out-of-the-way, private, quiet, remote, retired, secluded, unfrequented

seraphic angelic, beatific, blissful, celestial, divine, heavenly, holy, pure, sublime

serene 1. calm, composed, imperturbable, peaceful, placid, tranquil, undisturbed, unruffled, untroubled 2. bright, clear, cloudless, fair, halcyon, unclouded

serenity 1. calm, calmness, composure, peace, peacefulness, peace of mind, placidity, quietness, quietude, stillness, tranquillity 2. brightness, clearness, fairness

series arrangement, chain, course, line, order, progression, run, sequence, set, string, succession, train

serious 1. grave, humourless, long-faced, pensive, sedate, sober, solemn, stern, thoughtful, unsmiling 2. deliberate, determined, earnest, genuine, honest, in earnest, resolute, resolved, sincere 3. crucial, deep, difficult, far-reaching, fateful, grim, important, momentous, no laughing matter, of moment *or* consequence, pressing, significant, urgent, weighty, worrying 4. acute, alarming, critical, dangerous, grave, severe

seriously 1. all joking aside, earnestly, gravely, in all conscience, in earnest, no joking (*Inf.*), sincerely, solemnly, thoughtfully, with a straight face 2. acutely, badly, critically, dangerously, distressingly, gravely, grievously, severely, sorely

seriousness 1. earnestness, gravity, humourlessness, sedateness, sobriety, solemnity, staidness, sternness 2. danger, gravity, importance, moment, significance, urgency, weight

sermon 1. address, exhortation, homily 2. dressing-down (*Inf.*), harangue, lecture, talking-to (*Inf.*)

servant attendant, domestic, drudge, help, helper, lackey, maid, menial, retainer, servitor (*Archaic*), slave, vassal

serve 1. aid, assist, attend to, be in the service of, be of assistance, be of use, help, minister to, oblige, succour, wait on, work for 2. act, attend, complete, discharge, do, fulfil, go through, observe, offici~ ate, pass, perform 3. answer, an~ swer the purpose, be acceptable, be adequate, be good enough, con~ tent, do, do duty as, do the work of, fill the bill (*Inf.*), function as, satis~ fy, suffice, suit 4. arrange, deal, deliver, dish up, distribute, handle, present, provide, set out, supply

service *n.* 1. advantage, assistance, avail, benefit, help, ministrations, supply, use, usefulness, utility 2. check, maintenance, overhaul, servicing 3. business, duty, employ, employment, labour, office, work 4. ceremony, function, observance, rite, worship ~*v.* 5. check, fine tune, go over, maintain, overhaul, recondition, repair, tune (up)

serviceable advantageous, benefi~ cial, convenient, dependable, du~ rable, efficient, functional, hard~ wearing, helpful, operative, prac~ tical, profitable, usable, useful, utilitarian

session assembly, conference, dis~ cussion, get-together (*Inf.*), hear~ ing, meeting, period, sitting, term

set[1] *v.* 1. aim, apply, deposit, direct, embed, fasten, fix, install, lay, lo~ cate, lodge, mount, park, place, plant, plonk, plump, position, put, rest, seat, situate, station, stick, turn 2. agree upon, allocate, ap~ point, arrange, assign, conclude, decide (upon), designate, deter~ mine, establish, fix, fix up, name, ordain, regulate, resolve, schedule, settle, specify 3. arrange, lay, make ready, prepare, spread 4. adjust, coordinate, rectify, regu~ late, synchronize 5. cake, con~ dense, congeal, crystallize, gelati~ nize, harden, jell, solidify, stiffen, thicken 6. allot, decree, impose, lay down, ordain, prescribe, specify 7. decline, dip, disappear, go down, sink, subside, vanish ~*n.* 8. atti~ tude, bearing, carriage, fit, hang, position, posture, turn 9. *mise-en-scène*, scene, scenery, setting, stage set, stage setting ~*adj.* 10. agreed, appointed, arranged, cus~ tomary, decided, definite, estab~ lished, firm, fixed, prearranged, predetermined, prescribed, regu~

lar, scheduled, settled, usual 11. artificial, conventional, formal, hackneyed, rehearsed, routine, standard, stereotyped, stock, tra~ ditional, unspontaneous 12. en~ trenched, firm, hard and fast, hardened, hidebound, immovable, inflexible, rigid, strict, stubborn 13. *With* on *or* upon bent, determined, intent, resolute

set[2] *n.* 1. band, circle, class, clique, company, coterie, crew (*Inf.*), crowd, faction, gang, group, outfit (*Inf.*), sect 2. assemblage, assort~ ment, batch, collection, compen~ dium, coordinated group, kit, outfit, series

set about 1. address oneself to, attack, begin, get cracking (*Inf.*), get down to (*Inf.*), get to work, get weaving (*Inf.*), make a start on, put one's shoulder to the wheel (*Inf.*), roll up one's sleeves, sail into (*Inf.*), set to, start, tackle, take the first step, wade into 2. assail, assault, attack, belabour, lambaste, sail into (*Inf.*)

set aside 1. keep, keep back, put on one side, reserve, save, select, separate, set apart, single out 2. abrogate, annul, cancel, discard, dismiss, nullify, overrule, overturn, quash, reject, render null and void, repudiate, reverse

setback bit of trouble, blow, check, defeat, disappointment, hitch, hold~ up, misfortune, rebuff, reverse, upset

set off 1. depart, embark, leave, sally forth, set out, start out 2. detonate, explode, ignite, light, set in motion, touch off 3. bring out the highlights in, enhance, show off, throw into relief

set on assail, assault, attack, fall upon, fly at, go for, incite, instigate, let fly at, pitch into, pounce on, sail into (*Inf.*), set about, sic, spur on, urge

set out 1. arrange, array, describe, detail, display, dispose, elaborate, elucidate, exhibit, explain, expose to view, lay out, present, set forth 2. begin, embark, get under way, hit the road (Sl.), sally forth, set off, start out, take to the road

setting backdrop, background, context, frame, locale, location, mise en scène, mounting, perspective, scene, scenery, set, site, surround, surroundings

settle 1. adjust, dispose, order, put into order, regulate, set to rights, straighten out, work out 2. choose, clear up, complete, conclude, decide, dispose of, put an end to, reconcile, resolve 3. Often with **on** or **upon** agree, appoint, arrange, choose, come to an agreement, confirm, decide, determine, establish, fix 4. calm, compose, lull, pacify, quell, quiet, quieten, reassure, relax, relieve, sedate, soothe, tranquillize 5. alight, bed down, come to rest, descend, land, light, make oneself comfortable 6. dwell, inhabit, live, make one's home, move to, put down roots, reside, set up home, take up residence 7. colonize, found, people, pioneer, plant, populate 8. acquit oneself of, clear, discharge, liquidate, pay, quit, square (up) 9. decline, fall, sink, subside

settlement 1. adjustment, agreement, arrangement, completion, conclusion, confirmation, disposition, establishment, resolution, termination, working out 2. clearance, clearing, defrayal, discharge, liquidation, payment, satisfaction 3. colonization, colony, community, encampment, hamlet, outpost, peopling

settler colonist, colonizer, frontiersman, immigrant, pioneer, planter

set-to argument, argy-bargy (Brit. inf.), barney (Inf.), brush, disagreement, dust-up (Inf.), fight, quarrel, row, scrap (Inf.), slanging match (Brit.), spat, squabble, wrangle

setup arrangement, circumstances, conditions, organization, regime, structure, system

set up 1. arrange, begin, compose, establish, found, initiate, install, institute, make provision for, organize, prearrange, prepare 2. back, build up, establish, finance, promote, put some beef into (Inf.), strengthen, subsidize 3. assemble, build, construct, elevate, erect, put together, put up, raise

set upon ambush, assail, assault, attack, beat up, fall upon, go for, lay into, mug (Inf.), set about, turn on

several adj. assorted, different, disparate, distinct, divers (Archaic), diverse, indefinite, individual, many, particular, respective, single, some, sundry, various

severe 1. austere, cruel, Draconian, hard, harsh, inexorable, iron-handed, oppressive, pitiless, relentless, rigid, strict, unbending, unrelenting 2. cold, disapproving, dour, flinty, forbidding, grave, grim, serious, sober, stern, strait-laced, tight-lipped, unsmiling 3. acute, bitter, critical, dangerous, distressing, extreme, fierce, grinding, inclement, intense, violent 4. ascetic, austere, chaste, classic, forbidding, functional, plain, restrained, simple, Spartan, unadorned, unembellished, unfussy 5. arduous, demanding, difficult, exacting, fierce, hard, punishing, rigorous, stringent, taxing, tough, unrelenting 6. astringent, biting, caustic, cutting, harsh, satirical, scathing, unsparing

severely 1. harshly, rigorously, sharply, sternly, strictly, with an iron hand, with a rod of iron 2. acutely, badly, critically, dangerously, extremely, gravely, hard, sorely

severity austerity, gravity, hardness, harshness, plainness, rigour, seriousness, severeness, sternness, strictness, stringency, toughness

sex 1. gender 2. Inf. coition, coitus, copulation, fornication, going to bed (with someone), intimacy, lovemaking, (sexual) intercourse, sexual relations 3. desire, facts of life, libido, reproduction, sexuality, the birds and the bees (Inf.)

sexual 1. carnal, erotic, intimate, of the flesh, sensual, 2. genital, pro-

creative, reproductive, sex, ve~
nereal

sexual intercourse carnal knowl~
edge, coition, coitus, commerce
(*Archaic*), congress, copulation,
coupling, mating, union

sexuality bodily appetites, carnal~
ity, desire, eroticism, lust, sensual~
ity, sexiness (*Inf.*), voluptuousness

sexy arousing, beddable, bedroom,
come-hither (*Inf.*), cuddly, erotic,
flirtatious, inviting, kissable,
naughty, provocative, provoking,
seductive, sensual, sensuous,
slinky, suggestive, titillating, vo~
luptuous

shabby 1. dilapidated, down at
heel, faded, frayed, having seen
better days, mean, neglected, poor,
ragged, run-down, scruffy, seedy,
tattered, tatty, the worse for wear,
threadbare, worn, worn-out 2.
cheap, contemptible, despicable,
dirty, dishonourable, ignoble, low,
low-down (*Inf.*), mean, rotten
(*Inf.*), scurvy, shameful, shoddy,
ungentlemanly, unworthy

shade *n.* 1. coolness, dimness, dusk,
gloom, gloominess, obscurity,
screen, semidarkness, shadiness,
shadow, shadows 2. **put into the
shade** eclipse, make pale by com~
parison, outclass, outshine, over~
shadow 3. blind, canopy, cover,
covering, curtain, screen, shield,
veil 4. colour, hue, stain, tinge, tint,
tone 5. amount, dash, degree, dif~
ference, gradation, hint, nuance,
semblance, suggestion, suspicion,
trace, variety 6. apparition, ghost,
manes, phantom, shadow, spectre,
spirit ~*v.* 7. cast a shadow over,
cloud, conceal, cover, darken, dim,
hide, mute, obscure, protect,
screen, shadow, shield, shut out the
light, veil

shadow *n.* 1. cover, darkness, dim~
ness, dusk, gathering darkness,
gloaming, gloom, obscurity, pro~
tection, shade, shelter 2. hint, sug~
gestion, suspicion, trace 3. ghost,
image, phantom, remnant, repre~
sentation, spectre, vestige 4. blight,
cloud, gloom, sadness ~*v.* 5. cast a
shadow over, darken, overhang,

screen, shade, shield 6. dog, follow,
spy on, stalk, tail (*Inf.*), trail

shadowy 1. crepuscular, dark, dim,
dusky, gloomy, indistinct, murky,
obscure, shaded, shady, tenebrious,
tenebrous 2. dim, dreamlike, faint,
ghostly, illusory, imaginary, im~
palpable, intangible, nebulous, ob~
scure, phantom, spectral, unde~
fined, unreal, unsubstantial, vague,
wraithlike

shady 1. bosky (*Literary*), bowery,
cool, dim, leafy, shaded, shadowy,
umbrageous 2. *Inf.* crooked, dis~
reputable, dubious, fishy (*Inf.*),
questionable, shifty, slippery, sus~
pect, suspicious, unethical, unscru~
pulous, untrustworthy

shaft 1. handle, pole, rod, shank,
stem, upright 2. beam, gleam, ray,
streak 3. barb, cut, dart, gibe, sting,
thrust

shaggy hairy, hirsute, long-haired,
rough, unkempt, unshorn

shake *v.* 1. bump, fluctuate, jar,
joggle, jolt, jounce, oscillate, quake,
quiver, rock, shiver, shudder, sway,
totter, tremble, vibrate, waver,
wobble 2. brandish, flourish, wave
3. *Often with* **up** agitate, churn,
convulse, rouse, stir 4. discompose,
distress, disturb, frighten, intimi~
date, move, rattle (*Inf.*), shock, un~
nerve, upset 5. impair, pull the rug
out from under (*Inf.*), undermine,
weaken ~*n.* 6. agitation, convul~
sion, disturbance, jar, jerk, jolt,
jounce, pulsation, quaking, shiver,
shock, shudder, trembling, tremor,
vibration 7. *Inf.* instant, jiffy (*Inf.*),
moment, second, tick (*Brit. inf.*),
trice

shake off dislodge, elude, get away
from, get rid of, get shot of (*Sl.*),
give the slip, leave behind, lose, rid
oneself of, throw off

shake up agitate, churn (up), dis~
turb, mix, overturn, reorganize,
shock, stir (up), turn upside down,
unsettle, upset

shaky 1. all of a quiver (*Inf.*), fal~
tering, insecure, precarious, quiv~
ery, rickety, tottering, trembling,
tremulous, unstable, unsteady,
weak, wobbly 2. dubious, question~

able, suspect, uncertain, unde~
pendable, unreliable, unsound, un~
supported

shallow 1. *adj. Fig.* empty, flimsy,
foolish, frivolous, idle, ignorant,
meaningless, puerile, simple, skin-
deep, slight, superficial, surface,
trivial, unintelligent 2. *n. Often
plural* bank, flat, sandbank, sand
bar, shelf, shoal

sham 1. *n.* counterfeit, feint, for~
gery, fraud, hoax, humbug, imitation, impostor, imposture, phoney
(*Sl.*), pretence, pretender, pseud
(*Sl.*), wolf in sheep's clothing 2. *adj.*
artificial, bogus, counterfeit, er~
satz, false, feigned, imitation,
mock, phoney (*Sl.*), pretended,
pseud (*Sl.*), pseudo (*Inf.*), simulat~
ed, spurious, synthetic 3. *v.* affect,
assume, counterfeit, fake, feign,
imitate, play possum, pretend, put
on, simulate

shame *n.* 1. blot, contempt, degra~
dation, derision, disgrace, dishon~
our, disrepute, ill repute, infamy,
obloquy, odium, opprobrium, re~
proach, scandal, skeleton in the
cupboard, smear 2. abashment,
chagrin, compunction, embarrass~
ment, humiliation, ignominy, loss
of face, mortification, shamefac~
edness 3. **put to shame** disgrace,
eclipse, outclass, outdo, outstrip,
show up, surpass ~*v.* 4. abash,
confound, disconcert, disgrace,
embarrass, humble, humiliate,
mortify, reproach, ridicule, take
(someone) down a peg (*Inf.*) 5.
blot, debase, defile, degrade, dis~
credit, dishonour, smear, stain

shameful 1. atrocious, base, das~
tardly, degrading, disgraceful, dis~
honourable, ignominious, indecent,
infamous, low, mean, outrageous,
reprehensible, scandalous, unbe~
coming, unworthy, vile, wicked 2.
blush-making (*Inf.*), degrading,
embarrassing, humiliating, morti~
fying, shaming

shameless abandoned, audacious,
barefaced, brash, brazen, corrupt,
depraved, dissolute, flagrant,
hardened, immodest, improper,
impudent, incorrigible, indecent,
insolent, profligate, reprobate, un~
abashed, unashamed, unblushing,
unprincipled, wanton

shape *n.* 1. build, configuration,
contours, cut, figure, form, lines,
make, outline, profile, silhouette 2.
frame, model, mould, pattern 3.
appearance, aspect, form, guise,
likeness, semblance 4. condition,
fettle, health, kilter, state, trim ~*v.*
5. create, fashion, form, make,
model, mould, produce 6. accom~
modate, adapt, define, develop,
devise, frame, guide, modify, plan,
prepare, regulate, remodel

shapeless amorphous, asymmet~
rical, battered, embryonic, form~
less, indeterminate, irregular,
misshapen, nebulous, undeveloped,
unstructured

share 1. *v.* apportion, assign, dis~
tribute, divide, go Dutch (*Inf.*), go
fifty-fifty (*Inf.*), go halves, parcel
out, partake, participate, receive,
split, use in common 2. *n.* allot~
ment, allowance, contribution, cut
(*Inf.*), division, due, lot, part, por~
tion, proportion, quota, ration,
whack (*Inf.*)

sharp *adj.* 1. acute, cutting, honed,
jagged, keen, knife-edged, knife-
like, pointed, razor-sharp, serrated,
sharpened, spiky 2. abrupt, dis~
tinct, extreme, marked, sudden 3.
alert, apt, astute, bright, clever,
discerning, knowing, long-headed,
observant, penetrating, perceptive,
quick, quick-witted, ready, subtle 4.
artful, crafty, cunning, dishonest,
fly (*Sl.*), shrewd, sly, smart, un~
scrupulous, wily 5. acute, distress~
ing, excruciating, fierce, intense,
painful, piercing, severe, shooting,
sore, stabbing, stinging, violent 6.
clear, clear-cut, crisp, distinct,
well-defined 7. *Inf.* chic, classy
(*Sl.*), dressy, fashionable, natty
(*Inf.*), smart, snappy, stylish 8. ac~
rimonious, barbed, biting, bitter,
caustic, cutting, harsh, hurtful,
sarcastic, sardonic, scathing, se~
vere, trenchant, vitriolic 9. acer~
bic, acid, acrid, burning, hot, pi~
quant, pungent, sour, tart, vinegary
~*adv.* 10. exactly, on the dot, on
time, precisely, promptly, punctu~

ally **11.** abruptly, suddenly, unex~
pectedly, without warning

sharpen edge, grind, hone, put an
edge on, strop, whet

shatter 1. break, burst, crack,
crush, crush to smithereens, de~
molish, explode, implode, pulver~
ize, shiver, smash, split **2.** blast,
blight, bring to nought, demolish,
destroy, disable, exhaust, impair,
overturn, ruin, torpedo, wreck **3.**
break (someone's) heart, crush,
devastate, dumbfound, knock the
stuffing out of (someone) (*Inf.*),
upset

shave *v.* **1.** crop, pare, plane, shear,
trim **2.** brush, graze, touch

shed *v.* **1.** afford, cast, diffuse, drop,
emit, give, give forth, pour forth,
radiate, scatter, shower, spill,
throw **2.** cast off, discard, exuviate,
moult, slough

sheepish abashed, chagrined, em~
barrassed, foolish, mortified, self-
conscious, shamefaced, silly, un~
comfortable

sheer 1. abrupt, headlong (*Archa~
ic*), perpendicular, precipitous,
steep **2.** absolute, arrant, complete,
downright, out-and-out, pure, rank,
thoroughgoing, total, unadulterat~
ed, unalloyed, unmitigated, un~
qualified, utter **3.** *Of fabrics* di~
aphanous, fine, gauzy, gossamer,
seethrough, thin, transparent

sheet 1. coat, film, folio, lamina,
layer, leaf, membrane, overlay,
pane, panel, piece, plate, slab,
stratum, surface, veneer **2.** area,
blanket, covering, expanse,
stretch, sweep

shell *n.* **1.** carapace, case, husk, pod
~*v.* **2.** husk, shuck **3.** attack, bar~
rage, blitz, bomb, bombard, strafe,
strike ~*n.* **4.** chassis, frame,
framework, hull, skeleton, struc~
ture

shelter 1. *v.* cover, defend, guard,
harbour, hide, protect, safeguard,
seek refuge, shield, take in, take
shelter **2.** *n.* asylum, cover, covert,
defence, guard, haven, protection,
refuge, retreat, roof over one's
head, safety, sanctuary, screen,
security, shiel (*Scot.*), umbrella

sheltered cloistered, conventual,
ensconced, hermitic, isolated, pro~
tected, quiet, reclusive, retired,
screened, secluded, shaded,
shielded, withdrawn

shelve defer, dismiss, freeze, hold
in abeyance, hold over, lay aside,
mothball, pigeonhole, postpone,
put aside, put off, put on ice, table
(*U.S.*)

shepherd *v.* conduct, convoy,
guide, herd, marshal, steer, usher

shield *n.* **1.** buckler, escutcheon
(*Heraldry*), targe (*Archaic*) **2.**
aegis, bulwark, cover, defence,
guard, protection, rampart, safe~
guard, screen, shelter, ward (*Ar~
chaic*) ~*v.* **3.** cover, defend, guard,
protect, safeguard, screen, shelter,
ward off

shift *v.* **1.** alter, budge, change, dis~
place, fluctuate, move, move
around, rearrange, relocate, re~
move, reposition, swerve, switch,
transfer, transpose, vary, veer **2.**
As in shift for oneself assume re~
sponsibility, contrive, devise, fend,
get along, look after, make do,
manage, plan, scheme, take care
of ~*n.* **3.** about-turn, alteration,
change, displacement, fluctuation,
modification, move, permutation,
rearrangement, removal, shifting,
switch, transfer, veering **4.** artifice,
contrivance, craft, device, dodge,
equivocation, evasion, expedient,
move, resource, ruse, stratagem,
subterfuge, trick, wile

shifty contriving, crafty, deceitful,
devious, duplicitous, evasive, fly-
by-night (*Inf.*), furtive, scheming,
slippery, tricky, underhand, un~
principled, untrustworthy, wily

shimmer 1. *v.* dance, gleam, glis~
ten, phosphoresce, scintillate,
twinkle **2.** *n.* diffused light, gleam,
glimmer, glow, incandescence, iri~
descence, lustre, phosphorescence,
unsteady light

shine *v.* **1.** beam, emit light, flash,
give off light, glare, gleam, glim~
mer, glisten, glitter, glow, radiate,
scintillate, shimmer, sparkle,
twinkle **2.** be conspicuous (distin~
guished, outstanding, pre-eminent),

excel, stand out, stand out in a crowd, star **3.** brush, buff, burnish, polish, rub up ~*n.* **4.** brightness, glare, gleam, lambency, light, luminosity, radiance, shimmer, sparkle **5.** glaze, gloss, lustre, patina, polish, sheen

shining 1. beaming, bright, brilliant, effulgent, gleaming, glistening, glittering, luminous, radiant, resplendent, shimmering, sparkling **2.** *Fig.* brilliant, celebrated, conspicuous, distinguished, eminent, glorious, illustrious, leading, outstanding, splendid

shiny agleam, bright, burnished, gleaming, glistening, glossy, lustrous, nitid (*Poetic*), polished, satiny, sheeny

shirk avoid, dodge, duck (out of) (*Inf.*), evade, get out of, scrimshank (*Brit. military sl.*), shun, sidestep, skive (*Brit. sl.*), slack

shirker clock-watcher, dodger, gold brick (*U.S. sl.*), idler, malingerer, quitter, scrimshanker (*Brit. military sl.*), shirk, skiver (*Brit. sl.*), slacker

shiver *v.* break, crack, fragment, shatter, smash, smash to smithereens, splinter

shivery chilled, chilly, cold, quaking, quivery, shaking, trembly

shock *v.* **1.** agitate, appal, astound, disgust, disquiet, give (someone) a turn (*Inf.*), horrify, jar, jolt, nauseate, numb, offend, outrage, paralyse, revolt, scandalize, shake, shake out of one's complacency, shake up (*Inf.*), sicken, stagger, stun, stupefy, traumatize, unsettle ~*n.* **2.** blow, bolt from the blue, bombshell, breakdown, collapse, consternation, distress, disturbance, prostration, state of shock, stupefaction, stupor, trauma, turn (*Inf.*), upset **3.** blow, clash, collision, encounter, impact, jarring, jolt

shocking abominable, appalling, atrocious, detestable, disgraceful, disgusting, disquieting, distressing, dreadful, foul, frightful, ghastly, hideous, horrible, horrifying, loathsome, monstrous, nauseating,

odious, offensive, outrageous, repulsive, revolting, scandalous, sickening, stupefying, unspeakable

shoddy cheap-jack (*Inf.*), inferior, junky, poor, rubbishy, second-rate, slipshod, tacky (*Inf.*), tatty, tawdry, trashy

shoemaker bootmaker, cobbler, souter (*Scot.*)

shoot¹ *v.* **1.** bag, blast (*Sl.*), bring down, hit, kill, open fire, pick off, plug (*Sl.*), pump full of lead (*Sl.*), zap (*Sl.*) **2.** discharge, emit, fire, fling, hurl, launch, let fly, project, propel **3.** bolt, charge, dart, dash, flash, fly, hurtle, race, rush, scoot, speed, spring, streak, tear, whisk, whiz (*Inf.*)

shoot² **1.** *n.* branch, bud, offshoot, scion, slip, sprig, sprout, twig **2.** *v.* bud, burgeon, germinate, put forth new growth, sprout

shore 1. *n.* beach, coast, foreshore, lakeside, sands, seaboard (*Chiefly U.S.*), seashore, strand (*Poetic*), waterside **2.** *adj.* littoral

short *adj.* **1.** abridged, brief, compendious, compressed, concise, curtailed, laconic, pithy, sententious, succinct, summary, terse **2.** diminutive, dumpy, little, low, petite, small, squat, wee **3.** brief, fleeting, momentary, short-lived, short-term **4.** *Often with of* deficient, inadequate, insufficient, lacking, limited, low (on), meagre, poor, scant, scanty, scarce, shorthanded, slender, slim, sparse, tight, wanting **5.** abrupt, blunt, brusque, crusty, curt, discourteous, gruff, impolite, offhand, sharp, terse, testy, uncivil **6.** direct, straight **7.** *Of pastry* brittle, crisp, crumbly, friable ~*adv.* **8.** abruptly, by surprise, suddenly, unaware, without warning **9. cut short** abbreviate, arrest, butt in, curtail, cut in on, dock, halt, interrupt, reduce, stop, terminate **10. fall short** be inadequate, disappoint, fail, fall down on (*Inf.*), not come up to expectations *or* scratch (*Inf.*) **11. in short** briefly, in a nutshell, in a word, in essence, to come to the point, to cut a long story short, to put it briefly **12.**

short of a. apart from, except, other than, unless **b.** deficient in, in need of, lacking, low (on), missing, wanting

shortage dearth, deficiency, deficit, failure, inadequacy, insufficiency, lack, leanness, paucity, poverty, scarcity, shortfall, want

shortcoming defect, drawback, failing, fault, flaw, frailty, imperfection, weakness, weak point

shorten abbreviate, abridge, curtail, cut, cut back, cut down, decrease, diminish, dock, lessen, reduce, trim, turn up

short-sighted 1. myopic, near-sighted **2.** careless, ill-advised, ill-considered, impolitic, impractical, improvident, imprudent, injudicious, unthinking

short-staffed below strength, short-handed, undermanned, understaffed

short-tempered choleric, fiery, hot-tempered, impatient, irascible, peppery, quick-tempered, ratty (*Brit. sl.*), testy, touchy

shot *n.* **1.** discharge, lob, pot shot, throw **2.** ball, bullet, lead, pellet, projectile, slug **3.** marksman, shooter **4.** *Inf.* attempt, chance, conjecture, crack (*Inf.*), effort, endeavour, essay, go, guess, opportunity, stab, surmise, try, turn **5. by a long shot a.** by far, easily, far and away, indubitably, undoubtedly, without doubt **b.** by any means, in any circumstances, on any account **6. have a shot** *Inf.* attempt, have a go (bash (*Inf.*), crack (*Inf.*), stab), tackle, try, try one's luck **7. like a shot** at once, eagerly, immediately, like a flash, quickly, unhesitatingly **8. shot in the arm** *Inf.* boost, encouragement, fillip, impetus, lift, stimulus

shoulder *n.* **1. give (someone) the cold shoulder** cut (*Inf.*), ignore, ostracize, rebuff, shun, snub **2. put one's shoulder to the wheel** *Inf.* apply oneself, buckle down to (*Inf.*), exert oneself, get down to, make every effort, set to work, strive **3. rub shoulders with** *Inf.* associate with, consort with, frat-

ernize with, hobnob with, mix with, socialize with **4. shoulder to shoulder** as one, in cooperation, in partnership, in unity, jointly, side by side, together, united **5. straight from the shoulder** candidly, directly, frankly, man to man, outright, plainly, pulling no punches (*Inf.*), straight, unequivocally, with no holds barred ~*v.* **6.** accept, assume, bear, be responsible for, carry, take on, take upon oneself **7.** elbow, jostle, press, push, shove, thrust

shout 1. *n.* bellow, call, cry, roar, scream, yell **2.** *v.* bawl, bay, bellow, call (out), cry (out), holler (*Inf.*), hollo, raise one's voice, roar, scream, yell

shout down drown, drown out, overwhelm, silence

shove *v.* crowd, drive, elbow, impel, jostle, press, propel, push, shoulder, thrust

shovel *v.* convey, dredge, heap, ladle, load, move, scoop, shift, spoon, toss

show *v.* **1.** appear, be visible, disclose, display, divulge, evidence, evince, exhibit, indicate, make known, manifest, present, register, reveal, testify to **2.** assert, clarify, demonstrate, elucidate, evince, explain, instruct, point out, present, prove, teach **3.** accompany, attend, conduct, escort, guide, lead **4.** accord, act with, bestow, confer, grant ~*n.* **5.** array, demonstration, display, exhibition, expo (*Inf.*), exposition, fair, manifestation, pageant, pageantry, parade, representation, sight, spectacle, view **6.** affectation, air, appearance, display, illusion, likeness, ostentation, parade, pose, pretence, pretext, profession, semblance **7.** entertainment, presentation, production

showdown breaking point, clash, climax, confrontation, crisis, culmination, exposé, moment of truth

shower *n.* **1.** *Fig.* barrage, deluge, fusillade, plethora, rain, stream, torrent, volley **2.** *Brit. sl.* bunch of layabouts, crew, rabble ~*v.* **3.** deluge, heap, inundate, lavish, load, pour, rain, spray, sprinkle

showing n. 1. display, exhibition, presentation, staging 2. account of oneself, appearance, impression, performance, show, track record 3. evidence, representation, statement

showman entertainer, impresario, performer, publicist, stage manager

show off 1. advertise, demonstrate, display, exhibit, flaunt, parade, spread out 2. boast, brag, make a spectacle of oneself, shoot a line (Inf.), swagger

show up 1. expose, highlight, lay bare, pinpoint, put the spotlight on, reveal, unmask 2. appear, be conspicuous, be visible, catch the eye, leap to the eye, stand out 3. Inf. embarrass, let down, mortify, put to shame, shame, show in a bad light 4. Inf. appear, arrive, come, make an appearance, put in an appearance, turn up

shred n. 1. bit, fragment, piece, rag, ribbon, scrap, sliver, snippet, tatter 2. Fig. atom, grain, iota, jot, particle, scrap, trace, whit

shrewd acute, artful, astute, calculated, calculating, canny, clever, crafty, cunning, discerning, discriminating, far-seeing, far-sighted, fly (Sl.), intelligent, keen, knowing, long-headed, perceptive, perspicacious, sagacious, sharp, sly, smart, wily

shrewdly artfully, astutely, cannily, cleverly, far-sightedly, knowingly, perceptively, perspicaciously, sagaciously, with all one's wits about one, with consummate skill

shrewdness acumen, acuteness, astuteness, canniness, discernment, grasp, judgment, penetration, perspicacity, quick wits, sagacity, sharpness, smartness

shriek v./n. cry, howl, scream, screech, squeal, wail, whoop, yell

shrill acute, ear-piercing, ear-splitting, high, high-pitched, penetrating, piercing, piping, screeching, sharp

shrink 1. contract, decrease, deflate, diminish, drop off, dwindle, fall off, grow smaller, lessen, narrow, shorten, shrivel, wither, wrinkle 2. cower, cringe, draw back, flinch, hang back, quail, recoil, retire, shy away, wince, withdraw

shrivel 1. burn, dry (up), parch, scorch, sear 2. dehydrate, desiccate, dwindle, shrink, wilt, wither, wizen, wrinkle

shrivelled desiccated, dried up, dry, sere (Archaic), shrunken, withered, wizened, wrinkled

shroud v. 1. blanket, cloak, conceal, cover, envelop, hide, screen, swathe, veil ~n. 2. cerecloth, cerement, covering, grave clothes, winding sheet 3. cloud, mantle, pall, screen, veil

shudder 1. v. convulse, quake, quiver, shake, shiver, tremble 2. n. convulsion, quiver, spasm, trembling, tremor

shuffle 1. drag, scrape, scuff, scuffle, shamble 2. confuse, disarrange, disorder, intermix, jumble, mix, rearrange, shift 3. Usually with off or out of beat about the bush, beg the question, cavil, dodge, equivocate, evade, gloss over, hedge, prevaricate, pussyfoot (Inf.), quibble

shun avoid, cold-shoulder, elude, eschew, evade, fight shy of, give (someone or something) a wide berth, have no part in, keep away from, shy away from, steer clear of

shut 1. bar, close, draw to, fasten, push to, seal, secure, slam 2. With in, out, etc. cage, confine, enclose, exclude, imprison, wall off or up

shut down cease, cease operating, close, discontinue, halt, shut up, stop, switch off

shut out 1. bar, debar, exclude, keep out, lock out, ostracize 2. block out, conceal, cover, hide, mask, screen, veil

shuttle v. alternate, commute, ply, seesaw, shunt

shut up 1. bottle up, box in, cage, confine, coop up, immure, imprison, incarcerate, intern, keep in 2. Inf. be quiet, fall silent, gag, hold one's tongue, hush, keep one's trap shut (*Sl.*), muzzle, pipe down (*Sl.*), silence

shy 1. *adj.* backward, bashful, cautious, chary, coy, diffident, distrustful, hesitant, modest, mousy, nervous, reserved, reticent, retiring, self-conscious, self-effacing, shrinking, suspicious, timid, wary 2. *v. Sometimes with* off *or* away balk, buck, draw back, flinch, quail, rear, recoil, start, swerve, take fright, wince

shyness bashfulness, diffidence, lack of confidence, modesty, mousiness, nervousness, reticence, self-consciousness, timidity, timidness, timorousness

sick 1. green around the gills (*Inf.*), ill, nauseated, puking (*Sl.*), qualmish, queasy 2. ailing, diseased, feeble, indisposed, laid up (*Inf.*), on the sick list (*Inf.*), poorly (*Inf.*), under the weather (*Inf.*), unwell, weak 3. *Inf.* black, ghoulish, macabre, morbid, sadistic 4. *Inf. Often with* of blasé, bored, disgusted, displeased, fed up, jaded, revolted, satiated, tired, weary

sicken 1. disgust, make one's gorge rise, nauseate, repel, revolt, turn one's stomach 2. be stricken by, contract, fall ill, go down with (*Brit.*), show symptoms of, take sick

sickening disgusting, distasteful, foul, loathsome, nauseating, nauseous, noisome, offensive, putrid, repulsive, revolting, stomach-turning (*Inf.*), vile

sickly 1. ailing, bilious, bloodless, delicate, faint, feeble, indisposed, infirm, in poor health, lacklustre, languid, pallid, peaky, pining, unhealthy, wan, weak 2. bilious (*Inf.*), cloying, mawkish, nauseating, revolting (*Inf.*), syrupy (*Inf.*)

sickness 1. nausea, queasiness, (the) collywobbles (*Sl.*), vomiting 2. affliction, ailment, bug (*Inf.*), complaint, disease, disorder, illness, indisposition, infirmity, malady

side *n.* 1. border, boundary, division, edge, limit, margin, part, perimeter, periphery, rim, sector,

verge 2. aspect, face, facet, flank, hand, part, surface, view 3. angle, light, opinion, point of view, position, slant, stand, standpoint, viewpoint 4. camp, cause, faction, party, sect, team 5. *Brit. sl.* airs, arrogance, insolence, pretentiousness ~*adj.* 6. flanking, lateral 7. ancillary, incidental, indirect, lesser, marginal, minor, oblique, roundabout, secondary, subordinate, subsidiary ~*v.* 8. *Usually with* with ally with, associate oneself with, befriend, favour, go along with (*Inf.*), join with, second, support, take the part of, team up with (*Inf.*)

sidelong *adj.* covert, indirect, oblique, sideways

sidestep avoid, bypass, circumvent, dodge, duck (*Inf.*), elude, evade, skip, skirt

sidetrack deflect, distract, divert, lead off the subject

sideways 1. *adv.* crabwise, edgeways, laterally, obliquely, sidelong, sidewards, to the side 2. *adj.* oblique, side, sidelong, slanted

siesta catnap, doze, forty winks (*Inf.*), nap, rest, sleep, snooze (*Inf.*)

sieve 1. *n.* colander, riddle, screen, sifter, strainer, tammy cloth 2. *v.* bolt, remove, riddle, separate, sift, strain

sift 1. bolt, filter, pan, part, riddle, separate, sieve 2. analyse, examine, fathom, go through, investigate, pore over, probe, screen, scrutinize

sigh *v.* 1. breathe, complain, grieve, lament, moan, sorrow, sough, suspire (*Archaic*) 2. *Often with* for languish, long, mourn, pine, yearn

sight *n.* 1. eye, eyes, eyesight, seeing, vision 2. appearance, apprehension, eyeshot, field of vision, ken, perception, range of vision, view, viewing, visibility 3. display, exhibition, pageant, scene, show, spectacle, vista 4. *Inf.* blot on the landscape (*Inf.*), eyesore, fright (*Inf.*), mess, monstrosity, spectacle 5. **catch sight of** descry, espy, glimpse, recognize, spot, view ~*v.* 6. behold, discern, distinguish, make out, observe, perceive, see, spot

sign *n.* 1. clue, evidence, gesture, giveaway, hint, indication, manifestation, mark, note, proof, signal, spoor, suggestion, symptom, token, trace, vestige 2. board, notice, placard, warning 3. badge, character, cipher, device, emblem, ensign, figure, logo, mark, representation, symbol 4. augury, auspice, foreboding, forewarning, omen, portent, presage, warning, writing on the wall ~*v.* 5. autograph, endorse, initial, inscribe, set one's hand to, subscribe 6. beckon, gesticulate, gesture, indicate, signal, use sign language, wave

signal 1. *n.* beacon, cue, gesture, go-ahead (*Inf.*), green light, indication, indicator, mark, sign, token 2. *adj.* conspicuous, distinguished, eminent, exceptional, extraordinary, famous, memorable, momentous, notable, noteworthy, outstanding, remarkable, significant, striking 3. *v.* beckon, communicate, gesticulate, gesture, give a sign to, indicate, motion, nod, sign, wave

significance 1. force, implication(s), import, meaning, message, point, purport, sense, signification 2. consequence, consideration, importance, impressiveness, matter, moment, relevance, weight

significant 1. denoting, eloquent, expressing, expressive, indicative, knowing, meaning, meaningful, pregnant, suggestive 2. critical, important, material, momentous, noteworthy, serious, vital, weighty

signify 1. announce, be a sign of, betoken, communicate, connote, convey, denote, evidence, exhibit, express, imply, indicate, intimate, matter, mean, portend, proclaim, represent, show, stand for, suggest, symbolize 2. *Inf.* be of importance *or* significance, carry weight, count, matter

silence *n.* 1. calm, hush, lull, noiselessness, peace, quiescence, quiet, stillness 2. dumbness, muteness, reticence, speechlessness, taciturnity, uncommunicativeness ~*v.* 3. cut off, cut short, deaden, extinguish, gag, muffle, quell, quiet, quieten, stifle, still, strike dumb, subdue, suppress

silent 1. hushed, muted, noiseless, quiet, soundless, still, stilly (*Poetic*) 2. dumb, mum, mute, nonvocal, not talkative, speechless, struck dumb (*Inf.*), taciturn, tongue-tied, uncommunicative, unspeaking, voiceless, wordless 3. aphonic (*Phonetics*), implicit, implied, tacit, understood, unexpressed, unpronounced, unspoken

silently as quietly as a mouse (*Inf.*), dumbly, in silence, mutely, noiselessly, quietly, soundlessly, speechlessly, without a sound, wordlessly

silhouette 1. *n.* delineation, form, outline, profile, shape 2. *v.* delineate, etch, outline, stand out

silky silken, sleek, smooth, velvety

silly *adj.* 1. absurd, asinine, brainless, childish, fatuous, foolhardy, foolish, frivolous, giddy, idiotic, immature, imprudent, inane, inappropriate, irresponsible, meaningless, pointless, preposterous, puerile, ridiculous, senseless, stupid, unwise, witless 2. *Inf.* benumbed, dazed, groggy (*Inf.*), in a daze, muzzy, stunned, stupefied ~*n.* 3. *Inf.* clot (*Brit. sl.*), duffer (*Inf.*), goose (*Inf.*), ignoramus, ninny, silly-billy (*Inf.*), simpleton, twit (*Inf.*)

silver 1. *adj.* argent (*Poetic*), pearly, silvered, silvery 2. *n.* silver plate, silverware

similar alike, comparable, congruous, corresponding, in agreement, much the same, resembling, uniform

similarity affinity, agreement, analogy, closeness, comparability, concordance, congruence, correspondence, likeness, point of comparison, relation, resemblance, sameness, similitude

similarly by the same token, correspondingly, in like manner, likewise

simmer *v. Fig.* be angry (agitated,

tense, uptight (*Inf.*)), boil, burn, fume, rage, seethe, smart, smoul~der

simmer down calm down, collect oneself, contain oneself, control oneself, cool off *or* down, get down off one's high horse (*Inf.*), grow quieter, unwind (*Inf.*)

simple 1. clear, easy, elementary, intelligible, lucid, manageable, plain, straightforward, uncompli~cated, understandable, uninvolved **2.** classic, clean, natural, plain, Spartan, unadorned, uncluttered, unembellished, unfussy **3.** elemen~tary, pure, single, unalloyed, un~blended, uncombined, undivided, unmixed **4.** artless, childlike, frank, green, guileless, ingenuous, inno~cent, naive, natural, sincere, unaf~fected, unpretentious, unsophisti~cated **5.** bald, basic, direct, frank, honest, naked, plain, sincere, stark, undeniable, unvarnished **6.** home~ly, humble, lowly, modest, rustic, unpretentious **7.** brainless, credu~lous, dense, dumb (*Inf.*), feeble, feeble-minded, foolish, half-witted, moronic, obtuse, shallow, silly, slow, stupid, thick

simple-minded 1. a bit lacking (*Inf.*), addle-brained, backward, brainless, dead from the neck up (*Sl.*), dim-witted, feeble-minded, foolish, idiot, idiotic, moronic, re~tarded, simple, stupid **2.** artless, natural, unsophisticated

simpleton blockhead, booby, dolt, dope (*Sl.*), dullard, dunce, fool, goose (*Inf.*), greenhorn (*Inf.*), idiot, imbecile (*Inf.*), jackass, moron, nincompoop, ninny, numskull, Simple Simon, stupid (*Inf.*), twerp (*Inf.*)

simplicity 1. absence of complica~tions, clarity, clearness, ease, easi~ness, elementariness, obviousness, straightforwardness **2.** clean lines, lack of adornment, modesty, natu~ralness, plainness, purity, restraint **3.** artlessness, candour, directness, guilelessness, innocence, lack of sophistication, naivety, openness

simplify abridge, decipher, disen~tangle, facilitate, make intelligible, reduce to essentials, streamline

simply 1. clearly, directly, easily, intelligibly, modestly, naturally, plainly, straightforwardly, unaf~fectedly, unpretentiously, without any elaboration **2.** just, merely, only, purely, solely **3.** absolutely, altogether, completely, really, to~tally, unreservedly, utterly, wholly

simultaneous at the same time, coincident, coinciding, concurrent, contemporaneous, synchronous

simultaneously all together, at the same time, concurrently, in chorus, in concert, in the same breath, in unison, together

sin 1. *n.* crime, damnation, error, evil, guilt, iniquity, misdeed, of~fence, sinfulness, transgression, trespass, ungodliness, unright~eousness, wickedness, wrong, wrongdoing **2.** *v.* err, fall, fall from grace, go astray, lapse, offend, transgress, trespass (*Archaic*)

sincere artless, bona fide, candid, earnest, frank, genuine, guileless, heartfelt, honest, natural, no-nonsense, open, real, serious, straightforward, true, unaffected, unfeigned, wholehearted

sincerely earnestly, genuinely, honestly, in all sincerity, in good faith, really, seriously, truly, wholeheartedly

sincerity artlessness, bona fides, candour, frankness, genuineness, good faith, guilelessness, honesty, probity, seriousness, straight~forwardness, truth, wholehearted~ness

sinecure cushy number (*Sl.*), gravy train (*Sl., chiefly U.S.*), money for jam *or* old rope (*Inf.*), soft job (*Inf.*), soft option

sinful bad, corrupt, criminal, de~praved, erring, guilty, immoral, iniquitous, irreligious, morally wrong, ungodly, unholy, unright~eous, wicked

sing 1. carol, chant, chirp, croon, make melody, pipe, trill, vocalize, warble, yodel **2.** *Sl., chiefly U.S.* betray, blow the whistle (on) (*Inf.*), fink (on) (*Sl., chiefly U.S.*), grass

(*Brit. sl.*), inform (on), peach (*Sl.*), rat (on), spill the beans (*Inf.*), squeal (*Sl.*), turn in (*Inf.*) **3.** buzz, hum, purr, whine, whistle

singe burn, char, scorch, sear

singer chanteuse (*Fem.*), chorister, crooner, minstrel, songster, vocalist

single *adj.* **1.** distinct, individual, lone, one, only, particular, separate, singular, sole, solitary, unique **2.** free, unattached, unmarried, unwed **3.** exclusive, individual, separate, simple, unblended, uncompounded, undivided, unmixed, unshared ~*v.* **4.** *Usually with* out choose, cull, distinguish, fix on, pick, pick on *or* out, put on one side, select, separate, set apart, winnow

single-minded dedicated, determined, dogged, fixed, monomaniacal, steadfast, stubborn, tireless, undeviating, unswerving, unwavering

singly individually, one at a time, one by one, separately

singular **1.** conspicuous, eminent, exceptional, noteworthy, outstanding, prodigious, rare, remarkable, uncommon, unique, unparalleled **2.** atypical, curious, eccentric, extraordinary, odd, out-of-the-way, peculiar, puzzling, queer, strange, unusual **3.** individual, separate, single, sole

sinister dire, disquieting, evil, injurious, malevolent, malign, malignant, menacing, ominous, threatening

sink *v.* **1.** cave in, decline, descend, dip, disappear, droop, drop, drown, ebb, engulf, fall, founder, go down, go under, lower, merge, plummet, plunge, sag, slope, submerge, subside **2.** abate, collapse, drop, fall, lapse, relapse, retrogress, slip, slump, subside **3.** decay, decline, decrease, degenerate, depreciate, deteriorate, die, diminish, dwindle, fade, fail, flag, go downhill (*Inf.*), lessen, weaken, worsen **4.** bore, dig, drill, drive, excavate, lay, put down **5.** be the ruin of, defeat, destroy, finish, overwhelm, ruin,

scupper (*Brit. sl.*), seal the doom of **6.** be reduced to, debase oneself, lower oneself, stoop, succumb

sinner evildoer, miscreant, offender, reprobate, transgressor, trespasser (*Archaic*), wrongdoer

sip **1.** *v.* sample, sup, taste **2.** *n.* drop, swallow, taste, thimbleful

siren charmer, Circe, *femme fatale*, Lorelei, seductress, temptress, vamp (*Inf.*), witch

sit **1.** be seated, perch, rest, settle, take a seat, take the weight off one's feet **2.** assemble, be in session, convene, deliberate, meet, officiate, preside **3.** accommodate, contain, have space for, hold, seat

site **1.** *n.* ground, location, place, plot, position, spot **2.** *v.* install, locate, place, position, set, situate

sitting *n.* consultation, get-together (*Inf.*), hearing, meeting, period, session

situation **1.** locale, locality, location, place, position, seat, setting, site, spot **2.** ball game (*Inf.*), case, circumstances, condition, kettle of fish (*Inf.*), plight, state, state of affairs, status quo, the picture (*Inf.*) **3.** rank, sphere, station, status **4.** berth (*Inf.*), employment, job, office, place, position, post

size amount, bigness, bulk, dimensions, extent, greatness, hugeness, immensity, largeness, magnitude, mass, measurement(s), proportions, range, vastness, volume

size up appraise, assess, evaluate, get (something) taped (*Brit. inf.*), get the measure of, take stock of

sizzle crackle, frizzle, fry, hiss, spit, sputter

skeleton *Fig.* bare bones, bones, draft, frame, framework, outline, sketch, structure

sketch **1.** *v.* block out, delineate, depict, draft, draw, outline, paint, plot, portray, represent, rough out **2.** *n.* delineation, design, draft, drawing, outline, plan, skeleton

sketchy bitty, cobbled together, crude, cursory, inadequate, incomplete, outline, perfunctory, rough, scrappy, skimpy, slight, superficial, unfinished, vague

skilful able, accomplished, adept, adroit, apt, clever, competent, dexterous, experienced, expert, handy, masterly, practised, professional, proficient, quick, ready, skilled, trained

skill ability, accomplishment, adroitness, aptitude, art, cleverness, competence, dexterity, experience, expertise, expertness, facility, finesse, handiness, ingenuity, intelligence, knack, proficiency, quickness, readiness, skilfulness, talent, technique

skilled able, accomplished, a dab hand at (*Brit. inf.*), experienced, expert, masterly, practised, professional, proficient, skilful, trained

skim 1. cream, separate 2. brush, coast, dart, float, fly, glide, sail, soar 3. *Usually with* **through** glance, run one's eye over, scan, skip (*Inf.*), thumb *or* leaf through

skimp be mean with, be niggardly, be sparing with, pinch, scamp, scant, scrimp, stint, withhold

skin *n.* 1. fell, hide, integument, pelt, tegument 2. casing, coating, crust, film, husk, membrane, outside, peel, rind 3. **by the skin of one's teeth** by a hair's-breadth, by a narrow margin, by a whisker (*Inf.*), narrowly, only just 4. **get under one's skin** annoy, grate on, irk, irritate, needle (*Inf.*), nettle, rub up the wrong way ~*v.* 5. abrade, bark, excoriate, flay, graze, peel, scrape

skinny emaciated, lean, scraggy, skeletal, skin-and-bone (*Inf.*), thin, twiggy, undernourished

skip *v.* 1. bob, bounce, caper, cavort, dance, flit, frisk, gambol, hop, prance, trip 2. eschew, give (something) a miss, leave out, miss out, omit, pass over, skim over 3. *Inf.* cut (*Inf.*), dog it *or* dog off (*Dialect*), miss, play truant from, twag (*Dialect*)

skirmish 1. *n.* affair, affray (*Law*), battle, brush, clash, combat, conflict, contest, dust-up (*Inf.*), encounter, engagement, fracas, incident, scrap (*Inf.*), scrimmage, set-to (*Inf.*), spat, tussle 2. *v.* clash, collide, come to blows, scrap (*Inf.*), tussle

skirt *v.* 1. border, edge, flank, lie alongside 2. *Often with* **around** *or* **round** avoid, bypass, circumvent, detour, evade, steer clear of ~*n.* 3. *Often plural* border, edge, fringe, hem, margin, outskirts, periphery, purlieus, rim

skit burlesque, parody, sketch, spoof (*Inf.*), takeoff (*Inf.*), travesty, turn

skulk creep, lie in wait, loiter, lurk, pad, prowl, slink, sneak

sky *n.* 1. azure (*Poetic*), empyrean (*Poetic*), firmament, heavens, upper atmosphere, vault of heaven, welkin (*Archaic*) 2. **to the skies** excessively, extravagantly, fulsomely, highly, immoderately, inordinately, profusely

slab chunk, hunk, lump, piece, portion, slice, wedge, wodge (*Brit. inf.*)

slack *adj.* 1. baggy, easy, flaccid, flexible, lax, limp, loose, not taut, relaxed 2. asleep on the job (*Inf.*), easy-going, idle, inactive, inattentive, lax, lazy, neglectful, negligent, permissive, remiss, tardy 3. dull, inactive, quiet, slow, slow-moving, sluggish ~*n.* 4. excess, give (*Inf.*), leeway, looseness, play, room ~*v.* 5. dodge, flag, idle, neglect, relax, shirk, skive (*Brit. sl.*), slacken

slacken (off) abate, decrease, diminish, drop off, ease (off), lessen, let up, loosen, moderate, reduce, relax, release, slack off, slow down, tire

slacker dodger, do-nothing, gold brick (*U.S. sl.*), good-for-nothing, idler, loafer, passenger, scrimshanker (*Brit. military sl.*), shirker, skiver (*Brit. sl.*)

slam 1. bang, crash, dash, fling, hurl, smash, throw, thump 2. *Sl.* attack, castigate, criticize, damn, excoriate, lambaste, pan (*Inf.*), pillory, shoot down (*Inf.*), slate (*Inf.*), vilify

slander 1. *n.* aspersion, backbiting, calumny, defamation, detraction, libel, misrepresentation, muckraking, obloquy, scandal, smear 2. *v.* backbite, blacken (someone's) name, calumniate, decry, defame, detract, disparage, libel, malign, muckrake, slur, smear, traduce, vilify

slanderous abusive, calumnious, damaging, defamatory, libellous, malicious

slang v. abuse, berate, call names, hurl insults at, insult, inveigh against, malign, rail against, revile, vilify, vituperate

slant v. 1. angle off, bend, bevel, cant, incline, lean, list, shelve, skew, slope, tilt ~n. 2. camber, declination, diagonal, gradient, incline, pitch, rake, ramp, slope, tilt ~v. 3. angle, bias, colour, distort, twist, weight ~n. 4. angle, attitude, bias, emphasis, leaning, one-sidedness, point of view, prejudice, viewpoint

slanting angled, aslant, asymmetrical, at an angle, bent, canted, cater-cornered (U.S. inf.), diagonal, inclined, oblique, on the bias, sideways, slanted, slantwise, sloping, tilted, tilting

slap n. 1. bang, blow, clout (Inf.), cuff, smack, spank, wallop (Inf.), whack 2. **a slap in the face** blow, humiliation, insult, put-down, rebuff, rebuke, rejection, repulse, snub ~v. 3. bang, clap, clout (Inf.), cuff, hit, spank, strike, whack 4. Inf. daub, plaster, plonk, spread ~adv. 5. Inf. bang, directly, exactly, plumb (Inf.), precisely, slap-bang (Inf.), smack (Inf.)

slapdash careless, clumsy, disorderly, haphazard, hasty, hurried, last-minute, messy, negligent, perfunctory, slipshod, sloppy (Inf.), slovenly, thoughtless, thrown-together, untidy

slap down bring to heel, put (someone) in his place, rebuke, reprimand, restrain, squash

slash v. 1. cut, gash, hack, lacerate, rend, rip, score, slit ~n. 2. cut, gash, incision, laceration, rent, rip, slit ~v. 3. cut, drop, lower, reduce

slashing aggressive, biting, brutal, harsh, savage, searing, vicious

slate v. berate, blame, castigate, censure, criticize, haul over the coals (Inf.), lambaste, lay into (Inf.), pan (Inf.), pitch into, rail against, rap (someone's) knuckles (Inf.), rebuke, roast (Inf.), scold, slam (Sl.), slang, take to task, tear (someone) off a strip (Inf.)

slaughter n. 1. blood bath, bloodshed, butchery, carnage, extermination, killing, liquidation, massacre, murder, slaying ~v. 2. butcher, destroy, do to death, exterminate, kill, liquidate, massacre, murder, put to the sword, slay 3. Inf. crush, defeat, hammer (Inf.), overwhelm, rout, thrash, trounce, vanquish, wipe the floor with (Inf.)

slaughterhouse abattoir, butchery, shambles

slave 1. n. bondservant, bondsman, drudge, scullion (Archaic), serf, servant, skivvy, slavey (Brit. inf.), vassal, villein 2. v. drudge, grind (Inf.), skivvy (Brit.), slog, toil, work one's fingers to the bone

slavery bondage, captivity, enslavement, serfdom, servitude, subjugation, thraldom, thrall, vassalage

slavish 1. abject, base, cringing, despicable, fawning, grovelling, low, mean, menial, obsequious, servile, submissive, sycophantic 2. conventional, imitative, second-hand, unimaginative, uninspired, unoriginal

slay 1. annihilate, assassinate, butcher, destroy, dispatch, do away with, eliminate, exterminate, kill, massacre, mow down, murder, rub out (U.S. sl.), slaughter 2. Inf. amuse, be the death of (Inf.), impress, make a hit with (Inf.), wow (Sl., chiefly U.S.)

sleek glossy, lustrous, shiny, smooth, well-fed, well-groomed

sleep 1. v. be in the land of Nod, catnap, doze, drop off (Inf.), drowse, hibernate, nod off (Inf.), rest in the arms of Morpheus, slumber, snooze (Inf.), snore, take a nap, take forty winks (Inf.) 2. n. beauty sleep (Inf.), dormancy, doze, forty winks (Inf.), hibernation, nap, repose, rest, shuteye

(*Sl.*), siesta, slumber(s), snooze (*Inf.*)

sleepiness doziness, drowsiness, heaviness, lethargy, somnolence, torpor

sleepless 1. disturbed, insomniac, restless, unsleeping, wakeful 2. alert, unsleeping, vigilant, watch~ ful, wide awake

sleeplessness insomnia, wakeful~ ness

sleepwalker noctambulist, som~ nambulist

sleepwalking noctambulation, noctambulism, somnambulation, somnambulism

sleepy 1. drowsy, dull, heavy, inac~ tive, lethargic, sluggish, slumber~ some, somnolent, torpid 2. dull, hypnotic, inactive, quiet, sleep~ inducing, slow, slumberous, som~ nolent, soporific

slender 1. lean, narrow, slight, slim, svelte, sylphlike, willowy 2. inadequate, inconsiderable, insuf~ ficient, little, meagre, scanty, small, spare 3. faint, feeble, flimsy, fragile, poor, remote, slight, slim, tenuous, thin, weak

sleuth detective, dick (*U.S. sl.*), gumshoe (*U.S. sl.*), private eye (*Inf.*), (private) investigator, sleuthhound (*Inf.*), tail (*Inf.*)

slice 1. *n.* cut, helping, piece, por~ tion, segment, share, sliver, wedge 2. *v.* carve, cut, divide, sever

slick *adj.* 1. glib, meretricious, plausible, polished, smooth, so~ phistical, specious 2. adroit, deft, dextrous, polished, professional, sharp, skilful ~*v.* 3. make glossy, plaster down, sleek, smarm down (*Brit. inf.*), smooth

slide *v.* 1. coast, glide, glissade, skim, slip, slither, toboggan, veer 2. **let slide** forget, gloss over, ignore, let ride, neglect, pass over, push to the back of one's mind, turn a blind eye to

slight *adj.* 1. feeble, inconsiderable, insignificant, insubstantial, mea~ gre, minor, modest, negligible, paltry, scanty, small, superficial, trifling, trivial, unimportant, weak 2. delicate, feeble, fragile, lightly-

built, slim, small, spare ~*v.* 3. af~ front, cold-shoulder, despise, dis~ dain, disparage, give offence *or* umbrage to, ignore, insult, neglect, scorn, show disrespect for, snub, treat with contempt ~*n.* 4. affront, contempt, discourtesy, disdain, disregard, disrespect, inattention, indifference, insult, neglect, rebuff, slap in the face (*Inf.*), snub, (the) cold shoulder

slightly a little, marginally, on a small scale, somewhat, to some extent *or* degree

slim *adj.* 1. lean, narrow, slender, slight, svelte, sylphlike, thin, trim 2. faint, poor, remote, slender, slight ~*v.* 3. diet, lose weight, re~ duce, slenderize (*Chiefly U.S.*)

slimy 1. clammy, glutinous, miry, mucous, muddy, oozy, viscous 2. creeping, grovelling, obsequious, oily, servile, smarmy (*Brit. inf.*), soapy (*Sl.*), sycophantic, toadying, unctuous

sling *v.* 1. cast, chuck (*Inf.*), fling, heave, hurl, lob (*Inf.*), shy, throw, toss 2. dangle, hang, suspend, swing

slink creep, prowl, pussyfoot (*Inf.*), skulk, slip, sneak, steal

slip *v.* 1. glide, skate, slide, slither 2. fall, lose one's balance, miss *or* lose one's footing, skid, trip (over) 3. conceal, creep, hide, insinuate oneself, sneak, steal 4. *Sometimes with up* blunder, boob (*Brit. sl.*), err, go wrong, make a mistake, miscalculate, misjudge, mistake 5. break away from, break free from, disappear, escape, get away, get clear of, take French leave 6. **let slip** blurt out, come out with (*Inf.*), disclose, divulge, give away, leak, let out (*Inf.*), let the cat out of the bag, reveal ~*n.* 7. bloomer (*Brit. inf.*), blunder, boob (*Brit. sl.*), error, failure, fault, imprudence, indis~ cretion, mistake, omission, over~ sight, slip of the tongue, slip-up (*Inf.*) 8. **give (someone) the slip** dodge, elude, escape from, evade, get away from, lose (someone), outwit, shake (someone) off

slippery 1. glassy, greasy, icy, lu~

bricious (*Rare*), perilous, skiddy (*Inf.*), slippy (*Inf.*), smooth, unsafe, unstable, unsteady 2. crafty, cunning, devious, dishonest, duplicitous, evasive, false, foxy, shifty, sneaky, treacherous, tricky, two-faced, unpredictable, unreliable, untrustworthy

slipshod careless, loose, slapdash, sloppy (*Inf.*), slovenly, unsystematic, untidy

slit 1. *v.* cut (open), gash, knife, lance, pierce, rip, slash, split open 2. *n.* cut, fissure, gash, incision, opening, rent, split, tear

slither *v.* glide, skitter, slide, slink, slip, snake, undulate

slog *v.* 1. hit, hit for six, slosh (*Brit. sl.*), slug, sock (*Sl.*), strike, thump, wallop (*Inf.*) 2. apply oneself to, labour, peg away at, persevere, plod, plough through, slave, toil, tramp, trek, trudge, work ~*n.* 3. effort, exertion, hike, labour, struggle, tramp, trek, trudge

slogan catchword, jingle, motto, rallying cry

slope *v.* 1. drop away, fall, incline, lean, pitch, rise, slant, tilt ~*n.* 2. brae (*Scot.*), declination, declivity, descent, downgrade (*Chiefly U.S.*), gradient, inclination, incline, ramp, rise, scarp, slant, tilt ~*v.* 3. *With off, away, etc.* creep, make oneself scarce, skulk, slink, slip, steal

sloping bevelled, cant, inclined, inclining, leaning, oblique, slanting

sloppy 1. sludgy, slushy, splashy, watery, wet 2. *Inf.* amateurish, careless, clumsy, hit-or-miss (*Inf.*), inattentive, messy, slipshod, slovenly, unkempt, untidy, weak 3. banal, gushing, mawkish, mushy (*Inf.*), overemotional, sentimental, slushy (*Inf.*), soppy (*Brit. inf.*), trite, wet (*Brit. inf.*)

slot *n.* 1. aperture, channel, groove, hole, slit 2. *Inf.* niche, opening, place, position, space, time, vacancy ~*v.* 3. adjust, assign, fit, fit in, insert, pigeonhole

sloth faineance, idleness, inactivity, indolence, inertia, laziness, slackness, slothfulness, sluggishness, torpor

slothful do-nothing (*Inf.*), fainéant, idle, inactive, indolent, inert, lazy, skiving (*Brit. inf.*), slack, sluggish, torpid, workshy

slouch *v.* droop, loll, slump, stoop

slovenly careless, disorderly, heedless, loose, negligent, slack, slapdash, slatternly, slipshod, sloppy (*Inf.*), unkempt, untidy

slow *adj.* 1. creeping, dawdling, deliberate, easy, lackadaisical, laggard, lagging, lazy, leaden, leisurely, loitering, measured, plodding, ponderous, slow-moving, sluggardly, sluggish, tortoise-like, unhurried 2. backward, behind, behindhand, delayed, dilatory, late, long-delayed, tardy, unpunctual 3. gradual, lingering, long-drawn-out, prolonged, protracted, time-consuming 4. behind the times, boring, conservative, dead, dead-and-alive (*Brit.*), dull, inactive, one-horse (*Inf.*), quiet, slack, sleepy, sluggish, stagnant, tame, tedious, uneventful, uninteresting, unproductive, unprogressive, wearisome 5. blockish, bovine, dense, dim, dull, dull-witted, dumb (*Inf.*), obtuse, retarded, slow on the uptake (*Inf.*), slow-witted, stupid, thick, unresponsive 6. *With* to averse, disinclined, hesitant, indisposed, loath, reluctant, unwilling ~*v.* 7. *Often with* up *or* down brake, check, curb, decelerate, delay, detain, handicap, hold up, lag, reduce speed, rein in, relax, restrict, retard, slacken (off), spin out

slowly at a snail's pace, at one's leisure, by degrees, gradually, inchmeal, in one's own (good) time, leisurely, ploddingly, steadily, taking one's time, unhurriedly, with leaden steps

sluggish dull, heavy, inactive, indolent, inert, lethargic, lifeless, listless, phlegmatic, slothful, slow, slow-moving, torpid, unresponsive

sluggishness apathy, drowsiness, dullness, heaviness, indolence, inertia, languor, lassitude, lethargy, listlessness, slothfulness, somnolence, stagnation, torpor

slumber *v.* be inactive, doze, lie

dormant, nap, repose, sleep, snooze (*Inf.*)

slump v. 1. collapse, crash, decline, deteriorate, fall, fall off, go down~ hill (*Inf.*), plummet, plunge, reach a new low, sink, slip ~n. 2. col~ lapse, crash, decline, depreciation, depression, downturn, failure, fall, falling-off, low, recession, reverse, stagnation, trough ~v. 3. bend, droop, hunch, loll, sag, slouch

slur n. affront, aspersion, blot, brand, calumny, discredit, dis~ grace, innuendo, insinuation, insult, reproach, smear, stain, stigma

slut drab (*Archaic*), slattern, slov~ en, trollop

sly adj. 1. artful, astute, clever, con~ niving, covert, crafty, cunning, de~ vious, foxy, furtive, guileful, insidi~ ous, scheming, secret, shifty, stealthy, subtle, underhand, wily 2. arch, impish, knowing, mischie~ vous, roguish ~n. 3. **on the sly** behind (someone's) back, covertly, like a thief in the night, on the q.t. (*Inf.*), on the quiet, privately, se~ cretly, surreptitiously, underhand~ edly, under the counter (*Inf.*)

smack v. 1. box, clap, cuff, hit, pat, slap, sock (*Sl.*), spank, strike, tap ~n. 2. blow, crack, slap 3. **smack in the eye** blow, rebuff, repulse, setback, slap in the face, snub ~adv. 4. *Inf.* directly, exactly, plumb, point-blank, precisely, right, slap (*Inf.*), squarely, straight

small 1. diminutive, immature, lit~ tle, mini, miniature, minute, petite, pint-sized (*Inf.*), pocket-sized, puny, slight, tiny, undersized, wee, young 2. insignificant, lesser, minor, neg~ ligible, paltry, petty, trifling, triv~ ial, unimportant 3. inadequate, in~ considerable, insufficient, limited, meagre, scanty 4. humble, modest, small-scale, unpretentious 5. base, grudging, illiberal, mean, narrow, petty, selfish 6. **make (someone) feel small** chagrin, disconcert, humble, humiliate, make (some~ one) look foolish, mortify, put down (*Sl.*), show up (*Inf.*), take down a peg or two (*Inf.*)

small-minded bigoted, envious, grudging, hidebound, intolerant, mean, narrow-minded, petty, rigid, ungenerous

smart[1] adj. 1. acute, adept, agile, apt, astute, bright, brisk, canny, clever, ingenious, intelligent, keen, nimble, quick, quick-witted, ready, sharp, shrewd 2. chic, elegant, fashionable, fine, modish, natty (*Inf.*), neat, snappy, spruce, stylish, trim, well turned-out 3. effective, impertinent, nimble-witted, point~ ed, ready, saucy, smart-alecky (*Inf.*), witty 4. brisk, cracking (*Inf.*), jaunty, lively, quick, spank~ ing, spirited, vigorous

smart[2] 1. v. burn, hurt, pain, sting, throb, tingle 2. adj. hard, keen, painful, piercing, resounding, sharp, stinging 3. n. burning sensa~ tion, pain, pang, smarting, sore~ ness, sting

smash v. 1. break, collide, crash, crush, demolish, disintegrate, pul~ verize, shatter, shiver ~n. 2. acci~ dent, collision, crash, pile-up (*Inf.*), smash-up (*Inf.*) ~v. 3. defeat, de~ stroy, lay waste, overthrow, ruin, wreck ~n. 4. collapse, defeat, de~ struction, disaster, downfall, fail~ ure, ruin, shattering

smashing excellent, exhilarating, fab (*Sl.*), fabulous (*Inf.*), fantastic (*Inf.*), first-class, first-rate, great (*Inf.*), magnificent, marvellous, out of this world (*Inf.*), sensational, stupendous, super (*Inf.*), superb, superlative, terrific (*Inf.*), wonder~ ful

smattering bit, dash, elements, modicum, rudiments, smatter, sprinkling

smear v. 1. bedaub, bedim, be~ smirch, blur, coat, cover, daub, dirty, patch, plaster, rub on, smudge, soil, spread over, stain, sully ~n. 2. blot, blotch, daub, smudge, splotch, streak ~v. 3. as~ perse, besmirch, blacken, calum~ niate, drag (someone's) name through the mud (*Inf.*), malign, sully, tarnish, traduce, vilify ~n. 4. calumny, defamation, libel, mud~ slinging, slander, vilification, whis~ pering campaign

smell *n.* 1. aroma, bouquet, fragrance, odour, perfume, redolence, scent, whiff ~*v.* 2. get a whiff of (*Brit. sl.*), nose, scent, sniff ~*n.* 3. fetor, pong (*Brit. inf.*), stench, stink ~*v.* 4. be malodorous, hum (*Sl.*), pong (*Brit. inf.*), reek, stink, stink to high heaven (*Inf.*), whiff (*Brit. sl.*)

smirk *n.* grin, leer, simper, smug look, sneer

smitten 1. afflicted, beset, laid low, plagued, struck 2. beguiled, bewitched, bowled over (*Inf.*), captivated, charmed, enamoured, infatuated, swept off one's feet

smoky begrimed, black, caliginous (*Archaic*), grey, grimy, hazy, murky, reeky, smoke-darkened, sooty, thick

smooth *adj.* 1. even, flat, flush, horizontal, level, plain, plane, unwrinkled 2. glossy, polished, shiny, silky, sleek, soft, velvety 3. calm, equable, glassy, mirror-like, peaceful, serene, tranquil, undisturbed, unruffled 4. agreeable, bland, mellow, mild, pleasant, soothing 5. facile, glib, ingratiating, persuasive, silky, slick, smarmy (*Brit. inf.*), suave, unctuous, urbane 6. easy, effortless, flowing, fluent, frictionless, regular, rhythmic, steady, unbroken, uneventful, uniform, uninterrupted, untroubled, well-ordered ~*v.* 7. flatten, iron, level, plane, polish, press 8. allay, alleviate, appease, assuage, calm, ease, extenuate, facilitate, iron out the difficulties of, mitigate, mollify, palliate, pave the way, soften

smoothness 1. evenness, flushness, levelness, regularity, unbrokenness 2. silkiness, sleekness, smooth texture, softness, velvetiness 3. calmness, glassiness, placidity, serenity, stillness, unruffled surface 4. glibness, oiliness, smarminess (*Brit. inf.*), suavity, urbanity 5. ease, efficiency, effortlessness, felicity, finish, flow, fluency, polish, rhythm, slickness, smooth running

smother *v.* 1. choke, extinguish, snuff, stifle, strangle, suffocate 2. conceal, hide, keep back, muffle, repress, stifle, suppress 3. be swimming in, cocoon, cover, envelop, heap, inundate, overwhelm, shower, shroud, surround ~*n.* 4. fug (*Chiefly Brit.*), smog

smoulder *Fig.* be resentful, boil, burn, fester, fume, rage, seethe, simmer, smart under

smug complacent, conceited, holier-than-thou, priggish, self-opinionated, self-righteous, self-satisfied, superior

smuggler bootlegger, contrabandist, gentleman, moonshiner (*U.S.*), rum-runner, runner, wrecker

snack bite, bite to eat, break, elevenses (*Brit. inf.*), light meal, nibble, refreshment(s), titbit

snag 1. *n.* catch, complication, difficulty, disadvantage, drawback, hitch, inconvenience, obstacle, problem, stumbling block, the rub 2. *v.* catch, hole, rip, tear

snap *v.* 1. break, come apart, crack, give way, separate 2. bite, bite at, catch, grip, nip, seize, snatch 3. bark, flare out, flash, fly off the handle at (*Inf.*), growl, jump down (someone's) throat (*Inf.*), lash out at, retort, snarl, speak sharply 4. click, crackle, pop 5. **snap one's fingers at** cock a snook at (*Brit.*), defy, flout, pay no attention to, scorn, set at naught, wave two fingers at (*Sl.*) 6. **snap out of it** cheer up, get a grip on oneself, get over, liven up, perk up, pull oneself together (*Inf.*), recover ~*n.* 7. crackle, fillip, flick, pop 8. bite, grab, nip 9. *Inf.* energy, get-up-and-go (*Inf.*), go (*Inf.*), liveliness, pizazz (*Inf.*), vigour, zip (*Inf.*) ~*adj.* 10. abrupt, immediate, instant, on-the-spot, sudden, unpremeditated

snappy 1. apt to fly off the handle (*Inf.*), cross, edgy, hasty, irritable, like a bear with a sore head (*Inf.*), quick-tempered, snappish, tart, testy, touchy, waspish 2. chic, dapper, fashionable, modish, natty (*Inf.*), smart, stylish, trendy (*Brit. inf.*), up-to-the-minute 3. **look snappy** be quick, buck up (*Inf.*), get a move on (*Inf.*), get one's skates on, hurry (up), look lively, make haste

snap up avail oneself of, grab, grasp, nab (*Inf.*), pounce upon, seize, swoop down on, take advantage of

snare 1. *v.* catch, entrap, net, seize, springe, trap, trepan (*Archaic*), wire **2.** *n.* catch, gin, net, noose, pitfall, springe, trap, wire

snarl[1] *v.* complain, growl, grumble, mumble, murmur, show its teeth (*of an animal*)

snarl[2] *v. Often with* **up** complicate, confuse, embroil, enmesh, entangle, entwine, muddle, ravel, tangle

snarl-up confusion, entanglement, muddle, tangle, (traffic) jam

snatch 1. *v.* clutch, gain, grab, grasp, grip, make off with, pluck, pull, rescue, seize, take, win, wrench, wrest **2.** *n.* bit, fragment, part, piece, smattering, snippet, spell

sneak *v.* **1.** cower, lurk, pad, sidle, skulk, slink, slip, smuggle, spirit, steal **2.** *Inf.* grass on (*Brit. inf.*), inform on, peach (*Sl.*), tell on (*Inf.*), tell tales ~*n.* **3.** informer, snake in the grass, telltale ~*adj.* **4.** clandestine, furtive, quick, secret, stealthy, surprise

sneaking 1. hidden, private, secret, suppressed, unavowed, unconfessed, undivulged, unexpressed, unvoiced **2.** intuitive, nagging, niggling, persistent, uncomfortable, worrying **3.** contemptible, furtive, mean, sly, sneaky, surreptitious, two-faced, underhand

sneer 1. *v.* curl one's lip, deride, disdain, gibe, hold in contempt, hold up to ridicule, jeer, laugh, look down on, mock, ridicule, scoff, scorn, sniff at, snigger, turn up one's nose (*Inf.*) **2.** *n.* derision, disdain, gibe, jeer, mockery, ridicule, scorn, snidery, snigger

sniff *v.* breathe, inhale, smell, snuff, snuffle

snigger giggle, laugh, smirk, sneer, snicker, titter

snip *v.* **1.** clip, crop, cut, nick, nip off, notch, shave, trim ~*n.* **2.** bit, clipping, fragment, piece, scrap, shred, snippet **3.** *Inf.* bargain, giveaway, good buy

snivel blubber, cry, girn (*Dialect*), gripe (*Inf.*), grizzle (*Inf.*), mewl, moan, sniffle, snuffle, weep, whimper, whine, whinge (*Inf.*)

snobbery airs, arrogance, condescension, pretension, pride, side (*Brit. sl.*), snobbishness, snootiness (*Inf.*), uppishness (*Brit. inf.*)

snobbish arrogant, condescending, high and mighty (*Inf.*), high-hat (*Inf., chiefly U.S.*), hoity-toity (*Inf.*), patronizing, pretentious, snooty (*Inf.*), stuck-up (*Inf.*), superior, toffee-nosed (*Sl.*), uppish (*Brit. inf.*)

snoop interfere, poke one's nose in (*Inf.*), pry, spy

snooper busybody, meddler, nosy parker (*Inf.*), Paul Pry, pry, snoop (*Inf.*), stickybeak (*Aust. inf.*)

snooze 1. *v.* catnap, doze, drop off (*Inf.*), drowse, kip (*Brit. sl.*), nap, nod off (*Inf.*), take forty winks (*Inf.*) **2.** *n.* catnap, doze, forty winks (*Inf.*), kip (*Brit. sl.*), nap, siesta

snub 1. *v.* cold-shoulder, cut (*Inf.*), cut dead (*Inf.*), give (someone) the brush-off (*Sl.*), give (someone) the cold shoulder, humble, humiliate, mortify, rebuff, shame, slight **2.** *n.* affront, brushoff (*Sl.*), humiliation, insult, put-down, slap in the face

snug 1. comfortable, comfy (*Inf.*), cosy, homely, intimate, sheltered, warm **2.** close, compact, neat, trim

snuggle cuddle, nestle, nuzzle

soak *v.* **1.** bathe, damp, drench, immerse, infuse, marinate (*Cookery*), moisten, penetrate, permeate, saturate, steep, wet **2.** *With* **up** absorb, assimilate, drink in, take up *or* in

soaking drenched, dripping, drookit (*Scot.*), saturated, soaked, soaked to the skin, sodden, sopping, streaming, waterlogged, wet through, wringing wet

soar 1. ascend, fly, mount, rise, tower, wing **2.** climb, escalate, rise, rocket, shoot up

sob *v.* bawl, blubber, boohoo, cry, greet (*Dialect*), howl, shed tears, snivel, weep

sober *adj.* **1.** abstemious, abstinent,

moderate, on the wagon (*Inf.*), temperate 2. calm, clear-headed, cold, composed, cool, dispassion~ ate, grave, level-headed, lucid, peaceful, practical, rational, real~ istic, reasonable, sedate, serene, serious, solemn, sound, staid, steady, unexcited, unruffled 3. dark, drab, plain, quiet, severe, sombre, subdued ~*v.* 4. *Usually with up* bring (someone) back to earth, calm down, clear one's head, come *or* bring to one's senses, give (someone) pause for thought, make (someone) stop and think

sobriety 1. abstemiousness, absti~ nence, moderation, nonindulgence, self-restraint, soberness, temper~ ance 2. calmness, composure, coolness, gravity, level-headedness, reasonableness, re~ straint, sedateness, seriousness, solemnity, staidness, steadiness

so-called alleged, ostensible, pre~ tended, professed, self-styled, *soi-disant*, supposed

sociability affability, companion~ ability, congeniality, conviviality, cordiality, friendliness, gregari~ ousness, neighbourliness

sociable accessible, affable, ap~ proachable, companionable, con~ versable, convivial, cordial, famili~ ar, friendly, genial, gregarious, neighbourly, outgoing, social, warm

social *adj.* 1. collective, common, communal, community, general, group, organized, public, societal 2. companionable, friendly, gregari~ ous, neighbourly, sociable ~*n.* 3. do (*Inf.*), gathering, get-together (*Inf.*)

socialize be a good mixer, enter~ tain, fraternize, get about *or* around, get together, go out, mix

society 1. civilization, culture, hu~ manity, mankind, people, popula~ tion, social order, the community, the general public, the public, the world at large 2. camaraderie, companionship, company, fellow~ ship, friendship 3. association, brotherhood, circle, club, corpora~ tion, fellowship, fraternity, group,

guild, institute, league, organiza~ tion, sisterhood, union 4. beau monde, elite, gentry, *haut monde*, high society, polite society, the country set, the nobs (*Sl.*), the smart set, the swells (*Inf.*), the toffs (*Brit. sl.*), the top drawer, upper classes, upper crust (*Inf.*)

sodden boggy, drenched, drookit (*Scot.*), marshy, miry, saturated, soaked, soggy, sopping, water~ logged

soft 1. creamy, cushioned, cush~ iony, doughy, elastic, gelatinous, pulpy, quaggy, spongy, squashy, swampy, yielding 2. bendable, ductile (*of metals*), elastic, flexible, impressible, malleable, mouldable, plastic, pliable, supple 3. downy, feathery, fleecy, flowing, fluid, fur~ ry, like a baby's bottom (*Inf.*), rounded, silky, smooth, velvety 4. balmy, bland, caressing, delicate, diffuse, dim, dimmed, dulcet, faint, gentle, light, low, mellifluous, mel~ low, melodious, mild, murmured, muted, pale, pastel, pleasing, quiet, restful, shaded, soft-toned, sooth~ ing, subdued, sweet, temperate, twilight, understated, whispered 5. compassionate, gentle, kind, pity~ ing, sensitive, sentimental, sympa~ thetic, tender, tenderhearted 6. easy-going, indulgent, lax, lenient, liberal, overindulgent, permissive, spineless, weak 7. *Inf.* comfortable, cushy (*Sl.*), easy, undemanding 8. effeminate, flabby, flaccid, limp, namby-pamby, out of condition, out of training, overindulged, pam~ pered, podgy, weak 9. *Inf.* a bit lacking (*Inf.*), daft (*Inf.*), feeble-minded, foolish, silly, simple, soft in the head (*Inf.*), soppy (*Brit. inf.*)

soften abate, allay, alleviate, ap~ pease, assuage, calm, cushion, di~ minish, ease, lessen, lighten, lower, melt, mitigate, moderate, modify, mollify, muffle, palliate, quell, re~ lax, soothe, still, subdue, temper, tone down, turn down

soften up conciliate, disarm, melt, soft-soap (*Inf.*), weaken, win over, work on

softhearted charitable, compas~

sionate, generous, indulgent, kind, sentimental, sympathetic, tender, tenderhearted, warm-hearted

soil[1] *n.* 1. clay, dirt, dust, earth, ground, loam 2. country, land, region, terra firma

soil[2] *v.* bedraggle, befoul, begrime, besmirch, defile, dirty, foul, maculate (*Literary*), muddy, pollute, smear, spatter, spot, stain, sully, tarnish

solace 1. *n.* alleviation, assuagement, comfort, consolation, relief 2. *v.* allay, alleviate, comfort, console, mitigate, soften, soothe

soldier enlisted man (*U.S.*), fighter, GI (*U.S. inf.*), man-at-arms, military man, redcoat, serviceman, squaddy (*Brit. inf.*), Tommy (*Brit.*), trooper, warrior

sole alone, exclusive, individual, one, one and only, only, single, singular, solitary

solecism blunder, boo-boo (*Inf.*), breach of etiquette, cacology, faux pas, gaffe, gaucherie, impropriety, incongruity, indecorum, lapse, mistake

solely alone, completely, entirely, exclusively, merely, only, single-handedly, singly

solemn 1. earnest, glum, grave, portentous, sedate, serious, sober, staid, thoughtful 2. august, awe-inspiring, ceremonial, ceremonious, dignified, formal, grand, grave, imposing, impressive, majestic, momentous, stately 3. devotional, hallowed, holy, religious, reverential, ritual, sacred, sanctified, venerable

solemnity 1. earnestness, grandeur, gravity, impressiveness, momentousness, portentousness, sacredness, sanctity, seriousness 2. *Often plural* celebration, ceremonial, ceremony, formalities, observance, proceedings, rite, ritual

solemnize celebrate, commemorate, honour, keep, observe

solicit ask, beg, beseech, canvass, crave, entreat, implore, importune, petition, plead for, pray, seek, supplicate

solicitous anxious, apprehensive, attentive, careful, caring, concerned, eager, earnest, troubled, uneasy, worried, zealous

solicitude anxiety, attentiveness, care, concern, considerateness, consideration, regard, worry

solid *adj.* 1. compact, concrete, dense, firm, hard, massed, stable, strong, sturdy, substantial, unshakable 2. genuine, good, pure, real, reliable, sound 3. agreed, complete, continuous, unalloyed, unanimous, unbroken, undivided, uninterrupted, united, unmixed 4. constant, decent, dependable, estimable, law-abiding, level-headed, reliable, sensible, serious, sober, trusty, upright, upstanding, worthy

solidarity accord, camaraderie, cohesion, community of interest, concordance, esprit de corps, harmony, like-mindedness, singleness of purpose, soundness, stability, team spirit, unanimity, unification, unity

solidify cake, coagulate, cohere, congeal, harden, jell, set

solitary *adj.* 1. desolate, hidden, isolated, lonely, out-of-the-way, remote, retired, secluded, sequestered, unfrequented, unvisited 2. alone, lone, single, sole 3. cloistered, companionless, friendless, hermitical, lonely, lonesome, reclusive, unsociable, unsocial ~*n.* 4. hermit, introvert, loner (*Inf.*), lone wolf, recluse

solitude 1. isolation, loneliness, privacy, reclusiveness, retirement, seclusion 2. *Poetic* desert, emptiness, waste, wasteland, wilderness

solution 1. answer, clarification, elucidation, explanation, explication, key, resolution, result, solving, unfolding, unravelling 2. blend, compound, emulsion, mix, mixture, solvent, suspension (*Chem.*) 3. disconnection, dissolution, liquefaction, melting

solve answer, clarify, clear up, crack, decipher, disentangle, elucidate, explain, expound, get to the bottom of, interpret, resolve, unfold, unravel, work out

sombre dark, dim, dismal, doleful,

somebody drab, dull, dusky, funereal, gloomy, grave, joyless, lugubrious, melan~ choly, mournful, obscure, sad, se~ pulchral, shadowy, shady, sober

somebody n. big noise (Brit. sl.), big shot (Sl.), big wheel (Sl.), big~ wig (Sl.), celebrity, dignitary, heavyweight (Inf.), household name, luminary, name, notable, personage, person of note, public figure, star, superstar, V.I.P.

someday eventually, one day, one of these (fine) days, sooner or lat~ er, ultimately

somehow by fair means or foul, by hook or (by) crook, by some means or other, come hell or high water (Inf.), come what may, one way or another

sometimes at times, every now and then, every so often, from time to time, now and again, now and then, occasionally, off and on, once in a while, on occasion

somnolent comatose, dozy, drowsy, half-awake, heavy-eyed, nodding off (Inf.), sleepy, soporific, torpid

song air, anthem, ballad, canticle, canzonet, carol, chant, chorus, dit~ ty, hymn, lay, lyric, melody, num~ ber, pop song, psalm, shanty, strain, tune

soon anon (Archaic), any minute now, before long, betimes (Archa~ ic), in a little while, in a minute, in a short time, in the near future, shortly

soothe allay, alleviate, appease, assuage, calm, calm down, com~ pose, ease, hush, lull, mitigate, mollify, pacify, quiet, relieve, set~ tle, smooth down, soften, still, tranquillize

soothing balsamic, calming, de~ mulcent, easeful, emollient, leni~ tive, palliative, relaxing, restful

soothsayer augur, diviner, fore~ teller, prophet, seer, sibyl

sophisticated 1. blasé, citified, cosmopolitan, cultivated, cultured, jet-set, refined, seasoned, urbane, worldly, worldly-wise, world-weary 2. advanced, complex, complicat~ ed, delicate, elaborate, highly-

developed, intricate, multifaceted, refined, subtle

sophistication finesse, poise, savoir-faire, savoir-vivre, urbanity, worldliness, worldly wisdom

sophistry casuistry, fallacy, quib~ ble, sophism

soporific 1. adj. hypnotic, sedative, sleep-inducing, sleepy, somnifer~ ous (Rare), somnolent, tranquilliz~ ing 2. n. anaesthetic, hypnotic, narcotic, opiate, sedative, tran~ quillizer

soppy corny (Inf.), daft (Inf.), drip~ py (Inf.), gushy (Inf.), lovey-dovey, mawkish, overemotional, schmaltzy (Sl.), sentimental, silly, slushy (Inf.), soft (Inf.), weepy (Inf.)

sorcerer enchanter, mage (Archa~ ic), magician, magus, necroman~ cer, sorceress, warlock, witch, wizard

sorcery black art, black magic, charm, divination, enchantment, incantation, magic, necromancy, spell, witchcraft, witchery, wiz~ ardry

sordid 1. dirty, filthy, foul, mean, seamy, seedy, sleazy, slovenly, slummy, squalid, unclean, wretch~ ed 2. backstreet, base, debauched, degenerate, degraded, despicable, disreputable, low, shabby, shame~ ful, vicious, vile 3. avaricious, cor~ rupt, covetous, grasping, merce~ nary, miserly, niggardly, selfish, self-seeking, ungenerous, venal

sore adj. 1. angry, burning, chafed, inflamed, irritated, painful, raw, reddened, sensitive, smarting, ten~ der 2. annoying, distressing, griev~ ous, harrowing, severe, sharp, troublesome 3. acute, critical, des~ perate, dire, extreme, pressing, urgent 4. afflicted, aggrieved, an~ gry, annoyed, grieved, hurt, irked, irritated, pained, peeved (Inf.), re~ sentful, stung, upset, vexed ~n. 5. abscess, boil, chafe, gathering, in~ flammation, ulcer

sorrow n. 1. affliction, anguish, dis~ tress, grief, heartache, heartbreak, misery, mourning, regret, sadness, unhappiness, woe 2. affliction, blow, hardship, misfortune, trial, tribulation, trouble, woe, worry ~v. 3. agonize, bemoan, be sad, bewail, grieve, lament, moan, mourn, weep

sorrowful affecting, afflicted, dejected, depressed, disconsolate, distressing, doleful, grievous, heartbroken, heart-rending, heavy-hearted, lamentable, lugubrious, melancholy, miserable, mournful, painful, piteous, rueful, sad, sick at heart, sorry, tearful, unhappy, woebegone, woeful, wretched

sorry 1. apologetic, conscience-stricken, contrite, guilt-ridden, in sackcloth and ashes, penitent, regretful, remorseful, repentant, self-reproachful, shamefaced 2. disconsolate, distressed, grieved, melancholy, mournful, sad, sorrowful, unhappy 3. commiserative, compassionate, full of pity, moved, pitying, sympathetic 4. abject, base, deplorable, dismal, distressing, mean, miserable, paltry, pathetic, piteous, pitiable, pitiful, poor, sad, shabby, vile, wretched

sort n. 1. brand, breed, category, character, class, denomination, description, family, genus, group, ilk, kind, make, nature, order, quality, race, species, stamp, style, type, variety 2. out of sorts crotchety, down in the dumps (*Inf.*), down in the mouth (*Inf.*), grouchy (*Inf.*), in low spirits, mopy, not up to par, not up to snuff (*Inf.*), off colour, poorly (*Inf.*), under the weather (*Inf.*) 3. sort of as it were, in part, moderately, rather, reasonably, slightly, somewhat, to some extent ~v. 4. arrange, assort, catalogue, categorize, choose, class, classify, distribute, divide, file, grade, group, order, put in order, rank, select, separate, systematize

sort out 1. clarify, clear up, organize, put *or* get straight, resolve, tidy up 2. pick out, put on one side, segregate, select, separate, sift

soul 1. animating principle, essence, intellect, life, mind, psyche, reason, spirit, vital force 2. being,

body, creature, individual, man, mortal, person, woman 3. embodiment, essence, incarnation, personification, quintessence, type 4. animation, ardour, courage, energy, feeling, fervour, force, inspiration, nobility, vitality, vivacity

sound[1] n. 1. din, noise, report, resonance, reverberation, tone, voice 2. drift, idea, implication(s), impression, look, tenor 3. earshot, hearing, range ~v. 4. echo, resonate, resound, reverberate 5. appear, give the impression of, look, seem, strike one as being 6. announce, articulate, declare, enunciate, express, pronounce, signal, utter

sound[2] adj. 1. complete, entire, firm, fit, hale, hale and hearty, healthy, intact, perfect, robust, solid, sturdy, substantial, undamaged, unhurt, unimpaired, uninjured, vigorous, well-constructed, whole 2. correct, fair, just, level-headed, logical, orthodox, proper, prudent, rational, reasonable, reliable, responsible, right, right-thinking, sensible, true, trustworthy, valid, well-founded, well-grounded, wise 3. established, orthodox, proven, recognized, reliable, reputable, safe, secure, solid, solvent, stable, tried-and-true 4. deep, peaceful, unbroken, undisturbed, untroubled

sound[3] v. 1. fathom, plumb, probe 2. examine, inspect, investigate, test

sound out canvass, examine, probe, pump, question, see how the land lies

sour adj. 1. acetic, acid, acidulated, bitter, pungent, sharp, tart, unpleasant 2. bad, curdled, fermented, gone off, rancid, turned, unsavoury, unwholesome 3. acrid, acrimonious, churlish, crabbed, cynical, disagreeable, discontented, embittered, grouchy (*Inf.*), grudging, ill-natured, ill-tempered, jaundiced, peevish, tart, ungenerous, waspish ~v. 4. alienate, disenchant, embitter, envenom, exacerbate, exasperate, turn off (*Inf.*)

source 1. author, begetter, beginning, cause, commencement, derivation, fountainhead, origin, originator, rise, spring, wellspring 2. authority, informant

souse drench, dunk, immerse, marinate (*Cookery*), pickle, soak, steep

souvenir keepsake, memento, relic, remembrancer (*Archaic*), reminder, token

sovereign n. 1. chief, emperor, empress, king, monarch, potentate, prince, queen, ruler, shah, supreme ruler, tsar ~adj. 2. absolute, chief, dominant, imperial, kingly, monarchal, paramount, predominant, principal, queenly, regal, royal, ruling, supreme, unlimited 3. effectual, efficacious, efficient, excellent

sovereignty ascendancy, domination, kingship, primacy, supremacy, supreme power, suzerainty, sway

sow broadcast, disseminate, implant, inseminate, lodge, plant, scatter, seed

space 1. amplitude, capacity, elbowroom, expanse, extension, extent, leeway, margin, play, room, scope, spaciousness, volume 2. blank, distance, gap, interval, lacuna, omission 3. duration, interval, period, span, time, while 4. accommodation, berth, place, seat

spaceman or **spacewoman** astronaut, cosmonaut

spacious ample, broad, capacious, comfortable, commodious, expansive, extensive, huge, large, roomy, sizable, uncrowded, vast

spadework donkey-work, groundwork, labour, preparation

span n. 1. amount, distance, extent, length, reach, spread, stretch 2. duration, period, spell, term ~v. 3. arch across, bridge, cover, cross, extend across, link, range over, traverse, vault

spank v. belt (*Sl.*), cuff, give (someone) a hiding (*Inf.*), put (someone) over one's knee, slap, slipper (*Inf.*), smack, tan (*Sl.*), wallop (*Inf.*)

spar v. argue, bicker, dispute, exchange blows, fall out (*Inf.*), have a tiff, lead a cat-and-dog life, scrap (*Inf.*), skirmish, spat (*U.S.*), squabble, wrangle, wrestle

spare adj. 1. additional, emergency, extra, free, going begging (*Inf.*), in excess, in reserve, leftover, odd, over, superfluous, supernumerary, surplus, unoccupied, unused, unwanted 2. gaunt, lank, lean, meagre, slender, slight, slim, wiry 3. economical, frugal, meagre, modest, scanty, sparing 4. **go spare** *Brit. sl.* become angry (distracted, distraught, enraged, mad (*Inf.*), upset), blow one's top (*Inf.*), do one's nut (*Brit. sl.*), go up the wall (*Sl.*), have or throw a fit (*Inf.*) ~v. 5. afford, allow, bestow, dispense with, do without, give, grant, let (someone) have, manage without, part with, relinquish 6. be merciful to, deal leniently with, go easy on (*Inf.*), have mercy on, leave, let off (*Inf.*), pardon, refrain from, release, relieve from, save from

spare time free time, leisure, odd moments, time on one's hands, time to kill

sparing careful, chary, cost-conscious, economical, frugal, money-conscious, prudent, saving, thrifty

spark n. 1. flare, flash, flicker, gleam, glint, scintillation, spit 2. atom, hint, jot, scintilla, scrap, trace, vestige ~v. 3. *Often with* off animate, excite, inspire, kindle, precipitate, provoke, set in motion, set off, start, stimulate, stir, touch off, trigger (off)

sparkle v. 1. beam, coruscate, dance, flash, gleam, glint, glisten, glister (*Archaic*), glitter, glow, scintillate, shimmer, shine, spark, twinkle, wink 2. bubble, effervesce, fizz, fizzle ~n. 3. brilliance, coruscation, dazzle, flash, flicker, gleam, glint, radiance, spark, twinkle 4. animation, dash, élan, gaiety, life, panache, spirit, vim (*Sl.*), vitality, vivacity, zip (*Inf.*)

spartan 1. abstemious, ascetic, austere, bleak, disciplined, ex~

treme, frugal, plain, rigorous, self-denying, severe, stern, strict, stringent 2. bold, brave, courageous, daring, dauntless, doughty, fearless, hardy, heroic, intrepid, resolute, unflinching, valorous

spasm 1. contraction, convulsion, paroxysm, throe (*Rare*), twitch 2. access, burst, eruption, fit, frenzy, outburst, seizure

spasmodic convulsive, erratic, fitful, intermittent, irregular, jerky, sporadic

spate deluge, flood, flow, outpouring, rush, torrent

speak 1. articulate, communicate, converse, discourse, enunciate, express, make known, pronounce, say, state, talk, tell, utter, voice 2. address, argue, declaim, deliver an address, descant, discourse, harangue, hold forth, lecture, plead, speechify, spiel (*Inf.*) 3. *With of* advert to, allude to, comment on, deal with, discuss, make reference to, mention, refer to

speaker lecturer, mouthpiece, orator, public speaker, spieler (*Inf.*), spokesman, spokesperson, spokeswoman, word-spinner

speak for act for *or* on behalf of, appear for, hold a brief for, hold a mandate for, represent

speaking *adj.* eloquent, expressive, moving, noticeable, striking

speak out *or* **up** 1. make oneself heard, say it loud and clear, speak loudly 2. have one's say, make one's position plain, sound off, speak one's mind, stand up and be counted

speak to 1. accost, address, apostrophize, direct one's words at, talk to 2. admonish, bring to book, dress down (*Inf.*), lecture, rebuke, reprimand, scold, tell off (*Inf.*), tick off (*Inf.*), warn

spearhead *v.* be in the van, blaze the trail, head, initiate, launch, lay the first stone, lead, lead the way, pioneer, set in motion, set off

special 1. distinguished, especial, exceptional, extraordinary, festive, gala, important, memorable, momentous, out of the ordinary, red-letter, significant, uncommon, unique, unusual 2. appropriate, certain, characteristic, distinctive, especial, individual, particular, peculiar, precise, specialized, specific 3. chief, main, major, particular, primary

specialist *n.* authority, connoisseur, consultant, expert, master, professional

speciality claim to fame, distinctive *or* distinguishing feature, forte, *pièce de résistance*, special, specialty

species breed, category, class, collection, description, group, kind, sort, type, variety

specific *adj.* 1. clear-cut, definite, exact, explicit, express, limited, particular, precise, unambiguous, unequivocal 2. characteristic, distinguishing, especial, peculiar, special

specification condition, detail, item, particular, qualification, requirement, stipulation

specify be specific about, cite, define, designate, detail, enumerate, indicate, individualize, itemize, mention, name, particularize, spell out, stipulate

specimen copy, embodiment, example, exemplar, exemplification, exhibit, individual, instance, model, pattern, proof, representative, sample, type

specious casuistic, deceptive, fallacious, misleading, plausible, sophistic, sophistical, unsound

speck 1. blemish, blot, defect, dot, fault, flaw, fleck, mark, mote, speckle, spot, stain 2. atom, bit, dot, grain, iota, jot, mite, modicum, particle, shred, tittle, whit

speckled brindled, dappled, dotted, flecked, freckled, mottled, speckledy, spotted, spotty, sprinkled, stippled

spectacle 1. display, event, exhibition, extravaganza, pageant, parade, performance, show, sight 2. curiosity, laughing stock, marvel, phenomenon, scene, sight, wonder

spectacular 1. *adj.* breathtaking, daring, dazzling, dramatic, eye-catching, fantastic (*Inf.*), grand, impressive, magnificent, marked, remarkable, sensational, splendid, staggering, striking, stunning (*Inf.*) 2. *n.* display, extravaganza, show, spectacle

spectator beholder, bystander, eyewitness, looker-on, observer, onlooker, viewer, watcher, witness

speculate 1. cogitate, conjecture, consider, contemplate, deliberate, hypothesize, meditate, muse, scheme, suppose, surmise, theorize, wonder 2. gamble, have a flutter (*Inf.*), hazard, play the market, risk, take a chance with, venture

speculation 1. conjecture, consideration, contemplation, deliberation, guess, guesswork, hypothesis, opinion, supposition, surmise, theory 2. gamble, gambling, hazard, risk

speculative 1. abstract, academic, conjectural, hypothetical, notional, suppositional, tentative, theoretical 2. chancy (*Inf.*), dicey (*Sl.*), hazardous, risky, uncertain, unpredictable

speech 1. communication, conversation, dialogue, discussion, intercourse, talk 2. address, discourse, disquisition, harangue, homily, lecture, oration, spiel (*Inf.*) 3. articulation, dialect, diction, enunciation, idiom, jargon, language, lingo (*Inf.*), parlance, tongue, utterance, voice

speechless 1. dumb, inarticulate, mum, mute, silent, tongue-tied, unable to get a word out (*Inf.*), wordless 2. *Fig.* aghast, amazed, astounded, dazed, dumbfounded, dumbstruck, shocked, thunderstruck

speed *n.* 1. acceleration, celerity, expedition, fleetness, haste, hurry, momentum, pace, precipitation, quickness, rapidity, rush, swiftness, velocity ~*v.* 2. belt (along) (*Sl.*), bomb (along), bowl along, career, dispatch, exceed the speed limit, expedite, flash, gallop, get a move on (*Inf.*), go hell for leather (*Inf.*), go like a bat out of hell (*Inf.*), go

like the wind, hasten, hurry, lose no time, make haste, press on, put one's foot down (*Inf.*), quicken, race, rush, sprint, step on it (*Inf.*), tear, urge, zoom 3. advance, aid, assist, boost, expedite, facilitate, further, help, impel, promote

speed up accelerate, gather momentum, get moving, get under way, increase, increase the tempo, open up the throttle, put one's foot down (*Inf.*), put on speed

speedy expeditious, express, fast, fleet, fleet of foot, hasty, headlong, hurried, immediate, nimble, precipitate, prompt, quick, rapid, summary, swift, winged

spell[1] *n.* bout, course, interval, patch, period, season, stint, stretch, term, time, tour of duty, turn

spell[2] *n.* 1. abracadabra, charm, conjuration, exorcism, incantation, sorcery, witchery 2. allure, bewitchment, enchantment, fascination, glamour, magic, trance

spell[3] *v.* amount to, augur, herald, imply, indicate, mean, point to, portend, presage, promise, signify, suggest

spellbound bemused, bewitched, captivated, charmed, enthralled, entranced, fascinated, gripped, hooked (*Inf.*), mesmerized, possessed, rapt, transfixed, transported, under a spell

spelling orthography

spell out 1. clarify, elucidate, make clear *or* plain, make explicit, specify 2. discern, make out, puzzle out

spend 1. disburse, expend, fork out (*Sl.*), lay out, pay out, shell out (*Inf.*), splash out (*Brit. inf.*) 2. blow (*Sl.*), consume, deplete, dispense, dissipate, drain, empty, exhaust, fritter away, run through, squander, use up, waste 3. apply, bestow, concentrate, devote, employ, invest, lavish, put in, use 4. fill, occupy, pass, while away

spendthrift 1. *n.* big spender, prodigal, profligate, spender, squanderer, waster, wastrel 2. *adj.* extravagant, improvident, prodigal, profligate, wasteful

spent *adj.* **1.** all in (*Sl.*), burnt out, bushed (*U.S. inf.*), dead beat (*Inf.*), debilitated, dog-tired (*Inf.*), done in *or* up (*Inf.*), drained, exhausted, fagged (out) (*Inf.*), knackered (*Sl.*), played out (*Inf.*), prostrate, ready to drop (*Inf.*), shattered (*Inf.*), tired out, weakened, wearied, weary, whacked (*Brit. inf.*), worn out **2.** consumed, expended, finished, gone, used up

sphere 1. ball, circle, globe, glob~ule, orb **2.** capacity, compass, de~partment, domain, employment, field, function, pale, province, range, rank, realm, scope, station, stratum, territory, walk of life

spherical globe-shaped, globular, orbicular, rotund, round

spice *n.* **1.** relish, savour, seasoning **2.** colour, excitement, gusto, kick (*Inf.*), pep, piquancy, tang, zap (*Sl.*), zest, zip (*Inf.*)

spike *n.* **1.** barb, point, prong, spine ~*v.* **2.** impale, spear, spit, stick **3.** block, foil, frustrate, render inef~fective, thwart

spill *v.* **1.** discharge, disgorge, over~flow, overturn, scatter, shed, slop over, spill *or* run over, throw off, upset **2. spill the beans** *Inf.* betray a secret, blab, blow the gaff (*Brit. sl.*), give the game away, inform, let the cat out of the bag, split (*Sl.*), squeal (*Sl.*), talk out of turn, tattle ~*n.* **3.** *Inf.* accident, cropper (*Inf.*), fall, tumble

spin *v.* **1.** gyrate, pirouette, reel, revolve, rotate, turn, twirl, twist, wheel, whirl **2.** concoct, develop, invent, narrate, recount, relate, tell, unfold **3.** be giddy, be in a whirl, grow dizzy, reel, swim, whirl ~*n.* **4.** gyration, revolution, roll, twist, whirl **5.** (flat) **spin** *Inf.* agita~tion, commotion, flap (*Inf.*), panic, state (*Inf.*), tiz-woz (*Inf.*), tizzy (*Inf.*) **6.** *Inf.* drive, hurl (*Scot.*), joy ride (*Inf.*), ride, turn, whirl

spine 1. backbone, spinal column, vertebrae, vertebral column **2.** barb, needle, quill, rachis, ray, spike, spur

spine-chilling bloodcurdling, eerie, frightening, hair-raising,

horrifying, scary (*Inf.*), spooky (*Inf.*), terrifying

spineless cowardly, faint-hearted, feeble, gutless (*Inf.*), inadequate, ineffective, irresolute, lily-livered, soft, spiritless, squeamish, submis~sive, vacillating, weak, weak-kneed (*Inf.*), weak-willed, without a will of one's own, yellow (*Inf.*)

spin out amplify, delay, drag out, draw out, extend, lengthen, pad out, prolong, prolongate, protract

spiral 1. *adj.* circular, cochlear, cochleate (*Biol.*), coiled, cork~screw, helical, scrolled, voluted, whorled, winding **2.** *n.* coil, cork~screw, curlicue, gyre (*Literary*), helix, screw, volute, whorl

spirit *n.* **1.** air, breath, life, life force, psyche, soul, vital spark **2.** attitude, character, complexion, disposition, essence, humour, out~look, quality, temper, tempera~ment **3.** animation, ardour, back~bone, courage, dauntlessness, ear~nestness, energy, enterprise, en~thusiasm, fire, force, gameness, grit, guts (*Inf.*), life, liveliness, mettle, resolution, sparkle, spunk (*Inf.*), stoutheartedness, vigour, warmth, zest **4.** motivation, resolu~tion, resolve, will, willpower **5.** at~mosphere, feeling, gist, humour, tenor, tone **6.** essence, intent, in~tention, meaning, purport, purpose, sense, substance **7.** *Plural* feelings, frame of mind, humour, mood, morale **8.** apparition, ghost, phan~tom, shade (*Literary*), shadow, spectre, spook (*Inf.*), sprite, vision ~*v.* **9.** *With* **away** *or* **off** abduct, abstract, carry, convey, make away with, purloin, remove, seize, snaffle (*Brit. inf.*), steal, whisk

spirited active, animated, ardent, bold, courageous, energetic, game, high-spirited, lively, mettlesome, plucky, sparkling, sprightly, spunky (*Inf.*), vigorous, vivacious

spiritual devotional, divine, ethe~real, ghostly, holy, immaterial, in~corporeal, nonmaterial, other~worldly, pure, religious, sacred

spit 1. *v.* discharge, eject, expecto~rate, hiss, spew, splutter, sputter, throw out 2. *n.* dribble, drool, saliva, slaver, spittle, sputum

spite *n.* 1. animosity, bitchiness (*Sl.*), gall, grudge, hate, hatred, ill will, malevolence, malice, malignity, pique, rancour, spitefulness, spleen, venom 2. **in spite of** despite, in defiance of, notwithstanding, regardless of ~*v.* 3. annoy, discomfit, gall, harm, hurt, injure, needle (*Inf.*), nettle, offend, pique, provoke, put out, put (someone's) nose out of joint (*Inf.*), vex

spiteful barbed, bitchy (*Inf.*), catty (*Inf.*), cruel, ill-disposed, ill-natured, malevolent, malicious, malignant, rancorous, snide, splenetic, venomous, vindictive

splash *v.* 1. bespatter, shower, slop, slosh (*Inf.*), spatter, splodge, spray, spread, sprinkle, squirt, strew, wet 2. bathe, dabble, paddle, plunge, wade, wallow 3. batter, break, buffet, dash, plash, plop, smack, strike, surge, wash 4. blazon, broadcast, flaunt, headline, plaster, publicize, tout, trumpet ~*n.* 5. burst, dash, patch, spattering, splodge, touch 6. *Inf.* display, effect, impact, sensation, splurge, stir 7. **make a splash** be ostentatious, cause a stir, cut a dash, go overboard (*Inf.*), go to town (*Inf.*), splurge

splash out be extravagant, lash out (*Inf.*), push the boat out (*Brit. inf.*), spare no expense, spend, splurge

spleen acrimony, anger, animosity, animus, bad temper, bile, bitterness, gall, hatred, hostility, ill humour, ill will, malevolence, malice, malignity, peevishness, pique, rancour, resentment, spite, spitefulness, venom, vindictiveness, wrath

splendid 1. admirable, brilliant, exceptional, glorious, grand, heroic, illustrious, magnificent, outstanding, rare, remarkable, renowned, sterling, sublime, superb, supreme 2. costly, dazzling, gorgeous, imposing, impressive, lavish, luxurious, magnificent, ornate, resplendent, rich, sumptuous, superb 3. excellent, fantastic (*Inf.*), fine, first-class, glorious, great

(*Inf.*), marvellous, wonderful 4. beaming, bright, brilliant, glittering, glowing, lustrous, radiant, refulgent

splendour brightness, brilliance, ceremony, dazzle, display, effulgence, glory, gorgeousness, grandeur, lustre, magnificence, majesty, pomp, radiance, refulgence, renown, resplendence, richness, show, solemnity, spectacle, stateliness, sumptuousness

splice *v.* braid, entwine, graft, interlace, intertwine, intertwist, interweave, join, knit, marry, mesh, plait, unite, wed, yoke

splinter 1. *n.* chip, flake, fragment, needle, paring, shaving, sliver 2. *v.* break into smithereens, disintegrate, fracture, shatter, shiver, split

split *v.* 1. bifurcate, branch, break, break up, burst, cleave, come apart, come undone, crack, disband, disunite, diverge, fork, gape, give way, go separate ways, open, part, pull apart, rend, rip, separate, slash, slit, snap, splinter 2. allocate, apportion, carve up, distribute, divide, divvy up (*Inf.*), dole out, halve, parcel out, partition, share out, slice up 3. **With on** *Sl.* betray, give away, grass (*Brit. sl.*), inform on, peach (*Sl.*), squeal (*Sl.*) ~*n.* 4. breach, crack, damage, division, fissure, gap, rent, rip, separation, slash, slit, tear 5. breach, break, break-up, difference, discord, disruption, dissension, disunion, divergence, division, estrangement, partition, rift, rupture, schism ~*adj.* 6. ambivalent, bisected, broken, cleft, cracked, divided, dual, fractured, ruptured, twofold

split up break up, disband, divorce, go separate ways, part, part company, separate

spoil *v.* 1. blemish, damage, debase, deface, destroy, disfigure, harm, impair, injure, mar, mess up, ruin, upset, wreck 2. baby, cocker (*Rare*), coddle, cosset, indulge, kill with kindness, mollycoddle, overindulge, pamper, spoon-feed 3. addle, become tainted, curdle, decay, decompose, go bad, go off (*Brit. inf.*), mildew, putrefy, rot, turn **4. spoiling for** bent upon, desirous of, eager for, enthusiastic about, keen to, looking for, out to get (*Inf.*), raring to

spoilsport damper, dog in the manger, kill-joy, misery (*Brit. inf.*), party-pooper (*U.S. sl.*), wet blanket (*Inf.*)

spoken expressed, oral, phonetic, put into words, said, told, unwritten, uttered, verbal, viva voce, voiced, by word of mouth

spongy absorbent, cushioned, cushiony, elastic, light, porous, springy

sponsor 1. *n.* angel (*Inf.*), backer, godparent, guarantor, patron, promoter **2.** *v.* back, finance, fund, guarantee, lend one's name to, patronize, promote, put up the money for, subsidize

spontaneous extempore, free, impromptu, impulsive, instinctive, natural, unbidden, uncompelled, unconstrained, unforced, unpremeditated, unprompted, voluntary, willing

spontaneously extempore, freely, impromptu, impulsively, instinctively, off one's own bat, off the cuff (*Inf.*), of one's own accord, on impulse, quite unprompted, voluntarily

sporadic infrequent, intermittent, irregular, isolated, occasional, on and off, random, scattered, spasmodic

sport *n.* **1.** amusement, diversion, entertainment, exercise, game, pastime, physical activity, play, recreation **2.** badinage, banter, frolic, fun, jest, joking, kidding (*Inf.*), merriment, mirth, raillery, teasing **3.** buffoon, butt, derision, fair game, game, laughing stock, mockery, plaything, ridicule ~*v.* **4. With with** amuse oneself, dally, flirt, play, take advantage of, toy, treat lightly *or* cavalierly, trifle **5.** *Inf.* display, exhibit, show off, wear **6.** caper, disport, frolic, gambol, play, romp

sporting fair, game (*Inf.*), gentlemanly, sportsman-like

spot *n.* **1.** blemish, blot, blotch, daub, discoloration, flaw, mark, pimple, plook (*Scot.*), pustule, smudge, speck, stain, taint **2.** locality, location, place, point, position, scene, site, situation **3.** *Inf.* bit, little, morsel, splash **4.** *Inf.* difficulty, mess, plight, predicament, quandary, trouble ~*v.* **5.** catch sight of, descry, detect, discern, espy, identify, make out, observe, pick out, recognize, see, sight **6.** besmirch, blot, dirty, dot, fleck, mark, mottle, soil, spatter, speckle, splodge, splotch, stain, sully, taint, tarnish

spotless above reproach, blameless, chaste, faultless, flawless, gleaming, immaculate, innocent, irreproachable, pure, shining, snowy, unblemished, unimpeachable, unstained, unsullied, untarnished, virgin, virginal, white

spotlight *Fig.* **1.** *v.* accentuate, draw attention to, feature, focus attention on, give prominence to, highlight, illuminate, point up, throw into relief **2.** *n.* attention, fame, interest, limelight, notoriety, public attention, public eye

spotted dappled, dotted, flecked, mottled, pied, polka-dot, specked, speckled

spouse better half (*Inf.*), companion, consort, helpmate, husband, mate, partner, wife

spout *v.* **1.** discharge, emit, erupt, gush, jet, shoot, spray, spurt, squirt, stream, surge **2.** *Inf.* declaim, expatiate, go on (*Inf.*), hold forth, orate, pontificate, rabbit on (*Brit. sl.*), ramble (on), rant, speechify, spiel (*Inf.*), talk

sprawl *v.* flop, loll, lounge, ramble, slouch, slump, spread, straggle, trail

spray¹ *v.* **1.** atomize, diffuse, scatter, shower, sprinkle ~*n.* **2.** drizzle, droplets, fine mist, moisture, spindrift, spoondrift **3.** aerosol, atomizer, sprinkler

spray² *n.* bough, branch, corsage, floral arrangement, shoot, sprig

spread v. **1.** be displayed, bloat, broaden, dilate, expand, extend, fan out, open, open out, sprawl, stretch, swell, unfold, unfurl, unroll, widen **2.** escalate, multiply, mushroom, proliferate **3.** advertise, blazon, broadcast, bruit, cast, circulate, cover, diffuse, disseminate, distribute, make known, make public, proclaim, promulgate, propagate, publicize, publish, radiate, scatter, shed, strew, transmit **4.** arrange, array, cover, furnish, lay, prepare, set ~n. **5.** advance, advancement, development, diffusion, dispersion, dissemination, escalation, expansion, increase, proliferation, spreading, suffusion, transmission **6.** compass, extent, period, reach, span, stretch, sweep, term **7.** *Inf.* array, banquet, blowout (*Sl.*), feast, repast

spree bacchanalia, bender (*Inf.*), binge (*Inf.*), carouse, debauch, fling, jag (*Sl.*), junketing, orgy, revel, splurge

sprightly active, agile, airy, alert, animated, blithe, brisk, cheerful, energetic, frolicsome, gay, jaunty, joyous, lively, nimble, perky, playful, spirited, sportive, spry, vivacious

spring v. **1.** bounce, bound, hop, jump, leap, rebound, recoil, vault **2.** *Often with* **from** arise, be derived, be descended, come, derive, descend, emanate, emerge, grow, issue, originate, proceed, start, stem **3.** *With* **up** appear, burgeon, come into existence *or* being, develop, mushroom, shoot up ~n. **4.** bound, buck, hop, jump, leap, saltation, vault **5.** bounce, bounciness, buoyancy, elasticity, flexibility, give (*Inf.*), recoil, resilience, springiness **6.** beginning, cause, fountainhead, origin, root, source, well, wellspring ~adj. **7.** *Of the season* vernal

sprinkle v. dredge, dust, pepper, powder, scatter, shower, spray, strew

sprinkling admixture, dash, dusting, few, handful, scatter, scattering, smattering, sprinkle

sprint v. dart, dash, go at top speed, hare (*Brit. inf.*), hotfoot, put on a burst of speed, race, scamper, shoot, tear, whiz (*Inf.*)

sprite apparition, brownie, dryad, elf, fairy, goblin, imp, leprechaun, naiad, nymph, pixie, spirit, sylph

sprout v. bud, develop, germinate, grow, push, shoot, spring, vegetate

spruce as if one had just stepped out of a bandbox, dainty, dapper, elegant, natty (*Inf.*), neat, smart, trig (*Archaic*), trim, well-groomed, well turned out

spry active, agile, alert, brisk, nimble, nippy (*Brit. inf.*), quick, ready, sprightly, supple

spur v. **1.** animate, drive, goad, impel, incite, press, prick, prod, prompt, stimulate, urge ~n. **2.** goad, prick, rowel **3.** impetus, impulse, incentive, incitement, inducement, motive, stimulus **4. on the spur of the moment** impetuously, impromptu, impulsively, on impulse, on the spot, unpremeditatedly, unthinkingly, without planning, without thinking

spurious artificial, bogus, contrived, counterfeit, deceitful, fake, false, feigned, forged, imitation, mock, phoney (*Sl.*), pretended, pseudo (*Inf.*), sham, simulated, specious, unauthentic

spurn cold-shoulder, contemn, despise, disdain, disregard, rebuff, reject, repulse, scorn, slight, snub, turn one's nose up at (*Inf.*)

spurt 1. v. burst, erupt, gush, jet, shoot, spew, squirt, surge **2.** n. access, burst, fit, rush, spate, surge

spy n. **1.** double agent, fifth columnist, foreign agent, mole, secret agent, secret service agent, undercover agent ~v. **2.** *Usually with* **on** follow, keep under surveillance, keep watch on, shadow, tail (*Inf.*), trail, watch **3.** catch sight of, descry, espy, glimpse, notice, observe, set eyes on, spot

spying n. espionage, secret service

squabble 1. v. argue, bicker, brawl, clash, dispute, fall out (*Inf.*), fight, have words, quarrel, row, scrap (*Inf.*), wrangle **2.** n. argument, barney (*Inf.*), difference of opinion, disagreement, dispute, fight, row, scrap (*Inf.*), set-to (*Inf.*), spat, tiff

squad band, company, crew, force, gang, group, team, troop

squalid broken-down, decayed, dirty, disgusting, fetid, filthy, foul, low, nasty, poverty-stricken, re~pulsive, run-down, seedy, sleazy, slovenly, slummy, sordid, unclean

squalor decay, filth, foulness, meanness, sleaziness, slumminess, squalidness, wretchedness

squander be prodigal with, blow (*Sl.*), consume, dissipate, expend, fritter away, frivol away, lavish, misspend, misuse, run through, scatter, spend, spend like water, throw away, waste

square *Fig. v.* 1. *Often with* with accord, agree, conform, corre~spond, fit, harmonize, match, rec~oncile, tally 2. *Sometimes with* up balance, clear (up), discharge, liq~uidate, make even, pay off, quit, satisfy, settle 3. accommodate, adapt, adjust, align, even up, level, regulate, suit, tailor, true (up) 4. *Sl.* bribe, buy off, corrupt, fix (*Inf.*), rig, suborn ~*adj.* 5. aboveboard, decent, equitable, ethical, fair, fair and square, genuine, honest, just, on the level (*Inf.*), straight, straightforward, upright 6. *Inf.* be~hind the times (*Inf.*), bourgeois, conservative, conventional, old-fashioned, out of date, straight (*Sl.*), strait-laced, stuffy ~*n.* 7. *Inf.* ante~diluvian, back number (*Inf.*), con~servative, die-hard, fuddy-duddy (*Inf.*), old buffer (*Brit. inf.*), (old) fogy, stick-in-the-mud (*Inf.*), tradi~tionalist

squash *v.* 1. compress, crush, dis~tort, flatten, mash, pound, press, pulp, smash, stamp on, trample down 2. annihilate, crush, humili~ate, put down (*Sl.*), put (someone) in his (*or* her) place, quash, quell, silence, sit on (*Inf.*), suppress

squawk *v.* 1. cackle, crow, cry, hoot, screech, yelp 2. *Inf.* com~plain, kick up a fuss (*Inf.*), protest, raise Cain (*Sl.*), squeal (*Inf.*)

squeak *v.* peep, pipe, shrill, squeal, whine, yelp

squeal *n.* 1. scream, screech, shriek, wail, yell, yelp, yowl ~*v.* 2. scream, screech, shout, shriek, shrill, wail, yelp 3. *Sl.* betray, blab, grass (*Brit. sl.*), inform on, peach (*Sl.*), rat on, sell (someone) down the river (*Inf.*), sing (*Sl.*), snitch (*Sl.*) 4. *Inf.* complain, kick up a fuss (*Inf.*), moan, protest, squawk (*Inf.*)

squeamish 1. delicate, fastidious, finicky, nice (*Rare*), particular, prissy (*Inf.*), prudish, punctilious, scrupulous, strait-laced 2. nau~seous, qualmish, queasy, queer, sick, sickish

squeeze *v.* 1. clutch, compress, crush, grip, nip, pinch, press, squash, wring 2. cram, crowd, force, jam, jostle, pack, press, ram, stuff, thrust, wedge 3. clasp, cuddle, embrace, enfold, hold tight, hug 4. bleed (*Inf.*), bring pressure to bear on, extort, lean on (*Inf.*), milk, op~press, pressurize, put the screws on (*Inf.*), put the squeeze on (*Inf.*), wrest ~*n.* 5. clasp, embrace, hand~clasp, hold, hug 6. congestion, crowd, crush, jam, press, squash

squire *v.* accompany, attend, com~panion, escort

squirm agonize, fidget, flounder, shift, twist, wiggle, wriggle, writhe

stab *v.* 1. bayonet, cut, gore, injure, jab, knife, pierce, puncture, run through, spear, stick, thrust, trans~fix, wound 2. stab in the back be~tray, break faith with, deceive, do the dirty on (*Brit. sl.*), double-cross (*Inf.*), give the Judas kiss to, inform on, let down, play false, sell, sell out (*Inf.*), slander ~*n.* 3. gash, inci~sion, jab, puncture, rent, thrust, wound 4. ache, pang, prick, twinge 5. make a stab at attempt, en~deavour, essay, have a go (crack, shot) (*Inf.*), try, try one's hand at, venture

stability constancy, durability, firmness, permanence, solidity, soundness, steadfastness, steadi~ness, strength

stable abiding, constant, deep-rooted, durable, enduring, estab~

lished, fast, firm, fixed, immutable, invariable, lasting, permanent, reliable, secure, sound, steadfast, steady, strong, sturdy, sure, unalterable, unchangeable, unwavering, well-founded

stack 1. *n.* clamp (*Brit. agriculture*), cock, heap, hoard, load, mass, mound, mountain, pile 2. *v.* accumulate, amass, assemble, bank up, heap up, load, pile, stockpile

staff *n.* 1. employees, lecturers, officers, organization, personnel, teachers, team, workers, work force 2. cane, pole, prop, rod, stave, wand

stage 1. *n.* division, juncture, lap, leg, length, level, period, phase, point, step 2. *v.* arrange, do, engineer, give, lay on, mount, orchestrate, organize, perform, play, present, produce, put on

stagger *v.* 1. falter, hesitate, lurch, reel, sway, teeter, totter, vacillate, waver, wobble 2. amaze, astonish, astound, bowl over (*Inf.*), confound, dumbfound, flabbergast, give (someone) a shock, nonplus, overwhelm, shake, shock, strike (someone) dumb (*Inf.*), stun, stupefy, surprise, take (someone) aback, take (someone's) breath away, throw off balance 3. alternate, overlap, step, zigzag

stagnant brackish, motionless, quiet, sluggish, stale, standing, still

stagnate decay, decline, deteriorate, fester, go to seed, idle, languish, lie fallow, rot, rust, stand still, vegetate

staid calm, composed, decorous, demure, grave, quiet, sedate, self-restrained, serious, sober, solemn, steady

stain *v.* 1. blemish, blot, colour, dirty, discolour, dye, mark, soil, spot, tarnish, tinge 2. besmirch, blacken, contaminate, corrupt, defile, deprave, disgrace, drag through the mud, sully, taint ~*n.* 3. blemish, blot, discoloration, dye, spot, tint 4. blemish, blot on the escutcheon, disgrace, dishonour,

infamy, reproach, shame, slur, stigma

stake¹ *n.* 1. pale, paling, picket, pole, post, spike, stave, stick ~*v.* 2. brace, prop, secure, support, tether, tie up 3. *Often with* out define, delimit, demarcate, lay claim to, mark out, outline, reserve

stake² *n.* 1. ante, bet, chance, hazard, peril, pledge, risk, venture, wager 2. claim, concern, interest, investment, involvement, share ~*v.* 3. bet, chance, gamble, hazard, imperil, jeopardize, pledge, put on, risk, venture, wager

stale 1. decayed, dry, faded, fetid, flat, fusty, hard, insipid, musty, old, sour, stagnant, tasteless 2. antiquated, banal, cliché-ridden, common, commonplace, drab, effete, flat, hackneyed, insipid, old hat, overused, platitudinous, repetitious, stereotyped, threadbare, trite, unoriginal, worn-out

stalk *v.* 1. creep up on, follow, haunt, hunt, pursue, shadow, tail (*Inf.*), track 2. flounce, march, pace, stride, strut

stalwart athletic, beefy (*Inf.*), brawny, daring, dependable, hefty (*Inf.*), husky (*Inf.*), indomitable, intrepid, lusty, manly, muscular, redoubtable, robust, rugged, sinewy, staunch, stout, strapping, strong, sturdy, valiant, vigorous

stamina energy, force, grit (*Inf.*), indefatigability, lustiness, power, power of endurance, resilience, resistance, staying power, strength, vigour

stammer *v.* falter, hem and haw, hesitate, pause, splutter, stumble, stutter

stamp *v.* 1. beat, crush, trample 2. engrave, fix, impress, imprint, inscribe, mark, mould, print 3. betray, brand, categorize, exhibit, identify, label, mark, pronounce, reveal, show to be, typecast ~*n.* 4. brand, cast, earmark, hallmark, imprint, mark, mould, signature 5. breed, cast, character, cut, description, fashion, form, kind, sort, type

stampede *n.* charge, flight, rout, rush, scattering

stamp out crush, destroy, eliminate, eradicate, extinguish, extirpate, put down, put out, quell, quench, scotch, suppress

stance 1. bearing, carriage, deportment, posture 2. attitude, position, stand, standpoint, viewpoint

stand *v.* 1. be upright, be vertical, erect, mount, place, position, put, rank, rise, set 2. be in force, belong, be situated *or* located, be valid, continue, exist, halt, hold, obtain, pause, prevail, remain, rest, stay, stop 3. abide, allow, bear, brook, cope with, countenance, endure, experience, handle, put up with (*Inf.*), stomach, submit to, suffer, support, sustain, take, thole (*Dialect*), tolerate, undergo, wear (*Brit. sl.*), weather, withstand ~*n.* 4. halt, rest, standstill, stay, stop, stopover 5. attitude, determination, firm stand, opinion, position, stance, standpoint 6. base, booth, bracket, dais, frame, grandstand, place, platform, rack, rank, stage, staging, stall, stance (*Chiefly Scot.*), support, table

standard[1] *n.* 1. average, benchmark, canon, criterion, example, gauge, grade, guide, guideline, measure, model, norm, pattern, principle, requirement, rule, sample, specification, touchstone, type, yardstick 2. *Often plural* code of honour, ethics, ideals, moral principles, morals, principles ~*adj.* 3. accepted, average, basic, customary, normal, orthodox, popular, prevailing, regular, set, staple, stock, typical, usual 4. approved, authoritative, classic, definitive, established, official, recognized

standard[2] *n.* banner, colours, ensign, flag, pennant, pennon, streamer

standardize assimilate, bring into line, institutionalize, mass-produce, regiment, stereotype

stand by 1. back, befriend, be loyal to, champion, defend, stick up for (*Inf.*), support, take (someone's) part, uphold 2. be prepared, wait, wait in the wings

stand for 1. betoken, denote, exemplify, indicate, mean, represent, signify, symbolize 2. *Inf.* bear, brook, endure, lie down under (*Inf.*), put up with, suffer, tolerate, wear (*Brit. inf.*)

stand in for cover for, deputize for, do duty for, hold the fort for, replace, take the place of, understudy

standing *n.* 1. condition, credit, eminence, estimation, footing, position, rank, reputation, repute, station, status 2. continuance, duration, existence, experience ~*adj.* 3. fixed, lasting, permanent, perpetual, regular, repeated 4. erect, perpendicular, rampant (*Heraldry*), upended, upright, vertical

stand out attract attention, be highlighted, be prominent (conspicuous, distinct, striking), be thrown into relief, bulk large, catch the eye, leap to the eye, project, stare one in the face (*Inf.*), stick out a mile (*Inf.*)

standpoint angle, point of view, position, post, stance, station, vantage point, viewpoint

stand up for champion, come to the defence of, defend, side with, stick up for (*Inf.*), support, uphold

star 1. *n.* celebrity, draw (*Inf.*), idol, lead, leading man *or* lady, luminary, main attraction, name 2. *adj.* brilliant, celebrated, illustrious, leading, major, paramount, principal, prominent, talented, wellknown

stare *v.* gape, gawk, gawp (*Brit. sl.*), gaze, goggle, look, rubberneck (*Sl.*), watch

stark *adj.* 1. absolute, arrant, bald, bare, blunt, consummate, downright, entire, flagrant, out-and-out, palpable, patent, pure, sheer, simple, unalloyed, unmitigated, utter 2. austere, bare, barren, bleak, cold, depressing, desolate, drear (*Literary*), dreary, forsaken, grim, harsh, plain, severe, solitary, unadorned ~*adv.* 3. absolutely, altogether, clean, completely, entirely, quite, utterly, wholly

stark-naked in a state of nature, in one's birthday suit (*Inf.*), in the altogether (*Inf.*), in the buff (*Inf.*), in the raw (*Inf.*), naked, nude, stark, starkers (*Inf.*), stripped, unclad, undressed, without a stitch on (*Inf.*)

start *v.* 1. appear, arise, begin, come into being, come into existence, commence, depart, first see the light of day, get on the road, get under way, go ahead (*Inf.*), hit the road (*Inf.*), issue, leave, originate, pitch in (*Inf.*), sally forth, set off, set out 2. activate, embark upon, engender, enter upon, get going, initiate, instigate, kick off (*Inf.*), make a beginning, open, originate, put one's hand to the plough (*Inf.*), set about, set in motion, start the ball rolling, take the first step, take the plunge (*Inf.*), turn on 3. begin, create, establish, father, found, inaugurate, initiate, institute, introduce, launch, lay the foundations of, pioneer, set up 4. blench, flinch, jerk, jump, recoil, shy, twitch ~*n.* 5. beginning, birth, commencement, dawn, first step(s), foundation, inauguration, inception, initiation, kickoff (*Inf.*), onset, opening, outset 6. advantage, edge, head start, lead 7. backing, break (*Inf.*), chance, helping hand, introduction, opening, opportunity, sponsorship 8. convulsion, jar, jump, spasm, twitch

startle agitate, alarm, amaze, astonish, astound, frighten, give (someone) a turn (*Inf.*), make (someone) jump, scare, shock, surprise, take (someone) aback

startling alarming, astonishing, astounding, extraordinary, shocking, staggering, sudden, surprising, unexpected, unforeseen

starving faint from lack of food, famished, hungering, hungry, ravenous, ready to eat a horse (*Inf.*), sharp-set, starved

state[1] *v.* 1. affirm, articulate, assert, asseverate, aver, declare, enumerate, explain, expound, express, present, propound, put, report, say, specify, voice ~*n.* 2. case, category, circumstances, condition, mode, pass, plight, position, predicament, shape, situation, state of affairs 3. attitude, frame of mind, humour, mood, spirits 4. ceremony, dignity, display, glory, grandeur, majesty, pomp, splendour, style 5. *Inf.* bother, flap (*Inf.*), panic, pother, tiz-woz (*Inf.*), tizzy (*Inf.*) 6. in a state *Inf.* agitated, all steamed up (*Sl.*), anxious, distressed, disturbed, flustered, het up, panic-stricken, ruffled, upset

state[2] *n.* body politic, commonwealth, country, federation, government, kingdom, land, nation, republic, territory

stately august, ceremonious, deliberate, dignified, elegant, grand, imperial, imposing, impressive, lofty, majestic, measured, noble, pompous, regal, royal, solemn

statement account, announcement, communication, communiqué, declaration, explanation, proclamation, recital, relation, report, testimony, utterance

static changeless, constant, fixed, immobile, inert, motionless, stagnant, stationary, still, unmoving, unvarying

station *n.* 1. base, depot, headquarters, location, place, position, post, seat, situation 2. appointment, business, calling, employment, grade, occupation, position, post, rank, situation, sphere, standing, status ~*v.* 3. assign, establish, fix, garrison, install, locate, post, set

stationary at a standstill, fixed, inert, moored, motionless, parked, standing, static, stock-still, unmoving

status condition, consequence, degree, distinction, eminence, grade, position, prestige, rank, standing

stay *v.* 1. abide, continue, delay, establish oneself, halt, hang around (*Inf.*), hover, linger, loiter, pause, put down roots, remain, reside, settle, sojourn, stand, stay put, stop, tarry, wait 2. *Often with* **at** be accommodated at, lodge, put up at, sojourn, visit 3. adjourn, defer, discontinue, hold in abeyance, hold over, prorogue, put off, suspend 4. *Archaic* arrest, check, curb, delay, detain, hinder, hold, impede, obstruct, prevent ~*n.* 5. holiday, sojourn, stop, stopover, visit 6. deferment, delay, halt, pause, postponement, remission, reprieve, stopping, suspension

steadfast constant, dedicated, dependable, established, faithful, fast, firm, fixed, intent, loyal, persevering, reliable, resolute, single-minded, stable, staunch, steady, unfaltering, unflinching, unswerving, unwavering

steady *adj.* 1. firm, fixed, immovable, safe, stable, substantial, unchangeable, uniform 2. balanced, calm, dependable, equable, having both feet on the ground, imperturbable, level-headed, reliable, sedate, sensible, serene, serious-minded, settled, sober, staid, steadfast 3. ceaseless, confirmed, consistent, constant, continuous, even, faithful, habitual, incessant, nonstop, persistent, regular, rhythmic, unbroken, unfaltering, unfluctuating, uninterrupted, unremitting, unvarying, unwavering ~*v.* 4. balance, brace, secure, stabilize, support 5. compose *or* calm oneself, cool down, sober (up), get a grip on oneself (*Inf.*)

steal 1. appropriate, be light-fingered, embezzle, filch, half-inch (*Inf.*), heist (*U.S. sl.*), lift (*Inf.*), misappropriate, nick (*Sl.*), peculate, pilfer, pinch (*Inf.*), pirate, plagiarize, poach, prig (*Brit. sl.*), purloin, shoplift, snitch (*Sl.*), swipe (*Sl.*), take, thieve, walk *or* make off with 2. creep, flit, insinuate oneself, slink, slip, sneak, tiptoe

stealing embezzlement, larceny, misappropriation, pilferage, pilfering, plagiarism, robbery, shoplifting, theft, thievery, thieving

stealth furtiveness, secrecy, slyness, sneakiness, stealthiness, surreptitiousness, unobtrusiveness

stealthy clandestine, covert, furtive, secret, secretive, skulking, sly, sneaking, sneaky, surreptitious, underhand

steep *adj.* 1. abrupt, headlong, precipitous, sheer 2. *Inf.* excessive, exorbitant, extortionate, extreme, high, overpriced, stiff, uncalled-for, unreasonable

steer 1. be in the driver's seat, conduct, control, direct, govern, guide, pilot 2. **steer clear of** avoid, circumvent, eschew, evade, give a wide berth to, sheer off, shun

stem[1] 1. *n.* axis, branch, peduncle, shoot, stalk, stock, trunk 2. *v. Usually with* **from** arise, be caused (bred, brought about, generated) by, derive, develop, emanate, flow, issue, originate

stem[2] *v.* bring to a standstill, check, contain, curb, dam, hold back, oppose, resist, restrain, stanch, stay (*Archaic*), stop, withstand

step *n.* 1. footfall, footprint, footstep, gait, impression, pace, print, stride, trace, track, walk 2. act, action, deed, expedient, manoeuvre, means, measure, move, procedure, proceeding 3. **take steps** act, intervene, move in, prepare, take action, take measures, take the initiative 4. advance, advancement, move, phase, point, process, progression, stage 5. degree, level, rank, remove 6. doorstep, round, rung, stair, tread 7. **in step** coinciding, conforming, in harmony (agreement, conformity, unison), in line 8. **out of step** erratic, incongruous, in disagreement, out of harmony, out of line, out of phase, pulling different ways 9. **watch one's step** be discreet (canny, careful, cautious), be on one's guard, have one's wits about one, look out, mind how one goes, mind one's p's and q's, take care, take heed, tread carefully ~*v.* 10. move, pace, tread, walk

step in become involved, chip in (*Inf.*), intercede, intervene, take action, take a hand

step up accelerate, augment,

boost, escalate, increase, intensify, raise, speed up, up

stereotype 1. *n.* formula, mould, pattern, received idea 2. *v.* categorize, conventionalize, dub, pigeonhole, standardize, take to be, typecast

sterile 1. abortive, bare, barren, dry, empty, fruitless, infecund, unfruitful, unproductive, unprofitable, unprolific 2. antiseptic, aseptic, disinfected, germ-free, sterilized

sterilize autoclave, disinfect, fumigate, purify

sterling authentic, excellent, first-class, genuine, pure, real, sound, standard, substantial, superlative, true

stern austere, authoritarian, bitter, cruel, flinty, forbidding, frowning, grim, hard, harsh, inflexible, relentless, rigid, rigorous, serious, severe, steely, strict, unrelenting, unsparing, unyielding

stick[1] *v.* 1. adhere, affix, attach, bind, bond, cement, cleave, cling, fasten, fix, fuse, glue, hold, hold on, join, paste, weld 2. dig, gore, insert, jab, penetrate, pierce, pin, poke, prod, puncture, spear, stab, thrust, transfix 3. *With* out, up *etc.* bulge, extend, jut, obtrude, poke, project, protrude, show 4. *Inf.* deposit, drop, fix, install, lay, place, plant, plonk, position, put, set, store, stuff 5. be bogged down, become immobilized, be embedded, catch, clog, come to a standstill, jam, lodge, snag, stop 6. linger, persist, remain, stay 7. *Sl.* abide, bear up under, endure, get on with, stand, stomach, take, tolerate 8. **stick it out** *Inf.* bear, endure, grin and bear it (*Inf.*), last out, put up with (*Inf.*), see it through, see through to the bitter end, soldier on, take it (*Inf.*), weather 9. **stick up for** *Inf.* champion, defend, stand up for, support, take the part *or* side of, uphold

stick[2] *n.* 1. baton, birch, cane, pole, rod, staff, stake, switch, twig, wand 2. *Inf.* fuddy-duddy (*Inf.*), (old) fogy, pain (*Inf.*), prig, stick-in-the-mud (*Inf.*) 3. *Brit. sl.* abuse, blame,

criticism, flak (*Inf.*), hostility, punishment

stick to adhere to, cleave to, continue in, honour, keep, persevere in, remain loyal (faithful, true), stick at

sticky 1. adhesive, claggy (*Dialect*), clinging, gluey, glutinous, gooey (*Inf.*), gummy, syrupy, tacky, tenacious, viscid, viscous 2. *Inf.* awkward, delicate, difficult, discomforting, embarrassing, hairy (*Sl.*), nasty, painful, thorny, tricky, unpleasant 3. clammy, close, humid, muggy, oppressive, sultry, sweltering

stiff 1. brittle, firm, hard, hardened, inelastic, inflexible, rigid, solid, solidified, taut, tense, tight, unbending, unyielding 2. artificial, austere, ceremonious, chilly, cold, constrained, forced, formal, laboured, mannered, pompous, priggish, prim, punctilious, standoffish, starchy (*Inf.*), stilted, uneasy, unnatural, unrelaxed, wooden 3. arthritic, awkward, clumsy, creaky (*Inf.*), crude, graceless, inelegant, jerky, rheumaticky (*Inf.*), ungainly, ungraceful, unsupple 4. arduous, difficult, exacting, fatiguing, formidable, hard, laborious, tough, trying, uphill 5. austere, cruel, drastic, extreme, great, hard, harsh, heavy, inexorable, oppressive, pitiless, rigorous, severe, sharp, strict, stringent 6. brisk, fresh, powerful, strong, vigorous

stiffen brace, coagulate, congeal, crystallize, harden, jell, reinforce, set, solidify, starch, tauten, tense, thicken

stifle 1. asphyxiate, choke, smother, strangle, suffocate 2. check, choke back, cover up, curb, extinguish, hush, muffle, prevent, repress, restrain, silence, smother, stop, suppress

still 1. *adj.* at rest, calm, hushed, inert, lifeless, motionless, noiseless, pacific, peaceful, placid, quiet, restful, serene, silent, smooth, stationary, stilly (*Poetic*), tranquil, undisturbed, unruffled, unstirring 2. *v.* allay, alleviate, appease, calm, hush, lull, pacify, quiet, quieten, settle, silence, smooth, smooth over, soothe, subdue, tranquillize 3. *conj.* but, for all that, however, nevertheless, notwithstanding, yet 4. *n. Poetic* hush, peace, quiet, silence, stillness, tranquillity

stilted artificial, bombastic, con~ strained, forced, grandiloquent, high-flown, high-sounding, inflated, laboured, pedantic, pompous, pre~ tentious, stiff, unnatural, wooden

stimulant analeptic, bracer (*Inf.*), energizer, excitant, pep pill (*Inf.*), pick-me-up (*Inf.*), restorative, re~ viver, tonic, upper (*Sl.*)

stimulate animate, arouse, en~ courage, fan, fire, foment, goad, impel, incite, inflame, instigate, prompt, provoke, quicken, rouse, spur, turn on (*Inf.*), urge, whet

stimulating exciting, exhilarating, galvanic, inspiring, intriguing, provocative, provoking, rousing, stirring, thought-provoking

stimulus encouragement, fillip, goad, incentive, incitement, in~ ducement, provocation, shot in the arm (*Inf.*), spur

sting *v.* 1. burn, hurt, pain, smart, tingle, wound 2. anger, gall, in~ cense, inflame, infuriate, nettle, pique, provoke, rile 3. *Inf.* cheat, defraud, do (*Sl.*), fleece, over~ charge, rip off (*Sl.*), swindle, take for a ride (*Inf.*)

stint 1. *n.* assignment, bit, period, quota, share, shift, spell, stretch, term, time, tour, turn 2. *v.* be~ grudge, be sparing (frugal, mingy (*Brit. inf.*), parsimonious), econo~ mize, hold back, save, scrimp, skimp on, spoil the ship for a ha'porth of tar, withhold

stipulate agree, contract, cov~ enant, engage, guarantee, insist upon, lay down, lay down *or* im~ pose conditions, make a point of, pledge, postulate, promise, require, settle, specify

stipulation agreement, clause, condition, contract, engagement, precondition, prerequisite, provi~ sion, proviso, qualification, re~

quirement, restriction, settlement, *sine qua non*, specification, term

stir *v.* 1. agitate, beat, disturb, flut~ ter, mix, move, quiver, rustle, shake, tremble 2. *Often with up* animate, arouse, awaken, excite, incite, inflame, instigate, kindle, prompt, provoke, quicken, raise, spur, stimulate, urge 3. affect, electrify, excite, fire, inspire, move, thrill, touch 4. bestir, be up and about (*Inf.*), budge, exert one~ self, get a move on (*Inf.*), get mov~ ing (*Inf.*), hasten, look lively (*Inf.*), make an effort, mill about, move, shake a leg (*Inf.*) ~*n.* 5. activity, ado, agitation, bustle, commotion, disorder, disturbance, excitement, ferment, flurry, fuss, movement, to-do, tumult, uproar

stirring animating, dramatic, emo~ tive, exciting, exhilarating, heady, impassioned, inspiring, intoxicat~ ing, lively, moving, rousing, spirit~ ed, stimulating, thrilling

stock *n.* 1. array, assets, assort~ ment, cache, choice, commodities, fund, goods, hoard, inventory, merchandise, range, reserve, res~ ervoir, selection, stockpile, store, supply, variety, wares 2. *Animals* beasts, cattle, domestic animals, flocks, herds, horses, livestock, sheep 3. ancestry, background, breed, descent, extraction, family, forebears, house, line, lineage, line of descent, parentage, pedigree, race, strain, type, variety 4. *Money* capital, funds, investment, proper~ ty 5. **take stock** appraise, estimate, review the situation, see how the land lies, size up (*Inf.*), weigh up ~*adj.* 6. banal, basic, common~ place, conventional, customary, formal, hackneyed, ordinary, overused, regular, routine, run-of-the-mill, set, standard, staple, ste~ reotyped, traditional, trite, usual, worn-out ~*v.* 7. deal in, handle, keep, sell, supply, trade in 8. *With up* accumulate, amass, buy up, gather, hoard, lay in, put away, replenish, save, store (up), supply 9. equip, fill, fit out, furnish, kit out, provide with, provision, supply

stocky chunky, dumpy, mesomor~

phic, solid, stubby, stumpy, sturdy, thickset

stodgy 1. filling, heavy, leaden, starchy, substantial 2. boring, dull, dull as ditchwater, formal, fuddy-duddy (*Inf.*), heavy going, laboured, staid, stuffy, tedious, turgid, unexciting, unimaginative, uninspired

stoical calm, cool, dispassionate, impassive, imperturbable, indifferent, long-suffering, philosophic, phlegmatic, resigned, stoic, stolid

stoicism acceptance, calmness, dispassion, fatalism, forbearance, fortitude, impassivity, imperturbability, indifference, long-suffering, patience, resignation, stolidity

stolid apathetic, bovine, doltish, dull, heavy, lumpish, obtuse, slow, stupid, unemotional, wooden

stomach *n.* 1. abdomen, belly, breadbasket (*Sl.*), gut (*Inf.*), inside(s) (*Inf.*), paunch, pot, potbelly, spare tyre (*Inf.*), tummy (*Inf.*) 2. appetite, desire, inclination, mind, relish, taste ~*v.* 3. abide, bear, endure, put up with (*Inf.*), reconcile *or* resign oneself to, submit to, suffer, swallow, take, tolerate

stony *Fig.* adamant, blank, callous, chilly, expressionless, frigid, hard, heartless, hostile, icy, indifferent, inexorable, merciless, obdurate, pitiless, unfeeling, unforgiving, unresponsive

stoop *v.* 1. be bowed *or* round-shouldered, bend, bow, crouch, descend, duck, hunch, incline, kneel, lean, squat 2. *Often with to* condescend, deign, demean oneself, descend, lower oneself, resort, sink, vouchsafe ~*n.* 3. bad posture, droop, round-shoulderedness, sag, slouch, slump

stop *v.* 1. be over, break off, bring *or* come to a halt, bring *or* come to a standstill, call it a day (*Inf.*), cease, come to an end, conclude, cut out (*Inf.*), cut short, desist, discontinue, draw up, end, finish, halt, leave off, pack in (*Brit. inf.*), pause, peter out, pull up, put an end to, quit, refrain, run down, run its course, shut down, stall, terminate

2. arrest, bar, block, break, check, close, forestall, frustrate, hinder, hold back, impede, intercept, interrupt, obstruct, plug, prevent, rein in, repress, restrain, seal, silence, staunch, stem, suspend 3. break one's journey, lodge, put up, rest, sojourn, stay, tarry ~*n.* 4. cessation, conclusion, discontinuation, end, finish, halt, standstill 5. break, rest, sojourn, stay, stopover, visit 6. bar, block, break, check, control, hindrance, impediment, plug, stoppage 7. depot, destination, halt, stage, station, termination, terminus

stopgap 1. *n.* improvisation, makeshift, resort, shift, substitute, temporary expedient 2. *adj.* emergency, impromptu, improvised, makeshift, provisional, rough-and-ready, temporary

stoppage 1. abeyance, arrest, close, closure, cutoff, deduction, discontinuance, halt, hindrance, lay-off, shutdown, standstill, stopping 2. blockage, check, curtailment, interruption, obstruction, occlusion, stopping up

store *v.* 1. accumulate, deposit, garner, hoard, husband, keep, keep in reserve, lay by *or* in, lock away, put aside, put aside for a rainy day, put by, put in storage, reserve, salt away, save, stash (*Inf.*), stock, stockpile ~*n.* 2. abundance, accumulation, cache, fund, hoard, lot, mine, plenty, plethora, provision, quantity, reserve, reservoir, stock, stockpile, supply, wealth 3. chain store, department store, emporium, market, mart, outlet, shop, supermarket 4. depository, repository, storehouse, storeroom, warehouse 5. set store by appreciate, esteem, hold in high regard, prize, think highly of, value

storm *n.* 1. blast, blizzard, cyclone, gale, gust, hurricane, squall, tempest, tornado, whirlwind 2. *Fig.* agitation, anger, clamour, commotion, disturbance, furore, hubbub, outbreak, outburst, outcry, passion, roar, row, rumpus, stir, strife, tumult, turmoil, violence ~*v.* 3. assail, assault, beset, charge, rush,

take by storm ~*n.* **4.** assault, at~
tack, blitz, blitzkrieg, offensive,
onset, onslaught, rush ~*v.* **5.** blus~
ter, complain, fly off the handle
(*Inf.*), fume, rage, rant, rave, scold,
thunder **6.** flounce, fly, rush, stalk,
stamp, stomp (*Inf.*)

stormy blustering, blustery, bois~
terous, dirty, foul, gusty, raging,
rough, squally, tempestuous, tur~
bulent, wild, windy

story 1. account, anecdote, chroni~
cle, fictional account, history, leg~
end, narration, narrative, novel,
recital, record, relation, romance,
tale, version, yarn **2.** *Inf.* falsehood,
fib, fiction, lie, untruth, white lie **3.**
article, feature, news, news item,
report, scoop

stout 1. big, bulky, burly, corpulent,
fat, fleshy, heavy, obese, on the
large *or* heavy side, overweight,
plump, portly, rotund, substantial,
tubby **2.** able-bodied, athletic, beefy
(*Inf.*), brawny, hardy, hulking,
husky (*Inf.*), lusty, muscular, ro~
bust, stalwart, strapping, strong,
sturdy, substantial, tough, vigorous
3. bold, brave, courageous, daunt~
less, doughty, fearless, gallant, in~
trepid, lion-hearted, manly, plucky,
resolute, valiant, valorous

straggle drift, lag, loiter, ramble,
range, roam, rove, spread, stray,
string out, trail, wander

straight *adj.* **1.** direct, near, short,
undeviating, unswerving **2.** aligned,
erect, even, horizontal, in line, lev~
el, perpendicular, plumb, right,
smooth, square, true, upright, ver~
tical **3.** blunt, candid, forthright,
frank, honest, outright, plain, point-
blank, straightforward, unqualified
4. above board, accurate, authen~
tic, decent, equitable, fair, fair and
square, honest, honourable, just,
law-abiding, reliable, respectable,
trustworthy, upright **5.** arranged,
in order, neat, orderly, organized,
put to rights, shipshape, sorted out,
tidy **6.** consecutive, continuous,
nonstop, running, solid, successive,
sustained, through, uninterrupted,
unrelieved **7.** *Sl.* bourgeois, con~
servative, conventional, orthodox,

square (*Inf.*), traditional **8.** neat,
pure, unadulterated, undiluted, un~
mixed ~*adv.* **9.** as the crow flies, at
once, directly, immediately, in~
stantly **10.** candidly, frankly, hon~
estly, in plain English, point-blank,
pulling no punches (*Inf.*), with no
holds barred

straightaway at once, directly,
immediately, instantly, now, on the
spot, right away, straightway (*Ar~
chaic*), there and then, this minute,
without any delay, without more
ado

straighten arrange, neaten, order,
put in order, set *or* put to rights,
smarten up, spruce up, tidy (up)

straighten out become clear,
clear up, correct, disentangle, put
right, rectify, regularize, resolve,
settle, sort out, unsnarl, work out

straightforward 1. above board,
candid, direct, forthright, genuine,
guileless, honest, open, sincere,
truthful **2.** clear-cut, easy, elemen~
tary, routine, simple, uncomplicat~
ed, undemanding

strain[1] *v.* **1.** distend, draw tight, ex~
tend, stretch, tauten, tighten **2.**
drive, exert, fatigue, injure, over~
exert, overtax, overwork, pull,
push to the limit, sprain, tax, tear,
tire, twist, weaken, wrench **3.** en~
deavour, go all out for (*Inf.*), la~
bour, make a supreme effort,
strive, struggle **4.** filter, percolate,
purify, riddle, screen, seep, sepa~
rate, sieve, sift ~*n.* **5.** effort, exer~
tion, force, injury, pull, sprain,
struggle, tautness, tension, tensity
(*Rare*), wrench **6.** anxiety, burden,
pressure, stress, tension **7.** *Often
plural* air, lay, measure (*Poetic*),
melody, song, theme, tune

strain[2] *n.* **1.** ancestry, blood, de~
scent, extraction, family, lineage,
pedigree, race, stock **2.** streak,
suggestion, suspicion, tendency,
trace, trait **3.** humour, manner,
spirit, style, temper, tone, vein,
way

strained artificial, awkward, con~
strained, difficult, embarrassed,
false, forced, laboured, put on, self-

conscious, stiff, tense, uncomfort~
able, uneasy, unnatural, unrelaxed

strait-laced moralistic, narrow,
narrow-minded, of the old school,
old-maidish (*Inf.*), overscrupulous,
prim, proper, prudish, puritanical,
strict, Victorian

straits *n. Sometimes singular* 1.
crisis, difficulty, dilemma, distress,
embarrassment, emergency, ex~
tremity, hardship, hole (*Sl.*), mess,
pass, perplexity, plight, predica~
ment, pretty *or* fine kettle of fish
(*Inf.*) 2. channel, narrows, sound

strand *n.* fibre, filament, length,
lock, rope, string, thread, tress,
twist

stranded 1. aground, ashore,
beached, cast away, grounded,
marooned, wrecked 2. *Fig.* aban~
doned, helpless, high and dry,
homeless, left in the lurch, penni~
less

strange 1. abnormal, astonishing,
bizarre, curious, eccentric, excep~
tional, extraordinary, fantastic,
funny, irregular, marvellous, mys~
tifying, odd, out-of-the-way, pecu~
liar, perplexing, queer, rare, re~
markable, singular, unaccountable,
uncanny, uncommon, unheard of,
weird, wonderful 2. alien, exotic,
foreign, new, novel, outside one's
experience, remote, unexplored,
unfamiliar, unknown, untried 3.
Often with to a stranger to, igno~
rant of, inexperienced, new to, un~
accustomed, unpractised, unsea~
soned, unused, unversed in 4. awk~
ward, bewildered, disoriented, ill at
ease, lost, out of place, uncomfort~
able

stranger alien, foreigner, guest, in~
comer, new arrival, newcomer,
outlander, unknown, visitor

strangle 1. asphyxiate, choke, gar~
rotte, smother, strangulate, suffo~
cate, throttle 2. gag (*Inf.*), inhibit,
repress, stifle, suppress

strap *n.* 1. belt, leash, thong, tie ~*v.*
2. bind, buckle, fasten, lash, secure,
tie, truss 3. beat, belt, flog, lash,
scourge, whip

stratagem artifice, device, dodge,
feint, intrigue, manoeuvre, plan,

plot, ploy, ruse, scheme, subter~
fuge, trick, wile

strategic 1. cardinal, critical, cru~
cial, decisive, key, vital 2. calcu~
lated, deliberate, diplomatic,
planned, politic

strategy approach, grand design,
manoeuvring, plan, planning, poli~
cy, procedure, programme,
scheme

stray *v.* 1. deviate, digress, diverge,
get off the point, get sidetracked,
go off at a tangent, ramble 2. be
abandoned *or* lost, drift, err, go
astray, lose one's way, meander,
range, roam, rove, straggle, wan~
der ~*adj.* 3. abandoned, homeless,
lost, roaming, vagrant 4. acciden~
tal, chance, erratic, freak, odd,
random, scattered

streak *n.* 1. band, layer, line, slash,
smear, strip, stripe, stroke, vein 2.
dash, element, strain, touch, trace,
vein ~*v.* 3. band, daub, fleck, slash,
smear, striate, stripe 4. dart, flash,
fly, hurtle, move like greased
lightning (*Inf.*), speed, sprint,
sweep, tear, whistle, whiz (*Inf.*),
zoom

stream 1. *n.* beck, brook, burn,
course, creek (*U.S.*), current, drift,
flow, freshet, outpouring, rill, river,
rivulet, run, rush, surge, tide, tor~
rent, tributary 2. *v.* cascade,
course, emit, flood, flow, glide,
gush, issue, pour, run, shed, spill,
spout

streamlined efficient, modernized,
organized, rationalized, sleek,
slick, smooth, smooth-running,
time-saving, well-run

street 1. avenue, boulevard, lane,
road, roadway, row, terrace,
thoroughfare 2. (**right**) **up one's
street** acceptable, compatible,
congenial, familiar, one's cup of
tea (*Inf.*), pleasing, suitable, to
one's liking, to one's taste

strength 1. backbone, brawn,
brawniness, courage, firmness,
fortitude, health, lustiness, might,
muscle, robustness, sinew, stami~
na, stoutness, sturdiness, toughness
2. cogency, concentration, effec~
tiveness, efficacy, energy, force,

intensity, potency, power, resolu~
tion, spirit, vehemence, vigour,
virtue (*Archaic*) 3. advantage, an~
chor, asset, mainstay, security,
strong point, succour, tower of
strength

strengthen 1. animate, brace up,
consolidate, encourage, fortify,
give new energy to, harden, heart~
en, invigorate, nerve, nourish, re~
juvenate, restore, stiffen, toughen
2. bolster, brace, build up, buttress,
confirm, corroborate, enhance,
establish, give a boost to, harden,
heighten, increase, intensify, justi~
fy, reinforce, steel, substantiate,
support

strenuous 1. arduous, demanding,
exhausting, hard, Herculean, labo~
rious, taxing, toilsome, tough,
tough going, unrelaxing, uphill 2.
active, bold, determined, eager,
earnest, energetic, persistent,
resolute, spirited, strong, tireless,
vigorous, zealous

stress *n.* 1. emphasis, force, im~
portance, significance, urgency,
weight 2. anxiety, burden, hassle
(*Inf.*), nervous tension, oppression,
pressure, strain, tautness, tension,
trauma, worry 3. accent, accen~
tuation, beat, emphasis ~*v.* 4. ac~
centuate, belabour, dwell on, em~
phasize, harp on, lay emphasis
upon, point up, repeat, rub in,
underline, underscore

stretch *v.* 1. cover, extend, put
forth, reach, spread, unfold, unroll
2. distend, draw out, elongate, ex~
pand, inflate, lengthen, pull, pull
out of shape, rack, strain, swell,
tighten ~*n.* 3. area, distance, ex~
panse, extent, spread, sweep, tract
4. bit, period, run, space, spell,
stint, term, time

strict 1. austere, authoritarian,
firm, harsh, no-nonsense, rigid,
rigorous, severe, stern, stringent 2.
accurate, close, exact, faithful,
meticulous, particular, precise, re~
ligious, scrupulous, true 3. absolute,
complete, perfect, total, utter

strident clamorous, clashing, dis~
cordant, grating, harsh, jangling,
jarring, rasping, raucous, screech~

ing, shrill, stridulant, stridulous,
unmusical, vociferous

strife animosity, battle, bickering,
clash, clashes, combat, conflict,
contention, contest, controversy,
discord, dissension, friction, quar~
rel, rivalry, row, squabbling, strug~
gle, warfare, wrangling

strike *v.* 1. bang, beat, box, buffet,
chastise, clobber (*Sl.*), clout (*Inf.*),
clump (*Sl.*), cuff, hammer, hit,
knock, lay a finger on (*Inf.*), pound,
punish, slap, smack, smite, sock
(*Sl.*), thump, wallop (*Inf.*) 2. be in
collision with, bump into, clash,
collide with, come into contact
with, dash, hit, knock into, run into,
smash into, touch 3. drive, force,
hit, impel, thrust 4. affect, come to,
come to the mind of, dawn on *or*
upon, hit, impress, make an impact
on, occur to, reach, register (*Inf.*),
seem 5. *Sometimes with* **upon**
come upon *or* across, discover, en~
counter, find, happen *or* chance
upon, hit upon, light upon, reach,
stumble upon *or* across, turn up,
uncover, unearth 6. affect, assail,
assault, attack, deal a blow to,
devastate, fall upon, hit, invade, set
upon, smite 7. achieve, arrange,
arrive at, attain, effect, reach 8.
down tools, mutiny, revolt, walk
out

striking astonishing, conspicuous,
dazzling, extraordinary, forcible,
impressive, memorable, notice~
able, out of the ordinary, outstand~
ing, stunning (*Inf.*), wonderful

string *n.* 1. cord, fibre, twine 2.
chain, file, line, procession, queue,
row, sequence, series, strand, suc~
cession ~*v.* 3. festoon, hang, link,
loop, sling, stretch, suspend, thread
4. *With* **out** disperse, extend, fan
out, lengthen, protract, space out,
spread out, straggle

stringent binding, demanding, ex~
acting, inflexible, rigid, rigorous,
severe, strict, tight, tough

strings *Fig.* catches (*Inf.*), compli~
cations, conditions, obligations,
prerequisites, provisos, qualifica~
tions, requirements, stipulations

strip[1] *v.* 1. bare, denude, deprive,

despoil, dismantle, divest, empty, gut, lay bare, loot, peel, pillage, plunder, ransack, rob, sack, skin, spoil 2. disrobe, unclothe, uncover, undress

strip² n. band, belt, bit, fillet, piece, ribbon, shred, slip, swathe, tongue

stripling adolescent, boy, fledgling, hobbledehoy (*Archaic*), lad, shaver (*Inf.*), young fellow, youngster, youth

strive attempt, compete, contend, do all one can, do one's best, do one's utmost, endeavour, exert oneself, fight, go all out (*Inf.*), labour, leave no stone unturned, make every effort, strain, struggle, toil, try, try hard

stroke n. 1. accomplishment, achievement, blow, feat, flourish, hit, knock, move, movement, pat, rap, thump 2. apoplexy, attack, collapse, fit, seizure, shock ~v. 3. caress, fondle, pat, pet, rub

stroll 1. v. amble, make one's way, mooch (*Inf.*), mosey (*Inf.*), promenade, ramble, saunter, stooge (*Inf.*), stretch one's legs, take a turn, toddle, wander 2. n. airing, breath of air, constitutional, excursion, promenade, ramble, turn, walk

strong 1. athletic, beefy (*Inf.*), brawny, burly, capable, hale, hardy, healthy, Herculean, lusty, muscular, powerful, robust, sinewy, sound, stalwart, stout, strapping, sturdy, tough, virile 2. aggressive, brave, courageous, determined, firm in spirit, forceful, hard as nails, hard-nosed (*Inf.*), high-powered, plucky, resilient, resolute, resourceful, self-assertive, steadfast, stouthearted, tenacious, tough, unyielding 3. acute, dedicated, deep, deep-rooted, eager, fervent, fervid, fierce, firm, intense, keen, severe, staunch, vehement, violent, zealous 4. clear, clear-cut, cogent, compelling, convincing, distinct, effective, formidable, great, marked, overpowering, persuasive, potent, redoubtable, sound, telling, trenchant, unmistakable, urgent, weighty, well-established, well-founded 5. Draconian, drastic, extreme, forceful, severe 6. durable, hard-wearing, heavy-duty, on a firm foundation, reinforced, sturdy, substantial, well-armed, well-built, well-protected 7. bold, bright, brilliant, dazzling, glaring, loud, stark 8. biting, concentrated, heady, highly-flavoured, highly-seasoned, hot, intoxicating, piquant, pungent, pure, sharp, spicy, undiluted

stronghold bastion, bulwark, castle, citadel, fastness, fort, fortress, keep, refuge

strong-minded determined, firm, independent, iron-willed, resolute, strong-willed, unbending, uncompromising

structure n. 1. arrangement, configuration, conformation, construction, design, fabric, form, formation, interrelation of parts, make, make-up, organization 2. building, construction, edifice, erection, pile ~v. 3. arrange, assemble, build up, design, organize, put together, shape

struggle v. 1. exert oneself, go all out (*Inf.*), labour, make every effort, strain, strive, toil, work, work like a Trojan ~n. 2. effort, exertion, grind (*Inf.*), labour, long haul, pains, scramble, toil, work ~v. 3. battle, compete, contend, fight, grapple, lock horns, scuffle, wrestle ~n. 4. battle, brush, clash, combat, conflict, contest, encounter, hostilities, skirmish, strife, tussle

strut v. parade, peacock, prance, stalk, swagger

stub n. butt, counterfoil, dog-end (*Inf.*), end, fag end (*Inf.*), remnant, stump, tail, tail end

stubborn bull-headed, contumacious, cross-grained, dogged, dour, fixed, headstrong, inflexible, intractable, mulish, obdurate, obstinate, opinionated, persistent, pigheaded, recalcitrant, refractory, self-willed, stiff-necked, tenacious, unbending, unmanageable, unshakable, unyielding, wilful

stuck 1. cemented, fast, fastened, firm, fixed, glued, joined 2. *Inf.* at a loss, at a standstill, at one's wits' end, baffled, beaten, bereft of ideas, nonplussed, stumped, up against a brick wall (*Inf.*) **3.** *Sl.* **With on** enthusiastic about, hung up on (*Sl.*), infatuated, keen, mad, obsessed with, wild about (*Inf.*) **4.** **get stuck into** *Inf.* get down to, make a start on, set about, tackle

stud *v.* bejewel, bespangle, dot, fleck, ornament, spangle, speckle, spot, sprinkle

student apprentice, disciple, learner, observer, pupil, scholar, undergraduate

studied calculated, conscious, deliberate, intentional, planned, premeditated, purposeful, well-considered, wilful

studio atelier, workshop

studious academic, assiduous, attentive, bookish, careful, diligent, eager, earnest, hard-working, intellectual, meditative, reflective, scholarly, sedulous, serious, thoughtful

study *v.* **1.** apply oneself (to), bone up (on) (*Inf.*), burn the midnight oil, cogitate, con (*Archaic*), consider, contemplate, cram (*Inf.*), examine, go into, hammer away at, learn, lucubrate (*Rare*), meditate, mug up (*Brit. sl.*), ponder, pore over, read, read up, swot (up) (*Brit. inf.*) **2.** analyse, deliberate, examine, investigate, look into, peruse, research, scrutinize, survey ~*n.* **3.** academic work, application, book work, cramming (*Inf.*), learning, lessons, reading, research, school work, swotting (*Brit. inf.*), thought **4.** analysis, attention, cogitation, consideration, contemplation, examination, inquiry, inspection, investigation, review, scrutiny, survey

stuff *v.* **1.** compress, cram, crowd, fill, force, jam, load, pack, pad, push, ram, shove, squeeze, stow, wedge **2.** gobble, gorge, gormandize, guzzle, make a pig of oneself (*Inf.*), overindulge, sate, satiate ~*n.* **3.** belongings, bits and pieces, clobber (*Brit. sl.*), effects, equipment, gear, goods and chattels, impedimenta, junk, kit, luggage, materials, objects, paraphernalia, possessions, tackle, things, trappings **4.** cloth, fabric, material, raw material, textile **5.** essence, matter, pith, quintessence, staple, substance **6.** balderdash, baloney (*Inf.*), bosh (*Inf.*), bunk (*Inf.*), bunkum, claptrap (*Inf.*), foolishness, humbug, nonsense, poppycock (*Inf.*), rot, rubbish, stuff and nonsense, tommyrot, tripe (*Inf.*), twaddle, verbiage

stuffing **1.** filler, kapok, packing, quilting, wadding **2.** farce, farcemeat, forcemeat

stuffy **1.** airless, close, fetid, frowsty, fuggy, heavy, muggy, oppressive, stale, stifling, suffocating, sultry, unventilated **2.** conventional, deadly, dreary, dull, fusty, humourless, musty, old-fashioned, old-fogyish, pompous, priggish, prim, prim and proper, staid, stilted, stodgy, strait-laced, uninteresting

stumble **1.** blunder about, come a cropper (*Inf.*), fall, falter, flounder, hesitate, lose one's balance, lurch, reel, slip, stagger, trip **2.** *With on or* **upon** blunder upon, chance upon, come across, discover, encounter, find, happen upon, light upon, run across, turn up **3.** falter, fluff (*Inf.*), stammer, stutter

stump *v.* **1.** baffle, bewilder, bring (someone) up short, confound, confuse, dumbfound, flummox, foil, mystify, outwit, perplex, puzzle, stop, stymie **2.** clomp, clump, lumber, plod, stamp, stomp (*Inf.*), trudge

stump up chip in (*Inf.*), come across with (*Inf.*), contribute, cough up (*Inf.*), donate, fork out (*Sl.*), hand over, pay, shell out (*Inf.*)

stun *Fig.* amaze, astonish, astound, bewilder, confound, confuse, daze, dumbfound, flabbergast (*Inf.*), hit (someone) like a ton of bricks (*Inf.*), knock out, knock (someone) for six (*Inf.*), overcome, overpower, shock, stagger, strike (someone) dumb (*Inf.*), stupefy, take (someone's) breath away

stunned *Fig.* astounded, at a loss for words, bowled over (*Inf.*), dazed, devastated, dumbfounded, flabbergasted (*Inf.*), numb, shocked, staggered, struck dumb (*Inf.*)

stunning beautiful, brilliant, dazzling, devastating (*Inf.*), gorgeous, great (*Inf.*), heavenly, impressive, lovely, marvellous, out of this world (*Inf.*), ravishing, remarkable, sensational, smashing (*Inf.*), spectacular, striking, wonderful

stunt *n.* act, deed, exploit, feat, feature, gest (*Archaic*), *tour de force*, trick

stunted diminutive, dwarfed, dwarfish, little, small, tiny, undersized

stupefaction amazement, astonishment, awe, wonder, wonderment

stupefy amaze, astound, bewilder, confound, daze, dumbfound, knock senseless, numb, shock, stagger, stun

stupendous amazing, astounding, breathtaking, colossal, enormous, fabulous (*Inf.*), fantastic (*Inf.*), gigantic, huge, marvellous, mindblowing (*Sl.*), mind-boggling (*Inf.*), out of this world (*Inf.*), overwhelming, phenomenal, prodigious, staggering, stunning (*Inf.*), superb, surpassing belief, surprising, tremendous (*Inf.*), vast, wonderful

stupid 1. Boeotian, brainless, cretinous, deficient, dense, dim, doltish, dopey (*Sl.*), dozy (*Brit. inf.*), dull, dumb (*Inf., chiefly U.S.*), foolish, gullible, half-witted, moronic, naive, obtuse, simple, simple-minded, slow, slow on the uptake (*Inf.*), slow-witted, sluggish, stolid, thick, thickheaded, unintelligent, witless, woodenheaded (*Inf.*) 2. crackbrained, futile, half-baked (*Inf.*), idiotic, ill-advised, imbecilic, inane, indiscreet, irrelevant, irresponsible, laughable, ludicrous, meaningless, mindless, nonsensical, pointless, puerile, rash, senseless, short-sighted, trivial, unintelligent, unthinking 3. dazed, groggy, in a daze, insensate, punch-drunk, semiconscious, senseless, stunned, stupefied

stupidity 1. asininity, brainlessness, denseness, dimness, dopiness (*Sl.*), doziness (*Brit. inf.*), dullness, dumbness (*Inf., chiefly U.S.*), feeble-mindedness, imbecility, lack of brain, lack of intelligence, naivety, obtuseness, puerility, simplicity, slowness, thickheadedness, thickness 2. absurdity, fatuity, fatuousness, folly, foolhardiness, foolishness, futility, idiocy, impracticality, inanity, indiscretion, ineptitude, irresponsibility, ludicrousness, lunacy, madness, pointlessness, rashness, senselessness, silliness

sturdy athletic, brawny, built to last, determined, durable, firm, flourishing, hardy, hearty, lusty, muscular, powerful, resolute, robust, secure, solid, stalwart, staunch, steadfast, stouthearted, substantial, vigorous, well-built, well-made

stutter *v.* falter, hesitate, speak haltingly, splutter, stammer, stumble

style *n.* 1. cut, design, form, hand, manner, technique 2. fashion, mode, rage, trend, vogue 3. approach, custom, manner, method, mode, way 4. *bon ton*, chic, cosmopolitanism, dash, dressiness (*Inf.*), élan, elegance, fashionableness, flair, grace, panache, polish, refinement, savoir-faire, smartness, sophistication, stylishness, taste, urbanity 5. affluence, comfort, ease, elegance, gracious living, grandeur, luxury 6. appearance, category, characteristic, genre, kind, pattern, sort, spirit, strain, tenor, tone, type, variety 7. diction, expression, mode of expression, phraseology, phrasing, treatment, turn of phrase, vein, wording ~*v.* 8. adapt, arrange, cut, design, dress, fashion, shape, tailor 9. address, call, christen, denominate, designate, dub, entitle, label, name, term

stylish à la mode, chic, classy (*Sl.*),

dapper, dressy (*Inf.*), fashionable, in fashion, in vogue, modish, natty (*Inf.*), polished, smart, snappy, snazzy (*Inf.*), trendy (*Brit. inf.*), urbane, voguish, well turned-out

subconscious *adj.* hidden, inner, innermost, intuitive, latent, repressed, subliminal, suppressed

subdue 1. beat down, break, conquer, control, crush, defeat, discipline, gain ascendancy over, get the better of, get the upper hand over, get under control, humble, master, overcome, overpower, overrun, put down, quell, tame, trample, triumph over, vanquish 2. check, control, mellow, moderate, quieten down, repress, soften, suppress, tone down

subdued 1. chastened, crestfallen, dejected, downcast, down in the mouth, grave, out of spirits, quiet, repentant, repressed, restrained, sad, sadder and wiser, serious, sobered, solemn 2. dim, hushed, low-key, muted, quiet, shaded, sober, soft, subtle, toned down, unobtrusive

subject *n.* 1. affair, business, field of enquiry *or* reference, issue, matter, object, point, question, subject matter, substance, theme, topic 2. case, client, guinea pig (*Inf.*), participant, patient, victim 3. citizen, dependant, liegeman, national, subordinate, vassal ~*adj.* 4. at the mercy of, disposed, exposed, in danger of, liable, open, prone, susceptible, vulnerable 5. conditional, contingent, dependent 6. answerable, bound by, captive, dependent, enslaved, inferior, obedient, satellite, subjugated, submissive, subordinate, subservient ~*v.* 7. expose, lay open, make liable, put through, submit, treat

subjective biased, emotional, idiosyncratic, instinctive, intuitive, nonobjective, personal, prejudiced

sublime elevated, eminent, exalted, glorious, grand, great, high, imposing, lofty, magnificent, majestic, noble, transcendent

submerge deluge, dip, drown, duck, dunk, engulf, flood, immerse, inundate, overflow, overwhelm, plunge, sink, swamp

submerged drowned, immersed, subaquatic, subaqueous, submarine, submersed, sunk, sunken, undersea, underwater

submission 1. acquiescence, assent, capitulation, giving in, surrender, yielding 2. compliance, deference, docility, meekness, obedience, passivity, resignation, submissiveness, tractability, unassertiveness 3. argument, contention, proposal 4. entry, handing in, presentation, submitting, tendering

submissive abject, accommodating, acquiescent, amenable, biddable, bootlicking (*Inf.*), compliant, deferential, docile, dutiful, humble, ingratiating, lowly, malleable, meek, obedient, obeisant, obsequious, passive, patient, pliant, resigned, subdued, tractable, uncomplaining, unresisting, yielding

submit 1. accede, acquiesce, agree, bend, bow, capitulate, comply, defer, endure, give in, hoist the white flag, knuckle under, lay down arms, put up with (*Inf.*), resign oneself, stoop, succumb, surrender, throw in the sponge, toe the line, tolerate, yield 2. commit, hand in, present, proffer, put forward, refer, table, tender 3. advance, argue, assert, claim, contend, move, propose, propound, put, state, suggest, volunteer

subordinate *adj.* 1. dependent, inferior, junior, lesser, lower, minor, secondary, subject, subservient 2. ancillary, auxiliary, subsidiary, supplementary ~*n.* 3. aide, assistant, attendant, dependant, inferior, junior, second, subaltern, underling

subordination inferior *or* secondary status, inferiority, servitude, subjection, submission

subscribe 1. chip in (*Inf.*), contribute, donate, give, offer, pledge, promise 2. acquiesce, advocate, agree, consent, countenance, endorse, support

subscription annual payment,

contribution, donation, dues, gift, membership fee, offering

subsequent after, consequent, consequential, ensuing, following, later, succeeding, successive

subsequently afterwards, at a lat~ er date, consequently, in the after~ math (of), in the end, later

subside 1. abate, decrease, de~ escalate, diminish, dwindle, ease, ebb, lessen, let up, level off, melt away, moderate, peter out, quiet~ en, recede, slacken, wane 2. cave in, collapse, decline, descend, drop, ebb, lower, settle, sink

subsidence 1. decline, descent, ebb, settlement, settling, sinking 2. abatement, decrease, de~ escalation, diminution, easing off, lessening, slackening

subsidiary aiding, ancillary, assis~ tant, auxiliary, contributory, co~ operative, helpful, lesser, minor, secondary, serviceable, subordi~ nate, subservient, supplemental, supplementary, useful

subsidize finance, fund, promote, put up the money for, sponsor, support, underwrite

subsidy aid, allowance, assistance, contribution, financial aid, grant, help, subvention, support

subsist be, continue, eke out an existence, endure, exist, keep go~ ing, last, live, make ends meet, re~ main, stay alive, survive, sustain oneself

subsistence aliment, existence, food, keep, livelihood, living, maintenance, provision, rations, support, survival, sustenance, up~ keep, victuals

substance 1. body, element, fabric, material, stuff, texture 2. burden, essence, gist, gravamen (*Law*), import, main point, matter, mean~ ing, pith, significance, subject, sum and substance, theme 3. actuality, concreteness, entity, force, reality 4. affluence, assets, estate, means, property, resources, wealth

substantial 1. ample, big, consid~ erable, generous, goodly, impor~ tant, large, significant, sizable, tidy (*Inf.*), worthwhile 2. bulky, durable, firm, hefty, massive, solid, sound, stout, strong, sturdy, well-built 3. actual, existent, material, positive, real, true, valid, weighty

substantially essentially, in es~ sence, in essentials, in substance, in the main, largely, materially, to a large extent

substantiate affirm, attest to, authenticate, bear out, confirm, corroborate, establish, prove, sup~ port, validate, verify

substitute v. 1. change, commute, exchange, interchange, replace, swap (*Inf.*), switch 2. *With* **for** act for, be in place of, cover for, depu~ tize, double for, fill in for, hold the fort for, relieve, stand in for, take over ~n. 3. agent, depute (*Chiefly Scot.*), deputy, equivalent, expedi~ ent, locum, locum tenens, make~ shift, proxy, relief, replacement, representative, reserve, stand-by, stopgap, sub, supply, surrogate, temp (*Inf.*), temporary ~adj. 4. acting, additional, alternative, proxy, replacement, reserve, sec~ ond, surrogate, temporary

substitution change, exchange, interchange, replacement, swap (*Inf.*), switch

subterfuge artifice, deception, de~ viousness, dodge, duplicity, eva~ sion, excuse, machination, ma~ noeuvre, ploy, pretence, pretext, quibble, ruse, shift, stall, strata~ gem, trick

subtle 1. deep, delicate, discrimi~ nating, ingenious, nice, penetrat~ ing, profound, refined, sophisticat~ ed 2. delicate, faint, implied, indi~ rect, insinuated, slight, understated 3. artful, astute, crafty, cunning, designing, devious, intriguing, keen, Machiavellian, scheming, shrewd, sly, wily

subtlety 1. acumen, acuteness, cleverness, delicacy, discernment, fine point, intricacy, nicety, re~ finement, sagacity, skill, sophisti~ cation 2. discernment, discrimina~ tion, finesse, penetration 3. artful~ ness, astuteness, craftiness, cun~ ning, deviousness, guile, slyness, wiliness

subtract deduct, detract, diminish, remove, take away, take from, take off, withdraw

suburbs dormitory area (*Brit.*), environs, faubourgs, neighbour~ hood, outskirts, precincts, purlieus, residential areas, suburbia

subversive 1. *adj.* destructive, in~ cendiary, inflammatory, insurrec~ tionary, overthrowing, perversive, riotous, seditious, treasonous, underground, undermining 2. *n.* deviationist, dissident, fifth col~ umnist, insurrectionary, quisling, saboteur, seditionary, seditionist, terrorist, traitor

subvert 1. demolish, destroy, in~ validate, overturn, raze, ruin, sabotage, undermine, upset, wreck 2. confound, contaminate, corrupt, debase, demoralize, deprave, per~ vert, poison, vitiate

succeed 1. arrive (*Inf.*), be suc~ cessful, come off (*Inf.*), do all right for oneself (*Inf.*), do the trick (*Inf.*), flourish, gain one's end, get to the top (*Inf.*), make good, make it (*Inf.*), prosper, thrive, triumph, turn out well, work 2. be subse~ quent, come next, ensue, follow, result, supervene 3. *Usually with* to accede, assume the office of, come into, come into possession of, enter upon, inherit, replace, take over

succeeding ensuing, following, next, subsequent, successive

success 1. ascendancy, eminence, fame, favourable outcome, fortune, happiness, hit (*Inf.*), luck, prosper~ ity, triumph 2. best seller, big name, celebrity, hit (*Inf.*), market leader, sensation, smash hit (*Inf.*), somebody, star, V.I.P., winner

successful acknowledged, at the top of the tree, best-selling, boom~ ing, efficacious, favourable, flour~ ishing, fortunate, fruitful, lucky, lucrative, moneymaking, out in front (*Inf.*), paying, profitable, prosperous, rewarding, thriving, top, unbeaten, victorious, wealthy

successfully famously (*Inf.*), fa~ vourably, in triumph, swimmingly, victoriously, well, with flying col~ ours

succession 1. chain, continuation, course, cycle, flow, order, proces~ sion, progression, run, sequence, series, train 2. **in succession** con~ secutively, one after the other, one behind the other, on the trot (*Inf.*), running, successively 3. accession, assumption, elevation, entering upon, inheritance, taking over 4. descendants, descent, line, lineage, race

successive consecutive, following, in a row, in succession, sequent, succeeding

succinct brief, compact, compen~ dious, concise, condensed, gnomic, in a few well-chosen words, lacon~ ic, pithy, summary, terse, to the point

succour 1. *v.* aid, assist, befriend, comfort, encourage, foster, give aid and encouragement to, help, minister to, nurse, relieve, render assistance to, support 2. *n.* aid, as~ sistance, comfort, help, relief, sup~ port

succulent juicy, luscious, lush, mellow, moist, mouthwatering, rich

succumb capitulate, die, fall, fall victim to, give in, give way, go under, knuckle under, submit, sur~ render, yield

sucker butt, cat's paw, dupe, easy game *or* mark (*Inf.*), fool, mug (*Sl.*), pushover (*Sl.*), sap (*Sl.*), sit~ ting duck (*Inf.*), victim

sudden abrupt, hasty, hurried, im~ pulsive, quick, rapid, rash, swift, unexpected, unforeseen, unusual

suddenly abruptly, all at once, all of a sudden, on the spur of the moment, out of the blue (*Inf.*), un~ expectedly, without warning

sue 1. *Law* bring an action against (someone), charge, have the law on (someone) (*Inf.*), indict, insti~ tute legal proceedings against (someone), prefer charges against (someone), prosecute, summon, take (someone) to court 2. appeal for, beg, beseech, entreat, petition, plead, solicit, supplicate

suffer 1. ache, agonize, be affected, be in pain, be racked, feel wretch~

ed, go through a lot (*Inf.*), grieve, have a thin *or* bad time, hurt 2. bear, endure, experience, feel, go through, put up with (*Inf.*), support, sustain, tolerate, undergo 3. appear in a poor light, be handicapped, be impaired, deteriorate, fall off, show to disadvantage 4. *Archaic* allow, let, permit

suffering *n.* affliction, agony, anguish, discomfort, distress, hardship, martyrdom, misery, ordeal, pain, torment, torture

suffice answer, be sufficient (adequate, enough), content, do, fill the bill (*Inf.*), meet requirements, satisfy, serve

sufficient adequate, competent, enough, enow (*Archaic*), satisfactory

suffocate asphyxiate, choke, smother, stifle, strangle

suffuse bathe, cover, flood, imbue, infuse, mantle, overspread, permeate, pervade, spread over, steep, transfuse

suggest 1. advise, advocate, move, offer a suggestion, propose, put forward, recommend 2. bring to mind, connote, evoke, put one in mind of 3. hint, imply, indicate, insinuate, intimate, lead one to believe

suggestion 1. motion, plan, proposal, proposition, recommendation 2. breath, hint, indication, insinuation, intimation, suspicion, trace, whisper

suggestive 1. *With* of evocative, expressive, indicative, redolent, reminiscent 2. bawdy, blue, immodest, improper, indecent, indelicate, off colour, provocative, prurient, racy, ribald, risqué, rude, smutty, spicy (*Inf.*), titillating, unseemly

suit *v.* 1. agree, agree with, answer, be acceptable to, become, befit, be seemly, conform to, correspond, do, go with, gratify, harmonize, match, please, satisfy, tally 2. accommodate, adapt, adjust, fashion, fit, modify, proportion, tailor ~*n.* 3. addresses, appeal, attentions, courtship, entreaty, invocation, petition, prayer, request 4. *Law* action, case, cause, lawsuit, proceeding, prosecution, trial 5. clothing, costume, dress, ensemble, habit, outfit 6. **follow suit** accord with, copy, emulate, run with the herd, take one's cue from

suitability appropriateness, aptness, fitness, opportuneness, rightness, timeliness

suitable acceptable, applicable, apposite, appropriate, apt, becoming, befitting, convenient, cut out for, due, fit, fitting, in character, in keeping, opportune, pertinent, proper, relevant, right, satisfactory, seemly, suited

suite 1. apartment, collection, furniture, rooms, series, set 2. attendants, entourage, escort, followers, retainers, retinue, train

suitor admirer, beau, follower (*Obsolete*), swain (*Archaic*), wooer

sulk be in a huff, be put out, brood, have the hump (*Brit. inf.*), look sullen, pout

sulky aloof, churlish, cross, disgruntled, ill-humoured, in the sulks, moody, morose, perverse, petulant, put out, querulous, resentful, sullen, vexed

sullen brooding, cheerless, cross, dismal, dull, gloomy, glowering, heavy, moody, morose, obstinate, out of humour, perverse, silent, sombre, sour, stubborn, surly, unsociable

sultry 1. close, hot, humid, muggy, oppressive, sticky, stifling, stuffy, sweltering 2. come-hither (*Inf.*), erotic, passionate, provocative, seductive, sensual, sexy (*Inf.*), voluptuous

sum aggregate, amount, entirety, quantity, reckoning, score, sum total, tally, total, totality, whole

summarily arbitrarily, at short notice, expeditiously, forthwith, immediately, on the spot, peremptorily, promptly, speedily, swiftly, without delay, without wasting words

summarize abridge, condense, encapsulate, epitomize, give a rundown of, give the main points of, outline, précis, put in a nutshell, review, sum up

summary 1. *n.* abridgment, abstract, compendium, digest, epitome, essence, extract, outline, précis, recapitulation, résumé, review, rundown, summing-up, synopsis 2. *adj.* arbitrary, brief, compact, compendious, concise, condensed, cursory, hasty, laconic, perfunctory, pithy, succinct

summit acme, apex, crown, crowning point, culmination, head, height, peak, pinnacle, top, zenith

summon 1. arouse, assemble, bid, call, call together, cite, convene, convoke, invite, rally, rouse, send for 2. *Often with* **up** call into action, draw on, gather, invoke, mobilize, muster

sumptuous costly, dear, de luxe, expensive, extravagant, gorgeous, grand, lavish, luxurious, magnificent, opulent, plush (*Inf.*), posh (*Inf.*), rich, ritzy (*Sl.*), splendid, superb

sum up 1. close, conclude, put in a nutshell, recapitulate, review, summarize 2. estimate, form an opinion of, get the measure of, size up (*Inf.*)

sun 1. *n.* daystar (*Poetic*), eye of heaven, Helios (*Greek myth*), Phoebus (*Greek myth*), Phoebus Apollo (*Greek myth*), Sol (*Roman myth*) 2. *v.* bake, bask, sunbathe, tan

sunburnt bronzed, brown, brown as a berry, burnt, like a lobster, peeling, red, ruddy, scarlet, tanned

sundry assorted, different, divers (*Archaic*), miscellaneous, several, some, varied, various

sunken 1. concave, drawn, haggard, hollow, hollowed 2. at a lower level, below ground, buried, depressed, immersed, lower, recessed, submerged

sunless bleak, cheerless, cloudy, dark, depressing, gloomy, grey, hazy, overcast, sombre

sunny 1. bright, brilliant, clear, fine, luminous, radiant, summery, sunlit, sunshiny, unclouded, without a cloud in the sky 2. *Fig.*

beaming, blithe, buoyant, cheerful, cheery, genial, happy, joyful, light-hearted, optimistic, pleasant, smiling

sunrise aurora (*Poetic*), break of day, cockcrow, dawn, daybreak, daylight, dayspring (*Poetic*), sunup

sunset close of (the) day, dusk, eventide, gloaming, nightfall, sundown

superb admirable, breathtaking, choice, excellent, exquisite, fine, first-rate, gorgeous, grand, magnificent, marvellous, of the first water, splendid, superior, unrivalled

supercilious arrogant, condescending, contemptuous, disdainful, haughty, high and mighty (*Inf.*), hoity-toity (*Inf.*), imperious, insolent, lofty, lordly, overbearing, patronizing, proud, scornful, snooty (*Inf.*), stuck-up (*Inf.*), toffee-nosed (*Sl.*), uppish (*Brit. inf.*), vainglorious

superficial 1. exterior, external, on the surface, peripheral, shallow, skin-deep, slight, surface 2. casual, cosmetic, cursory, desultory, hasty, hurried, inattentive, nodding, passing, perfunctory, sketchy, slapdash 3. empty, empty-headed, frivolous, lightweight, shallow, silly, trivial 4. apparent, evident, ostensible, outward, seeming

superficiality emptiness, lack of depth, lack of substance, shallowness, triviality

superficially apparently, at first glance, externally, on the surface, ostensibly, to the casual eye

superfluous excess, excessive, extra, in excess, left over, needless, on one's hands, pleonastic (*Rhetoric*), redundant, remaining, residuary, spare, superabundant, supererogatory, supernumerary, surplus, surplus to requirements, uncalled-for, unnecessary, unneeded, unrequired

superhuman 1. herculean, heroic, phenomenal, prodigious, stupendous, valiant 2. divine, paranormal, preternatural, supernatural

superintend administer, control,

direct, inspect, look after, manage, overlook, oversee, run, supervise

superintendence care, charge, control, direction, government, guidance, inspection, management, supervision, surveillance

superintendent administrator, chief, conductor, controller, director, governor, inspector, manager, overseer, supervisor

superior *adj.* 1. better, grander, greater, higher, more advanced (expert, extensive, skilful), paramount, predominant, preferred, prevailing, surpassing, unrivalled 2. a cut above (*Inf.*), admirable, choice, de luxe, distinguished, excellent, exceptional, exclusive, fine, first-class, first-rate, good, good quality, high calibre, highclass, of the first order 3. airy, condescending, disdainful, haughty, lofty, lordly, patronizing, pretentious, snobbish, stuck-up (*Inf.*), supercilious ~*n.* 4. boss (*Inf.*), chief, director, manager, principal, senior, supervisor

superiority advantage, ascendancy, excellence, lead, predominance, pre-eminence, preponderance, prevalence, supremacy

superlative *adj.* consummate, crack (*Sl.*), excellent, greatest, highest, magnificent, matchless, of the first water, of the highest order, outstanding, peerless, supreme, surpassing, transcendent, unparalleled, unrivalled, unsurpassed

supernatural abnormal, dark, ghostly, hidden, miraculous, mysterious, mystic, occult, paranormal, phantom, preternatural, psychic, spectral, supranatural, uncanny, unearthly, unnatural

supervise administer, be on duty at, be responsible for, conduct, control, direct, handle, have or be in charge of, inspect, keep an eye on, look after, manage, oversee, preside over, run, superintend

supervision administration, auspices, care, charge, control, direction, guidance, instruction, management, oversight, stewardship, superintendence, surveillance

supervisor administrator, boss (*Inf.*), chief, foreman, inspector, manager, overseer, steward, superintendent

supervisory administrative, executive, managerial, overseeing, superintendent

supplant displace, oust, overthrow, remove, replace, supersede, take over, take the place of, undermine, unseat

supple bending, elastic, flexible, limber, lithe, plastic, pliable, pliant

supplement 1. *n.* added feature, addendum, addition, appendix, codicil, complement, extra, insert, postscript, pull-out, sequel 2. *v.* add, augment, complement, extend, fill out, reinforce, supply, top up

supplementary accompanying, additional, ancillary, auxiliary, complementary, extra, secondary, supplemental

suppliant 1. *adj.* begging, beseeching, craving, entreating, imploring, importunate, on bended knee 2. *n.* applicant, petitioner, suitor, supplicant

supplication appeal, entreaty, invocation, petition, plea, pleading, prayer, request, solicitation, suit

supply *v.* 1. afford, cater to or for, come up with, contribute, endow, fill, furnish, give, grant, minister, outfit, produce, provide, purvey, replenish, satisfy, stock, store, victual, yield ~*n.* 2. cache, fund, hoard, quantity, reserve, reservoir, source, stock, stockpile, store 3. *Usually plural* equipment, food, foodstuff, items, materials, necessities, provender, provisions, rations, stores

support *v.* 1. bear, bolster, brace, buttress, carry, hold, hold up, prop, reinforce, shore up, sustain, underpin, uphold 2. be a source of strength to, buoy up, cherish, finance, foster, fund, keep, look after, maintain, nourish, provide for, strengthen, subsidize, succour, sustain, take care of, underwrite 3. advocate, aid, assist, back, boost (someone's) morale, champion, defend, forward, go along with, help, promote, second, side with, stand behind, stand up for, stick up for (*Inf.*), take (someone's) part, take up the cudgels for, uphold 4. attest to, authenticate, bear out, confirm, corroborate, document, endorse, lend credence to, substantiate, verify 5. bear, brook, countenance, endure, put up with (*Inf.*), stand (for), stomach, submit, suffer, thole (*Dialect*), tolerate, undergo ~*n.* 6. abutment, back, brace, foundation, lining, pillar, post, prop, shore, stanchion, stay, stiffener, underpinning 7. aid, approval, assistance, backing, blessing, championship, comfort, encouragement, friendship, furtherance, help, loyalty, moral support, patronage, protection, relief, succour, sustenance 8. keep, livelihood, maintenance, subsistence, sustenance, upkeep 9. backbone, backer, comforter, mainstay, prop, second, stay, supporter, tower of strength

supporter adherent, advocate, ally, apologist, champion, co-worker, defender, fan, follower, friend, helper, patron, sponsor, upholder, well-wisher

suppose 1. assume, calculate (*U.S. dialect*), conjecture, dare say, expect, guess (*Inf.*), imagine, infer, judge, opine, presume, presuppose, surmise, take as read, take for granted, think 2. believe, conceive, conclude, conjecture, consider, fancy, hypothesize, imagine, postulate, pretend

supposed 1. accepted, alleged, assumed, hypothetical, presumed, presupposed, professed, putative, reputed, rumoured 2. *With* to expected, meant, obliged, ought, required

supposedly allegedly, at a guess, avowedly, by all accounts, hypothetically, ostensibly, presumably, professedly, purportedly, theoretically

supposition conjecture, doubt, guess, guesswork, hypothesis, idea, notion, postulate, presumption, speculation, surmise, theory

suppress 1. beat down, check, clamp down on, conquer, crack down on, crush, drive underground, extinguish, overpower, overthrow, put an end to, quash, quell, quench, snuff out, stamp out, stop, subdue, trample on 2. censor, conceal, contain, cover up, curb, hold in *or* back, hold in check, keep secret, muffle, muzzle, repress, restrain, silence, smother, stifle, withhold

suppression check, clampdown, crackdown, crushing, dissolution, elimination, extinction, inhibition, prohibition, quashing, smothering, termination

supremacy absolute rule, ascendancy, dominance, domination, dominion, lordship, mastery, paramountcy, predominance, pre-eminence, primacy, sovereignty, supreme authority, sway

supreme cardinal, chief, crowning, culminating, extreme, final, first, foremost, greatest, head, highest, incomparable, leading, matchless, paramount, peerless, predominant, pre-eminent, prevailing, prime, principal, sovereign, superlative, surpassing, top, ultimate, unsurpassed, utmost

sure 1. assured, certain, clear, confident, convinced, decided, definite, free from doubt, persuaded, positive, satisfied 2. accurate, dependable, effective, foolproof, honest, indisputable, infallible, never-failing, precise, reliable, sure-fire (*Inf.*), tried and true, trustworthy, trusty, undeniable, undoubted, unerring, unfailing, unmistakable, well-proven 3. assured, bound, guaranteed, ineluctable, inescapable, inevitable, irrevocable 4. fast, firm, fixed, safe, secure, solid, stable, steady

surely assuredly, beyond the shadow of a doubt, certainly, come what may, definitely, doubtlessly, for certain, indubitably, inevitably, inexorably, undoubtedly, unquestionably, without doubt, without fail

surface *n.* 1. covering, exterior, fa~cade, face, facet, outside, plane, side, skin, superficies (*Rare*), top, veneer 2. **on the surface** appar~ently, at first glance, ostensibly, outwardly, superficially, to all ap~pearances, to the casual eye ~*adj.* 3. apparent, exterior, external, outward, superficial ~*v.* 4. appear, come to light, come up, crop up (*Inf.*), emerge, materialize, rise, transpire

surfeit 1. *n.* excess, glut, overindul~gence, plethora, satiety, super~abundance, superfluity 2. *v.* cram, fill, glut, gorge, overfeed, overfill, satiate, stuff

surge 1. *v.* billow, eddy, gush, heave, rise, roll, rush, swell, swirl, tower, undulate, well forth 2. *n.* billow, breaker, efflux, flood, flow, gush, intensification, outpouring, roller, rush, swell, uprush, upsurge, wave

surly bearish, brusque, churlish, crabbed, cross, crusty, curmudg~eonly, grouchy (*Inf.*), gruff, ill-natured, morose, perverse, sulky, sullen, testy, uncivil, ungracious

surmise 1. *v.* come to the conclu~sion, conclude, conjecture, consid~er, deduce, fancy, guess, hazard a guess, imagine, infer, opine, pre~sume, speculate, suppose, suspect 2. *n.* assumption, conclusion, con~jecture, deduction, guess, hypoth~esis, idea, inference, notion, pos~sibility, presumption, speculation, supposition, suspicion, thought

surmount conquer, exceed, mas~ter, overcome, overpower, over~top, pass, prevail over, surpass, triumph over, vanquish

surpass beat, best, eclipse, exceed, excel, go one better than (*Inf.*), outdo, outshine, outstrip, override, overshadow, top, tower above, transcend

surpassing exceptional, extraor~dinary, incomparable, matchless, outstanding, phenomenal, rare, su~preme, transcendent, unrivalled

surplus 1. *n.* balance, excess, re~

mainder, residue, superabundance, superfluity, surfeit 2. *adj.* excess, extra, in excess, left over, odd, re~maining, spare, superfluous, un~used

surprise *v.* 1. amaze, astonish, astound, bewilder, bowl over (*Inf.*), confuse, disconcert, flabbergast (*Inf.*), leave open-mouthed, non~plus, stagger, stun, take aback 2. burst in on, catch in the act *or* red-handed, catch napping, catch una~wares *or* off-guard, come down on like a bolt from the blue, discover, spring upon, startle ~*n.* 3. amaze~ment, astonishment, bewilder~ment, incredulity, stupefaction, wonder 4. bolt from the blue, bombshell, eye-opener (*Inf.*), jolt, revelation, shock, start (*Inf.*)

surprised amazed, astonished, at a loss, caught on the hop (*Brit. inf.*), caught on the wrong foot (*Inf.*), disconcerted, incredulous, non~plussed, open-mouthed, speechless, startled, taken aback, taken by surprise, thunderstruck, unable to believe one's eyes

surprising amazing, astonishing, astounding, extraordinary, incred~ible, marvellous, remarkable, staggering, startling, unexpected, unlooked-for, unusual, wonderful

surrender *v.* 1. abandon, cede, concede, deliver up, forego, give up, part with, relinquish, renounce, resign, waive, yield 2. capitulate, give in, give oneself up, give way, lay down arms, quit, show the white flag, submit, succumb, throw in the towel, yield ~*n.* 3. capitula~tion, delivery, relinquishment, re~nunciation, resignation, submis~sion, yielding

surreptitious clandestine, covert, fraudulent, furtive, secret, sly, sneaking, stealthy, unauthorized, underhand, veiled

surround 1. close in on, encircle, enclose, encompass, envelop, en~viron, fence in, girdle, hem in, ring 2. *Military* besiege, invest (*Rare*), lay siege to

surrounding nearby, neighbouring

surroundings background, envi~

ronment, environs, location, mi~
lieu, neighbourhood, setting

surveillance care, control, direc~
tion, inspection, observation, scru~
tiny, superintendence, supervision,
vigilance, watch

survey v. 1. contemplate, examine,
inspect, look over, observe, recon~
noitre, research, review, scan,
scrutinize, study, supervise, view 2.
appraise, assess, estimate, meas~
ure, plan, plot, prospect, size up,
take stock of, triangulate ~n. 3.
examination, inquiry, inspection,
overview, perusal, random sample,
review, scrutiny, study

survive be extant, endure, exist,
hold out, keep body and soul to~
gether (Inf.), last, live, live on, out~
last, outlive, pull through, remain
alive, subsist

susceptibility liability, predisposi~
tion, proneness, propensity, re~
sponsiveness, sensitivity, suggest~
ibility, vulnerability, weakness

susceptible 1. Usually with to dis~
posed, given, inclined, liable, open,
predisposed, prone, subject, vul~
nerable 2. alive to, easily moved,
impressionable, receptive, respon~
sive, sensitive, suggestible, tender

suspect v. 1. distrust, doubt, har~
bour suspicions about, have one's
doubts about, mistrust, smell a rat
(Inf.) 2. believe, conclude, conjec~
ture, consider, fancy, feel, guess,
have a sneaking suspicion, hazard
a guess, speculate, suppose, sur~
mise, think probable ~adj. 3.
doubtful, dubious, fishy (Inf.), open
to suspicion, questionable

suspend 1. append, attach, dangle,
hang, swing 2. adjourn, arrest,
cease, cut short, debar, defer, de~
lay, discontinue, hold off, interrupt,
lay aside, pigeonhole, postpone,
put off, shelve, stay, withhold

suspense 1. anticipation, anxiety,
apprehension, doubt, expectancy,
expectation, indecision, insecurity,
irresolution, tension, uncertainty,
wavering 2. in suspense anxious,
in an agony of doubt, keyed up, on
edge, on tenterhooks

suspension abeyance, adjourn~

ment, break, breaking off, defer~
ment, delay, disbarment, discon~
tinuation, interruption, morato~
rium, postponement, remission,
respite, stay

suspicion 1. bad vibes (Inf.),
chariness, distrust, doubt, funny
feeling (Inf.), jealousy, lack of con~
fidence, misgiving, mistrust,
qualm, scepticism, wariness 2.
above suspicion above reproach,
blameless, honourable, like Cae~
sar's wife, pure, sinless, unim~
peachable, virtuous 3. conjecture,
guess, gut feeling (Inf.), hunch,
idea, impression, notion, supposi~
tion, surmise 4. glimmer, hint,
shade, shadow, soupçon, strain,
streak, suggestion, tinge, touch,
trace

suspicious 1. apprehensive, dis~
trustful, doubtful, jealous, mis~
trustful, sceptical, suspecting, un~
believing, wary 2. doubtful, dubi~
ous, fishy (Inf.), funny, irregular, of
doubtful honesty, open to doubt or
misconstruction, queer, question~
able, shady (Inf.), suspect

sustain 1. bear, carry, keep from
falling, keep up, support, uphold 2.
bear, bear up under, endure, ex~
perience, feel, suffer, undergo,
withstand 3. aid, assist, comfort,
foster, help, keep alive, nourish,
nurture, provide for, relieve 4. ap~
prove, confirm, continue, keep
alive, keep going, keep up, main~
tain, prolong, protract, ratify 5.
endorse, uphold, validate, verify

sustained constant, continuous,
nonstop, perpetual, prolonged,
steady, unremitting

sustenance 1. aliment, comes~
tibles, daily bread, eatables, ed~
ibles, food, nourishment, proven~
der, provisions, rations, refection,
refreshments, victuals 2. liveli~
hood, maintenance, subsistence,
support

swagger 1. v. bluster, boast, brag,
bully, gasconade (Rare), hector,
parade, prance, show off (Inf.),
strut, swank (Inf.) 2. n. arrogance,
bluster, braggadocio, display, gas~
conade (Rare), ostentation, pom~

posity, show, showing off (*Inf.*), swank (*Inf.*), swashbuckling

swallow v. 1. absorb, consume, devour, down (*Inf.*), drink, eat, gulp, ingest, swig (*Inf.*), swill, wash down 2. *Often with* up absorb, assimilate, consume, engulf, envelop, overrun, overwhelm, use up, waste 3. choke back, hold in, repress 4. *Inf.* accept, believe, buy (*Inf.*), fall for

swamp n. 1. bog, everglade(s) (*U.S.*), fen, marsh, mire, morass, moss (*Scot., & northern English dialect*), quagmire, slough ~v. 2. capsize, drench, engulf, flood, inundate, overwhelm, sink, submerge, swallow up, upset, wash over, waterlog 3. beset, besiege, deluge, flood, inundate, overload, overwhelm, snow under

swampy boggy, fenny, marish (*Obsolete*), marshy, miry, quaggy, waterlogged, wet

swap, swop v. bandy, barter, exchange, interchange, switch, trade, traffic

swarm n. 1. army, bevy, concourse, crowd, drove, flock, herd, horde, host, mass, multitude, myriad, shoal, throng ~v. 2. congregate, crowd, flock, mass, stream, throng 3. *With* with abound, be alive (infested, overrun), bristle, crawl, teem

swarthy black, brown, dark, dark-complexioned, dark-skinned, dusky, swart (*Archaic*), tawny

swashbuckling bold, daredevil, dashing, flamboyant, gallant, mettlesome, roisterous, spirited, swaggering

swastika fylfot

swathe bandage, bind, bundle up, cloak, drape, envelop, enwrap, fold, furl, lap, muffle up, sheathe, shroud, swaddle, wrap

sway v. 1. bend, fluctuate, incline, lean, lurch, oscillate, rock, roll, swing, wave 2. affect, control, direct, dominate, govern, guide, induce, influence, persuade, prevail on, win over ~n. 3. ascendency, authority, clout (*Inf.*), command, control, dominion, government, influence, jurisdiction, power, pre-

dominance, rule, sovereignty 4. **hold sway** predominate, prevail, reign, rule, run

swear 1. affirm, assert, attest, avow, declare, depose, give one's word, pledge oneself, promise, state under oath, take an oath, testify, vow, warrant 2. be foul-mouthed, blaspheme, curse, cuss (*Inf.*), imprecate, take the Lord's name in vain, turn the air blue, utter profanities 3. *With* by depend on, have confidence in, rely on, trust

swearing bad language, blasphemy, cursing, cussing (*Inf.*), foul language, imprecations, malediction, profanity

sweat n. 1. diaphoresis (*Medical*), exudation, perspiration, sudor (*Medical*) 2. *Inf.* agitation, anxiety, distress, flap (*Inf.*), panic, strain, worry 3. *Inf.* backbreaking task, chore, drudgery, effort, labour ~v. 4. break out in a sweat, exude moisture, glow, perspire 5. *Inf.* agonize, be on pins and needles (*Inf.*), be on tenterhooks, chafe, fret, lose sleep over, suffer, torture oneself, worry 6. **sweat it out** *Inf.* endure, see (something) through, stay the course, stick it out (*Inf.*)

sweaty clammy, drenched (bathed, soaked) in perspiration, glowing, perspiring, sticky, sweating

sweep v. 1. brush, clean, clear, remove 2. career, flounce, fly, glance, glide, hurtle, pass, sail, scud, skim, tear, zoom ~n. 3. arc, bend, curve, gesture, move, movement, stroke, swing 4. compass, extent, range, scope, span, stretch, vista

sweeping 1. all-embracing, all-inclusive, bird's-eye, broad, comprehensive, extensive, global, radical, thoroughgoing, wide, wide-ranging 2. across-the-board, blanket, exaggerated, indiscriminate, overdrawn, overstated, unqualified, wholesale

sweet adj. 1. cloying, honeyed, luscious, melting, saccharine, sugary, sweetened, syrupy, toothsome 2.

affectionate, agreeable, amiable, appealing, attractive, beautiful, charming, delightful, engaging, fair, gentle, kind, lovable, sweet-tempered, taking, tender, unself-ish, winning, winsome 3. beloved, cherished, darling, dear, dearest, pet, precious, treasured 4. aromat-ic, balmy, clean, fragrant, fresh, new, perfumed, pure, redolent, sweet-smelling, wholesome 5. dul-cet, euphonic, euphonious, harmo-nious, mellow, melodious, musical, silver-toned, silvery, soft, sweet-sounding, tuneful 6. **sweet on** en-amoured of, gone on (*Sl.*), head over heels in love with, infatuated by, in love with, keen on, obsessed *or* bewitched by, taken with, wild *or* mad about (*Inf.*) ~n. 7. afters (*Brit. inf.*), dessert, pudding, sweet course 8. *Usually plural* bonbon, candy (*U.S.*), confectionery, sweetie, sweetmeats

sweeten 1. honey, sugar, sugar-coat 2. alleviate, appease, mollify, pacify, soften up, soothe, sugar the pill

sweetheart admirer, beau, belov-ed, boyfriend, darling, dear, flame (*Inf.*), follower (*Obsolete*), girl-friend, inamorata, inamorato, love, lover, steady (*Inf.*), suitor, swain (*Archaic*), sweetie (*Inf.*), truelove, valentine

swell *v.* 1. balloon, become bloated *or* distended, become larger, be inflated, belly, billow, bloat, bulge, dilate, distend, enlarge, expand, extend, fatten, grow, increase, protrude, puff up, rise, round out, tumefy, well up 2. add to, aggra-vate, augment, enhance, heighten, intensify, mount, surge ~n. 3. bil-low, rise, surge, undulation, wave 4. *Inf.* beau, blade (*Archaic*), cockscomb (*Inf.*), dandy, fashion plate, fop, nob (*Sl.*), toff (*Brit. sl.*) ~adj. 5. *Inf.* de luxe, exclusive, fashionable, grand, plush *or* plushy (*Inf.*), posh (*Inf.*), ritzy (*Sl.*), smart, stylish

swelling *n.* blister, bruise, bulge, bump, dilation, distension, en-largement, inflammation, lump,

protuberance, puffiness, tumes-cence

swerve *v.* bend, deflect, depart from, deviate, diverge, incline, sheer off, shift, skew, stray, swing, turn, turn aside, veer, wander, wind

swift abrupt, expeditious, express, fast, fleet, fleet-footed, flying, hur-ried, nimble, nippy (*Brit. inf.*), prompt, quick, rapid, ready, short, short-lived, spanking, speedy, sud-den, winged

swiftly as fast as one's legs can carry one, (at) full tilt, double-quick, fast, hotfoot, hurriedly, in less than no time, nippily (*Brit. inf.*), posthaste, promptly, rapidly, speedily, without losing time

swiftness alacrity, celerity, dis-patch, expedition, fleetness, promptness, quickness, rapidity, speed, speediness, velocity

swill *v.* 1. consume, drain, drink (down), gulp, guzzle, imbibe, pour down one's gullet, quaff, swallow, swig (*Inf.*), toss off 2. *Often with* out drench, flush, rinse, sluice, wash down, wash out ~n. 3. hog-wash, mash, mush, pigswill, scour-ings, slops, waste

swindle 1. *v.* bamboozle (*Inf.*), bilk (of), cheat, con (*Sl.*), deceive, de-fraud, diddle (*Inf.*), do (*Sl.*), dupe, fleece, hornswoggle (*Sl.*), over-charge, pull a fast one (on some-one) (*Inf.*), put one over on (some-one) (*Inf.*), rip (someone) off (*Sl.*), rook (*Sl.*), take (someone) for a ride (*Inf.*), take to the cleaners (*Inf.*), trick 2. *n.* con trick (*Inf.*), deceit, deception, double-dealing, fiddle (*Brit. inf.*), fraud, imposition, knavery, racket, rip-off (*Sl.*), ro-guery, sharp practice, swizz (*Brit. inf.*), swizzle (*Brit. inf.*), trickery

swindler charlatan, cheat, confi-dence man, con man (*Sl.*), fraud, impostor, knave (*Archaic*), moun-tebank, rascal, rogue, rook (*Sl.*), shark, sharper, trickster

swing *v.* 1. be pendent, be sus-pended, dangle, hang, move back and forth, suspend 2. fluctuate, os-cillate, rock, sway, vary, veer, vibrate, wave 3. *Usually with round* curve, pivot, rotate, swivel, turn, turn on one's heel, wheel ~*n*. 4. fluctuation, oscillation, stroke, sway, swaying, vibration 5. in full swing animated, at its height, live~ ly, on the go (*Inf.*), under way

swinging dynamic, fashionable, full of go *or* pep (*Inf.*), groovy (*Sl.*), hip (*Sl.*), in the swim (*Inf.*), lively, trendy (*Brit. inf.*), up-to-date, up to the minute, with it (*Inf.*)

swirl agitate, boil, churn, eddy, spin, surge, twirl, twist, whirl

switch v. 1. change, change course, deflect, deviate, divert, exchange, interchange, rearrange, replace by, shift, substitute, swap (*Inf.*), trade, turn aside ~*n*. 2. about-turn, alteration, change, change of di~ rection, exchange, reversal, shift, substitution, swap (*Inf.*) ~*v*. 3. lash, swish, twitch, wave, whip

swollen bloated, distended, dropsi~ cal, enlarged, inflamed, puffed up, puffy, tumescent, tumid

swoop 1. *v*. descend, dive, pounce, rush, stoop, sweep 2. *n*. descent, drop, lunge, plunge, pounce, rush, stoop, sweep

sword 1. blade, brand (*Archaic*), trusty steel 2. cross swords argue, come to blows, dispute, fight, spar, wrangle

syllabus course of study, curricu~ lum

symbol badge, emblem, figure, im~ age, logo, mark, representation, sign, token, type

symbolic, symbolical allegorical, emblematic, figurative, repre~ sentative, significant, token, typi~ cal

symbolize betoken, body forth, connote, denote, exemplify, mean, personify, represent, signify, stand for, typify

symmetrical balanced, in propor~ tion, proportional, regular, well-proportioned

symmetry agreement, balance, correspondence, evenness, form, harmony, order, proportion, regu~ larity

sympathetic 1. affectionate, car~ ing, commiserating, compassion~ ate, concerned, condoling, feeling, interested, kind, kindly, pitying, responsive, supportive, tender, understanding, warm, warm-hearted 2. *Often with* to agreeable, approving, encouraging, favour~ ably disposed, friendly, in sympa~ thy with, pro, well-disposed 3. agreeable, appreciative, compan~ ionable, compatible, congenial, friendly, like-minded, responsive, well-intentioned

sympathize 1. bleed for, commis~ erate, condole, empathize, feel for, feel one's heart go out to, grieve with, have compassion, offer con~ solation, pity, share another's sor~ row 2. agree, be in accord, be in sympathy, go along with, identify with, side with, understand

sympathizer fellow traveller, par~ tisan, supporter, well-wisher

sympathy 1. commiseration, com~ passion, condolence(s), empathy, pity, tenderness, thoughtfulness, understanding 2. affinity, agree~ ment, congeniality, correspond~ ence, fellow feeling, harmony, rapport, union, warmth

symptom expression, indication, mark, note, sign, syndrome, token, warning

synthesis 1. amalgamation, coa~ lescence, combination, integration, unification, welding 2. amalgam, blend, combination, composite, compound, fusion, union

synthetic artificial, ersatz, fake, man-made, manufactured, mock

system 1. arrangement, classifica~ tion, combination, coordination, organization, scheme, setup (*Sl.*), structure 2. fixed order, frame of reference, method, methodology, modus operandi, practice, pro~ cedure, routine, technique, theory, usage 3. definite plan, logical pro~ cess, method, methodicalness, or~ derliness, regularity, systematiza~ tion

systematic businesslike, efficient, methodical, orderly, organized, precise, standardized, systema~ tized, well-ordered

T

table *n.* 1. bench, board, counter, slab, stand 2. board, diet, fare, food, spread (*Inf.*), victuals 3. flat, flat~ land, plain, plateau, tableland 4. agenda, catalogue, chart, diagram, digest, graph, index, inventory, list, plan, record, register, roll, sched~ ule, synopsis, tabulation ~*v.* 5. en~ ter, move, propose, put forward, submit, suggest

tableau picture, representation, scene, spectacle

taboo 1. *adj.* anathema, banned, beyond the pale, disapproved of, forbidden, frowned on, not allowed, not permitted, outlawed, prohibit~ ed, proscribed, ruled out, unaccep~ table, unmentionable, unthinkable 2. *n.* anathema, ban, disapproval, interdict, prohibition, proscription, restriction

tabulate arrange, catalogue, cat~ egorize, chart, classify, codify, in~ dex, list, order, range, systematize, tabularize

tacit implicit, implied, inferred, si~ lent, taken for granted, unde~ clared, understood, unexpressed, unspoken, unstated, wordless

taciturn aloof, antisocial, close-lipped, cold, distant, dumb, mute, quiet, reserved, reticent, silent, tight-lipped, uncommunicative, unforthcoming, withdrawn

tack *n.* 1. drawing pin, nail, pin, staple, thumbtack (*U.S.*), tintack 2. approach, bearing, course, direc~ tion, heading, line, method, path, plan, procedure, tactic, way ~*v.* 3. affix, attach, fasten, fix, nail, pin, staple 4. baste, stitch 5. add, annex, append, attach, tag

tackle *n.* 1. accoutrements, appa~ ratus, equipment, gear, imple~ ments, outfit, paraphernalia, rig, rigging, tools, trappings 2. block, challenge, stop ~*v.* 3. apply oneself to, attempt, begin, come *or* get to grips with, deal with, embark upon, engage in, essay, get stuck into

(*Inf.*), have a go at (*Inf.*), set about, take on, try, turn one's hand to, undertake 4. block, bring down, challenge, clutch, confront, grab, grasp, halt, intercept, seize, stop, take hold of, throw

tact address, adroitness, consid~ eration, delicacy, diplomacy, dis~ cretion, finesse, judgment, percep~ tion, savoir-faire, sensitivity, skill, thoughtfulness, understanding

tactful careful, considerate, deli~ cate, diplomatic, discreet, judi~ cious, perceptive, polished, polite, politic, prudent, sensitive, subtle, thoughtful, understanding

tactic 1. approach, course, device, line, manoeuvre, means, method, move, ploy, policy, scheme, strata~ gem, tack, trick, way 2. *Plural* campaign, generalship, manoeu~ vres, plans, strategy

tactical adroit, artful, clever, cun~ ning, diplomatic, politic, shrewd, skilful, smart, strategic

tactician brain (*Inf.*), campaigner, coordinator, director, general, mastermind, planner, strategist

tactless blundering, boorish, care~ less, clumsy, discourteous, gauche, harsh, impolite, impolitic, impru~ dent, inconsiderate, indelicate, in~ discreet, inept, injudicious, insen~ sitive, maladroit, rough, rude, sharp, thoughtless, uncivil, undip~ lomatic, unfeeling, unkind, unsub~ tle

tail *n.* 1. appendage, conclusion, empennage, end, extremity, rear end, tailpiece, train 2. file, line, queue, tailback, train 3. *Of hair* braid, pigtail, plait, ponytail, tress 4. *Inf.* backside (*Inf.*), behind (*Inf.*), bottom, buttocks, croup, posterior, rear (*Inf.*), rear end, rump 5. **turn tail** cut and run, escape, flee, make off, retreat, run away, run for it (*Inf.*), run off, scarper (*Brit. sl.*), show a clean pair of heels, ske~ daddle (*Inf.*), take off (*Inf.*), take to

one's heels ~v. 6. *Inf.* dog the foot~
steps of, follow, keep an eye on,
shadow, stalk, track, trail

tail off *or* **away** decrease, die out,
drop, dwindle, fade, fall away, pe~
ter out, wane

tailor 1. *n.* clothier, costumier, cou~
turier, dressmaker, garment mak~
er, outfitter, seamstress 2. *v.* ac~
commodate, adapt, adjust, alter,
convert, cut, fashion, fit, modify,
mould, shape, style, suit

taint *v.* 1. adulterate, blight, con~
taminate, corrupt, dirty, foul, in~
fect, poison, pollute, soil, spoil 2.
besmirch, blacken, blemish, blot,
brand, damage, defile, disgrace,
dishonour, muddy, ruin, shame,
smear, stain, stigmatize, sully, tar~
nish, vitiate ~n. 3. black mark,
blemish, blot, blot on one's es~
cutcheon, defect, disgrace, dishon~
our, fault, flaw, shame, smear, spot,
stain, stigma 4. contagion, con~
tamination, infection, pollution

take *v.* 1. abduct, acquire, arrest,
capture, carry off, catch, clutch,
ensnare, entrap, gain possession
of, get, get hold of, grasp, grip,
have, help oneself to, lay hold of,
obtain, receive, secure, seize, win
2. abstract, appropriate, carry off,
filch, misappropriate, nick (*Brit.
sl.*), pinch (*Inf.*), pocket, purloin,
run off with, steal, swipe (*Sl.*), walk
off with 3. book, buy, engage, hire,
lease, pay for, pick, purchase, rent,
reserve, select 4. abide, bear,
brave, brook, endure, go through,
pocket, put up with (*Inf.*), stand,
stomach, submit to, suffer, swal~
low, thole (*Scot.*), tolerate, under~
go, weather, withstand 5. consume,
drink, eat, imbibe, ingest, inhale,
swallow 6. accept, adopt, assume,
enter upon, undertake 7. do, effect,
execute, have, make, perform 8.
assume, believe, consider, deem,
hold, interpret as, perceive, pre~
sume, receive, regard, see as, think
of as, understand 9. be efficacious,
do the trick (*Inf.*), have effect, op~
erate, succeed, work 10. bear,
bring, carry, cart, convey, ferry,
fetch, haul, tote (*Inf.*), transport 11.
accompany, bring, conduct, con~

voy, escort, guide, lead, usher 12.
attract, become popular, captivate,
charm, delight, enchant, fascinate,
please, win favour 13. call for, de~
mand, necessitate, need, require
14. deduct, eliminate, remove,
subtract 15. accept, accommodate,
contain, have room for, hold 16. *Sl.*
bilk, cheat, con (*Inf.*), deceive, de~
fraud, do (*Sl.*), dupe, fiddle (*Inf.*),
gull (*Archaic*), pull a fast one on
(*Inf.*), swindle ~n. 17. catch, gate,
haul, proceeds, profits, receipts,
return, revenue, takings, yield

take back 1. disavow, disclaim, re~
cant, renounce, retract, unsay,
withdraw 2. get back, recapture,
reclaim, reconquer, regain, repos~
sess, retake 3. accept back, ex~
change, give one a refund for

take down 1. make a note of, min~
ute, note, put on record, record, set
down, transcribe, write down 2.
depress, drop, haul down, let down,
lower, pull down, remove, take off
3. demolish, disassemble, disman~
tle, level, raze, take apart, take to
pieces, tear down 4. deflate, hum~
ble, humiliate, mortify, put down
(*Sl.*)

take in 1. absorb, assimilate, com~
prehend, digest, grasp, understand
2. comprise, contain, cover, em~
brace, encompass, include 3. ac~
commodate, admit, let in, receive
4. *Inf.* bilk, cheat, con (*Inf.*), de~
ceive, do (*Sl.*), dupe, fool, gull (*Ar~
chaic*), hoodwink, mislead, pull the
wool over (someone's) eyes (*Inf.*),
swindle, trick

takeoff 1. departure, launch, liftoff
2. *Inf.* caricature, imitation, lam~
poon, mocking, parody, satire,
send-up (*Brit. inf.*), spoof (*Inf.*),
travesty

take off 1. discard, divest oneself
of, doff, drop, peel off, remove,
strip off 2. become airborne, leave
the ground, lift off, take to the air
3. *Inf.* beat it (*Sl.*), decamp, depart,
disappear, go, hit the road (*Sl.*),
leave, set out, split (*Sl.*), strike out
4. *Inf.* caricature, hit off, imitate,
lampoon, mimic, mock, parody,

satirize, send up (*Brit. inf.*), spoof (*Inf.*), travesty

take on 1. employ, engage, enlist, enrol, hire, retain 2. acquire, assume, come to have 3. accept, address oneself to, agree to do, have a go at (*Inf.*), tackle, undertake 4. compete against, contend with, enter the lists against, face, fight, match oneself against, oppose, pit oneself against, vie with 5. *Inf.* break down, get excited, get upset (*Inf.*), give way, make a fuss

take over assume control of, become leader of, come to power, gain control of, succeed to, take command of

take to 1. flee to, head for, make for, man, run for 2. become friendly, be pleased by, be taken with, conceive an affection for, get on with, like, warm to 3. have recourse to, make a habit of, resort to

take up 1. adopt, assume, become involved in, engage in, start 2. begin again, carry on, continue, follow on, go on, pick up, proceed, recommence, restart, resume 3. absorb, consume, cover, extend over, fill, occupy, use up

taking *adj.* 1. attractive, beguiling, captivating, charming, compelling, delightful, enchanting, engaging, fascinating, fetching (*Inf.*), intriguing, pleasing, prepossessing, winning 2. *Inf.* catching, contagious, infectious ~*n.* 3. *Plural* earnings, gain, gate, income, pickings, proceeds, profits, receipts, returns, revenue, take, yield

tale 1. account, anecdote, *conte*, fable, fiction, legend, narration, narrative, novel, relation, report, romance, saga, short story, story, yarn (*Inf.*) 2. cock-and-bull story (*Inf.*), fabrication, falsehood, fib, lie, rigmarole, rumour, spiel (*Inf.*), tall story (*Inf.*), untruth

talent ability, aptitude, bent, capacity, endowment, faculty, flair, forte, genius, gift, knack, parts, power

talented able, artistic, brilliant, gifted, well-endowed

talk *v.* 1. articulate, chat, chatter, communicate, converse, crack (*Scot.*), express oneself, gab (*Inf.*), give voice to, gossip, natter, prate, prattle, rap (*Sl.*), say, speak, utter, verbalize, witter (*Inf.*) 2. chew the rag (*Inf.*), confabulate, confer, have a confab (*Inf.*), hold discussions, negotiate, palaver, parley 3. blab, crack, give the game away, grass (*Sl.*), inform, reveal information, sing (*Inf.*), spill the beans (*Inf.*), squeak (*Inf.*), squeal (*Sl.*) ~*n.* 4. address, discourse, disquisition, dissertation, harangue, lecture, oration, sermon, speech 5. blather, blether, chat, chatter, chitchat, conversation, crack (*Scot.*), gab (*Inf.*), gossip, hearsay, jaw (*Sl.*), natter, rap (*Sl.*), rumour, tittle-tattle 6. colloquy, conclave, confab (*Inf.*), confabulation, conference, consultation, dialogue, discussion, meeting, negotiation, palaver, parley, seminar, symposium 7. argot, dialect, jargon, language, lingo (*Inf.*), patois, slang, speech, words

talkative big-mouthed (*Sl.*), chatty, effusive, gabby (*Inf.*), garrulous, gossipy, long-winded, loquacious, mouthy, prolix, verbose, voluble, wordy

talker conversationalist, lecturer, orator, speaker, speechmaker

talking-to criticism, dressing-down (*Inf.*), lecture, rap on the knuckles (*Inf.*), rebuke, reprimand, reproach, reproof, row, scolding, slating (*Inf.*), telling-off (*Inf.*), ticking-off (*Inf.*), wigging (*Brit. sl.*)

tall 1. big, elevated, giant, high, lanky, lofty, soaring, towering 2. *Inf.* absurd, embellished, exaggerated, far-fetched, implausible, incredible, overblown, preposterous, steep (*Brit. inf.*), unbelievable 3. *Inf.* demanding, difficult, exorbitant, hard, unreasonable, well-nigh impossible

tally *v.* 1. accord, agree, coincide, concur, conform, correspond, fit, harmonize, jibe (*Inf.*), match, parallel, square, suit 2. compute, count up, keep score, mark, reckon, record, register, total ~*n.* 3. count, mark, reckoning, record, running total, score, total 4. counterfoil, counterpart, duplicate, match, mate, stub

tame *adj.* 1. amenable, broken, cultivated, disciplined, docile, domesticated, gentle, obedient, tractable 2. fearless, unafraid, used to human contact 3. compliant, docile, manageable, meek, obedient, spiritless, subdued, submissive, unresisting 4. bland, boring, dull, flat, humdrum, insipid, lifeless, prosaic, tedious, unexciting, uninspiring, uninteresting, vapid, wearisome ~*v.* 5. break in, domesticate, gentle, house-train, make tame, pacify, train 6. break the spirit of, bridle, bring to heel, conquer, curb, discipline, enslave, humble, master, repress, subdue, subjugate, suppress 7. mitigate, mute, soften, soft-pedal (*Inf.*), subdue, temper, tone down, water down

tamper 1. alter, damage, fiddle (*Inf.*), fool about (*Inf.*), interfere, intrude, meddle, mess about, monkey around, muck about (*Brit. sl.*), poke one's nose into (*Inf.*), tinker 2. bribe, corrupt, fix (*Inf.*), get at, influence, manipulate, rig

tangible actual, concrete, corporeal, definite, discernible, evident, manifest, material, objective, palpable, perceptible, physical, positive, real, solid, substantial, tactile, touchable

tangle *n.* 1. coil, confusion, entanglement, jam, jungle, knot, mass, mat, mesh, snarl, twist, web 2. complication, entanglement, fix (*Inf.*), imbroglio, labyrinth, maze, mess, mix-up ~*v.* 3. coil, confuse, entangle, interlace, interlock, intertwist, interweave, jam, kink, knot, mat, mesh, snarl, twist 4. *Often with* with come into conflict, come up against, contend, contest, cross swords, dispute, lock horns 5. catch, drag into, embroil, enmesh, ensnare, entangle, entrap, implicate, involve

tangled 1. entangled, jumbled, knotted, knotty, matted, messy, scrambled, snarled, tousled, twist-

ed 2. complex, complicated, confused, convoluted, involved, knotty, messy, mixed-up

tantalize baffle, balk, disappoint, entice, frustrate, keep (someone) hanging on, lead on, make (someone's) mouth water, provoke, taunt, tease, thwart, titillate, torment, torture

tantamount as good as, commensurate, equal, equivalent, synonymous, the same as

tantrum fit, flare-up, hysterics, ill humour, outburst, paddy (*Brit. inf.*), storm, temper, wax (*Inf.*)

tap[1] 1. *v.* beat, drum, knock, pat, rap, strike, touch 2. *n.* beat, knock, light blow, pat, rap, touch

tap[2] *n.* 1. faucet (*U.S.*), spigot, spout, stopcock, valve 2. bung, plug, spile, stopper 3. bug (*Inf.*), listening device 4. *Inf.* at hand, available, in reserve, on hand, ready b. on draught ~*v.* 5. bleed, broach, drain, draw off, open, pierce, siphon off, unplug 6. draw on, exploit, make use of, milk, mine, put to use, turn to account, use, utilize 7. bug (*Inf.*), eavesdrop on, listen in on

tape *n.* 1. band, ribbon, strip ~*v.* 2. bind, seal, secure, stick, wrap 3. record, tape-record, video

taper 1. come to a point, narrow, thin 2. *With off* decrease, die away, die out, dwindle, fade, lessen, reduce, subside, thin out, wane, weaken, wind down

target 1. aim, ambition, bull's-eye, end, goal, intention, mark, object, objective 2. butt, quarry, scapegoat, victim

tariff 1. assessment, duty, excise, impost, levy, rate, tax, toll 2. bill of fare, charges, menu, price list, schedule

tarnish 1. *v.* befoul, blacken, blemish, blot, darken, dim, discolour, drag through the mud, dull, lose lustre *or* shine, rust, soil, spot, stain, sully, taint 2. *n.* blackening, black mark, blemish, blot, discoloration, rust, spot, stain, taint

tarry abide, bide, dally, dawdle, delay, dwell, hang around (*Inf.*), linger, lodge, loiter, lose time, pause, remain, rest, sojourn, stay, take one's time, wait

tart¹ 1. pastry, pie, tartlet 2. call girl, fallen woman, *fille de joie*, floozy (*Sl.*), harlot, hooker (*U.S. sl.*), loose woman, prostitute, slut, streetwalker, strumpet, trollop, whore, woman of easy virtue

tart² 1. acid, acidulous, astringent, bitter, piquant, pungent, sharp, sour, tangy, vinegary 2. acrimonious, astringent, barbed, biting, caustic, crusty, cutting, harsh, nasty, scathing, sharp, short, snappish, testy, trenchant, wounding

task n. 1. assignment, business, charge, chore, duty, employment, enterprise, exercise, job, labour, mission, occupation, toil, undertaking, work 2. **take to task** blame, censure, criticize, lecture, reprimand, reproach, reprove, scold, tell off (*Inf.*), upbraid ~v. 3. assign to, charge, entrust 4. burden, exhaust, load, lumber (*Brit. inf.*), oppress, overload, push, saddle, strain, tax, test, weary

taste n. 1. flavour, relish, savour, smack, tang 2. bit, bite, dash, drop, morsel, mouthful, nip, sample, sip, soupçon, spoonful, swallow, titbit, touch 3. appetite, bent, desire, fancy, fondness, inclination, leaning, liking, palate, partiality, penchant, predilection, preference, relish 4. appreciation, cultivation, culture, discernment, discrimination, elegance, grace, judgment, perception, polish, refinement, style 5. correctness, decorum, delicacy, discretion, nicety, politeness, propriety, restraint, tact, tactfulness ~v. 6. differentiate, discern, distinguish, perceive 7. assay, nibble, relish, sample, savour, sip, test, try 8. have a flavour of, savour of, smack 9. come up against, encounter, experience, feel, have knowledge of, know, meet with, partake of, undergo

tasteful aesthetically pleasing, artistic, beautiful, charming, cultivated, cultured, delicate, discriminating, elegant, exquisite, fastidious, graceful, handsome, harmonious, in good taste, polished, refined, restrained, smart, stylish

tasteless 1. bland, boring, dull, flat, flavourless, insipid, mild, stale, tame, thin, uninspired, uninteresting, vapid, watered-down, weak 2. cheap, coarse, crass, crude, flashy, garish, gaudy, graceless, gross, impolite, improper, indecorous, indelicate, indiscreet, inelegant, low, rude, tactless, tawdry, uncouth, unseemly, vulgar

tasty appetizing, delectable, delicious, flavourful, flavoursome, full-flavoured, good-tasting, luscious, palatable, sapid, savoury, scrumptious (*Inf.*), toothsome, yummy (*Sl.*)

taunt 1. v. deride, flout, gibe, guy (*Inf.*), insult, jeer, mock, provoke, reproach, revile, ridicule, sneer, tease, torment, twit, upbraid 2. n. barb, censure, cut, derision, dig, gibe, insult, jeer, provocation, reproach, ridicule, sarcasm, teasing

taut 1. flexed, rigid, strained, stressed, stretched, tense, tight 2. *Nautical* in good order, neat, orderly, shipshape, spruce, tidy, tight, trim, well-ordered, well-regulated

tavern alehouse (*Archaic*), bar, boozer (*Brit. inf.*), hostelry, inn, pub (*Brit. inf.*), public house

tawdry brummagem, cheap, cheap-jack (*Inf.*), flashy, gaudy, gimcrack, glittering, meretricious, plastic (*Sl.*), raffish, showy, tacky, tasteless, tatty, tinsel, tinselly, vulgar

tax n. 1. assessment, charge, contribution, customs, duty, excise, imposition, impost, levy, rate, tariff, tithe, toll, tribute 2. burden, demand, drain, load, pressure, strain, weight ~v. 3. assess, charge, demand, exact, extract, impose, levy a tax on, rate, tithe 4. burden, drain, enervate, exhaust, load, make heavy demands on, overburden, push, put pressure on, sap, strain, stretch, task, try, weaken, wear out, weary, weigh heavily on 5. accuse, arraign, blame, charge, impeach, impugn, incriminate, lay at one's door

taxing burdensome, demanding, enervating, exacting, heavy, onerous, punishing, sapping, stressful, tiring, tough, trying, wearing, wearisome

teach advise, coach, demonstrate, direct, discipline, drill, edify, educate, enlighten, give lessons in, guide, impart, implant, inculcate, inform, instil, instruct, school, show, train, tutor

teacher coach, dominie (*Scot.*), don, educator, guide, guru, instructor, lecturer, master, mentor, mistress, pedagogue, professor, schoolmaster, schoolmistress, schoolteacher, trainer, tutor

team *n.* 1. band, body, bunch, company, crew, gang, group, line-up, set, side, squad, troupe 2. pair, span, yoke ~*v.* 3. *Often with up* band together, cooperate, couple, get together, join, link, unite, work together, yoke

tear *v.* 1. claw, divide, lacerate, mangle, mutilate, pull apart, rend, rip, rive, run, rupture, scratch, sever, shred, split, sunder 2. belt (*Sl.*), bolt, career, charge, dart, dash, fly, gallop, hurry, race, run, rush, shoot, speed, sprint, zoom 3. grab, pluck, pull, rip, seize, snatch, wrench, wrest, yank ~*n.* 4. hole, laceration, mutilation, rent, rip, run, rupture, scratch, split

tearful 1. blubbering, crying, in tears, lachrymose, sobbing, weeping, weepy (*Inf.*), whimpering 2. distressing, dolorous, lamentable, mournful, pathetic, pitiable, pitiful, poignant, sad, sorrowful, upsetting, woeful

tears 1. blubbering, crying, distress, lamentation, mourning, pain, regret, sadness, sobbing, sorrow, wailing, weeping, whimpering, woe 2. in tears blubbering, crying, distressed, sobbing, visibly moved, weeping, whimpering

tease aggravate (*Inf.*), annoy, badger, bait, bedevil, chaff, gibe, goad, guy (*Inf.*), lead on, mock, needle, pester, plague (*Inf.*), provoke, rag, rib (*Inf.*), ridicule, tan-

talize, taunt, torment, twit, vex, worry

technique 1. approach, course, fashion, manner, means, method, mode, modus operandi, procedure, style, system, way 2. address, adroitness, art, artistry, craft, craftsmanship, delivery, execution, facility, knack, know-how (*Inf.*), performance, proficiency, skill, touch

tedious annoying, banal, boring, deadly dull, drab, dreary, dull, fatiguing, humdrum, irksome, laborious, lifeless, long-drawn-out, monotonous, prosaic, prosy, soporific, tiring, unexciting, uninteresting, vapid, wearisome

tedium banality, boredom, deadness, drabness, dreariness, dullness, ennui, lifelessness, monotony, routine, sameness, tediousness, the doldrums

teem abound, be abundant, bear, be crawling with, be full of, be prolific, brim, bristle, burst at the seams, overflow, produce, pullulate, swarm

teeming abundant, alive, brimful, brimming, bristling, bursting, chock-a-block, chock-full, crawling, fruitful, full, numerous, overflowing, packed, replete, swarming, thick

teenager adolescent, boy, girl, juvenile, minor, youth

teetotaller abstainer, nondrinker, Rechabite

telegram cable, radiogram, telegraph, telex, wire (*Inf.*)

telegraph *n.* 1. tape machine (*Stock Exchange*), teleprinter, telex 2. cable, radiogram, telegram, telex, wire (*Inf.*) ~*v.* 3. cable, send, telex, transmit, wire (*Inf.*)

telepathy mind-reading, sixth sense, thought transference

telephone 1. *n.* blower (*Inf.*), handset, line, phone 2. *v.* buzz (*Inf.*), call, call up, dial, get on the blower (*Inf.*), give (someone) a buzz (*Inf.*), give (someone) a call, give (someone) a ring (*Brit.*), give someone a tinkle (*Brit. inf.*), phone, put a call through to, ring (*Brit.*)

telescope *n.* 1. glass, spyglass ~*v.* 2. concertina, crush, squash 3. abbreviate, abridge, compress, condense, consolidate, contract, curtail, cut, shorten, shrink, trim, truncate

television gogglebox (*Brit. sl.*), idiot box (*Sl.*), receiver, small screen (*Inf.*), telly (*Brit. inf.*), the box (*Brit. inf.*), the tube (*Sl.*), TV, TV set

tell *v.* 1. acquaint, announce, apprise, communicate, confess, disclose, divulge, express, impart, inform, let know, make known, mention, notify, proclaim, reveal, say, speak, state, utter 2. authorize, bid, call upon, command, direct, enjoin, instruct, order, require, summon 3. chronicle, depict, describe, give an account of, narrate, portray, recount, rehearse, relate, report 4. comprehend, discern, discover, make out, see, understand 5. differentiate, discern, discriminate, distinguish, identify 6. carry weight, count, have *or* take effect, have force, make its presence felt, register, take its toll, weigh 7. calculate, compute, count, enumerate, number, reckon, tally

telling considerable, decisive, effective, effectual, forceful, forcible, impressive, influential, marked, potent, powerful, significant, solid, striking, trenchant, weighty

temper *n.* 1. attitude, character, constitution, disposition, frame of mind, humour, mind, mood, nature, temperament, tenor, vein 2. bad mood, fit of pique, fury, paddy (*Brit. inf.*), passion, rage, tantrum, wax (*Inf.*) 3. anger, annoyance, heat, hot-headedness, ill humour, irascibility, irritability, irritation, passion, peevishness, petulance, resentment, surliness 4. calm, calmness, composure, cool (*Sl.*), coolness, equanimity, good humour, moderation, self-control, tranquillity ~*v.* 5. abate, admix, allay, assuage, calm, lessen, mitigate, moderate, mollify, palliate,

restrain, soften, soft-pedal (*Inf.*), soothe, tone down 6. anneal, harden, strengthen, toughen

temperament 1. bent, cast of mind, character, complexion, constitution, disposition, frame of mind, humour, make-up, mettle, nature, outlook, personality, quality, soul, spirit, stamp, temper, tendencies, tendency 2. anger, excitability, explosiveness, hotheadedness, impatience, mercurialness, moodiness, moods, petulance, volatility

temperamental 1. capricious, easily upset, emotional, erratic, excitable, explosive, fiery, highly strung, hot-headed, hypersensitive, impatient, irritable, mercurial, moody, neurotic, passionate, petulant, sensitive, touchy, volatile 2. congenital, constitutional, inborn, ingrained, inherent, innate, natural 3. erratic, inconsistent, undependable, unpredictable, unreliable

temperance 1. continence, discretion, forbearance, moderation, restraint, self-control, self-discipline, self-restraint 2. abstemiousness, abstinence, prohibition, sobriety, teetotalism

temperate 1. agreeable, balmy, calm, clement, cool, fair, gentle, mild, moderate, pleasant, soft 2. calm, composed, dispassionate, equable, even-tempered, mild, moderate, reasonable, self-controlled, self-restrained, sensible, stable 3. abstemious, abstinent, continent, moderate, sober

tempest 1. cyclone, gale, hurricane, squall, storm, tornado, typhoon 2. commotion, disturbance, ferment, furore, storm, tumult, upheaval, uproar

tempestuous 1. agitated, blustery, boisterous, breezy, gusty, raging, squally, stormy, turbulent, windy 2. agitated, boisterous, emotional, excited, feverish, furious, heated, hysterical, impassioned, intense, passionate, stormy, turbulent, uncontrolled, violent, wild

temple church, holy place, place of worship, sanctuary, shrine

temporarily briefly, fleetingly, for a little while, for a moment, for a short time, for a short while, for the moment, for the time being, momentarily, pro tem

temporary brief, ephemeral, evanescent, fleeting, fugacious, fugitive, here today and gone tomorrow, impermanent, interim, momentary, passing, pro tem, *pro tempore*, provisional, short-lived, transient, transitory

tempt 1. allure, appeal to, attract, coax, decoy, draw, entice, inveigle, invite, lead on, lure, make one's mouth water, seduce, tantalize, whet the appetite of, woo 2. bait, dare, fly in the face of, provoke, risk, test, try

temptation allurement, appeal, attraction, attractiveness, bait, blandishments, coaxing, come-on (*Inf.*), decoy, draw, enticement, inducement, invitation, lure, pull, seduction, snare, tantalization

tempting alluring, appetizing, attractive, enticing, inviting, mouth-watering, seductive, tantalizing

tenable arguable, believable, defendable, defensible, justifiable, maintainable, plausible, rational, reasonable, sound, viable

tenacious 1. clinging, fast, firm, forceful, iron, strong, tight, unshakable 2. retentive, unforgetful 3. adamant, determined, dogged, firm, inflexible, intransigent, obdurate, obstinate, persistent, pertinacious, resolute, staunch, steadfast, strong-willed, stubborn, sure, unswerving, unyielding 4. coherent, cohesive, solid, strong, tough 5. adhesive, clinging, gluey, glutinous, mucilaginous, sticky

tenacity 1. fastness, firmness, force, forcefulness, power, strength 2. firm grasp, retention, retentiveness 3. application, determination, diligence, doggedness, firmness, inflexibility, intransigence, obduracy, obstinacy, perseverance, persistence, pertinacity, resoluteness, resolution, resolve, staunchness, steadfastness, strength of purpose, strength of

will, stubbornness 4. coherence, cohesiveness, solidity, solidness, strength, toughness 5. adhesiveness, clingingness, stickiness

tenancy 1. holding, lease, occupancy, occupation, possession, renting, residence 2. incumbency, period of office, tenure, time in office

tenant holder, inhabitant, leaseholder, lessee, occupant, occupier, renter, resident

tend[1] 1. be apt, be biased, be disposed, be inclined, be liable, be likely, gravitate, have a leaning, have an inclination, have a tendency, incline, lean, trend 2. aim, bear, be conducive, conduce, contribute, go, head, influence, lead, make for, move, point

tend[2] attend, care for, cater to, control, cultivate, feed, guard, handle, keep, keep an eye on, look after, maintain, manage, minister to, nurse, nurture, protect, see to, serve, take care of, wait on, watch, watch over

tendency 1. bent, disposition, inclination, leaning, liability, partiality, penchant, predilection, predisposition, proclivity, proneness, propensity, readiness, susceptibility 2. bearing, bias, course, direction, drift, drive, heading, movement, purport, tenor, trend, turning

tender[1] 1. breakable, delicate, feeble, fragile, frail, soft, weak 2. callow, green, immature, impressionable, inexperienced, new, raw, sensitive, unripe, vulnerable, wet behind the ears (*Inf.*), young, youthful 3. affectionate, amorous, benevolent, caring, compassionate, considerate, fond, gentle, humane, kind, loving, merciful, pitiful, sentimental, softhearted, sympathetic, tenderhearted, warm, warm-hearted 4. emotional, evocative, moving, poignant, romantic, touching 5. complicated, dangerous, difficult, risky, sensitive, ticklish, touchy, tricky 6. aching, acute, bruised, inflamed, irritated, painful, raw, sensitive, smarting, sore

tender² v. 1. extend, give, hand in, offer, present, proffer, propose, put forward, submit, suggest, volunteer ~n. 2. bid, estimate, offer, proffer, proposal, submission, suggestion 3. currency, medium, money, payment, specie

tenderness 1. delicateness, feebleness, fragility, frailness, sensitiveness, sensitivity, softness, vulnerability, weakness 2. callowness, greenness, immaturity, impressionableness, inexperience, newness, rawness, sensitivity, vulnerability, youth, youthfulness 3. affection, amorousness, attachment, benevolence, care, compassion, consideration, devotion, fondness, gentleness, humaneness, humanity, kindness, liking, love, mercy, pity, sentimentality, softheartedness, sympathy, tenderheartedness, warm-heartedness, warmth 4. ache, aching, bruising, inflammation, irritation, pain, painfulness, rawness, sensitiveness, sensitivity, smart, soreness

tense adj. 1. rigid, strained, stretched, taut, tight 2. anxious, apprehensive, edgy, fidgety, jittery (Inf.), jumpy, keyed up, nervous, on edge, overwrought, restless, strained, strung up (Inf.), under pressure, uptight (Sl.), wound up (Inf.), wrought up 3. exciting, moving, nerve-racking, stressful, worrying ~v. 4. brace, flex, strain, stretch, tauten, tighten

tension 1. pressure, rigidity, stiffness, straining, stress, stretching, tautness, tightness 2. anxiety, apprehension, edginess, hostility, ill feeling, nervousness, pressure, restlessness, strain, stress, suspense, the jitters (Inf.), unease

tentative 1. conjectural, experimental, indefinite, provisional, speculative, unconfirmed, unsettled 2. backward, cautious, diffident, doubtful, faltering, hesitant, timid, uncertain, undecided, unsure

tepid 1. lukewarm, slightly warm, warmish 2. apathetic, cool, half-hearted, indifferent, lukewarm, unenthusiastic

term n. 1. appellation, denomination, designation, expression, locution, name, phrase, title, word 2. duration, interval, period, season, space, span, spell, time, while 3. course, session 4. bound, boundary, close, conclusion, confine, culmination, end, finish, fruition, limit, terminus ~v. 5. call, denominate, designate, dub, entitle, label, name, style

terminal adj. 1. bounding, concluding, extreme, final, last, limiting, ultimate, utmost 2. deadly, fatal, incurable, killing, lethal, mortal ~n. 3. boundary, end, extremity, limit, termination, terminus 4. depot, end of the line, station, terminus

terminate abort, bring or come to an end, cease, close, complete, conclude, cut off, discontinue, end, expire, finish, issue, lapse, put an end to, result, run out, stop, wind up

termination abortion, cessation, close, completion, conclusion, consequence, cut-off point, discontinuation, effect, end, ending, expiry, finale, finis, finish, issue, result, wind-up (Inf.)

terminology argot, cant, jargon, language, lingo (Inf.), nomenclature, patois, phraseology, terms, vocabulary

terminus 1. boundary, close, end, extremity, final point, goal, limit, target, termination 2. depot, end of the line, garage, last stop, station

terms 1. language, manner of speaking, phraseology, terminology 2. conditions, particulars, premises (Law), provisions, provisos, qualifications, specifications, stipulations 3. charges, fee, payment, price, rates 4. footing, position, relations, relationship, standing, status 5. **come to terms** be reconciled, come to an agreement, come to an understanding, conclude agreement, learn to live with, reach acceptance, reach agreement

terrible 1. bad, dangerous, desperate, extreme, serious, severe 2. Inf.

abhorrent, awful, bad, beastly (*Inf.*), dire, dreadful, duff (*Brit. sl.*), foul, frightful, hateful, hideous, loathsome, obnoxious, odious, offensive, poor, repulsive, revolting, rotten (*Inf.*), unpleasant, vile 3. appalling, awful, dread, dreaded, dreadful, fearful, frightful, gruesome, harrowing, horrendous, horrible, horrid, horrifying, monstrous, shocking

terribly awfully (*Inf.*), decidedly, desperately, exceedingly, extremely, gravely, greatly, much, seriously, thoroughly, very

terrific 1. awesome, awful, dreadful, enormous, excessive, extreme, fearful, fierce, gigantic, great, harsh, horrific, huge, intense, monstrous, severe, terrible, tremendous 2. *Inf.* ace (*Inf.*), amazing, breathtaking, excellent, fabulous (*Inf.*), fantastic (*Inf.*), fine, great (*Inf.*), magnificent, marvellous, outstanding, sensational (*Inf.*), smashing (*Inf.*), stupendous, super (*Inf.*), superb, very good, wonderful

terrified alarmed, appalled, awed, dismayed, frightened, frightened out of one's wits, horrified, horror-struck, intimidated, panic-stricken, petrified, scared, scared stiff, scared to death, shocked, terror-stricken

terrify alarm, appal, awe, dismay, fill with terror, frighten, frighten out of one's wits, horrify, intimidate, make one's blood run cold, make one's flesh creep, make one's hair stand on end, petrify, put the fear of God into, scare, scare to death, shock, terrorize

territory area, bailiwick, country, district, domain, land, province, region, sector, state, terrain, tract, zone

terror 1. alarm, anxiety, awe, consternation, dismay, dread, fear, fear and trembling, fright, horror, intimidation, panic, shock 2. bogeyman, bugbear, devil, fiend, monster, scourge

terrorize 1. browbeat, bully, coerce, intimidate, menace, oppress, strong-arm (*Inf.*), threaten 2.

alarm, appal, awe, dismay, fill with terror, frighten, frighten out of one's wits, horrify, inspire panic in, intimidate, make one's blood run cold, make one's flesh creep, make one's hair stand on end, petrify, put the fear of God into, scare, scare to death, shock, strike terror into, terrify

terse 1. aphoristic, brief, clipped, compact, concise, condensed, crisp, elliptical, epigrammatic, gnomic, incisive, laconic, neat, pithy, sententious, short, succinct, summary, to the point 2. abrupt, brusque, curt, short, snappy

test 1. *v.* analyse, assay, assess, check, examine, experiment, investigate, prove, put to the proof, put to the test, try, try out, verify 2. *n.* analysis, assessment, attempt, catechism, check, evaluation, examination, investigation, ordeal, probation, proof, trial

testament 1. last wishes, will 2. attestation, demonstration, earnest, evidence, exemplification, proof, testimony, tribute, witness

testify affirm, assert, attest, bear witness, certify, corroborate, declare, depone (*Scots Law*), depose (*Law*), evince, give testimony, show, state, swear, vouch, witness

testimonial certificate, character, commendation, credential, endorsement, recommendation, reference, tribute

testimony 1. affidavit, affirmation, attestation, avowal, confirmation, corroboration, declaration, deposition, evidence, information, profession, statement, submission, witness 2. corroboration, demonstration, evidence, indication, manifestation, proof, support, verification

text 1. body, contents, main body, matter 2. wording, words 3. *Bible* paragraph, passage, sentence, verse 4. argument, matter, motif, subject, theme, topic 5. reader, reference book, source, textbook

texture character, composition, consistency, constitution, fabric, feel, grain, make, quality, structure, surface, tissue, weave

thank express gratitude, say thank you, show gratitude, show one's appreciation

thankful appreciative, beholden, grateful, indebted, obliged, pleased, relieved

thankless 1. fruitless, unappreciated, unprofitable, unrequited, unrewarding, useless 2. inconsiderate, unappreciative, ungracious, ungrateful, unmindful, unthankful

thanks 1. acknowledgment, appreciation, credit, gratefulness, gratitude, recognition, thanksgiving 2. **thanks to** as a result of, because of, by reason of, due to, owing to, through

thaw defrost, dissolve, liquefy, melt, soften, unfreeze, warm

theatrical 1. dramatic, dramaturgic, melodramatic, scenic, Thespian 2. affected, artificial, ceremonious, dramatic, exaggerated, hammy (*Inf.*), histrionic, mannered, ostentatious, overdone, pompous, showy, stagy, stilted, unreal

theft embezzlement, fraud, larceny, pilfering, purloining, rip-off (*Sl.*), robbery, stealing, swindling, thievery, thieving

theme 1. argument, burden, idea, keynote, matter, subject, subject matter, text, thesis, topic 2. leitmotiv, motif, recurrent image, unifying idea 3. composition, dissertation, essay, exercise, paper

theological divine, doctrinal, ecclesiastical, religious

theorem deduction, dictum, formula, hypothesis, principle, proposition, rule, statement

theoretical abstract, academic, conjectural, hypothetical, ideal, impractical, pure, speculative

theorize conjecture, formulate, guess, hypothesize, project, propound, speculate, suppose

theory 1. assumption, conjecture, guess, hypothesis, presumption, speculation, supposition, surmise, thesis 2. philosophy, plan, proposal, scheme, system

therapeutic ameliorative, analep-

tic, beneficial, corrective, curative, good, healing, remedial, restorative, salubrious, salutary, sanative

therapy cure, healing, remedial treatment, remedy, treatment

therefore accordingly, as a result, consequently, ergo, for that reason, hence, so, then, thence, thus, whence

thesis 1. composition, disquisition, dissertation, essay, monograph, paper, treatise 2. contention, hypothesis, idea, line of argument, opinion, proposal, proposition, theory, view 3. area, subject, theme, topic 4. assumption, postulate, premiss, proposition, statement, supposition, surmise

thick *adj.* 1. broad, bulky, deep, fat, solid, substantial, wide 2. close, clotted, coagulated, compact, concentrated, condensed, crowded, deep, dense, heavy, impenetrable, opaque 3. abundant, brimming, bristling, bursting, chock-a-block, chock-full, covered, crawling, frequent, full, numerous, packed, replete, swarming, teeming 4. blockheaded, brainless, dense, dimwitted (*Inf.*), dopey (*Sl.*), dull, insensitive, moronic, obtuse, slow, slow-witted, stupid, thickheaded 5. dense, heavy, impenetrable, soupy 6. distorted, guttural, hoarse, husky, inarticulate, indistinct, throaty 7. broad, decided, distinct, marked, pronounced, rich, strong 8. *Inf.* chummy (*Inf.*), close, confidential, devoted, familiar, friendly, hand in glove, inseparable, intimate, matey (*Brit. inf.*), on good terms, pally (*Inf.*), well in (*Inf.*) 9. **a bit thick** excessive, over the score (*Inf.*), too much, unfair, unjust, unreasonable ~*n.* 10. centre, heart, middle, midst

thicken cake, clot, coagulate, condense, congeal, deepen, gel, inspissate (*Archaic*), jell, set

thickset 1. beefy (*Inf.*), brawny, bulky, burly, heavy, muscular, powerfully built, stocky, strong, stubby, sturdy, well-built 2. closely packed, dense, densely planted, solid, thick

thick-skinned callous, case-hardened, hard-boiled (*Inf.*), hardened, impervious, insensitive, stolid, tough, unfeeling, unsusceptible

thief bandit, burglar, cheat, cracksman (*Sl.*), crook (*Inf.*), embezzler, housebreaker, larcenist, mugger (*Inf.*), pickpocket, pilferer, plunderer, purloiner, robber, shoplifter, stealer, swindler

thieve cheat, embezzle, filch, half-inch (*Inf.*), knock off (*Sl.*), lift (*Inf.*), misappropriate, nick (*Brit. sl.*), peculate, pilfer, pinch (*Inf.*), plunder, poach, purloin, rip off (*Sl.*), rob, run off with, snitch (*Sl.*), steal, swipe (*Sl.*)

thin *adj.* 1. attenuate, attenuated, fine, narrow, threadlike 2. delicate, diaphanous, filmy, fine, flimsy, gossamer, seethrough, sheer, translucent, transparent, unsubstantial 3. bony, emaciated, lank, lanky, lean, light, meagre, scraggy, scrawny, skeletal, skinny, slender, slight, slim, spare, spindly, thin as a rake, undernourished, underweight 4. deficient, meagre, scanty, scarce, scattered, skimpy, sparse, wispy 5. dilute, diluted, rarefied, runny, watery, weak, wishy-washy (*Inf.*) 6. feeble, flimsy, inadequate, insufficient, lame, poor, scant, scanty, shallow, slight, superficial, unconvincing, unsubstantial, weak ~*v.* 7. attenuate, cut back, dilute, diminish, emaciate, prune, rarefy, reduce, refine, trim, water down, weaken, weed out

thing 1. affair, article, being, body, circumstance, concept, entity, fact, matter, object, part, portion, something, substance 2. act, deed, event, eventuality, feat, happening, incident, occurrence, phenomenon, proceeding 3. apparatus, contrivance, device, gadget, implement, instrument, machine, means, mechanism, tool 4. aspect, detail, facet, factor, feature, item, particular, point, statement, thought 5. *Plural* baggage, belongings, bits and pieces, clobber (*Brit. sl.*), clothes, effects, equipment, gear (*Inf.*), goods, impedimenta, luggage, odds and ends, paraphernalia, possessions, stuff 6. *Inf.* attitude, bee in one's bonnet, fetish, fixation, hang-up (*Inf.*), *idée fixe*, mania, obsession, phobia, preoccupation, quirk

think *v.* 1. believe, conceive, conclude, consider, deem, determine, esteem, estimate, hold, imagine, judge, reckon, regard, suppose, surmise 2. brood, cerebrate, chew over (*Inf.*), cogitate, consider, contemplate, deliberate, have in mind, meditate, mull over, muse, ponder, reason, reflect, revolve, ruminate, turn over in one's mind, weigh up 3. call to mind, recall, recollect, remember 4. anticipate, envisage, expect, foresee, imagine, plan for, presume, suppose 5. **think better of** change one's mind about, decide against, go back on, have second thoughts about, reconsider, repent, think again, think twice about 6. **think much of** admire, attach importance to, esteem, have a high opinion of, hold in high regard, rate (*Sl.*), respect, set store by, think highly of, value 7. **think nothing of** consider unimportant, have no compunction about, have no hesitation about, regard as routine, set no store by, take in one's stride ~*n.* 8. assessment, consideration, contemplation, deliberation, look, reflection

thinker brain (*Inf.*), intellect (*Inf.*), mastermind, philosopher, sage, theorist, wise man

thinking 1. *n.* assessment, conclusions, conjecture, idea, judgment, opinion, outlook, philosophy, position, reasoning, theory, thoughts, view 2. *adj.* contemplative, cultured, intelligent, meditative, philosophical, ratiocinative, rational, reasoning, reflective, sophisticated, thoughtful

think over chew over (*Inf.*), consider, consider the pros and cons of, contemplate, give thought to, mull over, ponder, reflect upon, turn over in one's mind, weigh up

think up come up with, concoct, contrive, create, devise, dream up, imagine, improvise, invent, visualize

thin-skinned easily hurt, hypersensitive, quick to take offence, sensitive, soft, susceptible, tender, touchy, vulnerable

third-rate bad, duff (*Brit. sl.*), indifferent, inferior, low-grade, mediocre, poor, poor-quality, ropy (*Brit. inf.*), shoddy

thirst *n.* 1. craving to drink, drought, dryness, thirstiness 2. appetite, craving, desire, eagerness, hankering, hunger, keenness, longing, lust, passion, yearning, yen (*Inf.*)

thirsty 1. arid, dehydrated, dry, parched 2. athirst, avid, burning, craving, desirous, dying, eager, greedy, hankering, hungry, itching, longing, lusting, thirsting, yearning

thorn 1. barb, prickle, spike, spine 2. affliction, annoyance, bane, bother, curse, irritant, irritation, nuisance, pest, plague, scourge, torment, torture, trouble

thorny 1. barbed, bristling with thorns, bristly, pointed, prickly, sharp, spiky, spinous, spiny 2. awkward, difficult, harassing, hard, irksome, problematic, sticky (*Inf.*), ticklish, tough, troublesome, trying, unpleasant, upsetting, vexatious, worrying

thorough *or* **thoroughgoing** 1. all-embracing, all-inclusive, assiduous, careful, complete, comprehensive, conscientious, efficient, exhaustive, full, in-depth, intensive, leaving no stone unturned, meticulous, painstaking, scrupulous, sweeping 2. absolute, arrant, complete, downright, entire, out-and-out, perfect, pure, sheer, total, unmitigated, unqualified, utter

thoroughbred blood, full-blooded, of unmixed stock, pedigree, pure-blooded, purebred

thoroughfare access, avenue, highway, passage, passageway, road, roadway, street, way

thoroughly 1. assiduously, carefully, completely, comprehensively, conscientiously, efficiently, exhaustively, from top to bottom, fully, inside out, intensively, leaving no stone unturned, meticulously, painstakingly, scrupulously, sweepingly, through and through, throughout 2. absolutely, completely, downright, entirely, perfectly, quite, totally, to the full, utterly, without reservation

though 1. *conj.* albeit, allowing, although, despite the fact that, even if, even supposing, granted, notwithstanding, while 2. *adv.* all the same, for all that, however, nevertheless, nonetheless, notwithstanding, still, yet

thought 1. brainwork, cerebration, cogitation, consideration, contemplation, deliberation, introspection, meditation, musing, reflection, regard, rumination, thinking 2. assessment, belief, concept, conception, conclusion, conjecture, conviction, estimation, idea, judgment, notion, opinion, thinking, view 3. attention, consideration, heed, regard, scrutiny, study 4. aim, design, idea, intention, notion, object, plan, purpose 5. anticipation, aspiration, dream, expectation, hope, prospect 6. dash, jot, little, small amount, soupçon, touch, trifle, whisker (*Inf.*) 7. anxiety, attentiveness, care, compassion, concern, kindness, regard, solicitude, sympathy, thoughtfulness

thoughtful 1. attentive, caring, considerate, helpful, kind, kindly, solicitous, unselfish 2. astute, canny, careful, cautious, circumspect, deliberate, discreet, heedful, mindful, prudent, wary, well thought-out 3. contemplative, deliberative, in a brown study, introspective, lost in thought, meditative, musing, pensive, rapt, reflective, ruminative, serious, studious, thinking, wistful

thoughtless 1. impolite, inconsiderate, indiscreet, insensitive, rude, selfish, tactless, uncaring, undiplomatic, unkind 2. absent-minded, careless, foolish, heedless, ill-considered, imprudent, inadvertent, inattentive, injudicious, mindless, neglectful, negligent, rash, reckless, regardless, remiss, silly, stupid, unmindful, unobservant, unthinking

thrash 1. beat, belt, birch, cane, chastise, drub, flagellate, flog, give (someone) a (good) hiding (*Inf.*), hide (*Inf.*), horsewhip, lambaste, leather, paste (*Sl.*), punish, scourge, spank, take a stick to, tan (*Sl.*), whip 2. beat, beat (someone) hollow (*Brit. inf.*), clobber (*Brit. sl.*), crush, defeat, drub, hammer (*Inf.*), maul, overwhelm, paste (*Sl.*), rout, slaughter (*Inf.*), trounce, wipe the floor with (*Inf.*) 3. flail, heave, jerk, plunge, squirm, thresh, toss, toss and turn, writhe

thrashing 1. beating, belting, caning, chastisement, drubbing, flogging, hiding (*Inf.*), lashing, pasting (*Sl.*), punishment, tanning (*Sl.*), whipping 2. beating, defeat, drubbing, hammering (*Inf.*), hiding (*Inf.*), mauling, pasting (*Sl.*), rout, trouncing

thrash out argue out, debate, discuss, have out, resolve, settle, solve, talk over

thread *n.* 1. cotton, fibre, filament, line, strand, string, yarn 2. course, direction, drift, motif, plot, story line, strain, tenor, theme, train of thought ~*v.* 3. ease, inch, loop, meander, pass, pick (one's way), squeeze through, string, wind

threadbare 1. down at heel, frayed, old, ragged, scruffy, shabby, tattered, tatty, used, worn, worn-out 2. clichéd, cliché-ridden, common, commonplace, conventional, corny (*Inf.*), familiar, hackneyed, overused, stale, stereotyped, stock, tired, trite, well-worn

threat 1. commination, intimidatory remark, menace, threatening remark, warning 2. foreboding, foreshadowing, omen, portent, presage, warning, writing on the wall 3. danger, hazard, menace, peril, risk

threaten 1. endanger, imperil, jeopardize, put at risk, put in jeopardy 2. be imminent, be in the air, be in the offing, forebode, foreshadow, hang over, impend, loom over, portend, presage, warn 3.

browbeat, bully, cow, intimidate, lean on (*Sl.*), make threats to, menace, pressurize, terrorize, warn

threatening 1. bullying, cautionary, comminatory, intimidatory, menacing, minatory, terrorizing, warning 2. baleful, grim, inauspicious, ominous, sinister

threesome triad, trilogy, trine, trinity, trio, triple, triplet, triplex, triptych, triumvirate, triune, troika

threshold 1. door, doorsill, doorstep, doorway, entrance, sill 2. beginning, brink, dawn, inception, opening, outset, start, starting point, verge 3. lower limit, minimum

thrift carefulness, economy, frugality, good husbandry, parsimony, prudence, saving, thriftiness

thrifty careful, economical, frugal, parsimonious, provident, prudent, saving, sparing

thrill *n.* 1. adventure, buzz (*Sl.*), charge (*Sl.*), flush of excitement, glow, kick (*Inf.*), pleasure, sensation, stimulation, tingle, titillation 2. flutter, fluttering, quiver, shudder, throb, tremble, tremor, vibration ~*v.* 3. arouse, electrify, excite, flush, get a charge (*Sl.*), get a kick (*Inf.*), glow, move, send (*Sl.*), stimulate, stir, tingle, titillate 4. flutter, quake, quiver, shake, shudder, throb, tremble, vibrate

thrilling 1. electrifying, exciting, gripping, hair-raising, rip-roaring (*Inf.*), riveting, rousing, sensational, stimulating, stirring 2. quaking, shaking, shivering, shuddering, trembling, vibrating

thrive advance, bloom, boom, burgeon, develop, do well, flourish, get on, grow, grow rich, increase, prosper, succeed, wax

thriving blooming, booming, burgeoning, developing, doing well, flourishing, going strong (*Inf.*), growing, healthy, prosperous, successful, wealthy, well

throb 1. *v.* beat, palpitate, pound, pulsate, pulse, thump, vibrate 2. *n.* beat, palpitation, pounding, pulsat~

ing, pulse, thump, thumping, vibration

throng 1. *n.* assemblage, concourse, congregation, crowd, crush, horde, host, jam, mass, mob, multitude, pack, press, swarm 2. *v.* bunch, congregate, converge, cram, crowd, fill, flock, hem in, herd, jam, mill around, pack, press, swarm around, troop

throttle *v.* 1. choke, garrotte, strangle, strangulate 2. control, gag (*Inf.*), inhibit, silence, stifle, suppress

through *prep.* 1. between, by, from end to end of, from one side to the other of, in and out of, past 2. as a consequence *or* result of, because of, by means of, by virtue of, by way of, using, via, with the help of 3. during, in, in the middle of, throughout 4. *With* with at the end of, done, finished, having completed, having had enough of ~*adj.* 5. completed, done, ended, finished, terminated, washed up (*Inf.*) ~*adv.* 6. **through and through** altogether, completely, entirely, fully, thoroughly, totally, to the core, unreservedly, utterly, wholly

throughout all over, all the time, all through, during the whole of, everywhere, for the duration of, from beginning to end, from end to end, from start to finish, from the start, over the length and breadth of, right through, the whole time, through the whole of

throw *v.* 1. cast, chuck (*Inf.*), fling, heave, hurl, launch, lob (*Inf.*), pitch, project, propel, put, send, shy, sling, toss 2. *Inf.* astonish, baffle, confound, confuse, disconcert, dumbfound, put one off one's stroke, throw off, throw one off one's stride, throw out 3. bring down, dislodge, fell, floor, hurl to the ground, overturn, unseat, upset ~*n.* 4. cast, fling, heave, lob (*Inf.*), pitch, projection, put, shy, sling, toss 5. *Inf.* attempt, chance, essay, gamble, hazard, try, venture, wager

throw away 1. cast off, discard, dispense with, dispose of, ditch (*Sl.*), dump (*Inf.*), get rid of, jettison, reject, scrap, throw out 2. blow (*Sl.*), fail to exploit, fritter away, lose, make poor use of, squander, waste

throw off 1. abandon, cast off, discard, drop, free oneself of, rid oneself of, shake off 2. elude, escape from, evade, get away from, give (someone) the slip, leave behind, lose, outdistance, outrun, shake off, show a clean pair of heels to 3. confuse, disconcert, disturb, put one off one's stroke, throw (*Inf.*), throw one off one's stride, unsettle, upset

throw out 1. cast off, discard, dismiss, dispense with, ditch (*Sl.*), dump (*Inf.*), eject, evict, expel, get rid of, jettison, kick out (*Inf.*), reject, scrap, show the door to, throw away, turf out (*Brit. inf.*), turn down 2. confuse, disconcert, disturb, put one off one's stroke, throw (*Inf.*), throw one off one's stride, unsettle, upset 3. diffuse, disseminate, emit, give off, put forth, radiate

thrust *v.* 1. butt, drive, elbow *or* shoulder one's way, force, impel, jam, plunge, poke, press, prod, propel, push, ram, shove, urge 2. jab, lunge, pierce, stab, stick ~*n.* 3. drive, lunge, poke, prod, push, shove, stab 4. impetus, momentum, motive force, motive power, propulsive force

thud *n./v.* clonk, clump, clunk, crash, knock, smack, thump, wallop (*Inf.*)

thug assassin, bandit, bruiser (*Inf.*), bully boy, cutthroat, gangster, hooligan, killer, mugger (*Inf.*), murderer, robber, ruffian, tough

thumb *n.* 1. pollex 2. **all thumbs** butterfingered (*Inf.*), cack-handed (*Inf.*), clumsy, ham-fisted (*Inf.*), inept, maladroit 3. **thumbs down** disapproval, negation, no, rebuff, refusal, rejection 4. **thumbs up** acceptance, affirmation, approval, encouragement, go-ahead (*Inf.*), green light, O.K. (*Inf.*), yes ~*v.* 5. hitch (*Inf.*), hitchhike 6. *Often with* **through** browse through, flick through, flip through, glance at, leaf through, riffle through, run one's eye over, scan the pages of, skim through, turn over 7. dog-ear, finger, handle, mark 8. **thumb one's nose at** be contemptuous of, cock a snook at, deride, flout, jeer at, laugh at, laugh in the face of, mock, ridicule, show contempt for, show disrespect to

thump 1. *n.* bang, blow, clout (*Inf.*), clunk, crash, knock, rap, smack, thud, thwack, wallop (*Inf.*), whack 2. *v.* bang, batter, beat, belabour, clout (*Inf.*), crash, hit, knock, lambaste (*Sl.*), pound, rap, smack, strike, thrash, throb, thud, thwack, wallop (*Inf.*), whack

thumping colossal, enormous, excessive, exorbitant, gargantuan, gigantic, great, huge, impressive, mammoth, massive, monumental, terrific, thundering (*Sl.*), titanic, tremendous, whopping (*Inf.*)

thunder *n.* 1. boom, booming, cracking, crash, crashing, detonation, explosion, pealing, rumble, rumbling ~*v.* 2. blast, boom, clap, crack, crash, detonate, explode, peal, resound, reverberate, roar, rumble 3. bark, bellow, declaim, roar, shout, yell 4. curse, denounce, fulminate, rail, threaten, utter threats

thunderous booming, deafening, ear-splitting, loud, noisy, resounding, roaring, tumultuous

thunderstruck aghast, amazed, astonished, astounded, bowled over (*Inf.*), dazed, dumbfounded, flabbergasted (*Inf.*), floored (*Inf.*), knocked for six (*Inf.*), left speechless, nonplussed, open-mouthed, paralysed, petrified, rooted to the spot, shocked, staggered, struck dumb, stunned, taken aback

thus 1. as follows, in this fashion (manner, way), like so, like this, so, to such a degree 2. accordingly, consequently, ergo, for this reason, hence, on that account, so, then, therefore

thwart baffle, balk, check, defeat, foil, frustrate, hinder, impede, obstruct, oppose, outwit, prevent, stop, stymie

tick¹ *n.* 1. clack, click, clicking, tap, tapping, ticktock 2. *Brit. inf.* flash, half a mo (*Brit. inf.*), instant, jiffy (*Inf.*), minute, moment, sec (*Inf.*), second, shake (*Inf.*), split second, trice, twinkling, two shakes of a lamb's tail (*Inf.*) 3. dash, mark, stroke ~*v.* 4. clack, click, tap, ticktock 5. check off, choose, indicate, mark, mark off, select 6. **what makes someone tick** drive, motivation, motive, *raison d'être*

tick² account, credit, deferred payment, the slate (*Brit. inf.*)

ticket 1. card, certificate, coupon, pass, slip, token, voucher 2. card, docket, label, marker, slip, sticker, tab, tag

tickle *Fig.* amuse, delight, divert, entertain, excite, gratify, please, thrill, titillate

ticklish awkward, critical, delicate, difficult, nice, risky, sensitive, thorny, touchy, tricky, uncertain, unstable, unsteady

tick off 1. check off, mark off, put a tick at 2. *Inf.* berate, censure, chide, haul over the coals (*Inf.*), lecture, rebuke, reprimand, reproach, reprove, scold, take to task, tear off a strip (*Inf.*), tell off (*Inf.*), upbraid

tide 1. course, current, ebb, flow, stream 2. course, current, direction, drift, movement, tendency, trend

tide over aid, assist, bridge the gap, help, keep one going, keep one's head above water, keep the wolf from the door, see one through

tidings advice, bulletin, communication, greetings, information, intelligence, message, news, report, word

tidy *adj.* 1. businesslike, clean, cleanly, methodical, neat, ordered, orderly, shipshape, spick-and-span, spruce, systematic, trim, well-groomed, well-kept, well-ordered 2. *Inf.* ample, considerable, fair, generous, good, goodly, handsome, healthy, large, largish, respectable, sizable, substantial ~*v.* 3. clean, groom, neaten, order, put in order, put in trim, put to rights, spruce up, straighten

tie *v.* 1. attach, bind, connect, fasten, interlace, join, knot, lash, link, make fast, moor, rope, secure, tether, truss, unite 2. bind, confine, hamper, hinder, hold, limit, restrain, restrict 3. be even, be neck and neck, draw, equal, match ~*n.* 4. band, bond, connection, cord, fastening, fetter, joint, knot, ligature, link, rope, string 5. affiliation, allegiance, bond, commitment, connection, duty, kinship, liaison, obligation, relationship 6. encumbrance, hindrance, limitation, restraint, restriction 7. dead heat, deadlock, draw, stalemate 8. *Brit.* contest, fixture, game, match

tier bank, echelon, file, layer, level, line, order, rank, row, series, storey, stratum

tie up 1. attach, bind, pinion, restrain, tether, truss 2. lash, make fast, moor, rope, secure 3. engage, engross, keep busy, occupy 4. bring to a close, conclude, end, finish off, settle, terminate, wind up, wrap up (*Inf.*)

tight 1. close, close-fitting, compact, constricted, cramped, fast, firm, fixed, narrow, rigid, secure, snug, stiff, stretched, taut, tense 2. hermetic, impervious, proof, sealed, sound, watertight 3. harsh, inflexible, rigid, rigorous, severe, stern, strict, stringent, tough, uncompromising, unyielding 4. close, grasping, mean, miserly, niggardly, parsimonious, penurious, sparing, stingy, tightfisted 5. dangerous, difficult, hazardous, perilous, precarious, problematic, sticky (*Inf.*), ticklish, tough, tricky, troublesome, worrisome 6. close, even, evenly-balanced, near, well-matched 7. *Inf.* drunk, half cut (*Brit. sl.*), half seas over (*Brit. inf.*), inebriated, in one's cups, intoxicated, pickled (*Inf.*), pie-eyed (*Sl.*), plastered (*Sl.*), smashed (*Sl.*), sozzled (*Inf.*), stewed (*Sl.*), stoned (*Sl.*), three sheets in the wind (*Sl.*), tiddly (*Brit. sl.*), tipsy, under the influence (*Inf.*)

tighten close, constrict, cramp, fasten, fix, narrow, rigidify, screw, secure, squeeze, stiffen, stretch, tauten, tense

till[1] cultivate, dig, plough, turn over, work

till[2] cash box, cash drawer, cash register

tilt *v.* 1. cant, incline, lean, list, slant, slope, tip 2. attack, break a lance, clash, contend, cross swords, duel, encounter, fight, joust, overthrow, spar ~*n.* 3. angle, cant, inclination, incline, list, pitch, slant, slope 4. *Medieval history* clash, combat, duel, encounter, fight, joust, lists, set-to (*Inf.*), tournament, tourney 5. (at) **full tilt** for dear life, full force, full speed, headlong, like a bat out of hell (*Inf.*), like the clappers (*Brit. inf.*)

timber beams, boards, forest, logs, planks, trees, wood

time *n.* 1. age, chronology, date, duration, epoch, era, generation, hour, interval, period, season, space, span, spell, stretch, term, while 2. instance, juncture, occasion, point, stage 3. allotted span, day, duration, life, life span, lifetime, season 4. heyday, hour, peak 5. *Mus.* beat, measure, metre, rhythm, tempo 6. **all the time** always, at all times, constantly, continually, continuously, ever, for the duration, perpetually, throughout 7. **at one time a.** for a while, formerly, hitherto, once, once upon a time, previously **b.** all at once, at the same time, simultaneously, together 8. **at times** every now and then, every so often, from time to time, now and then, occasionally, once in a while, on occasion, sometimes 9. **behind the times** antiquated, dated, obsolete, old-fashioned, old hat, outdated, outmoded, out of date, out of fashion, out of style, passé, square (*Inf.*) 10. **for the time being** for now, for the moment, for the present, in the meantime, meantime, meanwhile, pro tem, temporarily 11. **from time to time** at times, every now and then, every so often, now and then, occasionally, once in a while, on occasion, sometimes 12. **in good time a.** early, on time, with time to spare b. quickly, rapidly, speedily, swiftly, with dispatch 13. **in no time** before one knows it, before you can say Jack Robinson, in an instant, in a trice (flash, jiffy, moment), in two shakes of a lamb's tail (*Inf.*), quickly, rapidly, speedily, swiftly 14. **in time a.** at the appointed time, early, in good time, on schedule, on time, with time to spare b. by and by, eventually, one day, someday, sooner or later, ultimately 15. **on time** in good time, on the dot, punctually 16. **time and again** frequently, many times, often, on many occasions, over and over again, repeatedly, time after time ~v. 17. clock, control, count, judge, measure, regulate, schedule, set

timeless abiding, ageless, ceaseless, changeless, deathless, endless, enduring, eternal, everlasting, immortal, immutable, imperishable, indestructible, lasting, permanent, persistent, undying

timely appropriate, at the right time, convenient, judicious, opportune, prompt, propitious, punctual, seasonable, suitable, well-timed

timetable agenda, calendar, curriculum, diary, list, order of the day, programme, schedule

timid afraid, apprehensive, bashful, cowardly, coy, diffident, faint-hearted, fearful, irresolute, modest, mousy, nervous, pusillanimous, retiring, shrinking, shy, timorous

timorous afraid, apprehensive, bashful, cowardly, coy, diffident, faint-hearted, fearful, frightened, irresolute, mousy, nervous, pusillanimous, retiring, shrinking, shy, timid, trembling

tinge n. 1. cast, colour, dye, shade, stain, tincture, tint, wash 2. bit, dash, drop, pinch, smack, smattering, soupçon, sprinkling, suggestion, touch, trace ~v. 3. colour, dye, imbue, shade, stain, suffuse, tinge, tint

tingle 1. v. have goose pimples, itch, prickle, sting, tickle 2. n. goose pimples, itch, itching, pins and needles (*Inf.*), prickling, quiver, shiver, stinging, thrill, tickle, tickling

tinker v. dabble, fiddle (*Inf.*), meddle, mess about, monkey, muck about (*Brit. sl.*), play, potter, toy

tint n. 1. cast, colour, hue, shade, tone 2. dye, rinse, stain, tincture, tinge, wash 3. hint, shade, suggestion, tinge, touch, trace ~v. 4. colour, dye, rinse, stain, tincture, tinge 5. affect, colour, influence, taint, tinge

tiny diminutive, dwarfish, infinitesimal, insignificant, Lilliputian, little, microscopic, mini, miniature, minute, negligible, petite, pint-sized (*Inf.*), puny, pygmy, slight, small, trifling, wee

tip[1] 1. n. apex, cap, crown, end, extremity, head, peak, point, summit, top 2. v. cap, crown, finish, surmount, top

tip[2] v. 1. cant, capsize, incline, lean, list, overturn, slant, spill, tilt, topple over, upend, upset 2. *Brit.* ditch (*Sl.*), dump, empty, pour out, unload ~n. 3. *Brit.* dump, midden (*Dialect*), refuse heap, rubbish heap

tip[3] n. 1. baksheesh, gift, gratuity, perquisite, *pourboire* 2. *Also* tip-off clue, forecast, gen (*Brit. inf.*), hint, information, inside information, pointer, suggestion, warning, word, word of advice ~v. 3. remunerate, reward 4. *Also* tip off advise, caution, forewarn, give a clue, give a hint, suggest, tip (someone) the wink (*Brit. inf.*), warn

tipple 1. v. bend the elbow (*Inf.*), drink, imbibe, indulge (*Inf.*), quaff, swig, take a drink, tope 2. n. alcohol, booze (*Inf.*), drink, John Barleycorn, liquor, poison (*Inf.*)

tire 1. drain, droop, enervate, exhaust, fag (*Inf.*), fail, fatigue, flag, jade, knacker (*Sl.*), sink, take it out of (*Inf.*), wear down, wear out, weary, whack (*Brit. inf.*) 2. annoy, bore, exasperate, harass, irk, irritate, weary

tired 1. all in (*Sl.*), asleep *or* dead on

one's feet, dead beat (*Inf.*), dog~
tired (*Inf.*), done in (*Inf.*), drained,
drooping, drowsy, enervated, ex~
hausted, fagged (*Inf.*), fatigued,
flagging, jaded, knackered (*Sl.*),
ready to drop, sleepy, spent, wea~
ry, whacked (*Brit. inf.*), worn out 2.
With of annoyed with, bored with,
exasperated by, fed up with, irked
by, irritated by, sick of, weary of 3.
clichéd, conventional, corny (*Inf.*),
familiar, hackneyed, old, outworn,
stale, stock, threadbare, trite, well-
worn

tireless determined, energetic, in~
defatigable, industrious, resolute,
unflagging, untiring, unwearied,
vigorous

tiresome annoying, boring, dull,
exasperating, flat, irksome, irritat~
ing, laborious, monotonous, tedi~
ous, trying, uninteresting, vexa~
tious, wearing, wearisome

tiring arduous, demanding, enerva~
tive, exacting, exhausting, fatigu~
ing, laborious, strenuous, tough,
wearing, wearying

tissue 1. fabric, gauze, mesh,
structure, stuff, texture, web 2. pa~
per, paper handkerchief, wrapping
paper 3. accumulation, chain, col~
lection, combination, concatena~
tion, conglomeration, fabrication,
mass, network, pack, series, web

titbit *bonne bouche*, choice item,
dainty, delicacy, goody (*Inf.*), juicy
bit, morsel, scrap, snack, treat

title *n.* 1. caption, heading, inscrip~
tion, label, legend, name, style 2.
appellation, denomination, desig~
nation, epithet, handle (*Sl.*), moni~
ker (*Inf.*), name, nickname, nom
de plume, pseudonym, sobriquet,
term 3. championship, crown, lau~
rels 4. claim, entitlement, owner~
ship, prerogative, privilege, right
~*v.* 5. call, designate, label, name,
style, term

titter chortle (*Inf.*), chuckle, giggle,
laugh, snigger, te-hee

toady 1. *n.* apple polisher (*U.S. sl.*),
bootlicker (*Inf.*), crawler (*Sl.*),
creep (*Sl.*), fawner, flatterer,
flunkey, groveller, hanger-on,
jackal, lackey, lickspittle, minion,

parasite, spaniel, sycophant,
truckler, yes man 2. *v.* be obsequi~
ous to, bow and scrape, butter up,
crawl, creep, cringe, curry favour
with, fawn on, flatter, grovel, kiss
the feet of, kowtow to, lick the
boots of (*Inf.*), suck up to (*Inf.*)

toast[1] *v.* brown, grill, heat, roast,
warm

toast[2] *n.* 1. compliment, drink,
health, pledge, salutation, salute,
tribute 2. darling, favourite, hero~
ine ~*v.* 3. drink to, drink (to) the
health of, pledge, salute

together *adv.* 1. as a group, as one,
cheek by jowl, closely, collectively,
hand in glove, hand in hand, in a
body, in concert, in cooperation, in
unison, jointly, mutually, shoulder
to shoulder, side by side 2. all at
once, as one, at one fell swoop, at
the same time, concurrently, con~
temporaneously, en masse, in uni~
son, simultaneously, with one ac~
cord 3. consecutively, continuous~
ly, in a row, in succession, one
after the other, on end, succes~
sively, without a break, without in~
terruption 4. *Inf.* arranged, fixed,
ordered, organized, settled, sorted
out, straight, to rights ~*adj.* 5. *Sl.*
calm, composed, cool, stable, well-
adjusted, well-balanced, well-
organized

toil 1. *n.* application, donkey-work,
drudgery, effort, elbow grease
(*Inf.*), exertion, graft (*Inf.*), hard
work, industry, labour, pains, slog,
sweat, travail 2. *v.* drag oneself,
drudge, graft (*Inf.*), grind (*Inf.*),
grub, knock oneself out, labour,
push oneself, slave, slog, strive,
struggle, sweat (*Inf.*), work, work
like a dog, work like a Trojan,
work one's fingers to the bone

toilet 1. ablutions (*Military inf.*),
bathroom, bog (*Brit. sl.*), closet,
convenience, gents (*Brit. inf.*), la~
dies' room, latrine, lavatory, loo
(*Brit. inf.*), outhouse, powder room,
privy, urinal, washroom, water
closet, W.C. 2. ablutions, bathing,
dressing, grooming, toilette

token *n.* 1. badge, clue, demonstra~
tion, earnest, evidence, expression,

index, indication, manifestation, mark, note, proof, representation, sign, symbol, warning 2. keepsake, memento, memorial, remem~ brance, reminder, souvenir ~*adj.* 3. hollow, minimal, nominal, per~ functory, superficial, symbolic

tolerable 1. acceptable, allowable, bearable, endurable, sufferable, supportable 2. acceptable, ad~ equate, all right, average, fair, fairly good, fair to middling, good enough, indifferent, mediocre, middling, not bad (*Inf.*), O.K. (*Inf.*), ordinary, passable, run-of-the-mill, so-so (*Inf.*), unexceptional

tolerance 1. broad-mindedness, charity, forbearance, indulgence, lenity, magnanimity, open~ mindedness, patience, permissive~ ness, sufferance, sympathy 2. en~ durance, fortitude, hardiness, hardness, resilience, resistance, stamina, staying power, toughness 3. fluctuation, play, swing, vari~ ation

tolerant 1. broad-minded, catholic, charitable, fair, forbearing, latitu~ dinarian, liberal, long-suffering, magnanimous, open-minded, pa~ tient, sympathetic, unbigoted, understanding, unprejudiced 2. complaisant, easy-going, free and easy, indulgent, kind-hearted, lax, lenient, permissive, soft

tolerate abide, accept, admit, al~ low, bear, brook, condone, counte~ nance, endure, indulge, permit, pocket, put up with (*Inf.*), receive, sanction, stand, stomach, submit to, suffer, swallow, take, thole (*Scot.*), turn a blind eye to, under~ go, wink at

toleration 1. acceptance, allow~ ance, condonation, endurance, in~ dulgence, permissiveness, sanc~ tion, sufferance 2. freedom of con~ science, freedom of worship, reli~ gious freedom

toll[1] *v.* 1. chime, clang, knell, peal, ring, sound, strike 2. announce, call, signal, summon, warn ~*n.* 3. chime, clang, knell, peal, ring, ringing, tolling

toll[2] 1. assessment, charge, cus~ toms, demand, duty, fee, impost, levy, payment, rate, tariff, tax, tribute 2. cost, damage, inroad, loss, penalty

tomb burial chamber, catacomb, crypt, grave, mausoleum, sepul~ chre, vault

tombstone gravestone, headstone, marker, memorial, monument

tome book, volume, work

tomfoolery 1. buffoonery, childish~ ness, clowning, fooling around (*Inf.*), foolishness, horseplay, idio~ cy, larks (*Inf.*), messing around (*Inf.*), shenanigans (*Inf.*), silliness, skylarking (*Inf.*), stupidity 2. bal~ derdash, baloney (*Inf.*), bilge (*Inf.*), bosh (*Inf.*), bunk (*Inf.*), bunkum, claptrap (*Inf.*), hogwash, hooey (*Sl.*), inanity, nonsense, poppycock (*Inf.*), rot, rubbish, stuff and non~ sense, tommyrot, tosh, trash, twaddle

tone *n.* 1. accent, emphasis, force, inflection, intonation, modulation, pitch, strength, stress, timbre, to~ nality, volume 2. air, approach, as~ pect, attitude, character, drift, ef~ fect, feel, frame, grain, manner, mood, note, quality, spirit, style, temper, tenor, vein 3. cast, colour, hue, shade, tinge, tint ~*v.* 4. blend, go well with, harmonize, match, suit

tone down dampen, dim, mitigate, moderate, modulate, play down, reduce, restrain, soften, soft-pedal (*Inf.*), subdue, temper

tongue 1. argot, dialect, idiom, language, lingo (*Inf.*), parlance, patois, speech, talk, vernacular 2. articulation, speech, utterance, verbal expression, voice

tongue-tied at a loss for words, dumb, dumbstruck, inarticulate, mute, speechless, struck dumb

tonic analeptic, boost, bracer (*Inf.*), cordial, fillip, livener, pick-me-up (*Inf.*), refresher, restorative, ro~ borant, shot in the arm (*Inf.*), stimulant

too 1. also, as well, besides, further, in addition, into the bargain, like~ wise, moreover, to boot 2. exces~ sively, exorbitantly, extremely, immoderately, inordinately, over-, overly, unduly, unreasonably, very

tool *n.* **1.** apparatus, appliance, contraption, contrivance, device, gadget, implement, instrument, machine, utensil **2.** agency, agent, intermediary, means, medium, vehicle, wherewithal **3.** cat's-paw, creature, dupe, flunkey, hireling, jackal, lackey, minion, pawn, puppet, stooge (*Sl.*) ~*v.* **4.** chase, cut, decorate, ornament, shape, work

top *n.* **1.** acme, apex, apogee, crest, crown, culmination, head, height, high point, meridian, peak, pinnacle, summit, vertex, zenith **2.** cap, cork, cover, lid, stopper **3.** first place, head, highest rank, lead **4. blow one's top** *Inf.* blow up (*Inf.*), do one's nut (*Brit. sl.*), explode, fly into a temper, fly off the handle (*Inf.*), go spare (*Brit. sl.*), have a fit (*Inf.*), lose one's temper, see red (*Inf.*), throw a tantrum **5. over the top** a bit much (*Inf.*), excessive, going too far, immoderate, inordinate, over the limit, too much, uncalled-for ~*adj.* **6.** best, chief, crack (*Inf.*), crowning, culminating, dominant, elite, finest, first, foremost, greatest, head, highest, lead, leading, pre-eminent, prime, principal, ruling, sovereign, superior, topmost, upper, uppermost ~*v.* **7.** cap, cover, crown, finish, garnish, roof, tip **8.** ascend, climb, crest, reach the top of, scale, surmount **9.** be first, be in charge of, command, head, lead, rule **10.** beat, best, better, eclipse, exceed, excel, go beyond, outdo, outshine, outstrip, surpass, transcend

topic issue, matter, point, question, subject, subject matter, text, theme, thesis

topical 1. contemporary, current, newsworthy, popular, up-to-date, up-to-the-minute **2.** local, parochial, regional, restricted

topmost dominant, foremost, highest, leading, loftiest, paramount, principal, supreme, top, upper, uppermost

topple 1. capsize, collapse, fall, fall headlong, fall over, keel over, knock down, knock over, overbalance, overturn, tip over, totter, tumble, upset **2.** bring down, bring low, oust, overthrow, overturn, unseat

topsy-turvy chaotic, confused, disarranged, disorderly, disorganized, inside-out, jumbled, messy, mixed-up, untidy, upside-down

torment *v.* **1.** afflict, agonize, crucify, distress, excruciate, harrow, pain, rack, torture **2.** annoy, bedevil, bother, chivvy, devil (*Inf.*), harass, harry, hound, irritate, nag, persecute, pester, plague, provoke, tease, trouble, vex, worry ~*n.* **3.** agony, anguish, distress, hell, misery, pain, suffering, torture **4.** affliction, annoyance, bane, bother, harassment, irritation, nag, nagging, nuisance, pain in the neck (*Inf.*), persecution, pest, plague, provocation, scourge, thorn in one's flesh, trouble, vexation, worry

torn *adj.* **1.** cut, lacerated, ragged, rent, ripped, slit, split **2.** divided, in two minds (*Inf.*), irresolute, split, uncertain, undecided, unsure, vacillating, wavering

tornado cyclone, gale, hurricane, squall, storm, tempest, twister (*U.S. inf.*), typhoon, whirlwind, windstorm

torpor accidie, acedia, apathy, dormancy, drowsiness, dullness, inactivity, inanition, indolence, inertia, inertness, languor, laziness, lethargy, listlessness, numbness, passivity, sloth, sluggishness, somnolence, stagnancy, stupor, torpidity

torrent cascade, deluge, downpour, effusion, flood, flow, gush, outburst, rush, spate, stream, tide

tortuous 1. bent, circuitous, convoluted, crooked, curved, indirect, mazy, meandering, serpentine, sinuous, twisted, twisting, winding, zigzag **2.** ambiguous, complicated, convoluted, cunning, deceptive, devious, indirect, involved, mazy, misleading, roundabout, tricky

torture 1. *v.* afflict, agonize, crucify, distress, excruciate, harrow, lacerate, martyr, pain, persecute, put on the rack, rack, torment 2. *n.* affliction, agony, anguish, distress, hell, laceration, martyrdom, misery, pain, pang(s), persecution, rack, suffering, torment

toss *v.* 1. cast, chuck (*Inf.*), fling, flip, hurl, launch, lob (*Inf.*), pitch, project, propel, shy, sling, throw 2. agitate, disturb, jiggle, joggle, jolt, rock, roll, shake, thrash, tumble, wriggle, writhe 3. heave, labour, lurch, pitch, roll, wallow ~*n.* 4. cast, fling, lob (*Inf.*), pitch, shy, throw

tot[1] *n.* 1. baby, child, infant, little one, mite, toddler, wean (*Scot.*) 2. dram, finger, measure, nip, shot (*Inf.*), slug, snifter (*Inf.*), toothful

tot[2] *v.* add up, calculate, count up, reckon, sum (up), tally, total

total 1. *n.* aggregate, all, amount, entirety, full amount, mass, sum, totality, whole 2. *adj.* absolute, all-out, complete, comprehensive, consummate, downright, entire, full, gross, integral, out-and-out, outright, perfect, sheer, sweeping, thorough, thoroughgoing, unconditional, undisputed, undivided, unmitigated, unqualified, utter, whole 3. *v.* add up, amount to, come to, mount up to, reach, reckon, sum up, tot up

totalitarian authoritarian, despotic, dictatorial, monolithic, one-party, oppressive, tyrannous, undemocratic

totally absolutely, completely, comprehensively, consummately, entirely, fully, perfectly, quite, thoroughly, unconditionally, unmitigatedly, utterly, wholeheartedly, wholly

totter falter, lurch, quiver, reel, rock, shake, stagger, stumble, sway, teeter, tremble, walk unsteadily, waver

touch *n.* 1. feel, feeling, handling, palpation, physical contact, tactility 2. blow, brush, caress, contact, fondling, hit, pat, push, stroke, tap 3. bit, dash, detail, drop, hint, intimation, jot, pinch, smack, small amount, smattering, *soupçon*, speck, spot, suggestion, suspicion,

taste, tincture, tinge, trace, whiff 4. direction, effect, hand, influence 5. approach, characteristic, handiwork, manner, method, style, technique, trademark, way 6. ability, adroitness, art, artistry, command, deftness, facility, flair, knack, mastery, skill, virtuosity 7. acquaintance, awareness, communication, contact, correspondence, familiarity, understanding ~*v.* 8. brush, caress, contact, feel, finger, fondle, graze, handle, hit, lay a finger on, palpate, pat, push, strike, stroke, tap 9. abut, adjoin, be in contact, border, brush, come together, contact, converge, graze, impinge upon, meet 10. affect, disturb, get through to, get to (*Inf.*), have an effect on, impress, influence, inspire, make an impression on, mark, melt, move, soften, stir, strike, upset 11. be a party to, concern oneself with, consume, deal with, drink, eat, get involved in, handle, have to do with, partake of, use, utilize 12. *With* **on** allude to, bring in, cover, deal with, mention, refer to, speak of 13. bear upon, concern, have to do with, interest, pertain to, regard 14. be a match for, be in the same league as, be on a par with, come near, come up to, compare with, equal, hold a candle to (*Inf.*), match, parallel, rival 15. arrive at, attain, come to, reach

touchiness bad temper, crabbedness, fretfulness, grouchiness, irascibility, irritability, peevishness, pettishness, petulance, surliness, testiness, tetchiness, ticklishness

touching affecting, emotive, heartbreaking, melting, moving, pathetic, piteous, pitiable, pitiful, poignant, sad, stirring, tender

touchstone criterion, guage, measure, norm, standard, yardstick

touch up 1. finish off, perfect, put the finishing touches to, round off 2. brush up, enhance, fake (up), falsify, give a face-lift to, gloss over, improve, patch up, polish up, renovate, retouch, revamp, titivate, whitewash (*Inf.*)

touchy bad-tempered, captious, crabbed, cross, easily offended, grouchy, grumpy, irascible, irritable, oversensitive, peevish, pettish, petulant, querulous, quick-tempered, splenetic, surly, testy, tetchy, thin-skinned, ticklish

tough *adj.* 1. cohesive, durable, firm, hard, inflexible, leathery, resilient, resistant, rigid, rugged, solid, stiff, strong, sturdy, tenacious 2. brawny, fit, hard as nails, hardened, hardy, resilient, seasoned, stalwart, stout, strapping, strong, sturdy, vigorous 3. hard-bitten, pugnacious, rough, ruffianly, ruthless, vicious, violent 4. adamant, callous, exacting, firm, hard, hardboiled (*Inf.*), hard-nosed (*Sl.*), inflexible, intractable, merciless, obdurate, obstinate, refractory, resolute, severe, stern, strict, stubborn, unbending, unforgiving, unyielding 5. arduous, baffling, difficult, exacting, exhausting, hard, intractable, irksome, knotty, laborious, perplexing, puzzling, strenuous, thorny, troublesome, uphill 6. *Inf.* bad, hard cheese (*Brit. sl.*), hard lines (*Brit. inf.*), hard luck, lamentable, regrettable, too bad (*Inf.*), unfortunate, unlucky ~*n.* 7. bravo, bruiser (*Inf.*), brute, bully, bully boy, hooligan, rough (*Inf.*), roughneck (*Sl.*), rowdy, ruffian, thug

tour *n.* 1. excursion, expedition, jaunt, journey, outing, peregrination, progress, trip 2. circuit, course, round ~*v.* 3. explore, go on the road, go round, holiday in, journey, sightsee, travel round, travel through, visit

tourist excursionist, globetrotter, holiday-maker, journeyer, sightseer, traveller, tripper, voyager

tournament 1. competition, contest, event, match, meeting, series 2. *Medieval* joust, the lists, tourney

tow *v.* drag, draw, haul, lug, pull, trail, trawl, tug

towards 1. en route for, for, in the direction of, in the vicinity of, on the road to, on the way to, to 2. about, concerning, for, regarding, with regard to, with respect to 3. almost, close to, coming up to, getting on for, just before, nearing, nearly, not quite, shortly before

tower *n.* 1. belfry, column, obelisk, pillar, skyscraper, steeple, turret 2. castle, citadel, fort, fortification, fortress, keep, refuge, stronghold ~*v.* 3. ascend, be head and shoulders above, dominate, exceed, loom, mount, overlook, overtop, rear, rise, soar, surpass, top, transcend

toxic baneful (*Archaic*), deadly, harmful, lethal, noxious, pernicious, pestilential, poisonous, septic

toy *n.* 1. doll, game, plaything 2. bauble, gewgaw, knick-knack, trifle, trinket ~*v.* 3. amuse oneself, dally, fiddle (*Inf.*), flirt, play, sport, trifle, wanton

trace *n.* 1. evidence, indication, mark, record, relic, remains, remnant, sign, survival, token, vestige 2. bit, dash, drop, hint, iota, jot, shadow, *soupçon*, suggestion, suspicion, tincture, tinge, touch, trifle, whiff 3. footmark, footprint, footstep, path, slot, spoor, track, trail ~*v.* 4. ascertain, detect, determine, discover, ferret out, find, follow, hunt down, pursue, search for, seek, shadow, stalk, track, trail, unearth 5. chart, copy, delineate, depict, draw, map, mark out, outline, record, show, sketch

track *n.* 1. footmark, footprint, footstep, mark, path, scent, slot, spoor, trace, trail, wake 2. course, flight path, line, orbit, path, pathway, road, track, trajectory, way 3. line, permanent way, rail, rails 4. **keep track of** follow, keep an eye on, keep in sight, keep in touch with, keep up to date with, keep up with, monitor, oversee, watch 5. **lose track of** lose, lose sight of, misplace ~*v.* 6. chase, dog, follow, follow the trail of, hunt down, pursue, shadow, stalk, tail (*Inf.*), trace, trail

track down apprehend, bring to light, capture, catch, dig up, discover, expose, ferret out, find, hunt down, run to earth, sniff out, trace, unearth

tracks 1. footprints, impressions, imprints, tyremarks, tyreprints, wheelmarks 2. **make tracks** beat it (*Sl.*), depart, disappear, get going, get moving, go, head off, hit the road (*Sl.*), leave, set out, split (*Sl.*), take off (*Inf.*) 3. **stop in one's tracks** bring to a standstill, freeze, immobilize, petrify, rivet to the spot, stop dead, transfix

tract[1] area, district, estate, ex~ panse, extent, lot, plot, quarter, re~ gion, stretch, territory, zone

tract[2] booklet, brochure, disquisi~ tion, dissertation, essay, homily, leaflet, monograph, pamphlet, tractate, treatise

tractable 1. amenable, biddable, compliant, controllable, docile, governable, manageable, obedient, persuadable, submissive, tame, willing, yielding 2. ductile, fictile, malleable, plastic, pliable, pliant, tractile, workable

traction adhesion, drag, draught, drawing, friction, grip, haulage, pull, pulling, purchase, resistance

trade *n.* 1. barter, business, buying and selling, commerce, dealing, exchange, traffic, transactions, truck 2. avocation, business, call~ ing, craft, employment, job, line, line of work, métier, occupation, profession, pursuit, skill 3. deal, exchange, interchange, swap 4. clientele, custom, customers, mar~ ket, patrons, public ~*v.* 5. bargain, barter, buy and sell, deal, do busi~ ness, exchange, have dealings, peddle, traffic, transact, truck 6. barter, exchange, swap, switch

trader broker, buyer, dealer, mar~ keter, merchandiser, merchant, seller

tradesman 1. dealer, merchant, retailer, seller, shopkeeper, vendor 2. artisan, craftsman, journeyman, skilled worker, workman

tradition convention, custom, cus~ toms, established practice, folk~ lore, habit, institution, lore, praxis, ritual, unwritten law, usage

traditional accustomed, ancestral, conventional, customary, estab~ lished, fixed, folk, historic, long-established, old, oral, time-honoured, transmitted, unwritten, usual

traffic *n.* 1. coming and going, freight, movement, passengers, transport, transportation, vehicles 2. barter, business, buying and selling, commerce, communica~ tion, dealing, dealings, doings, ex~ change, intercourse, peddling, re~ lations, trade, truck ~*v.* 3. bargain, barter, buy and sell, deal, do busi~ ness, exchange, have dealings, have transactions, market, peddle, trade, truck

tragedy adversity, affliction, ca~ lamity, catastrophe, disaster, grievous blow, misfortune

tragic anguished, appalling, awful, calamitous, catastrophic, deadly, dire, disastrous, doleful, dreadful, fatal, grievous, heartbreaking, heart-rending, ill-fated, ill-starred, lamentable, miserable, mournful, pathetic, pitiable, ruinous, sad, shocking, sorrowful, unfortunate, woeful, wretched

trail *v.* 1. dangle, drag, draw, hang down, haul, pull, stream, tow 2. chase, follow, hunt, pursue, shad~ ow, stalk, tail (*Inf.*), trace, track 3. bring up the rear, dawdle, drag oneself, fall behind, follow, hang back, lag, linger, loiter, straggle, traipse (*Inf.*) 4. dangle, droop, ex~ tend, hang, straggle ~*n.* 5. foot~ prints, footsteps, mark, marks, path, scent, spoor, trace, track, wake 6. beaten track, footpath, path, road, route, track, way 7. ap~ pendage, stream, tail, train

train *v.* 1. coach, discipline, drill, educate, guide, improve, instruct, prepare, rear, rehearse, school, teach, tutor 2. exercise, improve, prepare, work out 3. aim, bring to bear, direct, focus, level, line up, point ~*n.* 4. chain, concatenation, course, order, progression, se~ quence, series, set, string, succes~ sion 5. caravan, column, convoy, file, procession 6. appendage, tail, trail 7. attendants, cortege, court, entourage, followers, following, household, retinue, staff, suite

trainer coach

training 1. coaching, discipline, education, grounding, guidance, instruction, schooling, teaching, tuition, tutelage, upbringing **2.** body building, exercise, practice, preparation, working-out

trait attribute, characteristic, feature, idiosyncrasy, lineament, mannerism, peculiarity, quality, quirk

traitor apostate, back-stabber, betrayer, deceiver, defector, deserter, double-crosser (*Inf.*), fifth columnist, informer, Judas, miscreant, quisling, rebel, renegade, snake in the grass (*Inf.*), turncoat

trajectory course, flight, flight path, line, path, route, track

tramp *v.* **1.** footslog, hike, march, ramble, range, roam, rove, slog, trek, walk, yomp **2.** march, plod, stamp, stump, toil, traipse (*Inf.*), trudge, walk heavily **3.** crush, stamp, stomp (*Inf.*), trample, tread, walk over ~*n.* **4.** derelict, dosser (*Brit. sl.*), down-and-out, drifter, hobo (*Chiefly U.S.*), vagabond, vagrant **5.** hike, march, ramble, slog, trek **6.** footfall, footstep, stamp, tread

trample 1. crush, flatten, run over, squash, stamp, tread, walk over **2.** do violence to, encroach upon, hurt, infringe, ride roughshod over, show no consideration for, violate

trance abstraction, daze, dream, ecstasy, hypnotic state, muse, rapture, reverie, spell, stupor, unconsciousness

tranquil at peace, calm, composed, cool, pacific, peaceful, placid, quiet, restful, sedate, serene, still, undisturbed, unexcited, unperturbed, unruffled, untroubled

tranquillity ataraxia, calm, calmness, composure, coolness, equanimity, hush, imperturbability, peace, peacefulness, placidity, quiet, quietness, quietude, repose, rest, restfulness, sedateness, serenity, stillness

tranquillize calm, compose, lull, pacify, quell, quiet, relax, sedate, settle one's nerves, soothe

tranquillizer barbiturate, bromide, downer (*Sl.*), opiate, red (*Sl.*), sedative

transact accomplish, carry on, carry out, conclude, conduct, discharge, do, enact, execute, handle, manage, negotiate, perform, prosecute, see to, settle, take care of

transaction 1. action, affair, bargain, business, coup, deal, deed, enterprise, event, matter, negotiation, occurrence, proceeding, undertaking **2.** *Plural* affairs, annals, doings, goings-on (*Inf.*), minutes, proceedings, record

transcend eclipse, exceed, excel, go above, go beyond, leave behind, leave in the shade (*Inf.*), outdo, outrival, outshine, outstrip, outvie, overstep, rise above, surpass

transcendent consummate, exceeding, extraordinary, incomparable, matchless, peerless, pre-eminent, second to none, sublime, superior, transcendental, unequalled, unique, unparalleled, unrivalled

transcribe 1. copy out, engross, note, reproduce, rewrite, set out, take down, transfer, write out **2.** interpret, render, translate, transliterate **3.** record, tape, tape-record

transcript carbon, carbon copy, copy, duplicate, manuscript, note, notes, record, reproduction, transcription, translation, transliteration, version

transfer 1. *v.* carry, change, consign, convey, displace, hand over, make over, move, pass on, relocate, remove, shift, translate, transmit, transplant, transport, transpose, turn over **2.** *n.* change, displacement, handover, move, relocation, removal, shift, transference, translation, transmission, transposition

transfix 1. engross, fascinate, halt *or* stop in one's tracks, hold, hypnotize, mesmerize, paralyse, petrify, rivet the attention of, root to the spot, spellbind, stop dead, stun **2.** fix, impale, pierce, puncture, run

through, skewer, spear, spit, trans~
pierce

transform alter, change, convert,
make over, metamorphose, recon~
struct, remodel, renew, revolu~
tionize, transfigure, translate,
transmogrify (*Jocular*), transmute

transformation alteration, change,
conversion, metamorphosis, radi~
cal change, renewal, revolution,
revolutionary change, sea change,
transfiguration, transmogrification
(*Jocular*), transmutation

transgress break, break the law,
contravene, defy, disobey, do *or* go
wrong, encroach, err, exceed, fall
from grace, go astray, go beyond,
infringe, lapse, misbehave, offend,
overstep, sin, trespass, violate

transgression breach, contraven~
tion, crime, encroachment, error,
fault, infraction, infringement, in~
iquity, lapse, misbehaviour, mis~
deed, misdemeanour, offence, sin,
trespass, violation, wrong, wrong~
doing

transgressor criminal, culprit, de~
linquent, evildoer, felon, law~
breaker, malefactor, miscreant,
offender, sinner, trespasser, villain,
wrongdoer

transient brief, ephemeral, eva~
nescent, fleeting, flying, fugacious,
fugitive, here today and gone to~
morrow, impermanent, momen~
tary, passing, short, short-lived,
short-term, temporary, transitory

transit *n.* 1. carriage, conveyance,
crossing, motion, movement, pas~
sage, portage, shipment, transfer,
transport, transportation, travel,
traverse 2. alteration, change,
changeover, conversion, shift,
transition 3. **in transit** during pas~
sage, en route, on the journey, on
the move, on the road, on the way,
while travelling ~*v.* 4. cross, jour~
ney, move, pass, travel, traverse

transition alteration, change,
changeover, conversion, develop~
ment, evolution, flux, metamor~
phosis, metastasis, passage, pass~
ing, progression, shift, transit,
transmutation, upheaval

transitional changing, develop~

mental, fluid, intermediate, pass~
ing, provisional, temporary, tran~
sitionary, unsettled

transitory brief, ephemeral, eva~
nescent, fleeting, flying, fugacious,
here today and gone tomorrow,
impermanent, momentary, pass~
ing, short, short-lived, short-term,
temporary, transient

translate 1. construe, convert, de~
cipher, decode, interpret, para~
phrase, render, transcribe, trans~
literate 2. elucidate, explain, make
clear, paraphrase, put in plain
English, simplify, spell out, state in
layman's language 3. alter, change,
convert, metamorphose, transfig~
ure, transform, transmute, turn 4.
carry, convey, move, remove,
send, transfer, transplant, trans~
port, transpose

translation 1. construction, decod~
ing, gloss, interpretation, para~
phrase, rendering, rendition, tran~
scription, transliteration, version 2.
elucidation, explanation, para~
phrase, rephrasing, rewording,
simplification 3. alteration,
change, conversion, metamorpho~
sis, transfiguration, transforma~
tion, transmutation 4. conveyance,
move, removal, transference,
transposition

translator interpreter, linguist,
metaphrast, paraphrast

transmission 1. carriage, commu~
nication, conveyance, diffusion,
dispatch, dissemination, remission,
sending, shipment, spread, trans~
fer, transference, transport 2.
broadcasting, dissemination, put~
ting out, relaying, sending, showing
3. broadcast, programme, show

transmit 1. bear, carry, communi~
cate, convey, diffuse, dispatch, dis~
seminate, forward, hand down,
hand on, impart, pass on, remit,
send, spread, take, transfer, trans~
port 2. broadcast, disseminate, put
on the air, radio, relay, send, send
out

transparency 1. clarity, clearness,
diaphaneity, diaphanousness,
filminess, gauziness, limpidity,
limpidness, pellucidity, pellucid~

ness, sheerness, translucence, translucency, transparence 2. apparentness, distinctness, explicitness, obviousness, patentness, perspicuousness, plainness, unambiguousness, visibility 3. candidness, directness, forthrightness, frankness, openness, straightforwardness 4. photograph, slide

transparent 1. clear, crystal clear, crystalline, diaphanous, filmy, gauzy, limpid, lucent, lucid, pellucid, seethrough, sheer, translucent, transpicuous 2. apparent, as plain as the nose on one's face (*Inf.*), distinct, easy, evident, explicit, manifest, obvious, patent, perspicuous, plain, recognizable, unambiguous, understandable, undisguised, visible 3. candid, direct, forthright, frank, open, plainspoken, straight, straightforward, unambiguous, unequivocal

transpire 1. *Inf.* arise, befall, chance, come about, come to pass (*Archaic*), happen, occur, take place, turn up 2. become known, be disclosed, be discovered, be made public, come out, come to light, emerge

transplant displace, relocate, remove, resettle, shift, transfer, uproot

transport *v.* 1. bear, bring, carry, convey, fetch, haul, move, remove, run, ship, take, transfer 2. banish, deport, exile, sentence to transportation 3. captivate, carry away, delight, electrify, enchant, enrapture, entrance, move, ravish, spellbind ~n. 4. conveyance, transportation, vehicle 5. carriage, conveyance, removal, shipment, shipping, transference, transportation 6. cloud nine (*Inf.*), enchantment, euphoria, heaven, rapture, seventh heaven 7. bliss, delight, ecstasy, happiness, ravishment

transpose alter, change, exchange, interchange, move, rearrange, relocate, reorder, shift, substitute, swap (*Inf.*), switch, transfer

transverse athwart, crossways, crosswise, diagonal, oblique

trap *n.* 1. ambush, gin, net, noose, pitfall, snare, springe, toils 2. ambush, artifice, deception, device, ruse, stratagem, subterfuge, trick, wile ~v. 3. catch, corner, enmesh, ensnare, entrap, snare, take 4. ambush, beguile, deceive, dupe, ensnare, inveigle, trick

trapped ambushed, at bay, beguiled, caught, cornered, cut off, deceived, duped, ensnared, in a tight corner, in a tight spot, inveigled, netted, snared, stuck (*Inf.*), surrounded, tricked, with one's back to the wall

trappings accoutrements, adornments, decorations, dress, equipment, finery, fittings, fixtures, fripperies, furnishings, gear, livery, ornaments, panoply, paraphernalia, raiment (*Archaic*), things, trimmings

trash 1. balderdash, drivel, foolish talk, hogwash, inanity, nonsense, rot, rubbish, tripe (*Inf.*), trumpery, twaddle 2. dregs, dross, garbage, junk, litter, offscourings, refuse, rubbish, sweepings, waste

trashy brummagem, catchpenny, cheap, cheap-jack (*Inf.*), flimsy, inferior, meretricious, rubbishy, shabby, shoddy, tawdry, thrown together, tinsel, worthless

traumatic agonizing, damaging, disturbing, hurtful, injurious, painful, scarring, shocking, upsetting, wounding

travel *v.* 1. cross, go, journey, make a journey, make one's way, move, proceed, progress, ramble, roam, rove, take a trip, tour, traverse, trek, voyage, walk, wander, wend 2. be transmitted, carry, get through, move ~n. 3. *Usually plural* excursion, expedition, globetrotting, journey, movement, passage, peregrination, ramble, tour, touring, trip, voyage, walk, wandering

traveller 1. excursionist, explorer, globetrotter, gypsy, hiker, holidaymaker, journeyer, migrant, nomad, passenger, tourist, tripper, voyager, wanderer, wayfarer 2. agent, commercial traveller, rep, repre~

sentative, salesman, travelling salesman

travelling *adj.* itinerant, migrant, migratory, mobile, moving, no~ madic, peripatetic, restless, roam~ ing, roving, touring, unsettled, wandering, wayfaring

traverse 1. bridge, cover, cross, cut across, go across, go over, make one's way across, negotiate, pass over, ply, range, roam, span, travel over, wander **2.** balk, contravene, counter, counteract, deny, frus~ trate, go against, hinder, impede, obstruct, oppose, thwart **3.** check, consider, examine, eye, inspect, investigate, look into, look over, pore over, range over, review, scan, scrutinize, study

travesty 1. *n.* burlesque, carica~ ture, distortion, lampoon, mockery, parody, perversion, send-up (*Brit. inf.*), sham, spoof (*Inf.*), takeoff (*Inf.*) **2.** *v.* burlesque, caricature, deride, distort, lampoon, make a mockery of, make fun of, mock, parody, pervert, ridicule, send up (*Brit. inf.*), sham, spoof (*Inf.*), take off (*Inf.*)

treacherous 1. deceitful, disloyal, double-crossing (*Inf.*), double-dealing, duplicitous, faithless, false, perfidious, recreant (*Archaic*), traitorous, treasonable, unfaithful, unreliable, untrue, untrustworthy **2.** dangerous, deceptive, hazardous, icy, perilous, precarious, risky, slippery, slippy (*Inf.*), tricky, unre~ liable, unsafe, unstable

treachery betrayal, disloyalty, double-cross (*Inf.*), double-dealing, duplicity, faithlessness, infidelity, perfidiousness, perfidy, stab in the back, treason

tread *v.* **1.** hike, march, pace, plod, stamp, step, stride, tramp, trudge, walk **2.** crush underfoot, squash, trample **3.** bear down, crush, op~ press, quell, repress, ride rough~ shod over, subdue, subjugate, sup~ press **4. tread on someone's toes** affront, annoy, bruise, disgruntle, get someone's back up (*Sl.*), hurt, hurt someone's feelings, infringe, injure, irk, offend, vex ~*n.* **5.** foot~

fall, footstep, gait, pace, step, stride, walk

treason disaffection, disloyalty, duplicity, lese-majesty, mutiny, perfidy, sedition, subversion, trai~ torousness, treachery

treasonable disloyal, false, muti~ nous, perfidious, seditious, subver~ sive, traitorous, treacherous, trea~ sonous

treasure *n.* **1.** cash, fortune, funds, gold, jewels, money, riches, valu~ ables, wealth **2.** apple of one's eye, darling, gem, jewel, nonpareil, paragon, pearl, precious, pride and joy, prize ~*v.* **3.** adore, cherish, dote upon, esteem, hold dear, idol~ ize, love, prize, revere, value, ven~ erate, worship **4.** accumulate, cache, collect, garner, hoard, hus~ band, lay up, salt away, save, stash (away) (*Inf.*), store up

treasury 1. bank, cache, hoard, re~ pository, store, storehouse, vault **2.** assets, capital, coffers, exchequer, finances, funds, money, resources, revenues

treat *n.* **1.** banquet, celebration, en~ tertainment, feast, gift, party, re~ freshment **2.** delight, enjoyment, fun, gratification, joy, pleasure, satisfaction, surprise, thrill ~*v.* **3.** act towards, behave towards, con~ sider, deal with, handle, look upon, manage, regard, use **4.** apply treatment to, attend to, care for, doctor, medicate, nurse **5.** buy for, entertain, feast, foot *or* pay the bill, give, lay on, pay for, provide, re~ gale, stand (*Inf.*), take out, wine and dine **6.** be concerned with, contain, deal with, discourse upon, discuss, go into, touch upon **7.** bar~ gain, come to terms, confer, have talks, make terms, negotiate, par~ ley

treatise disquisition, dissertation, essay, exposition, monograph, pamphlet, paper, study, thesis, tract, work, writing

treatment 1. care, cure, healing, medication, medicine, remedy, surgery, therapy **2.** action towards, behaviour towards, conduct, deal~

ing, handling, management, manipulation, reception, usage

treaty agreement, alliance, bargain, bond, compact, concordat, contract, convention, covenant, entente, pact

trek 1. *n.* expedition, footslog, hike, journey, long haul, march, odyssey, slog, tramp 2. *v.* footslog, hike, journey, march, plod, range, roam, rove, slog, traipse (*Inf.*), tramp, trudge, yomp

tremble 1. *v.* oscillate, quake, quiver, rock, shake, shake in one's shoes, shiver, shudder, teeter, totter, vibrate, wobble 2. *n.* oscillation, quake, quiver, shake, shiver, shudder, tremor, vibration, wobble

tremendous 1. appalling, awesome, awful, colossal, deafening, dreadful, enormous, fearful, formidable, frightful, gargantuan, gigantic, great, huge, immense, mammoth, monstrous, prodigious, stupendous, terrible, terrific, titanic, towering, vast, whopping (*Inf.*) 2. *Inf.* ace (*Inf.*), amazing, excellent, exceptional, extraordinary, fabulous (*Inf.*), fantastic (*Inf.*), great, incredible, marvellous, super (*Inf.*), terrific (*Inf.*), wonderful

tremor 1. agitation, quaking, quaver, quiver, quivering, shake, shaking, shiver, tremble, trembling, trepidation, vibration, wobble 2. earthquake, quake (*Inf.*), shock

trench channel, cut, ditch, drain, earthwork, entrenchment, excavation, fosse, furrow, gutter, pit, trough, waterway

trenchant 1. acerbic, acid, acidulous, acute, astringent, biting, caustic, cutting, hurtful, incisive, keen, mordant, penetrating, piquant, pointed, pungent, sarcastic, scathing, severe, sharp, tart 2. driving, effective, effectual, emphatic, energetic, forceful, potent, powerful, strong, vigorous 3. clear, clear-cut, crisp, distinct, distinctly defined, explicit, salient, unequivocal, well-defined

trend *n.* 1. bias, course, current, direction, drift, flow, inclination, leaning, tendency 2. craze, fad (*Inf.*), fashion, look, mode, rage, style, thing, vogue ~*v.* 3. bend, flow, head, incline, lean, run, stretch, swing, tend, turn, veer

trepidation agitation, alarm, anxiety, apprehension, blue funk (*Inf.*), butterflies (*Inf.*), cold feet (*Inf.*), cold sweat (*Inf.*), consternation, dismay, disquiet, disturbance, dread, emotion, excitement, fear, fright, jitters (*Inf.*), nervousness, palpitation, perturbation, quivering, shaking, the heebie-jeebies (*Sl.*), trembling, tremor, uneasiness, worry

trespass *v.* 1. encroach, infringe, intrude, invade, obtrude, poach 2. *Archaic* offend, sin, transgress, violate, wrong ~*n.* 3. encroachment, infringement, intrusion, invasion, poaching, unlawful entry, wrongful entry 4. breach, crime, delinquency, error, evildoing, fault, infraction, iniquity, injury, misbehaviour, misconduct, misdeed, misdemeanour, offence, sin, transgression, wrongdoing

trespasser 1. infringer, interloper, intruder, invader, poacher, unwelcome visitor 2. *Archaic* criminal, delinquent, evildoer, malefactor, offender, sinner, transgressor, wrongdoer

tress braid, curl, lock, plait, ringlet

triad threesome, trilogy, trine, trinity, trio, triple, triplet, triptych, triumvirate, triune

trial *n.* 1. assay, audition, check, dry run (*Inf.*), examination, experience, experiment, probation, proof, test, testing, test-run 2. contest, hearing, judicial examination, litigation, tribunal 3. attempt, crack (*Inf.*), effort, endeavour, go, shot (*Inf.*), stab, try, venture, whack (*Inf.*) 4. adversity, affliction, burden, cross to bear, distress, grief, hardship, hard times, load, misery, ordeal, pain, suffering, tribulation, trouble, unhappiness, vexation, woe, wretchedness 5. bane, bother, hassle (*Inf.*), irritation, nuisance, pain in the neck (*Inf.*), pest, plague (*Inf.*), thorn in one's flesh, vexation ~*adj.* 6. experimental, exploratory, pilot, probationary, provisional, testing

tribe blood, caste, clan, class, division, dynasty, ethnic group, family, gens, house, people, race, seed, sept, stock

tribulation adversity, affliction, bad luck, blow, burden, care, cross to bear, curse, distress, grief, heartache, ill fortune, misery, misfortune, ordeal, pain, reverse, sorrow, suffering, trial, trouble, unhappiness, vexation, woe, worry, wretchedness

tribunal bar, bench, court, hearing, judgment seat, judicial examination, trial

tribute 1. accolade, acknowledgment, applause, commendation, compliment, encomium, esteem, eulogy, gift, gratitude, honour, laudation, panegyric, praise, recognition, respect, testimonial 2. charge, contribution, customs, duty, excise, homage, impost, offering, payment, ransom, subsidy, tax, toll

trick *n.* 1. artifice, con (*Sl.*), deceit, deception, device, dodge, feint, fraud, gimmick, hoax, imposition, imposture, manoeuvre, ploy, ruse, stratagem, subterfuge, swindle, trap, wile 2. antic, cantrip (*Scot.*), caper, device, feat, frolic, gag (*Sl.*), gambol, jape, joke, juggle, legerdemain, leg-pull (*Brit. inf.*), practical joke, prank, put-on (*Sl.*), sleight of hand, stunt 3. art, command, craft, device, expertise, gift, hang (*Inf.*), knack, know-how (*Inf.*), secret, skill, technique 4. characteristic, crotchet, foible, habit, idiosyncrasy, mannerism, peculiarity, practice, quirk, trait 5. **do the trick** *Inf.* be effective *or* effectual, have effect, produce the desired result, work ~*v.* 6. bamboozle (*Inf.*), cheat, con (*Sl.*), deceive, defraud, delude, dupe, fool, gull (*Archaic*), have (someone) on, hoax, hoodwink, impose upon, mislead, pull the wool over (someone's) eyes, put one over on (someone) (*Inf.*), swindle, take in (*Inf.*), trap

trickery cheating, chicanery, con (*Sl.*), deceit, deception, dishonesty, double-dealing, fraud, funny business, guile, hanky-panky (*Inf.*), hoax, imposture, jiggery-pokery (*Inf.*), monkey business (*Inf.*), pretence, skulduggery (*Inf.*), swindling

trickle 1. *v.* crawl, creep, dribble, drip, drop, exude, ooze, percolate, run, seep, stream 2. *n.* dribble, drip, seepage

tricky 1. complicated, delicate, difficult, knotty, problematic, risky, sticky (*Inf.*), thorny, ticklish, touch-and-go 2. artful, crafty, cunning, deceitful, deceptive, devious, foxy, scheming, slippery, sly, subtle, wily

trifle *n.* 1. bagatelle, bauble, child's play, gewgaw, knick-knack, nothing, plaything, toy, triviality 2. bit, dash, drop, jot, little, pinch, spot, touch, trace ~*v.* 3. amuse oneself, coquet, dally, dawdle, flirt, fritter, idle, mess about, palter, play, toy, wanton, waste, waste time

trifling empty, frivolous, idle, inconsiderable, insignificant, minuscule, negligible, paltry, petty, piddling (*Inf.*), puny, shallow, silly, slight, small, tiny, trivial, unimportant, valueless, worthless

trigger *v.* activate, bring about, cause, elicit, generate, give rise to, produce, prompt, provoke, set in motion, set off, spark off, start

trim 1. compact, dapper, natty (*Inf.*), neat, nice, orderly, shipshape, smart, soigné, soignée, spick-and-span, spruce, tidy, well-groomed, well-ordered, well turned-out 2. fit, shapely, sleek, slender, slim, streamlined, svelte, willowy ~*v.* 3. barber, clip, crop, curtail, cut, cut back, dock, even up, lop, pare, prune, shave, shear, tidy 4. adorn, array, beautify, bedeck, deck out, decorate, dress, embellish, embroider, garnish, ornament, trick out 5. adjust, arrange, balance, distribute, order, prepare, settle ~*n.* 6. adornment, border, decoration, edging, embellishment, frill, fringe, garnish, ornamentation, piping, trimming 7. condition, fettle, fitness, form, health, order, repair, shape (*Inf.*), situation, state 8. clipping, crop, cut, pruning, shave, shearing, tidy~ ing up, trimming 9. array, attire, dress, equipment, gear, trappings

trimming 1. adornment, border, braid, decoration, edging, embel~ lishment, frill, fringe, garnish, or~ namentation, piping 2. *Plural* ac~ cessories, accompaniments, ap~ purtenances, extras, frills, garnish, ornaments, paraphernalia, trap~ pings 3. *Plural* brash, clippings, cuttings, ends, parings, shavings

trinity threesome, triad, trilogy, trine, trio, triple, triplet, triptych, triumvirate, triune

trinket bagatelle, bauble, bibelot, gewgaw, gimcrack, kickshaw, knick-knack, nothing, ornament, piece of bric-a-brac, toy, trifle

trio threesome, triad, trilogy, trine, trinity, triple, triplet, triptych, tri~ umvirate, triune

trip *n.* 1. errand, excursion, expedi~ tion, foray, jaunt, journey, outing, ramble, run, tour, travel, voyage 2. blunder, boob (*Brit. sl.*), error, fall, false move, false step, faux pas, indiscretion, lapse, misstep, slip, stumble ~*v.* 3. blunder, boob (*Brit. sl.*), err, fall, go wrong, lapse, lose one's balance, lose one's footing, make a false move, make a faux pas, miscalculate, misstep, slip, slip up (*Inf.*), stumble, tumble 4. catch out, confuse, disconcert, put off one's stride, throw off, trap, unset~ tle 5. go, ramble, tour, travel, voy~ age 6. caper, dance, flit, frisk, gambol, hop, skip, spring, tread lightly 7. *Inf.* get high (*Inf.*), get stoned (*Sl.*), take drugs, turn on (*Sl.*) 8. activate, engage, flip, pull, release, set off, switch on, throw, turn on

tripe balderdash, bunkum, claptrap (*Inf.*), drivel, foolish talk, garbage, guff (*Sl.*), hogwash, inanity, non~ sense, poppycock (*Inf.*), rot, rub~ bish, trash, trumpery, twaddle

triple 1. *adj.* threefold, three times as much, three-way, tripartite 2. *n.* threesome, triad, trilogy, trine, trinity, trio, triplet, triumvirate,

triune 3. *v.* increase threefold, tre~ ble, triplicate

triplet threesome, triad, trilogy, trine, trinity, trio, triple, triumvi~ rate, triune

tripper excursionist, holiday~ maker, journeyer, sightseer, tour~ ist, voyager

trite banal, bromidic, clichéd, com~ mon, commonplace, corny (*Sl.*), dull, hack, hackneyed, ordinary, pedestrian, routine, run-of-the-mill, stale, stereotyped, stock, thread~ bare, tired, uninspired, unoriginal, worn

triumph *n.* 1. elation, exultation, happiness, joy, jubilation, pride, rejoicing 2. accomplishment, achievement, ascendancy, attain~ ment, conquest, coup, feat, hit (*Inf.*), mastery, sensation, smash (*Inf.*), smash-hit (*Inf.*), success, *tour de force*, victory, walkover (*Inf.*) ~*v.* 3. *Often with over* best, carry the day, come out on top (*Inf.*), dominate, flourish, get the better of, overcome, overwhelm, prevail, prosper, subdue, succeed, take the honours, thrive, vanquish, win 4. celebrate, crow, exult, gloat, glory, jubilate, rejoice, revel, swagger

triumphant boastful, celebratory, cock-a-hoop, conquering, domi~ nant, elated, exultant, glorious, ju~ bilant, proud, rejoicing, successful, swaggering, triumphal, undefeat~ ed, victorious, winning

trivia details, minutiae, petty de~ tails, trifles, trivialities

trivial commonplace, everyday, frivolous, incidental, inconsequen~ tial, inconsiderable, insignificant, little, meaningless, minor, negli~ gible, paltry, petty, puny, slight, small, trifling, trite, unimportant, valueless, worthless

triviality 1. frivolity, inconsequen~ tiality, insignificance, littleness, meaninglessness, negligibility, paltriness, pettiness, slightness, smallness, triteness, unimpor~ tance, valuelessness, worthlessness 2. detail, no big thing, no great

matter, nothing, petty detail, tech~
nicality, trifle

troop n. 1. assemblage, band, body,
bunch (Inf.), company, contingent,
crew (Inf.), crowd, drove, flock,
gang, gathering, group, herd,
horde, multitude, pack, squad,
swarm, team, throng, unit 2. Plural
armed forces, army, fighting men,
men, military, servicemen, sol~
diers, soldiery ~v. 3. crowd, flock,
march, parade, stream, swarm,
throng, traipse (Inf.)

trophy award, bays, booty, cup,
laurels, memento, prize, souvenir,
spoils

tropical hot, humid, lush, steamy,
stifling, sultry, sweltering, torrid

trot v. 1. canter, go briskly, jog,
lope, run, scamper ~n. 2. brisk
pace, canter, jog, lope, run 3. **on
the trot** Inf. consecutively, in a
row, in succession, one after the
other, without break, without in~
terruption

trot out bring forward, bring up,
come out with, drag up, exhibit,
recite, rehearse, reiterate, relate,
repeat

trouble n. 1. agitation, annoyance,
anxiety, disquiet, distress, grief,
heartache, irritation, misfortune,
pain, sorrow, suffering, torment,
tribulation, vexation, woe, worry 2.
agitation, bother (Inf.), commotion,
discontent, discord, disorder, dis~
satisfaction, disturbance, row,
strife, tumult, unrest 3. ailment,
complaint, defect, disability, dis~
ease, disorder, failure, illness,
malfunction, upset 4. bother, con~
cern, danger, difficulty, dilemma,
dire straits, hot water (Inf.), mess,
nuisance, pest, pickle (Inf.), pre~
dicament, problem, scrape (Inf.),
spot (Inf.) 5. attention, bother,
care, effort, exertion, inconven~
ience, labour, pains, struggle,
thought, work ~v. 6. afflict, agitate,
annoy, bother, discompose, dis~
concert, disquiet, distress, disturb,
fret, grieve, harass, inconvenience,
pain, perplex, perturb, pester,
plague, sadden, torment, upset,
vex, worry 7. be concerned, both~

er, burden, discomfort, discom~
mode, disturb, impose upon, in~
commode, inconvenience, put out
8. exert oneself, go to the effort of,
make an effort, take pains, take
the time

troublemaker agent provocateur,
agitator, firebrand, incendiary, in~
stigator, meddler, mischief-maker,
rabble-rouser, stormy petrel

troublesome 1. annoying, arduous,
bothersome, burdensome, de~
manding, difficult, harassing, hard,
importunate, inconvenient, irk~
some, irritating, laborious, oppres~
sive, pestilential, plaguy (Inf.),
taxing, tiresome, tricky, trying,
upsetting, vexatious, wearisome,
worrisome, worrying 2. disorderly,
insubordinate, rebellious, recalci~
trant, refractory, rowdy, turbulent,
uncooperative, undisciplined, un~
ruly, violent

trough 1. crib, manger, water
trough 2. canal, channel, depres~
sion, ditch, duct, flume, furrow,
gully, gutter, trench, watercourse

trounce beat, clobber (Brit. sl.),
crush, defeat heavily or utterly,
drub, give a hiding (Inf.), give a
pasting (Sl.), hammer (Inf.), lick
(Inf.), make mincemeat of, over~
whelm, paste (Sl.), rout, slaughter
(Inf.), thrash, walk over (Inf.), wipe
the floor with (Inf.)

troupe band, cast, company

trouper actor, artiste, entertainer,
performer, player, theatrical,
thespian

truancy absence, absence without
leave, malingering, shirking, skiv~
ing (Brit. sl.)

truant n. 1. absentee, delinquent,
deserter, dodger, malingerer, run~
away, shirker, skiver (Brit. sl.),
straggler 2. adj. absent, absent
without leave, A.W.O.L., missing,
skiving (Brit. sl.) ~v. 3. absent
oneself, desert, dodge, go missing,
malinger, play truant, run away,
shirk, skive (Brit. sl.), twag (Dia~
lect)

truce armistice, break, ceasefire,
cessation, cessation of hostilities,
intermission, interval, let-up (Inf.),

lull, moratorium, peace, respite, rest, stay, treaty

truck *n.* 1. commercial goods, commodities, goods, merchandise, stock, stuff, wares 2. barter, business, buying and selling, commerce, communication, connection, contact, dealings, exchange, relations, trade, traffic ~*v.* 3. bargain, barter, buy and sell, deal, do business, exchange, have dealings, negotiate, swap, trade, traffic, transact business

truculent aggressive, antagonistic, bad-tempered, bellicose, belligerent, combative, contentious, cross, defiant, fierce, hostile, ill-tempered, itching *or* spoiling for a fight (*Inf.*), obstreperous, pugnacious, scrappy (*Inf.*), sullen, violent

trudge 1. *v.* clump, drag oneself, footslog, hike, lumber, march, plod, slog, stump, traipse (*Inf.*), tramp, trek, walk heavily, yomp 2. *n.* footslog, haul, hike, march, slog, traipse (*Inf.*), tramp, trek, yomp

true *adj.* 1. accurate, actual, authentic, bona fide, correct, exact, factual, genuine, legitimate, natural, precise, pure, real, right, truthful, valid, veracious, veritable 2. confirmed, constant, dedicated, devoted, dutiful, faithful, fast, firm, honest, honourable, loyal, pure, sincere, staunch, steady, true-blue, trustworthy, trusty, unswerving, upright 3. accurate, correct, exact, on target, perfect, precise, proper, spot-on (*Brit. inf.*), unerring ~*adv.* 4. honestly, rightly, truthfully, veraciously, veritably 5. accurately, correctly, on target, perfectly, precisely, properly, unerringly 6. **come true** become reality, be granted, be realized, come to pass, happen, occur

truism axiom, bromide, cliché, commonplace, platitude, stock phrase, trite saying

truly 1. accurately, authentically, beyond doubt, beyond question, correctly, exactly, factually, genuinely, in actuality, in fact, in reality, in truth, legitimately, precisely, really, rightly, truthfully, veraciously, veritably, without a doubt 2. confirmedly, constantly, devotedly, dutifully, faithfully, firmly, honestly, honourably, loyally, sincerely, staunchly, steadily, with all one's heart, with dedication, with devotion 3. exceptionally, extremely, greatly, indeed, of course, really, to be sure, verily, very

trumped-up concocted, contrived, cooked-up (*Inf.*), fabricated, fake, false, falsified, invented, made-up, phoney (*Sl.*), untrue

trumpery *n.* 1. balderdash, bilge (*Inf.*), bunkum, claptrap (*Inf.*), drivel, foolishness, foolish talk, garbage, guff (*Sl.*), hogwash, idiocy, inanity, nonsense, poppycock (*Inf.*), rot, rubbish, stuff, trash, tripe (*Inf.*), twaddle 2. bagatelle, bauble, gewgaw, kickshaw, knick-knack, toy, trifle, trinket ~*adj.* 3. brummagem, cheap, flashy, meretricious, nasty, rubbishy, shabby, shoddy, tawdry, trashy, trifling, useless, valueless, worthless

trumpet *n.* 1. bugle, clarion, horn 2. bay, bellow, call, cry, roar 3. **blow one's own trumpet** boast, brag, crow, sing one's own praises, vaunt ~*v.* 4. advertise, announce, broadcast, extol, noise abroad, proclaim, publish, shout from the rooftops, sound loudly, tout (*Inf.*)

trump up concoct, contrive, cook up (*Inf.*), create, fabricate, fake, invent, make up

truncate abbreviate, clip, crop, curtail, cut, cut short, lop, pare, prune, shorten, trim

truncheon baton, club, cudgel, staff

trunk 1. bole, stalk, stem, stock 2. body, torso 3. proboscis, snout 4. bin, box, case, chest, coffer, crate, kist (*Scot.*), locker, portmanteau

truss *v.* 1. bind, bundle, fasten, make fast, pack, pinion, secure, strap, tether, tie ~*n.* 2. beam, brace, buttress, joist, prop, shore, stanchion, stay, strut, support 3. *Medical* bandage, support 4. bale, bundle, package, packet

trust *n.* 1. assurance, belief, certainty, certitude, confidence, conviction, credence, credit, expectation, faith, hope, reliance 2. duty, obligation, responsibility 3. care, charge, custody, guard, guardianship, protection, safekeeping, trusteeship ~v. 4. assume, believe, expect, hope, presume, suppose, surmise, think likely 5. bank on, believe, count on, depend on, have faith in, lean on, pin one's faith on, place confidence in, place one's trust in, place reliance on, rely upon, swear by, take at face value 6. assign, command, commit, confide, consign, delegate, entrust, give, put into the hands of, sign over, turn over

trustful, trusting confiding, credulous, gullible, innocent, naive, optimistic, simple, unguarded, unsuspecting, unsuspicious, unwary

trustworthy dependable, ethical, honest, honourable, level-headed, mature, principled, reliable, responsible, righteous, sensible, steadfast, to be trusted, true, trusty, truthful, upright

trusty dependable, faithful, firm, honest, reliable, responsible, solid, staunch, steady, straightforward, strong, true, trustworthy, upright

truth 1. accuracy, actuality, exactness, fact, factuality, factualness, genuineness, legitimacy, precision, reality, truthfulness, validity, veracity, verity 2. candour, constancy, dedication, devotion, dutifulness, faith, faithfulness, fidelity, frankness, honesty, integrity, loyalty, naturalism, realism, uprightness 3. axiom, certainty, fact, law, maxim, proven principle, reality, truism, verity

truthful accurate, candid, correct, exact, faithful, forthright, frank, honest, literal, naturalistic, plainspoken, precise, realistic, reliable, sincere, straight, straightforward, true, trustworthy, veracious, veritable

try v. 1. aim, attempt, do one's best, do one's damnedest (Inf.), endeavour, essay, exert oneself, have a go (crack, shot, stab, whack), make an attempt, make an effort, seek, strive, struggle, undertake 2. appraise, check out, evaluate, examine, experiment, inspect, investigate, prove, put to the test, sample, taste, test 3. afflict, annoy, inconvenience, irk, irritate, pain, plague, strain, stress, tax, tire, trouble, upset, vex, weary 4. adjudge, adjudicate, examine, hear ~n. 5. attempt, crack (Inf.), effort, endeavour, essay, go, shot (Inf.), stab, whack (Inf.) 6. appraisal, evaluation, experiment, inspection, sample, taste, test, trial

trying aggravating (Inf.), annoying, arduous, bothersome, difficult, exasperating, fatiguing, hard, irksome, irritating, stressful, taxing, tiresome, tough, troublesome, upsetting, vexing, wearisome

try out appraise, check out, evaluate, experiment with, inspect, put into practice, put to the test, sample, taste, test

tsar, czar autocrat, despot, emperor, head, leader, overlord, ruler, sovereign, tyrant

tuck v. 1. fold, gather, insert, push ~n. 2. fold, gather, pinch, pleat 3. Inf. comestibles, eats (Sl.), food, grub (Sl.), nosh (Sl.), scoff (Sl.), victuals

tuck in 1. bed down, enfold, fold under, make snug, put to bed, swaddle, wrap up 2. eat heartily, get stuck in (Sl.)

tug 1. v. drag, draw, haul, heave, jerk, lug, pull, tow, wrench, yank 2. n. drag, haul, heave, jerk, pull, tow, traction, wrench, yank

tuition education, instruction, lessons, schooling, teaching, training, tutelage, tutoring

tumble 1. v. drop, fall, fall end over end, fall headlong, fall head over heels, flop, lose one's footing, pitch, plummet, roll, stumble, topple, toss, trip up 2. n. collapse, drop, fall, flop, headlong fall, plunge, roll, spill, stumble, toss, trip

tumble-down crumbling, decrepit, dilapidated, disintegrating, falling to pieces, ramshackle, rickety, ruined, shaky, tottering

tumour cancer, carcinoma (Medical), growth, lump, neoplasm

(*Medical*), sarcoma (*Medical*), swelling

tumult ado, affray (*Law*), agitation, altercation, bedlam, brawl, brou~ haha, clamour, commotion, din, disorder, disturbance, excitement, fracas, hubbub, hullabaloo, out~ break, pandemonium, quarrel, racket, riot, row, ruction (*Inf.*), stir, strife, turmoil, unrest, upheaval, uproar

tumultuous agitated, boisterous, clamorous, confused, disorderly, disturbed, excited, fierce, hectic, irregular, lawless, noisy, obstrep~ erous, passionate, raging, restless, riotous, rowdy, rumbustious, stormy, turbulent, unrestrained, unruly, uproarious, violent, vocif~ erous, wild

tune *n.* 1. air, melody, melody line, motif, song, strain, theme 2. agreement, concert, concord, con~ sonance, euphony, harmony, pitch, sympathy, unison 3. attitude, de~ meanour, disposition, frame of mind, mood 4. **call the tune** be in charge (command, control), call the shots (*Sl.*), command, dictate, govern, lead, rule, rule the roost 5. **change one's tune** change one's mind, do an about-face, have a change of heart, reconsider, take a different tack, think again ~*v.* 6. adapt, adjust, attune, bring into harmony, harmonize, pitch, regu~ late

tuneful catchy, consonant (*Music*), easy on the ear (*Inf.*), euphonious, harmonious, mellifluous, melodic, melodious, musical, pleasant, sym~ phonic

tuneless atonal, cacophonous, clashing, discordant, dissonant, harsh, unmelodic, unmelodious, unmusical

tunnel 1. *n.* burrow, channel, hole, passage, passageway, shaft, sub~ way, underpass 2. *v.* burrow, dig, dig one's way, excavate, mine, penetrate, scoop out, undermine

turbulence agitation, boiling, commotion, confusion, disorder, instability, pandemonium, rough~ ness, storm, tumult, turmoil, un~ rest, upheaval

turbulent 1. agitated, blustery, boiling, choppy, confused, disor~ dered, foaming, furious, raging, rough, tempestuous, tumultuous, unsettled, unstable 2. agitated, an~ archic, boisterous, disorderly, in~ subordinate, lawless, mutinous, obstreperous, rebellious, refrac~ tory, riotous, rowdy, seditious, tu~ multuous, unbridled, undisciplined, ungovernable, unruly, uproarious, violent, wild

turf 1. clod, divot, grass, green, sod, sward 2. **the turf** horse-racing, racecourse, racetrack, racing, the flat

turmoil agitation, bedlam, brouha~ ha, bustle, chaos, commotion, con~ fusion, disorder, disturbance, fer~ ment, flurry, hubbub, noise, pan~ demonium, row, stir, strife, trouble, tumult, turbulence, uproar, vio~ lence

turn *v.* 1. circle, go round, gyrate, move in a circle, pivot, revolve, roll, rotate, spin, swivel, twirl, twist, wheel, whirl 2. change course, change position, go back, move, return, reverse, shift, swerve, switch, veer, wheel 3. arc, come round, corner, go round, ne~ gotiate, pass, pass around, take a bend 4. adapt, alter, become, change, convert, divert, fashion, fit, form, metamorphose, mould, mutate, remodel, shape, transfig~ ure, transform, transmute 5. be~ come rancid, curdle, go bad, go off (*Brit. inf.*), go sour, make rancid, sour, spoil, taint 6. appeal, apply, approach, go, have recourse, look, resort 7. nauseate, sicken, upset 8. apostatize, bring round (*Inf.*), change one's mind, change sides, defect, desert, go over, influence, persuade, prejudice, prevail upon, renege, retract, talk into 9. con~ struct, deliver, execute, fashion, frame, make, mould, perform, shape, write 10. **turn tail** beat a hasty retreat, bolt, cut and run (*Inf.*), flee, run away, run off, show a clean pair of heels, take off (*Inf.*), take to one's heels ~*n.* 11. bend,

change, circle, curve, cycle, gyra~
tion, pivot, reversal, revolution,
rotation, spin, swing, turning, twist,
whirl 12. bias, direction, drift,
heading, tendency, trend 13. bend,
change of course, change of direc~
tion, curve, departure, deviation,
shift 14. chance, crack (*Inf.*), fling,
go, opportunity, period, round,
shift, shot (*Inf.*), spell, stint, suc~
cession, time, try, whack (*Inf.*) 15.
airing, circuit, constitutional, drive,
excursion, jaunt, outing, prom~
enade, ride, saunter, spin (*Inf.*),
stroll, walk 16. affinity, aptitude,
bent, bias, flair, gift, inclination,
knack, leaning, propensity, talent
17. cast, fashion, form, format,
guise, make-up, manner, mode,
mould, shape, style, way 18. act,
action, deed, favour, gesture, ser~
vice 19. bend, distortion, twist,
warp 20. *Inf.* fright, scare, shock,
start, surprise 21. **by turns** alter~
nately, in succession, one after an~
other, reciprocally, turn and turn
about

turn down 1. diminish, lessen,
lower, muffle, mute, quieten, re~
duce the volume of, soften 2. de~
cline, rebuff, refuse, reject, repu~
diate, say no to, spurn, throw out

turn in 1. go to bed, go to sleep, hit
the sack (*Sl.*), retire for the night 2.
deliver, give back, give up, hand in,
hand over, return, submit, surren~
der, tender

turning bend, crossroads, curve,
junction, side road, turn, turn-off

turning point change, climacteric,
crisis, critical moment, crossroads,
crux, decisive moment, moment of
decision, moment of truth

turn off 1. branch off, change di~
rection, depart from, deviate,
leave, quit, take another road, take
a side road 2. cut out, kill, put out,
shut down, stop, switch off, turn
out, unplug

turn on 1. activate, energize, ignite,
put on, set in motion, start, start
up, switch on 2. balance, be con~
tingent on, be decided by, depend,
hang, hinge, pivot, rest 3. assail,

assault, attack, fall on, lose one's
temper with, round on

turn out 1. put out, switch off, turn
off, unplug 2. bring out, fabricate,
finish, make, manufacture, pro~
cess, produce, put out 3. axe (*Inf.*),
banish, cashier, cast out, deport,
discharge, dismiss, dispossess,
drive out, drum out, evict, expel,
fire (*Inf.*), give one the sack (*Inf.*),
kick out (*Inf.*), oust, put out, sack
(*Inf.*), throw out, turf out (*Brit.
inf.*), unseat 4. become, come
about, come to be, come to light,
crop up (*Inf.*), develop, emerge,
end up, eventuate, evolve, happen,
prove to be, result, transpire (*Inf.*),
work out 5. accoutre, apparel (*Ar~
chaic*), attire, clothe, dress, fit,
outfit, rig out

turn up 1. appear, arrive, attend,
come, put in an appearance, show
(*Sl.*), show one's face, show up
(*Inf.*) 2. appear, become known, be
found, bring to light, come to light,
come to pass, come up with, crop
up (*Inf.*), dig up, disclose, discover,
expose, find, pop up, reveal, tran~
spire, unearth

tussle 1. *v.* battle, brawl, contend,
fight, grapple, scrap (*Inf.*), scuffle,
struggle, vie, wrestle 2. *n.* battle,
bout, brawl, competition, conflict,
contention, contest, fight, fracas,
fray, punch-up (*Inf.*), scrap (*Inf.*),
scuffle, set-to (*Inf.*), struggle

tutor 1. *n.* coach, educator, gover~
nor, guardian, guide, guru, instruc~
tor, lecturer, master, mentor, pre~
ceptor, schoolmaster, teacher 2. *v.*
coach, direct, discipline, drill, edi~
fy, educate, guide, instruct, lecture,
school, teach, train

twilight *n.* 1. dimness, dusk, eve~
ning, gloaming (*Scot.*), half-light,
sundown, sunset 2. decline, ebb,
last phase ~*adj.* 3. crepuscular,
darkening, dim, evening

twin 1. *n.* clone, corollary, counter~
part, double, duplicate, fellow,
likeness, lookalike, match, mate,
ringer (*Sl.*) 2. *adj.* corresponding,
double, dual, duplicate, geminate,
identical, matched, matching,
paired, parallel, twofold

twine *n.* 1. cord, string, yarn 2. coil, convolution, interlacing, twist, whorl 3. knot, snarl, tangle ~*v.* 4. braid, entwine, interlace, interweave, knit, plait, splice, twist, twist together, weave 5. bend, coil, curl, encircle, loop, meander, spiral, surround, twist, wind, wrap, wreathe

twinkling 1. blink, coruscation, flash, flashing, flicker, gleam, glimmer, glistening, glittering, scintillation, shimmer, shining, sparkle, twinkle, wink 2. flash, instant, jiffy (*Inf.*), moment, second, shake (*Inf.*), split second, tick (*Inf.*), trice, twinkle, two shakes of a lamb's tail (*Inf.*)

twirl *v.* 1. gyrate, pirouette, pivot, revolve, rotate, spin, turn, turn on one's heel, twiddle, twist, wheel, whirl, wind ~*n.* 2. gyration, pirouette, revolution, rotation, spin, turn, twist, wheel, whirl 3. coil, spiral, twist

twist *v.* 1. coil, corkscrew, curl, encircle, entwine, intertwine, screw, spin, swivel, twine, weave, wind, wrap, wreathe, wring 2. contort, distort, screw up 3. rick, sprain, turn, wrench 4. alter, change, distort, falsify, garble, misquote, misrepresent, pervert, warp 5. squirm, wriggle, writhe ~*n.* 6. coil, curl, spin, swivel, twine, wind 7. braid, coil, curl, hank, plug, quid, roll 8. change, development, revelation, slant, surprise, turn, variation 9. arc, bend, convolution, curve, meander, turn, undulation, zigzag 10. defect, deformation, distortion, flaw, imperfection, kink, warp 11. jerk, pull, sprain, turn, wrench 12. aberration, bent, characteristic, crotchet, eccentricity, fault, foible, idiosyncrasy, oddity, peculiarity, proclivity, quirk, trait 13. confusion, entanglement, kink, knot, mess, mix-up, snarl, tangle

twit ass, blockhead, chump (*Inf.*), clown, dope (*Sl.*), fool, halfwit, idiot, juggins (*Brit. inf.*), nincompoop, ninny, nitwit, silly-billy (*Inf.*), simpleton, twerp (*Inf.*)

twitch 1. *v.* blink, flutter, jerk, jump, pluck, pull, snatch, squirm, tug, yank 2. *n.* blink, flutter, jerk, jump, pull, spasm, tic, tremor, twinge

tycoon baron, big cheese (*Sl.*), big noise (*Sl.*), capitalist, captain of industry, fat cat (*Sl.*), financier, industrialist, magnate, merchant prince, mogul, plutocrat, potentate, wealthy businessman

type 1. breed, category, class, classification, form, genre, group, ilk, kidney, kind, order, sort, species, strain, subdivision, variety 2. case, characters, face, fount, print, printing 3. archetype, epitome, essence, example, exemplar, model, original, paradigm, pattern, personification, prototype, quintessence, specimen, standard

typhoon cyclone, squall, storm, tempest, tornado, tropical storm

typical archetypal, average, characteristic, classic, conventional, essential, illustrative, in character, indicative, in keeping, model, normal, orthodox, representative, standard, stock, true to type, usual

typify characterize, embody, epitomize, exemplify, illustrate, incarnate, personify, represent, sum up, symbolize

tyrannical absolute, arbitrary, authoritarian, autocratic, coercive, cruel, despotic, dictatorial, domineering, high-handed, imperious, inhuman, magisterial, oppressive, overbearing, overweening, peremptory, severe, tyrannous, unjust, unreasonable

tyranny absolutism, authoritarianism, autocracy, coercion, cruelty, despotism, dictatorship, harsh discipline, high-handedness, imperiousness, oppression, peremptoriness, reign of terror, unreasonableness

tyrant absolutist, authoritarian, autocrat, bully, despot, dictator, Hitler, martinet, oppressor, slavedriver

tyro apprentice, beginner, catechumen, greenhorn (*Inf.*), initiate, learner, neophyte, novice, novitiate, pupil, student, trainee

U

ubiquitous all-over, ever-present, everywhere, omnipresent, pervasive, universal

ugly 1. hard-favoured, hard-featured, homely (*Chiefly U.S.*), ill-favoured, misshapen, not much to look at, plain, unattractive, unlovely, unprepossessing, unsightly 2. disagreeable, disgusting, distasteful, frightful, hideous, horrid, monstrous, objectionable, offensive, repugnant, repulsive, revolting, shocking, terrible, unpleasant, vile 3. dangerous, forbidding, menacing, ominous, sinister, threatening 4. angry, bad-tempered, dark, evil, malevolent, nasty, spiteful, sullen, surly

ulcer abscess, boil, fester, gathering, gumboil, peptic ulcer, pustule, sore

ulterior concealed, covert, hidden, personal, secondary, secret, selfish, undisclosed, unexpressed

ultimate *adj.* 1. conclusive, decisive, end, eventual, extreme, final, furthest, last, terminal 2. extreme, greatest, highest, maximum, most significant, paramount, superlative, supreme, topmost, utmost 3. basic, elemental, fundamental, primary, radical ~*n.* 4. culmination, epitome, extreme, greatest, height, peak, perfection, summit, the last word

ultimately after all, at last, basically, eventually, finally, fundamentally, in due time, in the end, sooner or later

umbrage anger, chagrin, displeasure, grudge, high dudgeon, huff, indignation, offence, pique, resentment, sense of injury

umbrella 1. brolly (*Brit. inf.*), gamp (*Brit. inf.*) 2. aegis, agency, cover, patronage, protection

umpire 1. *n.* adjudicator, arbiter, arbitrator, judge, moderator, ref (*Inf.*), referee 2. *v.* adjudicate, arbitrate, call (*Sport*), judge, moderate, referee

unabashed blatant, bold, brazen, confident, unawed, unblushing, unconcerned, undaunted, undismayed, unembarrassed

unable impotent, inadequate, incapable, ineffectual, no good, not able, not equal to, not up to, powerless, unfit, unfitted, unqualified

unabridged complete, full-length, uncondensed, uncut, unexpurgated, unshortened, whole

unacceptable disagreeable, displeasing, distasteful, improper, inadmissible, insupportable, objectionable, offensive, undesirable, unpleasant, unsatisfactory, unwelcome

unaccompanied a cappella (*Music*), alone, by oneself, lone, on one's own, solo, unescorted

unaccountable 1. baffling, incomprehensible, inexplicable, inscrutable, mysterious, odd, peculiar, puzzling, strange, unexplainable, unfathomable, unintelligible 2. astonishing, extraordinary, uncommon, unheard-of, unusual, unwonted 3. clear, exempt, free, not answerable, not responsible, unliable

unaccustomed 1. With to a newcomer to, a novice at, green, inexperienced, not given to, not used to, unfamiliar with, unpractised, unused to, unversed in 2. new, out of the ordinary, remarkable, special, strange, surprising, uncommon, unexpected, unfamiliar, unprecedented, unusual, unwonted

unaffected[1] artless, genuine, honest, ingenuous, naive, natural, plain, simple, sincere, straightforward, unassuming, unpretentious, unsophisticated, unspoilt, unstudied, without airs

unaffected[2] aloof, impervious, not influenced, proof, unaltered, unchanged, unimpressed, unmoved, unresponsive, unstirred, untouched

unafraid confident, daring, daunt~ less, fearless, intrepid, unfearing, unshakable

unalterable fixed, fixed as the laws of the Medes and the Persians, im~ mutable, invariable, permanent, steadfast, unchangeable, unchang~ ing

unanimity accord, agreement, chorus, concert, concord, concur~ rence, consensus, harmony, like~ mindedness, one mind, unison, unity

unanimous agreed, agreeing, at one, common, concerted, concord~ ant, harmonious, in agreement, in complete accord, like-minded, of one mind, united

unanimously by common consent, nem. con., unitedly, unopposed, with one accord, without excep~ tion, without opposition

unanswerable 1. absolute, con~ clusive, incontestable, incontro~ vertible, indisputable, irrefutable, unarguable, undeniable 2. insol~ uble, insolvable, unascertainable, unexplainable, unresolvable

unanswered disputed, ignored, in doubt, open, undecided, undenied, unnoticed, unrefuted, unresolved, unsettled, up in the air, vexed

unappetizing distasteful, insipid, off-putting (*Brit. inf.*), tasteless, unappealing, unattractive, unin~ teresting, uninviting, unpalatable, unpleasant, unsavoury, vapid

unapproachable 1. aloof, chilly, cool, distant, frigid, offish (*Inf.*), remote, reserved, standoffish, un~ friendly, unsociable, withdrawn 2. inaccessible, out of reach, out-of- the-way, remote, un-get-at-able (*Inf.*), unreachable

unarmed assailable, defenceless, exposed, helpless, open, open to attack, unarmoured, unprotected, weak, weaponless, without arms

unasked 1. gratuitous, sponta~ neous, unbidden, undemanded, un~ desired, uninvited, unprompted, unrequested, unsought, unwanted 2. off one's own bat, of one's own accord, voluntarily, without prompting

unassailable 1. impregnable, in~ vincible, invulnerable, secure, well-defended 2. absolute, conclu~ sive, incontestable, incontrovert~ ible, indisputable, irrefutable, positive, proven, sound, undeniable

unassertive backward, bashful, diffident, meek, mousy, retiring, self-effacing, timid, timorous, un~ assuming

unassuming diffident, humble, meek, modest, quiet, reserved, re~ tiring, self-effacing, simple, unas~ sertive, unobtrusive, unostenta~ tious, unpretentious

unattached 1. autonomous, free, independent, nonaligned, unaffili~ ated, uncommitted 2. a free agent, available, by oneself, footloose and fancy-free, not spoken for, on one's own, single, unengaged, unmarried

unattended 1. abandoned, disre~ garded, ignored, left alone, not cared for, unguarded, unwatched 2. alone, on one's own, unaccom~ panied, unescorted

unauthorized illegal, unapproved, unconstitutional, unlawful, unoffi~ cial, unsanctioned, unwarranted

unavailing abortive, bootless, fruitless, futile, idle, ineffective, in~ effectual, of no avail, pointless, to no purpose, unproductive, unsuc~ cessful, useless, vain

unavoidable bound to happen, certain, compulsory, fated, ineluc~ table, inescapable, inevitable, in~ exorable, necessary, obligatory, sure

unaware heedless, ignorant, in~ cognizant, oblivious, unconscious, unenlightened, uninformed, un~ knowing, unmindful, unsuspecting

unawares 1. aback, abruptly, by surprise, off guard, on the hop (*Brit. inf.*), suddenly, unexpectedly, unprepared, without warning 2. accidentally, by accident, by mis~ take, inadvertently, mistakenly, unconsciously, unintentionally, un~ knowingly, unwittingly

unbalanced 1. asymmetrical, ir~ regular, lopsided, not balanced, shaky, unequal, uneven, unstable, unsymmetrical, wobbly 2. crazy, demented, deranged, disturbed, eccentric, erratic, insane, irrational, lunatic, mad, *non compos mentis*, not all there, touched, unhinged, unsound, unstable 3. biased, inequitable, one-sided, partial, partisan, prejudiced, unfair, unjust

unbearable insufferable, insupportable, intolerable, oppressive, too much (*Inf.*), unacceptable, unendurable

unbeatable indomitable, invincible, more than a match for, unconquerable, unstoppable, unsurpassable

unbeaten 1. triumphant, unbowed, undefeated, unsubdued, unsurpassed, unvanquished, victorious, winning 2. new, untouched, untried, untrodden, virgin

unbecoming 1. ill-suited, inappropriate, incongruous, unattractive, unbefitting, unfit, unflattering, unsightly, unsuitable, unsuited 2. discreditable, improper, indecorous, indelicate, offensive, tasteless, unseemly

unbelief atheism, disbelief, distrust, doubt, incredulity, scepticism

unbelievable astonishing, beyond belief, far-fetched, implausible, impossible, improbable, inconceivable, incredible, outlandish, preposterous, questionable, staggering, unconvincing, unimaginable, unthinkable

unbeliever agnostic, atheist, disbeliever, doubting Thomas, infidel, sceptic

unbending 1. aloof, distant, formal, inflexible, reserved, rigid, stiff, uptight (*Sl.*) 2. firm, hard-line, intractable, resolute, severe, strict, stubborn, tough, uncompromising, unyielding

unbiased disinterested, dispassionate, equitable, even-handed, fair, impartial, just, neutral, objective, open-minded, unprejudiced

unbidden 1. free, spontaneous, unforced, unprompted, voluntary, willing 2. unasked, uninvited, unwanted, unwelcome

unbind free, loosen, release, set

free, unchain, undo, unfasten, unfetter, unloose, unshackle, untie, unyoke

unblemished flawless, immaculate, perfect, pure, spotless, unflawed, unspotted, unstained, unsullied, untarnished

unborn 1. awaited, embryonic, expected, *in utero* 2. coming, future, hereafter, latter, subsequent, to come

unbounded absolute, boundless, endless, immeasurable, infinite, limitless, unbridled, unchecked, unconstrained, uncontrolled, unlimited, unrestrained, vast

unbreakable armoured, durable, indestructible, infrangible, lasting, nonbreakable, resistant, rugged, shatterproof, solid, strong, toughened

unbridled excessive, intemperate, licentious, rampant, riotous, unchecked, unconstrained, uncontrolled, uncurbed, ungovernable, ungoverned, unrestrained, unruly, violent, wanton

unbroken 1. complete, entire, intact, solid, total, unimpaired, whole 2. ceaseless, constant, continuous, endless, incessant, progressive, serried, successive, uninterrupted, unremitting 3. deep, fast, profound, sound, undisturbed, unruffled, untroubled 4. unbowed, unsubdued, untamed

unburden 1. disburden, discharge, disencumber, ease the load, empty, lighten, relieve, unload 2. come clean (*Inf.*), confess, confide, disclose, get (something) off one's chest (*Inf.*), lay bare, make a clean breast of, reveal, tell all, unbosom

uncalled-for gratuitous, inappropriate, needless, undeserved, unjust, unjustified, unnecessary, unprovoked, unwarranted, unwelcome

uncanny 1. creepy (*Inf.*), eerie, eldritch (*Poetic*), mysterious, preternatural, queer, spooky (*Inf.*), strange, supernatural, unearthly, unnatural, weird 2. astonishing, astounding, exceptional, extraordinary, fantastic, incredible, in-

spired, miraculous, prodigious, remarkable, singular, unheard-of,
unusual

unceasing ceaseless, constant,
continual, continuing, continuous,
endless, incessant, never-ending,
nonstop, perpetual, persistent, unending, unfailing, unremitting

uncertain 1. ambiguous, chancy,
conjectural, doubtful, incalculable,
indefinite, indeterminate, indistinct, questionable, risky, speculative, undetermined, unforeseeable,
unpredictable 2. ambivalent,
doubtful, dubious, hazy, in two
minds, irresolute, unclear, unconfirmed, undecided, undetermined,
unfixed, unresolved, unsettled, unsure, up in the air, vacillating,
vague 3. changeable, erratic, fitful,
hesitant, inconstant, insecure, irregular, precarious, unpredictable,
unreliable, vacillating, variable,
wavering

uncertainty ambiguity, bewilderment, confusion, dilemma, doubt,
hesitancy, hesitation, inconclusiveness, indecision, irresolution,
lack of confidence, misgiving,
mystification, perplexity, puzzlement, qualm, quandary, scepticism, state of suspense, unpredictability, vagueness

unchangeable changeless, constant, fixed, immutable, inevitable,
invariable, irreversible, permanent, stable, steadfast, strong, unalterable

unchanging abiding, changeless,
constant, continuing, enduring,
eternal, immutable, imperishable,
lasting, permanent, perpetual, unchanged, unfading, unvarying

uncharitable cruel, hardhearted,
insensitive, mean, merciless, stingy, unchristian, unfeeling, unforgiving, unfriendly, ungenerous, unkind, unsympathetic

uncharted not mapped, strange,
undiscovered, unexplored, unfamiliar, unknown, unplumbed, virgin

uncivil bad-mannered, bearish,
boorish, brusque, churlish, discourteous, disrespectful, gruff, ill-

bred, ill-mannered, impolite, rude,
surly, uncouth, unmannerly

uncivilized 1. barbarian, barbaric,
barbarous, illiterate, primitive,
savage, wild 2. beyond the pale,
boorish, brutish, churlish, coarse,
gross, philistine, uncouth, uncultivated, uncultured, uneducated, un-
mannered, unpolished, unsophisticated, vulgar

unclean contaminated, corrupt,
defiled, dirty, evil, filthy, foul, impure, nasty, polluted, soiled, spotted, stained, sullied, tainted

uncomfortable 1. awkward, causing discomfort, cramped, disagreeable, hard, ill-fitting, incommodious, irritating, painful, rough,
troublesome 2. awkward, confused,
discomfited, disquieted, distressed,
disturbed, embarrassed, ill at ease,
out of place, self-conscious, troubled, uneasy

uncommitted floating, free, free-
floating, neutral, nonaligned, nonpartisan, not involved, (sitting) on
the fence, unattached, uninvolved

uncommon 1. bizarre, curious, few
and far between, infrequent, novel,
odd, out of the ordinary, peculiar,
queer, rare, scarce, singular,
strange, unfamiliar, unusual 2. distinctive, exceptional, extraordinary, incomparable, inimitable,
notable, noteworthy, outstanding,
rare, remarkable, singular, special,
superior, unparalleled, unprecedented

uncommonly 1. hardly ever, infrequently, not often, occasionally,
only now and then, rarely, scarcely
ever, seldom 2. exceptionally, extremely, particularly, peculiarly,
remarkably, strangely, unusually,
very

uncommunicative close, curt,
guarded, reserved, reticent, retiring, secretive, short, shy, silent,
taciturn, tight-lipped, unforthcoming, unresponsive, unsociable,
withdrawn

uncompromising decided, firm,
hard-line, inexorable, inflexible,
intransigent, obdurate, obstinate,

rigid, steadfast, strict, stubborn, tough, unbending, unyielding

unconcern aloofness, apathy, detachment, indifference, insouciance, lack of interest, nonchalance, remoteness, uninterest, uninterestedness

unconcerned 1. aloof, apathetic, cool, detached, dispassionate, distant, incurious, indifferent, oblivious, uninterested, uninvolved, unmoved, unsympathetic 2. blithe, carefree, careless, easy, insouciant, nonchalant, not bothered, relaxed, serene, unperturbed, unruffled, untroubled, unworried

unconditional absolute, categorical, complete, downright, entire, explicit, full, out-and-out, outright, plenary, positive, thoroughgoing, total, unlimited, unqualified, unreserved, unrestricted, utter

uncongenial antagonistic, antipathetic, disagreeable, discordant, displeasing, distasteful, incompatible, not one's cup of tea (*Inf.*), unharmonious, uninviting, unpleasant, unsuited, unsympathetic

unconnected 1. detached, disconnected, divided, independent, separate 2. disconnected, disjointed, illogical, incoherent, irrelevant, meaningless, nonsensical, not related, unrelated

unconquerable 1. indomitable, invincible, unbeatable, undefeatable, unyielding 2. enduring, ingrained, innate, insurmountable, inveterate, irrepressible, irresistible, overpowering

unconscionable 1. amoral, criminal, unethical, unfair, unjust, unprincipled, unscrupulous 2. excessive, exorbitant, extravagant, extreme, immoderate, inordinate, outrageous, preposterous, unreasonable

unconscious 1. blacked out (*Inf.*), comatose, dead to the world, insensible, knocked out, numb, out, out cold, senseless, stunned 2. blind to, deaf to, heedless, ignorant, in ignorance, lost to, oblivious, unaware, unknowing, unmindful, unsuspecting 3. accidental, inadvertent, unintended, unintentional, unpremeditated, unwitting 4. automatic, gut (*Inf.*), inherent, innate, instinctive, involuntary, latent, reflex, repressed, subconscious, subliminal, suppressed, unrealized

uncontrollable beside oneself, carried away, frantic, furious, irrepressible, irresistible, like one possessed, mad, strong, ungovernable, unmanageable, unruly, violent, wild

uncontrolled boisterous, furious, lacking self-control, out of control, out of hand, rampant, riotous, running wild, unbridled, unchecked, uncurbed, undisciplined, ungoverned, unrestrained, unruly, unsubmissive, untrammelled, violent

unconventional atypical, bizarre, bohemian, different, eccentric, far-out (*Sl.*), freakish (*Inf.*), idiosyncratic, individual, individualistic, informal, irregular, nonconformist, odd, offbeat, original, out of the ordinary, uncustomary, unorthodox, unusual, way-out (*Inf.*)

unconvincing dubious, feeble, fishy (*Inf.*), flimsy, hard to believe, implausible, improbable, inconclusive, lame, questionable, specious, suspect, thin, unlikely, unpersuasive, weak

uncoordinated all thumbs, awkward, bumbling, bungling, butterfingered (*Inf.*), clodhopping (*Inf.*), clumsy, graceless, heavy-footed, inept, lumbering, maladroit, ungainly, ungraceful

uncounted countless, infinite, innumerable, legion, multitudinous, myriad, numberless, unnumbered, untold

uncouth awkward, barbaric, boorish, clownish, clumsy, coarse, crude, gawky, graceless, gross, ill-mannered, loutish, lubberly, oafish, rough, rude, rustic, uncivilized, uncultivated, ungainly, unrefined, unseemly, vulgar

uncover 1. bare, lay open, lift the lid, open, show, strip, take the wraps off, unwrap 2. bring to light, disclose, discover, divulge, expose,

lay bare, make known, reveal, un~
earth, unmask

uncritical easily pleased, indis~
criminate, undiscerning, undis~
criminating, unexacting, unfussy,
unperceptive, unselective, un~
thinking

undeceive be honest with, correct,
disabuse, disillusion, enlighten,
open (someone's) eyes (to), put
(someone) right, set (someone)
straight, shatter (someone's) illu~
sions

undecided 1. ambivalent, dither~
ing, doubtful, dubious, hesitant, in
two minds, irresolute, swithering
(*Scot.*), torn, uncertain, uncommit~
ted, unsure, wavering 2. debatable,
indefinite, in the balance, moot,
open, pending, tentative, uncon~
cluded, undetermined, unsettled,
up in the air, vague

undecipherable crabbed, cryptic,
hieroglyphic, illegible, impen~
etrable, incomprehensible, indeci~
pherable, indistinct, undistinguish~
able, unreadable, unrecognizable

undefended defenceless, exposed,
naked, open to attack, unarmed,
unfortified, unguarded, unprotect~
ed, vulnerable, wide open

undefiled chaste, clean, clear,
flawless, immaculate, pure, sinless,
spotless, unblemished, unsoiled,
unspotted, unstained, unsullied,
virginal

undefined 1. formless, hazy, in~
definite, indistinct, shadowy, tenu~
ous, vague 2. imprecise, indeter~
minate, inexact, unclear, unex~
plained, unspecified

undemonstrative aloof, cold, con~
tained, distant, formal, impassive,
reserved, restrained, reticent, stiff,
stolid, unaffectionate, uncommu~
nicative, unemotional, unrespon~
sive, withdrawn

undeniable beyond (a) doubt, be~
yond question, certain, clear, evi~
dent, incontestable, incontrovert~
ible, indisputable, indubitable, ir~
refutable, manifest, obvious, pa~
tent, proven, sound, sure, unassail~
able, undoubted, unquestionable

under *prep.* 1. below, beneath, on

the bottom of, underneath 2. di~
rected by, governed by, inferior to,
junior to, reporting to, secondary
to, subject to, subordinate to, sub~
servient to 3. belonging to, com~
prised in, included in, subsumed
under ~*adv.* 4. below, beneath,
down, downward, lower, to the
bottom

underclothes lingerie, smalls
(*Inf.*), underclothing, undergar~
ments, underlinen, underthings
(*Inf.*), underwear, undies (*Inf.*)

undercover clandestine, con~
cealed, confidential, covert, hid~
den, hush-hush (*Inf.*), intelligence,
private, secret, spy, surreptitious,
underground

undercurrent 1. crosscurrent, rip,
rip current, riptide, underflow,
undertow 2. atmosphere, aura,
drift, feeling, flavour, hidden feel~
ing, hint, murmur, overtone, sense,
suggestion, tendency, tenor, tinge,
trend, undertone, vibes (*Inf.*), vi~
brations

undercut 1. sacrifice, sell at a loss,
sell cheaply, undercharge, under~
price, undersell 2. cut away, cut
out, excavate, gouge out, hollow
out, mine, undermine

underdog fall guy (*Inf.*), little fel~
low (*Inf.*), loser, victim, weaker
party

underestimate belittle, hold
cheap, minimize, miscalculate,
misprize, not do justice to, rate too
low, sell short (*Inf.*), set no store
by, think too little of, underrate,
undervalue

undergo bear, be subjected to, en~
dure, experience, go through,
stand, submit to, suffer, sustain,
weather, withstand

underground *adj.* 1. below ground,
below the surface, buried, covered,
subterranean 2. clandestine, con~
cealed, covert, hidden, secret, sur~
reptitious, undercover 3. alterna~
tive, avant-garde, experimental,
radical, revolutionary, subversive
~*n.* **the underground** 4. the metro,
the subway, the tube (*Brit.*) 5. the
Maquis, partisans, the Resistance

undergrowth bracken, brambles,

briars, brush, brushwood, scrub, underbrush, underbush, under~ wood

underhand clandestine, crafty, crooked (*Inf.*), deceitful, deceptive, devious, dishonest, dishonourable, fraudulent, furtive, secret, secre~ tive, sly, sneaky, stealthy, surrep~ titious, treacherous, underhanded, unethical, unscrupulous

underline 1. italicize, mark, rule a line under, underscore **2.** accentu~ ate, bring home, call *or* draw at~ tention to, emphasize, give em~ phasis to, highlight, point up, stress

underling flunky, hireling, inferior, lackey, menial, minion, nonentity, retainer, servant, slave, subordi~ nate, understrapper

underlying 1. concealed, hidden, latent, lurking, veiled **2.** basal, ba~ sic, elementary, essential, funda~ mental, intrinsic, primary, prime, root

undermine 1. dig out, eat away at, erode, excavate, mine, tunnel, undercut, wear away **2.** debilitate, disable, impair, sabotage, sap, sub~ vert, threaten, weaken

underprivileged badly off, de~ prived, destitute, disadvantaged, impoverished, in need, in want, needy, poor

underrate belittle, discount, dis~ parage, fail to appreciate, mis~ prize, not do justice to, set (too) little store by, underestimate, undervalue

undersized atrophied, dwarfish, miniature, pygmy, runtish, runty, small, squat, stunted, tiny, under~ developed, underweight

understand 1. appreciate, appre~ hend, be aware, catch on (*Inf.*), comprehend, conceive, cotton on (*Inf.*), discern, fathom, follow, get, get the hang of (*Inf.*), get to the bottom of, grasp, know, make head or tail of (*Inf.*), make out, pen~ etrate, perceive, realize, recognize, savvy (*Sl.*), see, take in, tumble to (*Inf.*), twig (*Brit. inf.*) **2.** assume, be informed, believe, conclude, gath~ er, hear, learn, presume, suppose, take it, think **3.** accept, appreciate,

be able to see, commiserate, show compassion for, sympathize with, tolerate

understanding *n.* **1.** appreciation, awareness, comprehension, dis~ cernment, grasp, insight, intelli~ gence, judgment, knowledge, pen~ etration, perception, sense **2.** be~ lief, conclusion, estimation, idea, interpretation, judgment, notion, opinion, perception, view, view~ point **3.** accord, agreement, com~ mon view, gentlemen's agreement, meeting of minds, pact ~*adj.* **4.** accepting, compassionate, consid~ erate, discerning, forbearing, for~ giving, kind, kindly, patient, per~ ceptive, responsive, sensitive, sympathetic, tolerant

understood 1. implicit, implied, inferred, tacit, unspoken, unstated **2.** accepted, assumed, axiomatic, presumed, taken for granted

understudy *n.* double, fill-in, re~ placement, reserve, stand-in, sub, substitute

undertake 1. agree, bargain, com~ mit oneself, contract, covenant, engage, guarantee, pledge, prom~ ise, stipulate, take upon oneself **2.** attempt, begin, commence, em~ bark on, endeavour, enter upon, set about, tackle, take on, try

undertaker funeral director, mor~ tician (*U.S.*)

undertaking 1. affair, attempt, business, effort, endeavour, enter~ prise, game, operation, project, task, venture **2.** assurance, com~ mitment, pledge, promise, solemn word, vow, word, word of honour

undertone 1. low tone, murmur, subdued voice, whisper **2.** atmos~ phere, feeling, flavour, hint, sug~ gestion, tinge, touch, trace, under~ current

undervalue depreciate, hold cheap, look down on, make light of, minimize, misjudge, misprize, set no store by, underestimate, under~ rate

underwater submarine, sub~ merged, sunken, undersea

under way afoot, begun, going on,

in motion, in operation, in progress, started

underwear lingerie, smalls (*Inf.*), underclothes, underclothing, undergarments, underlinen, undies (*Inf.*), unmentionables

underweight half-starved, puny, skin and bone, skinny, undernourished, undersized

underworld 1. criminal element, criminals, gangland (*Inf.*), gangsters, organized crime 2. abode of the dead, Hades, hell, infernal region, nether regions, nether world, the inferno

underwrite 1. back, finance, fund, guarantee, insure, provide security, sponsor, subsidize 2. countersign, endorse, initial, sign, subscribe 3. agree to, approve, consent, okay (*Inf.*), sanction

undesirable disagreeable, disliked, distasteful, dreaded, objectionable, obnoxious, offensive, out of place, repugnant, (to be) avoided, unacceptable, unattractive, unpleasing, unpopular, unsavoury, unsuitable, unwanted, unwelcome, unwished-for

undeveloped embryonic, immature, inchoate, in embryo, latent, potential, primordial (*Biol.*)

undignified beneath one, beneath one's dignity, improper, inappropriate, indecorous, inelegant, infra dig (*Inf.*), lacking dignity, unbecoming, ungentlemanly, unladylike, unrefined, unseemly, unsuitable

undisciplined disobedient, erratic, fitful, obstreperous, uncontrolled, unpredictable, unreliable, unrestrained, unruly, unschooled, unsteady, unsystematic, untrained, wayward, wild, wilful

undisguised complete, evident, explicit, genuine, manifest, obvious, open, out-and-out, overt, patent, thoroughgoing, transparent, unconcealed, unfeigned, unmistakable, utter, wholehearted

undisputed accepted, acknowledged, beyond question, certain, conclusive, freely admitted, incontestable, incontrovertible, indis-

putable, irrefutable, not disputed, recognized, sure, unchallenged, uncontested, undeniable, undoubted, unquestioned

undistinguished commonplace, everyday, indifferent, mediocre, no great shakes (*Inf.*), nothing to write home about (*Inf.*), ordinary, pedestrian, prosaic, run-of-the-mill, so-so (*Inf.*), unexceptional, unexciting, unimpressive, unremarkable

undisturbed 1. not moved, quiet, uninterrupted, untouched, without interruption 2. calm, collected, composed, equable, even, motionless, placid, serene, tranquil, unagitated, unbothered, unperturbed, unruffled, untroubled

undivided combined, complete, concentrated, concerted, entire, exclusive, full, solid, thorough, unanimous, undistracted, united, whole, wholehearted

undo 1. disengage, disentangle, loose, loosen, open, unbutton, unfasten, unlock, untie, unwrap 2. annul, cancel, invalidate, neutralize, nullify, offset, reverse, wipe out 3. bring to naught, defeat, destroy, impoverish, invalidate, mar, overturn, quash, ruin, shatter, subvert, undermine, upset, wreck

undoing 1. collapse, defeat, destruction, disgrace, downfall, humiliation, overthrow, overturn, reversal, ruin, ruination, shame 2. affliction, blight, curse, fatal flaw, misfortune, the last straw, trial, trouble, weakness

undone incomplete, left, neglected, not completed, not done, omitted, outstanding, passed over, unattended to, unfinished, unfulfilled, unperformed

undoubted acknowledged, certain, definite, evident, incontrovertible, indisputable, indubitable, obvious, sure, undisputed, unquestionable, unquestioned

undoubtedly assuredly, beyond a shadow of (a) doubt, beyond question, certainly, definitely, doubtless, of course, surely, undeniably, unmistakably, unquestionably, without doubt

undreamed of astonishing, inconceivable, incredible, miraculous, undreamt, unexpected, unforeseen, unheard-of, unimagined, unsuspected, unthought-of

undress 1. *v.* disrobe, divest oneself of, peel off (*Sl.*), shed, strip, take off one's clothes 2. *n.* disarray, dishabille, nakedness, nudity

undue disproportionate, excessive, extravagant, extreme, immoderate, improper, inordinate, intemperate, needless, overmuch, too great, too much, uncalled-for, undeserved, unnecessary, unseemly, unwarranted

unduly disproportionately, excessively, extravagantly, immoderately, improperly, inordinately, out of all proportion, overly, overmuch, unjustifiably, unnecessarily, unreasonably

undying constant, continuing, deathless, eternal, everlasting, immortal, imperishable, indestructible, inextinguishable, infinite, perennial, permanent, perpetual, sempiternal (*Literary*), undiminished, unending, unfading

unearth 1. dig up, disinter, dredge up, excavate, exhume 2. bring to light, discover, expose, ferret out, find, reveal, root up, turn up, uncover

unearthly 1. eerie, eldritch (*Poetic*), ghostly, haunted, nightmarish, phantom, spectral, spooky (*Inf.*), strange, uncanny, weird 2. ethereal, heavenly, not of this world, preternatural, sublime, supernatural 3. abnormal, absurd, extraordinary, ridiculous, strange, ungodly (*Inf.*), unholy (*Inf.*), unreasonable

uneasiness agitation, alarm, anxiety, apprehension, apprehensiveness, disquiet, doubt, misgiving, nervousness, perturbation, qualms, suspicion, worry

uneasy 1. agitated, anxious, apprehensive, discomposed, disturbed, edgy, ill at ease, impatient, jittery (*Inf.*), nervous, on edge, perturbed, restive, restless, troubled, uncomfortable, unsettled, upset, worried 2. awkward, constrained, insecure, precarious, shaky, strained, tense, uncomfortable, unstable 3. bothering, dismaying, disquieting, disturbing, troubling, upsetting, worrying

uneconomic loss-making, nonpaying, non-profit-making, nonviable, unprofitable

uneducated 1. ignorant, illiterate, unlettered, unread, unschooled, untaught 2. benighted, lowbrow, uncultivated, uncultured

unemotional apathetic, cold, cool, impassive, indifferent, listless, passionless, phlegmatic, reserved, undemonstrative, unexcitable, unfeeling, unimpressionable, unresponsive

unemployed idle, jobless, laid off, on the dole (*Brit. inf.*), out of a job, out of work, redundant, resting (*of an actor*), workless

unending ceaseless, constant, continual, endless, eternal, everlasting, incessant, interminable, never-ending, perpetual, unceasing, unremitting

unendurable insufferable, insupportable, intolerable, more than flesh and blood can stand, unbearable

unenthusiastic apathetic, blasé, bored, half-hearted, indifferent, lukewarm, neutral, nonchalant, unimpressed, uninterested, unmoved, unresponsive

unenviable disagreeable, painful, thankless, uncomfortable, undesirable, unpleasant

unequal 1. different, differing, disparate, dissimilar, not uniform, unlike, unmatched, variable, varying 2. *With to* found wanting, inadequate, insufficient, not up to 3. asymmetrical, disproportionate, ill-matched, irregular, unbalanced, uneven

unequalled beyond compare, incomparable, inimitable, matchless, nonpareil, paramount, peerless, pre-eminent, second to none, supreme, transcendent, unmatched,

unparalleled, unrivalled, unsur~
passed, without equal

unequivocal absolute, certain,
clear, clear-cut, decisive, definite,
direct, evident, explicit, incontro~
vertible, indubitable, manifest,
plain, positive, straight, unambigu~
ous, uncontestable, unmistakable

unethical dirty, dishonest, dishon~
ourable, disreputable, illegal, im~
moral, improper, shady (*Inf.*),
underhand, unfair, unprincipled,
unprofessional, unscrupulous,
wrong

uneven 1. bumpy, not flat, not lev~
el, not smooth, rough 2. broken,
changeable, fitful, fluctuating,
intermittent, irregular, jerky,
patchy, spasmodic, unsteady, vari~
able 3. asymmetrical, lopsided, not
parallel, odd, out of true, unbal~
anced 4. disparate, ill-matched,
one-sided, unequal, unfair

uneventful boring, commonplace,
dull, humdrum, monotonous, ordi~
nary, quiet, routine, tedious, unex~
ceptional, unexciting, uninterest~
ing, unmemorable, unremarkable,
unvaried

unexceptional common or garden
(*Inf.*), commonplace, conventional,
insignificant, mediocre, normal,
ordinary, pedestrian, run-of-the-
mill, undistinguished, unimpres~
sive, unremarkable, usual

unexpected abrupt, accidental, a~
stonishing, chance, fortuitous, not
bargained for, out of the blue,
startling, sudden, surprising, unan~
ticipated, unforeseen, unlooked-for,
unpredictable

unfailing 1. bottomless, boundless,
ceaseless, continual, continuous,
endless, inexhaustible, never-
failing, persistent, unflagging, un~
limited 2. certain, constant, de~
pendable, faithful, infallible, loyal,
reliable, staunch, steadfast, sure,
tried and true, true

unfair 1. arbitrary, biased, bigoted,
discriminatory, inequitable, one-
sided, partial, partisan, prejudiced,
unjust 2. crooked (*Inf.*), dishonest,
dishonourable, uncalled-for, un~
ethical, unprincipled, unscrupu~

lous, unsporting, unwarranted,
wrongful

unfaithful 1. deceitful, disloyal,
faithless, false, false-hearted, per~
fidious, recreant (*Archaic*), trai~
torous, treacherous, treasonable,
unreliable, untrustworthy 2. adul~
terous, faithless, fickle, inconstant,
two-timing (*Inf.*), unchaste, untrue
3. distorted, erroneous, imperfect,
imprecise, inaccurate, inexact,
unreliable, untrustworthy

unfamiliar 1. alien, curious, differ~
ent, little known, new, novel, out-
of-the-way, strange, unaccustomed,
uncommon, unknown, unusual 2.
With **with** a stranger to, inexperi~
enced in, unaccustomed to, unac~
quainted, unconversant, unin~
formed about, uninitiated in, un~
practised in, unskilled at, unversed
in

unfashionable antiquated, behind
the times, dated, obsolete, old-
fashioned, old hat, out, outmoded,
out of date, out of fashion, passé,
unpopular

unfasten detach, disconnect, let
go, loosen, open, separate, uncou~
ple, undo, unlace, unlock, untie

unfathomable 1. bottomless, im~
measurable, unmeasured, un~
plumbed, unsounded 2. abstruse,
baffling, deep, esoteric, impen~
etrable, incomprehensible, indeci~
pherable, inexplicable, profound,
unknowable

unfavourable 1. adverse, bad,
contrary, disadvantageous, hostile,
ill-suited, infelicitous, inimical, low,
negative, poor, unfortunate, un~
friendly, unsuited 2. inauspicious,
inopportune, ominous, threatening,
unlucky, unpromising, unpropi~
tious, unseasonable, untimely, un~
toward

unfeeling 1. apathetic, callous,
cold, cruel, hardened, hardhearted,
heartless, inhuman, insensitive,
pitiless, stony, uncaring, unsympa~
thetic 2. insensate, insensible,
numb, sensationless

unfinished 1. deficient, half-done,
imperfect, incomplete, in the
making, lacking, unaccomplished,

uncompleted, undone, unfulfilled, wanting 2. bare, crude, natural, raw, rough, sketchy, unpolished, unrefined, unvarnished

unfit 1. ill-equipped, inadequate, incapable, incompetent, ineligible, no good, not cut out for, not equal to, not up to, unprepared, unqualified, untrained, useless 2. illadapted, inadequate, inappropriate, ineffective, not designed, not fit, unsuitable, unsuited, useless 3. debilitated, decrepit, feeble, flabby, in poor condition, out of kelter, out of shape, out of trim, unhealthy

unflappable calm, collected, composed, cool, impassive, imperturbable, level-headed, not given to worry, self-possessed, unruffled

unflattering 1. blunt, candid, critical, honest, uncomplimentary, warts and all 2. not shown in the best light, not shown to advantage, plain, unattractive, unbecoming, unprepossessing

unflinching bold, constant, determined, firm, resolute, stalwart, staunch, steadfast, steady, unfaltering, unshaken, unshrinking, unswerving, unwavering

unfold 1. disentangle, expand, flatten, open, spread out, straighten, stretch out, undo, unfurl, unravel, unroll, unwrap 2. *Fig.* clarify, describe, disclose, divulge, explain, illustrate, make known, present, reveal, show, uncover 3. bear fruit, develop, evolve, expand, grow, mature

unforeseen abrupt, accidental, out of the blue, startling, sudden, surprise, surprising, unanticipated, unexpected, unlooked-for, unpredicted

unforgettable exceptional, extraordinary, fixed in the mind, impressive, memorable, never to be forgotten, notable

unforgivable deplorable, disgraceful, indefensible, inexcusable, shameful, unjustifiable, unpardonable, unwarrantable

unfortunate 1. adverse, calamitous, disastrous, ill-fated, ill-starred, inopportune, ruinous, unfavour-able, untoward 2. cursed, doomed, hapless, hopeless, luckless, out of luck, poor, star-crossed, unhappy, unlucky, unprosperous, unsuccessful, wretched 3. deplorable, illadvised, inappropriate, infelicitous, lamentable, regrettable, unbecoming, unsuitable

unfounded baseless, fabricated, false, groundless, idle, spurious, trumped up, unjustified, unproven, unsubstantiated, vain, without basis, without foundation

unfrequented deserted, godforsaken, isolated, lone, lonely, off the beaten track, remote, sequestered, solitary, uninhabited, unvisited

unfriendly 1. aloof, antagonistic, chilly, cold, disagreeable, distant, hostile, ill-disposed, inhospitable, not on speaking terms, quarrelsome, sour, surly, uncongenial, unneighbourly, unsociable 2. alien, hostile, inauspicious, inhospitable, inimical, unfavourable, unpropitious

unfruitful barren, fruitless, infecund, infertile, sterile, unproductive, unprofitable, unprolific, unrewarding

ungainly awkward, clumsy, gangling, gawky, inelegant, loutish, lubberly, lumbering, slouching, uncoordinated, uncouth, ungraceful

ungodly 1. blasphemous, corrupt, depraved, godless, immoral, impious, irreligious, profane, sinful, vile, wicked 2. *Inf.* dreadful, horrendous, intolerable, outrageous, unearthly, unholy (*Inf.*), unreasonable, unseemly

ungovernable rebellious, refractory, uncontrollable, unmanageable, unrestrainable, unruly, wild

ungracious bad-mannered, churlish, discourteous, ill-bred, impolite, offhand, rude, uncivil, unmannerly

ungrateful heedless, ingrate (*Archaic*), selfish, thankless, unappreciative, unmindful, unthankful

unguarded 1. careless, foolhardy, heedless, ill-considered, impolitic, imprudent, incautious, indiscreet, rash, thoughtless, uncircumspect, undiplomatic, unthinking, unwary 2. defenceless, open to attack, undefended, unpatrolled, unprotected, vulnerable 3. artless, candid, direct, frank, guileless, open, straightforward

unhappy 1. blue, crestfallen, dejected, depressed, despondent, disconsolate, dispirited, down, downcast, gloomy, long-faced, melancholy, miserable, mournful, sad, sorrowful 2. cursed, hapless, ill-fated, ill-omened, luckless, unfortunate, unlucky, wretched 3. awkward, clumsy, gauche, ill-advised, ill-timed, inappropriate, inept, infelicitous, injudicious, malapropos, tactless, unsuitable, untactful

unharmed in one piece (*Inf.*), intact, safe, safe and sound, sound, undamaged, unhurt, uninjured, unscarred, unscathed, untouched, whole, without a scratch

unhealthy 1. ailing, delicate, feeble, frail, infirm, in poor health, invalid, poorly (*Inf.*), sick, sickly, unsound, unwell, weak 2. deleterious, detrimental, harmful, insalubrious, insanitary, noisome, noxious, unwholesome 3. bad, baneful (*Archaic*), corrupt, corrupting, degrading, demoralizing, morbid, negative, undesirable

unheard-of 1. little known, obscure, undiscovered, unfamiliar, unknown, unregarded, unremarked, unsung 2. inconceivable, never before encountered, new, novel, singular, unbelievable, undreamed of, unexampled, unique, unprecedented, unusual 3. disgraceful, extreme, offensive, outlandish, outrageous, preposterous, shocking, unacceptable, unthinkable

unhesitating 1. implicit, resolute, steadfast, unfaltering, unquestioning, unreserved, unswerving, unwavering, wholehearted 2. immediate, instant, instantaneous, prompt, ready, without delay

unhinge 1. confound, confuse, craze, derange, disorder, distemper (*Archaic*), drive out of one's mind, madden, unbalance, unsettle 2. detach, disconnect, disjoint, dislodge, remove

unholy 1. base, corrupt, depraved, dishonest, evil, heinous, immoral, iniquitous, irreligious, profane, sinful, ungodly, vile, wicked 2. *Inf.* appalling, awful, dreadful, horrendous, outrageous, shocking, unearthly, ungodly (*Inf.*), unnatural, unreasonable

unhoped-for beyond one's wildest dreams, incredible, like a dream come true, out of the blue, surprising, unanticipated, unbelievable, undreamed of, unexpected, unimaginable, unlooked-for

unhurried calm, deliberate, easy, easy-going, leisurely, sedate, slow, slow and steady, slow-paced

unidentified anonymous, mysterious, nameless, unclassified, unfamiliar, unknown, unmarked, unnamed, unrecognized, unrevealed

unification alliance, amalgamation, coalescence, coalition, combination, confederation, federation, fusion, merger, union, uniting

uniform n. 1. costume, dress, garb, habit, livery, outfit, regalia, regimentals, suit ~adj. 2. consistent, constant, equable, even, regular, smooth, unbroken, unchanging, undeviating, unvarying 3. alike, equal, identical, like, same, selfsame, similar

uniformity 1. constancy, evenness, homogeneity, invariability, regularity, sameness, similarity 2. drabness, dullness, flatness, lack of diversity, monotony, sameness, tedium

unify amalgamate, bind, bring together, combine, confederate, consolidate, federate, fuse, join, merge, unite

unimaginable beyond one's wildest dreams, fantastic, impossible, inconceivable, incredible, indescribable, ineffable, mind-boggling (*Inf.*), unbelievable, unheard-of, unthinkable

unimaginative barren, commonplace, derivative, dry, dull, hackneyed, lifeless, matter-of-fact, ordinary, pedestrian, predictable, prosaic, routine, tame, uncreative, uninspired, unoriginal, unromantic, usual

unimpassioned calm, collected, composed, controlled, cool, dispassionate, impassive, moderate, rational, sedate, temperate, tranquil, undemonstrative, unemotional, unmoved

unimpeachable above reproach, beyond criticism, beyond question, blameless, faultless, impeccable, irreproachable, perfect, unassailable, unblemished, unchallengeable, unexceptionable, unquestionable

unimportant immaterial, inconsequential, insignificant, irrelevant, low-ranking, minor, not worth mentioning, nugatory, of no account, of no consequence, of no moment, paltry, petty, slight, trifling, trivial, worthless

uninhabited abandoned, barren, desert, deserted, desolate, empty, unoccupied, unpopulated, unsettled, untenanted, vacant, waste

uninhibited 1. candid, frank, free, free and easy, informal, instinctive, liberated, natural, open, relaxed, spontaneous, unrepressed, unreserved, unselfconscious 2. free, unbridled, unchecked, unconstrained, uncontrolled, uncurbed, unrestrained, unrestricted

uninspired commonplace, dull, humdrum, indifferent, ordinary, prosaic, stale, stock, unexciting, unimaginative, uninspiring, uninteresting, unoriginal

unintelligent brainless, dense, dull, empty-headed, foolish, gormless (*Brit. inf.*), obtuse, slow, stupid, thick, unreasoning, unthinking

unintelligible double Dutch (*Brit. inf.*), illegible, inarticulate, incoherent, incomprehensible, indecipherable, indistinct, jumbled, meaningless, muddled, unfathomable

unintentional accidental, casual, fortuitous, inadvertent, involuntary, unconscious, undesigned, un-

intended, unpremeditated, unthinking, unwitting

uninterested apathetic, blasé, bored, distant, impassive, incurious, indifferent, listless, unconcerned, uninvolved, unresponsive

uninteresting boring, commonplace, drab, dreary, dry, dull, flat, humdrum, monotonous, tedious, tiresome, unenjoyable, uneventful, unexciting, uninspiring, wearisome

uninterrupted constant, continual, continuous, nonstop, peaceful, steady, sustained, unbroken, undisturbed, unending

uninvited not asked, not invited, unasked, unbidden, unwanted, unwelcome

uninviting disagreeable, offensive, off-putting (*Brit. inf.*), repellent, repulsive, unappealing, unappetizing, unattractive, undesirable, unpleasant, untempting, unwelcoming

union 1. amalgam, amalgamation, blend, combination, conjunction, fusion, junction, mixture, synthesis, uniting 2. alliance, association, Bund, coalition, confederacy, confederation, federation, league 3. accord, agreement, concord, concurrence, harmony, unanimity, unison, unity 4. coition, coitus, copulation, coupling, intercourse, marriage, matrimony, wedlock

unique 1. lone, one and only, only, single, solitary, sui generis 2. incomparable, inimitable, matchless, nonpareil, peerless, unequalled, unexampled, unmatched, unparalleled, unrivalled, without equal

unison accord, accordance, agreement, concert, concord, cooperation, harmony, unanimity, unity

unit 1. assembly, detachment, entity, group, section, system, whole 2. component, constituent, element, item, member, module, part, piece, portion, section, segment 3. measure, measurement, module, quantity

unite 1. amalgamate, blend, coalesce, combine, confederate, consolidate, couple, fuse, incorporate, join, link, marry, merge, unify, wed

2. ally, associate, band, close ranks, club together, cooperate, join forces, join together, league, pool, pull together

united 1. affiliated, allied, banded together, collective, combined, concerted, in partnership, leagued, pooled, unified **2.** agreed, in accord, in agreement, like-minded, of like mind, of one mind, of the same opinion, one, unanimous

unity 1. entity, integrity, oneness, singleness, undividedness, unification, union, wholeness **2.** accord, agreement, concord, concurrence, consensus, harmony, peace, solidarity, unanimity

universal all-embracing, catholic, common, ecumenical, entire, general, omnipresent, total, unlimited, whole, widespread, worldwide

universality all-inclusiveness, completeness, comprehensiveness, entirety, generality, generalization, totality, ubiquity

universally always, everywhere, in all cases, in every instance, invariably, uniformly, without exception

universe cosmos, creation, everything, macrocosm, nature, the natural world

unjust biased, inequitable, one-sided, partial, partisan, prejudiced, undeserved, unfair, unjustified, unmerited, wrong, wrongful

unjustifiable indefensible, inexcusable, outrageous, unacceptable, unforgivable, unjust, unpardonable, unwarrantable, wrong

unkind cruel, hardhearted, harsh, inconsiderate, inhuman, insensitive, malicious, mean, nasty, spiteful, thoughtless, uncaring, uncharitable, unchristian, unfeeling, unfriendly, unsympathetic

unknown 1. alien, concealed, dark, hidden, mysterious, new, secret, strange, unrecognized, unrevealed, untold **2.** anonymous, nameless, uncharted, undiscovered, unexplored, unidentified, unnamed **3.** humble, little known, obscure, undistinguished, unfamiliar, unheard-of, unrenowned, unsung

unlamented unbemoaned, unbe-

wailed, undeplored, unmissed, unmourned, unregretted, unwept

unlawful actionable, against the law, banned, criminal, forbidden, illegal, illegitimate, illicit, outlawed, prohibited, unauthorized, unlicensed

unlettered ignorant, illiterate, uneducated, unlearned, unschooled, untaught, untutored

unlike contrasted, different, dissimilar, distinct, divergent, diverse, ill-matched, incompatible, not alike, opposite, unequal, unrelated

unlikely 1. doubtful, faint, improbable, not likely, remote, slight, unimaginable **2.** implausible, incredible, questionable, unbelievable, unconvincing

unlimited 1. boundless, countless, endless, extensive, great, illimitable, immeasurable, immense, incalculable, infinite, limitless, unbounded, vast **2.** absolute, all-encompassing, complete, full, total, unconditional, unconstrained, unfettered, unqualified, unrestricted

unload disburden, discharge, dump, empty, off-load, relieve, unburden, unlade, unpack

unlock free, let loose, open, release, unbar, unbolt, undo, unfasten, unlatch

unlooked-for chance, fortuitous, out of the blue, surprise, surprising, unanticipated, undreamed of, unexpected, unforeseen, unhoped-for, unpredicted, unthought-of

unloved disliked, forsaken, loveless, neglected, rejected, spurned, uncared-for, uncherished, unpopular, unwanted

unlucky 1. cursed, disastrous, hapless, luckless, miserable, unfortunate, unhappy, unsuccessful, wretched **2.** doomed, ill-fated, ill-omened, ill-starred, inauspicious, ominous, unfavourable, untimely

unmanageable 1. awkward, bulky, cumbersome, difficult to handle, inconvenient, unhandy, unwieldy **2.** difficult, fractious, intractable, obstreperous, out of hand, refractory, stroppy (*Brit. sl.*), uncontrollable, unruly, wild

unmannerly badly behaved, bad-mannered, discourteous, disre~spectful, ill-bred, ill-mannered, im~polite, misbehaved, rude, uncivil, uncouth

unmarried bachelor, celibate, maiden, single, unattached, unwed, unwedded, virgin

unmask bare, bring to light, dis~close, discover, expose, lay bare, reveal, show up, uncloak, uncover, unveil

unmatched beyond compare, consummate, incomparable, matchless, paramount, peerless, second to none, supreme, un~equalled, unparalleled, unrivalled, unsurpassed

unmentionable disgraceful, dis~reputable, forbidden, frowned on, immodest, indecent, scandalous, shameful, shocking, taboo, un~speakable, unutterable

unmerciful brutal, cruel, hard, heartless, implacable, merciless, pitiless, relentless, remorseless, ruthless, uncaring, unfeeling, un~sparing

unmindful careless, forgetful, heedless, inattentive, indifferent, lax, neglectful, negligent, oblivious, remiss, slack, unheeding

unmistakable certain, clear, con~spicuous, decided, distinct, evident, glaring, indisputable, manifest, ob~vious, palpable, patent, plain, posi~tive, pronounced, sure, unambigu~ous, unequivocal

unmitigated 1. grim, harsh, in~tense, oppressive, persistent, re~lentless, unabated, unalleviated, unbroken, undiminished, unmodi~fied, unqualified, unredeemed, un~relieved 2. absolute, arrant, com~plete, consummate, downright, out-and-out, outright, perfect, rank, sheer, thorough, thoroughgoing, utter

unmoved 1. fast, firm, in place, in position, steady, unchanged, un~touched 2. cold, dry-eyed, impas~sive, indifferent, unaffected, un~feeling, unimpressed, unrespon~sive, unstirred, untouched 3. de~termined, firm, inflexible, resolute,

resolved, steadfast, undeviating, unshaken, unwavering

unnatural 1. aberrant, abnormal, anomalous, irregular, odd, per~verse, perverted, unusual 2. bi~zarre, extraordinary, freakish, outlandish, queer, strange, super~natural, unaccountable, uncanny 3. affected, artificial, assumed, con~trived, factitious, false, feigned, forced, insincere, laboured, man~nered, phoney (Sl.), self-conscious, stagy, stiff, stilted, strained, stud~ied, theatrical 4. brutal, callous, cold-blooded, evil, fiendish, heart~less, inhuman, monstrous, ruthless, savage, unfeeling, wicked

unnecessary dispensable, ex~pendable, inessential, needless, nonessential, redundant, super~erogatory, superfluous, surplus to requirements, uncalled-for, un~needed, unrequired, useless

unnerve confound, daunt, demor~alize, disarm, disconcert, discour~age, dishearten, dismay, dispirit, fluster, frighten, intimidate, rattle (Inf.), shake, throw off balance, unhinge, unman, upset

unnoticed disregarded, ignored, neglected, overlooked, undiscov~ered, unheeded, unobserved, un~perceived, unrecognized, unre~marked, unseen

unobtrusive humble, inconspicu~ous, keeping a low profile, low-key, meek, modest, quiet, restrained, retiring, self-effacing, subdued, un~assuming, unnoticeable, unosten~tatious, unpretentious

unoccupied 1. empty, tenantless, uninhabited, untenanted, vacant 2. at leisure, disengaged, idle, inac~tive, unemployed

unofficial informal, personal, pri~vate, unauthorized, unconfirmed, wildcat

unorthodox abnormal, heterodox, irregular, unconventional, uncus~tomary, unusual, unwonted

unpaid 1. due, not discharged, out~standing, overdue, owing, payable, unsettled 2. honorary, unsalaried, voluntary

unpalatable bitter, disagreeable,

displeasing, distasteful, offensive, repugnant, unappetizing, unattractive, uneatable, unpleasant, unsavoury

unparalleled beyond compare, consummate, exceptional, incomparable, matchless, peerless, rare, singular, superlative, unequalled, unique, unmatched, unprecedented, unrivalled, unsurpassed, without equal

unpardonable deplorable, disgraceful, indefensible, inexcusable, outrageous, scandalous, shameful, unforgivable, unjustifiable

unperturbed calm, collected, composed, cool, placid, poised, self-possessed, tranquil, undismayed, unflustered, unruffled, untroubled, unworried

unpleasant abhorrent, bad, disagreeable, displeasing, distasteful, ill-natured, irksome, nasty, objectionable, obnoxious, repulsive, troublesome, unattractive, unlikable, unlovely, unpalatable

unpopular avoided, detested, disliked, not sought out, out in the cold, out of favour, rejected, shunned, unattractive, undesirable, unloved, unwanted, unwelcome

unprecedented abnormal, exceptional, extraordinary, freakish, new, novel, original, remarkable, singular, unexampled, unheard-of, unparalleled, unrivalled, unusual

unpredictable chance, changeable, doubtful, erratic, fickle, fluky (*Inf.*), iffy, inconstant, random, unforeseeable, unreliable, unstable, variable

unprejudiced balanced, even-handed, fair, fair-minded, impartial, just, nonpartisan, objective, open-minded, unbiased, uninfluenced

unpremeditated extempore, impromptu, impulsive, offhand, off the cuff (*Inf.*), spontaneous, spur-of-the-moment, unplanned, unprepared

unprepared 1. half-baked (*Inf.*), ill-considered, incomplete, not thought out, unfinished, unplanned 2. caught napping, caught on the

hop (*Brit. inf.*), surprised, taken aback, taken off guard, unaware, unready, unsuspecting 3. ad-lib, extemporaneous, improvised, off the cuff (*Inf.*), spontaneous

unpretentious homely, honest, humble, modest, plain, simple, straightforward, unaffected, unassuming, unimposing, unobtrusive, unostentatious, unspoiled

unprincipled amoral, corrupt, crooked, deceitful, devious, dishonest, immoral, tricky, unconscionable, underhand, unethical, unprofessional, unscrupulous

unproductive 1. bootless, fruitless, futile, idle, ineffective, inefficacious, otiose, unavailing, unprofitable, unremunerative, unrewarding, useless, vain, valueless, worthless 2. barren, dry, fruitless, sterile, unprolific

unprofessional 1. improper, lax, negligent, unethical, unfitting, unprincipled, unseemly, unworthy 2. amateur, amateurish, incompetent, inefficient, inexperienced, inexpert, untrained

unpromising adverse, discouraging, doubtful, gloomy, inauspicious, infelicitous, ominous, unfavourable, unpropitious

unprotected defenceless, exposed, helpless, naked, open, open to attack, pregnable, unarmed, undefended, unguarded, unsheltered, vulnerable

unqualified 1. ill-equipped, incapable, incompetent, ineligible, not equal to, not up to, unfit, unprepared 2. categorical, downright, outright, unconditional, unmitigated, unreserved, unrestricted, without reservation 3. absolute, complete, consummate, downright, out-and-out, thorough, thoroughgoing, total, utter

unquestionable absolute, beyond a shadow of doubt, certain, clear, conclusive, definite, faultless, flawless, incontestable, incontrovertible, indisputable, indubitable, irrefutable, manifest, patent, perfect, self-evident, sure, undeniable, unequivocal, unmistakable

unravel 1. disentangle, extricate, free, separate, straighten out, undo, unknot, untangle, unwind 2. clear up, explain, figure out (*Inf.*), get straight, get to the bottom of, interpret, make out, puzzle out, resolve, solve, work out

unreadable 1. crabbed, illegible, undecipherable 2. badly written, dry as dust, heavy going, turgid

unreal 1. chimerical, dreamlike, fabulous, fanciful, fictitious, illusory, imaginary, make-believe, phantasmagoric, storybook, visionary 2. hypothetical, immaterial, impalpable, insubstantial, intangible, mythical, nebulous 3. artificial, fake, false, insincere, mock, ostensible, pretended, seeming, sham

unrealistic 1. half-baked (*Inf.*), impracticable, impractical, improbable, quixotic, romantic, starry-eyed, theoretical, unworkable 2. non-naturalistic, unauthentic, unlifelike, unreal

unreasonable 1. excessive, exorbitant, extortionate, extravagant, immoderate, steep (*Brit. inf.*), too great, uncalled-for, undue, unfair, unjust, unwarranted 2. arbitrary, biased, blinkered, capricious, erratic, headstrong, inconsistent, opinionated, quirky 3. absurd, far-fetched, foolish, illogical, irrational, mad, nonsensical, preposterous, senseless, silly, stupid

unrefined 1. crude, raw, unfinished, unpolished, unpurified, untreated 2. boorish, coarse, inelegant, rude, uncultured, unsophisticated, vulgar

unregenerate 1. godless, impious, profane, sinful, unconverted, unreformed, unrepentant, wicked 2. hardened, intractable, obdurate, obstinate, recalcitrant, refractory, self-willed, stubborn

unrelated 1. different, dissimilar, not kin, not kindred, not related, unconnected, unlike 2. beside the point, extraneous, inapplicable, inappropriate, irrelevant, not germane, unassociated, unconnected

unreliable 1. disreputable, irresponsible, not conscientious, treacherous, undependable, unstable, untrustworthy 2. deceptive, delusive, erroneous, fake, fallible, false, implausible, inaccurate, mistaken, specious, uncertain, unconvincing, unsound

unrepentant abandoned, callous, hardened, impenitent, incorrigible, not contrite, obdurate, shameless, unregenerate, unremorseful, unrepenting

unreserved 1. demonstrative, extrovert, forthright, frank, free, open, open-hearted, outgoing, outspoken, uninhibited, unrestrained, unreticent 2. absolute, complete, entire, full, total, unconditional, unlimited, unqualified, wholehearted, without reservation

unresolved doubtful, moot, open to question, pending, problematical, unanswered, undecided, undetermined, unsettled, unsolved, up in the air, vague, yet to be decided

unrest 1. agitation, disaffection, discontent, discord, dissatisfaction, dissension, protest, rebellion, sedition, strife, tumult, turmoil 2. agitation, anxiety, disquiet, distress, perturbation, restlessness, uneasiness, worry

unrestrained abandoned, boisterous, free, immoderate, inordinate, intemperate, natural, unbounded, unbridled, unchecked, unconstrained, uncontrolled, unhindered, uninhibited, unrepressed

unrestricted 1. absolute, free, free-for-all (*Inf.*), freewheeling (*Inf.*), open, unbounded, uncircumscribed, unhindered, unlimited, unregulated 2. clear, open, public, unobstructed, unopposed

unrivalled beyond compare, incomparable, matchless, nonpareil, peerless, supreme, unequalled, unexcelled, unmatched, unparalleled, unsurpassed, without equal

unruly disobedient, disorderly, fractious, headstrong, insubordinate, intractable, lawless, mutinous, obstreperous, rebellious, refractory, riotous, rowdy, turbulent, uncontrollable, ungovernable, un~manageable, wayward, wild, wilful

unsafe dangerous, hazardous, in~secure, perilous, precarious, risky, threatening, treacherous, uncer~tain, unreliable, unsound, unstable

unsaid left to the imagination, tac~it, undeclared, unexpressed, un~spoken, unstated, unuttered, un~voiced

unsatisfactory deficient, disap~pointing, displeasing, inadequate, insufficient, mediocre, not good enough, not up to par, not up to scratch (*Inf.*), poor, unacceptable, unsuitable, unworthy, weak

unsavoury 1. distasteful, nasty, ob~jectionable, obnoxious, offensive, repellent, repugnant, repulsive, revolting, unpleasant 2. disagree~able, distasteful, nauseating, sick~ening, unappetizing, unpalatable

unscrupulous conscienceless, corrupt, crooked (*Inf.*), dishonest, dishonourable, exploitative, im~moral, improper, knavish, roguish, ruthless, unconscientious, uncon~scionable, unethical, unprincipled

unseat 1. throw, unhorse, unsaddle 2. depose, dethrone, discharge, dismiss, displace, oust, overthrow, remove

unseemly discreditable, disrepu~table, improper, inappropriate, in~decorous, indelicate, in poor taste, out of keeping, out of place, unbe~coming, unbefitting, undignified, unrefined, unsuitable

unseen concealed, hidden, invis~ible, lurking, obscure, undetected, unnoticed, unobserved, unobtru~sive, unperceived, veiled

unselfish altruistic, charitable, de~voted, disinterested, generous, hu~manitarian, kind, liberal, mag~nanimous, noble, self-denying, selfless, self-sacrificing

unsettle agitate, bother, confuse, discompose, disconcert, disorder, disturb, fluster, perturb, rattle (*Inf.*), ruffle, throw (*Inf.*), throw into confusion (disorder, uproar), throw off balance, trouble, unbal~ance, upset

unsettled 1. disorderly, insecure, shaky, unstable, unsteady 2. changeable, changing, inconstant, uncertain, unpredictable, variable 3. agitated, anxious, confused, dis~turbed, flustered, on edge, per~turbed, restive, restless, shaken, tense, troubled, uneasy, unnerved 4. debatable, doubtful, moot, open, undecided, undetermined, unre~solved 5. due, in arrears, outstand~ing, owing, payable, pending 6. un~inhabited, unoccupied, unpeopled, unpopulated

unshakable absolute, constant, firm, fixed, resolute, staunch, steadfast, sure, unassailable, un~swerving, unwavering, well-founded

unshaken calm, collected, com~posed, impassive, unaffected, un~alarmed, undaunted, undismayed, undisturbed, unmoved, unper~turbed, unruffled

unsheltered exposed, open, out in the open, unprotected, unscreened, unshielded

unsightly disagreeable, hideous, horrid, repulsive, revolting (*Inf.*), ugly, unattractive, unpleasant, un~prepossessing

unskilled amateurish, inexperi~enced, uneducated, unprofessional, unqualified, untalented, untrained

unsociable chilly, cold, distant, hostile, inhospitable, introverted, reclusive, retiring, standoffish, un~congenial, unforthcoming, un~friendly, unneighbourly, unsocial, withdrawn

unsolicited free-will, gratuitous, spontaneous, unasked for, uncalled-for, unforced, uninvited, unrequested, unsought, unwel~come, voluntary, volunteered

unsophisticated 1. artless, child~like, guileless, inexperienced, in~genuous, innocent, naive, natural, unaffected, untutored, unworldly 2. plain, simple, straightforward, un~complex, uncomplicated, unin~volved, unrefined, unspecialized 3. genuine, not artificial, pure, un~adulterated

unsound 1. ailing, defective, deli~cate, deranged, diseased, frail, ill, in poor health, unbalanced, unhealthy, unhinged, unstable, unwell, weak 2. defective, erroneous, fallacious, false, faulty, flawed, ill-founded, illogical, invalid, shaky, specious, unreliable, weak 3. flimsy, insecure, not solid, rickety, shaky, tottering, unreliable, unsafe, unstable, unsteady, wobbly

unspeakable 1. beyond description, beyond words, inconceivable, indescribable, ineffable, inexpressible, overwhelming, unbelievable, unimaginable, unutterable, wonderful 2. abominable, appalling, awful, bad, dreadful, evil, execrable, frightful, heinous, horrible, loathsome, monstrous, odious, repellent, shocking, too horrible for words

unspoiled, unspoilt 1. intact, perfect, preserved, unaffected, unblemished, unchanged, undamaged, unharmed, unimpaired, untouched 2. artless, innocent, natural, unaffected, unassuming, unstudied, wholesome

unspoken 1. assumed, implicit, implied, left to the imagination, not put into words, not spelt out, tacit, taken for granted, undeclared, understood, unexpressed, unspoken, unstated 2. mute, silent, unsaid, unuttered, voiceless, wordless

unstable 1. insecure, not fixed, precarious, rickety, risky, shaky, tottering, unsettled, unsteady, wobbly 2. capricious, changeable, erratic, fitful, fluctuating, inconsistent, inconstant, irrational, unpredictable, unsteady, untrustworthy, vacillating, variable, volatile

unsteady 1. infirm, insecure, precarious, reeling, rickety, shaky, tottering, treacherous, unsafe, unstable, wobbly 2. changeable, erratic, flickering, flighty, fluctuating, inconstant, irregular, unreliable, unsettled, vacillating, variable, volatile, wavering

unsubstantial 1. airy, flimsy, fragile, frail, inadequate, light, slight, thin 2. erroneous, full of holes, ill-founded, superficial, tenuous, unsound, unsupported,

weak 3. dreamlike, fanciful, illusory, imaginary, immaterial, impalpable, visionary

unsubstantiated open to question, unattested, unconfirmed, uncorroborated, unestablished, unproven, unsupported

unsuccessful 1. abortive, bootless, failed, fruitless, futile, ineffective, unavailing, unproductive, useless, vain 2. balked, defeated, foiled, frustrated, hapless, ill-starred, losing, luckless, unfortunate, unlucky

unsuitable improper, inapposite, inappropriate, inapt, incompatible, incongruous, ineligible, infelicitous, out of character, out of keeping, out of place, unacceptable, unbecoming, unbefitting, unfitting, unseasonable, unseemly, unsuited

unsure 1. insecure, lacking in confidence, unassured, unconfident 2. distrustful, doubtful, dubious, hesitant, in a quandary, irresolute, mistrustful, sceptical, suspicious, unconvinced, undecided

unsurpassed consummate, exceptional, incomparable, matchless, nonpareil, paramount, peerless, second to none, superlative, supreme, transcendent, unequalled, unexcelled, unparalleled, unrivalled, without an equal

unsuspecting confiding, credulous, gullible, inexperienced, ingenuous, innocent, naive, off guard, trustful, trusting, unconscious, unsuspicious, unwarned, unwary

unswerving constant, dedicated, devoted, direct, firm, resolute, single-minded, staunch, steadfast, steady, true, undeviating, unfaltering, unflagging, untiring, unwavering

unsympathetic apathetic, callous, cold, compassionless (*Rare*), cruel, hard, harsh, heartless, indifferent, insensitive, soulless, stony-hearted, uncompassionate, unconcerned, unfeeling, unkind, unmoved, unpitying, unresponsive

untamed barbarous, feral, fierce, not broken in, savage, unbroken, uncontrollable, undomesticated, untameable, wild

untangle clear up, disentangle, ex~plain, extricate, solve, straighten out, unravel, unsnarl

untenable fallacious, flawed, groundless, illogical, indefensible, insupportable, shaky, unreason~able, unsound, unsustainable, weak

unthinkable 1. absurd, illogical, impossible, improbable, not on (*Inf.*), out of the question, prepos~terous, unlikely, unreasonable 2. beyond belief, beyond the bounds of possibility, implausible, incon~ceivable, incredible, insupportable, unbelievable, unimaginable

unthinking 1. blundering, incon~siderate, insensitive, rude, selfish, tactless, thoughtless, undiplomatic 2. careless, heedless, impulsive, inadvertent, instinctive, mechani~cal, negligent, oblivious, rash, senseless, unconscious, unmindful, vacant, witless

untidy bedraggled, chaotic, clut~tered, disorderly, higgledy-piggledy (*Inf.*), jumbled, littered, messy, muddled, muddly, mussy (*U.S. inf.*), rumpled, slatternly, slipshod, sloppy (*Inf.*), slovenly, topsy-turvy, unkempt

untie free, loosen, release, unbind, undo, unfasten, unknot, unlace

untimely awkward, badly timed, early, ill-timed, inappropriate, in~auspicious, inconvenient, inoppor~tune, mistimed, premature, unfor~tunate, unseasonable, unsuitable

untiring constant, dedicated, de~termined, devoted, dogged, inces~sant, indefatigable, patient, perse~vering, persistent, staunch, steady, tireless, unfaltering, unflagging, unremitting, unwearied

untold 1. indescribable, inexpress~ible, undreamed of, unimaginable, unspeakable, unthinkable, unut~terable 2. countless, incalculable, innumerable, measureless, myriad, numberless, uncountable, un~counted, unnumbered 3. hidden, private, secret, undisclosed, un~known, unpublished, unrecounted, unrelated, unrevealed

untouched 1. intact, safe and sound, undamaged, unharmed, un~hurt, uninjured, unscathed, without a scratch 2. dry-eyed, indifferent, unaffected, unconcerned, unim~pressed, unmoved, unstirred

untoward 1. annoying, awkward, disastrous, ill-timed, inconvenient, inimical, irritating, troublesome, unfortunate, vexatious 2. adverse, contrary, inauspicious, inoppor~tune, unfavourable, unlucky, un~timely 3. improper, inappropriate, indecorous, out of place, unbe~coming, unfitting, unseemly, un~suitable

untrained amateur, green, inexpe~rienced, raw, uneducated, unprac~tised, unqualified, unschooled, un~skilled, untaught, untutored

untroubled calm, composed, cool, peaceful, placid, serene, steady, tranquil, unagitated, unconcerned, undisturbed, unflappable (*Inf.*), unflustered, unperturbed, unruf~fled, unstirred, unworried

untrue 1. deceptive, dishonest, er~roneous, fallacious, false, inaccu~rate, incorrect, lying, misleading, mistaken, sham, spurious, untruth~ful, wrong 2. deceitful, disloyal, faithless, false, forsworn, incon~stant, perfidious, traitorous, treacherous, two-faced, unfaithful, untrustworthy 3. deviant, distorted, inaccurate, off, out of line, out of true, wide

untrustworthy capricious, deceit~ful, devious, dishonest, disloyal, fair-weather, faithless, false, fickle, fly-by-night (*Inf.*), not to be de~pended on, slippery, treacherous, tricky, two-faced, undependable, unfaithful, unreliable, untrue, un~trusty

untruth 1. deceitfulness, duplicity, falsity, inveracity (*Rare*), lying, mendacity, perjury, truthlessness, untruthfulness 2. deceit, fabrica~tion, falsehood, falsification, fib, fiction, lie, prevarication, story, tale, trick, whopper (*Inf.*)

untruthful crooked (*Inf.*), deceitful, deceptive, dishonest, dissembling, false, fibbing, hypocritical, lying, mendacious

unusual abnormal, atypical, bi~

zarre, curious, different, exceptional, extraordinary, odd, out of the ordinary, phenomenal, queer, rare, remarkable, singular, strange, surprising, uncommon, unconventional, unexpected, unfamiliar, unwonted

unutterable beyond words, extreme, indescribable, ineffable, overwhelming, unimaginable, unspeakable

unvarnished bare, candid, frank, honest, naked, plain, pure, pure and simple, simple, sincere, stark, straightforward, unadorned, unembellished

unveil bare, bring to light, disclose, divulge, expose, lay bare, lay open, make known, make public, reveal, uncover

unwanted *de trop*, going begging, outcast, rejected, superfluous, surplus to requirements, unasked, undesired, uninvited, unneeded, unsolicited, unwelcome, useless

unwarranted gratuitous, groundless, indefensible, inexcusable, uncalled-for, unjust, unjustified, unprovoked, unreasonable, wrong

unwary careless, hasty, heedless, imprudent, incautious, indiscreet, rash, reckless, thoughtless, uncircumspect, unguarded, unwatchful

unwavering consistent, dedicated, determined, resolute, single-minded, staunch, steadfast, steady, undeviating, unfaltering, unflagging, unshakable, unshaken, unswerving, untiring

unwelcome 1. excluded, rejected, unacceptable, undesirable, uninvited, unpopular, unwanted, unwished for 2. disagreeable, displeasing, distasteful, thankless, undesirable, unpleasant

unwell ailing, ill, indisposed, in poor health, off colour, out of sorts, poorly (*Inf.*), sick, sickly, under the weather (*Inf.*), unhealthy

unwholesome 1. deleterious, harmful, insalubrious, junk (*Inf.*), noxious, poisonous, tainted, unhealthy, unnourishing 2. bad, corrupting, degrading, demoralizing, depraving, evil, immoral, pervert-

ing, wicked 3. anaemic, pale, pallid, pasty, sickly, wan

unwieldy 1. awkward, burdensome, cumbersome, inconvenient, unhandy, unmanageable 2. bulky, clumsy, hefty, massive, ponderous, ungainly, weighty

unwilling averse, demurring, disinclined, grudging, indisposed, laggard (*Rare*), loath, not in the mood, opposed, reluctant, resistant, unenthusiastic

unwind 1. disentangle, slacken, uncoil, undo, unravel, unreel, unroll, untwine, untwist 2. calm down, let oneself go, loosen up, quieten down, relax, sit back, slow down, take a break, take it easy (*Inf.*), wind down

unwise foolhardy, foolish, ill-advised, ill-considered, ill-judged, impolitic, improvident, imprudent, inadvisable, indiscreet, injudicious, irresponsible, rash, reckless, senseless, short-sighted, silly, stupid

unwitting 1. ignorant, innocent, unaware, unconscious, unknowing, unsuspecting 2. accidental, chance, inadvertent, involuntary, undesigned, unintended, unintentional, unmeant, unplanned

unworldly 1. abstract, celestial, metaphysical, nonmaterialistic, religious, spiritual, transcendental 2. green, idealistic, inexperienced, innocent, naive, raw, trusting, unsophisticated 3. ethereal, extraterrestrial, otherworldly, unearthly

unworthy 1. *With* of beneath the dignity of, improper, inappropriate, out of character, out of place, unbecoming, unbefitting, unfitting, unseemly, unsuitable 2. base, contemptible, degrading, discreditable, disgraceful, dishonourable, disreputable, ignoble, shameful 3. ineligible, not deserving of, not fit for, not good enough, not worth, undeserving

unwritten 1. oral, unrecorded, vocal, word-of-mouth 2. accepted, conventional, customary, tacit, traditional, understood, unformulated

unyielding adamant, determined, firm, hardline, immovable, inexorable, inflexible, intractable, obdurate, obstinate, relentless, resolute, rigid, staunch, steadfast, stubborn, tough, unbending, uncompromising, unwavering

upbringing breeding, bringing-up, care, cultivation, education, nurture, raising, rearing, tending, training

upgrade advance, ameliorate, better, elevate, enhance, improve, promote, raise

upheaval cataclysm, disorder, disruption, disturbance, eruption, overthrow, revolution, turmoil, violent change

uphill adj. 1. ascending, climbing, mounting, rising 2. arduous, difficult, exhausting, gruelling, hard, laborious, punishing, Sisyphean, strenuous, taxing, tough, wearisome

uphold advocate, aid, back, champion, defend, encourage, endorse, hold to, justify, maintain, promote, stand by, support, sustain, vindicate

upkeep 1. conservation, keep, maintenance, preservation, repair, running, subsistence, support, sustenance 2. expenditure, expenses, oncosts (*Brit.*), operating costs, outlay, overheads, running costs

uplift v. 1. elevate, heave, hoist, lift up, raise 2. advance, ameliorate, better, civilize, cultivate, edify, improve, inspire, raise, refine, upgrade ~n. 3. advancement, betterment, cultivation, edification, enhancement, enlightenment, enrichment, improvement, refinement

upper 1. high, higher, loftier, top, topmost 2. elevated, eminent, greater, important, superior

upper-class aristocratic, blue-blooded, highborn, high-class, noble, patrician, top-drawer, well-bred

upper hand advantage, ascendancy, control, dominion, edge, mastery, superiority, supremacy, sway, whip hand

uppermost 1. highest, loftiest, most elevated, top, topmost, upmost 2. chief, dominant, foremost, greatest, leading, main, paramount, predominant, pre-eminent, primary, principal, supreme

uppish affected, arrogant, conceited, high and mighty (*Inf.*), hoity-toity (*Inf.*), overweening, presumptuous, putting on airs, self-important, snobbish, stuck-up (*Inf.*), supercilious, toffee-nosed (*Sl.*), uppity (*Inf.*)

upright 1. erect, on end, perpendicular, straight, vertical 2. *Fig.* above board, conscientious, ethical, faithful, good, high-minded, honest, honourable, incorruptible, just, principled, righteous, straightforward, true, trustworthy, unimpeachable, virtuous

uprising disturbance, insurgence, insurrection, mutiny, outbreak, putsch, rebellion, revolt, revolution, rising, upheaval

uproar brawl, brouhaha, clamour, commotion, confusion, din, furore, hubbub, hullabaloo, hurly-burly, mayhem, noise, outcry, pandemonium, racket, riot, ruckus (*Inf.*), ruction (*Inf.*), rumpus, turbulence, turmoil

uproarious 1. clamorous, confused, disorderly, loud, noisy, riotous, rowdy, tempestuous, tumultuous, turbulent, wild 2. convulsive (*Inf.*), hilarious, hysterical, killing (*Inf.*), rib-tickling, rip-roaring (*Inf.*), screamingly funny, side-splitting, very funny 3. boisterous, gleeful, loud, rollicking, unrestrained

upset v. 1. capsize, knock over, overturn, spill, tip over, topple over 2. change, disorder, disorganize, disturb, mess up, mix up, put out of order, spoil, turn topsy-turvy 3. agitate, bother, discompose, disconcert, dismay, disquiet, distress, disturb, fluster, grieve, perturb, ruffle, throw (someone) off balance, trouble 4. be victorious over, conquer, defeat, get the better of, overcome, overthrow, triumph over, win against the odds ~n. 5. defeat, reverse, shake-up (*Inf.*), sudden change, surprise **6.** bug (*Inf.*), complaint, disorder, disturb~ance, illness, indisposition, malady, queasiness, sickness **7.** agitation, bother, discomposure, disquiet, distress, disturbance, shock, trou~ble, worry ~*adj.* **8.** capsized, over~turned, spilled, tipped over, top~pled, tumbled, upside down **9.** dis~ordered, disturbed, gippy (*Sl.*), ill, poorly (*Inf.*), queasy, sick **10.** agi~tated, bothered, confused, discon~certed, dismayed, disquieted, dis~tressed, disturbed, frantic, grieved, hurt, overwrought, put out, ruffled, troubled, worried **11.** at sixes and sevens, chaotic, confused, disor~dered, in disarray *or* disorder, messed up, muddled, topsy-turvy **12.** beaten, conquered, defeated, overcome, overthrown, van~quished

upshot conclusion, consequence, culmination, end, end result, event, finale, issue, outcome, payoff (*Inf.*), result

upside down 1. bottom up, invert~ed, on its head, overturned, up~turned, wrong side up **2.** *Inf.* cha~otic, confused, disordered, higgledy-piggledy (*Inf.*), in confu~sion (chaos, disarray, disorder), jumbled, muddled, topsy-turvy

upstanding 1. ethical, good, hon~est, honourable, incorruptible, moral, principled, true, trust~worthy, upright **2.** firm, hale and hearty, hardy, healthy, robust, stalwart, strong, sturdy, upright, vigorous

upstart arriviste, nobody, *nouveau riche*, parvenu, social climber, status seeker

up-to-date all the rage, current, fashionable, in, in vogue, modern, newest, now (*Inf.*), stylish, trendy (*Brit. inf.*), up-to-the-minute, with it (*Inf.*)

urban city, civic, inner-city, metro~politan, municipal, oppidan (*Rare*), town

urbane civil, civilized, cosmopoli~tan, courteous, cultivated, cultured, debonair, elegant, mannerly, pol~ished, refined, smooth, sophisticat~

ed, suave, well-bred, well-mannered

urbanity charm, civility, courtesy, culture, elegance, grace, manner~liness, polish, refinement, sophisti~cation, suavity, worldliness

urchin brat, gamin, guttersnipe, mudlark (*Sl.*), ragamuffin, street Arab, waif, young rogue

urge *v.* **1.** appeal to, beg, beseech, entreat, exhort, implore, plead, press, solicit **2.** advise, advocate, champion, counsel, insist on, push for, recommend, support **3.** com~pel, constrain, drive, egg on, en~courage, force, goad, hasten, im~pel, incite, induce, instigate, press, propel, push, spur, stimulate ~*n.* **4.** compulsion, desire, drive, fancy, impulse, itch, longing, wish, yearn~ing, yen (*Inf.*)

urgency exigency, extremity, gravity, hurry, imperativeness, importance, importunity, neces~sity, need, pressure, seriousness, stress

urgent 1. compelling, critical, cru~cial, immediate, imperative, im~portant, instant, not to be delayed, pressing, top-priority **2.** clamorous, earnest, importunate, insistent, in~tense, persistent, persuasive

urinate leak (*Sl.*), make water, micturate, pass water, pee (*Sl.*), spend a penny (*Brit. inf.*), tinkle (*Brit. inf.*), wee (*Inf.*), wee-wee (*Inf.*)

usable at one's disposal, available, current, fit for use, functional, in running order, practical, ready for use, serviceable, utilizable, valid, working

usage 1. control, employment, handling, management, operation, regulation, running, treatment, use **2.** convention, custom, form, habit, matter of course, method, mode, practice, procedure, regime, rou~tine, rule, tradition, wont

use *v.* **1.** apply, avail oneself of, bring into play, employ, exercise, find a use for, make use of, oper~ate, ply, practise, profit by, put to use, turn to account, utilize, wield, work **2.** act towards, behave to~

wards, deal with, exploit, handle, manipulate, misuse, take advantage of, treat 3. consume, exhaust, expend, run through, spend, waste ~n. 4. application, employment, exercise, handling, operation, practice, service, treatment, usage, wear and tear 5. advantage, application, avail, benefit, good, help, mileage (*Inf.*), point, profit, service, usefulness, utility, value, worth 6. custom, habit, practice, usage, way, wont 7. call, cause, end, necessity, need, object, occasion, point, purpose, reason

used cast-off, hand-me-down (*Inf.*), nearly new, not new, reach-me-down (*Inf.*), second-hand, shop-soiled, worn

used to accustomed to, at home in, attuned to, familiar with, given to, habituated to, hardened to, in the habit of, inured to, tolerant of, wont to

useful advantageous, all-purpose, beneficial, effective, fruitful, general-purpose, helpful, of help, of service, of use, practical, profitable, salutary, serviceable, valuable, worthwhile

useless 1. bootless, disadvantageous, fruitless, futile, hopeless, idle, impractical, ineffective, ineffectual, of no use, pointless, profitless, unavailing, unproductive, unworkable, vain, valueless, worthless 2. *Inf.* hopeless, incompetent, ineffectual, inept, no good, stupid, weak

use up absorb, burn up, consume, deplete, devour, drain, exhaust, finish, fritter away, run through, squander, swallow up, waste

usher n. 1. attendant, doorkeeper, escort, guide, usherette ~v. 2. conduct, direct, escort, guide, lead, pilot, show in *or* out, steer 3. *Usually with* in bring in, herald, inaugurate, initiate, introduce, launch,

open the door to, pave the way for, precede, ring in

usual accustomed, common, constant, customary, everyday, expected, familiar, fixed, general, habitual, normal, ordinary, regular, routine, standard, stock, typical, wonted

usually as a rule, as is the custom, as is usual, by and large, commonly, for the most part, generally, habitually, in the main, mainly, mostly, most often, normally, on the whole, ordinarily, regularly, routinely

utility advantageousness, avail, benefit, convenience, efficacy, fitness, point, practicality, profit, service, serviceableness, use, usefulness

utilize appropriate, avail oneself of, employ, have recourse to, make the most of, make use of, profit by, put to use, resort to, take advantage of, turn to account, use

utmost *adj.* 1. chief, extreme, greatest, highest, maximum, paramount, pre-eminent, supreme 2. extreme, farthest, final, last, most distant, outermost, remotest, uttermost ~n. 3. best, greatest, hardest, highest, most

utter¹ *v.* 1. articulate, enunciate, express, pronounce, put into words, say, speak, verbalize, vocalize, voice 2. declare, divulge, give expression to, make known, proclaim, promulgate, publish, reveal, state

utter² *adj.* absolute, arrant, complete, consummate, downright, entire, out-and-out, perfect, sheer, stark, thorough, thoroughgoing, total, unmitigated, unqualified

utterly absolutely, completely, entirely, extremely, fully, perfectly, thoroughly, totally, to the core, wholly

V

vacancy 1. job, opening, opportun~ ity, position, post, room, situation 2. absent-mindedness, abstraction, blankness, inanity, inattentiveness, incomprehension, incuriousness, lack of interest, vacuousness 3. emptiness, gap, space, vacuum, void

vacant 1. available, disengaged, empty, free, idle, not in use, to let, unemployed, unengaged, unfilled, unoccupied, untenanted, void 2. absent-minded, abstracted, blank, dreaming, dreamy, expressionless, idle, inane, incurious, thoughtless, unthinking, vacuous

vacuum emptiness, free space, gap, nothingness, space, vacuity, void

vagabond 1. *n.* beggar, bum (*U.S. inf.*), down-and-out, hobo (*U.S.*), itinerant, knight of the road, mi~ grant, nomad, outcast, rascal, rov~ er, tramp, vagrant, wanderer, wayfarer 2. *adj.* destitute, down and out, drifting, fly-by-night (*Inf.*), footloose, homeless, idle, itinerant, journeying, nomadic, rootless, roving, shiftless, vagrant, wander~ ing

vagrant 1. *n.* beggar, bird of pas~ sage, bum (*U.S. inf.*), hobo (*U.S.*), itinerant, person of no fixed ad~ dress, rolling stone, tramp, wan~ derer 2. *adj.* itinerant, nomadic, roaming, rootless, roving, unset~ tled, vagabond

vague amorphous, blurred, dim, doubtful, fuzzy, generalized, hazy, ill-defined, imprecise, indefinite, indeterminate, indistinct, lax, loose, nebulous, obscure, shadowy, uncertain, unclear, unknown, un~ specified, woolly

vaguely absent-mindedly, dimly, evasively, imprecisely, in a gener~ al way, obscurely, slightly, through a glass darkly, vacantly

vagueness ambiguity, imprecise~ ness, inexactitude, lack of precise~ ness, looseness, obscurity

vain 1. arrogant, bigheaded (*Inf.*), cocky, conceited, egotistical, in~ flated, narcissistic, ostentatious, overweening, peacockish, pleased with oneself, proud, self-important, stuck-up (*Inf.*), swaggering, swanky (*Inf.*), swollen-headed (*Inf.*), vainglorious 2. abortive, empty, fruitless, futile, hollow, idle, nugatory, pointless, senseless, time-wasting, trifling, trivial, un~ availing, unimportant, unproduc~ tive, unprofitable, useless, worth~ less 3. **be vain** have a high opinion of oneself, have a swelled head (*Inf.*), have one's head turned, think a lot of oneself, think oneself it (*Inf.*), think oneself the cat's whiskers *or* pyjamas (*Sl.*) 4. **in vain** bootless, fruitless(ly), ineffectual~ (ly), to no avail, to no purpose, unsuccessful(ly), useless(ly), vain~ (ly), wasted, without success

valedictory *adj.* farewell, final, parting

valiant bold, brave, courageous, dauntless, doughty, fearless, gal~ lant, heroic, indomitable, intrepid, lion-hearted, plucky, redoubtable, stouthearted, valorous, worthy

valid 1. binding, cogent, conclusive, convincing, efficacious, efficient, good, just, logical, powerful, sound, substantial, telling, weighty, well-founded, well-grounded 2. authen~ tic, bona fide, genuine, in force, lawful, legal, legally binding, le~ gitimate, official

validity 1. cogency, force, founda~ tion, grounds, point, power, sound~ ness, strength, substance, weight 2. authority, lawfulness, legality, le~ gitimacy, right

valley coomb, cwm (*Welsh*), dale, dell, depression, dingle, glen, hol~ low, strath (*Scot.*), vale

valuable *adj.* 1. costly, dear, ex~ pensive, high-priced, precious 2.

beneficial, cherished, esteemed, estimable, held dear, helpful, im~portant, prized, profitable, ser~viceable, treasured, useful, valued, worthwhile, worthy ~n. 3. *Usually plural* heirloom, treasure(s)

value *n.* 1. cost, equivalent, market price, monetary worth, rate 2. ad~vantage, benefit, desirability, help, importance, merit, profit, service~ableness, significance, use, useful~ness, utility, worth 3. *Plural* code of behaviour, ethics, (moral) stand~ards, principles ~v. 4. account, ap~praise, assess, compute, estimate, evaluate, price, put a price on, rate, set at, survey 5. appreciate, cherish, esteem, hold dear, hold in high regard *or* esteem, prize, re~gard highly, respect, set store by, treasure

valued cherished, dear, esteemed, highly regarded, loved, prized, treasured

valueless miserable, no good, of no earthly use, of no value, unsale~able, useless, worthless

vanguard advance guard, fore~front, forerunners, front, front line, front rank, leaders, spearhead, trailblazers, trendsetters, van

vanish become invisible, be lost to sight, die out, disappear, disappear from sight *or* from the face of the earth, dissolve, evanesce, evapo~rate, exit, fade (away), melt (away)

vanity 1. affected ways, airs, arro~gance, bigheadedness (*Inf.*), con~ceit, conceitedness, egotism, nar~cissism, ostentation, pretension, pride, self-admiration, self-love, showing off (*Inf.*), swollen-headedness (*Inf.*), vainglory 2. emptiness, frivolity, fruitlessness, futility, hollowness, inanity, point~lessness, profitlessness, triviality, unproductiveness, unreality, un~substantiality, uselessness, worth~lessness

vanquish beat, conquer, crush, de~feat, get the upper hand over, master, overcome, overpower, overwhelm, put down, put to flight, put to rout, quell, reduce, repress, rout, subdue, subjugate, triumph over

vapour breath, dampness, exhala~tion, fog, fumes, haze, miasma, mist, smoke, steam

variable capricious, chameleonic, changeable, fickle, fitful, flexible, fluctuating, inconstant, mercurial, mutable, protean, shifting, tem~peramental, unstable, unsteady, vacillating, wavering

variance 1. difference, difference of opinion, disagreement, discord, discrepancy, dissension, dissent, divergence, inconsistency, lack of harmony, strife, variation 2. **at variance** at loggerheads, at odds, at sixes and sevens (*Inf.*), conflict~ing, in disagreement, in opposition, out of harmony, out of line

variant 1. *adj.* alternative, derived, different, divergent, exceptional, modified 2. *n.* alternative, derived form, development, modification, sport (*Biol.*), variation

variation alteration, break in rou~tine, change, departure, departure from the norm, deviation, differ~ence, discrepancy, diversification, diversity, innovation, modification, novelty, variety

varied assorted, different, diverse, heterogeneous, miscellaneous, mixed, motley, sundry, various

variety 1. change, difference, dis~crepancy, diversification, diver~sity, many-sidedness, multifarious~ness, variation 2. array, assort~ment, collection, cross section, intermixture, medley, miscellany, mixture, multiplicity, range 3. brand, breed, category, class, kind, make, order, sort, species, strain, type

various assorted, different, differ~ing, disparate, distinct, divers (*Ar~chaic*), diverse, diversified, heterogeneous, many, many-sided, miscellaneous, several, sundry, varied, variegated

varnish *v.* adorn, decorate, embel~lish, gild, glaze, gloss, japan, lac~quer, polish, shellac

vary alter, alternate, be unlike, change, depart, differ, disagree,

varying diverge, diversify, fluctuate, inter~mix, modify, permutate, reorder, transform

varying changing, different, dis~tinct, distinguishable, diverse, fluctuating, inconsistent

vast astronomical, boundless, co~lossal, enormous, extensive, gigan~tic, great, huge, illimitable, im~measurable, immense, limitless, mammoth, massive, measureless, monstrous, monumental, never-ending, prodigious, sweeping, tre~mendous, unbounded, unlimited, vasty (*Archaic*), voluminous, wide

vault[1] *v.* bound, clear, hurdle, jump, leap, spring

vault[2] *n.* 1. arch, ceiling, roof, span 2. catacomb, cellar, crypt, mauso~leum, tomb, undercroft 3. deposi~tory, repository, strongroom ~*v.* 4. arch, bend, bow, curve, overarch, span

vaunt boast about, brag about, crow about, exult in, flaunt, give oneself airs about, make a display of, make much of, parade, prate about, show off, talk big about (*Inf.*)

veer be deflected, change, change course, change direction, sheer, shift, swerve, tack, turn

vegetate 1. be inert, deteriorate, exist, go to seed, idle, languish, loaf, moulder, stagnate 2. burgeon, germinate, grow, shoot, spring, sprout, swell

vehemence ardour, eagerness, earnestness, emphasis, energy, enthusiasm, fervency, fervour, fire, force, forcefulness, heat, impetu~osity, intensity, keenness, passion, verve, vigour, violence, warmth, zeal

vehement ardent, eager, earnest, emphatic, enthusiastic, fervent, fervid, fierce, forceful, forcible, impassioned, impetuous, intense, passionate, powerful, strong, vio~lent, zealous

vehicle *Fig.* apparatus, channel, means, means of expression, mechanism, medium, organ

veil 1. *v.* cloak, conceal, cover, dim, disguise, hide, mantle, mask, ob~scure, screen, shield 2. *n.* blind, cloak, cover, curtain, disguise, film, mask, screen, shade, shroud

veiled concealed, covert, disguised, hinted at, implied, masked, sup~pressed

vein 1. blood vessel, course, cur~rent, lode, seam, stratum, streak, stripe 2. dash, hint, strain, streak, thread, trait 3. attitude, bent, char~acter, faculty, humour, mode, mood, note, style, temper, tenor, tone, turn

venal bent (*Sl.*), corrupt, corrup~tible, crooked (*Inf.*), dishonourable, grafting, mercenary, prostituted, purchasable, rapacious, simonia~cal, sordid, unprincipled

vendetta bad blood, blood feud, feud, quarrel

veneer *n. Fig.* appearance, façade, false front, finish, front, gloss, guise, mask, pretence, semblance, show

venerable august, esteemed, grave, honoured, respected, re~vered, reverenced, sage, sedate, wise, worshipped

venerate adore, esteem, hold in awe, honour, look up to, respect, revere, reverence, worship

veneration adoration, awe, defer~ence, esteem, respect, reverence, worship

vengeance 1. an eye for an eye, avenging, lex talionis, reprisal, re~quital, retaliation, retribution, re~venge, settling of scores 2. with a vengeance a. forcefully, furiously, vehemently, violently b. and no mistake, extremely, greatly, to the full, to the utmost, with no holds barred

venial allowable, excusable, for~givable, insignificant, minor, par~donable, slight, trivial

venom 1. bane, poison, toxin 2. acidity, acrimony, bitterness, gall, grudge, hate, ill will, malevolence, malice, maliciousness, malignity, rancour, spite, spitefulness, spleen, virulence

venomous 1. baneful (*Archaic*), envenomed, mephitic, noxious, poison, poisonous, toxic, virulent 2.

baleful, hostile, malicious, malig~
nant, rancorous, savage, spiteful,
vicious, vindictive, virulent

vent 1. *n.* aperture, duct, hole,
opening, orifice, outlet, split 2. *v.*
air, come out with, discharge, emit,
empty, express, give expression to,
give vent to, pour out, release, ut~
ter, voice

ventilate *Fig.* air, bring out into the
open, broadcast, debate, discuss,
examine, make known, scrutinize,
sift, talk about

venture *v.* 1. chance, endanger,
hazard, imperil, jeopardize, put in
jeopardy, risk, speculate, stake,
wager 2. advance, dare, dare say,
hazard, make bold, presume, stick
one's neck out (*Inf.*), take the lib~
erty, volunteer 3. *With* **out, forth,**
etc. embark on, go, plunge into, set
out ~*n.* 4. adventure, chance, en~
deavour, enterprise, fling, gamble,
hazard, jeopardy, project, risk,
speculation, undertaking

verbal literal, oral, spoken, unwrit~
ten, verbatim, word-of-mouth

verbally by word of mouth, orally

verbatim exactly, precisely, to the
letter, word for word

verbose circumlocutory, diffuse,
garrulous, long-winded, periphras~
tic, pleonastic, prolix, tautological,
windy, wordy

verbosity garrulity, logorrhoea,
long-windedness, loquaciousness,
prolixity, rambling, verbiage, ver~
boseness, windiness, wordiness

verdict adjudication, conclusion,
decision, finding, judgment, opin~
ion, sentence

verge 1. *n.* border, boundary, brim,
brink, edge, extreme, limit, lip,
margin, roadside, threshold 2. *v.*
approach, border, come near

verification authentication, confir~
mation, corroboration, proof, sub~
stantiation, validation

verify attest, attest to, authenticate,
bear out, check, confirm, corrobo~
rate, prove, substantiate, support,
validate

vernacular 1. *adj.* colloquial, com~
mon, indigenous, informal, local,
mother, native, popular, vulgar 2.

n. argot, cant, dialect, idiom, jar~
gon, native language, parlance,
patois, speech, vulgar tongue

versatile adaptable, adjustable, all-
purpose, all-round, flexible, func~
tional, handy, many-sided, multifaceted, protean, resourceful,
variable

versed accomplished, acquainted,
competent, conversant, experi~
enced, familiar, knowledgeable,
practised, proficient, qualified,
seasoned, skilled, well informed,
well up in (*Inf.*)

version 1. account, adaptation, ex~
ercise, interpretation, portrayal,
reading, rendering, side, transla~
tion 2. design, form, kind, model,
style, type, variant

vertical erect, on end, perpendicu~
lar, upright

vertigo dizziness, giddiness, light-
headedness, loss of equilibrium,
swimming of the head

verve animation, brio, dash, élan,
energy, enthusiasm, force, get-up-
and-go (*Inf.*), gusto, life, liveliness,
punch (*Inf.*), sparkle, spirit, vigour,
vim (*Sl.*), vitality, vivacity, zeal, zip
(*Inf.*)

very *adv.* 1. absolutely, acutely, aw~
fully (*Inf.*), decidedly, deeply, emi~
nently, exceedingly, excessively,
extremely, greatly, highly, jolly
(*Brit.*), noticeably, particularly,
profoundly, really, remarkably,
superlatively, surpassingly, terri~
bly, truly, uncommonly, unusually,
wonderfully ~*adj.* 2. actual, appro~
priate, exact, express, identical,
perfect, precise, real, same, self~
same, unqualified 3. bare, mere,
plain, pure, sheer, simple

vessel 1. barque (*Poetic*), boat,
craft, ship 2. container, pot, recep~
tacle, utensil

vest *v.* 1. *With* **in** *or* **with** authorize,
be devolved upon, bestow, confer,
consign, empower, endow, entrust,
furnish, invest, lodge, place, put in
the hands of, settle 2. apparel, be~
deck, clothe, cover, dress, envelop,
garb, robe

vestibule anteroom, entrance hall,
foyer, hall, lobby, porch, portico

vestige evidence, glimmer, hint, indication, relic, remainder, remains, remnant, residue, scrap, sign, suspicion, token, trace, track

vet *v.* appraise, check, check out, examine, give (someone *or* something) the once-over (*Inf.*), investigate, look over, pass under review, review, scan, scrutinize, size up (*Inf.*)

veteran 1. *n.* master, old hand, old stager, old-timer, past master, past mistress, pro (*Inf.*), trouper, warhorse (*Inf.*) 2. *adj.* adept, battle-scarred, expert, long-serving, old, proficient, seasoned

veto 1. *v.* ban, disallow, forbid, give the thumbs down to, interdict, kill (*Inf.*), negative, prohibit, put the kibosh on (*Sl.*), refuse permission, reject, rule out, turn down 2. *n.* ban, embargo, interdict, nonconsent, prohibition

vex afflict, aggravate (*Inf.*), agitate, annoy, bother, bug (*Inf.*), displease, distress, disturb, exasperate, fret, gall, grate on, harass, irritate, molest, needle (*Inf.*), nettle, offend, peeve (*Inf.*), perplex, pester, pique, plague, provoke, put out, rile, tease, torment, trouble, upset, worry

vexation 1. aggravation (*Inf.*), annoyance, displeasure, dissatisfaction, exasperation, frustration, irritation, pique 2. bother, difficulty, headache (*Inf.*), irritant, misfortune, nuisance, problem, thorn in one's flesh, trouble, upset, worry

vexatious afflicting, aggravating (*Inf.*), annoying, bothersome, burdensome, disagreeable, disappointing, distressing, exasperating, harassing, irksome, irritating, nagging, plaguy (*Archaic*), provoking, teasing, tormenting, troublesome, trying, unpleasant, upsetting, worrisome, worrying

vexed 1. afflicted, aggravated (*Inf.*), agitated, annoyed, bothered, confused, displeased, distressed, disturbed, exasperated, fed up, harassed, irritated, miffed (*Inf.*), nettled, out of countenance, peeved (*Inf.*), perplexed, provoked,

put out, riled, ruffled, tormented, troubled, upset, worried 2. contested, controversial, disputed, moot, much debated

viable applicable, feasible, operable, practicable, usable, within the bounds of possibility, workable

vibrant 1. aquiver, oscillating, palpitating, pulsating, quivering, trembling 2. alive, animated, colourful, dynamic, electrifying, full of pep (*Inf.*), responsive, sensitive, sparkling, spirited, vivacious, vivid

vibrate fluctuate, judder (*Inf.*), oscillate, pulsate, pulse, quiver, resonate, reverberate, shake, shiver, sway, swing, throb, tremble, undulate

vibration juddering (*Inf.*), oscillation, pulsation, pulse, quiver, resonance, reverberation, shaking, throb, throbbing, trembling, tremor

vice 1. corruption, degeneracy, depravity, evil, evildoing, immorality, iniquity, profligacy, sin, venality, wickedness 2. blemish, defect, failing, fault, imperfection, shortcoming, weakness

vicinity area, district, environs, locality, neck of the woods (*Inf.*), neighbourhood, precincts, propinquity, proximity, purlieus

vicious 1. abandoned, abhorrent, atrocious, bad, barbarous, corrupt, cruel, dangerous, debased, degenerate, degraded, depraved, diabolical, ferocious, fiendish, foul, heinous, immoral, infamous, monstrous, profligate, savage, sinful, unprincipled, vile, violent, wicked, worthless, wrong 2. backbiting, bitchy (*Sl.*), cruel, defamatory, malicious, mean, rancorous, slanderous, spiteful, venomous, vindictive

viciousness 1. badness, corruption, cruelty, depravity, ferocity, immorality, profligacy, savagery, wickedness 2. bitchiness (*Sl.*), malice, rancour, spite, spitefulness, venom

victim 1. casualty, fatality, injured party, martyr, sacrifice, scapegoat, sufferer 2. dupe, easy prey, fall guy

(*Inf.*), gull (*Archaic*), innocent, sit~
ting target, sucker (*Sl.*)

victimize 1. discriminate against,
have a down on (someone) (*Inf.*),
have it in for (someone) (*Inf.*),
have one's knife into (someone),
persecute, pick on 2. cheat, de~
ceive, defraud, dupe, exploit, fool,
gull (*Archaic*), hoodwink, prey on,
swindle, take advantage of, use

victor champ (*Inf.*), champion,
conquering hero, conqueror, first,
prizewinner, top dog (*Inf.*), van~
quisher, winner

victorious champion, conquering,
first, prizewinning, successful, tri~
umphant, vanquishing, winning

victory conquest, laurels, mastery,
success, superiority, the palm, the
prize, triumph, win

victuals bread, comestibles, eat~
ables, eats (*Sl.*), edibles, food, grub
(*Sl.*), meat, nosh (*Sl.*), provisions,
rations, stores, supplies, viands,
vittles (*Obsolete*)

view *n.* 1. aspect, landscape, out~
look, panorama, perspective, pic~
ture, prospect, scene, spectacle,
vista 2. range *or* field of vision,
sight, vision 3. *Sometimes plural*
attitude, belief, conviction, feeling,
impression, judgment, notion,
opinion, point of view, sentiment,
thought, way of thinking 4. con~
templation, display, examination,
inspection, look, scan, scrutiny,
sight, survey, viewing 5. **with a
view to** in order to, in the hope of,
so as to, with the aim *or* intention
of ~*v.* 6. behold, contemplate, ex~
amine, explore, eye, gaze at, in~
spect, look at, observe, regard,
scan, spectate, stare at, survey,
watch, witness 7. consider, deem,
judge, look on, regard, think about

viewer observer, one of an audi~
ence, onlooker, spectator, TV
watcher, watcher

viewpoint angle, frame of refer~
ence, perspective, point of view,
position, slant, stance, standpoint,
vantage point, way of thinking

vigilant alert, Argus-eyed, atten~
tive, careful, cautious, circum~
spect, keeping one's eyes peeled *or*
skinned (*Inf.*), on one's guard, on
one's toes, on the alert, on the
lookout, on the qui vive, on the
watch, sleepless, unsleeping,
wakeful, watchful, wide awake

vigorous active, brisk, dynamic,
effective, efficient, energetic, en~
terprising, flourishing, forceful,
forcible, full of energy, hale, hale
and hearty, hardy, healthy, in~
tense, lively, lusty, powerful, red-
blooded, robust, sound, spanking,
spirited, strenuous, strong, virile,
vital, zippy (*Inf.*)

vigorously all out, eagerly, ener~
getically, forcefully, hammer and
tongs, hard, like mad (*Sl.*), lustily,
strenuously, strongly, with a
vengeance, with might and main

vigour activity, animation, dash,
dynamism, energy, force, forceful~
ness, gusto, health, liveliness,
might, oomph (*Inf.*), pep, power,
punch (*Inf.*), robustness, snap
(*Inf.*), soundness, spirit, strength,
verve, vim (*Sl.*), virility, vitality, zip
(*Inf.*)

vile 1. abandoned, abject, appalling,
bad, base, coarse, contemptible,
corrupt, debased, degenerate, de~
grading, depraved, despicable, dis~
graceful, evil, humiliating, ignoble,
impure, loathsome, low, mean,
miserable, nefarious, perverted,
shocking, sinful, ugly, vicious, vul~
gar, wicked, worthless, wretched 2.
disgusting, foul, horrid, loathsome,
nasty, nauseating, noxious, offen~
sive, repellent, repugnant, repul~
sive, revolting, sickening

vilify abuse, asperse, bad-mouth
(*U.S. sl.*), berate, calumniate, de~
base, decry, defame, denigrate,
disparage, malign, pull to pieces
(*Inf.*), revile, run down, slander,
smear, speak ill of, traduce, vili~
pend (*Rare*), vituperate

villain 1. blackguard, caitiff (*Ar~
chaic*), criminal, evildoer, knave
(*Archaic*), libertine, malefactor,
miscreant, profligate, rapscallion,
reprobate, rogue, scoundrel,
wretch 2. antihero, baddy (*Inf.*) 3.
devil, monkey, rascal, rogue, scal~
lywag (*Inf.*), scamp

villainous atrocious, bad, base, blackguardly, criminal, cruel, debased, degenerate, depraved, detestable, diabolical, evil, fiendish, hateful, heinous, ignoble, infamous, inhuman, mean, nefarious, outrageous, ruffianly, scoundrelly, sinful, terrible, thievish, vicious, vile, wicked

villainy atrocity, baseness, crime, criminality, delinquency, depravity, devilry, iniquity, knavery, rascality, sin, turpitude, vice, wickedness

vindicate 1. absolve, acquit, clear, defend, do justice to, exculpate, excuse, exonerate, free from blame, justify, rehabilitate 2. advocate, assert, establish, maintain, support, uphold

vindication apology, assertion, defence, exculpating, exculpation, excuse, exoneration, justification, maintenance, plea, rehabilitation, substantiation, support

vindictive full of spleen, implacable, malicious, malignant, rancorous, relentless, resentful, revengeful, spiteful, unforgiving, unrelenting, vengeful, venomous

vintage 1. *n.* collection, crop, epoch, era, generation, harvest, origin, year 2. *adj.* best, choice, classic, mature, prime, rare, ripe, select, superior, venerable

violate 1. break, contravene, disobey, disregard, encroach upon, infract, infringe, transgress 2. abuse, assault, befoul, debauch, defile, desecrate, dishonour, invade, outrage, pollute, profane, rape, ravish

violation 1. abuse, breach, contravention, encroachment, infraction, infringement, transgression, trespass 2. defilement, desecration, profanation, sacrilege, spoliation

violence 1. bestiality, bloodshed, bloodthirstiness, brutality, brute force, cruelty, destructiveness, ferocity, fierceness, fighting, force, frenzy, fury, murderousness, passion, rough handling, savagery, strong-arm tactics (*Inf.*), terrorism, thuggery, vehemence, wildness 2. boisterousness, power, raging, roughness, storminess, tumult, turbulence, wildness 3. abandon, acuteness, fervour, force, harshness, intensity, severity, sharpness, vehemence

violent 1. berserk, bloodthirsty, brutal, cruel, destructive, fiery, forcible, furious, headstrong, homicidal, hot-headed, impetuous, intemperate, maddened, maniacal, murderous, passionate, powerful, raging, riotous, rough, savage, strong, uncontrollable, ungovernable, unrestrained, vehement, vicious, wild 2. blustery, boisterous, devastating, full of force, gale force, powerful, raging, ruinous, strong, tempestuous, tumultuous, turbulent, wild 3. acute, agonizing, biting, excruciating, extreme, harsh, inordinate, intense, outrageous, painful, severe, sharp

virgin 1. *n.* damsel (*Archaic*), girl, maid (*Archaic*), vestal, virgo intacta 2. *adj.* chaste, fresh, immaculate, maidenly, modest, new, pristine, pure, snowy, uncorrupted, undefiled, unsullied, untouched, unused, vestal, virginal

virile forceful, lusty, macho, male, manlike, manly, masculine, potent, red-blooded, robust, strong, vigorous

virility machismo, manhood, masculinity, potency, vigour

virtual essential, implicit, implied, in all but name, indirect, potential, practical, tacit, unacknowledged

virtually as good as, effectually, for all practical purposes, in all but name, in effect, in essence, nearly, practically, to all intents and purposes

virtue 1. ethicalness, excellence, goodness, high-mindedness, incorruptibility, integrity, justice, morality, probity, quality, rectitude, righteousness, uprightness, worth, worthiness 2. advantage, asset, attribute, credit, good point, good quality, merit, plus (*Inf.*), strength 3. chastity, honour, innocence, morality, purity, virginity 4. **by virtue of** as a result of, by dint of, by reason of, in view of, on account of, owing to, thanks to

virtuosity brilliance, éclat, exper~ tise, finish, flair, mastery, panache, polish, skill

virtuoso 1. *n.* artist, genius, maes~ tro, magician, master, master hand 2. *adj.* bravura (*Music*), brilliant, dazzling, masterly

virtuous 1. blameless, ethical, ex~ cellent, exemplary, good, high-principled, honest, honourable, in~ corruptible, moral, praiseworthy, pure, righteous, upright, worthy 2. celibate, chaste, clean-living, inno~ cent, pure, spotless, virginal

virulent 1. baneful (*Archaic*), deadly, infective, injurious, lethal, malignant, pernicious, poisonous, septic, toxic, venomous 2. acrimo~ nious, bitter, envenomed, hostile, malevolent, malicious, rancorous, resentful, spiteful, splenetic, ven~ omous, vicious, vindictive

visible anywhere to be seen, ap~ parent, clear, conspicuous, detect~ able, discernible, discoverable, distinguishable, evident, in sight, in view, manifest, not hidden, notice~ able, observable, obvious, palpable, patent, perceivable, perceptible, plain, to be seen, unconcealed, un~ mistakable

vision 1. eyes, eyesight, perception, seeing, sight, view 2. breadth of view, discernment, farsightedness, foresight, imagination, insight, in~ tuition, penetration, prescience 3. castle in the air, concept, concep~ tion, daydream, dream, fantasy, idea, ideal, image, mental picture, pipe dream 4. apparition, chimera, delusion, ghost, hallucination, illu~ sion, mirage, phantasm, phantom, revelation, spectre, wraith 5. dream, feast for the eyes, perfect picture, picture, sight, sight for sore eyes, spectacle

visionary *adj.* 1. dreaming, dreamy, idealistic, quixotic, romantic, starry-eyed, with one's head in the clouds 2. chimerical, delusory, fanciful, fantastic, ideal, idealized, illusory, imaginary, impractical, prophetic, speculative, unreal, un~

realistic, unworkable, utopian ~*n.* 3. daydreamer, Don Quixote, dreamer, enthusiast (*Archaic*), idealist, mystic, prophet, romantic, seer, theorist, utopian, zealot

visit *v.* 1. be the guest of, call in, call on, drop in on (*Inf.*), go to see, inspect, look (someone) up, pay a call on, pop in (*Inf.*), stay at, stay with, stop by, take in (*Inf.*) 2. af~ flict, assail, attack, befall, descend upon, haunt, smite, trouble 3. *With* **on** *or* **upon** bring down upon, ex~ ecute, impose, inflict, wreak ~*n.* 4. call, sojourn, stay, stop

visitation 1. examination, inspec~ tion, visit 2. bane, blight, calamity, cataclysm, catastrophe, disaster, infliction, ordeal, punishment, scourge, trial

visitor caller, company, guest, visi~ tant

visual 1. ocular, optic, optical 2. discernible, observable, percep~ tible, visible

visualize conceive of, conjure up a mental picture of, envisage, imag~ ine, picture, see in the mind's eye

vital 1. basic, cardinal, essential, fundamental, imperative, indis~ pensable, necessary, requisite 2. critical, crucial, decisive, impor~ tant, key, life-or-death, significant, urgent 3. animated, dynamic, en~ ergetic, forceful, full of the joy of living, lively, spirited, vibrant, vig~ orous, vivacious, zestful 4. alive, animate, generative, invigorative, life-giving, live, living, quickening

vitality animation, energy, exuber~ ance, go (*Inf.*), life, liveliness, lustiness, pep, robustness, sparkle, stamina, strength, vigour, vim (*Sl.*), vivaciousness, vivacity

vitriolic *Fig.* acerbic, acid, bitchy (*Sl.*), bitter, caustic, destructive, dripping with malice, envenomed, sardonic, scathing, venomous, virulent, withering

vituperation abuse, billingsgate, blame, castigation, censure, fault-finding, flak (*Inf.*), invective, oblo~ quy, rebuke, reprimand, reproach, scurrility, tongue-lashing, vilifica~ tion

vivacious animated, bubbling, cheerful, ebullient, effervescent, frolicsome, full of life, gay, high-spirited, jolly, light-hearted, lively, merry, scintillating, sparkling, spirited, sportive, sprightly, vital

vivacity animation, ebullience, effervescence, energy, gaiety, high spirits, life, liveliness, pep, quickness, sparkle, spirit, sprightliness

vivid 1. bright, brilliant, clear, colourful, glowing, intense, rich 2. distinct, dramatic, graphic, highly-coloured, lifelike, memorable, powerful, realistic, sharp, sharply-etched, stirring, strong, telling, true to life 3. active, animated, dynamic, energetic, expressive, flamboyant, lively, quick, spirited, striking, strong, vigorous

vixen *Fig.* fury, harpy, harridan, hellcat, scold, shrew, spitfire, termagant (*Rare*), virago, Xanthippe

vocabulary dictionary, glossary, language, lexicon, wordbook, word hoard, words, word stock

vocal *adj.* 1. articulate, articulated, oral, put into words, said, spoken, uttered, voiced 2. articulate, blunt, clamorous, eloquent, expressive, forthright, frank, free-spoken, noisy, outspoken, plain-spoken, strident, vociferous

vocation business, calling, career, employment, job, life's work, life work, métier, mission, office, post, profession, pursuit, role, trade

vociferous clamant, clamorous, loud, loudmouthed (*Inf.*), noisy, obstreperous, ranting, shouting, strident, uproarious, vehement

vogue *n.* 1. craze, custom, *dernier cri*, fashion, last word, mode, style, the latest, the rage, the thing (*Inf.*), trend, way 2. acceptance, currency, fashionableness, favour, popularity, prevalence, usage, use ~*adj.* 3. fashionable, in, modish, now (*Inf.*), popular, prevalent, trendy (*Brit. inf.*), up-to-the-minute, voguish, with it (*Inf.*)

voice *n.* 1. articulation, language, power of speech, sound, tone, utterance, words 2. decision, expression, part, say, view, vote, will, wish 3. agency, instrument, medium, mouthpiece, organ, spokesman, spokesperson, spokeswoman, vehicle ~*v.* assert, come out with (*Inf.*), declare, divulge, enunciate, express, give expression *or* utterance to, put into words, say, utter, ventilate

void *adj.* 1. bare, clear, drained, emptied, empty, free, tenantless, unfilled, unoccupied, vacant 2. *With of* destitute, devoid, lacking, without 3. dead, ineffective, ineffectual, inoperative, invalid, non-viable, nugatory, null and void, unenforceable, useless, vain, worthless ~*n.* 4. blank, blankness, emptiness, gap, lack, opening, space, vacuity, vacuum, want ~*v.* 5. discharge, drain, eject, eliminate (*Physiol.*), emit, empty, evacuate 6. abnegate, cancel, invalidate, nullify, rescind

volatile airy, changeable, erratic, explosive, fickle, flighty, gay, giddy, inconstant, lively, mercurial, sprightly, unsettled, unstable, unsteady, up and down (*Inf.*), variable, whimsical

volition choice, choosing, determination, discretion, election, free will, option, preference, purpose, resolution, will

volley *n.* barrage, blast, bombardment, burst, cannonade, discharge, explosion, fusillade, hail, salvo, shower

volubility fluency, garrulity, gift of the gab (*Inf.*), glibness, loquaciousness, loquacity

voluble articulate, blessed with the gift of the gab (*Inf.*), fluent, forthcoming, glib, loquacious, talkative

volume 1. aggregate, amount, body, bulk, capacity, compass, cubic content, dimensions, mass, quantity, total 2. book, publication, tome, treatise

voluminous ample, big, billowing, bulky, capacious, cavernous, copious, full, large, massive, prolific, roomy, vast

voluntarily by choice, freely, of one's own accord, of one's own free will, on one's own initiative, willingly, without being asked, without prompting

voluntary discretional, free, gratuitous, honorary, intended, intentional, optional, spontaneous, uncompelled, unconstrained, unforced, unpaid, volunteer, willing

volunteer v. advance, let oneself in for (*Inf.*), need no invitation, offer, offer one's services, present, proffer, propose, put forward, put oneself at (someone's) disposal, step forward, suggest, tender

voluptuous 1. epicurean, hedonistic, licentious, luxurious, pleasure-loving, self-indulgent, sensual, sybaritic 2. ample, buxom, curvaceous (*Inf.*), enticing, erotic, full-bosomed, provocative, seductive, shapely, well-stacked (*Brit. sl.*)

voluptuousness carnality, curvaceousness (*Inf.*), licentiousness, opulence, seductiveness, sensuality, shapeliness

vomit v. belch forth, be sick, bring up, disgorge, eject, emit, heave, puke (*Sl.*), regurgitate, retch, sick up (*Inf.*), spew out *or* up, throw up (*Inf.*)

voracious avid, devouring, gluttonous, greedy, hungry, insatiable, omnivorous, prodigious, rapacious, ravening, ravenous, uncontrolled, unquenchable

vote n. 1. ballot, franchise, plebiscite, poll, referendum, right to vote, show of hands, suffrage ~v. 2. ballot, cast one's vote, elect, go to the polls, opt, return 3. *Inf.* declare,

judge, pronounce, propose, recommend, suggest

vouch *Usually with* for affirm, answer for, assert, asseverate, attest to, back, certify, confirm, give assurance of, go bail for, guarantee, stand witness, support, swear to, uphold

vouchsafe accord, cede, condescend to give, confer, deign, favour (someone) with, grant, yield

vow 1. v. affirm, consecrate, dedicate, devote, pledge, promise, swear, undertake solemnly 2. n. oath, pledge, promise, troth (*Archaic*)

voyage n. crossing, cruise, journey, passage, travels, trip

vulgar 1. blue, boorish, cheap and nasty, coarse, common, crude, dirty, flashy, gaudy, gross, ill-bred, impolite, improper, indecent, indecorous, indelicate, low, nasty, naughty, off colour, ribald, risqué, rude, suggestive, tasteless, tawdry, uncouth, unmannerly, unrefined 2. general, native, ordinary, unrefined, vernacular

vulgarity bad taste, coarseness, crudeness, crudity, gaudiness, grossness, indecorum, indelicacy, lack of refinement, ribaldry, rudeness, suggestiveness, tastelessness, tawdriness

vulnerable accessible, assailable, defenceless, exposed, open to attack, sensitive, susceptible, tender, thin-skinned, unprotected, weak, wide open

W

wad ball, block, bundle, chunk, hunk, lump, mass, plug, roll

wadding filler, lining, packing, padding, stuffing

waddle rock, shuffle, sway, toddle, totter, wobble

wade 1. ford, paddle, splash, walk through 2. *With* **through** drudge, labour, peg away, plough through, toil, work one's way 3. *With* **in** or **into** assail, attack, get stuck in (*Sl.*), go for, launch oneself at, light into (*Inf.*), set about, tackle, tear into (*Inf.*)

waffle 1. *v.* blather, jabber, prate, prattle, rabbit on (*Brit. sl.*), verbalize, witter on (*Inf.*) 2. *n.* blather, jabber, padding, prating, prattle, prolixity, verbiage, verbosity, wordiness

waft 1. *v.* bear, be carried, carry, convey, drift, float, ride, transmit, transport 2. *n.* breath, breeze, current, draught, puff, whiff

wag 1. *v.* bob, flutter, nod, oscillate, quiver, rock, shake, stir, vibrate, waggle, wave, wiggle 2. *n.* bob, flutter, nod, oscillation, quiver, shake, toss, vibration, waggle, wave, wiggle

wage 1. *n. Also* wages allowance, compensation, earnings, emolument, fee, hire, pay, payment, recompense, remuneration, reward, stipend 2. *v.* carry on, conduct, engage in, practise, proceed with, prosecute, pursue, undertake

wager 1. *n.* bet, flutter (*Brit. inf.*), gamble, pledge, punt, stake, venture 2. *v.* bet, chance, gamble, hazard, lay, pledge, punt, put on, risk, speculate, stake, venture

waggle 1. *v.* flutter, oscillate, shake, wag, wave, wiggle, wobble 2. *n.* flutter, oscillation, shake, wag, wave, wiggle, wobble

waif foundling, orphan, stray

wail 1. *v.* bemoan, bewail, cry, deplore, grieve, howl, keen, lament, ululate, weep, yowl 2. *n.* complaint, cry, grief, howl, keen, lament, lamentation, moan, ululation, weeping, yowl

wait 1. *v.* abide, bide one's time, cool one's heels, dally, delay, hang fire, hold back, hold on (*Inf.*), linger, mark time, pause, remain, rest, stand by, stay, tarry 2. *n.* delay, halt, hold-up, interval, pause, rest, stay

waiter, waitress attendant, server, steward, stewardess

wait on or upon attend, minister to, serve, tend

waive abandon, defer, dispense with, forgo, give up, postpone, put off, refrain from, relinquish, remit, renounce, resign, set aside, surrender

waiver abandonment, abdication, disclaimer, giving up, relinquishment, remission, renunciation, resignation, setting aside, surrender

wake¹ *v.* 1. arise, awake, awaken, bestir, come to, get up, rouse, rouse from sleep, stir 2. activate, animate, arouse, awaken, enliven, excite, fire, galvanize, kindle, provoke, quicken, stimulate, stir up ~*n.* 3. deathwatch, funeral, vigil, watch

wake² aftermath, backwash, path, track, trail, train, wash, waves

wakeful 1. insomniac, restless, sleepless, unsleeping 2. alert, alive, attentive, heedful, observant, on guard, on the alert, on the lookout, on the qui vive, unsleeping, vigilant, wary, watchful

waken activate, animate, arouse, awake, awaken, be roused, come awake, come to, enliven, fire, galvanize, get up, kindle, quicken, rouse, stimulate, stir

walk *v.* 1. advance, amble, foot it, go, go by shanks's pony (*Inf.*), go on foot, hike, hoof it (*Sl.*), march, move, pace, perambulate, promenade, saunter, step, stride, stroll, traipse (*Inf.*), tramp, travel on foot, trek, trudge 2. accompany, convoy, escort, take ~*n.* 3. constitutional, hike, march, perambulation, promenade, ramble, saunter, stroll, traipse (*Inf.*), tramp, trek, trudge, turn 4. carriage, gait, manner of walking, pace, step, stride 5. aisle, alley, avenue, esplanade, footpath, lane, path, pathway, pavement, promenade, sidewalk, trail 6. area, arena, calling, career, course, field, line, métier, profession, sphere, trade, vocation

walker footslogger, hiker, pedes~ trian, rambler, wayfarer

walkout industrial action, protest, stoppage, strike

walk out 1. flounce out, get up and go, leave suddenly, storm out, take off (*Inf.*) 2. down tools, go on strike, stop work, strike, take industrial action, withdraw one's labour 3. *With* **on** abandon, chuck (*Inf.*), de~ sert, forsake, jilt, leave, leave in the lurch, pack in (*Inf.*), run away from, throw over

walkover child's play (*Inf.*), doddle (*Brit. sl.*), easy victory, picnic (*Inf.*), piece of cake (*Inf.*), push~ over (*Sl.*), snap (*Inf.*)

wall 1. divider, enclosure, panel, partition, screen 2. barricade, breastwork, bulwark, embank~ ment, fortification, palisade, para~ pet, rampart, stockade 3. barrier, block, fence, hedge, impediment, obstacle, obstruction 4. **go to the wall** *Inf.* be ruined, collapse, fail, fall, go bust (*Inf.*), go under 5. **drive up the wall** *Sl.* annoy, dement, de~ range, drive crazy, drive insane, exasperate, infuriate, irritate, madden, send off one's head (*Sl.*), try

wallet case, holder, notecase, pocketbook, pouch, purse

wallow 1. lie, roll about, splash around, tumble, welter 2. flounder, lurch, stagger, stumble, wade 3. bask, delight, glory, indulge one~ self, luxuriate, relish, revel, take pleasure

wan 1. anaemic, ashen, bloodless, cadaverous, colourless, discol~ oured, ghastly, livid, pale, pallid, pasty, sickly, washed out, waxen, wheyfaced, white 2. dim, faint, feeble, pale, weak

wand baton, rod, sprig, stick, twig, withe, withy

wander *v.* 1. cruise, drift, knock about, knock around, meander, mooch around (*Sl.*), peregrinate, ramble, range, roam, rove, strag~ gle, stravaig (*Scot.*), stray, stroll, traipse (*Inf.*) 2. depart, deviate, di~ gress, divagate (*Rare*), diverge, err, get lost, go astray, go off at a tangent, go off course, lapse, lose concentration, lose one's train of thought, lose one's way, swerve, veer 3. babble, be delirious, be in~ coherent, ramble, rave, speak in~ coherently, talk nonsense ~*n.* 4. cruise, excursion, meander, per~ egrination, ramble, traipse (*Inf.*)

wanderer bird of passage, drifter, gypsy, itinerant, nomad, rambler, ranger, rolling stone, rover, stroll~ er, traveller, vagabond, vagrant, voyager

wandering drifting, homeless, itinerant, migratory, nomadic, peripatetic, rambling, rootless, roving, strolling, travelling, vaga~ bond, vagrant, voyaging, wayfaring

wane *v.* 1. abate, atrophy, decline, decrease, die out, dim, diminish, draw to a close, drop, dwindle, ebb, fade, fade away, fail, lessen, sink, subside, taper off, weaken, wind down, wither ~*n.* 2. abatement, at~ rophy, decay, declension, de~ crease, diminution, drop, dwin~ dling, ebb, fading, failure, fall, fall~ ing off, lessening, sinking, subsid~ ence, tapering off, withering 3. **on the wane** at its lowest ebb, declin~ ing, dropping, dwindling, dying out, ebbing, fading, lessening, obsoles~ cent, on its last legs, on the decline, on the way out, subsiding, tapering off, weakening, withering

want *v.* 1. covet, crave, desire, feel a need for, hanker after, have a fancy for, have a yen for (*Inf.*), hunger for, long for, need, pine for, require, thirst for, wish, yearn for 2. be able to do with, be deficient in, be short of, be without, call for, demand, fall short in, have need of, lack, miss, need, require, stand in need of ~*n*. 3. appetite, craving, demand, desire, fancy, hankering, hunger, longing, necessity, need, requirement, thirst, wish, yearn~ ing, yen (*Inf.*) 4. absence, dearth, default, deficiency, famine, insuffi~ ciency, lack, paucity, scantiness, scarcity, shortage 5. destitution, indigence, need, neediness, pau~ perism, penury, poverty, privation

wanting 1. absent, incomplete, lacking, less, missing, short, shy 2. defective, deficient, disappointing, faulty, imperfect, inadequate, infe~ rior, leaving much to be desired, not good enough, not up to expec~ tations, not up to par, patchy, poor, sketchy, substandard, unsound

wanton *adj.* 1. abandoned, dissi~ pated, dissolute, fast, immoral, lecherous, lewd, libertine, libidi~ nous, licentious, loose, lustful, of easy virtue, promiscuous, rakish, shameless, unchaste 2. arbitrary, cruel, evil, gratuitous, groundless, malevolent, malicious, motiveless, needless, senseless, spiteful, uncalled-for, unjustifiable, unjusti~ fied, unprovoked, vicious, wicked, wilful 3. careless, devil-may-care, extravagant, heedless, immoder~ ate, intemperate, lavish, outra~ geous, rash, reckless, unrestrained, wild ~*n*. 4. Casanova, debauchee, Don Juan, harlot, lecher, libertine, loose woman, profligate, prostitute, rake, roué, slut, strumpet, tart (*Inf.*), trollop, voluptuary, whore, woman of easy virtue ~*v*. 5. de~ bauch, dissipate, revel, riot, sleep around (*Inf.*), wench (*Archaic*), whore 6. fritter away, misspend, squander, throw away, waste

war 1. *n*. armed conflict, battle, bloodshed, combat, conflict, con~ tention, contest, enmity, fighting, hostilities, hostility, strife, struggle, warfare 2. *v*. battle, campaign against, carry on hostilities, clash, combat, conduct a war, contend, contest, fight, make war, strive, struggle, take up arms, wage war

war cry battle cry, rallying cry, slogan, war whoop

ward 1. area, district, division, pre~ cinct, quarter, zone 2. apartment, cubicle, room 3. charge, depend~ ant, minor, protégé, pupil 4. care, charge, custody, guardianship, keeping, protection, safekeeping

warden administrator, caretaker, curator, custodian, guardian, jani~ tor, keeper, ranger, steward, superintendent, warder, watchman

warder, wardress custodian, gaoler, guard, jailer, keeper, prison officer, screw (*Sl.*), turnkey (*Ar~ chaic*)

ward off avert, avoid, beat off, block, deflect, fend off, forestall, keep at arm's length, keep at bay, parry, repel, stave off, thwart, turn aside, turn away

wardrobe 1. closet, clothes cup~ board, clothes-press 2. apparel, at~ tire, clothes, collection of clothes, outfit

warehouse depository, depot, stockroom, store, storehouse

wares commodities, goods, lines, manufactures, merchandise, pro~ duce, products, stock, stuff

warfare armed conflict, armed struggle, arms, battle, blows, cam~ paigning, clash of arms, combat, conflict, contest, discord, fighting, hostilities, passage of arms, strat~ egy, strife, struggle, war

warily cagily (*Inf.*), carefully, cau~ tiously, charily, circumspectly, distrustfully, gingerly, guardedly, suspiciously, vigilantly, watchfully, with care

wariness alertness, attention, caginess (*Inf.*), care, carefulness, caution, circumspection, discre~ tion, distrust, foresight, heedful~ ness, mindfulness, prudence, sus~ picion, vigilance, watchfulness

warlike aggressive, bellicose, bel~ ligerent, bloodthirsty, combative, hawkish, hostile, inimical, jingois~ tic, martial, militaristic, military, pugnacious, sabre-rattling, un~ friendly, warmongering

warm *adj.* 1. balmy, heated, luke~ warm, moderately hot, pleasant, sunny, tepid, thermal 2. affable, affectionate, amiable, amorous, cheerful, cordial, friendly, genial, happy, hearty, hospitable, kindly, loving, pleasant, tender 3. animated, ardent, cordial, earnest, effusive, emotional, enthusiastic, excited, fervent, glowing, heated, intense, keen, lively, passionate, spirited, stormy, vehement, vigorous, violent, zealous 4. irascible, irritable, passionate, quick, sensitive, short, touchy 5. *Inf.* dangerous, disagreeable, hazardous, perilous, tricky, uncomfortable, unpleasant ~*v.* 6. heat, heat up, melt, thaw, warm up 7. animate, awaken, excite, get going (*Inf.*), interest, make enthusiastic, put some life into, rouse, stimulate, stir, turn on (*Sl.*)

warm-blooded ardent, earnest, emotional, enthusiastic, excitable, fervent, impetuous, lively, passionate, rash, spirited, vivacious

warm-hearted affectionate, compassionate, cordial, generous, kindhearted, kindly, loving, sympathetic, tender, tender-hearted

warmonger belligerent, hawk, jingo, militarist, sabre-rattler

warmth 1. heat, hotness, warmness 2. animation, ardour, eagerness, earnestness, effusiveness, enthusiasm, excitement, fervency, fervour, fire, heat, intensity, passion, spirit, transport, vehemence, vigour, violence, zeal, zest 3. affability, affection, amorousness, cheerfulness, cordiality, happiness, heartiness, hospitableness, kindliness, love, tenderness

warn admonish, advise, alert, apprise, caution, forewarn, give fair warning, give notice, inform, make (someone) aware, notify, put one on one's guard, summon, tip off

warning 1. *n.* admonition, advice, alarm, alert, augury, caution, caveat, foretoken, hint, notice, notification, omen, premonition, presage, sign, signal, threat, tip, tip-off, token, word, word to the wise 2. *adj.* admonitory, cautionary, monitory, ominous, premonitory, threatening

warrant *n.* 1. assurance, authority, authorization, carte blanche, commission, guarantee, licence, permission, permit, pledge, sanction, security, warranty ~*v.* 2. affirm, answer for, assure, attest, avouch, certify, declare, guarantee, pledge, secure, stand behind, underwrite, uphold, vouch for 3. approve, authorize, call for, commission, demand, empower, entitle, excuse, give ground for, justify, license, necessitate, permit, require, sanction

warrantable accountable, allowable, defensible, justifiable, lawful, necessary, permissible, proper, reasonable, right

warrior champion, combatant, fighter, fighting man, man-at-arms, soldier

wary alert, attentive, cagey (*Inf.*), careful, cautious, chary, circumspect, distrustful, guarded, heedful, leery (*Sl.*), on one's guard, on the lookout, on the qui vive, prudent, suspicious, vigilant, watchful, wideawake

wash *v.* 1. bath, bathe, clean, cleanse, launder, moisten, rinse, scrub, shampoo, shower, wet 2. *With away* bear away, carry off, erode, move, sweep away, wash off 3. *Inf.* bear scrutiny, be convincing, be plausible, carry weight, hold up, hold water, stand up, stick 4. **wash one's hands of** abandon, accept no responsibility for, give up on, have nothing to do with, leave to one's own devices ~*n.* 5. ablution, bath, bathe, cleaning, cleansing, laundering, rinse, scrub, shampoo, shower, washing 6. ebb and flow, flow, roll, surge, sweep, swell, wave 7. coat, coating, film, layer, overlay, screen, stain, suffusion

washed out 1. blanched, bleached, colourless, etiolated, faded, flat, lacklustre, mat, pale 2. all in (*Sl.*), dead on one's feet, dog-tired (*Inf.*), done in (*Inf.*), drained, drawn, exhausted, fatigued, haggard, knackered (Sl.), pale, spent, tired-out, wan, weary, worn-out

washout 1. disappointment, disaster, dud (Inf.), failure, fiasco, flop (Inf.), mess **2.** failure, incompetent, loser

waspish bad-tempered, cantankerous, captious, crabbed, crabby, cross, crotchety (Inf.), fretful, grumpy, ill-tempered, irascible, irritable, peevish, peppery, pettish, petulant, snappish, splenetic, testy, touchy, waxy (Brit. sl.)

waste v. **1.** blow (Sl.), dissipate, fritter away, frivol away (Inf.), lavish, misuse, run through, squander, throw away **2.** atrophy, consume, corrode, crumble, debilitate, decay, decline, deplete, disable, drain, dwindle, eat away, ebb, emaciate, enfeeble, exhaust, fade, gnaw, perish, sap the strength of, sink, undermine, wane, wear out, wither **3.** despoil, destroy, devastate, lay waste, pillage, rape, ravage, raze, ruin, sack, spoil, wreak havoc upon ~n. **4.** dissipation, expenditure, extravagance, frittering away, loss, lost opportunity, misapplication, misuse, prodigality, squandering, unthriftiness, wastefulness **5.** desolation, destruction, devastation, havoc, ravage, ruin **6.** debris, dregs, dross, garbage, leavings, leftovers, litter, offal, offscourings, refuse, rubbish, scrap, sweepings, trash **7.** desert, solitude, void, wasteland, wild, wilderness ~adj. **8.** leftover, superfluous, supernumerary, unused, unwanted, useless, worthless **9.** bare, barren, desolate, devastated, dismal, dreary, empty, uncultivated, uninhabited, unproductive, wild **10.** lay waste depredate (Rare), despoil, destroy, devastate, pillage, rape, ravage, raze, ruin, sack, spoil, wreak havoc upon

wasteful extravagant, improvident, lavish, prodigal, profligate, ruinous, spendthrift, thriftless, uneconomical, unthrifty

wastrel 1. prodigal, profligate, spendthrift, squanderer **2.** drone, good-for-nothing, idler, layabout, loafer, loser, malingerer, ne'er-do-well, shirker, waster

watch v. **1.** contemplate, eye, gaze at, look, look at, look on, mark, note, observe, pay attention, peer at, regard, see, stare at, view **2.** attend, be on the alert, be on the lookout, be vigilant, be wary, be watchful, keep an eye open (Inf.), look out, take heed, wait **3.** guard, keep, look after, mind, protect, superintend, take care of, tend ~n. **4.** chronometer, clock, pocket watch, timepiece, wristwatch **5.** alertness, attention, eye, heed, inspection, lookout, notice, observation, supervision, surveillance, vigil, vigilance, watchfulness

watchdog 1. guard dog **2.** custodian, guardian, inspector, monitor, protector, scrutineer

watcher looker-on, lookout, observer, onlooker, spectator, spy, viewer, witness

watchful alert, attentive, circumspect, guarded, heedful, observant, on one's guard, on the lookout, on the qui vive, on the watch, suspicious, vigilant, wary, wide awake

watchman caretaker, custodian, guard, security guard, security man

watch out be alert, be careful, be on one's guard, be on the alert, be on (the) watch, be vigilant, be watchful, have a care, keep a sharp lookout, keep a weather eye open, keep one's eyes open, keep one's eyes peeled or skinned (Inf.), look out, mind out, watch oneself

watch over defend, guard, keep safe, look after, preserve, protect, shelter, shield, stand guard over

water n. **1.** Adam's ale or wine, aqua, H_2O **2. hold water** bear examination or scrutiny, be credible (logical, sound), make sense, pass the test, ring true, work **3. of the first water** excellent, of the best, of the best quality, of the finest quality, of the highest degree, of the highest grade ~v. **4.** damp, dampen, douse, drench, flood, hose, irrigate, moisten, soak, souse, spray, sprinkle **5.** add water to, adulterate, dilute, put water in, thin, water down, weaken

water down 1.add water to, adul~ terate, dilute, put water in, thin, water, weaken 2.adulterate, miti~ gate, qualify, soften, tone down, weaken

waterfall cascade, cataract, chute, fall, force (*Northern Brit.*), linn (*Scot.*)

watertight 1.sound, waterproof 2. airtight, firm, flawless, foolproof, impregnable, incontrovertible, sound, unassailable

watery 1.aqueous, damp, fluid, hu~ mid, liquid, marshy, moist, soggy, squelchy, wet 2. rheumy, tear-filled, tearful, weepy 3.adulterat~ ed, dilute, diluted, flavourless, in~ sipid, runny, tasteless, thin, washy, watered-down, waterish, weak, wishy-washy (*Inf.*)

wave v. 1.brandish, flap, flourish, flutter, move to and fro, oscillate, quiver, ripple, shake, stir, sway, swing, undulate, wag, waver, wield 2.beckon, direct, gesticulate, ges~ ture, indicate, sign, signal ~n. 3. billow, breaker, comber, ridge, ripple, roller, sea surf, swell, undu~ lation, unevenness 4.current, drift, flood, ground swell, movement, outbreak, rash, rush, stream, surge, sweep, tendency, trend, up~ surge

waver 1.be indecisive, be irreso~ lute, be unable to decide, be unable to make up one's mind, blow hot and cold (*Inf.*), dither, falter, fluc~ tuate, hesitate, hum and haw, see-saw, shillyshally (*Inf.*), swither (*Scot.*), vacillate 2.flicker, fluctu~ ate, quiver, reel, shake, sway, tot~ ter, tremble, undulate, vary, wave, weave, wobble

wax v. become fuller, become larger, develop, dilate, enlarge, expand, fill out, get bigger, grow, increase, magnify, mount, rise, swell

way 1.approach, course of action, fashion, manner, means, method, mode, plan, practice, procedure, process, scheme, system, tech~ nique 2. access, avenue, channel,

course, direction, highway, lane, path, pathway, road, route, street, thoroughfare, track, trail 3.elbow-room, opening, room, space 4.dis~ tance, journey, length, stretch, trail 5. advance, approach, journey, march, passage, progress 6.char~ acteristic, conduct, custom, habit, idiosyncrasy, manner, nature, per~ sonality, practice, style, trait, us~ age, wont 7.aspect, detail, feature, particular, point, respect, sense 8. aim, ambition, choice, demand, desire, goal, pleasure, will, wish 9. *Inf.* circumstance, condition, fettle, shape (*Inf.*), situation, state, status 10. forward motion, headway, movement, passage, progress 11. **by the way** by the bye, en passant, incidentally, in parenthesis, in passing 12. **give way a.** break down, cave in, collapse, crack, crumple, fall, fall to pieces, give, go to pieces, subside **b.** accede, acknowledge defeat, acquiesce, back down, concede, make con~ cessions, withdraw, yield 13. **under way** afoot, begun, going, in motion, in progress, moving, on the go (*Inf.*), on the move, started

wayfarer bird of passage, globe-trotter, Gypsy, itinerant, journeyer, nomad, rover, traveller, trekker, voyager, walker, wanderer

wayward capricious, changeable, contrary, contumacious, cross-grained, disobedient, erratic, fick~ le, flighty, froward, headstrong, in~ constant, incorrigible, insubordi~ nate, intractable, mulish, obdurate, obstinate, perverse, rebellious, re~ fractory, self-willed, stubborn, un~ dependable, ungovernable, un~ manageable, unpredictable, unru~ ly, wilful

weak 1.anaemic, debilitated, de~ crepit, delicate, effete, enervated, exhausted, faint, feeble, fragile, frail, infirm, languid, puny, shaky, sickly, spent, tender, unsound, un~ steady, wasted, weakly 2.coward~ ly, impotent, indecisive, ineffec~ tual, infirm, irresolute, namby-pamby, powerless, soft, spineless, timorous, weak-kneed (*Inf.*) 3.dis~ tant, dull, faint, imperceptible, low, muffled, poor, quiet, slight, small, soft 4. deficient, faulty, inadequate, lacking, poor, substandard, under-strength, wanting 5. feeble, flimsy, hollow, inconclusive, invalid, lame, pathetic, shallow, slight, uncon-vincing, unsatisfactory 6. defence-less, exposed, helpless, unguarded, unprotected, unsafe, untenable, vulnerable, wide open 7. diluted, insipid, milk-and-water, runny, tasteless, thin, under-strength, wa~terish, watery, wishy-washy (*Inf.*)

weaken 1. abate, debilitate, de-press, diminish, droop, dwindle, ease up, enervate, fade, fail, flag, give way, impair, invalidate, less-en, lower, mitigate, moderate, re-duce, sap, sap the strength of, sof-ten up, temper, tire, undermine, wane 2. adulterate, cut, debase, di-lute, thin, thin out, water down

weakling coward, doormat (*Sl.*), drip (*Inf.*), jellyfish (*Inf.*), milksop, mouse, sissy, wet (*Brit. inf.*), wimp (*Inf.*)

weakness 1. debility, decrepitude, enervation, faintness, feebleness, fragility, frailty, impotence, infir~mity, irresolution, powerlessness, vulnerability 2. Achilles heel, blemish, chink in one's armour, defect, deficiency, failing, fault, flaw, imperfection, lack, short~coming 3. fondness, inclination, liking, passion, penchant, predi-lection, proclivity, proneness, soft spot

wealth 1. affluence, assets, capital, cash, estate, fortune, funds, goods, lucre, means, money, opulence, pelf, possessions, property, pros~perity, resources, riches, substance 2. abundance, bounty, copiousness, cornucopia, fullness, plenitude, plenty, profusion, richness, store

wealthy affluent, comfortable, filthy rich (*Sl.*), flush (*Inf.*), in the money (*Inf.*), loaded (*Sl.*), made of money (*Inf.*), moneyed, on easy street (*Sl.*), opulent, prosperous, quids in (*Sl.*), rich, rolling in it (*Sl.*), stinking rich (*Sl.*), well-heeled (*Sl.*), well-off, well-to-do

wear *v.* 1. bear, be clothed in, be dressed in, carry, clothe oneself, don, dress in, have on, put on, sport 2. display, exhibit, fly, show 3. abrade, consume, corrode, de-teriorate, erode, fray, grind, im-pair, rub, use, wash away, waste 4. bear up, be durable, endure, hold up, last, stand up 5. annoy, drain, enervate, exasperate, fatigue, har-ass, irk, pester, tax, undermine, vex, weaken, weary 6. *Brit. sl.* ac-cept, allow, brook, countenance, fall for, permit, put up with (*Inf.*), stand for, stomach, swallow (*Inf.*), take ~*n.* 7. employment, mileage (*Inf.*), service, use, usefulness, util~ity 8. apparel, attire, clothes, cos-tume, dress, garb, garments, gear, habit, outfit, things 9. abrasion, at~trition, corrosion, damage, depre~ciation, deterioration, erosion, friction, use, wear and tear

wear down 1. abrade, be con-sumed, consume, corrode, erode, grind down, rub away 2. chip away at (*Inf.*), fight a war of attrition against, overcome gradually, re-duce, undermine

weariness drowsiness, enervation, exhaustion, fatigue, languor, lassi~tude, lethargy, listlessness, pros-tration, tiredness

wearing exasperating, exhausting, fatiguing, irksome, oppressive, taxing, tiresome, tiring, trying, wearisome

wearisome annoying, boring, bothersome, burdensome, dull, ex-asperating, exhausting, fatiguing, humdrum, irksome, monotonous, oppressive, pestilential, prosaic, tedious, troublesome, trying, unin~teresting, vexatious, wearing

wear off 1. abate, decrease, dimin-ish, disappear, dwindle, ebb, fade, lose effect, lose strength, peter out, subside, wane, weaken 2. abrade, disappear, efface, fade, rub away

wear out 1. become useless, be-come worn, consume, deteriorate, erode, fray, impair, use up, wear through 2. enervate, exhaust, fag out (*Inf.*), fatigue, frazzle (*Inf.*), knacker (*Brit. sl.*), prostrate, sap, tire, weary

weary *adj.* **1.** all in (*Sl.*), asleep *or* dead on one's feet (*Inf.*), dead beat (*Inf.*), dog-tired (*Inf.*), done in (*Inf.*), drained, drooping, drowsy, enervated, exhausted, fagged (*Inf.*), fatigued, flagging, jaded, knackered (*Sl.*), ready to drop, sleepy, spent, tired, wearied, whacked (*Brit. inf.*), worn out **2.** arduous, enervative, irksome, laborious, taxing, tiresome, tiring, wearing, wearisome **3.** bored, browned-off (*Inf.*), discontented, fed up, impatient, indifferent, jaded, sick (*Inf.*), sick and tired (*Inf.*) ~*v.* **4.** burden, debilitate, drain, droop, enervate, fade, fag (*Inf.*), fail, fatigue, grow tired, sap, take it out of (*Inf.*), tax, tire, tire out, wear out **5.** annoy, become bored, bore, exasperate, have had enough, irk, jade, make discontented, plague, sicken, try the patience of, vex

weather *n.* **1.** climate, conditions **2.** under the weather **a.** ailing, below par, ill, indisposed, nauseous, not well, off-colour, out of sorts, poorly (*Inf.*), seedy (*Inf.*), sick **b.** crapulent, crapulous, drunk, groggy (*Inf.*), hung over (*Inf.*), inebriated, intoxicated, one over the eight (*Sl.*), the worse for drink, three sheets in the wind (*Inf.*), under the influence (*Inf.*) ~*v.* **3.** expose, harden, season, toughen **4.** bear up against, brave, come through, endure, get through, live through, make it (*Inf.*), overcome, pull through, resist, ride out, rise above, stand, stick it out (*Inf.*), suffer, surmount, survive, withstand

weave **1.** blend, braid, entwine, fuse, incorporate, interlace, intermingle, intertwine, introduce, knit, mat, merge, plait, twist, unite **2.** build, construct, contrive, create, fabricate, make, make up, put together, spin **3.** crisscross, move in and out, weave one's way, wind, zigzag **4.** get weaving *Inf.* get a move on, get going, get one's finger out (*Brit. inf.*), get under way, hurry, make a start, shake a leg (*Sl.*), start

web **1.** cobweb, spider's web **2.** interlacing, lattice, mesh, net, net-ting, network, screen, tangle, toils, weave, webbing

wed **1.** become man and wife, be married to, espouse, get hitched (*Inf.*), get married, join, make one, marry, splice (*Inf.*), take as one's husband, take as one's wife, take to wife, tie the knot (*Inf.*), unite **2.** ally, blend, coalesce, combine, commingle, dedicate, fuse, inter-weave, join, link, marry, merge, unify, unite, yoke

wedding espousals, marriage, marriage ceremony, nuptial rite, nuptials, wedlock

wedge **1.** *n.* block, chock, chunk, lump, wodge (*Brit. inf.*) **2.** *v.* block, cram, crowd, force, jam, lodge, pack, ram, split, squeeze, stuff, thrust

wedlock marriage, matrimony

weed out dispense with, eliminate, eradicate, extirpate, get rid of, remove, root out, separate out, shed, uproot

weekly by the week, every week, hebdomadal, hebdomadally, heb-domadary, once a week

weep bemoan, bewail, blub (*Sl.*), blubber, boohoo, complain, cry, greet (*Dialect*), keen, lament, moan, mourn, shed tears, snivel, sob, ululate, whimper, whinge (*Inf.*)

weigh **1.** have a weight of, measure the weight of, put on the scales, tip the scales at (*Inf.*) **2.** apportion, deal out, dole out, measure **3.** consider, contemplate, deliberate upon, evaluate, examine, give thought to, meditate upon, mull over, ponder, reflect upon, study, think over **4.** be influential, carry weight, count, cut any ice (*Inf.*), have influence, impress, matter, tell **5.** bear down, burden, oppress, prey

weigh down bear down, burden, depress, get down, oppress, over-burden, overload, press down, trouble, weigh upon, worry

weight *n.* **1.** avoirdupois, burden, gravity, heaviness, heft (*Inf.*), load, mass, poundage, pressure, tonnage **2.** ballast, heavy object, load, mass

3. burden, load, millstone, oppres~ sion, pressure, strain 4. greatest force, main force, onus, prepon~ derance 5. authority, clout (*Inf.*), consequence, consideration, effi~ cacy, emphasis, impact, import, importance, influence, moment, persuasiveness, power, signifi~ cance, substance, value ~*v.* 6. add weight to, ballast, charge, freight, increase the load on, increase the weight of, load, make heavier 7. burden, encumber, handicap, im~ pede, oppress, overburden, weigh down 8. bias, load, unbalance

weighty 1. burdensome, cumber~ some, dense, heavy, hefty (*Inf.*), massive, ponderous 2. consequen~ tial, considerable, critical, crucial, forcible, grave, important, mo~ mentous, portentous, serious, sig~ nificant, solemn, substantial 3. backbreaking, burdensome, crushing, demanding, difficult, ex~ acting, onerous, oppressive, taxing, worrisome, worrying

weird bizarre, creepy (*Inf.*), eerie, eldritch (*Poetic*), far-out (*Sl.*), freakish, ghostly, grotesque, mys~ terious, odd, outlandish, queer, spooky (*Inf.*), strange, supernatu~ ral, uncanny, unearthly, unnatural

welcome *adj.* 1. acceptable, ac~ cepted, agreeable, appreciated, delightful, desirable, gladly re~ ceived, gratifying, pleasant, pleas~ ing, pleasurable, refreshing, want~ ed 2. at home, free, invited, under no obligation ~*n.* 3. acceptance, entertainment, greeting, hospital~ ity, reception, salutation ~*v.* 4. ac~ cept gladly, bid welcome, em~ brace, greet, hail, meet, offer hos~ pitality to, receive, receive with open arms, roll out the red carpet for, usher in

welfare advantage, benefit, good, happiness, health, interest, profit, prosperity, success, wellbeing

well[1] *adv.* 1. agreeably, capitally, famously (*Inf.*), happily, in a satis~ factory manner, nicely, pleasantly, satisfactorily, smoothly, splendidly, successfully 2. ably, adeptly, ad~ equately, admirably, conscien~

tiously, correctly, effectively, effi~ ciently, expertly, proficiently, properly, skilfully, with skill 3. ac~ curately, attentively, carefully, closely 4. comfortably, flourish~ ingly, prosperously 5. correctly, easily, fairly, fittingly, in all fair~ ness, justly, properly, readily, rightly, suitably 6. closely, com~ pletely, deeply, fully, intimately, personally, profoundly, thoroughly 7. approvingly, favourably, glow~ ingly, graciously, highly, kindly, warmly 8. abundantly, amply, completely, considerably, fully, greatly, heartily, highly, substan~ tially, sufficiently, thoroughly, very much 9. as well also, besides, in addition, into the bargain, to boot, too 10. as well as along with, at the same time as, in addition to, in~ cluding, over and above ~*adj.* 11. able-bodied, fit, hale, healthy, hearty, in fine fettle, in good health, robust, sound, strong, up to par 12. advisable, agreeable, bright, fine, fitting, flourishing, fortunate, good, happy, lucky, pleasing, profitable, proper, pru~ dent, right, satisfactory, thriving, useful

well[2] *n.* 1. fountain, pool, source, spring, waterhole 2. bore, hole, pit, shaft 3. fount, mine, repository, source, wellspring ~*v.* 4. flow, gush, jet, ooze, pour, rise, run, seep, spout, spring, spurt, stream, surge, trickle

well-balanced 1. graceful, harmo~ nious, proportional, symmetrical, well-proportioned 2. judicious, level-headed, rational, reasonable, sane, sensible, sober, sound, to~ gether (*Sl.*), well-adjusted

well-bred 1. aristocratic, blue-blooded, gentle, highborn, noble, patrician, well-born 2. civil, cour~ teous, courtly, cultivated, cultured, gallant, genteel, gentlemanly, ladylike, mannerly, polished, po~ lite, refined, urbane, well-brought-up, well-mannered

well-fed 1. healthy, in good condi~ tion, well-nourished 2. chubby, fat, fleshy, plump, podgy, portly, ro~ tund, rounded, stout

well-groomed dapper, neat, smart, spruce, tidy, trim, well-dressed, well turned out

well-known celebrated, familiar, famous, illustrious, notable, noted, popular, renowned, widely known

well-nigh all but, almost, just about, more or less, nearly, next to, practically, virtually

well-off 1. comfortable, flourishing, fortunate, lucky, successful, thriving 2. affluent, comfortable, flush (*Inf.*), loaded (*Sl.*), moneyed, prosperous, rich, wealthy, well-heeled (*Sl.*), well-to-do

well-to-do affluent, comfortable, flush (*Inf.*), loaded (*Sl.*), moneyed, prosperous, rich, wealthy, well-heeled (*Sl.*), well-off

wet *adj.* 1. aqueous, damp, dank, drenched, dripping, humid, moist, moistened, saturated, soaked, soaking, sodden, soggy, sopping, waterlogged, watery, wringing wet 2. clammy, dank, drizzling, humid, misty, pouring, raining, rainy, showery, teeming 3. *Brit. inf.* effete, feeble, foolish, ineffectual, irresolute, namby-pamby, silly, soft, spineless, timorous, weak, weedy (*Inf.*) 4. **wet behind the ears** *Inf.* born yesterday, callow, green, immature, inexperienced, innocent, naive, new, raw ~*n.* 5. clamminess, condensation, damp, dampness, humidity, liquid, moisture, water, wetness 6. damp weather, drizzle, rain, rains, rainy season, rainy weather 7. *Brit. inf.* drip (*Inf.*), milksop, weakling, weed (*Inf.*), wimp (*Inf.*) ~*v.* 8. damp, dampen, dip, douse, drench, humidify, irrigate, moisten, saturate, soak, splash, spray, sprinkle, steep, water

wharf dock, jetty, landing stage, pier, quay

wheedle butter up, cajole, charm, coax, court, draw, entice, flatter, inveigle, persuade, talk into, worm

wheel *n.* 1. circle, gyration, pivot, revolution, roll, rotation, spin, turn, twirl, whirl 2. **at the wheel** at the helm, driving, in charge, in command, in control, in the driving seat, steering ~*v.* 3. circle, gyrate, orbit, pirouette, revolve, roll, rotate, spin, swing, swivel, turn, twirl, whirl

wheeze *v.* 1. breathe roughly, catch one's breath, cough, gasp, hiss, rasp, whistle ~*n.* 2. cough, gasp, hiss, rasp, whistle 3. *Brit. sl.* expedient, idea, plan, ploy, ruse, scheme, stunt, trick, wrinkle (*Inf.*) 4. *Inf.* anecdote, chestnut (*Inf.*), crack (*Sl.*), gag (*Sl.*), joke, old joke, one-liner (*Sl.*), story

whereabouts location, position, site, situation

wherewithal capital, equipment, essentials, funds, means, money, ready (*Inf.*), ready money, resources, supplies

whet 1. edge, file, grind, hone, sharpen, strop 2. animate, arouse, awaken, enhance, excite, incite, increase, kindle, pique, provoke, quicken, rouse, stimulate, stir

whiff *n.* 1. aroma, blast, breath, draught, gust, hint, odour, puff, scent, smell, sniff ~*v.* 2. breathe, inhale, puff, smell, smoke, sniff, waft 3. *Brit. sl.* hum (*Sl.*), pong (*Brit. inf.*), reek, stink

whim caprice, conceit, craze, crotchet, fad (*Inf.*), fancy, freak, humour, impulse, notion, passing thought, quirk, sport, sudden notion, urge, vagary, whimsy

whimper 1. *v.* blub (*Sl.*), blubber, cry, grizzle (*Inf.*), mewl, moan, pule, snivel, sob, weep, whine, whinge (*Inf.*) 2. *n.* moan, snivel, sob, whine

whimsical capricious, chimerical, crotchety, curious, droll, eccentric, fanciful, fantastic, fantastical, freakish, funny, mischievous, odd, peculiar, playful, quaint, queer, singular, unusual, waggish, weird

whine *n.* 1. cry, moan, plaintive cry, sob, wail, whimper 2. beef (*Sl.*), complaint, gripe (*Inf.*), grouse, grumble, moan ~*v.* 3. beef (*Sl.*), bellyache (*Sl.*), carp, complain, cry, gripe (*Inf.*), grizzle (*Inf.*), grouse, grumble, moan, sob, wail, whimper, whinge (*Inf.*)

whip *v.* 1. beat, birch, cane, castigate, flagellate, flog, give a hiding (*Inf.*), lash, leather, punish, scourge, spank, strap, switch, tan (*Sl.*), thrash 2. exhibit, flash, jerk, produce, pull, remove, seize, show, snatch, whisk 3. *Inf.* dart, dash, dive, flit, flounce, fly, rush, shoot, tear, whisk 4. *Inf.* beat, best, clobber (*Sl.*), conquer, defeat, drub, hammer (*Inf.*), lick (*Inf.*), outdo, overcome, overpower, overwhelm, rout, take apart (*Sl.*), thrash, trounce, wipe the floor with (*Inf.*), worst 5. agitate, compel, drive, foment, goad, hound, incite, instigate, prick, prod, provoke, push, spur, stir, urge, work up 6. beat, whisk ~*n.* 7. birch, bullwhip, cane, cat-o'-nine-tails, crop, horsewhip, knout, lash, rawhide, riding crop, scourge, switch, thong

whipping beating, birching, caning, castigation, flagellation, flogging, hiding (*Inf.*), lashing, leathering, punishment, spanking, tanning (*Sl.*), the strap, thrashing

whirl *v.* 1. circle, gyrate, pirouette, pivot, reel, revolve, roll, rotate, spin, swirl, turn, twirl, twist, wheel 2. feel dizzy, reel, spin ~*n.* 3. birl (*Scot.*), circle, gyration, pirouette, reel, revolution, roll, rotation, spin, swirl, turn, twirl, twist, wheel 4. confusion, daze, dither, flurry, giddiness, spin 5. flurry, merry-go-round, round, series, succession 6. agitation, bustle, commotion, confusion, flurry, hurly-burly, stir, tumult, uproar 7. give(something) a whirl *Inf.* attempt, have a bash (crack, go, shot, stab, whack) (*Inf.*), try

whirlwind 1. *n.* dust devil, tornado, waterspout 2. *adj.* hasty, headlong, impetuous, impulsive, lightning, quick, rapid, rash, short, speedy, swift

whisk *v.* 1. brush, flick, sweep, whip, wipe 2. dart, dash, fly, hasten, hurry, race, rush, shoot, speed, sweep, tear 3. beat, fluff up, whip ~*n.* 4. brush, flick, sweep, whip, wipe 5. beater

whisky barley-bree (*Scot.*), bour-

bon, John Barleycorn, malt, rye, Scotch, usquebaugh

whisper *v.* 1. breathe, murmur, say softly, speak in hushed tones, utter under the breath 2. gossip, hint, insinuate, intimate, murmur, spread rumours 3. hiss, murmur, rustle, sigh, sough, susurrate (*Literary*), swish ~*n.* 4. hushed tone, low voice, murmur, soft voice, undertone 5. hiss, murmur, rustle, sigh, sighing, soughing, susurration *or* susurrus (*Literary*), swish 6. breath, fraction, hint, shadow, suggestion, suspicion, tinge, trace, whiff 7. *Inf.* buzz, gossip, innuendo, insinuation, report, rumour, word

white 1. ashen, bloodless, ghastly, grey, pale, pallid, pasty, wan, waxen, wheyfaced 2. grey, grizzled, hoary, silver, snowy 3. clean, immaculate, innocent, pure, spotless, stainless, unblemished, unsullied

white-collar clerical, executive, nonmanual, office, professional, salaried

whiten blanch, bleach, blench, etiolate, fade, go white, pale, turn pale

whitewash 1. *n.* camouflage, concealment, cover-up, deception, extenuation 2. *v.* camouflage, conceal, cover up, extenuate, gloss over, make light of, suppress

whole *adj.* 1. complete, entire, full, in one piece, integral, total, unabridged, uncut, undivided 2. faultless, flawless, good, in one piece, intact, inviolate, mint, perfect, sound, unbroken, undamaged, unharmed, unhurt, unimpaired, uninjured, unmutilated, unscathed, untouched 3. able-bodied, better, cured, fit, hale, healed, healthy, in fine fettle, in good health, recovered, robust, sound, strong, well ~*adv.* 4. in one, in one piece ~*n.* 5. aggregate, all, everything, lot, sum total, the entire amount, total 6. ensemble, entirety, entity, fullness, piece, totality, unit, unity 7. on the whole a. all in all, all things considered, by and large, taking everything into consideration b. as a rule, for the most part, generally, in the main, in general, mostly, predominantly

wholehearted committed, complete, dedicated, determined, devoted, earnest, emphatic, enthusiastic, genuine, heartfelt, hearty, real, sincere, true, unfeigned, unqualified, unreserved, unstinting, warm, zealous

wholesale 1. *adj.* all-inclusive, broad, comprehensive, extensive, far-reaching, indiscriminate, mass, sweeping, wide-ranging 2. *adv.* all at once, comprehensively, extensively, indiscriminately, on a large scale, without exception

wholesome 1. beneficial, good, healthful, health-giving, healthy, helpful, hygienic, invigorating, nourishing, nutritious, salubrious, salutary, sanitary, strengthening 2. clean, decent, edifying, ethical, exemplary, honourable, improving, innocent, moral, nice, pure, respectable, righteous, uplifting, virtuous, worthy

wholly 1. all, altogether, completely, comprehensively, entirely, fully, heart and soul, in every respect, one hundred per cent (*Inf.*), perfectly, thoroughly, totally, utterly 2. exclusively, only, solely, without exception

whore *n.* 1. brass (*Sl.*), call girl, cocotte, courtesan, demimondaine, demirep (*Rare*), fallen woman, *fille de joie*, harlot, hooker (*U.S. sl.*), hustler (*U.S. sl.*), lady of the night, loose woman, prostitute, streetwalker, strumpet, tart (*Inf.*), trollop, woman of easy virtue, woman of ill repute ~*v.* 2. be on the game (*Sl.*), hustle (*U.S. sl.*), prostitute oneself, sell one's body, sell oneself, solicit, walk the streets 3. fornicate, lech (*Inf.*), sleep around (*Inf.*), wanton, wench (*Archaic*), womanize

wicked 1. abandoned, abominable, amoral, atrocious, bad, blackhearted, corrupt, debased, depraved, devilish, dissolute, egregious, evil, fiendish, flagitious, foul, guilty, heinous, immoral, impious, iniquitous, irreligious, nefarious, scandalous, shameful, sinful, unprincipled, unrighteous, vicious, vile, villainous, worthless 2. arch, impish, incorrigible, mischievous, naughty, rascally, roguish 3. acute, agonizing, awful, crashing, destructive, dreadful, fearful, fierce, harmful, injurious, intense, mighty, painful, severe, terrible 4. bothersome, difficult, distressing, galling, offensive, troublesome, trying, unpleasant 5. *Sl.* adept, adroit, deft, expert, masterly, mighty, outstanding, powerful, skilful, strong

wide *adj.* 1. ample, broad, catholic, comprehensive, distended, encyclopedic, expanded, expansive, extensive, far-reaching, general, immense, inclusive, large, sweeping, vast 2. away, distant, off, off course, off target, remote 3. dilated, distended, expanded, fully open, outspread, outstretched 4. ample, baggy, capacious, commodious, full, loose, roomy, spacious ~*adv.* 5. as far as possible, completely, fully, right out, to the furthest extent 6. astray, nowhere near, off course, off target, off the mark, out

wide-awake 1. conscious, fully awake, roused, wakened 2. alert, aware, heedful, keen, observant, on one's toes, on the alert, on the ball (*Inf.*), on the qui vive, vigilant, wary, watchful

wide-eyed credulous, green, impressionable, ingenuous, innocent, naive, simple, trusting, unsophisticated, unsuspicious, wet behind the ears (*Inf.*)

widen broaden, dilate, enlarge, expand, extend, open out *or* up, open wide, spread, stretch

wide-open 1. fully extended, fully open, gaping, outspread, outstretched, splayed, spread 2. at risk, defenceless, exposed, in danger, in peril, open, susceptible, unprotected, vulnerable 3. anybody's guess (*Inf.*), indeterminate, uncertain, unpredictable, unsettled, up for grabs (*Inf.*)

widespread broad, common, epidemic, extensive, far-flung, far-reaching, general, pervasive, popular, prevalent, rife, sweeping, universal, wholesale

width breadth, compass, diameter, extent, girth, measure, range, reach, scope, span, thickness, wideness

wield 1. brandish, employ, flourish, handle, manage, manipulate, ply, swing, use 2. apply, be possessed of, command, control, exercise, exert, have, have at one's disposal, hold, maintain, make use of, manage, possess, put to use, utilize

wife better half (*Humorous*), bride, helpmate, helpmeet, little woman (*Inf.*), mate, old lady (*Inf.*), old woman (*Inf.*), partner, spouse, (the) missis *or* missus (*Inf.*), woman (*Inf.*)

wild *adj.* 1. feral, ferocious, fierce, savage, unbroken, undomesticated, untamed 2. free, indigenous, native, natural, uncultivated 3. desert, deserted, desolate, empty, godforsaken, trackless, uncivilized, uncultivated, uninhabited, unpopulated, virgin 4. barbaric, barbarous, brutish, ferocious, fierce, primitive, rude, savage, uncivilized 5. boisterous, chaotic, disorderly, impetuous, lawless, noisy, riotous, rough, rowdy, self-willed, turbulent, unbridled, uncontrolled, undisciplined, unfettered, ungovernable, unmanageable, unrestrained, unruly, uproarious, violent, wayward 6. blustery, choppy, furious, howling, intense, raging, rough, tempestuous, violent 7. dishevelled, disordered, straggly, tousled, unkempt, untidy, windblown 8. at one's wits' end, berserk, beside oneself, crazed, crazy, delirious, demented, excited, frantic, frenzied, hysterical, irrational, mad, maniacal, rabid, raving 9. extravagant, fantastic, flighty, foolhardy, foolish, giddy, ill-considered, impracticable, imprudent, madcap, outrageous, preposterous, rash, reckless 10. *Inf.* agog, avid, crazy (*Inf.*), daft (*Inf.*), eager, enthusiastic, excited, mad (*Inf.*), nuts (*Sl.*), potty (*Inf.*) ~*adv.* 11. **run wild a.** grow unchecked, ramble, spread, straggle b. abandon all restraint, cut loose, go on the rampage, kick over the traces, rampage, run free, run riot, stray ~*n.* 12. *Often plural* back of beyond (*Inf.*), desert, middle of nowhere (*Inf.*), uninhabited area, wasteland, wilderness

wilderness 1. desert, jungle, waste, wasteland, wild 2. clutter, confused mass, confusion, congeries, jumble, maze, muddle, tangle, welter

wildlife flora and fauna

wile 1. artfulness, artifice, cheating, chicanery, craft, craftiness, cunning, fraud, guile, slyness, trickery 2. *Usually plural* artifice, contrivance, device, dodge, imposition, lure, manoeuvre, ploy, ruse, stratagem, subterfuge, trick

wilful 1. adamant, bull-headed, determined, dogged, froward, headstrong, inflexible, intractable, intransigent, mulish, obdurate, obstinate, persistent, perverse, pigheaded, refractory, self-willed, stubborn, uncompromising, unyielding 2. conscious, deliberate, intended, intentional, purposeful, volitional, voluntary, willed

will *n.* 1. choice, decision, determination, discretion, option, prerogative, volition 2. declaration, last wishes, testament 3. choice, decision, decree, desire, fancy, inclination, mind, pleasure, preference, wish 4. aim, determination, intention, purpose, resolution, resolve, willpower 5. attitude, disposition, feeling 6. **at will** as one pleases, as one thinks fit, as one wishes, at one's desire (discretion, inclination, pleasure, whim, wish) ~*v.* 7. bid, bring about, cause, command, decree, determine, direct, effect, ordain, order, resolve 8. choose, desire, elect, opt, prefer, see fit, want, wish 9. bequeath, confer, give, leave, pass on, transfer

willing agreeable, amenable, compliant, consenting, content, desirous, disposed, eager, enthusiastic, favourable, game (*Inf.*), happy, inclined, in favour, in the mood, nothing loath, pleased, prepared, ready, so-minded

willingly by choice, cheerfully, eagerly, freely, gladly, happily, of one's own accord, of one's own free will, readily, voluntarily, with all one's heart, without hesitation, with pleasure

willingness agreeableness, agreement, consent, desire, disposition, enthusiasm, favour, good will, inclination, volition, will, wish

willpower determination, drive, firmness of purpose *or* will, fixity of purpose, force *or* strength of will, grit, resolution, resolve, self-control, self-discipline, single-mindedness

wilt 1. become limp *or* flaccid, droop, sag, shrivel, wither 2. diminish, dwindle, ebb, fade, fail, flag, languish, lose courage, melt away, sag, sink, wane, weaken, wither

wily arch, artful, astute, cagey (*Inf.*), crafty, crooked, cunning, deceitful, deceptive, designing, fly (*Sl.*), foxy, guileful, intriguing, scheming, sharp, shifty, shrewd, sly, tricky, underhand

win *v.* 1. achieve first place, achieve mastery, be victorious, carry all before one, carry the day, come first, conquer, finish first, gain victory, overcome, prevail, succeed, take the prize, triumph 2. accomplish, achieve, acquire, attain, bag (*Inf.*), catch, collect, come away with, earn, gain, get, net, obtain, pick up, procure, receive, secure 3. *Often with* over allure, attract, bring *or* talk round, carry, charm, convert, convince, disarm, induce, influence, persuade, prevail upon, sway ~*n.* 4. *Inf.* conquest, success, triumph, victory

wince 1. *v.* blench, cower, cringe, draw back, flinch, quail, recoil, shrink, start 2. *n.* cringe, flinch, start

wind¹ 1. *n.* air, air-current, blast, breath, breeze, current of air, draught, gust, zephyr 2. *Inf.* clue, hint, inkling, intimation, notice, report, rumour, suggestion, tidings, warning, whisper 3. babble, blath-er, bluster, boasting, empty talk, gab (*Inf.*), hot air, humbug, idle talk, talk, verbalizing 4. breath, puff, respiration 5. *Inf.* flatulence, flatus, gas 6. **get** *or* **have the wind up** *Inf.* be afraid (alarmed, frightened, scared), fear, take fright 7. **in the wind** about to happen, approaching, close at hand, coming, imminent, impending, in the offing, near, on the cards (*Inf.*), on the way 8. **put the wind up** *Inf.* alarm, discourage, frighten, frighten off, scare, scare off

wind² *v.* 1. coil, curl, encircle, furl, loop, reel, roll, spiral, turn around, twine, twist, wreathe 2. bend, curve, deviate, meander, ramble, snake, turn, twist, zigzag ~*n.* 3. bend, curve, meander, turn, twist, zigzag

winded breathless, gasping for breath, out of breath, out of puff, panting, puffed, puffed out

windfall bonanza, find, godsend, jackpot, manna from heaven, stroke of luck

winding 1. *n.* bend, convolution, curve, meander, turn, twist, undulation 2. *adj.* anfractuous, bending, circuitous, convoluted, crooked, curving, flexuous, indirect, meandering, roundabout, serpentine, sinuous, spiral, tortuous, turning, twisting

wind up 1. bring to a close, close, close down, conclude, end, finalize, finish, liquidate, settle, terminate, tie up the loose ends (*Inf.*), wrap up 2. *Inf.* excite, make nervous, make tense, put on edge, work up 3. *Inf.* be left, end one's days, end up, find oneself, finish up

windy 1. blowy, blustering, blustery, boisterous, breezy, gusty, squally, stormy, tempestuous, wild, windswept 2. boastful, bombastic, diffuse, empty, garrulous, long-winded, loquacious, meandering, pompous, prolix, rambling, turgid, verbose, wordy 3. *Sl.* afraid, chicken (*Sl.*), cowardly, fearful, frightened, nervous, scared, timid

wing *n.* 1. organ of flight, pennon (*Poetic*), pinion (*Poetic*) 2. arm,

branch, circle, clique, coterie, fac~
tion, group, grouping, section, seg~
ment, set, side 3. adjunct, annexe,
ell, extension ~v. 4. fly, glide, soar
5. fleet, fly, hasten, hurry, race,
speed, zoom 6. clip, hit, nick,
wound

wink v. 1. bat, blink, flutter, nictate,
nictitate 2. flash, gleam, glimmer,
sparkle, twinkle ~n. 3. blink, flut~
ter, nictation 4. flash, gleam, glim~
mering, sparkle, twinkle 5. instant,
jiffy (*Inf.*), moment, second, split
second, twinkling

winkle out dig out, dislodge, draw
out, extract, extricate, force out,
prise out, smoke out, worm out

winner champ (*Inf.*), champion,
conquering hero, conqueror, first,
master, vanquisher, victor

winning 1. alluring, amiable, at~
tractive, bewitching, captivating,
charming, delectable, delightful,
disarming, enchanting, endearing,
engaging, fascinating, fetching,
lovely, pleasing, prepossessing,
sweet, taking, winsome 2. con~
quering, successful, triumphant,
victorious

winnings booty, gains, prize(s),
proceeds, profits, spoils, takings

winnow comb, cull, divide, fan,
part, screen, select, separate,
separate the wheat from the chaff,
sift, sort out

wintry 1. brumal, chilly, cold,
freezing, frosty, frozen, harsh, hi~
bernal, hiemal, icy, snowy 2. bleak,
cheerless, cold, desolate, dismal

wipe v. 1. brush, clean, dry, dust,
mop, rub, sponge, swab 2. clean
off, erase, get rid of, remove, rub
off, take away, take off ~n. 3.
brush, lick, rub, swab

wipe out annihilate, blot out, de~
stroy, efface, eradicate, erase, ex~
punge, exterminate, extirpate, kill
to the last man, massacre, oblit~
erate

wiry 1. lean, sinewy, strong, tough
2. bristly, kinky, stiff

wisdom astuteness, circumspec~
tion, comprehension, discernment,
enlightenment, erudition, fore~
sight, insight, intelligence, judg~

ment, judiciousness, knowledge,
learning, penetration, prudence,
reason, sagacity, sapience, sense,
sound judgment, understanding

wise 1. aware, clever, discerning,
enlightened, erudite, informed, in~
telligent, judicious, knowing, per~
ceptive, politic, prudent, rational,
reasonable, sagacious, sage, sapi~
ent, sensible, shrewd, sound,
understanding, well-advised, well-
informed 2. **put wise** *Sl.* alert, ap~
prise, clue in *or* up, inform, let
(someone) into the secret, notify,
tell, tip off, warn

wisecrack 1. *n.* barb, funny (*Inf.*),
gag (*Sl.*), jest, jibe, joke, pithy re~
mark, quip, sardonic remark,
smart remark, witticism 2. *v.* be
facetious, jest, jibe, joke, quip, tell
jokes

wish v. 1. aspire, covet, crave, de~
siderate, desire, hanker, hope,
hunger, long, need, set one's heart
on, sigh for, thirst, want, yearn 2.
bid, greet with 3. ask, bid, com~
mand, desire, direct, instruct, or~
der, require ~n. 4. aspiration, de~
sire, hankering, hope, hunger, in~
clination, intention, liking, longing,
thirst, urge, want, whim, will,
yearning 5. bidding, command, de~
sire, order, request, will

wistful contemplative, disconso~
late, dreaming, dreamy, forlorn,
longing, meditative, melancholy,
mournful, musing, pensive, reflec~
tive, sad, thoughtful, yearning

wit 1. badinage, banter, drollery,
facetiousness, fun, humour, jocu~
larity, levity, pleasantry, raillery,
repartee, wordplay 2. card (*Inf.*),
comedian, epigrammatist, *farceur*,
humorist, joker, punster, wag 3.
acumen, brains, cleverness, com~
mon sense, comprehension, dis~
cernment, ingenuity, insight, intel~
lect, judgment, mind, nous (*Brit.
sl.*), perception, practical intelli~
gence, reason, sense, understand~
ing, wisdom

witch enchantress, magician,
necromancer, occultist, sorceress

witchcraft enchantment, incanta~
tion, magic, necromancy, occult~

ism, sorcery, sortilege, spell, the black art, the occult, voodoo, witchery, witching, wizardry

withdraw 1. draw back, draw out, extract, pull out, remove, take away, take off 2. abjure, disavow, disclaim, recall, recant, rescind, retract, revoke, take back, unsay 3. absent oneself, back out, depart, detach oneself, disengage, drop out, fall back, go, leave, make one~ self scarce (*Inf.*), pull back, pull out, retire, retreat, secede

withdrawal 1. extraction, removal 2. abjuration, disavowal, disclaim~ er, recall, recantation, repudiation, rescission, retraction, revocation 3. departure, disengagement, exit, exodus, retirement, retreat, seces~ sion

withdrawn 1. aloof, detached, dis~ tant, introverted, quiet, reserved, retiring, shrinking, shy, silent, taciturn, timorous, uncommunica~ tive, unforthcoming 2. hidden, iso~ lated, out-of-the-way, private, re~ mote, secluded, solitary

wither 1. blast, blight, decay, de~ cline, desiccate, disintegrate, droop, dry, fade, languish, perish, shrink, shrivel, wane, waste, wilt 2. abash, blast, humiliate, mortify, put down (*Sl.*), shame, snub

withering 1. blasting, blighting, devastating, humiliating, hurtful, mortifying, scornful, snubbing 2. deadly, death-dealing, destructive, devastating, killing, murderous, slaughterous

withhold 1. check, conceal, deduct, hide, hold back, keep, keep back, keep secret, refuse, repress, re~ serve, resist, restrain, retain, sit on (*Inf.*), suppress 2. *With* from for~ bear, keep oneself, refrain, stop oneself

withstand 1. bear, brave, combat, confront, cope with, defy, endure, face, grapple with, hold off, hold out against, oppose, put up with (*Inf.*), resist, stand up to, suffer, take, take on, thwart, tolerate, weather 2. endure, hold *or* stand one's ground, hold out, remain firm, stand, stand fast, stand firm

witness *n.* 1. beholder, bystander, eyewitness, looker-on, observer, onlooker, spectator, viewer, watcher 2. attestant, corroborator, deponent, testifier 3. bear witness a. depone, depose, give evidence, give testimony, testify b. attest to, bear out, be evidence of, be proof of, betoken, confirm, constitute proof of, corroborate, demonstrate, evince, prove, show, testify to, vouch for ~ *v.* 4. attend, be present at, look on, mark, note, notice, ob~ serve, perceive, see, view, watch 5. attest, authenticate, bear out, bear witness, confirm, corroborate, de~ pone, depose, give evidence, give testimony, testify 6. countersign, endorse, sign

wits 1. acumen, astuteness, brains (*Inf.*), cleverness, comprehension, faculties, ingenuity, intelligence, judgment, nous (*Brit. sl.*), reason, sense, understanding 2. **at one's wits' end** at a loss, at the end of one's tether, baffled, bewildered, in despair, lost, stuck (*Inf.*), stumped

witticism bon mot, clever remark, epigram, one-liner (*Sl.*), play on words, pleasantry, pun, quip, rep~ artee, riposte, sally, witty remark

witty amusing, brilliant, clever, droll, epigrammatic, facetious, fanciful, funny, gay, humorous, in~ genious, jocular, lively, original, piquant, sparkling, waggish, whimsical

wizard 1. conjurer, enchanter, mage (*Archaic*), magician, magus, necromancer, occultist, shaman, sorcerer, thaumaturge (*Rare*), warlock, witch 2. ace (*Inf.*), adept, expert, genius, hotshot (*Inf.*), maestro, master, prodigy, star, virtuoso, whiz (*Inf.*), whizz kid (*Inf.*), wiz (*Inf.*)

wizened dried up, gnarled, lined, sere (*Archaic*), shrivelled, shrunk~ en, withered, worn, wrinkled

wobble *v.* 1. quake, rock, seesaw, shake, sway, teeter, totter, trem~ ble, vibrate, waver 2. be unable to make up one's mind, be undecided, dither, fluctuate, hesitate, shilly~ shally (*Inf.*), swither (*Scot.*), vacil~

late, waver ~n. 3. quaking, shake, tremble, tremor, unsteadiness, vibration

woe adversity, affliction, agony, anguish, burden, curse, dejection, depression, disaster, distress, gloom, grief, hardship, heartache, heartbreak, melancholy, misery, misfortune, pain, sadness, sorrow, suffering, trial, tribulation, trouble, unhappiness, wretchedness

woeful 1. afflicted, agonized, anguished, calamitous, catastrophic, cruel, deplorable, disastrous, disconsolate, distressing, doleful, dreadful, gloomy, grieving, grievous, heartbreaking, heart-rending, lamentable, miserable, mournful, pathetic, piteous, pitiable, pitiful, plaintive, sad, sorrowful, tragic, unhappy, wretched 2. appalling, awful, bad, deplorable, disappointing, disgraceful, dreadful, duff (*Brit. Sl.*), feeble, hopeless, inadequate, lousy (*Inf.*), mean, miserable, paltry, pathetic, pitiable, pitiful, poor, rotten (*Inf.*), shocking, sorry, terrible, wretched

wolf n. 1. *Fig.* devil, fiend, killer, mercenary, pirate, predator, robber, savage, shark 2.*Inf.* Casanova, Don Juan, lady-killer, lecher, Lothario, philanderer, seducer, womanizer ~v. 3. *With* down bolt, cram, devour, gobble, gollop, gorge, gulp, pack away (*Inf.*), scoff (*Sl.*), stuff

woman 1. bird (*Sl.*), chick (*Sl.*), dame (*Sl.*), female, girl, lady, lass, lassie, maid (*Archaic*), maiden (*Archaic*), miss, she 2. chambermaid, char (*Inf.*), charwoman, domestic, female servant, handmaiden, housekeeper, lady-in-waiting, maid, maidservant 3. *Inf.* bride, girl, girlfriend, ladylove, mate, mistress, old lady (*Inf.*), partner, spouse, sweetheart, wife

womanizer Casanova, Don Juan, lady-killer, lecher, Lothario, philanderer, seducer, wolf (*Inf.*)

womanly female, feminine, ladylike, matronly, motherly, tender, warm

wonder n. 1. admiration, amaze-

ment, astonishment, awe, bewilderment, curiosity, fascination, stupefaction, surprise, wonderment 2. curiosity, marvel, miracle, nonpareil, phenomenon, portent, prodigy, rarity, sight, spectacle, wonderment ~v. 3. ask oneself, be curious, be inquisitive, conjecture, cudgel one's brains (*Inf.*), doubt, inquire, meditate, ponder, puzzle, query, question, speculate, think 4. be amazed (astonished, awed, dumbstruck), be flabbergasted (*Inf.*), boggle, gape, gawk, marvel, stand amazed, stare

wonderful 1. amazing, astonishing, astounding, awe-inspiring, awesome, extraordinary, fantastic, incredible, marvellous, miraculous, odd, peculiar, phenomenal, remarkable, staggering, startling, strange, surprising, unheard-of, wondrous 2. ace (*Inf.*), admirable, brilliant, excellent, fabulous (*Inf.*), fantastic (*Inf.*), great (*Inf.*), magnificent, marvellous, outstanding, sensational, smashing (*Inf.*), stupendous, super (*Inf.*), superb, terrific, tiptop, tremendous

woo chase, court, cultivate, importune, pay court to, pay one's addresses to, pay suit to, press one's suit with, pursue, seek after, seek the hand of, seek to win, solicit the good will of, spark (*Rare*)

wood 1. *Also* woods coppice, copse, forest, grove, thicket, trees, woodland 2. out of the wood(s) clear, home an dry (*Brit. sl.*), in the clear, out of danger, safe, safe and sound, secure 3. planks, timber

wooded forested, sylvan (*Poetic*), timbered, tree-clad, tree-covered, woody

wooden 1. ligneous, made of wood, of wood, timber, woody 2. awkward, clumsy, gauche, gawky, graceless, inelegant, maladroit, rigid, stiff, ungainly 3. blank, colourless, deadpan, dull, emotionless, empty, expressionless, glassy, lifeless, spiritless, unemotional, unresponsive, vacant 4. inflexible, obstinate, rigid, stiff, unbending, unyielding 5. dense, dim, dim-witted

(*Inf.*), dull, dull-witted, obtuse, slow, stupid, thick, witless, wooden~ headed (*Inf.*) 6. dull, muffled

wool 1. fleece, hair, yarn 2. **dyed in the wool** confirmed, diehard, fixed, hardened, inflexible, inveterate, settled, unchangeable, uncompro~ mising, unshakable 3. **pull the wool over someone's eyes** bam~ boozle (*Inf.*), con (*Sl.*), deceive, de~ lude, dupe, fool, hoodwink, lead (someone) up the garden path (*Inf.*), pull a fast one (on someone) (*Inf.*), put one over on (*Sl.*), take in (*Inf.*), trick

woolly *adj.* 1. fleecy, flocculent, hairy, made of wool, shaggy, wool~ len 2. blurred, clouded, confused, foggy, fuzzy, hazy, ill-defined, in~ definite, indistinct, muddled, nebu~ lous, unclear, vague

word *n.* 1. brief conversation, chat, chitchat, colloquy, confab (*Inf.*), confabulation, consultation, dis~ cussion, talk, tête-à-tête 2. brief statement, comment, declaration, expression, remark, utterance 3. expression, locution, name, term, vocable 4. account, advice, bul~ letin, communication, communi~ qué, dispatch, gen (*Brit. inf.*), in~ formation, intelligence, intimation, message, news, notice, report, tid~ ings 5. command, go-ahead (*Inf.*), green light, order, signal 6. affir~ mation, assertion, assurance, guarantee, oath, parole, pledge, promise, solemn oath, solemn word, undertaking, vow, word of honour 7. bidding, command, com~ mandment, decree, edict, man~ date, order, ukase (*Rare*), will 8. countersign, password, slogan, watchword 9. **in a word** briefly, concisely, in a nutshell, in short, succinctly, to put it briefly, to sum up ~*v.* 10. couch, express, phrase, put, say, state, utter

wordplay punning, puns, repartee, wit, witticisms

words 1. lyrics, text 2. altercation, angry exchange, angry speech, argument, barney (*Inf.*), bickering, disagreement, dispute, falling-out

(*Inf.*), quarrel, row, run-in (*Inf.*), set-to (*Inf.*), squabble

wordy diffuse, discursive, garru~ lous, long-winded, loquacious, pleonastic, prolix, rambling, ver~ bose, windy

work *n.* 1. drudgery, effort, elbow grease (*Inf.*), exertion, grind (*Inf.*), industry, labour, slog, sweat, toil, travail (*Literary*) 2. business, call~ ing, craft, duty, employment, job, line, livelihood, métier, occupation, office, profession, pursuit, trade 3. assignment, chore, commission, duty, job, stint, task, undertaking 4. achievement, composition, crea~ tion, handiwork, *oeuvre*, opus, per~ formance, piece, production 5. art, craft, skill, workmanship 6. **out of work** idle, jobless, on the dole (*Brit. inf.*), on the street, out of a job, unemployed ~*v.* 7. drudge, ex~ ert oneself, labour, peg away, slave, slog (away), sweat, toil 8. be employed, be in work, do business, earn a living, have a job 9. act, control, direct, drive, handle, manage, manipulate, move, oper~ ate, ply, use, wield 10. function, go, operate, perform, run 11. cultivate, dig, farm, till 12. fashion, form, handle, knead, make, manipulate, mould, process, shape 13. be agi~ tated, convulse, move, twitch, writhe 14. *Often with* up arouse, excite, move, prompt, provoke, rouse, stir 15. accomplish, achieve, bring about, carry out, cause, con~ trive, create, effect, encompass, execute, implement 16. force, make one's way, manoeuvre, move, progress 17. *Inf.* arrange, bring off, contrive, exploit, fiddle (*Inf.*), fix (*Inf.*), handle, manipu~ late, pull off, swing (*Inf.*)

workable doable, feasible, possible, practicable, practical, viable

workaday common, common~ place, everyday, familiar, hum~ drum, mundane, ordinary, practi~ cal, prosaic, routine

worker artisan, craftsman, em~ ployee, hand, labourer, proletar~ ian, tradesman, wage earner, working man, working woman, workman

working *n.* 1. action, functioning, manner, method, mode of operation, operation, running 2. *Plural* diggings, excavations, mine, pit, quarry, shaft ~*adj.* 3. active, employed, in a job, in work, labouring 4. functioning, going, operative, running 5. effective, practical, useful, viable

workman artificer, artisan, craftsman, employee, hand, journeyman, labourer, mechanic, operative, tradesman, worker

workmanlike, workmanly adept, careful, efficient, expert, masterly, painstaking, professional, proficient, satisfactory, skilful, skilled, thorough

workmanship art, artistry, craft, craftsmanship, execution, expertise, handicraft, handiwork, manufacture, skill, technique, work

work out 1. accomplish, achieve, attain, win 2. calculate, clear up, figure out, find out, puzzle out, resolve, solve 3. arrange, construct, contrive, develop, devise, elaborate, evolve, form, formulate, plan, put together 4. be effective, flourish, go as planned, go well, prosper, prove satisfactory, succeed 5. come out, develop, evolve, go, happen, pan out (*Inf.*), result, turn out 6. do exercises, drill, exercise, practise, train, warm up 7. add up to, amount to, come to, reach, reach a total of

works 1. factory, mill, plant, shop, workshop 2. canon, *oeuvre*, output, productions, writings 3. actions, acts, deeds, doings 4. action, guts (*Sl.*), innards (*Inf.*), insides (*Inf.*), machinery, mechanism, movement, moving parts, parts, workings

workshop 1. atelier, factory, mill, plant, shop, studio, workroom, works 2. class, discussion group, seminar, study group

work up agitate, animate, arouse, enkindle, excite, foment, generate, get (someone) all steamed up (*Sl.*), incite, inflame, instigate, move, rouse, spur, stir up, wind up (*Inf.*)

world 1. earth, earthly sphere, globe 2. everybody, everyone, humanity, humankind, human race, man, mankind, men, the public, the race of man 3. cosmos, creation, existence, life, nature, universe 4. heavenly body, planet, star 5. area, domain, environment, field, kingdom, province, realm, sphere, system 6. age, days, epoch, era, period, times 7. **for all the world** exactly, in every respect, in every way, just as if, just like, precisely, to all intents and purposes 8. **on top of the world** *Inf.* beside oneself with joy, ecstatic, elated, exultant, happy, in raptures, on cloud nine (*Inf.*), overjoyed, over the moon (*Inf.*) 9. **out of this world** *Inf.* excellent, fabulous (*Inf.*), fantastic (*Inf.*), great (*Inf.*), incredible, indescribable, marvellous, superb, unbelievable, wonderful

worldly 1. carnal, earthly, fleshly, lay, mundane, physical, profane, secular, sublunary, temporal, terrestrial 2. avaricious, covetous, grasping, greedy, materialistic, selfish, worldly-minded 3. blasé, cosmopolitan, experienced, knowing, politic, sophisticated, urbane, well versed in the ways of the world, worldly-wise

worldwide general, global, international, omnipresent, pandemic, ubiquitous, universal

worn 1. frayed, ragged, shabby, shiny, tattered, tatty, the worse for wear, threadbare 2. careworn, drawn, haggard, lined, pinched, wizened 3. exhausted, fatigued, jaded, played-out (*Inf.*), spent, tired, tired out, wearied, weary, worn-out

worn-out 1. broken-down, clapped-out (*Brit. inf.*), decrepit, done, frayed, on its last legs, ragged, run-down, shabby, tattered, tatty, threadbare, used, used-up, useless, worn 2. all in (*Sl.*), dead *or* out on one's feet (*Inf.*), dog-tired (*Inf.*), done in (*Inf.*), exhausted, fatigued, fit to drop, jiggered (*Dialect*), knackered (*Brit. sl.*), played-out, prostrate, spent, tired, tired out, weary

worried afraid, anxious, apprehensive, bothered, concerned, distracted, distraught, distressed, disturbed, fearful, fretful, frightened, ill at ease, nervous, on edge, overwrought, perturbed, tense, tormented, troubled, uneasy, unquiet, upset

worry *v.* 1. agonize, annoy, badger, be anxious, bother, brood, disquiet, distress, disturb, feel uneasy, fret, harass, harry, hassle (*Inf.*), hector, importune, irritate, make anxious, perturb, pester, plague, tantalize, tease, torment, trouble, unsettle, upset, vex 2. attack, bite, gnaw at, go for, harass, harry, kill, lacerate, savage, tear ~*n.* 3. annoyance, care, irritation, pest, plague, problem, torment, trial, trouble, vexation 4. annoyance, anxiety, apprehension, care, concern, disturbance, fear, irritation, misery, misgiving, perplexity, torment, trouble, unease, vexation, woe

worsen aggravate, damage, decay, decline, degenerate, deteriorate, exacerbate, get worse, go downhill (*Inf.*), go from bad to worse, retrogress, sink, take a turn for the worse

worship 1. *v.* adore, adulate, deify, exalt, glorify, honour, idolize, laud, love, praise, pray to, put on a pedestal, respect, revere, reverence, venerate 2. *n.* adoration, adulation, deification, devotion, exaltation, glorification, glory, homage, honour, laudation, love, praise, prayer(s), regard, respect, reverence

worst *v.* beat, best, conquer, crush, defeat, gain the advantage over, get the better of, master, overcome, overpower, overthrow, subdue, subjugate, vanquish

worth 1. aid, assistance, avail, benefit, credit, desert(s), estimation, excellence, goodness, help, importance, merit, quality, usefulness, utility, value, virtue, worthiness 2. cost, price, rate, valuation, value

worthless 1. futile, ineffectual, insignificant, inutile, meaningless, miserable, no use, nugatory, paltry, pointless, poor, rubbishy, trashy, trifling, trivial, unavailing, unimportant, unusable, useless, valueless, wretched 2. abandoned, abject, base, contemptible, depraved, despicable, good-for-nothing, ignoble, useless, vile

worthwhile beneficial, constructive, gainful, good, helpful, justifiable, productive, profitable, useful, valuable, worthy

worthy 1. *adj.* admirable, commendable, creditable, decent, dependable, deserving, estimable, excellent, good, honest, honourable, laudable, meritorious, praiseworthy, reliable, reputable, respectable, righteous, upright, valuable, virtuous, worthwhile 2. *n.* big shot (*Sl.*), bigwig (*Sl.*), dignitary, luminary, notable, personage

wound *n.* 1. cut, damage, gash, harm, hurt, injury, laceration, lesion, slash 2. anguish, distress, grief, heartbreak, injury, insult, offence, pain, pang, sense of loss, shock, slight, torment, torture, trauma ~*v.* 3. cut, damage, gash, harm, hit, hurt, injure, irritate, lacerate, pierce, slash, wing 4. annoy, cut (someone) to the quick, distress, grieve, hurt, hurt the feelings of, mortify, offend, pain, shock, sting, traumatize

wrangle 1. *v.* altercate, argue, bicker, brawl, contend, disagree, dispute, fall out (*Inf.*), fight, have words, quarrel, row, scrap, squabble 2. *n.* altercation, angry exchange, argy-bargy (*Brit. inf.*), barney (*Inf.*), bickering, brawl, clash, contest, controversy, dispute, falling-out (*Inf.*), quarrel, row, set-to (*Inf.*), slanging match (*Brit.*), squabble, tiff

wrap 1. *v.* absorb, bind, bundle up, cloak, cover, encase, enclose, enfold, envelop, fold, immerse, muffle, pack, package, roll up, sheathe, shroud, surround, swathe, wind 2. *n.* cape, cloak, mantle, shawl, stole

wrapper case, cover, envelope,

jacket, packaging, paper, sheath, sleeve, wrapping

wrap up 1. bundle up, enclose, en~wrap, giftwrap, pack, package 2. dress warmly, muffle up, put warm clothes on, wear something warm 3. *Sl.* be quiet, be silent, hold one's tongue, put a sock in it (*Brit. sl.*), shut one's face (*Brit. sl.*), shut one's mouth (*Sl.*), shut one's trap (*Sl.*), shut up 4. *Inf.* bring to a close, conclude, end, finish off, polish off, round off, terminate, tidy up, wind up

wrath anger, choler, displeasure, exasperation, fury, indignation, ire, irritation, passion, rage, resent~ment, temper

wrathful angry, beside oneself with rage, displeased, enraged, furious, incensed, indignant, infuriated, irate, on the warpath (*Inf.*), raging, wroth (*Archaic*)

wreath band, chaplet, coronet, crown, festoon, garland, loop, ring

wreathe adorn, coil, crown, encir~cle, enfold, entwine, envelop, en~wrap, festoon, intertwine, inter~weave, surround, twine, twist, wind, wrap, writhe

wreck *v.* 1. break, dash to pieces, demolish, destroy, devastate, mar, play havoc with, ravage, ruin, shatter, smash, spoil 2. founder, go *or* run aground, run onto the rocks, shipwreck, strand ~*n.* 3. derelict, hulk, shipwreck, sunken vessel 4. desolation, destruction, devasta~tion, disruption, mess, overthrow, ruin, undoing

wreckage debris, fragments, hulk, pieces, remains, rubble, ruin, wrack

wrench *v.* 1. force, jerk, pull, rip, tear, tug, twist, wrest, wring, yank 2. distort, rick, sprain, strain ~*n.* 3. jerk, pull, rip, tug, twist, yank 4. sprain, strain, twist 5. ache, blow, pain, pang, shock, upheaval, up~rooting 6. adjustable spanner, shifting spanner, spanner

wrestle battle, combat, contend, fight, grapple, scuffle, strive, struggle, tussle

wretch 1. blackguard, cur, good-

for-nothing, miscreant, outcast, profligate, rascal, rat (*Inf.*), rogue, rotter (*Sl.*), ruffian, scoundrel, swine, vagabond, villain, worm 2. poor thing, unfortunate

wretched 1. abject, broken-hearted, cheerless, comfortless, crestfallen, dejected, deplorable, depressed, disconsolate, distressed, doleful, downcast, forlorn, gloomy, hapless, hopeless, melancholy, miserable, pathetic, pitiable, piti~ful, poor, sorry, unfortunate, un~happy, woebegone, woeful, worth~less 2. calamitous, deplorable, in~ferior, miserable, paltry, pathetic, poor, sorry, worthless 3. base, con~temptible, despicable, low, low-down (*Inf.*), mean, paltry, scurvy, shabby, shameful, vile

wriggle *v.* 1. jerk, jiggle, squirm, turn, twist, wag, waggle, wiggle, writhe 2. crawl, slink, snake, twist and turn, worm, zigzag 3. crawl, dodge, extricate oneself, manoeu~vre, sneak, talk one's way out, worm ~*n.* 4. jerk, jiggle, squirm, turn, twist, wag, waggle, wiggle

wring 1. coerce, extort, extract, force, screw, squeeze, twist, wrench, wrest 2. distress, hurt, lacerate, pain, pierce, rack, rend, stab, tear at, wound

wrinkle[1] 1. *n.* corrugation, crease, crinkle, crow's-foot, crumple, fold, furrow, gather, line, pucker, rum~ple 2. *v.* corrugate, crease, crinkle, crumple, fold, furrow, gather, line, pucker, ruck, rumple

wrinkle[2] device, dodge, gimmick, idea, plan, ploy, ruse, scheme, stunt, tip, trick, wheeze (*Brit. sl.*)

writ court order, decree, document, summons

write author (*Nonstandard*), com~mit to paper, compose, copy, cor~respond, create, draft, draw up, in~dite, inscribe, jot down, pen, put down in black and white, put in writing, record, scribble, set down, take down, tell, transcribe

write off 1. cancel, cross out, dis~regard, forget about, give up for lost, score out, shelve 2. *Inf.* crash, damage beyond repair, destroy, smash up, total (*U.S. sl.*), wreck

writer author, columnist, essayist, hack, littérateur, man of letters, novelist, penman, penny-a-liner (*Rare*), penpusher, scribbler, scribe, wordsmith

writhe contort, distort, jerk, squirm, struggle, thrash, thresh, toss, twist, wiggle, wriggle

writing 1. calligraphy, chirography, hand, handwriting, penmanship, print, scrawl, scribble, script 2. book, composition, document, letter, opus, publication, work 3. belles-lettres, letters, literature

wrong *adj.* 1. erroneous, fallacious, false, faulty, inaccurate, incorrect, in error, mistaken, off beam (*Inf.*), off target, out, unsound, untrue, wide of the mark 2. bad, blameworthy, criminal, crooked, dishonest, dishonourable, evil, felonious, illegal, illicit, immoral, iniquitous, reprehensible, sinful, unethical, unfair, unjust, unlawful, wicked, wrongful 3. funny, improper, inappropriate, inapt, incongruous, incorrect, indecorous, infelicitous, malapropos, not done, unacceptable, unbecoming, unconventional, undesirable, unfitting, unhappy, unseemly, unsuitable 4. amiss, askew, awry, defective, faulty, not working, out of commission, out of order 5. inside, inverse, opposite, reverse ~*adv.* 6. amiss, askew, astray, awry, badly, erroneously, inaccurately, incorrectly, mistakenly, wrongly 7. **go wrong a.** come to grief (*Inf.*), come to nothing, fail, fall through, flop (*Inf.*), miscarry,

misfire **b.** boob (*Brit. sl.*), err, go astray, make a mistake, slip up (*Inf.*) **c.** break down, cease to function, conk out (*Inf.*), fail, go kaput (*Inf.*), go on the blink (*Sl.*), go phut (*Inf.*), malfunction, misfire **d.** err, fall from grace, go astray, go off the straight and narrow (*Inf.*), go to the bad, lapse, sin ~*n.* 8. abuse, bad *or* evil deed, crime, error, grievance, immorality, inequity, infraction, infringement, iniquity, injury, injustice, misdeed, offence, sin, sinfulness, transgression, trespass, unfairness, wickedness 9. **in the wrong** at fault, blameworthy, guilty, in error, mistaken, off beam (*Inf.*), off course, off target, to be blamed ~*v.* 10. abuse, cheat, discredit, dishonour, harm, hurt, ill-treat, ill-use, impose upon, injure, malign, maltreat, misrepresent, mistreat, oppress, take advantage of

wrongdoer criminal, culprit, delinquent, evildoer, lawbreaker, malefactor, miscreant, offender, sinner, transgressor, trespasser (*Archaic*)

wrongful blameworthy, criminal, dishonest, dishonourable, evil, felonious, illegal, illegitimate, illicit, immoral, improper, reprehensible, unethical, unfair, unjust, unlawful, wicked

wry 1. askew, aslant, awry, contorted, crooked, deformed, distorted, off the level, twisted, uneven, warped 2. droll, dry, ironic, mocking, pawky (*Scot.*), sarcastic, sardonic

XYZ

X-rays Röntgen rays (*Old name*)

yank *v./n.* hitch, jerk, pull, snatch, tug, wrench

yardstick benchmark, criterion, gauge, measure, standard, touchstone

yarn *n.* 1. fibre, thread 2. *Inf.* anecdote, cock-and-bull story (*Inf.*), fable, story, tale, tall story

yawning cavernous, chasmal, gaping, vast, wide, wide-open

yearly annual, annually, every year, once a year, per annum

yearn ache, covet, crave, desire, hanker, have a yen for (*Inf.*), hunger, itch, languish, long, lust, pant, pine, set one's heart upon

yell 1. *v.* bawl, holler (*Inf.*), howl, scream, screech, shout, shriek, squeal 2. *n.* cry, howl, scream, screech, shriek, whoop

yet 1. as yet, so far, thus far, until now, up to now 2. however, nevertheless, notwithstanding, still 3. additionally, as well, besides, further, in addition, into the bargain, moreover, over and above, still, to boot 4. already, just now, now, right now, so soon

yield *v.* 1. afford, bear, bring forth, bring in, earn, furnish, generate, give, net, pay, produce, provide, return, supply ~*n.* 2. crop, earnings, harvest, income, output, produce, profit, return, revenue, takings ~*v.* 3. abandon, abdicate, admit defeat, bow, capitulate, cave in (*Inf.*), cede, cry quits, give in, give up the struggle, give way, knuckle under, lay down one's arms, part with, raise the white flag, relinquish, resign, resign oneself, submit, succumb, surrender, throw in the towel 4. accede, agree, allow, bow, comply, concede, consent, go along with, grant, permit

yielding 1. accommodating, acquiescent, biddable, compliant, docile, easy, flexible, obedient, pliant, submissive, tractable 2. elastic,

pliable, quaggy, resilient, soft, spongy, springy, supple, unresisting

yoke *n.* 1. bond, chain, coupling, ligament, link, tie 2. bondage, burden, enslavement, helotry, oppression, serfdom, service, servility, servitude, slavery, thraldom, vassalage ~*v.* 3. bracket, connect, couple, harness, hitch, join, link, tie, unite

yokel boor, bucolic, clodhopper (*Inf.*), (country) bumpkin, country cousin, countryman, hick (*Inf., chiefly U.S.*), hillbilly, hind (*Obsolete*), peasant (*Inf.*), rustic

young *adj.* 1. adolescent, callow, green, growing, immature, infant, in the springtime of life, junior, juvenile, little, unfledged, youthful 2. at an early stage, early, fledgling, new, newish, not far advanced, recent, undeveloped ~*n.* 3. babies, brood, family, issue, litter, little ones, offspring, progeny

youngster boy, cub, girl, juvenile, kid (*Inf.*), lad, lass, pup (*Inf.*), teenager, teenybopper (*Sl.*), urchin, young adult, young hopeful, young person, young shaver (*Inf.*), young 'un (*Inf.*), youth

youth 1. adolescence, boyhood, early life, girlhood, immaturity, juvenescence, salad days, young days 2. adolescent, boy, kid (*Inf.*), lad, shaveling (*Archaic*), stripling, teenager, young man, young shaver (*Inf.*), youngster 3. teenagers, the rising generation, the young, younger generation, young people

youthful 1. boyish, childish, girlish, immature, inexperienced, juvenile, pubescent, puerile, young 2. active, fresh, spry, vigorous, young at heart, young looking

zeal ardour, devotion, eagerness, earnestness, enthusiasm, fanaticism, fervency, fervour, fire, gusto, keenness, militancy, passion, spirit, verve, warmth, zest

ι, enthusiast, extremist, ⁓end (*Inf.*), maniac, mili~

afire, ardent, burning, de~ eager, earnest, enthusiastic, ⁓ical, fervent, fervid, impas~ ⁓ned, keen, militant, passionate, ⁓bid, spirited

⁓enith acme, apex, apogee, climax, height, high noon, high point, me~ ridian, peak, pinnacle, summit, top, vertex

zero 1. cipher, naught, nil, nothing, nought 2. bottom, lowest point *or* ebb, nadir, nothing, rock bottom

zero hour appointed hour, crisis, moment of decision, moment of truth, turning point, vital moment

zest 1. appetite, delectation, enjoy~ ment, gusto, keenness, relish, zeal, zing (*Inf.*) 2. charm, flavour, inter~ est, kick (*Inf.*), piquancy, pungen~ cy, relish, savour, smack, spice, tang, taste

zone area, belt, district, region, section, sector, sphere